McDougal Littell

WORLD HISTORY

PATTERNS OF INTERACTION

Portrait of a woman from
first-century Pompeii

Young girl from Dali, Yunnan
Province, China

A young European nobleman
of the 1400s

Sculpted Moche figure from
around A.D. 100, Trujillo, Peru

A woman in ceremonial
headdress, Kenya, Africa

A local fisherman, Peru

Funerary mask, Tomb of
Tutankhamen, around 1300 B.C.

A farmer in Turkey

A woman in traditional dress,
Rajasthan, India

McDougal Littell

WORLD HISTORY

PATTERNS OF INTERACTION

Roger B. Beck

Linda Black

Larry S. Krieger

Phillip C. Naylor

Dahia Ibo Shabaka

*"The history of
civilizations, in fact,
is the history of
continual mutual
borrowings over many
centuries."*

—Fernand Braudel

McDougal Littell
A HOUGHTON MIFFLIN COMPANY
Evanston, Illinois • Boston • Dallas

Senior Consultants

Roger B. Beck, Ph.D.

Roger B. Beck is a Professor of African History, World History, History of the Third World, and Social Studies Methods at Eastern Illinois University. He is also a Social Studies Student Teacher Supervisor at that university. Dr. Beck recently served as Associate Dean of the Graduate School and International Programs at Eastern Illinois University. In addition to his distinguished teaching career at high school, college, and graduate school levels, Dr. Beck is a contributing author to several books and has written numerous articles, reviews, and papers. He is also an active member of the National Council for the Social Studies, the World History Association, and the African Studies Association. Dr. Beck was a key contributor to the National Standards for World History.

Linda Black, B.A., M.Ed.

Linda Black teaches World History at Cypress Falls High School in Houston, Texas, and has had a distinguished career in education as a teacher of world history, American history, and Texas history. In 1993–1994, Mrs. Black was named an Outstanding Secondary Social Studies Teacher in the United States by the National Council for the Social Studies. In 1996, she was elected to the Board of Directors of the National Council for the Social Studies. As an active member of that Council, the Texas Council for the Social Studies, the Texas Humanities Alliance, and the World History Association, Mrs. Black frequently presents and directs workshops at the local, state, and national levels.

Larry S. Krieger, B.A., M.A., M.A.T.

Larry S. Krieger is the Social Studies Supervisor for Grades K-12 in Montgomery Township Public Schools in New Jersey. For 26 years he has taught world history in public schools. He has also introduced many innovative in-service programs, such as "Putting the Story Back in History," and has co-authored several successful history textbooks. Mr. Krieger earned his B.A. and M.A.T. from the University of North Carolina and his M.A. from Wake Forest University.

Phillip C. Naylor, Ph.D.

Phillip C. Naylor is an Associate Professor of History at Marquette University and teaches Modern European and non-Western history courses on both graduate and undergraduate levels. He is also the Director of the Western Civilization Program at Marquette University. He has co-authored and co-edited several books, including *State and Society in Algeria* and *Western Receptions/Perceptions: A Trans-Cultural Anthology*. In addition, Dr. Naylor is a contributing author to several history texts and study programs and has published numerous articles, papers, reviews, and CD-ROM projects. In 1996, Dr. Naylor received the Reverend John P. Raynor, S.J., Faculty Award for Teaching Excellence at Marquette University. In 1992, he received the Edward G. Roddy Teaching Award at Merrimack College.

Dahia Ibo Shabaka, B.A., M.A., Ed.S.

Dahia Ibo Shabaka is the Director of Social Studies and African-Centered Education in the Detroit Public Schools system. She has an extensive educational and scholarly background in the disciplines of history, political science, economics, law, and reading, and also in secondary education, curriculum development, and school administration and supervision. Ms. Shabaka has been a teacher, a curriculum coordinator, and a supervisor of Social Studies in the Detroit Secondary Schools. In 1991 she was named Social Studies Educator of the Year by the Michigan Council for the Social Studies. Ms. Shabaka is the recipient of a Fulbright Fellowship at the Hebrew University in Israel and has served as an executive board member of the National Social Studies Supervisors Association.

Acknowledgments begin on page 1072.

ISBN 0-618-10823-8

Printed in the United States of America.

2 3 4 5 6 7 8 9–DWO–03 02 01

This text contains material that appeared originally in *World History: Perspectives on the Past* (D.C. Heath and Company) by Larry S. Krieger, Kenneth Neill, and Dr. Edward Reynolds.

Content Consultants

The content consultants reviewed the manuscript for historical depth and accuracy and for clarity of presentation.

Jerry Bentley
Department of History
University of Hawaii
Honolulu, Hawaii

Marc Brettler
Department of Near Eastern
  and Judaic Studies
Brandeis University
Waltham, Massachusetts

Steve Gosch
Department of History
University of Wisconsin at Eau Claire
Eau Claire, Wisconsin

Don Holsinger
Department of History
Seattle Pacific University
Seattle, Washington

Patrick Manning
World History Center
Department of History
Northeastern University
Boston, Massachusetts

Richard Saller
Department of History
University of Chicago
Chicago, Illinois

Wolfgang Schlauch
Department of History
Eastern Illinois University
Charleston, Illinois

Susan Schroeder
Department of History
Loyola University of Chicago
Chicago, Illinois

Scott Waugh
Department of History
University of California, Los Angeles
Los Angeles, California

Multicultural Advisory Board Consultants

The multicultural advisors reviewed the manuscript for appropriate historical content.

Pat A. Brown
Director of the Indianapolis
  Public Schools
  Office of African Centered
  Multicultural Education
Indianapolis Public Schools
Indianapolis, Indiana

Ogle B. Duff
Associate Professor of English
University of Pittsburgh
Pittsburgh, Pennsylvania

Mary Ellen Maddox
Black Education Commission
  Director
Los Angeles Unified School District
Los Angeles, California

Jon Reyhner
Associate Professor and Coordinator of
  the Bilingual Multicultural
  Education Program
Northern Arizona University
Flagstaff, Arizona

Ysidro Valenzuela
Fresno High School
Fresno, California

Teacher Review Panels

The following educators provided ongoing review during the development of prototypes, the table of contents, and key components of the program.

Texas Teacher Panel

Patrick Adams
Pasadena High School
Pasadena, Texas

Ellen Bell
Bellaire High School
Bellaire, Texas

Craig Grace
Lanier High School
Austin, Texas

Katie Ivey
Dimmit High School
Dimmitt, Texas

Pat Knapp
Burgess High School
El Paso, Texas

Eric R. Larson
Clark High School
Plano, Texas

Linda Marrs
Naaman Forest High School
Garland, Texas

Terry McRae
Robert E. Lee High School
Tyler, Texas

Sherrie Prahl
The Woodlands High School
The Woodlands, Texas

Dorothy Schulze
Health Careers High School
San Antonio, Texas

Liz Silva
Townview Magnet Center
Dallas, Texas

Linda Stevens
Central High School
San Angelo, Texas

Midwest Teacher Panel

Bruce Bekemeyer
Marquette High School
Chesterfield, Missouri

Margaret Campbell
Central High School
St. Louis, Missouri

Nancy Coates
Belleville East High School
Belleville, Illinois

Kim Coil
Francis Howell North High School
St. Charles, Missouri

Gary Kasprovich
Granite City High School
Granite City, Illinois

Harry McCown
Hazelwood West High School
Hazelwood, Missouri

Joseph Naumann
McCluer North High School
Florissant, Missouri

Leonard Sullivan
Pattonville High School
Maryland Hts., Missouri

Carole Weeden
Fort Zumwalt South High School
St. Peters, Missouri

Rita Wylie
Parkway West Sr. High School
Ballwin, Missouri

Teacher Reviewers

Glenn Bird
Springville High School
Springville, Utah

Michael Cady
North High School
Phoenix, Arizona

William Canter
Guilford High School
Rockford, Illinois

Nancy Coates
Belleville East High School
Belleville, Illinois

Paul Fitzgerald
Estancia High School
Costa Mesa, California

Tom McDonald
Phoenix Union HSD
Phoenix, Arizona

Myras Osman
Homewood Flossmoor High School
Flossmoor, Illinois

Dorothy Schulze
Health Careers High School
Dallas, Texas

Student Board

The following students reviewed prototype materials for the textbook.

LaShaunda Allen
Weston High School
Greenville, MS

Brandy Andreas
Rayburn High School
Pasadena, TX

Adam Bishop
Jordan High School
Sandy, UT

Jennifer Bragg
Midlothian High School
Midlothian, VA

Nicole Fevry
Midwood High School
Brooklyn, NY

Phillip Gallegos
Hilltop High School
Chula Vista, CA

Matt Gave
Stevenson Senior High School
Sterling Heights, MI

Blair Hogan
Leesville Road High School
Raleigh, NC

Ngoc Hong
Watkins Mill Senior High School
Gaithersburg, MD

Iman Jalali
Glenbrook North High School
Northbrook, IL

Vivek Makhijani
Durfee High School
Fall River, MA

Todd McDavitt
Derby High School
Derby, KS

Teniqua Mitchell
Linden-McKinley High School
Columbus, OH

Cicely Nash
Edmond Memorial High School
Edmond, OK

Brian Nebrensky
Hillsboro High School
Hillsboro, OR

Jesse Neumyer
Cumberland Valley High School
Mechanicsburg, PA

Nora Patronas
Alba High School
Bayou La Batre, LA

Lindsey Petersen
Stoughton High School
Stoughton, WI

Nicholas Price
Central Lafourche Senior
High School
Mathews, LA

Ben Richey
Fort Vancouver High School
Vancouver, WA

Karen Ryan
Silver Creek High School
San Jose, CA

Matt Shaver
Weatherford High School
Weatherford, TX

Richie Spitler
Atlantic High School
Port Orange, FL

Jessie Stoneberg
Burnsville High School
Burnsville, MN

Kelly Swick
Ocean Township High School
Oakhurst, NJ

Jason Utzig
Kenmore East High School
Tonawanda, NY

Justin Woodly
North Cobb High School
Kennesaw, GA

Beginnings of Civilization

Introduction

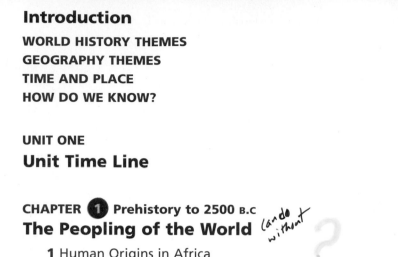

New Directions in Government and Society

Unit 3
500–1500

An Age of Exchange and Encounter

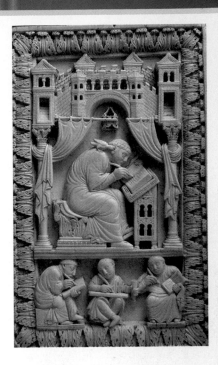

Unit 4
900–1800

Connecting Hemispheres

Absolutism to Revolution

Unit 5
1500–1900

Unit 6
1700–1914

Industrialism and the Race for Empire

The World at War

Unit 8
1945–Present

Perspectives on the Present

Skillbuilder Handbook

The Skillbuilder Handbook is at the back of the book on pages 990–1014. Refer to it when you need help in answering Think Through History questions, doing the activities entitled Interact with History, or answering questions in Section Assessments and Chapter Assessments.

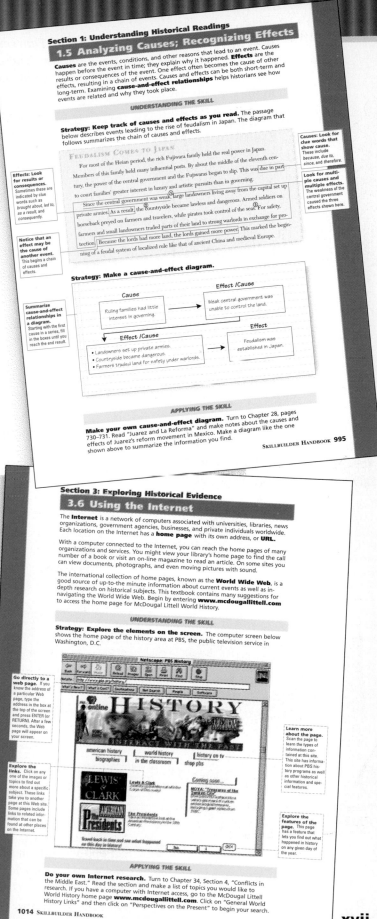

VIDEO Each video in the series *Patterns of Interaction* relates to a *Global Impact* feature in the text. These eight exciting videos show how cultural interactions have shaped our world and how patterns in history continue to the present day.

Volume 1

Building Empires
The Rise of the Persians and the Inca
Watch the Persian and Incan empires expand and rule other peoples, with unexpected results for both conquered and conquering cultures.

Trade Connects the World
Silk Roads and the Pacific Rim
Explore the legendary trade routes of the Silk Roads and the modern trade of the Pacific Rim, and notice how both affected much more than economics.

Volume 2

The Spread of Epidemic Disease
Bubonic Plague and Smallpox
Look for sweeping calamities and incredible consequences when interacting peoples bring devastating diseases to one another.

The Geography of Food
The Impact of Potatoes and Sugar
Notice how the introduction of new foods to a region provides security to some and spells disaster for millions.

Volume 3

Struggling Toward Democracy
Revolutions in Latin America and South Africa
Examine the impact of democratic ideas that incite people to join revolutions in 19th century Latin America and 20th century South Africa.

Technology Transforms an Age
The Industrial and Electronic Revolutions
See how another kind of revolution, caused by inventions in industry and communication, affects people not only a century ago but today as well.

Volume 4

Arming for War
Modern and Medieval Weapons
Watch how warring peoples' competition in military technology has resulted in a dangerous game of bigger, better, and faster throughout the ages.

Cultural Crossroads
The United States and the World
Observe how universal enjoyments like music, sports, and fashion become instruments of cultural blending across the world.

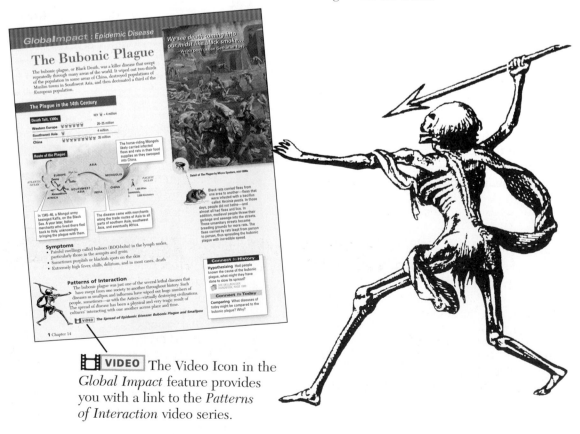

VIDEO The Video Icon in the *Global Impact* feature provides you with a link to the *Patterns of Interaction* video series.

Major Features

Features

CONNECT *to* TODAY

HISTORY THROUGH ART

Marie Antoinette, **Jacques Gautier d'Agoty**

Fresco detail by José Clemente Orozco

The sphinx of Nubia's King Taharqa

Features

**Padre José Morelos
1765–1815**

Born into poverty, Padre José Morelos did not begin to study for the priesthood until he was 25. In his parish work, he mainly served poor Indians and mestizos. In 1811, he joined Father Hidalgo, along with his parishioners. After Hidalgo's death, Morelos took skillful command of the peasant army.

By 1813, his army controlled all of southern Mexico except for the largest cities. Morelos then called a Mexican congress to set up a democratic government. The supporters of Spain, however, finally caught up with the congress. As the rebels fled, Morelos stayed behind to fight. The Spanish finally captured and shot Morelos in 1815. Napoleon knew of this priest-revolutionary and said: "Give me three generals like him and I can conquer the world."

Historical and Political Maps

Historical and Political Maps

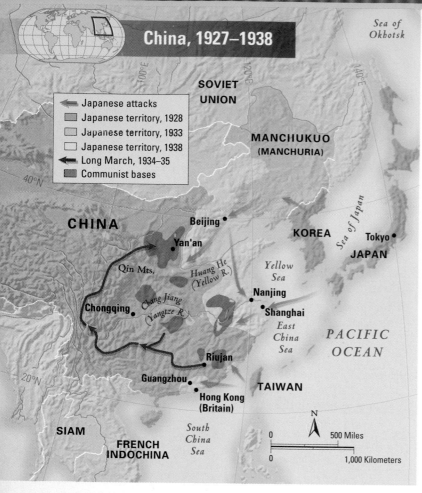

China, 1927–1938

Japanese attacks
Japanese territory, 1928
Japanese territory, 1933
Japanese territory, 1938
Long March, 1934–35
Communist bases

Sea of Okhotsk

SOVIET UNION

MANCHUKUO (MANCHURIA)

CHINA

Beijing
Yan'an
Qin Mts.
Huang He (Yellow R.)
Chongqing
Chang Jiang (Yangtze R.)
Nanjing
Shanghai

KOREA
Tokyo
JAPAN
Sea of Japan

Yellow Sea
East China Sea
PACIFIC OCEAN

Riujan
Guangzhou
Hong Kong (Britain)
TAIWAN
South China Sea

SIAM
FRENCH INDOCHINA

0 — 500 Miles
0 — 1,000 Kilometers

Charts, Graphs, and Time Lines

Infographics and Focus On

Infographics

FOCUS ON

Primary Sources and Personal Voices

VOICE FROM THE PAST
. . . one who has been an emperor
cannot endure to be a fugitive.
THEODORA, quoted in *History of the Wars*

Primary Sources and Personal Voices

VOICE FROM THE PAST
For even though some of the Western methods are different from our own, and may even be an improvement, there is little about them that is new.

KANGXI, quoted in *Emperor of China: Self-Portrait of K'ang-hsi*

World History Themes

While historical events are unique, they often are driven by similar, repeated forces. In telling the history of our world, this book pays special attention to eight significant and recurring themes. These themes are presented to show that from America, to Africa, to Asia, people are more alike than they realize. Throughout history humans have confronted similar obstacles, have struggled to achieve similar goals, and continually have strived to better themselves and the world around them.

Power and Authority

History is often made by the people and institutions in power. As you read about the world's powerful people and governments, try to answer several key questions.

- Who holds the power?
- How did that person or group get power?
- What system of government provides order in this society?
- How does the group or person in power keep or lose power?

Religious and Ethical Systems

Throughout history, humans around the world have been guided by, as much as anything else, their religious and ethical beliefs. As you examine the world's religious and ethical systems, pay attention to several important issues.

- What beliefs are held by a majority of people in a region?
- How do these major religious beliefs differ from one another?
- How do the various religious groups interact with one another?
- How do religious groups react toward nonmembers?

Revolution

Often in history, great change has been achieved only through force. As you read about the continuous overthrow of governments, institutions, and even ideas throughout history, examine several key questions.

- What long-term ideas or institutions are being overthrown?
- What caused people to make this radical change?
- What are the results of the change?

Interaction with Environment

Since the earliest of times, humans have had to deal with their surroundings in order to survive. As you read about our continuous interaction with the environment, keep in mind several important issues.

- How do humans adjust to the climate and terrain where they live?
- How have changes in the natural world forced people to change?
- What positive and negative changes have people made to their environment?

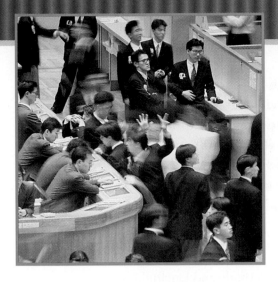

Economics

Economics has proven to be a powerful force in human history. From early times to the present, human cultures have been concerned with how to use their scarce resources to satisfy their needs. As you read about different groups, note several key issues regarding the role of economics in world history.

- What goods and services does a society produce?
- Who controls the wealth and resources of a society?
- How does a society obtain more goods and services?

Cultural Interaction

Today, people around the world share many things, from music, to food, to ideas. Human cultures actually have interacted with each other since ancient times. As you read about how different cultures have interacted, note several significant issues.

- How have cultures interacted (trade, migration, or conquest)?
- What items have cultures passed on to each other?
- What political, economic, and religious ideas have cultures shared?
- What positive and negative effects have resulted from cultural interaction?

Empire Building

Since the beginning of time, human cultures have shared a similar desire to grow more powerful—often by dominating other groups. As you read about empire building through the ages, keep in mind several key issues.

- What motivates groups to conquer other lands and people?
- How does one society gain control of others?
- How does a dominating society control and rule its subjects?

Science and Technology

All humans share an endless desire to know more about their world and to solve whatever problems they encounter. The development of science and technology has played a key role in these quests. As you read about the role of science and technology in world history, try to answer several key questions.

- What tools and methods do people use to solve the various problems they face?
- How do people gain knowledge about their world? How do they use that knowledge?
- How do new discoveries and inventions change the way people live?

Geography Themes

Geography is the study of the earth and its features. It is also an important part of human history. Since the beginning of time, all civilizations have had to control their surroundings in order to survive. In addition, geography has played a vital role in many historical events. Like history itself, geography reflects several key themes. These themes help us to understand the different ways in which geography has helped shape the story of world history.

Location

Location tells us where in the world a certain area is. Geographers describe location in two ways: *absolute* location and *relative* location. An area's absolute location is its point of latitude and longitude. Latitude is the distance in degrees north or south of the equator. Longitude is the degree distance east or west of an imaginary vertical line that runs through Greenwich, England, called the prime meridian. An area's relative location describes where it is in terms of other areas.

In absolute terms, the middle of Singapore lies at 1°20' north latitude and 103°50' east longitude. This information allows you to pinpoint Singapore on a map. In relative terms, Singapore is an island country on the southern tip of the Malay Peninsula near where the South China Sea and the Indian Ocean meet. How might Singapore's location on the sea have helped it develop into an economic power?

Human/Environment Interaction

Throughout history, humans have changed and have been changed by their environment. Because they live on an island, the people of Singapore have built a bridge in order to travel more easily to mainland Malaysia. In addition, Singapore residents have carved an inviting harbor out of parts of its coastline in order to accommodate the island's busy ocean traffic.

Singapore is one of the most densely populated countries in the world. Many of its nearly three million citizens live in the capital city, Singapore. The country's population density is about 12,000 persons per square mile. In contrast, the United States has a population density of 71 persons per square mile. What environmental challenges does this situation pose?

Region

A region is any area that has common characteristics. These characteristics may include physical factors, such as landforms or climate. They also may include cultural aspects, such as language or religion. Singapore is part of a region known as Southeast Asia. The countries of this region share such characteristics as rich, fertile soil, as well as a strong influence of Buddhism and Islam.

Because regions share similar characteristics, they often share similar concerns. In 1967, Singapore joined with the other countries of Southeast Asia to form the Association of Southeast Asian Nations. This body was created to address the region's concerns. What concerns might Singapore have that are unique?

Place

Place, in geography, indicates what an area looks like in both physical and human terms. The physical setting of an area—its landforms, soil, climate, and resources—are aspects of place. So are the different cultures which inhabit an area.

The physical characteristics of Singapore include a hot, moist climate with numerous rain forests. In human terms, Singapore's population is mostly Chinese. How does Singapore's human characteristic tie it to other countries?

Movement

In geography, movement is the transfer of people, goods, and ideas from one place to another. In many ways, history is the story of movement. Since early times, people have migrated in search of better places to live. They have traded with distant peoples to obtain new goods. And they have spread a wealth of ideas from culture to culture.

Singapore, which is a prosperous center of trade and finance, attracts numerous people in search of greater wealth and new goods. What about Singapore's geography makes it the ideal place for the trading of goods?

Time

While history is the story of people, it is also the examination of when events occurred. Keeping track of the order of historical events will help you to better retain and understand the material. To help you remember the order and dates of important events in history, this book contains numerous time lines. Below is some instruction on how to read a time line, as well as a look at some terms associated with tracking time in history.

How to Read a Time Line

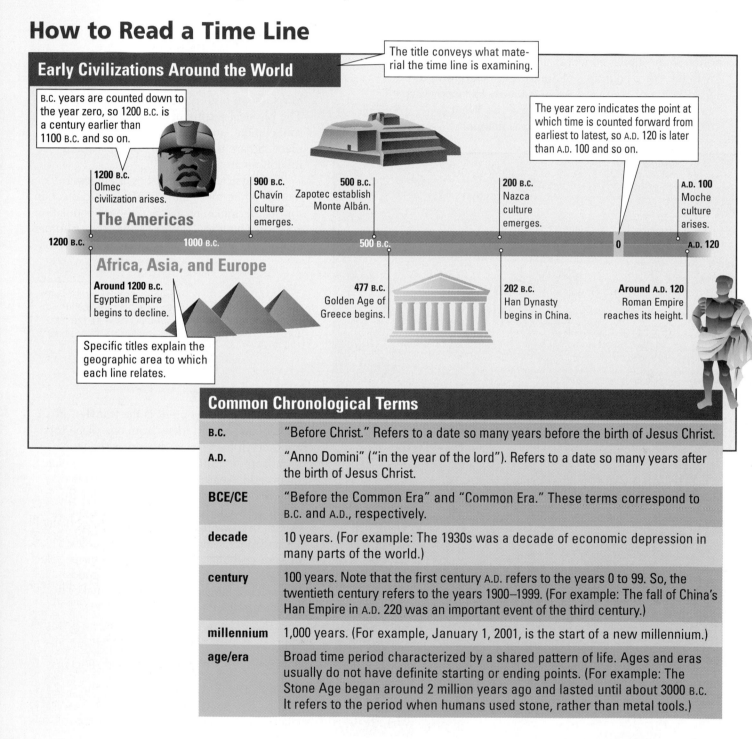

Early Civilizations Around the World

The title conveys what material the time line is examining.

B.C. years are counted down to the year zero, so 1200 B.C. is a century earlier than 1100 B.C. and so on.

The year zero indicates the point at which time is counted forward from earliest to latest, so A.D. 120 is later than A.D. 100 and so on.

The Americas

1200 B.C. Olmec civilization arises.

900 B.C. Chavín culture emerges.

500 B.C. Zapotec establish Monte Albán.

200 B.C. Nazca culture emerges.

A.D. 100 Moche culture arises.

1200 B.C. — 1000 B.C. — 500 B.C. — 0 — A.D. 120

Africa, Asia, and Europe

Around 1200 B.C. Egyptian Empire begins to decline.

477 B.C. Golden Age of Greece begins.

202 B.C. Han Dynasty begins in China.

Around A.D. 120 Roman Empire reaches its height.

Specific titles explain the geographic area to which each line relates.

Common Chronological Terms

B.C.	"Before Christ." Refers to a date so many years before the birth of Jesus Christ.
A.D.	"Anno Domini" ("in the year of the lord"). Refers to a date so many years after the birth of Jesus Christ.
BCE/CE	"Before the Common Era" and "Common Era." These terms correspond to B.C. and A.D., respectively.
decade	10 years. (For example: The 1930s was a decade of economic depression in many parts of the world.)
century	100 years. Note that the first century A.D. refers to the years 0 to 99. So, the twentieth century refers to the years 1900–1999. (For example: The fall of China's Han Empire in A.D. 220 was an important event of the third century.)
millennium	1,000 years. (For example, January 1, 2001, is the start of a new millennium.)
age/era	Broad time period characterized by a shared pattern of life. Ages and eras usually do not have definite starting or ending points. (For example: The Stone Age began around 2 million years ago and lasted until about 3000 B.C. It refers to the period when humans used stone, rather than metal tools.)

Place

You are about to examine not only thousands of years of history, but nearly every region of the globe. To help you visualize the faraway places you read about, this book contains numerous maps. Many of these maps contain several layers of information that provide a better understanding of how and why events in history occurred. Below is a look at how to read a map in order to obtain all of the rich information it offers.

How to Read a Map

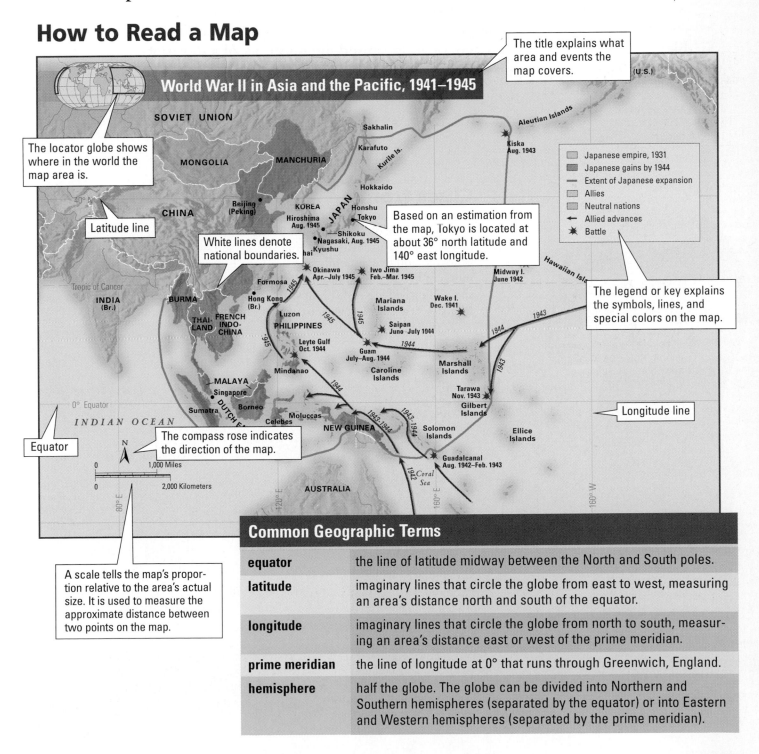

The title explains what area and events the map covers.

The locator globe shows where in the world the map area is.

Latitude line

White lines denote national boundaries.

Based on an estimation from the map, Tokyo is located at about 36° north latitude and 140° east longitude.

The legend or key explains the symbols, lines, and special colors on the map.

Longitude line

Equator

The compass rose indicates the direction of the map.

A scale tells the map's proportion relative to the area's actual size. It is used to measure the approximate distance between two points on the map.

World War II in Asia and the Pacific, 1941–1945

Legend:
- Japanese empire, 1931
- Japanese gains by 1944
- Extent of Japanese expansion
- Allies
- Neutral nations
- Allied advances
- Battle

Common Geographic Terms

equator	the line of latitude midway between the North and South poles.
latitude	imaginary lines that circle the globe from east to west, measuring an area's distance north and south of the equator.
longitude	imaginary lines that circle the globe from north to south, measuring an area's distance east or west of the prime meridian.
prime meridian	the line of longitude at 0° that runs through Greenwich, England.
hemisphere	half the globe. The globe can be divided into Northern and Southern hemispheres (separated by the equator) or into Eastern and Western hemispheres (separated by the prime meridian).

Do you like puzzles? If so, you are in luck. You are about to encounter the greatest puzzle there is: history. The study of history is much more than the recollection of dates and names. It is an attempt to answer a continuous and puzzling question: what really happened?

In their effort to solve this puzzle, historians and researchers use a variety of methods. From digging up artifacts, to uncovering eyewitness accounts, experts collect and analyze mountains of data in numerous ways. As a result, the history books you read more accurately depict what life was like in a culture 5,000 years ago, or what caused the outbreak of a devastating war. The following two pages examine some of the pieces used to solve the puzzle of history.

Clues from an Ancient Girl

In 1995, an anthropologist discovered the mummified and frozen remains of a teenage girl in the Andes Mountains of South America. Scientists believe that she is about 500 years old and was a member of the Inca Empire. Because much of her remains are well preserved, scientists hope she will provide them with new information about one of the Americas' most powerful ancient cultures.

An analysis of her stomach content may provide information about the Inca diet.

Her clothing, believed to belong to the upper class, should shed new light on how noble Inca women dressed.

Some of her DNA remains intact, which will help scientists determine whether she has any living descendants.

Modern Science

The ever-improving field of science has lent its hand in the search to learn more about the past. Using everything from microscopes to computers, researchers have shed new light on many historical mysteries. Here, a researcher uses computer technology to determine what the owner of a prehistoric human skull may have looked like.

Written Sources

Historians often look to written documents for insight into the past. There are various types of written sources. Documents written during the same time period as an event are known as *primary* sources. They include such things as diaries and newspapers. They also include drawings, such as the one shown here by Italian painter and inventor, Leonardo da Vinci. His rough sketch of a helicopter-type machine tells us that as early as the late 1400s, humans considered mechanical flight. Material written about an event later, such as books, are known as *secondary* sources. Some written sources began as oral tradition—legends, myths, and beliefs passed on by spoken word from generation to generation.

Digging Up History

Researchers have learned much about the past by discovering the remains of ancient societies. Spearheads like these, which date back to around 9,500 B.C., were found throughout North America. They tell us among other things that the early Americans were hunters. These spearheads were once considered to be the earliest evidence of humankind in the Americas. However, as an example of how history continues to change, scientists recently found evidence of human life in South America as early as 10,500 B.C.

Rising out of the sands of Egypt are the enduring signs of the ancient world. Pictured here are two of the three major pyramids of Giza, which are thought to be about 4,500 years old. Scholars believe that the early Egyptians built these and other pyramids as elaborate tombs for their rulers.

	3500 B.C.	3000 B.C.	2500 B.C.	2000 B.C.

CHAPTER ➊ Prehistory to 2500 B.C.

The Peopling of the World

4,000,000 B.C. to 8000 B.C.

4,000,000 B.C. *Africa*
Early hominids appear

2,500,000 B.C.
Paleolithic Age begins

1,600,000 B.C. *Africa, Asia, Europe* Homo erectus appears

200,000 B.C. *Europe, Southwest Asia*
Neanderthals appear

40,000 B.C. *Europe*
Cro-Magnons appear

8000 B.C. Last Ice Age ends; Neolithic Age begins

8000 B.C. *Africa, Asia*
Agriculture begins

3000 B.C. *Mesopotamia*
Bronze Age begins

3000 B.C. *Mesopotamia*
Civilization emerges in Sumer

2600 B.C. *Mesopotamia* ▶

CHAPTER ➋ 3500 B.C.–450 B.C.

Early River Valley Civilizations

3100 B.C. *Egypt*
Upper and Lower Egypt unite

2600 B.C. *Egypt*
Great Pyramid is built

3000 B.C. *Mesopotamia*
City-states rise in Sumer

2500 B.C. *Indus Valley*
Planned cities rise

2350 B.C. *Mesopotamia*
Sargon of Akkad builds empire

2080 B.C. *Egypt*
Middle Kingdom begins

◀ 2600 B.C. *Egypt*

CHAPTER ➌ 3500 B.C.–259 B.C.

People and Ideas on the Move

CHAPTER ➍ 1570 B.C.–200 B.C.

First Age of Empires

3500 B.C.	3000 B.C.	2500 B.C.	2000 B.C.

Living History
Unit 1 Portfolio Project

THEME Interaction with Environment

Your portfolio for this unit will track the ways early humans adjusted to survive in their many environments, as well as the changes they made to those environments. You will show the earliest peoples' surroundings and the technology they created to help them solve basic problems of survival.

Living History Project Choices

Each Chapter Assessment offers you choices of ways to show how the early humans interacted with their environment in that chapter. Activities include the following:

Chapter ❶ field notes, bio board, top 10 list

Chapter ❷ interviews, poems, maps

Chapter ❸ map, dialogue, myth

Chapter ❹ mural, map, short story

2000 B.C. *China*
Xia Dynasty emerges

1790 B.C. *Mesopotamia*
Hammurabi codifies laws

1640 B.C. *Egypt*
Hyksos invade Egypt

1532 B.C. *China*
Shang Dynasty begins

1500 B.C. *Indus Valley*
Indus Valley cities decline

1027 B.C. *China*
Zhou Dynasty begins

771 B.C. *China*
Nomads sack Hao, Zhou capital; dynasty moves to Luoyang

256 B.C. *China*
Zhou dynasty ends

2000 B.C. *Anatolia*
Hittites settle

1700 B.C. *Asian Steppes*
Indo-Europeans begin massive migrations

1500 B.C. *India*
Aryans move into Indus River Valley

1100 B.C. *Mediterranean*
Phoenicians begin to dominate trade

1020 B.C. *Canaan*
King Saul unites Hebrews

922 B.C. *Canaan*
Hebrew kingdom divides into Israel and Judah

750–550 B.C. *India*
Hindus compose the *Upanishads*

722 B.C. *Mesopotamia*
Assyrians conquer Israel

445 B.C. *Canaan*
Jews rebuild walls of Jerusalem

483 B.C. *India*
The Buddha dies

◄ **Statue of Dying Buddha**

2000 B.C. *Nubia*
First Nubian kingdom, Kerma, arises

1570 B.C. *Egypt*
New Kingdom arises

◄ **521 B.C. *Persia***

1472 B.C. *Egypt*
Hatshepsut becomes pharoah

1285 B.C. *Egypt*
Battle of Kadesh between Egyptians and Hittites

850 B.C. *Assyria* Assyria builds a large empire

751 B.C. *Kush* Kushite king Piankhi conquers Egypt

550 B.C. *Persia* Cyrus builds Persian Empire

538 B.C. *Persia* Cyrus allows Jews to return to Jerusalem

521 B.C. *Persia* Darius claims throne of Persia

479 B.C. *China*
Confucius dies

250 B.C. *Africa* Kingdom of Meroë prospers

221 B.C. *China*
Shi Huangdi becomes emperor

202 B.C. *China*
Han Dynasty replaces Qin Dynasty

CHAPTER 1

The Peopling of the World, Prehistory—2500 B.C.

PREVIEWING THEMES

Interaction with Environment

As early humans spread out over the world, they adapted to each environment they encountered. They learned to fashion tools, to master fire, and to make clothing from animal skins. As time progressed, they learned to harness natural resources.

Science and Technology

Even the earliest prehistoric peoples came up with new ideas, tools, and inventions to solve problems of survival. As people began to live in settlements, they continued to develop new technology to control the environment.

Economics

Early humans hunted animals and gathered wild plant foods. Then about 10,000 years ago, they learned to tame animals and to plant crops. Gradually, more complex economies developed. Extra food supplies freed some people to learn special crafts and to become traders.

🡒 **INTERNET CONNECTION**

Visit us at **www.mcdougallittell.com** to learn more about human prehistory, the development of civilization, and related topics.

PREHISTORIC WORLD TO 2500 B.C.

UKRAINE

Black Sea

Caspian Sea

Catal Huyuk

ATLANTIC OCEAN

Mediterranean Sea

Ur

Red Sea

Nile River

Tropic of Cancer

0° Prime Meridian

AFRICA

Niger River

ETHIOPIA

Bones from mammoths—gigantic woolly creatures—made unique building materials. Around **20,000 B.C.**, prehistoric hunters in the **Ukraine** used such bones to construct an elaborate hut weighing 23 tons. A pair of huge tusks formed a curved entranceway.

40°W · 40°E

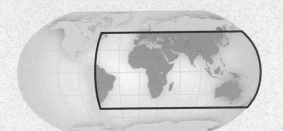

ASIA

PACIFIC OCEAN

40°N

Around **2600 B.C.** in **Ur,** an ancient city located in present-day Iraq, the queen went to her grave in style. Buried in a royal tomb, she wore a magnificent gold headdress that would show her power in the next life. Her large hoop earrings were a fashion trend among Ur's wealthy women.

Equator 0°

INDIAN OCEAN

In **1974**, Donald Johanson discovered a 3.5 million-year-old fossil, nicknamed **Lucy.** He explained Lucy's claim to fame: "She is the oldest, most complete, best-preserved skeleton of any erect-walking human ancestor that has ever been found." About 47 of her 207 bones made up her reconstructed skeleton.

Tropic of Capricorn

◻ Early civilizations

N

0   1000 Miles
0   2000 Kilometers

80°E   120°E   160°E

5

You have joined a team of scientists on an expedition to an ancient site where early humans once lived. The scientists' goal is to search for evidence that might unlock the mysteries of the past.

You're an eyewitness to their astounding discovery—human-made tools around 5,000 years old.

This small sharp-tipped tool is made of bone.

X-rays indicate that the wedge-shaped blade of this tool is made of copper. Birch tar, a gummy substance from the bark of a tree, binds the blade to a 2-foot-long wooden handle partially wrapped with strips of animal hide.

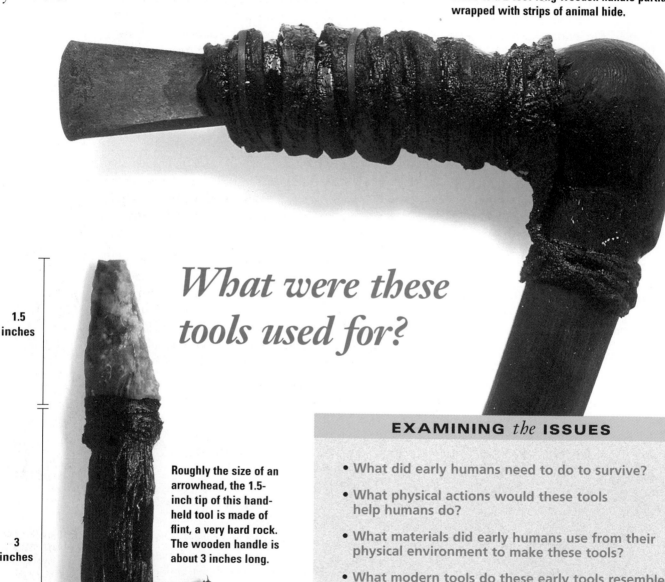

What were these tools used for?

1.5 inches

3 inches

Roughly the size of an arrowhead, the 1.5-inch tip of this hand-held tool is made of flint, a very hard rock. The wooden handle is about 3 inches long.

EXAMINING *the* ISSUES

• What did early humans need to do to survive?

• What physical actions would these tools help humans do?

• What materials did early humans use from their physical environment to make these tools?

• What modern tools do these early tools resemble?

As a class, discuss these questions. In your discussion, think about recent tools and inventions that have dramatically changed people's daily lives.

As you read about the ancestors of present-day humans, notice how early toolmakers applied their creativity and problem-solving skills.

Human Origins in Africa

TERMS & NAMES
- artifact
- culture
- hominid
- Paleolithic Age
- Neolithic Age
- technology
- *Homo sapiens*

MAIN IDEA

Fossil evidence shows that the earliest humans originated in Africa.

WHY IT MATTERS NOW

Early humans' discoveries helped them survive, grow in numbers, and spread across the globe.

SETTING THE STAGE What were the earliest humans like? Many people have asked themselves this question. Because there are no written records of prehistoric peoples, scientists have to piece together information about the past. Teams of scientists use a variety of research methods and techniques to learn more about how, where, and when early humans developed. Interestingly, recent discoveries provide the most knowledge about human origins and the way prehistoric people lived. Yet the picture of prehistory is still far from complete.

Scientists Search for Human Origins

Written documents provide a window to the distant past. For several thousand years, people have recorded information about their beliefs, activities, and important events. Prehistory, however, dates back to the time before the invention of writing—roughly 5,000 years ago. Without access to written records, scientists investigating the lives of prehistoric peoples face special challenges.

Vocabulary
excavating: uncovering by digging

Scientists Discover Clues Specially trained scientists work like detectives to uncover the story of prehistoric peoples. Archaeologists are scientists who learn about early people by excavating and studying the traces of early settlements. An excavated site, called an archaeological dig, provides one of the richest sources of clues to the prehistoric way of life. Archaeologists sift through the dirt in a small plot of land. They analyze all existing evidence, such as bones and artifacts. Bones might reveal what the people looked like, how tall they were, and how long they lived. **Artifacts** are remains, such as tools, jewelry, and other human-made objects. These items might hint at how people dressed, what work they did, or how they worshiped.

THINK THROUGH HISTORY
A. Making Inferences Why are scientists who study prehistory so important in providing knowledge about the distant past?

Scientists called anthropologists study **culture,** or people's unique way of life. Anthropologists examine the artifacts at archaeological digs. From these, they re-create a picture of early people's cultural behavior, including customs, family life, and social relationships.

Other scientists, called paleontologists, study fossils—evidence of early life preserved in rocks. Human fossils often consist of small fragments of teeth, skulls, or other bones. Paleontologists use complex techniques to date ancient fossil remains and rocks. Archaeologists, anthropologists, paleontologists, and other scientists work as a team to make new discoveries about how prehistoric people lived.

This artifact from around 200,000 B.C. is a hand ax made of flint. An all-purpose tool, the hand ax was probably a hunting weapon, chopper, scraper, and slicer.

Mary Leakey Finds Footprints In the mid-1970s, Mary Leakey, an archaeologist, led a scientific expedition to the region of Laetoli in Tanzania, an East African nation. There she and her team looked for new clues about human origins. In 1978, they made an amazing discovery. They found prehistoric footprints that resembled those of modern humans. These footprints were made by humanlike beings now called australopithecines (aw·STRAY·loh·PIHTH·ih·SYNZ). Humans and other creatures that walk

The Peopling of the World **7**

Australopithecines
• 4 million to 1 million B.C.
• found in southern and eastern Africa
• brain size 500 cm³ (cubic centimeters)
• first humanlike creature to walk upright

Homo habilis
• 2.5 million to 1.5 million B.C.
• found in East Africa
• brain size 700 cm³
• first to make stone tools

4 million years ago
Australopithecines

3 million years ago

Homo habilis

HISTORY MAKERS

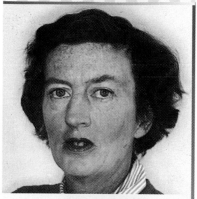

**Mary Leakey
1913–1996**

Born in London, England, Mary Leakey left a remarkable legacy in the fields of archaeology and anthropology. "She was one of the world's great originals," said a scientist who worked with the Leakey family on fossil hunts. Mary earned respect for her excavations and well-documented findings.

At 22, she made her first visit to East Africa. In her autobiography she reflected on her experiences there:

"I am lucky enough to have been involved for half a century with work, mostly in East Africa, that very much belongs to everyone, since it concerns the human origins that are common to the whole human race."

---

upright, such as australopithecines, are called **hominids.** The Laetoli footprints provided striking evidence about the origins of humans:

A VOICE FROM THE PAST

What do these footprints tell us? First, . . . that at least 3,600,000 years ago, what I believe to be man's direct ancestor walked fully upright with a . . . free-striding gait. Second, that the form of the foot was exactly the same as ours. . . . [The footprints produced] a kind of poignant time wrench. At one point, . . . she [the female hominid] stops, pauses, turns to the left to glance at some possible threat or irregularity, and then continues to the north. This motion, so intensely human, transcends time. . . .

MARY LEAKEY, quoted in *National Geographic*

Johanson Discovers "Lucy" While Mary Leakey was working in East Africa, American anthropologist Donald Johanson and his team were also searching for fossils. They were exploring sites in Ethiopia, 1,000 miles to the north. In 1974, Johanson's team made a remarkable find—an unusually complete skeleton of an adult female hominid. They nicknamed her "Lucy" after the Beatles song "Lucy in the Sky with Diamonds." She had lived around 3.5 million years ago—the oldest hominid found to date.

Hominids in Motion Lucy and the hominids who left their footprints in East Africa were species of australopithecines. Walking upright helped them travel distances more easily. They were also able to spot threatening animals and carry food and children.

These early hominids had already developed the opposable thumb. This means that the tip of the thumb can cross the palm of the hand. The opposable thumb was crucial for tasks such as picking up small objects and making tools. (To see its importance, try picking up a coin with just the index and middle fingers. Imagine all the other things that cannot be done without the opposable thumb.)

**THINK THROUGH HISTORY
B. Drawing Conclusions**
Why were the discoveries of hominid footprints and "Lucy" important?

Progress During the Old Stone Age

The invention of tools, mastery over fire, and the development of language are some of the most impressive achievements in human history. These occurred during the prehistoric period known as the Stone Age. It spanned an enormous length of time. The earlier and longer part of the Stone Age, called the Old Stone Age or **Paleolithic Age,** lasted from about 2.5 million to 8000 B.C. The oldest stone chopping tools date back to this era. The New Stone Age, or **Neolithic Age,** began about 8000 B.C. and ended as early as 3000 B.C. in some areas. People who lived during this second phase of the Stone Age learned to polish stone tools, make pottery, grow crops, and raise animals.

Much of the Paleolithic Age occurred during the period in the earth's history known as the Ice Age. During this time, glaciers alternately advanced and retreated as many as 18 times. The last of these ice ages ended about 10,000 years ago. By the beginning of the Neolithic Age, glaciers had retreated to roughly the same area they now occupy.

Vocabulary
glaciers: huge masses of slowly moving ice

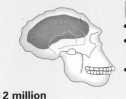

Homo erectus
- 1.6 million to 30,000 B.C.
- found in Africa, Asia, and Europe
- brain size 1,000 cm³

Neanderthal
- 200,000 to 30,000 B.C.
- found in Europe and Southwest Asia
- brain size 1,450 cm³
- first to have ritual burials

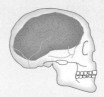

Cro-Magnon
- 40,000 to 8000 B.C.
- found in Europe
- brain size 1,400 cm³
- fully modern humans
- created art

2 million years ago — Homo erectus — **1 million years ago** — **Present** — Neanderthal — Cro-Magnon

Homo Habilis: **The First Toolmaker?** Before the australopithecines eventually vanished, new hominids appeared in East Africa around 2.5 million years ago. In 1960, Mary Leakey and her husband, Louis, discovered a hominid fossil at Olduvai (OHL·duh·vy) Gorge in northern Tanzania. The Leakeys named the fossil *Homo habilis,* which means "man of skill." Scientists jokingly called this hominid "Handy Man." The Leakeys and other researchers found tools made of lava rock. They believed *Homo habilis* used these tools to cut meat and crack open bones. Modern archaeologists have shown that these stone blades could butcher elephant meat.

Homo Erectus **Is More Intelligent** About 1.6 million years ago, before *Homo habilis* left the scene, another species of hominids appeared in East Africa. This species is now known as *Homo erectus,* or "upright man." Some anthropologists believe *Homo erectus* was a more intelligent and adaptable species than *Homo habilis. Homo erectus* people used intelligence to develop **technology**—ways of applying knowledge, tools, and inventions to meet their needs. Tools made the task of survival easier. These hominids gradually became skillful hunters and invented more sophisticated tools for digging, scraping, and cutting. They also eventually became the first hominids to migrate, or to move, from Africa. Fossils and stone tools show that bands of *Homo erectus* hunters settled in India, China, Southeast Asia, and Europe.

According to anthropologists, *Homo erectus* was the first to use fire. Fire provided warmth in cold climates, cooked food, and frightened away attacking animals. A band of hunters may have carried torches to drive herds of animals into marshes in order to slaughter them. The control of fire also probably helped *Homo erectus* settle new lands.

Homo erectus might also have developed the beginnings of spoken language. Language, like technology, probably gave *Homo erectus* greater control over the environment and boosted chances for survival. The teamwork needed to plan hunts and cooperate in other tasks probably relied on language. *Homo erectus* might have named objects, places, animals, and plants and exchanged ideas.

THINK THROUGH HISTORY
C. Recognizing Effects How did *Homo erectus* use fire to control the environment?

CONNECT *to* TODAY

Cheddar Man

In 1997, scientists at Oxford University tested samples of DNA from a Stone Age skeleton nicknamed "Cheddar Man." This young hunter from around 7150 B.C. was found buried in the Cheddar Caves in England.

Scientists then compared the skeleton's samples to samples from people whose families had lived in the area for generations. The results of the genetic tests surprised Adrian Targett, a 42-year-old history teacher who participated in the study. He discovered that Cheddar Man was his ancient relative. Cheddar Man's and Targett's DNA were nearly identical. Scientists believe that the DNA match also proves that Britain's native population is descended from Stone Age humans.

The Dawn of Modern Humans

Many scientists believe *Homo erectus* eventually developed into **Homo sapiens**—the species name for modern humans. *Homo sapiens* means "wise men." While they physically resembled *Homo erectus, Homo sapiens* had much larger brains. Scientists have traditionally classified Neanderthals and Cro-Magnons as early groups of *Homo sapiens.* However, in 1997, DNA tests on a Neanderthal skeleton indicated that Neanderthals were not ancestors of modern humans. They were, however, affected by the arrival of Cro-Magnons, who may have competed with Neanderthals for land and food.

Neanderthals' Way of Life In 1856, as quarry workers were digging for limestone in the Neander Valley in Germany, they spotted fossilized bone fragments. These were the remains of Neanderthals, whose bones were discovered elsewhere in

Background
Thal (as in *Neanderthal*) is the German word for valley.

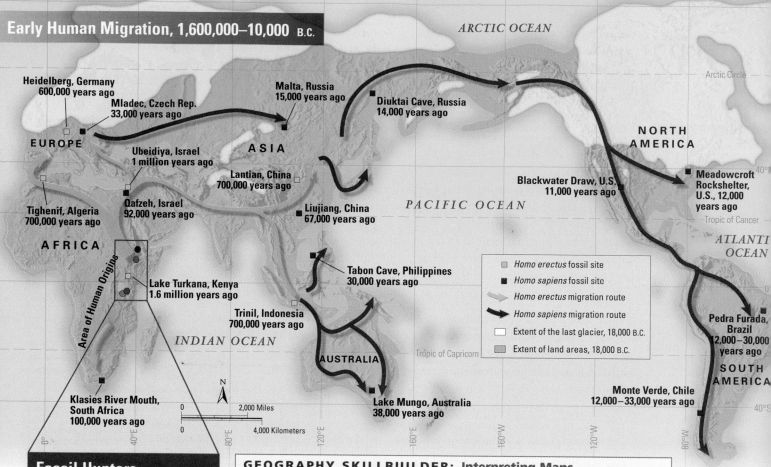

Early Human Migration, 1,600,000–10,000 B.C.

ARCTIC OCEAN

Arctic Circle

EUROPE

Heidelberg, Germany
600,000 years ago

Mladec, Czech Rep.
33,000 years ago

Malta, Russia
15,000 years ago

Diuktai Cave, Russia
14,000 years ago

NORTH AMERICA

Meadowcroft
Rockshelter,
U.S., 12,000
years ago

40°N

ASIA

Ubeidiya, Israel
1 million years ago

Lantian, China
700,000 years ago

Blackwater Draw, U.S.
11,000 years ago

PACIFIC OCEAN

Tropic of Cancer

Tighenif, Algeria
700,000 years ago

Qafzeh, Israel
92,000 years ago

Liujiang, China
67,000 years ago

ATLANTIC OCEAN

AFRICA

Area of Human Origins

Lake Turkana, Kenya
1.6 million years ago

Tabon Cave, Philippines
30,000 years ago

Pedra Furada,
Brazil
12,000–30,000
years ago

SOUTH AMERICA

Trinil, Indonesia
700,000 years ago

INDIAN OCEAN

AUSTRALIA

Tropic of Capricorn

- ☐ *Homo erectus* fossil site
- ■ *Homo sapiens* fossil site
- *Homo erectus* migration route
- *Homo sapiens* migration route
- ☐ Extent of the last glacier, 18,000 B.C.
- ▨ Extent of land areas, 18,000 B.C.

Klasies River Mouth,
South Africa
100,000 years ago

N

0   2,000 Miles

0   4,000 Kilometers

Lake Mungo, Australia
38,000 years ago

Monte Verde, Chile
12,000–33,000 years ago

40°S

Fossil Hunters

Famous Finds

● **1960** At Olduvai Gorge, Louis Leakey finds 2 million-year-old stone tools.

● **1974** In Ethiopia, Donald Johanson finds "Lucy," a 3.5 million-year-old hominid skeleton.

● **1978** At Laetoli, Mary Leakey finds 3.6-million-year-old hominid footprints.

● **1994** In Ethiopia, an international team of scientists finds 2.33 million-year-old hominid jaw.

GEOGRAPHY SKILLBUILDER: Interpreting Maps

1. **Movement** *To what continents did* Homo erectus *groups migrate after leaving Africa?*

2. **Human-Environment Interaction** *What do the migration routes of* Homo sapiens *reveal about their survival skills and ability to adapt?*

Europe and Southwest Asia. These people were powerfully built. They had heavy slanted brows, well-developed muscles, and thick bones. To many people, the name "Neanderthal" calls up the comic-strip image of a club-carrying caveman. However, archaeological discoveries reveal a more realistic picture of these early hominids, who lived between 200,000 and 30,000 years ago.

Evidence suggests that Neanderthals tried to explain and control their world. They developed religious beliefs and performed rituals. About 60,000 years ago, Neanderthals held a funeral for a man in Shanidar Cave, located in northeastern Iraq. Archaeologists theorize that during the funeral, the Neanderthal's family covered his body with flowers. The prehistoric funeral points to a belief in a world beyond the grave. Fossil hunter Richard Leakey, the son of Mary and Louis Leakey, wrote about the meaning of this Neanderthal burial:

A VOICE FROM THE PAST

The Shanidar events . . . speak clearly of a deep feeling for the spiritual quality of life. A concern for the fate of the human soul is universal in human societies today, and it was evidently a theme of Neanderthal society too. There is also reason to believe that the Neanderthals cared for the old and the sick of their group. A number of individuals buried at the Shanidar Cave, for instance, showed signs of injury during life, and in one case a man was severely crippled. . . . These people lived for a long time, although they needed constant support and care to do so.

RICHARD E. LEAKEY, *The Making of Mankind*

THINK THROUGH HISTORY
D. Comparing
How were Neanderthals similar to people today?

Neanderthals were also resourceful. They survived harsh Ice Age winters by living in caves or temporary shelters made of wood and animal skins. Animal bones found with fossils of Neanderthals indicate their ability to hunt in subarctic regions of Europe. To cut up and skin their prey, Neanderthals fashioned stone blades, scrapers, and other tools.

The Neanderthals survived for some 170,000 years and then vanished about 30,000 years ago. Their disappearance remains a mystery.

Cro-Magnons Emerge About 40,000 years ago, a group of prehistoric humans called Cro-Magnons appeared. Their skeletal remains show that they are identical to modern humans.

Unlike the Neanderthals, Cro-Magnons planned their hunts. They studied animals' habits and stalked their prey. Evidently, Cro-Magnons' superior hunting strategies allowed them to survive more easily. This may have caused Cro-Magnon populations to grow at a slightly faster rate and eventually replace the Neanderthals. Cro-Magnons' advanced skill in spoken language may also have helped them to plan more difficult projects. This cooperation perhaps gave them an edge over the Neanderthals.

THINK THROUGH HISTORY
E. Contrasting
Why did Cro-Magnons have a better chance of survival than Neanderthals?

Recent Findings Add New Knowledge The story of human origins is constantly changing with new discoveries. Reports of such findings continue to update when and where various species of hominids are believed to have originated. In 1994, two fossil hunters in Ethiopia found a 2.33 million-year-old jaw. It was the oldest fossil belonging to the species that includes modern humans. They also unearthed stone tools at the same site. This find suggests that the first toolmakers emerged earlier than previously thought.

In 1996, a team of researchers from Canada and the United States, including a high school student from New York, dated a Neanderthal bone flute. They believe it is between 43,000 and 82,000 years old. This discovery hints at a previously unknown talent of the Neanderthals—their gift of musical expression.

Each new scientific discovery helps add further details to the still sketchy picture of human prehistory. As time progressed, early humans' skills and tools for surviving and adapting to their environment became more sophisticated. These technological advances would help launch a revolution in the way people lived.

SPOTLIGHT ON

Time Line of Planet Earth
Imagine the 102 stories of the Empire State Building as a scale for a time line of the earth's history. Each story represents about 40 million years. Modern human beings have existed for just a tiny percentage of the life of this planet.

Present

1 billion years ago

2 billion years ago

3 billion years ago

40,000 years ago
Cro-Magnons appear.
200,000 years ago
Neanderthals appear.

4 million years ago
Australopithecines appear.

65 million years ago
Dinosaurs disappear; first mammals appear.

240 million years ago
First dinosaurs appear.

3.5 billion years ago First single-cell life appears.

4 billion years ago

4.4 billion years ago
Earth is formed.

Section 1 Assessment

1. TERMS & NAMES

Identify
- artifact
- culture
- hominid
- Paleolithic Age
- Neolithic Age
- technology
- *Homo sapiens*

2. TAKING NOTES

Create a chart like the one below, showing the advances, discoveries, and inventions of hominids.

Australo-pithecines	*Homo erectus*	Nean-derthals	Cro-Magnons

3. SYNTHESIZING

How do recent findings keep revising knowledge of the prehistoric past?

THINK ABOUT
- modern scientific methods
- the way various species of hominids are classified
- dates relating to hominids

4. ANALYZING THEMES

Interaction with Environment Which of the following skills—toolmaking, the use of fire, or the development of language—do you think gave hominids the most control over their environment? Why?

THINK ABOUT
- the kinds of tools early humans developed
- the various uses of fire
- the benefits of language

TERMS & NAMES
- nomad
- hunter-gatherer
- Neolithic Revolution
- slash-and-burn farming
- domestication

2 Humans Try to Control Nature

MAIN IDEA	WHY IT MATTERS NOW
The development of agriculture spurred an increase in population and the growth of a settled way of life.	New methods for obtaining food and the development of technology laid the foundations for modern civilizations.

SETTING THE STAGE By about 40,000 years ago, human beings had become fully modern in their physical appearance. With a shave, a haircut, and a suit, a Cro-Magnon man would have looked like a businessman. However, over the following thousands of years, the human way of life underwent incredible changes. People developed new technology, artistic skills, and most importantly, agriculture.

Achievements in Technology and Art

Early modern humans quickly distinguished themselves from their ancestors, who had devoted most of their time to the task of survival. As inventors and artists, more advanced humans stepped up the pace of cultural changes.

A New Tool Kit For thousands of years, men and women of the Old Stone Age were nomads. **Nomads** wander from place to place, rather than making permanent settlements. These highly mobile people were always searching for new sources of food. Nomadic groups whose food supply depends on hunting animals and collecting plant foods are called **hunter-gatherers.** Prehistoric hunter-gatherers, such as roving bands of Cro-Magnons, increased their food supply by inventing tools. For example, hunters crafted special spears that enabled them to kill game at greater distances. Digging sticks helped food gatherers pry plants loose at the roots.

Early modern humans had launched a technological revolution. They skillfully used stone, bone, and wood to fashion more than 100 different tools. These expanded tool kits included knives to kill and butcher game and fish hooks and harpoons to catch fish. A chisel-like cutter was designed to make other tools. Cro-Magnons used bone needles to sew clothing made of animal hides.

Paleolithic Art The tools of early modern humans explain how they met their survival needs. Yet their world best springs to life through their artistic creations. Necklaces of seashells, lion teeth, and bear claws adorned both men and women. People ground mammoth tusks into polished beads. They also carved small realistic sculptures of animals that inhabited their world.

The best-known Stone Age works of art are the paintings on the walls and ceilings of European caves, mainly in France and Spain. Here early artists drew lifelike images of wild animals. Cave artists made colored paints from charcoal, mud, and animal blood. In Africa, early artists engraved pictures on rocks or painted scenes in caves or rock shelters. In Australia, they created paintings on large rocks.

SPOTLIGHT ON

The Iceman's Tool Kit

In 1991, a German couple made an accidental discovery. It gave archaeologists a firsthand look at the technology of early toolmakers. Near the border of Austria and Italy, the two hikers spotted the mummified body of a prehistoric traveler, preserved in ice for some 5,000 years.

Nicknamed the "Iceman," this early human was not empty-handed. The tool kit found with him included a six-foot longbow and a deerskin case with 14 arrows. It also contained a stick with an antler tip for sharpening flint blades, a small flint dagger in a woven sheath, and a copper ax. Unfortunately, officials damaged both Iceman's belongings and his body as they tried to remove him from the ice.

THINK THROUGH HISTORY
A. Making Inferences How did Cro-Magnons' new tool kit make the task of survival easier?

Cave Painting

Prehistoric paintings probably served a more meaningful role than just showing vivid scenes from daily life. They may have represented religious beliefs. Early artists may have also hoped their images had magical power that would bring hunters good luck. Perhaps some paintings acted as a kind of textbook to help young hunters identify various animals. The use of pictures to communicate information represents an important first step in the development of writing.

Algeria

Farming and herding gradually replaced hunting as a means of getting food. This African cave painting from Algeria shows women and children tending cattle. The white rings—symbols for huts—illustrate an early version of signs used in writing.

Australia

This rock painting from Australia features two humanlike figures holding up their hands. Early artists used stencils to create these outstretched hands, which commonly appear in Australian rock art.

France

Stampeding wild horses and bison seem to come alive in this prehistoric painting below from Lascaux Cave in Francè. After viewing such striking scenes, the world-famous, 20th-century artist Picasso reportedly said, "We have learned nothing."

Connect *to* History

Comparing What do you think is the purpose of each of these paintings?

SEE SKILLBUILDER HANDBOOK, PAGE 996.

Connect *to* Today

Analyzing Motives Prehistoric artists painted images on the walls of caves. What motives do you think compel today's artists to paint murals on the walls of city buildings?

 INTERNET CONNECTION

Visit us at **www.mcdougallittell.com** to learn more about cave and rock paintings.

The Neolithic Revolution

For thousands upon thousands of years, humans survived by hunting game and gathering edible plants. They lived in bands of no more than two dozen to three dozen people. The men almost certainly did the hunting. The women gathered fruits, berries, roots, and grasses. Then about 10,000 years ago, some of the women may have scattered seeds near a regular campsite. When they returned the next season, they may have found new crops growing. This discovery would usher in the **Neolithic Revolution,** or the agricultural revolution—the far-reaching changes in human life resulting from the beginnings of farming. The shift from food-gathering to food-producing culture represents one of the great breakthroughs in history.

Vocabulary
edible: safe to eat

Causes of the Agricultural Revolution Scientists do not know exactly why the agricultural revolution occurred during this period. Change in climate was probably a key factor. Rising temperatures worldwide provided longer growing seasons and drier land for cultivating wild grasses. A rich supply of grain helped support a small population boom. As populations slowly rose, hunter-gatherers felt pressure to find new food sources. Farming offered an attractive alternative. Unlike hunting, farming provided a steady source of food.

Background
The agricultural revolution caused a dramatic change in human diet. Hunter-gatherers consumed about 80 percent meat and 20 percent plant foods. The agricultural revolution reversed these percentages.

Agricultural Revolution

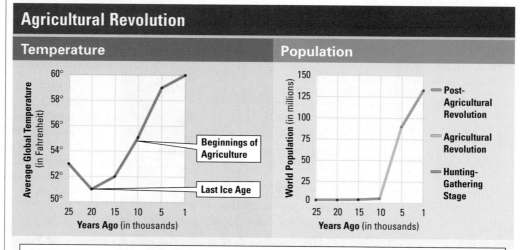

Temperature

Population

SKILLBUILDER: Interpreting Charts
1. *How was the agricultural revolution linked to a change in temperature?*
2. *What effect did the agricultural revolution have on population growth? Why?*

Early Farming Methods Some groups practiced **slash-and-burn farming,** in which they cut trees or grasses and burned them to clear a field. The remaining ashes fertilized the soil. Farmers planted crops for a year or two. Then they moved on to another area of land. After several years, the trees and grass grew back, and other farmers repeated the process of slashing and burning.

Domestication of Animals Food gatherers' understanding of plants probably spurred the development of farming. Meanwhile, hunters' expert knowledge of wild animals likely played a key role in the **domestication,** or the taming of animals. They tamed horses, dogs, goats, and pigs. Like farming, domestication of animals came slowly. Stone Age hunters may have driven herds of animals into rocky ravines to be slaughtered. It was then a small step to drive herds into human-made enclosures. From there, farmers could keep the animals as a constant source of food and gradually tame them.

Not only farmers domesticated animals. Pastoral nomads, or wandering herders, tended sheep, goats, camels, or other animals. These herders moved their animals to new pastures and watering places.

Background
Dogs were probably the first domesticated animals, serving as pets and hunting companions. The oldest discovery of human and dog fossils found together dates back to roughly 8000 B.C.

Revolution in Jarmo Today the eroded and barren rolling foothills of the Zagros Mountains in northeastern Iraq seem an unlikely site for the birthplace of agriculture.

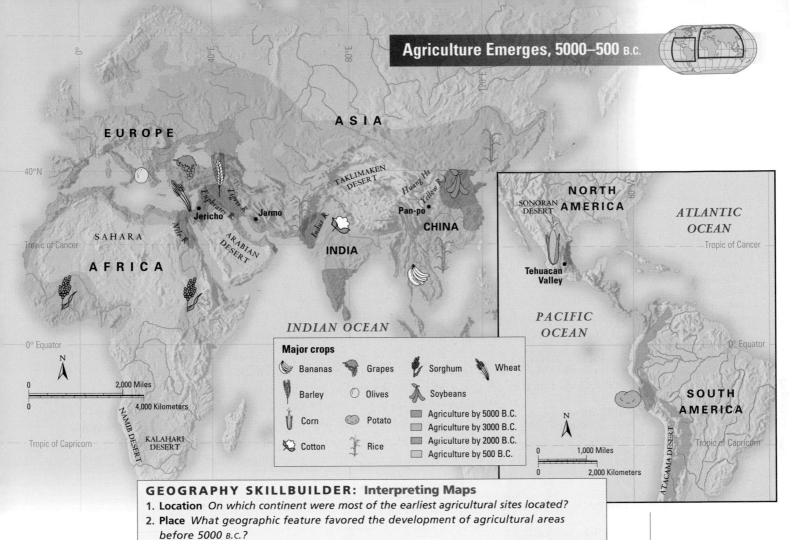

Major crops

Bananas	Grapes	Sorghum	Wheat
Barley	Olives	Soybeans	
Corn	Potato	Agriculture by 5000 B.C.	
Cotton	Rice	Agriculture by 3000 B.C.	
		Agriculture by 2000 B.C.	
		Agriculture by 500 B.C.	

GEOGRAPHY SKILLBUILDER: Interpreting Maps
1. **Location** *On which continent were most of the earliest agricultural sites located?*
2. **Place** *What geographic feature favored the development of agricultural areas before 5000 B.C.?*

According to archaeologist Robert Braidwood, thousands of years ago, the environmental conditions of this region favored the development of agriculture. Wild wheat and barley, along with wild goats, pigs, sheep, and horses, had once thrived near the Zagros Mountains.

During the early 1950s, Braidwood conducted an archaeological dig at a site called Jarmo. He concluded that its residents first established this agricultural settlement about 9,000 years ago:

A VOICE FROM THE PAST
We found weights for digging sticks, hoe-like [tools], flint-sickle blades, and a wide variety of milling stones. . . . We also discovered several pits that were probably used for the storage of grain. Perhaps the most important evidence of all was animal bones and the impressions left in the mud by cereal grains. . . . The people of Jarmo were adjusting themselves to a completely new way of life, just as we are adjusting ourselves to the consequences of such things as the steam engine. What they learned about living in a revolution may be of more than academic interest to us in our troubled times.

ROBERT BRAIDWOOD, quoted in *Scientific American*

THINK THROUGH HISTORY
B. Making Inferences
What evidence discovered at Jarmo shows how farming created new technological needs?

The farmers at Jarmo, and others like them in places as far apart as Mexico and Thailand, were pioneering a new way of life. Villages such as Jarmo marked the beginning of a new era and laid the foundation for modern life.

Villages Grow and Prosper

The changeover from hunting and gathering to farming and herding took place not once, but many times. Neolithic people in many parts of the world independently developed agriculture.

Farming Develops in Many Places Within a few thousand years, people in many other regions worldwide, especially in fertile river valleys, turned to farming:

- **Africa** The Nile River Valley developed into an important agricultural center for growing wheat, barley, and other crops.
- **China** About 8,000 years ago, farmers along the middle stretches of the Huang He cultivated a grain called millet. About 1,000 years later, Neolithic farmers first domesticated wild rice in the Chang Jiang River delta.
- **Mexico and Central America** Farmers cultivated corn, beans, and squash.
- **Peru** Farmers in the Central Andes were the first to grow tomatoes, sweet potatoes, and white potatoes.

From these early centers of agriculture, farming spread to surrounding regions.

Catal Huyuk The agricultural village now known as Catal Huyuk (chuh·TUL hoo·YOOK) was located on a fertile plain in south-central Turkey. The village showed the benefits of settled life. Farmers there produced large crops of wheat, barley, and peas. Villagers also raised sheep and cattle.

Many highly skilled workers, such as potters and weavers, worked in Catal Huyuk. The village was best known for its obsidian products. This dark volcanic rock looks like glass. It was used to make mirrors, jewelry, and knives for trade.

At its peak 8,000 years ago, Catal Huyuk was home to about 6,000 people. Its prosperity supported a varied cultural life. Archaeologists have uncovered colorful wall paintings depicting animals and hunting scenes. Many religious shrines were dedicated to a mother goddess. According to her worshipers, she controlled the supply of grain.

The new settled way of life also had its drawbacks. Floods, fire, drought, and other natural disasters could destroy a village. Diseases spread easily among people living close together. Jealous neighbors and roving nomadic bands might attack and loot a wealthy village like Catal Huyuk.

Despite these problems, some early villages expanded into cities that would become the setting for more complex cultures.

These cooking utensils—a pot, a bone spatula, and a fork—are from a kitchen in Catal Huyuk. They provide a glimpse of the settled life in new agricultural communities.

THINK THROUGH HISTORY
C. Evaluating
What advantages did farming and herding have over hunting and gathering?

Vocabulary
shrines: places where sacred relics are kept

Section ❷ Assessment

1. TERMS & NAMES

Identify
- nomad
- hunter-gatherer
- Neolithic Revolution
- slash-and-burn farming
- domestication

2. TAKING NOTES

Using a web diagram like the one below, show the effects of the development of agriculture.

```
        ( )        ( )
           \      /
         ( Development of )
         ( Agriculture   )
           /      \
        ( )        ( )
```

Choose one effect and write a paragraph about it.

3. HYPOTHESIZING

Why do you think the development of agriculture occurred around the same time in several different places?

THINK ABOUT
- the migrations of early peoples
- changes in the earth's climate
- a rise in human population

4. THEME ACTIVITY

Science and Technology
Create a chart explaining new tools, utensils, and other artifacts that archaeologists would likely find at the site of a permanent farming settlement. Use information from the text on Jarmo and Catal Huyuk to make your list of objects.

❸ Civilization

CASE STUDY: Ur in Sumer

TERMS & NAMES
- civilization
- specialization
- artisan
- institution
- scribe
- cuneiform
- Bronze Age
- barter
- ziggurat

MAIN IDEA	**WHY IT MATTERS NOW**
Prospering agricultural villages, food surpluses, and new technology led to the rise of civilizations.	Contemporary civilizations share the same characteristics typical of ancient civilizations.

SETTING THE STAGE Agriculture marked a dramatic change in how people lived together. They began dwelling in larger, more organized communities, such as farming villages and towns. Gradually, from some of these permanent settlements, cities emerged, forming the backdrop of a much more complex way of life—civilization.

Villages Grow into Cities

Over the centuries, people settled in stable communities that were based on agriculture. Domesticated animals became more common. The invention of new tools—hoes, sickles, and plow sticks—made the task of farming easier. As people gradually developed the technology to control their natural environment, they reaped larger harvests. Settlements with a plentiful supply of food could support more heavily populated communities.

As the population of some early farming villages increased, social relationships became more complex. The change from a nomadic hunting-gathering way of life to settled village life took a long time. Likewise, the change from village life to city life was a gradual process that spanned several generations.

Economic Changes To cultivate more land and to produce extra crops, ancient people in larger villages built elaborate irrigation systems. The resulting food surpluses freed some villagers to pursue other jobs and to develop skills besides farming. Individuals who learned to become craftspeople created valuable new products, such as pottery, metal objects, and woven cloth. In turn, people who became traders profited from a broader range of goods to exchange—craftwork, grains, and many raw materials. Two important inventions also fostered the expanded trade between villages. The wheel and the sail enabled traders to transport more goods over longer distances.

Social Changes A more complex and prosperous economy affected the social structure of village life. For example, building and operating large irrigation systems required the cooperation and labor of many people. As other special groups of workers formed, social classes with varying wealth, power and influence began to emerge. A system of social classes would later become more clearly defined as cities grew.

Religion also became more organized. During the Old Stone Age, prehistoric

This photograph shows the well-preserved remains of Skara Brae. This small agricultural village emerged around 3000 B.C. It is located on an island off the coast of northern Scotland.

peoples' religious beliefs centered around nature, animal spirits, and some idea of an afterlife. During the New Stone Age, farming peoples worshiped the many gods and goddesses who they believed had power over the rain, wind, and other forces of nature. Early city dwellers developed rituals founded on these earlier religious beliefs. As populations grew, common spiritual values became lasting religious traditions.

What Is Civilization?

Most historians believe that one of the first civilizations arose in Sumer, a region that is now part of modern Iraq. Sumer was located in Mesopotamia. Just what set the Sumerians apart from their neighbors? Most scholars define **civilization** as a complex culture with these five characteristics: (1) advanced cities, (2) specialized workers, (3) complex institutions, (4) record keeping, and (5) advanced technology.

Advanced Cities Cities were the birthplaces of the first civilizations. In fact, the word *civilization* comes from the Latin word for *city*. A city is more than a large group of people living together. The size of the population alone does not distinguish a village from a city. One of the key differences is that a city is a center of trade for a larger area. Like their modern-day counterparts, ancient city dwellers depended on trade. Farmers, merchants, and traders brought goods to market in the cities. The city dwellers themselves produced a variety of goods for exchange.

Specialized Workers As cities grew, so did the need for more specialized workers, such as traders, government officials, and priests. Food surpluses provided the opportunity for **specialization**—the development of skills in a specific kind of work. An abundant food supply allowed some people to become expert at jobs besides farming. In early civilizations, some city dwellers became **artisans**—skilled workers who make goods by hand. Specialization helped artisans develop their skill at designing jewelry, fashioning metal tools and weapons, or making pottery. The wide range of crafts that artisans produced helped cities become thriving centers of trade.

Complex Institutions The soaring populations of early cities made government, or a system of ruling, necessary. In civilizations, leaders emerged to maintain order among people and to establish laws. Government is an example of an **institution**—a long-lasting pattern of organization in a community. Complex institutions, such as government, religion, and the economy, are another characteristic of civilization.

With the growth of cities, religion became a formal institution. Most cities had great temples where dozens of priests took charge of religious duties. Sumerians believed that every city belonged to a god who lived in the temple and governed the city's activities. The temple became the hub of both government and religious affairs. It also served as the city's economic center. There food and trade items were distributed to the city's residents.

THINK THROUGH HISTORY
A. Drawing Conclusions
Why were cities essential to the growth of civilizations?

Record Keeping As government, religion, and the economy became more complex and structured, people recognized the need to keep records. In early civilizations, government officials had to document tax collections, the passage of laws, and the storage of grain. Priests needed some way to keep track of the yearly calendar and important rituals. Merchants had to record accounts of debts and payments.

Most civilizations developed a system of writing, though some devised other methods of record keeping. Around 3000 B.C., Sumerian **scribes**—or professional record keepers—invented a system of writing called **cuneiform** (KYOO·nee·uh·FAWRM), which means "wedge-shaped." (Earlier versions of Sumerian writing consisted of signs called pictographs—symbols of the objects or things

SPOTLIGHT ON

The Inca's System of Record Keeping

The empire of the ancient Inca civilization stretched along the western coast of South America. Though the Inca had no writing system, they kept records using a *quipu,* a complicated set of colored strings tied with different-sized knots at various intervals. Each knot represented a certain amount or its multiple. The colors of each cord represented the item being counted: people, animals, land, and so on.

The *quipucamayoc,* special officials who knew how to use the *quipu,* kept records of births, deaths, marriages, crops, and even important historical events.

they represented.) The scribe's tool, called a stylus, was a sharpened reed with a wedge-shaped point. It was pressed into moist clay to create symbols. Scribes baked their clay tablets in the sun to preserve the writing.

People soon began to use writing for other purposes besides record keeping. They also wrote about their cities' dramatic events—wars, natural disasters, the reign of kings. Thus, the beginning of civilization in Sumer also signaled the beginning of written history.

Advanced Technology New tools and techniques are always needed to solve the problems that emerge when large groups of people live together. In early civilizations, some farmers began to harness the powers of animals and nature. For example, they used ox-drawn plows to turn the soil. They created elaborate irrigation systems to expand planting areas.

Artisans relied on new technology to make their tasks easier. Around 3500 B.C., Sumerian artisans first used the potter's wheel to shape jugs, plates, and bowls. Sumerian metalworkers discovered that melting together certain amounts of copper and tin made bronze. After 2500 B.C., skilled metalworkers in Sumer's cities turned out bronze spearheads by the thousands. The period called the **Bronze Age** refers to the time when people began using bronze, rather than copper and stone, to fashion tools and weapons. The Bronze Age began in Sumer around 3000 B.C., but the starting date varied in different parts of Europe and Asia.

Background
Toolmakers discovered how to combine copper with a small amount of tin to make bronze. Bronze is harder than copper.

The wedge-shaped symbols of cuneiform are visible in this close-up of a clay tablet.

PATTERNS OF CHANGE: Key Traits of Civilizations

Characteristics	Examples from Sumer
Advanced Cities	• Uruk—population of about 10,000, which doubled in two centuries • Lagash—population of about 19,000 • Umma—population of about 16,000
Specialized Workers	• priests • metalworkers • scribes • soldiers • teachers • weavers • merchants • government officials • potters • farmers
Complex Institutions	• Formal governments with officials and laws • Priests with both religious and political power • A rigorous education system for training of scribes
Record Keeping	• Cuneiform tablets—records of business transactions, historical events, customs, and traditions
Advanced Technology	By around 3000 B.C.: • The wheel, the plow, and the sailboat probably in daily use • Bronze weapons and body armor that gave Sumerians a military advantage over their enemies

SKILLBUILDER: Interpreting Charts
1. *Based on the chart, what is one important feature of a city?*
2. *What kinds of social behavior are basic to the five characteristics of civilizations?*

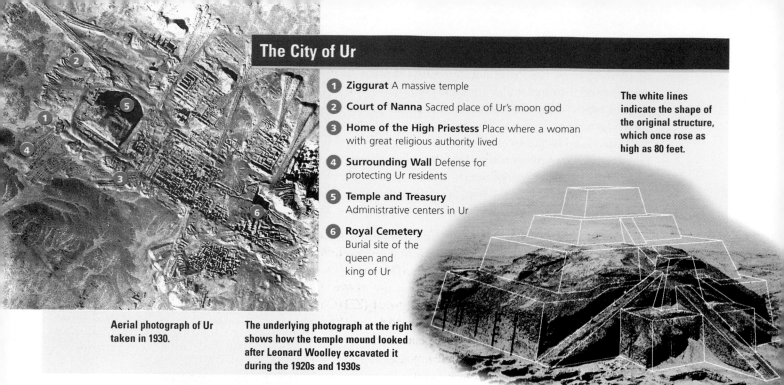

The City of Ur

1. **Ziggurat** A massive temple
2. **Court of Nanna** Sacred place of Ur's moon god
3. **Home of the High Priestess** Place where a woman with great religious authority lived
4. **Surrounding Wall** Defense for protecting Ur residents
5. **Temple and Treasury** Administrative centers in Ur
6. **Royal Cemetery** Burial site of the queen and king of Ur

The white lines indicate the shape of the original structure, which once rose as high as 80 feet.

Aerial photograph of Ur taken in 1930.

The underlying photograph at the right shows how the temple mound looked after Leonard Woolley excavated it during the 1920s and 1930s

CASE STUDY: Ur in Sumer

Civilization Emerges in Ur

Ur, one of the earliest cities in Sumer, stood on the banks of the Euphrates River in what is now southern Iraq. Some 30,000 people once lived in this ancient city. Ur was the site of a highly sophisticated civilization.

After a series of excavations from 1922 to 1934, English archaeologist Leonard Woolley and his team unraveled the mystery of this long-lost civilization. Woolley's archaeological dig at Ur revealed important clues about Ur's past. Woolley concluded that around 3000 B.C., Ur was a flourishing urban civilization. People in Ur lived in well-defined social classes. Priests and rulers wielded great power. Wealthy merchants profited from foreign trade. Artists and artisans created many extraordinary works, such as lavish ornaments and jewelry, musical instruments, and gold helmets and daggers. Woolley's finds have enabled historians to reconstruct scenes illustrating Ur's advanced culture.

An Agricultural Economy Imagine a time nearly 5,000 years ago. Outside the mud-brick walls surrounding Ur, ox-driven plows cultivate the fields. People are working barefoot in the irrigation ditches that run between patches of green plants. With stone hoes, the workers widen the ditches. The ditches carry water into their fields from the reservoir a mile away. The people of Ur have developed this large-scale irrigation system to provide Ur with food surpluses, which keep the economy thriving. The government officials who plan and direct this public works project ensure its smooth operation.

A Glimpse of City Life A broad dirt road leads from the fields up to the city's wall. Inside the city gate, the city dwellers go about their daily lives. Most people live in small, windowless, one-story, boxlike houses packed tightly together along the street. However, a few wealthy families live in two-story houses with an inner courtyard.

Down another street, accomplished artisans work full-time in their shops. A metalworker makes bronze by carefully mixing molten copper with just the right quantity of tin. Later he will hammer the bronze to make sharp spears—weapons to help Ur's well-organized armies defend the city. As a potter spins his potter's wheel, he expertly shapes the moist clay into a large bowl. These artisans and other craftworkers produce trade goods that help the city of Ur prosper.

THINK THROUGH HISTORY
B. Analyzing Causes
How did Ur's agricultural way of life foster the development of civilization there?

Ur's Thriving Trade The narrow streets open out into a broad avenue where merchants squat under their awnings and trade farmers' crops and artisans' crafts. This is the city's bazaar, or marketplace. People do not use coins to make purchases because money has not yet been invented. However, merchants and their customers know roughly how many pots of grain a farmer must give to buy a jug of wine. This way of trading goods and services without money is called **barter.** More complicated trades require the services of a scribe. He carefully forms cuneiform signs on a clay tablet. The signs show how much barley one farmer owes a merchant for a donkey.

The Temple: Center of City Life Farther down the main avenue stands Ur's tallest and most important building—the temple. Like a city within a city, the temple is surrounded by a heavy wall. Within the temple gate, a massive, tiered structure towers over the city. This pyramid-shaped monument is called a **ziggurat** (ZIHG·uh·RAT), which means "mountain of god." On the exterior of the ziggurat, a flight of perhaps 100 mud-brick stairs leads to the top. At the peak, priests conduct rituals to worship the city god who looms over Ur. Every day, priests with shaved heads climb these stairs. They often drag a plump goat or sheep for a sacrifice. The temple also houses storage areas for grains, woven fabrics, and gems—offerings to the city's god.

Background
The ziggurat of Ur was a huge temple dedicated to the moon god Nanna. The tiers are supposed to represent steps leading toward the heavens.

A Religious Ritual Recorded A poem preserved in cuneiform tablets reveals Sumerians' burial rituals and their belief in an afterlife. The following is a lament for a young woman's lover who was killed in a distant land. These lines describe what foods she will provide for his spirit when his body is returned home for his funeral:

> **A VOICE FROM THE PAST**
> I will offer him cakes and herbs of the grove,
> I will provide him with the fruits of the field,
> I will provide him with roasted barley and dates . . .
> I will provide him with grapes on the vine,
> I will provide him with apples of the wide earth,
> I will provide him with figs of the wide earth . . .
> I will provide him with dates on their cluster.
>
> Quoted in *From the Poetry of Sumer* by Samuel Kramer

The fruits, grains, and other foods mentioned in these lines also suggest the wide range of crops that Sumerians either grew themselves or received as trade goods.

The first early cities such as Ur represent a model of civilizations that continued to arise throughout history. While the Sumerians were advancing their culture, civilizations were also developing in Egypt, China, and other countries in Asia.

CONNECT *to* TODAY

Ziggurat's Role in Persian Gulf War

After 4,000 years, the city of Ur is still making history. During the Persian Gulf War in 1991, the Iraqi military established an air base near the site of the city of Ur. The ziggurat there had been reconstructed.

Hoping that U.S. and Allied forces would not risk destroying the ancient ziggurat, Iraqi forces parked aircraft next to the structure at Ur for protection. However, enemy planes targeted the city of Ur. Exploding bombs caused large craters at the site. Machine-gun attacks from enemy planes also left many bullet holes in the sides of the ziggurat itself.

Section 3 Assessment

1. TERMS & NAMES

Identify
- civilization
- specialization
- artisan
- institution
- scribe
- cuneiform
- Bronze Age
- barter
- ziggurat

2. TAKING NOTES

Create a two-column chart like the one below. List the five characteristics of civilization and give an example from Ur.

Characteristics of Civilization	Example from Ur
1.	
2.	
3.	
4.	
5.	

3. MAKING INFERENCES

In what ways does the ziggurat of Ur reveal that Sumerians had developed an advanced civilization?

THINK ABOUT
- the skills required to build the monument
- the various purposes of the ziggurat
- its location

4. THEME ACTIVITY

Economics Role-play a character from Ur who has a specialized skill, such as an artisan, a trader, or a scribe. Write a monologue explaining how you contribute to the economic welfare of the city.

Chapter **1** Assessment

TERMS & NAMES

Briefly explain the importance of each of the following to human prehistory.

1. artifact
2. culture
3. technology
4. hunter-gatherer
5. Neolithic Revolution
6. domestication
7. civilization
8. specialization
9. institution
10. Bronze Age

Interact *with* History

On page 6, you played the role of an amateur archaeologist as you tried to figure out the uses of three prehistoric tools. Now that you've read the chapter, what new clues have you discovered that would help you unravel the mystery of who made the tool with the wedge-shaped blade, and why? What evidence can you use to support your conclusions about its purpose? Discuss your ideas with a small group.

REVIEW QUESTIONS

SECTION 1 *(pages 7–11)*
Human Origins in Africa

11. What kinds of evidence do archaeologists, anthropologists, and paleontologists study to find out how prehistoric people lived?

12. Why did the ability to walk upright and the development of the opposable thumb represent important breakthroughs for early hominids?

13. Why is the prehistoric period called the Stone Age?

14. What evidence supports archaeologists' beliefs that Neanderthals developed a form of religion?

SECTION 2 *(pages 12–16)*
Humans Try to Control Nature

15. Why do some archaeologists believe that women were the first farmers?

16. What role did the food supply play in shaping the nomadic life of hunter-gatherers and the settled life of farmers?

17. In what areas of the world did agriculture first develop?

SECTION 3 *(pages 17–21)*
PATTERNS OF CHANGE: CIVILIZATION

18. What economic changes resulted from food surpluses in agricultural villages?

19. Why did the growth of civilization make government necessary?

20. Why did a system of record keeping develop in civilizations?

Visual Summary

The Peopling of the World

Social Organization

Hunting-Gathering Bands	Growth of Villages	Rise of Cities
Beginning about 2 million B.C.	Beginning about 8000 B.C.	Beginning about 3000 B.C.

Achievements

Key Achievements	Key Achievements	Key Achievements
• Invention of tools • Mastery over fire • Development of language • Creation of art	• Development of agriculture • Domestication of animals • Breakthroughs in farming technology • Food surpluses	• Specialized workers • Record keeping • Complex institutions • Advanced technology

CRITICAL THINKING

1. EFFECTS OF TRADE

THEME ECONOMICS What impact did trade have on the development of civilization?

2. STONE AGE CULTURES

Create a comparison chart like the one below to show the differences between Paleolithic and Neolithic cultures.

	Paleolithic	Neolithic
Source of food		
Means of living		
Technology		
Type of community		

3. THE ROLE OF RELIGION

What trends occurred in religious beliefs over the course of the Stone Age? Consider the religious practices of the Neanderthals, the villagers of Catal Huyuk, and the city dwellers of Ur.

4. ANALYZING PRIMARY SOURCES

The following quotation from Richard Leakey's book *The Making of Mankind* explains how archaeologists learn about the past. Read the paragraph and answer the questions that follow.

> **A VOICE FROM THE PAST**
> Litter of the past is the basis of archaeology. The coins, the pottery, the textiles and the buildings of bygone eras offer us clues as to how our [early ancestors] behaved, how they ran their economy, what they believed in and what was important to them. What archaeologists retrieve from excavations are images of past lives. . . . [These images] are pieced together slowly and painstakingly from the information contained in objects found.

- Why is the "litter" that humans leave behind so valuable to archaeologists?

- If archaeologists inspected a week's worth of your family's household trash, what conclusions might they draw about your way of life?

CHAPTER ACTIVITIES

1. LIVING HISTORY: Unit Portfolio Project

THEME INTERACTION WITH ENVIRONMENT Your unit portfolio project focuses on showing the ways in which hominids interacted with the environment. For Chapter 1, you might use one of the following ideas to add to your portfolio:

- Make a poster featuring how early humans adapted to the changing environment. Draw a series of pictures or cartoons showing how they used fire, built shelters, made clothing, and found new sources of food.

- Write a "Top 10" list of important steps that early humans took to control their environment. Read them aloud to your class. Be prepared to explain your rankings.

- Imagine you are an archaeologist working on the first dig of Ur at Sumer. Your job is to organize the artifacts and to discuss how Sumerians may have used them to adapt to their environment. Write your findings as field notes.

2. CONNECT TO TODAY: Cooperative Learning

THEME SCIENCE AND TECHNOLOGY In early civilizations, ox-drawn plows turned the soil, and elaborate irrigation systems expanded planting areas. Today, breakthroughs in technology continue to revolutionize farming methods in the United States and other countries.

Work with a team to create a chart explaining the latest high-tech equipment and machines used on a modern industrialized farm.

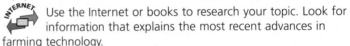 Use the Internet or books to research your topic. Look for information that explains the most recent advances in farming technology.

- Find diagrams that illustrate how farm machines work. You may wish to focus on computerized farm equipment.

- Make comparisons between these labor-saving farm machines and the simple farming tools and methods of early farmers.

3. INTERPRETING A TIME LINE

Revisit the unit time line on pages 2–3. Think of two or more events to add to the Chapter 1 segment of the time line.

FOCUS ON **FINE ART**

Study this cave painting created during the Stone Age in Argentina.

- What is depicted in the painting?

- What do you think the hands represent?

Connect to History Do you think the painting portrays a scene from daily life, represents religious beliefs, or shows an illustrated story about an important event? Support your answer with reasons.

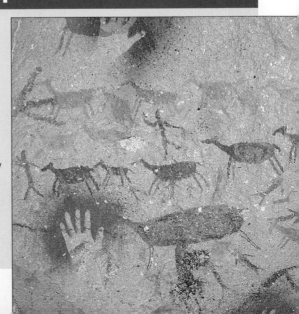

CHAPTER 2

Early River Valley Civilizations, 3500 B.C.–450 B.C.

PREVIEWING THEMES

Interaction with Environment

The earliest civilizations formed on river plains. While fertile, these lands also presented challenges, such as seasonal flooding and a limited growing area. To deal with these problems, people created irrigation systems, which produced surplus food. Surpluses supported the rise of cities.

Power and Authority

Projects such as irrigation systems required planning, leadership, and laws—the beginnings of organized government. In some societies, priests controlled the first governments. Over time, power and authority shifted to military leaders and kings.

Science and Technology

Early civilizations depended on breakthroughs in science and technology, including bronze tools, the wheel, the sail, the plow, writing, and mathematics. These innovations spread from one civilization to the next through trade, wars, and the movement of peoples.

INTERNET CONNECTION

Visit us at **www.mcdougallittell.com** to learn more about ancient Sumer, Egypt, India, and China.

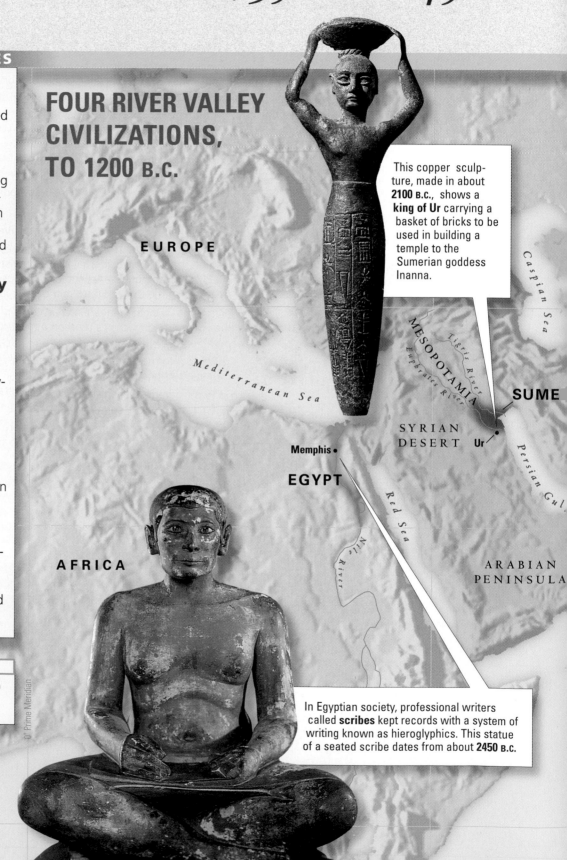

FOUR RIVER VALLEY CIVILIZATIONS, TO 1200 B.C.

EUROPE

Mediterranean Sea

Caspian Sea

MESOPOTAMIA

Tigris River

Euphrates River

SYRIAN DESERT

Memphis •

EGYPT

Ur •

SUME

Persian Gul

Red Sea

Nile River

AFRICA

ARABIAN PENINSULA

0° Prime Meridian

This copper sculpture, made in about **2100 B.C.**, shows a **king of Ur** carrying a basket of bricks to be used in building a temple to the Sumerian goddess Inanna.

In Egyptian society, professional writers called **scribes** kept records with a system of writing known as hieroglyphics. This statue of a seated scribe dates from about **2450 B.C.**

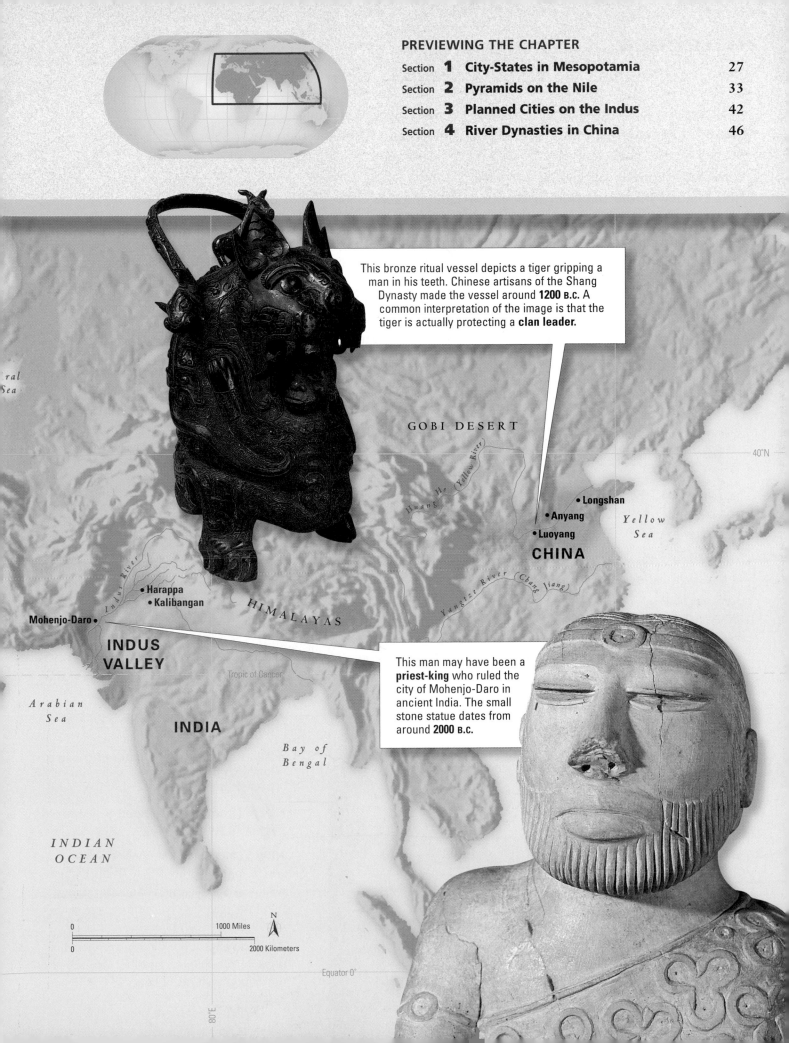

This bronze ritual vessel depicts a tiger gripping a man in his teeth. Chinese artisans of the Shang Dynasty made the vessel around **1200 B.C.** A common interpretation of the image is that the tiger is actually protecting a **clan leader.**

This man may have been a **priest-king** who ruled the city of Mohenjo-Daro in ancient India. The small stone statue dates from around **2000 B.C.**

GOBI DESERT

40°N

Huang He (Yellow River)

• Longshan

• Anyang   Yellow
• Luoyang   Sea

CHINA

Yangtze River (Chang Jiang)

Indus River

• Harappa
• Kalibangan   HIMALAYAS

Mohenjo-Daro •

**INDUS
VALLEY**

Tropic of Cancer

Arabian
Sea

INDIA

Bay of
Bengal

ral
Sea

INDIAN
OCEAN

0   1000 Miles

0   2000 Kilometers   N

Equator 0°

80°E

Interact *with* History

It has been a tough year ever since the harvest failed. Many times, you've cursed the name of Mummar, the government official responsible for overseeing the harvest. But now that you've heard about the king's punishment for Mummar, you're not sure what to think.

The law of the Babylonian Empire—Hammurabi's Code—holds people responsible for their actions. It usually applies retaliation as punishment. That is, if you put out the eye of another, your own eye will be put out. Mummar had hired a substitute to handle the harvest this year, and the harvest was a disaster. Because of Mummar's decision, your city has suffered through a serious food shortage. Some people may die. Therefore, the king has sentenced Mummar to die.

Does Mummar's punishment fit the crime?

A scribe records the proceedings against Mummar.

The Babylonian ruler Hammurabi, accompanied by his judges, sentences Mummar to death.

Mummar pleads for mercy.

EXAMINING *the* ISSUES

- Does the king's decision represent justice or revenge?

- What should be the main purpose of laws: to promote good behavior or to punish bad behavior?

- Do all communities need a system of laws to guide them?

Hold a class debate on these questions. As you prepare for the debate, think about what you have learned about the changes that take place as civilizations grow and become more complex.

As you read about the growth of civilizations in this chapter, consider why societies developed systems of laws.

TERMS & NAMES
- **Fertile Crescent**
- **silt**
- **irrigation**
- **city-state**
- **dynasty**
- **cultural diffusion**
- **polytheism**
- **empire**
- **Hammurabi**

1 City-States in Mesopotamia

MAIN IDEA

The earliest civilization in Asia arose in Mesopotamia and organized into city-states.

WHY IT MATTERS NOW

The development of this civilization reflects a pattern that has occurred repeatedly throughout history.

SETTING THE STAGE Two rivers flow from the mountains of what is now Turkey, down through Syria and Iraq, and finally to the Persian Gulf. Six thousand years ago, the waters of these rivers provided the lifeblood that allowed the formation of farming settlements. These grew into villages and then cities. This pattern would also occur along other river systems in northern Africa, India, and China, as the world's first civilizations developed.

Geography of the Fertile Crescent

A desert climate dominates the landscape between the Persian Gulf and the Mediterranean Sea in Southwest Asia. Yet within this dry region lies an arc of land that provides some of the best farming in Southwest Asia. The region's curved shape and the richness of its land led scholars to call it the **Fertile Crescent.**

The Zagros Mountains in Iran lie to the east of Mesopotamia. Melting snows from this and other ranges swelled the Tigris and Euphrates rivers each spring.

Fertile Plains In the eastern part of the Fertile Crescent, the Tigris (TY·grihs) and Euphrates (yoo·FRAY·teez) rivers flow southeastward to the Persian Gulf. (See the map on page 28.) Between them lies a plain that became known as Mesopotamia (MEHS·uh·puh·TAY·mee·uh), which in Greek means "land between the rivers."

The Tigris and Euphrates rivers flooded Mesopotamia at least once a year. As the floodwater receded, it left a thick bed of mud called **silt.** In this rich, new soil, farmers could plant and harvest enormous quantities of wheat and barley. The surpluses from their harvests allowed villages to grow.

THINK THROUGH HISTORY
A. Clarifying Why was silt so important to the inhabitants of Mesopotamia?

Environmental Challenges People first began to settle and farm in southern Mesopotamia before 4500 B.C. Around 3500 B.C., the people called the Sumerians, whom you read about in Chapter 1, arrived on the scene. The Sumerians mixed with the local farmers, and their language became dominant in the region. No one knows for sure where the Sumerians came from. Good soil was the advantage that attracted these settlers to the flat, swampy land of Sumer. There were, however, three disadvantages to their new environment.

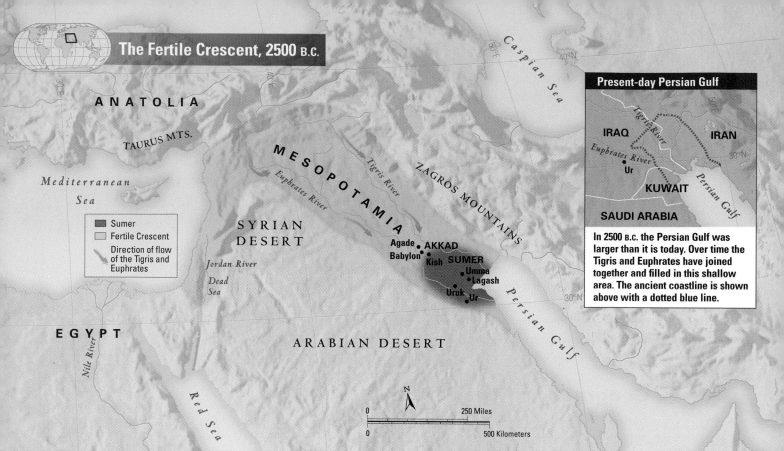

ANATOLIA

TAURUS MTS.

Mediterranean Sea

Caspian Sea

MESOPOTAMIA

Tigris River

Euphrates River

ZAGROS MOUNTAINS

SYRIAN DESERT

Jordan River

Dead Sea

Agade · AKKAD
Babylon · Kish · SUMER
· Umma
· Lagash
Uruk · Ur

Persian Gulf

EGYPT

Nile River

ARABIAN DESERT

Red Sea

Sumer
Fertile Crescent
Direction of flow of the Tigris and Euphrates

N

0   250 Miles

0   500 Kilometers

Present-day Persian Gulf

IRAQ   IRAN

Euphrates River   *Tigris River*

· Ur

KUWAIT

SAUDI ARABIA

In 2500 B.C. the Persian Gulf was larger than it is today. Over time the Tigris and Euphrates have joined together and filled in this shallow area. The ancient coastline is shown above with a dotted blue line.

GEOGRAPHY SKILLBUILDER: Interpreting Maps
1. **Place** *What major rivers flow through the Fertile Crescent?*
2. **Human-Environment Interaction** *What were some advantages of Sumer's location?*

First, the flooding of the rivers was unpredictable. Sometimes it came as early as April, sometimes as late as June. After the flood receded, the hot sun quickly dried out the mud. Little or no rain fell, and the land became almost a desert. How could Sumerian farmers water their fields during the dry summer months in order to make their barley grow?

Second, Sumer was a small region, only about the size of Massachusetts. The villages were little clusters of reed huts standing in the middle of an open plain. With no natural barriers for protection, a Sumerian village was almost defenseless. How could the villagers protect themselves?

Third, the natural resources of Sumer were extremely limited. Without a good supply of stone, wood, and metal, what were the Sumerians to use for tools or buildings?

Creating Solutions Over a long period of time, the people of Sumer created solutions to deal with these problems. To provide water, they dug **irrigation** ditches that carried river water to their fields and allowed them to produce a surplus of crops. For defense, they built city walls with mud bricks. Finally, Sumerians traded with the peoples of the mountains and the desert for the products they lacked. Sumerians traded their grain, cloth, and crafted tools for the stone, wood, and metal they needed to make their tools and buildings.

These activities required organization, cooperation, and leadership. It took many people working together, for example, for the Sumerians to construct their large irrigation systems. Leaders were needed to plan the projects and supervise the digging. These projects also created a need for laws to settle disputes over how land and water would be distributed. These leaders and laws were the beginning of organized government.

THINK THROUGH HISTORY
B. Clarifying How did the Sumerians overcome their lack of resources?

Sumerians Create City-States

The Sumerians stand out in history as one of the first groups of people to form a civilization. Five key characteristics set Sumer apart from earlier human societies: (1) advanced cities, (2) specialized workers, (3) complex institutions, (4) record keeping, and (5) advanced technology. All the later peoples who lived in this region of the world built upon the innovations of Sumerian civilization.

By 3000 B.C., the Sumerians had built a number of cities, each surrounded by fields of barley and wheat. Although these cities shared the same culture, they developed their own governments, each with its own rulers. Each city and the surrounding land it controlled formed a **city-state.** A city-state functioned much as an independent country does today. Sumerian city-states included Uruk, Kish, Lagash, Umma, and Ur. As in Ur, which Chapter 1 describes, the center of all Sumerian cities was the walled temple with a ziggurat at its center. There the priests appealed to the gods for the well-being of the city-state.

The Power of Priests Sumer's earliest governments were controlled by the temple priests. The farmers believed that the success of their crops depended upon the blessings of the gods, and the priests acted as go-betweens with the gods. In addition to being a place of worship, the ziggurat was like a city hall. From the ziggurat the priests managed the irrigation system. They also demanded a portion of every farmer's crop as taxes.

Monarchs Take Control In time of war, however, the priests did not lead the city. Instead, the men of the city chose a tough fighter who could command the city's soldiers. At first, a commander's power ended as soon as the war was over. After 3000 B.C., wars between cities became more and more frequent. Gradually, Sumerian priests and people gave commanders permanent control of standing armies.

In time, some military leaders became full-time rulers, or monarchs. These rulers usually passed their power on to their sons, who eventually passed it on to their own heirs. Such a series of rulers from a single family is called a **dynasty.** Between 3000 and 2500 B.C., many Sumerian city-states came under the rule of dynasties.

THINK THROUGH HISTORY
C. Analyzing Causes How did monarchs gain power in the city-states?

The Spread of Cities Sumer's city-states grew prosperous from the surplus food produced on their farms. These surpluses allowed Sumerians to increase long-distance trade, exchanging the extra food and other goods for items they needed but did not have.

As their population and trade expanded, the Sumerians came into contact with other peoples, and their ideas—such as living in cities—spread. By 2500 B.C., new cities were arising all over the Fertile Crescent, in what is now Syria, northern Iraq, and Turkey. So, too, did the Sumerians absorb ideas such as religious beliefs from neighboring cultures. This process of a new idea or a product spreading from one culture to another is called **cultural diffusion.**

Sumerian Culture

The belief systems, social structure, technology, and arts of the Sumerians reflected their civilization's triumph over its harsh environment.

A Religion of Many Gods Like many peoples in the Fertile Crescent, the Sumerians believed that many different gods controlled the various forces in nature. The belief in many gods is called **polytheism** (PAHL·ee·thee·IHZ·uhm). Enlil, the god of clouds and air, was among the most powerful gods. Sumerians feared him as "the raging flood that has no rival." Lowest of all the gods were demons known as Wicked Udugs, who caused disease, misfortune, and every kind

The writing on this Sumerian copper figurine from about 2100 B.C. tells that a king of Ur erected a temple for the goddess Inanna.

This panel made of shells and stone comes from the Sumerian city of Ur. It shows people and livestock captured in war being presented to the victorious king.

of human trouble. Altogether, the Sumerians believed in roughly 3,000 gods.

Sumerians described their gods as doing many of the same things humans do—falling in love, having children, quarreling, and so on. Yet the Sumerians also believed that their gods were both immortal and all-powerful. Humans were nothing but their servants. At any moment, the mighty anger of the gods might strike, sending a fire, a flood, or an enemy to destroy a city. To keep the gods happy, the Sumerians built impressive ziggurats for them and offered rich sacrifices of animals, food, and wine.

Sumerians worked hard to earn the gods' protection in this life. Yet they expected little help from the gods after death. The Sumerians believed that the souls of the dead went to the "land of no return," a dismal, gloomy place between the earth's crust and the ancient sea. No joy awaited souls there. A passage in a Sumerian poem describes the fate of dead souls: "Dust is their fare and clay their food."

Some of the richest accounts of Mesopotamian myths and legends appear in a long poem called the *Epic of Gilgamesh*. It is one of the earliest works of literature in the world. Through the heroic adventures of Gilgamesh, a legendary king, the narrative offers a glimpse into the beliefs and concerns of the ancient Sumerians. The epic tells of Gilgamesh's unsuccessful quest for immortality, a theme that recurs in ancient literature.

Vocabulary
epic: a long heroic poem that tells the story of a historical or legendary figure.

A VOICE FROM THE PAST
Gilgamesh, whither are you wandering?
Life, which you look for, you will never find.
For when the gods created man, they let
Death be his share, and withheld life
In their own hands.

Epic of Gilgamesh

Sumerian beliefs and legends such as those in the *Epic of Gilgamesh* greatly influenced other ancient cultures, including the Hebrews and the Greeks.

Life in Sumerian Society With civilization came greater differences between groups in society, or the beginning of what we call social classes. Priests and kings made up the highest level in Sumerian society. Wealthy merchants ranked next. The vast majority of ordinary Sumerian people worked with their hands in fields and workshops. At the lowest level of Sumerian society were the slaves. Some slaves were foreigners who had been captured in war. Others were Sumerians who had been sold into slavery as children to pay the debts of their poor parents. By working obediently day and night, Sumerian slaves could hope to earn freedom.

Social class affected the lives of both men and women. On the whole, Sumerian women could pursue most of the occupations of city life, from merchant to farmer to artisan. They could hold property in their own name. Women could also join the lower ranks of the priesthood. However, Sumer's written records mention few female

explain w/ more detail
why have they reached this conclusion?

scribes. Therefore, scholars have concluded that girls were not allowed to attend the schools where upper-class boys learned to read and write. Even so, Sumerian women had more rights than women in many later civilizations.

Sumerian Science and Technology

Sumerians invented the wheel, the sail, and the plow; they were the first to use bronze; and they developed the first system of writing, cuneiform. Cuneiform tablets provide evidence of other Mesopotamian innovations. One of the first known maps was made on a clay tablet in about 2300 B.C. Other tablets contain some of the oldest written records of scientific investigations in the areas of astronomy, chemical substances, and symptoms of disease.

Many other new ideas arose from the Sumerians' practical needs. In order to erect city walls and buildings, plan irrigation systems, and survey flooded fields, they needed arithmetic and geometry. They developed a number system in base 60, from which stem the modern units for measuring time (60 seconds = 1 minute) and the 360 degrees of a circle. Sumerian building techniques, including the use of mud bricks and mortar, made the most of the resources available. Their architectural innovations—such as arches, columns, ramps, and the pyramid-shaped design of the ziggurat—permanently influenced Mesopotamian civilization.

The First Empire Builders

From 3000 to 2000 B.C., the city-states of Sumer were almost constantly at war with one another. The weakened city-states could no longer ward off attacks from the peoples of the surrounding deserts and hills. Although the Sumerians never recovered from the attacks on their cities, their civilization did not die. Succeeding sets of rulers adapted the basic ideas of Sumerian culture to meet their own needs.

Sargon of Akkad About 2350 B.C., a conqueror named Sargon defeated the city-states of Sumer. Sargon led his army from Akkad (AK·ad), a city-state north of Sumer. Unlike the Sumerians, the Akkadians were a Semitic (suh·MIHT·ihk) people—that is, they spoke a language related to Arabic and Hebrew. The Akkadians had long before adopted most aspects of Sumerian culture. Sargon's conquests helped to spread that culture even farther, beyond the Tigris-Euphrates Valley.

THINK THROUGH HISTORY
D. Contrasting How does an empire differ from a city-state?

By taking control of both northern and southern Mesopotamia, Sargon created the world's first empire. An **empire** brings together several peoples, nations, or previously independent states under the control of one ruler. At its height, the Akkadian Empire extended from the Mediterranean Coast in the west to present-day Iran in the east. Sargon's dynasty lasted only about 200 years, after which it declined due to internal fighting, invasions, and a severe famine.

Babylonian Empire In about 2000 B.C., nomadic warriors known as Amorites, another Semitic group, invaded Mesopotamia. Within a short time, the Amorites overwhelmed the Sumerians and established their capital at Babylon, on the Euphrates River. The Babylonian Empire reached its peak during the reign of **Hammurabi,** from 1792 B.C.to 1750 B.C. Hammurabi's most enduring legacy is the code of laws he put together.

This bronze head depicts Sargon of Akkad, who created the world's first empire.

2350
2150

Early River Valley Civilizations **31**

HISTORY MAKERS

Hammurabi
? –1750 B.C.

The noted lawgiver Hammurabi was also an able military leader, diplomat, and administrator of a vast empire. Hammurabi himself described some of his accomplishments:

> When [the gods] Anu and Bel gave me the land of Sumer and Akkad to rule, . . . I dug out the Hammurabi-canal named Nuhus-nisi, which bringeth abundance of water unto the land of Sumer and Akkad. Both the banks thereof I changed to fields for cultivation, and I garnered piles of grain, and I procured unfailing water for the land. . . .
>
> As for the land of Sumer and Akkad, I collected the scattered peoples thereof, and I procured food and drink for them. In abundance and plenty I pastured them, and I caused them to dwell in peaceful habitation.

Hammurabi's Code Although individual Sumerian cities had developed codes of laws, Hammurabi recognized that a single, uniform code would help to unify the diverse groups within his empire. He therefore collected existing rules, judgments, and laws into the Code of Hammurabi. Hammurabi had the code engraved in stone, and copies were placed all over his empire.

The code lists 282 specific laws dealing with everything that affected the community, including family relations, business conduct, and crime. The laws tell us a great deal about the Mesopotamians' beliefs and what they valued. Since many were merchants and traders, for example, many of the laws related to property issues.

Although the code applied to everyone, it set different punishments for rich and poor and for men and women. It frequently applied the principle of retaliation (an eye for an eye and a tooth for a tooth) to punish crimes. Following are two of the laws:

A VOICE FROM THE PAST

- If a man has stolen an ox, a sheep, a pig, or a boat that belonged to a temple or palace, he shall repay thirty times its cost. If it belonged to a private citizen, he shall repay ten times. If the thief cannot pay, he shall be put to death.

- If a woman hates her husband and says to him "You cannot be with me," the authorities in her district will investigate the case. If she has been chaste and without fault, even though her husband has neglected or belittled her, she will be held innocent and may return to her father's house. . . . If the woman is at fault, she shall be thrown into the river.

Code of Hammurabi, adapted from a translation by L. W. King

Despite its severity, Hammurabi's Code carried forward an important idea in Mesopotamian civilization. It reinforced the principle that government had a responsibility for what occurred in society. For example, if a man was robbed and the thief was not caught, the government was required to compensate the victim for his loss.

Two centuries after Hammurabi's reign, the Babylonian Empire fell to nomadic warriors. Over the years, new groups dominated the Fertile Crescent. Yet many ideas of the early Sumerians would be adopted by the later peoples, including the Assyrians, Phoenicians, and Hebrews. Meanwhile, a similar pattern of development, rise, and fall, was taking place to the west, along the Nile River in Egypt. Egyptian civilization is described in Section 2.

THINK THROUGH HISTORY
E. Recognizing Effects How did Hammurabi's law code advance civilization?

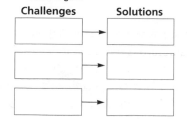

Section ① Assessment

1. TERMS & NAMES

Identify
- Fertile Crescent
- silt
- irrigation
- city-state
- dynasty
- cultural diffusion
- polytheism
- empire
- Hammurabi

2. TAKING NOTES

Recreate the chart below on your paper. List three environmental challenges the Sumerians faced and their solutions to these challenges.

Challenges		Solutions
	→	
	→	
	→	

3. MAKING INFERENCES

What advantages did living in cities offer the people of ancient Mesopotamia? Do modern cities offer any of the same advantages? Support your answer with references to the text.

THINK ABOUT
- characteristics of Sumer's city-states
- characteristics of Sumer's economy and society
- development of organized government

4. ANALYZING THEMES

Interaction with Environment
Do you think that living in a river valley with little rainfall helped or hurt the development of civilization in Mesopotamia? Explain your response.

TERMS & NAMES
- cataract
- delta
- Menes
- pharaoh
- theocracy
- pyramid
- mummification
- hieroglyphics
- papyrus

MAIN IDEA

Along the Nile River, civilization emerged in Egypt and became united into a kingdom ruled by pharaohs.

WHY IT MATTERS NOW

Many of the monuments built by the Egyptians stand as a testament to their ancient civilization.

SETTING THE STAGE To the west of the Fertile Crescent in Africa, another river makes its way to the sea. While Sumerian civilization was on the rise, a similar process took place along the banks of this river, the Nile in Egypt. Yet the Egyptian civilization turned out to be very different from the collection of city-states in Mesopotamia. Early on, Egypt was united into a single kingdom, which allowed it to enjoy a high degree of unity, stability, and cultural continuity over a period of 3,000 years.

The Geography of Egypt

From the highlands of east-central Africa to the Mediterranean Sea, the Nile River flows northward for over 4,100 miles, making it the longest river in the world. (See the map on page 34.) A thin ribbon of water in a parched desert land, the great river brings its water to Egypt from distant mountains, plateaus, and lakes in present-day Burundi, Tanzania, Uganda, and Ethiopia.

Egypt's settlements arose along the Nile on a narrow strip of land made fertile by the river. The change from fertile soil to desert—from the Black Land to the Red Land—was so abrupt that a person could stand with one foot in each.

A traditional sailboat sails the Nile River in Egypt.

The Gift of the Nile As in Mesopotamia, yearly flooding brought the water and rich soil that allowed settlements to grow. Every year in July, rains and melting snow from the mountains of east-central Africa caused the Nile River to rise and spill over its banks. When the river receded in October, it left behind a rich deposit of fertile black mud.

Before the scorching sun could dry out the soil, the peasants would hitch their cattle to plows and prepare their fields for planting. All fall and winter, they tended the wheat and barley plants. They watered their crops from an intricate network of irrigation ditches. At last came the welcome harvest. This cycle repeated itself year after year—flood, plant, harvest; flood, plant, harvest.

In an otherwise parched land, the abundance brought by the Nile was so great that the Egyptians worshiped it as a god who gave life and seldom turned against them. As the ancient Greek historian Herodotus (hih·RAHD·uh·tuhs) remarked in the fifth century B.C., Egypt was the "gift of the Nile."

Upper Egypt and Lower Egypt For most of their history, ancient Egyptians knew only the lower part of the Nile—the last 750 miles before the river empties north into the Mediterranean Sea. Their domain ended at a point where jagged granite cliffs and boulders turn the river into churning rapids called a **cataract** (KAT·uh·rakt). Riverboats could not pass this spot, known as the First Cataract, to continue upstream to the south.

Early River Valley Civilizations **33**

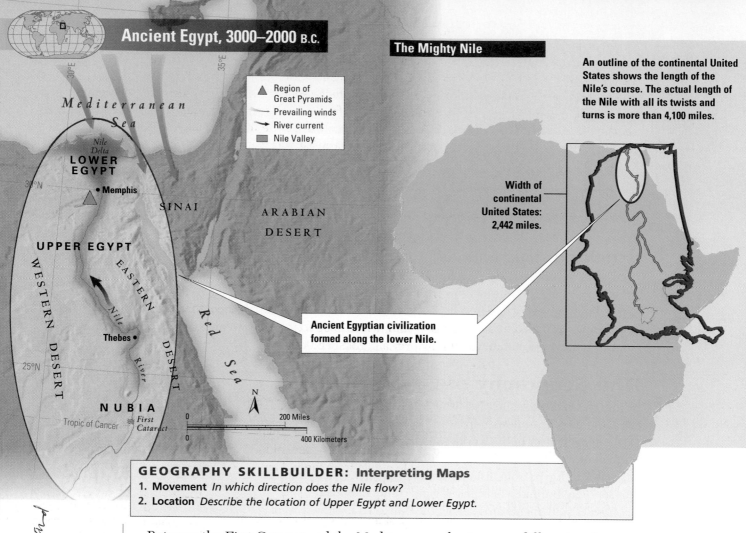

Ancient Egypt, 3000–2000 B.C.

The Mighty Nile

Region of Great Pyramids
Prevailing winds
River current
Nile Valley

Mediterranean Sea

Nile Delta

LOWER EGYPT

• Memphis

SINAI

ARABIAN DESERT

UPPER EGYPT

WESTERN DESERT

EASTERN DESERT

Nile River

Thebes •

Red Sea

NUBIA

Tropic of Cancer — First Cataract

0   200 Miles
0   400 Kilometers

N

Ancient Egyptian civilization formed along the lower Nile.

An outline of the continental United States shows the length of the Nile's course. The actual length of the Nile with all its twists and turns is more than 4,100 miles.

Width of continental United States: 2,442 miles.

GEOGRAPHY SKILLBUILDER: Interpreting Maps
1. **Movement** *In which direction does the Nile flow?*
2. **Location** *Describe the location of Upper Egypt and Lower Egypt.*

North and South Egypt

Between the First Cataract and the Mediterranean lay two very different regions. Upper Egypt (to the south) was a skinny strip of land from the First Cataract to the point where the river starts to fan out into many branches. Lower Egypt (to the north, near the sea) consisted of the Nile **delta** region, which begins about 100 miles before the river enters the Mediterranean. The delta is a broad, marshy, triangular area of land formed by deposits of silt at the mouth of the river. This rich land provided a home for many birds and wild animals.

The Nile provided a reliable system of transportation between Upper and Lower Egypt. The Nile flows north, so northbound boats simply drifted with the current. Southbound boats hoisted a wide sail. The prevailing winds of Egypt blow from north to south, carrying sailboats against the river current. The ease of contact made possible by this watery highway helped unify Egypt's villages and promote trade.

Environmental Challenges Egyptian farmers were much more fortunate than the villagers of Mesopotamia. Compared to the unpredictable Tigris and Euphrates rivers, the Nile was as regular as clockwork. Even so, life in Egypt had its risks. If the Nile's floodwaters were just a few feet lower than normal, the amount of fresh silt and water for crops was greatly reduced. Thousands of people might starve. If the floodwaters were a few feet higher than usual, the water would spread beyond the fields to the mud-brick villages nearby. The unwanted water might destroy houses, granaries, and the precious seeds that farmers needed for planting.

The vast and forbidding deserts on either side of the Nile acted as natural barriers between Egypt and other lands. They forced Egyptians to stay close to the river, their lifeline, which reduced their interaction with other peoples. At the same time, the deserts also shut out invaders. For much of its early history, Egypt was spared the constant warfare that plagued the Fertile Crescent.

THINK THROUGH HISTORY
A. Contrasting
What was the main difference between the flooding of the Nile and that of the rivers in Mesopotamia?

Movement of Goods and Ideas By 3200 B.C., Egyptians were coming into contact with the people of Mesopotamia. Caravans loaded with goods for trade were traveling between the two regions. By about 2000 B.C., Egyptian traders were also traveling up the Nile on barges to the lands of Nubia and Kush to the south. They were in search of such goods as gold, ivory, cattle, and granite blocks for their massive temples and tombs.

Whole groups of people seem to have moved freely from one region to another in search of better land for farming or grazing. The early Egyptians may have borrowed some ideas from the Mesopotamians in the early development of their cities and in their system of writing. However, the period of Mesopotamian influence ended quickly. From then on, Egypt followed its own cultural path, which was very different from Mesopotamia's. Egypt blended the cultures of the Nile Valley peoples with the cultures of peoples who migrated into the valley from other parts of Africa and from the Fertile Crescent. Egypt thus was a land of cultural, ethnic, and racial diversity throughout its 3,000-year history.

Egypt Unites into a Kingdom

Egyptians lived in farming villages as far back as 5000 B.C., perhaps even earlier. Each village had its own rituals, gods, and chieftain. By 3200 B.C., the villages of Egypt were under the rule of two separate kingdoms, Lower Egypt and Upper Egypt.

According to legend, the king of Lower Egypt wore a red crown, and the king of Upper Egypt wore a tall white crown shaped like a bowling pin. About 3100 B.C., a strong-willed king of Upper Egypt named **Menes** (MEE-neez) united all of Egypt. As a symbol of his united kingdom, Menes created a double crown from the red and white crowns. Menes shrewdly established his capital, Memphis, near the spot where Upper and Lower Egypt met, and established the first Egyptian dynasty. Eventually, the history of ancient Egypt would consist of 31 dynasties, spanning 2,600 years.

Little is known of Egypt's first two dynasties, but records improve with the Third Dynasty. The Third Dynasty begins the period historians call the Old Kingdom, which lasted from 2660 to 2180 B.C. The Old Kingdom set the pattern for Egypt's great civilization.

Pharaohs Rule as Gods The role of the king was one striking difference between Egypt and Mesopotamia. In Mesopotamia, kings were considered to be representatives of the gods. To the Egyptians, kings *were* gods, almost as splendid and powerful as the gods of the heavens. The Egyptian god-kings came to be called **pharaohs** (FAIR-ohz).

THINK THROUGH HISTORY
B. Making Inferences Why were Egypt's pharaohs unusually powerful rulers?

The pharaoh stood at the center of Egypt's religion as well as its government and army. This type of government in which the ruler is a divine figure is called a **theocracy.** Egyptians believed that the pharaoh bore full responsibility for the kingdom's well-being. It was the pharaoh who caused the sun to rise, the Nile to flood, and the crops to grow. It was the pharaoh's duty to promote truth and justice.

Builders of the Pyramids Egyptians believed that their king ruled even after his death. He had an eternal spirit, or *ka* (kah), which continued to take part in the governing of Egypt. In the Egyptian's mind, the *ka* remained much like a living king in its needs and pleasures. Since kings expected to reign forever, their tombs were even more important than their palaces. For the kings of the Old Kingdom, the resting place after death was an immense structure called a **pyramid.** The Old Kingdom was the great age of pyramid building in ancient Egypt.

crown of
Upper Egypt

crown of Upper
and Lower Egypt

crown of
Lower Egypt

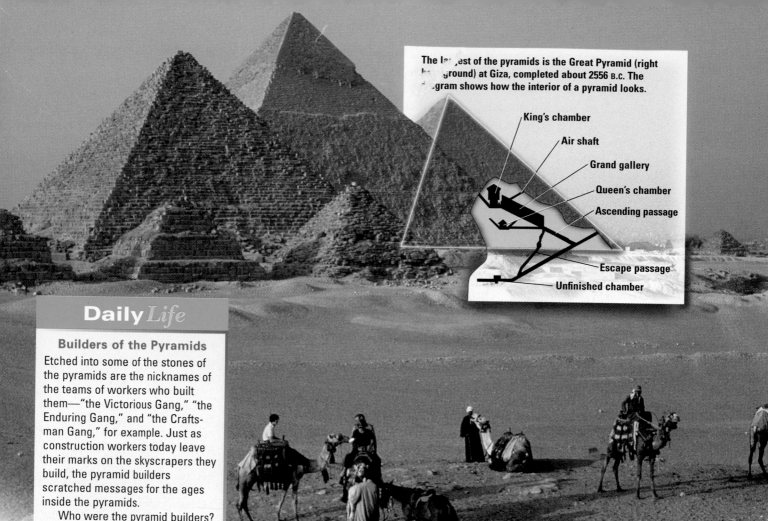

The largest of the pyramids is the Great Pyramid (right background) at Giza, completed about 2556 B.C. The diagram shows how the interior of a pyramid looks.

- King's chamber
- Air shaft
- Grand gallery
- Queen's chamber
- Ascending passage
- Escape passage
- Unfinished chamber

These magnificent monuments were remarkable engineering achievements, built by people who had not even begun to use the wheel. Unlike the Sumerians, however, the Egyptians did have a good supply of stone, both granite and limestone. For the Great Pyramid of Giza, for example, the limestone facing was quarried 400 miles upriver. Each perfectly cut stone block weighed at least 2 1/2 tons. Some weighed 15 tons. More than 2 million of these blocks were stacked with precision to a height of 481 feet. The entire structure covered more than 13 acres.

The pyramids also reflect the strength of the Egyptian civilization. They show that Old Kingdom dynasties had developed the economic strength to support massive public works projects, as well as the leadership and government organization to carry them out.

Egyptian Culture

With nature so much in their favor, Egyptians tended to approach life more confidently and optimistically than their neighbors in the Fertile Crescent.

Religion and Life Like the Mesopotamians, the early Egyptians were polytheistic, believing in many gods. The most important gods were Ra, the sun god, and Horus, the god of light. The most important goddess was Isis, who represented the ideal mother and wife. In all, Egyptians worshiped more than 2,000 gods and goddesses. They built huge temples to honor the major deities.

In contrast to the Mesopotamians, with their bleak view of death, Egyptians believed in an afterlife, a life that continued after death. Egyptians believed they would be judged for their deeds when they died. Osiris (oh·SY·rihs), the powerful god of the dead, would weigh each dead person's heart. To win eternal life, the heart could be no heavier than a feather. If the heart tipped the scale, showing that it was heavy with sin, a fierce beast known as the Devourer of Souls would pounce on the impure heart and gobble it up. But if the soul passed this test for purity and truth, it would live forever in the beautiful Other World.

People of all classes planned for their burials, so that they might safely reach the Other World. Kings and queens built great tombs, such as the pyramids, and other Egyptians built smaller tombs. Egyptians preserved a dead person's body by **mummification**—embalming and drying the corpse to prevent it from decaying. (See Something in Common, pages 40–41.) Scholars still accept Herodotus' description of the process of mummification.

THINK THROUGH HISTORY
C. Analyzing Motives Why do you think the Egyptians used mummification? How does it reflect their religious beliefs?

A VOICE FROM THE PAST
First, they draw out the brains through the nostrils with an iron hook. . . . Then with a sharp stone they make an incision in the side, and take out all the bowels. . . . Then, having filled the belly with pure myrrh, cassia, and other perfumes, they sew it up again; and when they have done this they steep it in natron [a mineral salt], leaving it under for 70 days. . . . At the end of 70 days, they wash the corpse, and wrap the whole body in bandages of waxen cloth.

HERODOTUS, *The History of Herodotus*

Attendants placed the mummy in a coffin inside a tomb. Then they filled the tomb with items the dead person could use in the afterlife, such as clothing, food, cosmetics, and jewelry. Many Egyptians purchased scrolls that contained hymns, prayers, and magic spells intended to guide the soul in the afterlife. This collection of texts is known as the *Book of the Dead*. These texts often contained declarations intended to prove the soul was worthy of eternal life.

A VOICE FROM THE PAST
Behold, I have come to you, I have brought you truth, I have repelled falsehood for you. I have not done falsehood against men, I have not impoverished my associates, I have done no wrong in the Place of Truth, I have not learnt that which is not, I have done no evil. . . . I have not caused pain, I have not made hungry, I have not made to weep, I have not killed, I have not commanded to kill, I have not made suffering for anyone. . . . I am pure, pure, pure, pure!

Book of the Dead, translated by Raymond O. Faulkner

Life in Egyptian Society Like the grand monuments to the kings, Egyptian society formed a pyramid. The king, queen, and royal family stood at the top. Below them were the other members of the upper class, which included wealthy landowners, government officials, priests, and army commanders. The next tier of the pyramid was the middle class, which included merchants and artisans. At the base of the pyramid was the lower class, by far the largest class. It consisted of peasant farmers and unskilled laborers.

In the later periods of Egyptian history, slavery became a widespread source of labor. Slaves, usually captives from foreign wars, served in the homes of the rich or toiled endlessly in the gold mines of Upper Egypt.

The Egyptians were not locked into their social classes. Lower- and middle-class Egyptians could gain higher status through

Daily Life

Egyptian Cosmetics
The dark-lined eyes that look out at us from the artwork of ancient Egypt were the height of fashion 3,000 years ago. Men and women applied the makeup, called kohl, to their eyes with small sticks. They made kohl from powdered minerals mixed with water.

The Egyptians also wore lipstick, made from powdered red ocher (iron oxide) mixed with oil. They soaked flowers and fragrant woods in oil and rubbed the oil into their skin. Sometimes they decked their hairdos with cones of scented wax, which melted slowly in the heat.

These cosmetics were more than just beauty aids. The dark eye makeup softened the glare of the desert sun. The oils protected skin, lips, and hair from the dry desert air. Egyptians kept their cosmetics in chests such as the one shown above, which was found in an Egyptian tomb.

marriage or success in their jobs. Even some slaves could hope to earn their freedom as a reward for their loyal service. To win the highest positions, people had to be able to read and write. Once a person had these skills, many careers were open in the army, the royal treasury, the priesthood, and the king's court.

Women in Egypt held many of the same rights as men. For example, a wealthy or middle-class woman could own and trade property. She could propose marriage or seek divorce. If she were granted a divorce, she would be entitled to one-third of the couple's property.

THINK THROUGH HISTORY
D. Comparing How was the status of women similar in Egyptian and Sumerian society?

Egyptian Writing As in Mesopotamia, the development of writing was one of the keys to the growth of Egyptian civilization. Crude pictographs were the earliest form of writing in Egypt, but scribes quickly developed a more flexible writing system called **hieroglyphics** (HY·ur·uh·GLIHF·ihks). This term comes from the Greek words *hieros* and *gluphē*, meaning "sacred carving."

As with Sumerian cuneiform writing, in the earliest form of hieroglyphics a picture stood for an idea. For instance, a picture of a man stood for the idea of a man; a picture of a bird stood for the idea of a bird. In time, the system changed so that pictures stood for sounds as well as ideas. The owl, for example, stood for an *m* sound. Hieroglyphics could be used almost like letters of the alphabet.

Although hieroglyphics were first written on stone and clay, as in Mesopotamia, the Egyptians soon invented a better writing surface. They used another gift of the Nile, the tall stalks of the **papyrus** (puh·PY·ruhs) reeds that grew in the marshy delta. The Egyptians split the reeds into narrow strips, dampened them, and then pressed them. As the papyrus dried, the plant's sap glued the strips together into a paperlike sheet.

Egyptian Science and Technology Practical needs led to many Egyptian inventions. In order to assess and collect taxes, the Egyptians developed a system of written numbers for counting, adding, and subtracting. Farmers used an early form of geometry to survey and reset property boundaries after the annual floods.

Mathematical knowledge helped Egypt's skillful engineers and architects as well. Builders needed to make accurate calculations and measurements to construct their remarkable pyramids and palaces. Egyptian architects were also the first to use stone columns in homes, palaces, and temples.

To help them keep track of the time between floods and plan their planting season, the Egyptians developed a calendar. Egyptian priests had

SPOTLIGHT ON

The Rosetta Stone

Although it lasted more than 2,500 years, Egyptian civilization eventually declined. Soon after, the ability to read hieroglyphics was lost and remained so for many centuries.

In 1799, near the delta village of Rosetta, some French soldiers found a polished black stone inscribed with a message in three languages. One version was written in hieroglyphics (top inset). A second version was in a simpler form of hieroglyphics and the third was in Greek (both are shown in the bottom inset).

Since ancient Greek was a well-known language, it provided clues to the meaning of the hieroglyphics. Still, deciphering the Rosetta Stone took many years. In 1822, a French scholar named Jean François Champollion (shahm·paw·LYAWN) finally broke the code of the hieroglyphics.

observed that a very bright star, now known as Sirius, began to appear above the eastern horizon just before the floods came. The time between one rising of Sirius and the next was 365 days. They divided this year into 12 months of 30 days each and added five days for holidays and feasting. This calendar was so accurate that it fell short of the true solar year by only six hours.

Egyptian medicine was also famous in the ancient world. Although Egyptian medical writings contain all sorts of magic charms and chants, Egyptian doctors also relied on practical knowledge. They knew how to check a person's heart rate by feeling for a pulse in different parts of the body. They set splints for broken bones and had effective treatments for wounds and fevers. They also used surgery to treat some conditions. All in all, the Egyptians approached their study of medicine in a remarkably scientific way.

THINK THROUGH HISTORY
E. Summarizing
What were the main achievements of the ancient Egyptians?

This detail from a tomb painting shows how the Egyptians grew their grain.

Chariot Riders Invade Egypt

The power of the pharaohs declined about 2180 B.C., marking the end of the Old Kingdom. Historians call the period of weakness and turmoil that followed the First Intermediate Period. Strong pharaohs regained control during the Middle Kingdom (2080–1640 B.C.) and restored law and order. They improved trade and transportation by having a canal dug from the Nile to the Red Sea. With the wealth from new trade, the kings undertook other public projects. They had huge dikes built to trap and channel the Nile's floodwaters for irrigation. They also created thousands of new acres of farmland by draining the swamps of Lower Egypt.

The prosperity of the Middle Kingdom did not last. In about 1640 B.C., a group of Asian nomads swept across the Isthmus of Suez into Egypt in horse-drawn chariots. These chariot-riders were the Hyksos (HIHK·sahs), which meant "the rulers of the uplands." The Hyksos ruled much of Egypt from 1640 to 1570 B.C. This 70-year period is sometimes called the Second Intermediate Period.

Egypt fell to the Hyksos at roughly the same time other nomads were invading Mesopotamia and the Indus Valley farther to the east. But Egypt would rise again for a new period of power and glory, the New Kingdom, which is discussed in Chapter 4.

general migration cast continuing theme

Section 2 Assessment

1. TERMS & NAMES

Identify
- cataract
- delta
- Menes
- pharaoh
- theocracy
- pyramid
- mummification
- hieroglyphics
- papyrus

2. TAKING NOTES

Recreate the web below on your paper and fill in examples related to the main idea in the center.

Egyptian
Achievements

Which would you consider most important? Why?

3. DRAWING CONCLUSIONS

Look at the map on page 34. Three natural features determined the boundaries of ancient Egyptian civilization: the Nile River, the First Cataract, and the surrounding desert. In your judgment, which of these features was most important to Egypt's history? Explain your conclusion.

4. THEME ACTIVITY

Interaction with Environment
Using information from Sections 1 and 2, create a chart, sketch, or drawing to show how Sumerians and Egyptians made use of their environment. Then tell which group you think made better use of what they had. Be prepared to defend your opinions.

Early River Valley Civilizations **39**

Dealing with Death

All humans face death. Anthropologists believe that religious beliefs grew out of humanity's attempts to explain what happens after death. The Egyptians wrapped their dead as mummies to preserve the body for an afterlife. The ways other cultures treat their dead reveal their own beliefs about God and the soul. As you compare and contrast the customs on these pages, look for how they are influenced by the religious beliefs of the people who practice them.

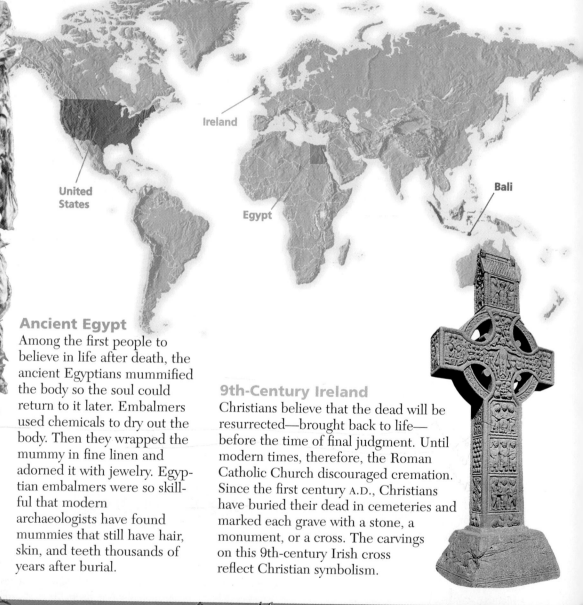

Ireland

United States

Egypt

Bali

Ancient Egypt

Among the first people to believe in life after death, the ancient Egyptians mummified the body so the soul could return to it later. Embalmers used chemicals to dry out the body. Then they wrapped the mummy in fine linen and adorned it with jewelry. Egyptian embalmers were so skillful that modern archaeologists have found mummies that still have hair, skin, and teeth thousands of years after burial.

9th-Century Ireland

Christians believe that the dead will be resurrected—brought back to life—before the time of final judgment. Until modern times, therefore, the Roman Catholic Church discouraged cremation. Since the first century A.D., Christians have buried their dead in cemeteries and marked each grave with a stone, a monument, or a cross. The carvings on this 9th-century Irish cross reflect Christian symbolism.

a closer look EGYPTIAN MUMMIES

The Egyptians also mummified the pets of the deceased. These are mummies of a cat and a dog.

These clay vessels are called Canopic jars. After preparing the mummy, embalmers placed the brain, liver, and other internal organs of the mummy in these jars.

Modern Bali

Hindus cremate, or burn, their dead. They consider the body as just a container for a soul that never dies. After a person dies, they believe the soul is reborn in another person. Hindu cremations are sacred rituals. On the Indonesian island of Bali, these rituals involve an elaborate celebration. Several bodies are put in a tall tower made of wood and bamboo, such as the one pictured at right. The whole tower is burned and the ashes scattered in the ocean.

19th-Century Native Americans

Just as Native American languages and lifestyles varied widely, so did Native American customs for dealing with the dead. Many 19th-century Plains Indians, such as the Sioux and the Blackfeet (pictured below), placed their dead on raised platforms. This protected the bodies from wild animals and also lifted the dead closer to the sky, where many spirits were believed to dwell.

This solid gold death mask of the pharaoh Tutankhamen covered the head of his mummy. The mask, which weighs 22.5 pounds, is part of a popular exhibit in the Egyptian Museum in Cairo, Egypt.

Connect *to* History

Recognizing Effects Which groups believed in preserving the body after death? How did those religious beliefs affect their customs?

 SEE SKILLBUILDER HANDBOOK, PAGE 995

Connect *to* Today

Reporting Find out about modern Jewish and Muslim burial practices. Illustrate each of these with a picture and a caption like those above. Then write a paragraph comparing them to either Christian or Hindu practices.

3 Planned Cities on the Indus

MAIN IDEA	WHY IT MATTERS NOW
The first Indian civilization built well-planned cities on the banks of the Indus River.	The culture of India today has it roots in the civilization of the early Indus cities.

SETTING THE STAGE The great civilizations of Mesopotamia and Egypt rose and fell. They left behind rich histories, but the current cultures in those areas have few links to their predecessors' ancient glories. Farther east, in India, another civilization arose about 2500 B.C. Historians know less about its origins and the reasons for its eventual decline than they do about the origins and decline of Mesopotamia and Egypt. Yet many characteristics of modern Indian culture can be traced to that early civilization.

The Geography of South Asia

A wall of mountains—the Hindu Kush, Karakoram, and Himalaya ranges—separates South Asia from the rest of the continent. As a result, geographers often refer to the land mass that includes what is now India, Pakistan, Nepal, and Bangladesh as a **subcontinent**—the Indian subcontinent.

Rivers, Mountains, and Monsoons The mountains guard an enormous flat and fertile plain formed by two rivers—the Indus and the Ganges (GAN·jeez). These two rivers and the lands they water make up a large area that stretches 1,500 miles across northern India and is called the Indus-Ganges Plain. Below this plain, the southern part of the subcontinent is a peninsula that thrusts south into the Indian Ocean. The center of the peninsula is a high plateau cut by twisting rivers. This region is called the Deccan (DEK·uhn). A narrow border of lush, tropical land lies along the coasts of southern India.

Seasonal winds called **monsoons** dominate India's climate. From October to May, winter monsoons from the northeast blow dry air across the country. Then, in the middle of June, the winds shift. Spring monsoons blow from the southwest, carrying moisture from the ocean in great rain clouds.

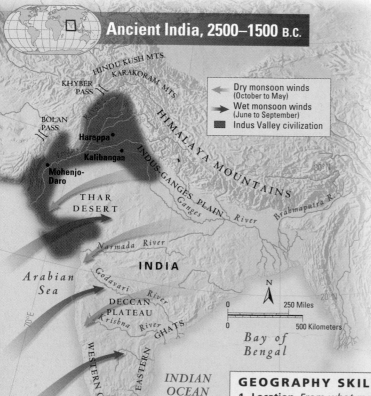

Ancient India, 2500–1500 B.C.

→ Dry monsoon winds (October to May)
→ Wet monsoon winds (June to September)
■ Indus Valley civilization

HINDU KUSH MTS.
KARAKORAM MTS.
KHYBER PASS
BOLAN PASS
Harappa
Kalibangan
Mohenjo-Daro
THAR DESERT
HIMALAYA MOUNTAINS
INDUS-GANGES PLAIN
Ganges River
Brahmaputra R.
Narmada River
INDIA
Arabian Sea
Godavari River
DECCAN PLATEAU
Krishna River
WESTERN GHATS
EASTERN GHATS
INDIAN OCEAN
Bay of Bengal

N
0   250 Miles
0   500 Kilometers

GEOGRAPHY SKILLBUILDER: Interpreting Maps
1. **Location** *From what mountain ranges do the Indus River and its branches flow?*
2. **Human-Environment Interaction** *What landforms presented natural barriers around the Indus Valley?*

THINK THROUGH HISTORY
A. Identifying Problems What environmental challenge did the farmers of the Indus Valley face that the Sumerians and Egyptians did not?

Environmental Challenges The civilization that emerged along the Indus River faced many of the same challenges as the ancient Mesopotamian and Egyptian civilizations. The Indus River flows southwest from the Himalayas to the Arabian Sea. As in Mesopotamia and Egypt, yearly floods spread deposits of rich soil over a wide area. Unlike the Nile floods, however, the floods along the Indus were unpredictable. The river sometimes changed its course. Unlike both the Mesopotamians and the Egyptians, the people of the Indus Valley had to cope with the cycle of wet and dry seasons brought by the monsoon winds. If there was too little rain, plants withered in the fields and people went hungry. Too much rain, and floods swept away whole villages.

The world's tallest mountains to the north and a large desert to the west presented natural boundaries between the Indus Valley and other areas. As in Egypt, the natural barriers helped protect the Indus Valley from invasion. At the same time, the Indus River provided a link to the sea. The river allowed valley inhabitants to develop trade with distant peoples, including the Mesopotamians.

Civilization Emerges on the Indus

Historians know less about the civilization in the Indus Valley than about those to the west. They have not yet deciphered the Indus system of writing. Evidence comes largely from archaeological digs, although many sites remain unexplored, and floods probably washed away others long ago. At its height, however, the civilization of the Indus Valley influenced an area much larger than either Mesopotamia or Egypt.

Earliest Arrivals No one is sure how human settlement began in India. Perhaps people who arrived by sea from Africa settled the south. Northern migrants may have made their way through the Khyber Pass in the Hindu Kush mountains. Archaeologists have found evidence in the highlands of agriculture and domesticated sheep and goats dating to about 7000 B.C. By about 3200 B.C., people were farming in villages along the Indus River.

Planned Cities Around 2500 B.C., while Egyptians were building pyramids, people in the Indus Valley were laying the bricks for India's first cities. Archaeologists have found the ruins of more than 100 settlements along the Indus. The largest cities were Kalibangan, Mohenjo-Daro, and Harappa. (Indus Valley civilization is sometimes called Harappan civilization, because of the many archaeological discoveries made at that site.)

One of the most remarkable achievements of the Indus Valley people was their sophisticated city planning. The cities of the early Mesopotamians were a jumble of buildings connected by a maze of winding streets. In contrast, the people of the Indus laid out their cities on a precise grid system. Cities featured a fortified area called a citadel, which contained the major buildings of the city. There were also separate residential districts. Buildings were constructed of oven-baked bricks cut in standard

The citadel arises out of the ruins of Mohenjo-Daro.

Plumbing in Mohenjo-Daro

maybe assignment with "Civilization"

From the time people began living in cities, they have faced the problem of plumbing: how to obtain clean water and remove human wastes? In most ancient cities, people retrieved water from the river or a central well. They dumped wastes into open drainage ditches or carted them out of town. Only the rich had separate bathrooms in their homes.

By contrast, the Indus peoples built extensive and modern-looking plumbing systems. In Mohenjo-Daro, almost every house had a private bathroom and toilet. No other civilization achieved this level of convenience until the 19th and 20th centuries. The toilets were neatly built of brick with a wooden seat. Pipes connected to each house carried wastewater into an underground sewer system.

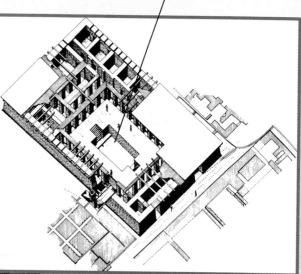

The swimming pool–sized Great Bath in Mohenjo-Daro was probably used for ritual bathing or other religious purposes. Private dressing rooms, some with their own toilets, surrounded the pool.

In their private baths, people took showers by pouring pitchers of water over their head.

Plumbing Facts

- The ancient Romans also built sophisticated plumbing and sewage systems. Aqueducts supplied Roman cities with water.

- In the 17th century, engineers installed a series of water wheels to pump water for the fountains of Versailles, the palace of French king Louis XIV. The water was pumped from a river ten miles away. This was the first water-supply system powered by machine rather than gravity.

- The first flush toilet was patented in 1775 by Alexander Cumming, a British mathematician and watchmaker.

Wastes drained though clay pipes into brick sewers running below the streets. These sewers had manholes, through which sanitation workers could inspect the drains and clean out the muck.

Connect *to* History

Making Inferences What does the attention the Indus people gave to the plumbing and sewer systems suggest about their culture?

SEE SKILLBUILDER HANDBOOK, PAGE 1005

Connect *to* Today

Researching Find out how water is supplied and wastewater disposed of in your home or community. Is your home connected to a municipal system? If so, when was this system built and how does it function? If not, how does your home system work? How does the system in your home or community compare to what was used in Mohenjo-Daro?

sizes, unlike the simpler, irregular, sun-dried mud bricks of the Mesopotamians. Early engineers also created sophisticated plumbing and sewage systems. These systems could rival any urban drainage systems built before the 19th century. The uniformity in the cities' planning and construction suggests that the Indus peoples had developed a strong central government. → explain

Culture and Trade Archaeological evidence shows that Indus civilization was generally stable. The uniform housing suggests that social divisions in the society were not great. Artifacts such as clay and wooden children's toys suggest a relatively prosperous society that could afford to produce nonessential goods. Finally, few weapons of warfare have been found, suggesting that conflict was limited.

Religious artifacts reveal links to modern Hindu culture. Figures show what may be early representations of Shiva, a major Indian god. Other figures relate to a mother goddess, fertility images, and the worship of cattle. All of these became part of later Indian civilization.

Stamps and seals made of carved stone were probably used by Indus merchants to identify their goods. These show that the Indus peoples conducted long-distance trade. Indus seals found in Sumer, and Sumerian objects found in the Indus Valley ruins, reveal that the two civilizations traded a great deal. Trading began as early as the reign of Sargon of Akkad, around 2350 B.C., and continued until 2000 B.C.

Many Indus seals depict animals, especially cattle. This seal depicts a long-horned bull.

Mysterious End to Indus Valley Culture

Mysterious Extinction / drought

Around 1750 B.C., the quality of building in the Indus Valley cities declined. Gradually, the great cities fell into decay. What happened? Some historians think that the Indus River changed course, as it tended to do, so that its floods no longer fertilized the fields near the cities. Other scholars suggest that people wore out the valley's land. They overgrazed it, overfarmed it, and overcut its trees, brush, and grass.

As the Indus Valley civilization neared its end, around 1500 B.C., a sudden catastrophe may have helped cause the cities' downfall. Archaeologists have found the remains of 38 bodies in the ruins of Mohenjo-Daro, seemingly never buried. Their presence suggests that residents may have abandoned the city after a natural disaster or an attack from human enemies. As Chapter 3 explains, the Aryans, a nomadic people from north of the Hindu Kush mountains, swept into the Indus Valley at about this time. Whether they caused the collapse of the first Indus civilization or followed later is not known.

Indian civilization would later grow again under the influence of these nomads. At this same time, farther to the east, another civilization was arising. It too was isolated from outside influences, as you will learn in Section 4.

THINK THROUGH HISTORY
B. Analyzing Causes What factors may have contributed to the decline of the Indus Valley civilization?

Section ③ Assessment

1. TERMS & NAMES

Identify
• subcontinent
• monsoon

2. TAKING NOTES

Create a two-column chart like the one below. In the left column, list the environmental conditions faced by the people of the Indus Valley. Next to each condition, in the right column, put a plus sign (+) if it was a benefit or a minus sign (–) if it was a drawback.

Environmental Condition	Benefit or Drawback

3. DRAWING CONCLUSIONS

What evidence has led historians to the following beliefs about Indus civilization?

(a) The cities were run by a strong central government.

(b) Indus people carried on trade with Sumer.

(c) Society was generally peaceful and stable.

Choose one of these conclusions and provide a different explanation based on the evidence.

4. THEME ACTIVITY

Science and Technology
Create a "Wall of Remarkable Indus Valley Achievements." Working in teams, write a paragraph about how your team's designated achievement simplified or complicated the Indus people's lives. Include an illustration or a cartoon.

4 River Dynasties in China

TERMS & NAMES
- loess
- oracle bone
- Mandate of Heaven
- dynastic cycle
- feudalism

MAIN IDEA

The early rulers introduced ideas about government and society that shaped Chinese civilization.

WHY IT MATTERS NOW

The culture that took root during ancient times still affects Chinese ways of life today.

SETTING THE STAGE The walls of China's first cities were built 1,500 years after the walls of Ur, 1,000 years after the great pyramids of Egypt, and 1,000 years after the planned cities of the Indus valley. Though a late starter, the civilization that began along one of China's river systems 3,500 years ago continues to thrive today. The reason for this endurance lies partly in China's geography.

The Geography of China

Natural barriers isolated ancient China from all other civilizations. To China's east lay the Pacific Ocean. To the west lay the Taklimaken (TAH·kluh·muh·KAHN) desert and the icy 14,000-foot Plateau of Tibet. To the southwest were the Himalaya Mountains. And to the north was the desolate Gobi Desert and the Mongolian Plateau. Two major river systems flow from the mountainous west to the Pacific Ocean. They are the Huang He (hwahng·HUH) in the north and the Yangtze (yang·SEE), in central China.

China's Heartland China's geography helps explain why early settlements developed along these main river systems. Mountain ranges and deserts dominate about two-thirds of China's land mass. About 90 percent of the remaining land that is suitable for farming lies within the comparatively small plain between the Huang He and Yangtze in eastern China. This plain was China's heartland.

Throughout China's long history, its political boundaries have expanded and contracted depending on the strength or weakness of its ruling families. Yet China remained a center of civilization. In the Chinese view, people who lived outside of Chinese civilization were barbarians. Because the Chinese saw their country as the center of the civilized world, their own name for China was the Middle Kingdom.

Environmental Challenges Like the other ancient civilizations in this chapter, China's first civilization arose in a river valley. Then as now, the Huang He, whose name means "yellow river," deposited huge amounts of dusty yellowish silt when it overflowed its banks. This silt is actually fertile soil called **loess** (LOH·uhs) that is blown by the winds from deserts to the west. Like the Tigris, Euphrates, and Indus, the Huang He's floods could be generous or ruinous. At its worst, the floods devoured whole villages, earning the river the nickname "China's Sorrow." (One great flood in A.D. 1887 killed nearly a million people.)

Because of China's relative geographic isolation, early settlers had to supply their own goods rather than trading with outside peoples. However, China's natural boundaries did not completely protect these settlers from outsiders. Invasions from the west and north occurred again and again in Chinese history.

Background
With a few exceptions, this book uses the Pinyin system for writing Chinese names, which is now standard in most publications.

Background
The Yangtze is also called the Chang Jiang (chahng jyahng).

CONNECT to TODAY

Three Gorges Project

The world's largest dam is being built between the dramatic granite cliffs that overlook the Yangtze River in central China. The dam, which is slated to open in 2003, promises to provide China with electrical power equivalent to ten nuclear power plants. However, no one is certain how control of the river's flooding will affect the plains downstream from the dam, which provide one-third of China's food.

Chinese officials hail the dam as an engineering achievement that ranks with the 2,000-year-old Great Wall of China. Yet its impact will affect both the future and the past. The lake created by the dam will displace more than a million Chinese residents. It will also drown forever the archaeological sites of some of China's earliest settlements.

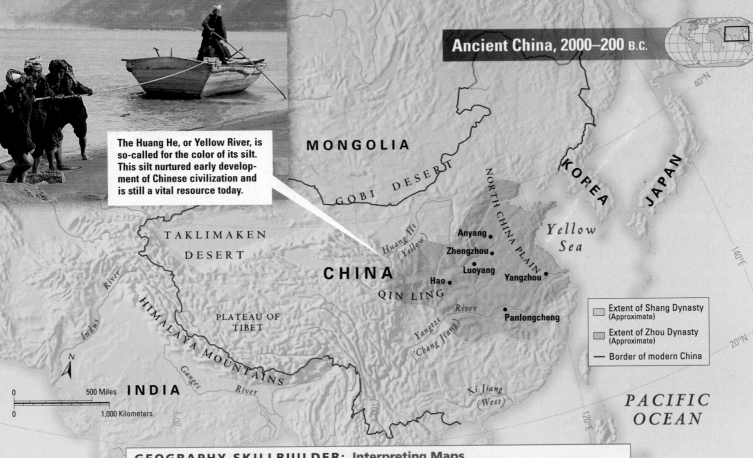

The Huang He, or Yellow River, is so-called for the color of its silt. This silt nurtured early development of Chinese civilization and is still a vital resource today.

Ancient China, 2000–200 B.C.

MONGOLIA

GOBI DESERT

TAKLIMAKEN DESERT

CHINA

QIN LING

HIMALAYA MOUNTAINS

PLATEAU OF TIBET

INDIA

Indus River

Ganges River

Huang He (Yellow)

Hao

Luoyang

Zhengzhou

Anyang

Yangzhou

NORTH CHINA PLAIN

Yellow Sea

KOREA

JAPAN

Yangtze (Chang Jiang) River

Panlongcheng

Xi Jiang (West)

PACIFIC OCEAN

Extent of Shang Dynasty (Approximate)

Extent of Zhou Dynasty (Approximate)

Border of modern China

0 500 Miles
0 1,000 Kilometers

GEOGRAPHY SKILLBUILDER: Interpreting Maps
1. **Location** Describe the location of the Huang He and Yangtze River in terms of where they rise and end.
2. **Region** What area did the Shang and Zhou dynasties control?

Civilization Emerges in Shang Times

Although Chinese civilization arose later than the others discussed in this chapter, humans have inhabited China for about a million years. Fossil remains show that ancestors of modern humans lived in southwest China about 1.7 million years ago. In northern China near Beijing, a *Homo erectus* skeleton was found. Known as Peking man, his remains show that people settled the river valley about 500,000 years ago.

The First Dynasties Even before the Sumerians settled in southern Mesopotamia, early Chinese cultures were building farming settlements along the Huang He. Around 2000 B.C., some of these settlements grew into China's first cities. According to legend, the first Chinese dynasty, the Xia (shyah) Dynasty, emerged about this time. Its leader was an engineer and mathematician named Yu. Yu's flood-control and irrigation projects helped tame the Huang He and its tributaries so settlements could grow. Since there are no written records from this period, the actual events of this time are unknown. During this period, however, farm surpluses allowed cities to grow. However, the legend of Yu reflects the level of technology of a society making the transition to civilization.

About the time the civilizations of Mesopotamia, Egypt, and the Indus Valley fell to outside invaders, a people called the Shang rose to power in northern China. The Shang Dynasty, which lasted from about 1532 to 1027 B.C., became the first family of Chinese rulers to leave written records. The Shang kings also built elaborate palaces and tombs that have been uncovered by archaeologists. Artifacts found among the remains have revealed a great deal about Shang society.

Early Cities Among the oldest and most important Shang cities was Anyang (ahn·YAHNG), one of the capitals of the Shang Dynasty. Unlike the cities of the Indus Valley or Fertile Crescent, Anyang was built mainly of wood. The city stood in a forest

Lady Hao's Tomb

Archaeologists have discovered several Shang royal tombs near Anyang. While most of these vast underground tombs had been robbed over the centuries, a significant one was unearthed intact—the tomb of Fu Hao.

Lady Hao was a wife of king Wu Ding, who ruled during the 1200s B.C. Her relatively small grave contained some 460 bronze artifacts, 750 jade objects, and more than 6,880 cowry shells. The other, far larger Shang royal tombs must have contained even greater wealth.

Writings found in other places reveal a remarkable figure in Lady Hao. On behalf of her husband, she led more than one military campaign, once with a force of 13,000 troops. She also took charge of rituals dedicated to the spirits of Shang ancestors, a duty reserved for the most distinguished members of the royal family.

clearing. The higher classes lived in timber-framed houses with walls of clay and straw. These houses lay inside the city walls. The peasants lived in hovels outside the city.

The Shang surrounded their cities with massive earthen walls for protection. The archaeological remains of one city include a wall of packed earth 118 feet wide at its base that encircled an area of 1.2 square miles. It likely took 10,000 men more than 12 years to build such a structure. Like the pyramids of Egypt, these walls demonstrate the Shang rulers' ability to raise and control large forces of workers.

Shang peoples needed walled cities because they were constantly waging war. The chariot, one of the major tools of war, was probably first introduced by contact with cultures from western Asia. The professional warriors, who made up the noble class, underwent lengthy training to learn the techniques of driving and shooting from horse-drawn chariots.

Social Classes Shang society was sharply divided between nobles and peasants. The Shang were governed by a ruling class of warrior-nobles headed by a king. These noble families owned the land. They governed the scattered villages within the Shang lands and sent tribute to the Shang ruler in exchange for local control.

Meanwhile, peasants tilled the soil for their overlords. The farmers had no plows, only wooden digging sticks, and hoes and sickles made of stone. (The Shang made magnificent bronze weapons and ceremonial vessels, but they believed bronze was too precious to be used for mere tools.) The soil was so rich, though, that it yielded two crops a year of millet, rice, and wheat.

> **THINK THROUGH HISTORY**
> **A. Compare** What did Shang cities have in common with those of Sumer?

The Origins of Chinese Culture

The culture that grew up in China had strong bonds that made for unity. From earliest times, the group seems to have been more important than the individual. Above all, people's lives were governed by their duties to two important authorities—their family and their king or emperor.

Family and Society The family was central to Chinese society. The most important virtue was respect for one's parents. The elder men in the family controlled the family's property and made important decisions. Women, on the other hand, were treated as inferiors. They were expected to obey their fathers, their husbands, and later, their own sons. When a girl was between 13 and 16 years old, her marriage was arranged, and she moved into the house of her husband. Only by bearing sons for her husband's family could she hope to improve her status.

A person's chief loyalty throughout life was to the family. Beyond this, people owed obedience and respect to the ruler of the Middle Kingdom, just as they did to the elders in their family.

Religious Beliefs In China, the family was closely linked to religion. The Chinese believed that the spirits of family ancestors had the power to bring good fortune or disaster to living members of the family. The Chinese did not regard these spirits as mighty gods. Rather, the spirits were more like troublesome or helpful neighbors who demanded attention and respect. Every family paid respect to the father's ancestors and made sacrifices in their honor.

Through the spirits of the ancestors, the Shang consulted the gods. The Shang worshiped a supreme god, Shang Di, as well as many lesser gods. Shang kings consulted the gods through the use of **oracle bones,**

This Shang oracle bone was found in the city of Anyang.

Chinese Writing

The earliest writing systems in the world—including Chinese, Sumerian, and Egyptian—developed from pictographs, or simplified drawings of objects. The writing system used in China today is directly related to the pictographic writing found on Shang oracle bones. As you can see in the chart below, the ancient pictographs can still be recognized in many modern Chinese characters.

	ox	goat, sheep	tree	moon	earth	water	field	heaven	to pray
Ancient symbol	𜵵	𜵶	𜵷	𜵸	𜵹	𜵺	田	𜵻	𜵼
Modern character	牛	羊	木	月	土	水	田	天	祝

animal bones and tortoise shells on which priests had scratched questions for the gods. After inscribing a question on the bone, a priest applied a hot poker to it, which caused it to crack. The priests then interpreted the cracks to see how the gods had answered.

Development of Writing The earliest evidence of Chinese writing comes from the oracle bones. In the Chinese method of writing, each character stands for an idea, not a sound. Recall that many of the Egyptian hieroglyphs stood for sounds in the spoken language. In contrast, there were practically no links between China's spoken language and its written language. One could read Chinese without being able to speak a word of it. (This seems less strange when you think of our own number system. Both a French person and an American can understand the written equation 2 + 2 = 4. But an American may not understand the spoken statement "Deux et deux font quatre.")

The Chinese system of writing had one major advantage. People in all parts of China could learn the same system of writing, even if their spoken languages were very different. Thus, the Chinese written language helped unify a large and diverse land.

The disadvantage of the Chinese system was the enormous number of written characters to be memorized—a different one for each idea. A person needed to know over 1,000 characters to be barely literate. To be a true scholar, one needed to know at least 10,000 characters. For centuries, this severely limited the number of literate, educated Chinese. As a general rule, a noble's children learned to write, but a peasant's children did not.

Shang Technology and Artistry People who were skilled in special crafts made up a separate class in Chinese society. Like other commoners, this group lived outside the walls of cities such as Anyang. They manufactured weapons, jewelry, and religious items for the city's nobles.

Bronzeworking was the leading craft in which Shang artisans excelled. Beautiful bronze objects were used in religious rituals and were also symbols of royal power. Some of these objects were small and graceful, such as bronze bells. Others were massive caldrons, weighing almost a ton.

In earliest Shang times, the Chinese also learned how to make silk cloth by drawing the fine threads from a silkworm's cocoon and weaving them into a light, beautiful fabric. Nobles prided themselves on their finely embroidered silk shoes, which they regarded as a symbol of civilization.

THINK THROUGH HISTORY
B. Recognizing Effects How did writing help unite China?

This detail from the ritual vessel shown on page 25 reveals the artistry of Shang bronze workers.

Early River Valley Civilizations **49**

Zhou Bring New Ideas

Around 1027 B.C., a people called the Zhou (joh) overthrew the Shang and established their own dynasty. Due to their prior contact with the Shang, the Zhou had adopted much of the Shang culture. Therefore, the change in dynasty did not bring a new culture. Nevertheless, Zhou rule brought new ideas to Chinese civilization.

To justify their conquest, the Zhou leaders declared that the final Shang king had been such a poor ruler that the gods had taken away the Shang's rule and given it to the Zhou. This justification developed over time into a broader view that royal authority came from heaven. A just ruler had divine approval, known as the **Mandate of Heaven.** A wicked or foolish king could lose the Mandate of Heaven and so lose the right to rule. The Duke of Shao, an aide of the Zhou leader who conquered the Shang, described the mandate:

perhaps connect to France and Europe "Divine Right"

Vocabulary
mandate: a command or instruction from a higher authority.

A VOICE FROM THE PAST

Heaven, unpitying, has sent down ruin on Yin [another name for Shang]. Yin has lost the Mandate, and we Zhou have received it. I dare not say that our fortune would continue to prosper, even though I believe that heaven favors those who are sincere in their intentions. I dare not say, either that it would end in certain disaster. . . .

The Mandate of Heaven is not easy to gain. It will be lost when men fail to live up to the reverent and illustrious virtues of their forefathers.

DUKE OF SHAO, quoted in *The Chinese Heritage*

Strong dynasty establishes peace and prosperity; it is considered to have Mandate of Heaven.

New dynasty gains power, restores peace and order, and claims to have Mandate of Heaven.

In time, dynasty declines and becomes corrupt; taxes are raised; power grows weaker.

Dynastic Cycle in China

Role of Mandate of Heaven

Dynasty is overthrown through rebellion and bloodshed; new dynasty emerges.

Disasters such as floods, famines, peasant revolts, and invasions occur.

Old dynasty is seen as having lost Mandate of Heaven; rebellion is justified.

The Mandate of Heaven became central to the Chinese view of government. Floods, riots, and other calamities might be signs that the ancestral spirits were displeased with a king's rule. In that case, the Mandate of Heaven might pass to another noble family. This was the Chinese explanation for rebellion, civil war, and the rise of a new dynasty.

Chinese history is marked by a succession of dynasties until dynastic rule was finally overthrown in the early 1900s. Historians describe the pattern of rise, decline, and replacement of dynasties as the **dynastic cycle.**

Control Through Feudalism The Zhou Dynasty controlled lands that stretched far beyond the Huang He in the north to the Yangtze in the south. In response to the challenge of governing this vast area, they gave control over different regions to members of the royal family and other trusted nobles. This established a system called feudalism. **Feudalism** is a political system in which nobles, or lords, are granted the use of lands that legally belong to the king. In return, the nobles owe loyalty and military service to the king and protection to the people who live on their estates. (Similar systems would arise centuries later in both Japan and Europe.)

At first, the local lords lived in small walled towns and had to submit to the superior strength and control of the Zhou rulers. Gradually, however, the lords grew stronger as the towns grew into cities and expanded into the surrounding territory. Peoples who had been hostile toward the lords gradually accepted their rule and adopted Zhou ways. As a result, the local lords became less dependent on the king. More and more, they fought among themselves and with neighboring peoples for wealth and territory.

THINK THROUGH HISTORY
C. Synthesizing
According to Chinese beliefs, what role did the Mandate of Heaven play in the dynastic cycle?

Improvements in Technology and Trade Although warfare was common throughout the Zhou Dynasty, the era also produced many innovations. As large cities grew, the Zhou built roads and canals to supply them. These in turn stimulated trade and agriculture. The Zhou also introduced coined money, which further improved trade. To run the daily operations of the cities, a new class of civil servants, or government administrative workers, emerged.

The major technological advancement was the use of iron. The Zhou developed blast furnaces that allowed them to produce cast iron. This skill would not be matched in Europe until the Middle Ages. The Zhou used iron to create weapons, especially dagger-axes and swords. They also used it for common agricultural tools such as sickles, knives, and spades. Since iron is stronger than bronze, iron tools made farm work easier and more productive. The ability to grow more food helped Zhou farmers support thriving cities.

Background
By about 1000 B.C., most advanced civilizations produced iron tools and weapons. The cast iron of the Chinese was produced by a special process in which molten iron was poured into molds and allowed to harden.

A Period of Warring States The Zhou ruled from around 1027 to 256 B.C. For the first 300 years of this long period, the Zhou empire was generally peaceful and stable. Gradually, however, Zhou rule weakened. In 771 B.C., nomads from the north and west sacked the city of Hao, the Zhou capital. They murdered the Zhou monarch, but a few members of the royal family escaped eastward to the city of Luoyang (lwoh-YAHNG). Here in this new capital on the Huang He, the Zhou Dynasty pretended to rule for another 500 years.

In fact, the Zhou kings at Luoyang were almost powerless, and they could not control the noble families. Trained as warriors, the lords sought every opportunity to pick fights with neighboring lords. As their power grew, these warlords claimed to be kings in their own territory. As a result, the later years of the Zhou are often called "the time of the warring states."

Even the style of warfare changed. Under feudalism, nobles had fought according to an honorable code of conduct. With the decline of law and order, professional warriors and mercenaries set the rules of battle. Peasant foot soldiers, supported by cavalry, replaced chariots as the main force on the battlefield. New weapons came into use, such as the crossbow, which would not be introduced in Europe until the Middle Ages.

Vocabulary
mercenary: a soldier who will fight in any army for pay.

In this time of bloodshed, traditional values collapsed. At the very heart of Chinese civilization was a love of order, harmony, and respect for authority. Now there was chaos, arrogance, and defiance. How could China be saved? The dynastic cycle was about to bring a new start at a time when migrations and invasions were changing the lands of all the early civilizations.

These Chinese coins shaped like a hoe and a knife come from the Zhou period. Their shapes may reflect the practice of using tools such as hoes and knives for payment before coins existed.

Section 4 Assessment

1. TERMS & NAMES

Identify
• loess
• oracle bone
• Mandate of Heaven
• dynastic cycle
• feudalism

2. TAKING NOTES

Create a time line of the major developments in the early Chinese dynasties, using a form such as the one below.

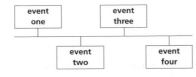

Which event do you think was the most critical turning point? Why?

3. ANALYZING

The group was often more important than the individual in Chinese culture. In your judgment, what are the benefits and drawbacks of this belief?

THINK ABOUT
• family roles
• the characteristics of a ruler
• role of spirit gods

4. ANALYZING THEMES

Power and Authority Do you think that the Zhou Dynasty's downfall resulted because of their method of control? Why or why not?

THINK ABOUT
• feudalism
• the large division of rich and poor
• the vast controlled lands
• the noble-king relationship

Early River Valley Civilizations **51**

TERMS & NAMES

Briefly explain the importance of each of the following to early river valley civilizations, 3500–450 B.C.

1. irrigation
2. city-state
3. polytheism
4. empire
5. mummification
6. hieroglyphics
7. subcontinent
8. monsoon
9. Mandate of Heaven
10. feudalism

Interact *with* History

On page 26, you looked at the justice of Hammurabi's Code. Now that you have read about the development of four civilizations, think about how laws differ from place to place. How have they developed and changed over time? What similarities do you see between Hammurabi's Code and the laws you live under today? How are they different? Discuss your opinions with a small group.

REVIEW QUESTIONS

SECTION 1 (*pages 27–32*)
City-States in Mesopotamia

11. What is the Fertile Crescent and why is it called that?
12. Name three disadvantages of Sumer's natural environment.
13. What circumstances led to the beginning of organized government?

SECTION 2 (*pages 33–41*)
Pyramids on the Nile

14. Why did the Egyptians build pyramids?
15. Herodotus remarked that Egypt was the "gift of the Nile." What did he mean by this?

SECTION 3 (*pages 42–45*)
Planned Cities on the Indus

16. What does the uniformity of Indus Valley cities tell us about their government?
17. Give two reasons historians use to explain the downfall of Indus Valley cities.

SECTION 4 (*pages 46–51*)
River Dynasties in China

18. Why is it not surprising that China's early settlements developed where they did?
19. What was the great advantage of the Chinese written language?
20. Explain the dynastic cycle in China.

Visual Summary

Early River Valley Civilizations

	Environment	Power & Authority	Science & Technology
Sumer	• Flooding of Tigris and Euphrates unpredictable • No natural barriers • Limited natural resources for making tools or buildings	• Independent city-states, often warring • City-states governed first by priests, then by generals who became kings • City-states eventually united into first empires by conquerors	• Irrigation • Cuneiform • Bronze • Wheel, sail, plow
Egypt	• Flooding of the Nile predictable • Nile an easy transportation link between Egypt's villages • Deserts were natural barriers	• Kingdom with strong government organization • Theocracy, with pharaohs ruling as gods • Pharaohs built pyramids	• Hieroglyphics • Pyramids • Mathematics, geometry • Medicine
Indus Valley	• Indus flooding unpredictable • Monsoon winds • Mountains, deserts were natural barriers	• Strong centralized government • Planned cities • Social divisions not significant	• Writing (not yet deciphered) • Cities built on precise grid • Plumbing and sewage systems
China	• Huang He flooding unpredictable • Mountains, deserts natural barriers • Geographically isolated from other ancient civilizations	• Community and family more important than individual • Sharp divisions between nobles and peasants • Mandate of Heaven	• Writing • Silk • Coined money • Cast iron

CRITICAL THINKING

1. RELIGIOUS BELIEFS

Create a Venn diagram like the one shown below to indicate differences and similarities in religious beliefs among these ancient civilizations.

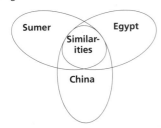

2. PUBLIC WORKS

THEME **POWER AND AUTHORITY** Think about a massive public project that might take place today, such as building a new subway system or a large dam. In terms of government power and authority, how would this be similar to the building of the pyramids? How would it be different?

3. WOMEN IN ANCIENT SOCIETIES

Women were treated differently in the four civilizations discussed in this chapter. If you had been a woman during this time, in which civilization would you have preferred to live? Why?

4. ANALYZING PRIMARY SOURCES

The following is an excerpt from an ancient Egyptian hymn praising the Nile. Read the paragraph and answer the questions below it.

> **A VOICE FROM THE PAST**
> The Lord of Fishes, He Who Makes the marsh birds to Go Upstream. There are no birds which come down because of the hot winds. He who makes barley and brings emmer [a kind of wheat] into being, that he may make the temples festive. If he is sluggish, then nostrils are stopped up, and everybody is poor. If there be thus a cutting down in the food offerings of the gods, then a million men perish among mortals, covetousness is practiced, the entire land is in a fury, and great and small are on the execution-block. . . . When he rises, then the land is in jubilation, then every belly is in joy, every backbone takes on laughter, and every tooth is exposed.
>
> "Hymn to the Nile," from *Ancient Near Eastern Texts*

- How does this quote show the importance of the Nile?
- What does the hymn show about ancient Egyptian culture?

CHAPTER ACTIVITIES

1. LIVING HISTORY: Unit Portfolio Project

THEME **INTERACTION WITH ENVIRONMENT** Your unit portfolio project focuses on showing how people in history have interacted with the environment (see page 3). For Chapter 2, you might use one of the following ideas to add to your portfolio.

- You are a news reporter reporting on the flood conditions in early Sumer. Ask classmates to role-play citizens before and after the invention of irrigation ditches. Tape-record your interviews.
- Write four poems, one for each civilization in the chapter. Include some reference to how each civilization interacted with the environment.
- Make a map of China showing how natural barriers helped to isolate Chinese civilization from other areas. Create your map on paper using an outline map, or make a salt map to show the features in three-dimensional relief.

2. CONNECT TO TODAY: Cooperative Learning

THEME **SCIENCE AND TECHNOLOGY** Indus Valley cities were laid out on a precise grid system. They were planned cities. Most cities without a grid system probably developed over a long period of time. Work with a team to create a street map of your hometown.

- Look at street maps of Washington, D.C. and Boston. Boston was not a planned city. Washington, D.C. was planned. How can you tell?

 Using the Internet, the library, or government resources, research the structure of your hometown, then draw it. Was it a planned city?

3. INTERPRETING A TIME LINE

Revisit the unit time line on pages 2–3 and study the segment for Chapter 2. Which of the events are examples of a well-organized government? Why?

FOCUS ON GEOGRAPHY

Look at the four ancient cities shown on the following climate map.

- Which cities are located in desert climates?
- Which city is not located in a dry climate? What is its climate region called?

Connect to History Identify which civilization each city belongs to. Which of these civilizations developed the latest?

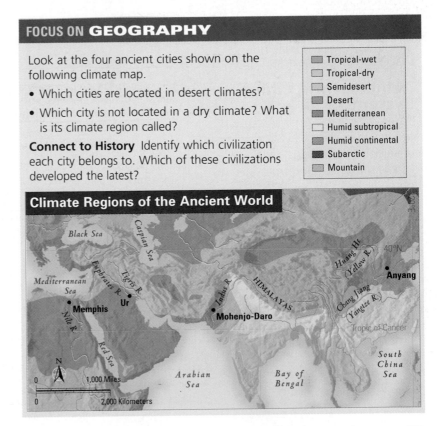

Climate Regions of the Ancient World

Legend:
- Tropical-wet
- Tropical-dry
- Semidesert
- Desert
- Mediterranean
- Humid subtropical
- Humid continental
- Subarctic
- Mountain

People and Ideas on the Move, 3500 B.C.–259 B.C.

PREVIEWING THEMES

Interaction with Environment

Early peoples often migrated from their lands both to escape hostile circumstances and to find new homes that promised a better life. Many times they responded to changing climates that hindered their way of life. Once resettled, they had to deal with the environment of their new homeland.

Economics

Traders long ago went to sea to transport their goods to other parts of the world. Among the most expert of early trading peoples were the Phoenicians. They so dominated the Mediterranean that it was called their lake. Sea traders also traveled between India and Arabia, spreading ideas as well as merchandise.

Religious and Ethical Systems

Three major world religions practiced by millions today developed during this time. Hinduism and Buddhism originated in India, while Judaism developed in Southwest Asia. Each has deeply influenced the way that people look at their world and judge human behavior.

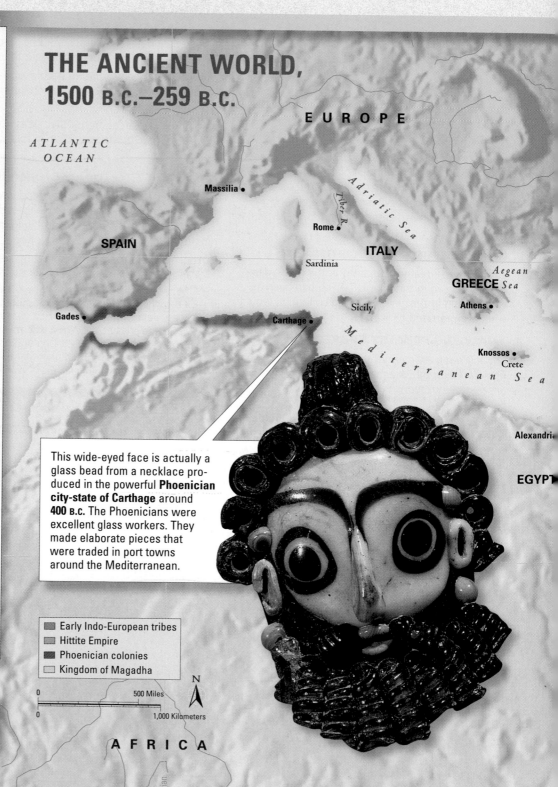

THE ANCIENT WORLD, 1500 B.C.–259 B.C.

ATLANTIC OCEAN

EUROPE

Massilia

Adriatic Sea

Tiber R.

Rome

SPAIN

ITALY

Sardinia

Aegean Sea

GREECE

Athens

Gades

Sicily

Knossos

Crete

Carthage

Mediterranean Sea

Alexandria

EGYPT

AFRICA

This wide-eyed face is actually a glass bead from a necklace produced in the powerful **Phoenician city-state of Carthage** around **400 B.C.** The Phoenicians were excellent glass workers. They made elaborate pieces that were traded in port towns around the Mediterranean.

- ▦ Early Indo-European tribes
- ▦ Hittite Empire
- ▦ Phoenician colonies
- ▦ Kingdom of Magadha

0   500 Miles

0   1,000 Kilometers

N

0° Prime Meridian

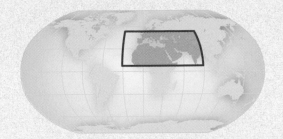

Reverence for cows, particularly milk cows, stretches back to the earliest days of the **Hindu religion.** Hindu scriptures call the cow Devi, or goddess. They also associate cows with Aditi, the mother of the gods herself. Cows still enjoy a special status in Hindu religion. In **India** today, killing or harming cows is forbidden. The animals are also free to wander about in cities—like these cows sitting in the middle of a busy street.

In one of the most famous episodes in the Bible, the Queen of Sheba visits **Israel's King Solomon.** The Arabian queen had heard of Solomon's great wisdom and had come to test it with difficult questions. When Solomon answered them all, the queen exclaimed: ". . . I did not believe the reports until I had come and my own eyes had seen it; your wisdom and prosperity far surpass the report that I had heard." This fresco by the 15th-century Italian artist Piero della Francesca illustrates the queen's visit.

STEPPES

Black Sea

CAUCASUS MOUNTAINS

Caspian Sea

Hittite Empire
• **Hattusas**

ASIA MINOR

Assyria

Euphrates River

Tigris River

yprus

Byblos
Sidon
Tyre

Phoenicia

Babylon •

Babylonia

erusalem •
Canaan

Ur •

emphis

• **Thebes**

ile River

ASIA

Indus River

Harappa •

• **Delhi (Yudhisthira)**

Ganges River

• **Kapilavastu**

• **Mohenjo-Daro**

Magadha

Tropic of Cancer

INDIA

Arabian Sea

INDIAN OCEAN

40°N

80°E

Interact *with* History

Yου are drawing water from your well when, without warning, a magnificent white horse appears on the horizon. You have heard stories about this horse. You know that, once a year, it is sent out by a foreign king to roam freely outside his land. The armed soldiers who are following the horse will claim all the land it travels through for their king.

You have three choices. You could stay and fight for your land. However, there are so many soldiers that it is unlikely that you and the other villagers would win. You can stay and accept the domination of the new ruler from the north. Or you can gather up your family and flee, as many others have done before you.

Will the invaders capture and enslave you? Or will they allow you to continue to live as you have?

Will you stay or flee?

Will the invaders take your land?

What new laws and beliefs will these invaders bring? How will they affect you?

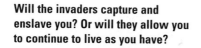

EXAMINING *the* ISSUES

- If you stay, will you be able to live in peace with the conquerors?

- Can you pretend to accept their rules and go about your life as before, perhaps practicing your religion in secret?

- If you leave, will you be welcomed in the land you flee to? Will you have to adopt the customs of the people living there? How will you acquire farmland?

As a class, discuss these options. In your discussion, weigh the advantages and disadvantages of both choices.

As you read about migration in this chapter, see how old and new ways of doing things can blend together when groups of people move.

1 Indo-European Migrations

TERMS & NAMES
- Indo-Europeans
- steppes
- migration
- Hittites
- Anatolia
- Aryans
- *Vedas*
- Brahmin
- caste
- *Mahabharata*

MAIN IDEA	WHY IT MATTERS NOW
Indo-European peoples migrated into Europe, India, and Southwest Asia and interacted with peoples living there.	Half the people living today speak languages that stem from the original Indo-European languages.

SETTING THE STAGE In India and in Mesopotamia, civilizations first developed along lush river valleys. Even as large cities such as Mohenjo-Daro and Harappa declined, agriculture and small urban communities flourished. These wealthy river valleys attracted seminomadic tribes. These peoples may have left their own homelands because of politics or changes in the environment.

Indo-Europeans Migrate

Background
This steppe area included parts of present-day Romania, Moldova, Ukraine, southern Russia, and Kazakhstan.

The **Indo-Europeans** were a group of seminomadic peoples who came from the **steppes**—dry grasslands that stretched north of the Caucasus (KAW·kuh·suhs). The Caucasus are the mountains between the Black and Caspian seas. (See the map on pages 54–55.) These primarily pastoral people herded cattle, sheep, and goats. The Indo-Europeans also tamed horses and rode into battle in light, two-wheeled chariots. They lived in tribes that spoke forms of a language that we call Indo-European.

The Indo-European Language Family The languages of the Indo-Europeans were the ancestors of many of the modern languages of Europe, Southwest Asia, and South Asia. English, Spanish, Persian, and Hindi all trace their origins back to different forms of the original Indo-European language.

Vocabulary
Slavic-speakers: speakers of a language that developed into most of today's eastern European languages.

Historians can actually tell where different Indo-European tribes settled by the languages they spoke. Some Slavic-speakers moved north and west. Others, who spoke early Celtic, Germanic, and Italic languages, moved west through Europe. Still others, Greek- and Persian-speakers, went south. The Aryans (AIR·ee·uhnz), who spoke an early form of Sanskrit, penetrated the mountain passes of the Hindu Kush and entered India.

Notice the similarities of words within the Indo-European family of languages.

Language Family Resemblances

English	mother	father/papa	daughter	new	six
Sanskrit	mātár	pitár	duhitá	návas	sát
Persian	muhdáhr	puhdáhr	dukhtáhr	now	shahsh
Spanish	madre	padre	hija	nuevo	seis
German	Mutter	Vater	Tochter	neu	sechs

An Unexplained Migration No one is quite sure why these people left their homelands in the steppes. The lands where their animals grazed may have dried up. Their human or animal population may have grown too large to feed. They may also have tried to escape from invaders, or from an outbreak of disease.

Whatever the reason, Indo-European nomads began to migrate outward in all directions between 1700 and 1200 B.C. These **migrations,** movements of a people from one region to another, did not happen all at once, but in waves over a long period of time.

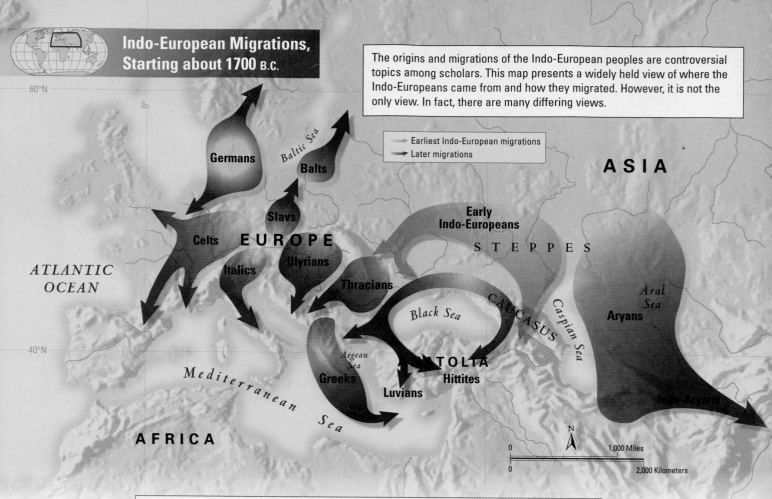

Indo-European Migrations, Starting about 1700 B.C.

The origins and migrations of the Indo-European peoples are controversial topics among scholars. This map presents a widely held view of where the Indo-Europeans came from and how they migrated. However, it is not the only view. In fact, there are many differing views.

→ Earliest Indo-European migrations
→ Later migrations

60°N

Germans
Baltic Sea
Balts
Slavs
Celts
EUROPE
Italics
Illyrians
Thracians
ATLANTIC OCEAN
40°N
Aegean Sea
Greeks
Luvians
ANATOLIA
Hittites
Black Sea
CAUCASUS
STEPPES
Early Indo-Europeans
ASIA
Caspian Sea
Aral Sea
Aryans
Indo-Aryans
Mediterranean Sea
AFRICA

N

0   1,000 Miles
0   2,000 Kilometers

GEOGRAPHY SKILLBUILDER: Interpreting Maps
1. **Location** *Which Indo-European people reached the farthest west?*
2. **Movement** *Describe the movement of the Indo-Europeans in their earliest migrations.*

Hittites Blend Empire and Technology

By about 2000 B.C., one group of Indo-European speakers, the **Hittites,** occupied **Anatolia** (AN·uh·TOH·lee·ah), also called Asia Minor. Anatolia is a huge peninsula in modern-day Turkey that juts out into the Black and Mediterranean seas. Anatolia was a high, rocky plateau, rich in timber and agriculture. Nearby mountains held important mineral deposits. Separate Hittite city-states came together to form an empire there in about 1650 B.C. The city of Hattusas (hah·TOO·sahs) was its capital.

The Hittite empire went on to dominate Southwest Asia for 450 years. Hittites occupied Babylon, the chief city in the Tigris-Euphrates Valley, and struggled with Egypt for control of northern Syria. Neither the Hittites nor the Egyptians were able to get the upper hand. So, the two peoples ended their conflicts by signing an unusual peace treaty. In it, they each pledged to help the other fight off future invaders. ✳

Hittites Adopt and Adapt The Hittites used their own Indo-European language with one another. However, for international use, they adopted Akkadian, the language of the Babylonians they had conquered. Akkadian was already widely spoken in Mesopotamia, and Babylonian culture was more advanced. The Hittites thus blended their own traditions with those of other, more advanced peoples. In the process, they spread many innovative ideas throughout Southwest Asia.

The Hittites borrowed ideas about literature, art, politics, and law from the Mesopotamian peoples they encountered. However, they always managed to give these ideas a distinctive twist. Their own legal code, for example, was similar to Hammurabi's Code but was more forgiving. Murderers were not automatically punished by death. A convicted murderer could make up for the crime by giving the victim's family a slave or a child from his own family.

Chariots and Iron Bring Victory The Hittites excelled in the technology of war. They conquered an empire even against Egyptian opposition—largely through their superior chariots and their iron weapons. The Hittite war chariot was light and easy to maneuver even at high speeds. The chariot had two wheels and a wooden frame covered with leather and was pulled by two or sometimes four horses. On the battlefield, the Hittite chariot proved itself a superb fighting machine. It helped make the Hittites conquerors.

The Hittites used iron in their chariots, and they owed many of their military victories to the skill of their ironworkers. Ancient peoples had long known that iron was stronger than bronze. They also knew that it could hold a sharper edge. However, the process of purifying iron ore and working it into weapons and tools is complex. For centuries, prehistoric people used only the purified iron they obtained from meteorites. Around 1500 B.C., the Hittites were the first in Southwest Asia to smelt iron and harden it into weapons of war. The raw materials they needed—iron ore and wood to make charcoal— were easily available to them in the mountains of Anatolia. Knowledge of iron technology traveled widely with the Hittites—in both their trade and conquests.

Despite its military might, the powerful Hittite empire fell quite suddenly around the year 1190 B.C. As part of a great wave of invasions, tribes attacked from the north and burned the Hittite capital city. Hittite supremacy in Southwest Asia had ended.

THINK THROUGH HISTORY
A. Analyzing Effects
How did environmental features in Anatolia help the Hittites advance technologically?

Aryan Invaders Transform India

In about 1500 B.C., the Hittites were establishing themselves in Anatolia. At the same time, another Indo-European people, the **Aryans**, crossed over the northwest mountain passes into the Indus River Valley of India. Though they left almost no archaeological record, their sacred literature, the **Vedas** (VAY-duhz), left a fairly reliable picture of Aryan life. The *Vedas* are four collections of prayers, magical spells, and instructions for performing rituals. The most important of the collections is the *Rig Veda*. The *Rig Veda* contains 1028 hymns, all devoted to Aryan gods.

For many years, no written form of the *Vedas* existed. Instead, elders of one generation passed on this tradition orally to men of the next generation. If a prayer was uttered incorrectly, they believed terrible consequences might result. So accuracy was crucial.

A Caste System Develops The Aryans ("the nobles" in their language) called the people they found in India *dasas* ("dark"), referring to the color of their skin. (*Dasa* eventually became the Aryan word for slave.) The Aryans differed from the *dasas* in many ways. Aryans were taller, lighter in skin color, and spoke a different language. Unlike the earlier inhabitants of the Indus Valley, the Aryans had not developed a writing system. They were also a pastoral people and counted their wealth in cows. The *dasas*, on the other hand, were town dwellers who lived in communities protected by walls. The Aryans offered sacrifices to heroic nature gods, such as Indra, the thunder god, and Agni, the fire god. Archaeological evidence seems to show that the *dasas* worshiped life-giving principles, such as the "Great God" Shiva and various mother goddesses.

When they first arrived in India, Aryans were divided into three social classes: **Brahmins** (priests), warriors, and peasants or traders. The class that an Aryan belonged to determined his or her role in society. At first, the three classes mixed freely. Eventually, non-Aryan laborers or craftsmen (*shudras*) formed a fourth group.

Background
Indra was the most popular god in the *Rig Veda*. Indra hurled thunderbolts, ate bulls, and raced his chariot across the sky.

Hittites sometimes owned small gold statues of their gods—probably intended to protect them from danger or bad fortune.

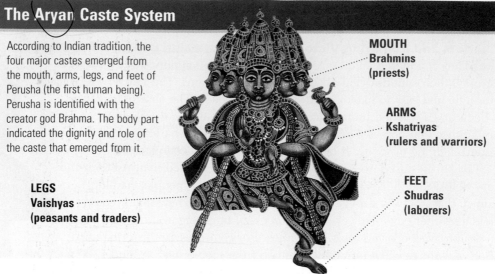

The Aryan Caste System

According to Indian tradition, the four major castes emerged from the mouth, arms, legs, and feet of Perusha (the first human being). Perusha is identified with the creator god Brahma. The body part indicated the dignity and role of the caste that emerged from it.

MOUTH
Brahmins
(priests)

ARMS
Kshatriyas
(rulers and warriors)

LEGS
Vaishyas
(peasants and traders)

FEET
Shudras
(laborers)

As the Aryans settled in India, they developed closer contacts with non-Aryans. To regulate those contacts, the Aryans made class restrictions more rigid. *Shudras* did work that Aryans did not want to do. V*arna*, or skin color, was a distinguishing feature of this system. So the four major groups came to be known as the *varnas*. Much later—in the fifteenth century A.D.— explorers from Portugal encountered this social system and called these groups **castes** (kasts).

As time went on, the four basic castes gradually grew more complex—with hundreds of subdivisions. People were born into their caste for life. Their caste membership determined the work they did, the man or woman they could marry, and the people with whom they could eat. Ritual purity—for example, habits of eating and washing that made a person physically and spiritually clean— became all-important. Those who were the most impure because of their work (butchers, gravediggers, collectors of trash) lived outside the caste structure. They were known as "untouchables," since even their touch endangered the ritual purity of others.

Aryan Kingdoms Arise Over the next few centuries, Aryans extended their settlements east, along the Ganges and Yamuna river valleys. (See map on page 61.) Progress was slow because of difficulties clearing the jungle for farming. This task grew easier when iron came into use in India about 1000 B.C.

When the Aryans first arrived in India, chiefs were elected by the entire tribe. Around 1000 B.C., however, minor kings who wanted to set up territorial kingdoms arose among the Aryans. They struggled with one another for land and power. And each claimed his authority as a right from the gods. Out of this strife emerged a major kingdom: Magadha. Under a series of ambitious kings, Magadha began expanding in the sixth century B.C. by taking over surrounding kingdoms. By the second century B.C., Magadha had expanded south to occupy almost all of the Indian subcontinent.

One of the great epics of India, the **Mahabharata** (muh·HAH·BAHR·ah·tuh), reflects the struggles that took place in India as the Aryans moved relentlessly south. The poem is the story of a great war between two sets of cousins, the Pandavas and the Kauravas. The *Mahabharata*'s 106,000 verses make it the longest single poem in the world. For several hundred years, it survived as an oral tradition.

CONNECT *to* TODAY

Untouchables Then and Now
In the sixth century B.C., ritual purity was so important to upper-caste Indians that untouchables had to ring a bell to warn that they were coming near. Even the shadow of an untouchable falling on upper-caste Hindus would contaminate them. They would have to bathe before worshiping or eating.

In the 20th century, the great Indian leader Mahatma Gandhi called the untouchables *harijans*, or "children of God." Through his efforts, caste distinctions were outlawed by the Indian constitution. Later, the 1955 Untouchability Act provided penalties for discrimination. However, 3,000-year-old traditions do not die easily. Most former untouchables in India today still suffer from extreme poverty and caste discrimination.

THINK THROUGH HISTORY
B. Making Inferences How were the more physical forms of work viewed by Aryans?

Elements of the *Mahabharata* indicate that a blending of cultures was taking place between Aryan and non-Aryan peoples. For example, Krishna, a semi-divine hero of the *Mahabharata,* is described as dark-faced. This suggests that he is non-Aryan.

One of the most famous incidents in all of Indian literature occurs when Krishna instructs one of the Pandavas, Arjuna (ahr·JUH·nuh), on the proper way to live one's life. Arjuna loses the will to fight when he sees his cousins lined up among the enemies he faces. He asks Krishna how we can find joy in killing our own kinsmen. Krishna answers that the eternal spirit (or Self) of every human being cannot kill or be killed. However, Arjuna must still do his duty and wage war:

A VOICE FROM THE PAST

He who thinks this Self [eternal spirit] to be a slayer, and he who thinks this Self to be slain, are both without discernment; the Soul slays not, neither is it slain. . . . But if you will not wage this lawful battle, then will you fail your own (caste) law and incur sin. . . . The people will name you with dishonor; and to a man of fame dishonor is worse than death.

KRISHNA, speaking in the *Mahabharata*

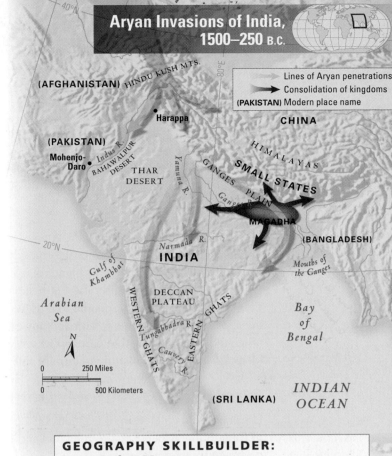

Aryan Invasions of India, 1500–250 B.C.

Lines of Aryan penetrations
Consolidation of kingdoms
(PAKISTAN) Modern place name

GEOGRAPHY SKILLBUILDER:
Interpreting Maps

1. **Location** *What waterway served as the focal point for the Aryan kingdom of Magadha?*
2. **Human-Environment Interaction** *Why do you think the Aryans migrated to the east of the Western Ghats?*

The violence and confusion of the time led many, like Krishna himself, to speculate about the place of the gods and human beings in the world. As a result of these speculations, religion in India gradually changed. New religions were born, which you will read about in Section 2.

Section 1 Assessment

1. TERMS & NAMES

Identify
- Indo-Europeans
- steppes
- migration
- Hittites
- Anatolia
- Aryans
- *Vedas*
- Brahmin
- caste
- *Mahabharata*

2. TAKING NOTES

Re-create the web below on your own paper, and fill in the names of some modern languages that stem from Indo-European roots.

Indo-European

Why did so many languages originate from Indo-European roots?

3. FORMING OPINIONS

What important contributions did the Aryan invaders make to the culture and way of life in India?

THINK ABOUT
- roles in society
- religion
- literature

4. ANALYZING THEMES

Interaction with Environment For what environmental reasons might the Indo-Europeans have migrated?

THINK ABOUT
- weather
- occupational needs
- health

PUSH
lack of resources
invasion
natural disasters
disease

PULL
resources
culture
religion
social
freedom

People and Ideas on the Move **61**

TERMS & NAMES
- reincarnation
- karma
- Jainism
- Siddhartha Gautama
- enlightenment
- nirvana

2 Roots of Hinduism and Buddhism

MAIN IDEA

The religious beliefs of the Vedic Age eventually developed into Hinduism and Buddhism.

WHY IT MATTERS NOW

Almost one-fifth of the world's people today practice one of these two religions.

What are the similarities between Christianity, Judaism, and Islam?

SETTING THE STAGE At first, the Aryans and non-Aryans followed their own forms of religion. Then as the two groups intermingled, the gods and forms of their religions also tended to blend together. This blending resulted in the worship of thousands of gods. Different ways of living and different beliefs made life more complex for both groups. This complexity led some people to question the world and their place in it. They even questioned the enormous wealth and power held by the Brahmin priests. These priests officiated at elaborate state ceremonies and sacrifices. Out of this turmoil, new religious ideas arose that have continued to influence millions of people today.

Hinduism Develops Over Centuries

Hinduism is a collection of religious beliefs that developed slowly over a long period of time. Some aspects of the religion can be traced back to ancient times. In a Hindu marriage today, for example, the bride and groom marry in the presence of the sacred fire as they did centuries ago. Verses from the *Vedas* are recited daily by the faithful. Also, some non-Aryan gods known in Vedic times, such as Krishna of the *Mahabharata,* continue to be worshiped.

From time to time, scholars have tried to organize the many popular cults, gods, and traditions into one grand system of belief. However, Hinduism—unlike religions such as Buddhism, Christianity, or Islam—cannot be traced back to one founder with a single set of ideas.

Vishnu grew to become a major Hindu god after the age of the *Vedas.* He is seen here as the whole Universe in all its variety. He is blue, the color of infinity.

Origins and Beliefs Hindus share a common world-view. They see religion as a way of liberating the soul from the illusions, disappointments, and mistakes of everyday existence. Sometime between 750 and 550 B.C., Hindu teachers tried to interpret and explain the hidden meaning of the Vedic hymns. As they meditated on the *Vedas,* they asked: What is the nature of reality? What is morality? Is there eternal life? What is the soul? The teachers' comments were later written down and became known as the *Upanishads* (oo·PAHN·ih·shahdz).

The *Upanishads* are written as dialogues, or discussions, between a student and a teacher. In the course of the dialogues, the two explore how a person can achieve liberation from desires and suffering. This is described as *moksha* (MOHK·shah), a state of perfect understanding of all things. The teacher distinguishes between atman, the individual soul of a living being, and Brahman, the world soul that contains and

Background
Both the *Vedas* and the *Upanishads* are counted among Hinduism's sacred books.

unites all atmans. The interconnectedness of all life is a basic concept in all Indian religions. Here is how one teacher explains the unifying spirit of Brahman:

A VOICE FROM THE PAST
Thou art woman, Thou art man, Thou art the lad and the maiden too. Thou art the old man tottering on his staff: Once born thou comest to be, thy face turned every way! A dark-blue moth art Thou, green [parrot] with red eyes. Pregnant with lightning—seasons, seas: Thyself beginningless, all things dost Thou pervade. From thee all worlds were born.

Svetasvatara Upanishad. IV. 3–4

When a person understands the relationship between atman and Brahman, that person achieves perfect understanding *(moksha)* and a release from life in this world. This understanding does not usually come in one lifetime. By the process of **reincarnation** (rebirth), an individual soul or spirit is born again and again until *moksha* is achieved. A soul's **karma**—good or bad deeds—follows from one reincarnation to another. Karma influences specific life circumstances, such as the caste one is born into, one's state of health, wealth or poverty, and so on.

Hinduism Changes and Develops Hinduism has gone through many changes over the last 2,500 years. The world soul, Brahman, was sometimes seen as having the personalities of three gods: Brahma, the creator; Vishnu, the protector; and Shiva, the destroyer. Vishnu also took on many forms or personalities, for example, as Krishna, the divine cowherder, and as Rama, the perfect king. Over the centuries, Brahma gradually faded into the background, while the many forms of a great Mother Goddess grew in importance.

Hindus today are free to choose the deity they worship or to choose none at all. Most, however, follow a family tradition that may go back centuries. They are also free to choose among three different paths for achieving *moksha*. They are the path of right thinking, the path of right action, or the path of religious devotion.

Hinduism and Society Hindu ideas about karma and reincarnation strengthened the caste system. If a person was born as an upper-caste male—a Brahmin, warrior, or merchant—his good fortune was said to come from good karma earned in a former life. However, a person who was born as a female, a laborer, or an untouchable might be getting the results of bad deeds in a former life. With some exceptions, only men of the top three varnas could hope to achieve *moksha* in their present life. The laws of karma worked with the same certainty as the world's other natural laws. Good karma brought good fortune and bad karma resulted in bad fortune.

Together, the beliefs of Hinduism and its caste structure dominated every aspect of a person's life. These beliefs determined what one could eat and how one ate it, personal cleanliness, the people one could associate with, how one dressed, and so on. Today, even in the most ordinary activities of daily life, Hindus turn to their religion for guidance.

New Religions Arise The same period of speculation reflected in the *Upanishads* also led to the rise of two other religions: Jainism (JY·nihz·uhm) and Buddhism. Mahavira, the founder of **Jainism,** was born about 599 B.C. and died in 527 B.C. Mahavira believed that everything in the universe has a soul and so should not be harmed. Jain monks carry the doctrine of nonviolence to its logical conclusion. They sweep ants off their path and wear gauze masks over their mouths to avoid breathing in an insect accidentally.

THINK THROUGH HISTORY
A. Making Inferences How might the lack of a single founder result in Hinduism changing more over time than other religions?

A Jain man wears a mask and carries a brush to prevent harm to small creatures.

Background
The doctrine of nonviolence *(ahimsa)* is important both to Hindus and Jains.

In keeping with this nonviolence, followers of Jainism looked for occupations that would not harm any creature. So they have a tradition of working in trade and commerce.

Because of their business activities, Jains today make up one of the wealthiest communities in India. Jains have traditionally preached tolerance of all religions. As a result, they have made few efforts to convert followers of other faiths. Because of this tolerance, Jains have not sent out missionaries. So, almost all the nearly 5 million Jains in the world today live in India.

THINK THROUGH HISTORY
B. Synthesizing
How far might the Jain respect for life extend?

HISTORY MAKERS

**Siddhartha Gautama
c. 563–483 B.C.**

According to Buddhist tradition, signs predicted even before his birth that Siddhartha Gautama would be a great man. His mother Mahamaya had dreamt of a beautiful elephant that was bright as silver. When asked to interpret the dream, Brahmin priests declared that the child to be born would either be a great monarch or a Buddha (an enlightened one).

Tradition also relates that at Gautama's birth, he exhibited the signs of a child destined for greatness. There were 32 such signs, including golden-tinged skin, webbed fingers and toes, a knob on the top of his skull, a long tongue, a tuft of hair between his eyebrows, and a thousand-spoked wheel on each foot. Some images of the Buddha display these traits.

The Buddha Seeks Enlightenment

Buddhism developed out of the same period of religious questioning that shaped modern Hinduism and Jainism. The founder of Buddhism, **Siddhartha Gautama** (sihd·DAHR·tuh GOW·tuh·muh) was born into a noble family that lived in Kapilavastu, in the foothills of the Himalayas in Nepal. According to Buddhist legend, the baby exhibited the marks of a great man. A prophecy indicated that if the child stayed at home he was destined to become a world ruler. If the child left home, however, he would become a universal spiritual leader. To make sure the boy would be a great king, his father isolated him in his palace. Separated from the world, Siddhartha married and had a son.

Siddhartha's Quest Siddhartha never ceased thinking about the world that lay outside the palace, which he had never seen. When he was 29, he ventured outside the palace four times. First he saw an old man, next a sick man, then a corpse being carried to the cremation grounds, and finally a wandering holy man who seemed at peace with himself. Siddhartha understood these events to mean that every living thing experiences old age, sickness, and death and that only a religious life offers a refuge from this inevitable suffering. Siddhartha decided to spend his life searching for religious truth and an end to suffering. So, soon after learning of his son's birth, he left the palace.

Siddhartha wandered through the forests of India for six years seeking **enlightenment,** or wisdom. He tried many ways of reaching an enlightened state. He first debated with other religious seekers. Then he fasted, eating only six grains of rice a day. (It was said that his stomach became so empty that by poking a finger into it, he could touch his backbone.) Yet none of these methods brought him to the truth, and he continued to suffer. Finally, he sat in meditation under a large fig tree. After 49 days of meditation, he achieved an understanding of the cause of suffering in this world. From then on, he was known as the Buddha, meaning "the enlightened one."

Vocabulary
fasted: did not eat.

Origins and Beliefs The Buddha preached his first sermon to five companions who had accompanied him on his wanderings. That first sermon became a landmark in the history of the world's religions. In it, he laid out the four main ideas that he had understood in his enlightenment. He called those ideas the Four Noble Truths:

First Noble Truth	Everything in life is suffering and sorrow.
Second Noble Truth	The cause of all suffering is people's selfish desire for the temporary pleasures of this world.
Third Noble Truth	The way to end all suffering is to end all desires.
Fourth Noble Truth	The way to overcome such desires and attain enlightenment is to follow the Eightfold Path, which is called the Middle Way between desires and self-denial.

The Eightfold Path was like a staircase. For the Buddha, those who were seeking enlightenment had to master one step at a time. Most often, this mastery would occur over many lifetimes. Here is how he described the Middle Way and its Eightfold Path:

A VOICE FROM THE PAST
What is the Middle Way? . . . It is the Noble Eightfold Path—Right Views, Right Resolve, Right Speech, Right Conduct, Right Livelihood, Right Effort, Right Mindfulness, and Right Concentration. This is the Middle Way.

The Buddha, from Samyutta Nikaya

By following the Eightfold Path, anyone could reach **nirvana,** the Buddha's word for release from selfishness and pain. The Buddha's teachings included many ideas from the Hindu tradition. However, they also differed sharply from that tradition.

THINK THROUGH HISTORY
C. Comparing In what ways are Buddhism and Hinduism similar?

As in Hinduism, the Buddha accepted the idea of reincarnation. He also accepted a cyclical, or repetitive, view of history, where the world is created and destroyed over and over again. However, the Buddha rejected the many gods of Hinduism. Instead, he taught a way of enlightenment. Like many of his time, the Buddha reacted against the privileges of the Brahmin priests, and thus he rejected the caste system. The final goals of both religions—*moksha* for Hindus and nirvana for Buddhists—are similar. Both involve a perfect state of understanding and a break from the chain of reincarnations.

The Religious Community The five disciples who heard the Buddha's first sermon were the first monks admitted to a *sangha,* or Buddhist religious order. At first, the *sangha* was a community of Buddhist monks and nuns. However, *sangha* eventually referred to the entire religious community. It included Buddhist laity (those who hadn't devoted their entire life to religion). The religious community, together with the Buddha and the *dharma* (Buddhist doctrine or law), make up the "Three Jewels" of Buddhism. Every day, Buddhists all over the world recognize the importance of the Three Jewels of their faith by declaring: "I take refuge in the Buddha. I take refuge in the law. I take refuge in the community." *The Three Jewels*

Buddhism and Society Because of his rejection of the caste system, many of the Buddha's early followers included laborers and craftspeople. He also gained a large following in northeast India, where the Aryans had less influence. The Buddha reluctantly admitted women to religious orders. He feared, however, that women's presence would distract men from their religious duties.

Monks and nuns took vows (solemn promises) to live a life of poverty, to be nonviolent, and not to marry. They wandered throughout India spreading the Buddha's teachings. Missionaries carried only a begging bowl to receive daily charity offerings from people. During the rainy season, they retreated to caves high up in the hillsides. Gradually, these seasonal retreats became permanent monasteries—some for men, others for women. One monastery, Nalanda, developed into a great university that also attracted non-Buddhists.

The teachings of the Buddha were written down shortly after his death. Buddhist sacred literature also includes commentaries, rules about monastic life, manuals on how to meditate,

Buddhist tradition tells that just before he died, the Buddha lay peacefully on his right side between two trees. Reclining Buddhas, like this one in Laos, point to this calm acceptance of death as the ideal.

65

and legends about the Buddha's previous reincarnations (the *Jatakas*). This sacred literature was first written down in the first century B.C.

Buddhism in India During the centuries following the Buddha's death, missionaries were able to spread his faith over large parts of Asia. Buddhist missionaries went to Sri Lanka and Southeast Asia in the third century B.C. Buddhist ideas also traveled along Central Asian trade routes to China. However, Buddhism never gained a significant foothold in India, the country of its origin. Several theories exist about Buddhism's gradual disappearance in India. One theory states that Hinduism simply absorbed Buddhism. The two religions constantly influenced each other. Over time, the Buddha came to be identified by Hindus as one of the ten incarnations (reappearances on earth) of the god Vishnu. Hindus, thus, felt no need to convert to Buddhism. They believed it had already become a part of their own religion.

Nonetheless, despite the small number of Buddhists in India, the region has always been an important place of pilgrimages for Buddhists. Today, as they have for centuries, Buddhist pilgrims flock to visit spots associated with the Buddha's life. These sites include his birthplace at Kapilavastu, the fig tree near Gaya, and the site of his first sermon near Varanasi. Buddhists also visit the *stupas*, or sacred mounds, that are said to contain his relics. The pilgrims circle around the sacred object or sanctuary, moving in a clockwise direction. They also lie face down on the ground and leave flowers. These three actions—circling a shrine, lying face down as a sign of humility, and offering flowers—are important rituals in Buddhist worship.

Vocabulary
pilgrimages: travels to holy places.

CONNECT to TODAY

Buddhism in the West
Throughout the 20th century, large numbers of Asians have immigrated to live in the West, particularly in North America. Many of them naturally brought their Buddhist religion with them. Today, Buddhist temples have become a common feature of many large cities in the West.

Since the 1950s, many non-Asians who were dissatisfied with the religions of the West have turned to Buddhism for insight into life's meaning and for peace of mind. They have particularly responded to Zen Buddhism, which stresses everyone's ability to reach enlightenment during this lifetime. Today, Buddhism can claim 920,000 Asian and non-Asian believers in North America alone.

Trade and the Spread of Buddhism As important as missionaries were to the spread of Buddhism, traders played an even more crucial role in this process. Along with their products, traders carried Buddhism beyond India to Sri Lanka. Buddhist religion was also brought southeast along trade routes to Burma, Thailand, and the island of Sumatra. Likewise, Buddhism followed the Central Asian trade routes, called the Silk Roads, all the way to China. From China, Buddhism spread to Korea—and from Korea to Japan. The movement of trade thus succeeded in making Buddhism the most widespread religion of East Asia. Throughout human history, trade has been a powerful force for the spread of ideas. Just as trade spread Buddhism in East Asia, it helped spread cultural influences in another major region of the world: the Mediterranean basin, as you will learn in Section 3.

Section 2 Assessment

1. TERMS & NAMES
Identify
- reincarnation
- karma
- Jainism
- Siddhartha Gautama
- enlightenment
- nirvana

2. TAKING NOTES
Compare Hindu and Buddhist beliefs and practices using a Venn diagram like the one below.

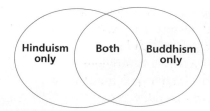

Hinduism only | Both | Buddhism only

3. MAKING INFERENCES
How might the belief in reincarnation provide a form of social control?

THINK ABOUT
- karma
- the belief in the interrelatedness of all life
- caste

4. THEME ACTIVITY
Religious and Ethical Systems Create an illustrated information board showing the life of Siddhartha Gautama. Include family background, accomplishments, and a list of his religious and ethical beliefs.

3 Seafaring Traders Extend Boundaries

TERMS & NAMES
- Minoans
- Aegean Sea
- Knossos
- King Minos
- Phoenicians

MAIN IDEA	WHY IT MATTERS NOW
Trading societies extended the development of civilizations beyond the Fertile Crescent region.	Traders spread knowledge of reading and writing, including an ancient form of the alphabet that we use today.

SETTING THE STAGE Buddhism spread to Southeast Asia and to East Asia partly through missionaries, but even more importantly through Buddhist traders. In the Mediterranean, the same process took place: traders in the region carried many new ideas from one society to another. They carried new ways of writing, of governing, and of worshiping their gods.

Minoans Trade Far and Wide

THINK THROUGH HISTORY
A. Drawing Conclusions How do you think archaeologists can identify places in the Mediterranean where Minoans traded?

A powerful seafaring people, the **Minoans** (mih·NOH·uhnz) dominated trade in the eastern Mediterranean from about 2000 to 1400 B.C. They lived on Crete, a large island on the southern edge of the **Aegean Sea** (ee·JEE·uhn). The Minoans produced some of the finest painted pottery of the time. They traded that pottery, along with swords, figurines, and vessels of precious metals, over a large area.

Along with their goods, Minoans also exported their art and culture. These included a unique architectural style, burial customs, and religious ritual. Minoan culture had an enormous influence on Greece, for example. Trading turned Crete into a kind of "stepping stone" for cultural exchange throughout the Mediterranean world.

Unearthing a Brilliant Civilization Archaeologists in the 19th century excavated **Knossos,** the Minoan capital city. There, they found the remains of an advanced and thriving culture. It must have been a peaceful one as well, since Minoan cities did not seem to need fortifications to protect them. The archaeologists named the civilization they found in Crete *Minoa* after **King Minos** (MY·nuhs). According to a legend, Minos was a king who kept a half-human, half-bull monster, called the Minotaur (MIHN·uh·TAWR). He kept the monster locked inside a labyrinth, a complicated maze from which no one could escape. MYTHOLOGY

Background
A Greek legend says that every year, King Minos sacrificed 14 Athenian boys and girls to the Minotaur. The mythical hero Theseus finally killed the Minotaur and ended the slaughter.

The excavation of Knossos and its colorful painted walls produced a great deal of information about Minoans. The wall paintings, as well as the official seals and painted vases, show the Minoans as graceful, athletic people who loved nature and beautiful objects. They also enjoyed vigorous sports such as boxing, wrestling, and bull-leaping.

Many Minoan artworks depict women and their role in religious ceremonies. The art suggests that women held a higher rank than in most neighboring cultures. A great Mother Earth Goddess seems to have ruled over the other gods of Crete. Also, priestesses took charge of some shrines, aided by male assistants.

Daily *Life*

Bull Leapers of Knossos

The bronze statue above captures the death-defying jump of a Minoan bull leaper in mid-flight. Many works of Minoan art show young men performing incredible acrobatic leaps over the horns of angry bulls. In one case, the gymnast jumps over the bull's horns, makes a somersault off its back, and lands behind its tail.

In another gymnastic feat, some team members hang on to the horns of a bull, using their bodies to cushion its horns and to force its head low, while another team member jumps over its back.

What was the reason for this bull-leaping? Was it a sport? Just a "fun" activity? An initiation for young warriors? Or a religious ritual? Most likely it was all of those. It probably also expressed a deep link between Minoans and nature, symbolized by the bull.

The Minoans sacrificed bulls and other animals to their gods. In at least one case, a young man was sacrificed. Excavation of a mountain temple revealed the bones of a 17-year-old boy on an altar, along with the skeletons of three priests. The positions of the skeletons suggest that the priests carried out the human sacrifice just before the building collapsed.

Minoan Culture's Mysterious End The Minoan civilization finally ended about 1200 B.C. The reasons for its end are unclear. Could it have been the result of some natural disaster? Did the island become overpopulated? Or was it overrun by invaders?

The civilization had withstood previous disasters. In about 1700 B.C., a great disaster, perhaps an earthquake, destroyed most Minoan towns and cities. The Minoans rebuilt the cities with equal richness. Then again in 1470 B.C. a series of earthquakes rocked Crete. The quakes were followed by a violent volcanic eruption on the neighboring island of Thera. Imagine the frightening catastrophe: first the shaking of the earth, then the fiery volcanic blast, next a huge tidal wave on Crete's northern coast, and finally a dense rain of white volcanic ash.

The disaster of 1470 B.C. was a blow from which the Minoans did not recover. This time, the Minoans did not succeed in rebuilding their cities. Nonetheless, Minoan civilization did linger on for almost 300 years. After that, invaders from Greece may have taken advantage of their weakened condition to destroy them. Some Minoans fled to the mountains to escape the ruin of the kingdom. Crete's influence as a major sea power and cultural force was over.

THINK THROUGH HISTORY
B. Summarizing
What adjectives might describe Minoan civilization?

Phoenicians Spread Trade and Civilization

About 1100 B.C., after Crete's decline, the most powerful traders along the Mediterranean were the **Phoenicians** (fih·NIHSH·uhnz). Phoenicia was mainly the area now known as Lebanon. Phoenicians never united into a country. Instead, they founded a number of wealthy city-states around the Mediterranean that sometimes competed with one another. (See the map on pages 54–55.) The first cities in Phoenicia, such as Byblos, Tyre (tyr), and Sidon (SYD·uhn), were important trading centers.

The Phoenicians were remarkable shipbuilders and seafarers. They were the first Mediterranean people to venture beyond the Strait of Gibraltar. Some scholars believe that the Phoenicians traded for tin with inhabitants of the southern coast of Britain. Some evidence exists for an even more remarkable feat—sailing around the continent of Africa by way of the Red Sea and back through the Strait of Gibraltar.

Phoenicians made vows to their cruel gods and goddesses, shown in statues like these from Byblos. The Phoenicians would sacrifice their first-born children and animals to please these deities.

Background
Lebanon is found on the eastern end of the Mediterranean Sea. The Straits of Gibraltar are on the western end.

Such a trip was not repeated again for 2,000 years. The Greek historian Herodotus (hih·RAHD·uh·tuhs) relates the feat.

A VOICE FROM THE PAST

The Phoenicians set out from the Red Sea and sailed the southern sea [the Indian Ocean]; whenever autumn came they would put in and sow the land, to whatever part of Libya [Africa] they might come, and there await the harvest; then, having gathered in the crop, they sailed on, so that after two years had passed, it was in the third that they rounded the Pillars of Heracles [Strait of Gibraltar] and came to Egypt. There they said (what some may believe, though I do not) that in sailing round Libya they had the sun on their right hand [in reverse position].

HERODOTUS, in *History*, Book IV (5th century B.C.).

Commercial Outposts Around the Mediterranean The Phoenicians' most important city-states in the eastern Mediterranean were Sidon and Tyre, both known for their production of purple dye; Berytus (now Beirut, in Lebanon); and Byblos, a trading center for papyrus. Phoenicians built colonies along the northern coast of Africa and the coasts of Sicily, Sardinia, and Spain. The colonies strung out like beads on a chain about 30 miles apart—about the distance a Phoenician ship could sail in a day. The greatest Phoenician colony was at Carthage (KAHR·thihj), in North Africa. Settlers from Tyre founded Carthage in about 725 B.C.

The Phoenicians traded goods they got from other lands—wine, weapons, precious metals, ivory, and slaves. They also were known as superb craftsmen who worked in wood, metal, glass, and ivory. Their famous purple dye was produced from the murex, a kind of snail that lived in the waters off Sidon and Tyre. One snail, when left to rot, produced just a drop or two of a liquid of a deep purple color. Some 60,000 snails were needed to produce one pound of dye.

Phoenicia's Great Legacy: The Alphabet As merchants, the Phoenicians needed a way of recording transactions clearly and quickly. So, the Phoenicians developed a writing system that used symbols to represent sounds. The Phoenician system was phonetic—that is, one sign was used for one sound. In fact, the word *alphabet* comes directly from the first two letters of the Phoenician alphabet: *aleph* and *beth.* As they traveled around the Mediterranean, the Phoenicians introduced this writing system to their trading partners. The Greeks, for example, adopted the Phoenician alphabet and changed the form of some of the letters.

Few examples of Phoenician writing exist. Most was on papyrus, which crumbled easily over time. However, the Phoenician contribution to the world was enormous. With a simplified alphabet, learning was now accessible to many more people.

Phoenician trade was upset when their eastern cities were captured by Assyrians in 842 B.C. However, these defeats encouraged exiles to set up city-states like Carthage to the west. The Phoenician homeland later came under the control of the Babylonians, and still later, of the Persian empire of King Cyrus I. Their conquerors recognized the Phoenicians' superb ability both as shipbuilders and as seamen. Nonetheless, one of their most lasting contributions remains the spread of the alphabet.

Background
Byblos was so famous for its papyrus that it gave the Greeks their word for book, *biblos,* from which the English word *Bible* comes.

Background
Though not the first, the Phoenician alphabet was one of the earliest. And because they were traders, the Phoenicians spread the idea of the alphabet far and wide.

Alphabets—Ancient and Modern

Phoenician	Greek	English
	A	A
	B	B
	Γ	C
	Δ	D
	E	E
		F
		G
	Z	H
	H	I
	Θ	
	I	J
	K	K
	Λ	L
	M	M
	N	N
	Ξ	
	O	O
	Π	P
		Q
	P	R
	Σ	S
	T	T
	Υ	U
	Φ	V
	X	W
	Ψ	X
		Y
	Ω	Z

SKILLBUILDER: Interpreting Charts
1. *Which letters show the most similarity across the three alphabets?*
2. *Why might one language have fewer letters in its alphabet than another?*

Phoenician Financial News

Dye Prices Go Up!

Murex, the snail from which the famous purple dye is made, is now an exclusive Phoenician monopoly.

Workers break the murex shell, then take out the shellfish and put it in large vats. When the snails have died and rotted, they excrete a yellow liquid. When exposed to the sun for long periods, the liquid turns purple. The small amount of dye extracted from huge numbers of snails means that only the richest Romans can afford to use the dye for their robes. Thus the dye has been named "royal purple."

Residents living near dye centers complain of the stench of rotting snails and the huge piles of empty shells left near the factories.

This bronze plaque from the gates in the city of Balawat shows sailors leaving Tyre on yet another profitable trading expedition.

Shipping News

As usual, Phoenician shipping fleets are exploring new territories. The latest trip has taken our vessels past the Rock of Gibraltar into the Atlantic Ocean. Consider the danger faced by our sailors as they row past the placid Mediterranean . . . into who-knows-what. These brave mariners have only the gods and their skill to rely on.

Home Construction
Carthage, Tyre, Sidon

Crowded conditions within these walled towns have led to the construction of two-story homes. Many are adding balconies onto the second story, so residents can look out over the city wall. Walls are still being constructed of brick or clay and covered with stucco. Some of the latest homes sport bathrooms, with tubs featuring a bath seat.

Glassmaking

The glass manufacturing and export business is growing by leaps and bounds. The sands of Lebanon are rich in silica and make the best glass in the Mediterranean area. Borrowing techniques from Palestine has resulted in the creation of window glass. Romans are extremely interested in this process and are also experimenting with glassblowing techniques. Less expensive glass is quickly replacing metal in Roman home decoration.

The horse and date palm have been chosen as official symbols on Carthaginian coins.

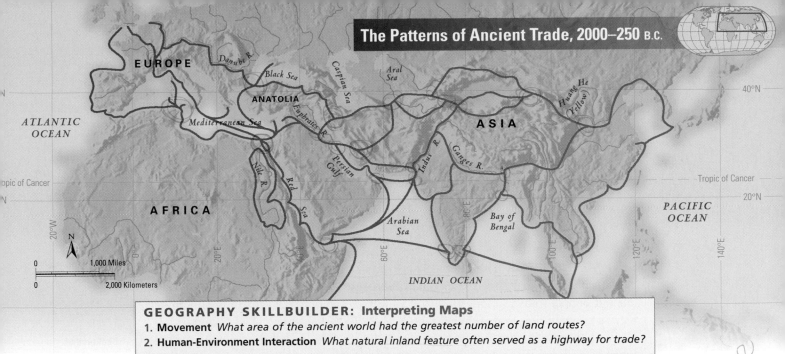

The Patterns of Ancient Trade, 2000–250 B.C.

EUROPE
Danube R.
Black Sea
ANATOLIA
ATLANTIC OCEAN
Mediterranean Sea
Euphrates R.
Caspian Sea
Aral Sea
ASIA
Huang He (Yellow)
Tropic of Cancer
AFRICA
Nile R.
Red Sea
Persian Gulf
Arabian Sea
Indus R.
Ganges R.
Bay of Bengal
PACIFIC OCEAN
Tropic of Cancer
INDIAN OCEAN

0   1,000 Miles
0   2,000 Kilometers

40°N
20°N
20°W
20°E
60°E
80°E
100°E
120°E
140°E

GEOGRAPHY SKILLBUILDER: Interpreting Maps
1. **Movement** *What area of the ancient world had the greatest number of land routes?*
2. **Human-Environment Interaction** *What natural inland feature often served as a highway for trade?*

The Long Reach of Ancient Trade

Trading in ancient times also connected the Mediterranean Sea with other centers of world commerce, such as South and East Asia. Several land routes crossed Central Asia and connected to India through Afghanistan. Two sea routes began by crossing the Arabian Sea to ports on the Persian Gulf and the Red Sea. From there, traders either went overland to Egypt, Syria, and Mediterranean countries, or they continued to sail up the Red Sea. To cross the Arabian Sea, sailors learned to make use of the monsoon winds. These winds blow from the southwest during the hot months and from the northeast during the cool season.

To widen the variety of their exports, Indian traders used other monsoon winds to travel to Southeast Asia and Indonesia. Once there, they obtained spices and other products not native to India.

Though traveling was difficult in ancient times, trading networks like those of the Phoenicians assured the exchange of products and information. Along with their goods, traders carried ideas, religious beliefs, art, and ways of living. They helped with the process of cultural diffusion as well as with moving merchandise.

Phoenician traders by their travels made crucial contributions to world civilization. At nearly the same time, another eastern Mediterranean people, the Jews, were creating a religious tradition that has lasted for more than 3,000 years. This is discussed in Section 4.

Vocabulary
monsoon: a wind that affects climate by changing direction in certain seasons.

used monsoons to advantage

trading spread culture

Section ❸ Assessment

1. TERMS & NAMES

Identify
• Minoans
• Aegean Sea
• Knossos
• King Minos
• Phoenicians

2. TAKING NOTES

Below is a list of accomplishments. Copy the chart beneath the list on your paper. Then fill in the chart, identifying feats that were Minoan and those that were Phoenician.

• dominated trade (2000–1400 B.C.)
• set up numerous city-states
• developed an alphabet
• produced a famous purple dye
• jumped over bulls for fun
• produced fine painted pottery

Minoan	Phoenician

3. EVALUATING SOURCES

Go back to page 69. Read Herodotus's account of how the Phoenicians sailed around Africa. What words show Herodotus's doubt? Why do you think he expresses doubts?

THINK ABOUT
• the sources that reported the feat
• Herodotus as a historian
• the Phoenicians' seafaring skills
• the fact that the trip was not repeated for 2000 years

4. ANALYZING THEMES

Economics The Phoenicians founded wealthy city-states around the Mediterranean. These city-states often competed with one another. Do you think it would have made more sense for the city-states to cooperate or did competition make them stronger? Explain your reasons.

THINK ABOUT
• advantages of a unified country
• advantages of independence
• benefits of competition

The Origins of Judaism

TERMS & NAMES
- Palestine
- Canaan
- Torah
- Abraham
- monotheism
- covenant
- Moses
- Israel
- Judah
- tribute

MAIN IDEA	WHY IT MATTERS NOW
The Hebrews maintained monotheistic religious beliefs that were unique in the ancient world.	From this tradition, Judaism, the religion of the Jews, evolved. Judaism is one of the world's major religions.

SETTING THE STAGE The Phoenicians lived in a region at the eastern end of the Mediterranean Sea that was later called **Palestine**. The Phoenicians were not the only ancient people to live in Palestine. Nor were they the only Palestinian people to make a great contribution to world civilization. The area of Palestine called **Canaan** (KAY·nuhn) was the ancient home of the Hebrews, later called the Jews. Their history, legends, and moral laws are a major influence on Western culture, and they began a tradition also shared by Christianity and Islam.

Background
Many scholars use the name *Israelite*, instead of *Hebrew*.

The Search for a Promised Land

Ancient Palestine's location made it a cultural crossroads of the ancient world. By land, it connected Asia and Africa and two great empires, both eager to expand. To the east lay Assyria and Babylonia and to the west Egypt. Palestine's seaports opened onto the two most important waterways of that time: the Mediterranean, which connected to the Atlantic Ocean, and the Red Sea, which flowed into the Indian Ocean. The Hebrews settled in Canaan, the part of ancient Palestine that lay between the Jordan River and the Mediterranean Sea. In fact, Hebrews often used the word *Canaan* to refer to all of ancient Palestine. According to the Bible, Canaan was the land God had promised to the Hebrew people.

From Ur to Egypt Most of what we know about the early history of the Hebrews is contained in the first five books of the Hebrew Bible. Jews call these books the **Torah** (TAWR·uh) and consider them the most sacred writings in their tradition. Christians respect them as part of the Old Testament. As in other sacred literatures, the books of the Torah describe some events that actually happened. However, those books also contain stories told to teach important lessons.

In the Torah, God chose **Abraham** (AY·bruh·HAM) to be the "father," or first, of the Hebrew people. God's first words to Abraham expressed a promise of land and a pledge: "Go from your country and your kindred and your father's house to the land that I will show you. I will make of you a great nation, and I will bless you, and make your name great. . . ." (Genesis 12:1–2)

Vocabulary
Bible: the name given to the sacred books of Judaism, as well as to those of Christianity.

The Torah says that Abraham was a shepherd who lived in the city of Ur, in Mesopotamia. The Torah tells that God commanded him to move his people and their flocks to Canaan. This would have occurred around 2000 B.C. The story of how and why he moved to Canaan is told in the Book of Genesis. Abraham, his family, and their herds made their way from the lower Tigris and Euphrates region to Canaan. Then, possibly around 1650 B.C., the descendants of Abraham moved again—this time to Egypt.

Background
The Book of Genesis is the first book of the Bible. *Genesis* means "beginning."

The God of Abraham The Bible tells how Abraham and his family roamed for many years from Mesopotamia to Canaan to Egypt and back to Canaan. All the while, their

SPOTLIGHT ON

Philistines

The Philistines were another ancient people who settled in Canaan. The Greeks called the area where they lived "Palestine" after the Philistines. Much of what we know about the Philistines comes from their neighbors, the Hebrews, who disliked them and fought with them over control of the land.

The Philistines enjoyed definite military advantages over the Hebrews. They had a fleet of ships and swift chariots. More importantly, they knew how to forge iron into swords and shields. Over time, Hebrews learned the secret of smelting iron and were able to fight the Philistines on more even terms.

Background
The name *Yahweh* later became *Jehovah* to some Christians.

God, whose name was Yahweh, went with them. Gods worshiped by other people at that time were often local, associated with a specific place. Because the God of the Hebrews did not belong to any one place, the Hebrews could carry their worship of him wherever they went.

Unlike the other groups around them, who were polytheists, the Hebrews were monotheists. They prayed only to one God. **Monotheism** (MAHN·uh·thee·IHZ·uhm), a belief in a single god, comes from the Greek words *mono*, meaning "one" and *theism*, meaning "god-worship." The Hebrews had made a startling leap. They proclaimed Yahweh as the one and only God. In their eyes, Yahweh had power not only over the Hebrews, but over all peoples, everywhere. To the Hebrews, God was not a physical being, and no physical images were to be made of him.

The Hebrews asked Yahweh for protection from their enemies, just as other people prayed to their gods to defend them. According to the Bible, Yahweh looked after the Hebrews not so much because of ritual ceremonies and sacrifices, but because Abraham had promised to obey him. In return, Yahweh had promised to protect Abraham and his descendants. This mutual promise between God and the founder of the Hebrew people is called a **covenant** (KUHV·uh·nuhnt). This was the first of a series of covenants that Yahweh and the Hebrews would make together.

On Moses' return from Mount Sinai, he saw the Hebrews worshiping a golden calf and angrily broke the tablets of the Law. The 17th-century Italian painter Guido Reni depicts this dramatic moment.

Background
In the Book of Exodus, God strikes down the first-born of the Egyptians, but he "passes over" the homes of the Hebrews. Passover celebrates this episode.

"Let My People Go." The Bible says the Hebrews migrated to Egypt because of a drought and threat of a famine. At first, the Hebrews were given places of honor in the Egyptian kingdom. Later, however, they were forced into slavery, their lives made "bitter with hard service, in mortar and brick, and in all kinds of work in the field." (Exodus 1:14)

The Hebrews fled Egypt—perhaps between 1300 and 1200 B.C. Jews call this event "the Exodus," and they remember it every year during the festival of Passover. The Torah says that the man who led the Hebrews out of slavery was named **Moses**. At Passover, it is told that at the time of Moses' birth, the Egyptian pharaoh felt threatened by the number of Hebrews in Egypt. He thus ordered all Hebrew male babies to be killed. Moses'

Canaan, the Crossroads, 2000–600 B.C.

Kingdom of Judah, 980 B.C.
Kingdom of Israel, 980 B.C.
Assyrian Empire, 650 B.C.
Babylonian Empire, 600 B.C.
— Wanderings of Abraham
— Route of Hebrews out of Egypt

GEOGRAPHY SKILLBUILDER: Interpreting Maps
1. **Movement** Along what waterway did Abraham begin his wanderings away from his native city?
2. **Location** How did Canaan's location make it a true crossroads of the eastern Mediterranean?

mother hid her baby in the reeds along the banks of the Nile. There, an Egyptian princess found and adopted him. Though raised in luxury, he did not forget his Hebrew birth. When God commanded him to lead the Jews out of Egypt, he obeyed. From that time on, Moses has been considered the greatest figure in Jewish history.

The Ten Commandments*

The first four commandments concerned the Hebrews' relationship with God:

- I am the Lord thy God. . . . Thou shalt have no other gods before me.
- Thou shalt not make unto thee any graven image. . . .
- Thou shalt not take the name of the Lord thy God in vain. . . .
- Remember the Sabbath day to keep it holy.

The last six commandments concerned the Hebrews' relationship with one another:

- Honor thy father and thy mother. . . .
- Thou shalt not kill.
- Thou shalt not commit adultery.
- Thou shalt not steal.
- Thou shalt not bear false witness against thy neighbor.
- Thou shalt not covet . . . anything that is thy neighbor's.

*Jews and Catholics word the commandments in ways slightly different from this version.

A New Covenant While the Hebrews were traveling across the Sinai (SY·ny) Peninsula, Moses climbed to the top of a mountain—Mount Sinai—to pray. The Bible says he spoke with God. When Moses came down from Mount Sinai, he brought down two stone tablets on which Yahweh had written ten laws, the Ten Commandments of the Bible.

These commandments and the other teachings that Moses delivered to his people became the basis for the civil and religious laws of Judaism. The Hebrews believed that these laws formed a new covenant between God and the Hebrew people. God promised to protect the Hebrews. They, in turn, promised to keep God's commandments. The covenant was based on the idea that God is just—and not arbitrary. In addition, the laws given to Moses required a high standard of moral conduct.

Background
The Hebrew word for these ten laws, *devarím*, actually means "words" or "utterances," not "commandments."

The Land and People of the Bible The Torah reports that the Hebrews wandered for 40 years in the Sinai Desert. Later books of the Bible tell about the history of the Hebrews after their wanderings. After the death of Moses, they returned to Canaan, where Abraham had lived. The Hebrews frequently fought with their neighbors over land. They were also making a change from a nomadic, tribal society to settled herders, farmers, and city dwellers. They were learning new technologies from neighboring peoples in ancient Palestine. These changes in their previously simple way of life made settling down a difficult experience for the Hebrews.

Tradition dictates that the Torah should be written on a scroll and kept at the synagogue in an ornamented chest called an ark.

**THINK THROUGH HISTORY
A. Contrasting** How did the religion of the Hebrews differ from many of the religions of their neighbors?

The Hebrews Are Ruled by Judges When the Hebrews arrived in Canaan, they were loosely organized into twelve tribes. These tribes lived in separate territories and were self-governing. In times of emergency, the Bible reports that God would raise up judges. They would unite the tribes and provide judicial and military leadership during a crisis. What the judges had in common was charisma, a personal magnetism that attracted many followers to their cause. In the course of time, God chose a series of judges, one of the most prominent of whom was a woman, Deborah.

Hebrew Law Deborah's leadership was unusual for a Hebrew woman. The roles of men and women were quite separate in Hebrew society. This was generally the case among peoples of the region. Women could not officiate at religious ceremonies. In general, a Hebrew woman's most important duty was to raise her children and provide moral leadership for them.

The Ten Commandments were part of a code of laws delivered to Moses. The code included other rules regulating social and religious behavior. In some ways, this code resembled Hammurabi's Code with its attitude of "an eye for an eye and a tooth for a tooth." However, its strict justice was softened by expressions of God's mercy. The code was later interpreted by religious teachers called prophets. The prophets believed that they had been chosen as messengers to reveal God's will to his people. They constantly urged the Hebrews to stay true to their covenant with God.

The prophets taught that the Hebrews had a duty both to worship God and to live justly with one another. The goal was a moral life lived in accordance with God's laws. In the words of the prophet Micah, "He has told you, O mortal/ what is good;/ and what does the Lord require/of you/but to do justice, and to love/kindness,/ and to walk humbly with your/God?" This emphasis on right conduct and the worship of one God is called ethical monotheism—a Hebrew idea that has influenced human behavior for thousands of years through Judaism, Christianity, and Islam. From ethical monotheism, the three religions derive much of the moral force that characterizes them.

THINK THROUGH HISTORY
B. Summarizing
What does Hebrew law require of believers?

The Kingdom of Israel

Canaan—the land that the Hebrews believed had been promised them by God—combined largely harsh features such as arid desert, rocky wilderness, grassy hills, and the dry, hot valley of the Jordan River. Water was never plentiful; even the numerous limestone formations soaked up any excess rainfall. After first settling in the south-central area of ancient Palestine, the Hebrews expanded south and north.

Saul and David Establish a Kingdom The judges occasionally pulled together the widely scattered tribes for a united military effort. Nonetheless, Philistines continued to threaten the Hebrews' position in ancient Palestine. The Hebrews got along somewhat better with their Canaanite neighbors. After the exile, the only large tribe left was the tribe of Judah. As a result, Hebrews came to be called Jews and their religion Judaism.

From about 1020 to 922 B.C., the Hebrews united under three able kings: Saul, David, and Solomon. The new kingdom was called **Israel** (IIIZ·ree·uhl). For 100 years, Israel enjoyed its greatest period of power and independence.

Saul, the first of the three kings, was chosen largely because of his success in driving out the Philistines from the central hills of ancient Palestine. Saul is portrayed in the Bible as a tragic man, who was given to bouts of jealousy. After his death, he was succeeded by his son-in-law, David. King David, an extremely popular leader, united the tribes, established Jerusalem as the capital, and founded a dynasty.

Solomon Builds the Kingdom About the year 962 B.C., David was succeeded by his son Solomon, whose mother was Bathsheba. Solomon was the most powerful of the Hebrew kings. He built a trading empire with the help of his friend Hiram, the king of the Phoenician city of Tyre. Solomon also beautified the capital city of Jerusalem. The crowning achievement of his extensive building program in Jerusalem was a great temple, which he built to glorify God. The temple was also to be a permanent home for the Ark of the Covenant, which contained the tablets of Moses's law.

The temple that Solomon built was not large, but it gleamed like a precious gem. Bronze pillars stood at its entrance. The temple was stone on the outside, while its inner walls were made of cedar covered in gold. The main hall was richly decorated with brass and gold. Solomon also built a royal palace even more costly and more magnificent than the temple.

CONNECT to TODAY

The State of Israel
On May 14, 1948, Jews and many non-Jews around the world celebrated the birth of the modern state of Israel. Israel owes its existence in part to the idea of the Promised Land. Jewish tradition kept that idea alive for almost 18 centuries after Jewish rule had ended in Palestine. By the 1800s, persecution of Jews in Europe led many to believe that Jews should return to the land given to them by God—to Palestine.

In the late 1800s, a movement called *Zionism* called for "a (Jewish) home in Palestine secured by law." In 1947, after the horrors of Nazism, the United Nations answered that call. It established Israel as a Jewish homeland. Jews had regained their Promised Land.

Background
Solomon formed alliances by marrying the sisters or daughters of other kings. The Bible says that he had 700 wives, who turned him away from God. (I Kings 11:3–4)

HISTORY MAKERS

**King Solomon
962?–922? B.C.**

Solomon's fame as a wise man became a legend. In the Bible, he prays to God for "an understanding mind," which God grants him.

Soon after, the story goes, two women and a baby boy were brought before him. Each woman claimed the baby was hers. After hearing their testimony, Solomon declared, "Divide the living boy in two; then give half to the one and half to the other." He then waited for the women's reactions.

One said: "Please, my lord, give her the living boy; certainly do not kill him!" However, the other woman accepted: "It shall be neither mine nor yours; divide it."

By his great wisdom, Solomon knew that the woman who would give up the child to save it was the real mother.

The Kingdom Divides Solomon's building projects required high taxes and badly strained the kingdom's finances. In addition, men were forced to spend one month out of every three working on the temple. The expense and forced labor caused much discontent. As a result, after Solomon's death, the Jews in the northern part of the kingdom—geographically distant from the south—revolted. By 922 B.C., the kingdom had divided in two—with Israel in the north and **Judah** (JOO·duh) in the south.

The next 200 years was a period of confusing ups and downs for the two kingdoms. Sometimes they fought each other; sometimes they joined together to fight common enemies. Each of the kingdoms had periods of prosperity, followed by low periods.

The Babylonian Captivity

Disaster finally struck as the independence of the two kingdoms was lost. In 738 B.C., both Israel and Judah began paying **tribute**—peace money paid by a weaker power to a stronger—to Assyria. By paying tribute, Israel and Judah hoped to assure that the mighty Assyrian empire would not attack. Then everything began to fall apart. The Assyrians began the siege of Samaria, the capital of Israel, in 725. By 722, the whole northern kingdom had fallen to the Assyrians.

The southern kingdom of Judah resisted for another 150 years before it too was destroyed. The destruction of Judah was to come at the hands of the Babylonians. After conquering Israel, the Assyrians rapidly lost power to a rising Babylonian empire. The Babylonian king Nebuchadnezzar (nehb·uh·kuhd·NEHZ·uhr) ran the Egyptians out of Syria and ancient Palestine, and he twice attacked Jerusalem. The city finally fell in 586 B.C. Solomon's Temple was destroyed in the Babylonian victory. Many of the survivors were exiled to Babylon. During their exile in Babylon, the Bible describes how the prophet Ezekiel urged his people to keep their religion alive in a foreign land.

Then about 50 years after the fall of Judah, another change of fortune occurred: in 539 B.C., the Persian king Cyrus the Great conquered Babylon. The next year, Cyrus allowed some 40,000 exiles to return to Jerusalem to rebuild the Temple. Many, however, were kept in Babylonia.

Work on the Second Temple was completed in 515 B.C. The walls of Jerusalem were rebuilt in 445 B.C. Soon, however, other empires would rise and fall in Southwest Asia. These new empires would take control both of ancient Palestine and the destiny of the Jewish people.

Assyrians attacked

**THINK THROUGH HISTORY
C. Drawing Conclusions** How might geographical distance make the split of Israel and Judah more likely?

**THINK THROUGH HISTORY
D. Making Inferences** The Temple was rebuilt before the walls of Jerusalem. What does this fact indicate about the Jews after the Babylonian captivity?

Section **4** Assessment

1. TERMS & NAMES

Identify
• Palestine
• Canaan
• Torah
• Abraham
• monotheism
• covenant
• Moses
• Israel
• Judah
• tribute

2. TAKING NOTES

On your own paper, create a time line showing major Hebrew leaders. Then, below the time line, give one piece of information about each.

2000 B.C.
|_____|_____|

Abraham:
Father of Jewish people

3. IDENTIFYING PROBLEMS

What were the main problems faced by the Hebrews between 2000 B.C. and 700 B.C.?

THINK ABOUT
• the quest for a homeland
• other peoples
• hardships
• problems among Hebrews

4. THEME ACTIVITY

Interaction with Environment You are the leader of a Hebrew tribe. Write a short speech explaining to your people why Palestine is the best choice as a homeland.

The Flood Story

The tale of a devastating flood appears among the legends of ancient peoples throughout the world. In some versions, the story of the flood serves to explain how the world came to be. In others, the flood is heaven's punishment for evil deeds committed by humans. At the right is a fifth-century A.D. view of Noah and his ark in the Hebrew flood story.

HEBREW LITERATURE

The Torah

When Yahweh saw how wickedly humans were acting, he was sorry that he had created them. Only one man, Noah, found favor in God's eyes.

And God said to Noah, "I have determined to make an end of all flesh, for the earth is filled with violence because of them. . . . Make yourself an ark of cypress wood; make rooms in the ark, and cover it inside and out with pitch. . . . And of every living thing, of all flesh, you shall bring two of every kind in the ark, to keep them alive with you; they shall be male and female. . . .

The rain fell on the earth forty days and forty nights. . . . At the end of the forty days Noah opened the window of the ark . . . and . . . sent out the dove from the ark; and the dove came back in the evening and there in its beak was a freshly plucked olive leaf; so Noah knew the waters had subsided from the earth. . . .

Then God said to Noah, "Go out of the ark, you and your wife, and your sons and your sons' wives with you. Bring out with you every living thing that is with you. . . . I establish my covenant with you, that . . . never again shall there be a flood to destroy the earth."

MESOPOTAMIAN MYTH

The Epic of Gilgamesh

In this legend, Utnapishtim, like Noah, escapes a worldwide flood by building an ark. The gods are unable to sleep because of the uproar caused by humans. To have peace, they agree to destroy the human race in a great flood. However, Ea, the god of wisdom, warns Utnapishtim of the coming catastrophe in a dream.

O man of Shurrupak, son of Ubara-Tutu; tear down your house and build a boat, abandon possessions and look for life. . . .

I loaded into (the boat) all that I had of gold and of living things, my family, my kin, the beasts of the field both wild and tame, and all the craftsmen. I sent them on board. . . .

For six days and six nights the winds blew, torrent and tempest and flood overwhelmed the world. . . . When the seventh day dawned the storm from the south subsided, the sea grew calm, the flood was stilled; I looked at the face of the world and there was silence, all mankind was turned to clay. . . . I opened a hatch and the light fell on my face. Then I bowed low, I sat down and I wept, the tears streamed down my face, for on every side was the waste of water.

A RETELLING OF AN INDIAN TALE

The Fish Incarnation of Vishnu

The Hindu god Vishnu is said to have reappeared on earth many times. In his first earthly incarnation, he took the form of Matsya, the fish, and saved mankind.

One day, as the sage Manu was praying at the river Ganges, a small fish asked for his protection. Manu put the fish in an earthen jar, but soon the fish was too big for the jar. So Manu put it into the river, but soon it outgrew the river. So Manu put the fish in the ocean. By now Manu began to suspect the divine nature of this fish.

The fish told Manu there would be a great deluge [flood]. He advised Manu to build a large boat and take seven Rishis (saints), the seeds of various kinds of plants and one of each type of animal. When the deluge came, the fish said, he would take the ark and its inhabitants to safety.

Sure enough, when the deluge occurred, the fish was there. Manu tied the boat to the horns of the fish, using the divine snake Vasuki as a rope. The fish then pulled the boat through the waters until it reached a mountain peak.

Connect *to* History

Drawing Conclusions List the similarities among the different versions. Why do you think that stories from such different geographical areas and time periods are so similar?

SEE SKILLBUILDER
HANDBOOK, PAGE 1006

Connect *to* Today

Researching Look in newspapers and magazines for accounts of people fleeing a great flood. Share what you find with the class.

CD-ROM   For another perspective on the Flood Story, see World History: Electronic Library of Primary Sources.

TERMS & NAMES

Briefly explain the importance of each of the following in the years 3500 B.C. to 259 B.C.

1. Indo-Europeans
2. caste
3. reincarnation
4. karma
5. Siddhartha Gautama
6. Minoans
7. Phoenicians
8. Torah
9. monotheism
10. Moses

Interact *with* History

On page 56, you considered staying or fleeing from a foreign invader before you knew what some of the consequences of your decision might be. Now that you've read the chapter, reconsider your decision to stay or flee. Would you still make the same choice, or have you changed your mind? Discuss the consequences of your decision on your life.

Visual Summary

REVIEW QUESTIONS

SECTION 1 *(pages 57–61)*
Indo-European Migrations

11. Name three reasons that historians give to explain why Indo-Europeans migrated.
12. What are two technologies that helped the Hittites build their empire?
13. How were the Aryans different from the non-Aryans *(dasas)* that they encountered when migrating to India?

SECTION 2 *(pages 62–66)*
Roots of Hinduism and Buddhism

14. In Hinduism, how are the ideas of karma, reincarnation, and *moksha* connected?
15. Why were lower castes more likely to convert to Buddhism?

SECTION 3 *(pages 67–71)*
Seafaring Traders Extend Boundaries

16. What did the Minoans export?
17. What is Phoenicia's greatest legacy to the world?

SECTION 4 *(pages 72–77)*
The Origins of Judaism

18. What is ethical monotheism and why is it important?
19. What caused the division of Solomon's kingdom?
20. Name two ways that early Judaism differed from other religions of the time.

People and Ideas on the Move

	Hinduism	Buddhism	Judaism
Number of Gods	Many gods, all faces of Brahman	Originally, no gods	One God
Holy Books	*Vedas; Upanishads, Mahabharata,* and others	Books on the teachings and life of the Buddha	The Torah and other books of the Hebrew Bible
Moral Law	Karma	Eightfold Path	Ten Commandments
Leaders	Brahmins	Monks	Priests, judges, kings, prophets
Final Goal	*Moksha*	Enlightenment, Nirvana	A moral life through obedience to God's law

CRITICAL THINKING

1. EFFECTS OF MIGRATION

How important were the migrations of the Indo-European peoples? How lasting were the changes that they brought to their new homelands? Explain your conclusion.

2. WORLD RELIGIONS

THEME RELIGIOUS AND ETHICAL SYSTEMS Using a chart like the one below, fill in the information about the three world religions listed.

Religion	Founder	Approximate Time Originated	Area Originated
Hinduism Buddhism Judaism			

3. SOLOMON'S KINGDOM

How would you evaluate King Solomon's reign? Was he a good king? Support your opinion with evidence from the chapter.

4. ANALYZING PRIMARY SOURCES

The following passage tells how the Hebrews came to the prophet Samuel to ask him to appoint a king to rule over them. Read the paragraph and answer the questions below it.

> **THE BIBLE**
> Then all the elders of Israel gathered together and came to Samuel at Ramah and said to him, ". . . Appoint for us then a king to govern us, like other nations. . . ." Samuel prayed to the Lord, and the Lord said to Samuel, "Listen to the voice of the people in all that they say to you; for they have not rejected you, but they have rejected me from being king over them. Just as they have done to me from the day I brought them out of Egypt to this day forsaking me and serving other gods, so also they are doing to you."
> **I SAMUEL 8:4–8**

- How does the writer present the idea of choosing a king? What words give you that impression?
- According to this passage, who was Israel's real king?

CHAPTER ACTIVITIES

1. LIVING HISTORY: Unit Portfolio Project

THEME INTERACTION WITH ENVIRONMENT Your unit portfolio project focuses on showing how people in history have interacted with the environment. For Chapter 3, you might use one of the following ideas to add to your portfolio.

- You are an Indo-European scout. Draw a map showing your chief the route to the place where you want your people to migrate. Then, explain to the chief why you have chosen this place.
- Write a dialogue between King Minos and a Minoan sailor describing the dangers of seagoing trade routes. Be specific. Include possible ways to minimize these dangers.
- Write a myth telling about events that might have occurred as the Phoenicians sailed around Africa. The events can clearly be imaginary, but they should be based on the geography of the route that the Phoenicians reportedly took.

2. CONNECT TO TODAY: Cooperative Learning

THEME ECONOMICS Although the caste system was officially abolished by the Indian government in 1955, a castelike system based on occupations still exists in India today. Work with a team to research and create a bar graph. In the bar graph, compare the percentage of people in certain occupations in today's India with the percentage of the wealth they own. For example, 2% of the working population in today's India are government officials and white collar workers; they own, say, 25% of the country's wealth.

INTERNET Use the Internet, magazines, or your library to research statistics about the topic. Look for statistics that answer such questions as: What percentage of working people in today's India belong to each major occupational group? What percentage of the country's wealth is owned by people in these occupational groups?

- Look for statistics. Figure out how to show those figures visually in a bar graph.
- Label the graph clearly.
- Compare the working population in India today with the ownership of wealth in the country.

FOCUS ON TIME LINES

Review the time line below. It shows the development of new ideas in the ancient world. Then make two charts.
- In the first chart, group the new ideas by category.
- In the second chart, list the new ideas by order of importance.

Connect to History
How could ironworking help Aryans to carry out their migrations in India? To conquer territory? To settle territory?

1500 B.C. Egyptians invent a method for raising water from rivers to irrigate fields. Hittites begin smelting iron

280 B.C. First lighthouse built in Alexandria, Egypt

3000 B.C. Writing invented in Mesopotamia

2000 B.C. First Minoan palace built on Crete

1000 B.C. Ironworking arrives in India

2650 B.C. The "step" pyramid designed in Egypt

1640 B.C. Chariots introduced into Egypt

1400 B.C. Invention of the Phoenician alphabet

600 B.C. First official coins of fixed weight produced in Anatolia

First Age of Empires, 1570 B.C.–200 B.C.

PREVIEWING THEMES

Interaction with Environment

In this first age of empires, different cultures engaged in monumental projects. These included the Royal Road in Persia, the Great Wall of China, fortified walled cities such as Nineveh, and extensive irrigation ditches and canals. The projects demonstrated these cultures' ability to adapt to and control the environment.

Empire Building

Throughout this period, people from Africa to China spread their influence across vast regions and built the world's earliest great empires.

Science & Technology

Advanced weaponry helped Assyria conquer its neighbors. A network of roads connected the far-flung Persian Empire. Other technology also played a key role in establishing and maintaining history's early empires.

INTERNET CONNECTION

Visit us at **www.mcdougallittell.com** to learn more about Egypt, Nubia, Assyria, Persia, and China.

ANCIENT EMPIRES, 650 B.C.–200 B.C.

Ashurbanipal, an Assyrian monarch who reigned from **668–627 B.C.,** fights a lion. The lion hunt was a royal sport of Assyrian kings. The king is portrayed as a mighty warrior, a conqueror of nature, even of the lion.

EUROPE

Black Sea

Caspian Sea

Royal Road

Sardis

Nineveh

Mediterranean Sea

Euphrates R.

Mesopotamia

Tigris R.

Babylon

Susa

Persepolis

SYRIAN DESERT

Persian Gulf

Memphis

Cairo

AFRICA

Nile River

Red Sea

ARABIAN PENINSULA

Napata

Meroë

Arabian Sea

Niger R.

The Nubian king **Taharqa,** who reigned from **690–664 B.C.,** celebrated with inscriptions and proclamations his military victories. He added inscriptions about sporting events, and even his mother's visit on his coronation. He also commissioned statues of himself, such as this one ordered for his temple.

0° Prime Meridian

40°E

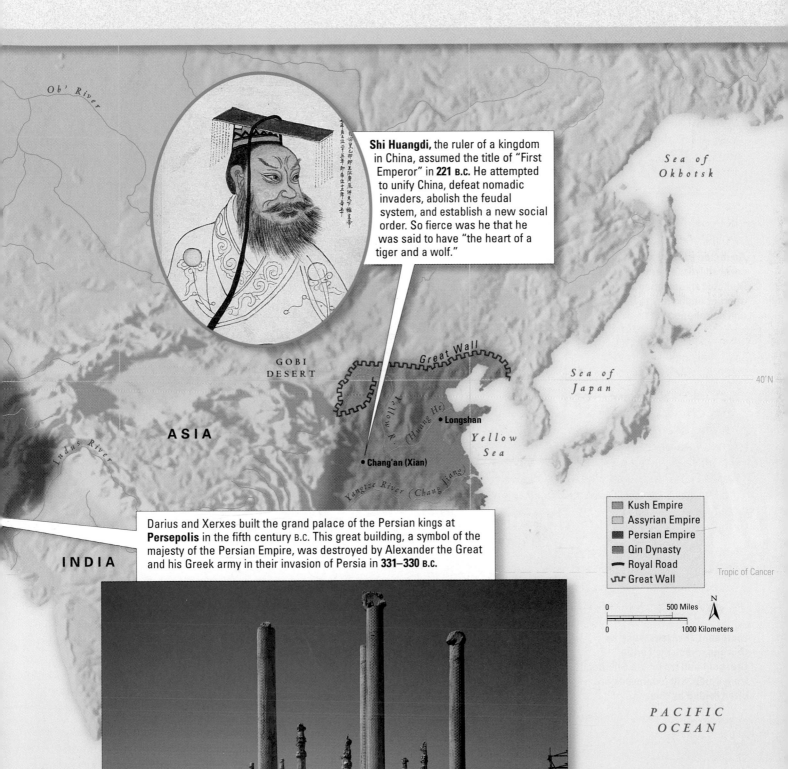

Shi Huangdi, the ruler of a kingdom in China, assumed the title of "First Emperor" in **221 B.C.** He attempted to unify China, defeat nomadic invaders, abolish the feudal system, and establish a new social order. So fierce was he that he was said to have "the heart of a tiger and a wolf."

Darius and Xerxes built the grand palace of the Persian kings at **Persepolis** in the fifth century B.C. This great building, a symbol of the majesty of the Persian Empire, was destroyed by Alexander the Great and his Greek army in their invasion of Persia in **331–330 B.C.**

Kush Empire
Assyrian Empire
Persian Empire
Qin Dynasty
Royal Road
Great Wall

0   500 Miles
0   1000 Kilometers

You are a merchant who travels great distances with your camel caravan in order to sell and trade goods. Your life has become increasingly difficult because bandits and thieves plague the roads. They ambush and rob unwary travelers, particularly merchants selling their wares. There is a new military power expanding its empire throughout the region of your travels that is suppressing the worst of the outlaw bands. At the same time that it is putting down lawlessness and disorder, however, the military empire is imposing harsh laws and heavy taxes on the regions that it conquers.

Empire—Good or Bad?

An armed cavalry escort protects a caravan from an armed raiding party. Mounted troops bring a new sense of order and safety to travelers and merchants.

A raiding party plans to attack a caravan. The caravan carries a fortune in exotic goods, including silks and spices from distant lands.

Merchant caravans, such as this one, cross the Fertile Crescent and travel the Silk Road from China. Such caravans are often raided by thieves.

EXAMINING *the* ISSUES

- Why might a merchant or other common person favor the establishment of a strong empire?

- Why might such a person oppose a strong empire?

- Why might a victorious army enslave a subject people?

- What advantages or abuses might a strong military power bring to a region?

In small groups, answer the questions, then report back to the class. In your discussion, remember what you've learned about military conquest and the behavior of such groups as the Sumerians, Egyptians, and Hittites.

As you read about the empires in this chapter, consider how the winners treat the people under their power and how the conquered people respond.

1 The Empires of Egypt and Nubia Collide

TERMS & NAMES
- Hyksos
- New Kingdom
- Hatshepsut
- Thutmose III
- Nubia
- Ramses II
- Kush
- Piankhi
- Meroë

MAIN IDEA	WHY IT MATTERS NOW
Two empires along the Nile, Egypt and Nubia, forged commercial, cultural, and political connections.	Neighboring civilizations participate in cultural exchange as well as conflict.

SETTING THE STAGE During the Middle Kingdom (about 2080–1640 B.C.), trade with Mesopotamia and the Indus Valley enriched Egypt, located in northeastern Africa. Meanwhile, up the Nile River, less than 600 miles south of the Egyptian city of Thebes, a major kingdom had developed in the region of Nubia. For centuries, the Nubian kingdom of Kush traded with Egypt. The two kingdoms influenced each other.

The New Kingdom of Egypt

Egyptians did not know about chariots

After the prosperity of the Middle Kingdom, Egypt descended into war and violence. This was caused by a succession of weak pharaohs and power struggles among rival nobles. The weakened country fell to invaders who swept across the Isthmus of Suez in chariots, a weapon of war unknown to the Egyptians. These invaders, nomads called **Hyksos** (HIHK·sohs), ruled Egypt from 1640 to 1570 B.C. The Hyksos invasion shook the Egyptians' confidence in the desert barriers that had protected their kingdom.

Around 1600 B.C., a series of warlike rulers began to restore Egypt's power. Among those who helped drive out the Hyksos was Queen Ahhotep (ah·HOH·tehp). The queen took over when her husband died in battle. The next pharaoh, Kamose (KAH·mohs), won a great victory over the hated Hyksos. His successors drove the Hyksos completely out of Egypt and pursued them across the Sinai Peninsula into Palestine.

After overthrowing the Hyksos rulers, the pharaohs of the **New Kingdom** (about 1570–1075 B.C.) sought to strengthen Egypt by building an empire. Egypt now entered its third period of glory in the New Kingdom. During this time it was wealthier and more powerful than ever before.

Egypt's Empire Builders in the New Kingdom Equipped with bronze weapons and two-wheeled chariots, the Egyptians became conquerors. The pharaohs of the Eighteenth Dynasty (1570–1365 B.C.) set up an army including archers, charioteers, and infantry, or foot soldiers. The symbols of royal power had always been the red crown and the white crown. Now the pharaohs added a new piece of royal headgear—the blue crown, a war crown shaped like a battle helmet.

Among the rulers of the New Kingdom, **Hatshepsut** (hat·SHEHP·soot), who boldly declared herself pharaoh around 1472 B.C., was unique. She took over because her stepson, the male heir to the throne, was a young child at the time. Unlike other New Kingdom rulers, Hatshepsut spent her reign encouraging trade rather than just waging war.

Vocabulary
dynasty: a series of rulers from a single family.

HISTORY MAKERS

Hatshepsut
reigned 1472–1458 B.C.
Hatshepsut was an excellent ruler of outstanding achievement who made Egypt more prosperous. As pharaoh, she sent traders down the Red Sea to bring back gold, ebony, baboons, and myrrh trees.

As male pharaohs had done, Hatshepsut planned a tomb for herself in the Valley of the Kings. Carved reliefs on the walls of the temple reveal the glories of her reign.

The inscription from Hatshepsut's obelisk (tall stone shaft) at Karnak trumpets her glory and her feelings about herself:

"I swear as Re loves me, as my father Amon favors me, as my nostrils are filled with satisfying life, as I wear the white crown, as I appear in the red crown, . . . as I rule this land like the son of Isis . . ."

Hatshepsut's stepson, **Thutmose III** (thoot·MOH·suh), proved to be a much more warlike ruler. In fact, in his eagerness to ascend to the throne, Thutmose III may even have murdered his stepmother, Hatshepsut. Between the time he took power and his death around 1425 B.C., Thutmose III led a number of victorious invasions into Palestine and Syria.

Under Thutmose's rule, Egyptian armies also pushed farther south into **Nubia,** a region of Africa that straddled the upper Nile River. From the Blue Nile, the southern boundary of Nubia, to the shores of the Mediterranean was a distance of approximately 1,000 miles. From Nubia, Egyptian soldiers returned carrying gold, cattle, ivory, and many captives whom they enslaved. The destinies of Egypt and Nubia would be connected for hundreds of years.

Egypt was now a mighty empire. It controlled lands around the Nile and far beyond. In addition, it drew boundless wealth from them. Contact with other cultures brought Egypt new ideas as well as material goods. Egypt had never before—nor has it since—commanded such power and wealth as during the reigns of the New Kingdom pharaohs.

The Egyptians and the Hittites By about 1400 B.C., Egyptian armies had crossed the Sinai Peninsula and conquered parts of Syria and Palestine. These conquests brought the Egyptians into conflict with the Hittites. The Hittites had moved into Asia Minor around 1900 B.C. and later expanded southward into Palestine.

After several battles, the Egyptian and Hittite armies met at the Battle of Kadesh around 1285 B.C. There the two armies fought each other to a standstill. The pharaoh, **Ramses II** (RAM·SEEZ), and a Hittite king later made a treaty that promised "peace and brotherhood between us forever." Their alliance lasted for the rest of the century.

An Age of Builders Like the Old Kingdom with its towering pyramids, rulers of the New Kingdom erected magnificent palaces, temples, and tombs. In search of security in the afterlife, they hid their splendid tombs beneath desert cliffs. In this way, they would not be plundered by grave robbers and looters. The site they chose was the remote Valley of the Kings near Thebes. Besides royal tombs, the pharaohs of this period also built great palaces and magnificent temples. Indeed, the word *pharaoh* means "great house" and comes from this time period. The word became a royal title.

Ramses II, whose reign extended from approximately 1290 to 1224 B.C., stood out among the great builders of the New Kingdom. He lived to the age of 99 and was the father of 150 children. At Karnak, he added to a monumental temple to Amon (AH·muhn), Egypt's chief god. Ramses also ordered a temple to be carved into the red sandstone cliffs above the Nile River at Abu Simbel (AH·boo SIHM·buhl). Egypt's last great pharaoh ordered these temples decorated with enormous statues of himself. The ears alone measured over three feet. Although these buildings are huge and impressive, they were not as skillfully built as those of the Old Kingdom.

The Empire Declines

The empire that Thutmose III had built and Ramses II had ruled came apart slowly after 1200 B.C. as other strong civilizations rose to challenge Egypt's power. Shortly after Ramses died, the entire eastern Mediterranean suffered a wave of invasions around 1200 B.C. These invasions destroyed many kingdoms.

Invasions by Land and Sea Both the Egyptian empire and the Hittite kingdom were attacked by "the People of the Sea." Scholars have not conclusively identified these invaders, although they may well have been the Philistines often mentioned

---

In this wall painting from an Egyptian tomb, Nubians bring tribute to the pharaoh.

THINK THROUGH HISTORY
A. Recognizing Effects What were some of the political and economic effects of Egypt's conquests?

Background The word *pharaoh* became a royal title because the ruler's own name was considered too sacred to use.

in the Bible. Whoever they were, the People of the Sea caused great destruction.

From the east, the tribes of Palestine often rebelled against their Egyptian overlords. From the west, even the vast desert no longer stopped Libyans from raiding Egyptian villages.

Egypt's Empire Fades After these invasions, Egypt never recovered its previous power. Egypt broke apart into regional units. Isolated rural populations erected their own walled defenses. In Egypt's former empire numerous small kingdoms arose. Each was eager to protect its independence. As the empire faded to a distant memory, princes of these small kingdoms treated Egyptian officials with contempt.

Powerless at home and abroad, Egypt fell to its neighbors' invasions. Libyans crossed the desert to the Nile delta. There they established independent dynasties. From 950 to 730 B.C., Libyan pharaohs ruled Egypt and erected cities. Far from imposing their own culture, the Libyans embraced the Egyptian way of life. When the Nubians came north to seize power, they, too, would adopt the Egyptian religion, manners, and culture.

The Kushites Conquer the Nile Region

For centuries, Nubia, the area along the upper Nile River south of Egypt, had been a source of products and slaves for Egypt. Egypt's domination of Nubia and the Nubian kingdom of **Kush** lasted for about a thousand years, between 2000 B.C. and 1000 B.C. During this time, Egyptian armies raided and even occupied Kush for a brief period. But as Egypt fell into decline around 1000 B.C., Kush was emerging as a regional power. Nubia would now establish its own Kushite dynasty on the throne of Egypt.

Napata, the capital of Kush, was a center of trade in the Nubian and Egyptian empires. Goods traded in Napata included pottery such as the vessel with giraffes shown above. This jug was probably used for wine storage.

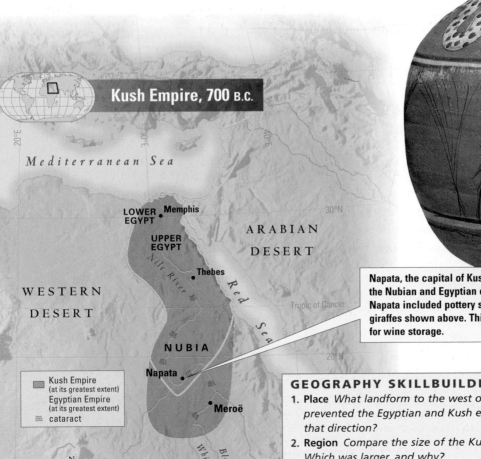

Kush Empire, 700 B.C.

Mediterranean Sea

LOWER EGYPT • Memphis

UPPER EGYPT

ARABIAN DESERT

30°N

• Thebes

WESTERN DESERT

Red Sea

Nile River

Tropic of Cancer

NUBIA

20°N

Napata •

• Meroë

Kush Empire (at its greatest extent)
Egyptian Empire (at its greatest extent)
cataract

White Nile

Blue Nile

10°N

N

0   500 Miles
0   1,000 Kilometers

GEOGRAPHY SKILLBUILDER: Interpreting Maps
1. **Place** What landform to the west of the Nile might have prevented the Egyptian and Kush empires from expanding in that direction?
2. **Region** Compare the size of the Kush and Egyptian empires. Which was larger, and why?

The People of Nubia Nubia lay south of Egypt between the first cataract of the Nile and the division of the river into the Blue and White Niles. Despite several cataracts around which boats had to be carried, the lengthy Nile provided the best north-south trade route. Several Nubian kingdoms (including Kush) served as a trade corridor. They linked Egypt and the Mediterranean world to the north with the interior of Africa to the south and to the Red Sea. Along the river, goods and ideas flowed back and forth for centuries. The first Nubian kingdom, Kerma, arose shortly after 2000 B.C. Kerma's kings were buried in chambers larger than those in any Egyptian pyramid. Red-and-black Kerma pottery of great beauty fetched high prices from Egyptian nobles. Kerma prospered during Egypt's Hyksos period.

The Interaction of Egypt and Nubia With Egypt's revival during the New Kingdom, pharaohs forcefully imposed Egyptian rule on Nubia's next great kingdom, Kush. During a long period, Egypt ruled Kush. Egyptian governors, priests, soldiers, and artists strongly influenced the Nubians. Indeed, Kush's capital, Napata, became the center for the spread of Egyptian culture to Kush's other African trading partners.

Kushite princes went to Egypt. They learned the Egyptian language and worshiped Egyptian gods. They adopted the customs and clothing styles of the Egyptian upper class. When they returned home, the Kushite nobles brought back royal rituals and hiero-glyphic writing. They built pyramids based on Egyptian models, but with steeper sides.

With Egypt's decline, beginning about 1100 B.C., Kush regained its independence. The Kushites viewed themselves as the guardians of Egyptian values. They sought to restore the Egyptian way of life. They tried to do this by conquering Egypt and ousting its Libyan rulers.

Piankhi Captures the Egyptian Throne In 751 B.C., a Kushite king named **Piankhi** led an army down the Nile and overthrew the Libyan dynasty that had ruled Egypt for over 200 years. He united the entire Nile Valley from the delta in the north to Napata in the south. Piankhi and his descendants became Egypt's Twenty-fifth Dynasty. After his victory, Piankhi erected a monument in his homeland of Kush. It tells the story of his military triumph, which he viewed as the restoration of Egypt's glory.

adopted & adapted

THINK THROUGH HISTORY
B. Making Inferences Why might the Kushites have viewed themselves as guardians of Egyptian values?

HISTORY THROUGH ART: Sculpture

The interaction of Egypt and Nubia can be seen in the art and sculpture of the two kingdoms. The portrait of the Egyptian pharaoh to the left is over a thousand years older than that of the Nubian king to the right.

Granite sculpture of Amenemhat III of Egypt as a sphinx dates back to the Twelfth Dynasty, 1844–1797 B.C.

Connect *to* History

Comparing What similarities can you see between the two portraits? What qualities do they suggest in the rulers?

SEE SKILLBUILDER HANDBOOK, PAGE 996

Connect *to* Today

Planning a Portrait What are some elements that you would include in a portrait of a powerful person in today's society?

This granite sphinx of King Taharqa of Nubia comes from the Amon Temple at Kawa, 690–664 B.C.

On the monument he had words inscribed that celebrated his victory. The inscription provided a catalog of the riches of the north, including those of Egypt and Syria:

A VOICE FROM THE PAST
Then the ships were laden with silver, gold, copper, clothing, and everything of the Northland, every product of Syria and all sweet woods of God's-Land. His Majesty sailed upstream [south], with glad heart, the shores on his either side were jubilating. West and east were jubilating in the presence of His Majesty.

PIANKHI, monument in Cairo Museum

However, Piankhi's dynasty proved short-lived. In 671 B.C., the Assyrians, a warlike people from Southwest Asia, conquered Egypt. The Kushites fought bravely, but they were forced to retreat south up the Nile by the Assyrians. There the Kushites would experience a golden age, despite their loss of Egypt.

ONLY 120 year

The Golden Age of Meroë

After their defeat by the Assyrians, the Kushite royal family eventually moved south to **Meroë** (MEHR·oh·EE). Far enough away from Egypt to provide security, Meroë lay closer to the Red Sea than Napata did. It became active in the booming trade between Africa, Arabia, and India.

The Wealth of Kush It was here that Kush made use of rich natural resources to thrive independently of Egypt for several hundred years. Unlike Egyptian cities along the Nile, Meroë enjoyed significant rainfall. And, unlike Egypt, Meroë boasted abundant supplies of iron ore. Meroë became a major center for the manufacture of iron weapons and tools.

Background
The use of iron weapons favored people who could forge iron and paved the way for an age of empires.

In Meroë, ambitious merchants loaded iron bars, tools, and spearheads onto their donkeys. They then transported the goods to the Red Sea, where they exchanged these goods for jewelry, fine cotton cloth, silver lamps, and glass bottles. As the mineral wealth of the central Nile valley flowed out of Meroë, luxury goods from India and Arabia flowed in. The Kushite kings lived like pharaohs, ruling from palaces and spending the afterlife in splendid stone-faced pyramids. Unlike the Egyptian pharaohs, their succession was determined by the agreement of the leaders and nobles.

The Decline of Meroë After four centuries of prosperity, from about 250 B.C. to A.D. 150, Meroë began to decline. The rise of Aksum, a rival power located 400 miles southeast, contributed to Meroë's fall. With a seaport along the Red Sea, Aksum now dominated North African trade. Aksum defeated Meroë around A.D. 350.

Centuries earlier, around the time the Kushite pharaoh sat on Egypt's throne, a new empire had gathered in the north. Like Kush, Assyria would come to dominate Egypt.

This armlet dates from Meroë in the late first century B.C. It is made of gold with fused-glass inlays. On the hinge is a goddess wearing a vulture headdress and a double crown.

Section 1 Assessment

1. TERMS & NAMES

Identify
- Hyksos
- New Kingdom
- Hatshepsut
- Thutmose III
- Nubia
- Ramses II
- Kush
- Piankhi
- Meroë

2. TAKING NOTES

Create a time line showing important events in the history of Egypt and Kush.

1570 B.C.   A.D. 350

Egyptian   Aksum
New   defeats
Kingdom   Meroë

Which empire was invaded more often? Why?

3. RECOGNIZING BIAS

Read the temple inscription written by Piankhi and quoted at the top of this page. Explain how an Egyptian might have written the inscription differently.

THINK ABOUT
- what bias Piankhi had
- how Egyptians benefited from Piankhi's invasion
- why Egyptians might have disagreed with Piankhi

4. ANALYZING THEMES

Empire Building How did Egypt and Nubia strengthen each other at various times in their histories?

THINK ABOUT
- the role of trade and the movement of goods
- the impact of military movements
- the influence of cultural developments

TERMS & NAMES
- Assyria
- Sennacherib
- Nineveh
- Ashurbanipal
- Medes
- Chaldeans
- Nebuchadnezzar

2 Assyria Dominates the Fertile Crescent

MAIN IDEA	WHY IT MATTERS NOW
Assyria developed a military machine, conquered an empire, and established imperial administration.	Some leaders still use military force to extend their rule, stamp out opposition, and gain wealth and power.

SETTING THE STAGE For more than two centuries, the Assyrian army advanced across Southwest Asia. It overwhelmed foes with its military strength. After the Assyrians seized control of Egypt, the Assyrian king Esarhaddon proclaimed, "I tore up the root of Kush, and not one therein escaped to submit to me." The last Kushite pharaoh retreated to Napata, Kush's capital city.

A Mighty Military Machine

Beginning around 850 B.C., **Assyria** (uh·SEER·ee·uh) acquired a large empire. It accomplished this by means of a sophisticated military organization and state-of-the-art weaponry. For a time, this campaign of conquest made Assyria the greatest power in Southwest Asia.

The Rise of a Warrior People The Assyrians came from the northern part of Mesopotamia. Their flat, exposed farmland made them easy to attack. Invaders swept down from the nearby mountains. The Assyrians may have developed their warlike behavior in response to these invasions. Lacking natural barriers such as mountains or deserts, they repelled invaders by developing a strong army. Through constant warfare, Assyrian kings built an empire that stretched from east and north of the Tigris River all the way to central Egypt.

One of these Assyrian kings, **Sennacherib** (sih·NAK·uhr·ihb), bragged that he had sacked 89 cities and 820 villages, burned Babylon, and ordered most of its inhabitants killed. Centuries later, in the 1800s, the English poet George Gordon, Lord Byron, romanticized the Assyrians' bloody exploits in a poem:

> **A VOICE ABOUT THE PAST**
> The Assyrian came down like a wolf on the fold,
> And his cohorts were gleaming in purple and gold;
> And the sheen of their spears was like stars on the sea,
> When the blue wave rolls nightly on deep Galilee.
>
> GEORGE GORDON, LORD BYRON, "The Destruction of Sennacherib"

**THINK THROUGH HISTORY
A. Analyzing Causes** What caused the Assyrians to develop a strong army and large empire?

always take higher ground

Military Organization and Conquest Assyria was a society which glorified military strength. Its soldiers were well equipped for conquering an empire. Making use of the iron-working technology of the time, the soldiers covered themselves in stiff leather and metal armor. They wore copper or iron helmets, padded loincloths, and leather skirts layered with metal scales. Their weapons were iron swords and iron-pointed spears. Infantry, archers, and spear throwers protected themselves with huge shields.

Advance planning and technical skill allowed the Assyrians to lay siege to enemy cities. When deep water blocked their passage, engineers would bridge the rivers with pontoons, or floating structures used to support a bridge. Tying inflated animal skins

This detail of a sandstone relief shows an Assyrian soldier with a shield and iron-tipped spear.

**Vocabulary
siege:** a military blockade to force a city to surrender.

Assyrian Military Power

Assyrian warriors were ferocious in combat. In this relief—sculpture that has figures standing out from a flat background—they are shown launching an assault on a fortified city. The Assyrian war machine included a variety of weapons and methods of attack.

❶ Ladders
While Assyrian archers launched waves of arrows against their opponents defending the city walls, Assyrian troops threw their ladders up against the walls and began their climb into the enemy's stronghold.

❷ Weapons
Troops were armed with the best weapons of the time, iron-tipped spears, as well as iron daggers and swords. They were also protected with armor and large shields.

❸ Tactics
The Assyrians were savage in their treatment of defeated opponents. Those who weren't slaughtered in the initial attack were often impaled or beheaded, while women and children were sometimes murdered or sold into slavery.

❹ Tunnels
The Assyrian army used sappers—soldiers who dug tunnels to sap, or undermine, the foundations of the enemy's walls so that they would fall.

together, they connected these pontoons to the shore with beams. Then they erected a raised dirt roadway at both ends. An armed guard protected the soldiers who installed a support structure of stones, brush, and clay.

Before attacking, the Assyrians dug beneath the city's walls to weaken them. Then, with disciplined organization, foot soldiers marched shoulder to shoulder. A trained cavalry, or troops riding horses, galloped into battle, following their generals, who rode in chariots. With courage and coordination, foot soldiers approached to within an arrow's shot of the city walls. At a signal from their commander, they stopped, strung their bows, and released a shower of arrows. Wave upon wave of arrows hissed over the walls of the besieged city. Meanwhile, another group of troops hammered the city's gates with massive, iron-tipped battering rams. When at last the city gates splintered, the Assyrians showed no mercy. They killed or enslaved their victims. Because soldiers received a bounty for severed heads, many of the defeated were beheaded.

One Assyrian king bragged of burning 3,000 captives to death. Another told how "all the chiefs who had revolted I flayed, with their skins I covered the pillar, some in the midst I walled up, others on stakes I impaled, still others I arranged around the pillar on stakes." To prevent later rebellions, the Assyrians forced groups of captives to leave their homelands. They were forced to settle far away as exiles in the empire's distant provinces and dependent states.

Background
Assyrian archers served as a kind of early form of artillery, clearing the enemy's walls of defenders so Assyrian troops could storm them.

An Expanding Empire

Between 850 and 650 B.C., the kings of Assyria defeated Syria, Palestine, and Babylonia. Reaching beyond the Fertile Crescent, Assyrian rule extended into Egypt and Anatolia. With the conquest of Egypt, the Assyrian Empire had established itself in North Africa.

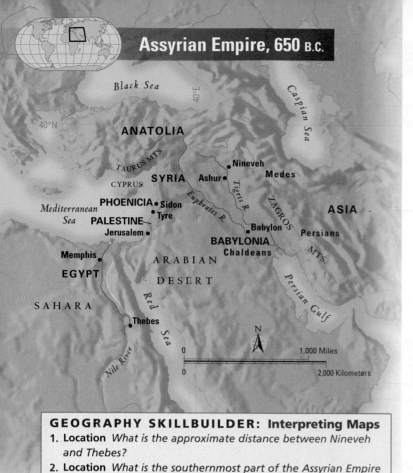

Assyrian Empire, 650 B.C.

GEOGRAPHY SKILLBUILDER: Interpreting Maps
1. **Location** *What is the approximate distance between Nineveh and Thebes?*
2. **Location** *What is the southernmost part of the Assyrian Empire and to what other empire did it previously belong?*

Assyrian Rule At its peak around 650 B.C., this empire included almost all of the old centers of civilization and power in Southwest Asia. With great efficiency, the Assyrians organized their conquered territories into an empire. Assyrian officials governed lands closest to Assyria as provinces and made them dependent territories. Assyrian kings influenced these dependent regions by choosing their rulers. Or, they supported kings who aligned themselves with Assyria. Assyrian armies protected the dependent territories from invasion by other enemies.

In addition, the military campaigns added new territory to the empire. This brought in taxes and tribute to the Assyrian treasury. These became an instrument of control. If a conquered people refused to pay, the Assyrians destroyed their cities and sent the people into exile. By these means the Assyrians developed an effective method of governing an extended empire.

Assyrian Culture Some of Assyria's most fearsome warriors earned a reputation as great builders. For example, the same King Sennacherib who had burned Babylon also established Assyria's capital at **Nineveh** (NIHN·uh·vuh) along the Tigris River. This great walled city, about three miles long and a mile wide, was famous as the largest city of its day. In the ruins of Nineveh and other Assyrian cities, archaeologists found finely carved sculptures. Two artistic subjects particularly fascinated the Assyrians: brutal military campaigns and the lion hunt.

In addition to the treasures of empire, Nineveh also held one of the ancient world's largest libraries. King **Ashurbanipal** (AH·shur·BAH·nuh·PAHL) prided himself on his ability to read in several languages: "The beautiful writings in Sumerian that are obscure, in Akkadian that are difficult to bear in mind, it was my joy to repeat!" This kingly reader collected more than 25,000 clay tablets from throughout the Fertile Crescent. Some were dictionaries containing the same words in several languages. When archaeologists uncovered the library's remains in the mid-1800s, the dictionary tablets enabled scholars to better understand Mesopotamian writing.

The Empire Crumbles

Ashurbanipal proved to be one of the last of the mighty Assyrian kings. Assyrian power had spread itself too thin. Also, the cruelty displayed by the Assyrians had earned them many enemies. Shortly after Ashurbanipal's death, Nineveh fell.

Decline and Fall Just as Assyrians had destroyed so many cities, Assyria's enemies demolished Nineveh. In 612 B.C. a combined army of **Medes** (meedz), **Chaldeans** (kal·DEE·uhnz), and others rammed open the city's gates. Their armies burned and leveled Nineveh. The fire glazed the tablets in the library, which preserved them for archaeologists to study centuries later. So thoroughly did the armies destroy Nineveh that two centuries later only mounds remained.

THINK THROUGH HISTORY
B. Recognizing Causes What methods enabled the Assyrians to rule their empire effectively?

THINK THROUGH HISTORY
C. Making Inferences Why might the Assyrian warrior kings have had such a great interest in writing and reading?

Many people in the region rejoiced at Nineveh's destruction. The Hebrew prophet Nahum (NAY·huhm) gave voice to the feelings of many:

THE BIBLE
And it shall come to pass, that all they that look upon thee shall flee from thee, and say, Nineveh is laid waste: who will bemoan her? Whence shall I seek comforters for thee? . . . Thy shepherds slumber, O king of Assyria: thy nobles shall dwell in the dust: thy people is scattered upon the mountains, and no man gathereth them.
NAHUM 3:7,18

THINK THROUGH HISTORY
D. Clarifying What was Nahum's opinion about the collapse of the Assyrian Empire?

Rebirth of Babylon Under the Chaldeans After defeating the Assyrians, the Chaldeans made Babylon their capital. Around 600 B.C., Babylon became the center of a new empire, more than 1,000 years after Hammurabi had ruled there. A Chaldean king named **Nebuchadnezzar** (NEHB·uh·kuhd·NEHZ·uhr) restored Babylon. The most impressive part of his palace may have been the famous hanging gardens. Greek scholars later listed them as one of the Seven Wonders of the World. According to legend, one of Nebuchadnezzar's wives missed the flowering shrubs of her mountain homeland. To please her, the king had fragrant trees and mountain shrubs planted on terraces. They rose 75 feet above Babylon's flat, dry plain. Slaves watered the plants from hidden pumps.

Indeed, the entire city was a wonder. Its walls were so thick that, according to one report, a four-horse chariot could wheel around on top of them. To ensure that the world knew who ruled Babylon, even the bricks were inscribed, "I am Nebuchadnezzar, King of Babylon."

The highest building in Babylon was a great, seven-tiered ziggurat more than 300 feet high. It was visible for miles. At night, priests observed the stars from the top of this tower and others in the city. They kept detailed records of how the stars and planets seemed to change position in the night sky. The Chaldeans' observations formed the basis for both astronomy and astrology.

Nebuchadnezzar's empire fell shortly after his death. The Persians who next came to power adopted many Assyrian military, political, and artistic inventions. The Persians would use the organization the Assyrians had developed to stabilize the region.

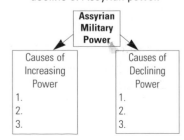
Lions made of glazed bricks decorated walls along the broad road that passed the Ishtar Gate of Nebuchadnezzar in Babylon.

Section ❷ Assessment

1. TERMS & NAMES
Identify
- Assyria
- Sennacherib
- Nineveh
- Ashurbanipal
- Medes
- Chaldeans
- Nebuchadnezzar

2. TAKING NOTES
Create a diagram showing the causes of the rise and of the decline of Assyrian power.

Assyrian Military Power	
Causes of Increasing Power	Causes of Declining Power
1.	1.
2.	2.
3.	3.

3. FORMING AND SUPPORTING OPINIONS
The Assyrians relied almost exclusively on military power in building, maintaining, and ruling their empire. Explain whether you think this was a good strategy.

THINK ABOUT
- the causes of Assyrian military power
- the stability of the empire
- the methods that empires use to become stronger

4. THEME ACTIVITY
Science and Technology
Work with a partner to draw a mural highlighting how developments in technology influenced the rise and decline of the Assyrian Empire.

TERMS & NAMES
- Cyrus
- Cambyses
- Darius
- satrap
- Royal Road
- Zoroaster

3 Persia Unites Many Lands

MAIN IDEA	WHY IT MATTERS NOW
The Persian Empire ruled with tolerance and wise government.	Tolerance and wise government are characteristics of the most successful methods of rule.

SETTING THE STAGE The Medes, along with the Chaldeans, helped to overthrow the Assyrian Empire in 612 B.C. The Medes marched to Nineveh from their homeland in the area of present-day northern Iran. Meanwhile, the Medes' close neighbor to the south, Persia, began to expand its horizons and territorial ambitions.

The Rise of Persia

The Assyrians employed military force to control a vast empire. In contrast, the Persians would base their empire on tolerance and diplomacy. They relied on a strong military to back up their policies. Ancient Persia included what is today Iran.

The Persian Homeland About 1000 B.C., Indo-Europeans first migrated from Central Europe and southern Russia to the mountains and plateaus east of the Fertile Crescent. This area extended from the Caspian Sea in the north to the Persian Gulf in the south. In addition to prosperous farmland, ancient Iran boasted a wealth of minerals. These included copper, lead, gold, silver, and gleaming blue lapis lazuli. A thriving trade put the settlers in contact with their neighbors to the east and the west.

At first, dozens of tiny kingdoms ruled in the region. The Medes and others joined forces to overthrow the Assyrian Empire in 612 B.C. Eventually two major powers emerged: the Medes and the Persians. A remarkable ruler would soon lead Persia to dominate not only the Medes but also a huge empire.

Cyrus the Great Founds an Empire The rest of the world paid little attention to the Persians until 550 B.C. That year, **Cyrus** (SY·ruhs), Persia's king, began his conquest of several neighboring kingdoms in Iran. A new power was rising in the region. Eventually, the Persians extended their rule from the Indus River in the east to Anatolia in the west. This empire spanned over two thousand miles.

Cyrus's soldiers wore leather pants and thick felt boots. Riding mountain ponies, they shot arrows from the short bows that their ancestors had used on the steppes of Russia. Their leader proved to be a military genius. He led his army from victory to victory between 550 and 539 B.C. Cyrus and his armies conquered the entire Fertile Crescent and most of Anatolia.

Even more than his military genius, though, Cyrus's most enduring legacy was his method of governing. His kindness toward conquered peoples revealed a wise and tolerant view of empire. For example, when Cyrus's army marched into a city, his generals enforced strict discipline against looting and burning. Unlike other conquerors, Cyrus believed in honoring local customs and religions. Instead of destroying the local temple, Cyrus would kneel there to pray.

Vocabulary
legacy: something handed down from the past.

Under Persian rule, subject peoples enjoyed remarkable freedom. Indeed, Babylon peacefully opened its gates for Cyrus in 539 B.C. Thankful for the bloodless victory, Cyrus offered prayers to Babylon's chief god, Marduk. According to Persian accounts, "all the inhabitants of Babylon . . . princes and governors included, bowed to Cyrus and kissed his feet, jubilant and with shining faces."

Cyrus also allowed the Jews, who had been deported from their homeland by the Babylonians, to return to Jerusalem in 538 B.C. Under Persian rule, the Jews rebuilt their city and temple. They also resumed their sacred rituals. Many portions of the Old Testament first appeared in written form during this period. The Jews were forever grateful to Cyrus, whom they considered one of God's anointed ones. The Hebrew prophet Ezra tells of Cyrus's kindness:

The tomb of Cyrus the Great still stands. It is notable for its simplicity when compared with other royal tombs of the ancient world.

THE BIBLE
This is the word of Cyrus king of Persia: The Lord the God of heaven has given me all the kingdoms of the earth, and he himself has charged me to build him a house at Jerusalem in Judah. To every man of his people now among you I say, God be with him, and let him go up to Jerusalem in Judah, and rebuild the house of the Lord the God of Israel, the God whose city is Jerusalem.

EZRA 1:2–3.

THINK THROUGH HISTORY
A. Summarizing
What are some examples of Cyrus's tolerant method of governing?

This wise and tolerant ruler was above all a warrior. Cyrus lost his life in battle, fighting nomadic invaders on the eastern border of his empire. According to the Greek historian Arrian, his simple, house-shaped tomb bore these poignant words: "O man, I am Cyrus the son of Cambyses. I established the Persian Empire and was king of Asia. Do not begrudge me my memorial."

Persian Rule and Religion

The task of organizing and unifying conquered territories fell to rulers who followed Cyrus. They succeeded by combining Persian control with local self-government.

Cambyses and Darius Cyrus died in 530 B.C. His son **Cambyses** (kam·BY·seez), named after Cyrus's father, extended the Persian Empire by conquering Egypt. However, the son neglected to follow his father's wise example. Cambyses publicly scorned the Egyptian religion. He ordered the images of Egyptian gods to be burned. After ruling for only eight years, Cambyses died. Immediately, widespread rebellions broke out across the empire. Persian control had seemed strong a decade earlier. It now seemed surprisingly fragile.

This stone relief of Darius on his throne shows him receiving his heir, the royal prince, Xerxes.

Cambyses's successor, **Darius** (duh·RY·uhs), a noble of the ruling dynasty, had begun his career as a member of the king's bodyguard. An elite group of Persian soldiers, the Ten Thousand Immortals, helped Darius seize the throne in 522–521 B.C. Darius spent the first three years of his reign putting down revolts. He spent the next few years establishing an unusually efficient and well-organized administration.

Soon the new king extended Persian conquests in the east. He led armies up into the mountains of present-day Afghanistan and down into the river valleys of India. The immense Persian Empire now embraced Egypt and Anatolia in the west, part of India in the east, and the Fertile Crescent in the center. This vast empire extended over 2,500 miles from east to west. Darius's only failure, and that of his son, was his inability to conquer Greece.

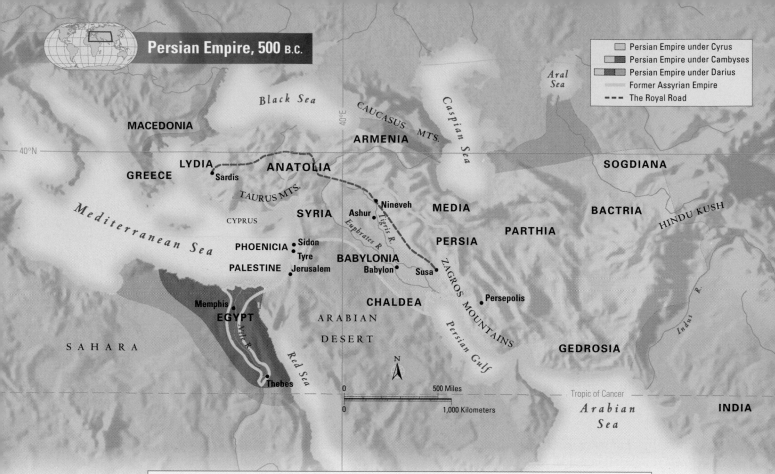

Persian Empire, 500 B.C.

Legend:
- Persian Empire under Cyrus
- Persian Empire under Cambyses
- Persian Empire under Darius
- Former Assyrian Empire
- The Royal Road

GEOGRAPHY SKILLBUILDER: Interpreting Maps

1. **Region** *What part of the ancient world did Cambyses add to the Persian Empire?*
2. **Region** *Compare the map of the Persian Empire with that of the Assyrian Empire. What areas did the Persians rule that the Assyrians did not?*

Provinces and Satraps Although a great warrior, Darius's greatest genius lay in administration. To govern his sprawling empire, the king divided it into 20 provinces. These provinces were roughly similar to the homelands of the many groups of people within the Persian Empire. Under Persian rule, the people of each province still practiced their own religion. They also spoke their own language and followed many of their own laws. This administrative policy of many groups—sometimes called "nationalities"—living by their own laws within one empire would be repeatedly practiced in Southwest Asia. This continued in the early 1900s in the Ottoman Empire.

Although tolerant of the many groups within his empire, Darius still ruled with absolute power. In each province of the Persian Empire, Darius installed a governor called a **satrap** (SAY·TRAP), who ruled locally. To ensure his satraps' loyalty, Darius sent out inspectors known as the "King's Eyes and Ears." They checked up on the administration of each province in every corner of the kingdom. Darius also appointed an army leader and a tax collector for each province.

Two other tools helped the Persian king hold his empire together. An excellent road system and the use of standard money helped unite the empire. The famous **Royal Road** of the Persian Empire ran from Susa in Persia to Sardis in Anatolia, a distance of 1,677 miles.

Darius borrowed his second idea, manufacturing metal coins, from the Lydians of Asia Minor. For the first time, coins of a standard value circulated throughout an extended empire. No longer did people have to weigh and measure odd pieces of gold or silver to pay for what they bought. Like the road system, the wider use of standardized coins promoted trade. Trade, in turn, helped to hold the empire together.

The Royal Road

One of the ways in which societies build and maintain empires is by establishing systems of communication and transportation. The Royal Road built by the Persian Empire connected Susa in Persia to Sardis in Anatolia. Because of this road, royal commands could quickly reach most parts of the empire.

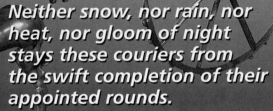

This four-horse chariot dates from the 6th–4th century B.C. It is the type of vehicle that would have traveled the Royal Road in the time of Darius. The studs on the wheels were designed to help prevent the chariot from slipping. The large wheels provided a smoother ride over rough ground.

Neither snow, nor rain, nor heat, nor gloom of night stays these couriers from the swift completion of their appointed rounds.
Greek historian Herodotus, writing in the 400s B.C. about the Persian messengers on the Royal Road.

A Ride Along the Royal Road

EUROPE
Black Sea
Caspian Sea
Sardis ANATOLIA Nineveh
ASIA
Mediterranean Sea
Susa
AFRICA
N
SOUTHWEST ASIA
INDIA
0 500 Miles
0 1,000 Kilometers
Arabian Sea

The Road
The road was 1,677 miles in length. There were 111 post or relay stations spaced about 15 miles apart along the road, similar to the American Pony Express system. Other roads branched off the main road to distant parts of the empire.

The Ride
Relay stations were equipped with fresh horses for the king's messengers. Royal messengers could cover the length of the Royal Road in seven days. Normal travel time along the road was longer. A caravan, for example, might take three months to travel the whole distance.

Patterns of Interaction
"There is nothing in the world which travels faster than these Persian couriers," Herodotus wrote about the messengers of the Royal Road. Strong road networks like the Royal Road enabled empires to expand and maintain control over people and places. Like the Persians, the Inca of South America created a road system thousands of miles long. These roads allowed the Inca to extend their rule over as many as 16 million people. Empires throughout history have shared characteristics such as efficient communication systems, effective leaders, and powerful armies.

A bronze figure of a Persian horseman, 5th–4th century B.C.

 VIDEO *Building Empires: The Rise of the Persians and the Inca*

Connect *to* **History**

Recognizing Effects How would the Royal Road enable the ruler to maintain power in the empire?

SEE SKILLBUILDER HANDBOOK, PAGE 995

Connect *to* **Today**

Comparing What systems of communication and transportation today might be compared to the Royal Road of the Persians?

Persian Religion By the time of Darius's rule, about 2,500 years had passed since the first Sumerian city-states had been built. During those years, people of the Fertile Crescent had endured war, conquest, and famine. This gave rise to a basic question: Why should so much suffering and chaos exist in the world? A Persian prophet and religious reformer named **Zoroaster** (ZAWR·oh·AS·tuhr), who lived around 600 B.C., offered an answer.

Background
Scholars know almost nothing about the life of Zoroaster. Even the date of his birth is unknown, with some historians dating it as early as the 1100s B.C., although most date it around the sixth century B.C.

This stone relief from the royal palace at Persepolis depicts the Persian god Ahura Mazda. The ancient Persians believed that this god embodied light and truth.

Zoroaster taught that two spiritual armies fight for possession of a person's soul. The god of truth and light, Ahura Mazda (ah·HUR·uh MAZ·duh), leads one army. The god of evil and darkness, Ahriman (AH·rih·muhn), leads the other. At the end of time, Zoroaster preached, all souls would be judged according to which side they had chosen. Followers of Ahura Mazda would be lifted into paradise. Followers of Ahriman would suffer forever in a fiery pit. A collection of books called the *Avesta* became the holy writings of the Zoroastrian religion. In Zoroaster's religion, people's own choices controlled their fate. At the final judgment, those who had chosen the side of goodness would not be doomed to a dismal underworld. Instead, they would ascend to paradise.

The Zoroastrian religion developed ideas about heaven, hell, and a final judgment that were similar to concepts in Judaism, Christianity, and Islam. The faith of Zoroaster spread eastward into India. There, it became the Parsi sect, the largest group of Zoroastrians in the world today. Zoroastrianism also was an important influence in the development of Manicheanism, a religious system that competed with early Christianity for believers. The cult of Mithra, a Zoroastrian god, spread westward to become a popular religion among the military legions in the Roman Empire.

THINK THROUGH HISTORY
B. Comparing What ideas and world view did Zoroastrianism share with other religions?

The Persian Legacy Through their tolerance and good government, the Persians brought political order to Southwest Asia. They preserved ideas from earlier civilizations and found new ways to live and rule. Their respect for other cultures helped to preserve those cultures for the future. The powerful dynasty Cyrus established in Persia lasted 200 years and grew into a huge empire. Likewise in China, as you will learn in Section 4, great empires arose that dominated their regions.

Section 3 Assessment

1. TERMS & NAMES

Identify
• Cyrus
• Cambyses
• Darius
• satrap
• Royal Road
• Zoroaster

2. TAKING NOTES

Create a Venn diagram to show the similarities and differences between Cyrus and Darius.

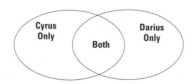

Cyrus Only | Both | Darius Only

Which of the differences do you consider most important? Why?

3. HYPOTHESIZING

Why do you think Persians and other peoples were able to turn their thoughts to religion?

THINK ABOUT
• past history of peoples in the Fertile Crescent
• living conditions in the Persian Empire
• role of leaders in the Persian Empire

4. ANALYZING THEMES

Empire Building How did Darius's methods of administration give stability to his empire?

THINK ABOUT
• the structure of the empire
• policy of tolerance
• the role of the satrap

An Empire Unifies China

TERMS & NAMES
- Confucius
- filial piety
- bureaucracy
- Daoism
- Legalism
- *I Ching*
- yin and yang
- Qin dynasty
- Shi Huangdi
- autocracy

MAIN IDEA

The social disorder of the warring states contributed to Chinese philosophy and unification.

WHY IT MATTERS NOW

The people, events, and ideas that shaped China's early history continue to influence China's role in today's world.

SETTING THE STAGE The Zhou Dynasty, as you read in Chapter 2, endured for at least eight centuries, from approximately 1027 B.C. to 256 B.C. For the first 300 years of their long reign, the Zhou kings controlled a large empire, including both eastern and western lands. Local rulers represented the king, but he had the ultimate power. By the latter years of the Zhou Dynasty, the lords of dependent territories began to think of themselves as independent kings. Their bloody warfare led to the decline of the Zhou Dynasty.

Philosophy and the Social Order

China's ancient values of social order, harmony, and respect for authority were put aside toward the end of the Zhou Dynasty. To restore these values, Chinese scholars and philosophers developed different solutions.

Confucius Urges Harmony China's most influential scholar was **Confucius** (kuhn·FYOO·shuhs). Born in 551 B.C., Confucius lived at a time when the Zhou Dynasty was being torn apart by warring lords. He led a scholarly life, studying and teaching history, music, and moral character.

Confucius believed that social order, harmony, and good government could be restored in China if society was organized around five basic relationships. These were the relationships between: 1) ruler and subject, 2) father and son, 3) husband and wife, 4) older brother and younger brother, and 5) friend and friend. A code of proper conduct regulated each of these relationships. For example, rulers should practice kindness and virtuous living. In return, subjects should be loyal and law-abiding.

Three of Confucius's five relationships were based upon the family. Confucius stressed that children should practice what he called **filial piety,** or respect for their parents and elders:

> **A VOICE FROM THE PAST**
> In serving his parents, a filial son renders utmost respect to them at home; he supports them with joy; he gives them tender care in sickness; he grieves at their death; he sacrifices to them with solemnity . . .
> **CONFUCIUS,** the *Analects*

Confucius was not content to be merely a great teacher. He wanted to reform Chinese society by showing a prince or duke how to govern wisely. Impressed by Confucius's wisdom, the duke of Lu appointed him Minister of Justice. According to legend, Confucius so overwhelmed people by his kindness and courtesy that almost overnight, crime vanished from Lu. When the duke's ways changed, however, Confucius felt compelled to resign.

This 18th-century painting shows Chinese students taking an examination on the Confucian classics. They wish to advance in the government. Written tests for civil servants in China go back to the Han Dynasty.

First Age of Empires **97**

Confucius spent the remainder of his life teaching. The only record of his ideas are the writings of his students. His students later collected his words in a book called the *Analects*. A disciple named Mencius (MEHN·shee·uhs) also spread Confucius's ideas. Both Confucius and Mencius taught that leaders should be virtuous.

Confucian Ideas About Government Confucius said that education could transform a humbly born person into a gentleman. In saying this, he laid the groundwork for the creation of a **bureaucracy**, a trained civil service, or those who run the government. According to Confucius, a gentleman had four virtues: "In his private conduct he was courteous, in serving his master he was punctilious [precise], in providing for the needs of the people he gave them even more than their due; in exacting service from the people, he was just." Education became critically important to career advancement in the bureaucracy.

Confucianism was never a religion, but it was an ethical system. It became the foundation for Chinese government and social order. In addition, the ideas of Confucius spread beyond China and influenced civilizations throughout East Asia.

Daoists Seek Harmony For Confucius, the social order of family and government was most important. For another Chinese thinker named Laozi, who may have lived during the sixth century B.C., only the natural order was important. His book *Dao De Ching* (*The Way of Virtue*) expressed Laozi's belief. He said that a universal force called the Dao (tow), meaning "the Way," guides all things.

If you seek order and harmony, said Laozi, go up into the hills, sit by a stream, and observe a drifting cloud or a soft breeze. Observe that nothing in nature strives for fame, power, or even wisdom. The cloud, the breeze, and the stream move without effort because they follow the Dao or way.

Of all the creatures of nature, according to Laozi, only humans fail to follow the Dao. They argue about questions of right and wrong, good manners and bad. According to Laozi, such arguments are pointless.

The philosophy of Laozi came to be known as **Daoism**. Its search for knowledge and understanding of nature led Daoism's followers to pursue scientific studies. Daoists made contributions to the sciences of alchemy, astronomy, and medicine.

Legalists Urge Harsh Rule In sharp contrast to the followers of Confucius was a group of practical political thinkers called the Legalists. They believed that a highly efficient and powerful government was the key to restoring order. They got their

Background
The *Analects* was compiled around 400 B.C. It became a fundamental part of traditional education in China. The word *analects* means "selections from a literary work."

Vocabulary
social order: having to do with relations between people.
natural order: having to do with relations between all living things.

Vocabulary
legend: a story handed down from earlier times, especially one believed to be historical.

HISTORY MAKERS

Confucius
551–479 B.C.

Born to a poor family, Confucius earned his living as a teacher. But he longed to put his principles into action by advising political leaders. Finally, at around age 50, Confucius won a post as minister in his home state.

According to legend, he set such a virtuous example that a purse lying in the middle of the street would lie untouched for days. As Confucius said, "If a ruler himself is upright, all will go well without orders. But if he himself is not upright, even though he gives orders, they will not be obeyed."

Driven from office by political intrigue, Confucius returned to teaching. He considered himself a failure because he had never held high office. Yet Confucius's ideas have molded Chinese thought for centuries.

Laozi
6th century B.C.

Legend has it that Laozi's mother carried him in her womb for 62 years and that he was born with white hair and wrinkled skin. Laozi's followers claimed that he was a contemporary of Confucius.

Unlike Confucius and the Legalists, however, Laozi believed that government should do as little as possible and leave the people alone:

Therefore in governing the people, the sage empties their minds but fills their bellies, weakens their wills but strengthens their bones. He always keeps them innocent of knowledge and free from desire, and ensures that the clever never dare to act.

Laozi thought that people could do little to influence the outcome of events. Daoism offered communion with nature as an alternative to political chaos.

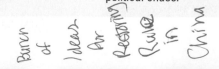

Chinese Ethical Systems

Confucianism	Daoism	Legalism
• Social order, harmony, and good government should be based on family relationships.	• The natural order is more important than the social order.	• A highly efficient and powerful government is the key to social order.
• Respect for parents and elders is important to a well-ordered society.	• A universal force guides all things.	• Punishments are useful to maintain social order.
• Education is important both to the welfare of the individual and to society.	• Human beings should live simply and in harmony with nature.	• Thinkers and their ideas should be strictly controlled by the government.

> **SKILLBUILDER: Interpreting Charts**
> 1. *Which of these three systems stress the importance of government and a well-ordered society?*
> 2. *Which system emphasizes the natural order over the social order?*
> 3. *Which of these systems seems to be most moderate and balanced? Explain.*

name from their belief that government should use the law to end civil disorder and restore harmony. Among the founders of **Legalism** were Hanfeizi and Li Si.

The Legalists taught that a ruler should provide rich rewards for people who carried out their duties well. Likewise, the disobedient should be harshly punished. In practice, the Legalists stressed punishment more than rewards. For example, anyone caught outside his own village without a travel permit should have his ears or nose chopped off, said the Legalists.

THINK THROUGH HISTORY
A. Summarizing
How did the Legalists think that a society could be made to run well?

The Legalists believed in controlling ideas as well as actions. They suggested that a ruler burn all writings that might encourage people to think critically about government. After all, it was for the prince to govern and the people to obey. Eventually, Legalist ideas gained favor with a prince of a new dynasty that replaced the Zhou. That powerful ruler was soon to put an end to China's long period of disorder.

***I Ching* and Yin and Yang** People with little interest in these philosophical debates consulted a book of oracles called *I Ching* (also spelled *Yi Jing*) to answer ethical or practical problems. Readers used the book by throwing a set of coins, interpreting the results, and then reading the appropriate oracle. The *I Ching (The Book of Changes)* helped people to lead a happy life by dispensing good advice and simple common sense.

Ancient thinkers developed the concept of **yin and yang,** two powers that together represented the natural rhythms of life. Yang represents the masculine qualities in the universe, yin the feminine. Both forces represent the rhythm of the universe and complement each other. Both the *I Ching* and yin and yang helped Chinese people understand how they fit into the world.

The Qin Dynasty

A short-lived dynasty replaced the Zhou Dynasty in the third century B.C. It emerged from the western state of Qin (chihn). The 13-year-old **Qin Dynasty** ruler who came to the throne in the third century B.C. employed Legalist ideas to subdue warring states and unify his country.

A New Emperor Takes Control After ruling for over 20 years, in 221 B.C., the Qin ruler assumed the name **Shi Huangdi** (shihr hwahng·dee), which means "First Emperor." The new emperor had

SPOTLIGHT ON

Yin and Yang

The symbol of yin and yang is a circle divided into halves, as shown in the emblem above. The circle represents the harmony of yin (earth, female, passive) and yang (heaven, male, active). Yin is represented by the tiger and the color orange; yang is represented by the dragon and the color blue.

Ancient Chinese thinkers believed that pain is caused by an imbalance in the body between the forces of yin and yang. They believed that acupuncture helped to restore this balance by releasing blocked energy.

civil wars

begun his reign by halting the internal battles that had sapped China's strength. Next he turned his attention to defeating invaders and crushing internal resistance to his rule. Shi Huangdi's armies attacked the invaders north of the Yellow River and south as far as what is now Vietnam. His victories doubled China's size. Shi Huangdi was determined to unify China.

The Qin emperor acted decisively to crush political opposition at home. To destroy the power of rival warlords, Shi Huangdi instituted a policy called "strengthening the trunk and weakening the branches." He commanded all the noble families to live at the capital city under his suspicious gaze. This edict, according to tradition, uprooted 120,000 noble families. Seizing their land, the emperor carved China into 36 administrative districts. He sent Qin officials to control them.

To silence criticism, the emperor and his prime minister, the Legalist philosopher Li Su, murdered hundreds of Confucian scholars. They also ordered "useless" books burned. These books were the works of Confucian thinkers and poets who disagreed with the Legalists. Practical books about medicine and farming were spared. Through measures such as these, Shi Huangdi established an **autocracy**—a government in which the ruler has unlimited power and uses it in an arbitrary manner.

A Program of Centralization Shi Huangdi's sweeping program of centralization included the building of a highway network of over 4,000 miles. He forced peasants to work on roads against their will. He also set uniform standards for Chinese writing, law, currency, and weights and measures, down to the length of cart axles. This last standard ensured that all vehicles could fit into the ruts of China's main roads.

Under Shi Huangdi's rule, irrigation projects increased farm production. Trade blossomed, thanks to the new road system. Trade pushed a new class—merchants—into prominence. Despite these social advances, harsh taxes and repressive government made the Qin regime unpopular. Shi Huangdi had unified China at the expense of human freedom.

EXTREMIST

Dictator

THINK THROUGH HISTORY
B. Recognizing Effects What were the positive and negative effects of Shi Huangdi's rule?

he is hated

Great Wall of China Scholars hated Shi Huangdi for his book burning; poor people hated him for their forced labor in building a unified wall. Earlier, Zhou rulers had erected smaller walls to discourage attacks by northern nomads. Shi Huangdi determined to close the gaps and unify the wall 1,400 miles to the west. Now enemies would have to gallop halfway to Tibet to get around it.

The Great Wall of China arose on the backs of hundreds of thousands of peasants. The wall builders worked neither for wages nor for love of empire. They faced a terrible choice: work on the wall or die. Many of the laborers worked on the wall and died anyway, victims of the crushing labor or the winter winds. The Great Wall of China is so huge that it is one of the few human-made features on Earth visible from space.

The Fall of the Qin The Qin Dynasty proved short-lived. Though fully as cruel as his father, Shi Huangdi's son proved less able. Peasants rebelled just three

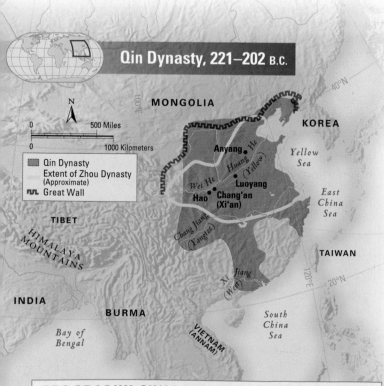

Qin Dynasty, 221–202 B.C.

MONGOLIA
KOREA
Anyang
Yellow Sea
Wei He
Luoyang
Hao
Chang'an (Xi'an)
East China Sea
TIBET
HIMALAYA MOUNTAINS
TAIWAN
INDIA
BURMA
Xi Jiang (West)
South China Sea
Bay of Bengal
VIETNAM (ANNAM)

N
0 500 Miles
0 1000 Kilometers

Qin Dynasty
Extent of Zhou Dynasty (Approximate)
Great Wall

GEOGRAPHY SKILLBUILDER: Interpreting Maps
1. **Region** How far south did the Qin empire extend?
2. **Human-Environment Interaction** How does the wall's location reflect its function?

From the Yellow Sea in the east to the Gobi Desert in the west, the Great Wall twisted like a dragon's tail for thousands of miles. Watch towers rose every 200 to 300 yards along the wall.

Slabs of cut stone on the outside of the wall enclosed a heap of pebbles and rubble on the inside. Each section of the wall rose to a height of 20 to 25 feet.

Although Shi Huangdi built the earliest unified wall, the wall as it exists today dates from the later Ming Dynasty (1368–1644).

In the time of Shi Huangdi, hundreds of thousands of peasants collected, hauled, and dumped millions of tons of stone, dirt, and rubble to fill the core of the Great Wall. Many who died working on the wall were buried in the core.

Han Dynasty

years after the second Qin emperor took office. One of their leaders, a peasant from the land of Han, marched his troops into the capital city. By 202 B.C., the harsh Qin Dynasty gave way to the Han Dynasty.

While the Chinese explored the best ways to govern, ancient Greece was experimenting with different forms of government, as you will read in Chapter 5.

Section 4 Assessment

1. TERMS & NAMES

Identify
- Confucius
- filial piety
- bureaucracy
- Daoism
- Legalism
- *I Ching*
- yin and yang
- Qin Dynasty
- Shi Huangdi
- autocracy

2. TAKING NOTES

Create a web like the one below, and indicate how the chaos of the warring states affected Chinese philosophy, politics, and the growth of cities.

3. HYPOTHESIZING

In 1776, the American Declaration of Independence declared that "all men are created equal." How would followers of the three philosophical traditions in China react to that statement?

THINK ABOUT
- their views on equality
- views on opposition to government

4. THEME ACTIVITY

Interaction with Environment Make a chart that compares and contrasts the monumental projects of the Persian Royal Road and the Great Wall of China. Include their purposes, how they changed the environment, and how they affected the peoples living there.

Chapter **4** Assessment

TERMS & NAMES

Briefly explain the importance of each of the following to the first great age of empires.

1. Ramses II
2. Kush
3. Assyria
4. Ashurbanipal
5. Cyrus
6. Royal Road
7. Zoroaster
8. Confucius
9. Daoism
10. Shi Huangdi

Interact *with* History

On page 82, you thought about the advantages and disadvantages of empire before studying the rise of the first great empires. Now that you've read the chapter, rethink the advantages and disadvantages of empire. Do empires benefit conquered peoples? Do empires impose penalties on those they conquer? Which outweighs the other? Discuss your opinions with a small group.

Visual Summary

REVIEW QUESTIONS

SECTION 1 *(pages 83–87)*
The Empires of Egypt and Nubia Collide

11. How were the reigns of Thutmose III and Piankhi alike?
12. Explain how the declines of the New Kingdom in Egypt and the Kushite empire in Meroë were similar.

SECTION 2 *(pages 88–91)*
Assyria Dominates the Fertile Crescent

13. Why was the Assyrian military so powerful?
14. What were the positive achievements of the Assyrian Empire?

SECTION 3 *(pages 92–96)*
Persia Unites Many Lands

15. Give two examples to show the enlightened view of empire held by Cyrus.
16. How was Darius able to rule such a large empire with absolute power?
17. Summarize the beliefs of Zoroaster.

SECTION 4 *(pages 97–101)*
An Empire Unifies China

18. Why are the later years of the Zhou Dynasty called "the time of the warring states"?
19. Summarize differences in how Confucius, the Legalists, and Laozi viewed government.
20. How did the Great Wall help to unify China?

First Age of Empires

Egypt 1570–1075 B.C.

- Pharaohs set up a professional army.
- Pharaohs invaded surrounding territories in Africa and Southwest Asia.
- Egypt drew vast wealth from the lands it controlled around the Nile and far beyond.

Nubia 751 B.C.–A.D. 350

- Nubia and Egypt interacted and spread their culture to their trading partners.
- The kings of Nubia conquered Egypt, ousted Libyan rulers, and restored Egyptian way of life.
- Nubia made use of abundant natural resources to establish trade between Africa, Arabia, and India.

EMPIRE BUILDING

Assyria 850–612 B.C.

- Assyria developed a sophisticated military organization and state-of-the-art weaponry to conquer an empire.
- The empire engaged in brutal treatment of its conquered peoples.
- Kings used harsh taxes as well as military power to control conquered peoples.

Persia 550–330 B.C.

- Persian kings were tolerant in their treatment of peoples and cultures that made up their empire.
- Kings permitted a high degree of local self-government, so that conquered peoples enjoyed remarkable freedom.
- The empire was divided into 20 provinces, each ruled by a satrap (or governor).

China 221–202 B.C.

- Confucian and Legalist ideas laid the groundwork for a strong central government and a bureaucracy.
- Chinese emperors of the Qin Dynasty defeated invaders and crushed internal resistance.
- China crushed political opposition at home in a sweeping program of centralization.

CRITICAL THINKING

1. IMPACT OF EMPIRES

THEME EMPIRE BUILDING With the creation of large empires, local leaders lost power. What was good and bad about this shift in power from local to empire rulers? Explain.

2. EVALUATING RULERS

Copy the table below and complete it by evaluating the military, economic, and political conditions in the empire under each leader. Then explain which leader you consider the most successful.

Leader	Military Strengths	Economic Growth	Political Stability
Thutmose III			
Sennacherib			
Cyrus			
Darius			
Shi Huangdi			

3. HISTORICAL CONTEXT

Compare the conditions that led to Zoroastrianism to the conditions that led to Confucianism. How were they similar?

4. ANALYZING PRIMARY SOURCES

The following quotation from Confucius reflects his beliefs about human nature and politics. Read the paragraph and answer the questions below it.

> **A VOICE FROM THE PAST**
> Guide the people with governmental measures and control or regulate them by the threat of punishment, and the people will try to keep out of jail, but will have no sense of honor or shame. Guide the people by virtue and control or regulate them by *li* [moral rules and customs], and the people will have a sense of honor and respect.
>
> **CONFUCIUS**, the *Analects*

- How might Ramses II, Sennacherib, and Cyrus respond to this statement? Explain.

- Do you think the U. S. government should follow this advice?

CHAPTER ACTIVITIES

1. LIVING HISTORY: Unit Portfolio Project

THEME INTERACTION WITH ENVIRONMENT Your unit portfolio tracks the ways early peoples adjusted to their environments (see page 3). For Chapter 4, you might use one of the following ideas to add to your portfolio:

- Create a mural that shows how plains, rivers, roads, walls, and other elements of the natural and human environment influenced the developments of Egypt, Assyria, Persia, and China.

- Create a map highlighting how the climates and geographic features of Egypt, Assyria, Persia, and China are similar and different. Write a short analysis of how climate and geography affected these empires.

- Write a short story set in one of the empires described in this chapter. In your story, include descriptions of the environment and demonstrate how it influenced the lives of people.

2. CONNECT TO TODAY: Cooperative Learning

THEME SCIENCE AND TECHNOLOGY The Assyrians and the Chinese built their power on technological innovation. Today, countries continue to compete to develop improved military technology. Work with a team to find out how much the United States and one other country spend on their militaries today.

Using the Internet or magazines, research statistics about the topic. Look for statistics that answer such questions as: How much money does each country spend on its military? What percentage of the country's total government spending goes to the military? What is the total world spending for military?

- Present the statistics in a table, bar graph, or other visual.

- Consider whether the money is spent for current conflicts, for maintaining a peacetime military, for research and development, or for other uses. Note any patterns in military spending by region, by level of economic prosperity, or by any other trait. Write a summary of your findings.

3. INTERPRETING A TIME LINE

Revisit the unit time line on pages 2–3. Compare three events listed on the Chapter 4 time line. How were they similar?

FOCUS ON ART

The relief below comes from Ashurbanipal's palace at Nineveh. It depicts the king and queen at a garden party. The queen is sitting on a throne and the king is reclining on a couch. In the tree hangs the head (circled in yellow) of one of the defeated opponents of the Assyrian conqueror.

- What elements in the relief suggest that the monarchs are relaxing?

- What characteristics of the Assyrians does this relief seem to express?

Connect to History What details in the relief show causes of the Assyrian Empire's downfall?

New Directions in Government and Society
2000 B.C.–A.D. 700

In this 19th century painting, *Cicerone denuncia Catilina*, by Cesare Maccari, the Roman senate watches as Cicero denounces Catiline for plotting to overthrow the government. The Romans, who valued the notion of law and order, lived under an early form of democracy.

New Directions in Government and Society

	2000 B.C.	1750 B.C.	1500 B.C.	1250 B.C.	1000 B.C.	750 B.C.

CHAPTER 5 2000 B.C.–300 B.C.
Classical Greece

2000 B.C. *Crete*
Minoan civilization thrives

1600 B.C. *Greece*
Mycenaean kings dominate Greece

1450 B.C. *Crete*
Mycenaeans invade Crete

1400 B.C. *Crete*
Minoan civilization disappears

1200 B.C. *Anatolia*
Trojan War is fought

1200 B.C. *Greece*
Dorian Age begins

800 B.C. *Greece*
City-states begin to rise

800 B.C. *Greece*
Homer composes epics

CHAPTER 6 500 B.C.–A.D. 500
Ancient Rome and Early Christianity

◄ **Roman painting from Pompeii**

CHAPTER 7 300 B.C.–A.D. 550
India and China Establish Empires

CHAPTER 8 1500 B.C.–A.D. 500
African Civilizations

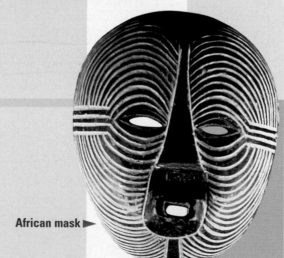

1000 B.C. *East Africa*
Kingdom of Aksum arises

African mask ►

CHAPTER 9 40,000 B.C.–A.D. 700
The Americas: A Separate World

10,500 B.C. to 9500 B.C.

10,500 B.C. *Chile* Monte Verde shows evidence of human life

10,000 B.C. *North America* Ice Age ends and land bridge disappears

9,500 B.C. *New Mexico* Humans gather at Clovis site

1200 B.C. *Mexico*
Olmec culture arises in southern Mexico

1000 B.C. *Mexico*
Zapotec civilization arises

900 B.C. *South America* Chavín civilization emerges

2000 B.C.	1750 B.C.	1500 B.C.	1250 B.C.	1000 B.C.	750 B.C.

Living History
Unit 2 Portfolio Project

THEME Power and Authority

Much of world history is the story of the ups and downs in the endless struggle for power. Your portfolio will compare and contrast the groups and individuals in this unit who grasp power and establish their authority. How do those people get the power, and how do they keep it? What systems of government do they establish? You can compare and contrast city-states, kingdoms, empires, even democracies.

Living History Project Choices
Each Chapter Assessment offers you choices of ways to track power and authority in that chapter. Activities include the following:

Chapter 5 epic poem, museum exhibit, talk show

Chapter 6 diagrams, persuasive argument, role-play

Chapter 7 bar chart, collage, editorial

Chapter 8 speech, dialogue, game

Chapter 9 historical fiction, time capsule, picture

600 B.C. Greece
Sparta develops strong military

594 B.C. Greece
Solon reforms Athens

461 B.C. Greece
Age of Pericles begins

338 B.C. Macedonia
Philip conquers Greece

334 B.C. Greece
Alexander begins to build empire

◀ 338 B.C. Macedonia

500 B.C. Rome
Republic thrives

451 B.C. Rome
Roman laws are carved on Twelve Tables

264 B.C. Carthage
Punic Wars with Rome begin

146 B.C. Rome Rome destroys Carthage

44 B.C. Rome Julius Caesar is killed

27 B.C. Rome
Octavian rules Roman Empire; *Pax Romana* begins

A.D. 29 Jerusalem
Jesus is crucified

A.D. 285 Rome
Empire divides into East and West

A.D. 330 Constantinople New capital of Roman Empire established

A.D. 476 Rome
Western Roman Empire falls

▼ A.D. 100s China

321 B.C. India
Chandragupta founds Mauryan Empire

269 B.C. India
Asoka builds Mauryan Empire

202 B.C. China
Liu Bang founds Han Dynasty

141 B.C. China
Wudi rules Han Dynasty

A.D. 65 China
First Buddhist monastery built

A.D. 105 China
Chinese invent paper

A.D. 220 China
Han Dynasty declines

A.D. 320 India
Chandra Gupta I starts Gupta Empire

A.D. 500 India
Mathematician calculates value of pi

500 B.C. West Africa
Nok develop iron-making technology

250 B.C. East Africa
Kingdom of Meroë at height

250 B.C. West Africa
Djenné-Djeno established

A.D. 100s Africa
Bantu speakers begin massive migrations throughout Africa

A.D. 100 East Africa
Zoskales becomes first king of Aksum

A.D. 250 West Africa Djenné-Djeno reaches its height

A.D. 325 East Africa King Ezana converts to Christianity and expands Aksum

◀ 900 B.C. South America

500 B.C. Mexico
Zapotec build Monte Albán

400 B.C. Mexico
Olmec civilization begins to decline

200 B.C. South America
Nazca culture arises

A.D. 100 South America
Moche civilization emerges

CHAPTER 5

Classical Greece, 2000 B.C.—300 B.C.

PREVIEWING THEMES

Power and Authority

In Egypt, Persia, and China, rulers had claimed their earthly power as a divine right. In the Greek city-state of Athens, a new form of government developed—democracy—in which citizens had the authority to exercise power.

Cultural Interaction

The Minoans of Crete had introduced Egyptian and Southwest Asian cultural ideas to Greek-speaking peoples. In turn, the conqueror Alexander the Great spread Greek culture throughout much of Asia. Greek and Asian cultures then blended to create Hellenistic culture.

Empire Building

Earlier conquerors, such as the Persians, had created empires that contained many diverse peoples. Alexander conquered the Persian Empire to create a vast new empire of his own.

INTERNET CONNECTION

Visit us at **www.mcdougallittell.com** to learn more about ancient Greece, Alexander, and related topics.

ALEXANDER'S EMPIRE, 323 B.C.

▨ Empire of Alexander the Great
▨ Greece (modern-day)

0   500 Miles
0   1,000 Kilometers

N

Dnieper River

Danube River

Black Sea

MACEDONIA
Pella •
    Granicus •
GREECE   • Pergamum   ASIA MINOR
    Athens •
Sparta •   Issus •

SYRIA
Mediterranean Sea   Damascus •

Alexandria •
Memphis •
EGYPT   *Nile River*   Red Sea
Thebes •

Athena was the goddess for whom Athens was named. As the goddess of wisdom and warfare, Athena was often shown wearing a helmet. According to legend, Athena sprang full grown from the forehead of her father, Zeus. He was known as the king of the Greek gods. In **447 B.C.**, the Athenians began building a new temple to honor her.

0° Dame Marsdam

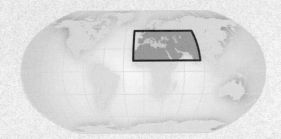

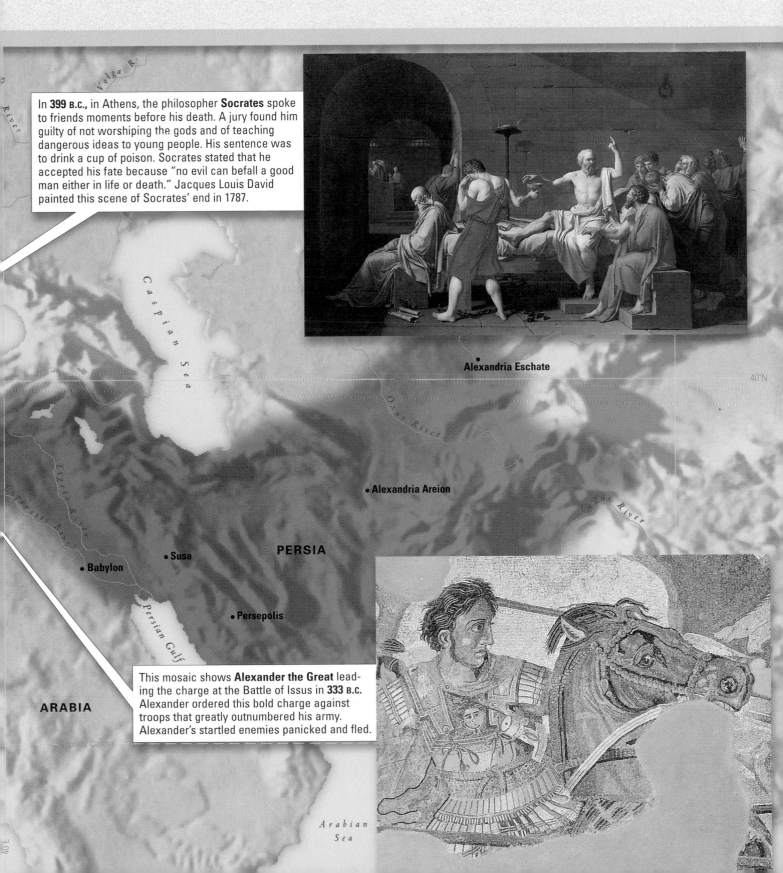

In **399 B.C.**, in Athens, the philosopher **Socrates** spoke to friends moments before his death. A jury found him guilty of not worshiping the gods and of teaching dangerous ideas to young people. His sentence was to drink a cup of poison. Socrates stated that he accepted his fate because "no evil can befall a good man either in life or death." Jacques Louis David painted this scene of Socrates' end in 1787.

This mosaic shows **Alexander the Great** leading the charge at the Battle of Issus in **333 B.C.** Alexander ordered this bold charge against troops that greatly outnumbered his army. Alexander's startled enemies panicked and fled.

Interact *with* History

The Greeks often used sculptures of graceful maidens, called caryatids, as building support columns.

"For we are lovers of the beautiful, yet simple in our tastes. . . ."
Thucydides, a historian

What is the first thing that comes to mind when you think of ancient Greece? You can learn much about what a culture values from its works of art, literature, and from the statements of its leaders and philosophers. Look at these famous works of art from Greece and read the quotations.

What did the Greeks value?

This stone relief panel of Democracy crowning Athens was placed in the marketplace, where citizens could see it daily.

"Our constitution is called a democracy because power is in the hands not of a minority but of the whole people."
Pericles, an Athenian statesman

"The river-god . . . Achelous took the form of a bull and attacked him fiercely . . . but Hercules . . . conquered him and broke off one of his horns."
Edith Hamilton, in *Mythology* (from Apollodorus)

This Greek vase depicts the mythological hero Hercules, noted for his strength and courage, battling Achelous.

EXAMINING *the* ISSUES

- What does the relief panel suggest about the role of democracy in Greek society?

- What special qualities do heroes and athletes possess?

- Why would the Greeks carve a statue of a lovely woman onto a building column or decorate their pottery with a heroic scene?

Break into small groups and talk about what common elements you see in these artworks. Also discuss what the quotes tell you about Greek culture and ideals. In what ways do you think Greek values still influence us today?

As you read about ancient Greece—its history, culture, and forms of government—note what roles these ideals played in Greek society.

1
Cultures of the Mountains and the Sea

TERMS & NAMES
- Mycenaeans
- Trojan War
- Dorians
- Homer
- epics
- myths

MAIN IDEA	WHY IT MATTERS NOW
Physical geography caused separate groups of Greek-speaking peoples to develop isolated societies.	The seeds of much of Western cultural heritage were planted during this time period.

SETTING THE STAGE In ancient times, Greece was not a united country. It was a collection of separate lands where Greek-speaking people lived. By 2000 B.C., the Minoans lived on the large Greek island of Crete. The Minoans created an elegant civilization that had great power in the Mediterranean world. At the same time, Indo-European peoples migrated from the plains along the Black Sea and Anatolia. The Indo-Europeans settled in mainland Greece. Seaborne commercial networks spread ideas as well as resources throughout the eastern Mediterranean.

Geography Shapes Greek Life

Vocabulary
peninsula: a piece of land that extends into a body of water and is connected to the mainland

Ancient Greece consisted mainly of a mountainous peninsula jutting out into the Mediterranean Sea. It also included approximately 1,400 islands in the Aegean (ih·JEE·uhn) and Ionian (eye·OH·nee·uhn) seas. Lands on the western coast of Anatolia were also part of ancient Greece. (See the map on page 112.) The region's physical geography directly shaped Greek traditions and customs.

The Sea The sea shaped Greek civilization just as rivers shaped the ancient civilizations of Egypt, the Fertile Crescent, India, and China. In one sense, the Greeks did not live *on* a land but *around* a sea. Greeks rarely traveled more than 85 miles to reach the coastline. The Aegean Sea, the Ionian Sea, and the neighboring Black Sea were important transportation routes for the Greek people. These liquid highways linked most parts of Greece. As the Greeks became skilled sailors, sea travel also connected Greece with other societies. Sea travel and trade were also important because Greece itself was poor in natural resources. Greece lacked timber, precious metals, and usable farmland.

The Land Rugged mountains covered about three-fourths of ancient Greece. Mountains divided the land into a number of different regions. The mountain chains ran mainly from northwest to southeast along the Balkan peninsula. They significantly influenced Greek political life. Unlike the Egyptians or the Chinese, it was difficult to unite the ancient Greeks under a single government. Greece developed small, independent communities within each little valley and its surrounding mountains. Most Greeks gave their loyalty to these local communities.

Nestled at the base of a mountain range, this coastal Greek city has a rugged shoreline.

THINK THROUGH HISTORY
A. Analyzing Causes In what ways did Greece's location by the sea and its mountainous land affect the development of its society?

In ancient times, the uneven terrain also made land transportation difficult. Early Greek roads were little more than dirt paths. For example, the city-state of Sparta was only about 60 miles from Olympia, the site of the Olympic Games. Yet it took Spartans almost seven days to travel that distance.

Much of the land itself was stony and only a small part of it—approximately 20 percent—was arable, or suitable for farming.

111

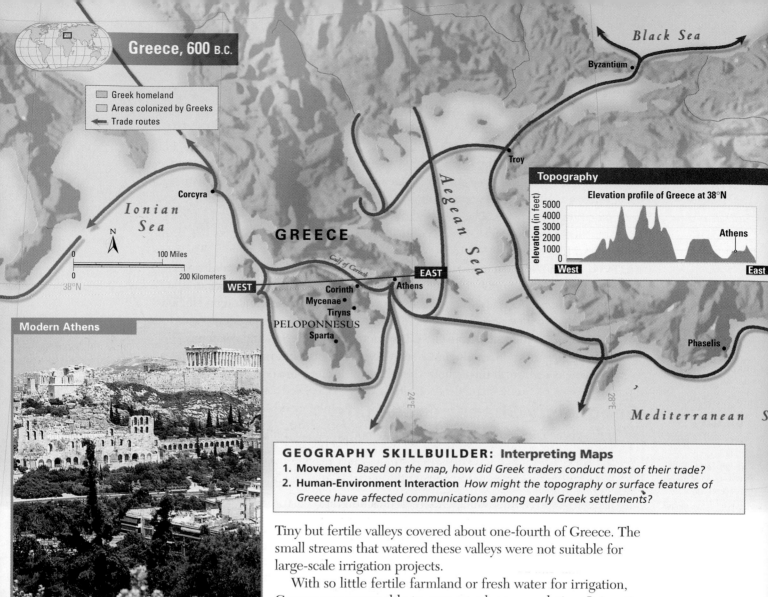

Greece, 600 B.C.

Greek homeland
Areas colonized by Greeks
Trade routes

Black Sea

Byzantium

Ionian Sea

Corcyra

Troy

Aegean Sea

GREECE

Topography

Elevation profile of Greece at 38°N

5000
4000
3000
2000
1000
0

elevation (in feet)

Athens

West   **East**

Gulf of Corinth

WEST   EAST   Athens

Corinth
Mycenae
Tiryns
PELOPONNESUS
Sparta

N

0   100 Miles
0   200 Kilometers
38°N

Phaselis

24°E   28°E

Mediterranean S

Modern Athens

GEOGRAPHY SKILLBUILDER: Interpreting Maps
1. **Movement** *Based on the map, how did Greek traders conduct most of their trade?*
2. **Human-Environment Interaction** *How might the topography or surface features of Greece have affected communications among early Greek settlements?*

Tiny but fertile valleys covered about one-fourth of Greece. The small streams that watered these valleys were not suitable for large-scale irrigation projects.

With so little fertile farmland or fresh water for irrigation, Greece was never able to support a large population. It is estimated that no more than a few million people lived in ancient Greece at any given time. Even this small population couldn't expect the land to support a life of luxury. As a result, the Greeks based their diet on basic staple crops such as grains, grapes, and olives. A desire for more living space, grassland for raising livestock, and adequate farmland may have been factors that motivated the Greeks to seek new sites for colonies.

The Climate Climate was the third important environmental influence on Greek civilization. Greece has a varied climate with temperatures averaging 48 degrees Fahrenheit in the winter and 80 degrees Fahrenheit in the summer. In ancient times, these moderate temperatures supported an outdoor life for many Greek citizens. Men spent much of their leisure time at outdoor public events. They met often to discuss public issues, exchange news, and take an active part in civic life.

Mycenaean Civilization Develops

As Chapter 3 explained, a large wave of Indo-Europeans migrated from the Eurasian steppes to Europe, India, and Southwest Asia. Some of these people who settled on the Greek mainland around 2000 B.C. were later known as **Mycenaeans.** The name came from their leading city, Mycenae (my·SEE·nee).

Mycenae was located on a steep, rocky ridge and surrounded by a protective wall up to 20 feet thick. The fortified city of Mycenae could withstand almost any attack. From

Mycenae, a warrior-king ruled the surrounding villages and farms. Similar Mycenaean palace-forts dotted the southern part of Greece. Influential and militaristic rulers controlled the Mycenaean communities in towns such as Tiryns and Athens. These kings dominated Greece from about 1600 to 1200 B.C.

Culture and Trade The nobles who lived within the fortresses enjoyed a life of surprising splendor. They feasted in great halls 35 feet wide and 50 feet long. During banquets, the firelight from a huge circular hearth glittered on a dazzling variety of gold pitchers and silver cups. When the royal Mycenaeans died, they were buried with their richest treasures. Warrior-kings won their enormous wealth by controlling local production and commercial trade. They also led their armies in search of plunder. However, few other Mycenaeans had the wealth of the warrior-kings. Wealthy kings of the Bronze Age (2000–1100 B.C.) wielded bronze weapons and drank from cups of gold. The common people used tools made from less expensive materials such as stone and wood. Most were farmers, but others worked as weavers, goat herders, or stonemasons.

The warrior-kings of Mycenae also invaded Crete. The Minoan civilization had flourished on Crete for 600 years. The civilization ended abruptly and mysteriously in 1400 B.C. The Mycenaean invasions prevented the Minoans from rebuilding. However, the Mycenaeans preserved elements of Minoan culture by making it part of their own lives.

From their contact with the Minoans, the Mycenaeans saw the value of seaborne trade. Mycenaean traders sailed to islands in the Aegean, coastal towns of Anatolia, and to cities in Syria, Egypt, Italy, and Crete. The Minoans influenced Mycenaean culture in other ways as well. The Mycenaeans adapted the Minoan writing system to the Greek language and decorated vases with Minoan designs. Their legacy survived in the form of legends. These legends later formed the core of Greek religious practice, art, politics, and literature. Western civilization has roots in these early Greek civilizations.

The Trojan War About 1200 B.C. the Mycenaean kings fought a ten-year war against Troy, an independent trading city located in Anatolia. According to legend, a Greek army besieged and destroyed Troy because a Trojan youth had kidnapped Helen, the beautiful wife of a Greek king.

For many years, historians thought that the legendary stories told of the **Trojan War** were totally fictional. Then around 1870, a German archaeologist, Heinrich Schliemann, began excavating a hill in northwestern Turkey. He found the remains of nine layers of city life, one of which may date from this time period. His discoveries suggest that the stories of the Trojan War may have been based on real cities, people, and events.

In 1988, another German historian, Manfred Korfmann, excavated an ancient maritime cemetery near the hill believed to be the site of ancient Troy. Although some scholars disagree, Korfmann believes the Trojan War was a struggle for control of a crucial waterway in the Aegean Sea. In any event, the attack on Troy was probably one of the last campaigns of the Mycenaeans.

Greek Culture Declines Under the Dorians

Not long after the Trojan War, Mycenaean civilization collapsed. Around 1200 B.C., sea raiders attacked and burned palace after palace. At Mycenae, a layer of ashes from a terrible fire covered the entire palace site. According to tradition, a new group of people, the **Dorians** (DAWR·ee·uhnz), moved into this war-torn countryside. The Dorians spoke a dialect of Greek and were distant relatives of the Bronze Age Greeks.

The Dorians were far less advanced than the Mycenaean Greeks. The centralized economy collapsed and trade eventually came to a standstill with their arrival. Most

Background
On the Aegean island of Thera, near Crete, a volcano erupted around 1470 B.C. This event may have helped to bring about the end of Minoan civilization.

Vocabulary
Western civilization: the culture that evolved in Europe and spread to the Americas

Greek stories tell of their army's capture of the legendary city of Troy. Some scholars think that the hollow wooden horse of Western literature may actually have been a gigantic siege engine or battering ram.

important to historians, Greeks appear to have temporarily forgotten the art of writing during the Dorian Age. No written record exists from the 400-year period between 1150 and 750 B.C. Without written records, little is known about this period of decline.

Epics of Homer Lacking writing, the Greeks of this time learned about the Trojan War through the spoken word. Their greatest storyteller, according to Greek tradition, was a blind man named **Homer.** Little is known of his personal life. Some historians believe Homer composed his **epics,** narrative poems celebrating heroic deeds, between 750 and 700 B.C. The Trojan War forms the backdrop for Homer's two great epic poems, *The Iliad* and *The Odyssey.*

The heroes of *The Iliad* are warriors: the fierce Greek, Achilles (uh·KIHL·eez), and the courageous and noble Hector of Troy. In the following dramatic excerpt, Hector's wife begs him not to fight Achilles:

A VOICE FROM THE PAST

"O Hector, your courage will be your destruction; and you have no pity on your little son or on me, who will soon be your widow. . . if I lose you, it would be better for me to die. . . ."

Then tall Hector. . . answered, "Wife, I too have thought upon all this. But I would feel deep shame if like a coward I stayed away from battle. All my life I have learned to be brave and to fight always in the front ranks of the Trojans, winning glory for myself. . . ."

HOMER, *The Iliad*

This is a marble sculpture of Polyphemus, a cyclops, or one-eyed monster, in Homer's *The Odyssey.*

Hector's response to his wife gives insight into the Greek heroic ideal of *aretē* (ar·uh·TAY), meaning virtue and excellence. A Greek could display this ideal on the battlefield, in combat, or in athletic contests.

Homer's other epic, *The Odyssey,* concerns the adventures of Odysseus (oh·DIH·see·uhs). Odysseus uses his wits and trickery to defeat the Trojans. Much of this epic is set after the war. It concerns his ten-year journey home and the strange and mysterious lands Odysseus visits along the way.

Greeks Create Myths The Greeks developed a rich set of **myths,** or traditional stories, about their gods. Through these myths, the Greeks sought to understand the mysteries of nature and the power of human passions. Myths explained the changing of the seasons, for example.

Greeks attributed human qualities, such as love, hate, and jealousy, to their gods. The gods quarreled and competed with each other constantly. However, unlike humans, the gods lived forever. Zeus, the ruler of the gods, lived on Mount Olympus with his wife, Hera. Hera was often jealous of Zeus' relationships with other women. Athena, goddess of wisdom, was Zeus' daughter and his favorite child. The Greeks thought of Athena as the guardian of cities, especially of Athens, which was named in her honor. You will learn about Athens and other cities in Section 2.

Section 1 Assessment

1. TERMS & NAMES

Identify
- Mycenaeans
- Trojan War
- Dorians
- Homer
- epics
- myths

2. TAKING NOTES

Re-create the graph below on your paper and fill in examples of how geography affected early Greek civilization.

Geographic Feature	Effects
sea	
land	
climate	

3. DRAWING CONCLUSIONS

Why did the lack of writing represent a setback to the development of Greek civilization?

THINK ABOUT
- Minoan and Mycenaean accomplishments
- uses of writing
- other forms of communication

4. ANALYZING THEMES

Cultural Interaction Why do you think that early Greek epics and myths are so well known and studied in today's society?

THINK ABOUT
- *aretē*
- Greek ideals compared to ideals in today's world
- early Greeks' purpose of storytelling

TERMS & NAMES
- polis
- acropolis
- monarchy
- aristocracy
- oligarchy
- phalanx
- tyrant
- helot
- democracy
- Persian Wars

2 Warring City-States

MAIN IDEA	WHY IT MATTERS NOW
The growth of city-states in Greece led to the development of several political systems, including democracy.	Many political systems in today's world mirror the varied forms of government that evolved in Greece.

SETTING THE STAGE After the sea peoples invaded mainland Greece around 1200 B.C., the Dorians moved into the area. Greek civilization experienced a period of decline during the Dorian period. After many centuries, Dorians and Mycenaeans alike identified less with the culture of their ancestors and more with their local city-state. By 750 B.C. the Greeks saw the rise of powerful city-states.

Rule and Order in Greek City-States

By 750 B.C., the city-state, or **polis,** was the fundamental political unit in ancient Greece. A polis was made up of a city and its surrounding countryside, which included numerous villages. Most city-states controlled between 50 and 500 square miles of territory. They were often home to fewer than 20,000 residents. At the agora (the public center), or on a fortified hilltop called an **acropolis** (uh·KRAHP·uh·lihs), male citizens gathered to conduct business.

[handwritten: → public center]

[handwritten: only men]

Greek Political Structures There were many ways to rule a Greek polis. In some city-states, much like river-valley civilizations, kings or monarchs ruled in a government called a **monarchy.** In time, some city-states adopted an **aristocracy** (AR·uh·STAHK·ruh·see), a government ruled by a small group of noble, land-owning families. These very rich families often gained political power after working in a king's military cavalry.

[handwritten: king]

Later, as trade expanded, a new class of wealthy merchants and artisans emerged in some cities. When these groups became dissatisfied with aristocratic rule, they sometimes took power or shared it with the nobility. They formed an **oligarchy,** a government ruled by a few powerful people. The idea of representative government also began to take root in many city-states. Regardless of its political structure, each polis enjoyed a close-knit community. Most Greeks looked down on all non-Greek foreigners, whom they considered barbarians.

[handwritten: 1/5 of total pop.]

A New Kind of Army Emerges During the Dorian Age, only the rich could afford bronze spears, shields, breastplates, and chariots. Iron later replaced bronze in the manufacture of weapons. Harder than bronze, iron was more common and therefore cheaper. Soon, ordinary citizens could afford to arm and defend themselves.

The shift from bronze to iron weapons made possible a new kind of army composed of merchants, artisans, and small landowners. Citizens were expected to defend the polis. Foot soldiers, called hoplites, stood side by side, holding a spear in one hand and a shield in the other. This fearsome formation, or **phalanx** (FAY·lanks), was the most powerful fighting force in the ancient world.

[handwritten: phlanEs, battle line]

Tyrants Seize Power No ruler could ignore the power of the citizen-soldiers. In many city-states, unemployed farmers and debt-ridden artisans joined in revolt against the

Armed with spears, shields, and protective headgear, Greek foot soldiers marched into battle. Artists often re-created scenes like the one pictured above on Greek pottery.

nobles. Powerful individuals, called **tyrants,** gained control of the government by appealing to the poor and the discontented for support.

The rule of some city-states passed from one tyrant to the next as competing groups took power. Other cities, however, found new ways of governing. Among these city-states were two of the most powerful, Sparta and Athens.

Sparta Builds a Military State

Located in the southern part of Greece known as the Peloponnesus (PEHL·uh·puh·NEE·sus), Sparta was nearly cut off from the rest of Greece by the Gulf of Corinth. (See the map on page 112.) Unlike other city-states, Sparta built a military state.

Sparta Dominates Messenians While other city-states founded colonies abroad, Sparta conquered neighboring Messenia around 725 B.C. and took over the land. The Messenians became **helots** (HEHL·uhts), peasants forced to stay on the land they worked. Each year, the Spartans demanded half of the helots' yearly crop. Around 600 B.C., the Messenians, who outnumbered the Spartans eight to one, revolted. The Spartans just barely put down the revolt, and then dedicated themselves to the creation of a strong city-state.

Sparta's Government and Society Two groups governed Sparta. An assembly, composed of all free adult males, elected officials and voted on major issues. The second group was the Council of Elders. It proposed laws on which the assembly voted. Five elected officials called ephors carried out the laws the council passed. These men controlled education and prosecuted court cases. In addition, two kings ruled over Sparta's military.

Like its political structure, Sparta's population was diverse and consisted of several social groups. The first were citizens descended from the original inhabitants of the region. This group included the ruling families who owned the land. A second group, noncitizens but free, worked in commerce and industry. The helots, near the bottom of Spartan society, were a little higher than slaves. Some also served as household servants or worked for the citizen hoplite warriors.

Spartan Education For men, daily life centered around military training. Training was rigorous. At the age of seven, boys left home and moved into army barracks. Wearing no shoes, they marched in light tunics during the day and slept on hard benches at night. Trainees gulped down meager meals of coarse black porridge. Such schooling produced tough soldiers.

Spartan girls also led hardy lives. Although they did not receive military training, they ran, wrestled, and played sports. Like the boys, they also learned to put service to Sparta above even love of family. As adults, women managed the family estates while their husbands served the polis. Although Spartan women did not have the right to vote, their roles in Spartan society surprised men from other Greek city-states. This was particularly true in Athens, where citizens expected women to remain out of sight and quietly raise children.

From around 600 until 371 B.C., the Spartans had the most powerful army in Greece, but they paid a high price for that position. All forms of individual expression were discouraged. As a result, Spartans did not value the arts and had practically no time for artistic expression. Spartans valued duty, strength, and discipline over individuality, beauty, and freedom.

Background
The kings of Sparta were not monarchs in the traditional sense but hereditary military leaders.

Spartan women, such as the runner below, took part in athletic contests.

Athens Builds a Limited Democracy

Located on a rocky hill in eastern Greece, Athens lay to the north of Sparta. (See the map on page 112.) In outlook and values, Athens contrasted sharply with Sparta. An ambassador from the city-state of Corinth once compared the Spartans to the Athenians in a speech to the Spartan assembly. He told the Spartans that though they had the strongest army in Greece, they were too cautious. He also said that the Spartans lacked imagination and curiosity. Athenians, he said, were always eager to learn new ideas because they had been educated to think and act as free people. *NOT GOOD?*

Political Developments in Athens Like other city-states, Athens went through a power struggle between rich and poor. However, Athenians avoided civil war by making timely reforms. Athenian reformers tried to create **democracy,** rule by the people. In Athens, citizens participated directly in political decision making.

NOT VOTE

Not everyone in Athens had a part in this new form of political participation. Only free adult males counted as citizens. Women, slaves, and foreigners living in Athens were excluded from citizenship and had few rights. Slaves formed about one-third of the Athenian population. They worked in mines, farmed fields, and did housework.

In general, Athenian women focused their attention on child rearing, weaving cloth, preparing meals, and managing the household. In this excerpt, a Greek historian describes what a husband expected from his wife:

> ### A VOICE FROM THE PAST
> You will need to stay indoors. . . . The greatest joy of all will be to prove yourself . . . a better helpmate to myself and to the children, a better guardian of our home, so will your honor increase. . . . [By being dutiful] you will enjoy your food, grow vigorous in health, and your complexion will in very truth be lovelier.
>
> **XENOPHON,** *Oeconomicus*

In addition to having no part in government, women had very little to do with the city's intellectual life. *NOT EDUCATED?*

Solon's Political and Economic Reforms Repeated clashes occurred between the aristocrats who governed Athens and the common people. A group of peasants foiled an attempt by an Athenian nobleman named Cylon (SI·luhn) to establish a tyranny. In return, they demanded a written code of laws. In 621 B.C., the Greek lawmaker Draco wrote the first legal code, dealing mainly with contracts and property ownership. Draco's code included such unfair practices as debt slavery, in which small farmers worked as slaves to repay their debts. As a result, conflicts between the aristocrats and the poor continued. To prevent civil war, in 594 B.C. the aristocrats chose a trusted statesman named Solon (SO·luhn) to head the government. Athenians gave him full power to reform the law.

MADE PROFIT FOR GREECE

Solon outlawed debt slavery. He allowed all citizens to participate and debate policies in the Athenian assembly. In another political move, Solon introduced the legal concept that any citizen could bring charges against wrongdoers. In addition, his economic reforms benefited many. For example, by encouraging the export of grapes and olives, Solon initiated a profitable overseas trade and demand for these products.

Although Solon initiated political and economic changes, he neglected land reforms. At the end of his rule, fighting erupted between wealthy landowners and the poor

For Athenian women, life centered around home and the family.

Background
The legal code prepared by Draco was so harsh that the word *draconian* has become a synonym for "extreme cruelty or severity."

Forms of Government

Monarchy
- State ruled by a king
- Rule is hereditary
- Some rulers claim divine right
- Practiced in Mycenae (1450 B.C.)

Aristocracy
- State ruled by nobility
- Rule is hereditary and based on land ownership
- Social status and wealth support rulers' authority
- Practiced in Athens (594 B.C.)

Oligarchy
- State ruled by a small group of citizens
- Rule is based on wealth
- Ruling group controls military
- Practiced in Sparta (800–600 B.C.)

Direct Democracy
- State ruled by its citizens
- Rule is based on citizenship
- Majority rule decides vote
- Practiced in Athens (461 B.C.)

SKILLBUILDER:
Interpreting Charts
1. *Which forms of government feature rule based on wealth or property ownership?*
2. *In which form of government do citizens have the most power?*

farmers. Around 546 B.C., a nobleman and military leader named Pisistratus (py·SIS·truh·tuhs) seized power and became one of Athens' first tyrants. Seeking power at the expense of the nobles, he provided funds to help peasants buy farm equipment. He financed this reform by a tax on agricultural production. Pisistratus also launched a massive building program that gave jobs to the poor and earned him their support.

Reforms of Cleisthenes Beginning in 508 B.C., the Athenian leader Cleisthenes (KLYS·thuh·NEEZ) introduced further reforms. He worked to make Athens a full democracy by reorganizing the assembly to break up the power of the nobility. He also increased the power of the assembly by allowing all citizens to submit laws for debate and passage. Cleisthenes then created the Council of Five Hundred. This body proposed laws and counseled the assembly. Council members were chosen by lot, or at random. While these reforms allowed Athenian citizens to participate in a limited democracy, only one-fifth of Athenian residents were actual citizens.

THINK THROUGH HISTORY
B. Contrasting How would you compare the ideals of Spartan and Athenian society?

The Persian Wars

Danger of a helot revolt led to Sparta becoming a military state. Danger of revolution among poverty-stricken farmers led to Athens becoming a democracy. The greatest danger of all—invasion by Persian armies—moved Sparta and Athens alike to their greatest glory.

Battle at Marathon The **Persian Wars,** between Greece and the Persian Empire, began in Ionia on the coast of Anatolia. Greeks had long been settled there, but around 520 B.C., the Persians conquered the area. When Ionian Greeks revolted, Athens sent ships and soldiers to their aid. The Persian king Darius defeated the rebels and then vowed to destroy Athens in revenge.

In 490 B.C., a Persian fleet carried 25,000 men across the Aegean Sea and landed northeast of Athens on a plain called Marathon. There, 10,000 Athenians, neatly arranged in phalanxes, waited for them. Vastly outnumbered, the Greek soldiers charged. The Persians, who wore light armor and lacked training in this kind of land combat, were no match for the disciplined Greek phalanx. After several hours, the Persians fled the battlefield. The casualties reportedly numbered 6,400 Persians and only 192 Athenians.

Though the Athenians won the land battle, their city now stood defenseless. According to tradition, army leaders chose a young runner named Pheidippides (fy·DIP·uh·DEEZ) to race back to Athens. He brought news of the Persian defeat so that Athenians would not give up the city without a fight. Sprinting the distance from Marathon to Athens, Pheidippides delivered his message, collapsed, and died. The Greek army soon set off rapidly and were actually waiting in Athens when the Persian ships sailed into the harbor. The Persians quickly sailed away in retreat.

Thermopylae and Salamis Ten years later, in 480 B.C., Darius the Great was dead. His son and successor Xerxes (ZURK·seez) tried to crush Greece. Xerxes assembled an enormous invasion force of ships and men. By then, however, the Greeks were badly divided. Some city-states agreed to fight the Persians. Others thought it wiser to let Xerxes destroy Athens and return home. Some Greeks even fought on the Persian side. Consequently, Xerxes' army met no resistance as it marched down the eastern coast of Greece.

When Xerxes came to a narrow mountain pass at Thermopylae (thur·MAHP·uh·lee), 7,000 Greeks, including 300 Spartans, blocked his way. The Persian king underestimated their power. They fought for three days before a traitor told the Persians about

CONNECT to TODAY

Modern Marathons

Today, the word *marathon* refers to a foot race of 26 miles, 385 yards. One of the largest and best known is the Boston Marathon. The history of this grueling race dates back to the Persian Wars and Pheidippides' run from Marathon to Athens.

After running at top speed for approximately 25 miles, Pheidippides arrived in Athens. He gasped "Rejoice, we conquer," and instantly died. His heroic run inspired officials at the 1896 Olympic Games in Athens to add a 26-mile marathon to their competition.

In 1908, officials in London further lengthened the race. King Edward VII decided he wanted it to begin at Windsor Castle—385 yards from the city's Olympic Stadium. The photo below shows Lameck Aquita of Kenya, who won the 1997 Boston Marathon with a time of 2 hours, 10 minutes, 34 seconds.

a secret path around the cliffs. Fearing defeat, the Spartans held the pass while the other Greek forces retreated. The Spartans' valiant sacrifice—all were killed—made a great impression on all Greeks.

Meanwhile, in Athens, the citizens debated how best to defend the city. Themistocles, an Athenian statesman, convinced Athenians to evacuate the city and fight at sea. He positioned the Greek fleet in a narrow channel near the island of Salamis (SAL·uh·mihs), a few miles southwest of Athens. After setting fire to Athens, Xerxes sent his warships to block both ends of the channel. However, the channel was too narrow to permit the Persian fleet to maneuver well. Greek ships drove their battering rams straight into the wooden hulls, punching holes in the Persian warships. Xerxes watched in horror as more than one-third of his fleet sank. The Spartans defeated the rest of the Persian army at a third battle on the plain of Plataea (pluh·TEE·uh) in 479 B.C.

Consequences of the Persian Wars

With the Persian threat ended, all the Greek city-states felt a new sense of confidence and freedom. Athens, in particular, basked in the glory of the Persian defeat. After the war, Athens became the leader of an alliance of 140 city-states called the Delian (DEE·lee·uhn) League. The league drove the Persians from the territories surrounding Greece and ended the threat of future attacks. Soon thereafter, Athens began to use its powerful navy to control the other league members. The prestige of victory and the wealth of the empire set the stage for a dazzling burst of creativity in Athens. The city was entering its brief, golden age.

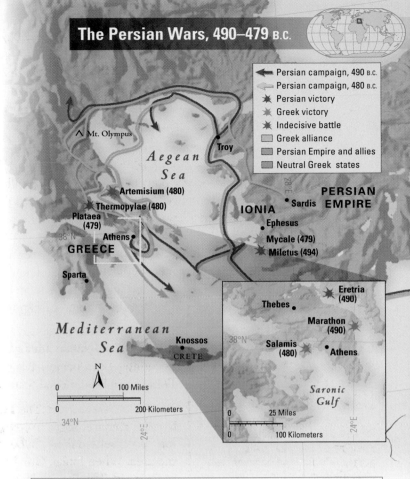

The Persian Wars, 490–479 B.C.

← Persian campaign, 490 B.C.
← Persian campaign, 480 B.C.
✱ Persian victory
✱ Greek victory
✱ Indecisive battle
■ Greek alliance
■ Persian Empire and allies
■ Neutral Greek states

Mt. Olympus
Aegean Sea
Troy
Artemisium (480)
Thermopylae (480)
Plataea (479)
Athens
GREECE
Sparta
Mediterranean Sea
Knossos
CRETE
PERSIAN EMPIRE
IONIA
Sardis
Ephesus
Mycale (479)
Miletus (494)

Thebes
Eretria (490)
Marathon (490)
Salamis (480)
Athens
Saronic Gulf

N
0   100 Miles
0   200 Kilometers

0   25 Miles
0   100 Kilometers

GEOGRAPHY SKILLBUILDER: Interpreting Maps
1. **Movement** By what routes did the Persians choose to attack Greece? Explain why.
2. **Location** Where did most of the battles of the Persian Wars occur? How might their citizens be affected?

THINK THROUGH HISTORY
C. Recognizing Effects How did the Persian Wars affect the Greek people, especially the Athenians?

Section 2 Assessment

1. TERMS & NAMES
Identify
• polis
• acropolis
• monarchy
• aristocracy
• oligarchy
• phalanx
• tyrant
• helot
• democracy
• Persian Wars

2. TAKING NOTES
Create a time line of the major battles of the Persian Wars in Greece, using a chart such as the one below. For each battle, include the victor.

first battle		third battle
	second battle		fourth battle

Pretend that you are a newspaper reporter in ancient Greece. Write appropriate headlines for each battle.

3. CONTRASTING
How was living in Athens different from living in Sparta?

THINK ABOUT
• roles of citizens
• type/form of government
• societal values

4. THEME ACTIVITY
Power and Authority Draw a cartoon or write a political monologue about democracy from an Athenian slave's point of view.

Classical Greece **119**

TERMS & NAMES
- **direct democracy**
- **classical art**
- **tragedy**
- **comedy**
- **Peloponnesian War**
- **philosophers**
- **Socrates**
- **Plato**
- **Aristotle**

3 Democracy and Greece's Golden Age

MAIN IDEA	WHY IT MATTERS NOW
Democratic principles and classical culture flourished during Greece's golden age.	At its height, Greece set lasting standards in art, politics, literature, and philosophy that are still adhered to today.

SETTING THE STAGE During Athens' golden age, drama, sculpture, poetry, philosophy, architecture, and science all reached new heights. For 50 years (from 480 to 430 B.C.), Athens experienced a growth in intellectual and artistic learning. The artistic and literary legacies of this time continue to inspire and instruct people around the world.

Pericles' Three Goals for Athens

A wise and able statesman named Pericles led Athens during its golden age. Honest and fair, Pericles held onto popular support for 32 years. He was a skillful politician, an inspiring speaker, and a respected general. He so dominated the life of Athens from 461 to 429 B.C. that this period often is called the Age of Pericles. He had three goals: (1) to strengthen Athenian democracy, (2) to hold and strengthen the empire, and (3) to glorify Athens.

Stronger Democracy To strengthen democracy, Pericles increased the number of paid public officials. Earlier, only wealthier citizens could afford to hold public office because most positions were unpaid. Pericles increased the number of officials who were paid salaries. Now even the poorest could serve if elected or chosen by lot. Consequently, Athens had more citizens engaged in self-government than any other city-state. This reform made Athens one of the most democratic governments in history. However, political rights were still limited to those with citizenship status.

The introduction of **direct democracy,** a form of government in which citizens rule directly and not through representatives, was an important legacy of Periclean

Athenian and United States Democracy

Athenian Democracy	Both	U. S. Democracy
• Citizens: male; 18 years old; born of citizen parents	• Political power exercised by citizens	• Citizens: born in United States or completed citizenship process
• Laws voted on and proposed directly by assembly of all citizens	• Three branches of government	• Representatives elected to propose and vote on laws
• Leader chosen by lot	• Legislative branch passes laws	• Elected president
• Executive branch composed of a council of 500 men	• Executive branch carries out laws	• Executive branch made up of elected and appointed officials
• Juries varied in size	• Judicial branch conducts trials with paid jurors	• Juries composed of 12 jurors
• No attorneys; no appeals; one-day trials		• Defendants and plaintiffs have attorneys; long appeals process

SKILLBUILDER: Interpreting Charts
1. *What does this chart suggest to you about the origins of U. S. democracy?*
2. *What is the main difference between Athenian democracy and democracy in the United States?*

Athens. Few other city-states practiced this style of government. In Athens, male citizens who served in the assembly established all the important government policies that affected the polis. In a speech for the slain soldiers killed in the first year of the Peloponnesian War, Pericles expressed his great pride in Athenian democracy:

THINK THROUGH HISTORY
A. Distinguishing Fact from Opinion
How accurate do you consider Pericles' statement that Athenian democracy was in the hands of "the whole people"?

A VOICE FROM THE PAST

Our constitution is called a democracy because power is in the hands not of a minority but of the whole people. When it is a question of settling private disputes, everyone is equal before the law; when it is a question of putting one person before another in positions of public responsibility, what counts is not membership in a particular class, but the actual ability which the man possesses. No one, so long as he has it in him to be of service to the state, is kept in political obscurity because of poverty.

PERICLES, *Funeral Oration*

Athenian Empire Pericles tried to enlarge the wealth and power of Athens. He used the money from the Delian League's treasury to build Athens' 200-ship navy into the strongest in the Mediterranean. A strong navy was important because it helped Athens strengthen the safety of its empire. Athenian prosperity depended on gaining access to its surrounding waterways. It needed overseas trade to obtain supplies of grain and other raw materials.

Glorifying Athens Pericles also used money from the empire to beautify Athens. Without the Delian League's approval, he persuaded the Athenian assembly to vote huge sums of the league's money to buy gold, ivory, and marble. Still more money went to a small army of artisans who worked for 15 years (447–432 B.C.) to build one of architecture's noblest works—the Parthenon.

Greek Styles in Art

The Parthenon, a masterpiece of craftsmanship and design, was not novel in style. Rather, Greek artisans built the 23,000-square-foot building in the traditional style that had been used to create Greek temples for 200 years. In ancient times, this temple built to honor Athena contained examples of Greek art that set standards for future generations of artists around the world.

Greek Sculpture Within the Parthenon stood a giant statue of Athena, the goddess of wisdom and the protector of Athens. Pericles entrusted much of the work on the temple, including the statue of Athena, to the sculptor Phidias (FIDH·ee·uhs). The great statue of the goddess not only contained precious materials such as gold and ivory, it stood 38 feet tall!

Phidias and other sculptors during this golden age aimed to create figures that were graceful, strong, and perfectly formed. Their faces showed neither laughter nor anger, only serenity. Greek sculptors also tried to capture the grace of the idealized human body in motion. Their values of order, balance, and proportion became the standard of what is called **classical art.**

Classical works such as the Parthenon and the statue of Athena showcased the pride that Athenians had for their city. (See History Through Art, page 122.)

Greek Drama

The Greeks invented drama and built the first theaters in the west. Theatrical productions in Athens were both an expression of civic pride and a tribute to the gods.

HISTORY MAKERS

Pericles
494?–429 B.C.

Pericles came from a rich and high-ranking noble family. His aristocratic father had led the Athenian assembly and fought at the Battle of Salamis in the Persian Wars. His mother was the niece of Cleisthenes, an influential statesman.

Well known for his political achievements as a leader of Athens, some historians say Pericles the man was harder to know. One historian wrote,

[Pericles] no doubt, was a lonely man. Among the politicians, including his supporters, he had no friend. He avoided all social activity . . . [and] he only went out [of his home] for official business. . . .

Architecture and Sculpture

The Parthenon, the most magnificent building on the Acropolis, shows the classical Greek ideals of balance and proportion in art. The Parthenon is so harmonious with its site, it appears to grow directly out of solid rock. Its architects knew geometrical principles and how to modify them to please the eye. Its 46 support columns lean slightly inward. Brightly painted sculptural friezes (decorative relief panels) and statues adorned the rectangular building.

Athena in the Parthenon

Greek statues depicted their gods in idealized human form. Inside the marble temple stood a huge statue of Athena, nearly 40 feet high. It portrayed the goddess in full battle armor, holding a six-foot high figure of victory. This is a copy of the original statue, which vanished during the fifth century A.D.

Theater at Delphi

Public theater performances during the fifth century B.C. were sponsored by the state. Hundreds of theaters were built, such as this one preserved at Delphi in central Greece. Notice how this theater is set directly into the natural setting of the hillside. The masks used by the actors in tragedies and comedies became favorite subjects in Greek art.

Connect to History

Summarizing What are the main things you associate with classical Greek art? Give examples from buildings and sculpture shown on this page.

SEE SKILLBUILDER HANDBOOK, PAGE 992

Connect to Today

Researching Look around your local community to find buildings and artworks that show Greek influences. Work in small groups to develop a guidebook to these treasures.

 INTERNET CONNECTION

Visit us at **www.mcdougallittell.com** to learn more about Greek art.

Actors used colorful costumes, masks, and sets to dramatize stories about leadership, justice, and the duties owed to the gods. As part of their civic duty, wealthy citizens bore the cost for producing the plays. The Greeks wrote two kinds of drama—tragedy and comedy.

Tragedy A **tragedy** was a serious drama about common themes such as love, hate, war, or betrayal. These dramas featured a main character, or tragic hero. The hero usually was an important person and often gifted with extraordinary abilities. A tragic flaw—an error in judgment or personality defect—usually caused the hero's downfall. Often this flaw was hubris, or excessive pride.

In ancient times, Greece had three notable dramatists who wrote tragedies: Aeschylus (EHS·kuh·luhs), Sophocles (SAHF·uh·kleez), and Euripides (yoo·RIP·uh·DEEZ). Aeschylus wrote more than 80 plays, of which seven survive. His most famous work is the trilogy *The Oresteia* (ohr·es·STEE·uh), based on the family of Agamemnon, commander of the Greeks at Troy. Sophocles wrote about 100 plays, including the tragedies *Oedipus the King* and *Antigone*. Euripides, author of the play *Medea*, often featured sympathetic portrayals of women in his plays.

Comedy In contrast to Greek tragedies, a **comedy** contained scenes filled with slapstick situations and crude humor. Many Greek comedies were satires, or works that poked fun at a subject. Playwrights often made fun of customs, politics, respected people, or ideas of the time. Aristophanes (AR·ih·STAHF·uh·neez) wrote the first great comedies of the stage, including *The Birds* and *Lysistrata*. For example, *Lysistrata*, named for its female lead, portrayed the women of Athens forcing their husbands to end the Peloponnesian War. The fact that Athenians could listen to criticism of themselves showed the freedom and openness of public discussion that existed in democratic Athens.

Spartans and Athenians Go to War

Tensions between Athens and Sparta had been building for years. Hostilities became especially strong as Athens evolved from a limited city-state to a vast naval empire. Many people in both cities thought war was inevitable. Instead of trying to avoid conflict, leaders in both Athens and Sparta pressed for a war to begin, as both groups of leaders believed their own city had the advantage.

Peloponnesian War Sparta declared war against Athens in 431 B.C. When the **Peloponnesian War** between the two city-states began, Athens had the strongest sea power in Greece. Sparta had the advantage on land because the inland city could not easily be attacked by sea. Pericles' strategy was to avoid land battles with the superior Spartan army and wait for an opportunity to strike Sparta's allies from the sea.

Eventually the Spartans marched into Athenian territory. They swept over the countryside, burning the Athenians' local food supply. Pericles responded by bringing residents from the surrounding countryside inside the safety of Athens' city walls. The city was safe from hunger as long as ships could sail into port with food from Athenian colonies and other foreign states.

Sparta Gains the Edge However, two events spelled disaster for Athens. In the second year of the war, a frightful plague killed roughly one-third to two-thirds of Athens' population, including Pericles. In 415 B.C., Athens suffered a second disaster. The Athenian assembly sent a huge fleet carrying 27,000 soldiers to destroy the polis of

SPOTLIGHT ON

The Plague
An unidentified disease struck Athens during the height of the war. The disease caused a terrible plague in 430 B.C.

According to Thucydides (thoo·SID·ih·DEEZ), the plague's symptoms included high fever, inflamed eyes, sore throat, coughing, extreme thirst, vomiting, and red blisters on the skin. As the disease spread, some victims lost their eyes or their fingers or toes. Many thousands died.

The following excerpt is from Thucydides' account of the Peloponnesian Wars:

They became infected by nursing one another and died like sheep. . . . Bodies of dying men lay one upon another. . . . The temples . . . were full of corpses of those who had died in them.

Syracuse, one of Sparta's wealthiest allies. The expedition suffered an unmistakable defeat in 413 B.C. The Athenian historian Thucydides recalled: "They [the Athenians] were destroyed with a total destruction—their fleet, their army—there was nothing that was not destroyed, and few out of many returned home." Somehow, a terribly weakened Athens fended off Spartan attacks for another nine years. Finally, in 404 B.C., Athens and its allies surrendered.

War Brings Political Changes After 27 years of war, Athens had lost its empire, power, and wealth. In addition, general confidence in democratic government began to falter. One leader after another proved weak, corrupt, or traitorous. The assembly often changed its decisions and did not stick to a single political program.

Philosophers Search for Truth

In this time of questioning and uncertainty, several great thinkers appeared. They were determined to seek the truth, no matter where the search led them. The Greeks called such thinkers **philosophers,** meaning "lovers of wisdom." These Greek thinkers based their philosophy on the following two assumptions: (1) The universe (land, sky, and sea) is put together in an orderly way, and subject to absolute and unchanging laws, and (2) people can understand these laws through logic and reason.

One group of philosophers, the Sophists, questioned people's unexamined beliefs and ideas about justice, and other traditional values. One of the most famous Sophists was Protagoras, who took a position questioning the existence of the traditional Greek gods. He also argued that there was no universal standard of truth, saying "Man [the individual] is the measure of all things. . . ." These were radical and dangerous ideas to many of the citizens of Athens.

Socrates One of the strongest critics of the Sophists was **Socrates** (SAHK·ruh·TEEZ). Unlike the Sophists, he believed that absolute standards did exist for truth and justice. However, he encouraged Greeks to go further and question themselves and their moral character. Historians believe that it was Socrates who once said, "The unexamined life is not worth living." Those who understood Socrates admired him deeply. The majority of citizens, however, could not understand this strange old man and his ideas.

In 399 B.C., when Socrates was about 70 years old, he was brought to trial for "corrupting the youth of Athens" and "neglecting the city's gods." In his own defense, Socrates said that his teachings were good for Athens because they forced people to think about their values and actions. The jury disagreed and condemned him to death. Later, he died after drinking a slow-acting poison.

Plato A student of Socrates, **Plato** (PLAY·toh), was approximately 28 years old when his teacher died. Later, Plato wrote down the conversations of Socrates "as a means of philosophical investigation." Sometime between 385 and 380 B.C., Plato wrote his most famous work, *The Republic.* In it, he set forth his vision of a perfectly governed society. It was not a democracy. In his ideal society, all citizens would fall naturally into three groups: farmers and artisans, warriors, and the ruling class. The person with the greatest

This Pompeiian mosaic from the first century A.D. pays tribute to the philosopher Plato (third from the left) as he teaches his followers.

THINK THROUGH HISTORY
C. Making Inferences Why would philosophers start questioning traditional beliefs at this particular time in Athens' history?

Socrates
469–399 B.C.

Socrates was one of the most powerful thinkers in history. He encouraged his students to examine their beliefs. Socrates asked them a series of leading questions to show that people hold many contradictory opinions. This method of teaching by a question-and-answer approach is known as the *Socratic method*. He devoted his life to gaining self-knowledge and once said, "There is only one good, knowledge; and one evil, ignorance."

Plato
427–347 B.C.

Born into a wealthy Athenian family, Plato had careers as a wrestler and a poet before he became a philosopher. He studied with Socrates. After his teacher died in 399 B.C., Plato left Greece and traveled to North Africa and Italy. He later returned to Athens and founded a school called The Academy in 387 B.C. The school lasted for approximately 900 years. It was Plato who once stated, "Philosophy begins in wonder."

Aristotle
384–322 B.C.

Aristotle, the son of a physician, was one of the brightest students at Plato's academy. He came there as a young man and stayed for 20 years until Plato's death. In 335 B.C., Aristotle opened his own school in Athens called the Lyceum. The school eventually rivaled the Academy. Aristotle once argued, "He who studies how things originated and came into being . . . will achieve the clearest view of them."

insight and intellect from the ruling class would be chosen philosopher-king. Plato's writings dominated philosophic thought in Europe for nearly 1,500 years. His only rivals in importance were Socrates and his own pupil, Aristotle (AR·ih·STAHT·uhl).

Aristotle The philosopher **Aristotle** questioned the nature of the world and of human belief, thought, and knowledge. Aristotle came close to summarizing all the knowledge up to his time. He invented a method for arguing according to rules of logic. He later applied his method to problems in the fields of psychology, physics, and biology. His work provides the basis of the scientific method used today.

One of Aristotle's most famous pupils was Alexander, son of King Philip of Macedonia. Around 343 B.C., Aristotle accepted the king's invitation to tutor the 13-year-old prince. Alexander's status as a student abruptly ended in 336 B.C., when he became the ruler of Macedonia. You will learn about Alexander the Great in Section 4.

Section 3 Assessment

1. TERMS & NAMES

Identify
• direct democracy
• classical art
• tragedy
• comedy
• Peloponnesian War
• philosophers
• Socrates
• Plato
• Aristotle

2. TAKING NOTES

Using a diagram like the one below, show Pericles' three goals for Athens, giving examples.

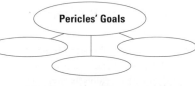

Pericles' Goals

Which goal had the greatest impact on the modern world?

3. FORMING AND SUPPORTING OPINIONS

Socrates believed in absolute standards for truth and justice. Sophists believed that standards of truth and justice are in the eye of the beholder. What is your opinion? Support your opinion with reasons and examples.

THINK ABOUT
• differences in values
• purpose of law
• circumstances

4. ANALYZING THEMES

Empire Building How does the concept of "hubris" from Greek tragedy apply to the Peloponnesian War?

THINK ABOUT
• Spartans' and Athenians' opinion of themselves
• why "hubris" is a tragic flaw
• why the war started

Sports Through Time

Throughout history, communities worldwide have valued athletes who possess great physical strength, agility, and balance. In ancient times, the Greeks believed that athletic competitions were a way to please the gods and honor dead heroes. One of Greece's many athletic festivals—the Olympic Games—continues today. Dedicated to the god Zeus, the Olympics began in 776 B.C. The Greeks even suspended wars between city-states so that athletes could compete. This love of sport lives on among different people and cultures throughout the world today.

Olympics in Greece

Every four years, some 40,000 Greeks crowded into the stadium built in Olympia to watch the competitions. The earliest games featured foot races of about 200 yards. Later, athletes also competed in wrestling, boxing, jumping, javelin-and discus-throwing events. Athletes were proud of their bodies and emphasized physical fitness. Myron's famous marble sculpture of a discus thrower is dated about 450 B.C. The sculpture survives in this Roman copy (left) of the Greek bronze.

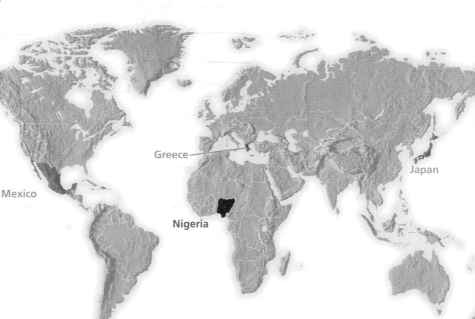

Mexico

Greece

Japan

Nigeria

a closer look GREEK SPORTS

126 Chapter 5

Victorious Olympians received a crown made of wild olive leaves.

Olympic chariot racing began in the seventh century B.C. Prizes went to the chariot's owner, not the driver.

Sumo Wrestling in Japan

Sumo wrestling is a sport that is native to Japan. Originally sponsored by imperial families, it dates back to the eighth century. Sumo's popularity remains strong and today is considered the national sport of Japan. During a match, wrestlers wear loincloths and battle each other inside a 15-foot circle. Many of these athletes weigh more than 300 pounds. All use their size and strength to overpower an opponent.

Soccer in Nigeria

Soccer is one of the most popular sports in the world. Known as football in some countries, soccer developed in England during the 1800s. Few items are needed to play the game: a ball, an open field, and players who are willing to run. The Nigerian soccer player pictured above was a participant in the 1994 World Cup, an international soccer competition. The World Cup attracts all-star teams from around the world.

Mayan Ball Courts in Mexico

This photograph of a site at Chichen Itza in Mexico shows a stone ring Mayans once used when playing an ancient game. During the seventh century, Mayan athletes played a ball game on walled I-shaped courts. Participants wore protective padding around their waist and on one knee. The object was to get a rubber ball through the stone ring without touching it with their hands. The ball court game had close ties to the Mayans' religious beliefs. While the exact rules are unknown, the losers were usually sacrificed to the gods.

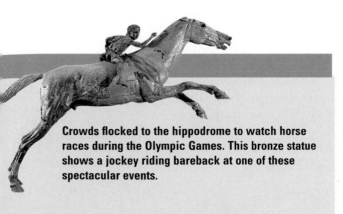

Crowds flocked to the hippodrome to watch horse races during the Olympic Games. This bronze statue shows a jockey riding bareback at one of these spectacular events.

Connect *to* History

Compare/Contrast Choose two of the sports or games illustrated on this page, such as modern soccer and the Mayan ball game. Then compare and contrast them.

SEE SKILLBUILDER HANDBOOK, PAGE 996

Connect *to* Today

Analyzing Issues Consider the ancient Greek practice of interrupting conflicts to allow athletes to compete. Write a brief editorial (paragraph) discussing the role of sports and games as a way to promote world peace or reduce hostile behavior.

Classical Greece **127**

Alexander— Empire Builder

TERMS & NAMES
- Philip II
- Macedonia
- Demosthenes
- Alexander the Great
- Darius III

MAIN IDEA	WHY IT MATTERS NOW
Alexander the Great conquered Persia and Egypt and extended his empire to the Indus River in northwest India.	Alexander's empire extended across three continents that today consist of many nations and diverse cultures.

SETTING THE STAGE The Peloponnesian War severely weakened several Greek city-states. This caused a rapid decline in their military and economic power. To make matters worse, in the 50 years after Sparta defeated Athens in 404 B.C., the two city-states had continued to fight each other. In the nearby kingdom of Macedonia, King **Philip II** took note. Philip dreamed of first taking control of Greece. Then Philip planned to move against Persia and seize its vast wealth. Philip also hoped to avenge the Persian invasion of Greece in 480 B.C.

Philip Builds Macedonia's Power

MACEDONIA

Aegean Sea

Thebes
Athens

Just north of Greece, the kingdom of **Macedonia** had rough mountains and a cold climate. The Macedonians were a tough people who lived in mountain villages rather than city-states. The Macedonian language was related to Greek. Most Macedonian nobles thought of themselves as Greeks. The Greeks, however, looked down on the Macedonians as uncivilized foreigners who had no great philosophers, sculptors, or writers. They did, however, have an important resource in their shrewd and fearless kings.

Philip's Army In 359 B.C., Philip II became king of Macedonia. Though only 23 years old, he quickly proved to be a brilliant general and a ruthless politician. Philip transformed the rugged peasants under his command into a well-trained professional army. He organized his troops into phalanxes that were 16 men across and 16 deep. Philip used this heavy phalanx formation armed with 18-foot pikes to pave the way for cavalry strikes through enemy lines.

Once his phalanx had broken through, Philip used the fast-moving cavalry to crush his disorganized opponents. When he first used these tactics against northern opponents who had invaded Macedonia, Philip's powerful army proved unbeatable. Within a short time, he was preparing to invade Greece.

Conquest of Greece The Athenian orator **Demosthenes** (dee·MAHS·thuh·NEEZ) tried to warn the Greeks of the threat Philip and his army posed. He urged them to unite against him. However, the Greek cities could not agree on any single policy. Finally, in 338 B.C., Athens and Thebes—two Greek city-states—joined forces against Philip. By then it was too late. The Macedonians soundly defeated the Greeks at the battle of Chaeronea (KAIR·uh·NEE·uh). Philip's 18-year-old son Alexander led a successful cavalry charge that helped win the battle. The defeat at Chaeronea ended Greek freedom and independence. The city-states retained self-government in local affairs. However, Greece itself remained firmly under the control of a succession of foreign powers—the first of which was Philip's Macedonia.

Although Philip planned to invade Persia next, he never got the chance. At his daughter's wedding in 336 B.C., a former guardsman stabbed him to death. With the support of the army, Philip's son Alexander immediately proclaimed himself king of Macedonia.

This bust of King Philip II dates from the 4th century B.C. Under Philip's leadership, Macedonia became a major power in the Greek-speaking world.

THINK THROUGH HISTORY
A. Analyzing Causes How did the Peloponnesian War pave the way for Philip's conquest of Greece?

Because of his accomplishments over the next 13 years, he became known in history as **Alexander the Great.**

Alexander Defeats Persia

[handwritten: student of Aristotle]

Although Alexander was only 20 years old when he became king in 336 B.C., he was well prepared to lead. Under Aristotle's teaching, Alexander had learned science, geography, and literature. Alexander especially enjoyed Homer's description of the heroic deeds performed by Achilles during the Trojan War. To inspire himself, he kept a copy of the *Iliad* under his pillow.

[handwritten margin: did anything to keep control]

As a young boy, Alexander learned to ride a horse, use weapons, and command troops. Once he became king, Alexander promptly demonstrated that his military training had not been wasted. When Thebes, a city in central Greece, rebelled, he destroyed the city. About 6,000 people were killed. The survivors were sold into slavery. Frightened by his cruelty, the other Greek cities quickly gave up any idea of rebellion.

Invasion of Persia With Greece now secure, Alexander felt free to carry out Philip's plan to invade Persia. In 334 B.C., he led 35,000 soldiers across the Hellespont into Anatolia. Persian messengers raced along the Royal Road to spread the alarm about the invasion. Within a short time, a Persian army of about 40,000 men rushed to defend Persia. The two forces met at the Granicus River. Instead of waiting for the Persians to make the first move, Alexander ordered an elite cavalry unit to attack. Leading his troops into battle, Alexander smashed the Persian defenses. *[handwritten: control over Persia]*

Background

The Hellespont is the ancient name for the Dardanelles, the narrow straits that separate Europe from Asia Minor.

Alexander's victory at Granicus alarmed the Persian king, **Darius III.** Vowing to crush the Macedonians, he raised a huge army of between 50,000–75,000 men to face the Macedonians near Issus. Realizing that he was outnumbered, Alexander surprised his enemies. He ordered his finest troops to break through a weak point in the Persian lines. The army then charged straight at Darius. To avoid capture, the frightened king fled, followed by his panicked army. This victory gave Alexander control over Anatolia. *[handwritten: clever]*

Alexander's Ambitions Grow Shaken by his defeat, Darius tried to negotiate a peace settlement. He offered Alexander the western third of his empire. Alexander's advisers urged him to accept. However, the rapid collapse of Persian resistance fired Alexander's ambition. He rejected Darius's offer and confidently announced his plan to conquer the entire Persian Empire.

Then Alexander marched into Egypt, a Persian territory, in 332 B.C. The Egyptians welcomed Alexander as a liberator. During his stay, he visited the temple of the god Zeus-Ammon. Alexander was crowned pharaoh—a title that Ptolemy used later to begin the Ptolemic pharaoh line. Alexander also founded the city of Alexandria at the mouth of the Nile. *[handwritten: ruled by Persia]*

Conquering the Persian Empire After leaving Egypt, Alexander moved east into Mesopotamia to confront Darius. The desperate Persian king assembled an army of 250,000 men. The Persian chariots were armed with deadly scythes protruding from the wheel hubs. The two armies collided at Gaugamela (GAW·guh·MEE·luh), a small village near the ruins of ancient Nineveh. Alexander launched a massive phalanx attack followed by a cavalry charge. As the Persian lines crumbled, Darius again panicked and fled. Alexander's victory at Gaugamela ended Persia's power. The Macedonian army now marched unopposed into Persia's wealthiest provinces.

[handwritten: ★ battle]

Vocabulary

scythes: razor-sharp knives or blades.

HISTORY MAKERS

**Alexander
356–323 B.C.**

When Alexander was only eight or nine years old, he tamed a horse that none of his father's grooms could manage. Alexander had noticed that the horse, Bucephalus, acted wild because he was afraid of his shadow. By speaking to the horse gently and turning him to face the sun, Alexander was able to ride him. Seeing this, Philip told his son, "You'll have to find another kingdom; Macedonia isn't going to be big enough for you."

Alexander took his father's advice. Riding Bucephalus at the head of an army, he conquered a region from Greece to the Indus Valley. When the horse died in what is now Pakistan, Alexander named the city of Bucephala after it. Maybe he was tired of the name *Alexandria.* He'd already named at least a dozen cities after himself!

Within a short time, Alexander's army occupied the capitals of Babylon, Susa, and Persepolis. These cities yielded a huge treasure, which Alexander distributed among his army. After a stay of several months, a fire broke out in Persepolis, Persia's royal capital. Some historians say Alexander left the city in ashes to signal the total destruction of the Persian Empire. The Greek historian Arrian wrote about Alexander's expeditions about 500 years later. Arrian explains that the fire was set in revenge for the Persian burning of Athens 150 years before. But others doubt that the fire was planned.

Alexander's Other Conquests

Alexander now reigned as the unchallenged ruler of southwest Asia. He was more interested in expanding his empire than in governing it. He left the ruined Persepolis to pursue Darius and conquer Persia's remote Asian provinces. Darius's trail led Alexander to a deserted spot south of the Caspian Sea. There he found Darius already dead, murdered by one of his provincial governors. Rather than return to Babylon, Alexander continued east. During the next three years, his army fought its way across the desert wastes and mountains of Central Asia. He pushed on, hoping to reach the farthest edge of the continent.

Alexander in India In 327 B.C., Alexander and his army reached and crossed into the Indus Valley. At the Hydaspes River, a powerful Indian army that included 200 elephants blocked their path. After winning a fierce battle, Alexander's soldiers marched some 200 miles farther, but their morale was low. They had been fighting for 11 years and had marched more than 11,000 miles. They had endured both scorching

Alexander and Darius (riding horses, near bottom) fight face to face in this Persian painting. The two rulers never battled this closely in real life.

BIG EMPIRE

EXPANDING GOVERNING

THINK THROUGH HISTORY
B. Analyzing Motives Why did Alexander continue his conquests after Darius was dead?

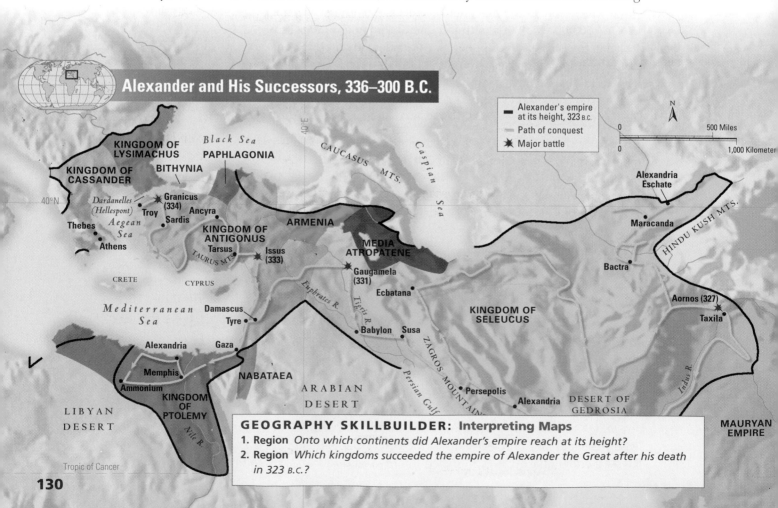

Alexander and His Successors, 336–300 B.C.

- Alexander's empire at its height, 323 B.C.
- Path of conquest
- ✴ Major battle

0 – 500 Miles
0 – 1,000 Kilometers

KINGDOM OF LYSIMACHUS
KINGDOM OF CASSANDER
Black Sea
PAPHLAGONIA
BITHYNIA
CAUCASUS MTS.
Caspian Sea
Alexandria Eschate
Dardanelles (Hellespont)
Granicus (334)
Troy
Ancyra
Sardis
Thebes
Aegean Sea
Athens
KINGDOM OF ANTIGONUS
Tarsus
TAURUS MTS.
Issus (333)
ARMENIA
MEDIA ATROPATENE
HINDU KUSH MTS.
Maracanda
CRETE
CYPRUS
Gaugamela (331)
Ecbatana
Bactra
Aornos (327)
Mediterranean Sea
Damascus
Tyre
Euphrates R.
Tigris R.
Babylon
Susa
KINGDOM OF SELEUCUS
ZAGROS MOUNTAINS
Taxila
Alexandria
Gaza
NABATAEA
ARABIAN DESERT
Persian Gulf
Persepolis
Alexandria
DESERT OF GEDROSIA
Indus R.
Memphis
Ammonium
KINGDOM OF PTOLEMY
Nile R.
LIBYAN DESERT
Tropic of Cancer
MAURYAN EMPIRE
40°N
40°E

GEOGRAPHY SKILLBUILDER: Interpreting Maps
1. **Region** Onto which continents did Alexander's empire reach at its height?
2. **Region** Which kingdoms succeeded the empire of Alexander the Great after his death in 323 B.C.?

Alexander's Empire and Its Legacy 336-306 B.C.

ALEXANDER'S EMPIRE

332 B.C.
Alexander entered Egypt and founded the city of Alexandria.

336 B.C.
Philip II was assassinated. Alexander became king of Macedonia at age 20.

334 B.C.
Alexander led 35,000 soldiers across the Hellespont or Dardanelles into Anatolia.

327 B.C.
Alexander's army reached the Indus Valley.

323 B.C.
Alexander caught fever and died at age 32. His generals began a power struggle.

MACEDONIA

PERSIA

EGYPT

323 B.C.
Ptolemy seized Egypt and became a pharaoh.

312 B.C.
Seleucus took Persian Empire.

306 B.C.
Antigonus I became king of Macedonia.

deserts and drenching monsoon rains. The exhausted soldiers yearned to go home. Bitterly disappointed, Alexander agreed to turn back.

On their homeward journey, Alexander and his troops crossed a brutally hot desert. Everyone was desperately thirsty. Some of the men collected water in a helmet—which they offered to their general. According to Arrian, Alexander saw an opportunity to inspire his discouraged men by sharing their hardship:

A VOICE FROM THE PAST
He received it [the water], and thanked those who had brought it; and . . . poured it out in the sight of all the troops; and at this . . . the whole army was so much heartened that you would have said that each and every man had drunk that water which Alexander thus poured out.

ARRIAN, *Anabasis*

By the spring of 323 B.C., Alexander and his army had returned west to Babylon. Restless as always, Alexander announced plans to organize and unify his empire. He would construct new cities, roads, and harbors and conquer Arabia. However, Alexander never carried out his plans. One year after his return, he became seriously ill with a fever. Eleven days later, Alexander died—a month short of his 33rd birthday.

Alexander's Legacy As he lay dying, Alexander correctly predicted that his empire would go to the strongest general. His Macedonian generals fought among themselves until three ambitious generals won out. Antigonus (an·TIG·uh·nus) became king of Macedonia and took control of the Greek city-states. Ptolemy (TAHL·uh·mee) seized Egypt, took the title of pharaoh, and established a dynasty. Seleucus (sih·LOO·kuhs) took most of the old Persian Empire, which became known as the Seleucid empire. Ignoring the democratic traditions of the Greek polis, these rulers and their descendants governed with complete power over their subjects.

Alexander's conquests ended the era of independent Greek city-states. As he and his army marched through the Persian Empire, thousands of Greek artists, merchants, and officials followed. Alexander himself adopted Persian dress and customs and married a Persian woman. He included Persians and people from other lands in his army. As time passed, Greek settlers throughout the empire also adopted new ways. A vibrant new culture emerged from the blend of Greek, Egyptian, and Eastern customs.

THINK THROUGH HISTORY
C. Hypothesizing
Was the power struggle that followed Alexander's death inevitable?

Section 4 Assessment

1. TERMS & NAMES

Identify
- Philip II
- Macedonia
- Demosthenes
- Alexander the Great
- Darius III

2. TAKING NOTES

Using a diagram like the one below, label how far north, south, east, and west Alexander ruled.

north

west — **Alexander's Rule** — east

south

Which conquests do you think was the most significant? Why?

3. HYPOTHESIZING

If Alexander had lived, do you think he would have been as successful in ruling his empire as he was in building it?

THINK ABOUT
- skills needed for military leadership
- skills needed to govern an empire
- Alexander's demonstrated abilities

4. THEME ACTIVITY

Empire Building In small groups, create an illustrated time line of Alexander's conquests. Include at least five main events.

The Spread of Hellenistic Culture

TERMS & NAMES
- Hellenistic
- Alexandria
- Euclid
- Archimedes
- Colossus of Rhodes

MAIN IDEA	WHY IT MATTERS NOW
Hellenistic culture, a blend of Greek and other influences, flourished throughout Greece, Egypt, and Asia.	Western civilization today continues to be influenced by diverse cultures.

SETTING THE STAGE Alexander the Great's ambitions were cultural as well as military and political. He started new cities as outposts of Greek culture. These cities, from Egyptian Alexandria in the south to the Asian Alexandrias in the east, adopted many Greek patterns and customs. After Alexander's death, trade, a shared Greek culture, and the Greek language continued to link these cities together. But each region had its own traditional ways of life, religion, and government that no ruler could afford to overlook. Alexander's successors gradually began dynasties in each of these lands. They encouraged local traditions while transplanting Greek culture.

Hellenistic Culture in Alexandria

This is a 19th-century illustration of the great Lighthouse of Alexandria. A fire at the top of the over 400-foot building guided ships into the Egyptian harbor.

After Alexander's death, a vibrant new culture emerged. Greek (Hellenic) culture blended with Egyptian, Persian, and Indian influences. This blending became known as **Hellenistic** culture. Koine (koy·NAY), the popular spoken language used in Hellenistic cities such as Alexandria, was the direct result of cultural blending. The word *koine* came from the Greek word for common. The language was a dialect of Greek. This language enabled educated people and traders from diverse backgrounds to communicate in cities throughout the Hellenistic world.

Trade and Cultural Diversity Among the many cities of the Hellenistic world, the African city of **Alexandria** became the foremost center of commerce and Hellenistic civilization. Alexandria occupied a strategic site on the western edge of the Nile delta. Ships from all around the Mediterranean docked in its spacious harbor. Its warehouses bulged with wheat and other products from the Nile Valley. Alexandria's thriving commerce enabled it to grow and prosper. By the third century B.C., its diverse population exceeded half a million people. Greek officials, Jewish merchants, and Egyptian priests mingled in crowded marketplaces with visitors from the rest of Africa, Persia, and India. Alexandria became an international community, with a rich mixture of customs and traditions from Egypt and from the Aegean.

Alexandria's Greatest Attractions Both residents and visitors admired Alexandria's great beauty. Broad avenues lined with statues of Greek gods divided the city into blocks. Rulers built magnificent royal palaces overlooking the harbor. A much visited tomb contained Alexander's elaborate glass coffin. Soaring more than 400 feet over the harbor stood an enormous stone lighthouse called the Pharos. This lighthouse contained a polished bronze mirror that reflected the light from a blazing fire.

Alexandria's greatest attractions were its famous museum and library. The museum was a temple dedicated to the Muses, the Greek goddesses of arts and sciences. (The word *museum* comes from muse.) It contained art

THINK THROUGH HISTORY
A. Recognizing Causes Why was the culture of the Hellenistic period so different from that of classical Greece?

galleries, a zoo, botanical gardens, and even a dining hall. The museum was an institute of advanced study.

Teachers and students were only a short distance from the nearby Alexandrian Library. Its collection of half a million papyrus scrolls included many of the masterpieces of ancient literature. As the first true research library in the world, it helped promote the work of a gifted group of scholars. These scholars greatly respected the earlier works of classical literature and learning. They produced commentaries that explained these works.

Science and Technology

During the Hellenistic period, the center of scholarship gradually shifted away from Athens. Hellenistic scholars, particularly in Alexandria, succeeded brilliantly in preserving Greek and Egyptian learning in the sciences. Until the scientific advances of the 16th and 17th centuries, scholars in Alexandria provided most of the scientific knowledge available to the West.

Astronomy Alexandria's museum contained a small observatory in which astronomers could study the planets and stars. One astronomer, Aristarchus (AR·ih·STAHR·kuhs) of Samos, reached two significant scientific conclusions. In one conclusion, he estimated that the sun was at least 300 times larger than the earth. Although he greatly underestimated the sun's true size, Aristarchus disproved the widely held belief that the sun was smaller than Greece. In another conclusion, Aristarchus proposed that the earth and other planets revolve around the sun. Unfortunately for science, other astronomers refused to support Aristarchus' theories. By the second century A.D., Alexandria's last renowned astronomer, Ptolemy, incorrectly placed the earth at the center of the solar system. Astronomers accepted this view for the next 14 centuries.

Hipparchus invented the system of longitude and latitude used on maps and sky charts. Here he is shown marking the position of a star.

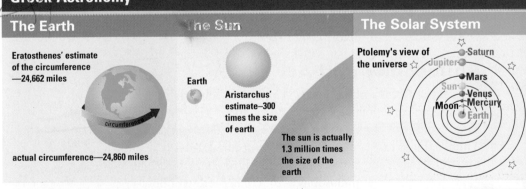

Greek Astronomy

The Earth

Eratosthenes' estimate of the circumference —24,662 miles

circumference

actual circumference—24,860 miles

The Sun

Earth

Aristarchus' estimate—300 times the size of earth

The sun is actually 1.3 million times the size of the earth

The Solar System

Ptolemy's view of the universe

Saturn
Jupiter
Mars
Sun
Venus
Mercury
Moon
Earth

SKILLBUILDER: Interpreting Charts
The foundations of modern scientific thought were laid during the Hellenistic period.
1. *Where were Greek astronomers' ideas most incorrect compared with modern concepts?*
2. *Which estimate is closest to modern measurements? How could the Hellenists be so accurate?*

While Hellenistic astronomers debated the earth's position in the solar system, a scholar named Eratosthenes (EHR·uh·TAHS·thuh·NEEZ) closely calculated the earth's true size. Eratosthenes was the director of the Alexandrian Library. He was also a highly regarded astronomer, poet, historian, and mathematician. He skillfully used geometry to compute the earth's circumference at 24,662 miles. Today, we compute the earth's circumference at 24,860 miles. His estimate was within 1 percent of our modern calculations.

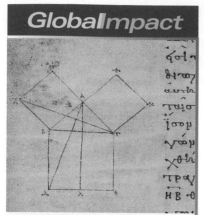

Greece, A.D. 800

Pythagorean Theorem

Geometry students remember Pythagoras for his theorem on the triangle but its principles were known earlier. This formula states that the square of a right triangle's hypotenuse equals the sum of the squared lengths of the two remaining sides. Chinese mathematicians knew this theory perhaps as early as 1100 B.C. Egyptian surveyors put it to practical use even earlier.

However, the work of the school Pythagoras founded caught the interest of later mathematicians. Shown is Euclid's proof in Greek along with a Chinese and an Arabic translation. The Arabs who conquered much of Alexander's empire spread Greek mathematical learning to the West. The formula became known as the Pythagorean theorem throughout the world.

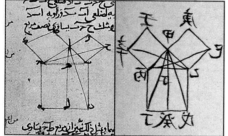

Arabic, A.D. 1250   **Chinese, A.D. 1607**

Mathematics and Physics Both Eratosthenes and Aristarchus used a geometry text compiled by **Euclid** (YOO·klihd). Euclid was a highly regarded mathematician who opened a school of geometry in Alexandria. His best-known book, the *Elements*, contained 465 carefully presented geometry propositions and proofs. Muslim and European universities used the *Elements* until well into the 1900s. It is sometimes said that only the Bible has been more widely used and studied. Euclid's work is still the basis for courses in geometry.

Another important Hellenistic scientist, **Archimedes** (AHR·kuh·MEE·deez) of Syracuse, studied at Alexandria. He accurately estimated the value of pi (π)—the ratio of the circumference of a circle to its diameter. He showed its value to be between $3^{10}/_{71}$ and $3\frac{1}{7}$. Archimedes also explained the law of the lever and invented the compound pulley to lift heavy objects. The writer Plutarch described how Archimedes demonstrated to an audience of curious onlookers how something heavy can be moved by a small force:

> **A VOICE FROM THE PAST**
> Archimedes took a . . . ship . . . which had just been dragged up on land with great labor and many men; in this he placed her usual complement of men and cargo, and then sitting at some distance, without any trouble, by gently pulling with his hand the end of a system of pulleys, he dragged it towards him with as smooth and even a motion as if it were passing over the sea.
>
> PLUTARCH, *Parallel Lives: Marcellus*

Gifted in both geometry and physics, Archimedes also put his genius to practical use. He invented the Archimedes screw, a device that raised water from the ground, and a catapult or missile-throwing machine. Building on the knowledge of Archimedes, Hellenistic scientists later built a force pump, pneumatic machines, and even a steam engine.

Philosophy and Art

Like earlier Greek philosophers, Hellenistic scholars believed that the universe followed rational principles. They felt that philosophy offered the best way to understand these principles. The teachings of Plato and Aristotle continued to be very influential in Hellenistic philosophy. In the third century B.C., however, new schools of philosophy were concerned with how people should live their lives. Two major philosophies developed during the Hellenistic period—Stoicism and Epicureanism.

Stoicism and Epicureanism A Greek philosopher named Zeno (335–263 B.C.) founded the school of philosophy called Stoicism (STOH·ih·SIHZ·uhm). Stoics believed in a divine power who controlled the universe. They proposed that people should live a virtuous life in harmony with natural law. Stoics also preached that vices such as human desires, power, and wealth were dangerous distractions that should be controlled. Stoicism explained nature and provided an ethical approach to life. The philosophy also promoted social unity and encouraged its followers to focus on things they could control. Its ethical doctrine appealed to people of many different races, cultures, and economic backgrounds.

(handwritten margin notes) live w/ nature / Deism

THINK THROUGH HISTORY
B. Summarizing
What were some of the main achievements of the scientists of the Hellenistic period?

Background
A *stoic* has come to mean someone who is indifferent to or unaffected by pain.

Epicurus (EHP·uh·KYUR·uhs) founded the school of thought called Epicureanism. He taught that the universe was composed of atoms and ruled by gods who had no interest in humans. Epicurus believed that the only real objects were those that the five senses perceived. He taught that the greatest good and the highest pleasure came from virtuous conduct and the absence of pain. Epicureans proposed that the main goal of humans was to achieve harmony of body and mind. Today, the word *epicurean* means one devoted to pursuing human pleasures. However, during his lifetime, Epicurus advocated moderation in all things.

Realism in Sculpture Like science, sculpture flourished during the Hellenistic age. Rulers, wealthy merchants, and cities all purchased statues to honor the gods, commemorate heroes, and portray ordinary people in everyday situations. The largest known Hellenistic statue was created on the island of Rhodes. Known as the **Colossus of Rhodes,** this bronze statue stood more than 100 feet high. The colossal statue could not have stood with its feet straddling the harbor entrance, as legend suggests.

One of the seven wonders of the ancient world, the Colossus of Rhodes was toppled by an earthquake about 225 B.C. Later, the bronze was sold for scrap. Another great Hellenistic statue was discovered by archaeologists in 1863, the famous Winged Victory of Samothrace. It commemorates a naval victory by the Greeks against foes who would have enslaved them.

Hellenistic sculpture moved away from the harmonic balance and idealized forms of the classical age. Sculptors created more realistic and emotional works. Instead of the serene face and perfect body of an idealized man or woman, Hellenistic sculptors created more natural works. They felt free to explore new subjects, carving ordinary people such as an old, wrinkled peasant woman.

By 150 B.C., the Hellenistic world was in decline. A new city, Rome, was growing and gaining strength. Through Rome, Greek-style drama, architecture, sculpture, religion, and philosophy were preserved and eventually became the core of Western civilization.

Winged Victory of Samothrace is one of the few surviving examples of Hellenistic art. The dramatic statue is now in the Louvre in Paris. It shows a winged figure standing on the bow of a ship. Notice how the deep relief makes the wind appear to ripple through her gown.

Section 5 Assessment

1. TERMS & NAMES

Identify
- Hellenistic
- Alexandria
- Euclid
- Archimedes
- Colossus of Rhodes

2. TAKING NOTES

Using a chart like the one below, list Hellenistic achievements in each of the following categories.

Category	Achievements
astronomy	
geometry	
philosophy	
art	

Select one category from the chart and make a poster highlighting Hellenistic achievements in that area.

3. SYNTHESIZING

Describe how the growth of Alexander's empire spread Greek culture.

THINK ABOUT
- public vs. private art
- realistic vs. ideal representations
- the decline of the polis

4. ANALYZING THEMES

Cultural Interaction The Hellenistic culture brought together Egyptian, Greek, Persian, and Indian influences. How is American culture a combination of different influences? Give examples of those influences.

THINK ABOUT
- American immigration
- geographic regions/influences
- your own cultural background

TERMS & NAMES

Briefly explain the importance of each of the following to Classical Greece.

1. Trojan War
2. Homer
3. polis
4. phalanx
5. classical art
6. Aristotle
7. Macedonia
8. Alexander the Great
9. Hellenistic
10. Archimedes

Interact *with* History

On page 110, you drew certain conclusions about what qualities Greeks valued without knowing details about their history. Now that you have read the chapter, reexamine the artworks and reread the Greeks' words. Conduct a class debate about how the values and heritage of Greece have influenced modern society.

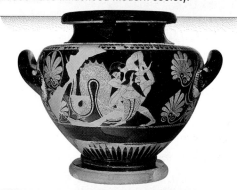

REVIEW QUESTIONS

SECTION 1 *(pages 111–114)*
Cultures of the Mountains and the Sea

11. Why was sea travel so important to early Greece?
12. Why did the Greeks develop myths?

SECTION 2 *(pages 115–119)*
Warring City-States

13. What were the two most powerful city-states in early Greece?
14. What were the consequences of the Persian Wars?

SECTION 3 *(pages 120–125)*
Democracy and Greece's Golden Age

15. What were Pericles' three goals for Athens?
16. Who were the three renowned philosophers of the golden age?

SECTION 4 *(pages 128–131)*
Alexander—Empire Builder

17. Why was Greece so easily conquered by Macedonia?
18. What was the full extent of Alexander's empire before his death?

SECTION 5 *(pages 132–135)*
The Spread of Hellenistic Culture

19. What four influences blended to form Hellenistic culture?
20. What did the Epicureans believe?

Visual Summary

The Legacy of Greece

Government
- Direct democracy; citizens rule by majority vote
- Written code of laws
- Citizens bring charges of wrongdoing; trial by jury
- Expansion of citizenship to all free adult males, except foreigners

Arts
- Drama and poetry
- Sculpture portraying ideals of beauty
- Painted pottery showing scenes of Greek life
- Classical architecture

Culture
- Greek language
- Mythology about gods and goddesses
- Olympic Games
- Philosophers search for truth

Greek Civilization

Science and Technology
- Disagreement whether sun or earth at center of universe
- Accurate estimate of circumference of earth
- Euclid's geometry textbook
- Development of lever, pulley, pump

CRITICAL THINKING

1. POWERFUL MEN

There is a saying that "the measure of man is what he does with power." Would you consider Alexander the Great or Pericles a "better" man? Why?

2. CLASSICAL GREEK INFLUENCES

THEME CULTURAL INTERACTION Copy the web below on your paper. Fill in examples of how classical Greece has influenced the United States.

Classical Greece

3. EMPIRE BUILDERS

THEME EMPIRE BUILDING Thinking back to Pericles and Alexander the Great, what qualifications or characteristics do you think are needed for a leader to build an empire? Why?

4. ANALYZING PRIMARY SOURCES

In the following selection from *Politics,* Aristotle presents his views on where the power of the state should reside. His conclusions reflect the idea that moderation is the best path to civic virtue. Read the paragraph and then answer the questions that follow.

> **A VOICE FROM THE PAST**
> Where ought the sovereign power of the state to reside? . . . The state aims to consist as far as possible of those who are alike and equal, a condition found chiefly among the middle section. . . . The middle class is also the steadiest element, the least eager for change. They neither covet, like the poor the possessions of others, nor do others covet theirs, as the poor covet those of the rich. . . . Tyranny often emerges from an over-enthusiastic democracy or from an oligarchy, but much more rarely from middle class constitutions . . .

- What is Aristotle arguing here?
- How closely does this model of an ideal state correspond to the reality of Athenian democracy?
- Do you agree with Aristotle? Support your opinion.

CHAPTER ACTIVITIES

1. LIVING HISTORY: Unit Portfolio Project

THEME POWER AND AUTHORITY Your unit portfolio project focuses on how people in history have gained power and authority. For Chapter 5, you might use one of the following ideas.

- Write an epic poem (about 2–3 pages) about a legendary battle or hero that you read about in Chapter 5. Use Homer's *The Iliad* or *The Odyssey* as a reference.
- Design a museum exhibit with the title POWER AND AUTHORITY IN CLASSICAL GREECE. Include a sketch of the exhibit layout and a one-page description of the exhibit.
- Create an imaginary television talk show about this topic: What makes a leader successful? Guests should include people mentioned in this chapter. Prepare a list of questions the host will ask. Videotape the show.

2. CONNECT TO TODAY: Cooperative Learning

THEME CULTURAL INTERACTION Like many other facets of classical Greek culture, the influence of classical Greek art and architecture spread throughout the world, including the United States.

Create a "Then and Now" board showing examples of art and architecture in the United States that were influenced by classical Greek styles.

 Using the Internet or the library, find examples from classical Greece and then compare them with contemporary buildings and art.

- Find examples from classical Greece. Sketch, photocopy, or otherwise render them on a poster board.
- Find buildings or other art that show evidence of a classical Greek influence. Photograph or render them on the poster board.
- Label the board clearly. Include at least four examples.

3. INTERPRETING A TIME LINE

Revisit the unit time line on page 106. Look at the Chapter 5 section of the time line. Can you find evidence of how geography or a natural phenomenon might have influenced an event? Explain your conclusion.

FOCUS ON **GEOGRAPHY**

Notice the present-day boundaries that appear on this map of Alexander's empire.

- What modern nations were once part of this empire?
- How did the physical characteristics of the empire block its unification and lead to the formation of separate nations?

Connect to History
Compare Greece's size to the area it once controlled. How did it influence such a large area?

CHAPTER 6

Ancient Rome and Early Christianity, 500 B.C.—A.D. 500

PREVIEWING THEMES

Power and Authority

The government of Rome began with kings, who were eventually displaced. Under the republic, government was based on laws and rule was by elected officials. Eventually, power was taken over by absolute rulers, called emperors, who exercised unlimited authority.

Empire Building

The Romans created a vast and powerful empire. At its height, it extended into three continents—Europe, Asia, and Africa. For several centuries, Rome brought Roman civilization and peace and prosperity to its empire. By the fifth century, internal weaknesses and outside invaders caused the empire to decline and eventually collapse.

Religious and Ethical Systems

Religion was important in the life of ancient Rome. Early Romans worshiped many gods, as had the Greeks. Jews in the Roman province of Judea were monotheistic, believing in only one god. From the home of the Jews arose another monotheistic religion, Christianity, based on the teachings of Jesus of Nazareth. Christianity grew and spread throughout Roman lands and beyond.

INTERNET CONNECTION

Visit us at www.mcdougallittell.com to learn more about ancient Rome and early Christianity.

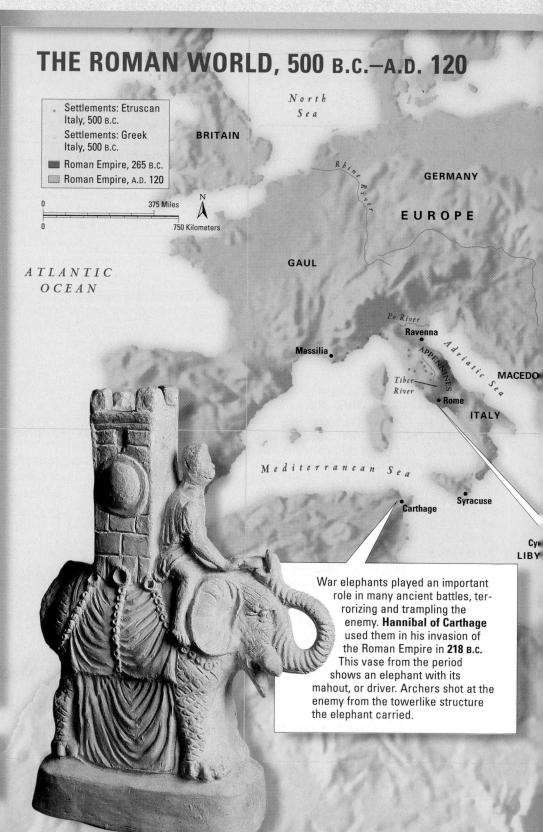

THE ROMAN WORLD, 500 B.C.—A.D. 120

- Settlements: Etruscan Italy, 500 B.C.
- Settlements: Greek Italy, 500 B.C.
- Roman Empire, 265 B.C.
- Roman Empire, A.D. 120

0   375 Miles
0   750 Kilometers

N

North Sea

BRITAIN

Rhine River

GERMANY

EUROPE

GAUL

ATLANTIC OCEAN

Po River

Ravenna

Massilia

APPENNINES

Adriatic Sea

MACEDO

Tiber River

• Rome

ITALY

Mediterranean Sea

Syracuse

Carthage

Cy
LIBY

War elephants played an important role in many ancient battles, terrorizing and trampling the enemy. **Hannibal of Carthage** used them in his invasion of the Roman Empire in **218 B.C.** This vase from the period shows an elephant with its mahout, or driver. Archers shot at the enemy from the towerlike structure the elephant carried.

138

The life and teachings of **Jesus** gave rise in the **first century A.D.** to one of the world's major religions—Christianity. Jesus appears here in a detail from a Roman mosaic of the fifth century.

DACIA

THRACE

Byzantium •

Black Sea

Aegean Sea

GREECE

Athens

Ankara •

ASIA MINOR

Tarsus •

Antioch •

SYRIA

JUDEA

• Jerusalem

Alexandria •

• Petra

EGYPT

ARABIA

Caspian Sea

Volga R.

Ural River

Euphrates River

Tigris River

Indus River

Danube R.

40°N

The Roman army—the best organized, trained, and disciplined fighting force of its time—brought the rule and civilization of Rome to three continents. The **Roman soldier** shown here in a sculpture from the **second century A.D.** was a member of the elite Praetorian Guard, the emperor's bodyguard.

Interact *with* History

"Brilliant orator"   "Manipulates people"

"Decisive"   "Too ambitious"

"Shrewd"   "Devious"

"Fair"   "Ruthless"

"The poor adore him."

"Yes, but he bought their support with huge sums for public entertainments."

You are a senator in ancient Rome. You have listened to hours of heated debate about a powerful leader who wants to be ruler. As you consider whether to support or oppose him, you recall some of the arguments.

"He is a military genius who added vast territory and wealth to Rome."

"Yes, but he disobeyed orders in his quest for personal glory."

"He has a great vision for the future of Rome."

"But he wants absolute power and would override the law to get it."

Before you decide, you must consider:

What qualities make a good leader?

EXAMINING *the* ISSUES

- What are the qualities of a good leader?

- Should leaders always be measured by the results they achieve?

- Have the qualities of good leaders changed over time?

As a class, discuss these questions. Based on the qualities you have discussed, think about what you have learned about other leaders in history, such as Alexander the Great and Darius of Persia. What qualities helped them to be successful or caused them to fail?

As you read about Rome, see how the qualities of its leaders helped or hindered its development. See also what happened to its most famous leader—Julius Caesar.

The Romans Create a Republic

TERMS & NAMES
- republic
- patrician
- plebeian
- tribune
- consul
- senate
- dictator
- legion
- Hannibal
- Scipio

MAIN IDEA

The early Romans established a republic, which grew powerful and spread its influence.

WHY IT MATTERS NOW

Some of the most fundamental values and institutions of Western civilization began in the Roman Republic.

SETTING THE STAGE While the great civilization of Greece was in decline, a new civilization to the west was developing and increasing its power. The city of Rome grew from a small village to a mighty empire. It adopted and preserved much of Greek art, philosophy, religion, and drama. And it created a lasting legacy of its own.

The Beginnings of Rome

According to Roman legend, the city was founded in 753 B.C. by Romulus and Remus, twin sons of the god Mars and a Latin princess. The twins were abandoned on the Tiber River as infants and raised by a she-wolf. They decided to build a city near the spot. In reality, Rome developed because of its strategic location and its fertile soil. Rome was built on seven rolling hills at a curve on the Tiber River, near the center of the Italian peninsula. It was midway between the Alps and Italy's southern tip. Rome also was near the midpoint of the Mediterranean Sea. The historian Livy wrote about the city's site:

> **A VOICE FROM THE PAST**
> Not without reason did gods and men choose this spot for the site of our city—the [salubrious] hills, the river to bring us produce from the inland regions and sea-borne commerce from abroad, the sea itself, near enough for convenience yet not so near as to bring danger from foreign fleets, our situation in the very heart of Italy—all these advantages make it of all places in the world the best for a city destined to grow great.
> **LIVY,** *The Early History of Rome*

THINK THROUGH HISTORY
A. Making Inferences Why was the geographical location of Rome an advantage?

The earliest settlers on the Italian peninsula arrived in prehistoric times. From about 1000 to 500 B.C., three groups inhabited the region and eventually battled for control. They were the Latins, the Greeks, and the Etruscans. The Latins were farmers and shepherds who wandered into Italy across the Alps around 1000 B.C. They settled on either side of the Tiber River in a region they called Latium. They built the original settlement at Rome, a cluster of wooden huts atop one of its seven hills, Palatine Hill. These settlers were the first Romans. (See the map on pages 138–139.)

Between 750 and 600 B.C., Greek settlers established about 50 colonies on the coasts of southern Italy and Sicily. The cities became prosperous and commercially active. They brought all of Italy, including Rome, into closer contact with Greek civilization. The Greeks also taught the Romans how to grow grapes and olives.

The Etruscans were native to northern Italy. They were skilled metalworkers and engineers. The Etruscans strongly influenced the development of Roman civilization. They had a system of writing, and the Romans adopted their alphabet. They also influenced Rome's architecture, especially the use of the arch. Romans borrowed religious ideas from both the Greeks and the Etruscans. The Romans adopted Etruscan rituals that they believed helped them to win the favor of the gods. Roman gods even took on the personalities and legends of the Greek gods. Romans, however, gave their gods different names. Thus Zeus, the king of the Greek gods, became Jupiter in Rome, and Hera, the queen of the gods, became Juno.

Background
The name *Rome* is Etruscan in origin.

The Early Republic

Around 600 B.C., an Etruscan became king. However, Rome was not controlled by the Etruscan cities. Under its Etruscan kings, Rome grew from a collection of hilltop villages to a city that covered nearly 500 square miles. Much of Rome was rich agricultural land. Various kings ordered the construction of Rome's first temples and public buildings. By royal order, the swampy valley below the Palatine Hill was drained, making a public meeting place. Later it became the Forum, the heart of Roman political life.

The last king of Rome was Tarquin the Proud. A harsh tyrant, he was driven from power in 509 B.C. Roman aristocrats, wealthy landowners who resented the Etruscan kings, overthrew him. The Romans declared they would never again be ruled by a king. They swore to put to death anyone who plotted to make himself king.

Having deposed the monarch, the Romans established a new government. They called it a republic, from the Latin phrase res publica, which means "public affairs." A **republic** is a form of government in which power rests with citizens who have the right to vote to select their leaders. In Rome, citizenship with voting rights was granted only to free-born male citizens.

Patricians and Plebeians In the early republic, different groups of Romans struggled for power. One group was the **patricians,** the aristocratic landowners who held most of the power. The other important group was the **plebeians,** the common farmers, artisans, and merchants who made up the majority of the population.

The patricians inherited their power and social status. They claimed that their ancestry gave them the authority to make laws for Rome and its people. The plebeians were citizens of Rome with the right to vote. They, however, were barred by law from holding most important government positions. In time, the Senate allowed them to form their own assembly and elect representatives called **tribunes.** Tribunes protected the rights of the plebeians from unfair acts of patrician officials. Eventually, plebeian pressure on the patricians gained them additional political power.

Twelve Tables An important victory for the plebeians was to force the creation of a written law code. With laws unwritten, patrician officials often interpreted the law to suit themselves. In 451 B.C. a group of ten officials began writing down Rome's laws. The laws were carved on twelve tablets, or tables, and hung in the Forum. They became the basis for later Roman law. The Twelve Tables established the idea that all free citizens, patricians and plebeians, had a right to the protection of the law.

Government Under the Republic In the first century B.C., Roman writers boasted that Rome had achieved a balanced government. What they meant was that their government had taken the best features of a monarchy (government by a king), an aristocracy (government by nobles), and a democracy (government by the people). In place of a king, Rome had two officials called **consuls.** Like kings, they commanded the army and directed the government. However, their power was limited. First, a consul's

Once the center of political power and intrigue, the Forum now lies in ruin in the center of modern Rome.

Comparing Republican Governments

	Rome	United States of America
Executive	Two consuls, elected by the assembly for one year—chief executives of the government and commanders-in-chief of the army.	A president, elected by the people for four years—chief executive of the government and commander-in-chief of the army.
Legislative	Senate of 300 members, chosen from aristocracy for life—controls foreign and financial policies, advises consuls.	Senate of 100 members, elected by the people for six-year terms—makes laws, advises president on foreign policy.
	Centuriate Assembly, all citizen-soldiers are members for life—selects consuls, makes laws.	House of Representatives of 435 members, elected by the people for two years—makes laws, originates revenue bills.
	Tribal Assembly, citizens grouped according to where they live are members for life—elects tribunes and makes laws.	
Judicial	Praetors, eight judges chosen for one year by Centuriate Assembly—two oversee civil and criminal courts (the others govern provinces).	Supreme Court, nine justices appointed for life by president—highest court, hears civil and criminal appeals cases.
Legal Code	Twelve Tables—a list of rules that were the basis of Roman legal system	U.S. Constitution—basic law of the United States
Citizenship	All adult male landowners	All native-born or naturalized persons

---

SKILLBUILDER: Interpreting Charts

1. *What similarities do you see in the governments of the Roman Republic and the United States?*
2. *Which government seems more democratic? Why?*

Vocabulary
veto: comes from the Latin for "I forbid."

term was only one year long. The same person could not be elected consul again for ten years. Second, one consul could always overrule, or veto, the other's decisions.

The **senate** was the aristocratic branch of Rome's government. It had both legislative and administrative functions in the republic. By tradition, there were 300 members, chosen from the upper class of Roman society. Later, plebeians were allowed in the senate. Because membership was for life, the senate provided continuity. It also exercised enormous influence over both foreign and domestic policy.

The assemblies were the more democratic side of the government. All citizen-soldiers were members of the Centuriate Assembly. In the early days of the republic, this patrician-controlled assembly appointed the consuls and made laws. It had less power than the senate. An assembly organized by the plebeians, the Tribal Assembly, elected the tribunes and made laws for the common people. Later, it won the right to make laws for the republic.

In times of crisis, the republic could appoint a **dictator**—a leader who had absolute power to make laws and command the army. A dictator's power lasted for only six months. Dictators were chosen by the consuls and then elected by the senate.

The Roman Army All citizens who owned land were required to serve in the army. To secure certain public offices, ten years of military service were required. Roman soldiers were organized into large military units called legions. The Roman **legion** was made up of some 5,000 heavily armed foot soldiers (infantry). A

Vocabulary
legion: also means a multitude.

SPOTLIGHT ON

Roman Legions
The legions were the fighting force that spread Rome's power around the Mediterranean. Each legion had a nickname and a flag, called its eagle. Losing the eagle in battle was a disgrace.

Legions were self-sufficient and could live off the land. They did their own construction and even built roads and bridges.

Each soldier had armor, a helmet, a shield, a sword, and a dagger. He also carried tools for digging and stakes that became part of a wall around the camp. In addition, each soldier brought a cooking pot, clothing, and any other items he needed.

Ancient Rome and Early Christianity **143**

group of soldiers on horseback (cavalry) supported each legion. Legions were divided into smaller groups of 80 men, each of which was called a century. In battle, the strength of the legion was its flexibility. Each century in a legion could act independently. The military organization and fighting skill of the Roman army were key factors in Rome's rise to greatness.

Rome Spreads Its Power

For hundreds of years after the founding of the republic, Rome sought to expand its territories through conquest and trade.

Rome Conquers Italy Roman power grew slowly but steadily as the legions battled for control of the Italian peninsula. By the fourth century B.C., Rome dominated central Italy. Then it suffered a major defeat. In 390 B.C., the Gauls, a Celtic people from the Po River Valley, north of the Apennines, sacked Rome. However, the Romans quickly recovered and rebuilt the city. They reestablished control by subduing one rival after another. They defeated the Etruscans to the north and the Greek city-states to the south. By 265 B.C., the Romans were masters of all Italy except the Po Valley.

Rome had different laws and treatment for different parts of its conquered territory. The neighboring Latins on the Tiber became full citizens of Rome. In territories farther from Rome, conquered peoples were given all the rights of Roman citizenship except the vote. All other conquered groups fell into a third category, allies of Rome. Rome did not interfere with its allies, as long as they sent troops to the Roman army and did not make treaties of friendship with any other state. The new citizens and allies became partners in Rome's growth. This lenient policy toward defeated enemies helped Rome to succeed in building a long-lasting empire. For the 250 years after 265 B.C., Roman power spread far beyond Italy.

Rome's Commercial Network Rome's location gave it easy access to the riches of the lands ringing the Mediterranean Sea. Roman merchants moved by land and sea. They traded Roman wine and olive oil for a variety of foods, raw materials, and manufactured goods from other lands. However, other large and powerful cities interfered with Roman access to the Mediterranean. The dominant city on the Mediterranean was Carthage, once a colony of Phoenicia. Carthage was located on a peninsula on the North African coast. Eventually Rome and Carthage fought bitterly for control of the Mediterranean.

War with Carthage In 264 B.C., Rome and Carthage went to war. This was the beginning of the long struggle known as the Punic Wars. Between 264 and 146 B.C., Rome and Carthage fought three wars. The first, for control of Sicily and the western Mediterranean, lasted 23 years (264–241 B.C.). It ended in the defeat of Carthage. Rome took the rich, grain-growing island of Sicily as the chief prize of victory. It thus gained its first province, or administrative unit, overseas. An uneasy peace followed. The Second Punic War began in 218 B.C. The mastermind behind the war was a 29-year-old Carthaginian general named **Hannibal.** Hannibal was a brilliant military strategist who wanted to avenge Carthage's earlier defeat.

Hannibal assembled an army of 50,000 infantry, 9,000 cavalry, and 60 elephants with the intent of capturing Rome. To surprise the Romans, he led his army on a long trek from Spain across France and through the Alps. Although he had lost more than half his men and most of his elephants, Hannibal invaded northern Italy. For more than a decade, he marched his forces up and down the Italian peninsula at

HISTORY MAKERS

**Hannibal
247–183 B.C.**

When Hannibal was only a boy of nine, his father, Hamilcar Barca, a general in Carthage's army, made him swear that he would always hate Rome and seek to destroy it. Hannibal became a lifelong foe of Rome. His war cry was "conquer or die!"

After his defeat at the battle of Zama and Carthage's loss in the Second Punic War, Hannibal took refuge among Rome's enemies. He fought against Roman forces as an ally of the kings of Syria and Bithynia. When Roman agents came for him in Bithynia on the Black Sea in Anatolia in 183 B.C., he committed suicide rather than submit to Rome.

THINK THROUGH HISTORY
C. Recognizing Effects How did its treatment of conquered people affect Rome's expansion?

Vocabulary
Punic: comes from the Latin word for Phoenician.

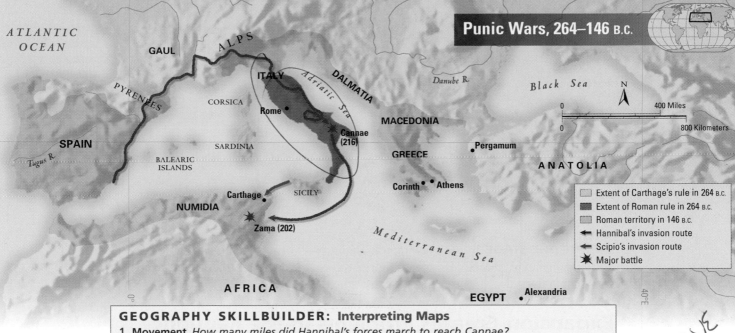

Punic Wars, 264–146 B.C.

ATLANTIC OCEAN

GAUL · ALPS · ITALY · DALMATIA · Danube R. · Black Sea

PYRENEES · CORSICA · Adriatic Sea · MACEDONIA

SPAIN · Rome · Cannae (216) · Pergamum

Tigus R. · SARDINIA · GREECE · ANATOLIA

BALEARIC ISLANDS · Corinth · Athens

Carthage · SICILY

NUMIDIA · Zama (202) · Mediterranean Sea

AFRICA · EGYPT · Alexandria

Extent of Carthage's rule in 264 B.C.
Extent of Roman rule in 264 B.C.
Roman territory in 146 B.C.
Hannibal's invasion route
Scipio's invasion route
Major battle

GEOGRAPHY SKILLBUILDER: Interpreting Maps
1. **Movement** How many miles did Hannibal's forces march to reach Cannae?
2. **Region** What territory did Rome add between 264 B.C. and 146 B.C.?

DESTRUCTIVE

Vocabulary
pillaged: took goods by force in wartime.

will. His soldiers lived off the land. They seized crops and cattle and pillaged farmhouses. Hannibal won his greatest victory at Cannae, in 216 B.C. There his army inflicted enormous losses on the Romans. However, the Romans regrouped and with the aid of many allies stood firm. They prevented Hannibal from capturing Rome.

FROM CARTHAGE

ROMAN

Finally the Romans found a daring military leader to match Hannibal's boldness. A general named **Scipio** (SIHP·ee·oh) devised a plan to attack Carthage. This strategy forced Hannibal to return to defend his native city. In 202 B.C., at Zama near Carthage, the Romans finally defeated Hannibal.

By the time of the Third Punic War (149–146 B.C.), Carthage was no longer a threat to Rome. Yet some Romans remembered the devastation Carthage had brought to Italy and were angered by its return to prosperity. An aged and influential senator named Cato ended all his speeches with the same message: "Carthage must be destroyed." In 149 B.C., Rome laid siege to Carthage. In 146 B.C., the city was set afire and its 50,000 inhabitants sold into slavery. Its territory was made the new province of Africa.

THINK THROUGH HISTORY
D. Recognizing Effects Why were the Punic Wars important?

Rome Controls the Mediterranean Rome's victories in the Punic Wars gave it domination over the western Mediterranean. The Romans went on to conquer the eastern half. Rome took control of Macedonia, Greece, and parts of Anatolia. By about 70 B.C., Rome's Mediterranean empire stretched from Anatolia on the east to Spain on the west.

Section 1 Assessment

1. TERMS & NAMES
Identify
• republic
• patrician
• plebeian
• tribune
• consul
• senate
• dictator
• legion
• Hannibal
• Scipio

2. TAKING NOTES
Using a time line like the one below, show the main events that mark the growth of Rome into a powerful republic.

509 B.C.—Romans overthrow Etruscan king

What was the most important event, and why do you think so?

3. FORMING OPINIONS
Do you think the Roman Republic owed its success more to its form of government or to its army? Why?

THINK ABOUT
• the structure of the republic
• how citizenship spread
• Rome's policies toward conquered peoples

4. ANALYZING THEMES
Power and Authority How did the office of dictator contribute to the balance and stability of the Roman Republic?

THINK ABOUT
• the role of the dictator
• the power of consuls
• the need for speedy decisions in a crisis

The Roman Empire Brings Change

TERMS & NAMES
- civil war
- Julius Caesar
- triumvirate
- absolute ruler
- Augustus
- *Pax Romana*
- gladiator

MAIN IDEA

The creation of the Roman Empire transformed Roman government, society, economy, and culture.

WHY IT MATTERS NOW

The Roman Empire has served throughout history as a model of political organization and control.

SETTING THE STAGE Rome grew rapidly, and growth brought political, economic, and social changes. Some leaders attempted reforms, but the republican government was unable to deal with the problems caused by these changes.

Expansion Creates Problems in the Republic

The Punic Wars and Rome's increasing wealth and expanding empire brought many problems. The most serious was the widening gap between rich and poor.

Rich landowners lived on huge estates called latifundia. Many of these estates had been created by occupying conquered lands and by taking farms left untended by soldiers serving in the army. Romans had made slaves of thousands of captured peoples during the wars. These slaves were made to work on the latifundia. By 100 B.C., slaves formed perhaps one-third of Rome's population.

Small farmers found it difficult to compete with the large estates run by slave labor. Some could not afford to repair the damage caused by Hannibal's invasion. They sold their lands to wealthy landowners. Many of these farmers, a large number of whom were returning soldiers, became homeless and jobless. Most stayed in the countryside and worked as seasonal migrant laborers. Some headed to Rome and other cities looking for work. The landless and unskilled in the cities found few jobs. They joined the ranks of the urban poor, a group that totaled about one-fourth of Roman society.

While wealthy Romans became corrupted by money and luxury, discontent arose among the slaves. Resentment also grew among the poor. Class tensions planted the seeds of the republic's collapse.

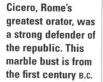

Cicero, Rome's greatest orator, was a strong defender of the republic. This marble bust is from the first century B.C.

THINK THROUGH HISTORY
A. Making Inferences What problems did increasing wealth bring to Rome?

The Republic Collapses

Two brothers, Tiberius and Gaius Gracchus (GRAK·us), attempted to help Rome's poor. As tribunes, they proposed reforms. The reforms included limiting the size of estates and giving land to the poor. Tiberius spoke eloquently about the plight of the landless former soldiers:

A VOICE FROM THE PAST

The savage beasts have their . . . dens . . . , but the men who bear arms and expose their lives for the safety of their country, enjoy . . . nothing more in it but the air and light . . . and wander from place to place with their wives and children.

TIBERIUS GRACCHUS quoted in Plutarch, *The Lives of Noble Greeks and Romans*

The brothers were strongly opposed by senators who felt threatened by their ideas. Both met violent deaths—Tiberius in 133 B.C. and Gaius in 121 B.C. A period of **civil war,** or conflict between groups within the same country, followed their deaths.

Changes in the character of the army had led to the rise of politically powerful military leaders. Generals began recruiting soldiers from the landless poor by promising them land. These soldiers fought for pay and owed allegiance only to their commander. They replaced the citizen-soldiers whose loyalty had been to the republic. It now was possible for a politician supported by his own troops to take over by force. → *tyranny*

Two such generals were Gaius Marius and Lucius Cornelius Sulla. During 88–82 B.C., their supporters fought a bloody civil war. The war ended with Sulla being named dictator. Rivalries between generals continued to threaten the republic. Eventually an ambitious and daring leader, **Julius Caesar** (SEE·zuhr), emerged to bring order to Rome.

Julius Caesar Takes Control In 60 B.C., Julius Caesar joined forces with Crassus, a wealthy Roman, and Pompey, a popular general. With their help, Caesar was elected consul in 59 B.C. For the next ten years, these men dominated Rome as a **triumvirate,** a group of three rulers.

Caesar was a strong leader and a genius at military strategy. Abiding by tradition, he served only one year as consul. He then appointed himself governor of Gaul (now France). During 58–50 B.C., Caesar led his legions in a grueling but successful campaign to conquer all of Gaul. Because he shared fully in the hardships of war, he won his men's loyalty and devotion. Here he speaks of rallying his troops in battle:

> **A VOICE FROM THE PAST**
> I had no shield with me but I snatched one from a soldier in the rear ranks and went forward to the front line. Once there, I called to all the centurions by name and shouted encouragement to the rest of the men. . . . My arrival gave the troops fresh hope. . . .
>
> **JULIUS CAESAR,** *Commentaries*

The reports of Caesar's successes in Gaul made him very popular with the people of Rome. Pompey, who had become his political rival, feared Caesar's ambitions. In 50 B.C., the senate, at Pompey's urgings, ordered Caesar to disband his legions and return home.

Caesar's next move led to civil war. He defied the senate's order. On the night of January 10, 49 B.C., he took his army across the Rubicon River in Italy, the southern limit of the area he commanded. He marched his army swiftly toward Rome, and Pompey fled. Caesar's troops defeated Pompey's armies in Greece, Asia, Spain, and Egypt. In 46 B.C., Caesar returned to Rome, where he had the support of the army and the masses. That same year, the senate appointed him dictator; in 44 B.C., he was named dictator for life.

Caesar's Reforms Caesar governed as an **absolute ruler,** one who has total power. He made sweeping changes. He granted Roman citizenship to many people in the provinces. He expanded the senate, adding friends and supporters from Italy and the provinces. Caesar helped the poor by creating jobs, especially through the construction of new public buildings. He started colonies where the landless could own land and increased pay for soldiers.

Many nobles and senators were troubled by Caesar's growing power, success, and popularity. Some feared losing their influence. Others considered him a tyrant. A number of important senators, led by Marcus Brutus and Gaius Cassius, plotted his assassination. On March 15, 44 B.C., they stabbed him to death in the senate chamber. *IDES OF MARCH)*

Beginning of the Empire After Caesar's death, civil war broke out again and destroyed what was left of the Roman Republic. Three of Caesar's supporters banded

HISTORY MAKERS

Julius Caesar
100–44 B.C.

In 44 B.C, on March 15 (known to Romans as the Ides of March), Caesar prepared to go to speak to the Senate, unaware that important senators plotted his death. According to legend, his wife, Calpurnia, begged him not to go. She said she had seen him in a dream dying in her arms of stab wounds. He earlier had been warned of danger by a soothsayer (fortune teller).

When Caesar arrived at the Senate chamber, he sat in his chair. Soon the plotters encircled him, took knives hidden in their togas, and stabbed him 23 times. They were led by Gaius Cassius and Caesar's friend Marcus Brutus. Caesar's last words were "Et tu, Brute?" ("You, too, Brutus?")

Background
All future Roman emperors would take the name "Caesar" as a title, and the word would be adopted in other languages: kaiser (German) and czar (Russian).

THINK THROUGH HISTORY
B. Analyzing Motives Why did Caesar's rivals feel they had to kill him?

together to crush the assassins. Caesar's 18-year-old grand-nephew and adopted son Octavian (ahk·TAY·vee·uhn) joined with an experienced general named Mark Antony and a powerful politician named Lepidus. In 43 B.C., they took control of Rome and ruled for ten years as the Second Triumvirate. Among those killed in the Triumvirate's purge of Caesar's enemies was Cicero, a defender of the republic in the senate.

The Second Triumvirate ended in jealousy and violence. Octavian forced Lepidus to retire. He and Mark Antony then became rivals. While leading troops against Rome's enemies in Anatolia, Mark Antony met Queen Cleopatra of Egypt. He fell in love with her and followed her to Egypt. Octavian accused Antony of plotting to rule Rome from Egypt, and another civil war erupted. Octavian defeated the combined forces of Antony and Cleopatra at the naval battle of Actium in 31 B.C. Later, Antony and Cleopatra committed suicide.

Cleopatra, who appears here in a marble sculpture from the first century B.C., was Egypt's last queen. In her quest for power, she allied herself first with Julius Caesar and then with Mark Antony.

Octavian claimed he would restore the republic, and, in fact, did retain some of its forms and traditions. The senate, for example, continued to meet, and Octavian consulted it on important matters. However, Octavian became the unchallenged ruler of Rome. Eventually he accepted the title of **Augustus** (aw·GUHS·tuhs), or "exalted one." He also kept the title *imperator*, or "supreme military commander," a term from which *emperor* is derived. Rome was now an empire ruled by one man.

A Vast and Powerful Empire

Rome was at the peak of its power from the beginning of Augustus' rule in 27 B.C. to A.D. 180. For 207 years, peace reigned throughout the empire, except for some fighting with tribes along the borders. This period of peace and prosperity is known as the ***Pax Romana***—"Roman peace."

During this time, the Roman Empire included more than 3 million square miles. Its population numbered between 60 and 80 million people. About 1 million people lived in the city of Rome itself.

An Economy Based on Agriculture and Trade Agriculture was the most important industry in the empire. All else depended on it. About 90 percent of the people were engaged in farming. Most Romans survived on the produce from their local area. Additional foodstuffs (when needed) and luxury items for the rich were obtained through trade. In Augustus' time, a silver coin called a denarius was in use throughout the empire. Having common coinage made trade between different parts of the empire much easier.

Rome had a vast trading network. Ships from the east traveled the Mediterranean protected by the Roman navy. Cities such as Corinth in Greece, Ephesus in Anatolia, and Antioch on the eastern coast of the Mediterranean grew wealthy. Rome also traded with China and India.

A complex network of roads linked the empire to such far-flung places as Persia and southern Russia. These roads were originally built by the Roman army for military purposes. The most important of the roads were the Silk Roads, named for the overland routes on which silk from China came through Asia to the Romans. Other luxury goods traveled along the same routes. Trade also brought Roman ways to the provinces and beyond.

trade "cultural diffusion"

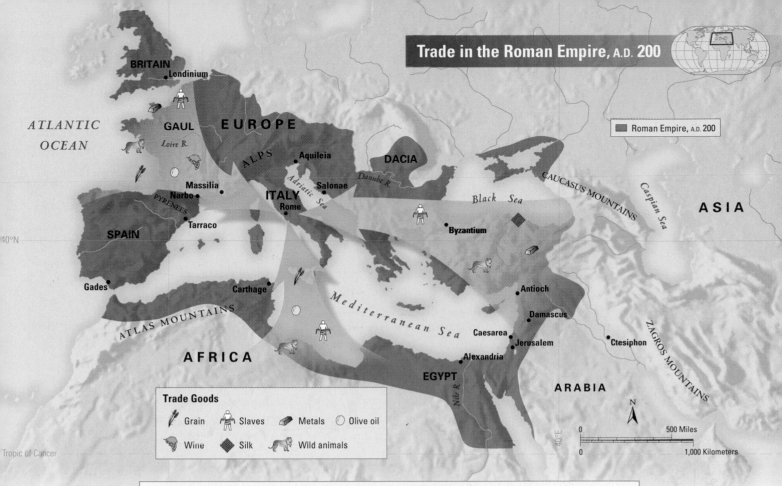

Roman Empire, A.D. 200

ATLANTIC OCEAN

BRITAIN
• Londinium

GAUL
EUROPE
Loire R.
ALPS
Aquileia
DACIA
Danube R.
CAUCASUS MOUNTAINS
Caspian Sea
ASIA

Massilia
Salonae
Adriatic Sea
ITALY
Rome
Black Sea
Byzantium

Narbo
PYRENEES
40°N
Tarraco
SPAIN

Gades
Carthage
Mediterranean Sea
Antioch
Damascus
Caesarea
Jerusalem
Ctesiphon
ZAGROS MOUNTAINS

ATLAS MOUNTAINS

AFRICA
Alexandria
EGYPT
Nile R.
ARABIA

Tropic of Cancer

Trade Goods

| Grain | Slaves | Metals | Olive oil |
| Wine | Silk | Wild animals | |

N

0   500 Miles
0   1,000 Kilometers

GEOGRAPHY SKILLBUILDER: Interpreting Maps
1. **Movement** *From what three continents did trade goods come to Rome?*
2. **Location** *Which goods were supplied by all three areas?*

Managing a Huge Empire The borders of the Roman Empire measured some 10,000 miles. By the second century A.D., the empire reached from Spain to Mesopotamia, from North Africa to Britain. Included in its provinces were people of many languages, cultures, and customs.

THINK THROUGH HISTORY
C. Summarizing
Summarize how Roman culture spread to the provinces.

The Roman army drew upon the men of the provinces as auxiliary, or support, forces. They were not citizens of Rome. But they learned Roman customs and became citizens when they were discharged from military service. In this way, the army also spread the Roman way of life to the provinces and Roman rights to non-Romans.

A Sound Government Augustus was Rome's ablest emperor. He stabilized the frontier, glorified Rome with splendid public buildings, and created a system of government that survived for centuries. He set up a civil service. That is, he paid workers to manage the affairs of government, such as the grain supply, tax collection, and the postal system. Although the senate still functioned, civil servants drawn from plebeians and even former slaves actually administered the empire.

Vocabulary
civil service: persons employed in the civil administration of government

After Augustus died in A.D. 14, the senate chose his adopted son Tiberius as his successor. During the *Pax Romana*, some of Rome's emperors were able and intelligent. Some were cruel. Two, Caligula and Nero, were either insane or unstable. Yet the system of government set up by Augustus proved to be stable. This was due mainly to the effectiveness of the civil service in carrying out day-to-day operations.

The Emperors and Succession Rome's peace and prosperity depended upon the orderly transfer of power. Because Rome had no written law for selecting a new emperor, a crisis or a civil war was always a possibility when an emperor died. The succession problem was temporarily solved by the leaders known as the Five Good Emperors. Beginning with Nerva in A.D. 96, each of them adopted as his heir a

Ancient Rome and Early Christianity **149**

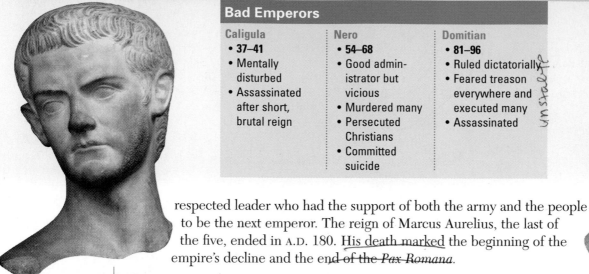

Bad Emperors

Caligula	Nero	Domitian
• 37–41	• 54–68	• 81–96
• Mentally disturbed	• Good administrator but vicious	• Ruled dictatorially
• Assassinated after short, brutal reign	• Murdered many	• Feared treason everywhere and executed many
	• Persecuted Christians	• Assassinated
	• Committed suicide	

unstable

respected leader who had the support of both the army and the people to be the next emperor. The reign of Marcus Aurelius, the last of the five, ended in A.D. 180. His death marked the beginning of the empire's decline and the end of the *Pax Romana*.

Caligula

Nero

Life in Imperial Rome

Merchants, soldiers, slaves, foreigners, and philosophers all shared the crowded, noisy streets of Rome. However, most people in the Roman Empire did not live in the cities and towns. They lived in the countryside and worked on farms. For all Romans, life changed as Rome moved from republic to empire.

power / grace

Men and Women Throughout its history, Rome emphasized the values of discipline, strength, and loyalty. A person with these qualities was said to have the important virtue of *gravitas*. The Romans were a practical people. They honored strength more than beauty, power more than grace, and usefulness more than elegance.

At the heart of Roman society was the family. By law and custom, the eldest man, known as the paterfamilias, or "father of the family," had power to rule the household. He controlled all property and had authority over all family members. He could disown newborn children, banish family members, or even sell them into slavery.

By the time of the empire's establishment, Roman women, both rich and poor, had become nearly the social equals of men. Upper-class women ran the household and were given authority and respect. They had more personal freedom than the women of Greece and than most women would have until the 19th century. Roman women could own property and testify in court. However, they could not vote. Officially they were expected to remain in the background. But they frequently attended the public baths (where most Romans went to bathe), plays, festivals, and games. Lower-class women could work at such jobs as spinners, weavers, shopkeepers, midwives, entertainers, and waitresses.

Vocabulary
gravitas: Latin for weightiness.

This Roman husband and wife from first-century Pompeii show their pride at being able to read and write. Their portrait includes writing implements and a scroll.

boy 9/11/15

Children and Education Romans favored boy children over girls. Boys would become citizens with the right to vote and would carry on family traditions. Girls were not even given their own names. Daughters received the feminine form of the father's name, with "the elder" or "the younger" or a number added, such as Octavia II.

Few children went to school. Those who did were usually boys from noble or wealthy families. Their schooling continued until they officially became adults at 16. Girls from these families most

Good Emperors

Trajan

Nerva	Trajan	Hadrian	Antoninus Pius	Marcus Aurelius
• 96–98	• 98–117	• 117–138	• 138–161	• 161–180
• Began custom of adopting heir	• Empire reached its greatest extent • Undertook vast building program • Enlarged social welfare	• Consolidated earlier conquests • Reorganized the bureaucracy	• Reign largely a period of peace and prosperity	• Brought empire to height of economic prosperity • Defeated invaders • Wrote philosophy

THINK THROUGH HISTORY
D. Contrasting How did the lives of Roman girls differ from those of boys?

often were educated at home and were prepared for marriage and motherhood. They were usually married at the age of 12 to 15, to much older husbands. MISTRESS

Poor children, whether they lived in the city or on a farm, had to work. They did not go to school and generally remained illiterate.

Slaves and Captivity Slavery was a significant part of Roman life. It was widespread and important to the economy. The Romans made more use of slaves than any previous civilization. Numbers of slaves may have reached as high as one-third of the population.

Most slaves were conquered peoples brought back by victorious Roman armies and included men, women, and children. Children born to slaves also became slaves. Slaves could be bought and sold. According to Roman law, slaves were the property of their owner. They could be punished, rewarded, set free, or put to death as their master saw fit. Slaves worked both in the city and on the farm. Many were treated cruelly and worked at hard labor all day long. Some—strong, healthy males—were forced to become **gladiators,** or professional fighters, who fought to the death in public contests. Other slaves, particularly those who worked in wealthy households, were better treated.

Occasionally, slaves would rebel. None of the slave revolts succeeded. More than a million slaves lost their lives attempting to gain their freedom.

Gods and Goddesses The earliest Romans worshipped powerful spirits or divine forces, called *numina,* that they thought resided in everything around them. Closely related to these spirits were the Lares (LAIR·eez), who were the guardian spirits of each family. After the Romans came into contact with Etruscans and Greeks, they began to think of these powerful spirits as having humanlike forms and individual personalities. They were given Roman names. Romans honored these powerful gods and goddesses through various rituals, hoping to gain favor and avoid misfortune.

In Rome, government and religion were linked. The deities were symbols of the state. Romans were expected to honor them not only in private rituals at shrines in their homes but also in public worship ceremonies conducted by priests in temples. Among the most important Roman gods and goddesses were Jupiter, father of the gods; Juno, his wife, who supposedly watched over women; and Minerva, goddess of wisdom and of the arts and crafts. During the empire, worship of the emperor also became part of the official religion of Rome.

By A.D. 100, many Romans had become interested in the religions of Asia. These religions had practices and beliefs that were more personal and emotional than the somber rituals connected with Rome's deities.

"Bread and Circuses"—Food and Entertainment By the time of the empire, wealth and social status had made huge differences in how people lived. Classes had little in common. The rich lived extravagantly. They spent large sums of money on homes, gardens, slaves, and luxuries. They gave banquets that lasted for many hours and included foods that were rare and costly, such as boiled ostrich and parrot-tongue pie.

Ancient Rome and Early Christianity **151**

Charioteers race their chariots in this ancient wall painting from Pompeii.

CONNECT *to* TODAY

Charioteers—Professional Athletes

Professional athletes are well-known personalities in the United States. In addition to the large salaries paid by their teams, athletes earn extra money endorsing products from athletic shoes to fast food. Some athletes even become actors; a few have become politicians.

Charioteers were popular athletes in ancient Rome. They were usually slaves or freed slaves. They raced for one of four "factions" (something like a modern team)—the whites, greens, reds, or blues. They competed for large cash prizes. When a charioteer won a big race, his portrait would appear on walls all over the city.

However, most people in Rome barely had the necessities of life. During the time of the empire, much of the city's population was unemployed. The government supported these people with daily rations of grain. In the shadow of Rome's great temples and public buildings, poor people crowded into rickety, sprawling tenements. Fire was a constant danger.

To distract and control the masses of Romans, the government provided free games, races, mock battles, and gladiator contests. By A.D. 250, there were 150 holidays a year. On these days of celebration, the Colosseum, a huge arena that could hold 50,000, would fill with the rich and the poor alike. The spectacles they watched combined bravery and cruelty, honor and violence. In the animal shows, wild creatures brought from distant lands, such as tigers, lions, and bears, fought to the death. In other contests, gladiators engaged in combat with animals or with each other, often until one of them was killed.

The *Pax Romana* had brought 200 years of peace and prosperity to Rome. During this time, a new religion called Christianity developed and began to spread throughout the empire.

Hunger Games

Background
Many Roman cities had arenas similar to the Colosseum that were used for public entertainment.

Section 2 Assessment

1. TERMS & NAMES

Identify
- civil war
- Julius Caesar
- triumvirate
- absolute ruler
- Augustus
- *Pax Romana*
- gladiator

2. TAKING NOTES

Make a bulleted chart like the one below, showing how Rome changed during the *Pax Romana*.

Changes in Rome
•
•
•

Which changes do you consider negative? Why?

3. ANALYZING CAUSES

What role did Julius Caesar play in the decline of the republic and the rise of the empire?

THINK ABOUT
- the problems facing the republic
- how Caesar helped restore order
- Caesar's defiance of the senate
- Caesar's rule as dictator

4. THEME ACTIVITY

Empire Building Role-play a discussion in the Roman Forum, in which various members of society comment on conditions in the Roman Empire during the *Pax Romana*. Participants might include a senator, a civil servant, a slave, a merchant, and a landless and jobless former soldier. Working in small teams, one for each participant, focus on the changes that have come with the rise of the empire.

The Rise of Christianity

TERMS & NAMES
- **Jesus**
- **apostle**
- **Peter**
- **Paul**
- **Diaspora**
- **bishop**
- **pope**
- **Constantine**
- **heresy**

MAIN IDEA

Christianity arose in Roman-occupied Judea and spread throughout the Roman Empire.

WHY IT MATTERS NOW

As the world's most widespread religion, Christianity guides the lives of millions today.

SETTING THE STAGE The worship of Roman gods was impersonal, practiced without a great deal of emotion. Priests used sacred rites to intercede on behalf of worshippers. A new religion called Christianity, born as a movement within Judaism, emphasized the personal relationship between God and people. It attracted many Romans.

Jews Come Under Roman Rule

Roman power spread to Judea, the home of the Jews, around 63 B.C. At first the Jewish kingdom remained independent, at least in name. Jewish kings ruled as representatives of Rome. Some Jews allied with the Romans and accepted their plans to "Romanize" Jerusalem. The ruler Herod, for example, was a Romanized Jew. His loyalties were divided between Rome and the Jewish people, but he ruled with an iron hand and angered many Jews. When he died, the Jews began a revolt against Roman influence that lasted for ten years. Rome finally took control of the Jewish kingdom and made it the province of Judea in A.D. 6.

In an attempt to restore order in Judea, the Romans gave control of religious matters and local affairs to the Jewish court called the Sanhedrin. Jews were divided into two major factions. One group, called the Zealots, wanted to rid their homeland of the Romans. Another group believed that the Messiah, or savior, was soon to appear. According to biblical tradition, God had promised that the Messiah would restore the kingdom of the Jews.

Vocabulary
Zealot: has come to mean a fanatically committed person.

The Life and Teachings of Jesus

Jesus was born in the town of Bethlehem in Judea. The date is uncertain but is thought to have been around 6 to 4 B.C. Jesus was both a Jew and a Roman subject. He was raised in the village of Nazareth in northern Palestine. Jesus was baptized by the prophet known as John the Baptist. As a young man, he took up the trade of carpentry.

Background
The original dating of the birth of Jesus made in the sixth century A.D. is now generally recognized as being four to six years in error.

Jesus' Message At the age of 30 Jesus began his public ministry. For the next three years, he preached, taught, did good works, and reportedly performed miracles. His teachings contained many ideas from Jewish tradition, such as monotheism, or belief in only one god, and the principles of the Ten Commandments. Jesus emphasized God's personal relationship to each human being. He stressed the importance of people's love for God, their neighbors, their enemies, and even themselves. He also taught that God would end wickedness in the world and would establish an eternal kingdom after death for people who sincerely repented their sins.

Jesus gathered about himself twelve special disciples, or pupils. Historical records of the time mention very little about Jesus. The main source of information about Jesus' life and teachings are the Gospels, the first four books of the New Testament of the Bible. Some of the Gospels are thought to have been written by one or more of Jesus' disciples, who later came to be called **apostles**.

Vocabulary
Gospel: means good news.

The cross became the universal symbol of Christianity. This jewel-studded cross was made by a goldsmith centuries after the death of Jesus.

Jesus is portrayed in this glass mosaic from the fifth century as "the good shepherd," tending his flock, watching over the faithful.

As Jesus preached from town to town, his fame grew. He attracted large crowds, and many people were touched by his message. Many believed him to be the long-awaited Messiah, the son of God. Because Jesus ignored wealth and status, his message had special appeal to the poor. "Blessed are the meek: for they shall inherit the earth," he said. His words, as related in the Gospels, are simple and direct:

> Love your enemies, do good to those who hate you, bless those who curse you, and pray for those who mistreat you. If anyone hits you on the cheek, let him hit the other one too; if someone takes your coat, let him have your shirt as well. Give to everyone who asks you for something, and when someone takes what is yours, do not ask for it back. Do for others just what you want them to do for you.
>
> The Gospel of Luke, 6:27–31

THINK THROUGH HISTORY
A. Hypothesizing
Why did the followers of Jesus think he was the Messiah?

Jesus' Death Jesus' growing popularity concerned both Roman and Jewish leaders. When Jesus visited Jerusalem about A.D. 29, enthusiastic crowds greeted him as the Messiah, or king. The chief priests of the Jews denied that Jesus was the Messiah. They said his teachings were blasphemy, or contempt for God. The Roman governor Pontius Pilate thought that Jesus, whom the Romans mockingly called "King of the Jews," challenged the authority of Rome. Pilate arrested Jesus and sentenced him to be crucified, or nailed to a large wooden cross to die.

After Jesus' death, his body was placed in a tomb. According to the Gospels, three days later his body was gone, and a living Jesus began appearing to his followers. Then one day it was said that he ascended into heaven. The apostles were more than ever convinced that Jesus was the Messiah. It was from this belief that Jesus came to be referred to as Jesus Christ. *Christos* is a Greek word meaning "messiah" or "savior." The name Christianity was derived from "Christ."

The followers of Jesus were strengthened by their conviction that he had triumphed over death. Led by **Peter,** the first apostle, they spread the teachings of Jesus throughout Palestine and Syria. The cross on which he had been crucified became a symbol for their beliefs.

Christianity Spreads Through the Empire

Jesus' teachings did not contradict Jewish law, and his first followers were Jews. Soon, however, these followers began to create a new religion based on his messages. Despite political and religious opposition, the new religion of Christianity spread slowly but steadily throughout the Roman Empire.

Paul's Mission One man, the apostle **Paul**, had enormous influence on Christianity's development. Paul was a Jew whose Hebrew name was Saul. He had never met Jesus and at first was an enemy of Christianity. While traveling to Damascus in Syria, he reportedly had a vision of Christ. He then began using his Roman name, Paul, and spent the rest of his life spreading and interpreting Christ's teachings.

The *Pax Romana*, which made travel and the exchange of ideas fairly safe, provided the ideal conditions for Christianity to spread. The excellent Roman road system made passage by land easy, and common languages—Latin and Greek—allowed the message to be easily understood. Paul was able to travel freely from city to city around the eastern Mediterranean to preach. He wrote influential letters, called Epistles, to groups of believers. In his teaching, Paul stressed that Jesus was the son of God who died for people's sins. He also declared that Christianity should welcome all converts, Jew or Gentile (non-Jew). He said: "There is neither Jew nor Greek, there is neither slave nor free, there is neither male nor female; for you are all one in Christ Jesus." It was this universality that enabled Christianity to become more than just a local religion.

THINK THROUGH HISTORY
B. Recognizing Effects How did conditions in the Roman Empire contribute to the spread of Christianity?

Jewish Rebellion During the early years of Christianity, much Roman attention was focused on the land of Jesus' birth and on the Jews. In A.D. 66, a band of Zealots rebelled against Rome. In A.D. 70, the Romans stormed Jerusalem and destroyed the Temple complex. All that remained was a western portion of the wall, which today is the holiest Jewish shrine. The Jewish fortress near Masada held out until A.D. 73. About a half million Jews were killed in the course of this rebellion.

The Jews made another attempt to break free of the Romans in A.D. 132. Another half-million Jews died in three years of fighting. Although the Jewish religion survived, the Jewish political state ceased to exist for more than 1,800 years. Most Jews were driven from their homeland into exile. This dispersal of the Jews is called the **Diaspora.**

Persecution of the Christians Christians also posed a problem for Roman rulers because Christians refused to worship Roman gods. This refusal was seen as opposition to Roman rule. Some Roman rulers also used Christians as scapegoats for political and economic troubles. In A.D. 64, for example, when the emperor Nero was blamed for a disastrous fire in Rome, he said Christians were responsible and ordered them to be persecuted. Both the apostles Peter and Paul were put to death in Rome sometime after A.D. 60.

Vocabulary
scapegoats: groups or individuals that innocently bear the blame for others

The emperors who followed Nero in the first century did not continue the persecutions. Later, however, as the *Pax Romana* began to crumble, the Romans exiled, imprisoned, or executed Christians for refusing to worship Roman gods. Thousands were crucified, burned, or killed by wild animals in the circus arenas. Other Christians and even some non-Christians regarded persecuted Christians as martyrs. Martyrs were people willing to sacrifice their lives for the sake of a belief or a cause.

Despite persecution, Christianity became a powerful religious force. By the late third century A.D., there were millions of Christians in the Roman Empire. Missionaries spread the faith throughout the empire and beyond.

GlobalImpact

The Jewish Diaspora

Centuries of Jewish exile followed the destruction of their Temple and the fall of Jerusalem in A.D. 70. This period is called the Diaspora, from the Greek word for "dispersal." Jews fled to many parts of the world. Some moved to Babylonia and the Arabian Desert. Others went to Syria, Egypt, and Spain.

Eventually, Jews spread into France, England, and the Rhineland, where they lived in small groups. In the 1100s, many European Jews were expelled from their homes. Some moved to Turkey, Palestine, and Syria. Others went to Poland and nearby neighboring areas.

The statelessness of the Jews did not end until the creation of Israel in 1948.

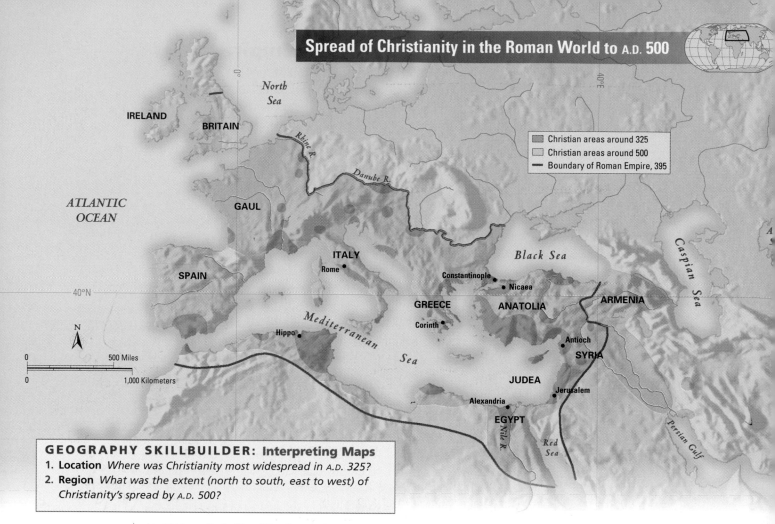

Spread of Christianity in the Roman World to A.D. 500

North
Sea

IRELAND

BRITAIN

Rhine R.

Danube R.

ATLANTIC
OCEAN

GAUL

- Christian areas around 325
- Christian areas around 500
- Boundary of Roman Empire, 395

Black Sea

ITALY
Rome •

Constantinople •
• Nicaea

SPAIN

Caspian Sea

ARMENIA

40°N

GREECE

ANATOLIA

Mediterranean

Corinth •

Hippo •

Sea

Antioch •

SYRIA

N

0   500 Miles

0   1,000 Kilometers

JUDEA

Jerusalem •

Alexandria •

EGYPT

Nile R.

*Red
Sea*

Persian Gulf

GEOGRAPHY SKILLBUILDER: Interpreting Maps
1. **Location** *Where was Christianity most widespread in* A.D. *325?*
2. **Region** *What was the extent (north to south, east to west) of
Christianity's spread by* A.D. *500?*

A World Religion

The widespread appeal of Christianity was the result of a variety of reasons.
Christianity grew because it:

- embraced all people—men and women; slaves, the poor, and nobles.
- gave hope to the powerless.
- appealed to those who were repelled by the extravagances of imperial Rome.
- offered a personal relationship with a loving God.
- promised eternal life after death.

Early Christian Church Christians soon began to give their religion a structure,
much as the Roman Empire had a hierarchy. At the local level, a priest led each small
group of Christians. A **bishop,** who was also a priest, supervised several local
churches. The apostle Peter had traveled to Rome from Jerusalem and became the
first bishop there. According to tradition, Jesus referred to Peter as the "rock" on
which the Christian Church would be built. As a result, all priests and bishops traced
their authority to him.

Eventually, every major city had its own bishop. However, later bishops of Rome
claimed to be the heirs of Peter. These bishops said that Peter was the first **pope,** the
father or head of the Christian Church. They said that whoever was bishop of Rome
was also the leader of the whole Church. Also, as Rome was the capital of the empire,
it seemed the logical choice to be the center of the Church.

Constantine Accepts Christianity A critical moment in Christianity occurred in A.D.
312, when the Roman emperor **Constantine** was fighting three rivals for his title. He
had marched to the Tiber River at Rome to battle his chief rival. On the day before the
battle at Milvian Bridge, Constantine prayed for divine help. He reported that he then

THINK THROUGH HISTORY
**C. Making
Inferences** Why
were the citizens of
the Roman Empire so
receptive to a new
religion at this time?

Vocabulary
hierarchy: a group of
persons organized in
order of ranks, with
each level subject to
the authority of the
one above.

saw a cross of light in the heavens bearing the inscription, "In this sign, conquer." Constantine ordered artisans to put the Christian symbol on his soldier's shields. Constantine and his troops were victorious in battle. He gave credit for his success to the help of the Christian God.

In the next year, A.D. 313, Constantine announced an end to the persecution of Christians. In the Edict of Milan, he declared Christianity to be one of the religions approved by the emperor. The edict granted "both to the Christians and to all men freedom to follow the religion that they choose." Christianity continued to gain strength. In 380, the emperor Theodosius made it the empire's official religion.

Vocabulary
edict: decree or proclamation.

Discord and Harmony As Christianity grew, disagreements about beliefs developed among its followers. Church leaders called any belief that appeared to contradict the basic teachings a **heresy.** Dispute over beliefs became intense. In an attempt to end conflicts, Church leaders sought to set a single, official standard of belief. These beliefs were compiled in the New Testament, which contained the four Gospels, the Epistles of Paul, and other documents. In A.D. 325, Constantine decided to end the disputes and the disorder they caused. He called Church leaders to Nicaea in Anatolia. There they wrote the Nicene Creed, which defined the basic beliefs of the Church.

DECLARATION

Background
The New Testament was added to the Hebrew Bible, which Christians called the Old Testament.

The Fathers of the Church Also influential in defining Church teachings were several early writers and scholars who have been called the Fathers of the Church. One of the most important was Augustine, who became bishop of the city of Hippo in North Africa in 396. Augustine taught that while humans needed the grace of God to be saved, God was merciful and gave his grace freely.

One of Augustine's most famous books is *The City of God.* It was written after Rome was plundered in the fifth century. Augustine wrote that the fate of cities such as Rome was not important because the heavenly city, the city of God, could never be destroyed:

Constantine
A.D. 285?–337

Constantine was a deeply religious man. He initially believed in the traditional Roman gods. He identified with the god Apollo, whom he claimed to have seen in a vision.

Sometime after his conversion to Christianity in A.D. 312, Constantine reportedly remarked that "God is the cause of the exploits I have performed." He maintained that he received revelations and instructions from God.

Although he legalized Christianity throughout the empire and took a leading role in the affairs of the Christian Church, Constantine was not formally baptized until he was on his deathbed in 337.

THINK THROUGH HISTORY
D. Analyzing Motives What do you think was St. Augustine's motive for writing *The City of God* right after Rome had been attacked?

A VOICE FROM THE PAST
The one consists of those who live by human standards, the other of those who live according to God's will. . . . By two cities I mean two societies of human beings, one of which is predestined to reign with God for all eternity, the other is doomed to undergo eternal punishment with the Devil.
ST. AUGUSTINE, *The City of God*

Christianity increased in both power and wealth despite the empire's growing internal and external problems.

Section ❸ Assessment

1. TERMS & NAMES

Identify
- Jesus
- apostle
- Peter
- Paul
- Diaspora
- bishop
- pope
- Constantine
- heresy

2. TAKING NOTES

Using a sequence graphic like the one below, show the five or six events that led to the spread of Christianity throughout the Roman Empire.

Rome takes over Jewish kingdom.

Which event do you think had the biggest impact? Explain.

3. HYPOTHESIZING

Do you think Christianity would have developed in the same way if it had arisen in an area outside the Roman Empire? Explain.

THINK ABOUT
- Jesus' growing popularity
- the effect of actions Rome took against Jesus and his followers
- the depth of belief of Jesus' followers
- the advantages of being part of a vast empire

4. ANALYZING THEMES

Religious and Ethical Systems Who do you think did more to spread Christianity—Paul or Constantine?

THINK ABOUT
- Paul's travels
- the opening of Christianity to the Gentiles
- Constantine's power as an emperor

4 The Decline of the Roman Empire

TERMS & NAMES
- inflation
- mercenary
- Diocletian
- Constantinople
- Alaric
- Attila

MAIN IDEA

Internal problems and nomadic invasions spurred the division and decline of the Roman empire.

WHY IT MATTERS NOW

The decline and fall of great civilizations is a repeating pattern in world history.

SETTING THE STAGE In the third century A.D., Rome faced many problems. They came both from within the empire and from outside. Drastic economic, military, and political reforms would be needed to hold off collapse.

A Century of Crisis

Historians generally agree that the Roman Empire began its decline at the end of the reign of the last of the Five Good Emperors, Marcus Aurelius (A.D. 161–180). The rulers that followed in the next century had little or no idea of how to deal with the problems facing the empire. Most, like Aurelius' son Commodus, were brutal and incompetent. They left the empire greatly weakened.

Rome's Economy Declines During the *Pax Romana,* bustling trade flowed over routes patrolled by Roman legions and ships. Rome's treasuries were enriched by gold and silver taken from conquered territories. Most important of all, the empire's farms grew enough grain to feed the population of the cities. During the third century A.D., all three sources of prosperity evaporated.

Hostile tribes outside the boundaries of the empire and pirates on the Mediterranean Sea disrupted trade. Frequent wars were costly. The wealthy spent money on luxury goods from China, India, and Arabia. This spending drained the empire of gold and silver. Since the empire's expansion had come to an end, there were no new sources of precious metals.

Desperate to pay its mounting expenses, including the rising cost of defense, the government raised taxes. It also started minting coins that contained less and less silver. It hoped to create more money with the same amount of precious metal. However, the economy soon suffered from **inflation,** a drastic drop in the value of money coupled with a rise in prices.

Agriculture faced equally serious problems. Harvests in Italy and western Europe became increasingly meager because overworked soil had lost its fertility. Farmland was destroyed by warfare. The higher taxes imposed by the government caused many poor farmers to abandon their lands. The use of cheap slave labor had discouraged improvements in technology. Serious food shortages resulted for all these reasons. Eventually, disease spread and the population declined.

Rome Faces Military Upheaval The empire's economic crisis was worsened by its growing military troubles. Throughout the third century, Germanic tribes repeatedly overwhelmed the Roman legions guarding the northern frontiers. At the same time, Persia threatened Roman territory in Syria and Anatolia. (Romans

This Roman road, still in use in Manchester, England, was part of a 53,000-mile network of paved roads that connected the far-flung empire.

THINK THROUGH HISTORY
A. Analyzing Causes What caused the weakening of the Roman economy?

158 Chapter 6

called all invaders "barbarians," a term that they used to refer to non-Romans.) Rome's most humiliating defeat occurred in A.D. 260, when the Persians captured the emperor Valerian.

In the army, discipline and loyalty had collapsed. Soldiers gave their loyalty not to Rome but to their commanders, who fought among themselves for the throne. To defend against the increasing threats to the empire, the government began to recruit **mercenaries,** foreign soldiers who fought for money. While mercenaries would accept lower pay than Romans, they felt little sense of loyalty to the empire.

Roman Politics Decay Loyalty was in fact a key problem, perhaps the most serious of all. In the past, Romans cared so deeply about their republic that they willingly sacrificed their lives for it. Conditions in the later centuries of the empire caused citizens to lose their sense of patriotism. They became indifferent to the empire's fate.

Romans had once considered holding political office to be an honor. It was also an opportunity to gain wealth. By the 200s, however, local officials usually lost money because they were required to pay for the costly public circuses and baths out of their own pockets. Few people chose to serve the government under those conditions.

Only the armies remained actively interested in politics. In a 50-year period (A.D. 235–284), armies in the provinces and in Rome proclaimed 50 generals to be emperors of Rome. Of these "barracks emperors," 26 briefly won the approval of the Roman senate; 25 died violently.

Emperors Attempt Reform

Remarkably, the empire survived intact for another 200 years. Its life was prolonged by reforming emperors and by its division into two parts: eastern and western.

Diocletian Reforms the Empire In A.D. 284, **Diocletian,** a strong-willed army leader, became the new emperor. With amazing boldness, he restored order in the empire and increased its strength. To accomplish this, he governed as an absolute ruler and severely limited personal freedoms.

Diocletian doubled the size of the Roman armies, drafting prisoners of war and hiring German mercenaries. He attempted to control inflation by setting fixed prices for goods. He also ordered farmers to remain on their lands and other workers to stay in their jobs for life. To restore the prestige of the office of emperor, Diocletian claimed descent from the ancient Roman gods. He viewed Christianity as a threat and passed decrees to persecute the Christians.

Diocletian believed that the empire had grown too large and too complex for one ruler. In his most significant reform, he divided the empire into the Greek-speaking East (Greece, Anatolia, Syria, and Egypt) and the Latin-speaking West (Italy, Gaul, Britannia, and Spain). He took the eastern half for himself and appointed a co-ruler for the West, General Maximian. Each emperor also selected an assistant, who was to be his successor. While Diocletian shared authority, he kept overall control. His half of the empire, the East, included most of the empire's great cities and trade centers and was far wealthier than the West.

Diocletian's reforms slowed the decline of the empire. The borders became safe again, and the emperor's prestige was restored. Because of ill health, Diocletian took the extraordinary step of retiring in A.D. 305.

However, his plans for orderly succession failed. Civil war broke out immediately. By 311, four rivals were competing for power.

THINK THROUGH HISTORY
B. Supporting Opinions Do you think Diocletian was a good emperor?

HISTORY MAKERS

Diocletian
A.D. 245?–313

Diocletian, who may have been born the son of a slave in the province of Dalmatia, raised the office of emperor to a form of divine monarch. He declared himself to be a son of Jupiter, the father of the gods. He devised elaborate ceremonies to present himself in a godlike aura.

When he appeared in public, trumpets heralded his entrance. Anyone who approached the imperial presence had to kneel and kiss the hem of the his robe. He had his clothing and shoes decorated with precious gems. By his actions, Diocletian sought to restore the dignity of the emperor. He also hoped to give himself greater security by making assassination appear to be a crime against the gods.

Among them was an ambitious young commander named Constantine, the same Constantine who would later end the persecution of Christians.

Constantine Moves the Capital Constantine gained control of the western part of the empire in A.D. 312 and continued many of the social and economic policies of Diocletian. In 324 Constantine also secured control of the East, thus restoring the concept of a single ruler.

In A.D. 330, Constantine took a step that would have great consequence for the empire. He moved the capital from Rome to the Greek city of Byzantium (bih·ZAN·shee·uhm), in what is now Turkey. The new capital stood on the Bosporus Strait, strategically located for trade and defense purposes on a crossroads between West and East.

With Byzantium as its capital, the center of power in the empire shifted from Rome to the East. Soon the new capital was protected by massive walls and filled with imperial buildings modeled after those in Rome. The city was given a new name— **Constantinople** (KAHN·stan·tuhn·OH·puhl), city of Constantine. After Constantine's death, the empire would again be divided. The East would survive; the West would fall.

THINK THROUGH HISTORY
C. Analyzing Motives Why did Constantine choose the location of Byzantium for his new capital?

Invaders Overrun the Western Empire

The decline of the Western Roman Empire took place over many years. Its final collapse was the result of worsening internal problems, the separation of the Western Empire from the wealthier Eastern part, and outside invasions.

Since the days of Julius Caesar, Germanic peoples had gathered on the northern borders of the Empire. Some groups settled into a peaceful farming life. Eventually they adopted Roman ways, such as speaking Latin and becoming Christians. Other groups remained nomads. From A.D. 376 to 476, huge numbers of Germans poured

Multiple Causes: Fall of the Western Roman Empire

Contributing Factors

Political	Social	Economic	Military
• Political office seen as burden, not reward	• Decline in interest in public affairs	• Poor harvests	• Threat from northern European tribes
• Military interference in politics	• Low confidence in empire	• Disruption of trade	• Low funds for defense
• Civil war and unrest	• Disloyalty, lack of patriotism, corruption	• No more war plunder	• Problems recruiting Roman citizens; recruiting of non-Romans
• Division of empire	• Contrast between rich and poor	• Gold and silver drain	
• Moving of capital to Byzantium		• Inflation	• Decline of patriotism and loyalty among soldiers
		• Crushing tax burden	
		• Widening gap between rich and poor and increasingly impoverished Western empire	

Immediate Causes

• Pressure from Huns	• Invasion by Germanic tribes and by Huns	• Sack of Rome	• Conquest by invaders

FALL OF ROMAN EMPIRE

SKILLBUILDER: Interpreting Charts
1. *Could changes in any contributing factors have reversed the decline of the empire?*
2. *Which contributing factors—political, economic, or military—were the most significant in the fall of the Western Roman Empire?*

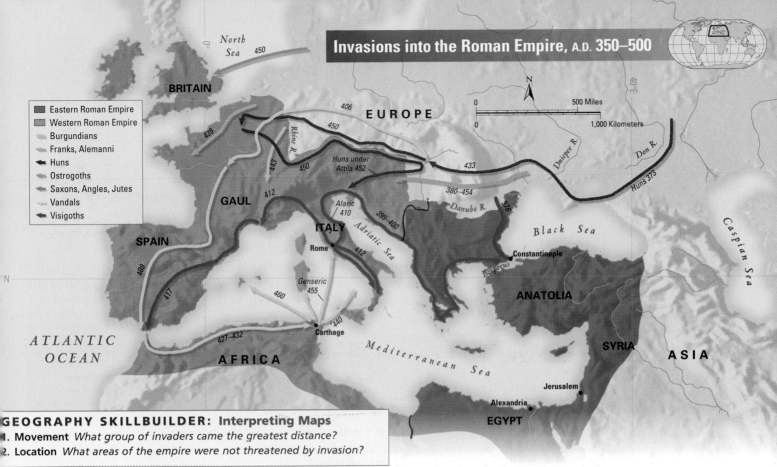

Invasions into the Roman Empire, A.D. 350–500

Eastern Roman Empire
Western Roman Empire
Burgundians
Franks, Alemanni
Huns
Ostrogoths
Saxons, Angles, Jutes
Vandals
Visigoths

GEOGRAPHY SKILLBUILDER: Interpreting Maps
1. **Movement** *What group of invaders came the greatest distance?*
2. **Location** *What areas of the empire were not threatened by invasion?*

INVASION APOCOLYPSE

into Roman territory—Ostrogoths, Visigoths, Franks, Angles, Saxons, Burgundians, Alemanni, and Vandals. Gradually, they overwhelmed the structures of Roman society. Finally, they drove the last Roman emperor from the throne.

The Huns Move West The main reason for the Germanic invasions of the Empire was the movement into Europe of the Huns. The Huns were fierce Mongol nomads from central Asia. They began invading the frontier regions of the Rhine and Danube rivers around A.D. 370, destroying all in their path. The pressure from the Huns forced other groups to move as well—into the Roman Empire.

The following description from a fourth-century Roman historian shows how intensely the Huns were feared and scorned:

A VOICE FROM THE PAST
The nation of the Huns . . . surpasses all other barbarians in wildness of life. . . . And though [the Huns] do just bear the likeness of men (of a very ugly pattern), they are so little advanced in civilization that they . . . feed upon the . . . half-raw flesh of any sort of animal. . . . When attacked, . . . they fill the air with varied and discordant cries . . . they fight in no regular order of battle, but by being extremely swift and sudden in their movements, they disperse . . . spread havoc over vast plains, and . . . pillage the camp of their enemy almost before he has become aware of their approach.
AMMIANUS MARCELLINUS, *The Chronicle of Events (Rerum gestarum libri)*

Background
Most of the Germanic invaders were Christians.

Germanic Invasions Germanic people near the Rhine River—Franks, Burgundians, and Vandals—fled the invading Huns and sought refuge in Roman lands. When the Rhine River froze during an especially cold winter in 406, Vandal warriors and their families swarmed across the ice. They met little resistance and kept moving through the Roman province of Gaul. The Western Empire was now so disorganized that it was unable to field an army to stop them.

By the early fifth century, the city of Rome itself was vulnerable to attack. More than 600 years had passed since a foreign army, that of Hannibal, had threatened

Ancient Rome and Early Christianity **161**

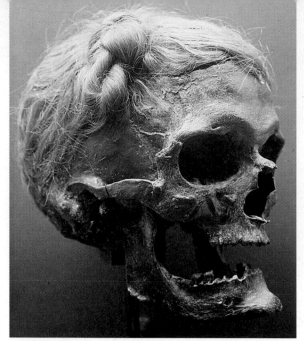

This skull from the period, still retaining its hair, shows a kind of topknot in the hair that some Germanic peoples fashioned to identify themselves.

Rome. Then in 408 Visigoths, led by their king, ~~Alaric~~ (AL·ur·ihk), marched across the Alps toward Rome. After putting the city under siege, hordes of Germans stormed Rome in 410 and plundered it for three days.

Attila the Hun Meanwhile, the Huns, who were indirectly responsible for the Germanic assault on the Empire, became a direct threat. In 444 they united for the first time under a powerful chieftain named **Attila** (AT·uhl·uh). With his 100,000 soldiers, Attila terrorized both halves of the empire. In the East, his armies attacked and plundered 70 cities. (They failed, however, to scale the high walls of Constantinople.)

The Huns then swept into the West. In A.D. 452, Attila's forces advanced against Rome, but they were weakened by famine and disease. As a result, Pope Leo I was able to negotiate their withdrawal. Although the Huns were no longer a threat to the empire after Attila's death in 453, the Germanic invasions continued. In 455 Vandals, under Gaiseric, sacked Rome, leaving it in chaos. Famine struck, and its population eventually dropped from about one million to 20,000.

Rome's Last Emperor The Roman emperor in the West had become practically powerless. Germanic tribes now fought one another for possession of the Western provinces. Spain belonged to the Visigoths, North Africa to the Vandals. Gaul was overrun by competing tribes—Franks, Burgundians, and Visigoths. Britannia was invaded by Angles and Saxons. Italy was falling victim to raids by the Ostrogoths.

The last Roman emperor was a 14-year-old boy named Romulus Augustulus. In 476 he was deposed by a German general named Odoacer (oh·doh·AY·sur) and sent into exile. After that, no emperor even pretended to rule Rome and its western provinces. Roman power in the western half of the Empire had disappeared.

The eastern half of the Empire, which came to be called the Byzantine Empire, not only survived but flourished. It preserved the great heritage of Greek and Roman culture for another 1,000 years. (See Chapter 11.) The Byzantine emperors ruled from Constantinople and saw themselves as heirs to the power of Augustus Caesar. The empire endured until 1453, when it fell to the Ottoman Turks.

Even though Rome's political power in the West ended, its cultural influence, through its ideas, customs, and institutions, continued to be deeply embedded in Western civilization.

THINK THROUGH HISTORY
D. Hypothesizing Do you think that Rome would have been taken by invaders if the Huns had not moved into the west?

Vocabulary
sacked: looted or plundered a captured city or town

Background
Vandals gave their name to the word for those who willfully destroy property.

Section 4 Assessment

1. TERMS & NAMES

Identify
• inflation
• mercenary
• Diocletian
• Constantinople
• Alaric
• Attila

2. TAKING NOTES

Identify the causes of each of the effects listed in the chart below.

Decline of the Roman Empire	
Effects	Causes
Inflation	
Untrustworthy army	
Decreased citizen interest in government	

How did these problems open the empire to invading peoples?

3. DRAWING CONCLUSIONS

How do you think the splitting of the empire into two parts helped it survive for another 200 years?

THINK ABOUT
• the differences between the eastern and western halves of the empire
• the advantages of a smaller empire

4. THEME ACTIVITY

Empire Building Imagine you are a journalist in the Roman Empire. Write an editorial in which you comment—favorably or unfavorably—on Constantine's decision to move the capital of the empire. Present the facts of the move, but focus the editorial on the effects you think the move will have on Rome and its citizens.

The Fall of the Roman Empire

Since the fifth century, historians and others have argued over the empire's fall. They have attributed it to a variety of causes, coming both from within and outside the empire. The following excerpts are examples of the differing opinions.

HISTORICAL COMMENTARY
Edward Gibbon

In the 1780s Gibbon published *The History of the Decline and Fall of the Roman Empire*. In this passage, Gibbon explains that a major cause of the collapse was that the empire was simply just too large.

The decline of Rome was the natural and inevitable effect of immoderate greatness. Prosperity ripened the principle of decay; the causes of destruction multiplied with the extent of conquest; and, as soon as time or accident had removed the artificial supports, the stupendous fabric yielded to the pressure of its own weight. The story of its ruin is simple and obvious; and instead of inquiring why the Roman Empire was destroyed, we should rather be surprised that it had subsisted so long.

HISTORICAL COMMENTARY
Arther Ferrill

In his book *The Fall of the Roman Empire* (1986), Arther Ferrill argues that the fall of Rome was a military collapse.

In fact the Roman Empire of the West did fall. Not every aspect of the life of Roman subjects was changed by that, but the fall of Rome as a political entity was one of the major events of the history of Western man. It will simply not do to call that fall a myth or to ignore its historical significance merely by focusing on those aspects of Roman life that survived the fall in one form or another. At the opening of the fifth century a massive army, perhaps more than 200,000 strong, stood at the service of the Western emperor and his generals. The destruction of Roman military power in the fifth century was the obvious cause of the collapse of Roman government in the West.

HISTORICAL COMMENTARY
Finley Hooper

In this passage from his *Roman Realities* (1967), Hooper argues against the idea of a "fall."

The year was 476. For those who demand to know the date Rome fell, that is it. Others will realize that the fall of Rome was not an event but a process. Or, to put it another way, there was no fall at all—ancient Roman civilization simply became something else, which is called medieval. [It evolved into another civilization, the civilization of the Middle Ages.]

EYEWITNESS ACCOUNT
St. Jerome

This early Church leader did not live to see the empire's end, but he vividly describes his feelings after a major event in Rome's decline—the attack and plunder of the city by Visigoths in 410. He said:

"It is the end of the world ... Words fail me. My sobs break in ... The city which took captive the whole world has itself been captured."

Connect *to* History

Comparing Compare the reasons given in these excerpts for the fall of Rome. Which seem the most valid to you? Why?

SEE SKILLBUILDER HANDBOOK, PAGE 996

Connect *to* Today

Comparing In 1991, the Union of Soviet Socialist Republics collapsed after nearly 70 years of existence. Research that fall and discuss one way in which the Soviet Union's decline can be compared to the fall of Rome.

 For more information about the fall of the Roman Empire, see the World History Electronic Library of Primary Sources.

TERMS & NAMES
- Greco-Roman culture
- Pompeii
- Virgil
- Tacitus
- aqueduct

MAIN IDEA

The Romans developed many ideas and institutions that became fundamental to Western civilization.

WHY IT MATTERS NOW

Evidence of Roman culture is found throughout Europe and North America and in Asia and Africa.

SETTING THE STAGE Romans borrowed and adapted cultural elements freely, especially from the Greek and Hellenistic cultures. Rome created a great civilization, whose art and architecture, language and literature, engineering, and law became its legacy to the world.

The Legacy of Greco-Roman Civilization

Under the Roman Empire, hundreds of territories were knitted into a single state. Each Roman province and city was governed in the same way. The Romans were proud of their ability to rule, but they acknowledged Greek leadership in the fields of art, architecture, literature, and philosophy.

By the second century B.C., Romans had conquered Greece and had come to greatly admire Greek culture. Educated Romans learned the Greek language. As Horace, a Roman poet said, "Greece, once overcome, overcame her wild conqueror." The mixing of elements of Greek, Hellenistic, and Roman culture produced a new culture, called **Greco-Roman culture.** This is also often called classical civilization.

Roman artists, philosophers, and writers did not merely copy their Greek and Hellenistic models. They adapted them for their own purposes and created a style of their own. Roman art and literature came to convey the Roman ideals of strength, permanence, solidity.

Roman Fine Arts Romans learned the art of sculpture from the Greeks. However, while the Greeks were known for the beauty and idealization of their sculpture, Roman sculptors created realistic portraits in stone. Much Roman art was practical in purpose, intended for public education.

The reign of Augustus was a period of great artistic achievement. At that time the Romans further developed a type of sculpture called bas-relief. In bas-relief, or low-relief, images project from a flat background. Roman sculptors used bas-relief to tell stories and to represent crowds of people, soldiers in battle, and landscapes. (See Trajan's Column on page 169.)

Roman artists were particularly skilled in creating mosaics. Mosaics were pictures or designs made by setting small pieces of stone, glass, or tile onto a surface. Most Roman villas, the country houses of the wealthy, had at least one colored mosaic.

THINK THROUGH HISTORY
A. Summarizing
What were the origins of Greco-Roman culture?

Gladiators and leopards fight to the death in this third-century mosaic.

Romans also excelled at the art of painting. Most wealthy Romans had bright, large murals, called frescoes, painted directly on their walls. Few have survived. The best examples of Roman painting are found in the Roman town of **Pompeii,** and date from as early as the second century B.C. In A.D. 79, Mount Vesuvius erupted, covering Pompeii in a thick layer of ash and killing about 2,000. The ash acted to preserve many buildings and works of art.

Learning and Literature Romans borrowed much of their philosophy from the Greeks. Stoicism, the philosophy of the Greek teacher Zeno, was especially influential. Stoicism encouraged virtue, duty, moderation, and endurance. One of the most noted Stoics was the emperor Marcus Aurelius. His steadfastness is shown in his *Meditations:* "In the midst of it all, you must take your stand, good-temperedly and without disdain."

In literature, as in philosophy, the Romans found inspiration in the works of the Greeks. Writers used Roman themes and ideas while following Greek forms and models.

The poet **Virgil** spent ten years writing the most famous work of Latin literature, the *Aeneid* (ih·NEE·ihd), the epic of the legendary Aeneas. Virgil modeled the *Aeneid*, written in praise of Rome and Roman virtues, after the Greek epics of Homer. Here he speaks of government as being Rome's most important contribution to civilization:

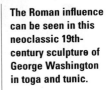

THINK THROUGH HISTORY
B. Supporting Opinions What is your opinion of Virgil's statement that government was Rome's most important contribution to civilization? Support your opinion.

A VOICE FROM THE PAST
. . . Romans, never forget that government is your medium! Be this your art:—to practice men in habit of peace, Generosity to the conquered, and firmness against aggressors.

VIRGIL, *Aeneid*

While Virgil's writing carries all the weight and seriousness of the Roman character, the poet Ovid wrote light, witty poetry for enjoyment. In the *Amores,* Ovid relates that he can only compose when he is in love: "When I was from Cupid's passions free, my Muse was mute and wrote no elegy."

The Romans also wrote excellent prose, especially history. Livy compiled a multivolume history of Rome from its origins to 9 B.C. He used legends freely, creating more of a national myth of Rome than a true history. Tacitus (TAS·ih·tuhs), another Roman historian, is notable among ancient historians because he presented the facts accurately. He also was concerned about the Romans' lack of morality. In his *Annals* and *Histories,* he wrote about the good and bad of imperial Rome.

Roman Achievements

The presence of Rome is still felt daily in the languages, the institutions, and the thought of the Western world.

Latin, the Language of Rome Latin remained the language of learning in the West long after the fall of Rome. It was the official language of the Roman Catholic Church into the 20th century.

Latin was adopted by different peoples and developed into French, Spanish, Portuguese, Italian, and Romanian. These languages are called Romance languages because of their common Roman heritage. Latin also influenced other languages. For example, more than half the words in English have a basis in Latin.

Architecture, Engineering, and Technology Visitors from all over the empire marveled at the architecture of Rome. The arch, the dome, and concrete were combined to build spectacular structures, such as the Colosseum.

The Roman influence can be seen in this neoclassic 19th-century sculpture of George Washington in toga and tunic.

The Colosseum

The Colosseum was one of the greatest feats of Roman engineering and a model for the ages. The name comes from the Latin word *colossus*, meaning "gigantic." Its construction was started by the Emperor Vespasian and was completed by his sons, emperors Titus and Domitian. For centuries after its opening in A.D. 80, excited spectators, both rich and poor, cheered a variety of free, bloody spectacles presented for their entertainment. Gladiator fought gladiator to the death. Wild animals were hunted and slaughtered. Christians were devoured by lions. The poor sat in the higher seats, the rich and powerful closer to the action.

The Colosseum in Rome as it appears today.

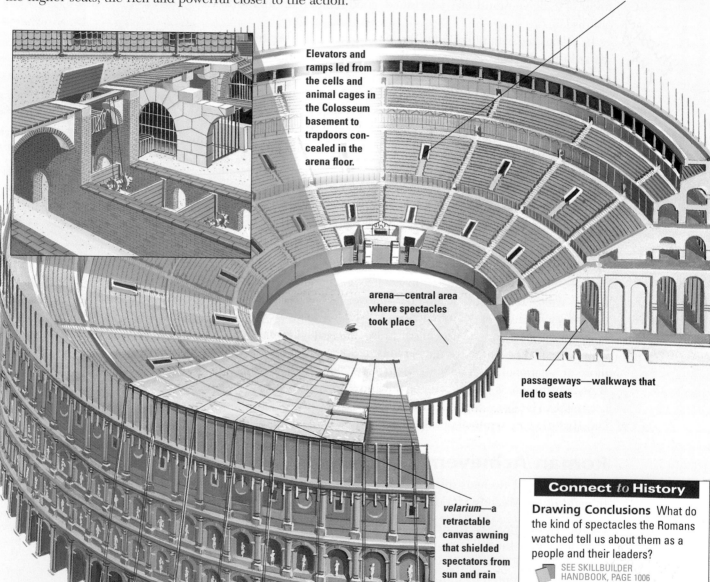

exits—giant staircases that allowed the building to be emptied in minutes

Elevators and ramps led from the cells and animal cages in the Colosseum basement to trapdoors concealed in the arena floor.

arena—central area where spectacles took place

passageways—walkways that led to seats

velarium—a retractable canvas awning that shielded spectators from sun and rain

entrances— eighty in all

Facts About the Colosseum

- Built—A.D. 72–81
- Capacity—45,000–50,000
- Materials—stone and concrete
- Size—157 feet high, 620 feet long
- Arena—287 feet long, 180 feet wide

Connect *to* History

Drawing Conclusions What do the kind of spectacles the Romans watched tell us about them as a people and their leaders?

SEE SKILLBUILDER HANDBOOK, PAGE 1006

Connect *to* Today

Comparing The Colosseum has been the model for sports stadiums worldwide. How is the design of modern stadiums patterned after that of the Colosseum? What are the similarities?

Arches also supported bridges and aqueducts. **Aqueducts** were designed by Roman engineers to bring water into cities and towns. When the water channel spanned a river or ravine, the aqueduct was lifted high up on arches.

Because Roman architectural forms were so practical, they have remained popular. Thomas Jefferson began a Roman revival in the United States in the 18th century. Many large public buildings, such as the U.S. Capitol and numerous state capitols, include Roman features.

Roman roads were also technological marvels. The army built a vast network of roads constructed of stone, concrete, and sand that connected Rome to all parts of the empire. Many lasted into the Middle Ages; some are still used.

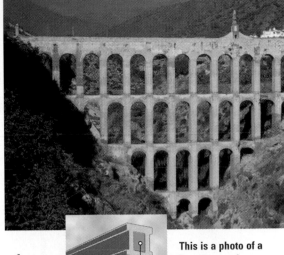

This is a photo of a Roman aqueduct in modern Spain that has survived. The cross section shows how the water moved within the aqueduct.

Roman System of Law Rome's most lasting and widespread contribution was its law. Early Roman law dealt mostly with the rights of Roman citizens. As the empire grew, however, the Romans came to believe that laws should be fair and apply equally to all people, rich and poor. Slowly, judges began to recognize certain standards of justice. These standards were influenced largely by the teachings of Stoic philosophers and were based on common sense and practical ideas. Some of the most important principles of Roman law were:

- All persons had the right to equal treatment under the law.
- A person was considered innocent until proven guilty.
- The burden of proof rested with the accuser rather than the accused.
- A person should be punished only for actions, not thoughts.
- Any law that seemed unreasonable or grossly unfair could be set aside.

The principles of Roman law endured to form the basis of legal systems in many European countries and of places influenced by Europe, including the United States.

THINK THROUGH HISTORY
C. Hypothesizing
How would the world be different if Rome had not existed?

Rome's Enduring Influence By preserving and adding to Greek civilization, Rome strengthened the Western cultural tradition. The world would be a very different place had Rome not existed. Historian R. H. Barrow has stated that Rome never fell because it turned into something even greater—an idea—and achieved immortality.

Around the same time that Rome was developing its enduring culture, different but equally complex empires were growing in India and China, as you will see in Chapter 7.

Section 5 Assessment

1. TERMS & NAMES

Identify
- Greco-Roman culture
- Pompeii
- Virgil
- Tacitus
- aqueduct

2. TAKING NOTES

Using a chart like the one below, list the accomplishments of Roman culture.

Fine Arts	Literature	Engineering	Law

Choose one and write a few paragraphs on its importance.

3. DRAWING CONCLUSIONS

Which principle of law do you think has been Rome's greatest contribution to modern legal systems?

THINK ABOUT
- equality before the law
- innocent until proven guilty
- unfair laws could be set aside

4. ANALYZING THEMES

Power and Authority Why do you think the Greek philosophy of Stoicism was so appealing to Romans?

THINK ABOUT
- Stoic philosophy
- the Roman citizen-soldier
- Roman law

Ancient Rome and Early Christianity

Chapter 6 Assessment

Early Rome

- 1000 B.C. Latins enter region
- 753 B.C. Rome founded

Roman Republic

- 509 B.C. Republic created
- 451 B.C. Twelve Tables written
- 405–265 B.C. Italy conquered
- 264–146 B.C. Punic Wars fought
- 44 B.C. **Julius Caesar** assassinated

Roman Empire

- 27 B.C. Empire and *Pax Romana* begin with reign of **Augustus**
- A.D. 29 **Jesus** crucified
- A.D. 64 Christian persecution begins
- A.D. 79 Pompeii destroyed
- A.D. 180 *Pax Romana* ends
- A.D. 253 Germanic tribes enter frontier regions
- A.D. 285 **Diocletian** divides empire into East and West
- A.D. 313 Christianity given recognition
- A.D. 324 **Constantine** reunites empire
- A.D. 370 Huns invade frontier
- A.D. 380 Christianity made official religion
- A.D. 395 Empire permanently split
- A.D. 410 Visigoths attack Rome
- A.D. 455 Vandals sack Rome
- A.D. 476 Last emperor deposed

Timeline (left margin): 1000 B.C., 900 B.C., 800 B.C., 700 B.C., 600 B.C., 500 B.C., 400 B.C., 300 B.C., 200 B.C., 100 B.C., 0, A.D. 100, A.D. 200, A.D. 300, A.D. 400, A.D. 500 — labeled Early Rome, Roman Republic, Roman Empire

TERMS & NAMES

Briefly explain the importance of each of the following to ancient Rome or to the rise of Christianity.

1. republic
2. senate
3. Hannibal
4. Julius Caesar
5. Augustus
6. Jesus
7. Paul
8. Constantine
9. inflation
10. Virgil

REVIEW QUESTIONS

SECTION 1 (*pages 141–145*)
The Romans Create a Republic

11. Name the three main parts of government under the Roman republic.
12. How did Rome treat different sections of its conquered territory?

SECTION 2 (*pages 146–152*)
The Roman Empire Brings Change

13. How did Augustus change Roman government?
14. How did Rome's population fare during the golden age of the *Pax Romana*?

SECTION 3 (*pages 153–157*)
The Rise of Christianity

15. How did the apostle Paul encourage the spread of Christianity?
16. Why did the Roman emperors persecute Christians?

SECTION 4 (*pages 158–162*)
The Decline of the Roman Empire

17. What was the most important reform that the Emperor Diocletian made?
18. How did the western Roman Empire fall?

SECTION 5 (*pages 164–167*)
Roman Culture and the Roots of Western Civilization

19. Why did so much of Roman culture have a Greek flavor?
20. How might Western civilization be different today without the cultural legacy of the Roman Empire?

Interact *with* History

On page 140, you considered the qualities that made a good leader before knowing what the Romans thought about leadership. Now that you have read the chapter, reevaluate your decision. What qualities were needed for Roman leaders to be effective? What qualities hindered their success? How would you rate the overall leadership of the Roman Empire? Discuss your opinions with a small group.

CRITICAL THINKING

1. FROM REPUBLIC TO EMPIRE

On a large sheet of paper, create a Venn diagram like the one below. Use the diagram to compare the Roman Republic with the Roman Empire when both were at the peak of their power.

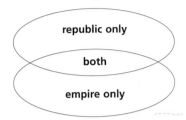

republic only

both

empire only

2. PERSECUTION OF CHRISTIANS

THEME RELIGIOUS AND ETHICAL SYSTEMS Many Christians sacrificed their lives rather than give up their beliefs during the periods of Roman persecution. What kind of person do you think became a martyr? Consider the personal characteristics of individuals who refused to renounce their faith even in the face of death.

3. DIOCLETIAN

What do you think of Diocletian's decision to divide the Roman Empire into two parts? Was it wise? Consider Diocletian's possible motives and the results of his actions.

4. ANALYZING PRIMARY SOURCES

The rule of Augustus began a long period of peace and prosperity that spread from Rome into the provinces. The following decree from the Roman province of Asia, which appeared in 9 B.C., suggests how the governing class felt about their first emperor.

> **A VOICE FROM THE PAST**
> Whereas the divine providence that guides our life has displayed its zeal and benevolence by ordaining for our life the most perfect good, bringing to us Augustus, whom it has filled with virtue for the benefit of mankind, employing him as a saviour for us and our descendants, him who has put an end to wars and adorned peace; . . . and the birthday of the god [Augustus] is the beginning of all the good tidings brought by him to the world.

- How did the officials of this province feel toward Augustus? What descriptive words and phrases support your conclusion?
- Do you think Augustus deserved this evaluation? Why or why not?

CHAPTER ACTIVITIES

1. LIVING HISTORY: Unit Portfolio Project

THEME POWER AND AUTHORITY Your unit portfolio project focuses on tracing the development and decline of power and authority (see page 107). For Chapter 6, you might use one of the following ideas to add to your portfolio.

- Draw two diagrams, side by side, to compare the balance of government achieved by the Roman Republic with the balance of power achieved by the Constitution of the United States.
- As an adviser to Octavian, write a persuasive argument convincing him to become the sole ruler of Rome but not to abolish the Senate.
- With another student, role-play the meeting of Pope Leo and Attila in A.D. 452, in which the pope persuades the Hun to withdraw his forces. Record the meeting on videotape or audiotape or as a written dialogue.

2. CONNECT TO TODAY: Cooperative Learning

THEME EMPIRE BUILDING The spread of the Roman Republic owed much to strategic alliances made with territories distant from Rome. The United States, too, has used alliances to bolster its strength in the world. Work with a team to prepare and present a short television documentary about the relationship between the United States and one of its allies today.

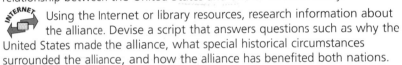 Using the Internet or library resources, research information about the alliance. Devise a script that answers questions such as why the United States made the alliance, what special historical circumstances surrounded the alliance, and how the alliance has benefited both nations.

- Make comparisons with the Roman Republic. Do additional research on the republic's system of alliances if needed.
- Draw a conclusion about whether or not the United States used its alliances for building a kind of "empire" or for other reasons.

3. INTERPRETING A TIME LINE

Revisit the time line on pages 106–107. Did Christianity arise before, during, or after the *Pax Romana*? Explain your reasoning.

FOCUS ON ART

Trajan's Column in Rome is a monument that shows the Emperor Trajan's victories against Dacia (modern Romania) on a relief spiral 650 feet long. This detail depicts Roman soldiers defeating the Dacians.

- What kinds of equipment do the Roman soldiers have?

Connect to History Public monuments like Trajan's Column appeared all over the empire.

- Why do you think the Romans told their history with images on monuments rather than with words?
- What values are the Romans celebrating on monuments like Trajan's Column?

CHAPTER 7

India and China Establish Empires, 300 B.C.—A.D. 550

PREVIEWING THEMES

Power and Authority
Alexander the Great used military power to invade India. In China, rival kings fought for power after the Qin Dynasty ended. In both countries, generals seized power and used their authority to strengthen government.

Cultural Interaction
From the time of the Aryan nomads, Indian civilization was a product of interacting cultures. Starting in the 100s B.C., new invaders changed Indian culture. In China, the government pressured conquered peoples to adopt Chinese culture.

Religious and Ethical Systems
By 250 B.C., Hinduism and Buddhism were India's two main religions. Both changed over time to have more popular appeal. In China, government officials began to be educated in the ethical teachings of Confucius.

INTERNET CONNECTION
Visit us at **www.mcdougallittell.com** to learn more about India and China.

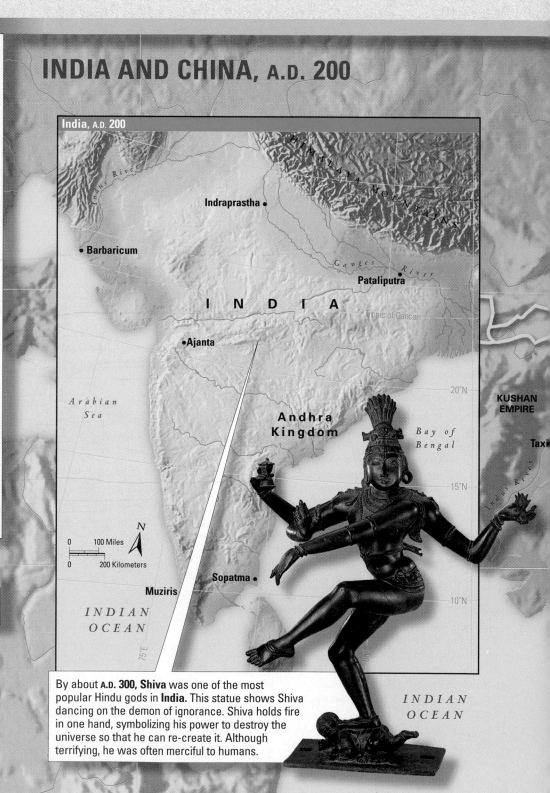

INDIA AND CHINA, A.D. 200

By about **A.D. 300**, **Shiva** was one of the most popular Hindu gods in **India**. This statue shows Shiva dancing on the demon of ignorance. Shiva holds fire in one hand, symbolizing his power to destroy the universe so that he can re-create it. Although terrifying, he was often merciful to humans.

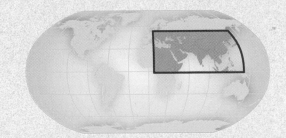

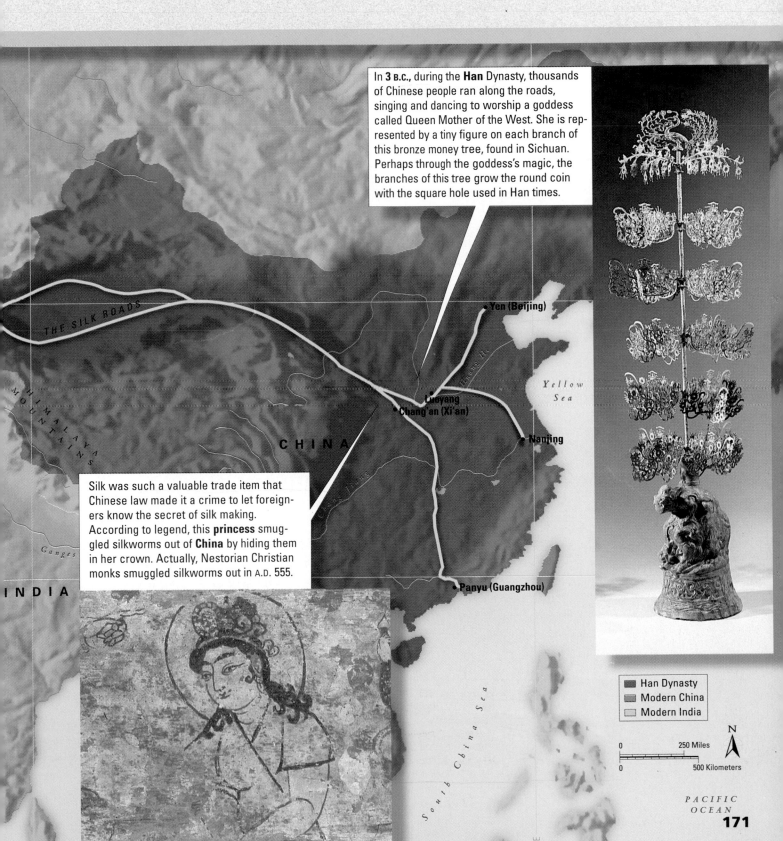

In **3 B.C.**, during the **Han** Dynasty, thousands of Chinese people ran along the roads, singing and dancing to worship a goddess called Queen Mother of the West. She is represented by a tiny figure on each branch of this bronze money tree, found in Sichuan. Perhaps through the goddess's magic, the branches of this tree grow the round coin with the square hole used in Han times.

Silk was such a valuable trade item that Chinese law made it a crime to let foreigners know the secret of silk making. According to legend, this **princess** smuggled silkworms out of **China** by hiding them in her crown. Actually, Nestorian Christian monks smuggled silkworms out in A.D. 555.

THE SILK ROADS

HIMALAYA MOUNTAINS

Ganges

INDIA

CHINA

Yen (Beijing)

Luoyang
Chang'an (Xi'an)

Nanjing

Yellow Sea

Panyu (Guangzhou)

South China Sea

PACIFIC OCEAN

Han Dynasty
Modern China
Modern India

N

| 0 | 250 Miles |
| 0 | 500 Kilometers |

You are a weaver working at your loom when a stranger enters your shop. You fear it is one of the emperor's inspectors, coming to check the quality of your cloth. The man eyes you sternly and then, in a whisper, asks if you will spy on other weavers in your neighborhood. If you take the job, you will be paid the equivalent of four years' earnings. But you would have to turn in one of your friends, whom you suspect is not paying enough sales tax to the government.

Would you be a spy?

This man sits by the window and writes down what he sees. He may be a spy for the emperor.

This person points toward something in the street. He comments on the scene to his friend.

This soldier's job is to check that everyone pays taxes. He seems to be suspicious of the man carrying bananas.

Two people duck behind this woman to gossip about their neighbors

EXAMINING *the* ISSUES

- Do citizens have the responsibility to turn in people who are committing crimes?

- What kinds of tensions might exist in a society where people spy on each other?

- Is it right for a government to control people by spying on them?

As a class, discuss these questions. In your discussion, review what you know about how other emperors exercised power in places such as Persia and Rome.

As you read about the emperors of India and China, notice how they try to control their subjects' lives.

First Empires of India

TERMS & NAMES
- Mauryan Empire
- Asoka
- religious toleration
- Tamil
- Gupta Empire
- patriarchal
- matriarchal

MAIN IDEA

The Mauryas and the Guptas established Indian empires, but neither unified India permanently.

WHY IT MATTERS NOW

The diversity of peoples, cultures, beliefs, and languages in India continues to pose challenges to Indian unity today.

SETTING THE STAGE By 600 B.C., almost 1,000 years after the Aryan migrations, many small kingdoms were scattered throughout India. In 326 B.C., Alexander the Great brought the Indus Valley in the northwest under Greek control—but left the region almost immediately. Soon after, a great Indian military leader, Chandragupta Maurya (CHUHN·druh·GUP·tuh MAH·oor·yuh), seized power for himself.

Chandragupta Maurya Builds an Empire

Background
Chandragupta may have been a younger son of the Nanda king.

Chandragupta Maurya may have been born in the powerful kingdom of Magadha. Centered on the lower Ganges River, the kingdom had been ruled for centuries by the Nanda family. Chandragupta gathered an army, killed the Nanda king, and in about 321 B.C. claimed the throne. This began the **Mauryan Empire.**

Chandragupta Unifies North India Chandragupta moved northwest, seizing all the land from Magadha to the Indus. Around 305 B.C., Chandragupta began to battle Seleucus I, one of Alexander the Great's generals. Seleucus had inherited the eastern part of Alexander's empire. He wanted to reestablish Greek control over the Indus Valley. After several years of fighting, however, Chandragupta defeated Seleucus, who gave up some of his territory to Chandragupta. By 303 B.C., the Mauryan Empire stretched more than 2,000 miles, uniting north India politically for the first time. (See the map on page 175.)

THINK THROUGH HISTORY
A. Evaluating Decisions
Explain whether Chandragupta was wise to use heavy taxes to finance his army.

To win his wars of conquest, Chandragupta raised a vast army: 600,000 soldiers on foot, 30,000 soldiers on horseback, and 9,000 elephants. To clothe, feed, and pay these troops, the government levied high taxes. For example, farmers had to pay up to one half the value of their crops to the king. The government heavily taxed income from trading, mining, and manufacturing.

Running the Empire Chandragupta relied on an adviser named Kautilya (kow·TIHL·yuh), who was a member of the priestly caste. Kautilya wrote a ruler's handbook called the *Arthasastra* (AHR·thuh·SHAHS·truh). This book teaches how to hold a vast empire together.

Following Kautilya's advice, Chandragupta created a highly bureaucratic government. He carefully chose his officials and had them closely supervised. Chandragupta divided the empire into four provinces, each headed by a royal prince. Each province was then divided into local districts, whose officials assessed taxes and enforced the law.

City Life and Country Life Eager to stay at peace with the Indian emperor, Seleucus sent an ambassador, Megasthenes (muh·GAS·thuh·neez), to Chandragupta's capital. In his diary, Megasthenes wrote glowing descriptions of Chandragupta's palace. The palace was filled

SPOTLIGHT ON

Kautilya's *Arthasastra*

The *Arthasastra* states,

> The welfare of the king does not lie in the fulfillment of what is dear to him; whatever is dear to the subjects constitutes his welfare.

Although this sounds noble, the *Arthasastra* is better known for proposing tough-minded policies. For example, the manual suggests that the king hire an army of spies to gather information about his subjects by posing as priests, students, beggars, or merchants. The *Arthasastra* also urges the king to make war against neighboring kingdoms that are weak.

Although Kautilya began the *Arthasastra*, other royal advisers added to it for centuries to come. The manual is often compared to a 16th-century European book on how to rule: *The Prince* by Machiavelli, which also offers hardheaded political advice.

with gold-covered pillars, numerous fountains, and imposing thrones. His capital city featured beautiful parks and bustling markets.

Megasthenes also described the countryside and how farmers lived:

A VOICE FROM THE PAST

[Farmers] are exempted from military service and cultivate their lands undisturbed by fear. They do not go to cities, either on business or to take part in their tumults. It therefore frequently happens that at the same time, and in the same part of the country, men may be seen marshaled for battle and risking their lives against the enemy, while other men are ploughing or digging in perfect security under the protection of these soldiers.

MEGASTHENES, in *Geography* by Strabo

THINK THROUGH HISTORY
B. Making Inferences
Did Mauryan India place a high value on agriculture? What information in this quotation indicates that?

In 301 B.C., Chandragupta's son assumed the throne and ruled for 32 years. Then Chandragupta's grandson, **Asoka** (uh·SOH·kuh), brought the Mauryan Empire to its greatest heights.

Asoka Promotes Buddhism Asoka became king of the Mauryan Empire in 269 B.C. At first, he followed Kautilya's philosophy of waging war to expand his power. He led a long campaign against his neighbors to the southeast in the state of Kalinga. During this bloody war, 100,000 soldiers were slain and even more civilians perished.

Although victorious, Asoka felt sorrow over the slaughter at Kalinga. As a result, he studied Buddhism and decided to rule by Buddha's teaching of nonviolence and "peace to all beings." Throughout the empire, Asoka erected huge stone pillars inscribed with his new policies. Some edicts guaranteed that Asoka would treat his subjects fairly and humanely. Others preached nonviolence. Still others urged **religious toleration**—acceptance of people who held different beliefs—and acceptance of people of all cultural backgrounds.

Vocabulary
edicts: official, public announcements of policy.

This carved set of three lions appeared on top of one of Asoka's pillars. This trio of lions is still used as a symbol of India.

HISTORY MAKERS

Chandragupta Maurya
?–298 B.C.

Chandragupta feared being assassinated—maybe because he had killed a king to get his throne. To avoid being poisoned, he made servants taste all his food. To avoid being murdered in bed, he slept in a different room every night. A guard of armed women surrounded him at all times and killed anyone who came inside their lines.

Although Chandragupta was a fierce warrior for most of his life, in 301 B.C., he voluntarily gave up his throne and converted to Jainism. Jainists taught nonviolence and respect for all life. With a group of monks, he traveled to southern India. There he followed the Jainist custom of fasting until he starved to death.

Asoka
?–232 B.C.

One of Asoka's edicts states,

If one hundredth part or one thousandth of those who died in Kalinga . . . should now suffer similar fate, [that] would be a matter of pain to His Majesty.

Even though Asoka wanted to be a loving, peaceful ruler, he still had to control a huge empire. To do so, he had to balance Kautilya's methods of keeping power and Buddha's urgings to be unselfish.

After converting to Buddhism, Asoka softened Chandragupta's harsher policies. Instead of spies, he employed officials to look out for his subjects' welfare. He kept his army but sought to rule humanely. In addition, Asoka sent missionaries to Southeast Asia to spread Buddhism.

Asoka had extensive roads built so that he could visit the far corners of India. He also improved conditions along these roads to make travel easier for his officials and to improve communication in the vast empire. For example, he had trees planted to provide shade. Every nine miles, he had wells dug and rest houses built. This allowed travelers to stop and refresh themselves. Asoka even ordered the creation of watering places for animals. Such actions demonstrated Asoka's concern for his subjects' well-being.

Noble as Asoka's policies of toleration and nonviolence were, they failed to hold the empire together once Asoka was gone. Soon after he died in 232 B.C., the empire began to break up.

THINK THROUGH HISTORY
C. Clarifying Which of Asoka's actions show the influence of Buddha's teaching of "peace to all beings"?

A Period of Turmoil

Asoka's death left a power vacuum that was felt through the entire subcontinent. In northern and central India, regional kings challenged the imperial government. The kingdoms of central India, which had only been loosely held in the Mauryan Empire, regained their independence soon after the death of Asoka. The Andhra (AHN·druh) Dynasty arose and dominated the region for hundreds of years. Because of their central position, the Andhras profited from the extensive trade between north and south India and also built up trade with Rome, Sri Lanka, and Southeast Asia.

At the same time, northern India had to absorb a flood of new people fleeing political instability in other regions of Asia. For 500 years, wave after wave of Greeks, Persians, and Central Asians poured through the mountain passes into northern India. Without a doubt, these invaders disrupted Indian society. But they also introduced new languages and customs that added to the already rich blend of Indian culture.

Southern India also experienced turmoil. Some rulers in southern India broke away from the empire after Asoka's death. In addition, India's southern tip was home to three kingdoms that had never been conquered by the Mauryans. The people who lived in this region spoke the **Tamil** (TAM·uhl) language and are called the Tamil people. These three kingdoms often were at war with one another and with other states.

Background
When the Aryans entered India about 1500 B.C., they drove many of the pre-Aryans south to this region.

Indian Empires, 250 B.C.–A.D. 400

- Mauryan Empire, 250 B.C.
- Gupta Empire, A.D. 400
- Areas under Gupta influence
- Tamil kingdoms

CHINA

HINDU KUSH MTS.

HIMALAYAS

Indus R.

THAR DESERT

Mathura

Ayodhya

Prayaga

Ganges R.

Pataliputra

Brahmaputra R.

20°N

Narmada R.

Mouths of the Ganges

Arabian Sea

Godavari R.

WESTERN GHATS

Cauvery R.

EASTERN GHATS

Bay of Bengal

INDIAN OCEAN

N

0   500 Miles
0   1,000 Kilometers

30°E

GEOGRAPHY SKILLBUILDER: Interpreting Maps
1. **Region** *Compare the region occupied by the Gupta Empire to that occupied by the Mauryan Empire. Discuss size, location, and physical characteristics.*
2. **Place** *The two empires had one boundary—the northeast boundary—that was roughly the same. Explain why neither empire expanded further in this direction.*

The Gupta Empire

After 500 years of invasion and turmoil, a strong leader again arose in the northern state of Magadha. His name was Chandra Gupta (GUP· tuh), but he was no relation to India's first emperor, Chandragupta Maurya. India's second empire, the **Gupta Empire,** oversaw a great flowering of Indian civilization, especially Hindu culture.

Chandra Gupta Builds an Empire The first Gupta emperor came to power, not through battle, but by marrying the daughter of an old, influential royal family. After this useful marriage, Chandra Gupta I took the title of "Great King of Kings" in A.D. 320. His empire included Magadha and the area just to the north of it, with the central region of the Ganges River as a power base.

Chandra Gupta I's son, Samudra (suh·MU·druh) Gupta, became king in A.D. 335. Although he was a lover of poetry and music, Samudra also had a warlike side. He expanded the empire with 40 years of war and conquest. This gave him control over most of the lands immediately surrounding his father's empire.

Daily Life in India The Gupta era is the first period about which historians have much information concerning daily life in India. Most Indians lived in small villages, where life followed a stable rhythm that beat steadily on for centuries. Craftspeople and merchants clustered in specific districts. They had shops on the street level and lived in the rooms above.

Mauryan Empire

Gupta Empire

320 B.C.

321 B.C. Chandragupta kills the king and claims the throne.

301 B.C. Chandragupta's son assumes the throne.

269 B.C. Chandragupta's grandson Asoka becomes king. Height of the Mauryan Empire.

232 B.C. Asoka dies.

500 years of turmoil follow Asoka's death.

A.D. 335 Chandra Gupta's son Samudra becomes king.

A.D. 320 Chandra Gupta I becomes king.

A.D. 375 Chandra Gupta II becomes king. Gupta Empire reaches its height.

A.D. 415 Chandra Gupta II dies.

A.D. 420

women lead

The majority of villagers, however, were farmers, who walked daily from their homes to the fields outlying the town. Most Indian families were **patriarchal,** headed by the eldest male. Parents, grandparents, uncles, aunts, and children all worked together to raise their crops. Because drought was common, farmers often had to irrigate their crops. There was a tax on water, and every month, people had to donate a day's worth of labor to maintain wells, irrigation ditches, reservoirs, and dams. As in Mauryan times, farmers owed a large part of their earnings to the king.

Southern India followed a different cultural pattern. Some Tamil groups were **matriarchal,** which meant that the mother, rather than the father, was head of the family. Property, and sometimes the throne, was passed through the female line. One famous Tamil ruler was the queen of the Pandyas, whom Megasthenes described as having an army of 500 elephants, 4,000 cavalry, and 13,000 infantry.

THINK THROUGH HISTORY
D. Contrasting
How were the family systems of north and south India different?

Height of the Gupta Empire While village life followed unchanging traditional patterns, the royal court of the third Gupta emperor was a place of excitement and growth. Many Indians consider this emperor, Chandra Gupta II, to be the prince of princes among the Guptas because of his heroic and gallant qualities.

Chandra Gupta II defeated the Shakas—an enemy kingdom to the west. He added their west coast territory to his empire. This allowed the Guptas to take part in the profitable trade between India and the Mediterranean world. Chandra Gupta II also strengthened his empire through peaceful means by negotiating diplomatic and marriage alliances. For example, he arranged for his daughter to marry a king who controlled the western Deccan (a plateau in south-central India).

Chandra Gupta II ruled for 40 years. Faxian, a Chinese Buddhist who traveled in India during Chandra Gupta II's reign, recorded that his subjects seemed generally happy. During the reign of the first three Guptas, India experienced a period of great achievement in art, literature, religious thought, science, and mathematics. These will be discussed in Section 2. After the death of Chandra Gupta II, another wave of invaders again threatened northern India. These fierce fighters, called the Hunas, were cousins to the Huns who were disrupting the Roman Empire at the same time. Over the next 100 years, the Gupta Empire broke into small separate kingdoms. Many of these were overrun by the Huns and other Central Asian nomads.

Section 1 Assessment

1. TERMS & NAMES

Identify
• Mauryan Empire
• Asoka
• religious toleration
• Tamil
• Gupta Empire
• patriarchal
• matriarchal

2. TAKING NOTES

Create a Venn diagram comparing the Mauryan and Gupta empires.

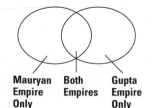

Mauryan Empire Only — Both Empires — Gupta Empire Only

Which similarity do you consider most important? Explain.

3. SUPPORTING OPINIONS

Which of the Indian rulers described in this section would you rather live under? Explain your opinion.

THINK ABOUT
• whether the ruler maintained peace and order—and how
• what methods the ruler used to influence his subjects
• developments in art and culture during the ruler's reign

4. THEME ACTIVITY

Power and Authority With a partner, prepare an exhibit called "Symbols of Power." For three of the rulers described in this section, choose an object or image that symbolizes how that ruler exercised power. Write captions explaining why the symbols are appropriate.

TERMS & NAMES
- **Mahayana**
- **Theravada**
- **Brahma**
- **Vishnu**
- **Shiva**
- **Kalidasa**
- **Silk Roads**

② Trade Spreads Indian Religions and Culture

MAIN IDEA	WHY IT MATTERS NOW
Indian religions, culture, and science evolved and spread to other regions through trade.	The influence of Indian culture and religions is very evident throughout Southeast Asia today.

SETTING THE STAGE The 500 years between the Mauryan and Gupta empires was a time of upheaval. Invaders poured into India, bringing new ideas and customs. In response, Indians began to change their own culture.

Changes in Religious Thought

By 250 B.C., Hinduism and Buddhism were India's two main faiths. (See Chapter 3.) Hinduism is a complex polytheistic religion that blended Aryan and pre-Aryan beliefs. Buddhism teaches that desire causes suffering and that humans should overcome desire by following the Eightfold Path. Over the centuries, both religions had become increasingly removed from the people. Hinduism became dominated by priests, while the Buddhist ideal of self-denial was difficult to follow.

A More Popular Form of Buddhism The Buddha had stressed that each person could reach a state of peace called nirvana. Nirvana was achieved by rejecting the sensory world and embracing spiritual discipline. After the Buddha died, his followers developed many different interpretations of his teachings.

Although the Buddha had forbidden people to worship him, some began to teach that he was a god. Some Buddhists also began to believe that many people could become Buddhas. These potential Buddhas, called bodhisattvas (BOH·dih·SUHT·vuhs), could choose to give up nirvana and work to save humanity through good works and self-sacrifice. The new ideas changed Buddhism from a religion that emphasized individual discipline. It became a mass religion that offered salvation to all and allowed popular worship. By the first century A.D., Buddhists had divided over the new doctrines. Those who accepted them belonged to the **Mahayana** (MAH·huh·YAH·nuh) sect. Those who held to the Buddha's stricter, original teachings belonged to the **Theravada** (THEHR·uh·VAH·duh) sect. This is also called the Hinayana (HEE·nuh·YAH·nuh) sect, but *Theravada* is preferred.

These new trends in Buddhism inspired Indian art. For example, artists carved huge statues of the Buddha for people to worship. Wealthy Buddhist merchants who were eager to do good deeds paid for the construction of stupas—mounded stone structures built over holy relics. Buddhists walked the paths circling the stupas as a part of their meditation. Merchants also commissioned the carving of cave temples out of solid rock. Artists then adorned these temples with beautiful sculptures and paintings.

A Hindu Rebirth Like Buddhism, Hinduism had become remote from the people. By the time of the Mauryan Empire, Hinduism had developed a complex set of sacrifices that could be performed only by the priests. People who weren't priests had less and less direct connection with the religion.

Gradually, through exposure to other cultures and in response to the popularity of Buddhism, Hinduism changed. Although the religion continued to

THINK THROUGH HISTORY
A. Making Inferences Would the Buddha have approved of the new art? Explain.

This Buddha is carved in the Gandharan artistic style—a blend of Greco-Roman and Indian styles. For example, the flowing robes are similar to those seen on Roman imperial statues.

India and China Establish Empires **177**

embrace hundreds of gods, a trend toward monotheism was growing. Many people began to believe that there was only one divine force in the universe. The various gods represented parts of that force. The three most important gods were **Brahma** (BRAH·muh), creator of the world; **Vishnu** (VIHSH·noo), preserver of the world; and **Shiva** (SHEE·vuh), destroyer of the world. Of the three, Vishnu and Shiva were by far the favorites. Many Indians began to devote themselves to these two gods. As Hinduism evolved to a more personal religion, its appeal to the masses grew.

THINK THROUGH HISTORY
B. Drawing Conclusions Why did the changes in Buddhism and Hinduism make them more popular?

Flowering of Indian Culture

Just as Hinduism and Buddhism underwent changes, so did Indian culture and learning. India entered a highly productive period in literature, art, science, and mathematics that continued until roughly A.D. 500.

Literature and the Performing Arts One of India's greatest writers, **Kalidasa** (KAHL·ee·DAHS·uh), may have been the court poet for Chandra Gupta II, who reigned from A.D. 375 to 415. Kalidasa's most famous play is *Shakuntala.* It tells the story of a beautiful girl who falls in love with and marries a middle-aged king. After Shakuntala and her husband are separated, they suffer tragically because of a curse that prevents the king from recognizing his wife when they meet again. Generations of Indians have continued to admire Kalidasa's plays because they are skillfully written and emotionally stirring.

theatrical

Southern India also has a rich literary tradition. In the second century A.D., the city of Madurai in southern India became a site of writing academies. More than 2,000 Tamil poems from this period still exist. In the following excerpt from a third-century poem, a young man describes his sweetheart cooking him a meal:

A VOICE FROM THE PAST
There dwells my sweetheart, curving and lovely,
languid of gaze, with big round earrings,
and little rings on her tiny fingers.
  She has cut the leaves of the garden plantain
and split them in pieces down the stalk
to serve as platters for the meal.
Her eyes are filled with the smoke of cooking.
Her brow, as fair as the crescent moon,
is covered now with drops of sweat.
  She wipes it away with the hem of her garment
and stands in the kitchen, and thinks of me.
ANONYMOUS TAMIL POET, quoted in *The Wonder That Was India*

In addition to literature, drama was very popular. In southern India, traveling acting troupes put on performances in cities across the region. Women as well as men took part in these shows that combined drama and dance. Many of the classical dance forms in India today are based on techniques explained in a book written between the first century B.C. and the first century A.D.

Astronomy, Mathematics, and Medicine The expansion of trade spurred the advance of science. Because sailors on trading ships used the stars to help them figure their position at sea, knowledge of astronomy increased. From Greek invaders, Indians adapted Western methods of keeping time. They began to use a calendar based on the cycles of the sun rather than the moon, adopted a seven-day week, and divided each day into hours.

During the Gupta Empire (A.D. 320 to about 500), knowledge of astronomy increased further. Almost 1,000 years before Columbus, Indian astronomers proved

CONNECT *to* TODAY

Entertainment in India
Today, drama remains hugely popular in India. India has the largest movie industry in the world. About twice as many full-length feature films are released yearly in India as in the United States.

India produces both popular and serious films. Indian popular films are often love stories that blend music, dance, drama, and action adventure. India's serious films have received worldwide critical praise. In 1992, the Indian director Satyajit Ray received a lifetime achievement Academy Award for making artistic films. His films brought Indian culture to a worldwide audience.

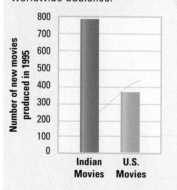

Source: *International Motion Picture Almanac,* 1997

Arabic Numerals

that the earth was round by observing a lunar eclipse. During the eclipse, the earth's shadow fell across the face of the moon. The astronomers noted that the earth's shadow was curved, indicating that the earth itself was round.

Indian mathematics was among the most advanced in the world. Modern numerals, the zero, and the decimal system were invented in India. Around A.D. 500, an Indian named Aryabhata (AHR·yuh· BUHT·uh) calculated the value of pi (Π) to four decimal places. He also calculated the length of the solar year as 365.3586805 days. This figure is very close to modern calculations made with an atomic clock.

In medicine, two important medical guides were compiled. These works classified more than 1,000 diseases and described more than 500 medicinal plants. Hindu physicians knew how to perform surgery—including plastic surgery—and possibly gave inoculations.

The Spread of Indian Trade

In addition to knowledge, India has always been rich in precious resources. Spices, diamonds, sapphires, gold, pearls, and beautiful woods—including ebony, teak, and fragrant sandalwood—have always been valuable items of exchange. Trade between India and regions as distant as Africa and Sumeria began more than 4,000 years ago. Trade continued to expand even after the Mauryan Empire ended around 185 B.C.

Overland Trade, East and West The groups who invaded India after the end of Mauryan rule helped to expand India's trade to new regions. For example, Central Asian nomads brought Indians information about the caravan routes that crisscrossed central Asia.

These caravan routes were known as **Silk Roads** because traders used them to bring silk from China to Western Asia and on to Rome. Once Indians learned of the Silk Roads, they realized that they could make great profits by acting as middlemen.

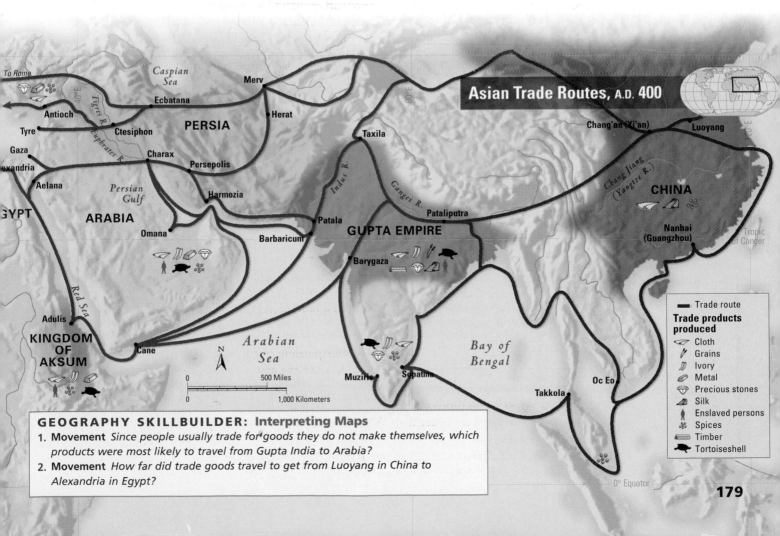

Asian Trade Routes, A.D. 400

Trade route

Trade products produced
- Cloth
- Grains
- Ivory
- Metal
- Precious stones
- Silk
- Enslaved persons
- Spices
- Timber
- Tortoiseshell

GEOGRAPHY SKILLBUILDER: Interpreting Maps

1. **Movement** *Since people usually trade for goods they do not make themselves, which products were most likely to travel from Gupta India to Arabia?*

2. **Movement** *How far did trade goods travel to get from Luoyang in China to Alexandria in Egypt?*

Middlemen are go-betweens in business transactions. For example, Indian traders would buy goods from traders coming out of China and sell those goods to traders who were traveling to Rome. To aid their role as middlemen, Indians built trading stations at oases all along the Silk Roads.

Vocabulary
oases: plural of oasis, which is a watering place in a desert.

Sea Trade, East and West Sea trade also increased. Traders used coastal routes around the rim of the Arabian Sea and up the Persian Gulf to bring goods from India to Rome. In addition, traders from southern India would sail to Southeast Asia to collect spices. They bought the spices back to India and sold them to merchants from Rome.

Archaeologists have found hoards of Roman gold coins in southern India. Records show that some Romans were upset about the amount of gold their countrymen spent on Indian luxuries. They believed that a state with a healthy economy must collect gold rather than spend it.

Rome wasn't India's only trading partner. India imported African ivory and gold and exported cotton cloth. Rice and wheat went to Arabia in exchange for dates and horses. After trade with Rome declined around the third century A.D., India's sea trade with China increased. The Chinese imported Indian cotton cloth, monkeys, parrots, and elephants and sent India silk.

Effects of Indian Trade Increased trade led to the rise of banking in India. Commerce was quite profitable. Bankers were willing to lend money to merchants and charge them interest on the loans. Interest rates varied, depending on how risky business was. During Mauryan times, the annual interest rate on loans used for overseas trade had been 240 percent! During the Gupta Empire, bankers no longer considered sea trade so dangerous, so they charged only 15 to 20 percent interest a year.

A number of Indian merchants went to live abroad and brought Indian culture with them. As a result, people throughout Asia picked up and adapted a variety of Indian traditions. For example, Indian culture affected styles in art, architecture, and dance throughout Southeast Asia. Indian influence was especially strong in Thailand, Cambodia, and on the Indonesian island of Java.

Traders also brought Indian religions to new regions. Hinduism spread to Nepal, a region northeast of India; to Sri Lanka, an island off southeastern India; and to Borneo, an island in Indonesia. Buddhism spread because of traveling Buddhist merchants and monks. In time, Buddhism even influenced China. You will learn about this in Section 3.

THINK THROUGH HISTORY
D. Analyzing Causes Why would dangerous conditions make bankers charge higher interest on loans for trade?

Global Impact

The Spread of Buddhism

Buddhism became a missionary religion during Asoka's reign. From his capital city (1), Asoka sent out Buddhist missionaries. After Indians began trading along the Silk Roads, Buddhist monks travelled these routes and converted people on the way.

Buddhist monks from India established their first monastery in China (2) in A.D. 65, and many Chinese became Buddhists. From China, Buddhism reached Korea in the fourth century and Japan in the sixth century.

Today, Buddhism is a major religion throughout East and Southeast Asia. The Theravada school is strong in Myanmar, Cambodia (3), Sri Lanka (4), and Thailand. The Mahayana school is strong in Japan and Korea.

Section 2 Assessment

1. TERMS & NAMES

Identify
- Mahayana
- Theravada
- Brahma
- Vishnu
- Shiva
- Kalidasa
- Silk Roads

2. TAKING NOTES

Create a diagram like the one shown. For each category, list one or more specific developments in Indian culture.

Indian Culture	
Religion	
Literature/Arts	
Science/Math	
Trade	

3. RECOGNIZING EFFECTS

What do you think was the most significant effect of the changes in Buddhism and Hinduism? Explain.

THINK ABOUT
- the effect on people who practiced the religion
- the effect on art and culture
- the effect on other countries

4. ANALYZING THEMES

Cultural Interaction Cite three of the cultures that interacted with India. Explain the result of each cultural interaction.

THINK ABOUT
- interaction because of trade
- the influence of art, science, religion

TERMS & NAMES
- **Han Dynasty**
- **centralized government**
- **civil service**
- **monopoly**
- **assimilation**

3 Han Emperors in China

MAIN IDEA	WHY IT MATTERS NOW
The Han Dynasty expanded China's borders and developed a system of government that lasted for centuries.	The pattern of a strong central government has remained a permanent part of Chinese life.

SETTING THE STAGE Under Shi Huangdi, the Qin Dynasty had unified China. Shi Huangdi conquered the rival kings who ruled small states throughout China and established a strong government. After Shi Huangdi died in 210 B.C., his son proved to be a weak, ineffective leader. China's government fell apart.

The Han Restore Unity to China

Rumblings of discontent during the Qin Dynasty grew to roars in the years after Shi Huangdi's death. The peasants—bitter over years of high taxes, harsh labor quotas, and a severe penal system—rebelled. The rival kings—eager to regain control of the regions they had held before Shi Huangdi—raised armies and fought over territory.

The Founding of the Han Dynasty During the civil war that followed, two powerful leaders emerged. Xiang Yu (shee·ANG yoo) was an aristocratic general who was willing to allow the warlords to keep their territories if they would acknowledge him as their feudal lord. Liu Bang (LEE·oo bahng) was one of Xiang Yu's generals.

Eventually, Liu Bang turned against Xiang Yu. The two fought their final battle in 202 B.C. Liu Bang won and declared himself the first emperor of the Han Dynasty. The **Han Dynasty**, which ruled China for more than 400 years, is divided into two periods. The Former Han ruled for about two centuries, until A.D. 9. After a brief period when the Han were out of power, the Later Han ruled for almost another two centuries. The Han Dynasty so influenced China that even today many Chinese call themselves "people of the Han."

Liu Bang's first goal was to destroy the rival kings' power. He followed Shi Huangdi's policy of establishing **centralized government,** in which a central authority controls the running of a state. Reporting to Liu Bang's central government were hundreds of local officials of provinces called commanderies.

To win popular support, Liu Bang departed from Shi Huangdi's strict legalism. He lowered taxes and softened harsh punishments. People throughout the empire appreciated the peace and stability that Liu Bang brought to China.

The Empress Lü When Liu Bang died in 195 B.C., his son became emperor—in name only. The real ruler was his mother, Empress Lü. Although Lü had not been Liu Bang's only wife, she had powerful friends at court who helped her seize power. The empress outlived her son and retained control of the throne by naming first one infant and then another as emperor. Because the infants were too young to rule, she remained in control. When Empress Lü died in 180 B.C., people who remained loyal to Liu Bang's

HISTORY MAKERS

Liu Bang
256–195 B.C.

Although Liu Bang was born a peasant, legend says that dragons attended his birth. According to Chinese belief, this meant he would rise to great power.

Liu Bang was a village official who turned rebel general after Shi Huangdi died. He wasn't a great military leader. According to one story, nomads once captured him and held him for ransom.

However, Liu Bang had other skills that made him a successful emperor. Wisely, he chose educated advisers. He strengthened the central government. With foreign powers, he knew when to negotiate and when to use force. He was such a strong leader that Chinese historians call him "Gaozu," which means exalted founder.

India and China Establish Empires **181**

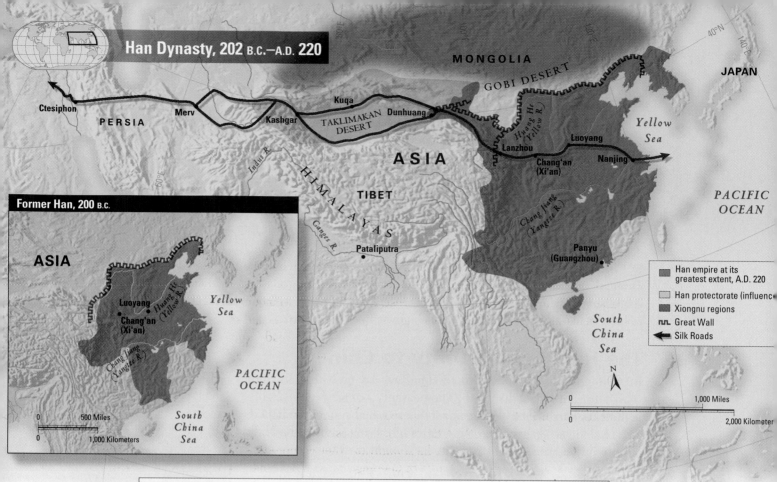

Han Dynasty, 202 B.C.–A.D. 220

Former Han, 200 B.C.

Han empire at its greatest extent, A.D. 220
Han protectorate (influence)
Xiongnu regions
Great Wall
Silk Roads

GEOGRAPHY SKILLBUILDER: Interpreting Maps
1. **Place** *What was the approximate size, in square miles, of the Han empire at its greatest extent?*
2. **Location** *Along which border did the Chinese build the Great Wall? Why did they build it there and not in other places?*

family, rather than to Lü's family, came back into power. They rid the palace of the old empress's relatives by executing them.

Such palace plots occurred often throughout the Han Dynasty. Traditionally, the emperor chose the favorite among his wives as the empress and appointed one of her sons as successor. Because of this, the palace women and their families competed fiercely for the emperor's notice. The families would make alliances with influential people in the court. The resulting power plays distracted the emperor and his officials so much that they sometimes could not govern efficiently.

The Martial Emperor When Liu Bang's great-grandson took the throne, he continued Liu Bang's centralizing policies. Wudi (woo·dee), who reigned from 141 to 87 B.C., held the throne longer than any other Han emperor. He is called the martial emperor because he adopted the policy of expanding the Chinese empire through war.

Wudi's first set of enemies were the Xiongnu (shee·UNG·noo), a nomadic people known for their fierceness as arrow-shooting warriors on horseback. The Xiongnu roamed the steppes to the north and west of China. They made raids into China's settled farmland and stole grain, farm animals, valuable items, and hostages. The early Han emperors tried to buy off the Xiongnu by sending them thousands of pounds of silk, rice, alcohol, and money. Usually, the Xiongnu just accepted these gifts and continued their raids.

Vocabulary
martial: warlike.

GlobalImpact

Xiongnu and the Huns

Eventually, Wudi defeated the Xiongnu. After their defeat, the nomads moved deeper into Asia. This had long-range effects. As the Xiongnu pushed south and west, they displaced other nomadic peoples. Because of this, successive waves of central Asian invaders pushed into northwestern India.

In addition, some historians theorize that over the centuries, the Xiongnu wandered thousands of miles westward across central Asia into Europe. The fierce horse-riding Huns who invaded the Roman Empire may have been the distant grandsons of the Xiongnu.

When Wudi realized that the bribes were simply making the Xiongnu stronger, he sent more than 100,000 soldiers to fight them. To help defeat the Xiongnu, Wudi also made allies of their enemies:

A VOICE FROM THE PAST
The Xiongnu had defeated the king of the Yuezhi people and had made his skull into a drinking vessel. As a result the Yuezhi . . . bore a constant grudge against the Xiongnu, though as yet they had been unable to find anyone to join them in an attack on their enemy. . . . When the emperor [Wudi] heard this, he decided to try to send an envoy to establish relations with the Yuezhi.

SIMA QIAN, *Records of the Grand Historian*

After his army forced the nomads to retreat into Central Asia, Wudi attempted to make his northwest border safe by settling his troops on the Xiongnu's former pastures. Although this tactic succeeded for a time, nomadic raiders continued to cause problems during much of China's later history.

Wudi also colonized areas to the northeast, now known as Manchuria and Korea. He sent his armies south, where they conquered mountain tribes and set up Chinese colonies all the way into what is now Vietnam. By the end of Wudi's reign, the empire had expanded nearly to the bounds of present-day China.

A Highly Structured Government

Just as Han emperors tried to control the people they conquered, they exerted vast control over the Chinese themselves. Because the Chinese considered their emperor to be semidivine, they accepted his exercise of power. He was in charge of keeping order on a cosmic level. If the emperor did his job well, China had peace and prosperity. If he failed, the heavens showed their displeasure with earthquakes, floods, and famines. However, the emperor did not rule alone.

Background
According to the Mandate of Heaven, divine forces appointed Chinese emperors to rule—and would take away the throne if they governed badly.

Structures of Han Government The Chinese emperor relied on a complex bureaucracy to help him rule. Running the bureaucracy and maintaining the imperial army were expensive. To raise money, the government levied taxes. Like the farmers in India, Chinese peasants owed part of their yearly crops to the government. Merchants also paid taxes.

Besides taxes, the peasants owed the government a month's worth of labor or military service every year. With this source of labor, the Han emperors built roads, canals, and irrigation ditches. The emperors also filled the ranks of China's vast armies and expanded the Great Wall that stretched across the northern frontier.

Confucianism, the Road to Success Wudi's government employed more than 130,000 people. The bureaucracy included 18 different ranks of **civil service** jobs—government jobs that civilians obtained by taking examinations. At times, Chinese emperors rewarded loyal followers with government posts. However, another way to fill government posts evolved under the Han. This method involved testing applicants' knowledge of Confucianism—the teachings of Confucius, who had lived 400 years before.

The early Han emperors had employed some Confucian scholars as court advisers, but it was Wudi who began actively to favor them. Confucius had taught that gentlemen should practice "reverence [respect], generosity, truthfulness, diligence [hard work], and kindness." Because these were exactly the qualities he wanted his government officials to have, Wudi set up a school where hopeful job applicants from all over China could come to study Confucius's works.

THINK THROUGH HISTORY
A. Making Inferences
Why would Wudi want his officials to have qualities such as diligence?

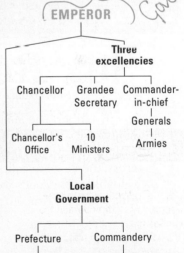

SPOTLIGHT ON

Chinese Bureaucracy
The Chinese bureaucracy reflected top-down rule. Each level of officials had authority over the officials below them. The emperor had authority over all.

EMPEROR

Three excellencies

Chancellor   Grandee Secretary   Commander-in-chief

Chancellor's Office   10 Ministers   Generals

Armies

Local Government

Prefecture   Commandery

District   Inspecting Secretary
Commandery Administrator
Commune   Commandery Commandant
Prison Commandant
Village   Specialists

India and China Establish Empires **183**

After their studies, job applicants took formal examinations in history, law, literature, and Confucianism. In theory, anyone could take the exams. In practice, few peasants could afford to educate their sons. So only sons of wealthy landowners had a chance at a government career. In spite of this flaw, the civil service system begun by Wudi worked so efficiently that it continued in China until 1912.

Han Technology, Commerce, and Culture

The 400 years of Han rule saw not only improvements in education but also great advances in Chinese technology and culture. In addition, the centralized government began to exert more control over commerce and manufacturing.

Technology Revolutionizes Chinese Life Advances in technology influenced all aspects of Chinese life. Paper was invented in A.D. 105. Before that, books were usually written on silk. But paper was cheaper, so books became more readily available. This helped spread education in China. The invention of paper also affected Chinese government. Formerly, all government documents had been recorded on strips of wood. Paper was much more convenient to use for record-keeping, so Chinese bureaucracy expanded.

Other technological advances included a collar harness that made it possible for horses to pull heavy loads. The Chinese perfected a plow that was more efficient because it had two blades, improved iron tools, and invented the wheelbarrow. In addition, the Chinese began to use watermills to grind grain.

Agriculture Versus Commerce During the Han Dynasty, the population of China swelled to 60 million. Because there were so many people to feed, Confucian scholars and ordinary Chinese people considered agriculture the most important and

Vocabulary
commerce: the buying and selling of goods.

THINK THROUGH HISTORY
B. Making Inferences
Which of the inventions discussed here helped the task of feeding China's huge population?

GlobalImpact: Trade Networks

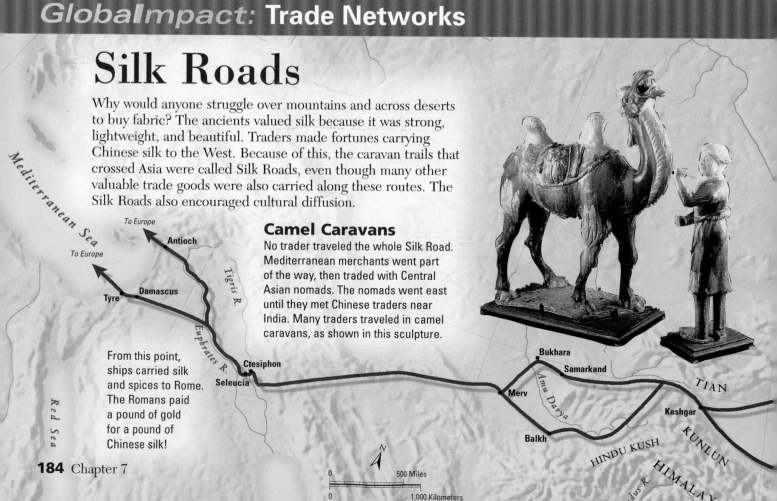

Silk Roads

Why would anyone struggle over mountains and across deserts to buy fabric? The ancients valued silk because it was strong, lightweight, and beautiful. Traders made fortunes carrying Chinese silk to the West. Because of this, the caravan trails that crossed Asia were called Silk Roads, even though many other valuable trade goods were also carried along these routes. The Silk Roads also encouraged cultural diffusion.

Camel Caravans
No trader traveled the whole Silk Road. Mediterranean merchants went part of the way, then traded with Central Asian nomads. The nomads went east until they met Chinese traders near India. Many traders traveled in camel caravans, as shown in this sculpture.

From this point, ships carried silk and spices to Rome. The Romans paid a pound of gold for a pound of Chinese silk!

184 Chapter 7

0   500 Miles

0   1,000 Kilometers

honored occupation. An imperial edict, written in 167 B.C., stated this philosophy quite plainly:

A VOICE FROM THE PAST

Agriculture is the foundation of the world. No duty is greater. Now if [anyone] personally follows this pursuit diligently, he has yet [to pay] the impositions of the land tax and tax on produce. . . . Let there be abolished the land tax and the tax on produce levied upon the cultivated fields.

BAN GU and **BAN ZHAO** in *History of the Former Han Dynasty*

Although the same decree dismissed commerce as the least important occupation, manufacturing and commerce were actually very important to the Han empire. The government established monopolies on the mining of salt, the forging of iron, the minting of coins, and the brewing of alcohol. A **monopoly** occurs when a group has exclusive control over the production and distribution of certain goods.

control over one trade

For a time, the government also ran huge silk mills—competing with private silk weavers in making this luxurious cloth. As contact with people from other lands increased, the Chinese realized how valuable their silk was as an item of trade. Because of this, the techniques of silk production became a closely guarded state secret. Spurred by the worldwide demand for silk, Chinese commerce expanded along the Silk Roads to most of Asia and, through India, all the way to Rome.

Unifying Chinese Culture As the Han empire expanded its trade networks, the Chinese began to learn about the foods, animals, and fashions that were common in foreign lands. Similarly, the expansion of the Han empire through conquest brought people of many different cultures under Chinese rule. To unify the empire, the Chinese government encouraged **assimilation**, or the process of making these conquered peoples part of Chinese culture. To accomplish this, the government sent

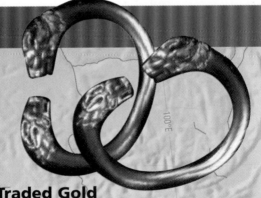

Traded Gold
First-century traders near Samarkand traded for these gold and turquoise bracelets. The lion heads show Persian influence. Many artifacts found in the same site as the bracelets show a mix of Greek, Central Asian, and Indian styles. This shows that ideas as well as objects traveled the Silk Roads.

Patterns of Interaction

Throughout history, the desire for material goods led to the development of long-distance trade routes like the Silk Roads. In turn, trade caused cultural diffusion. Similarly today, trade in the Pacific Rim has helped spread many products across the globe.

VIDEO *Trade Connects the World: Silk Roads and the Pacific Rim*

Connect *to* History

Hypothesizing If the Romans had learned the secret of making silk, how might patterns of trade and cultural diffusion have changed?

SEE SKILLBUILDER HANDBOOK, PAGE 1000

Connect *to* Today

Researching What are China's top three exports today? What countries buy those products? Cite the sources of your information.

The Silk Road split in two to skirt the edges of the Taklimaken Desert. Both routes had oases along the way.

Silk sold for so much money that the Chinese were willing to go through a difficult process to make it. The cocoons of silk worms like these had to be soaked in water and unraveled to get silk thread. It took more than 2,000 cocoons to make a pound of silk!

SHAN
Turfan
Anxi
Dunhuang

TAKLIMAKEN
DESERT
SHAN
TIBET

Lanzhou
Chang'an (Xi'an)
Luoyang
Huang
To Japan
Nanjing

CHINA

This is the lid of a Chinese bronze vessel from Han times. The figures on top are women who are weaving cloth, perhaps silk.

Chinese farmers to settle newly colonized areas. The government also encouraged them to intermarry with local peoples. Government officials set up schools to train local people in the Confucian philosophy and then appointed local scholars to government posts.

Several writers also helped to unify Chinese culture by recording China's history. Sima Qian (SU·MAH chee·YEHN), who lived from 145 to 85 B.C., is called the "Grand Historian" for his work in compiling a history of China from the ancient dynasties to Wudi. To write accurately, Sima Qian visited historical sites, interviewed eyewitnesses, researched official records, and examined artifacts. The resulting book is called *Records of the Grand Historian.*

Another famous Chinese book was the *History of the Former Han Dynasty.* Ban Biao (BAHN bee·OW), who lived from A.D. 3 to 54, started the project. After his death, his son Ban Gu (bahn goo) and later his daughter Ban Zhao (bahn jow) worked on it. Ban Zhao also wrote a guide called *Lessons for Women.*

Background
In China, the family name comes first and the personal name comes second. These historians belong to the Ban family.

Wives, Nuns, and Scholars Although Ban Zhao gained fame as a historian, most women during the Han Dynasty led quiet lives at home. Confucian teachings dictated that women were to devote themselves to their families. They were supposed to obey their parents in childhood and their husband and husband's parents after they married. To add to their family's honor, women were to be faithful, pure, and modest.

A few upper-class women broke out of this mold. As explained earlier, some empresses wielded great power. Daoist and later Buddhist nuns were able to gain an education and lead lives apart from their families. Women in aristocratic and land-owning families also sometimes pursued education and culture.

Rebellion and Restoration

In spite of economic and cultural advances, the Han emperors faced grave problems. One of the main problems was an economic imbalance caused by customs that allowed the rich to gain more wealth at the expense of the poor.

The Rich Take Advantage of the Poor According to custom, a family's land was divided equally among all of the father's male heirs. Unless a farmer could afford to buy more land during his lifetime, each generation inherited smaller plots. With such small plots of land, farmers had a hard time raising enough food to sell or even to feed the family. Because of this, small farmers often went into debt and had to borrow money from large landowners, who charged very high interest rates. If the farmer couldn't pay back the debt, the landowner took possession of the farmer's land.

Large landowners were not required to pay taxes, so when their land holdings increased, the amount of land that was left for the government to tax decreased. With less money coming in, the government pressed harder to collect money from the small farmers. As a result, the gap between rich and poor increased.

Wang Mang Overthrows the Han During this time of economic change, political instability grew. At the palace, court advisers, palace servants, and rival influential families wove complex plots to influence the emperor's choice of who would succeed him as ruler. From about 32 B.C. until A.D. 9, one inexperienced emperor replaced another. Chaos reigned in the palace, and with peasant revolts, unrest spread across the land as well.

Finally, Wang Mang (wahng mahng), a Confucian scholar and member of the court, decided that a strong ruler was needed to restore order. For six years he had been acting as regent for the infant who had been crowned emperor. In A.D. 9, Wang Mang took the imperial title for himself and overthrew the Han, thus ending the first half of the Han Dynasty known as the Former Han.

Vocabulary
regent: a person who rules temporarily while a monarch is too young

more land → tax

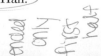

Two Great Empires: Han China and Rome

Han Dynasty—202 B.C. to A.D. 220	Roman Empire—27 B.C. to A.D. 476
• Empire replaced rival kingdoms	• Empire replaced republic
• Centralized, bureaucratic government	• Centralized, bureaucratic government
• Built roads and defensive walls	• Built roads and defensive walls
• Conquered many diverse peoples in regions bordering China	• Conquered many diverse peoples in regions of three continents
• At its height—area of 1,500,000 square miles and a population of 60,000,000	• At its height—area of 3,400,000 square miles and a population of 55,000,000
• Chinese became common written language throughout empire	• Latin did not replace other written languages in empire
• Ongoing conflict with nomads	• Ongoing conflict with nomads
• Empire fell apart; restored by Tang dynasty in 618	• Empire fell apart; never restored

SKILLBUILDER: Interpreting Charts
1. *How long did each empire last? During what years were they both in existence?*
2. *How were Han China and the Roman Empire similar? How were they different?*

Silk was the trade good that linked the Han and Roman Empires. Han artists often did beautiful paintings on silk, such as this one.

Wang Mang tried to bring the country under control. He minted new money to relieve the treasury's shortage. He set up public granaries to help feed China's poor. He took away large landholdings from the rich and planned to redistribute the land to farmers who had lost their land. This plan angered powerful landholders. And Wang Mang's larger supply of money disrupted the economy because it allowed people to increase their spending, which encouraged merchants to raise prices.

Then, in A.D. 11, a great flood left thousands dead and millions homeless. The public granaries did not hold enough to feed the displaced, starving people. Huge peasant revolts rocked the land. The wealthy, opposed to Wang Mang's land policies, joined in the rebellion. The rebels assassinated Wang Mang in A.D. 23. Within two years, a member of the old imperial family took the throne and began the second period of Han rule—called the Later Han.

THINK THROUGH HISTORY
C. Recognizing Effects How did Wang Mang's policies help cause his own downfall?

The Later Han Years With peace restored to China, the first decades of the Later Han Dynasty were quite prosperous. The government sent soldiers and merchants westward to regain control of posts along the Silk Roads. But this expansion couldn't make up for social, political, and economic weaknesses within the empire itself. Within a century, China suffered from the same economic imbalances, political intrigues, and social unrest that had toppled the Former Han. By 220, the Later Han Dynasty had disintegrated into three rival kingdoms.

Section 3 Assessment

1. TERMS & NAMES

Identify
- Han Dynasty
- centralized government
- civil service
- monopoly
- assimilation

2. TAKING NOTES

Create a spider map like the one shown to record the methods that Han rulers used to centralize the government.

Centralized Government

Explain which method you think was most important and why.

3. IDENTIFYING PROBLEMS

What problem do you think was most responsible for weakening the Han Dynasty's power?

THINK ABOUT
- problems at court
- problems with non-Chinese peoples
- economic and social problems

4. THEME ACTIVITY

Religious and Ethical Systems Review the five qualities that Confucius said all gentlemen should practice (see page 183). Working with a small team, think of actions that government officials could take to demonstrate each of those qualities. Choose the best actions and illustrate them on a motivational poster that could hang in a government office.

India and China Establish Empires

321 B.C.
300 B.C.

Mauryan Empire

- 321 B.C.—**Chandragupta Maurya** seized throne and began Mauryan Empire

200 B.C.

- 269 B.C.—**Asoka** began rule; conquered Kalinga; regretted slaughter and converted to Buddhism; sent out missionaries

- 232 B.C.—**Asoka** died; empire started to break apart

100 B.C.

- 185 B.C.—Greeks invaded India, beginning five centuries of turmoil

Mauryan Empire

Han Dynasty

1 B.C.
A.D. 1

- 202 B.C.—**Liu Bang** started Han Dynasty; strengthened central government

- 141 B.C.—**Wudi** began reign; conquered neighboring regions; started civil service

A.D. 100

- Chinese invented paper, collar harness, watermill

- A.D. 9—**Wang Mang** temporarily overthrew the Han

- 1st century A.D.— Later Han rulers encouraged Silk Road trade with West

A.D. 200

Han Dynasty

Gupta Empire

A.D. 300

- Buddhism and Hinduism developed more popular forms

- A.D. 320—**Chandra Gupta** began empire

- A.D. 375—**Chandra Gupta II** started reign; Indian art, literature, and dance flowered

A.D. 400

- A.D. 500—Indian astronomers realized earth was round; mathematician calculated value of pi and length of solar year

- Trade spread Indian culture, Hinduism, and Buddhism

Gupta Empire

A.D. 500

188 Chapter 7

TERMS & NAMES

Briefly explain the importance of each of the following to the empires in India and China between 321 B.C. and A.D. 550.

1. Mauryan Empire
2. Asoka
3. religious toleration
4. Gupta Empire
5. Kalidasa
6. Silk Roads
7. Han Dynasty
8. centralized government
9. civil service
10. assimilation

REVIEW QUESTIONS

SECTION 1 (pages 173–176)

First Empires of India

11. List three significant accomplishments of the Mauryan rulers.
12. How did India change during the 500 years between the decline of the Mauryan Empire and the rise of the Gupta Empire?
13. How did the southern tip of India differ from the rest of India?

SECTION 2 (pages 177–180)

Trade Spreads Indian Religions and Culture

14. How did changes in Buddhism influence art in India?
15. Summarize the main advances in science and mathematics by Indians prior to A.D. 500.
16. Describe the economic and cultural links between India and Southeast Asia.

SECTION 3 (pages 181–187)

Han Emperors in China

17. Explain why Wudi was one of China's most significant rulers.
18. Under the Chinese civil service system, who could become government officials?
19. How did silk influence China's government, economy, and culture during the Han period?
20. How did economic problems lead to the decline of the Han?

Interact *with* History

On page 172, you looked at a situation in which a government hired people to spy on each other. Now that you have read the chapter, reevaluate your decision about being a spy. What do you think are the best methods for a government to use to control large numbers of people? Consider the methods used by Chandragupta, Asoka, and the Han emperors.

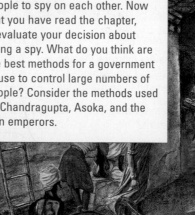

CRITICAL THINKING

1. INFLUENCING GOVERNMENT

THEME **RELIGIOUS AND ETHICAL SYSTEMS** Contrast Buddhism's influence on India's government with Confucianism's influence on China's government. Contrast the teachings, the motive of the rulers who tried to implement those teachings, and how long the influence lasted.

2. COMPARING EMPIRES

Create a table such as the one below and fill in the information about each empire.

Empire	Period of Influence	Key Leaders	Significant Achievements
Mauryan			
Gupta			
Han			

3. EVALUATING SUCCESS

Was the Mauryan, Gupta, or Han empire most successful? Identify the standards you used to evaluate success and how each empire measured up to these standards.

4. ANALYZING PRIMARY SOURCES

The following quotation, from one of Asoka's edicts, describes Asoka's reaction after he conquered Kalinga. Read the quotation and answer the questions below it.

> **A VOICE FROM THE PAST**
> Kalinga was conquered by his Sacred and Gracious Majesty when he had been conse-crated eight years. 150,000 persons were thence carried away captive, 100,000 were slain, and many times that number died. . . . Thus arose his Sacred Majesty's remorse for having conquered the Kalingas, because the conquest of a country previously uncon-quered involves the slaughter, death, and car-rying away captive of the people.
>
> **ASOKA,** in *A History of Modern India*
> by Percival Spear

- Judging from this edict, what did the conquest of Kalinga cause Asoka to realize about the nature of war?
- Why would this realization have motivated him to investigate Buddhism? Support your answer with details from the text.
- If more rulers had shared Asoka's belief, how might world history have been different?

CHAPTER ACTIVITIES

1. LIVING HISTORY: Unit Portfolio Project

THEME **POWER AND AUTHORITY** Your unit portfolio project focuses on people who grab power and establish their authority (see page 107). For Chapter 7, you might use one of the following ideas to add to your portfolio.

- Draw a bar chart comparing how long five different rulers held power. In a paragraph below the bar chart, explain which three rulers you think were most significant and why. Is length of rule the main element in deciding how significant a ruler was?
- Create a collage of sketches and photocopies showing the methods of exercising power used by rulers of the Mauryan, Gupta, and Han empires.
- Write a newspaper editorial either praising or criticizing Asoka and his methods of governing. Use historical examples to show the wisdom or the foolishness of his actions.

2. CONNECT TO TODAY: Cooperative Learning

THEME **CULTURAL INTERACTION** Throughout its history, India has been strongly affected by the many cultural groups who migrated onto the subcontinent. Work with a team to research the different peoples living in India today and how they interact with one another.

Using the Internet, reference books, or magazines, research information about the different peoples of India. Look for statistics and data that answer such questions as, How many different languages are spoken in India? How many different religions are practiced in India? Are any groups of people in India currently in conflict with each other?

As a team, create an encyclopedia article about the peoples of India today. Include graphs to show how India's population is distributed among various groups and text that describes those groups and how they interact today.

3. INTERPRETING A TIME LINE

Revisit the unit time line on pages 106-107. On the Chapter 7 time line, which events named reflect cultural achievements? Explain which of these events influenced India or China.

FOCUS ON ART

Look carefully at this 16-inch high, bronze sculpture from Han China.

- Would you describe this sculpture as realistic or not? Why?
- Do you think the scene depicted by the sculpture was typical of Han life? Why or why not?

Connect to History Think about the different classes that made up Han society. Which do you think is most likely the subject of this sculpture? Explain.

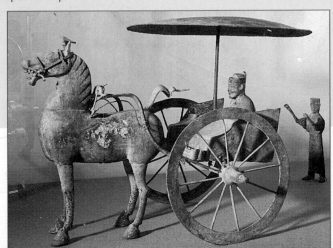

CHAPTER 8

African Civilizations, 1500 B.C.–A.D. 500

PREVIEWING THEMES

Interaction with Environment

To survive in the diverse, often harsh, environments of Africa, early peoples learned to adjust and adapt. Various cultures evolved as Africans developed ways of life suited to their particular geography and climate.

Power and Authority

All African societies developed means of providing their members with stability and order. These methods ranged from simple family ties to complex kingships.

Cultural Interaction

Migration—and the resulting mingling of peoples—is one of the major ways cultures spread and change. Mass migrations, such as those of the Bantu-speaking peoples, changed the face of the world and have had an ongoing influence on world culture.

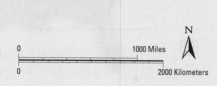

INTERNET CONNECTION

Visit us at **www.mcdougallittell.com** to learn more about African civilizations.

AFRICA, A.D. 350

Vegetation Regions
- Mediterranean
- Desert
- Savanna
- Rain Forest

N

| 0 | | 1000 Miles |
| 0 | | 2000 Kilometers |

Tropic of Cancer

Although largely barren, the **Sahara** is a major source of an important trading commodity—salt. Africans extract it by adding water to hollows dug in the salty soil. As harvesters like this one pour water from the larger to the smaller holes, the salt becomes more concentrated. When the water finally evaporates, the harvesters collect the precious crystals.

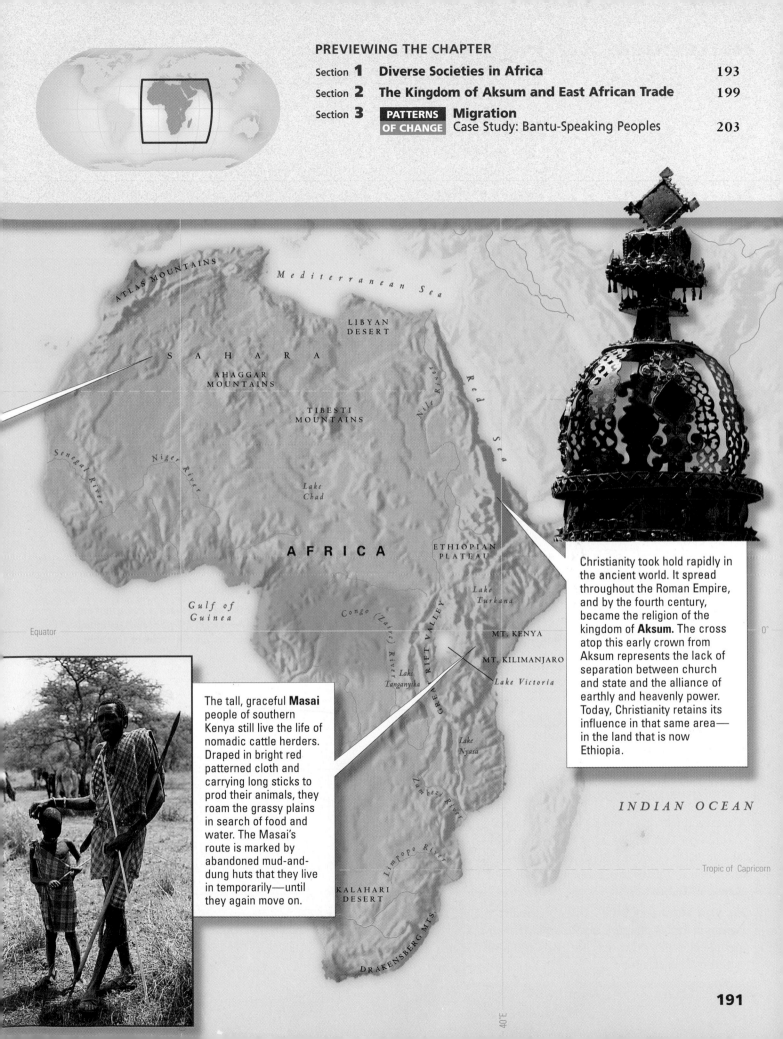

Mediterranean Sea

ATLAS MOUNTAINS

LIBYAN
DESERT

S A H A R A

AHAGGAR
MOUNTAINS

TIBESTI
MOUNTAINS

Nile River

Red Sea

Senegal River

Niger River

Lake
Chad

A F R I C A

ETHIOPIAN
PLATEAU

Gulf of
Guinea

Congo (Zaïre) River

Lake
Turkana

GREAT RIFT VALLEY

MT. KENYA

Equator   0°

MT. KILIMANJARO

Lake
Tanganyika

Lake Victoria

Lake
Nyasa

Zambezi River

INDIAN OCEAN

Limpopo River

Tropic of Capricorn

KALAHARI
DESERT

DRAKENSBERG MTS.

40° E

The tall, graceful **Masai** people of southern Kenya still live the life of nomadic cattle herders. Draped in bright red patterned cloth and carrying long sticks to prod their animals, they roam the grassy plains in search of food and water. The Masai's route is marked by abandoned mud-and-dung huts that they live in temporarily—until they again move on.

Christianity took hold rapidly in the ancient world. It spread throughout the Roman Empire, and by the fourth century, became the religion of the kingdom of **Aksum**. The cross atop this early crown from Aksum represents the lack of separation between church and state and the alliance of earthly and heavenly power. Today, Christianity retains its influence in that same area— in the land that is now Ethiopia.

191

Interact *with* History

Y ou belong to a small band of hunter-gatherers living in southern Africa around 100 B.C. You eat edible roots and plants the women and children in your group find in the forest, and animals the men trap or kill. One evening as you are sitting around the fire listening to a storyteller, you see a large group of people approaching. They are carrying iron spears and driving animals and are chanting in an unfamiliar language.

Your first reaction to these newcomers is fear. But you are also curious. Who are they? What do they want? How do they live? As they draw closer, you go to meet them.

What effects will these newcomers have on the community?

Having traveled large distances, these people might have valuable survival skills to share.

Their spears could indicate that the newcomers are good hunters or that they are hostile invaders—or both.

The hunter-gatherer community is small and tightly knit. There is, however, room to expand to accommodate the newcomers.

EXAMINING *the* ISSUES

- What problems, such as language, food, and shelter, might people face in dealing with newcomers?

- How might both native people and newcomers benefit from their interaction?

- In what ways would such interactions change everyone involved?

Discuss these questions as a class. In your discussion, remember what you've learned about other peoples who dealt with foreigners, such as the Indo-European invaders of Asia and India.

As you read about the early African civilizations in this chapter, notice how African peoples developed varied lifestyles and interacted with each other.

Diverse Societies in Africa

TERMS & NAMES
- Sahara
- savanna
- Sahel
- desertification
- extended family
- clan
- animism
- griot
- Djenné-Djeno
- Nok

MAIN IDEA	WHY IT MATTERS NOW
African peoples developed diverse societies as they adapted to varied environments.	Differences among modern societies are also based on people's interactions with their environments.

SETTING THE STAGE "Geography is the mother of history. Nowhere in the world is this more powerfully illustrated than in Africa. The most [powerful] force in Africa's experience is Africa's environment—the combined elements of geophysical features, location, and climate. . . . Africa has been a continent of abundant life but speedy death. Partly because of this . . . Africa has been the first habitat of man but the last to become truly [livable]." That is how Ali A. Mazrui, African scholar and creator of the television series *The Africans,* summed up his homeland. In the continent's widely varied environments, Africans developed unique cultures and societies—including the great civilizations of Egypt, Carthage, and Kush.

A Land of Geographic Contrasts

Africa is the second largest continent in the world. It stretches 4,600 miles from east to west and 5,000 miles from north to south. With a total of 11.7 million square miles, it occupies about one-fifth of the earth's land surface. The elevation of the continent is like a plate turned upside down. Narrow coastlines (50 to 100 miles) lie on either side of a central plateau. Waterfalls and rapids often form as rivers drop down to the coast from the plateau, making navigation impossible to or from the coast. Africa's coastline has few harbors, ports, or inlets. Because of this, the coastline is actually shorter than that of Europe, a land one-third Africa's size.

Vocabulary
tropics: the area of the globe that lies between the Tropic of Capricorn and the Tropic of Cancer.

As the map on the next page shows, Africa straddles the equator, and most of the continent is in the tropics. But it includes a large range of the earth's environments—from steamy coastal plains to snow-capped mountain peaks. Some parts of Africa suffer from constant drought, while others receive over 400 inches of rain a year. Vegetation varies from sand dunes and rocky wastes to dense green rain forests.

From Deserts to Rain Forests Each African environment offers its own challenges to people and wildlife. Deserts make up about 40 percent of the continent. They are largely uninhabitable and also hamper people's movement to more welcoming climates. During the day, temperatures can reach 136°F, and any rain that falls evaporates quickly. The largest deserts are the **Sahara** in the north and the Kalahari (kahl·uh·HAHR·ee) in the south. Stretching from the Atlantic Ocean to the Red Sea, the Sahara covers an area roughly the size of the United States. Only a small part of the Sahara consists of sand dunes. The rest is mostly a flat, gray wasteland of scattered rocks and gravel.

Vocabulary
uninhabitable: unsuitable for human life.

Another very different—but also partly uninhabitable—African environment is the rain forest. This densely wooded region stretches across about half of the middle of Africa, and covers about 5 percent of the continent. The rain forest

SPOTLIGHT ON

Tsetse Fly

The deadliest creature lurking in the gloom of the rain forests is neither the Congo python nor the wild leopard. It is a small fly called the tsetse (TSHET·see). Tsetse flies carry a disease that is deadly to livestock and can cause fatal sleeping sickness in humans.

The tsetse fly has played a major role in African history. Its presence prevented Africans from using cattle, donkeys, and horses to farm near the rain forests. This destructive insect also prevented invaders—especially Europeans—from colonizing fly-infested territories.

(shown at 3 to 7 times life size)

African Civilizations **193**

is hot and humid and receives enormous amounts of rain. Sometimes called "nature's greenhouse," it produces mahogany and teak trees up to 150 feet tall. Their leaves and branches form a dense canopy that keeps sunlight from reaching the forest floor. As a result, there are few small plants in the rain forest, despite the fact that movies often portray it as a vegetation-clogged jungle.

From Fertile Farmlands to Grassy Plains The northern coast and the southern tip of Africa, on the other hand, have welcoming climates and fertile soil. Summers are sunny, dry, and hot, while winters are mild. Rainfall is moderate. Because these coastal areas with Mediterranean vegetation are so fertile, they are densely populated with farmers and herders.

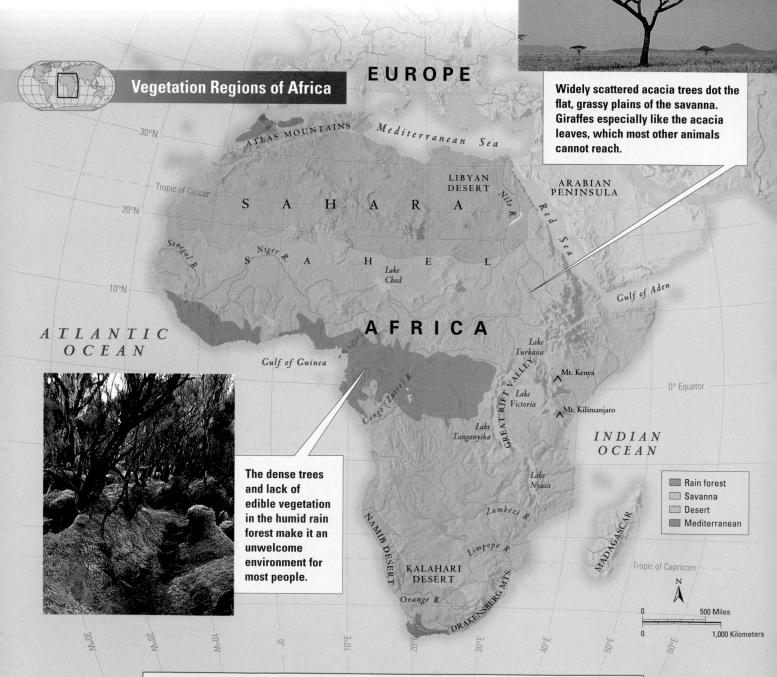

Vegetation Regions of Africa

Widely scattered acacia trees dot the flat, grassy plains of the savanna. Giraffes especially like the acacia leaves, which most other animals cannot reach.

The dense trees and lack of edible vegetation in the humid rain forest make it an unwelcome environment for most people.

Rain forest
Savanna
Desert
Mediterranean

500 Miles

1,000 Kilometers

GEOGRAPHY SKILLBUILDER: Interpreting Maps

1. **Location** *About what percent of Africa is desert? savanna?*
2. **Region** *If you were to fold a map of Africa in half along the equator, what do you notice about the similar vegetation zones above and below the fold?*

The largest number of people in Africa, however, live on the **savannas,** or grassy plains. Covered with tall grasses and dotted with acacia trees, the savannas cover over 40 percent of the continent. Dry seasons alternate with rainy seasons—often, two of each a year. The topsoil throughout Africa is thin, and heavy rains strip away minerals. In most years, however, the savannas support abundant agriculture. Major crops are grains such as sorghum and millet, rice, wheat, and maize (corn).

Africa's savanna is not just an endless plain, however. It includes mountainous highlands, swampy tropical stretches, and the land at the southern edge of the Sahara Desert, the **Sahel** (suh·HAYL). Sahel means "coastline" in Arabic, and the ancient north African people may have named it this because the Sahara seemed to them a vast ocean of sand. Each year, however, the desert takes over more and more of the Sahel. This steady process of drying of the soil is called **desertification.**

Early Humans Adapt to Their Environments

The first humans appeared in the Great Rift Valley, a deep gash in the earth's crust that runs through the floor of the Red Sea and across eastern Africa. People moved outward from this area in the world's first migration, adapting to the vastly different environments they encountered. They developed technologies that helped them survive in—and then alter—their surroundings. For example, first using pointed sticks as spears, they progressed to shaping spear points out of stone, and later, iron.

Nomadic Lifestyle Africa's earliest peoples were nomadic hunter-gatherers who roamed from place to place seeking sources of food. Today, some of the San of the Kalahari Desert and the BaMbuti (bah·uhm·BOO·tee) of the rain forests of Congo are still hunter-gatherers. The San, for example, travel in small bands of a few related families. The men hunt with spears and bows and arrows, and the women and children gather roots and berries. As shown in the Daily Life feature on page 196, they know and use the resources of their environment well.

Africans who lived in areas that supported a variety of animals eventually learned to domesticate and raise them for food. Called herders, or pastoralists, these people kept cattle, goats, or sheep. Like the hunter-gatherers, they were nomads, driving their animals to find water and good pastures for grazing during the dry season. Millions of modern Africans are pastoral herders as well. The Masai (mah·SEYE) of Tanzania and southern Kenya, for example, still measure their wealth by the size of their herds.

Transition to a Settled Lifestyle Most early Africans continued to hunt, although they eventually learned to grow their own food, rather than gathering what grew wild. Experts believe that agriculture probably began by 10,000 B.C. in Africa. Between 8000 and 4000 B.C., the Sahara received increased rainfall and turned into a savanna. But about 4000 B.C., the Sahara began to dry up again. To survive, many early farmers moved east into the Nile Valley and south into West Africa. Many settled on the savannas, which had the best agricultural land. Some peoples also learned to farm in the rain forest, where they planted root crops, such as yams, that needed little sun.

Agriculture drastically changed the way Africans lived on the savannas. Growing their own food enabled them to settle in one location, where they built permanent shelters. Settlements expanded because reliable food supplies meant longer, healthier lives and an increased birthrate. The increased food supply also freed some members of the community to practice activities other than farming. These activities included working metal, making pottery, or crafting jewelry.

THINK THROUGH HISTORY
A. Making Inferences Why might herders have remained nomadic?

CONNECT to TODAY

Nomads in Nairobi

In the drought of 1997, Masai herders traveled hundreds of miles in search of grass for their starving cattle. They drove their animals through plains and along modern highways onto land near the Kenyan capital, Nairobi. The cattle ate whatever grass they could find, including several acres surrounding the transmitters of the Kenya Broadcasting Corporation.

In a tense confrontation, company officials finally allowed the Masai to use the land for grazing—possibly because it saved them the cost of hiring people to cut the grass.

Nomad Nutritional News

A Movable Feast

San women make a picnic of it when they take their children out to gather food for their families. The women carry sharp wooden digging sticks as well as net bags holding ostrich eggshells filled with water. Around her body, each woman fastens a two-compartment bag called a *kaross,* which carries more than 20 pounds of food—fruits, nuts, melons, roots, tubers, termites, caterpillars, and locusts. These foods satisfy about three-quarters of the San's daily caloric needs.

Making a Bee-Line

Once the rains begin to fall, San men and women know that they will soon get their fill of honey. During the short rainy season, the San note where the bees fly at sunset, when they return to their hives. A San who finds a good hive immediately smokes out the bees and removes the sticky, sweet treat. He doesn't bypass unripe hives, though. He marks them with a small heap of stones and returns later to retrieve the honey. Tampering with marked hives is a serious crime, one that the San may punish by death. So bee-ware.

Thirsty? Look for a three-pronged leaf and dig down about a foot. You'll find a juicy *bi* bulb like this one that you can mash and mix with chewed leaves for a refreshing drink.

Ate Too Much? See a Shaman

Shamans, or healers, often beat drums and chant to create the right atmosphere for healing. To cure indigestion and other illnesses, they use sacred objects and medicine in a ceremony attended by the patient's family. Don't visit a shaman unless you're willing to believe in his or her powers, though. Your trust is the shaman's most important medicine.

The Gourmet Corner:

A One-Egg Omelet
One ostrich egg is the equivalent of two dozen hens' eggs, a handy fact to know if you're an omelet fan. A San cook shares her recipe: Take one ostrich egg. To save the shell for carrying water, tap a hole in the crown. With a twig, remove the membrane. To scramble the egg, twirl the stick in the hole. Pour the scrambled egg into a tortoise-shell pan and then into a hole lined with hot coals. Build the fire up around the hole to cook the top of your omelet. Dust the ash off the completed omelet, clean the bottom, and serve it to 15 or 20 friends.

An empty ostrich eggshell and the omelet in progress.

Connect *to* History

Drawing Conclusions How do the San use their extensive knowledge of their environment?
SEE SKILLBUILDER HANDBOOK PAGE 1006

Connect *to* Today

Researching Gather information about a modern nomadic culture, such as the Masai of southern Kenya and Tanzania, by using the library or Internet. In what ways is this culture similar to that of the San? How does it differ?

These increasingly large and complex settlements of people required more organization and regulation than smaller communities. Various types of governing bodies developed to fill this need. Some governments consisted of a village chief and/or a council of the leaders of individual family groups. As strong groups moved to extend their land and conquered weaker settlements, they centralized their power and their governments. Some of these societies eventually developed into great kingdoms.

Africans Share Common Characteristics No matter what environment they lived in and what style of life they adopted, the societies south of the Sahara—like all human cultures—shared common elements. One of these elements was the importance of the basic social unit, the family. Besides parents and children, this primary group often included grandparents, aunts, uncles, and cousins in an **extended family.** Ties often expanded to the **clan,** a group that shared common ancestors.

African peoples not only organized themselves into family groups. They also developed belief systems that helped them understand and organize information about their world. Nearly all of these local religions involved a belief in one creator, or god. They generally also included elements of **animism,** a religion in which spirits played an important role in regulating daily life. Animists believe that these spirits are present in animals, plants, and other natural forces, and also take the form of the souls of their dead ancestors.

Although all African societies had a language, most were not written down. History, literature, and culture were shared orally by specialized storytellers. In West Africa, for example, these storytellers, or **griots** (gree·OHZ), kept this history alive, passing it from parent to child:

THINK THROUGH HISTORY
B. Summarizing
What common characteristics did all African societies share?

Early Societies in West Africa

To add to information provided by Africa's oral historians, archaeologists have continued to look for evidence of the history of Africa south of the Sahara. Recent discoveries in West Africa have proved how old and extensive that history is. Archaeologists believe that early peoples moved into this area from the north as desertification forced them to find better farmland. Discoveries in the areas of modern Mali and Nigeria reveal that West Africans developed advanced societies and cities long before outsiders came to the continent.

Djenné-Djeno Archaeologists uncovered the remains of one of these cities, **Djenné-Djeno**

(jeh·NAY jeh·NOH), or ancient Djenné, in 1977 on a tributary of the Niger River. In excavating a huge tell, or mound covering the remains of a series of civilizations, they discovered hundreds of thousands of artifacts. These objects included pottery, copper hair ornaments, clay toys, glass beads, stone bracelets, and iron knives. The oldest objects dated from 250 B.C., making Djenné-Djeno the oldest known city

The water that surrounded Djenné-Djeno provided food and also offered a transportation route, which made the city a bustling trade center.

197

in Africa south of the Sahara. The city was abandoned some time after A.D. 1400. About that time, another city, Djenné, arose about two miles away.

At its height, Djenné-Djeno had some 50,000 residents. They lived in round reed huts plastered with mud. Later, they built enclosed houses made of mud bricks. They fished in the Niger River, raised rice on its fertile floodplains, and herded cattle. By the third century B.C., they had discovered how to smelt iron. They exchanged their rice, fish, and pottery for copper, gold, and salt with other peoples who lived along the river. Djenné-Djeno was linked to other towns not only by the Niger, but also by overland camel routes. For that reason, it became a bustling trading center.

The Nok Culture Although Djenné-Djeno was its oldest town, West Africa's earliest known culture was that of the **Nok** (nahk) people. They lived in what is now Nigeria

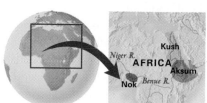

This terra cotta elephant head reveals both the artistry of its Nok creator and the fact that elephants played a role in that people's daily lives.

between 500 B.C. and A.D. 200. Their name came from the village where the first artifacts from their culture were discovered. Like the residents of Djenné-Djeno, the Nok were farmers. They were also the first West African people known to smelt iron. They used it to make tools for farming and weapons for hunting. These iron implements lasted longer than ones made of wood or stone, and vastly improved the lives of the Nok.

The Nok developed iron-making technology about 500 B.C., nearly 300 years before it arose in Djenné-Djeno. In fact, they may have brought the technology to Djenné-Djeno. The similarity of artifacts found in these two distant places suggests that the Nok may have settled in Djenné-Djeno at one time.

Nok artifacts have been found in an area stretching for 300 miles between the Niger and Benue rivers. Many are sculptures made of terra cotta, a reddish-brown clay. They often depict human or animal heads in great artistic detail, showing the Nok's skill. The features of some of the heads reveal more about history than just the skill of their creators, however. One of the heads, for example, shows a distinctive hairdo arranged in six buns, a style that is still worn by some people in Nigeria. This similarity suggests that the Nok may have been the direct ancestors of some modern Africans.

THINK THROUGH HISTORY
C. Comparing In what ways were the cultures of Djenné-Djeno and the Nok alike?

While the early inhabitants of West Africa were developing cities, cultures, and technologies that would write their name on the pages of history, East Africa was undergoing its own cultural evolution.

Section ① Assessment

1. TERMS & NAMES

Identify
- Sahara
- savanna
- Sahel
- desertification
- extended family
- clan
- animism
- griot
- Djenné-Djeno
- Nok

2. TAKING NOTES

Use a flow chart like the one below to trace the main events that followed the development of agriculture on the African savannas.

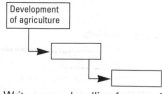

Development of agriculture

Write a news headline for one of these developments.

3. ANALYZING CAUSES

How does adapting to different environments lead to the development of diverse cultures?

THINK ABOUT
- natural resources
- Nok accomplishments
- migrations of different groups of people

4. THEME ACTIVITY

Interaction with Environment Take an imaginary journey to one of the four African vegetation zones. Then write a short diary entry or letter describing what you see and experience. Explain your difficulties adapting to this environment and tell what you learn.

2 The Kingdom of Aksum and East African Trade

MAIN IDEA

The kingdom of Aksum became an international trading power and adopted Christianity.

WHY IT MATTERS NOW

Ancient Aksum, which is now Ethiopia, is still a center of Eastern Christianity.

SETTING THE STAGE In the eighth century B.C., before the Nok were spreading their culture throughout West Africa, the kingdom of Kush in East Africa had become powerful enough to conquer Egypt. (See Chapter 4.) However, fierce Assyrians swept into Egypt during the next century and drove the Kushite pharaohs south. Kush nevertheless remained a powerful kingdom for over 1,000 years—until it was conquered by another even more powerful kingdom.

The Rise of the Kingdom of Aksum

The kingdom that arose was **Aksum** (AHK·soom). It was located south of Kush on a rugged plateau on the Red Sea, in what is now Eritrea and Ethiopia. A legend traces the founding of the kingdom of Aksum and the Ethiopian royal dynasty to the son of King Solomon of ancient Israel and the Queen of Sheba. That dynasty includes the 20th-century ruler Haile Selassie. In fact, the history of Aksum may have begun as early as 1000 B.C., when Arab peoples crossed the Red Sea into Africa. There they mingled with Kushite herders and farmers and passed along their written language, Ge'ez (GEE·ehz). They also shared their skills of working stone and building dams and aqueducts.

The first mention of Aksum was in a Greek guidebook written around A.D. 100, *Periplus of the Erythraean Sea*. It describes Zoskales (ZAHS·kuh·leez), thought to be the first king of Aksum. He was "a stickler about his possessions and always [greedy] for getting more, but in other respects a fine person and well versed in reading and writing Greek." Greece was not the only country to interact with Aksum, however. Under Zoskales and other rulers, Aksum began conquering people in other lands. The Aksumites seized areas along the Red Sea and the Blue Nile in Africa. They also crossed the Red Sea and took control of lands on the southwestern Arabian Peninsula.

Aksum Controls International Trade Aksum's location and expansion into surrounding areas

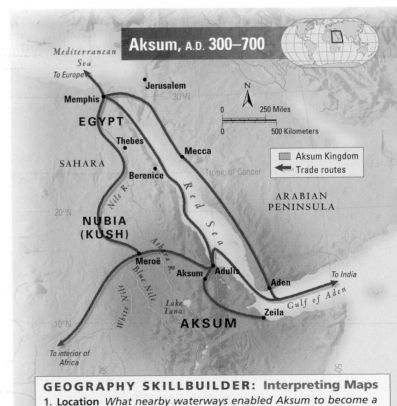

Aksum, A.D. 300–700

GEOGRAPHY SKILLBUILDER: Interpreting Maps
1. **Location** What nearby waterways enabled Aksum to become a major trading center?
2. **Movement** What continents or countries did Aksum's trade routes give it access to?

made it an important trading center. It was a hub for caravan routes to Egypt and Meroë, the capital of Kush. Its miles of coastline and ports on the Red Sea gave it influence over sea trade on the Mediterranean Sea and Indian Ocean as well. Traders from Egypt, Arabia, Persia, India, and the Roman Empire crowded Aksum's chief seaport, **Adulis** (AHD·uh·luhs), near present-day Massawa. As a result, Aksum soon became an international trading power.

Aksumite merchants traded necessities such as salt and luxuries such as rhinoceros horns, tortoise shells, ivory, emeralds, and gold. In return, they chose from items such as imported cloth, glass, olive oil, wine, brass, iron, and copper. Around A.D. 550, an Egyptian merchant named Cosmas described how Aksumite agents bargained for gold from the people in southern Ethiopia:

A VOICE FROM THE PAST

They take along with them to the mining district oxen, lumps of salt, and iron, and when they reach its neighborhood they . . . halt . . . and form an encampment, which they fence round with a great hedge of thorns. Within this they live, and having slaughtered the oxen, cut them in pieces and lay the pieces on top of the thorns along with the lumps of salt and the iron. Then come the natives bringing gold in nuggets like peas . . . and lay one or two or more of these upon what pleases them. . . . Then the owner of the meat approaches, and if he is satisfied he takes the gold away, and upon seeing this its owner comes and takes the flesh or the salt or the iron.

COSMAS, quoted in *Travellers in Ethiopia*

A Strong Ruler Expands the Kingdom The kingdom of Aksum reached its height between A.D. 325 and 360, when an exceptionally strong ruler, **Ezana** (AY·zah·nah), occupied the throne. Determined to establish and expand his authority, Ezana first conquered the part of the Arabian peninsula that is now Yemen. Then, in 330, Ezana turned his attention to Kush, which already had begun to decline. In 350, he conquered the Kushites and burned Meroë to the ground:

A VOICE FROM THE PAST

I carried war against [them] when they had rebelled. . . . I burnt their towns of stone and their towns of straw. At the same time, my men plundered [stole] their grain, their bronze, their iron and their copper, destroyed the idols in their homes, their stocks of corn and of cotton; and they threw themselves into the river. . . .

KING EZANA OF AKSUM, quoted in *Africa: Past and Present*

A Cosmopolitan Culture Develops

From the beginning, Aksumites had a diverse cultural heritage. This blend included traditions of the Arab peoples who crossed the Red Sea into Africa and those of the Kushite peoples they settled among. As the kingdom expanded and became a powerful trading center, it attracted people from all over the ancient world.

The port city of Adulis was particularly cosmopolitan. It included people from Aksum's widespread trading partners, such as Egypt, Arabia, Greece, Rome, Persia, India, and even Byzantium. In the babble of tongues heard in Aksum, Greek stood out as the international language of the time, much as English does in the world today.

The Spread of Christianity The Aksumites, like other ancient Africans, traditionally believed in one god. They called their god Mahrem and believed that their king was directly descended from him. They were also animists, however, and worshipped the spirits of nature and honored their dead ancestors. They offered sacrifices—often as many as a dozen oxen at a time—to those spirits, to Mahrem, and often, to the Greek god of war, Ares.

Vocabulary
cosmopolitan: including elements from many parts of the world.

Merchants exchanged more than raw materials and finished goods in Aksum. They shared ideas as well. One of these ideas was a new religion, Christianity. Based on the teachings of Jesus and a belief in one God—monotheism—Christianity began in Palestine about A.D. 30. It spread throughout the Roman Empire and then to Aksum. King Ezana's conversion and his devout practice of Christianity strengthened its hold in Aksum.

In A.D. 451, a dispute arose over the nature of Christ—whether he was solely divine, or both divine and human. This dispute led to a split between Egypt and Ethiopia on the one hand and the church of Constantinople and Rome on the other. The Egyptian and Ethiopian churches, which believed in the wholly divine nature of Christ, followed their separate paths. They became the Coptic Church of Egypt and the Ethiopian Orthodox Church. The influence of these churches has continued. The Ethiopian Orthodox Church today boasts a membership of more than 22 million people—over half the population of the country.

Aksumite Architecture The establishment of Christianity was just one lasting achievement of the Aksumites. They also developed a unique architecture. They used stone instead of mud bricks to construct vast royal palaces and public buildings. Like the Egyptians, the Aksumites used no mortar. Instead, they carved stones to fit together tightly. Aksum's kings also built huge stone pillars called stelae (STEE·lee). These presumably were meant to celebrate the kings' conquests and to demonstrate Aksum's greatness. Some are 60 feet tall and were among the largest structures in the ancient world. Ezana left a lasting reminder of Aksum's spiritual and structural achievements in his last stele. He dedicated this soaring stone to the Christian God, "the Lord of heaven, who in heaven and upon earth is mightier than everything that exists."

Language and Agriculture The inscription on Ezana's stele is written in Ge'ez, the language brought to Aksum by its early Arab inhabitants. Aside from Egypt and Meroë, Aksum was the only ancient African kingdom known to have developed a written language. It was also the first state south of the Sahara to mint its own coins. Made of bronze, silver, and gold, these coins were imprinted with the saying, "May the country be satisfied." Ezana apparently hoped that this inscription would make him popular with the people. Every time they used a coin, it would remind them that he had their interests at heart.

In addition to these cultural achievements, the Aksumites adapted creatively to their rugged, hilly environment. They created a new method of agriculture, terrace farming. This enabled them to greatly increase the productivity of their land. Terraces, or steplike ridges constructed on mountain slopes, helped the soil retain water and prevented its being washed downhill in heavy rains. The Aksumites dug canals to channel water from mountain streams into the fields. They also built dams and cisterns, or holding tanks, to store water.

The Fall of Aksum

Aksum's cultural and technological achievements enabled it to last for 800 years. The kingdom finally declined, however, under invaders who practiced the religion called Islam (ihs·LAHM). Its founder was the prophet Muhammad, and by the time of his death in 632, his followers had conquered all of Arabia. This territory included Aksum's lands on the Arabian coast of the Red Sea. The Islamic invaders went on to conquer vast territories in the Mediterranean world, spreading their religion as they went. Because Aksum had protected

This towering stone pillar, or stele, was built to celebrate Aksum's achievements. Still standing today, its size and elaborate inscriptions make it an achievement in its own right.

Global Impact

A Road Paved with Gold: Aksum to Rome

The kingdom of Aksum had a tremendous impact on the ancient Mediterranean world. It particularly influenced one of the most important powers of the time, the Roman Empire. Roman ships came to Adulis weekly to trade with the Aksumites. Many Roman merchants lived in Adulis, and in the capital city, Aksum.

One of the chief commodities that linked the two powers was gold. The Aksumites had access to it from inland gold mines, and the Romans needed it to support the monetary system of their growing empire. Rome and Aksum were linked not only by gold, however. They also shared a spiritual link in their commitment to Christianity.

African Civilizations **201**

*[Handwritten margin note: *Maghrib: N. africa which has been converted islam to]*

This 15th-century Ethiopian fan shows the Christian influence that began in Aksum and continues in the area today. It may have been used during the church service to keep flies from settling on the communion bread and wine.

Muhammad's family and followers during his rise to power, however, his followers initially did not invade Aksum's territories on the African coast of the Red Sea. Retaining control of that coastline enabled Aksum to remain a trading power.

Before long, though, the invaders seized footholds on the African coast as well. In 710 they destroyed Adulis. This conquest cut Aksum off from the major ports along both the Red Sea and the Mediterranean. As a result, the kingdom declined as an international trading power. But it was not only Aksum's political power that weakened. Its spiritual identity and environment were also endangered.

As the invaders spread Islam to the lands they conquered, Aksum became isolated from other Christian settlements. To escape the advancing wave of Islam, Aksum's rulers moved their capital over the mountains into what is now northern Ethiopia. There, depletion of the forests and soil erosion as well as Aksum's new geographic isolation led to its decline as a world power.

Although the kingdom of Aksum reached tremendous heights and left a lasting legacy in its religion, architecture, and agriculture, it lived out its lifespan within a fairly small area. Other cultures, both in Africa and around the world, have developed not by expanding locally, but by moving over great distances. As their living circumstances changed, they adapted to the other peoples and environments they encountered.

Section 2 Assessment

1. TERMS & NAMES

Identify
- Aksum
- Adulis
- Ezana

2. TAKING NOTES

Use a web like the one below to list the achievements of Aksum.

Aksum's achievements

Write a paragraph comparing Aksum's achievements with those of another empire, such as Egypt or Rome.

3. ANALYZING CAUSES

Why did the kingdom of Aksum decline?

THINK ABOUT
- the rise and spread of Islam
- Aksum's relocation
- changes in the environment

4. ANALYZING THEMES

Power and Authority Do you think that the kingdom of Aksum would have reached the same heights if Ezana had not become king? Explain your answer.

THINK ABOUT
- Ezana's accomplishments
- Aksum's importance as a trading center
- Ezana's conversion to Christianity
- the decline of Aksum

❸ Migration

CASE STUDY: Bantu-Speaking Peoples

MAIN IDEA	WHY IT MATTERS NOW
Throughout history, people have been driven to uproot themselves and explore their world.	Migration continues to shape the modern world.

SETTING THE STAGE Human history is a motion picture, a vibrating spectacle of movement, collision, settlement, and more movement. Human beings have always been driven to search for new opportunities. The desire to move on in search of a better life seems to be built into human nature.

Migrations Through History

Aside from the general human desire for change, migrations have many specific causes. Some of these are listed in the chart below.

PATTERNS OF CHANGE: Migration

Cause	Example	Effect
Environmental change	Shift in climate, depletion of natural resources, drought, earthquake	Redistribution of world's population, blending of cultures
Economic pressure	Increasing population, famine, unemployment	Shifts in population
Political and religious persecution	Slave trade, war, ethnic cleansing, repression	Dislocation and oppression of peoples, spread of ideas and religions
Technological development	Tools, agriculture, iron smelting, communications and transportation networks	Development of civilizations and empires

SKILLBUILDER: Interpreting Charts
1. *Which causes of migration have remained important throughout history? Explain.*
2. *Which cause do you think is most important in modern migrations? Why?*

As an important pattern in human culture, migrations have influenced world history from its outset. The first human beings began populating the globe as they were pushed to move on by environmental change, population growth, and technological advances, such as the smelting of iron. In the 15th century, the Ottomans' drive for power pushed them to move all over the ancient world to create a massive empire. Seventeenth-century European settlers were pulled to America by the hope of religious tolerance and improving their lives economically.

One way experts can trace the patterns of this movement of people through history is by studying the spread of languages. People bring their languages with them when they move to new places. And languages, like the people who speak them, are living things that evolve and change in regular ways. If two languages have similar words for a particular object or idea, for example, it is likely that the people who spoke them were in close contact at one time.

Massive Migrations

Language is one major element that unites or divides people. One group of African languages, the Niger-Congo, includes over 900 individual languages. A family of languages in this group developed from a single parent tongue, Proto-Bantu. The speakers of these related languages belong to many different ethnic groups, but often are referred to collectively as **Bantu-speaking peoples.** (The word *Bantu* itself means "the people.") These early Africans made one of the greatest migrations in history and populated the southern third of the continent. The Bantu-speaking people lived in the savanna south of the Sahara in the area that is now southeastern Nigeria. Starting in the first few centuries A.D. and continuing until recent times, a small number of Bantu speakers moved southward throughout Africa, spreading their language and culture.

Bantu Culture Bantu speakers were not one people, but a group of peoples who shared certain cultural characteristics. They were farmers and nomadic herders who developed and passed along the skill of ironworking. Many experts believe they were related to the Nok peoples.

Beginning at least 2,000 years ago or earlier, small groups of Bantu speakers began spreading south and east. They shared their skills with the people they met, adapted their methods to suit each new environment, and learned new ways. They followed the Congo River through the rain forests. There they farmed the riverbanks—the only place that received enough sunlight to support agriculture.

As they moved eastward into the savannas, they adapted their techniques for herding goats and sheep to raising cattle. Passing through what is now Kenya and Tanzania, they learned to cultivate new crops. One such crop was the banana, which came from Southeast Asia via Indonesian travelers. In this way, they were able to expand and vary their food supply. Within 1,500 years or so—a short time in the span of history—the Bantu speakers reached the southern tip of Africa.

Some of their farming methods quickly exhausted the land, however. The search for new, fertile soil kept the migrating people on the move. A 19th-century Scottish missionary and explorer, David Livingstone, described the farming methods of one group of Bantu speakers, which had probably changed little over time:

A VOICE FROM THE PAST

Food abounds, and very little labor is required for its cultivation. . . . When a garden becomes too poor for good crops . . . the owner removes a little farther into the forest, applies fire around the roots of the larger trees to kill them, cuts down the smaller, and a new, rich garden is ready for the seed.

DAVID LIVINGSTONE, quoted in *History of World Societies*

Effects of the Migration Although it isn't possible to know exactly what caused the Bantu-speaking peoples to migrate, anthropologists have proposed a logical explanation. These experts suggest that once these peoples developed agriculture, they were able to produce more food than they could by hunting and gathering. As a result, the population in West Africa increased. Because this enlarged population required more food, the earliest Bantu speakers planted more land, and soon there wasn't enough land to go around. They couldn't go north in search of land, because the area was densely populated and the Sahara was slowly advancing toward them. The areas that

This carved wood mask mingles human and animal features. It probably was used by Bantu speakers in a ceremony to communicate with natural or ancestral spirits.

THINK THROUGH HISTORY
A. Clarifying How did the Bantu deal with the problems they encountered in their migrations?

once had been savanna were undergoing desertification. So the people moved southward. *REASON FOR MIGRATION*

Within only 1,500 years, the Bantu speakers had populated much of the southern half of Africa. The area was sparsely populated with peoples like the BaMbuti and the San. These Africans were not Bantu speakers and lived then, as they still do, by hunting and gathering.

Territorial wars often broke out as the Bantu speakers spread south into these peoples' lands. Fighting with iron-tipped spears, the newcomers easily drove off the BaMbuti and the San, who were armed only with stone *NOT ADVANCED* weapons. Today, the BaMbuti are confined to a corner of the Congo Basin. The San live only around the Kalahari Desert in northwestern South Africa, Namibia, and Botswana.

The Bantu speakers also exchanged ideas and intermarried with the people they joined, however. This intermingling created new cultures with unique customs and traditions. Although the Bantu migrations produced a great diversity of cultures, they also left a unifying influence on the continent. As a result of these migrations, in Africa today there are at least 60 million people who speak one of the hundreds of Bantu languages. *BROADENS*

Migration continues to shape the modern world as new factors make living conditions difficult. For example, political refugees leave or are forced out of countries for places that offer them safe haven. A worldwide process of urbanization also sets people in motion. It draws them from rural areas where there is little opportunity for advancement to cities such as Mexico City. In the next chapter, you will see how early Americans underwent a process of growth similar to that of early Africans.

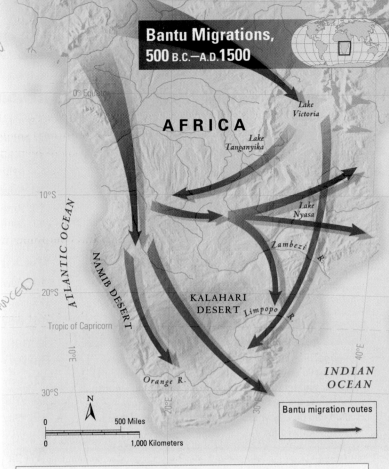

Bantu Migrations, 500 B.C.–A.D. 1500

AFRICA

Lake Victoria
Lake Tanganyika
Lake Nyasa
Zambezi R.
NAMIB DESERT
KALAHARI DESERT
Limpopo R.
Orange R.
ATLANTIC OCEAN
INDIAN OCEAN

0° Equator
10°S
20°S
Tropic of Capricorn
30°S
10°E
20°E
30°E
40°E

N

0 ____ 500 Miles
0 ____ 1,000 Kilometers

Bantu migration routes

GEOGRAPHY SKILLBUILDER: Interpreting Maps
1. **Human-Environment Interaction** *What geographic features did the Bantu speakers encounter in the course of their migrations?*
2. **Movement** *Compare this map with the one on page 194. Why didn't the Bantu speakers migrate northward?*

Section 3 Assessment

1. TERMS & NAMES
Identify
• Bantu-speaking peoples

2. TAKING NOTES
In a chart like the one below, list three reasons why people migrate. Give an example of a migration that occurred for each reason.

Reason for migration	Example
1.	
2.	
3.	

3. COMPARING AND CONTRASTING
How might the migrating Bantu speakers and the peoples they encountered have reacted to each other?

THINK ABOUT
• Bantu culture
• territorial wars
• cultural adaptation

4. THEME ACTIVITY
Cultural Interaction With a classmate, act out an encounter between a native of southern Africa and a Bantu speaker who has just migrated into the area.

Chapter **8** Assessment

TERMS & NAMES

Briefly explain the importance of each of the following to African civilizations in the period from 1500 B.C. to A.D. 500.

1. Sahara
2. desertification
3. extended family
4. animism
5. griot
6. Djenné-Djeno
7. Nok
8. Aksum
9. Ezana
10. Bantu-speaking peoples

Interact *with* History

On page 192, you considered the effects newcomers would have on a community. Now that you've read the chapter and learned about people's interactions with their environments and with other cultures, how would you modify your answer? Discuss your ideas with a small group.

REVIEW QUESTIONS

SECTION 1 *(pages 193–198)*

Diverse Societies in Africa

11. Which two vegetation zones of Africa are welcoming to human habitation? Which two are not?
12. How did agriculture develop in Africa?
13. What circumstances enabled Djenné-Djeno to become a bustling trade center?

SECTION 2 *(pages 199–202)*

The Kingdom of Aksum and East African Trade

14. Why was Aksum able to control international trade?
15. In what ways did Ezana contribute to the rise of his kingdom?
16. Why did Aksum fall?

SECTION 3 *(pages 203–205)*

Patterns of Change: Migration

17. Why is language important in the study of migrations?
18. What caused the Bantu-speaking peoples to migrate?
19. Why were the migrations of Bantu speakers so extensive and successful?
20. Name three conditions that cause people to migrate.

Visual Summary

African Civilizations

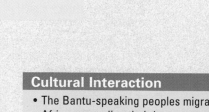

Power and Authority

- Some cultures were governed by family clan leaders or village chiefs.
- Migratory peoples, such as the Bantu speakers, exerted their power by spreading their beliefs and influence to other cultures.
- Aksum became so large and strong that it centralized its power and became a great kingdom.

Interaction with Environment

- The Bantu-speaking peoples left environments that could not support them and migrated to more welcoming lands.
- The location of Djenné-Djeno on a tributary of the Niger enabled it to become a bustling center of trade.
- The Aksumites developed techniques such as terrace farming to harness their environment.

Cultural Interaction

- The Bantu-speaking peoples migrated throughout southern Africa, spreading their language and culture.
- Since Aksum was a major trading center, its people interacted constantly with cultures from throughout the ancient world.
- The Nok shared their ironworking and agricultural skills with other peoples they came in contact with, such as those of Djenné-Djeno.

CRITICAL THINKING

1. GRIOTS—STILL GOING STRONG?

Reread the quote on page 197 by Djeli Mamadou Kouyate. Why does he consider his job as griot so important? Who or what takes the place of griots in the modern world?

2. MOVING ON AND MORE

Environmental change, technological development, economic pressure, and political and religious persecution give rise to migrations. These conditions also can affect each other, however. For example, technological developments such as industrialization can contribute to environmental change. Using a diagram like the one below, list examples of mutual effects of these conditions in the boxes.

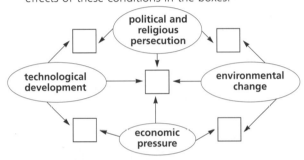

3. REACTING TO MIGRATION

THEME **CULTURAL INTERACTION** People have different cultural characteristics and personal qualities. Which of these might determine how individuals react to and interact with migrating people who settle among them?

4. ANALYZING PRIMARY SOURCES

Pliny, a scholar and naturalist, lived in Rome during the first century A.D. The following paragraph expresses his thoughts about the peoples who lived in central Africa at that time. Read the quotation and answer the questions below it.

A VOICE FROM THE PAST

The Atlas tribe is primitive and subhuman.... When they observe the rising and setting sun they utter terrible curses against it, as the cause of disaster to themselves and their fields. Nor do they have dreams in their sleep like the rest of mankind.... The Blemmyae are reported as being without heads; their mouth and eyes are attached to their chest .... The Strapfeet are people with feet like thongs who naturally move by crawling.

PLINY THE ELDER, *Natural History*

- What was Pliny's biased view of Africans?
- How might he have developed that view?
- What does his point of view suggest about how people should read history?

CHAPTER ACTIVITIES

1. LIVING HISTORY: Unit Portfolio Project

THEME **POWER AND AUTHORITY** Your unit portfolio project focuses on showing how people in history have exercised and been affected by power and authority (see page 107). For Chapter 8, you might use one of the following ideas to add to your portfolio.

- Write a speech in which Ezana expresses his belief in Christianity to Aksum's citizens.
- Present a dialogue in which two Aksumites discuss how the presence of foreigners and foreign products affects their daily lives.
- Design a game called "Power Play." Set the game in fourth-century Africa. Include situations that helped or hindered the rise of kingdoms, such as desertification, development of ironworking technology, and the spread of religions. Have players do whatever they have to do—migrate, trade, seize territories, or adjust and adapt—to gain power.

2. CONNECT TO TODAY: Cooperative Learning

THEME **INTERACTION WITH ENVIRONMENT** Modern Africans still face many of the same environmental issues that their ancestors dealt with. Drought, overuse of land, and desertification are problems that affect the present and will help determine the future.

 Use the Internet or magazines to research the ways a current African ethnic group or country is struggling to survive in its environment. Then write a short report of your findings.

- Describe the group or country and its current problems and indicate how the people are trying to solve them.
- Draw comparisons with problems Africans faced in the past.

3. INTERPRETING A TIME LINE

Look back at the unit time line on pages 106–107. Which group or kingdom of peoples in Africa from 1500 B.C. to A.D. 500 do you think had the most lasting influence on the world? Explain your answer.

FOCUS ON GEOGRAPHY

Look at the size of Africa compared with that of several other major continents and countries.

- How does the size of the Sahara compare with that of the United States?
- How do you think the population of Africa compares with that of the countries shown?

Connect to History How does the map clarify the extent of the migrations of Bantu speakers?

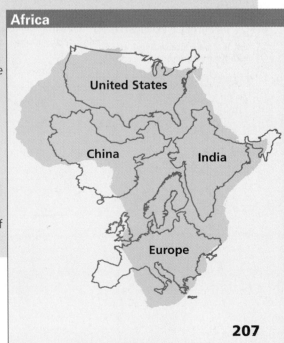

Africa

The Americas: A Separate World, 40,000 B.C.—A.D. 700

PREVIEWING THEMES

Power and Authority

In southern Mexico and later around modern-day Peru, the first civilizations in the Americas arose as people came together to create more powerful and structured societies.

Interaction with Environment

The Olmec in Mesoamerica took advantage of their fertile surroundings, while the groups in South America carved societies out of rough, mountainous terrain. The early American civilizations flourished only after controlling their environment.

Cultural Interaction

From their art to their technology, the early Mesoamerican and South American civilizations influenced the better-known empires that followed them.

⇦⇨ **INTERNET CONNECTION**

Visit us at **www.mcdougallittell.com** to learn more about early American cultures.

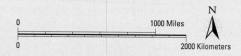

AMERICAN CIVILIZATIONS
1200 B.C.—A.D. 700

0 ——————— 1000 Miles
0 ——————— 2000 Kilometers
N

The Olmec, the Americas' oldest known civilization, emerged around **1200 B.C.** Among other things, they were master sculptors. Archaeologists found these seven-inch-high stone figures, arranged as shown here, buried beneath an Olmec ceremonial court.

This miniature warrior is one of the many treasures uncovered from the **Moche** culture, which arose around **A.D. 100.** This tiny trinket shows both the Moche's expert craftsmanship and their skill in using a variety of stones and metals. The headdress is made from thinly hammered gold, the eyes from turquoise, and the pupils from black stone. Amazingly, the piece weighs only three ounces and is believed to have been used as a nose ornament!

Fiji

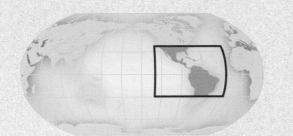

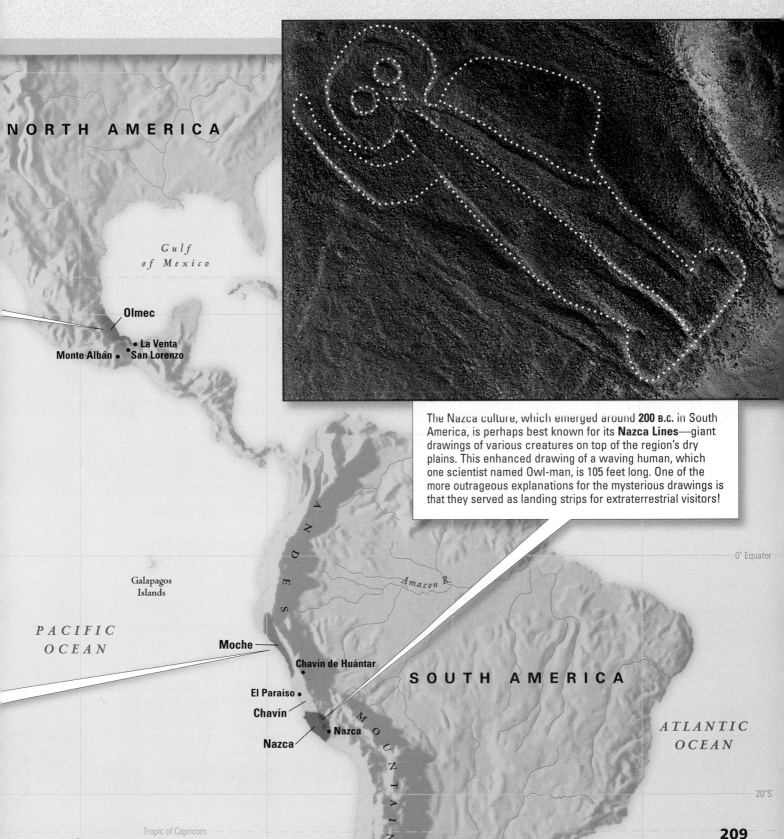

NORTH AMERICA

Gulf of Mexico

Olmec

• **La Venta**
Monte Albán • • **San Lorenzo**

The Nazca culture, which emerged around **200 B.C.** in South America, is perhaps best known for its **Nazca Lines**—giant drawings of various creatures on top of the region's dry plains. This enhanced drawing of a waving human, which one scientist named Owl-man, is 105 feet long. One of the more outrageous explanations for the mysterious drawings is that they served as landing strips for extraterrestrial visitors!

0° Equator

Amazon R.

Galapagos
Islands

PACIFIC
OCEAN

Moche

• **Chavín de Huántar**

SOUTH AMERICA

El Paraíso •

Chavín

• **Nazca**

Nazca

ATLANTIC
OCEAN

20°S

Tropic of Capricorn

100°W   80°W   60°W   40°W

209

Interact *with* History

You live in ancient North America, where most people must hunt for their food. Along with several members of your group, you have been hunting the mastodon for days. The giant beast is a challenging but rewarding prey. While the animal stands more than 14 feet high and weighs more than a ton, it will provide much meat, as well as hides for clothing and shelter.

Suddenly in the clearing you spot the massive creature. Aside from spears, your only weapons are some crude tools and your superior intelligence.

How would you kill a mastodon?

As the group determines its strategy, its members seek protection behind boulders and loose rocks.

Your group carries several shovels for digging holes.

Should a hunter get too close, the mastodon might crush him under his large feet, or stab him with his sharp tusks.

EXAMINING *the* ISSUES

• How might the group use the shovels to trap the mastodon?

• Aside from spears and tools, what else could be used as a weapon against the animal?

As a class, discuss these questions. In your discussion, consider how this situation speaks to the difficulties of life in a hunter-gatherer society.

As you read about the growth of civilizations in the Americas, notice how the old hunting and gathering way of life dramatically changed with the development of agriculture.

1 Hunters and Farmers in the Americas

TERMS & NAMES
• Beringia
• Ice Age
• maize

MAIN IDEA

Although isolated, the first Americans developed in ways similar to the other earliest humans.

WHY IT MATTERS NOW

The Americas' first inhabitants developed the basis for American civilizations to come.

SETTING THE STAGE While civilizations were developing in Africa, Asia, and Europe, they were also emerging in the Americas. Human settlement in the Americas is relatively recent compared to that in other parts of the world. However, it followed a similar pattern. At first the ancient people of the Americas survived mainly by hunting. Over time, they developed farming methods that ensured a more reliable supply of food. This in turn led to the growth of the first civilizations in the Americas.

The Earliest Americans

The American continents include North and South America. They are connected and span two hemispheres, from the frigid Arctic Circle in the north to the icy waters around Antarctica in the south. Although this land mass narrows greatly around modern-day Panama, it stretches unbroken for more than 10,000 miles. This large and rugged land is isolated from the rest of the world by vast oceans. Yet, at one time, thousands of years ago, the Americas were connected by a land bridge to Asia. Most experts believe that the first people came to the Americas from Asia over this land bridge. The land bridge is known as **Beringia.**

Peopling the Americas The first Americans arrived sometime toward the end of the last **Ice Age,** which lasted from roughly 1.6 million to 10,000 B.C. During this period huge sheets of moving ice, called glaciers, spread southward from the Arctic Circle. They covered large portions of North America. The buildup of glaciers locked up huge amounts of the earth's water. It lowered sea levels and created a land corridor between Asia and Alaska across what is now the Bering Strait.

Herds of wild animals from Siberia, including the mastodon, migrated across the flat, treeless plains of the Beringia land bridge. Gradually, Siberian hunters followed these animals into North America. They most likely were unaware that they were entering a new continent. These migrants became the first Americans.

Thomas Canby, a writer for *National Geographic* magazine, spent a year with archaeologists as they searched for ancient burial sites throughout the Americas. From his experience, Canby envisioned the type of world that might have greeted the first Americans:

A VOICE ABOUT THE PAST
What a wild world it was! To see it properly, we must board a time machine and travel back into the Ice Age. The northern half of North America has vanished, buried beneath ice sheets two miles thick. Stretching south to Kentucky, they buckle the earth's crust with their weight. . . . Animals grow oversize. . . . Elephant-eating jaguars stand tall as lions, beavers grow as big as bears, South American sloths as tall as giraffes. With arctic cold pushing so far southward, walrus bask on Virginia beaches, and musk-oxen graze from Maryland to California.

THOMAS CANBY, "The Search for the First Americans"

No one knows for sure when the first Americans arrived. Some scholars contend that the migration across the land bridge began as early as 40,000 B.C. Others argue it occurred as late as 12,000 B.C. For years, many researchers have regarded the discovery of spearheads dating back to 9500 B.C. near Clovis, New Mexico, to be the earliest evidence of humankind in the Americas.

However, recent discoveries of possible pre-Clovis sites have challenged this theory. One such discovery was made at Monte Verde, Chile, near the southern tip of the Americas. Researchers there have found evidence of human life dating back to 10,500 B.C. Underneath this site—a sandy bank near a creek—archaeologists discovered pieces of animal hide and various tools. They also found a preserved chunk of mastodon meat and a child's single footprint. The evidence at Monte Verde suggests

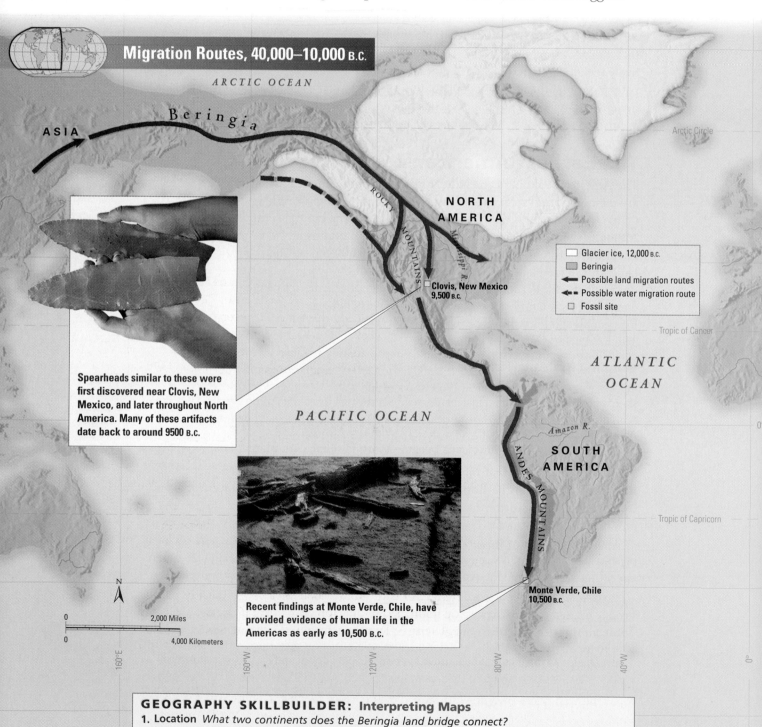

Migration Routes, 40,000–10,000 B.C.

ARCTIC OCEAN

ASIA

Beringia

NORTH AMERICA

ROCKY MOUNTAINS

Mississippi R.

☐ Clovis, New Mexico
9,500 B.C.

☐ Glacier ice, 12,000 B.C.
▨ Beringia
← Possible land migration routes
◄- - Possible water migration route
☐ Fossil site

Arctic Circle

Tropic of Cancer

ATLANTIC OCEAN

PACIFIC OCEAN

Amazon R.

SOUTH AMERICA

ANDES MOUNTAINS

Tropic of Capricorn

Spearheads similar to these were first discovered near Clovis, New Mexico, and later throughout North America. Many of these artifacts date back to around 9500 B.C.

Monte Verde, Chile
10,500 B.C.

Recent findings at Monte Verde, Chile, have provided evidence of human life in the Americas as early as 10,500 B.C.

N

0   2,000 Miles
0   4,000 Kilometers

GEOGRAPHY SKILLBUILDER: Interpreting Maps
1. **Location** *What two continents does the Beringia land bridge connect?*
2. **Movement** *From where do scholars believe the first Americans came? How did they come?*

that the first Americans arrived well before the Clovis era. To reach southern Chile at such an early date, experts believe, humans would have had to cross the land bridge at least 20,000 years ago.

They also could have come by boat. Most experts believe the earliest Americans traveled by foot across the land bridge. However, some scholars think they also may have paddled from Asia to the Pacific Coast in small boats.

Hunters and Gatherers Questions remain about how and when the first Americans arrived. What appears more certain—from the discovery of chiseled spearheads and charred bones at ancient sites—is that the earliest Americans lived as hunters. Perhaps their most challenging and rewarding prey was the mastodon. Weighing more than a ton, this animal provided meat, hide, and bones for making food, clothing, shelters, and tools.

Eventually, large animals like the mastodon became extinct. Hunters soon turned to smaller prey, such as deer and rabbits, for their survival. They also fished and gathered edible plants and fruits. Because they were hunters, the earliest Americans found it necessary to move regularly in search of food. Whenever they did settle in one place for a short time, prehistoric Americans lived in caves or temporary shelters in the open air.

With the end of the Ice Age, around 12,000 to 10,000 years ago, came the end of land travel across Beringia. As the great glaciers melted, sea levels rose. The ancient land bridge disappeared under the Bering Strait. By this time, however, humans inhabited most regions of the Americas. Wherever they roamed, from the grassy plains of the modern-day United States to the steamy tropical forests of Central America, the first Americans adapted to the variety of environments they inhabited. In doing so, they carved out unique ways of life.

THINK THROUGH HISTORY
A. Recognizing Effects How did the earliest Americans adapt to the loss of large animals?

Agriculture Prompts a New Way of Life

Gradually, the earliest Americans became more familiar with plant foods. They began to experiment with simple methods of farming. Their efforts at planting and harvesting eventually led to the birth of agriculture. This in turn dramatically changed their way of life.

The Development of Farming Around 7000 B.C., a revolution quietly began in what is now central Mexico. There, people began to rely more on wild edible plants, raising some of them from seeds. By 5000 B.C. many had begun to grow these preferred plants. They included squashes, gourds, beans, avocados, and chilies. By 3400 B.C., these early farmers grew **maize,** or corn. Maize soon became the most important crop. This highly nourishing crop flourished in the tropical climate of Mexico. There, a family of three could raise enough corn in four months to feed themselves for up to two years.

Gradually, people settled in permanent villages in the Tehuacan (TAY·wuh·KAHN) Valley, south of present-day Mexico City. There, they raised corn and other crops. Eventually the techniques of agriculture spread over most of North and South America. However, it is believed that people in some areas, such as Peru and eastern North America, may have discovered the secrets of cultivating local edible plants independently.

Digging Up the Past

It is mainly through the work of archaeologists and paleontologists that we know as much as we do about ancient America, as well as the other ancient lands of the world. Archaeology is the study of prehistoric human cultures. Paleontology is the study of ancient animals and plants. Both are sciences, requiring specialized skills and techniques. The men and women in both fields must show patience, precision, and a careful touch. Their job is to extract from the earth the fragile fossils and artifacts of the past.

Below is a dig at the La Brea tar pits, in what is now downtown Los Angeles. There, paleontologists found the remains of numerous prehistoric animals. They included saber-toothed tigers, mammoths, bison, and birds.

Where To Dig?

How do researchers know where to dig in the first place? One way is by using an instrument called a soil-resistivity meter. This device transmits electric currents into the soil and registers any abnormalities in the currents—usually caused by buried objects.

Using such tools as picks and brushes, workers clear away soil without damaging the animal remains.

Unearthed remains must be covered for protection from the sun and rain.

A digger uses a jackhammer-type instrument to loosen the extremely hard dried tar.

Diggers use a sieve to shake free tiny fossils that may be lodged in soil.

Tools of the Trade

The most commonly used tool on the site is a bricklayer's trowel (far left). Workers use the durable instrument for a variety of tasks, including digging and scraping. To recover fragile remains, diggers must use delicate, tiny tools, such as dental picks (left).

Connect *to* History

Analyzing Issues What things are paleontologists concerned with during a dig?

SEE SKILLBUILDER HANDBOOK, PAGE 1001

Connect *to* Today

Examining a Dig Read an account of a dig at a prehistoric site. Then write a brief report explaining what researchers found as well as some of the specific methods they used.

**white and
black maize**

The Effects of Agriculture

Before Agriculture

- People hunted or gathered what they ate.
- Families continually moved in search of big game.
- Groups remained small due to the scarcity of reliable sources of food.
- Humans devoted much of their time to obtaining food.

After Agriculture

- People enjoyed a more reliable and steady source of food.
- Families settled down and formed larger communities.
- Humans concentrated on new skills: arts and crafts, architecture, social organization.
- Complex societies eventually arose.

beans

avocados

peppers

potatoes

SKILLBUILDER: Interpreting Charts
1. *How did the early Americans' way of life change after the development of agriculture?*
2. *How might the establishment of agriculture have helped humans to develop new skills and interests?*

Over the next several centuries, farming methods became increasingly advanced. In central Mexico, for example, native farmers created small islands in swamps and shallow lakes by stacking layers of vegetation, dirt, and mud. They then planted crops on top of the island soil. The surrounding water provided continuous irrigation. These floating gardens, known as chinampas, were very productive, yielding up to three harvests a year.

Farming Brings Great Change "[The] . . . transition from a foraging to a farming way of life," noted American scientist Bruce Smith, "was a major turning point in the long evolutionary history of our species." Indeed, in the Americas as in other regions of the world, agriculture brought great and lasting change to peoples' way of life.

The cultivation of corn and other crops provided a more reliable and expanding food supply. This encouraged population growth and the establishment of large, settled communities. As the population grew, and as farming became more efficient and productive, more people turned their attention to nonagricultural pursuits. They developed specialized skills in arts and crafts, building trades, and other fields. Differences between social classes—between rich and poor, ruler and subject—began to emerge. With the development of agriculture, society became more complex and sophisticated. The stage was set for the rise of more advanced civilizations.

THINK THROUGH HISTORY
B. Making Inferences
Why might the development of agriculture be characterized by some as a turning point in human history?

Section ❶ Assessment

1. TERMS & NAMES

Identify
- Beringia
- Ice Age
- maize

2. TAKING NOTES

The events listed in the following chart had important effects on the development of the Americas. Identify the main effects for each.

Cause	Effects
Beringia land bridge forms.	
Large animals become extinct.	
Early Americans experiment with farming.	
Crops provide a reliable food supply.	

3. FORMING OPINIONS

Why do you think early Americans, isolated from the rest of the world, developed in ways similar to other early humans?

THINK ABOUT
- similarities among all human beings
- availability of similar resources
- the development from hunting to farming

4. ANALYZING THEMES

Power and Authority What type of person might hold power in a hunter-gatherer society? in a settled, agricultural society?

THINK ABOUT
- qualities needed to succeed in a hunting society
- qualities most admired in a settled, farming society

Early Mesoamerican Civilizations

TERMS & NAMES
• **Mesoamerica**
• **Olmec**
• **Zapotec**
• **Monte Albán**

MAIN IDEA

The Olmec created the Americas' first civilization, which in turn influenced later civilizations in the region.

WHY IT MATTERS NOW

Later American civilizations relied on the technology and achievements of earlier cultures to move forward.

SETTING THE STAGE The story of developed civilizations in the Americas begins in a region archaeologists and historians refer to as **Mesoamerica.** This area stretches south from central Mexico to the northern reaches of modern-day Honduras. It was here, more than 3,000 years ago, that the first complex societies in the Americas arose.

Mesoamerica's Mother Culture

Mesoamerica's first known civilization builders were a people known as the **Olmec.** They began carving out a thriving society around 1200 B.C. in the humid jungles of southern Mexico. The Olmec influenced neighboring groups, as well as the later civilizations of the region. Thus, they often are called Mesoamerica's "mother culture."

The Rise of Olmec Civilization Around 1860, a worker clearing a field in the hot coastal plain of southeastern Mexico uncovered an extraordinary stone sculpture. It stood five feet tall and weighed an estimated eight tons. The sculpture was of an enormous head, wearing a headpiece that resembled a football helmet. The head was carved in a strikingly realistic style, with thick lips, a flat nose, and large oval eyes. (See History Through Art on page 219.) Archaeologists had never seen anything like it in the Americas.

This head, along with others that were discovered later, was a remnant of the Olmec civilization. The Olmec flourished from 1200 B.C. to 400 B.C. They lived along the Gulf Coast of Mexico, in the modern-day Mexican states of Veracruz and Tabasco.

On the surface, the Gulf Coast seemed an unlikely site for a high culture to take root. The region was hot and humid and covered with swamps and jungle. In some places, giant trees formed a thick cover that prevented most sunlight from reaching the ground. Up to 100 inches of rain fell every year. The rainfall swelled rivers and caused severe flooding.

However, the region also had certain advantages. There were abundant deposits of salt and tar, as well as fine clay used in making pottery. There was also wood and rubber from the rain forest. The hills to the north provided hard stone from which the Olmec could make tools and monuments. The rivers that laced the region provided a ready means of transport. Perhaps most important, the flood plains of these rivers provided fertile land for farming.

The Olmec used their abundant resources to build thriving communities. The oldest site, San Lorenzo, dates back to around 1150 B.C. Here, and at other sites, archaeologists uncovered important clues that offered a glimpse into the Olmec world.

Olmec Society At San Lorenzo archaeologists discovered earthen mounds, courtyards, and pyramids. Set among these earthworks were large stone monuments. They included columns, altars, and more colossal, sculpted heads, which may have represented particular Olmec rulers. These giant monuments weigh as much as 44 tons. Researchers are left to wonder how the Olmec moved them to various centers of

This Olmec figure represents either a wrestler or ball player. The Olmec played a game in which two opponents battled to place a ball in a goal. The loser often was sacrificed.

THINK THROUGH HISTORY
A. Making Inferences In what ways did the Olmec's environment help in the creation of its civilization?

worship. Some scholars suspect that Olmec workers moved these sculptures over land on rolling logs to the river banks. From there, they rafted the monuments along numerous waterways to various sites.

The organization needed for such an undertaking is one reason scholars think San Lorenzo was home to a small ruling class of priests and nobles. These rulers may have commanded a much larger group of peasant farmers living in the surrounding country.

To the east of San Lorenzo, another significant Olmec site, La Venta, rose around 900 B.C. Here, researchers discovered a 100-foot-high mound of earth and clay. This structure may have served as the tomb of a great Olmec ruler. Known as the Great Pyramid, the mound also may have been the center of the Olmec religion. Based on other artifacts found at sites like La Venta, experts believe the Olmec prayed to a variety of nature gods.

Jaguar Worship Most of all they probably worshiped the jaguar spirit. Numerous Olmec sculptures and carvings depict a half-human, half-jaguar creature. Some scholars believe that the jaguar represented a powerful rain god. Others contend that there were several jaguar gods, representing such vital things as the earth, fertility, and maize. As anthropologist Peter Furst points out, the jaguar was central to Olmec religion:

A VOICE ABOUT THE PAST
You can almost call the Olmec the people of the jaguar. In tropical America, jaguars were the shamans [medicine men] of the animal world, the alter ego [other identity] of the shaman. They are the most powerful predators. That's why in Olmec art you get these combinations of jaguars and humans.

PETER FURST, quoted in "New Light on the Olmec"

Trade and Commerce Archaeologists once believed that sites such as La Venta were ceremonial centers where important rituals were performed but few people lived. In recent years, however, experts have begun to revise that view. According to Mexican archaeologist Rebecca González, "La Venta was not just an empty ceremonial spot visited by Olmec priests and nobles, but a prosperous community of fishers, farmers, traders, and specialists, such as the artisans and the sculptors."

Indeed, the Olmec appear to have been a prosperous people who directed a large trading network throughout Mesoamerica. Olmec goods traveled as far as Mexico City to the north and Honduras to the south. In addition, raw materials—including iron ore and various stones—reached San Lorenzo from faraway regions. This trade network helped boost the Olmec economy and spread Olmec influence to other parts of Mesoamerica.

THINK THROUGH HISTORY
B. Clarifying What is the jaguar believed to have represented to the Olmec?

Vocabulary
artisan: a skilled worker or craftsman.

Olmec Civilization, 900 B.C.

EASTERN SIERRA MADRE

Tropic of Cancer

Gulf of Mexico

YUCATAN PENINSULA

Bay of Campeche

San Lorenzo **La Venta**

Oaxaca Valley

N

PACIFIC OCEAN

0 — 250 Miles
0 — 500 Kilometers

Legend:
- Olmec homeland
- Oaxaca Valley
- Possible trade routes
- Centers of Olmec civilization
- Other Olmec sites
- Limit of Mesoamerica

GEOGRAPHY SKILLBUILDER: Interpreting Maps
1. **Movement** Judging from the map, what was one way in which the Olmec spread their influence?
2. **Movement** What difficulties might the Olmec have encountered in developing their trade routes?

CONNECT *to* TODAY

Jaguar Worship

Some descendants of the Olmec and other Mesoamerican peoples still practice jaguar worship. In the spring, villagers in Acatlan, Mexico, put on jaguar masks and draw blood in mock combat. They do this in the hope that the jaguar will shed its own blood, in the form of rain, to water the fields. In another ritual, shown here, a boy becomes a jaguar dancer to bring rain.

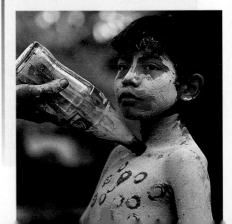

Decline of the Olmec For reasons that are not fully understood, Olmec civilization eventually collapsed. Scholars believe San Lorenzo was destroyed around 900 B.C. La Venta may have fallen sometime around 400 B.C. Some experts speculate that outside invaders caused the destruction. Others believe the Olmec may have destroyed their own monuments upon the death of their rulers.

Because the Olmec apparently left no written records, scholars may never know the full truth. Nevertheless, Olmec artifacts continue to offer up tantalizing clues about this first known Mesoamerican civilization.

Zapotec Civilization Arises

By the time Olmec civilization had collapsed, another people—the **Zapotec**—were developing an advanced society to the southwest, in what is now the Mexican state of Oaxaca (wuh·HAH·kah). Though they showed traces of Olmec influence, the Zapotec built a unique civilization. This ancient group dominated Oaxaca for more than a thousand years.

Peoples of the Oaxaca Valley Oaxaca is a rugged region of mountains and valleys in southern Mexico. In the center of the state, three valleys meet to form a large open area known as the Oaxaca Valley. (See map on page 217.) Though much of Oaxaca is hot and dry, this valley has fertile soil, a mild climate, and enough rainfall to support agriculture. As a result, various peoples have made the Oaxaca Valley their home, including the ancient Zapotec.

For centuries the Zapotec lived in scattered villages throughout the valley. By 1000 B.C., however, one site—San José Mogote—was emerging as the main power in the region. At this site, the Zapotec constructed stone platforms. They also built temples and began work on monumental sculptures. By 500 B.C. they also had developed early forms of hieroglyphic writing and a calendar system.

THINK THROUGH HISTORY
C. Hypothesizing
What things might lead to the disappearance of an entire civilization?

HISTORY THROUGH ART: Sculpture

A Legacy of Sculpture

More than 2,000 years after the Olmec's collapse, the ancient society's sculpture remains its most lasting legacy. From the colossal stone heads to the tiny jade figures, these carvings reveal the Olmec's expert craftsmanship and commitment to detail. They also provide a glimpse of the values and beliefs of the Americas' oldest known civilization.

Giant Altars
The Olmec carved a number of impressive altars. Like the one pictured to the right, they often depicted a priest or shaman emerging from the structure. In numerous altars, the priest cradles a child. Some scholars believe that this may have signified the importance of the notion of dynasty—with the child representing the heir to the throne—in Olmec society.

The Zapotec Flourish at Monte Albán Around 500 B.C., Zapotec civilization took a major leap forward. High atop a mountain at the center of the Oaxaca Valley, the Zapotec built the first real urban center in the Americas: **Monte Albán.** This city, with its commanding view of the entire valley, grew and prospered over the next several centuries. By 200 B.C., Monte Albán was home to around 15,000 people. The city eventually would reach a peak population of 25,000.

From A.D. 250 to A.D. 700, Monte Albán was truly impressive. At the heart of the city was a giant plaza paved with stones. Towering pyramids, temples, and palaces, all made out of stone, surrounded this plaza. There was even a building that may have acted as an observatory for gazing at the stars. Nearby was a series of stone carvings of corpses. Their thick lips and flat noses show a clear influence of Olmec style.

For more than a thousand years the Zapotec controlled the Oaxaca Valley and the surrounding region. Sometime after A.D. 600, however, the Zapotec began to decline. Some scholars believe they may have suffered a loss of trade or other economic difficulties. As with the Olmec, the fall of Zapotec civilization remains a puzzle.

The Early Mesoamericans' Legacy

Although both the Zapotec and Olmec civilizations eventually collapsed, each culture left its mark on the Mesoamerican civilizations that followed.

The Olmec Leave Their Mark The Olmec contributed much to later Mesoamerican civilizations. They influenced the powerful Maya, who will be discussed in Chapter 16. Olmec art styles, especially the use of the jaguar motif, can be seen in the pottery and sculpture of later peoples in the region. In addition, future Mesoamerican societies copied the Olmec pattern of urban design. Like the Olmec, later civilizations built cities by combining pyramids, plazas, and monumental sculpture.

Jade Figures
With little technology at their disposal, the Olmec mastered the difficult art of carving jade. Jade is a hard and tough but highly colorful stone. "The tough material was mastered as though it were a plastic," one scholar said of the Olmec's work. As shown here, the Olmec often carved jaguar figures out of jade. The jaguar-god was a powerful deity in Olmec society.

Colossal Heads
Perhaps the most recognizable Olmec sculptures are the giant stone heads. Researchers have uncovered more than a dozen Olmec heads. The largest one stands 11 feet tall. Some scholars say that the heads represent idolized warriors or ball players. However, most experts believe they depict individual rulers.

Connect *to* History

Analyzing Issues What characteristics of Olmec society does each of these sculptures convey?

SEE SKILLBUILDER HANDBOOK, PAGE 1001

Connect *to* Today

Comparing Consider the better-known sculptures and monuments in your country. What do they say about your civilization?

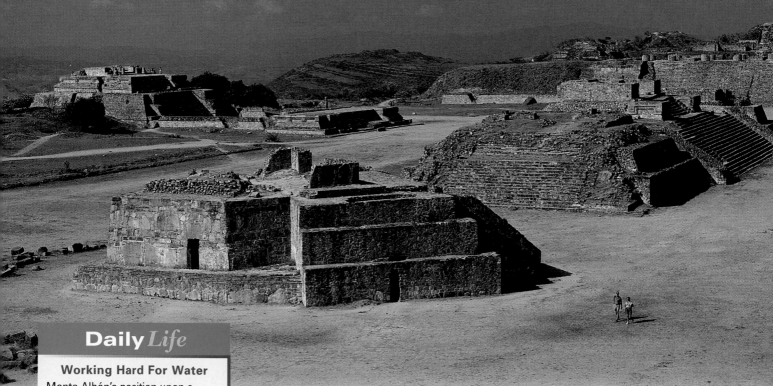

Daily *Life*

Working Hard For Water

Monte Albán's position upon a mountain top (depicted in this photograph of its ruins) added to its magnificence. But it also presented a daily problem for the city's residents: limited access to water.

Perched so high above the valley, Monte Albán had no natural waterways leading into the city. Scholars believe that city leaders may have organized citizens to carry drinking water up the mountain—as far as 1,500 feet—in jars.

The Olmec also left behind the notions of planned ceremonial centers, ritual ball games, and an elite ruling class. And while there is no clear evidence that the Olmec used a written language, their descendants or a related people carved out stone symbols that may have influenced later glyph writing.

Zapotec Contributions The Zapotec left behind their own legacy. It included a hieroglyphic language and a calendar system based on the movement of the sun. In addition, the Zapotec are noted as the Americas' first city builders. Monte Albán combined ceremonial grandeur with residential living space. This style influenced the development of future urban centers and became a hallmark of Mesoamerican civilizations.

As the Zapotec and Olmec flourished and then declined, civilizations were also taking shape in South America. Along the rough and mountainous terrain in what is now Peru, ancient peoples came together. There, they created more advanced and complex societies.

THINK THROUGH HISTORY
E. Forming Opinions
What do you consider to be the Olmec's and Zapotec's most important contributions to later cultures? Why?

Section ❷ Assessment

1. TERMS & NAMES

Identify
• Mesoamerica
• Olmec
• Zapotec
• Monte Albán

2. TAKING NOTES

Compare the Olmec and Zapotec cultures by using a Venn diagram similar to the one below.

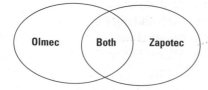

Design another way to show this same information.

3. DRAWING CONCLUSIONS

Why do you think the Olmec are called Mesoamerica's "mother culture"? Consider the Olmec's influence on later groups in the region.

THINK ABOUT
• architecture
• religion
• art

4. THEME ACTIVITY

Cultural Interaction As a trader from a small Mesoamerican village, you have just returned from your first visit to the Olmec site at La Venta. Write a description of what you might tell your family about the wondrous things you saw in and around the site. Prepare to present the description orally to the class.

3 Early Civilizations of the Andes

MAIN IDEA

Around the harsh terrain of the Andes Mountains in South America, various groups created flourishing civilizations.

WHY IT MATTERS NOW

Like the early Andean civilizations, people today must adapt to their environment in order to survive.

SETTING THE STAGE While civilizations were emerging in Mesoamerica, advanced societies were also arising in South America. The early cultures of South America arose in difficult environs, namely the rugged terrain of the Andes Mountains. However, like the peoples of Mesoamerica, the early Andean cultures controlled their surroundings and created flourishing civilizations.

Societies Grow in the Andes Region

The Andes Mountains stretch some 4,000 miles down the western edge of South America, from Colombia in the north to Chile in the south. After the Himalayas in southern Asia, the Andes is the highest mountain range in the world. The Andes has a number of peaks over 20,000 feet in elevation. It was in the northern Andes region, in what is now Peru, that South America's first advanced civilizations emerged.

Early Settlements Along the Coast Peru was a difficult place to launch a civilization. The Andes are steep and rocky, with generally poor soil. Ice and snow cover the highest elevations year-round. Overland travel often is difficult. The climate is also severe: hot and dry during the day, and often freezing at night.

Between the mountains and the Pacific Ocean lies a narrow coastal plain. Most of this plain is harsh desert where rain seldom falls. In some places, however, rivers cross the desert on their path from the mountains to the sea. It was in these river valleys that the first settlements occurred.

Between 3600 and 2500 B.C. people began to establish temporary villages along the Pacific coast. These first inhabitants were hunter-gatherers who relied on seafood and small game for their survival. Eventually, around 3000 B.C., these people began to farm. By 1800 B.C., a number of thriving communities existed along the coast.

The Chavín Period The first influential civilization in South America arose not on the coast, however, but in the mountains. This culture, known as the **Chavín** (sha·VEEN), flourished from around 900 B.C. to 200 B.C. Archaeologists named the culture after a major ruin, Chavín de Huántar, in the northern highlands of Peru. This site is situated more than 10,000 feet above sea level. It features pyramids, plazas, and massive earthen mounds.

Chavín culture spread quickly across much of northern and central Peru. Archaeologists have found no evidence of political or economic organization within the culture. Thus, they conclude that the Chavín were primarily a religious civilization. According to this theory, Chavín de Huántar and other similar sites were important religious centers rather than outposts of a powerful empire. Nevertheless, the spread of Chavín art styles and religious images—as seen in stone carving, pottery, and textiles—demonstrates the powerful influence of this culture. Ancient Peruvians may have visited Chavín temples to pay their respects. They then carried ideas back to their communities. The Chavín are believed to

THINK THROUGH HISTORY
A. Contrasting
How did the environment of the Andes region differ from that of much of Mesoamerica?

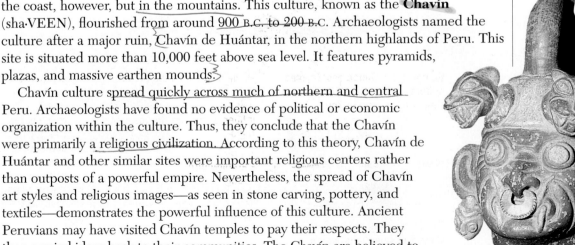

The Chavín's artistic styles influenced peoples throughout the Andes region. Here, a Chavín ceramic vessel depicts images of snarling cats.

have established certain patterns that helped unify Andean culture and lay the foundation for later civilizations in Peru. Thus, like the Olmec, the Chavín may have acted as a "mother culture."

Other Andean Civilizations Flourish

Around the time Chavín culture declined, other civilizations were emerging in Peru. First the Nazca and then the Moche (MO·chay) built advanced societies that flourished for centuries in the Andes region.

Nazca Achievements The **Nazca** culture flourished along the southern coast of Peru from around 200 B.C. to A.D. 600. This area is extremely dry. The Nazca developed extensive irrigation systems, including underground canals, that allowed them to farm the land. The Nazca are known for their beautiful textiles and pottery. Both feature images of animals and mythological beings.

They are even more famous, however, for an extraordinary but puzzling set of creations known as the Nazca Lines. On a large, rock-strewn plain, the Nazca made huge drawings by scraping away stones to reveal the lighter soil underneath. The drawings depict various plants and animals, including a monkey, birds, and other creatures. These drawings are so huge, however, that they can be seen only from the air. Scientists believe that the Nazca made these drawings for their gods.

Moche Culture Meanwhile, on the northern coast of Peru, another civilization was reaching great heights. This was the **Moche** culture, which lasted from about A.D. 100 to A.D. 700. The Moche took advantage of the rivers that flowed from the Andes Mountains. They built impressive irrigation systems to water their wide range of

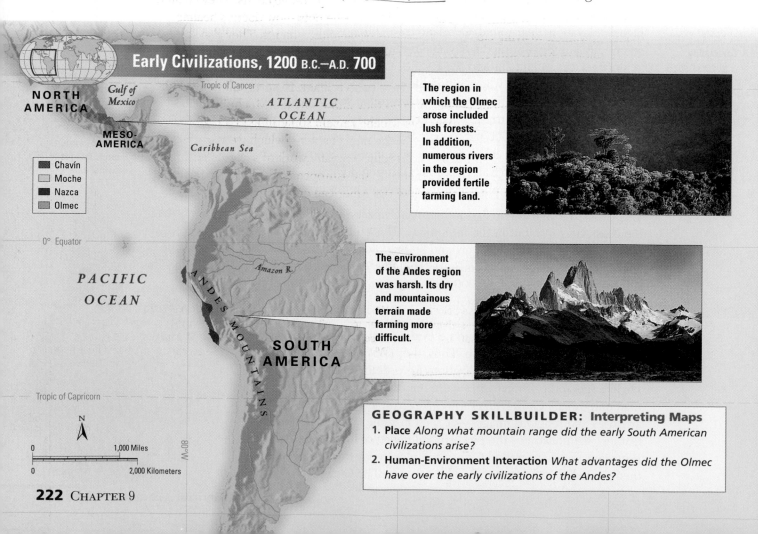

Early Civilizations, 1200 B.C.–A.D. 700

NORTH AMERICA
Gulf of Mexico
Tropic of Cancer
ATLANTIC OCEAN
MESO-AMERICA
Caribbean Sea

- Chavín
- Moche
- Nazca
- Olmec

0° Equator

PACIFIC OCEAN

Amazon R.

ANDES MOUNTAINS

SOUTH AMERICA

Tropic of Capricorn

N

0   1,000 Miles
0   2,000 Kilometers

80°W

The region in which the Olmec arose included lush forests. In addition, numerous rivers in the region provided fertile farming land.

The environment of the Andes region was harsh. Its dry and mountainous terrain made farming more difficult.

GEOGRAPHY SKILLBUILDER: Interpreting Maps
1. **Place** Along what mountain range did the early South American civilizations arise?
2. **Human-Environment Interaction** What advantages did the Olmec have over the early civilizations of the Andes?

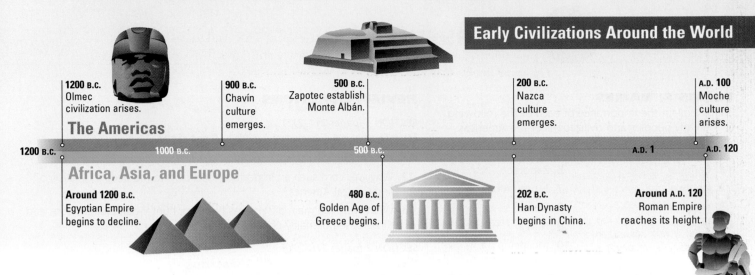

1200 B.C.
Olmec
civilization arises.

The Americas

900 B.C.
Chavín
culture
emerges.

500 B.C.
Zapotec establish
Monte Albán.

200 B.C.
Nazca
culture
emerges.

A.D. 100
Moche
culture
arises.

1200 B.C.   1000 B.C.   500 B.C.   A.D. 1   A.D. 120

Africa, Asia, and Europe

Around 1200 B.C.
Egyptian Empire
begins to decline.

480 B.C.
Golden Age of
Greece begins.

202 B.C.
Han Dynasty
begins in China.

Around A.D. 120
Roman Empire
reaches its height.

crops, which included corn, beans, potatoes, squash, and peanuts. According to Peruvian archaeologist Walter Alva, the Moche enjoyed a variety of foods:

A VOICE ABOUT THE PAST
The Moche enjoyed a diet rich in protein and probably better balanced than that of many modern Peruvians. Fish from the nearby Pacific were eaten fresh or sun dried. They ate Muscovy ducks and guinea pigs. To drink, there was potent *chicha*, a cloudy beverage fermented from corn that had been ground and boiled. Deer, now rare, were abundant. . . . Crayfish in irrigation ditches supplemented seafood from the coast.
WALTER ALVA, "Richest Unlooted Tomb of a Moche Lord"

THINK THROUGH HISTORY
B. Analyzing Issues
How were archaeologists able to gain so much information about the Moche without the help of a written language?

Moche tombs uncovered in the recent past have revealed a civilization with enormous wealth. Archaeologists have found beautiful jewelry crafted from gold, silver, and semiprecious stones. The Moche were also brilliant ceramic artists. They created pottery that depicted scenes from everyday life. Moche pots show doctors healing patients, women weaving cloth, and musicians playing instruments. They also show fierce soldiers armed with spears, leading enemy captives. Although the Moche never developed a written language, their pottery provides a wealth of detail about Moche life.

Nevertheless, many questions about the Moche remain. Experts still do not fully understand Moche religious beliefs. Nor do they know why the Moche fell. Like many early cultures of the Americas, the Moche remain something of a mystery.

Unlike the lands you will read about in the next chapter—which were unified by the spread of Islam—the Americas would remain a patchwork of separate civilizations until the early 16th century. Around that time the Europeans would begin to arrive and bring dramatic and lasting changes to the American continents.

Section 3 Assessment

1. TERMS & NAMES
Identify
• Chavín
• Nazca
• Moche

2. TAKING NOTES
Use a chart like the one below to record important details about the earliest Andean civilizations.

Culture	Time Span	Location	Achievements
Chavín			
Nazca			
Moche			

What achievements, if any, did all three cultures share?

3. HYPOTHESIZING
Would the Chavín culture have been more influential if it had arisen along the Peruvian coast? Why or why not?

THINK ABOUT
• the harsh environment of the Andes Mountain region
• the effect of environment on the spread of culture
• the nature of Chavín influence

4. ANALYZING THEMES
Interaction with Environment Describe how the Nazca and the Moche adapted to their environment in order to build flourishing societies.

The Americas: A Separate World **223**

TERMS & NAMES

Briefly explain the importance of each of the following to the early peoples and civilizations of the Americas.

1. Beringia
2. Ice Age
3. maize
4. Mesoamerica
5. Olmec
6. Zapotec
7. Monte Albán
8. Chavín
9. Nazca
10. Moche

Interact *with* History

On page 210 you examined ways to kill the mastodon and discussed the difficulties of living in a hunter-gatherer society. Now that you have read the chapter, discuss why the early Americans moved from a hunting to a farming existence. In what ways was food gathering easier in an agricultural society?

REVIEW QUESTIONS

SECTION 1 *(pages 211–215)*
Hunters and Farmers in the Americas

11. How do archaeologists know that the first Americans lived as hunters?
12. Why was corn such an important food crop to the people of Mexico and Central America?
13. What were the main differences between hunter-gatherer societies and those based primarily on agriculture?

SECTION 2 *(pages 216–220)*
Early Mesoamerican Civilizations

14. Where did the Olmec, the Americas' first known civilization, arise?
15. How did the Olmec's location contribute to the development of their civilization?
16. How did the Olmec influence the Zapotec civilization?
17. How do archaeologists know that the Zapotec city of Monte Albán was more than just a ceremonial center?

SECTION 3 *(pages 221–223)*
Early Civilizations of the Andes

18. In what ways did the Chavín influence other peoples of the Andes region?
19. What do scholars believe the Nazca Lines represented?
20. How were the Nazca and Moche able to develop productive farmland?

Visual Summary

The Americas: A Separate World

The Earliest Americans

- Hunted big game and later fished and gathered berries and plants
- Lived in small groups, as they had to move continually in search of food
- Eventually developed farming and settled down into large communities
- Developed various new skills, including arts and crafts, architecture, and social and political organization
- Gradually forged more complex societies

Early South American Societies

The Chavín
- Established powerful religious worship centers
- Created influential artistic styles

The Nazca and Moche
- Developed extensive irrigation systems for farming
- Crafted intricate ceramics and textiles and other decorative art

Early Mesoamerican Societies

The Olmec
- Designed and built pyramids, plazas, and monumental sculptures
- Developed ceremonial centers, ritual ball games, and a ruling class
- Directed a large trade network throughout Mesoamerica

The Zapotec
- Built a magnificent urban center at Monte Albán
- Developed early forms of hieroglyphic writing and a calendar system

CRITICAL THINKING

1. STAGES TO CIVILIZATION

The early Americans' way of life developed through several stages, starting with hunting. Use a sequence graphic like the one below to show the stages of this development up to and including the time of the first civilizations.

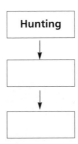

Hunting

2. CHALLENGING LOCATIONS

THEME **INTERACTION WITH ENVIRONMENT** What unique environmental challenges did the early Mesoamerican and South American peoples face as they built thriving civilizations?

3. EARLY WAYS OF LIFE

Would you rather have lived in a hunting society or a settled farming society? Explain your answer.

4. ANALYZING PRIMARY SOURCES

In his article "The Chavín Cult," historian Brian Fagan describes the mysterious shrine of Chavín de Huántar.

A VOICE ABOUT THE PAST

Its U-shaped temple opens east toward the nearby Mosna River and the rising sun. The sacred precinct faces away from the nearby prehistoric settlement, presenting a high, almost menacing, wall to the outside world. The entire effect is one of mystery and hidden power. . . . Worshippers entered the sacred precincts by a roundabout route, passing along the temple pyramid to the river, then up some low terraces that led into the heart of the shrine. Here they found themselves in a sacred landscape set against a backdrop of mountains. Ahead of them lay the hidden place where the axis of the world passed from the sky into the underworld, an oracle [a place for predicting the future] famous for miles around.

BRIAN FAGAN, quoted in *The Peru Reader*

- How might visitors have felt upon entering this shrine for the first time? Why?

- Do you think the mystery and majesty of this place helped spread the Chavín culture's influence? Explain.

CHAPTER ACTIVITIES

1. LIVING HISTORY: Unit Portfolio Project

THEME **POWER AND AUTHORITY** Your unit portfolio project focuses on the growth and use of power and authority in ancient history. (See page 107.) For Chapter 9 you might use one of the following ideas to add to your portfolio.

- Write a piece of historical fiction about an early American in which you describe how the first ruler gained power or how some people got rich.
- With a partner, design and prepare a time capsule that members of one of the first civilizations might have created to preserve the memory of their powerful and successful society.
- Speculate about why the Olmec or another civilization declined. Then draw a picture showing a key aspect of that decline. Include a caption.

2. CONNECT TO TODAY: Cooperative Learning

THEME **CULTURAL INTERACTION** One way that a culture's influence spread was by direct contact between people. Members of advanced civilizations, especially traders, carried their influential ideas with them as they traveled. Today, cultural influence is still spread in a similar way.

Work with a team to create and role-play two distinct meetings. In the first meeting, a trader from an ancient American civilization shares ideas and descriptions of his or her society with a farmer from a distant settlement. In the second meeting, an American salesperson from today shares similar information with a farmer in a distant land.

- Decide exactly what information you want the person from each of the dominant cultures to pass on.
- Establish a set of specific questions that the curious farmers will ask in order to draw out information about each culture.

3. INTERPRETING A TIME LINE

Revisit the time line on pages 106–107. Look above the Chapter 9 time line. Write about three other events that are happening in the world at this time.

FOCUS ON **GEOGRAPHY**

Notice the location of the early Mesoamerican and South American civilizations.

- How many miles apart by land do they appear to be?

- What geographic factors would have made interaction between the two regions difficult?

Connect to History
Based on the map, why do you think it took so many thousands of years to travel from the land bridge in upper North America to the southern tip of South America?

Early America, 1200 B.C.–A.D. 700

ATLANTIC OCEAN
Tropic of Cancer
Gulf of Mexico
MESOAMERICA
Early Mesoamerican Civilizations
Caribbean Sea
PACIFIC OCEAN
ANDES MOUNTAINS
SOUTH AMERICA
Early Andean Civilizations

0 1,000 Miles
0 2,000 Kilometers

225

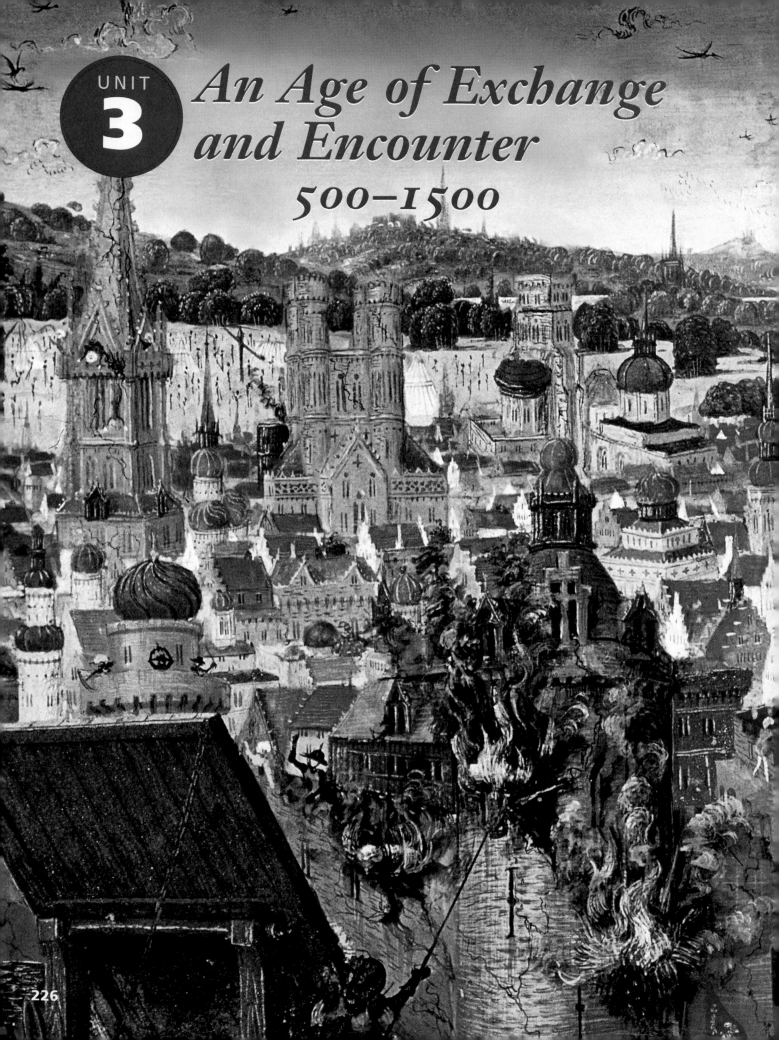

UNIT 3

An Age of Exchange and Encounter

500–1500

In this manuscript entitled *The Siege of Jerusalem by the Crusaders,* Christians battle Muslims for control of the holy city. Religion was just one of the issues over which empires fought as they tried to spread their influence.

227

An Age of Exchange and Encounter

	500	600	700	800	900	1000

CHAPTER 10 600–1250
The Muslim World

622 Arabia Muhammad makes the Hegira to Medina

661 Arabia Umayyad Dynasty leads Muslims

732 France Christians defeat Muslims at Battle of Tours

750 Persia Abbasids take control of Muslim Empire

800s Baghdad House of Wisdom is built

800s Baghdad Al-Khwarizmi invents algebra

909 North Africa Fatimid Dynasty established

911 France Vikings establish Normandy under Rollo

CHAPTER 11 500–1500
Byzantines, Russians, and Turks Interact

527 Constantinople Justinian I becomes Byzantine emperor

671 Constantinople Greek fire invented

862 Russia Viking chief Rurik founds Novgorod

970 Anatolia Seljuk Turks migrate into Abbasid Empire

988 Russia Prince Vladimir chooses Eastern Christianity

CHAPTER 12 600–1350
Empires in East Asia

618 China Tang Dynasty begins

751 China Arabs defeat Chinese at Battle of Talas

850 China Gunpowder is invented

935 Korea Koryu Dynasty begins

939 Vietnam Vietnamese gain independence from China

960 China Song Dynasty begins

◄ **700s China**

CHAPTER 13 500–1200
European Middle Ages

520 Italy Benedict begins writing a set of rules for monasteries

732 France Charles Martel defeats Muslims at the Battle of Tours

800 Rome Pope Leo III crowns Charlemagne emperor

814 Carolingian Empire Charlemagne unites much of Europe

850–950 Europe Worst attacks by invaders throughout Europe

900s Western Europe Feudalism expands

CHAPTER 14 800–1500
The Formation of Western Europe

910 France Benedictine monastery at Cluny is founded

987 France Hugh Capet establishes Capetian Dynasty

1200s Italy ►

CHAPTER 15 800–1500
Societies and Empires of Africa

800s–900s West Africa Empire of Ghana thrives

Benin ►

500	600	700	800	900	1000

Living History
Unit 3 Portfolio Project

THEME | Religious and Ethical Systems

Your portfolio for Unit 3 will show how religious and ethical systems affect all aspects of the lives of people in this time period. The effects you track will be political, economic, social, and intellectual as well as spiritual. As the young religions grow, you will see the blending of cultures, power struggles between religions, and the blurring of the lines between politics and religion.

Living History Project Choices

Each Chapter Assessment offers you choices of ways to show the effects of religious and ethical systems in that chapter. Activities include the following:

Chapter 10 poster, talk show, letter

Chapter 11 documentary script, report, dialogue

Chapter 12 photo essay, mural, tour

Chapter 13 character sketch, poster, time line

Chapter 14 newscast, cartoon, speech

Chapter 15 interview, skit, diagram

1000s *Africa, Asia, Europe*
Abbasids, Fatimids, Umayyads rule Muslim Empire

1100s *Spain*
Muslim Ibn Rushd writes philosophy

◄ **1100s** *Baghdad*

1054 *Rome, Constantinople*
Christian Church divides

1071 *Turkey*
Seljuks defeat Byzantines

1100s *Turkey*
Seljuk Empire declines

1100s *Russia*
Moscow founded

1242 *Russia*
Kiev falls to the Mongols

◄ **1000s** *Russia*

1453 *Turkey*
Constantinople falls to the Turks

1480 *Russia*
Ivan III refuses to pay Mongol tribute

1020s *China*
Song Dynasty issues paper currency

1127 *China*
Dynasty of Southern Song flourishes

1192 *Japan*
Kamakura Shogunate begins

1209 *Mongolia*
Genghis Khan begins Mongol conquests

1279 *China*
Kublai Khan conquers Song Dynasty

1330s *Persia*
Ilkhanate government falls apart

1368 *China*
Chinese rebels overthrow Mongols

▼ **1400s** *France*

1075 *Holy Roman Empire*
Henry IV clashes with Pope Gregory VII

1122 *Holy Roman Empire* Concordat of Worms compromise reached

1152 *Holy Roman Empire*
Frederick I becomes king

1095 *France* Pope Urban II issues call for First Crusade

1187 *Palestine*
Jerusalem falls to Muslims led by Saladin

1204 *Byzantine Empire*
Crusaders loot city of Constantinople

1215 *England*
King John agrees to Magna Carta

1337 *France*
Hundred Years' War begins between England and France

1347 *Italy*
Bubonic plague spreads to Europe

1431 *France* Joan of Arc is burned at the stake

1453 *France* End of the Hundred Years' War

1076 *Ghana*
Muslim Almoravids conquer Ghana

1148 *Morocco*
Almohad Dynasty takes control of Muslim Morocco

1235 *Mali*
Sundiata founds Mali Empire

1324 *Mali*
Mansa Musa goes on a hajj

1352 *Mali*
Muslim traveler Ibn Battuta visits Mali

1420 *Southern Africa*
Mutota begins Mutapa Empire

1450 *Great Zimbabwe* City of Great Zimbabwe is abandoned

CHAPTER 10

The Muslim World, 600–1250

PREVIEWING THEMES

Religious and Ethical Systems

Islam, a monotheistic religion, developed during the 600s. The teachings of Muhammad were embraced by Arab peoples, who spread the religion through Southwest Asia and parts of Africa and Europe.

Empire Building

As Muslims spread the religion of Islam, they captured new lands and the people of those lands came under Muslim rule. The leaders following Muhammad built a huge empire that by A.D. 750 stretched from the Atlantic Ocean to India. It included millions of people from diverse ethnic, language, and religious groups.

Cultural Interaction

Muslim tolerance of conquered peoples and the emphasis on learning blended the cultural traits of people under Muslim rule. The ideas of ancient Greeks and Indians combined with new ideas. This began a brilliant age of learning and cultural sharing that marked the Muslim world between 750 and 1250.

INTERNET CONNECTION

Visit us at **www.mcdougallittell.com** to learn more about the Muslim world.

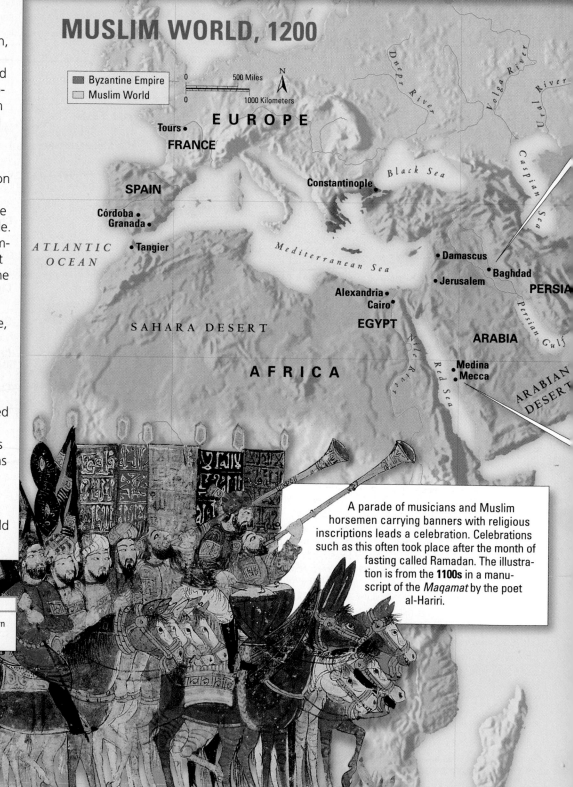

MUSLIM WORLD, 1200

- Byzantine Empire
- Muslim World

0 — 500 Miles
0 — 1000 Kilometers

EUROPE

Tours •
FRANCE

SPAIN

Córdoba •
Granada •

ATLANTIC OCEAN

• Tangier

SAHARA DESERT

AFRICA

Black Sea

Constantinople •

Mediterranean Sea

• Damascus
• Jerusalem   • Baghdad

Alexandria •
Cairo •

EGYPT

Dnepr River
Volga River
Ural River
Caspian Sea

PERSIA

Persian Gulf

ARABIA

Red Sea
Nile River

• Medina
• Mecca

ARABIAN DESERT

A parade of musicians and Muslim horsemen carrying banners with religious inscriptions leads a celebration. Celebrations such as this often took place after the month of fasting called Ramadan. The illustration is from the **1100s** in a manuscript of the *Maqamat* by the poet al-Hariri.

Following a dream in which he spoke with Aristotle, Caliph al-Ma'mun ordered a **House of Wisdom** to be built in **Baghdad** in the early **800s.** It contained a library, an academy, and translation facilities for scientific and philosophical works, especially those from Greece, Byzantium, Persia, and India. There was an observatory nearby. Pictured here are scholars studying in a library in Baghdad.

ASIA

INDIA

PACIFIC OCEAN

40°N

INDIAN OCEAN

Equator 0°

Tropic of Capricorn

This aerial view shows the holiest shrine of Islam, located in **Mecca.** Millions of pilgrims come to Mecca as part of their religious obligations. The cube located in the middle of the mosque is the Ka'aba. Muslims believe this house of worship was originally built by Abraham.

Interact *with* History

A round 825, an Arab mathematician, al-Khwarizmi of Baghdad, studied Indian math and wrote a book on using "Hindu" numerals. He suggested that not only mathematicians but also merchants should use the numerals.

You are an ambitious Italian merchant in the 1400s, visiting Muslim lands. You hear about these "Arabic" numerals that are widely used in transactions with Muslim traders. You wonder if they have any advantages for your business.

In the marketplace, you buy four necklaces at a cost of 23 dinars each. You ask the merchant to show you the calculation using Roman and then Arabic numerals. The problem is IV necklaces at XXIII dinars, or 4 × 23. You observe that computation with Arabic numerals is much easier and quicker.

Baker measures flour.

What makes an idea useful?

Jeweler sells customer four necklaces at 23 dinars each.

Apothecary weighs out medicinal products.

EXAMINING *the* ISSUES

- Do the math problem using both sets of numerals. What is the advantage of using the Arabic numerals?

- Of what use would this system of numbers be to a businessperson?

- In what ways is the Arabic numeral system like a universal language?

- The mathematical idea of Arabic numbers spread to many cultures. In what ways do ideas move from one culture to another?

Discuss these questions with your classmates. In your discussion, consider what makes an idea useful and what kinds of ideas spread fastest. Think about ideas that have to do with business, as well as ideas in such areas as religion and science.

As you read about the spread of Islam and the development of Muslim culture in this chapter, notice in what ways ideas are accepted and spread.

Butcher divides a carcass.

TERMS & NAMES
- **Allah**
- **Muhammad**
- **Islam**
- **Muslim**
- **Hijrah**
- **Qur'an**
- **mosque**
- **hajj**
- **Sunna**
- **shari'a**

① The Rise of Islam

MAIN IDEA	WHY IT MATTERS NOW
Muhammad unified the Arab people both politically and through the religion of Islam.	As the world's fastest growing major religion, Islam has a strong impact on the lives of millions today.

SETTING THE STAGE The cultures of the Arabian Peninsula were in constant contact with each other for centuries. Southwest Asia (often referred to as the Middle East) was a bridge between Africa, Asia, and Europe, where goods were traded and new ideas were shared. One set of shared ideas would become a powerful force for change in the world—the religion of Islam.

Deserts, Towns, and Travelers

The Arabian Peninsula is a crossroads of three continents—Africa, Europe, and Asia. At its longest and widest points, the peninsula is about 1,200 miles from north to south and 1,300 miles from east to west. Only a tiny strip of fertile land in south Arabia and Oman and a few oases can support agriculture. The remainder of the land is desert, which in the past was inhabited by nomadic Arab herders.

Vocabulary
oases: places in the desert made fertile by the presence of water.

Desert and Town Life On this desert, the nomads, called Bedouins (BEHD·oo·ihnz), were organized into tribes and groups called clans. These clans provided security and support for a life made difficult by the extreme conditions of the desert. The tribesmen took pride in their ability to adapt to the desert conditions and to defend themselves against raids by other clans seeking water, grazing territory, livestock, or food supplies. Because of the desert nomads' fighting ability, they eventually became the core of armies who would build a huge empire in the 600s and 700s. The Bedouin ideals of courage and loyalty to family, along with their warrior skills, would become part of the Islamic way of life.

The areas with more fertile soil and the larger oases had enough water to support farming communities. By the early 600s, many Arabs had chosen to settle in an oasis or in a market town. A few generations earlier, the town dwellers had themselves been nomads. They, however, left the Bedouin life behind for life in settled areas. Larger towns near the western coast of Arabia became market towns for local, regional, and long-distance trade goods.

Crossroads of Trade and Ideas By the early 600s, trade routes connected Arabia to the major ocean and land trade routes. Trade routes through Arabia ran from the extreme south of the peninsula to the Byzantine and Sassanid empires to the north. Merchants from these two empires moved along the caravan routes, trading for goods from the Silk Roads of the east. They transported spices and incense from Yemen and other products to the west. They also carried information and ideas from the world outside Arabia. By the early 600s, cities such as Petra and Palmyra had

Petra, one of the early Arab trading cities, was literally a rock city. Buildings were carved out of the red sandstone cliffs. The name Petra means "rock" in Greek.

The Muslim World **233**

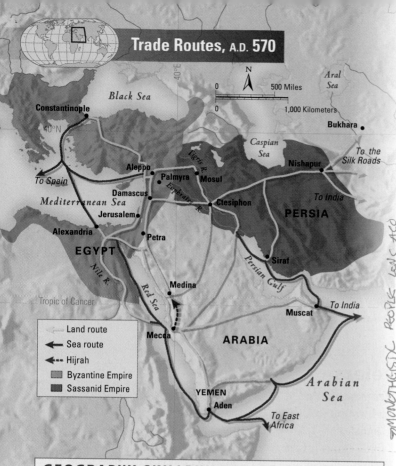

Trade Routes, A.D. 570

Black Sea

Constantinople

Mediterranean Sea

To Spain

Aleppo
Palmyra
Damascus
Jerusalem
Alexandria
Petra

EGYPT

Nile R.

Tropic of Cancer

Red Sea

Medina

Mecca

ARABIA

YEMEN
Aden

Tigris R.
Euphrates R.

Mosul
Ctesiphon

PERSIA

To India

Nishapur
Siraf

Caspian Sea

Aral Sea

Bukhara

To the
Silk Roads

To India

Muscat

Persian Gulf

Arabian Sea

To East
Africa

500 Miles

1,000 Kilometers

Land route
Sea route
Hijrah
Byzantine Empire
Sassanid Empire

GEOGRAPHY SKILLBUILDER: Interpreting Maps
1. **Location** Why is Arabia's location a good one for trade?
2. **Movement** Why was the location of Mecca ideal for the spread of ideas?

long been prosperous trading centers on the caravan routes.

The city of Mecca, in western Arabia, became an important stop on the trade route. During certain holy months, caravans stopped in Mecca. They brought religious pilgrims who came to worship at an ancient shrine in the city. Mecca housed a simple house of worship called the Ka'aba (KAH·buh). The Arabs associated this house of worship with Abraham, a believer in one God. Over the years, they had introduced the worship of many gods and spirits to the place. The Ka'aba contained over 360 idols brought here by many tribes. Many people traveled to this site as a pilgrimage.

The concept of belief in one God, called **Allah** (AL·luh) in Arabic, was no stranger to the Arabian Peninsula. A tradition of belief in one God had long been followed by a few people, known as *hanifs*. Many Christians and Jews lived in Arab lands and practiced monotheism. Into this mixed religious environment of Mecca, around A.D. 570, Muhammad was born.

THINK THROUGH HISTORY
A. Summarizing
What religious traditions were in practice in the Arabian Peninsula?

The Prophet Muhammad

Muhammad (mu·HAM·id) was born into the clan of a powerful Meccan family. Orphaned at the age of six, the boy was raised by his grandfather and uncle. He received little schooling and began working in the caravan trade as a very young man. Muhammad became a trader and business manager for Khadijah (kah·DEE·juh), a wealthy businesswoman. When Muhammad was 25, he and Khadijah married. Theirs was both a good marriage and a good business partnership.

Revelations Muhammad took great interest in religion and often spent time alone in prayer and meditation. At about the age of 40, Muhammad's life was changed overnight when a voice called to him while he meditated in a cave outside Mecca. According to Muslim belief, the voice was that of the angel Gabriel, who told Muhammad that he was a messenger of God. "What shall I proclaim?" asked Muhammad. The voice answered:

> **THE QUR'AN**
> Proclaim! In the name of thy Lord and Cherisher, who created man out of a (mere) clot of congealed blood. Proclaim! And thy Lord is most bountiful. He who taught (the use of) the pen taught man that which he knew not.
> Qur'an Surah 96:1–5

After much soul-searching, Muhammad came to believe that the Lord who spoke to him through Gabriel was Allah. Muhammad became convinced that he was indeed the last of the prophets. He taught that Allah was the one and only God and that all other gods must be abandoned. People who agreed to this basic principle of Islam were called Muslims. In Arabic, **Islam** (ihs·LAHM) means "submission to the will of Allah."

Background
Muhammad is often referred to as The Prophet.

Muslim (MOOZ·lim) means "one who has submitted." Muhammad's wife, Khadijah, and several close friends and relatives were his first followers.

By 613, Muhammad had begun to preach publicly in Mecca. At first, he had little success. Many Meccans believed his revolutionary ideas would lead to neglect of the traditional Arab gods. They feared that Mecca would lose its position as a pilgrimage center if people accepted Muhammad's monotheistic beliefs. Some of his followers were even beaten up or stoned in the streets.

The Hijrah Facing such hostility, Muhammad decided to leave Mecca. In 622, following a small band of supporters he sent ahead, Muhammad resettled in the town of Yathrib, over 200 miles to the north of Mecca. This migration became known as the **Hijrah** (hih·JEE·ruh). The Hijrah to Yathrib marked a turning point for Muhammad. He attracted many devoted followers. Later, Yathrib was renamed Medina, meaning "city of the Prophet." *FOR THE BETTER*

In Medina, Muhammad displayed impressive leadership skills. He fashioned an agreement that joined his own people with the Arabs and Jews of Medina as a single community. These groups accepted Muhammad as a political leader. As a religious leader, he drew many more converts who found the message and the Messenger appealing. Finally, Muhammad also became a military leader in the hostilities between Mecca and Medina. *HAD TO DEFEND BASIS OF RELIGION*

Returning to Mecca Many of the region's Bedouin tribes converted to Islam and joined Muhammad and his followers. During the years that the Muslims and the Meccans battled against each other, Mecca's power as a city declined. In 630, the Prophet and 10,000 of his followers marched to the outskirts of Mecca. Facing sure defeat, Mecca's leaders surrendered. The Prophet entered the city in triumph. *MUHAMMAD WON*

When he entered the city, Muhammad went to the Ka'aba and declared, "Truth has come and falsehood has vanished." Then he destroyed the idols in the Ka'aba and had the call to prayer made from the roof of the Ka'aba.

Most Meccans pledged their loyalty to Muhammad, and many converted to Islam. By doing so, they joined the *umma*, or Muslim religious community. Muhammad died two years later, at about the age of 62. However, he had taken great strides toward unifying the entire Arabian Peninsula under Islam. *UNIFIED ARABIA THROUGH ISLAM*

 MECCA →

THINK THROUGH HISTORY
B. Summarizing
Identify four major events in the life of Muhammad.

SPOTLIGHT ON

The Dome of the Rock

The Dome of the Rock, located in Jerusalem, is the earliest surviving Islamic monument. It was completed in 691. It is situated on Mount Moriah, the site of a Jewish temple destroyed by Romans in A.D. 70.

The rock on the site is the spot from which Muslims say Muhammad ascended to heaven to learn of Allah's will. With Allah's blessing, Muhammad returned to earth to bring God's message to all people. Jews identify the same rock as the site where Abraham was prepared to sacrifice his son Isaac.

The dome itself is wooden and about 60 feet in diameter. The supporting structure includes mosaic designs, columns, and many windows.

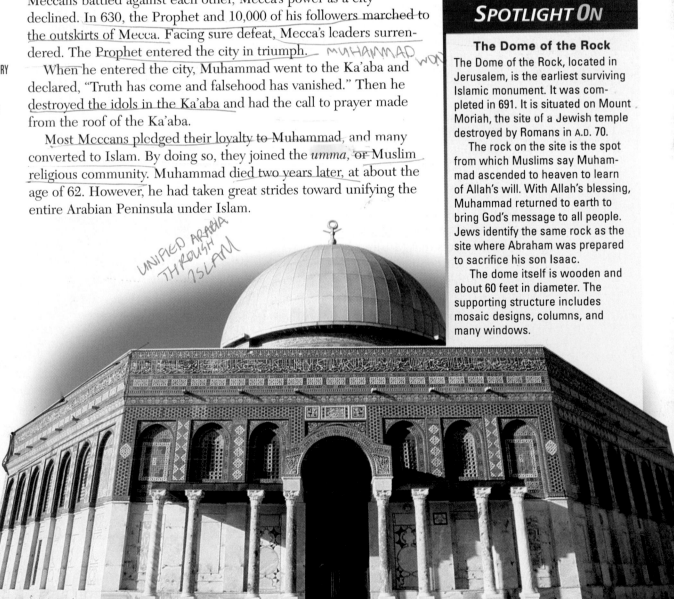

Beliefs and Practices of Islam

The main teaching of Islam is that there is only one God, Allah. All other beliefs and practices follow from this teaching. Islam teaches that there is good and evil, and that each individual is responsible for the actions of his or her life. The holy book of the Muslims, the **Qur'an** (kuh·RAN), states, "And if any one earns sin, he earns it against his own soul" (Surah 4:111). Muslims believe that each person will stand before Allah on a final judgment day and enter either heaven or hell.

Artists decorating the Qur'an do it as a holy act. The design is geometric and often repeats to show the infinite quality of Allah. Muslims use abstract designs because they are not permitted to picture Muhammad or the angels.

The Five Pillars To be a Muslim, all believers have to carry out five duties. These duties demonstrate a Muslim's submission to the will of God. These duties are known as the Five Pillars of Islam.

- **Faith** To become a Muslim, a person has to testify to the following statement of faith: "There is no God but Allah, and Muhammad is the Messenger of Allah." This simple statement is heard again and again in Islamic rituals and in Muslim daily life.

- **Prayer** Five times a day, Muslims face toward Mecca to pray. They may assemble at a **mosque** (mahsk), an Islamic house of worship. Or they may pray wherever they find themselves. The duty of praying serves to bring Muslims closer to God.

- **Alms** Muhammad taught that all Muslims have a responsibility to support the less fortunate. Muslims meet that social responsibility by giving alms, or money for the poor, through a special religious tax.

- **Fasting** During the Islamic holy month of Ramadan, Muslims fast. They eat and drink nothing between dawn and sunset. A simple meal is eaten at the end of the day. The duty of fasting reminds Muslims that they have "greater needs than bread."

- **Pilgrimage** All Muslims perform the **hajj** (haj), or pilgrimage to Mecca, at least once in a lifetime. In the past, this involved a grueling journey across deserts, mountains, and seas. Today, many pilgrims arrive by airplane. During the pilgrimage events in Mecca, pilgrims wear identical garments so that all stand as equals before God.

A Way of Life Muslims do not separate their personal life from their religious life. Carrying out the Five Pillars of Islam ensures that Muslims live their religion while serving in their community. Along with the Five Pillars, there are other customs, morals, and laws for Islamic society that affect Muslims' daily lives. Believers are forbidden to eat pork or to drink wine or other intoxicating beverages. Friday afternoons are set aside for communal worship and prayer. Muslims who are able to do so gather at a mosque to worship. Unlike many other religions, Islam has no priests or central religious authority. Every Muslim is expected to worship God directly. Islam does, however, have a scholar class called the *ulama*, who are concerned with learning and law. The ulama includes religious teachers who study the words and deeds of Muhammad and apply them to everyday life.

Sources of Authority The original source of authority for Muslims is Allah. According to Islamic belief, Allah expressed his will through the Angel Gabriel, who

This tenth-century Turkish prayer rug has a traditional design. The design has an arch at one end. The arch must point to Mecca while the prayers are taking place.

revealed it to Muhammad as the Qur'an. While Muhammad lived, his followers listened to his prayers and teachings and memorized and recited the Revelations. Soon after the Prophet's death, it was suggested that the revelations of Muhammad be collected in a book. This book is the Qur'an.

The Qur'an is written in Arabic, and Muslims consider only the Arabic version to be the true word of God. Only Arabic can be used in worship. Wherever Muslims carried the Qur'an, Arabic became the language of worshipers and scholars. Thus, the Arabic language spread widely as Muslim control expanded into different lands.

Muslims believe that Muhammad's mission as a prophet was to receive the Qur'an and to demonstrate how to apply it in life. To them, the **Sunna** (SOON·uh), or Muhammad's example, is the best model for proper living. The guidance of the Qur'an and Sunna was assembled in a practical form to aid Muslims in applying the will of Allah to their daily lives. This body of law is known as **shari'a** (shah·REE·ah). This system of law regulates the family life, moral conduct, and business and community life of Muslims. It does not separate religious matters from criminal or civil matters, but brings all aspects of life together. Because shari'a applies to all who follow the teachings of the Prophet, it brings a sense of unity to all Muslims.

Links to Judaism and Christianity To Muslims, Allah is the same God that is worshiped in Christianity and Judaism. However, Muslims view Jesus as a prophet, not the Son of God. The Qur'an is regarded as the word of God as revealed to Muhammad, in the same way that Jews and Christians believe the Torah and the Gospels were revealed to Moses and the New Testament writers. Muslims believe that the Qur'an perfects the earlier revelations from God. To them, it is the final book, and Muhammad was the final prophet. All three religions believe in heaven and hell and a day of judgment. The Muslims trace their ancestry to Abraham, as do the Jews and Christians.

The bonds among the three monotheistic religions were reflected in the way the Muslims treated Christians and Jews. Both Christians and Jews were known as "people of the book," because each religion had a holy book with teachings similar to those of the Qur'an. Shari'a law required Muslim leaders to extend religious tolerance to Christians and Jews. A huge Muslim empire, as you will learn in Section 2, grew to include people of many different cultures and religions.

THINK THROUGH HISTORY
C. Summarizing
What are the sources of authority for Muslims?

Background
Arab Muslims consider themselves descended from Abraham's son Ismail.

Daily Life

Muslim Prayer

Five times a day—dawn, noon, mid-afternoon, sunset, and evening—Muslims face toward Mecca to pray. Worshipers are called to prayer by a *muezzin*. The call to prayer sometimes is given from a *minaret* tower like those pictured above. In large cities, muezzins call worshipers to prayer using public address systems and even the radio.

Because they believe that standing before Allah places them on holy ground, Muslims perform a ritual cleansing before praying so that they will not contaminate the holy ground. They also remove their shoes.

Muslims may pray at a mosque, called a *masjid* in Arabic, meaning "place of kneeling to God." This term refers to the movements of prayer, which involve both the body and the mind in worship.

Section ❶ Assessment

1. TERMS & NAMES

Identify
• Allah
• Muhammad
• Islam
• Muslim
• Hijrah
• Qur'an
• mosque
• hajj
• Sunna
• shari'a

2. TAKING NOTES

Create a diagram like the one shown below. Fill in at least three details for each category.

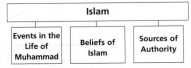

Islam		
Events in the Life of Muhammad	Beliefs of Islam	Sources of Authority

Based on your notes, write three paragraphs on Islam.

3. RECOGNIZING EFFECTS

Explain how the beliefs and practices of Islam created unity and strength among Muslims in the 600s.

THINK ABOUT
• why individuals felt they were part of a community
• what Muslims did to carry out the Five Pillars of Islam
• how Muslims viewed the relationship between religion and politics

4. THEME ACTIVITY

Religious and Ethical Systems With a small group, write a conversation that involves a supporter of Muhammad, a person who opposes Muhammad, and a pilgrim visiting Mecca who knows nothing about Muhammad. Place the conversation in a marketplace setting in Mecca. Read or perform your conversation for the class.

The Spread of Islam

TERMS & NAMES
- caliph
- Umayyads
- Shi'a
- Sunni
- Sufi
- Abbasids
- al-Andalus
- Fatimid

MAIN IDEA

In spite of internal conflicts, the Muslims created a huge empire that included lands on three continents.

WHY IT MATTERS NOW

Muslims' influence on three continents produced cultural blending that has continued into the modern world.

SETTING THE STAGE When Muhammad died in 632, the community faced a crisis. Muslims, inspired by the message of Allah, believed they had a duty to carry the word of God to the world. However, they lacked a clear way to choose a new leader. Eventually, the issue of leadership would divide the Muslim world.

Muhammad's Successors Spread Islam

Muhammad had not named a successor or instructed his followers how to choose one. Relying on ancient tribal custom, the Muslim community elected as their leader Abu-Bakr, a loyal friend of Muhammad and a man respected for his devotion to Islam. In 632, Abu-Bakr became the first **caliph** (KAY·lihf), a title that means "successor" or "deputy."

"Rightly Guided" Caliphs Abu-Bakr and the next three elected caliphs—Umar, Uthman, and Ali—all had known Muhammad and supported his mission. They used the Qur'an and Muhammad's actions as guides to leadership. For this, they are known as the "rightly guided" caliphs. Their rule was called a caliphate (KAY·lih·FAYT).

Abu-Bakr had promised the Muslim community he would uphold what Muhammad stood for. Shortly after the Prophet's death, some tribes on the Arabian Peninsula abandoned Islam. Others refused to pay taxes, and a few individuals even declared themselves prophets. For two years, Abu-Bakr used military force to reassert the authority of Muhammad's successors in the Muslim community. In that time, his troops gained experience and organized themselves into an effective mobile army.

By the time Abu-Bakr died in 634, the Muslim state controlled all of Arabia. Under Umar, the second caliph, swift and highly disciplined armies conquered Syria and lower Egypt, which were part of the Byzantine Empire. They also took parts of the Persian Empire. The next two caliphs, Uthman and Ali, continued to expand Muslim territory both eastward and westward. The "rightly guided" caliphs were able to gain the support of military and naval forces of the conquered lands. They used these forces to aid in further conquests. By 750, from the Atlantic Ocean to the Indus River, the Muslim Empire stretched 6,000 miles—about two times the distance across the continental United States. (See the map on page 241.)

Reasons for Success The four "rightly guided" caliphs made great progress in their quest to spread Islam. Muslims of the day saw the victories as a sign of Allah's support of Islam. Muslims drew energy and inspiration from their faith and were willing to struggle to extend and defend Islam. Historians have identified many reasons for the Muslims' military success in addition to the faith of the Muslim soldiers. The Muslim armies were well disciplined and expertly commanded. Their tactics enabled them to overwhelm forces unaccustomed to their style of warfare.

From 632 to 750, highly mobile troops mounted on camels were successful in conquering lands in the name of Allah.

The success of the Muslim armies was also due to weakness in the two empires north of Arabia. The Byzantine and Persian empires had been in conflict for a long period of time. By the time the Muslim army invaded their lands, they were exhausted militarily. Another reason for Muslim success was the persecution of Byzantine or Persian populations who did not support the official state religions, Christianity or Zoroastrianism. The persecuted people often welcomed the invaders, seeing them as liberators.

Treatment of Conquered Peoples Many conquered peoples chose to accept Islam. They were attracted by the appeal of the message of Islam, as well as by the economic benefit for Muslims of not having to pay a poll tax. Because the Qur'an forbade forced conversion, Muslims allowed conquered peoples to retain their own religion. Christians and Jews, as "people of the book," received special consideration. They paid a poll tax each year in exchange for exemption from military duties. They were also subject to various restrictions on their lives. The following account by an Arab army officer shows how he treated people in Persia:

A VOICE FROM THE PAST
In the name of God, the Merciful and the Compassionate. This is what Suwayd ibn Muqarrin gave to the inhabitants of Qumis and those who are dependent on them, concerning safe-conduct for themselves, their religions, and their property, on condition they pay the *jizya* [a poll tax] from the hand for every adult male, according to his capacity, that they show goodwill and do not deceive, that they guide [the Muslim traveler], and that they accommodate Muslims who make a halt with them for a day and a night with their average food. If they change this or make light of their obligations, the pact [*dhimma*] with them is void.

SUWAYD IBN MUQARRIN quoted in *Islam: From the Prophet Muhammad to the Capture of Constantinople*

In practice, tolerance like this was extended to other groups as well. Though they were not allowed to spread their religion, Christians and Jews played important roles as officials, scholars, and bureaucrats in the Muslim state.

Ceremonial weapons such as this battle-ax were often decorated with fine artistic designs.

Internal Conflict Creates a Crisis

Despite spectacular gains on the battlefield, the Muslim community had difficulty maintaining a unified rule. The murder of Uthman in 656 triggered a civil war, with various groups struggling for power. Ali, as Muhammad's cousin and son-in-law, was the natural choice as a successor to Uthman. However, his right to rule was challenged by Muawiya, a governor of Syria. Then, in 661, Ali too was assassinated. The elective system of choosing a caliph died with him.

A family known as the **Umayyads** (oo·MYE·yadz) came to power. They set up a hereditary system of succession. The Umayyads also made another important change. The Muslim capital was moved to Damascus, a distant city in the recently conquered province of Syria. This location, away from Mecca, made controlling conquered territories easier. However, the Arab Muslims felt it was too far away from their lands. In addition, the Umayyads abandoned the simple life of previous caliphs and began to surround themselves with wealth and ceremony similar to that of non-Muslim rulers. These actions, along with the leadership issue, gave rise to a fundamental division in the Muslim community.

Sunni–Shi'a Split In the interest of peace, the majority of Muslims accepted the Umayyads' rule. A minority did continue to resist, and around some of these groups an alternate view of the office of caliph developed. In this view, the caliph—the person most responsible for spreading Muhammad's message—needed to be a relative of the Prophet. This group was called **Shi'a,** meaning the "party" of Ali. Those who did not outwardly resist the rule of the Umayyads later became known as **Sunni,** meaning followers of Muhammad's example. Among those who did not actively resist Umayyad rule were many who believed that the Umayyads had become too concerned with worldly affairs and had lost touch with their religion.

Another group, the **Sufi** (SOO·fee), reacted to the luxurious life of the Umayyads by pursuing a life of poverty and devotion to a spiritual path. They tried to achieve direct personal contact with God through mystical means, such as meditation and chanting. In some ways they were similar to Christian and Buddhist monks. The Sufis played an important role in keeping Muslims focused on the Qur'an and tradition. Later, they became very active as missionaries in newly conquered lands. Another religious development was the growth of scholarship in various branches of Islamic learning and law. The study of the traditions of Muhammad, Arabic language, and the development of schools of shari'a established standards of Islamic conduct.

Vigorous religious and political opposition to the Umayyad caliphate led to its downfall. Rebel groups overthrew the Umayyads in the year 750. The most powerful of those groups, the **Abbasids** (AB·uh·SIHDZ), took control of the empire.

THINK THROUGH HISTORY
B. Summarizing
What are three groups within Islam and how do they differ?

Muslims Control Areas of Three Continents

When the Abbasids came to power in 750, they ruthlessly murdered the remaining members of the Umayyad family. One prince named Abd al-Rahman escaped the slaughter and fled to Spain. There he set up an Umayyad dynasty. Spain had already been conquered and settled by Muslims from North Africa, who were known as Berbers. The Berbers were led by Tariq, a powerful military figure. So revered was Tariq that a famous rock peninsula was named for him. The name today reflects his presence: Jabal Tariq—Gibraltar. The Berber armies advanced north to within 100 miles of Paris before being halted at the Battle of Tours in 732. The Berbers then settled back into southern Spain, where they helped form an extraordinary Muslim state called **al-Andalus** (al·AN·duh·LUS).

Background
The Spanish name for Arabs and Berbers was Moors, because they came from the old Roman province of Mauritania.

Global Impact

Elephant Diplomacy

The Abbasids ruled a huge empire and were constantly searching for ways to hold it together and hold off outside attacks. The Abbasids viewed their relationship with the Kingdom of the Franks, ruled by Charlemagne, as essential to their ability to remain strong. They saw the Franks as possible allies against the Umayyads in al-Andalus (Spain).

To cement the relationship with Charlemagne, Caliph Harun al-Rashid sent an envoy with gifts to the court of Charlemagne. Among the gifts sent to the Frankish king was an elephant named Abu al-Abbas. It was the only elephant the caliph possessed.

The diplomatic trip was successful. Charlemagne marched against the Umayyad lands early in his reign.

Abbasids Consolidate Power The Abbasids' strength lay in the former Persian lands, including Iraq, Iran, and central Asia. To solidify power, in 762 they moved the capital of the empire to a newly created city, Baghdad, in southern Iraq. The location on key trade routes gave the caliph access to trade goods, gold, and information about parts of the empire in Asia, Africa, and Europe.

The Abbasids developed a strong bureaucracy to conduct the huge empire's affairs. A treasury kept track of the money flow. A chancery prepared letters and documents. A special department managed the business of the army. Diplomats from the empire were sent to courts in Europe (for example, Charlemagne's court), Africa, and Asia to conduct imperial business. To support this bureaucracy, the Abbasids taxed land, imports, and exports, and non-Muslims' wealth.

Rival Groups Divide Muslim Lands The Abbasid caliphate lasted from 750 to 1258. During that time, the Abbasids increased their authority by consulting religious leaders. But they failed to keep complete political control of the immense territory. Independent Muslim states sprang up, and local leaders dominated many smaller regions. The **Fatimid** (FAT·uh·MIHD) Dynasty, named after

Muhammad's daughter Fatima, began in North Africa and spread across the Red Sea to western Arabia and Syria. Although politically divided, the Abbasid Empire and the smaller powers remained unified in other ways. Religion, language, trade, and the economy tied the lands together.

Muslim Trade Network The two major sea-trading zones—those of the Mediterranean Sea and the Indian Ocean—linked the Muslim Empire into a world system of trade by sea. The land network connected the Silk Roads of China and India with Europe and Africa. Muslim merchants needed only a single language, Arabic, and a single currency, the Abbasid dinar, to travel from Córdoba to Baghdad and on to China.

THINK THROUGH HISTORY
C. Recognizing Effects Why would a single language and a single currency be such an advantage to a trader?

To encourage the flow of trade, Muslim money changers set up banks in cities throughout the empire. Banks offered letters of credit, called *sakks*, to merchants. A merchant with a *sakk* from a bank in Baghdad could exchange it for cash at a bank in any other major city in the empire. In Europe, the word *sakk* was pronounced "check." Thus, the practice of using checks dates back to the Muslim Empire.

At one end of the Muslim Empire was the city of Córdoba in al-Andalus. In the tenth century, this city had a population of 500,000; Paris, in contrast, had 38,000. The city's mix of Muslims, Christians, and Jews created a cosmopolitan atmosphere that attracted poets and philosophers as well as scientists and doctors. Many non-Muslims adopted the Arabic language and Muslim customs. Córdoba became a dazzling center of Muslim culture, boasting 70 libraries, 700 mosques, and 27 free schools.

In Córdoba, Damascus, Cairo, and Baghdad, a cultural blending of people fueled a period of immense achievements in the arts and the sciences.

Growth of Islam to 1200

EUROPE
ASIA
AFRICA
INDIA
ATLANTIC OCEAN
INDIAN OCEAN
Arabian Sea

40°N
Córdoba
Damascus
Baghdad
Cairo
Tropic of Cancer
Mecca
0° Equator
Tropic of Capricorn

N
0   1,500 Miles
0   2,500 Kilometers

- Muslim lands at the death of Muhammad, 632
- Lands conquered by Muslims under first four caliphs by 661
- Lands conquered by Muslims by 750
- Lands under Muslim influence in 1200

GEOGRAPHY SKILLBUILDER: Interpreting Maps
1. **Location** To which continents did Islam spread by 1200?
2. **Movement** In which time period was the largest amount of land conquered?

Section 2 Assessment

1. TERMS & NAMES

Identify
- caliph
- Umayyads
- Shi'a
- Sunni
- Sufi
- Abbasids
- al-Andalus
- Fatimid

2. TAKING NOTES

Create a table like the one below. For each group of rulers, identify the period of their rule and at least two developments that affected the growth or strength of Islam during that period.

Rulers	Period of Rule	Developments in Islam
Rightly Guided Caliphs		
Umayyads		
Abbasids		

3. HYPOTHESIZING

How do you think Shi'a Muslims felt about the Abbasids taking power in 750?

THINK ABOUT
- how the Shi'a viewed the Umayyads
- where the Shi'a lived
- actions of Abbasids while in power

4. ANALYZING THEMES

Empire Building What evidence supports the conclusion that the Islamic empires were well-run?

THINK ABOUT
- relationships between Muslims and non-Muslims
- efforts to promote trade
- the role of the military

3 Muslim Achievement

MAIN IDEA

Muslims combined and preserved the traditions of many peoples and also advanced learning in a variety of areas.

WHY IT MATTERS NOW

Many of the ideas developed during this time became the basis of today's scientific and academic disciplines.

SETTING THE STAGE The Abbasids governed during a prosperous age of Muslim history. Riches flowed into the empire from all over Europe, Asia, and Africa. Rulers could afford to build luxurious cities. They supported the scientists, mathematicians, and philosophers that those cities attracted. In the special atmosphere created by Islam, the scholars preserved existing knowledge and produced an enormous body of original learning.

Muslim Society

Over time, the influence of Muslims grew as the empire encompassed people from a variety of lands. Jobs in the bureaucracy and in the army were available to many different groups. At centers of learning in Syria, Persia, Spain, and Egypt, the halls echoed with the Arabic language, the language of the Qur'an. The many cultural traditions combined with the Arabic culture to create an international flavor. Muslim society had a sophistication matched at that time only by the Tang Empire of China. That cosmopolitan character was most evident in urban centers.

The Rise of Muslim Urban Centers Throughout the empire, market towns blossomed into cities. Migrants from the countryside and new converts came to cities looking for opportunities. Until the construction of Baghdad, Damascus was the leading city. Damascus was known for fine cloth called damask and for outstanding steel swords and armor. It was also the cultural center of Islamic learning. Other cities grew up around power centers, such as Córdoba, the Umayyad capital, and Cairo, the Fatimid capital. (See the map on page 241.) Urban centers, which symbolized the strength of the dynasty, grew to be impressive.

The Abbasid capital, Baghdad, impressed all who saw it. Caliph al-Mansur chose the site for his capital on the west bank of the Tigris River, in 762. Extensive planning went into the city's distinctive circular design, formed by three circular protective walls. The caliph's palace of marble and stone sat in the innermost circle, along with the grand mosque. Originally, the main streets between the middle wall and the palace were lined with shops. Later, the marketplace moved to a district outside the walls. Baghdad's population approached one million at its peak.

Four Social Classes Baghdad's population, made up of different cultures and social classes, was typical for a large Muslim city in the eighth and ninth centuries. Muslim society was made up of four classes. The upper class included those who were Muslims at birth. Converts to Islam were found in the second class. This class paid a higher tax than the upper class,

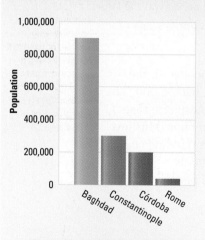

Urban Centers, A.D. 900

Population

1,000,000
800,000
600,000
400,000
200,000
0

Baghdad   Constantinople   Córdoba   Rome

Source: Tertius Chandler and Gerald Fox, *3,000 Years of Urban Growth.*

SKILLBUILDER: Interpreting Graphs

1. *How much larger in population was Baghdad than Córdoba?*
2. *How would the population of the largest city in your state compare to the population of Baghdad in A.D. 900?*

but lower than other classes of non-Muslim people. The third class consisted of the "protected people" and included Christians, Jews, and Zoroastrians. The lowest class was composed of slaves. Many slaves were prisoners of war, and all were non-Muslim. Slaves most frequently performed household work or fought in the military.

Role of Women The Qur'an states, "Men are the managers of the affairs of women," and "Righteous women are therefore obedient." However, the Qur'an also declares that men and women, as believers, are equal. The shari'a gave Muslim women specific legal rights concerning marriage, family, and property. Muslim women had more rights than European women of the same time period. The Qur'an provided for the care of widows and orphans, allowed divorce, and protected the woman's share of an inheritance.

Responsibilities of Muslim women varied with the income of their husbands. The wife of a poor man would often work in the fields with her husband. Wealthier women supervised the household and its servants. They had access to education, and among them were poets and scholars. Rich or poor, the woman was responsible for the raising of the children. In the early days of Islam, women could also participate in public life and gain an education.

THINK THROUGH HISTORY
A. Summarizing
What were the four classes of Muslim society?

In a miniature painting from Persia, women are shown having a picnic in a garden. Gardens were seen as earthly representations of paradise.

Muslim Scholarship Extends Knowledge

Muslims had practical reasons for supporting the advancement of science. Rulers wanted qualified physicians treating their ills. The faithful throughout the empire relied on mathematicians and astronomers to calculate the times for prayer and the direction of Mecca. The energy that Muslims devoted to preserving and extending knowledge, however, went beyond practical concerns. Their attitude reflected a deepseated curiosity about the world and a quest for truth that reached back as far as the Prophet. Muhammad himself believed strongly in the power of learning:

A VOICE FROM THE PAST

Acquire knowledge. It enableth its possessor to distinguish right from wrong; it lighteth the way to Heaven; it is our friend in the desert, our society in solitude, our companion when friendless; it guideth us to happiness; it sustaineth us in misery; it is an ornament amongst friends, and an armour against enemies.

MUHAMMAD, quoted in *The Sayings of Muhammad*

THINK THROUGH HISTORY
B. Recognizing Effects What are the nine valuable results of knowledge according to Muhammad?

The Prophet's emphasis on study and scholarship led to strong support of places of learning by Muslim leaders. After the fall of Rome in A.D. 476, Europe entered a period of upheaval and chaos, an era in which scholarship suffered. The scientific knowledge gained up to that time might have been lost. Thanks to Muslim leaders and scholars, much of that knowledge was preserved and expanded. Both Umayyads and Abbasids encouraged scholars to collect and translate scientific and philosophical texts. In the early 800s, Caliph al-Ma'mun opened in Baghdad a combination library, academy, and translation center called the **House of Wisdom.** There, scholars of

The Muslim World **243**

different cultures and beliefs worked side by side translating texts from Greece, India, Persia, and elsewhere into Arabic.

Arts and Sciences Flourish in the Muslim World

Scholars at the House of Wisdom included researchers, editors, linguists, and technical advisers. These scholars developed standards and techniques for research that are a part of the basic methods of today's research. Some Muslim scholars incorporated Greek ideas into their own work in fresh new ways. Others created original work of the highest quality. In these ways, Muslims in the Abbasid lands, especially in Córdoba and Baghdad, set the stage for a later revival of European learning. Muslim contributions in the sciences were most recognizable in medicine, mathematics, and astronomy.

Global Impact

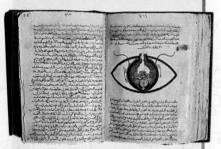

Medical Reference Books

When Europeans learned that Muslims had preserved important medical texts, they wanted to translate the texts into Latin. In the 11th century, scholars traveled to libraries in places such as Toledo, Spain, where they began translating —but only after they learned to read Arabic.

Through this process, European medical schools gained access to vital reference sources such as al-Razi's *Comprehensive Book* and Ibn Sina's *The Canon of Medicine*. Ibn Sina's five-volume encyclopedia guided doctors of Europe and Southwest Asia for six centuries. For nearly 500 years, al-Qasim's work, *The Method*, which contained original drawings of some 200 medical tools, was the foremost textbook on surgery in Europe.

Medical Advances A Persian scholar named al-Razi (Rhazes) was the greatest physician of the Muslim world and, more than likely, of world civilization between A.D. 500 and 1500. He wrote an encyclopedia called the *Comprehensive Book* that drew on knowledge from Greek, Syrian, Arabic, and Indian sources as well as on his own experience. Al-Razi also wrote a *Treatise on Smallpox and Measles*, which was translated into several languages. He believed patients would recover more quickly if they breathed cleaner air. To find that location, he hung shreds of meat all around Baghdad. He observed which shreds spoiled more slowly, perhaps because of cleaner air. Then he made a recommendation for the location of a hospital.

Math and Science Stretch Horizons Among the ideas that Muslim scholars introduced to modern math and science, two especially stand out. They are the reliance on scientific observation and experimentation, and the ability to find mathematical solutions to old problems. As for science, Muslims translated and studied Greek texts. But they did not follow the Greek method of solving problems. Aristotle, Pythagoras, and other Greek thinkers preferred logical reasoning over uncovering facts through observation. Muslim scientists preferred to solve problems by conducting experiments in laboratory settings.

Muslim scholars believed, as Aristotle did, that mathematics was the basis of all knowledge. Al-Khwarizmi, a mathematician born in Baghdad in the late 700s, studied Indian rather than Greek sources. He wrote a textbook in the 800s explaining "the art of bringing together unknowns to match a known quantity." He called this technique *al-jabr*—today called algebra.

Many of the advances in mathematics were related to the study of astronomy. The sciences of mathematics and optics, along with scientific observation, led to major advances in astronomy. Muslim observatories charted stars, comets, and planets. Ibn al-Haytham (Alhazen), a brilliant mathematician, produced a book called *Optics* that revolutionized ideas about vision. Through thoughtful experiments, Ibn al-Haytham showed that people see objects because rays pass from the objects to the eyes, not from the eyes to the objects as was commonly believed. His studies about optics were used in developing lenses for telescopes and microscopes.

Philosophy and Religion Blend Views In addition to scientific works, scholars at the House of Wisdom in Baghdad translated works of philosophers like Aristotle and Plato into Arabic. In the 1100s, Muslim philosopher Ibn Rushd (Averroës), who lived in Córdoba, tried in his writings to harmonize Aristotle's and Plato's views with those of Islam. Some Islamic religious thinkers attacked Ibn Rushd for using Greek philosophical methods to interpret the shari'a. However, Ibn Rushd

Background
Europeans changed Arabic names to ones they could pronounce. You will see the European names in parentheses.

Background
Ibn is a word used to mean "the son of."

Astronomy

Muslim interest in astronomy developed from the need to fulfill three of the Five Pillars of Islam—fasting during Ramadan, performing the hajj, and praying toward Mecca.

A correct lunar calendar was needed to mark religious periods such as the month of Ramadan and the month of the hajj. Studying the skies helped fix the locations of cities so that worshipers could face toward Mecca as they prayed. To correctly calculate the locations, Muslim mathematicians developed trigonometry. Cartographers (mapmakers) illustrated the information.

The cartographer al-Idrisi prepared this map as part of a series of maps for a ruler of Sicily. The maps were done in the 1100s. The map below of the world looks upside down to modern eyes because North is at the bottom. The body of water at the right is the Mediterranean, and the Arabian Peninsula juts out into the Indian Ocean.

Before telescopes, observations of the skies were made with the naked eye. The device shown above is called an armillary sphere. By aligning the top rings with various stars, astronomers could calculate the time of day or year. This aided in setting the calendar correctly. Muslims had a number of observatories. The most famous one was located at Samarkand, which is in modern Uzbekistan.

The astrolabe was an early scientific instrument used by Muslims and others to measure the angles of the sun and the stars above the horizon. It was like a very simple computer. The device was a brass disk engraved with a star map and having a movable bar used for sighting the angle of the sun or stars. To find the location north or south of the equator, the user rotated the rings to the positions of the stars on any given night.

Connect *to* History

Recognizing Effects How did fulfilling religious duties lead Muslims to astronomy and a better understanding of the physical world?

SEE SKILLBUILDER
HANDBOOK, PAGE 995.

Connect *to* Today

Researching Muslim astronomers developed instruments to improve their observations of the sky. Today, there are telescopes both on earth and in space. Do some research to find out what new information is being discovered from the Hubble telescope in space.

HISTORY MAKERS

Ibn Khaldun
1332–1406

Ibn Khaldun was literally a history maker. He produced a massive history of Muslim North Africa. However, Arnold Toynbee, a 20th-century historian, called Ibn Khaldun's Islamic history masterpiece *Muqaddimah* (an introduction to history) "the greatest work of its kind that has ever yet been created by any mind in any time or place."

In his six-volume study of world civilization, Ibn Khaldun introduced the ideas of sociology, economics, politics, and education and showed how they combined to create historical and social change.

He also established principles for writing about history that required historians to examine critically all facts they presented.

argued that Greek philosophy and Islam both had the same goal: to find the truth.

Moses Ben Maimon (Maimonides), a Jewish physician and philosopher, was born in Córdoba and lived in Egypt. Like Ibn Rushd, he faced strong opposition for his ideas, but he came to be recognized as the greatest Jewish philosopher. Writing during the same time as Ibn Rushd, Maimonides produced a book, *The Guide of the Perplexed*, that blended philosophy, religion, and science.

Muslim Literature Literature was a strong tradition in Arabia before Islam. Bedouin poets, reflecting the spirit of desert life, composed poems celebrating ideals such as bravery, love, generosity, and hospitality. Those themes continued to appear in poetry written after the rise of Islam.

The Qur'an, held sacred by Muslims, is the standard for all Arabic literature and poetry. Early Muslim poets sang the praises of the Prophet and of Islam and, later, of the caliphs and other patrons who supported them. During the age of the Abbasid caliphate, literary tastes expanded to include poems about nature and the pleasures of life and love.

The Sufis were especially known for their poetry that focused on mystical experiences with God. The following poem by the greatest of all Sufi poets, Rumi, describes an experience of sensing God:

A VOICE FROM THE PAST

As salt resolved in the ocean
I was swallowed in God's sea,
Past faith, past unbelieving,
Past doubt, past certainty.

Suddenly in my bosom
A star shone clear and bright;
All the suns of heaven
Vanished in that star's light.

JALAL AL-DIN RUMI, translated by A. J. Arberry, *Persian Poems*

Popular literature included *The Thousand and One Nights*, a collection of entertaining stories that included fairy tales, parables, and legends. The core of the collection has been linked to India and Persia, but peoples of the Muslim Empire added stories and arranged them, beginning around the 10th century.

Muslim Art and Architecture As they expanded, the Arabs entered regions that had rich artistic traditions. These traditions continued, with modifications inspired, and sometimes imposed, by Islam. For example, Islam forbade the depiction of living beings, based on the idea that only Allah can create life. Thus, picturing living beings was considered idolatry. With the drawing of such images prohibited, many artists turned to **calligraphy,** or the art of beautiful handwriting. Others expressed themselves through the decorative arts, such as woodwork, glass, ceramics, and textiles.

It is in architecture that the greatest cultural blending of the Muslim world can be seen. To some extent, the location of a building reflected the culture of people of the area. For example, the Great Mosque of Damascus was built on the site of a Christian church. In many ways, the huge dome and vaulted ceiling of the mosque blends Byzantine architecture with Muslim ideas. In Syrian areas, the architecture includes features that were very Roman, including baths using Roman heating systems. In Córdoba, the Great Mosque incorporated multi-lobed interwoven arches in a style unknown before. The style

Background
"Aladdin" and "Ali Baba and the Forty Thieves" are popular tales from *The Thousand and One Nights*.

This interior view of the Great Mosque of Córdoba shows a new architectural style. Two tiers of arches support the ceiling.

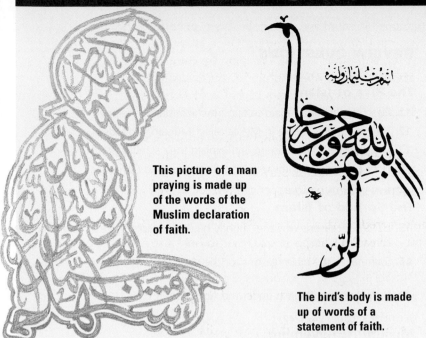

This picture of a man praying is made up of the words of the Muslim declaration of faith.

The bird's body is made up of words of a statement of faith.

Calligraphy, or ornamental writing, is important to Muslims because it is considered a way to reflect the glory of Allah. In pictorial calligraphy, pictures are formed using the letters of the alphabet. Prayers are written in the shape of a bird, plant, boat, or other object.

Connect to History

Clarifying How would these images help Muslims practice their religion?

SEE SKILLBUILDER HANDBOOK, PAGE 992.

Connect to Today

Comparing With what kinds of art do other religions in the modern age express their religious ideas?

was based on principles used in earlier mosques. These blended styles appear in all the lands occupied by the Muslims.

The values of many cultures were recognized by the Muslims and combined with Islamic values. A 9th-century Muslim philosophical society showed that it recognized the empire's diverse nature when it described its "ideal man":

A VOICE FROM THE PAST
The ideal and morally perfect man should be of East Persian derivation, Arabic in faith, of Iraqi education, a Hebrew in astuteness, a disciple of Christ in conduct, as pious as a Greek monk, a Greek in the individual sciences, an Indian in the interpretation of all mysteries, but lastly and especially a Sufi in his whole spiritual life.

IKHWAN AS-SAFA, quoted in *The World of Islam*

THINK THROUGH HISTORY
C. Drawing Conclusions What is the advantage of blending various traditions within a culture?

The elements of Muslim life remained and blended with local culture wherever Islam spread. Though the unified Muslim state broke up, Muslim culture continued. Three Muslim empires, the Ottoman, the Safavid, and the Mughal, would emerge that would reflect the blended nature of the culture of this time. The knowledge developed and preserved by the Muslim scholars would be drawn upon by European scholars in the time known as the Renaissance, beginning in the 14th century.

Section 3 Assessment

1. TERMS & NAMES
Identify
• House of Wisdom
• calligraphy

2. TAKING NOTES
Create a web diagram like the one below, showing the key elements of Muslim culture. In each circle write 3 aspects of that element.

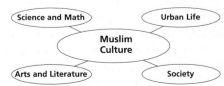

Science and Math — Urban Life — Muslim Culture — Arts and Literature — Society

Which of these most strengthened the Abbasid rule? Explain.

3. EVALUATING
List what you consider to be the five most significant developments in scholarship and the arts during the reign of the Abbasids. Explain the standards you used to make your selections.

THINK ABOUT
• reasons for each development
• immediate and practical impact
• long-term significance

4. THEME ACTIVITY
Cultural Interaction Look at the Voice from the Past above. On a map, mark the location of each of the specific places identified. Link the points together. Shade in the area. About how large an area in miles is covered? What might be learned about cultural blending from this map?

TERMS & NAMES

Briefly explain the importance of each of the following to the people in the Muslim world between 600 and 1200.

1. Islam
2. Allah
3. Hijrah
4. hajj
5. shari'a
6. caliph
7. Shi'a
8. Sufi
9. House of Wisdom
10. calligraphy

Interact *with* History

In this chapter, you learned that ideas spread through trade, war and conquest, and through scholarly exchange. With a partner, make a list of at least five ways to spread an idea in today's world—ways that were not available to Muslims in A.D. 600–1250.

REVIEW QUESTIONS

SECTION 1 *(pages 233–237)*
The Rise of Islam

11. Describe the geographic setting in which Islam developed.
12. Why did many people in Mecca reject Muhammad's ideas at first?
13. List the Five Pillars of Islam and explain their significance.
14. How did early Muslims view and treat Jews and Christians?

SECTION 2 *(pages 238–241)*
The Spread of Islam

15. List three reasons why the "rightly guided" caliphs were so successful in spreading Islam.
16. Summarize the main reasons for the split between the Sunni and the Shi'a.
17. Why did trade flourish under the Abbasids?

SECTION 3 *(pages 242–247)*
Muslim Achievement

18. In what ways did urban life in Muslim lands reflect Muslim culture?
19. Explain why Muslim scholars were so productive, particularly in the areas of mathematics, science, and medicine.
20. How did the art and the architecture of the Muslims differ from that of other cultures you have studied?

Visual Summary

The Muslim World

Islam

Empire Building

Four major Muslim dynasties build empires on parts of three continents.

- 661–750: Umayyad Dynasty
- 750–1258: Abbasid Dynasty
- 756–976: Umayyads of al-Andalus (Spain)
- 909–1171: Fatimid Dynasty (North Africa, Egypt, Western Arabia, and Syria)

Religion

- Muhammad receives revelations from Allah.
- The Five Pillars of Islam are Muslims' basic religious duties.
- The sources of authority—the Qur'an and the Sunna—guide daily life.
- Islam divides into several branches, including Sunni and Shi'a.

Achievements

Muslim scholars preserve, blend, and expand knowledge, especially in mathematics, astronomy, architecture, and medical science.

CRITICAL THINKING

1. ISLAM AND OTHER CULTURES

How did the development of Islam influence the blending of cultures in the region where Europe, Africa, and Asia come together? Consider ways that Islam encouraged or discouraged interaction among people of various cultures.

2. ISLAM'S EXPANSION

THEME EMPIRE BUILDING Create a time line listing the five most important events in the development and expansion of Islam between 570 and 1200. Explain the significance of each selection and why you left other important dates off the time line.

3. RELIGIOUS DUTIES

In what way did the religious duty of prayer affect the lives of Muslims everywhere?

4. ANALYZING PRIMARY SOURCES

Abd al-Latif, a legal and medical scholar who lived in Baghdad in the late 1100s and early 1200s, urged young people to become scholars. Among his suggestions is one urging people to learn history. Read the paragraph and answer the questions below it.

> **A VOICE FROM THE PAST**
> One should read histories, study biographies and the experiences of nations. By doing this, it will be as though, in his short life space, he lived contemporaneously with peoples of the past, was on intimate terms with them, and knew the good and the bad among them. . . . You should model your conduct on that of the early Muslims. Therefore, read the biography of the Prophet, study his deeds and concerns, follow in his footsteps, and try your utmost to imitate him.
>
> **ABD AL-LATIF,** quoted in *A History of the Arab Peoples*

- Why does al-Latif advocate studying history?

- Why does he want people to study the life of Muhammad?

- Do you agree with him about the importance of studying history? Explain. What about studying about Muhammad? Or other significant leaders? Explain your answer.

CHAPTER ACTIVITIES

1. LIVING HISTORY: Unit Portfolio Project

THEME RELIGIOUS AND ETHICAL SYSTEMS Your unit portfolio project focuses on how religious and ethical systems affected all aspects of the lives of people at this time. For Chapter 10, you might use one of the following ideas to add to your portfolio:

- Create a poster showing the Five Pillars of Islam. Draw, trace, or photocopy images that demonstrate the responsibilities of believers. Add notes to clarify these responsibilities.

- With several other students, create a talk show with members representing various religions—a Hindu, a Buddhist, a Jew, a Christian, and a Muslim. Discuss the issue of leading an ethical or proper life based on one's religious beliefs. Present the talk show to the class or videotape it for presentation.

- Write a letter to Muhammad, describing for him what happened in the centuries immediately following his death and telling about his legacy today.

2. CONNECT TO TODAY: Cooperative Learning

THEME CULTURAL INTERACTION Between 600 and 1200, Islam provided a powerful force of unity, eventually linking lands from Spain to Iran. Islam became established in many lands. Work with a team to create maps and charts showing countries where Muslims live in our world.

 Using the Internet or almanacs, do research to find the countries in which Islam is practiced today.

- Using a world map, identify by colors the countries of the world where Muslims can be found as a part of the culture. Devise a color code that shows countries where Islam spread between 600 and 1200.

3. INTERPRETING A TIME LINE

Revisit the Unit time line on pages 228–229. In the events for Chapter 10, find the date for the establishment of the House of Wisdom. What event was occurring about the same time in Europe? Which other areas experienced contact with the Muslims?

FOCUS ON CHARTS

The Muslim culture spread to Europe and the Americas. Here are some countries in those regions with Muslim populations.

- Which nations have a population of Muslims that is similar to that of the United States in terms of percentage?

- Which nations have approximately the same population of Muslims in actual numbers?

Connect to History
- Why is the percentage figure for Spain surprising?

Source: *The Cambridge Illustrated History of the Islamic World*

Country	Population	% of Total Population
Europe		
Albania	2,275,000	70.0
Bulgaria	1,200,000	13.0
France	3,500,000	6.1
Germany	1,700,000	2.1
Spain	300,000	0.8
United Kingdom	1,500,000	2.7
Americas		
Argentina	370,000	1.1
Brazil	500,000	0.3
Canada	350,000	1.3
Guyana	130,000	13.0
Surinam	150,000	30.0
USA	6,000,000	2.4

Muslim Population, 1990s

A Global View

Religion is defined as an organized system of beliefs, ceremonies, practices, and worship that centers on one or more gods. As numerous chapters in this book explain, religion has had a significant impact on world history. Throughout the centuries, religion has guided the beliefs and actions of millions around the globe. It has brought people together. But it has also torn them apart.

Religion continues to be a dominant force throughout the world—affecting everything from what people wear to how they behave. There are thousands of religions in the world. The following pages concentrate on five major religions, as well as Confucianism. They examine some of the characteristics and rituals that make these religions similar as well as unique. They also present some of each religion's sects and denominations.

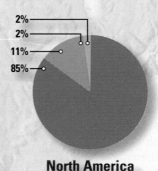

2%
2%
11%
85%

North America

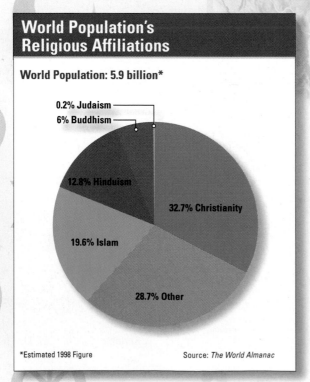

World Population's Religious Affiliations

World Population: 5.9 billion*

0.2% Judaism
6% Buddhism
12.8% Hinduism
32.7% Christianity
19.6% Islam
28.7% Other

*Estimated 1998 Figure   Source: *The World Almanac*

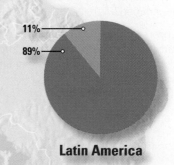

11%
89%

Latin America

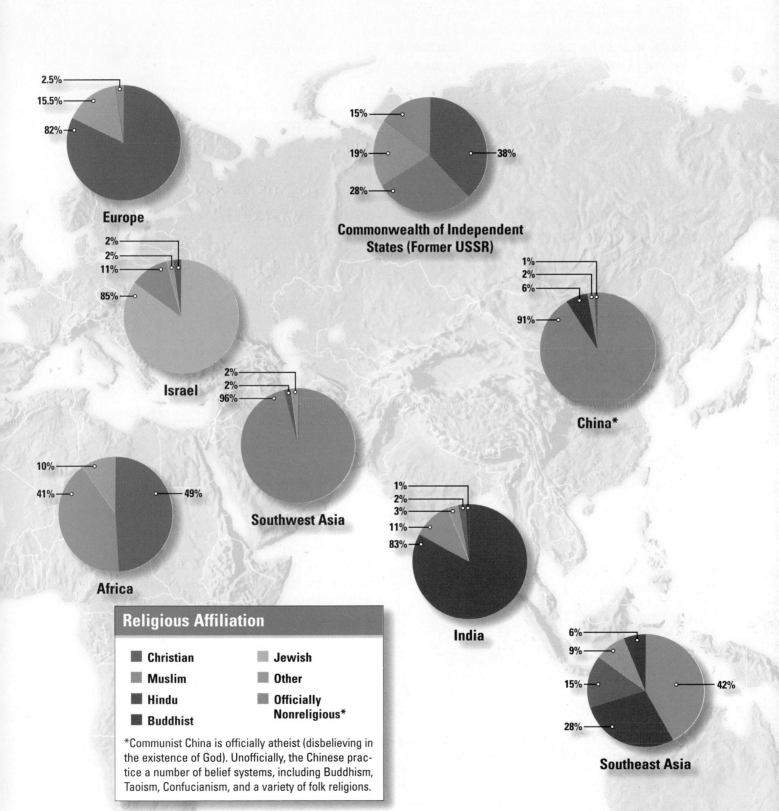

Europe

2.5%
15.5%
82%

Commonwealth of Independent States (Former USSR)

15%
19%
28%
38%

Israel

2%
2%
11%
85%

China*

1%
2%
6%
91%

Southwest Asia

2%
2%
96%

Africa

10%
41%
49%

India

1%
2%
3%
11%
83%

Southeast Asia

6%
9%
15%
28%
42%

Religious Affiliation

- ■ Christian
- ■ Muslim
- ■ Hindu
- ■ Buddhist
- ■ Jewish
- ■ Other
- ■ Officially Nonreligious*

*Communist China is officially atheist (disbelieving in the existence of God). Unofficially, the Chinese practice a number of belief systems, including Buddhism, Taoism, Confucianism, and a variety of folk religions.

Buddhism

Buddhism has been a dominant religious, cultural, and social force throughout Asia. Today, most Buddhists live in Sri Lanka, East and Southeast Asia, and Japan. Buddhism consists of several different sects. A religious sect is a group within a religion that distinguishes itself by one or more unique beliefs. Buddhists are united in their belief of the Buddha's teachings, known as the dharma.

Major Buddhist Sects

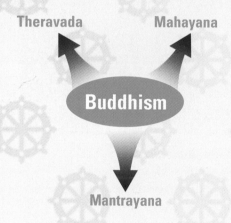

Theravada   Mahayana

Buddhism

Mantrayana

Chapter Connection
For a more in-depth examination of Buddhism, including a closer look at its origins and beliefs, see pages 64–66 of Chapter 3, and page 177 of Chapter 7.

Worship

Central to the Buddhist religion is its creator, Siddhartha Gautama, who became known as the Buddha, or "enlightened one." Statues of the Buddha, such as this one in Japan, appear in many forms and sizes throughout Asia. The Buddha preached that the key to happiness was detachment from all worldly goods and desires. This was achieved by following the Eightfold Path and the Middle Way, a life between earthly desires and extreme forms of self-denial.

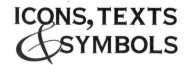

ICONS, TEXTS & SYMBOLS

Wheel of the Law
The Buddha is said to have "set in motion the wheel of the dharma" during his first sermon. His teaching often is symbolized by a wheel.

Leadership

Those who dedicate their entire life to the teachings of the Buddha are known as Buddhist monks and nuns. In many Buddhist sects, monks are expected to lead a life of poverty, meditation, and study. Here, Buddhist monks in Thailand carry what are known as begging bowls. To learn humility, monks must beg for food and money. They are not allowed to speak to or notice their donors. Any communication with donors is believed to lessen the spirituality of the act.

Ritual

Women in Rangoon, Myanmar, sweep the ground so that monks can avoid stepping on and killing any insects. Many Buddhists believe in rebirth. Rebirth is the notion that human beings, after death, are reborn and continue to exist in one form or another. This also applies to animals, birds, fish, and insects. Buddhists believe that all living beings possess the potential for spiritual growth—and the possibility of rebirth as humans. Because of this, Buddhists take special care not to kill any living being.

The Three Cardinal Faults

This image depicts what Buddhists consider the three cardinal faults of humanity: greed (the pig); hatred (the snake); and delusion (the rooster).

Sacred Writings

This palm leaf is part of an 11th-century text called the *Perfection of Wisdom Sutra*, which contains some 8,000 verses. The text, written in Sanskrit, relates the life and teachings of the Buddha.

Christianity

Christianity is the largest religion in the world, with about 1.9 billion followers. It is based on the life and teachings of Jesus Christ. Most Christians are members of one of three major groups: Roman Catholic, Protestant, or Eastern Orthodox. Christianity teaches the existence of only one God. All Christians regard Jesus as the son of God. They believe that Jesus entered the world and died to save humanity from sin. Christians believe that they reach salvation by following the teachings of Jesus Christ.

Major Christian Sects

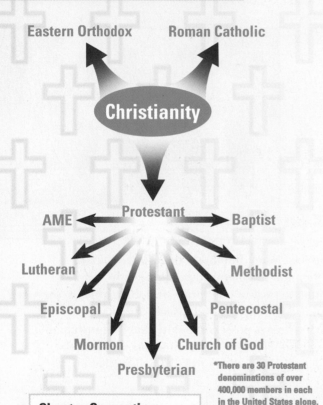

Eastern Orthodox   Roman Catholic

Christianity

AME   Protestant   Baptist

Lutheran   Methodist

Episcopal   Pentecostal

Mormon   Church of God

Presbyterian

*There are 30 Protestant denominations of over 400,000 members in each in the United States alone.

Chapter Connection

For more about Christianity, see pages 153–57 of Chapter 6. To learn about the Protestant and Catholic Reformations, see sections 3 and 4 of Chapter 17.

Ritual

Each year, hundreds of thousands of Christians from all over the world visit the Basilica of Guadalupe in northern Mexico City. The church is considered the holiest in Mexico. It is near the site where the Virgin Mary, the mother of Jesus Christ, is said to have appeared twice in 1531. Out of deep respect for Mary, some pilgrims approach the holy cathedral on their knees.

ICONS, TEXTS & SYMBOLS

The Cross

The cross, a symbol of the crucifixion of Jesus Christ, represents Jesus' love for humanity in dying for its sins.

Worship

Christians worship in many different ways. Pictured here is a Protestant worship service in the United States. Most Protestant services share several basic features. The service includes praying, singing, reading from the Bible, and a sermon by a minister. The laity, or church members who are not ministers, participate extensively in the service. Some services include baptism and communion.

Leadership

In some Christian churches, the person who performs services in the local church is known as a priest. Shown here is a priest of the Ethiopian Christian Church holding a picture of the Virgin Mary with her infant, Jesus. These priests, like those in other Christian sects, perform such duties as presiding over the liturgy, as well as over marriages and funerals. Rules of behavior for priests differ throughout the Christian world. For example, priests with the Ethiopian Church may marry, while Roman Catholic priests may not.

The Bible

The Bible is the most sacred book of the Christian religion. It is divided into two major parts. The Old Testament focuses on Jewish history and religion. The New Testament describes the teachings of Jesus Christ.

A Cross of Palms

Palm Sunday marks the beginning of Holy Week in the Christian calendar. On this day, palms are distributed in remembrance of the palms laid before Jesus' feet as he entered Jerusalem days before his death.

Hinduism

Hinduism, the world's oldest religion, is the major religion of India. It also has followers in Indonesia, as well as in parts of Africa, Europe, and the Western Hemisphere. Hinduism is a collection of religious beliefs that developed over thousands of years. Hindus worship several gods, which represent different forms of Brahman. Brahman is the most divine spirit in the Hindu religion. Hinduism, like Buddhism, stresses that persons reach true enlightenment and happiness only after they free themselves from their earthly desires. Followers of Hinduism achieve this goal through worship, the attainment of knowledge, and a lifetime of virtuous acts.

Major Hindu Sects

Shaktism

Reform Hinduism

Hinduism

Vaishnavites

Shaivites

Chapter Connection
For a closer look at the origins and beliefs of Hinduism, see pages 62–63 of Chapter 3, and pages 177–78 of Chapter 7.

Ritual
Each year, thousands of Hindus make a pilgrimage to India's Ganges River. The Ganges is considered a sacred site in the Hindu religion. Most Hindus come to bathe in the water, an act they believe will cleanse and purify them. The sick and disabled come in the belief that the holy water might cure their ailments. After most Hindus die, they are cremated. Some then have their ashes cast into the Ganges. According to traditional belief, this assures them an entry into Paradise.

ICONS, TEXTS & SYMBOLS

The Sacred Om
The sound *OM*, or *AUM*, represented here, is the most sacred syllable for Hindus. It often is used in prayers.

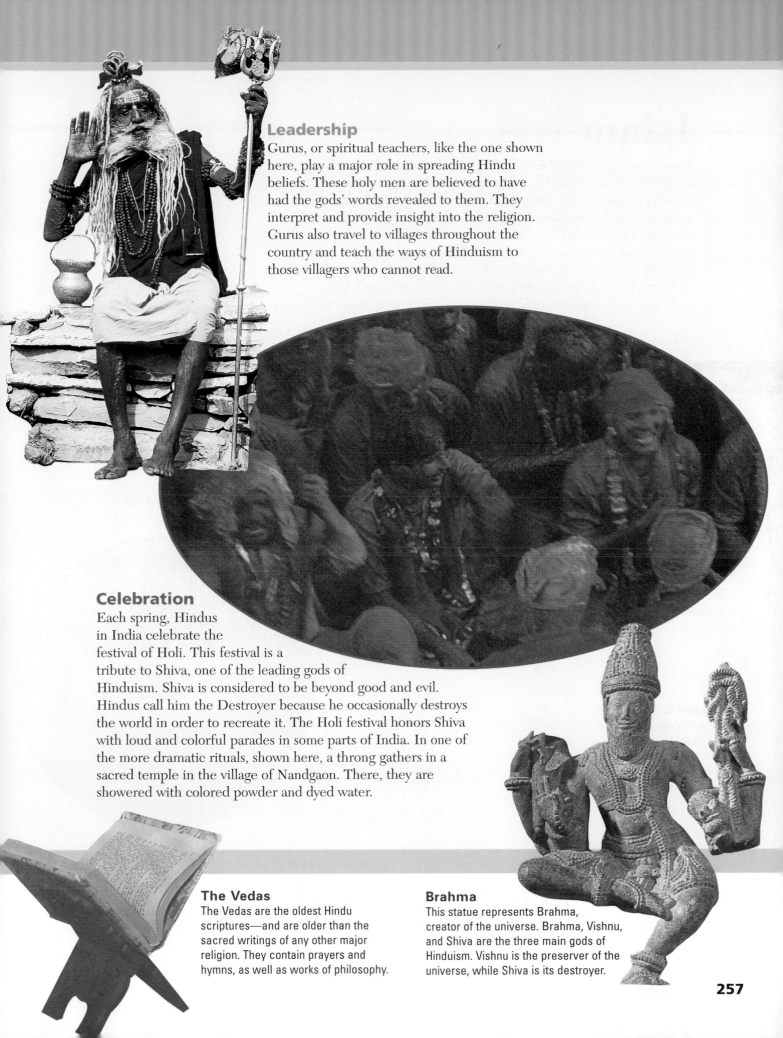

Leadership

Gurus, or spiritual teachers, like the one shown here, play a major role in spreading Hindu beliefs. These holy men are believed to have had the gods' words revealed to them. They interpret and provide insight into the religion. Gurus also travel to villages throughout the country and teach the ways of Hinduism to those villagers who cannot read.

Celebration

Each spring, Hindus in India celebrate the festival of Holi. This festival is a tribute to Shiva, one of the leading gods of Hinduism. Shiva is considered to be beyond good and evil. Hindus call him the Destroyer because he occasionally destroys the world in order to recreate it. The Holi festival honors Shiva with loud and colorful parades in some parts of India. In one of the more dramatic rituals, shown here, a throng gathers in a sacred temple in the village of Nandgaon. There, they are showered with colored powder and dyed water.

The Vedas

The Vedas are the oldest Hindu scriptures—and are older than the sacred writings of any other major religion. They contain prayers and hymns, as well as works of philosophy.

Brahma

This statue represents Brahma, creator of the universe. Brahma, Vishnu, and Shiva are the three main gods of Hinduism. Vishnu is the preserver of the universe, while Shiva is its destroyer.

257

Islam

Islam is a religion based on the teachings of the prophet Muhammad. Followers of Islam, known as Muslims, live throughout the world. They are concentrated from southwest to central Asia and parts of Africa. Islam also has many followers in Southeast Asia. Islam teaches the existence of only one God, called *Allah* in the Arabic language. Muslims believe in all prophets of Judaism and Christianity. They show their devotion by performing lifelong acts of worship known as the Five Pillars of Islam. These include faith, prayer, almsgiving (charity), fasting, and pilgrimage. Islam affects nearly every aspect of Muslims' lives.

Major Islamic Sects

Sunni

Islam

Shi'a

Chapter Connection
For a closer look at Islam, including the rise and spread of Islam, and significant Muslim achievements, see Chapter 10.

Celebration

During the sacred month known as Ramadan, Muslims fast, or abstain from food and drink, from dawn to sunset. They do this as a sign of obedience, humility, and self-control. The fasting traditionally ends with eating a few dates and milk or water, followed by the sunset prayer. These foods accompany the other dishes that families, such as the one shown here, eat each night during the month.

The most important night of Ramadan is called the Night of Power (Laylat al-Qadr). This is believed to be the night the angel Gabriel, the messenger of God, first spoke to Muhammad.

ICONS, TEXTS & SYMBOLS

Crescent Moon
The crescent moon has become a familiar symbol for Islam. It may be related to the new moon that begins each month in the Islamic lunar calendar, which orders religious life for Muslims.

Worship

At least once in their lifetime, all Muslims who are physically and financially able, go on hajj, or pilgrimage, to the holy city of Mecca in Saudi Arabia. There, pilgrims perform several rites, or acts of worship. One rite, shown here, is walking seven times around the Ka'aba—the house of worship that Muslims face in prayer.

The climax of the hajj is the day when millions of believers stand at a place named Arafat. There, they ask forgiveness of God on the same spot where Muhammad gave a farewell sermon.

Ritual

Five times a day Muslims throughout the world face Mecca and pray to Allah. This prayer ritual, known as Salat, occurs at dawn, noon, late afternoon, sunset, and evening. Muslims recite these prayers at work, or school, or wherever they happen to be. Pictured here are Muslims praying at an intersection in Alexandria, Egypt.

Prayer Rug

Muslims often pray by kneeling on a rug. The design of the rug includes a pointed or arch-shaped pattern. The rug must be placed so that the arch points toward Mecca.

The Qur'an

The Qur'an, the sacred book of Muslims, consists of verses grouped into 114 chapters, or surahs. The book is the spiritual guide on matters of faith and practice for all Muslims. In addition, it contains teachings that guide Muslim daily life.

Judaism

Judaism is the religion of the more than 13 million Jews throughout the world. Judaism was the first major religion to teach the existence of only one god. The basic laws and teachings of Judaism come from the Torah, the first five books of the Hebrew Bible. Judaism teaches that a person serves God by studying the Torah and living by its teachings.

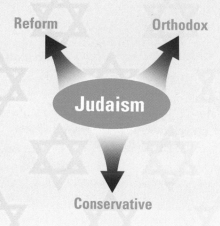

Major Jewish Sects

Reform   Orthodox

Judaism

Conservative

Chapter Connection
For an historical examination of Judaism, as well as the development of the Kingdom of Israel, see pages 72–76 of Chapter 3.

Celebration
Jews celebrate a number of holidays that honor their history as well as their God. Pictured here are Jews celebrating the holiday of Purim. Purim is a festival honoring the survival of the Jews who, in the fifth century B.C., were marked for death by their Persian rulers.

The story—found in the Book of Esther in the Hebrew Bible—describes how Esther, the Jewish queen of Persia, convinced the Persian king to spare her people. Jews celebrate Purim by sending food and gifts to friends, neighbors, and the poor. In addition, they dress in costumes and hold carnivals and dances.

ICONS, TEXTS & SYMBOLS

The Star of David
The Star of David, also called the Shield of David, is the universal symbol of Judaism. The emblem refers to King David, who ruled the kingdom of Israel from about 1000–962 B.C.

Ritual

Some Jews follow strict dietary laws based on passages from the Hebrew Bible. These laws have established what is kosher, or acceptable, for Jews to eat. Kosher laws forbid the eating of animals considered unclean. These animals include pigs and shellfish.

The preparation of food is a significant part of kosher law. Animals must be killed in a certain way—a single cut across the neck made with a knife absent of nicks. This is intended to kill the animal as quickly and painlessly as possible. Before the meat is cooked, it must be drained of its blood.

There are additional kosher laws that determine everything from the preparation of food to what foods may not be eaten together. Shown here, a rabbi inspects a kitchen in the United States to ensure that it follows kosher guidelines.

Worship

Several women worship at the Western Wall—a place of prayer and pilgrimage held sacred to the Jewish people. The ancient structure formed the western wall of the courtyard of the Second Temple of Jerusalem. The Romans destroyed the temple in A.D. 70. The wall, which dates back to the second century B.C., measures about 160 feet long and about 60 feet high. Located in Jerusalem, it is also known as the Wailing Wall. This term was coined by European travelers who witnessed some Jews loudly mourning the destruction of the temple.

Yarmulke

Out of respect for God, Jewish men are not supposed to leave their head uncovered. Therefore, many Orthodox and Conservative Jews wear a skullcap known as a yarmulke, or kippah.

The Torah Scroll

During a synagogue service, the Torah scroll is lifted, while the congregation declares: "This is the Law which Moses set before the children of Israel."

Confucianism

A look at the world's major religions would not be complete without an examination of Confucianism. With no clergy, or gods to worship, Confucianism is not considered a religion in the traditional sense. However, this ancient philosophy guides the actions and beliefs of millions of Chinese and other peoples of the East. Thus, it often is viewed as a major religion.

Confucianism is a way of life based on the teachings of the Chinese scholar Confucius. It stresses social and civic responsibility. It also provides people with an ethical system to follow. Over the centuries, however, Confucianism has greatly influenced people's spiritual beliefs as well. While East Asians declare themselves to follow any one of a number of religions, many also claim to be Confucian.

"Do not do unto others what you would not want others to do unto you."

CONFUCIUS'S GOLDEN RULE

Chapter Connection
For a closer look at the life and teachings of Confucius, see pages 97–99 of Chapter 4.

Celebration
While scholars remain uncertain of Confucius's date of birth, people throughout East Asia celebrate it on September 28. In Taiwan, it is an official holiday, known as Teachers' Day (shown above). Aside from honoring Confucius, the holiday pays tribute to teachers, who play a significant role in Confucianism. Confucius himself was a teacher, and he believed that education was an important part of a fulfilled life. In Confucianism, teachers are highly regarded, and their authority is just below that of a father.

ICONS, TEXTS & SYMBOLS

The Yin–Yang
The yin–yang symbol represents opposite forces in the world working together. It symbolizes the social order and harmony that Confucianism stresses.

Ritual

A key aspect of Confucianism is respect for family members and elders. This helped promote the religious practice throughout East Asia of honoring ancestors. In homes such as the one in China shown here, residents build shrines to honor their deceased relatives. The family offers prayers and food at the shrine. Family members then eat the meal—believing the ancestors have already tasted it. The Chinese believe showing respect for ancestors will ensure continued cooperation and aid from their deceased relatives.

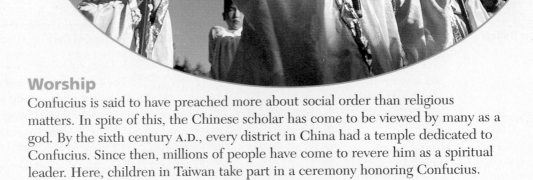

Worship

Confucius is said to have preached more about social order than religious matters. In spite of this, the Chinese scholar has come to be viewed by many as a god. By the sixth century A.D., every district in China had a temple dedicated to Confucius. Since then, millions of people have come to revere him as a spiritual leader. Here, children in Taiwan take part in a ceremony honoring Confucius.

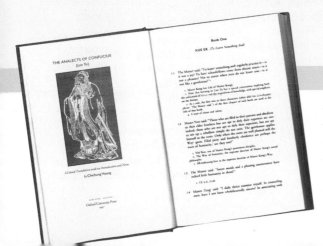

The Analects

The earliest and most authentic record of Confucius's ideas was recorded by his students. Around 400 B.C., they compiled Confucius's words in a book called the *Analects*.

WORLD RELIGIONS

A Comparison

	Buddhism	Christianity	Hinduism	Islam	Judaism	Confucianism
Followers Worldwide*	354 million	1.9 billion	762 million	1.2 billion	14 million	Not available
Name of Deity	The Buddha did not teach a personal deity.	God	Three main Gods: Brahma, Vishnu, Shiva	God (Allah)	God (Yahweh)	Confucius (viewed by many as a god)
Founder	The Buddha	Jesus Christ	No one founder	Muhammad	Abraham	Confucius
Holy Book	No one book—sacred texts, including the *Perfection of Wisdom Sutra*	Bible	No one book—sacred texts, including the Vedas, the Puranas	Qur'an	Hebrew Bible, including the Torah	the *Analects*, the Five Classics
Leadership	Buddhist monks and nuns	Clergy (priests/ministers)	Guru, Holy Man, Brahmin priest	No clergy	Rabbis	No Clergy
Basic Beliefs	•Persons achieve complete peace and happiness, known as nirvana, by eliminating their attachment to worldly things. •Nirvana is reached by following the Noble Eightfold Path: Right views; Right aspirations; Right speech; Right conduct; Right livelihood; Right endeavor; Right mindfulness; Right meditation.	•There is only one God, who watches over and cares for his people. •Jesus Christ was the son of God. He died to save humanity from sin. His death and resurrection made eternal life possible for others.	•The soul never dies, but is continually reborn. •Persons achieve happiness and enlightenment after they free themselves from their earthly desires. •Freedom from earthly desires comes from a lifetime of worship, knowledge, and virtuous acts.	•Persons achieve salvation by following the Five Pillars of Islam and living a just life. These pillars are: faith; almsgiving, or charity to the poor; fasting, which Muslims perform during Ramadan; pilgrimage (to Mecca); and prayer.	•There is only one God, who watches over and cares for his people. •God loves and protects his people, but also holds people accountable for their sins and shortcomings. •Persons serve God by studying the Torah and living by its teachings.	•Social order, harmony, and good government should be based on strong family relationships. •Respect for parents and elders is important to a well-ordered society. •Education is important both to the welfare of the individual and to society.

*estimated 1998 figures

Assessment

REVIEW QUESTIONS

Buddhism

1. According to the Buddha, how does one achieve happiness and fulfillment?

Christianity

2. Why is Jesus Christ central to the Christian religion?

Hinduism

3. Explain the importance of the Ganges River in Hinduism.

Islam

4. What is the most important night of Ramadan? Why?

Judaism

5. Why do Jews consider the Western Wall to be sacred?

Confucianism

6. How has Confucianism's emphasis on familial respect affected religious worship in East Asia?

ANALYZING PRIMARY SOURCES

In her book, *A History of God*, Karen Armstrong explains why religion is such a powerful force in people's lives:

> **A VOICE FROM THE PAST**
> . . . Human beings are spiritual animals. Indeed, there is a case for arguing that *Homo sapiens* is also *Homo religiosus*. Men and women started to worship gods as soon as they became recognizably human; they created religions at the same time they created works of art. . . . These early faiths expressed the wonder and mystery that seem always to have been an essential component of the human experience of this beautiful yet terrifying world. Like art, religion has been an attempt to find meaning and value in life, despite the suffering that flesh is heir to.

- Based on information from the previous pages, how might religion give life meaning and value?
- Do you agree or disagree with Ms. Armstrong? Explain.

CRITICAL THINKING

1. COMPARING AND CONTRASTING

Using information from the text and chart, choose two religions and identify their similarities and differences in a Venn diagram like the one below.

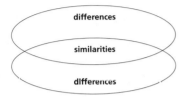

2. COMMON THREADS

The previous pages reveal items and activities that play an important role in more than one religion. Determine what some are and explain how each is significant to different religions.

ACTIVITIES

1. LIVING HISTORY: Unit Portfolio Project

THEME **RELIGIOUS AND ETHICAL SYSTEMS** Your unit portfolio project focuses on religious and ethical systems around the world (see page 229). You may want to include one of the following activities in your portfolio.

- Imagine you are a newspaper reporter who has been granted entrance to a Buddhist monastery. Write a brief article describing what you think a day in the life of a Buddhist monk might be like.
- Write a persuasive speech in order to convince someone that Confucianism can be considered a religion.
- Write a dialogue between two people in which each explains the workings of one of the major religions to the other.

2. CONNECT TO TODAY: Cooperative Learning

As the previous pages explained, the world's major religions contain various sects. Sects are smaller groups within a religion. These groups hold one or more unique beliefs, which make them slightly different from other followers.

Working in small groups, find out what makes the major sects of a particular religion different. As a group, report your findings to the class.

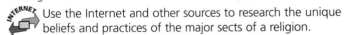 Use the Internet and other sources to research the unique beliefs and practices of the major sects of a religion.

- Each group member should be responsible for one sect. He or she should write a brief report detailing the beliefs and practices that make that sect unique.
- The group should then present its findings to the class by having each group member read aloud his or her report.

CHAPTER 11

Byzantines, Russians, and Turks Interact, 500–1500

PREVIEWING THEMES

Religious and Ethical Systems

Two world religions, Islam and Christianity, repeatedly met head-to-head as Arabs and Turks battled Byzantines and Crusaders. Both Islam and Christianity, meanwhile, attracted masses of converts. At the same time, disputes over doctrine split each religion into competing branches.

Cultural Interaction

Byzantine influence inspired the growth of a unique Russian culture. The Turks meanwhile adopted Islam. They also sponsored a rebirth of Persian culture and created a dynamic cultural blend.

Empire Building

The Byzantines, Slavs, Arabs, Turks, and Mongols waged bloody wars to expand their territories. However, each empire also brought together people of diverse traditions. In this way, they promoted the exchange of goods and ideas.

INTERNET CONNECTION

Visit us at **www.mcdougallittell.com** to learn more about the Byzantines, Slavs, and Turks between 500 and 1500.

THREE EMPIRES: BYZANTINE, RUSSIAN, SELJUK, 565–1100

- The Byzantine Empire c. 565
- Kievan Rus c. 1100
- The Seljuk Empire c. 1100

0 500 Miles
0 1000 Kilometers

N

Novgorod
Pakov
Vladimir
Smolensk
Minsk
Kiev
Don R.
Dnieper River

ALPS
Milan
Ravenna
Zara
Danube River
Silistra
Nicopolis
Brusa
Kossova
Ragusa
Rome
Bari
Naples   APULIA
CALABRIA
Palermo
Carthage
Adriatic Sea
Constantinople
Thessalonica
Black Sea
Sinope
Chalcedon Gangra Amasia
Nicaea Angora Siwas Trebizo
Brusa Tephrik Manzik
ANATOLIA SULTANATE Tephrik
OF RUM ARMENIA
Athens
Ephesus
Attalia Konia Hierapolis Edes
Antioch
Haleb
Tripoli   SYRIA
Beirut Damascus
Acre
Jerusalem
Mediterranean Sea
Alexandria
EGYPT
Nile R.
Aila
Red Sea
Medina
Mecc

40°E

In **678**, Byzantine ships broke the Arab siege of Constantinople with a secret weapon called **"Greek Fire."** Greek fire was a flammable liquid shot from a tube that turned any ship it hit into a blazing deathtrap. To this day, the chemical formula for Greek Fire remains unknown.

In **1049,** Kiev's grand prince **Yaroslav the Wise** arranged the marriage of his daughter Anna to the French king Henry I. As a citizen of sophisticated Kiev, Anna could write, and she signed her own name to the wedding contract. The French nobles, who could not write, signed with an X.

Completed in **537,** in the remarkably short time of six years, **Hagia Sophia** in Constantinople became the most splendid church in the Christian world. Nine hundred years later, in **1453,** Constantinople fell to Turkish armies. Shields bearing the names of Allah and the prophets testify to Hagia Sophia's conversion from church to mosque. The change occurred shortly after the Turkish victory.

267

Yͦou are a Byzantine diplomat working to serve the best interests of your emperor and your empire. Byzantium is threatened by a rampaging army moving from the north down to Constantinople. You know that diplomacy, or clever negotiating with foreign powers, has been important in preserving Byzantium from destruction.

Your mission is to convince the invading chief to stop advancing on the city. Will you threaten the chief with military retaliation, try to buy him off, or arrange a marriage between him and a Byzantine noblewoman to form an alliance?

How will you save the empire?

If shrewdness and good sense fail, a display of Byzantine military forces might scare the enemy away.

As the Byzantine ambassador, you may be proposing to pay yearly tribute to the invading chief if he will just leave the empire alone.

You may also be offering the chief a lavish, all-expense-paid trip to Constantinople. Such visits could impress potential invaders with Byzantine hospitality, wealth, and (above all) power.

EXAMINING *the* ISSUES

As you weigh your options, consider

- **the advantages of diplomacy over war**
- **new diplomatic strategies to stop the coming attack**
- **circumstances that might convince you to recommend war**

Which option(s) will you choose? Explain your choice(s).

As you read this chapter, think about how empires keep themselves alive over long periods of time.

Byzantium Becomes the New Rome

TERMS & NAMES
- Justinian Code
- Hagia Sophia
- patriarch
- icon
- iconoclast
- excommunication
- schism
- Cyrillic alphabet

MAIN IDEA	WHY IT MATTERS NOW
Constantinople ruled an eastern empire that survived for over a thousand years.	Byzantine culture deeply influenced Orthodox Christianity, a major branch of modern Christianity.

SETTING THE STAGE The western Roman Empire crumbled in the 5th century as it was overrun by invading Germanic tribes. (See Chapter 6.) The threat to the empire, however, was already apparent in the 4th century. Emperor Constantine rebuilt the old port city of Byzantium on the Bosporus strait for two reasons. In Byzantium, he could respond to the danger of the Germanic tribes. He could also be close to his rich eastern provinces. He renamed the city Constantinople and in the year 330, he made it the capital of the empire.

A New Rome in a New Setting

Constantine planned Constantinople as the new capital of the empire—the New Rome. As a result of his decision, the empire's center of power moved eastward. The eastern provinces then began to develop independently of the declining West. An eastern empire would gradually come into being.

Justinian: A New Line of Caesars Because of the difficulties of communication between the eastern and troubled western parts of the empire, they were officially divided in two in 395. Despite this separation, Constantine's successors in the East continued to see themselves as Roman emperors. In 527, a high-ranking Byzantine nobleman named Justinian succeeded his uncle to the throne of the eastern empire.

In his official writings, court historian Procopius (pruh·KOH·pee·uhs) described Justinian as a serious, even-tempered ruler who worked from dawn to midnight. But in *The Secret History* (a book of gossip published after Justinian's death), Procopius portrays Justinian as "deceitful, devious, false, hypocritical, two-faced, cruel, skilled in dissembling his thought, never moved to tears by either joy or pain . . . a liar always."

Whatever his true character, the new emperor quickly decided to make good on his claim to be the head of the whole Roman Empire—of both eastern and western parts. In 533, he sent his best general Belisarius (behl·uh·SAIR·ee·uhs) to recover North Africa from the Vandals. Belisarius got the job done in a few months. Two years later, Belisarius attacked Rome and took it from the Ostrogoths. But the city was repeatedly attacked by other Germanic tribes. In the next 16 years, Rome changed hands six times. After numerous campaigns, Justinian's armies won nearly all of Italy and parts of Spain. Justinian now ruled almost all the territory that Rome had ever ruled. He could honestly call himself a new Caesar.

The Absolute Power of the Emperors Like the last of the old Caesars, the Byzantine emperors ruled with absolute power. They headed not just the state but the Church as well. They appointed and dismissed bishops at will. The politics, however, were brutal, not spiritual. Emperors lived under constant risk of assassination. Of the 88 Byzantine emperors, 29 died violently, and 13 abandoned the throne to live in monasteries.

THINK THROUGH HISTORY
A. Drawing Conclusions How could a historian like Procopius give two such different accounts of the same person? Which do you believe?

Both sides of this gold medallion display Emperor Justinian as a military commander. But the coin really celebrates a victory by General Belisarius. The emperor often feared that the general's popularity would outshine his own.

SUCCESSFUL IN WARFARE

Building the New Rome

A separate government and difficult communications with the West gave the Byzantine Empire its own character—different from that of the western empire. The citizens thought of themselves as sharing in the Roman tradition, but few spoke Latin anymore. Most Byzantines spoke Greek. They also belonged to the eastern branch of the Christian Church.

To regulate a complex society, Justinian set up a panel of ten legal experts. Between 528 and 533, they combed through 400 years of Roman law and legal opinions. Some of those laws had become outdated. Some repeated or even contradicted other laws. The panel's task was to create a single, uniform code for Justinian's New Rome.

The result of the panel's work was a body of civil law known as the **Justinian Code**. After its completion, the code consisted of four works.

1. The *Code* contained nearly 5,000 Roman laws, which the experts still considered useful for the Byzantine Empire.

2. The *Digest* quoted and summarized the opinions of Rome's greatest legal thinkers about the laws. This massive work ran to a total of 50 volumes.

3. The *Institutes* was a textbook that told law students how to use the laws.

4. The *Novellae* (New Laws) presented legislation passed after 534.

The Justinian Code decided legal questions that regulated whole areas of Byzantine life. Marriage, slavery, property, inheritance, women's rights, and crimes were just some of those areas. Although Justinian himself died in 565, his code served the Byzantine Empire for 900 years.

Creating the Imperial Capital While his scholars were creating the legal code, Justinian launched into the most ambitious public building program ever seen in the Roman world. He rebuilt the crumbling fortifications of Constantinople. The city's coasts were ringed by a 14-mile stone wall. The city was also protected on its only land approach by a deep moat and three walls. The innermost of these was 25 feet thick and had towers 70 feet tall. Justinian saw to it that these massive fortifications were repaired.

Church building was the emperor's greatest passion. His beautiful churches also helped him show the close connection between church and state in his empire. The crowning glory of his reign was **Hagia Sophia** (HAY·ee·uh soh·FEE·uh), which means "Holy Wisdom" in Greek. A church of the same name had been destroyed in riots that swept Constantinople in 532. When Justinian rebuilt Hagia Sophia, he resolved to make it the most splendid church in the Christian world. Down through the centuries, rich mosaics glittered in the light of a thousand lamps and candles. In fact, more than 400 years after Justinian built his cathedral, the beauty of Hagia Sophia helped convince visiting Russian nobles that their country should adopt Byzantine Christianity.

As part of his building program, Justinian enlarged his palace into a vast complex. He also built baths, aqueducts, law courts, schools, and hospitals. By the time the emperor was finished with his projects, the city teemed with an excitement unmatched anywhere in the eastern and western empires.

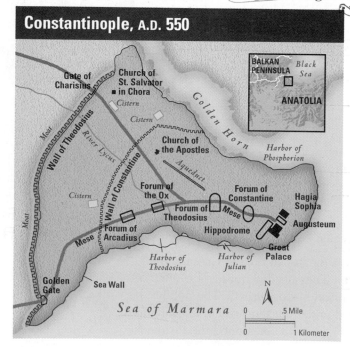

Constantinople, A.D. 550

The emperor often presided over wild chariot races at the Hippodrome, as this fourth-century ivory carving shows. When he dropped a white handkerchief, the races began.

Constantinople's Hectic Pace The main street running through Constantinople was the Mese (MEHS·ee) or "Middle Way." It ran from the imperial complex through a series of public squares and then in two branches to the outer walls. Merchant stalls lined the main street and filled the side streets. A stone roof sheltered the crowds shopping in this giant open-air market. Products from the most distant corners of Asia, Africa, and Europe passed through these stalls. Shoppers could buy tin from England, wine from France, cork from Spain, and ivory and gold from Africa. Fur, honey, and timber came from Russia, spices from India, and silk from China. Everywhere food stands filled the air with the smell of their delicacies, while acrobats and street musicians performed.

Meanwhile, citizens could enjoy free entertainment at the Hippodrome, which offered wild chariot races and circus acts. The Hippodrome (from Greek words meaning "horse" and "racecourse") held 60,000 spectators. Fans of the different teams formed rowdy gangs named for the colors worn by their heroes.

In 532, two such factions, the Blues and the Greens, sparked citywide riots called the Nika Rebellion (because the mob cried "Nika!" or "Victory!"). Both sides were angry at the government. They felt the city prefect (mayor) had been too severe in putting down a previous riot of Hippodrome fans. Even though Justinian dismissed the prefect, the mobs were not satisfied. They packed the Hippodrome and proclaimed a new emperor. Belisarius, however, broke in with his troops and slaughtered about 30,000 rebels.

Much credit for saving the day must go to Justinian's wife, Theodora. As her husband's steely adviser, Theodora had immense power. During the Nika Rebellion, when Justinian considered fleeing the city, Theodora rallied him with a fiery speech:

A VOICE FROM THE PAST
My opinion is that now is a poor time for flight, even though it bring safety. For any man who has seen the light of day will also die, but one who has been an emperor cannot endure to be a fugitive. If now you wish to go, Emperor, nothing prevents you. There is the sea, there are the steps to the boats. But take care that after you are safe, you do not find that you would gladly exchange that safety for death.

THEODORA, quoted by Procopius in *History of the Wars*

Byzantium Preserves Learning

Byzantine families valued education and sent their children to monastic or public schools or hired private tutors. Basic courses focused on Greek and Latin grammar, philosophy, and rhetoric. The classics of Greek and Roman literature served as textbooks. Students memorized Homer. They learned geometry from Euclid, history from Herodotus, and medicine from Galen. The modern world owes Byzantine scholars a huge debt for preserving many of the great works of Greece and Rome.

HISTORY MAKERS

**Empress Theodora
500–548**

The most powerful woman in Byzantine history rose from deep poverty. Theodora's father was a bear-keeper. Early in life, Theodora herself was an actress, a despised profession in Byzantium. But she caught Justinian's eye, and in 525, they married.

As empress, Theodora became a power in her own right. She met with foreign envoys, wrote to foreign leaders, passed laws, and built churches. During a political crisis, Theodora even confiscated the property of the general Belisarius. After she died in 548, Justinian was so depressed that he passed no major laws for the rest of his reign—a sign of Theodora's political influence.

The Empire Confronts Its Enemies

Constantinople remained rich and powerful for centuries. After Justinian's death in 565, however, the empire suffered countless setbacks. There were street riots, religious quarrels, palace intrigues, and foreign dangers. Each time the empire moved to the edge of collapse, it found some way to revive—only to face another crisis.

The Mysterious Plague of Justinian The first crisis actually began before Justinian's death. It was a disease that resembled what we now know as the bubonic plague. This horrifying illness hit Constantinople in the later years of Justinian's reign. The plague probably arrived from India on ships infested with rats. In 542, at its peak, it is estimated that 10,000 people were dying every day. The illness broke out every 8 to 12 years until around 700, when it finally faded out. By that time, it had destroyed a huge percentage of the Byzantine population. The smaller population left the empire exposed to its enemies.

Attacks from East and West Byzantium's enemies pressed in on all sides. Lombards overran Justinian's conquests in the west. Avars, Slavs, and Bulgars made frequent raids on the northern borders. The powerful Sassanid Persians attacked relentlessly in the east. The Persians and Avars struck against Constantinople itself in 626. With the rise of Islam, Arab armies attacked the city in 674 and once again in 717. Russians attempted invasions of the city three times between 860 and 1043. In the 11th century, the Turks took over the Muslim world and fought their way slowly into Anatolia. The Crusades brought armies of knights from Western Europe who pillaged Constantinople in 1204 on their way to fight the Turks.

As their first line of defense, the Byzantines used bribes, diplomacy, and political marriages to prop up their shaky empire. These strategies, however, were not enough. So, in the 7th century, Emperor Heraclius reorganized the empire along military lines. Provinces became *themes*, or military districts. Each theme was run by a general who reported directly to the emperor.

In spite of these measures, the Byzantine Empire slowly shrank under the impact of foreign attacks. By 1350, it was reduced to the tip of Anatolia and a strip of the Balkans. Yet thanks to its walls, its fleet, and its strategic location, the city held out for another 100 years. Finally, Constantinople fell to the Ottoman Turks in 1453.

Background

Except during Justinian's reign, the Byzantine Empire was relatively small for most of its 1,000-year history. The empire generally included most of Anatolia, Greece, and some of present-day Bulgaria and the former Yugoslavia.

The Church Divides

During those many centuries, the Eastern Church in Constantinople continued to flourish. At the same time, however, distance and lack of contact slowly caused the doctrines and rituals of Western and Eastern Christianity to diverge. The Church would eventually split into the Eastern Orthodox and Roman Catholic churches.

A Split Between Rome and Constantinople Eastern Christianity built its heritage on the works of early church fathers. One was Saint Basil, who, around 357, wrote rules for the life of monks. Another key figure was Saint John Chrysostom (KRIHS·uhs·tuhm). As bishop of Constantinople from 398 to 404, Chrysostom was the **patriarch** (PAY·tree·AHRK), or leading bishop of the East. But even the patriarch bowed to the emperor.

A controversy that tested the emperor's authority over religious matters broke out in the 8th century. In 730, Emperor Leo III banned the use of **icons**, religious images used by eastern Christians to aid their devotions. The emperor thought the use of icons amounted to idol worship. The army supported the emperor's view, and enthusiastic **iconoclasts** (eye·KAHN·uh·KLASTS), or "icon-breakers," broke into churches to destroy images. But the people rioted,

Background

Today, *iconoclast* means "someone who overthrows respected ideas and traditions."

CONNECT *to* **TODAY**

The Orthodox and Roman Catholic Churches Today

Today, the Orthodox Church has about 214 million members worldwide. Roman Catholics number about 1 billion. In 1965, the two churches met to discuss their differences and explore the possibilities of reunion.

Statements issued in the late 1980s outlined areas of agreement. Both churches believe that Jesus established seven sacraments, or ceremonies, for Christian worship. Of these sacraments, they consider Holy Communion the most important.

They also agree on the need for priests in the Church. However, as in the 11th century, they still disagree on the role of the pope, on the issue of divorce, and on whether priests may marry.

The 11th Century: Differences Between Two Christian Traditions

Roman Catholic	Eastern Orthodox
• Services are conducted in Latin.	• Services are conducted in Greek or local languages.
• The pope has authority over all other bishops.	• The patriarch and other bishops head the church as a group.
• The pope claims authority over all kings and emperors.	• The emperor claims authority over the patriarch and other bishops of the empire.
• Priests may not marry.	• Priests may be married.
• Divorce is not permitted.	• Divorce is allowed under certain conditions.

SKILLBUILDER: Interpreting Charts
1. *Which church seemed to allow for greater diversity among its members? Why?*
2. *Who would have more political power: the pope or the patriarch?*

A reliquary is a decorated container that holds the remains of holy persons, called saints. This tin reliquary, produced in the 12th century, contains pieces of the bones of Saints Cyril and Methodius.

and the clergy rebelled. In the West, the pope became involved in this eastern dispute and supported the use of icons. One pope even ordered the **excommunication** of a Byzantine emperor—that is, he declared that the emperor was an outcast from the Church. In 843, more than a hundred years after the controversy began, an order from an empress named Theodora restored icons to Eastern churches.

Differences between the Eastern and Western churches, however, continued to grow. (See the chart above.) In 1054, matters came to a head when the pope and the patriarch excommunicated each other in a dispute over religious doctrine. After this **schism** (SIHZ·uhm), or split, Christianity was permanently divided between the Roman Catholic Church in the West and the Orthodox Church in the East.

Byzantine Missionaries Convert the Slavs As West and East grew apart, the two traditions of Christianity competed for souls. Missionaries from the Orthodox Church, for example, took their form of Christianity north to the Slavs. Two of the most successful eastern missionaries, Saint Methodius and Saint Cyril (SEER·uhl), worked among the Slavs in the 9th century. Cyril and Methodius invented an alphabet for the Slavic languages. With an alphabet, Slavs would be able to read the Bible in their own tongues. Many Slavic languages, including Russian, are now written in what is called the **Cyrillic** (suh·RIHL·ihk) **alphabet**.

The Orthodox missionaries opened up highways for Byzantine influence in Slavic lands. As these missionaries were carrying out their work among the Slavs, an important new Slavic nation was forming.

Section ❶ Assessment

1. TERMS & NAMES

Identify
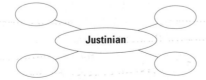
• Justinian Code
• Hagia Sophia
• patriarch
• icon
• iconoclast
• excommunication
• schism
• Cyrillic alphabet

2. TAKING NOTES

Using a cluster like the one below, show Justinian's accomplishments as emperor of the New Rome.

```
     ⬭        ⬭
      \      /
   ⬭—( Justinian )—⬭
      /      \
     ⬭        ⬭
```

In your opinion, was Justinian a great leader? Explain.

3. ANALYZING MOTIVES

Why do you think Justinian decided in the late 520s that it was the right time to reform Roman law?

THINK ABOUT
• the situation of the empire
• the role of laws in societies
• the state of Roman laws before reform

4. ANALYZING THEMES

Religious and Ethical Systems Do you think the differences between the Eastern and Western churches could have been reconciled before the Church split? Why? Working in small teams, brainstorm several reasons why the Church separated. For each reason, list two or three ways in which the problems might have been resolved.

Byzantines, Russians, and Turks Interact **273**

Russians Adapt Byzantine Culture

TERMS & NAMES
- **Slavs**
- **boyars**
- **Olga**
- **Vladimir**
- **Yaroslav the Wise**
- **Alexander Nevsky**
- **czar**

MAIN IDEA	WHY IT MATTERS NOW
Russia grew out of a blending of Slavic and Byzantine cultures with Eastern Orthodox traditions.	The early history of Russia separated it from the West, causing mutual misunderstandings that still exist today.

SETTING THE STAGE At the beginning of the 9th century, the Byzantines regarded the forests north of the Black Sea as a wilderness. In their minds, those forests were inhabited only by "barbarians," who sometimes made trouble along their borders. They would soon consider these Slavic peoples as fellow Byzantine Christians.

Background
Like the Greeks, the Byzantines labeled anyone who did not speak Greek as a "barbarian."

Both Slavic and Greek

Midway through the 9th century, the **Slavs**—the people from the forests north of the Black Sea—began trading with Constantinople. As they traded, they began absorbing Greek Byzantine ideas. Russian culture grew out of this blending of Slavic and Greek traditions.

The Land of Russia's Birth Russia's first unified territory originated west of the Ural Mountains in the region that runs from the Black Sea to the Baltic. Hilly grasslands are found in the extreme south of that area. The north, however, is densely forested, flat, and swampy. Slow-moving, interconnecting rivers allow boat travel across these plains in almost any direction. Three great rivers, the Dnieper (NEE·puhr), the Don, and the Volga, run from the heart of the forests to the Black Sea or the Caspian Sea.

In the early days of the Byzantine Empire, these forests were inhabited by tribes of Slavic farmers and traders. They spoke similar languages but had no political unity. Sometime in the 800s, small bands of adventurers came down among them from the north. These Varangians, or Rus as they were also called, were most likely Vikings. Eventually, the Vikings built forts along the rivers and settled among the Slavs.

THINK THROUGH HISTORY
A. Making Inferences Why might a territory with plains and rivers be difficult to defend against invaders?

Slavs and Vikings Russian legends say the Slavs invited the Viking chief Rurik to be their king. So in 862, he founded Novgorod (NAHV·guh·rahd), Russia's first important city. That account is given in *The Primary Chronicle,* a history of Russia written by monks

Many rivers in Russia are full of rocks and dangerous rapids. Vikings like the ones in this woodcut would lift up their boats and carry them past those dangers. Even so, many Vikings died in Russian rivers.

in the early 1100s. Around 880, a nobleman from Novgorod named Oleg moved south to Kiev (KEE·ehf), a city on the Dnieper River. From Kiev, the Vikings could sail by river and sea to Constantinople. There they could trade for the products from distant lands.

The merchandise they brought to Constantinople included timber, fur, wax, honey, and their Slavic subjects whom they sold as slaves. In fact, the word *slave* originates from *Slav*.

Kiev grew into a principality, a small state ruled by a prince. As it did, the Viking nobles intermarried with their Slavic subjects. They also adopted Slavic culture. The society remained strictly divided between peasant masses and the nobles, or **boyars.** Gradually, however, the line between Slavs and Vikings vanished.

Background
Vikings could dominate the Slavs partly because of superior weaponry. They used two-edged swords and battle axes.

Kiev Becomes Orthodox In 957, a member of the Kievan nobility paid a visit to Constantinople and publicly converted to Christianity. Her name was Princess **Olga.** From 945 to 955, she governed Kiev until her son was old enough to rule. Her son resisted Christianity. However, soon after Olga's grandson **Vladimir** (VLAD·uh·meer) came to the throne about 980, he considered conversion to Christianity. *The Primary Chronicle* reports that Vladimir sent out teams to observe the major religions of the times. Three of the teams returned with lukewarm accounts of Islam, Judaism, and Western Christianity. But the team from Byzantium told quite a different story:

A VOICE FROM THE PAST
. . . the Greeks led us to the buildings where they worship their God, and we knew not whether we were in heaven or on earth. For on earth there is no such splendor or such beauty, and we are at a loss how to describe it. We only know that God dwells there among men and . . . we cannot forget that beauty.

from *The Primary Chronicle*

THINK THROUGH HISTORY
B. Analyzing Motives Why do you think Vladimir thought it was important that all his subjects become Christian?

This report convinced Vladimir to convert to Byzantine Christianity and to make all his subjects convert, too. In 989 a baptism of all the citizens of Kiev was held in the Dnieper River. Kiev, already linked to Byzantium by trade, now looked to Constantinople for religious guidance. Vladimir imported teachers to instruct the people in the new faith. All the beliefs and traditions of Orthodox Christianity flourished in Kiev. Vladimir appreciated the Byzantine idea of the emperor as supreme ruler of the church. So the close link between Church and state took root in Russia as well.

Kiev's Power and Decline

Thanks to its Byzantine ties, Kiev grew from a cluster of crude wooden forts to the glittering capital of prosperous and educated people. The rise of Kiev marks the appearance of Russia's first important unified territory.

The Viking Invasions of Eastern Europe, 820–941

Vikings
Novgorod 820
Moscow
859–878
Baltic Sea
W. Dvina R.
Volga R.
Neman R.
RUSSIA
SAXONY
Vistula R.
Elbe R.
Oder R.
Kiev 882
Dnieper R.
BAVARIA
Odessa
LOMBARDY
Danube R.
866 907 941
Black Sea
Rome
Adriatic Sea
Constantinople
Thessalonica
Aegean Sea
Athens
N
0   500 Miles
0   1,000 Kilometers
Crete   Cyprus

Area of Viking control
Viking invasions
882 Year of invasion

GEOGRAPHY SKILLBUILDER: Interpreting Maps
1. **Human-Environment Interaction** *Which geographical feature of Russia did Vikings use to further their invasions?*
2. **Human-Environment Interaction** *Besides east, what is the other basic direction taken by Vikings in their Eastern European invasions? Why do you think they chose to attack in that direction?*

Kievan Russia Vladimir led the way in establishing Kiev's power. He expanded his state west into Poland and north almost to the Baltic Sea. He also fought off troublesome nomads from the steppes to the south.

In 1019, Vladimir's son **Yaroslav the Wise** came to the throne and led Kiev to even greater glory. Like the rulers of Byzantium, Yaroslav skillfully married off his daughters and sisters to the kings and princes of Western Europe. Those marriages helped him to forge important trading alliances. At the same time, he created a legal code tailored to Kiev's commercial culture. Many of its rules dealt with crimes against property. For example, Yaroslav's code called for a fine of three *grivnas* for cutting off a person's finger, but 12 *grivnas* for plowing over a property line. Yaroslav also built the first library in Kiev. Under his rule, Christianity prospered. By the 12th century, Kiev could even boast of having 400 churches. However, the wooden churches proved to be as temporary as Kiev's glory.

Power Struggles Bring on Kiev's Decline The decline of the Kievan state started with the death of Yaroslav in 1054. Yaroslav had made a crucial error. Yaroslav divided his realm among his sons—instead of following the custom of passing on the throne to the eldest son. His sons tore the state apart fighting for the choicest territories. And because this system of dividing among sons continued, each generation saw new struggles. The Crusades added to Kiev's troubles by disrupting trade. Then, just when it seemed that things could not get worse, they got far worse.

Background
Under Yaroslav's system, younger brothers were supposed to move up to better properties as their elders died. However, the brothers didn't always die in the right order!

Mongol Invasions Favor the Rise of Moscow

In the middle 1200s, a ferocious group of horsemen from central Asia slashed their way into Russia. These nomads were the Mongols. (See Chapter 12.) They had exploded onto the world scene at the beginning of the 1200s under Genghis Khan (JEHNG-gihs KAHN), one of the most feared warriors of all time.

Mongols may have been forced to move out by economic or military pressures. They may have been lured by the wealth of cities to the west. Whatever their reasons for leaving, Mongols rode their swift horses across the steppes of Asia and on into

HISTORY THROUGH ART: Fine Art

Madonna with Child and Angels (about 1463), Fra Filippo Lippi (Italy)

Christian religious art in the West strives to show the holy in realistic situations. Eastern Orthodox icons depict a spiritual world that is far removed from what some consider the "real" world. In Western art, the divine seems near and familiar. In the East, the divine looks far from our human level, but like windows, icons can help believers glimpse heaven.

Connect *to* History

Contrast What are the differences between the styles of these two paintings? Consider the mother, the child, and the background.

SEE SKILLBUILDER HANDBOOK, PAGE 1009

Connect *to* Today

Analyzing Go to a house of worship near you. See if and how the spiritual is portrayed there.

The Mother of God of Vladimir (12th century), icon commissioned by the grand duke of Kiev

Europe. Their savage killing and burning won them a reputation for ruthless brutality. When Genghis Khan died in 1227, his successors continued the conquering that he had begun. At its fullest extent, the Mongol Empire stretched from the Yellow Sea to the Baltic Sea and from the Himalayas to northern Russia.

In 1240, the Mongols attacked and demolished Kiev. They rode under the leadership of Batu Khan, Genghis's grandson. So many inhabitants were slaughtered, a Russian historian reported, that "no eye remained to weep." A Roman Catholic bishop traveling through Kiev five years later wrote, "When we passed through that land, we found lying in the field countless heads and bones of dead people." After the fall of Kiev, Mongols ruled all of southern Russia. For over 200 years, the Mongol Empire in Russia held power. The empire's official name was the Khanate of the Golden Horde. *Khanate*, from the Mongol word for "kingdom"; *Golden*, because gold was the royal color of the Mongols; *Horde*, from the Mongol word for "camp."

Mongol Rule in Russia Under Mongol rule, the Russians could follow all their usual customs, as long as they made no sign of rebellion. As fierce as they were, the Mongols tolerated all the religions in their realms. The Church acted as a mediator between the people and the Mongols. It also pacified the oppressors by praying for them. Church leaders found a religious meaning in the Mongol occupation of the country. They explained it as a punishment for the people's sins. Icons gained importance at this time, and Russians used the images to help escape their painful political realities.

The Mongols demanded just two things from Russians: slavish obedience and massive amounts of tribute. The Mongols themselves made sure Russians remained obedient. However, they made local nobles collect the tribute. As long as the money was delivered, the nobles could keep their titles. Novgorod's prince and military hero **Alexander Nevsky**, for example, advised his fellow princes to cooperate with the Mongols. The Russian nobles crushed revolts against the Mongols and collected oppressive taxes for the foreign rulers. At his death, Nevsky willed the principality of Moscow to his son Daniel. Daniel founded a line of princes there that in 200 years would rise to great prominence.

Mongol rule isolated the Russians more than ever from their neighbors in Western Europe, cutting them off from many new ideas and inventions. However, during this period, forces were at work that would eventually lead to Russia's liberation and to the rise of a new center of power, Moscow.

Mongol Rule Serves Moscow's Interests In some ways, the Mongols actually helped to unite Russia. Kievan Russia had been a collection of small independent principalities. Mongol rulers looked upon Russia as their unified empire, and all Russian principalities had to pay tribute to the Mongol Khan.

The rise of Moscow also began under the Mongols. The city was first founded in the 1100s. By 1156, it was a crude village protected by a log wall. Nonetheless, Moscow was located near three rivers: the Volga, Dnieper, and Don. From that strategic position, a prince of Moscow who could gain control of the three rivers could eventually control nearly all of European Russia.

That opportunity for expansion would not arise until the 14th century. In the late 1320s, Moscow's Prince Ivan I had earned the gratitude of the Mongols by helping to crush a Russian revolt against Mongol rule. For his services, the Mongols appointed Ivan I as tax collector of all the Slavic lands they had conquered. They also gave him the title of "Great Prince." Ivan had now become without any

HISTORY MAKERS

**Alexander Nevsky
1220?–1263**

Alexander of Novgorod was about 20 when he carved his name on Russian history. In 1240, the Swedes attacked the principality of Novgorod to stop its expansion. Alexander soundly defeated the invading Swedes at the Neva River. Grateful Russians called him Nevsky ("of the Neva") in honor of his victory.

In 1242, his fame grew even greater. In that year, the Teutonic Knights, a brotherhood of Germanic warriors, invaded the Baltics and Russia to convert them to Catholicism. Alexander cut the German armies to pieces on a frozen channel between two lakes—his famous "Battle on the Ice." For this victory and for his long protection of the Russian church, Alexander was declared a saint of the Russian Orthodox Church in 1547.

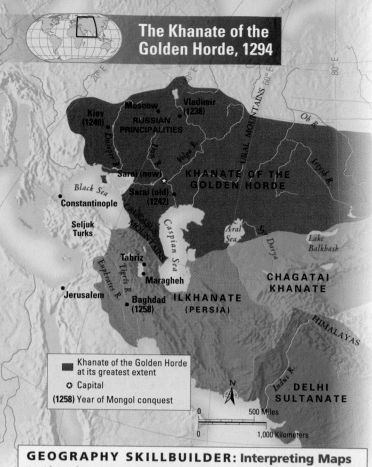

The Khanate of the Golden Horde, 1294

RUSSIAN PRINCIPALITIES
Kiev (1240)
Moscow
Vladimir (1238)
Sarai (new)
Sarai (old) (1242)
KHANATE OF THE GOLDEN HORDE
Black Sea
Constantinople
Seljuk Turks
CAUCASUS MOUNTAINS
Caspian Sea
Aral Sea
Lake Balkhash
CHAGATAI KHANATE
Tabriz
Maragheh
Jerusalem
Baghdad (1258)
ILKHANATE (PERSIA)
HIMALAYAS
DELHI SULTANATE

■ Khanate of the Golden Horde at its greatest extent
✪ Capital
(1258) Year of Mongol conquest

0 — 500 Miles
0 — 1,000 Kilometers

GEOGRAPHY SKILLBUILDER: Interpreting Maps
1. *About how many miles did the Khanate of the Golden Horde stretch from east to west?*
2. *What people controlled most of the kingdoms surrounding Mongol Russia?*

doubt the most powerful of all Russian princes. He also became the wealthiest and was known as "Ivan Moneybags."

Ivan was also able to convince the Patriarch of Kiev, the leading bishop of Eastern Europe, to move to Moscow. The move enhanced the city's prestige and gave Moscow's princes a powerful ally: the Church. Ivan I and his successors used numerous strategies to enlarge their territory: land purchases, wars, trickery, shrewd marriages. From generation to generation, they schemed to gain control over the small states around Moscow.

Vocabulary
enhanced: improved

An Empire Emerges The Russian state would become a genuine empire during the long, 43-year reign of Ivan III (1462–1505). This prince was only a boy of 13 when Constantinople fell to the Turkish Empire in 1453. In 1472, Ivan III managed to marry the niece of the last Byzantine emperor. He then began calling himself **czar** (zahr), the Russian version of Caesar. (The title became official only during the reign of Ivan IV.) By calling himself czar, however, Ivan III openly claimed to make Russia the "Third Rome."

Background
Rome itself was first; Constantinople was the Second Rome; the third was Russia, according to Ivan.

In 1480, Ivan made the final break with the Mongols. He refused to pay their tribute. Following his refusal, Russian and Mongol armies faced each other on either side of the Ugra River, about 150 miles southwest of Moscow. However, neither side wanted to fight. So, after a time, both armies turned around and marched home. Russians have traditionally considered this bloodless standoff as marking Russia's liberation from Mongol rule. After that liberation, the czars could openly pursue an empire.

The Mongols were not the only conquering people to emerge from central Asia. As you will learn in Section 3, Turks would begin establishing an empire in Southwest Asia. In one form or another, their empire would last from the 11th century to the 20th century.

Section ❷ Assessment

1. TERMS & NAMES
Identify
• Slavs
• boyars
• Olga
• Vladimir
• Yaroslav the Wise
• Alexander Nevsky
• czar

2. TAKING NOTES
Make a chart like the one below to show the effects of Mongol rule in Russia.

Nobles	Church	People	Moscow Princes

3. RECOGNIZING EFFECTS
How did Vladimir's conversion to Christianity affect the citizens, society, and government of Kiev?

THINK ABOUT
• the laws he passed
• the customs he encouraged
• the policies he followed

4. ANALYZING THEMES
Empire Building The Mongols were fierce conquerors, and their rule cut Russia off from the rest of the world. Even so, their policies helped to pull Russia together as a territory. How? Give reasons and examples from the text to support your opinion.

THINK ABOUT
• Mongol policies in Russia
• the Church's attitude toward the Mongols
• the role and power of the nobility

3 Turkish Empires Rise in Anatolia

MAIN IDEA

Turkish people converted to Islam and founded new empires that would renew Muslim civilization.

WHY IT MATTERS NOW

In the 20th century, the collapse of the Turkish empire left ethnic and religious hostilities that still affect the world.

SETTING THE STAGE To the east of Constantinople and south of Russia, the powerful Muslim empire of the Abbasids had ruled since the 8th century. (See Chapter 10.) By the late 10th century, however, their empire seemed ripe for conquest.

The Turks March from Central Asia

As early as 1300 B.C., Chinese records mention a people called the *Durko* living west of their borders. The *Durko* may well have been the Turks. For centuries, these nomads rode their horses over the vast plains. They herded goats and sheep, lived in tents, and used two-humped camels to carry their goods. The Islamic world first met them as raiders and traders along their northeastern frontiers. In the 10th century, the Turks began converting to Islam and slowly migrating into the Abbasid Empire.

From Slaves to Masters When the Abbasids first noticed the military skills of the Turks, they began buying Turkish children to raise as slaves, train as soldiers, and employ as bodyguards. The Abbasids came to prize the slaves for their skill and loyalty. On this subject, one author wrote: "One obedient slave is better than 300 sons; for the latter desire their father's death, the former [desires] long life for his master." Over time, Turkish military slaves, or **mamelukes,** became a powerful force in the Abbasid Empire. The mameluke forces soon became stronger than their Abbasid caliph masters in Baghdad.

This foreign influence could not have come at a worse time for the Abbasids. For 200 years, their empire had been losing significant stretches of territory. Spain broke away in 756, six years after the Abbasids came to power. After setting up their capital in Baghdad, the Abbasids saw other parts of their empire break away: Morocco in 788 and Tunisia in 800. In 809, some regions of Persia were lost. Then, in 868, the Abbasids lost control of Egypt.

Finally, in 945, Persian armies moved into Baghdad and put an end to the caliph's political power. Even though the caliph continued as the religious leader of Islam, he gave up all political power to the new Persian ruler.

The Rise of the Seljuks At this time of weakness and division, large numbers of Turks migrated into the Abbasid Empire around 970. One of the first of these migrating Turkish groups was known as the **Seljuks** (SEHL-JOOKS), after the family that led them. By the year 1000, the Seljuks had converted to the Sunni branch of Islam. Despite their conversion, however, they continued to make war on other Muslims. In 1055, they attacked and captured Baghdad from the Persians.

Twenty years later, the **Seljuk sultans** marched on the Byzantine Empire. At the Battle of Manzikert in 1071, the Turks crushed the Byzantines. Within ten years, the Seljuks occupied most of Anatolia, the eastern flank of Byzantium. This brought the

THINK THROUGH HISTORY
A. Recognizing Motives How would giving slaves position and power assure their loyalty?

Vocabulary
caliph: an Islamic religious and political leader.

Background
For a discussion of the split between Sunni and Shi'ite Muslims, see Chapter 10, page 240.

A mameluke horseman aims his bow at the enemy in this drawing from around the year 1300.

Byzantines, Russians, and Turks Interact **279**

Turks closer to Constantinople than the Arabs or Persians had ever come. This near conquest of the New Rome also inspired the name of the Seljuk sultanate of Rum (from "Rome"). Rum survived in Anatolia after the rest of the Seljuk Empire had crumbled.

The Turks Secure Persian Support Seljuk rulers wisely courted the support of their newly conquered Persian subjects. In fact, the founder of the Seljuk Dynasty, Toghril Beg, chose the Persian city of Isfahan (IHS·fuh·HAHN) as the capital of his kingdom. This favorable treatment made the Persians loyal supporters of the Seljuks, and the Turks often appointed them as government officials. The brilliant Nizam al-Mulk, for example, was a Persian who served as the **vizier**, or prime minister, of the most famous of Seljuk sultans, **Malik Shah.**

The bond between Turks and Persians also grew strong because of Turkish admiration of Persian learning. The nomadic Seljuks had arrived in Southwest Asia basically illiterate. They were unfamiliar with the traditions of Islam, which they had just adopted. As a result, they looked to their Persian subjects for both cultural and religious guidance. The Turks adopted Persian as the language of culture and adopted features of the Persian way of life that they so admired. Seljuk rulers were called *shahs,* from the Persian word for a king. They also promoted Persian writers like the mystical Islamic poet Jalaludin Rumi, whose poetry is widely read today. Rumi often wrote of his desire to achieve a personal experience of God. In this poem, he expresses that desire in passionate terms:

THINK THROUGH HISTORY
B. Contrasting
What advantages would a nomadic people like the Turks have in fighting settled people like the Persians or Byzantines?

HISTORY MAKERS

Malik Shah
1055–1092

Malik Shah, the third and greatest Seljuk sultan, was a conqueror like the sultans before him. However, he is remembered today for his love of art, science, and literature. Among his achievements, he built the great mosque Masjid-i-Jame (shown above) in Isfahan. Malik also established religious tolerance throughout his empire.

He patronized intellectuals and artists like Omar Khayyam (OH·mahr ky·YAHM), who is most famous today for the *Rubaiyat* (ROO·bee·AHT). The *Rubaiyat* is a collection of poems describing the poet's love of life's pleasures. Omar also created a more accurate calendar for Malik.

Malik Shah was also capable of great cruelty. When his brother Takash revolted against him, Malik punished Takash by blinding him. Malik Shah died suddenly at the age of 37, possibly poisoned by his wife.

A VOICE FROM THE PAST
Burning with longing-fire
Wanting to sleep with my head on your doorsill,
My living is composed only of this trying to be in your presence.
JALALUDIN RUMI, quoted in *Unseen Rain*

Seljuk shahs like the great Malik Shah took pride in supporting Persian artists and architects. Malik beautified the city of Isfahan, for example, by building many splendid mosques.

The Turks' political and cultural preference for the Persians caused the almost complete disappearance of the Arabic language from Persia. Only religious scholars studying the Qur'an used Arabic. As a result of their policy, the Seljuks won strong support from Persians, who were proud of their long heritage. Like other conquering peoples throughout history, the Seljuk Turks found that they had much to learn from those whom they had defeated.

Turks saw control of cities as the key to victory. This drawing from an early 13th-century manuscript illustrates a siege of a city that took place two centuries earlier. Notice the two soldiers being catapulted over the wall.

Seljuks Confront Crusaders and Mongols

Malik Shah ruled as the last of the strong Seljuk leaders. After his unexpected death in 1092, no capable shah appeared to replace him. So, the Seljuk Empire quickly disintegrated into a loose collection of minor kingdoms. Just at that point, the West launched a counterattack against the Turks. This series of military campaigns is called the Crusades.

Background
For a full discussion of the Crusades, see Chapter 14, page 343.

The Seljuks and the Crusaders Pope Urban II launched the First Crusade in 1095. He called for Christians to drive the Turks out of Anatolia and recover Jerusalem. Armies from Western Europe soon poured through Constantinople and proceeded on to Palestine. In 1099, the Crusaders captured Jerusalem and massacred its Jewish and Muslim inhabitants. They established a Latin Christian kingdom that lasted about a century.

Eventually, a fragment of the former Seljuk Empire gathered enough strength to fight back. Under their famous Kurdish captain Saladin, the Muslims recovered Jerusalem in 1187. Eventually, Saladin and his Western opponent King Richard I of England signed a truce. Their agreement gave Jerusalem to the Muslims but granted Western pilgrims access to Christian holy places.

Background
Christian holy places included sites believed to be connected with Jesus' life, death, and resurrection.

The popes called for further Crusades. But each new one was weaker than the last. The Western threat to the Turks was fading. However, just as the menace of the Crusades was subsiding, the Muslim world suffered another devastating shock. This time it came from the east.

Seljuks Face the Mongols The new threat to Turkish power was the Mongol army of conquest and destruction led by Genghis Khan. Early in the 1200s, Genghis Khan had forged his Mongol tribes into a unified force and conquered China.

In the course of their rampage west, the Mongol armies leveled any cities that dared to resist them. They slaughtered whole populations. In 1258, when Genghis's grandson Hulagu finally took Baghdad, he had tens of thousands of people killed. He burned down the caliph's palace. Mongol belief warned against the spilling of sacred blood. So Hulagu executed the last Abbasid caliph by having him wrapped in a carpet and trampled to death by horses.

With untold brutality, Genghis Khan and his successors shaped the biggest land empire in history. (See Chapter 12 for more about the Mongol Empire.) The warrior Mongols, however, knew little about administering their territory. As a result, their vast empire crumbled in just a few generations. And out of the rubble of the Mongol Empire rose another group of Turks—the Ottomans. They would build an empire that lasted into the 20th century. You will learn about more about the Ottoman Empire in Chapter 18.

Section 3 Assessment

1. TERMS & NAMES

Identify
- mamelukes
- Seljuks
- vizier
- Malik Shah

2. TAKING NOTES

Create a time line like the one below to show the events in the last 200 years of the Abassid Empire.

```
 +---------------+---------------+
756
Spain
breaks
away
```

3. ANALYZING ISSUES

In what ways would it be accurate to say that the Persians actually won over their Turkish conquerors?

THINK ABOUT
- religion
- culture
- political influence

4. THEME ACTIVITY

Empire Building Between Abbasid and Mongol rule, Baghdad was occupied and governed by four different powers. In a chart like the one below, summarize important events and features of those occupations.

Occupiers	Events/Features
Abbasids Persians Seljuks Mongols	

TERMS & NAMES

Briefly explain the importance of each of the following to the Byzantines, Russians, and Turks between 500 and 1500.

1. Justinian Code
2. Hagia Sophia
3. patriarch
4. icon
5. Slavs
6. boyars
7. Vladimir
8. Alexander Nevsky
9. Seljuks
10. Malik Shah

Interact *with* History

On page 268, you considered diplomatic ways of saving the Byzantine Empire from an invading army. Which non-military approach did you choose and why? Now that you've read about the Byzantine Empire, do you think that you chose the right strategy? Discuss your present ideas on handling the invader with the class.

REVIEW QUESTIONS

SECTION 1 *(pages 269–273)*

Byzantium Becomes the New Rome

11. Why did Constantine decide to create a new eastern capital for the Roman Empire?
12. Name and describe the contents of the four parts of the Justinian Code.
13. What were some important features of life in Constantinople?
14. Which peoples attacked the Byzantine Empire? What part of the empire did they invade?

SECTION 2 *(pages 274–278)*

Russians Adapt Byzantine Culture

15. What does *The Primary Chronicle* say about Rurik and the origin of Novgorod?
16. Describe the trade that developed between the Vikings and Constantinople.
17. According to *The Primary Chronicle*, how did Vladimir choose Byzantine Christianity?
18. How did each of the following contribute to the growth and prestige of Moscow: (a) its geography; (b) the Patriarch of Kiev; (c) Ivan I?

SECTION 3 *(pages 279–281)*

Turkish Empires Rise in Anatolia

19. Explain how Turkish children could move from slaves to masters.
20. List five ways the Turks showed respect for their Persian subjects.

Visual Summary

Byzantines, Russians, and Turks

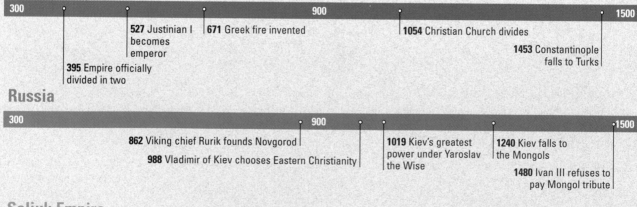

Byzantium

| 300 | | | 900 | | 1500 |

527 Justinian I becomes emperor

671 Greek fire invented

1054 Christian Church divides

1453 Constantinople falls to Turks

395 Empire officially divided in two

Russia

| 300 | 900 | 1500 |

862 Viking chief Rurik founds Novgorod

988 Vladimir of Kiev chooses Eastern Christianity

1019 Kiev's greatest power under Yaroslav the Wise

1240 Kiev falls to the Mongols

1480 Ivan III refuses to pay Mongol tribute

Seljuk Empire

| 300 | 900 | 1500 |

900s Turks begin converting to Islam

970 Seljuk Turks migrate into Abbasid Empire

1055 Seljuk armies capture Baghdad

1092 Malik Shah dies; Seljuk Empire declines

1071 Seljuks defeat Byzantines at Manzikert

CRITICAL THINKING

1. THE JUSTINIAN CODE

THEME **EMPIRE BUILDING** What were Justinian's goals in creating his law code? List several reasons why a leader might want to codify (organize) the laws. Explain the influence that the Justinian Code had in the Byzantine Empire.

2. LIVING UNDER THE MONGOLS

What advantages might Alexander Nevsky see in cooperating with the Mongols? What disadvantages can you see? Would you support such a policy? Why or why not?

3. THE VIKINGS, TURKS, AND MONGOLS

The Vikings, Turks, and Mongols moved into foreign lands. Where did they come from? Where did they settle? How did they interact with the native population? Recreate the chart below. Answer the questions above to fill in the chart. Show how these groups were similar or different.

	Where from?	Where settled?	Interactions with people
Vikings			
Turks			
Mongols			

4. ANALYZING PRIMARY SOURCES

The following is an account of Batu Khan's attack on the city of Riazan, in western Russia. *The Tale of the Destruction of Riazan* is found in church histories written during the 16th and 17th centuries. Partly fiction and partly fact, historians believe the description of the attack is generally accurate.

A VOICE FROM THE PAST
On the dawn of the sixth day the pagan warriors began to storm the city, some with firebrands [torches of burning wood], some with battering rams, and others with countless scaling ladders for ascending the walls of the city. . . . And the Tatars [Mongols] cut down many people, including women and children. Still others were drowned in the river. And they killed without exception all monks and priests. And they burned this holy city with all its beauty and wealth. . . . And churches of God were destroyed, and much blood was spilled on the holy altars. And not one man remained alive in the city. All were dead. . . . And this happened for our sins.

from ZENKOVSKY, Medieval Russia's Epics, Chronicles, and Tales

- How does the historian portray the Mongol invaders?
- According to the writer, why were the people of Riazan defeated by the Mongols?
- How does a historian's belief system influence the interpretation of history?

CHAPTER ACTIVITIES

1. LIVING HISTORY: Unit Portfolio Project

THEME **RELIGIOUS AND ETHICAL SYSTEMS** Your portfolio project shows how religions affected people's lives. For this chapter, you might choose to use one of the following ideas for your portfolio.

- Find a photograph of a holy place connected with the Byzantine, Russian, or Turkish empire. Write a two-minute documentary script explaining the meaning or importance of the religious site that you are focusing on. Record your documentary on audio- or videocassette and present it to the class.
- Meet in a team as Vladimir's delegates did to research different faiths. Each of you will investigate a different religious or ethical system. Combine the group's findings into a chart. Then write a personal report explaining which of these faiths best represents you and why.
- Write a dialogue between two advisers of an Abbasid caliph. One adviser gives reasons for training the mamelukes as soldiers to defend the empire. The other tries to convince the caliph that this policy is dangerous.

2. CONNECT TO TODAY Cooperative Learning

THEME **CULTURAL INTERACTION** When the Turks settled among the Persians, they took on Persian ways. When two peoples make contact, they tend to adopt aspects of each other's way of life. Today, contact among nations and peoples is occurring more frequently than at any other time in history.

Working in small groups, use the Internet, magazines, newspapers, or the library to find examples of how two peoples today have influenced each other. The group could focus on language, food, clothing, music, social customs, religion, system of government. The group should present the results of its research on an illustrated bulletin board with captions.

3. INTERPRETING A TIME LINE

Look at the time lines on page 282. How many years did the Byzantine Empire last? How long did Mongol rule last in Russia? How long did it take the Seljuk Empire to decline after the Seljuks took Baghdad?

FOCUS ON **CHARTS**

Study this chart of empires, their dates, territories, and populations.

- Which of the empires below lasted the longest time? the shortest?
- Which empire had the greatest territory and population?

Connect to History Is there any connection between how big an empire is or the number of people it rules and how long it lasts?

Seven Empires			
	Dates	Greatest Territory*	Greatest Population**
Egyptian	2780 B.C.–1075 B.C.	0.4	4.5
Persian	550 B.C.–330 B.C.	2.0	14.0
Roman	27 B.C.–A.D. 476	3.4	54.8
Byzantine	A.D. 395–A.D.1453	1.4	30.0
Mali	A.D. 1200–A.D. 1400	0.9	3.0
Mongol	A.D. 1206–A.D. 1380	11.7	125.0
Aztec	A.D. 1325–A.D. 1521	0.2	6.0

*Estimated in millions of square miles
**Estimated in millions of people

CHAPTER 12 *Empires in East Asia,* 600–1350

PREVIEWING THEMES

Religious and Ethical Systems

Buddhism, which had reached China from India, spread from China to Korea and Japan. In Japan, Buddhism mixed with the traditional religion, Shinto. Both Hindu and Buddhist missionaries from India spread their religions across Southeast Asia.

Empire Building

The Tang Dynasty built China into the most powerful and advanced empire in the world in the 700s and 800s. In the 1200s, China fell under the control of another group of empire builders, the Mongols. For a century, the Mongols controlled most of Eurasia in the largest unified land empire in history.

Cultural Interaction

Two trends dominated this period of history. First, Chinese culture spread to the rest of East Asia, influencing Korea, Japan, and mainland Southeast Asia. Second, the rise of the Mongols and their great conquests led to interaction between nomadic and settled peoples across all of Asia.

INTERNET CONNECTION

Visit us at **www.mcdougallittell.com** to learn more about East Asian history.

TANG AND SONG CHINA, 600–1279

- ▦ Tang Dynasty at furthest extent
- ▦ Song Dynasty to 1126
- ▦ Song Dynasty after 1126
- ⌁ Grand Canal
- ⌁ Great Wall, 814

Caspian Sea

Aral Sea

✳ Battle of Talas (751)

0   1,000 Miles
0   2,000 Kilometers

N

TAKI MAKE

HIMALAY

THAR DESERT

INDIA

Led by Genghis Khan, the fearsome **Mongol cavalry** swept out of Mongolia in **1209** and began a bloody conquest of Asia. By 1260, Genghis's successors controlled a vast empire extending from Korea to Kiev.

284

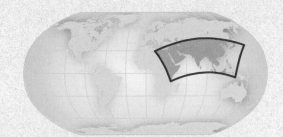

The man sitting behind the desk is a **Chinese scholar-official** in charge of a local district. In the **600s**, the rulers of the Tang Dynasty revived and expanded the civil service system begun by the Han emperors.

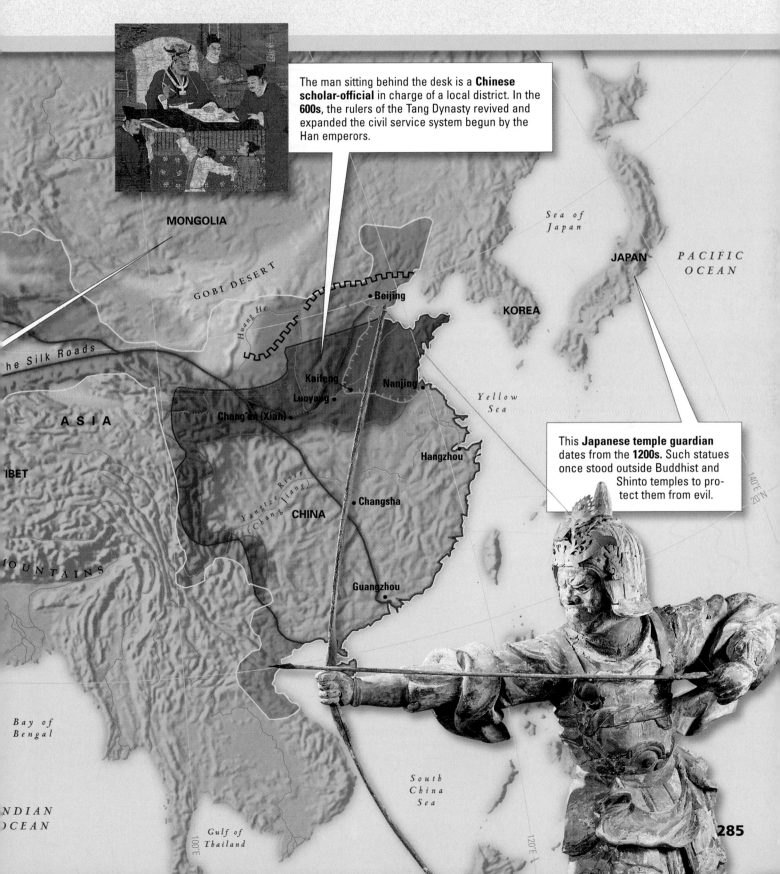

This **Japanese temple guardian** dates from the **1200s.** Such statues once stood outside Buddhist and Shinto temples to protect them from evil.

MONGOLIA

GOBI DESERT

Huang He

he Silk Roads

ASIA

TIBET

MOUNTAINS

Beijing

KOREA

Kaifeng

Luoyang

Nanjing

Chang'an (Xian)

Hangzhou

Yangtze River
(Chang Jiang)

CHINA

Changsha

Guangzhou

Bay of
Bengal

Sea of
Japan

JAPAN

PACIFIC
OCEAN

Yellow
Sea

140°E

20°N

South
China
Sea

INDIAN
OCEAN

Gulf of
Thailand

100°E

120°E

285

The magnetic compass can help sailors navigate the open sea.

Imagine it is the year 1292. You have spent the last 17 years traveling around the most advanced country in the world—China. The civilization you come from is on the other side of the world. It, too, is very sophisticated, but it lacks many of the innovations you have seen on your travels.

During your stay in China, you were of great assistance to the emperor. As a going-away present, he wants you to choose one of the inventions shown here to take back to your own society. After choosing one, you will receive the knowledge of how to create it.

Which one Chinese invention would you take back to your society? Why?

Paper is a relatively inexpensive and easy-to-produce surface for writing and printing.

Gunpowder can be used for fireworks or made into explosive weapons.

Silk makes a luxurious cloth—soft to the touch but also amazingly strong and warm.

EXAMINING *the* ISSUES

Use these questions to help you choose an invention:

- **Which item would be most useful to a society that currently has none of the items?**

- **Which would most improve the quality of life?**

- **Which might be the most profitable?**

- **What benefits and drawbacks might there be to introducing the item into your society?**

Discuss these questions with your classmates. In your discussion, remember what you've learned about the spread of new ideas.

As you read about China in this chapter, see how its ideas spread from the East to the West.

1 Two Great Dynasties in China

MAIN IDEA	WHY IT MATTERS NOW
During the Tang and Song dynasties, China experienced an era of prosperity and technological innovation.	Chinese inventions from this period, such as printing, gunpowder, and the compass, changed history.

SETTING THE STAGE After the Han Dynasty collapsed in A.D. 220, nomadic peoples from the northern steppe and Tibet conquered much of northern China. For 350 years, no emperor was strong to hold China together. More than 30 local dynasties rose and fell. By 589, an emperor named Sui Wendi had united northern and southern China once again. He restored a strong central government. Under the next two dynasties, the Tang and the Song, China experienced a golden age. It became the richest, most powerful, and most advanced country in the world.

The Tang Dynasty Expands China

Sui Wendi declared himself the first emperor of the Sui (sway) Dynasty. The dynasty lasted through only two emperors from 589 to 618. The Sui emperors' greatest accomplishment was the completion of the Grand Canal. This waterway connected the Huang He (Yellow River) and the Yangtze River. The canal provided a vital route for trade between the northern cities and the southern rice-producing region of the Yangtze delta.

To dig the 1,000-mile waterway, tens of thousands of peasant men and women *worked* toiled five years. Perhaps as many as half of the workers died on the job. Thousands more toiled and died to rebuild the Great Wall. The endless labor on state projects turned the people against the Sui Dynasty. Overworked and overtaxed, they finally revolted. In 618, a member of the imperial court strangled the second Sui emperor.

THINK THROUGH HISTORY
A. Synthesizing
What Sui accomplishments helped the Tang Dynasty become powerful?

Tang Rulers Create a Powerful Empire While short-lived, the Sui Dynasty built a strong foundation for the great achievements of the next dynasty, the Tang (tahng). The Tang Dynasty ruled for nearly 300 years (618–907). The Tang emperor who began these achievements was **Tang Taizong**, whose brilliant reign lasted from 627 to 649.

Under the Tang rulers, the empire expanded. Taizong's armies reconquered the northern and western lands that China had lost since the decline of the Han Dynasty. By 668, China had extended its influence over Korea as well. The ruler during the campaign in Korea was the empress **Wu Zhao** (woo jow). From about 660 on, she held the real power while weak emperors sat on the throne. Finally, in 690, Empress Wu assumed the title of emperor for herself—the only woman ever to do so in China. *General*

Tang rulers further strengthened the central government of China. They expanded the network of roads and canals begun by the Sui. This helped to pull the empire together. However, Tang Taizong also remembered the Sui emperors' mistake of overtaxing peasants. Therefore, he lowered taxes and took some lands from the wealthy to give to peasants. He and his successors also promoted foreign trade and improvements in agriculture. Tang China prospered.

Horses symbolized the power of the Tang Dynasty. Tang artists were famous for their glazed pottery horses such as this one, which was created in the early 700s.

Empires in East Asia **287**

Tang Taizong
600–649

The man who restored the Middle Kingdom to its glory was a distinguished general named Li Shimin. He seized the imperial throne in 626 after killing off his brothers as rivals and forcing his father, the first Tang emperor, to step aside. As emperor, Li Shimin took the title Taizong, meaning "Great Ancestor."

Taizong's military campaigns extended China's borders north to Manchuria, south to Vietnam, and west to the Aral Sea. China's power and influence reached much farther. At home, aided by his gifted advisers, Taizong reformed the government organization and law code. These became models for all of East Asia.

Wu Zhao
625–705

At the age of 13, the beautiful Wu Zhao arrived at the court of Tang Taizong to become one of the emperor's secondary wives. After Taizong's death, she became a favored wife of his son and successor. Wu Zhao soon rose above rival wives and became the emperor's chief wife, or empress.

For many years, Empress Wu virtually ruled China on behalf of the sickly emperor. After his death, two of their sons briefly held the throne. Frustrated by their lack of ability, she took the throne herself at the age of 65. She was 80 when she finally lost power.

A strong leader, Wu Zhao continued the work begun by Taizong to build and expand China.

Scholar-Officials To manage their large empire, the Tang rulers needed to restore China's vast bureaucracy. The civil service examination system begun by the Han Dynasty had fallen into disorder. The Tang rulers revived and expanded the system to recruit good officials. They opened schools around the country to train young scholars in Confucianism, poetry, and other subjects covered in the exams. The few who passed the tough exams became part of an elite group of scholar-officials.

In theory, the exams were open to all men, even commoners. However, only the wealthy could afford the necessary years of education. Also, men with political connections could obtain high positions without taking the exams.

Despite these flaws, the system created a remarkably intelligent and capable governing class in China. Before the Tang Dynasty, a few noble families dominated the country. As the examination system grew in importance, talent and education became more important than noble birth in winning power. As a result, many moderately wealthy families shared in China's government.

THINK THROUGH HISTORY
B. Recognizing Effects What resulted from the revival of the civil service system?

The Tang Lose Power By the mid-700s, the Tang Dynasty was weakening. To pay for military expansion, Tang rulers reimposed crushing taxes. These brought hardship to the people but still failed to meet the rising costs of government. In times of famine, peasants fled their villages and roved the countryside in bandit gangs.

Moreover, the Tang could not control the vast empire they had built. In 751, Arab armies soundly defeated the Chinese on China's western frontier at the Battle of Talas. (See the map on pages 284–285.) Central Asia passed out of Chinese control and into foreign hands. After this time, border attacks and internal rebellions steadily chipped away at the power of the imperial government. Finally, in 907, Chinese rebels sacked and burned the Tang capital at Chang'an and murdered the last Tang emperor, a child.

Background
Recall the Mandate of Heaven (page 50), a concept the Chinese held to explain the decline and fall of dynasties.

The Song Dynasty Restores China

After the end of the Tang Dynasty, rival warlords divided China into separate kingdoms. In 960, an able general reunited China and proclaimed himself Song Taizu, the first Song (sung) emperor. The Song Dynasty, like the Tang, lasted about three centuries (960–1279). Although the Song ruled a smaller empire than either the Han or the Tang, China remained stable, powerful, and prosperous.

Song armies never regained the western lands lost after 751. Nor did they regain northern lands that had been lost to nomadic tribes during the Tang decline. For a time, Song emperors tried to buy peace with their northern enemies. They paid hefty annual tributes of silver, silk, and tea. This policy, however, ultimately failed to stop their threat. In the early 1100s, a Manchurian people called the Jurchen conquered northern China and established the Jin empire. The Jurchen forced the Song to retreat south across the Huang He. After 1126, the Song emperors ruled only southern China.

The Song ruling family fled south. They established a grand new capital at Hangzhou, a coastal city south of the Yangtze. Despite its military troubles, the dynasty of the Southern Song (1127–1279) saw rapid economic growth. The south had become the economic heartland of China. Merchants in southern cities grew rich from trade with Chinese in the north, nomads of Central Asia, and people of western Asia and Europe.

An Era of Prosperity and Innovation

The period of the Tang and Song dynasties was one of intense growth. China grew in population, trade, wealth, new ideas, and artistic achievements. In the span of three or four centuries, China's population nearly doubled, soaring to 100 million. By the Song era, China had at least ten cities with a population of 1 million each. China was the most populous country in the world. It was also the most advanced.

Science and Technology Artisans and scholars made important technological advances during the Tang and Song eras. Among the most important inventions were movable type and gunpowder. With **movable type,** a printer could arrange blocks of individual characters in a frame to make up a page for printing. Previously, printers had carved the words of a whole page into one large block. The development of gunpowder led to the creation of explosive weapons such as bombs, grenades, small rockets, and cannons. Other important inventions of this period include porcelain, the mechanical clock, paper money, and the use of the magnetic compass for sailing.

Inventions of Tang and Song China

	Date	Description	Impact
Porcelain	Late 700s	Bone-hard, white ceramic made of a special clay and a mineral found only in China	Became a valuable export—so associated with Chinese culture that it is now called "china"; technology remained a Chinese secret for centuries
Mechanical clock	700s	Clock in which machinery (driven by running water) regulated the movements	Early Chinese clocks short-lived; idea for mechanical clock carried by traders to medieval Europe
Printing	Block printing: 700s Movable type: 1040	Block printing: one block on which a whole page is cut; movable type: individual characters arranged in frames, used over and over	Printing technology spread to Korea and Japan; movable type also developed later in Europe
Gunpowder	800s	Explosive powder made from mixture of saltpeter, sulfur, and charcoal	First used for fireworks, then weapons; technology spread west within 300 years
Paper money	1020s	Paper currency issued by Song government to replace cumbersome strings of metal cash used by merchants	Contributed to development of large-scale commercial economy in China
Magnetic compass (for navigation)	1100s	Floating magnetized needle that always points north-south; device had existed in China for centuries before it was adapted by sailors for use at sea	Helped China become a sea power; technology quickly spread west

> **SKILLBUILDER: Interpreting Charts**
> 1. *Which inventions eventually affected warfare and exploration?*
> 2. *Which of these inventions do you think had the greatest impact on history? Why?*

Agriculture The rapid growth of China resulted from advances in farming. Farmers especially improved the cultivation of rice. In about the year 1000, China imported from Vietnam a new variety of fast-ripening rice. This allowed the farmers to harvest two rice crops each year rather than one. To make sure that farmers knew about the improved variety, Chinese officials distributed seedlings throughout the country. The agricultural improvements enabled China's farmers to produce more food. This was necessary to feed the rapidly expanding population in the cities.

Trade and Foreign Contacts Under the Tang and Song emperors, foreign trade flourished. Tang imperial armies guarded the great Silk Roads, which linked China to the West. Eventually, however, China lost control over these routes during the long Tang decline. After this time, Chinese merchants relied increasingly on ocean trade. Chinese advances in sailing technology, including use of the magnetic compass, made it possible for sea trade to expand. During the Song period, China developed into the greatest sea power in the world.

Song artist Ju Ran painted this masterpiece, *Buddhist Monastery in Stream and Mountain Landscape,* in the late tenth century.

THINK THROUGH HISTORY
C. Analyzing Causes What factors contributed to the expansion of sea trade during the Song Dynasty?

Up and down China's long coastline, the largest port cities in the world bustled with international trade. Merchant ships carried trade goods to Korea and Japan. They sailed across the Indian Ocean to India, the Persian Gulf, and even the coast of Africa. Chinese merchants established trading colonies around Southeast Asia. Many foreign traders, mostly Arabs, resided in Chinese cities. Through trade and travel, Chinese culture spread throughout East Asia. One major cultural export was Buddhism. This religion spread from China to Japan, Korea, and Vietnam.

The exchange of goods and ideas was two-way. During Tang times, tea first arrived in China from Southeast Asia. The Chinese became avid tea drinkers as well as tea producers. New ideas in mathematics and astronomy developed from contact with India. Foreign religions, including Islam and some Eastern sects of Christianity, also spread to China and won followers there.

A Golden Age of Art The prosperity of the Tang and Song dynasties nourished an age of artistic brilliance. The spread of wealth, education, and urban culture stimulated a high level of artistic creativity. Scholar-officials, for example, were expected to write poetry and to own at least one fine painting.

The Tang period produced great poetry. Two of its most celebrated poets were Li Bo, who wrote about life's pleasures, and Du Fu, who praised orderliness and Confucian virtues. Du Fu also wrote critically about war and the hardships of soldiers. Once he himself was captured by rebels and taken to Chang'an, the capital city. He had sent his family to the village of Fuzhou for safety. Here he describes their separation.

A VOICE FROM THE PAST
The same moon is above Fuzhou tonight; From the open window she will be watching it alone, The poor children are too little To be able to remember Chang'an. Her perfumed hair will be dampened by the dew, The air may be too chilly on her delicate arms. When can we both lean by the wind-blown curtains And see the tears dry on each other's face?
DU FU, "Moonlight Night"

Chinese painting reached new heights of beauty and expression during the Song Dynasty. Painting of this era shows the influence of the Daoist love of nature. Artists emphasized the beauty of natural landscapes—lofty mountains, rippling brooks—and objects such as a single branch or flower. The artists did not use brightly colored paints. Black ink was their favorite paint. Said one Song artist, "Black is ten colors."

Changes in Chinese Society

China's prosperity produced many social changes during the Tang and Song periods. Chinese society became increasingly mobile. People moved to the cities in increasing numbers. The Chinese also experienced greater social mobility than ever before. The growing cities offered many opportunities for managers, professionals, and skilled workers. However, the most important avenue for social advancement was the civil service system.

Levels of Society During Tang and Song times the power of the old aristocratic families faded. A new, much larger upper class emerged, made up of scholar-officials and their families. Such a class of powerful, well-to-do people is called the **gentry.** The gentry attained their status through education and civil service positions, rather than through land ownership. However, many scholar-officials also became wealthy enough to own land.

Below the gentry was an urban middle class. It included merchants, shopkeepers, skilled artisans, minor officials, and others. At the bottom of urban society were laborers, soldiers, and servants. In the countryside lived the largest class by far, the peasants. They toiled for wealthy landowners as they had for centuries.

The Status of Women Women had always been subservient to men in Chinese society. Their status further declined during the Tang and Song periods. This was especially true among the upper classes in cities. There a woman's work was deemed less important to the family's prosperity and status. Changing attitudes affected peasant families less, however. Peasant women worked in the fields and helped produce their family's food and income.

One sign of the changing status of women was the custom of binding the feet of upper-class girls. The practice of foot binding began during this period and continued into the 20th century. When a girl was very young, her feet were bound tightly with cloth, which eventually broke the arch and curled all but the big toe under. This produced what was admiringly called a "lily-foot." Women with bound feet were crippled for life. To others in society, such a woman reflected the wealth and prestige of her husband, who could afford such a beautiful but impractical wife.

The social, economic, and technological transformations of the Tang and Song period permanently shaped Chinese civilization. They endured even as the Middle Kingdom fell to a group of nomadic outsiders, the Mongols, whom you will learn about in Section 2.

THINK THROUGH HISTORY
D. Making Inferences How did the practice of foot binding reflect the changing status of Chinese women?

Daily Life

A Scholar's Fingernails
Many scholar-officials eventually adopted the fashion of growing their fingernails long. A two-inch fingernail showed clearly that the owner did no manual labor. However, long nails did not prevent the scholar from following the pursuits of the gentry, such as writing poetry, painting, or practicing calligraphy. The photograph above is of a Chinese doctor in the late 19th century.

Section 1 Assessment

1. TERMS & NAMES

Identify
• Tang Taizong
• Wu Zhao
• movable type
• gentry

2. TAKING NOTES

Create a Venn diagram showing the similarities and differences between the Tang and Song dynasties.

Tang only

Both

Song only

3. RECOGNIZING EFFECTS

What impact did improvements in transportation have on Tang and Song China?

THINK ABOUT
• ways transportation was improved
• how these improvements were made
• relationships among regions in China
• trade with other countries

4. ANALYZING THEMES

Empire Building What actions taken by the Sui, Tang, and Song emperors strengthened China's empire? What actions weakened it?

THINK ABOUT
• military gains and losses
• changes to the government
• improvements in transportation and trade
• cultural changes

Healing Arts

Since illness is a part of living, every society has developed ways to treat health problems. For thousands of years, Chinese doctors have used acupuncture to relieve pain and cure diseases. During the Song Dynasty, the Chinese carefully studied human anatomy and created charts and models of the body. These improved the practice of acupuncture.

Acupuncture developed from traditional Chinese beliefs about the forces of nature. Likewise, in other cultures, the healing arts have been shaped by the cultures' beliefs about nature. Think about this connection as you read about the practices described here.

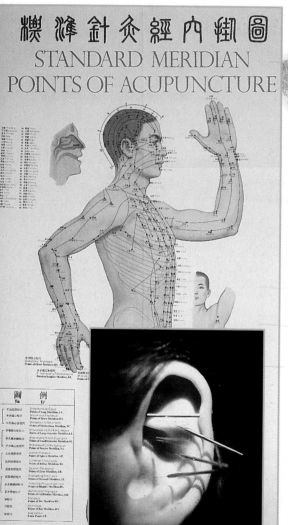

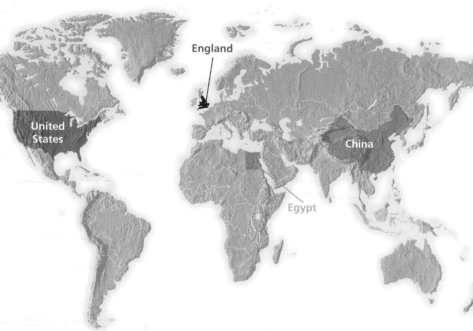

Chinese Acupuncture

Acupuncture is based on the belief that an energy force known as *qi* (chee) flows through the body and keeps people alive. According to this idea, *qi* flows along channels called meridians. Pain or illness arises when the *qi* does not flow properly. The treatment is to insert slender needles in the body at specific points (such as the ear) along the meridians, depending on the problem. This adjusts the flow of *qi* and restores health.

a closer look CHINESE MEDICINE

Qigong (chee·GONG) is a traditional Chinese healing art. It combines movement with deep breathing and meditation. These exercises are designed to maintain health by keeping the *qi* in proper balance.

A Physician, Ancient Egypt

Health care in ancient Egypt was remarkably complex. The Egyptians believed that gods and demons influenced health. Therefore, a doctor's treatment often called for certain spells, chants, or prayers. At the same time, doctors had a great deal of practical knowledge about symptoms and useful treatments and medicines. The Egyptians passed down their medical knowledge by recording it on scrolls and tablets. This stone tablet from about 2600 B.C. shows a portrait of Hesy-Re, one of the earliest known physicians.

Stone Age Surgery, England

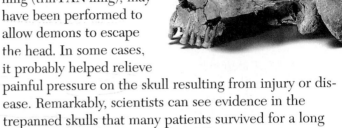

Archaeologists have discovered many Stone Age skulls, such as this one found in England, with portions deliberately removed. This procedure, called trepanning (trih·PAN·ihng), may have been performed to allow demons to escape the head. In some cases, it probably helped relieve painful pressure on the skull resulting from injury or disease. Remarkably, scientists can see evidence in the trepanned skulls that many patients survived for a long time after their operation.

Modern Surgery, U.S.A.

The scientific approach of Western medicine reflects the modern belief that technology can improve people's lives. Brain surgery, as shown below, has been transformed by high-tech equipment, specialized training, pain-killing drugs, and other advances. Today's scientific medicine has made some diseases less threatening and increased the human life span.

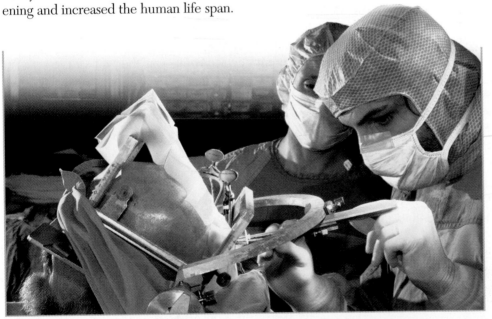

Connect *to* History

Making Inferences Look again at the healing arts of the four cultures described on these pages. How are each culture's beliefs about nature reflected in the culture's health practices?

SEE SKILLBUILDER HANDBOOK, PAGE 1005

Connect *to* Today

Interviewing Conduct a brief interview with someone who practices a non-Western or "alternative" type of medicine. Find out if this type of medicine has changed over time and, if so, how. Share what you learn with your classmates.

INTERNET CONNECTION

Visit us at **www.mcdougallittell.com** to learn more about the healing arts.

The tradition of Chinese herbal medicine dates back thousands of years. This modern pharmacy in Singapore dispenses Chinese medicines. Pharmacists may stock 1,500 herbs for use as remedies. Medicines can also include bark, twigs, and animal or insect parts.

The Mongol Conquests

MAIN IDEA	**WHY IT MATTERS NOW**
The Mongols, a nomadic people from the steppe, conquered settled societies across much of Asia.	The Mongols built the largest unified land empire in world history.

SETTING THE STAGE While the Chinese grew prosperous during the Song Dynasty, a great people far to the north were also gaining strength. The Mongols of the Asian steppe lived their lives on the move. They prided themselves on their skill on horseback, their discipline, their ruthlessness, and their courage in battle. They also wanted the wealth and glory that would come with conquering mighty empires. Conflict between these nomadic people and settled peoples across Eurasia was about to explode into violence. The Mongol conquests would forever transform Asia and Europe.

Nomads of the Asian Steppe

Across the landmass of Eurasia—from Manchuria to Hungary—stretches a vast belt of dry grassland called the steppe. The significance of the steppe to neighboring civilizations was twofold. First, it served as a land trade route connecting the East and the West. Second, it was home to nomadic peoples who frequently swept into the cities to plunder, loot, and conquer.

Geography of the Steppe There are two main expanses of the Eurasian steppe. The western steppe spans from Central Asia to eastern Europe. It was the original home of many of the ancient invaders you have read about, including the Hittites and the Aryans. The eastern steppe, covering the area of present-day Mongolia, was the first home of the Huns, the Turks, and the Mongols.

Very little rain falls on the steppe, but the dry, wind-swept plain supports short, hardy grasses. Temperature changes can be extreme. The temperature in Mongolia, for example, ranges from –57°F in winter to 96°F in the summer.

Rainfall is somewhat more plentiful and the climate milder in the western steppe than in the east. For this reason, movements of people have historically tended to be toward the west and the south.

The boundaries of the steppe were constantly shifting and were often less geographical than political. One way of defining where the steppe ended was to say where cultivated fields began. The Chinese, for example, were constantly trying to push back the line in order to extend the area under their cultivation.

The Nomadic Way of Life

Nomadic peoples were **pastoralists**—that is, they herded

THINK THROUGH HISTORY
A. Identifying Problems What conditions on the steppe might have discouraged agriculture?

The Steppe

SIBERIA

EUROPE

Moscow

Kiev

ASIA

WESTERN STEPPE

Aral Sea

EASTERN STEPPE

Constantinople

Caspian Sea

Tashkent

Karakorum

GOBI DESERT

Samarkand

Kashgar

Beijing

CHINA

INDIA

Kaifeng

0 1,000 Miles

0 2,000 Kilometers

N

80°E

40°N

GEOGRAPHY SKILLBUILDER: Interpreting Maps
1. **Region** *About how far does the western steppe extend from west to east?*
2. **Location** *About how far is Beijing from the edge of the eastern steppe?*

Many people on the Mongolian steppe still follow the nomadic way of life. This photograph shows modern Mongolians outside their yurt.

domesticated animals. They were constantly on the move, searching for good pasture to feed their herds. Nomads did not wander. Rather, they followed a familiar seasonal pattern and returned on a regular basis to the same campsites. Keeping claim to land that was not permanently occupied was difficult. Battles frequently arose among nomadic groups over grassland and water rights.

Asian nomads practically lived on horseback as they followed their huge herds over the steppe. They depended on their animals for food, clothing, and housing. Their diet consisted of meat and mare's milk. They wore clothing made of skins and wool, and they lived in portable felt tents called **yurts.**

Steppe nomads traveled together in kinship groups called **clans.** The members of each clan claimed to be descended from a common ancestor. Clans required good leaders to make decisions about when to leave one pasture for another and to devise military strategies. Different clans sometimes came together when they needed a large force to attack a common enemy or raid their settled neighbors.

Steppe Nomads and Settled Societies The differing ways of life of nomadic and settled peoples resulted in constant interaction between them. Often, they engaged in peaceful trade. The nomads exchanged horses, for example, for basic items they lacked, such as grain, metal, cloth, and tea. Nomads were accustomed to scarcity and hardship. They prided themselves on their toughness. However, they were sometimes tempted by the rich land and relative wealth of townspeople and took what they wanted by force. As a result, settled peoples lived in constant danger of raids.

Time and again in history, nomadic peoples rode out of the steppe to invade border towns and villages. When a state or empire was strong and organized, it could protect its frontier. The Chinese, for example, built and rebuilt the Great Wall in an attempt to keep out nomadic invaders. If the state or empire became divided and weak, this provided an opportunity for nomads to increase their attacks and gain more plunder. They might even take over a region and settle there.

Occasionally, a powerful group, such as the Mongols under Genghis Khan, was able to conquer a whole empire and become its rulers. Over generations, these nomadic rulers often became part of the civilization they conquered.

THINK THROUGH HISTORY
B. Making Inferences How might a strong, organized empire defend its frontier?

The Rise of the Mongols

For centuries, the Mongol people had roamed the eastern steppe in loosely organized clans. It took a military and political genius to unite the Mongols into a force with a single purpose—conquest.

Genghis Khan Unites the Mongols Around 1200, a Mongol khan, or clan leader, named Temujin sought to unify the clans under his leadership. Across the Mongolian steppe, he defeated his rivals one by one, showing no mercy. In 1206, Temujin accepted the title **Genghis Khan,** or "universal ruler" of the Mongol clans.

Over the next 21 years, Genghis led the Mongols in conquering much of Asia. His first goal was China. After invading the northern Jin empire in 1215, however, his attention turned to the Islamic region west of Mongolia. Angered by the murder of Mongol traders and an

HISTORY MAKERS

**Genghis Khan
1162?–1227**

Temujin, according to legend, was born with a blood clot in his fist. In his lifetime, his hands were often covered with the blood of others.

When he was about nine, his father was poisoned by the Tatars, a rival people. For a time, he and his family lived in extreme poverty, abandoned by their clan. When in manhood he fought and defeated the Tatars, he slaughtered every male taller than a cart axle. The survivors—the females and only the youngest male children—were brought up as his followers.

While driven by revenge, Genghis also loved conquest. He once remarked to his personal historian:

Man's greatest good fortune is to chase and defeat his enemy, seize his total possessions, leave his married women weeping and wailing, [and] ride his [horse]. . . .

ambassador at the hands of the Muslims, Genghis launched a campaign of terror across Central Asia. "In retribution for every hair on their heads it seemed that a hundred thousand heads rolled in the dust," wrote a court historian of Genghis's revenge. The Mongols destroyed one city after another—Utrar, Samarkand, Bukhara—and slaughtered many inhabitants. By 1221, Central Asia was under Mongol control.

Genghis the Conqueror Several characteristics lay behind Genghis Khan's stunning success as a conqueror. First, he was a brilliant organizer. He assembled his Mongol warriors into a mighty fighting force (see below). Following the model of the Chinese military, Genghis grouped his warriors in armies of 10,000. These in turn were organized into 1,000-man brigades, 100-man companies, and 10-man platoons. He put his most battle-proven and loyal men in command of these units.

Second, Genghis was a gifted strategist. He used various tricks to confuse his enemy. Sometimes, a small Mongol cavalry unit would attack, then pretend to gallop away in flight. The enemy usually gave chase. Then the rest of the Mongol army would appear suddenly and slaughter the exhausted enemy forces. Another strategy was to make the enemy believe that the Mongol army was bigger than it actually was. This was done by dressing prisoners or lifelike dummies as Mongol warriors. Genghis also used spies brilliantly to find out enemy weaknesses.

Third, Genghis adopted new weapons and technologies used by his enemies. For example, he put captured Chinese engineers to work building catapults and creating gunpowder charges. He then used the weapons to conquer other Chinese cities.

Finally, Genghis Khan used cruelty as a weapon. He believed in terrifying his enemies into surrender. If a city refused to open its gates to him, he might kill the entire population when he finally captured the place. The terror the Mongols inspired spread ahead of their armies, which led many towns to surrender without a fight. As one Arab historian wrote, "In the countries that have not yet been overrun by them, everyone spends the night afraid that they may appear there too."

THINK THROUGH HISTORY
C. Summarizing
What were some of the tactics Genghis Khan used in war?

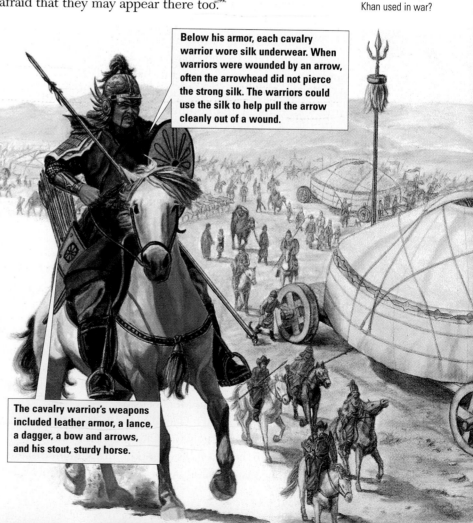

Below his armor, each cavalry warrior wore silk underwear. When warriors were wounded by an arrow, often the arrowhead did not pierce the strong silk. The warriors could use the silk to help pull the arrow cleanly out of a wound.

A Mighty Fighting Force

Mongol soldiers were superb horsemen, having spent all their lives in the saddle. Annual game roundups gave young men the chance to practice skills they would use in battle and gave their leaders the opportunity to spot promising warriors.

When on the move, each soldier was accompanied by three extra horses. By changing mounts, soldiers could stay in the saddle for up to ten days and nights at a time. When charging towards a target, they covered as much as 120 miles a day. If food was scarce, a Mongol soldier might make a small gash in the neck of one of his horses and sustain himself by drinking the blood.

A key to Mongol horsemanship was the stirrup, which was invented on the steppe in the second century B.C. Stirrups enabled a mounted warrior to stand, turn, and shoot arrows behind him.

The cavalry warrior's weapons included leather armor, a lance, a dagger, a bow and arrows, and his stout, sturdy horse.

The Mongol Empire

Genghis Khan died in 1227—not from violence, but from illness. His successors, however, continued to expand his empire. In less than 50 years, the Mongols conquered territory from China to Poland. In so doing, they created the largest unified land empire in history. (See the map on page 298.)

The Khanates Following the death of Genghis Khan, his son Ogadai became the Great Khan. The Great Khan headed the whole Mongol Empire. Under his leadership, Mongol armies commanded by Genghis's other sons and grandsons drove armies south, east and west out of Inner Asia. They completed their conquest of northern China and invaded Korea. They leveled the Russian city of Kiev and reached the banks of the Adriatic Sea. The cities of Venice and Vienna were within their grasp. No one knows how far west into Europe the Mongols might have penetrated. But Ogadai died in 1241. The commanders were called back to their capital to elect his successor. The westward campaign ended.

By 1260, the Mongol Empire was divided into four large khanates, each of them ruled by a descendant of Genghis. These four were the Khanate of the Great Khan (Mongolia and China), the Khanate of Chagatai (Central Asia), the Ilkhanate (Persia), and the Khanate of the Golden Horde (Russia). Kublai Khan, a grandson of Genghis Khan, named himself the Great Khan in 1260.

The Mongols as Rulers Many of the areas invaded by the Mongols never recovered. The populations of some cities were wiped out. Even worse, the Mongols destroyed ancient irrigation systems in areas such as the Tigris and Euphrates valleys. Thus the land could no longer support resettlement. One Persian assessed the destruction:

> ### A VOICE FROM THE PAST
> There can be no doubt that even if for a thousand years to come no evil befalls the country, yet will it not be possible to completely repair the damage, and bring back the land to the state in which it was formerly.
>
> **HAMD-ALLAH MUSTAWFI,** *The Geographical Part of the Nuzhat al-Qulub*

THINK THROUGH HISTORY
D. Identifying Problems What problems might the Mongols have faced in holding their vast empire together?

Over time, some Mongol rulers adopted aspects of the culture of the people they ruled. The Ilkhans and the Golden Horde became Muslims. The Great Khans made use of Chinese institutions. The growing cultural differences among the khanates contributed to the eventual splitting up of the empire.

The Mongol Peace From the mid-1200s to the mid-1300s, the Mongols imposed stability and law and order across much of Eurasia. This period is sometimes called the Mongol Peace. The Mongols guaranteed safe passage of trade caravans, travelers, and missionaries from one end of the empire to another. Trade between Europe and Asia had

Mongol women took primary responsibility for the needs of the camp, milked the livestock, and treated the wounded. Some also fought as warriors.

The khan and other leaders had great mobile yurts pulled by teams of oxen.

A Mongol army was like a moving city. The cavalry of 10,000 was accompanied by an even greater number of family members, and by tens of thousands of horses and livestock.

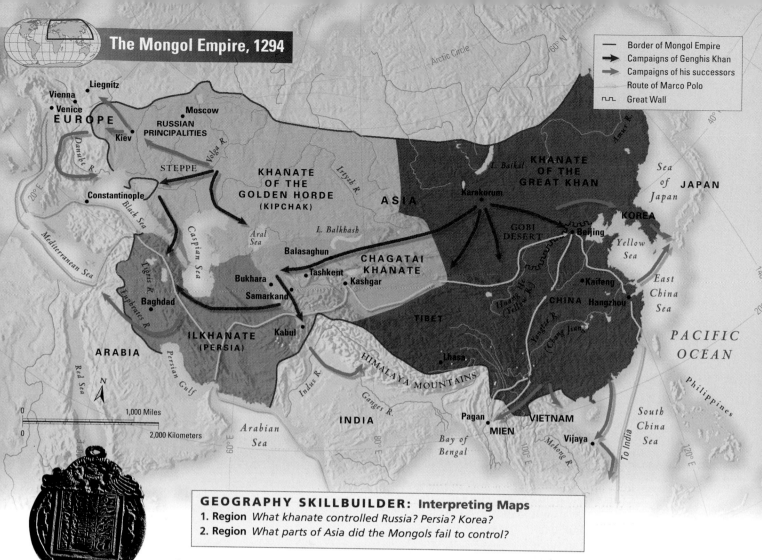

The Mongol Empire, 1294

Liegnitz
Vienna
Venice
EUROPE
Moscow
RUSSIAN PRINCIPALITIES
Kiev
Danube R.
Volga R.
STEPPE
Constantinople
Black Sea
Caspian Sea
Mediterranean Sea
Aral Sea
L. Balkbash
Irtysb R.
KHANATE OF THE GOLDEN HORDE (KIPCHAK)
ASIA
Balasaghun
Bukhara
Samarkand
Tashkent
Kashgar
CHAGATAI KHANATE
L. Baikal
Karakorum
KHANATE OF THE GREAT KHAN
Sea of Japan
JAPAN
KOREA
GOBI DESERT
Beijing
Yellow Sea
Kaifeng
Hangzhou
CHINA
East China Sea
Baghdad
Tigris R.
Euphrates R.
Persian Gulf
ILKHANATE (PERSIA)
Kabul
ARABIA
Red Sea
N
TIBET
Lhasa
Huang He (Yellow R.)
Yangtze R. (Chang Jiang)
PACIFIC OCEAN
Philippines
HIMALAYA MOUNTAINS
Indus R.
Ganges R.
INDIA
Arabian Sea
Bay of Bengal
Pagan
MIEN
VIETNAM
Vijaya
Mekong R.
South China Sea
To India

0   1,000 Miles
0   2,000 Kilometers

Legend:
— Border of Mongol Empire
→ Campaigns of Genghis Khan
→ Campaigns of his successors
— Route of Marco Polo
ᴖᴖ Great Wall

Arctic Circle

GEOGRAPHY SKILLBUILDER: Interpreting Maps
1. **Region** What khanate controlled Russia? Persia? Korea?
2. **Region** What parts of Asia did the Mongols fail to control?

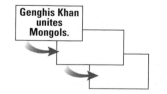

Messengers carried medallions like the one above as passports, so they could travel safely across the Mongol Empire.

never been more active. Ideas and inventions traveled along with the trade goods. Many Chinese innovations, such as gunpowder, reached Europe during this period.

Other things spread along with the goods and the ideas. Some historians speculate that the epidemic of bubonic plague that devastated Europe during the 1300s was first spread by the Mongols. (See Chapter 14.) The disease might have spread along trade routes or have been passed to others by infected Mongol troops.

For a brief period of history, the nomadic Mongols were the lords of city-based civilizations across Asia, including China. As you will read in Section 3, China continued to thrive under Mongol rule.

Section 2 Assessment

1. TERMS & NAMES

Identify
• pastoralist
• clan
• Genghis Khan

2. TAKING NOTES

Using a chart like the one below, list the series of events leading to the creation of the Mongol Empire.

```
Genghis Khan
unites
Mongols.
          →
              →
```

Write a news report describing the most important event you listed.

3. MAKING INFERENCES

What characteristics of Mongol culture do you think contributed to their military success? Explain your response.

THINK ABOUT
• how the nomadic way of life shaped Mongol culture
• the personality and leadership qualities of Genghis Khan
• Mongol weapons and tactics

4. THEME ACTIVITY

Cultural Interaction Draw a diagram showing the interaction between various cultures and the Mongols who conquered them. Consider influence on economic development, military tactics, and religious beliefs.

Empire of the Great Khan

MAIN IDEA	WHY IT MATTERS NOW
Kublai Khan ruled China and encouraged foreign trade, but the Yuan Dynasty was beset by problems.	The influence of Chinese ideas on Western civilization began with the Mongols' encouragement of trade.

SETTING THE STAGE Kublai Khan, the grandson of Genghis Khan, assumed the title Great Khan in 1260. In theory, the Great Khan ruled the entire Mongol Empire. In reality, the empire had split into four khanates. Other descendants of Genghis ruled Central Asia, Persia, and Russia as semi-independent states. The Great Khan focused instead on extending the power and range of his own khanate, which already included Mongolia, Korea, Tibet, and northern China. To begin, Kublai had to fulfill the goal of his grandfather to conquer all of China.

Kublai Khan Conquers China

It took three generations of Mongol leaders to complete the conquest of China begun by Genghis Khan. In 1234, Genghis's son Ogadai conquered northern China. This opened southern China to direct attack. Chinese soldiers in the south held off the Mongols for 40 years, but the armies of Kublai Khan finally overwhelmed them in 1279.

Throughout China's long history, the Chinese feared and fought off invasions of northern nomads. China sometimes lost territory to nomadic groups, but no foreigner had ever ruled the whole country. The first to do so was Kublai Khan.

This helmet was worn by a Mongol officer.

Beginning a New Dynasty As China's new emperor, **Kublai Khan** founded a new dynasty called the Yuan (yoo·AHN) Dynasty. It lasted less than a century, until 1368, when it was overthrown. However, the Yuan era was an important period in Chinese history for several reasons. First, Kublai Khan united China for the first time in 300 years. For this he is considered one of China's great emperors. Second, the control imposed by the Mongols across all of Asia opened China to greater foreign contacts and trade. Finally, Kublai and his successors tolerated Chinese culture and made few changes to the system of government.

Unlike his Mongol ancestors, Kublai spent almost his entire life in China. Far from the Mongolian steppe, he did not share his ancestors' hatred of civilization. On the contrary, he rather enjoyed living in the luxurious manner of a Chinese emperor. He maintained a beautiful summer palace at Shangdu, on the border between Mongolia and China. He also built a new square-walled capital at the site of modern Beijing. The size of Kublai's palace in Beijing greatly impressed the European traveler Marco Polo, who called it "the largest that was ever seen."

Background
Shangdu is the origin of the English word *Xanadu*, which means an idyllic, beautiful place.

A VOICE FROM THE PAST
The hall is so vast and so wide that a meal might well be served there for more than 6,000 men. . . . The whole building is at once so immense and so well constructed that no man in the world . . . could imagine any improvement in design or execution.

MARCO POLO, *The Travels of Marco Polo*

This detail from a 13th-century Japanese scroll depicts Japanese warriors fighting off a Mongol warship.

Kublai built this palace to enhance his prestige, but his new capital meant something more. Previously, the Great Khans had ruled their empire from Mongolia. Moving the capital from Mongolia to China was a sign that Kublai intended to make his mark as emperor of China.

Failure to Conquer Japan After conquering China, Kublai Khan tried to extend his rule to Japan. In 1274 and again in 1281, the Great Khan sent huge fleets against Japan. The Mongols forced Koreans to build, sail, and provide provisions for the boats, a costly task that almost ruined Korea. Both times the Japanese turned back the Mongol fleets.

The second fleet carried 150,000 Mongol, Chinese, and Korean warriors—the largest seaborne invasion force in history until World War II. After 53 days, Japanese warriors had fought the invaders to a standstill. Then, on the following day, the sky darkened and a typhoon swept furiously across the Sea of Japan. Mongol ships were upended, swamped, and dashed to bits against the rocky shore, despite their sailors' attempts to escape onto the open sea. Many Mongols drowned and the Japanese quickly slew many others. For centuries afterward, the Japanese spoke reverently of the *kamikaze*, or "divine wind," that had saved Japan.

Mongol Rule in China

Early in Kublai Khan's reign, one of his Chinese advisers told him, "I have heard that one can conquer the empire on horseback, but one cannot govern it on horseback." This advice illustrates the problems faced by Kublai Khan in ruling China. Mongol ways would not work in a sophisticated civilization like China's. Besides, the number of Mongols in China was few compared to the huge native population. Kublai would need to make use of Chinese institutions and non-Mongol officials to help him rule successfully.

The Mongols and the Chinese The Mongol rulers had little in common with their Chinese subjects. Because of their differences, the Mongols kept their separate identity. Mongols lived apart from the Chinese and obeyed different laws. They even kept the Chinese out of high government offices, although they retained as many Chinese officials as possible to serve on the local level. The Mongol rulers gave most of the highest government posts to Mongols and to foreigners. Foreigners included Muslims from western Asia and Christians such as Marco Polo of Venice. The Mongols believed that foreigners were more trustworthy than the Chinese since the foreigners had no local loyalties.

HISTORY MAKERS

Kublai Khan
1215–1294

As ruler of both China and the Mongol Empire, Kublai Khan straddled two worlds. He built luxurious palaces, dressed as a Chinese emperor, and supported the work of Chinese artists. However, he remained a Mongol warrior at heart.

The Great Khan is said to have planted a plot of grass from the steppe in the gardens at Beijing to remind himself of his home. He also loved to hunt and enclosed a large hunting ground at his palace at Shangdu.

Kublai also preserved the customs of his nomadic ancestors. Every August 28, he performed the Mongol ritual of the scattering of mare's milk to honor his ancestors and ensure a year of good luck. The rite involved calling out the name of Genghis Khan and scattering over the ground the milk that came from a special herd of white horses.

Despite his differences with the Chinese, Kublai Khan was an able leader. He restored the Grand Canal, which had been built during the Sui Dynasty, and extended it 135 miles north to Beijing. Along its banks a paved highway ran for 1,100 miles, from Hangzhou to Beijing. These routes ensured the north of a steady supply of grain and other goods from the southern heartland.

Background
Since the decline of the Tang Dynasty after 900, robbers and warring peoples had nearly shut down the caravan routes across Central Asia.

Encouragement of Foreign Trade Kublai Khan also encouraged foreign trade. The Mongol Peace made the caravan routes across Central Asia safe for trade and travel. Kublai Khan established post roads, or mail routes, that linked China to India and Persia and greatly improved trade. He invited foreign merchants to visit China. Most of them were Muslims from India, Central Asia, and Persia. Many European travelers, including Christian missionaries, also reached China.

Over the Silk Roads and other routes, traders transported Chinese silk and porcelain, which continued to be desired in Europe and western Asia. Other Chinese products and inventions that went west included printing, gunpowder, the compass, paper currency, and playing cards.

Marco Polo at the Mongol Court The most famous European to visit China in these years was a young Venetian trader, **Marco Polo.** With his father and uncle, he traveled by caravan on the Silk Roads, arriving at Kublai Khan's court around 1275. Marco had learned several Asian languages in his travels, and Kublai Khan sent him to various Chinese cities on government missions. Polo served the Great Khan well for 17 years. In 1292, two years before Kublai died, the Polos left China and made the long journey back to Venice. They traveled by sea around Southeast Asia and India.

THINK THROUGH HISTORY
B. Analyzing Motives Why do you think Kublai Khan employed Marco Polo?

Later, during a war against Venice's rival city, Genoa, Marco Polo was captured and imprisoned. In prison he had time to tell the full story of his travels and adventures. To his awed listeners, he spoke of China's fabulous cities, its fantastic wealth, and the strange things he had seen there. He mentioned the burning of "black stones" (coal) in Chinese homes. (Coal as a fuel was little known in Europe.) He also recorded the practical workings of the khan's government and aspects of Chinese life. Here is his description of trade in Beijing.

> **A VOICE FROM THE PAST**
> More precious and costly wares are imported into Khanbalik [Beijing] than into any other city in the world. . . . All the treasures that come from India—precious stones, pearls, and other rarities—are brought here. So too are the choicest and costliest products of Cathay [China] itself and every other province. . . . Every day more than 1,000 cart loads of silk enter the city; for much cloth of gold and silk is woven here.
>
> **MARCO POLO,** *The Travels of Marco Polo*

A fellow prisoner gathered Polo's stories into a book. It was an instant success in Europe, but most readers did not believe a word of it. They thought Polo's account was a marvelous collection of tall tales. It was clear to Marco Polo, however, that the civilization he had visited was the greatest in the world.

The End of Mongol Rule

During the last years of Kublai Khan's reign, cracks began to form under the surface of Mongol rule. In an attempt to further expand his empire, he sent several expeditions into Southeast Asia. His armies and navies suffered many humiliating defeats at a huge expense of lives and equipment. Heavy spending on fruitless wars, on public

HISTORY MAKERS

**Marco Polo
1254?–1324**
The man who described Kublai Khan to Europeans left behind very little information about himself. He was 17 when he set out from Venice with his father and uncle, who were on their second visit to Kublai's court. According to Marco, Kublai recognized his "merit and worth" and sent him on special missions around the empire. His impressions of China became the basis of his book, but he described few actual events about his life.

Since his book first appeared, people have debated whether or not Marco Polo actually saw all that he claimed to have seen. He is not mentioned in Chinese accounts of this time. His tales also fail to mention such common features of China as tea, acupuncture, or foot binding.

On his deathbed, Polo was asked if his travel stories were true. He replied that he had told barely half of what he had seen.

Empires in East Asia

850 Gunpowder invented

1215 Genghis Khan invades northern China

1275 Marco Polo reaches China

| Sui | Tang | | Song | Southern Song | Yuan |

500 A.D.   800 A.D.   WARFARE AND REVOLT   1100 A.D.   1400 A.D.

627 Tang Taizong becomes emperor

690 Empress Wu Zhao assumes throne

751 Chinese lose Battle of Talas

1024 Government issues paper money

1040 Movable type invented

1126 Song Dynasty retreats to south

1260 Kublai becomes Great Khan

works, and on the luxuries of the Yuan court burdened the treasury and created resentment among the overtaxed Chinese. This presented problems that Kublai's less able successors could not resolve.

Yuan Dynasty Overthrown Kublai Khan died in 1294. He was nearly 80. Mongol rule weakened after his death. Although the Yuan Dynasty remained in power for another 74 years, family members struggled among themselves over who would rule. In one 8-year period, four different khans took the throne.

Rebellions broke out in many parts of China in the 1300s. The Chinese had long resented their Mongol rulers, and the Mongol humiliation of the Chinese only increased under Kublai Khan's successors. The rebellions were also fueled by years of famine, flood, and disease, along with growing economic problems and official corruption. In 1368, Chinese rebels finally overthrew the Mongols and seized power. The rebel leader founded a new dynasty—the Ming—which you will read about in Chapter 19.

Some Mongols remained in China during the Ming Dynasty and were valued for their skill as cavalrymen. Many others, however, returned to their homelands on the Mongolian steppe.

Decline of the Mongol Empire By the end of the Yuan Dynasty in China, the entire Mongol Empire had disintegrated. The government of the Ilkhanate in Persia fell apart in the 1330s. The Chagatai khans ruled Central Asia until the 1370s. Only the Golden Horde in Russia stayed in power. The Golden Horde ruled Russia for 250 years. As discussed in Chapter 11, Ivan III finally asserted Russia's independence from the Mongols in 1480.

The rise and fall of Mongol rule affected civilizations from eastern Europe to China. Despite the efforts of Kublai Khan, Mongol domination never extended to Japan. However, several centuries earlier, the Japanese had embraced the influence of an outside culture—that of China—as its civilization developed. This development is described in Section 4.

THINK THROUGH HISTORY
C. Analyzing Causes What factors contributed to the decline and fall of the Yuan Dynasty?

Section ③ Assessment

1. TERMS & NAMES

Identify
• Kublai Khan
• Marco Polo

2. TAKING NOTES

Create a web diagram showing the impact of Kublai Khan on East Asia.

Choose an event from your diagram and explain how it affected China. Did the event make China stronger or weaker?

3. EVALUATING DECISIONS

Judging from the events of the Yuan Dynasty, do you think the Mongol policies toward the Chinese were effective?

THINK ABOUT
• the accomplishments of Kublai Khan as emperor of China
• the Mongols' policies towards the Chinese
• the military campaigns of Kublai Khan
• the fate of the Yuan Dynasty

4. ANALYZING THEMES

Cultural Interaction What evidence is there that the Chinese way of life influenced the Mongol conquerors?

THINK ABOUT
• the seat of Kublai Khan's empire
• Kublai's actions as emperor of China

4 Feudal Powers in Japan

MAIN IDEA	WHY IT MATTERS NOW
Japanese civilization was shaped by cultural borrowing from China and the rise of feudalism and military rulers.	An openness to adapting innovations from other cultures is still a hallmark of Japanese society.

SETTING THE STAGE Japan lies east of China, in the direction of the sunrise. In fact, the name *Japan* comes from the Chinese words *ri ben,* which mean "origin of the sun." From ancient times, Japan had borrowed ideas, institutions, and culture from the Chinese people. Japan's genius was its ability to take in new ideas and make them uniquely its own.

The Growth of Japanese Civilization

Japan's island location shaped the growth of its civilization. About 120 miles of water separate Japan from its closest neighbor, Korea, and 500 miles separate Japan from China. In their early history, the Japanese were close enough to feel the civilizing effect of China. Yet they were far enough away to be reasonably safe from invasion.

The Geography of Japan About 4,000 islands make up the Japanese archipelago (AHR·kuh·PEHL·uh·GOH), or island group, that extends in an arc about 1,200 miles long. If Japan were superimposed over eastern North America, the islands would extend from Montreal, Canada, to Tallahassee, Florida. Most Japanese people have always lived on the four largest islands: Hokkaido (hah·KY·doh), Honshu (HAHN·shoo), Shikoku (shih·KOH·koo), and Kyushu (kee·OO·shoo).

Japan's geography has both advantages and disadvantages. Southern Japan enjoys a mild climate with plenty of rainfall. The country is so mountainous, however, that only 15 percent of the land is suitable for farming. Natural resources such as coal, oil, and iron are in short supply. During the late summer and early fall, strong tropical storms called typhoons occur. Earthquakes and tidal waves are also threats.

Early Japan The first historic mention of Japan comes from Chinese writings of about A.D. 300. Japan at this time was not a united country. Instead, hundreds of clans controlled their own territories.

Each clan worshiped its own nature gods and goddesses. In different parts of Japan, people honored thousands of local deities. Their varied customs and beliefs eventually combined to form Japan's earliest religion. In later times, this religion was called **Shinto** (SHIHN·toh), meaning "way of the gods."

Shinto had no complex rituals or philosophy. Instead, it was based on respect for the forces of

Vocabulary
typhoons: tropical cyclones that occur in the western Pacific or Indian oceans. (Cyclones in the Atlantic and Caribbean are called hurricanes.)

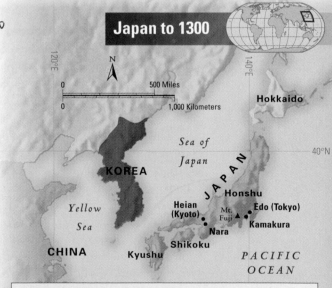

Japan to 1300

KOREA
Sea of Japan
JAPAN
Hokkaido
Honshu
Heian (Kyoto)
Mt. Fuji
Edo (Tokyo)
Nara
Kamakura
Shikoku
Yellow Sea
CHINA
Kyushu
PACIFIC OCEAN

500 Miles
1,000 Kilometers

GEOGRAPHY SKILLBUILDER: Interpreting Maps
1. **Location** How far is the southern end of Japan from Korea? from China?
2. **Location** On what island did Japan's major cities develop?

nature and on the worship of ancestors. Shinto worshipers believed in *kami,* divine spirits that dwelled in nature. Any unusual or especially beautiful tree, rock, waterfall, or mountain was considered the home of a *kami.*

The Yamato Emperors By the fifth century, the Yamato clan had established itself as the leading clan. The Yamato claimed to be descended from the sun goddess Amaterasu. By the seventh century, the Yamato chiefs called themselves the emperors of Japan. The early emperors did not control the entire country, or even much of it, but the Japanese gradually accepted the idea of an emperor.

Although many of the Yamato rulers lacked real power, the dynasty was never overthrown. When rival clans fought for power, the winning clan claimed control of the emperor and then ruled in the emperor's name. Japan had an emperor who reigned as a figurehead and a power behind the throne who actually ruled. This dual structure became an enduring characteristic of Japanese government.

The Japanese Adapt Chinese Ideas

About the year 500, the Japanese began to have more contact with mainland Asia. They were soon influenced by Chinese ideas and customs, which they first learned about from Korean travelers. During the sixth century, many Koreans migrated to Japan, bringing Chinese influences with them.

Buddhism in Japan One of the most important influences brought by Korean travelers was Buddhism. In the mid-700s, the Japanese imperial court officially accepted Buddhism in Japan. By the eighth or ninth century, Buddhist ideas and worship had spread through Japanese society. Buddhism was more complex than Shintoism. Its teachings, as well as the beauty and mystery of its ceremonies and art, impressed many Japanese. The Japanese, however, did not give up their Shinto beliefs. Some Buddhist rituals became Shinto rituals, and some Shinto gods and goddesses were worshipped in Buddhist temples.

Cultural Borrowing from China Interest in Buddhist ideas at the Japanese court soon grew into an enthusiasm for all things Chinese. The most influential convert to Buddhism was Prince Shotoku (shoh·toh·ku), who served as regent for his aunt, the empress Suiko. In 607, Prince Shotoku sent the first of three missions to Tang China. His people studied Chinese civilization firsthand. Some 600 scholars, painters, musicians, and monks traveled on each mission. Over the next 200 years, while the Tang Dynasty was at its height, the Japanese sent many such groups to learn about Chinese ways.

Vocabulary
regent: one who rules on behalf of another.

The Japanese adopted the Chinese system of writing, which first reached Japan through the Koreans. Japanese artists painted landscapes in the Chinese manner. The Japanese even followed Chinese styles in the simple arts of everyday living, such as cooking, gardening, drinking tea, and hairdressing.

For a time, Japan even modeled its government on China's. Prince Shotoku planned a strong central government like that of the Tang rulers. Shotoku also tried to introduce China's examination system. However, this attempt failed. In Japan, noble birth remained the key to winning a powerful position. Unlike China, Japan continued to be a country where a few great families held power.

THINK THROUGH HISTORY
A. Synthesizing
How did Chinese culture spread to Japan?

The Japanese adapted Chinese ways to suit their own needs. While they learned much, they still retained their own traditions. Eventually, the Japanese imperial court decided it had learned enough from Tang China. In the late ninth century, it ended formal missions to the Tang empire, which had fallen into decline. Although Chinese cultural influence would remain strong in Japan, Japan's own culture was about to bloom.

Life in the Heian Period

In 794, the imperial court moved its capital from Nara to Heian (HAY·ahn), the modern Kyoto (kee·OH·toh). Many of Japan's noble families also moved to Heian. Among the upper class in Heian, a highly refined court society arose. This era in Japanese history, from 794 to 1185, is called the Heian period.

Gentlemen and ladies of the court filled their days with elaborate ritual and artistic pursuits. Rules dictated every aspect of court life—the length of swords, the color of official robes, forms of address, even the number of skirts a woman wore. Etiquette was also extremely important. Loud laughter or mismatched clothing, for instance, caused deep embarrassment. Noble women wore their hair down to their ankles, blackened their teeth with cosmetics, and dyed their clothing to match the seasons. Everyone at court was expected to write poetry and to paint. Japanese aristocrats looked down on the common people, who could not share in court refinement.

The best accounts of Heian society come from the diaries, essays, and novels written by the women of the court. Two of the finest writers of the period were Lady Murasaki Shikibu and Sei Shonagon. Lady Murasaki's 11th-century masterpiece, *The Tale of Genji*, is an account of the life of a prince in the imperial court. This long prose narrative, full of detail and emotion, is considered the world's first novel. Sei Shonagon wrote vivid sketches of court life in her diary, called *The Pillow Book*. Here she lists some things that gave her pleasure:

One maid combs her lady's hair while another reads to her in this print depicting a scene from *The Tale of Genji*.

> **A VOICE FROM THE PAST**
> I greatly enjoy [conversing with] someone who is pleased with himself and who has a self-confident look, especially if he is a man. It is amusing to observe him as he alertly waits for my next repartee; but it is also interesting if he tries to put me off my guard by adopting an air of calm indifference as if there were not a thought in his head.
>
> I realize that it is very sinful of me, but I cannot help being pleased when someone I dislike has a bad experience.
>
> Entering the Empress's room and finding that ladies-in-waiting are crowded around her in a tight group, I go next to a pillar which is some distance from where she is sitting. What a delight it is when Her Majesty summons me to her side so that all the others have to make way!
>
> **SEI SHONAGON,** *The Pillow Book*

Feudalism Erodes Imperial Authority

During the Heian period, Japan's central government was relatively strong. However, this strength was soon to be challenged by great landowners and clan chiefs who acted more and more as independent local rulers.

Decline of Central Power For most of the Heian period, the rich Fujiwara family held the real power in Japan. Members of this family held many influential posts. By about the middle of the 11th century, however, the power of the central government and the Fujiwaras began to slip. Court families grew more interested in luxury and artistic pursuits than in governing.

Vocabulary
etiquette: the code governing correct behavior and appearance.

THINK THROUGH HISTORY
B. Making Inferences
Based on the excerpt from Shonagon's book, what personality characteristics does the writer admire?

Samurai Warrior News

Latest Uniforms

A samurai's armor consists of leather shin guards and thigh guards, billowing knickers, a kimono, metal-cased shoulder guards, a chest protector, an iron collar, a cotton skullcap, an iron facemask, and a visored helmet with leather horns.

This suit of armor is made of steel, wood, bronze, deerskin, and bear pelts.

Don't Leave Home Without It

A proper samurai would rather die than part with his sword. No wonder. Extraordinary craftsmanship goes into each weapon. Swordsmiths prepare themselves by undergoing purification rites.

Then they work dressed all in white. To give the blade superior strength, the swordsmith uses clay to protect the broad back of the sword from the hammering, heating, and cooling that produces the razor-sharp edge. For beauty, swordsmiths add inlaid hilt guards, scabbard ornaments, and handgrips made of sharkskin.

Lady Tomoe Gozen, a famous female warrior of the 1180s, enters bravely into battle.

The Zen Way

The Zen school of Buddhism is becoming popular among the samurai class. The Zen emphasis on spirituality through self-discipline and meditation appeals to this group of warriors.

Samurai vs. Knights

A class of elite warriors similar to the samurai is forming in Europe. Here is how the two groups compare.

Japanese Samurai	European Knights
• Live by code of honor called Bushido, which values bravery and loyalty to their lord above all else. Will commit ritual suicide rather than face defeat or dishonor.	• Live by code of honor called chivalry, which values bravery and loyalty to heavenly God, earthly lord, and chosen lady. Code also demands that knights show humility.
• Fight for lord in exchange for an allowance.	• Fight for lord in exchange for land.
• Expect women to live up to same values of honor and courage.	• Regard women as weak creatures to be idolized and defended.
• Enter into battle with iron and leather armor, swords, and bows and arrows.	• Enter into battle with chain mail or plate armor, broadsword, and lance.

Connect *to* History

Making Inferences What qualities did samurai most prize?

 SEE SKILLBUILDER HANDBOOK PAGE 1005

Connect *to* Today

Research Find out what happened to the samurai in Japan's later history. How long did this warrior class last? Did it change in any way?

Large landowners living away from the capital set up private armies. The countryside became lawless and dangerous. Armed soldiers on horseback preyed on farmers and travelers, and pirates took control of the seas. For safety, farmers and small landowners traded parts of their land to strong warlords in exchange for protection. With more land, the lords gained more power. This marked the beginning of a feudal system of localized rule like that of ancient China and medieval Europe.

Samurai Warriors Since wars between rival lords were commonplace, each lord surrounded himself with a bodyguard of loyal warriors called **samurai** (SAM·uh·RY). (*Samurai* means "one who serves.") Samurai lived according to a demanding code of behavior. In later centuries, this code was called **Bushido** (BUSH·ih·DOH), or "the way of the warrior." A samurai was expected to show reckless courage, reverence for the gods, fairness, and generosity toward those weaker than himself. Dying an honorable death was judged more important than living a long life.

The Kamakura Shogunate During the late 1100s, Japan's two most powerful clans fought for power. After almost 30 years of war, the Minamoto family emerged victorious. In 1192, the emperor gave a Minamoto leader named Yoritomo the title of **shogun,** meaning "supreme general of the emperor's army." In effect, the shogun had the powers of a military dictator. Officials, judges, taxes, armies, roads—all were under his authority.

THINK THROUGH HISTORY
C. Drawing Conclusions
What advantages were there to preserving the imperial dynasty, even if it lacked real power?

Following tradition, the emperor still reigned from Kyoto. (Kyoto was rebuilt on the ruins of Heian, which had been destroyed in war.) However, the real center of power was at the shogun's military headquarters at Kamakura (KAHM·uh·KUR·uh). The 1200s are known in Japanese history as the Kamakura shogunate. The pattern of government in which shoguns ruled through puppet emperors lasted in Japan until 1868.

Under the early shoguns, the local lords still held great power. A lord who loyally served the shogun received almost a free hand in ruling his own province. At the same time, the shoguns strengthened their own control by assigning a military governor to each province. These governors, called daimyo (DY·mee·OH), or "great lords," were responsible for maintaining peace and order. Over time, the daimyo came to exercise great power, as you will see in Chapter 19.

The Kamakura shoguns were strong enough to turn back the two naval invasions sent by the great Mongol ruler Kublai Khan in 1274 and 1281. However, the Japanese victory over the Mongols drained the shoguns' treasury. Loyal samurai were bitter when the government failed to pay them. The Kamakura shoguns lost prestige and power. Samurai attached themselves more closely to their local lords, who soon fought one another as fiercely as they had fought the Mongols.

Although feudal Japan no longer courted contact with China, it would continue to absorb Chinese ideas and shape them into the Japanese way. As you will read in Section 5, China's culture also influenced Korea and certain kingdoms of Southeast Asia.

Section 4 Assessment

1. TERMS & NAMES

Identify
- Shinto
- samurai
- Bushido
- shogun

2. TAKING NOTES

Create a time line showing the main periods and events in Japanese history between the years 300 and 1300.

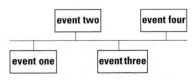

| event two | | event four |
| event one | | event three |

What event would you consider the most important turning point in Japan's early history? Why?

3. DRAWING CONCLUSIONS

Was the rise of the shogun beneficial for Japan overall? Explain.

THINK ABOUT
- problems developing in feudal Japan
- powers of the shogun
- achievements under the Kamakura shoguns

4. THEME ACTIVITY

Religious and Ethical Systems Work with a small group to create a short play, set in the 600s, about a Japanese family's decision to adopt Buddhism. Consider what changes occurring in Japanese society might make individuals more receptive to beliefs that came from China. Indicate how the family blends Buddhism with its traditional Shinto beliefs.

5 Kingdoms of Southeast Asia and Korea

MAIN IDEA	WHY IT MATTERS NOW
Several smaller kingdoms prospered in East and Southeast Asia, a region culturally influenced by China and India.	Chinese cultural influences still affect East and Southeast Asia today.

SETTING THE STAGE To the south of China lies the region called Southeast Asia. It includes the modern countries of Myanmar (Burma), Laos, Cambodia, Vietnam, Malaysia, Indonesia, Thailand, Singapore, Brunei, and the Philippines. Thousands of miles from this region, to China's northeast, lies the Korean peninsula. This peninsula is currently divided between North Korea and South Korea. In the shadow of powerful China, many small but prosperous kingdoms rose and fell in Southeast Asia and Korea.

Kingdoms of Southeast Asia

In Southeast Asia's river valleys and deltas and on its islands, many kingdoms had centuries of glory and left monuments of lasting beauty.

Geography of Southeast Asia Southeast Asia lies between the Indian and Pacific oceans and stretches from Asia almost to Australia. It consists of two main parts: (1) the mainland peninsula, which borders China to the north and India to the west, and (2) the islands, the largest of which include Sumatra, Borneo, and Java. All of Southeast Asia lies within the warm, humid tropics. Monsoon winds bring the region long annual rains.

Southeast Asia has never been united, either politically or culturally. Seas and straits separate the islands. On the mainland, five great rivers flow from the north and cut valleys to the sea. Between the valleys rise hills and mountains, making travel and communication difficult. Over time, many different peoples settled the region, so it was home to a great variety of languages and cultures.

Throughout Southeast Asia's history, the key to political power often has been control of trade routes and harbors. Powerful local lords

Background
The mainland peninsula of Southeast Asia is called Indochina.

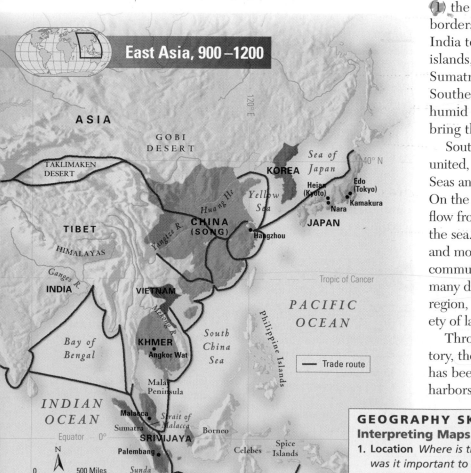

East Asia, 900–1200

GEOGRAPHY SKILLBUILDER:
Interpreting Maps
1. **Location** Where is the Strait of Malacca and why was it important to trade?
2. **Movement** Name one way Chinese culture might have spread around Southeast Asia.

charged merchants high fees to use their ports, pass through their waterways, or protect their ships from piracy. The lords could do this because Southeast Asia lies on the most direct sea route between the Indian Ocean and the South China Sea. Two important waterways connect the two seas: the Strait of Malacca, between the Malay Peninsula and Sumatra, and the Sunda Strait, between Sumatra and Java.

Influence of India and China Indian merchant boats sailing the monsoon winds began arriving in Southeast Asia by the first century A.D. In the period that followed, Hindu and Buddhist missionaries spread their faiths. Across the region, kingdoms arose that followed these religions and were modeled on Indian political ideas. Gradually, Indian influence shaped many aspects of the region's culture. The people of Southeast Asia adopted many Hindu practices. Southeast Asian poets wrote long, elegant poems in India's ancient language of Sanskrit. Many early Indian influences on Southeast Asian culture are evident today in its religions, languages, and art forms.

Chinese ideas and culture spread southward in the region through migration and trade. At different times, the Chinese also exerted political influence over parts of mainland Southeast Asia, either through direct rule or by demanding tributes from local rulers.

The Khmer Empire The **Khmer** (kmair) **Empire,** in what is now Cambodia, was for centuries the main power on the Southeast Asian mainland. An early Khmer kingdom, called Funan, dominated much of the sea trade between India and China. By around 800, the Khmer had expanded their state into an empire at the expense of neighboring kingdoms. They reached their peak of power around 1200.

Improved rice cultivation helped the Khmer become prosperous. The Khmer built elaborate irrigation systems and waterways. These advances made it possible to grow three or four crops of rice a year in an area that had previously produced only one.

THINK THROUGH HISTORY
**A. Making
Inferences** What does the size and splendor of Angkor Wat suggest about the empire that constructed it?

At their capital, Angkor, Khmer rulers built extensive city-and-temple complexes. One of these, called **Angkor Wat,** is among the world's greatest architectural achievements. The complex, which covers nearly a square mile, was built as a symbolic mountain dedicated to the Hindu god Vishnu. The Khmer also used it as an observatory.

Island Trading Kingdoms While the Khmer Empire expanded on the mainland, a dynasty called Sailendra ruled an agricultural kingdom on the island of Java. The Sailendra kings left behind another of the world's great architectural monuments, the Buddhist temple at Borobudur. The temple was built around 800. Like Angkor Wat, it reflects strong Indian influence. The massive complex has nine terraced levels like a stepped pyramid.

The Sailendra Dynasty eventually fell under the domination of the powerful island empire of Srivijaya. At its height from the 7th to the 13th centuries, Srivijaya ruled the Strait of Malacca and other waters around the islands of Sumatra, Borneo, and Java. It grew wealthy by taxing the trade that passed

Built in the 1100s, Angkor Wat is the world's largest religious structure. The vine-covered sculpture (inset) is the image of an ancient Khmer ruler.

Empires in East Asia **309**

through its waters. The Srivijayas established their capital, Palembang, on Sumatra. Palembang became a great center of Buddhist learning, where Chinese monks could study instead of traveling to India.

Vietnam The people of Southeast Asia least influenced by India were the Vietnamese. Located in the coastal region just south of China, Vietnam fell under Chinese domination. Around 100 B.C., during the mighty Han Dynasty, China took northern Vietnam.

This Vietnamese print depicts Trung Trac and Trung Nhi, two heroines in Vietnam's history. These sisters led a revolt against the Chinese occupation in A.D. 39.

The Vietnamese remained under Chinese control for 1,000 years. When China's Tang Dynasty grew weaker in the early 900s, Vietnam broke away. It became an independent kingdom in 939.

The Vietnamese absorbed many Chinese cultural influences, including Buddhism. However, they also preserved a strong spirit of independence and kept their own cultural identity. Vietnamese women, for example, traditionally had more freedom and influence than their Chinese counterparts.

Rulers of the Ly Dynasty (1009–1225) established their capital at Hanoi, on the Red River delta. They slowly expanded Vietnam by conquering neighboring peoples to the south. The Mongols tried to conquer Vietnam and captured Hanoi three times (in 1257, 1285, and 1287), but each time the Vietnamese forced them to withdraw.

Korean Dynasties

According to a Korean legend, the first Korean state was founded by the hero Tan'gun, whose father was a god and whose mother was a bear. Another legend relates that it was founded by a royal descendant of the Chinese Shang Dynasty. These legends reflect two sides to the development of Korean culture. On one side, the Koreans were a distinct people who developed their own native traditions. On the other side, their culture was shaped by Chinese influences since early dynastic times. However, like the Japanese, the Koreans adapted borrowed culture to fit their own needs and maintained a distinct way of life.

Geography of Korea Korea is located on a peninsula that juts out of the Asian mainland toward Japan. Its area is about the same size as the state of Utah. Korea's climate is hot in the summer and very cold in the winter. Like Japan, Korea is a mountainous land, and only a limited portion of the peninsula can be farmed. A mountainous barrier lies between Korea and its northern neighbor, Manchuria. Because of the mountains and the seas, Korea developed somewhat in isolation from its neighbors.

Early History In early Korea, as in early Japan, different clans or tribes controlled different parts of the country. In 108 B.C., the Han empire conquered much of Korea and established a military government there. Through the Chinese, Koreans learned about such ideas as centralized government, Confucianism, Buddhism, and writing.

During the period of Han rule, the various Korean tribes began to gather together into federations. Eventually, these federations developed into three rival kingdoms. In the mid-600s, one of these kingdoms, the Silla, defeated the other kingdoms and chased out the Chinese. The Silla gained control over the whole Korean peninsula.

Under Silla rule, the Koreans built Buddhist monasteries and produced elegant stone and bronze sculptures. They also developed a writing system suitable for writing Korean phonetically though still using Chinese characters.

The Koryu Dynasty By the tenth century, Silla rule had weakened. Around 935, a rebel officer named Wang Kon gained control of the country and became king. He named his new dynasty Koryu. The name is an abbreviation of Koguryo (one of the three kingdoms), and is the origin of the modern name Korea. The **Koryu Dynasty** lasted four and a half centuries, from 935 to 1392.

The Koryu Dynasty modeled its central government after China's. It established a Confucian civil service examination system and a university to train male scholars. However, this system did not provide the social mobility for Koreans that it did for many Chinese. Koryu society was sharply divided between a landed aristocracy and the rest of the population, including the military, commoners, and slaves. Despite the examination system, the sons of nobles received the best positions, and these positions became hereditary. Wealthy nobles built their land holdings into huge estates, which left the other groups to scrape by with little.

These problems spurred a series of rebellions in the 1100s. Although the Koryu Dynasty managed to remain in power, it soon faced a larger threat. In 1231, the Mongols swept into Korea. They demanded a crushing tribute from the Koryu rulers. The tribute included 20,000 horses, clothing for 1 million soldiers, and many children and artisans, who were to be taken away as slaves.

The harsh period of Mongol occupation lasted until the 1350s, when the Mongol empire collapsed. Mounting oppression and taxation of the people by Korea's wealthy landlords eventually led to a new round of revolts. In 1392, a group of scholar-officials and military leaders overthrew the Koryu Dynasty and instituted land reforms. They established a new dynasty, called the Choson (or Yi) Dynasty, which would rule for 518 years.

Koryu Culture The Koryu period produced great achievements in Korean culture. Inspired by Song porcelain artists, Korean artists produced the much-admired celadon pottery, famous for its milky green glaze. (Knowledge of the secret formula for celadon disappeared during the Mongol occupation.) Writers and scholars produced fine poetry and wrote the first national history of Korea.

Korean artisans produced one of the great treasures of the Buddhist world. Over a period of 60 years, Korean printers carved thousands of large wooden blocks for printing the entire canon of Buddhist scriptures. This set of blocks was destroyed by the Mongols, but the disaster sparked a national effort to re-create them. The more than 81,000 blocks in the new set remain in Korea today.

THINK THROUGH HISTORY
B. Comparing How did the Koryu government compare with the early imperial government of Japan (page 304)?

CONNECT *to* TODAY

Two Koreas
From the Koryu period until the end of World War II, Korea was united culturally and politically. In 1945, Japanese forces in North Korea surrendered to the Soviets. Those in South Korea surrendered to the U.S. military. This arbitrary division of Korea continues today.

Many Koreans look forward to a day when Korea is reunited. Hopes for such a day rose in 2000 when the presidents of each country sat down to discuss reunification in the first-ever meeting between leaders of the two nations. Observers caution, however, that the vast differences between the communist north and democratic south make the prospect of one Korea uncertain.

Section 5 Assessment

1. TERMS & NAMES

Identify
- Khmer Empire
- Angkor Wat
- Koryu Dynasty

2. TAKING NOTES

List five important kingdoms or dynasties covered in this section, and at least two major accomplishments of each.

Kingdom or Dynasty	Accomplishment

3. RECOGNIZING EFFECTS

Give examples to show how geography influenced the history and culture of Southeast Asia and of Korea.

THINK ABOUT
- the climate
- location relative to other countries
- natural features of water and land

4. THEME ACTIVITY

Religious and Ethical Systems Create a map showing how Hinduism and Buddhism entered Southeast Asia from China and India.

Chapter ⑫ Assessment

TERMS & NAMES

Briefly explain the importance of each of the following to East Asia between 600 and 1350.

1. Tang Taizong
2. Wu Zhao
3. pastoralist
4. Genghis Khan
5. Kublai Khan
6. Marco Polo
7. Shinto
8. samurai
9. Angkor Wat
10. Koryu Dynasty

Interact *with* History

Through the activity on page 286, you looked at the importance of Chinese inventions on world history. (After reading the chapter, you may have recognized that this imaginary situation was inspired by the travels of Marco Polo.) Now that you've read the chapter, consider the impact of Chinese inventions and how they spread. Would you now choose a different invention? Is there any other invention you would choose instead of those on page 286? Discuss these questions with a small group.

REVIEW QUESTIONS

SECTION 1 *(pages 287–291)*
Two Great Dynasties in China

11. Why was the reform of the civil service under the Tang so significant?
12. How did changes in agriculture support other developments during the Song dynasty?

SECTION 2 *(pages 294–298)*
The Mongol Conquests

13. Why were nomads and settled peoples often in conflict?
14. What were the most important accomplishments of the Mongol Empire?

SECTION 3 *(pages 299–302)*
Empire of the Great Khan

15. Explain how Kublai Khan treated his Chinese subjects.
16. How did China's economy improve during the Yuan Dynasty?

SECTION 4 *(pages 303–307)*
Feudal Powers in Japan

17. Describe the impact of Chinese culture on Japan in the 600s and 700s.
18. Explain how feudalism developed in Japan beginning in the 1200s.

SECTION 5 *(pages 308–311)*
Kingdoms of Southeast Asia and Korea

19. Describe the two sources of prosperity for Southeast Asian empires, and give examples of empires that prospered each way.
20. What were the major accomplishments of the Koryu Dynasty?

Visual Summary

Empires in East Asia

Japan	
• Distinct geography and culture • Shinto religion • Heian period • Feudal system	**Interaction with China** • Buddhism • Writing system • Civil service

Mongols	
• Nomadic way of life • Clan-based leadership	**Interaction with China** • Mongols' conquest of China • Spread of Chinese ideas through Mongol Empire across Eurasia

China
• Revival of civil service system
• Strengthening of central government
• Golden age of culture, science, and technology

Southeast Asia	
Interaction with China • Vietnam: Buddhism, civil service • Other areas: spread of ideas through migration and trade	• Location on trade routes between China and India • Indian cultural influence: political ideas and religions

Korea	
Interaction with China • Buddhism • Writing system • Civil service • Printing • Porcelain	• Distinct geography and culture • Divided society controlled by wealthy landowners

CRITICAL THINKING

1. HYPOTHESIZING

THEME **EMPIRE BUILDING** How might history have been different if the Mongols had conquered all or most of Europe? Discuss the possible immediate and long-term consequences for Europe and the rest of the Mongol Empire.

2. DEVELOPMENTS AND CHANGE

For each of the following developments, create a diagram like the one shown and identify two results from it: (a) construction of the Grand Canal, (b) stirrups, and (c) the compass.

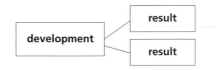

3. RISE AND FALL OF DYNASTIES

This chapter describes the rise and fall of three Chinese dynasties. What recurring patterns occur in the decline of these dynasties? What advice might you give a Chinese emperor, based on those patterns?

4. ANALYZING PRIMARY SOURCES

The following is part of a message sent by Kublai Khan to Japan's imperial court in 1266, as recorded by a Chinese historian. Read the passage and answer the questions below it.

> **A VOICE FROM THE PAST**
>
> The Emperor of the Great Mongols addresses the King of Japan as follows: . . . I am sending you my envoys bearing my personal message. It is my hope that the communication between our two countries be opened and maintained and that our mutual friendship be established. A sage regards the whole world as one family; how can different countries be considered one family if there is not friendly communication between them? Is force really necessary to establish friendly relations? I hope that you will give this matter your most careful attention.
>
> **SUNG LIEN,** quoted in *The Essence of Chinese Civilization*

- What is Kublai Khan asking of the Japanese?
- Based on what you have read about the Mongols and Japan, what do you think Kublai's real goal was?

CHAPTER ACTIVITIES

1. LIVING HISTORY: Unit Portfolio Project

THEME **RELIGIOUS AND ETHICAL SYSTEMS** Your unit portfolio project focuses on how belief systems have affected people's lives (see page 229). For Chapter 12, you might use one of the following ideas to add to your portfolio:

- Prepare a photo essay on one of the massive temple complexes of Southeast Asia, such as Angkor Wat or Borobudur. In the essay, show how the design of the complex reflected the religious influences on the region.
- Create a mural portraying the essential beliefs of Shintoism.
- Give a "virtual" guided tour of a traditional Buddhist temple in Korea, Japan, or Vietnam. Using slides or overhead images, show how the architecture relates to Buddhist practices and the country's culture.

2. CONNECT TO TODAY: Cooperative Learning

THEME **CULTURAL INTERACTION** For 100 years, the Mongols were the lords of settled societies across Eurasia. Today, modern civilization threatens to extinguish the nomadic way of life. Traditionally nomadic groups such as the Kurds, whose homeland includes parts of Turkey, Iraq, and Iran, have faced many challenges and changes. Work with a team to prepare a report on the challenges faced by the Kurds or another traditionally nomadic people today.

Using the Internet, magazines, or reference books, research the history of the Kurds or another group and their way of life today.

- How have modern political boundaries and population growth in their region affected their way of life?
- What is their political status in the countries in which they live? Are they treated the same as others? How has their status affected their way of life?

3. INTERPRETING A TIME LINE

Revisit the unit time line on pages 228–229, and study the segment for Chapter 12. Which events from East Asia had the greatest impact on developments outside of this region? Explain your response.

FOCUS ON **GEOGRAPHY**

Study the maps of China's population distribution in the Tang and Song dynasties.

- During the Tang Dynasty, which areas of China were most densely populated?
- Overall, how had China's population changed by the Song Dynasty?

Connect to History What political and economic developments in China were related to this population change?

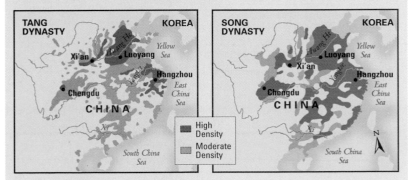

Source: John King Fairbank, *China: A New History*

CHAPTER 13 · European Middle Ages, 500–1200

Religious and Ethical Systems

During the Middle Ages, the Church was a unifying force. It shaped people's beliefs and guided their conduct. Most Europeans at this time shared a common bond of faith. Their religious beliefs affected their daily lives.

Empire Building

In western Europe, the Roman Empire fell apart into many small kingdoms. During the Middle Ages, two powerful leaders—Charlemagne and Otto the Great—tried to revive the idea of empire. They both allied with the Church.

Power and Authority

Weak rulers and the decline of central authority led to a feudal system of relationships. Under this system, local lords with large estates assumed power. The Church too played a growing role in government affairs. This led to power struggles between political leaders and popes.

INTERNET CONNECTION

Visit us at **www.mcdougallittell.com** to learn more about the European Middle Ages and related topics.

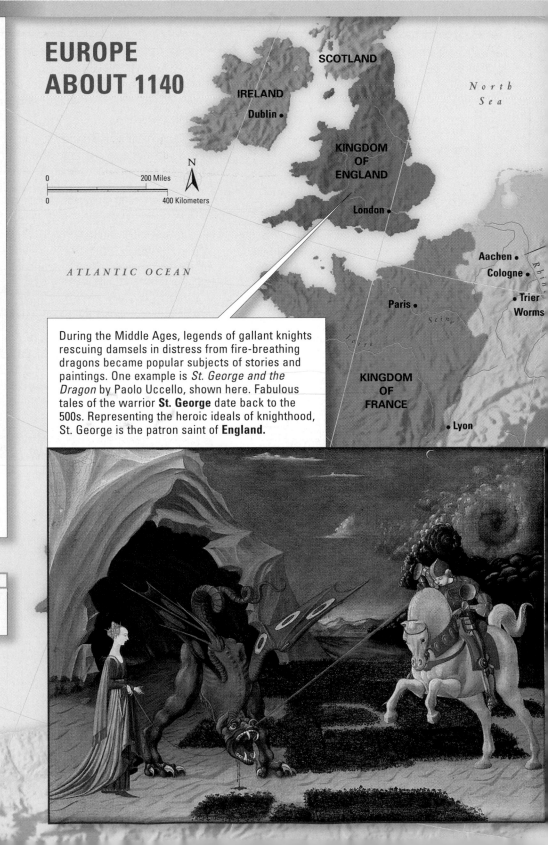

EUROPE ABOUT 1140

0 ——— 200 Miles
0 ——— 400 Kilometers

SCOTLAND

IRELAND
Dublin •

North Sea

KINGDOM OF ENGLAND

London •

ATLANTIC OCEAN

Aachen •
Cologne •

• Trier
Worms

Paris •

Seine

Loire

KINGDOM OF FRANCE

• Lyon

During the Middle Ages, legends of gallant knights rescuing damsels in distress from fire-breathing dragons became popular subjects of stories and paintings. One example is *St. George and the Dragon* by Paolo Uccello, shown here. Fabulous tales of the warrior **St. George** date back to the 500s. Representing the heroic ideals of knighthood, St. George is the patron saint of **England.**

From **768** to **814**, **Charlemagne** reigned over a vast kingdom later called the **Holy Roman Empire.** His biographer, Einhard, described what this mighty ruler wore at festivals: "a jeweled sword, . . . a garment woven in gold, and shoes studded with jewels, his cloak fastened with a golden clasp, and . . . a crown of gold set with precious stones."

KINGDOM OF SWEDEN

NGDOM OF ENMARK

Baltic Sea

PRUSSIA

Vistula River

Elbe River

Oder River

KINGDOM OF POLAND

Prague

HOLY ROMAN EMPIRE

Vienna

Danube

Buda •• Pest

KINGDOM OF HUNGARY

Drav River

Venice

Belgrade

APAL ATES

KINGDOM OF BULGARIA

SERBIA

Rome

BYZANTINE EMPIRE

While serving as pope from **590** to **604**, Gregory the Great wore only a monk's robe. He humbly called himself "the servant of the servants of god." Also an author, he wrote an influential book titled *The Dialogues.* It was a collection of simply told religious stories, full of miraculous events.

KINGDOM OF SICILY

MALTA

Mediterranean Sea

Black Sea

SELJUK KINGDOM OF ICONIUM

COUNTY OF EDESSA

ARMENIA

Euphrates River

Antioch
PRINCIPALITY OF ANTIOCH

COUNTY OF TRIPOLI

Nicosia
CYPRUS

KINGDOM OF JERUSALEM

Beirut / Damascus

315

Interact *with* History

You are living in the countryside of western Europe during the 1100s. Like about 90 percent of the population, you are a peasant working the land. Your family's hut is located in a small village on your lord's estate. The lord provides your basic needs, including housing, food, and protection.

Opportunities to leave the estate are rare. Within your lifetime, you will probably travel no more than 25 miles from your home.

What is good and bad about the small world of a peasant's life?

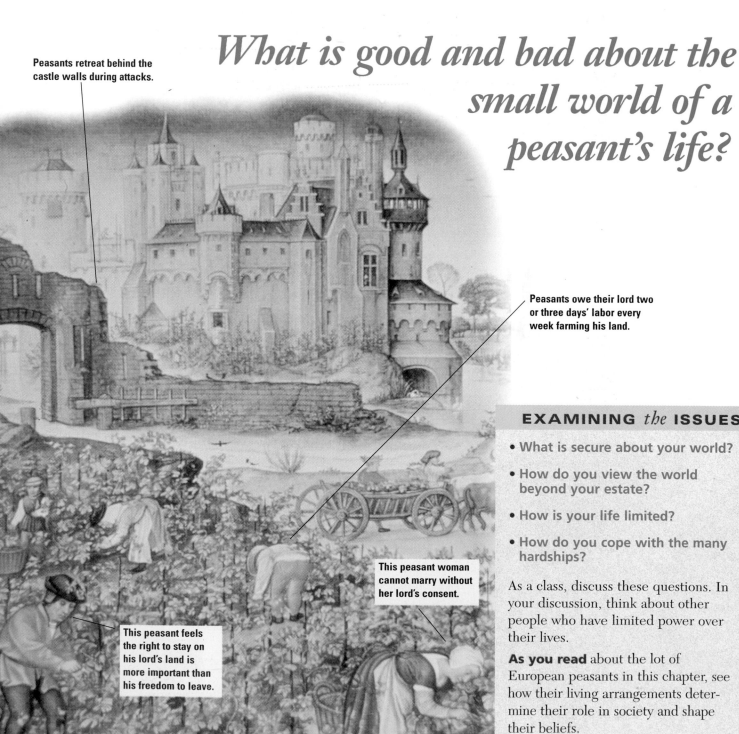

Peasants retreat behind the castle walls during attacks.

Peasants owe their lord two or three days' labor every week farming his land.

This peasant woman cannot marry without her lord's consent.

This peasant feels the right to stay on his lord's land is more important than his freedom to leave.

EXAMINING *the* ISSUES

- What is secure about your world?

- How do you view the world beyond your estate?

- How is your life limited?

- How do you cope with the many hardships?

As a class, discuss these questions. In your discussion, think about other people who have limited power over their lives.

As you read about the lot of European peasants in this chapter, see how their living arrangements determine their role in society and shape their beliefs.

Germanic Kingdoms Unite Under Charlemagne

TERMS & NAMES
• Middle Ages
• Franks
• monastery
• secular
• Carolingian Dynasty
• Charlemagne

MAIN IDEA

Many Germanic kingdoms that succeeded the Roman Empire were reunited under Charlemagne's empire.

WHY IT MATTERS NOW

Charlemagne spread Christian civilization through northern Europe, where it had a permanent impact.

SETTING THE STAGE The gradual decline of the Roman Empire ushered in an era of European history called the **Middle Ages,** or the medieval period. It spanned from around 500 to 1500. During these centuries, new institutions slowly emerged to replace those of the fallen Roman Empire. Unified civilizations flourished in China and Southwest Asia. Medieval Europe, though, remained fragmented.

Invasions Trigger Changes in Western Europe

By the end of the fifth century, invaders from many different Germanic groups over-ran the western half of the Roman Empire. Repeated invasions and constant warfare sparked new trends. A series of changes altered government, economy, and culture:

- **Disruption of Trade** Merchants faced invasions from both land and sea. Their businesses collapsed. The breakdown of trade destroyed Europe's cities as economic centers. Money became scarce.

- **Downfall of Cities** With the fall of the Roman Empire, cities were abandoned as centers of administration.

- **Population Shifts** As Roman centers of trade and government collapsed, nobles retreated to the rural areas. Roman cities were left without strong leader-ship. Other city dwellers also fled to the countryside, where they grew their own food. The population of western Europe became mostly rural.

**THINK THROUGH HISTORY
A. Recognizing Effects** How did the fall of the Roman Empire lead to disorder in western Europe?

The Decline of Learning The Germanic invaders who stormed Rome could not read or write. Among Roman subjects themselves, the level of learning sank sharply as more and more families left for rural areas. Few people except priests and other church officials were literate.

Knowledge of Greek, long important in Roman cul-ture, was almost lost. Few people could read Greek works of literature, science, and philosophy. The Germanic tribes, though, had a rich oral tradition of songs and leg-ends. However, they had no written language.

Loss of a Common Language As German-speaking peoples mixed with the Roman population, Latin began to change. It was no longer understood from region to region. Different dialects devel-oped as new words and phrases became part of everyday speech. By the 800s, French, Spanish, and other Roman-based languages had evolved from Latin. The development of various languages mirrored the continued breakup of a once unified empire.

**Vocabulary
dialects:** various ways words from the same language are pronounced or used in different regions.

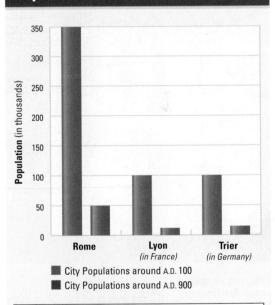

Population of Three Roman Cities

Population (in thousands): 0, 50, 100, 150, 200, 250, 300, 350

Rome   Lyon *(in France)*   Trier *(in Germany)*

■ City Populations around A.D. 100
■ City Populations around A.D. 900

**SKILLBUILDER:
Interpreting Graphs**
1. *How much did Rome's population decrease from around A.D. 100 to 900?*
2. *What does the bar graph suggest about trends that occurred after the fall of the Roman Empire?*

Germanic Kingdoms Emerge

In the years of upheaval between 400 and 600, small Germanic kingdoms replaced Roman provinces. The borders of those kingdoms changed constantly with the fortunes of war. The Church was an institution that survived the fall of the Roman Empire. During this time of political chaos, the Church provided order and security.

The Concept of Government Changes Along with shifting boundaries, the entire concept of government changed. Loyalty to public government and written law had unified Roman society. Family ties and personal loyalty, rather than citizenship in a public state, bound Germanic society together. Unlike the Romans, Germanic peoples lived in small communities. These were governed by unwritten rules and traditions.

Every Germanic chief led a band of warriors who had pledged their loyalty to him. In peacetime, these followers lived in their lord's hall. He gave them food, weapons, and treasure. In battle, warriors fought to the death at their lord's side. They considered it a disgrace to outlive him.

Germanic warriors willingly died for a leader they respected. Yet they felt no obligation to obey a king they didn't even know. Nor would they obey an official sent to collect taxes or administer justice in the name of an emperor they had never met. The Germanic stress on personal ties made it impossible to establish orderly government for large territories.

In the Roman province of Gaul, a Germanic people called the **Franks** held power. Their leader, Clovis (KLOH·vihs), would eventually bring Christianity to this region.

The Franks Under Clovis Clovis's wife, Clothilde, urged him to convert to her faith. She believed in a traditional form of Christianity. In 496 Clovis led his warriors into battle against another Germanic army. Fearing defeat, Clovis appealed to the Christian God. "For I have called on my gods," he prayed, "but I find they are far from my aid . . . Now I call on Thee. I long to believe in Thee. Only, please deliver me from my enemies." The tide of the battle shifted and the Franks triumphed. Afterward, Clovis and 3,000 of his warriors asked a bishop to baptize them.

The Church in Rome welcomed Clovis's conversion and supported his military campaigns against other Germanic peoples. By 511, Clovis had united the Franks into one kingdom. The strategic alliance between Clovis's Frankish kingdom and the Church marked the beginning of a special partnership between two powerful forces.

This ivory carving shows Clovis's conversion to Christianity in 496. A bishop baptizes him as his wife, Clothilde, looks on.

Germanic Peoples Adopt Christianity

Politics played a key role in spreading Christianity. By 600, the Church, with the help of Frankish rulers, had converted many Germanic peoples. These new converts had settled in Rome's former lands.

Missionaries also succeeded in spreading Christianity. These religious travelers often risked their lives to advance their beliefs. During the fourth and fifth centuries, they worked among the Germanic and Celtic groups that bordered the Roman Empire. In southern Europe, the fear of coastal attacks by Muslims also spurred many people to become Christians.

Monasteries and Convents To adapt to rural conditions, the Church built religious communities called **monasteries.** There Christian men called monks gave up all their private possessions. Monks became servants of God. Nuns, women who also followed this religious way of life, lived in convents.

Around 520, Benedict, an Italian monk, began writing a book describing a strict yet practical set of rules for monasteries. Benedict's sister, Scholastica (skuh·LAS·tik·uh), headed a convent. There she adapted the same rules for women. These guidelines became a model for many other religious communities in western Europe. Monks and nuns devoted their lives to prayer and good works.

Monasteries also became Europe's best-educated communities. Monks opened schools, maintained libraries, and copied books. In 731, Venerable Bede, an English monk, wrote a history of England. Scholars still consider it the best historical work of the early Middle Ages. In the 600s and 700s, monks made beautiful copies of religious writings, decorated with ornate letters and brilliant pictures. The monks' illuminated manuscripts preserved at least part of Rome's intellectual heritage.

Gregory I Expands Papal Power In 590, Gregory I, also called Gregory the Great, became pope. As head of the Church in Rome, Gregory broadened the authority of the papacy, or pope's office, beyond its spiritual role. Under Gregory, the papacy also became a **secular,** or worldly, power involved in politics. The pope's palace was the center of Roman government. Gregory used Church revenues to raise armies, repair roads, and help the poor. He also negotiated peace treaties with invaders such as the Lombards. Gregory had begun to act as the mayor of Rome. Yet his influence extended beyond the city's boundaries.

According to Gregory, the entire region from Italy to England, from Spain to western Germany, fell under his responsibility. Gregory strengthened the vision of Christendom. It was a spiritual kingdom that fanned out from Rome to the most distant churches. This idea of a churchly kingdom, ruled by a pope, would become a central theme of the Middle Ages. Meanwhile, secular rulers set their sights on expanding their own political kingdoms.

HISTORY MAKERS

Benedict
480?–543

At 15, Benedict left school and hiked up to the Sabine Hills, where he lived in a cave as a hermit. After learning about Benedict's deep religious conviction, a group of other monks persuaded Benedict to lead their monastery. Benedict declared:

We must prepare our hearts and bodies for combat under holy obedience to the divine commandments. . . . We are therefore going to establish a school in which one may learn the service of the Lord.

In his book describing the rules for monastic life, Benedict emphasized a balance between work and study. Such guidelines turned monasteries into centers of order, stability, and learning.

A European Empire Evolves

After the Roman Empire dissolved, small kingdoms sprang up all over Europe. For example, England splintered into seven tiny kingdoms. Some of them were no larger than the state of Connecticut. The Franks controlled the largest and strongest of Europe's kingdoms in an area that was formerly the Roman province of Gaul. The Franks' first Christian king, Clovis, laid down the foundations for this kingdom.

By the time Clovis died in 511, he had extended his rule over most of what is now France. Clovis greatly strengthened the Merovingian (MEHR·uh·VIHN·jee·uhn) Dynasty, which was named after his legendary ancestor.

Clovis's Descendants By 700, an official known as the *major domo,* or mayor of the palace, had become the most powerful person in the kingdom. Officially, the mayor of the palace had charge of the royal household and estates. Unofficially, he commanded armies and made policy. In effect, the mayor of the palace ruled the kingdom.

In 719, a mayor of the palace named Charles Martel (Charles the Hammer) held more power than the king. Charles Martel extended the Franks' reign to the north, south, and east. He also defeated a Muslim raiding party from Spain at the Battle of Tours in 732. The outcome of this battle held great significance for Christian Europeans. If the Muslims had won, western Europe might have become a part of

800 Pope Leo III crowns Charlemagne (below) emperor.

730	740	760	780	800

732 Charles Martel defeats the Muslims at the Battle of Tours.

751 Pepin the Short becomes the first king ever anointed by the pope.

771 Charlemagne becomes the sole king of the Franks and continues his conquest of Europe.

the Muslim Empire. Charles Martel's victory at the Battle of Tours halted the Muslim invasion. This conquest made him a Christian hero.

At his death, Charles Martel passed on his power to his son, Pepin the Short. Pepin wanted to become king. He shrewdly cooperated with the pope. On behalf of the Church, Pepin agreed to fight the Lombards. They were invading central Italy and threatening Rome. In exchange, the pope anointed Pepin "king by the grace of God." Thus began the reign of Frankish rulers called the **Carolingian** (KAR·uh·LIHN·juhn) **Dynasty.** It lasted from 751 to 987.

Charlemagne Extends Frankish Rule Pepin the Short died in 768. He left a greatly strengthened Frankish kingdom to his two sons, Carloman and Charles. After Carloman's death in 771, Charles, known as **Charlemagne** (SHAHR·luh·MAYN), or Charles the Great, quickly seized control of the entire kingdom.

Charlemagne was an imposing figure. He stood six feet four inches tall. His admiring secretary, a monk named Einhard, described Charlemagne's achievements:

> **A VOICE FROM THE PAST**
> [Charlemagne] was the most potent prince with the greatest skill and success in different countries during the forty-seven years of his reign. Great and powerful as was the realm of Franks, Karl [Charlemagne] received from his father Pippin, he nevertheless so splendidly enlarged it . . . that he almost doubled it.
>
> **EINHARD,** from *Life of Charlemagne*

Charlemagne Takes Center Stage

Charlemagne built an empire greater than any known since ancient Rome. Each summer Charlemagne led his armies against the enemies that surrounded his kingdom. He fought the Muslims in Spain and tribes from other Germanic kingdoms. Charlemagne conquered new lands to both the south and the east. Through these conquests, Charlemagne spread Christianity. He reunited western Europe for the first time since the Roman Empire. By 800, the Carolingian empire exceeded the Byzantine Empire. It included two-thirds of Italy, all of present-day France, a small part of Spain, and all of German Saxony. Charlemagne had become the most powerful king in western Europe.

In 800, Charlemagne traveled to Rome to crush an unruly mob that had attacked the pope. In gratitude, Pope Leo III crowned him emperor. The coronation was historic. A pope had claimed the political right to confer the title "Roman Emperor" on a European king. This event signaled the joining of Germanic power, the Church, and the heritage of the Roman Empire.

Charlemagne's Government Charlemagne strengthened his royal power by limiting the authority of the nobles. To govern his empire, Charlemagne sent out royal agents. They made sure that the powerful landholders, called counts, governed their counties justly. Charlemagne also regularly visited every part of his kingdom. He

Background
After his successful military campaign in Italy, Pepin gave the conquered territory around Rome to the pope. This gift of land was called the Papal States.

820   840

Charlemagne's Empire, 768–843

Frankish Kingdom before Charlemagne, 768

Areas conquered by Charlemagne, 814

— Division by Treaty of Verdun, 843

North Sea

0   250 Miles

0   500 Kilometers

Elbe R.

ENGLAND

ATLANTIC OCEAN

Aachen

Paris

EAST FRANKISH KINGDOM (Louis the German)

SLAVIC STATES

Rhine R.

Danube R.

Tours

WEST FRANKISH KINGDOM (Charles the Bald)

CENTRAL KINGDOM (Lothair)

Pavia

Ebro R.

SPAIN

Corsica

Mediterranean Sea

PAPAL STATES

Rome

judged cases, settled disputes, and rewarded faithful followers. He also kept a close watch on the management of his huge estates. They were the source of Carolingian wealth and power.

Cultural Revival One of Charlemagne's greatest accomplishments was his encouragement of learning. Charlemagne surrounded himself with English, German, Italian, and Spanish scholars. For his many sons and daughters and other children at the court, Charlemagne opened a palace school. He ordered monasteries to open schools that trained future monks and priests. Monasteries expanded their libraries. Monks labored to make handwritten copies of Latin books.

THINK THROUGH HISTORY
C. Evaluating What were Charlemagne's most notable achievements?

GEOGRAPHY SKILLBUILDER:
Interpreting Maps
1. **Region** By 814, what was the extent of Charlemagne's empire (north to south, east to west)?
2. **Region** Based on the map, why did the Treaty of Verdun signal the decline of Charlemagne's empire?

Charlemagne's Heirs Are Weak Rulers A year before Charlemagne died in 814, he crowned his only surviving son, Louis the Pious, as emperor. Louis was a devoutly religious man. He might have fared better as a monk. Louis proved an ineffective ruler.

Louis left three sons: Lothair (loh·THAIR), Charles the Bald, and Louis the German. Louis's sons fought one another for the empire. The civil war ended in 843 when the brothers signed the Treaty of Verdun. This pact divided Charlemagne's empire into three kingdoms. After the treaty, Carolingian kings lost power. As central authority broke down, the lack of strong rulers led to a new system of governing and landholding.

Section ❶ Assessment

1. TERMS & NAMES

Identify
• Middle Ages
• Franks
• monastery
• secular
• Carolingian Dynasty
• Charlemagne

2. TAKING NOTES

Create a chart like the one below to summarize how each person listed helped spread Christianity.

	Method of Spreading Christianity
Clovis	
Benedict	
Gregory I	
Charles Martel	
Charlemagne	

Which of these people do you think was the most influential in spreading Christianity? Why?

3. SYNTHESIZING

After the fall of the Roman Empire, learning declined. How was this trend offset during the early Middle Ages?

THINK ABOUT
• the establishment of monasteries
• Charlemagne's accomplishments

4. ANALYZING THEMES

Empire Building Why do you think Charlemagne succeeded in building such a vast empire?

THINK ABOUT
• Charlemagne's personality
• his military leadership
• his religious beliefs
• his relationship with the Church

TERMS & NAMES
- lord
- fief
- vassal
- knight
- serf
- manor
- tithe

2 Feudalism in Europe

MAIN IDEA	WHY IT MATTERS NOW
Europeans developed feudalism, a political and military system of protective alliances and relationships.	The rights and duties of feudal relationships helped shape today's forms of representative government.

SETTING THE STAGE After the Treaty of Verdun, Charlemagne's three feuding grandsons broke up the kingdom even further. Part of this territory also became a battleground as new waves of invaders attacked Europe. The political turmoil and constant warfare led to the rise of feudalism—a military and political system based on land ownership and personal loyalty.

New Invasions Trouble Western Europe

Between 800 and 1000, invasions completely destroyed the Carolingian Empire. Muslim invaders from the south seized Sicily and raided Italy. They sacked Rome in 846. Magyar invaders struck from the east. Like the earlier Huns and Avars, the Magyar warriors terrorized Germany and Italy. And from the north sailed the most dreaded attackers of all—the Vikings.

Vikings: Raiders, Traders, and Explorers The Vikings set sail from a wintry, wooded region called Scandinavia (SKAN·duh·NAY·vee·uh). The Vikings, a Germanic people, were also called Northmen or Norsemen. They worshiped warlike gods. The Vikings took pride in nicknames like Eric Bloodaxe and Thorfinn Skullsplitter.

The Vikings carried out their raids with terrifying speed. Clutching swords and heavy wooden shields, these helmeted warriors beached their ships. They struck and then quickly shoved out to sea again. By the time local troops arrived, the Vikings were gone. Viking warships were awesome. The largest of these long ships held 300 warriors. They took turns rowing the ship's 72 oars. The prow of each ship swept grandly upward, often ending with the carved head of a sea monster. A ship might weigh 20 tons when fully loaded. Yet it could sail in a mere three feet of water. Rowing up shallow creeks, the Vikings looted inland villages and monasteries.

The Vikings were not only warriors but also traders, farmers, and outstanding explorers. Vikings ventured far beyond western Europe. They journeyed down rivers into the heart of Russia, to Constantinople, and even across the icy waters of the North Atlantic. A Viking explorer named Leif (leef) Ericson most likely reached North America around 1000, almost 500 years before Columbus.

About the same time Ericson reached the Americas, the Viking terror in Europe faded away. As Vikings gradually accepted Christianity, they stopped raiding monasteries. Also, a warming trend in Europe's climate made farming easier in Scandinavia. As agricultural settlements in Iceland and Greenland prospered, fewer Scandinavians adopted the seafaring life of Viking warriors.

This curled oak prow is a model of a magnificent Viking ship found in Oseberg, Norway. Up to 30 Vikings rowed such ships, which were over 70 feet long.

Background
The Vikings in Russia, called Varangians, settled down to become traders and nation builders. Their earlier invasions of Russia led to the establishment of the first Russian state, in the mid-800s. (See Chapter 11.)

Viking invasion routes
Magyar invasion routes
Muslim invasion routes
Viking areas
Magyar areas
Muslim areas

GEOGRAPHY SKILLBUILDER: Interpreting Maps
1. **Location** *What lands did the Vikings raid?*
2. **Movement** *Why were the Viking, Magyar, and Muslim invasions so threatening to Europe?*

Magyars and Muslims As the Viking invasions declined, Europe became the target of new assaults. The Magyars, a group of nomadic people, attacked from the east. They were superb horseback riders. The Magyars swept across the plains of the Danube River and invaded western Europe in the late 800s. The Magyars did not settle conquered land. Instead, they captured people to sell as slaves. They attacked isolated villages and monasteries. The Magyars overran northern Italy and reached as far west as the Rhineland and Burgundy.

The Muslims struck from the south. From there, they controlled the Mediterranean Sea, and disrupted trade. In the 600s and 700s, the Muslims tried to conquer and settle in Europe. By the 800s and 900s, their goal was also plunder. The Muslims were excellent sailors. They attacked settlements on the Atlantic and Mediterranean coasts and as far inland as Switzerland.

The invasions of Vikings, Magyars, and Muslims caused widespread disorder and suffering. Most western Europeans were living in constant danger. Central authority proved powerless. They no longer looked to a central ruler for security. Instead, many turned to local rulers with their own armies. Leaders who could fight the invaders attracted followers and gained political strength.

THINK THROUGH HISTORY
A. Recognizing Effects What was the impact of Viking, Magyar, and Muslim invasions on medieval Europe?

Feudalism Structures Society

In 911, two former enemies faced each other in a peace ceremony. Rollo was the head of a Viking army. He had been plundering the rich Seine (sayn) River valley for years. Charles the Simple was the king of France but held little power. Charles granted the Viking leader a huge piece of French territory. It became known as Northmen's land, or Normandy. In return, Rollo placed his hands between the king's hands and swore a pledge of loyalty.

A New Social Order The worst years of the invaders' attacks roughly spanned from 850 to 950. During this time, rulers and warriors like Charles and Rollo made similar agreements in many parts of Europe. The system of governing and landholding called feudalism had emerged in Europe. A similar feudal system existed in China under the Zhou Dynasty that ruled from around the 11th century B.C. until 256 B.C. Feudalism in Japan began in A.D. 1192 and ended in the 19th century.

The feudal system was based on mutual obligations. In exchange for military protection and other services, a **lord**, or landowner, granted land called a **fief**. The person receiving a fief was called a **vassal**. Charles the Simple, the lord, and Rollo, the vassal, showed how this two-sided bargain worked. Feudalism depended on the control of land.

The Feudal Pyramid To visualize the structure of feudal society, think of a pyramid. At the peak reigned the king. Next came the most powerful vassals—wealthy landowners such as nobles and bishops. Serving beneath these vassals were knights. **Knights** were mounted warriors who pledged to defend their lords' lands in exchange for fiefs. At the base of the pyramid were landless peasants who toiled in the fields.

THINK THROUGH HISTORY
B. Summarizing
What are the key characteristics of feudalism?

Peasants

Peasants

Knights

Knights

Church Official

Noble

King

In practice, the feudal system did not work so simply. Relationships between various lords and their vassals were never clear-cut. The same noble might be a vassal to several different lords. The feudal pyramid often became a complex tangle of conflicting loyalties. Both lords and vassals tried to use these relationships to their own advantage.

Social Classes Are Well Defined In the feudal system, status determined a person's prestige and power. Medieval writers classified people into three groups: those who fought (nobles and knights), those who prayed (men and women of the Church), and those who worked (the peasants). Social class was usually inherited.

In Europe during the Middle Ages, the vast majority of people were peasants. Most peasants were serfs. **Serfs** were people who could not lawfully leave the place where they were born. Though bound to the land, serfs were not slaves. Their lords could not sell or buy them. The wealth of the feudal lords came from the labor of peasants.

Vocabulary
status: social ranking.

This medieval painting shows a noble and two workmen who live on a manor. During the Middle Ages, "fashion police" made sure that people dressed according to their social class. Peasants could not lawfully wear the clothes of a noble.

Connect *to* History

Contrasting How does the clothing of the three people in the painting reflect their status and responsibilities in medieval society?

 SEE SKILLBUILDER HANDBOOK, PAGE 1009

Connect *to* Today

Comparing How would you visually show that today's styles, especially among teenagers, blur the distinctions among various social classes?

March: Two Workmen in a Garden by Simon Bening (about 1515)

Manors: The Economic Side of Feudalism

The **manor** was the lord's estate. During the Middle Ages, the manor system was the basic economic arrangement. The manor system rested on a set of rights and obligations between a lord and his serfs. The lord provided the serfs with housing, strips of farmland, and protection from bandits. In return, serfs tended the lord's lands, cared for his animals, and performed other tasks to maintain the estate. Peasant women shared in the farmwork with their husbands. All peasants, whether free or serf, owed the lord certain duties. These included at least a few days' labor each week and a certain portion of their grain.

A Self-Contained World Peasants rarely traveled more than 25 miles from their own manor. By standing in the center of a plowed field, they could see their entire world at a glance. A manor usually covered only a few square miles of land. It typically consisted of the lord's manor house, a church, and workshops. Generally, 15 to 30 families lived in the village on a manor. Fields, pastures, and forests surrounded the village. Sometimes a stream wound through the manor. Streams and ponds provided fish, which served as an important source of food.

The manor was largely a self-sufficient community. The serfs and peasants raised or produced nearly everything that they and their lord needed for daily life—crops, fuel, cloth, leather goods, and lumber. The only outside purchases were salt, iron, and a few unusual objects such as millstones. These huge stones were used to grind flour.

The Harshness of Manor Life For the privilege of living on the lord's land, peasants paid a high price. They paid a tax on all grain ground in the lord's mill. Any attempt to dodge taxes by baking bread elsewhere was treated as a crime. Peasants also paid a tax on marriage. Weddings could take place only with the lord's consent. After all these payments to the lord, peasant families owed the village priest a **tithe,** or church tax. A tithe represented one-tenth of their income.

Background
Farming was the chief economic activity during the Middle Ages.

THINK THROUGH HISTORY
C. Analyzing Causes How might the decline of trade during the early Middle Ages have contributed to the self-sufficiency of the manor system?

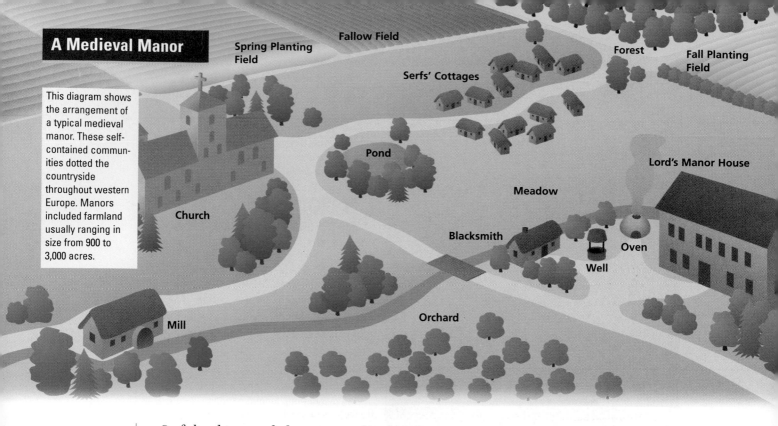

A Medieval Manor

This diagram shows the arrangement of a typical medieval manor. These self-contained communities dotted the countryside throughout western Europe. Manors included farmland usually ranging in size from 900 to 3,000 acres.

Fallow Field

Spring Planting Field

Forest

Fall Planting Field

Serfs' Cottages

Pond

Lord's Manor House

Meadow

Church

Blacksmith

Oven

Well

Mill

Orchard

Serfs lived in crowded cottages with only one or two rooms. They warmed their dirt-floor houses by bringing pigs inside. At night the family huddled on a pile of straw that often crawled with insects. Peasants' simple diet consisted mainly of vegetables, coarse brown bread, grain, cheese, and soup.

Piers Plowman, written by William Langland in 1362, reveals the hard life of English peasants:

A VOICE FROM THE PAST

What by spinning they save, they spend it in house-hire,
Both in milk and in meal to make a mess of porridge,
To cheer up their children who chafe for their food,
And they themselves suffer surely much hunger
And woe in the winter, with waking at nights
And rising to rock an oft restless cradle

WILLIAM LANGLAND, *Piers Plowman*

THINK THROUGH HISTORY
D. Making Inferences What does this excerpt suggest about the problems peasant families faced?

Despite the hardships they endured, serfs accepted their lot in life as part of the Church's teachings. They, like most Christians during medieval times, believed that God determined a person's place in society.

Section 2 Assessment

1. TERMS & NAMES

Identify
• lord
• fief
• vassal
• knight
• serf
• manor
• tithe

2. TAKING NOTES

Create a cause-and-effect chart like the one below. Show the reasons why feudalism developed and its consequences.

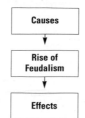

Causes
↓
Rise of Feudalism
↓
Effects

3. EVALUATING

What benefits do you think a medieval manor provided to the serfs who lived there? What were the drawbacks?

THINK ABOUT
• the duties and rights of serfs
• serfs' living conditions
• the diagram of the medieval manor on this page

4. THEME ACTIVITY

Power and Authority Work with a partner to draw up a contract between a lord and a vassal, such as a knight, or between the lord of a manor and a serf. Include the responsibilities, obligations, and rights of each party. Refer to information mentioned in the text.

3 The Age of Chivalry

MAIN IDEA	WHY IT MATTERS NOW
The code of chivalry for knights glorified combat and romantic love.	Chivalry has shaped modern ideas of romance in Western cultures.

SETTING THE STAGE During the Middle Ages, nobles constantly fought one another. Their feuding kept Europe in a fragmented state for centuries. Through warfare, feudal lords defended their estates, seized new territories, and increased their wealth. Lords and their armies lived in a violent society that prized combat skills. By the 1100s, a code of behavior arose. High ideals guided warriors' actions and glorified their roles.

Warriors on Horseback

Background
The Muslims who invaded Spain in the 700s and established a civilization there were called Moors.

Mounted soldiers became valuable in combat during the reign of Charlemagne's grandfather, Charles Martel, in the 700s. Charles Martel had observed that the Muslim cavalry often turned the tide of battles. As a result, he organized Frankish troops of armored horsemen, or knights.

Saddles and Stirrups The leather saddle was developed on the Asian steppes around 200 B.C. Stirrups were developed in India around the same time. Both changed the technology of warfare in Europe during the 700s. The saddle kept a warrior firmly seated on a moving horse. Stirrups allowed him to stand up while riding and to maneuver heavier weapons. Without stirrups to brace him, a charging warrior was likely to topple off his own horse.

Frankish knights, galloping full tilt, could knock over enemy foot soldiers and riders on horseback. Gradually, mounted knights became the most important part of an army. The horses they owned were status symbols. Warhorses played a key military role.

The Warrior's Role in Feudal Society By the 11th century, western Europe was a battleground of warring nobles vying for power. To defend their territories, feudal lords raised private armies. In exchange for military service, feudal lords used their most abundant resource—land. They rewarded knights, their most skilled warriors, with fiefs from their sprawling estates. Wealth from these fiefs allowed knights to devote their lives to war. Knights could afford to pay for costly weapons, armor, and warhorses.

As the lord's vassal, a knight's main obligation was to serve in battle. From each of his knights, a lord typically demanded about 40 days of mounted combat each year. Knights' pastimes also often revolved around training for war. Wrestling and hunting helped knights gain strength and practice the skills they would need on the battlefield.

These two-inch high iron spikes, called caltrops, were strewn over a battlefield or in front of a castle. They could maim galloping warhorses or enemy foot soldiers.

— 2 inches

— 0

327

PAGE The education of a young noble began early. At age 7, his parents sent him off to the castle of another lord. As a page, he waited on his hosts and learned courtly manners. He played chess to learn war strategies. To develop fighting skills, the page practiced sword fighting.

SQUIRE At around age 14, the page was raised to the rank of squire. A squire acted as a servant to a knight. The squire took care of the knight's armor, weapons, and warhorse. The squire also escorted the knight to battles.

KNIGHT At around age 21, a squire became a full-fledged knight. An English squire might have heard his lord say these words during the knighting ceremony: "In the name of God, Saint Michael, and Saint George, I dub thee knight. Be valiant."

Knighthood and Chivalry

Early in the Middle Ages, knights were expected to display courage in battle and loyalty to their lord. By the 1100s, the code of **chivalry** (SHIHV·uhl·ree), a complex set of ideals, demanded that a knight fight bravely in defense of three masters. He devoted himself to his earthly feudal lord, his heavenly Lord, and his chosen lady. The chivalrous knight also protected the weak and the poor. The ideal knight was loyal, brave, and courteous. Most knights, though, failed to meet these high standards. They treated the lower classes brutally.

A cowardly knight who disregarded the code of chivalry faced public shame. First, his armor was stripped off, and his shield was cracked. Next, his spurs were cut off, and his sword was broken over his head. People then threw the knight into a coffin and dragged him to church. There a priest would chant a mock funeral service.

War Games for Glory Sons of nobles began training for knighthood at an early age and learned the code of chivalry. After being dubbed a knight, most young men traveled with companions for a year or two. The young knights gained experience fighting in local wars. Some knights took part in mock battles called **tournaments**. Tournaments combined recreation with combat training. Two armies of knights charged each other. Trumpets blared, and lords and ladies cheered. Like real battles, tournaments were fierce and bloody competitions. Winners could usually demand large ransoms from defeated knights.

Brutal Reality of Warfare The small-scale violence of tournaments did not match the bloodshed of actual battles, especially those fought at castles. By the 1100s, stone castles were encircled by massive walls and guard towers. These castles dominated much of the countryside in western Europe. The castle was the home of the lord and lady, their family, knights and other men-at-arms, and servants. It also was a fortress, designed for defense.

A castle under siege was a gory sight. Attacking armies used a wide range of strategies and weapons to force castle residents to surrender. Defenders of a castle poured boiling water, hot oil, or molten lead on enemy soldiers. Expert archers were stationed on the roof of the castle. Armed with crossbows, they fired deadly bolts that could pierce full armor.

Background
The word *chivalry* comes from the French words *cheval* (horse) and *chevalier* (horse-riding knight).

THINK THROUGH HISTORY
A. Comparing How do medieval tournaments resemble modern sports competitions?

Vocabulary
siege: a military blockade staged by enemy armies trying to capture a fortress.

Castles and Siege Weapons

Attacking armies carefully planned how to capture a castle. Engineers would inspect the castle walls for weak points in the stone. Then enemy soldiers would try to ram the walls, causing them to collapse. At the battle site, attackers often constructed the heavy and clumsy weapons shown here.

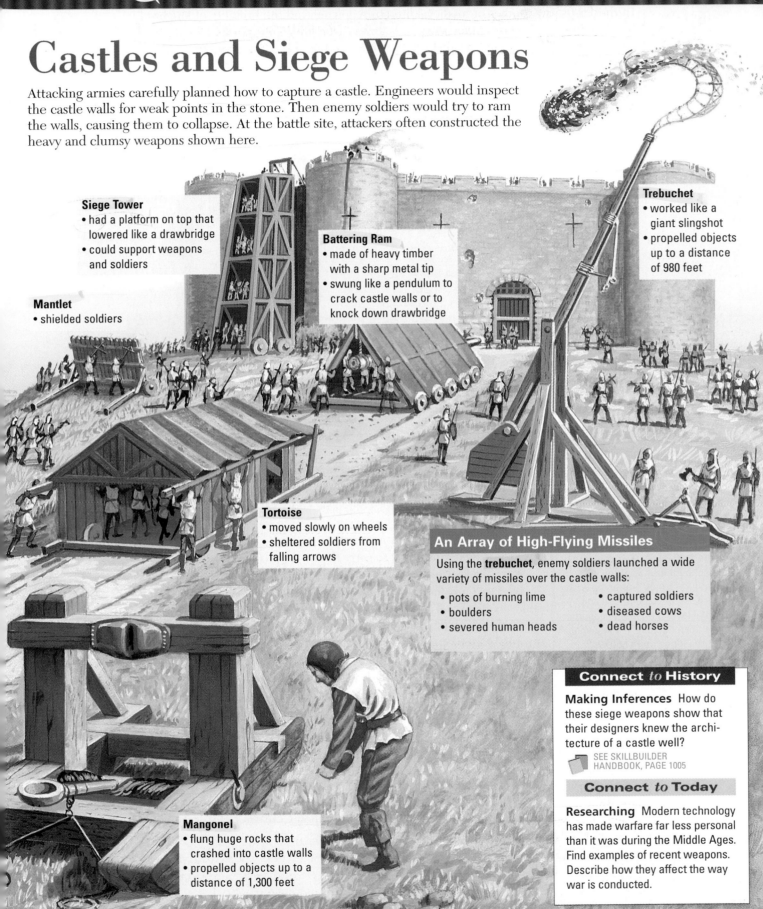

Siege Tower
- had a platform on top that lowered like a drawbridge
- could support weapons and soldiers

Mantlet
- shielded soldiers

Battering Ram
- made of heavy timber with a sharp metal tip
- swung like a pendulum to crack castle walls or to knock down drawbridge

Trebuchet
- worked like a giant slingshot
- propelled objects up to a distance of 980 feet

Tortoise
- moved slowly on wheels
- sheltered soldiers from falling arrows

Mangonel
- flung huge rocks that crashed into castle walls
- propelled objects up to a distance of 1,300 feet

An Array of High-Flying Missiles

Using the **trebuchet**, enemy soldiers launched a wide variety of missiles over the castle walls:

- pots of burning lime
- boulders
- severed human heads
- captured soldiers
- diseased cows
- dead horses

Connect *to* History

Making Inferences How do these siege weapons show that their designers knew the architecture of a castle well?

SEE SKILLBUILDER HANDBOOK, PAGE 1005

Connect *to* Today

Researching Modern technology has made warfare far less personal than it was during the Middle Ages. Find examples of recent weapons. Describe how they affect the way war is conducted.

The Literature of Chivalry

In the 1100s, the themes of medieval literature downplayed the brutality of knighthood and feudal warfare. Many stories idealized castle life. They glorified knighthood and chivalry, tournaments and real battles. Songs and poems about a knight's undying love for a lady were also popular.

Epic Poetry Feudal lords and their ladies enjoyed listening to epic poems. These poems recounted a hero's deeds and adventures. Many epics retold stories about legendary heroes of the early Middle Ages, such as King Arthur and Charlemagne.

The Song of Roland is one of the earliest and most famous medieval epic poems. It praises a band of French soldiers who perished in battle during Charlemagne's reign. The poem transforms the event into a struggle. A few brave French knights led by Roland battle an overwhelming army of Muslims from Spain. Roland's friend, Turpin the Archbishop, stands as a shining example of medieval ideals. Turpin represents courage, faith, and chivalry:

> ### A VOICE FROM THE PAST
> And now there comes the Archbishop.
> He spurs his horse, goes up into a mountain,
> summons the French; and he preached them a sermon:
> "Barons, my lords, [Charlemagne] left us in this place.
> We know our duty: to die like good men for our King.
> Fight to defend the holy Christian faith."
>
> from *The Song of Roland*

Love Poems and Songs Under the code of chivalry, a knight's duty to his lady became as important as his duty to his lord. In many medieval poems, the hero's difficulties resulted from a conflict between those two obligations.

Troubadours were poet-musicians at the castles and courts of Europe. They composed short verses and songs about the joys and sorrows of romantic love. Sometimes troubadours sang their own verses in the castles of their lady. They also sent roving minstrels to carry their songs to courts.

A troubadour might sing about love's disappointments: "My loving heart, my faithfulness, myself, my world she deigns to take/ Then leave me bare and comfortless to longing thoughts that ever wake."

Other songs told of lovesick knights who adored ladies they would probably never win: "Love of a far-off land/For you my heart is aching/And I can find no relief." The code of chivalry promoted a false image of knights. In turn, these love songs created an artificial image of women. In the troubadour's eyes, noblewomen were always beautiful and pure.

The most celebrated woman of the age was Eleanor of Aquitaine (1122–1204). Troubadours flocked to her court in the French duchy of Aquitaine. Later, as queen of England, Eleanor was the mother of Richard the Lion-Hearted and King John. Richard himself composed romantic songs and poems. Eleanor's daughter, Marie of Champagne, turned love into a subject of study like logic or law. She presided at a famed Court of Love. Troubled lovers came there to air their grievances.

Medieval musicians often played a harp or a lute, like the one shown here, to accompany recitals of poems celebrating warrior-heroes.

CONNECT to TODAY

Modern Love Songs

Many love songs played on the radio or cable TV share similarities with the love songs of troubadours from the 1100s and 1200s. Modern lyrics echo themes featured in troubadours' songs—happiness and heartbreaks, devoted lovers and unfaithful lovers, trust and jealousy.

The titles of modern love songs reflect the legacy of medieval troubadours' songs. Here are some examples:

- "Heartbreaker"
- "True Love"
- "Your Cheatin' Heart"
- "Power of Love"
- "Can't Help Falling in Love"

THINK THROUGH HISTORY
B. Making Inferences How was the code of chivalry like the idea of romantic love?

The Shifting Role of Women

The Church viewed women as inferior to men. In contrast, the idea of romantic love placed noblewomen on a pedestal where they could be worshipped. A true knight pledged to protect all women. He also might love, serve, and adore a particular lady, preferably from afar.

Yet as feudalism developed across western Europe, women's status actually declined. Their roles became increasingly limited to the home and convent.

For the vast majority of women life remained unchanged for centuries. During the Middle Ages, most women were still poor and powerless. Their roles were confined to performing endless labor, bearing children, and taking care of their families.

Women in Power Under the feudal system, a noblewoman could inherit an estate from her husband. Upon her lord's request, she could also send his knights to war. When her husband was off fighting, the lady of a medieval castle might act as military commander and a warrior. Noblewomen often played a key role in defending castles. They hurled rocks and fired arrows at attackers. Some women even dressed in armor, mounted warhorses, and mobilized a cavalry of knights.

However, unlike knights, women were not eligible to receive land as reward in exchange for military service. Women also held less property. Lords passed down their fiefs to their sons, not their daughters.

Women's Falling Status As the Middle Ages progressed, noblewomen wielded less real power than they had in earlier years. Eleanor of Aquitaine was a notable exception. As queen of England, she ruled at times for her husband, Henry II, and later for her sons, Richard and John. Few other women had such authority.

The Church played a part in medieval women's declining fortunes. The Church tried to regain control of religious appointments and organizations. It reclaimed convents and monasteries that noblewomen had founded or supported. As you will read in Section 4, the influence of the Church was far-reaching.

THINK THROUGH HISTORY
C. Summarizing
What privileges did noblewomen have in medieval society?

MS Bruxelles, B.R. 9961–62, fol. 91v. Copyright Bibliothèque Royale Albert Ier, Brussels, Belgium.

Knights were not the only warriors glorified in medieval paintings. These noblewomen show their courage and combat skills in defending a castle against enemies.

Section 3 Assessment

1. TERMS & NAMES

Identify
- chivalry
- tournament
- troubadour

2. TAKING NOTES

Using a web diagram like the one below, show ideas associated with chivalry.

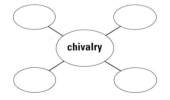

Which have remnants in today's society? Explain.

3. FORMING OPINIONS

Do you think the idea of romantic love helped or hindered women? Why?

THINK ABOUT
- pros and cons of placing women on a "pedestal"
- the Church's view of women
- the lyrics of love songs quoted in the text

4. ANALYZING THEMES

Religious and Ethical Systems What positive effects might the code of chivalry have had on feudal society?

THINK ABOUT
- the ideals of chivalry
- the education of a knight
- the importance of religious faith
- the violence and constant warfare during the Middle Ages

TERMS & NAMES
- clergy
- sacrament
- canon law
- Holy Roman Empire
- lay investiture

4 The Church Wields Power

MAIN IDEA	WHY IT MATTERS NOW
Church leaders and political leaders competed for power and authority.	Today many religious leaders still voice their opinions on political issues.

SETTING THE STAGE Amid the weak central governments in feudal Europe, the Church emerged as a powerful institution. It shaped the lives of people from all social classes. As the Church expanded its political role, strong rulers began to question the pope's authority. Dramatic power struggles unfolded in the Holy Roman Empire—the scene of mounting tensions between popes and emperors.

The Scope of Church Authority

In crowning Charlemagne emperor in 800, the Church sought to influence both spiritual and political matters. Three hundred years earlier, Pope Gelasius I recognized the conflicts that could arise between the two great forces—the Church and the state. He wrote, "There are two powers by which this world is chiefly ruled: the sacred authority of the priesthood and the authority of kings."

Gelasius suggested an analogy to solve such conflicts. God had created two symbolic swords. One sword was religious. The other was political. The pope held a spiritual sword. The emperor wielded a political one. Gelasius thought that the pope should bow to the emperor in political matters. In turn, the emperor should bow to the pope in religious matters. If each ruler kept the authority in his own realm, Gelasius suggested, the two leaders could share power in harmony.

In reality, though, the Church and state disagreed on the boundaries of either realm. Clashes erupted throughout the Middle Ages. The Church and various European governments competed for power.

This jeweled tiara, which a pope would wear in a procession, reflects the wealth, power, and authority of his office.

Church Structure Somewhat like the system of feudalism, the Church established its own organization. The distribution of power was based on status. Church structure consisted of different ranks of **clergy,** or religious officials. The pope headed the Church in Rome. All clergy, including bishops and priests, fell under his authority. Bishops supervised priests, the lowest ranking members of the clergy. Bishops also settled disputes over Church teachings and religious practices. For most people, local priests served as the main contact with the Church.

Religion as a Unifying Force Feudalism and the manor system created divisions among people. Shared beliefs in the teachings of the Church bonded people together. During an era of constant warfare and political turmoil, the Church was a stable force. The Church provided Christians with a sense of security and a religious community to which they might belong. The Middle Ages in Europe were aptly named the Age of Faith. Religion at this time occupied center stage.

Medieval Christians' everyday lives were often harsh. Still, they could all follow the same path to salvation—everlasting life in heaven. Priests and other religious officials administered the **sacraments,** or important religious ceremonies. These rites paved the

Background
The clergy was also part of the feudal system. In the early Middle Ages, some bishops, like other vassals, owed military service to their lord and fought courageously in battles.

way for achieving salvation. For example, through the sacrament of baptism, people became part of the Christian community. Through confirmation, baptized people of their own will publicly acknowledged their membership in the Church.

THINK THROUGH HISTORY
A. Analyzing Motives Why did medieval peasants support the Church?

At the local level, the village church was a unifying force in the daily lives of most people. It served as a religious and social center. People worshiped together at the church. They also met and talked with other villagers. Religious holidays, especially Christmas and Easter, were occasions for social gatherings and festive celebrations.

Church Justice The scope of the Church's authority was both religious and political. The Church provided a unifying set of spiritual beliefs and rituals. The Church also created a system of justice to guide people's conduct. All medieval Christians, kings and peasants alike, were subject to **canon law,** or the law of the Church, in matters such as marriage and religious practices. The Church also established courts to try people accused of violating canon law. Two of the harshest punishments that offenders faced were excommunication and interdict.

Popes used the threat of excommunication—banishment from the Church—to wield power over political rulers. For example, a disobedient king's quarrel with a pope might result in excommunication. This meant the king would be denied salvation. Excommunication also freed all the king's vassals from their duties to him. If an excommunicated king continued to disobey the pope, the pope, in turn, could use an even more frightening weapon—the interdict. Under an interdict, many sacraments and religious services could not be performed in the king's lands. As Christians, the king's subjects believed that without such sacraments they might be doomed to eternal suffering in hell. In the 11th century, excommunication and the possible threat of an interdict would force a German emperor to submit to the pope's commands.

The Church and the Holy Roman Empire

Background
The Holy Roman Empire was located in the region of present-day Germany.

After the death of Charlemagne, the **Holy Roman Empire** was the strongest kingdom that arose from the ruins of his empire. When Pope Leo III crowned Charlemagne emperor in 800, he unknowingly set the stage for future conflicts between popes and emperors.

Otto I Allies with the Church The most effective ruler of medieval Germany was Otto I. He was known as Otto the Great. Otto, crowned king in 936, consciously copied the policies of his boyhood hero, Charlemagne. Like Charlemagne, Otto formed a close alliance with the Church. To limit the nobles' strength, Otto sought help from the clergy. He built up his power base by gaining the support of the bishops and abbots, the heads of monasteries. Otto dominated the Church in Germany. He also used his power to defeat unruly German princes.

Following in Charlemagne's footsteps, Otto also invaded Italy on the pope's behalf. In 962, the pope rewarded Otto by crowning him emperor.

Signs of Future Conflicts The German-Italian empire Otto created was first called the Roman Empire of the German Nation. It later became known as the Holy Roman Empire. The Holy Roman Empire remained the strongest state in Europe until about 1100. However, Otto's attempt to revive Charlemagne's empire caused trouble for future German leaders. Italian nobles resented German rule. Popes too came to fear the political power that the German emperors held over Italy.

Daily Life

An Age of Superstition

Along with their devout Christian faith, many people during the Middle Ages also clung to superstitious beliefs. Medieval people expected the dead to reappear as ghosts. A friendly goblin might do a person a good deed, but an evil witch might cause great harm. Medieval people thought an evil witch had the power to exchange a healthy child for a sickly one.

The medieval Church frowned upon superstitions such as these:
- Preparing a table with three knives to please good fairies
- Making a vow by a tree, a pond, or any place but a church
- Believing that a person could change into the shape of a wolf
- Believing that the croak of a raven or meeting a priest would bring a person good or bad luck

---

Holy Roman Emperor Clashes with the Pope

The Church began to resent the control that kings, such as Otto, exercised over clergy and their offices. The focus of this resentment was **lay investiture**—a ceremony in which kings and nobles appointed church officials. Whoever controlled lay investiture wielded the real power in naming bishops. They were powerful clergy whom kings sought to control. Church reformers felt that bishops should not be under the power of any king. In 1075, Pope Gregory VII banned lay investiture.

The furious young German emperor, Henry IV, immediately called a meeting of the German bishops he had appointed. With their approval, the emperor sent a vicious letter to Gregory VII. Henry called Gregory "not pope, but false monk" and ordered him to step down from the papacy. Gregory fired back and excommunicated Henry. Afterward, German bishops and princes sided with the pope. Determined to save his throne, Henry tried to win the pope's forgiveness.

Showdown at Canossa In January 1077, Henry journeyed over the snowy Alps to the Italian town of Canossa (kuh·NAHS·uh). He approached the castle where Pope Gregory was a guest. Gregory later described the scene:

> **A VOICE FROM THE PAST**
> There, having laid aside all the belongings of royalty, wretchedly, with bare feet and clad in wool, he [Henry IV] continued for three days to stand before the gate of the castle. Nor did he desist from imploring with many tears the aid and consolation of the apostolic mercy until he had moved all of those who were present there. . . .
> **POPE GREGORY,** cited in *Basic Documents in Medieval History*

The Pope was obligated to forgive any sinner who begged so humbly. Still, Gregory kept Henry waiting in the snow for three days before ending his excommunication.

The meeting in Canossa was one of the most dramatic confrontations of the Middle Ages. Yet it actually solved nothing. A triumphant Henry rushed home to punish the nobles who had rebelled against him. The pope had gained an even greater victory by humiliating the proudest ruler in Europe. The key question of lay investiture remained undecided.

Concordat of Worms Gregory's and Henry's successors continued to fight over lay investiture until 1122. That year, representatives of the Church and the emperor met in the German city of Worms (wurms). There they reached a compromise known as the Concordat of Worms. By its terms, the Church alone could grant a bishop his ring and staff, symbols of Church office. Yet the emperor had the veto power to prevent the appointment of a bishop.

During Henry's struggle, German princes regained much of the power they had lost under Otto the Great. A later German ruler, Frederick I, would resume the battle to build up royal authority.

THINK THROUGH HISTORY
B. Making Inferences Why was Henry's journey to Canossa a political maneuver?

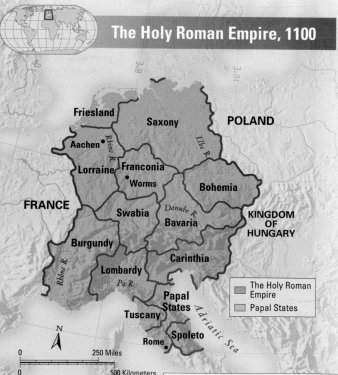

The Holy Roman Empire, 1100

Friesland
Saxony
POLAND
Aachen
Rhine R.
Elbe R.
Lorraine
Franconia
Worms
Bohemia
FRANCE
Swabia
Danube R.
Bavaria
KINGDOM OF HUNGARY
Burgundy
Carinthia
Rhône R.
Lombardy
Po R.
Papal States
Tuscany
Adriatic Sea
Rome
Spoleto

☐ The Holy Roman Empire
☐ Papal States

N

0   250 Miles
0   500 Kilometers

Mediterranean Sea

GEOGRAPHY SKILLBUILDER: Interpreting Maps
1. **Region** How many states make up the Holy Roman Empire? What does this suggest about ruling it as an empire?
2. **Location** How does the location of the Papal States make them an easy target for frequent invasions by Germanic rulers?

Ⓓ Renewed Church Conflicts Under Frederick I

Vocabulary
Barbarossa: "red
beard" in Italian.

By 1152, the seven German princes who elected the German king realized that Germany needed a strong ruler to keep the peace. The princes chose Frederick I. His red beard earned him the nickname "Barbarossa."

Frederick I was the first ruler to call his lands the Holy Roman Empire. However, this region was actually a patchwork of feudal territories. His forceful personality and military skills enabled him to dominate the German princes. Yet whenever he left the country, disorder returned.

Following Otto the Great's example, Frederick did not focus on building royal power in Germany. Instead, he repeatedly invaded the rich cities of Italy. Frederick's brutal tactics spurred Italian merchants to unite against him. Like Henry IV, Frederick angered the pope, who joined the merchants. Together, Frederick's enemies formed an alliance called the Lombard League.

In 1176, the foot soldiers of the Lombard League faced Frederick's army of mounted knights at the Battle of Legnano (lay·NYAHN·oh). In an astonishing victory, these foot soldiers used crossbows to defeat feudal knights for the first time in history.

In 1177, Frederick made peace with the pope and returned to Germany. Frederick's military defeat, though, had undermined his authority with the German princes. Their power continued to grow in spite of Frederick's efforts. After he drowned in 1190, Frederick's empire dissolved into an array of fragmented feudal states.

Ⓔ German States Remain Separate

THINK THROUGH HISTORY
**C. Analyzing
Causes** What long-lasting political trend kept German states separate during the Middle Ages?

By getting involved in Italian politics, German kings after Frederick continued their attempts to revive Charlemagne's empire and his alliance with the Church. This policy led to wars with Italian cities and to further clashes with the pope. These conflicts were among several reasons why the feudal states of Germany did not unify during the Middle Ages.

The system of German princes electing the king weakened royal authority. German rulers controlled fewer royal lands to use as a base of power than French and English kings, who were establishing strong central authority. These kings made changes in the legal system that would lay the foundation for modern unified nation-states.

As you will read in Chapter 14, feudalism in France and England spurred the rise of powerful leaders. They would create strong and enduring nations. Gradually, orderly government would replace the fighting and frequent warfare that characterized feudal societies, such as Germany.

This stained-glass portrait of Frederick I projects an image of imperial power. Yet like Henry IV, Frederick's clashes with the pope eroded the emperor's authority.

Section ④ Assessment

1. TERMS & NAMES

Identify
• clergy
• sacrament
• canon law
• Holy Roman Empire
• lay investiture

2. TAKING NOTES

Create a time line like the one below for the Holy Roman Empire. Write the significance of each date shown.

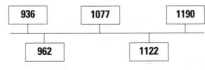

For which events did the Church and rulers engage in a power struggle? Why?

3. EVALUATING DECISIONS

Do you think the Concordat of Worms was a fair compromise for both the emperor and the Church? Why or why not?

THINK ABOUT
• the Church's authority in spiritual matters
• the emperor's political power
• the problems that remained unresolved

4. THEME ACTIVITY

Power and Authority Work with a partner to play the roles of Henry IV and Pope Gregory VII. Based on your role-play, write a dialogue about their meeting at Canossa.

TERMS & NAMES

Briefly explain the importance of each of the following during the Middle Ages from 500 to 1200.

1. monastery
2. Charlemagne
3. vassal
4. serf
5. manor

6. chivalry
7. troubadour
8. clergy
9. Holy Roman Empire
10. lay investiture

Interact *with* History

On page 316, you imagined what the world was like from the viewpoint of a peasant living on a medieval manor. Now that you've read the chapter, reconstruct a more accurate picture. What was a peasant's daily life like? Why did peasants cling to their religious beliefs and the teachings of the Church? Discuss your ideas in a small group.

REVIEW QUESTIONS

SECTION 1 (*pages 317–321*)
Germanic Kingdoms Unite Under Charlemagne

11. How did Gregory I increase the political power of the pope?
12. What was the outcome of the Battle of Tours?
13. What was the significance of the pope's declaring Charlemagne emperor?

SECTION 2 (*pages 322–326*)
Feudalism in Europe

14. Which invading peoples caused turmoil in Europe during the 800s?
15. What exchange took place between lords and vassals under the feudal system?
16. What duties did a lord of a manor and his serfs owe one another?

SECTION 3 (*pages 327–331*)
The Age of Chivalry

17. Briefly describe the stages of becoming a knight.
18. What were common subjects of troubadours' songs during the Middle Ages?

SECTION 4 (*pages 332–335*)
The Church Wields Power

19. What was Gelasius's two-swords theory?
20. Describe the conflict between Pope Gregory VII and Henry IV and its outcome.

Visual Summary

European Middle Ages

Feudalism
- Form of government based on landholding
- Alliances between lords and vassals
- Oaths of loyalty in exchange for land and military service
- Ranking of power and authority

POLITICAL SYSTEM

Chivalry
- Displays of courage and valor in combat
- Devotion to a feudal lord and heavenly lord
- Respect toward women

CODE OF BEHAVIOR

MEDIEVAL SOCIETY

ECONOMIC SYSTEM

Manors
- Lord's estate
- Set of rights and obligations between serfs and lords
- Self-sufficient community producing a variety of goods

BELIEF SYSTEM

The Church
- Unifying force of Christian faith
- Power over people's everyday lives
- Involvement in political affairs

CRITICAL THINKING

1. THE ROLE OF THE CHURCH

In what ways did the Church act as a system of government during the Middle Ages?

2. CHARLEMAGNE AND HIS LEGACY

THEME **EMPIRE BUILDING** Copy the three overlapping circles below to show how Otto I and Frederick I tried to imitate Charlemagne's approach to empire building.

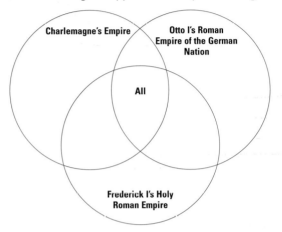

3. THE POWER OF LANDOWNERS

Why do you think the ownership of land became an increasing source of power for feudal lords?

4. ANALYZING PRIMARY SOURCES

In *The Canterbury Tales,* the English poet Geoffrey Chaucer tells a series of stories about characters from the Middle Ages. Read the following passage about a knight. Then answer the questions below it.

> **A VOICE FROM THE PAST**
> There was a *knight,* a most distinguished man,
> Who from the day on which he first began
> To ride abroad had followed chivalry,
> Truth, honor, generous, and courtesy.
> He had done nobly in sovereign's war
> And ridden in battle, no man more,
> As well as Christian in heathen places
> And ever honored for his noble graces.

- How does Chaucer characterize the knight?
- What qualities of knighthood do you think are missing from Chaucer's description? Use information from the text to support your answer.

CHAPTER ACTIVITIES

1. LIVING HISTORY: Unit Portfolio Projects

THEME **RELIGIOUS AND ETHICAL SYSTEMS** Your unit portfolio project focuses on showing the influence of the Church during the Middle Ages. For Chapter 13, you might use one of the following ideas to add to your portfolio.

- Write a character sketch of a religious or historical figure described in this chapter.
- Create a poster titled "The Age of Faith" focusing on the role that the Church played in the daily lives of Europeans.
- Create a time line tracing the most important power plays between religious and political leaders during the Middle Ages. Refer to the text for ideas.

2. CONNECT TO TODAY: Cooperative Learning

THEME **POWER AND AUTHORITY** Through warfare, knights helped feudal lords defend their estates, seize new territories, and gain more power. In mock battles called tournaments, knights developed their combat skills. Work with a team to design a video war game that imitates a medieval tournament between knights. Describe your ideas in a proposal that you might send to a video game company.

Use the Internet or books to find out more about medieval tournaments. Think about video games that are based on combat experiences. You might adapt some of the rules to your game. Use these questions to help you brainstorm ideas.

- What are the rules of the game?
- What is the system of keeping score of wins and losses?
- How should captured prisoners be treated?
- Which weapons should be used and which should be banned?

3. INTERPRETING A TIME LINE

Revisit the unit time line for Chapter 13 on pages 228–229. Which two important events in other parts of the world roughly coincide with the expansion of feudalism in western Europe? Give reasons to support your choices.

FOCUS ON **ART**

Chess was a popular game during the Middle Ages. The chess pieces portray important people from medieval society. Work with someone in class who plays chess to answer these questions:

- What element of medieval society do you think each chess piece represents?

- How do these chess pieces reflect the power of various members of medieval society?

Connect to History
Why do you think that learning to play chess was an important part of a knight's education?

The Formation of Western Europe, 800–1500

PREVIEWING THEMES

Religious and Ethical Systems

The Christian beliefs of the Middle Ages inspired the building of great cathedrals and helped shape the origins of European states. They also inspired the Crusades and guided the development of universities.

Economics

Medieval Europeans developed new methods of trade and new systems of finance and commerce. In response to population growth and territorial expansion, towns developed and learning revived.

Cultural Interaction

Although destructive in many ways, the Crusades resulted in a great deal of cultural exchange. The Christian world of medieval Europe learned and adopted much from the Muslim world and vice versa.

INTERNET CONNECTION

Visit us at **www.mcdougallittell.com** to learn more about medieval Europe, the Crusades, the medieval Muslim world, and related topics.

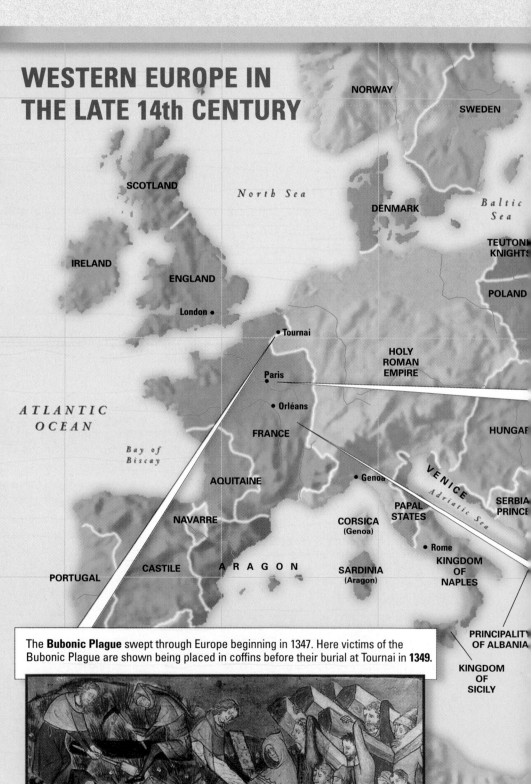

WESTERN EUROPE IN THE LATE 14th CENTURY

NORWAY
SWEDEN
SCOTLAND
North Sea
DENMARK
Baltic Sea
IRELAND
ENGLAND
TEUTONIC KNIGHTS
London
POLAND
Tournai
HOLY ROMAN EMPIRE
Paris
ATLANTIC OCEAN
Orléans
FRANCE
HUNGARY
Bay of Biscay
VENICE
Adriatic Sea
AQUITAINE
Genoa
PAPAL STATES
SERBIA PRINCE
NAVARRE
CORSICA (Genoa)
Rome
KINGDOM OF NAPLES
PORTUGAL
CASTILE
ARAGON
SARDINIA (Aragon)
PRINCIPALITY OF ALBANIA
KINGDOM OF SICILY

The **Bubonic Plague** swept through Europe beginning in 1347. Here victims of the Bubonic Plague are shown being placed in coffins before their burial at Tournai in **1349.**

20°W

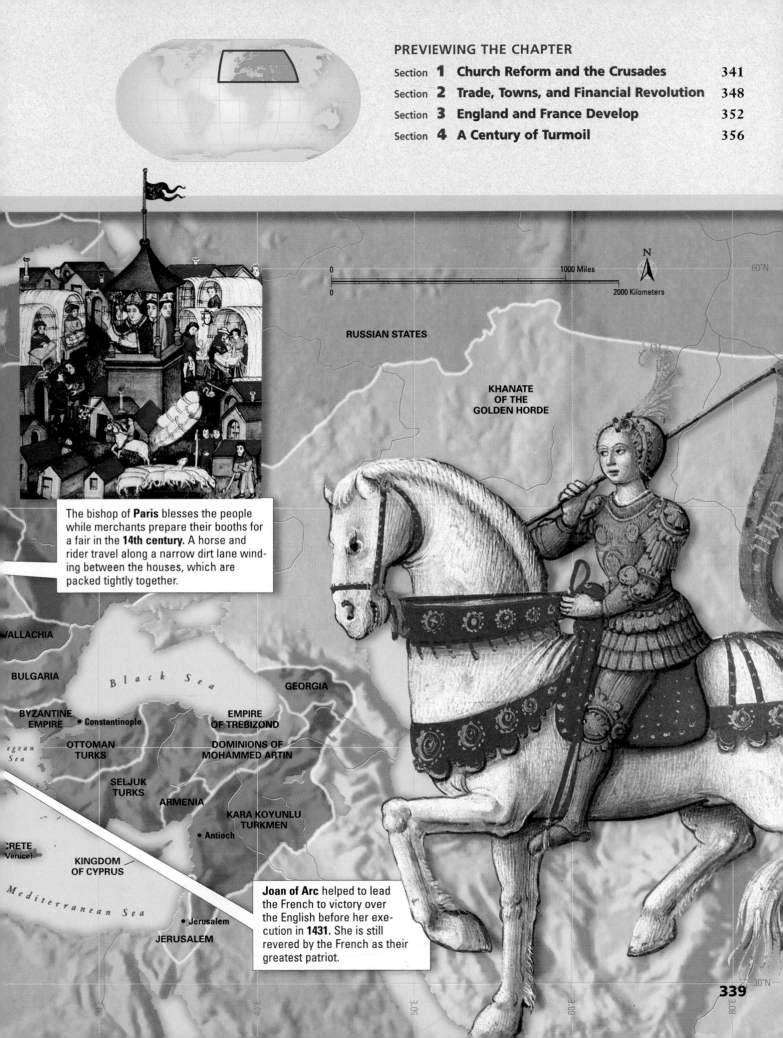

RUSSIAN STATES

KHANATE
OF THE
GOLDEN HORDE

0   1000 Miles

0   2000 Kilometers

60°N

The bishop of **Paris** blesses the people
while merchants prepare their booths for
a fair in the **14th century.** A horse and
rider travel along a narrow dirt lane winding between the houses, which are
packed tightly together.

WALLACHIA

Black Sea

BULGARIA

GEORGIA

BYZANTINE
EMPIRE   • Constantinople

EMPIRE
OF TREBIZOND

OTTOMAN
TURKS

DOMINIONS OF
MOHAMMED ARTIN

*Aegean
Sea*

SELJUK
TURKS

ARMENIA

KARA KOYUNLU
TURKMEN

• Antioch

CRETE
(Venice)

KINGDOM
OF CYPRUS

Mediterranean Sea

• Jerusalem

JERUSALEM

Joan of Arc helped to lead
the French to victory over
the English before her execution in **1431.** She is still
revered by the French as their
greatest patriot.

339

30°N

Interact *with* History

You are a squire in training to be a knight in France. The knight you serve has decided to join a Crusade to capture the city of Jerusalem from the Muslims. The knight has given you the choice of accompanying him on his expedition to the Holy Land (the biblical region of Palestine) or staying home to look after his family and manor. You would also look after your parents, who do not wish you to go. You are torn between the desire for adventure and possible riches that you might find on the Crusade, and fear of the hazards that await you on such a dangerous journey. On an earlier Crusade, the knight and his friends plundered towns and manors. They acquired jewels and precious objects. But some were also imprisoned, held for ransom, robbed, and murdered.

The knight as he went into battle was heavily armored. He wore a helmet and chain mail, and he carried various weapons, including a lance. He required assistance both in putting on his armor and in mounting his horse.

Would you join the Crusade?

While the knight went off on the Crusade, someone needed to look after his property in his absence. This task often fell to the lady of the manor, who exercised her authority through servants.

EXAMINING *the* ISSUES

- **What dangers might you face on the Crusade?**

- **What rewards, both material and personal, might come your way on the Crusade?**

- **What might be the advantages and disadvantages of staying home to defend the knight's family and estate?**

- **What arguments would you make to your parents to persuade them to agree to your participation in the Crusade?**

As a class, discuss these questions. In your discussion, remember what you've learned about other religious wars, sometimes called holy wars or crusades.

As you read about the Crusades in this chapter, see how events turned out for the Crusaders, especially the participants in the Children's Crusade.

A squire acted as a personal servant to the knight. A squire rode at his master's side in battle, in which he took an active part. One of his responsibilities in battle was to take charge of the prisoners.

Church Reform and the Crusades

TERMS & NAMES
- simony
- St. Francis of Assisi
- Gothic
- Urban II
- Crusade
- Saladin
- Richard the Lion-Hearted
- Reconquista
- Inquisition

MAIN IDEA

The Catholic Church underwent reform and launched Crusades (religious wars) against Muslims and others.

WHY IT MATTERS NOW

The Crusades resulted in trade and exploration between Christians and Muslims but left a legacy of distrust.

SETTING THE STAGE Between A.D. 500 and A.D. 1000, Vikings attacked and looted Church monasteries. They destroyed many of these centers of learning. At that time, the Church suffered severe problems. Some priests could barely read their prayers. Some popes were men of questionable morals. Many bishops and abbots cared more about their positions as feudal lords than about their duties as spiritual leaders. However, over the next 300 years the Church and medieval life changed dramatically.

Monastic Revival and Church Reform

Beginning in the 1000s, a spiritual revival spread across Europe. This revival was led by the monasteries. The reformers wanted to return to the basic principles of the Christian religion. New religious orders were founded. Influenced by the piety of the new monasteries, the popes began to reform the Church. They restored and expanded its power and authority. A new age of religious feeling was born—the Age of Faith.

Vocabulary
piety: religious devotion and reverence for God.

Problems in the Church Many problems troubled the Church at that time, but reformers were most distressed by three. First, many village priests married and had families. Such marriages were against Church rulings. Second, positions in the Church were sold by bishops, a practice called **simony** (SY·muh·nee). Third, the practice of lay investiture put kings in control of church bishops. Church reformers believed bishops should be appointed by the Church alone.

Reform Begins at Cluny Reforms began quietly in 910 with the founding of a Benedictine monastery at Cluny (KLOO·nee) in France. The monks there strictly followed the Benedictine rule. Soon Cluny's reputation for virtue inspired the founding of similar monasteries throughout western Europe. By the year 1000, there were 300 houses under Cluny's leadership. In 1098, another order was founded, the Cistercian (sih·STUR·shuhn) monks. The Cistercian life of hardship won many followers, helping to bring about further reforms.

Vocabulary
papacy: the position or office of the pope.

The reform movement, begun at Cluny, influenced the papacy. Pope Leo IX, who took office in 1049, enforced Church laws against simony and the marriage of priests. Pope Gregory VII was elected pope in 1073. He had spent time at Cluny and was determined to purify the Church. Gregory extended the reforms begun by Leo.

Reform and Church Organization The popes who followed Leo and Gregory reorganized the Church to continue the policy of reform. In the 1100s and 1200s the Church was restructured to resemble a kingdom, with the pope at its head. The pope's group of advisers was called the papal Curia. The Curia also acted as a court. It developed canon law (the law of the Church) on matters such as marriage, divorce, and inheritance. The Curia also decided cases based on these laws. Diplomats for the pope traveled through Europe dealing with bishops and kings. This extended the power of the pope.

This scene of monastic life comes from a Book of Hours, a book of prayers for private use that followed the hours of the day.

The Church collected taxes in the form of tithes. These consumed one-tenth the yearly income from every Christian family. The Church performed social services such as caring for the sick and the poor. Most hospitals in medieval Europe were operated by the Church. By the early 1200s, popes had achieved remarkable success in their reforms. The practice of simony and the marriage of clergy both declined dramatically. The popes established their authority throughout Europe.

Preaching Friars In the early 1200s, wandering friars traveled from place to place preaching and spreading the Church's ideas. Like monks, friars took vows of chastity, poverty, and obedience. Unlike monks, friars did not live apart from the world in monasteries. Instead, they preached to the poor throughout Europe's towns and cities. Friars owned nothing and lived by begging.

The Dominicans, one of the earliest orders of friars, were founded by Dominic, a Spanish priest. Because Dominic emphasized the importance of study, many Dominicans were scholars. Another order of friars, the Franciscans, was founded by the Italian **St. Francis of Assisi** (uh·SEE·zee). The son of a rich merchant, Francis gave up his wealth and turned to preaching when he was about 20 years old. He placed much less importance on scholarship than did Dominic. Francis treated all creatures as if they were his spiritual brothers and sisters.

Religious Orders for Women Women as well as men participated in the spiritual revival. Women joined the Dominicans. In 1212, the Franciscan order for women, known as the Poor Clares, was founded by Clare and her friend Francis of Assisi. In Germany, Hildegard of Bingen, a mystic and musician, founded a Benedictine convent in 1147. Unlike the men, women were not allowed to travel from place to place as preachers. However, they too lived in poverty and worked to help the poor and sick.

Cathedrals—Cities of God

Although the friars chose to live in poverty, evidence of the Church's wealth could be seen everywhere in the Middle Ages. This was especially true in the cathedrals that were built in Europe around this time.

A New Style of Church Architecture Between about 800 and 1100, churches were built in the Romanesque (ROH·muh·NEHSK) style. The churches had round arches and a heavy roof held up by thick walls and pillars. The thick walls had tiny windows that let in little light.

In the early 1100s, a new style of architecture, known as **Gothic**, evolved. The term *Gothic* comes from a Germanic tribe named the Goths. It describes the particular church architecture that spread throughout medieval Europe. Unlike the heavy, gloomy Romanesque buildings, Gothic cathedrals thrust upward as if reaching toward heaven. Light streamed in through huge stained-glass windows. Soon Gothic cathedrals were built in many towns of France. In Paris, the vaulted ceiling of the Cathedral of Notre Dame (NOH·truh DAHM) eventually rose to over 100 feet. Then Chartres, Reims, Amiens, and Beauvais built even higher cathedrals.

In all, nearly 500 Gothic churches were built between 1170 and 1270. Other arts of the medieval world clustered around the Gothic cathedral—sculpture, woodcarvings, and the stained-glass windows. The cathedral represented the City of God. As such, it was decorated with all the richness that people on earth could offer.

In this 13th-century painting, St. Clare (kneeling) is received by St. Francis (standing, with halo).

Background
Because of his love of nature, St. Francis was named the patron saint of ecology in 1979 by Pope John Paul II.

THINK THROUGH HISTORY
A. Making Inferences Why might women have preferred life in a religious order to secular life in the Middle Ages?

342 Chapter 14

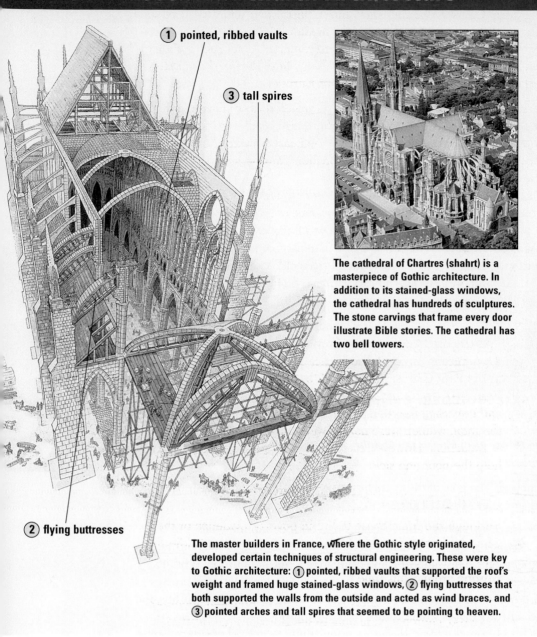

① pointed, ribbed vaults

③ tall spires

② flying buttresses

The master builders in France, where the Gothic style originated, developed certain techniques of structural engineering. These were key to Gothic architecture: ① pointed, ribbed vaults that supported the roof's weight and framed huge stained-glass windows, ② flying buttresses that both supported the walls from the outside and acted as wind braces, and ③ pointed arches and tall spires that seemed to be pointing to heaven.

The cathedral of Chartres (shahrt) is a masterpiece of Gothic architecture. In addition to its stained-glass windows, the cathedral has hundreds of sculptures. The stone carvings that frame every door illustrate Bible stories. The cathedral has two bell towers.

Chartres Cathedral has some of the most beautiful stained-glass windows of any Gothic cathedral in Europe. The windows illustrate stories from the Bible. As illiterate peasants walked past the 176 windows, they could view those stories. This window depicts the parable of the Good Samaritan.

Connect *to* History

Drawing Conclusions Gothic architecture was designed to achieve more height and light. What elements in the style of Gothic architecture might affect the sense of height and light inside?

SEE SKILLBUILDER HANDBOOK, PAGE 1006

Connect *to* Today

Taking a Tour Take a walk past the churches in your neighborhood. Notice the stained-glass windows. Do they tell a story? What figures or events do they illustrate?

The Crusades

The Age of Faith also inspired wars of conquest. In 1093, the Byzantine emperor Alexius Comnenus sent an appeal to Robert, Count of Flanders. That letter was also read by Pope **Urban II.** The emperor asked for help against the Muslim Turks. They were threatening to conquer his capital, Constantinople:

A VOICE FROM THE PAST
Come then, with all your people and give battle with all your strength, so that all this treasure shall not fall into the hands of the Turks. . . . Therefore act while there is still time lest the kingdom of the Christians shall vanish from your sight and, what is more important, the Holy Sepulchre [the tomb where Jesus was buried] shall vanish. And in your coming you will find your reward in heaven, and if you do not come, God will condemn you.

EMPEROR ALEXIUS COMNENUS, quoted in *The Dream and the Tomb*

Vocabulary
Holy Land: Palestine; the area where Jesus had lived and preached.

Shortly after this appeal, Pope Urban II issued a call for what he termed a "holy war," a **Crusade,** to gain control of the Holy Land. Over the next 200 years a number of such

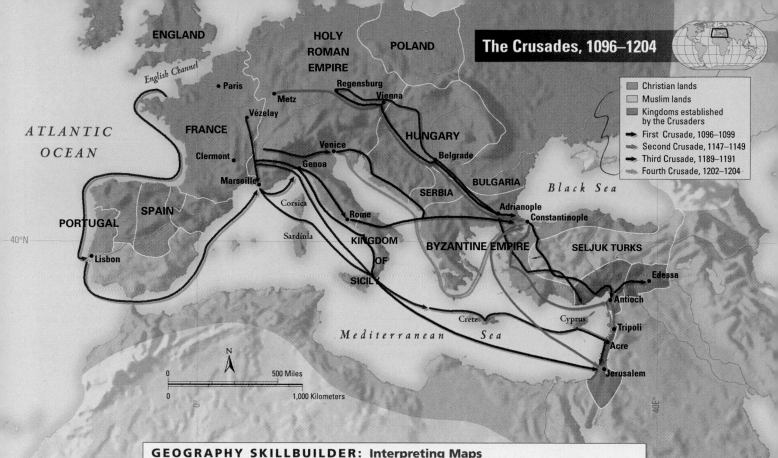

The Crusades, 1096–1204

Christian lands
Muslim lands
Kingdoms established by the Crusaders
First Crusade, 1096–1099
Second Crusade, 1147–1149
Third Crusade, 1189–1191
Fourth Crusade, 1202–1204

GEOGRAPHY SKILLBUILDER: Interpreting Maps
1. **Place** *What Muslim power ruled lands close to the Christian city of Constantinople?*
2. **Movement** *Which Crusade did not make it to Jerusalem? Where did this Crusade end?*
3. **Region** *Where in Europe were Muslim and Christian lands adjacent to one another?*

Crusades were launched. The goal of these military expeditions was to recover Jerusalem and the Holy Land from the Muslim Turks.

Causes of the Crusading Spirit The Crusades had both economic goals and religious motives. Pope Urban's call brought a tremendous outpouring of religious feeling and support for the Crusade. This support came from great lords and humble peasants alike. In 1096, between 50,000 and 60,000 knights became Crusaders. With red crosses sewn on tunics worn over their armor and the battle cry of "God wills it!" on their lips, the Crusaders marched eastward. Few would return from the journey.

Kings and the Church saw the Crusades as an opportunity to get rid of quarrelsome knights who fought each other. These knights threatened the peace of the kingdoms, as well as Church property. Others who participated were younger sons who, unlike their oldest brother, did not stand to inherit their father's property. They were looking for land and a position in society. Knights and commoners alike were fired by religious zeal. According to Pope Urban II, if the knights died on Crusade, they were assured of a place in heaven.

In later Crusades, merchants profited by making cash loans to finance the Crusade. They also leased their ships for a hefty fee to transport armies over the Mediterranean Sea. In addition, the merchants of Pisa, Genoa, and Venice hoped to win control of key trade routes to India, Southeast Asia, and China from Muslim traders.

The First and Second Crusades By early 1097, three armies of knights and people of all classes had gathered outside Constantinople. Most of the Crusaders were French. But Germans, Englishmen, Scots, Italians, and Spaniards came as well.

The Crusaders were ill-prepared for their holy war in this First Crusade. They knew nothing of the geography, climate, or culture of the Holy Land. They had no grand strategy to capture Jerusalem. The nobles argued among themselves and couldn't agree on a leader. Also, they had not set up adequate supply lines. Finally, however, an army of 12,000 (less than one-fourth the original army) approached Jerusalem. The Crusaders besieged the city for a month. On July 15, 1099, they captured the city.

All in all, the Crusaders had won a narrow strip of land. It stretched about 400 miles from Edessa in the north to Jerusalem in the south. Four feudal Crusader states were carved out of this territory, each ruled by a European noble.

THINK THROUGH HISTORY
B. Summarizing
What, if anything, had the Crusaders gained by the end of the Second Crusade?

The Crusaders' states were extremely vulnerable to Muslim counterattack. In 1144, Edessa was reconquered by the Turks. The Second Crusade was organized to recapture the city. But its armies straggled home in defeat. In 1187, Europeans were shocked to learn Jerusalem itself had fallen to the Muslim leader **Saladin** (SAL·uh·dihn).

The Third and Fourth Crusades

The Third Crusade to recapture Jerusalem was led by three of Europe's most powerful monarchs. These were the French king Philip Augustus, the German emperor Frederick I (Barbarossa), and the English king **Richard the Lion-Hearted.** Barbarossa drowned on the journey, and Philip Augustus argued with Richard and went home. Richard was left to regain the Holy Land from Saladin.

Both Richard and Saladin were ruthless fighters who respected each other. After many battles, the two agreed to a truce in 1192. Jerusalem remained under Muslim control. In return, Saladin promised that unarmed Christian pilgrims could freely visit the city's holy places.

In 1198, the powerful Pope Innocent III appealed for still another Crusade to capture Jerusalem. The knights who took part in this Fourth Crusade became entangled in Italian and Byzantine politics. They ended up looting the city of Constantinople in 1204, ending the Fourth Crusade. There was a breach (a split) between the Church in the east, whose capital was Constantinople, and the Church in the west, whose capital was Rome. This breach, caused in part by the Crusaders' actions, became permanent.

HISTORY MAKERS

Saladin
1138–1193

Saladin was the most famous Muslim leader of the 1100s. His own people considered him a most devout man. Even the Christians regarded him as honest and brave.

He wished to chase the Crusaders back into their own territories. He said:

> I think that when God grants me victory over the rest of Palestine, I shall divide my territories, make a will stating my wishes, then set sail on this sea for their far-off lands and pursue the Franks there, so as to free the earth from anyone who does not believe in Allah, or die in the attempt.

Richard the Lion-Hearted
1157–1199

Richard was noted for his good looks, charm, courage, grace—and ruthlessness. When he heard that Jerusalem had fallen to the Muslims, he was inspired with religious zeal. He joined the Crusade, leaving others to rule England in his place.

Richard mounted a siege on the city of Acre. Saladin's army was in the hills overlooking the city, but it was not strong enough to defeat the Crusaders. When finally the city fell, Richard had the Muslim survivors—some 3,000 men, women, and children—slaughtered. The Muslim army watched helplessly from the hills.

Background
In the looting of Constantinople, Crusaders stole the relics from the great cathedral. They loaded the jewel-studded communion table onto a Venetian ship. The ship sank, and its priceless cargo was never recovered.

The Crusading Spirit Dwindles

In the 1200s, Crusades became increasingly common and unsuccessful. The religious spirit of the First Crusade faded, replaced by a search for personal gain.

The Later Crusades In several later Crusades, armies marched not to the Holy Land but to North Africa. The French king who led the last two Crusades, Louis IX, won wide respect in Europe. He was later declared a saint. None of these attempts conquered much land, however.

The Children's Crusade took place in 1212. Thousands of children set out for the Holy Land. They were armed only with the belief that God would give them Jerusalem. On their march south to the Mediterranean, many died from cold and starvation. One group even turned back. The rest drowned at sea or were sold into slavery.

The Crusades

Causes

- Muslims control Palestine (the Holy Land) and threaten Constantinople.
- Byzantine emperor calls for help.
- Pope wants to reclaim Palestine and reunite Christendom.
- Pope appeals to Christian knights.
- Knights feel religious zeal and want land, riches, and adventure.
- Italian cities desire commercial power.

Effects

- Byzantine Empire is weakened.
- Pope's power declines.
- Power of feudal nobles weakens.
- Kings become stronger.
- Religious intolerance grows.
- Italian cities expand trade and grow rich.
- Muslims increasingly distrust Christians.
- Trade grows between Europe and the Middle East.
- European technology improves as Crusaders learn from Muslims.

A Spanish Crusade In Spain, Muslims (called Moors) had controlled most of the country until the 1100s. The **Reconquista** (ray·kawn·KEES·tuh) was a long effort to drive the Muslims out of Spain. By the late 1400s, the Muslims held only the tiny kingdom of Granada. In 1492, Granada fell to the Christian army of Ferdinand and Isabella, the Spanish monarchs.

Spain had a large Jewish population. Many achieved high positions in finance, government, and medicine. Many Jews (and Muslims) converted to Christianity during the late 1400s. To unify their country under Christianity and to consolidate their power, Isabella and Ferdinand made use of the **Inquisition.** This was a tribunal held by the Church to suppress heresy. Heretics were people whose religious beliefs differed from the teachings of the Church. The inquisitors suspected Jewish and Muslim converts of heresy. A person who was suspected of heresy might be questioned for weeks and even tortured. Once suspects confessed, they were often burned at the stake. Eventually, in 1492, the monarchs expelled all practicing Jews and Muslims from Spain.

The Effects of the Crusades The failure of later Crusades lessened the power of the pope. The Crusades weakened the feudal nobility. Thousands of knights lost their lives and fortunes.

On the positive side, the Crusades played a part in stimulating trade between Europe and Southwest Asia. The goods imported from Southwest Asia included spices, fruits, and cloth.

For Muslims, the Crusades also had both good and bad effects. The intolerance and prejudice displayed by Christians in the Holy Land left behind a legacy of bitterness and hatred. This legacy continues to the present. For Christians and Jews who remained in the region after the fall of the Crusader states, relations with their Muslim masters worsened. However, European merchants who lived and traded in the Crusader states were encouraged to continue their trading after the collapse of the states. This trade with the West benefited both Christians and Muslims.

The Crusades grew from the forces of religious fervor, feudalism, and chivalry as they came together with explosive energy. This same energy could be seen in the growth of trade, towns, and universities in medieval Europe.

THINK THROUGH HISTORY
C. Recognizing Effects What were the effects of the Reconquista?

Section ❶ Assessment

1. TERMS & NAMES

Identify
- simony
- St. Francis of Assisi
- Gothic
- Urban II
- Crusade
- Saladin
- Richard the Lion-Hearted
- Reconquista
- Inquisition

2. TAKING NOTES

Using a time line like the one below, show four or five key events that summarize the Age of Faith.

900 1000 1100 1200 1300 1400 1500

Write a paragraph describing one event in detail.

3. FORMING AND SUPPORTING OPINIONS

Which of the Church's problems—marriage of priests, simony, lay investiture—do you think was most harmful to the Church? Why?

THINK ABOUT
- the effects of each problem
- the reforms that corrected each problem

4. THEME ACTIVITY

Cultural Interaction With a partner, develop a scene from a play in which Richard the Lion-Hearted, in 1192, meets Saladin for the first time and the two warriors work out a truce. Include stage directions, but focus mainly on what the men say to each other. Be prepared to present the scene as a dialogue.

The Crusades

In the Crusades, both Christians and Muslims believed that God was on their side. They both felt justified in using violence to win or to keep the Holy Land. The following excerpts show their belief in God's approval for their deeds. The quotation from Norman Cantor explains where this attitude has led.

SPEECH
Pope Urban II

In 1095, Pope Urban II gave one of the most influential speeches of history when he issued a plea that resulted in the First Crusade. The pope assured his listeners that God was on their side.

Let the holy sepulcher of our Lord and Saviour, which is possessed by the unclean nations, especially arouse you. . . . This royal city [Jerusalem], situated at the center of the earth, is now held captive by the enemies of Christ and is subjected, by those who do not know God, to the worship of the heathen. Accordingly, undertake this journey eagerly for the remission of your sins, with the assurance of the reward of imperishable glory in the kingdom of heaven.

LETTER

Saladin

The German emperor Frederick I (Barbarossa) wrote the Muslim leader Saladin a letter threatening him if Saladin should attack Jerusalem. The following is an excerpt of Saladin's reply, written after he had recaptured Jerusalem.

Whenever your armies are assembled . . . we will meet you in the power of God. We will not be satisfied with the land on the seacoast, but we will cross over with God's good pleasure and take from you all your lands in the strength of the Lord. . . . And when the Lord, by His power, shall have given us victory over you, nothing will remain for us to do but freely to take your lands by His power and with His good pleasure. . . . By the virtue and power of God we have taken possession of Jerusalem and its territories; and of the three cities that still remain in the hands of the Christians . . . we shall occupy them also.

HISTORICAL ACCOUNT
William of Tyre

William of Tyre was a Christian bishop who drew upon eyewitness accounts of the capture of Jerusalem by the Crusaders in writing his account.

It was impossible to look upon the vast numbers of the slain without horror; everywhere lay fragments of human bodies, and the very ground was covered with the blood of the slain. It was not alone the spectacle of headless bodies and mutilated limbs strewn in all directions that roused horror in all who looked upon them. Still more dreadful was it to gaze upon the victors themselves, dripping with blood from head to foot, an ominous sight which brought terror to all who met them. It is reported that within the Temple enclosure alone about ten thousand infidels perished, in addition to those who lay slain everywhere throughout the city in the streets and squares, the number of whom was estimated as no less.

HISTORIAN'S COMMENTARY
Norman Cantor

Historian Norman Cantor explains the lasting legacy of the Crusades—even today when nation fights nation, each sincerely believes that God is on its side.

The most important legacy of the crusading movement was the sanctification [making holy] of violence in pursuit of [ideas]. This was not a new concept, but it took on new force when the pope and the flower of Christian chivalry acted it out in holy wars. The underlying concept outlived its religious origin, . . . and the state gradually replaced the Church as a holy cause.

Connect *to* History

Comparing Use specific phrases or passages from Urban's speech and from Saladin's letter to show how their attitudes are similar.

 SEE SKILLBUILDER HANDBOOK, PAGE 996

Connect *to* Today

Researching Find accounts in newspapers or magazines of how some groups today feel morally justified in using violence. Share your accounts with the class.

 CD-ROM For another perspective on the Crusades, see World History: Electronic Library of Primary Sources.

Trade, Towns, and Financial Revolution

TERMS & NAMES
- three-field system
- guild
- burgher
- vernacular
- Dante Alighieri
- Geoffrey Chaucer
- Thomas Aquinas
- scholastics

MAIN IDEA

European cities challenged the feudal system as agriculture, trade, finance, and universities developed.

WHY IT MATTERS NOW

The various changes in the Middle Ages laid the foundations for modern Europe.

SETTING THE STAGE While Church reform, cathedral building, and the Crusades were taking place, other important changes were occurring in medieval society. Between 1000 and 1300, agriculture, trade, and finance made remarkable progress. Towns and cities grew. This was in part due to the growing population and territorial expansion of western Europe. The creativity unleashed during this age also sparked the growth of learning and the birth of an institution new to Europe—the university.

A variety of farm chores is shown in this 14th-century agricultural almanac.

A Growing Food Supply

Europe's great revival would have been impossible without better ways of farming. Expanding civilization requires an increased food supply. Farming was helped by a warmer climate that lasted from about 800 to 1200. Farmers began to cultivate lands in regions once too cold to grow crops. They also developed new methods to take advantage of more available land.

Using Horsepower For hundreds of years, peasants depended on oxen to pull their plows. Oxen lived on the poorest straw and stubble. They were easy to keep, but they moved very slowly. Horses needed better food, but a team of horses could plow twice as much land in a day as a team of oxen.

Before they could use horses, however, people needed a new type of harness. Harnesses of the early Middle Ages went around the horse's neck. They nearly strangled the animal when it pulled. Sometime before 900, farmers in Europe began using a new technology. This was a harness that fitted across the horse's chest, taking pressure off its neck and windpipe. As a result, horses gradually replaced oxen for plowing and for pulling wagons.

The Three-Field System At the same time, villagers began to organize their land differently. Under the old, two-field system, peasants divided the village's land into two great fields. They planted one field with crops and left the other to lie fallow, or unplanted to avoid exhausting the soil, for a year. So if a village had 600 acres, each year farmers used 300 acres for raising food, leaving the other 300 acres fallow.

Around 800, some villages began to organize their land into three fields. With the same 600 acres, they used 200 acres for a winter crop of wheat or rye. In spring, they planted another 200 acres with oats, barley, peas, or beans. The remaining 200 acres lay fallow. Under this new, **three-field system,** farmers could grow crops on two-thirds of their land each year, not just on half of it. As a result, food production increased. Villagers had more to eat. The food was also better for them, because peas, beans, and lentils are good sources of vegetable protein. The result was an increase in population. People could raise larger families. Well-fed people could better resist disease and live longer. With horses, a farmer plowed more land in a day. This meant that teams cleared forests for new fields. All over Europe, axes rang as the great forests began to fall.

THINK THROUGH HISTORY
A. Recognizing Effects What were the main consequences of the three-field system?

Trade and Finance Expand

Just as agriculture was expanding, so were trade and finance. This was in part a response to population growth. By the 1000s, artisans and craftsmen were manufacturing goods by hand for local and long-distance trade. Trade routes spread across Europe from Flanders to Italy. Italian merchant ships traveled the Mediterranean to ports in Byzantium such as Constantinople. They also traveled to Muslim ports along the North African coast. Trade routes were opened to Asia, in part by the Crusades.

Fairs and Trade Most trade took place in towns. Peasants from nearby manors traveled to town on fair days, hauling items to trade. Cloth was the most common trade item. Other items included bacon, salt, honey, cheese, wine, leather, dyes, knives, and ropes. Such local fairs met all the needs of daily life for a small community. No longer was everything produced on a self-sufficient manor.

The Guilds Great fairs were made possible by the guilds, which controlled the crafts and trade. A **guild** was an association of people who worked at the same occupation. It was similar to a union today. In medieval towns, guilds controlled all wages and prices in their craft. Each guild usually met in its own guild hall. The first guilds were formed by merchants who controlled all the trade in their town.

As towns grew, skilled artisans—such as wheelwrights, glassmakers, winemakers, tailors, and druggists—began craft guilds. Guilds enforced standards of quality. Bakers, for example, were required to sell loaves of bread of a standard size and weight and at a fair price.

Only masters of the trade could be guild members. Becoming a master wasn't easy. First a child was apprenticed for five to nine years to a master to learn the trade. Then the apprentice became a journeyman and could go to work for wages. As the final step, a journeyman made an item—whether it was a shoe, a barrel, or a sword—that qualified as a "master piece." Journeymen whose product met guild standards were welcomed into the guild as masters.

A Financial Revolution This medieval world of fairs and guilds created a need for large amounts of cash. Before a merchant could make a profit selling his goods at a fair, he first had to purchase goods from distant places. Usually, this meant he had to borrow money, but the Church forbade Christians from lending money at interest, a sin called usury. Where, then, did merchants go for a loan?

Many of Europe's Jews lived in the growing towns and were moneylenders. Moneylending was one of the few ways of making a living allowed them. In this largely Christian world, Jews were kept on the fringes of society. Guilds excluded them. They had to live in segregated parts of towns called ghettos. Because Jews were forbidden to hold land, they had never become part of the feudal system. Over time, the Church relaxed its rule on usury. Banking became an important business, especially in Italy.

Urban Splendor Reborn

All over Europe, trade blossomed, and better farming methods caused a spurt of population growth. Scholars estimate that between 1000 and 1150, the population of western Europe rose from around 30 million to about 42 million. Towns grew and flourished. Compared to great cities like Constantinople, European towns were primitive and tiny. Europe's largest city, Paris, probably had no more than 60,000 people by the year 1200. A typical town in medieval Europe had only about 1,500 to 2,500 people. Nevertheless, these small communities became a powerful force for change.

Background
Great fairs were held several times a year, usually during religious festivals, when many people would be in town. People could visit the stalls set up by merchants from all parts of Europe.

Background
In most crafts, both husbands and wives worked at the family trade. In some guilds, especially for cloth-making, women formed the majority.

THINK THROUGH HISTORY
B. Recognizing Effects How did the exclusion of Jews from many aspects of life in medieval Europe affect their ways of earning a living?

Daily *Life*

Surnames

Many people can trace their last names, or surnames, back to a medieval occupation. For example, a man who made thatched roofs for cottages became Thatcher.

The name Smith refers to a man who "smites," or works, metal. There is also Brownsmith, one who works copper; Goldsmith, one who works gold; and Silversmith, one who works silver.

Someone who made things out of wood might be surnamed Carpenter. Someone who made or repaired wooden barrels might be called Cooper.

Place names also became surnames, such as Holland and Welsh (a person from Wales). Sometimes, a person new to the area simply received the surname Newman. Surnames can also derive from family relationships, as does Williamson.

Trade and Towns Grow Together By the later Middle Ages, trade was the very lifeblood of the new towns, which sprang up at ports, at crossroads, on hilltops, and along rivers. All over Europe, as trade grew, towns swelled with people. The excitement and bustle of towns drew many people. They were no longer content with their old feudal existence. Even though they were legally bound to their lord's manor, many serfs ran away. As people left life on the manor for life in towns, they challenged the traditional ways of feudal society in which everyone had his place. They did not return to the manor, and towns grew rapidly.

Most medieval towns developed haphazardly. Streets were narrow, filled with horses, pigs, oxen, and their refuse. With no sewers, most people dumped household waste, both animal and human, into the street in front of the house. Most people never bathed, and their houses lacked fresh air, light, and clean water. Because houses were built of wood with thatched roofs, they were a constant fire hazard. All in all, there were many drawbacks to living in a medieval town. Nonetheless, many people chose to move to such towns to pursue the economic and social opportunities they offered.

Towns and the Social Order So many serfs had left the manors by the 1100s that according to custom, a serf could now become free by living within a town for a year and a day. As the saying went, "Town air makes you free." Many of these runaway serfs, now free people, made better lives for themselves in towns.

The merchants and craftsmen of medieval towns did not fit into the traditional medieval social order of noble, clergy, and peasant. At first, towns came under the authority of feudal lords, who used their authority to levy fees, taxes, and rents. As trade expanded, the **burghers**, or town dwellers, resented this interference in their trade and commerce. They organized themselves and demanded privileges. These included freedom from certain kinds of tolls or the right to govern the town. At times they fought against their landlords and won these rights by force.

This drawing of the bishop of Paris blessing the people at a fair dates from the 14th century. The scene shows town dwellers going about their business, including merchants in their fair booths.

THINK THROUGH HISTORY
C. Summarizing
What were the advantages of town life for many former serfs?

The Revival of Learning

Growing trade and growing cities brought a new interest in learning. At the center of the growth of learning stood a new European institution—the university. Athens, Alexandria, Rome, and Constantinople had all been centers of learning, but never before had the world seen the university as it arose in western Europe.

Scholars and Writers The word *university* originally designated a group of scholars meeting wherever they could. People, not buildings, made up the medieval university. Universities arose at Paris and at Bologna, Italy, by the end of the 1100s. Others followed at the English town of Oxford and at Salerno, Italy. Most students were the sons of burghers or well-to-do artisans. For most students, the goal was a job in government or the Church. Earning a bachelor's degree in theology might take 5 to 7 years in school; becoming a master of theology took at least 12 years of study.

At a time when serious scholars and writers were writing in Latin, a few remarkable poets began using a lively **vernacular,** or the everyday language of their homeland. Some of these writers wrote masterpieces that are still read today. **Dante Alighieri** wrote *The Divine Comedy* (1321) in Italian. **Geoffrey Chaucer** wrote *The Canterbury Tales* (about 1387–1400) in English. Christine de Pisan wrote *The City of Ladies* (1405) in French. Since most people couldn't read or understand Latin, these writers brought literature to

Vocabulary

pilgrimage: a journey to a sacred place or shrine.

many people. For example, Chaucer's *Canterbury Tales* describes a pilgrimage to the shrine of St. Thomas à Becket. It was read aloud at gatherings:

A VOICE FROM THE PAST

It happened in that season that one day
In Southwark, at *The Tabard*, as I lay
Ready to go on pilgrimage and start
For Canterbury, most devout at heart,
At night there came into that hostelry
Some nine and twenty in a company
Of sundry folk happening then to fall
In fellowship, and they were pilgrims all
That towards Canterbury meant to ride.

GEOFFREY CHAUCER, the Prologue to *The Canterbury Tales*, translated by Nevill Coghill

SPOTLIGHT ON

Arab Scholars

A number of Islamic scholars had a great influence on European thought. The woodcut from 1584 above shows Ibn Sina, known in the West as Avicenna. He was a Persian philosopher, astronomer, poet, and physician. A book of his that greatly affected Western thought was *The Cure,* an interpretation of the philosophy of Aristotle. This work, translated into Latin, influenced the scholastics.

Another scholar was Ibn Rushd, known in the West as Averroes, who lived in Córdoba, Spain. He achieved fame for his commentaries on the works of Aristotle. These works were translated from Arabic into Latin and were used in universities throughout Christian Europe in the 1200s. Ibn Rushd's work greatly influenced Western thinkers.

The Muslim Connection The revival of learning sparked European interest in the works of ancient scholars. At the same time, the growth of trade was accelerated by the Crusades. This brought Europeans into contact with Muslims and Byzantines. These people had preserved in their libraries the writings of the old Greek philosophers. In the 1100s, Christian scholars from Europe began visiting Muslim libraries in Spain. Few Western scholars knew Greek. Jewish scholars translated Arabic versions of works by Aristotle and other Greek writers into Latin. All at once, Europeans acquired a huge new body of knowledge. This included science, philosophy, law, mathematics, and other fields. In addition, the Crusaders learned from, and brought back to Europe, superior Muslim technology in ships, navigation, and weapons.

Aquinas and Medieval Philosophy Christian scholars were excited by the Greek writings. Could a Christian scholar use Aristotle's logical approach to truth and still keep faith with the Bible?

In the mid-1200s, the scholar **Thomas Aquinas** (uh·KWY·nuhs) argued that the most basic religious truths could be proved by logical argument. Between 1267 and 1273, Aquinas wrote the *Summa Theologica*. Aquinas's great work, influenced by Aristotle, combined ancient Greek thought with the Christian thought of his time. Aquinas and his fellow scholars who met at the great universities were known as schoolmen, or **scholastics.** The scholastics used their knowledge of Aristotle to debate many issues of their time. Their teachings on law and government influenced the thinking of western Europeans, particularly the English and French. Accordingly, they began to develop democratic institutions and traditions.

THINK THROUGH HISTORY
D. Supporting Opinions Why do you suppose that Aristotle was called "the master of those who know" and "the philosopher" in medieval times?

Section 2 Assessment

1. TERMS & NAMES

Identify
- three-field system
- guild
- burgher
- vernacular
- Dante Alighieri
- Geoffrey Chaucer
- Thomas Aquinas
- scholastics

2. TAKING NOTES

Using a web diagram like the one below, show how medieval society changed between 1000 and 1300.

Changes in Medieval Society

3. ANALYZING CAUSES

What was the effect of towns on the feudal system?

THINK ABOUT
- where the new townsfolk came from
- the saying "Town air makes you free"
- the changes experienced by townspeople

4. ANALYZING THEMES

Economics How did guilds improve the quality of goods and business practices?

THINK ABOUT
- who enforced standards of quality
- who could become guild members

TERMS & NAMES
- **William the Conqueror**
- **Henry II**
- **Eleanor of Aquitaine**
- **Magna Carta**
- **parliament**
- **Philip II**
- **Louis IX**

3 England and France Develop

MAIN IDEA	WHY IT MATTERS NOW
As the kingdoms of England and France began to develop into nations, certain democratic traditions evolved.	Modern concepts of jury trials, common law, and legal rights developed during this period.

SETTING THE STAGE By the early 800s, small Anglo-Saxon kingdoms covered the former Roman province of Britain. In Europe, the decline of the Carolingian Empire in the 900s left a patchwork of feudal states controlled by local lords. Gradually, the rise of the burghers, the growth of towns and villages, and the breakup of the feudal system were leading to changes in government and the development of nations.

England Absorbs Waves of Invaders

For centuries, invaders from various regions in Europe landed on English shores. Many of them stayed, bringing their own ways and changing English culture.

Early Invasions In the 800s, Britain was battered by fierce raids of Danish Vikings. These invaders were so feared that a special prayer was said in churches: "God, deliver us from the fury of the Northmen." Only Alfred the Great, king from 871 to 899, managed to turn back the Viking invaders. Gradually he and his successors united the kingdom under one rule, calling it England—"land of the Angles." The Angles were one of the Germanic tribes that had invaded Britain.

In 1016, the Danish king Canute (kuh·NOOT) conquered England, molding Anglo-Saxons and Vikings into one people. In 1042, King Edward the Confessor, a descendant of the Anglo-Saxon Alfred the Great, took the throne. Edward died in January 1066 without an heir. A great struggle for the throne erupted, and that led to one last invasion.

The Norman Conquest The invader was William, duke of Normandy, who became known as **William the Conqueror.** Normandy is a region in the north of France that had been conquered by the Vikings. The Normans were descended from the Vikings, but they were French in language and in culture. As King Edward's cousin, William claimed the English crown and invaded England with a Norman army. William was ambitious, tough, and an imposing figure. An anonymous monk of the time described him:

A VOICE FROM THE PAST
[William was] great in body and strong, tall in stature but not ungainly. He was also temperate in eating and drinking. . . . In speech he was fluent and persuasive, being skilled at all times in making clear his will. If his voice was harsh, what he said was always suited to the occasion. . . .
ANONYMOUS MONK OF CAEN

William's rival was Harold Godwinson, the Anglo-Saxon who claimed the throne. And he was equally ambitious. On October 14, 1066, Normans and Saxons fought the battle that changed the course of English history—the Battle of Hastings. After Harold was killed by an arrow in his eye, the Normans won a decisive victory.

William the Conqueror, from a 13th-century English

Background
Through William's actions, England suddenly had a new ruling class of French-speaking nobles. William kept about one-fifth of England for himself, a powerful base for any king.

After his victory, William declared all England his personal property. The English lords who supported Harold lost their lands. William then granted fiefs to about 200 Norman lords who swore oaths of loyalty to him personally. In this way he laid the foundation for centralized government.

England's Evolving Government

William the Conqueror's descendants owned land both in Normandy and in England. The English King **Henry II** added to these holdings by marrying **Eleanor of Aquitaine.** She brought with her more lands from France. Over the next centuries English kings tried to achieve two goals. First, they wanted to hold and add on to their French lands. Second, they wanted to strengthen their own power over the nobles and the Church.

Monarchs, Nobles, and the Common Law Eleanor of Aquitaine was one of the most remarkable women in history. She was wife to two kings and mother to two kings. She married Louis VII of France when the Second Crusade began. In 1147, she accompanied him to the Holy Land. Shortly afterward their marriage was annulled. Eleanor then married Henry Plantagenet, who was to become Henry II of England. Their marriage produced four sons. Two became English kings—Richard the Lion-Hearted and John. The marriage also brought Henry a large territory in France called Aquitaine. He added Aquitaine to the lands in Normandy he had already inherited from William the Conqueror. Because Henry held lands in France, he was a vassal to the French king. But he was also a king in his own right.

Henry ruled England from 1154 to 1189. He strengthened the royal courts of justice by sending royal judges to every part of England at least once a year. They collected taxes, settled lawsuits, and punished crimes. Henry also introduced the use of the jury in English courts. A jury in medieval England was a group of loyal people—usually 12 neighbors of the accused—who answered a royal judge's questions about the facts of a case. Jury trials became a popular means of settling disputes. Only the king's courts were allowed to conduct them.

Over the centuries, case by case, the rulings of England's royal judges formed a unified body of law that became known as common law. Today these principles of English common law are the basis for law in many English-speaking countries, including the United States.

The Magna Carta Henry was succeeded first by his son Richard the Lion-Hearted, hero of the Third Crusade. When Richard died, his younger brother John took the throne. John ruled from 1199 to 1216. He failed as a military leader, earning the nickname John Softsword. John lost Normandy and all his lands in northern France to the French. This loss forced a confrontation with his own nobles.

Some of John's problems stemmed from his own character. He was mean to his subjects and tried to squeeze money out of them. John raised taxes to an all-time high to finance his wars. His nobles revolted. On June 15, 1215, they forced John to agree to the most celebrated document in English history, the **Magna Carta** (Great Charter). This document, drawn up by English nobles and reluctantly approved by King John, guaranteed certain basic political rights. The nobles wanted to safeguard their own feudal rights and limit the king's powers. In later years, however, English people of all classes argued that certain clauses in the Magna Carta applied to every citizen. Guaranteed rights included no taxation without representation, a jury trial, and the protection of the law. The Magna Carta guaranteed what are now considered basic legal rights both in England and in the United States.

THINK THROUGH HISTORY
A. Summarizing
What is the significance of the Magna Carta?

CONNECT to TODAY

Robin Hood in the Movies
During the time of King Richard and King John, Robin Hood was said to live in Sherwood Forest with his band of merry men. According to the stories about him, he was an outlaw who robbed from the rich and gave to the poor. He attempted to remedy some of the injustices committed under King John.

There have been many film versions of the story of Robin Hood. Douglas Fairbanks starred in a silent *Robin Hood* (1922). Errol Flynn (above right) starred in *The Adventures of Robin Hood* (1938), a version celebrated for its rousing action. Disney released an animated *Robin Hood* in 1973. Kevin Costner starred in the popular *Robin Hood: Prince of Thieves* (1991).

The Model Parliament Another important step toward democratic government resulted from Edward I's struggles to hang onto his last remaining French lands. In 1295, Edward needed to raise taxes for a war against the French. Edward summoned two burgesses (citizens of wealth and property) from every borough and two knights from every county to serve as a **parliament,** or legislative group. In November 1295, knights, burgesses, bishops, and lords met together at Westminster in London. This is now called the Model Parliament because its new makeup (commoners, or non-nobles, as well as lords) served as a model for later kings.

Over the next century, from 1300 to 1400, the king called the knights and burgesses whenever a new tax was needed. In Parliament, these two groups gradually formed an assembly of their own called the House of Commons. Nobles and bishops met separately as the House of Lords. Under Edward I, Parliament was in part a royal tool that weakened the great lords. As time went by, however, Parliament became strong. Like the Magna Carta, it provided a check on royal power.

Vocabulary
borough: a self-governing town.

THINK THROUGH HISTORY
B. Clarifying What was the Model Parliament and why did it come to be considered a model?

Capetian Dynasty Rules France

The kings of France, like those of England, looked for ways of increasing their power. After the breakup of Charlemagne's empire, French counts and dukes ruled their lands independently under the feudal system. By the year 1000, France was divided into about 30 feudal territories. In 987, the last member of the Carolingian family—Louis the Sluggard—died. Hugh Capet (kuh·PAY), an undistinguished duke from the middle of France, succeeded him. The Capet family ruled only a small territory, but at its heart stood Paris. Hugh Capet began the Capetian dynasty of French kings that ruled France from 987 to 1328.

France Becomes a Separate Kingdom Hugh Capet, his son, and his grandson all were weak rulers, but time and geography favored the Capetians. Their territory, though small, sat astride important trade routes in northern France. For 200 years, Capetian kings tightened their grip on this strategic area. The power of the king gradually spread outward from Paris. Eventually, the growth of royal power would unite France.

Philip II Expands His Power One of the most powerful Capetians was **Philip II,** called Philip Augustus, who ruled from 1180 to 1223. As a child, Philip had watched his father lose land to King Henry II of England. When Philip became king at the age of 15, he set out to weaken the power of the English kings in France. Philip was

The coronation of Philip II in the cathedral of Reims.

crafty, unprincipled, and willing to do whatever was necessary to achieve his goals.

Philip had little success against Henry II or Henry's son, Richard the Lion-Hearted. However, when King John seized the English throne, it was another matter. Philip earned the name Augustus (from the Latin word meaning "majestic"), probably because he greatly increased the territory of France. He seized Normandy from King John in 1204 and within two years had gained other territory. By the end of Philip's reign, he had tripled the lands under his direct control. For the first time, a French king had become more powerful than any of his vassals.

Philip Augustus not only wanted more land, he also wanted a stronger central government. He established royal officials called bailiffs. They were sent from Paris to every district in the kingdom to preside over the king's courts and collect the king's taxes.

The Development of England and France

England	France
• William the Conqueror, duke of Normandy, invades England in 1066.	• Hugh Capet establishes Capetian Dynasty in 987, which rules until 1328.
• Henry II (ruled 1154–1189) introduces use of the jury in English courts.	• Philip II (ruled 1180–1223) increases the territory of France.
• Under pressure from his nobles, King John agrees to Magna Carta in 1215.	• Louis IX (ruled 1226–1270) strengthens France's central government.
• Edward I calls Model Parliament in 1295.	• Philip IV (ruled 1285–1314) adds Third Estate to Estates-General.

SKILLBUILDER: Interpreting Charts
1. *Which French duke conquered England?*
2. *Which English king and French king contributed to the growth of a representative assembly?*

Philip II's Heirs France's central government was made even stronger during the reign of Philip's grandson, **Louis IX,** who ruled from 1226 to 1270. Unlike his grandfather, Louis was pious and saintly. He was known as the ideal king. After his death, he was made a saint by the Catholic Church. Louis created a French appeals court, which could overturn the decisions of local courts. These royal courts of France strengthened the monarchy while weakening feudal ties.

In 1302, Philip IV, who ruled France from 1285 to 1314, was involved in a quarrel with the pope. The pope refused to allow priests to pay taxes to the king. Philip disputed the right of the pope to control Church affairs in his kingdom. As in England, the French king usually called a meeting of his lords and bishops when he needed support for his policies. To win wider support against the pope, Philip IV decided to include commoners in the meeting.

In France, the Church leaders were known as the First Estate, and the great lords as the Second Estate. The commoners that Philip invited to participate in the council became known as the Third Estate. The whole meeting was called the Estates-General.

Like the English Parliament in its early years, the Estates-General helped to increase royal power against the nobility. Unlike Parliament, however, the Estates-General never became an independent force that limited the king's power. However, centuries later, the Third Estate would be the key to overthrowing the French monarchy. Now, in the 14th century, there was much turmoil. This included religious disputes, plague, and war. This disorder threatened the fragile achievements of England and France in beginning to establish a democratic tradition.

THINK THROUGH HISTORY
C. Summarizing
What three estates made up the Estates-General?

Section 3 Assessment

1. TERMS & NAMES

Identify
• William the Conqueror
• Henry II
• Eleanor of Aquitaine
• Magna Carta
• parliament
• Philip II
• Louis IX

2. TAKING NOTES

Using a graphic, name each major step toward a democratic government and describe why it was important. Add steps as needed.

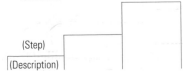

(Step)

(Description)

Which of the steps are similar to U.S. practices? Explain.

3. CONTRASTING

Contrast the way in which England and France began developing as nations.

THINK ABOUT
• the character of William, duke of Normandy, versus the character of Hugh Capet
• the rise of the Normans to power in England
• the rise of the Capetians to power in France

4. THEME ACTIVITY

Power and Authority
Imagine that you are an adviser to the king. Write him a letter in which you argue for or against including commoners in the Parliament or Estates-General. Tell the king the advantages and disadvantages of including commoners in the group.

A Century of Turmoil

TERMS & NAMES
- Avignon
- Great Schism
- John Wycliffe
- Jan Hus
- bubonic plague
- Hundred Years' War
- Joan of Arc

MAIN IDEA	WHY IT MATTERS NOW
During the 1300s, Europe was torn apart by religious strife, the bubonic plague, and the Hundred Years' War.	Events of the 1300s led to a change in attitudes toward religion and the state, a change reflected in modern attitudes.

SETTING THE STAGE At the turn of the century between the 1200s and 1300s, church and state seemed in good shape, but trouble was brewing. The Church seemed to be thriving. Ideals of fuller political representation seemed to be developing in France and England. However, the 1300s were filled with disasters, both natural and manmade. By the end of the century, the medieval way of life was beginning to disappear.

A Church Divided

At the beginning of the 1300s, the papacy seemed in some ways still strong. Soon, however, both pope and Church were in desperate trouble.

Pope and King Collide The pope in 1300 was an able but stubborn Italian. Pope Boniface VIII attempted to enforce papal authority on kings as previous popes had. When King Philip IV of France asserted his authority over French bishops, Boniface responded with a papal bull (an official document issued by the pope). It stated, "We declare, state, and define that subjection to the Roman Pontiff is absolutely necessary for the salvation of every human creature." In short, kings must always obey popes. Philip merely sneered at this bull. In fact one of Philip's ministers is said to have remarked that "my master's sword is made of steel, the pope's is made of [words]." Instead of obeying the pope, in September 1303 Philip had him held prisoner. The king planned to bring him to France for trial. The pope was rescued, but the elderly Boniface died a month later. Never again would a pope be able to force monarchs to obey him.

Boniface VIII served as pope from 1294 to 1303. This woodcut of Boniface was done in Venice in 1592.

Avignon and the Great Schism While Philip IV failed to keep Pope Boniface captive, in 1305 he persuaded the College of Cardinals to choose a French archbishop as the new pope. Clement V, the selected pope, shortly moved from Rome to the city of **Avignon** (av·vee·NYAWN) in France. Popes would live there for the next 67 years.

The move to Avignon badly weakened the Church. When reformers finally tried to move the papacy back to Rome, however, the result was even worse. In 1378, Pope Gregory XI died while visiting Rome. The College of Cardinals then met in Rome to choose a successor. As they deliberated, they could hear a mob outside screaming, "A Roman, a Roman, we want a Roman for pope, or at least an Italian!" Finally, the cardinals announced to the crowd that an Italian had been chosen: Pope Urban VI. Many cardinals regretted their choice almost immediately. Urban VI's passion for reform and his arrogant personality caused French cardinals to elect another pope a few months later. They chose Robert of Geneva, who spoke French. He took the name Clement VII.

Background
People outside France concluded that the Avignon popes were pawns of the French kings. They believed that the Church was held captive in Avignon just as, centuries before, the Jews had been held captive in Babylon. This period in Church history came to be called the Babylonian Captivity.

Now there were two popes. Each declared the other to be a false pope, excommunicating his rival. The French pope lived in Avignon, while the Italian pope lived in Rome. This began the split in the Church known as the **Great Schism** (SIHZ·uhm), or division.

The Council of Constance had as its major task to end the Great Schism by choosing a new pope. In 1414, when the Council of Constance began its meetings, there were a total of three popes: the Avignon pope, the Roman pope, and a third pope elected by an earlier council at Pisa. With the help of the Holy Roman Emperor, the council forced all three popes to resign. In 1417, the council chose a new pope, Martin V, ending the Great Schism.

A Scholarly Challenge to Church Authority The papacy was further challenged in the late 1300s and early 1400s by two professors. One was an Englishman named **John Wycliffe** (WIHK·lihf). He preached that Jesus Christ, not the pope, was the true head of the Church. He was much offended by the worldliness and wealth many clergy displayed. The pope himself, as Wycliffe noted, lived in shameful luxury, serving dinner on gold and silver plates to guests dressed in costly furs. Wycliffe believed that the clergy should own no land or wealth.

Wycliffe also taught that the Bible alone—not the pope—was the final authority for Christian life. He helped spread this idea by inspiring an English translation of the New Testament of the Bible, which at the time was available only in French or Latin. Wycliffe's radical ideas were discussed widely throughout England. Influenced by Wycliffe's writings, **Jan Hus,** a professor in Bohemia (now part of the Czech Republic), taught that the authority of the Bible was higher than that of the pope. Hus was excommunicated in 1412. In 1414, the German emperor Sigismund arranged the Council of Constance. He urged Hus to attend and even gave him safe conduct. When Hus arrived at the meeting, however, he was seized and tried as a heretic, then burned at the stake in 1415.

This scene from a 15th-century book shows Jan Hus being burned at the stake in 1415.

The Bubonic Plague Strikes

Artists of the 1300s depicted death as the Grim Reaper, a skeleton on horseback whose scythe cut people down. The image is appropriate—approximately one-third of the population of Europe died of the deadly disease known as the **bubonic plague.**

Origins and Symptoms of the Plague The plague began in Asia. Traveling the trade lanes, it infected most of Asia and the Muslim world. Inevitably it reached Europe. In 1347, a fleet of Genoese merchant ships arrived in Sicily carrying a dread cargo. This was the disease that became known as the Black Death. It got the name because of the purplish or blackish spots it produced on the skin. The disease swept through Italy. From there it followed trade routes to France, Germany, England, and other parts of Europe.

Unlike catastrophes that pull communities together, this epidemic was so terrifying that it ripped apart the very fabric of society. Giovanni Boccaccio, an Italian writer of the time, described its effect:

A VOICE FROM THE PAST
This scourge had implanted so great a terror in the hearts of men and women that brothers abandoned brothers, uncles their nephews, sisters their brothers, and in many cases wives deserted their husbands. But even worse, . . . fathers and mothers refused to nurse and assist their own children.

GIOVANNI BOCCACCIO, *The Decameron*

The Bubonic Plague

The bubonic plague, or Black Death, was a killer disease that swept repeatedly through many areas of the world. It wiped out two-thirds of the population in some areas of China, destroyed populations of Muslim towns in Southwest Asia, and then decimated a third of the European population.

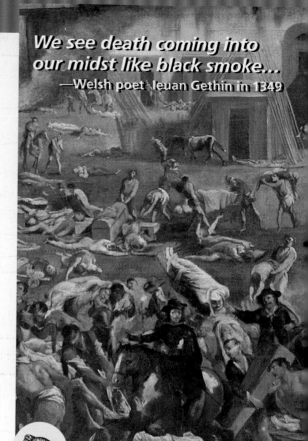

We see death coming into our midst like black smoke...
—Welsh poet Ieuan Gethin in 1349

The Plague in the 14th Century

Death Toll, 1300s   **KEY** ☠ = 4 million

Death Toll, 1300s	
Western Europe ☠☠☠☠☠	20–25 million
Southwest Asia ☠	4 million
China ☠☠☠☠☠☠☠☠☠	35 million

Route of the Plague

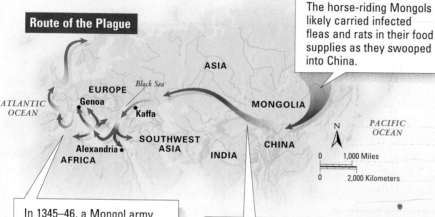

> The horse-riding Mongols likely carried infected fleas and rats in their food supplies as they swooped into China.

ASIA

Black Sea

EUROPE
Genoa

ATLANTIC OCEAN

Kaffa

MONGOLIA

PACIFIC OCEAN

SOUTHWEST ASIA

CHINA

INDIA

Alexandria

AFRICA

N

0   1,000 Miles
0   2,000 Kilometers

> In 1345–46, a Mongol army besieged Kaffa, on the Black Sea. A year later, Italian merchants who lived there fled back to Italy, unknowingly bringing the plague with them.

> The disease came with merchants along the trade routes of Asia to all parts of southern Asia, southwest Asia, and eventually Africa.

Detail of *The Plague* by Micco Spadaro, mid-1600s

Black rats carried fleas from one area to another—fleas that were infested with a bacillus called *Yersinia pestis*. In those days, people did not bathe—and almost all had fleas and lice. In addition, medieval people threw their garbage and sewage into the streets. These unsanitary streets became breeding grounds for more rats. The fleas carried by rats leapt from person to person, thus spreading the bubonic plague with incredible speed.

Symptoms

- Painful swellings called buboes (BOO·bohz) in the lymph nodes, particularly those in the armpits and groin
- Sometimes purplish or blackish spots on the skin
- Extremely high fever, chills, delirium, and in most cases, death

Patterns of Interaction

The bubonic plague was just one of the several lethal diseases that have swept from one society to another throughout history. Such diseases as smallpox and influenza have wiped out huge numbers of people, sometimes—as with the Aztecs—virtually destroying civilizations. The spread of disease has been a physical and very tragic result of cultures' interacting with one another across place and time.

 VIDEO *The Spread of Epidemic Disease: Bubonic Plague and Smallpox*

Connect *to* History

Hypothesizing Had people known the cause of the bubonic plague, what might they have done to slow its spread?

SEE SKILLBUILDER HANDBOOK, PAGE 1000

Connect *to* Today

Comparing What diseases of today might be compared to the bubonic plague? Why?

Frightened people looked around for a scapegoat. They found one in the Jews, who were blamed for bringing on the plague by poisoning the wells. All over Europe, Jews were driven from their homes or, worse, massacred.

The bubonic plague took about four years to reach almost every corner of Europe. In any given community, approximately three-quarters of those who caught the disease died. Before the bubonic plague ran its course, it killed almost 25 million Europeans and many more millions in Asia and North Africa.

Effects of the Plague The plague returned every few years, though it never struck as severely as in the first outbreak. However, the periodic attacks further reduced the population.

The economic effects of the plague were enormous. Town populations fell. Trade declined. Prices rose. Fewer people meant that workers were scarce everywhere. Farmland was abandoned or used to pasture sheep, which required less labor. Serfs had often been unpaid or poorly paid for their labor. They left the manor in search of better wages. The old manorial system began to crumble. Nobles fiercely resisted peasant demands for higher wages, causing peasant revolts in England, France, Italy, and Belgium.

The Church suffered a loss of prestige when its prayers and penances failed to stop the onslaught of the bubonic plague. In addition, many clergy deserted their flocks or charged high fees to perform services for the dying.

Many people who saw how abruptly life could end became pessimistic about life itself, fearing the future. As one poet of the time wrote, "Happy is he who has no children." Art and literature of the time reflect an unusual awareness of death. On the other hand, many people became occupied with pleasure and self-indulgence. They displayed the attitude of "Eat, drink, and be merry, for tomorrow you may die."

The bubonic plague and its aftermath disrupted medieval society, hastening changes that were already in the making. The society of the Middle Ages was collapsing. The century of war between England and France was that society's final death struggle.

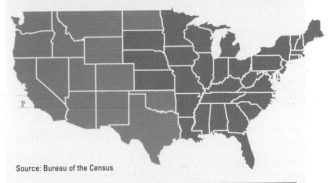

If the Plague Struck America Today

The bubonic plague reportedly wiped out about one-third of Europe's population in the 1300s. In the United States today, a one-third death toll would equal nearly 79 million people, or the number living in the states represented by the color ▨ .

Source: Bureau of the Census

SKILLBUILDER: Interpreting Charts
1. *How many states on the chart would have lost their entire population to the plague?*
2. *How might the chart help explain why many Europeans thought the world was ending?*

The Hundred Years' War

When the last Capetian king died without a successor, England's Edward III claimed the right to the French throne as grandson of Philip IV. The war that Edward III launched for that throne continued on and off from 1337 to 1453. It became known as the **Hundred Years' War** and added to the century's miseries. The war was a seesaw affair, fought on French soil. Victory passed back and forth between the two countries. Finally, between 1421 and 1453, the French rallied and drove the English out of France entirely, except for the port city of Calais.

The Battle of Crécy While the French eventually won the war, the English won three important battles in France. The first and most spectacular was the Battle of Crécy (KREHS-ee). Some of the combatants were still operating under medieval ideals of chivalry. They were anxious to perform noble deeds in war. They looked with contempt on the common foot soldiers and archers who fought alongside them. However, in the Battle of Crécy, it was the English archers who won the day.

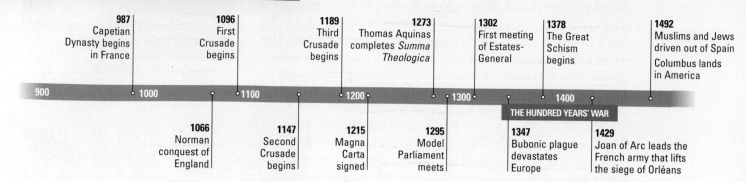

| 987 Capetian Dynasty begins in France | 1096 First Crusade begins | 1189 Third Crusade begins | 1273 Thomas Aquinas completes *Summa Theologica* | 1302 First meeting of Estates-General | 1378 The Great Schism begins | 1492 Muslims and Jews driven out of Spain · Columbus lands in America |

| 900 | 1000 | 1100 | 1200 | 1300 | 1400 |

THE HUNDRED YEARS' WAR

| 1066 Norman conquest of England | 1147 Second Crusade begins | 1215 Magna Carta signed | 1295 Model Parliament meets | 1347 Bubonic plague devastates Europe | 1429 Joan of Arc leads the French army that lifts the siege of Orléans |

English and French forces met near the town of Crécy on August 26, 1346. English men-at-arms and their longbowmen were outnumbered by a French army three times its size, including armored knights and a force of archers with crossbows. Mounted on warhorses and protected by heavy armor, French knights believed themselves invincible and attacked.

Meanwhile, English longbowmen let fly thousands of arrows at the oncoming French. The crossbowmen, out of range and peppered with English arrows, retreated in panic. A French noble, seeing the crossbowmen fleeing, shouted, "Slay these rascals who get in our way!" The knights trampled their own archers in an effort to cut a path through them. English longbowmen sent volley after volley of deadly arrows. They unhorsed knights who then lay helplessly on the ground in their heavy armor. Then, using long knives, the English foot soldiers attacked, slaughtering the French. At the end of the day, more than a third of the French force lay dead. Among them were some of the most honored in chivalry. The longbow, not chivalry, had won the day.

Poitiers and Agincourt The English repeated their victory ten years later at the Battle of Poitiers (pwah·TYAY). Near the town of Poitiers, France, the French believed they had caught the English at a disadvantage. When the overconfident knights charged on foot, English longbowmen greeted them with volleys of arrows so thick that the air grew dark. French knights were helpless. The French king John and his son Philip were captured and held for ransom.

The third English victory, the Battle of Agincourt (AJ·ihn·KAWRT), took place in 1415. Again the English army was outnumbered, with their 6,000 troops against a French force of 20,000 to 30,000. Led by King Henry V, English archers again won a victory over the heavily armored French knights. The success of the longbow in these battles spelled doom for chivalric warfare. The mounted, heavily armored medieval knight was soon to become extinct.

Joan of Arc Five years after Agincourt, the French and English signed a treaty stating that Henry V would inherit the French crown at the death of the French king Charles VI. The French had lost hope. Then, in 1429, a teenage French peasant girl named **Joan of Arc** felt moved by God to rescue France from its English conquerors. She believed that heavenly voices spoke to her. They told her to drive the English out of France and give the French crown to France's true king, Charles VI's son.

Joan convinced Charles that she was sincere. On May 7, 1429, Joan led the French army into battle against an English fort that blocked the roads to Orléans. The English had been besieging the city for over six months. Without help, the city's

Background
The English archers aimed for the horses' unprotected rumps. Wounded horses fell, causing chaos.

SPOTLIGHT ON

The Longbow

The bow and arrow reached one of its peaks from the 1200s through the early 1400s with the longbow. The string of the "short bow" was drawn back to the chest. The longbow was as tall as a man, or taller, and the string was pulled back to the archer's ear. A six-foot-tall man might have a bow seven feet tall.

English archers usually carried a case with extra bowstrings and a sheaf of 24 arrows with them into battle. The arrows were balanced in flight by feathers. The arrows were dangerous at a range of 300 yards. They were absolutely fatal within 100 yards. Writers of the time say that the sound of several thousand arrows whistling through the air was terrifying.

defenders could not hold out much longer. The English forts had to be taken in order to lift the siege. It was a hard-fought battle for both sides, and the French finally retreated in despair. But suddenly, Joan and a few soldiers charged back toward the fort. The entire French army stormed after her. The siege of Orléans was broken. Joan of Arc guided the French onto the path of victory.

After that victory, Joan persuaded Charles to go with her to Reims. There he was crowned king on July 17, 1429. Joan helped turn the tide for France. In 1430, she was captured in battle by the Burgundians, England's allies. They turned her over to the English. The English, in turn, handed her over to Church authorities to stand trial. Although the French king Charles VII owed his crown to Joan, he did nothing to rescue her. Condemned as a witch and a heretic because of her claim to hear voices, Joan was tied to a stake and burned to death on May 30, 1431.

The Impact of the Hundred Years' War The long, exhausting war finally ended in 1453, with the English left with only the French port of Calais. For France, the war—despite its terrible costs in lives, property, and money—ultimately raised the power and prestige of the French monarch. Nonetheless, it took a long time for some regions in France to recover.

The war gave birth in both countries to a feeling of nationalism. No longer did people think of the king as simply a feudal lord, but as a national leader fighting for the glory of the country.

Following the Hundred Years' War, the English suffered a period of internal turmoil known as the War of the Roses, in which two noble houses fought for the throne. Nevertheless, this war was responsible for strengthening the English Parliament. Edward III's constant need for money to finance the war led him to call Parliament as many as 27 times, asking for new taxes. Gradually, Parliament's "power of the purse" became firmly established, sowing another seed of democracy.

The end of the Hundred Years' War in 1453 is considered by some historians as the end of the Middle Ages. The twin pillars of the medieval world—intense religious devotion and the code of chivalry—both crumbled. The Age of Faith died a slow death. This death was caused by the Great Schism, the scandalous display of wealth by the Church, and the discrediting of the Church during the bubonic plague. The Age of Chivalry died on the battlefields of Crécy, Poitiers, and Agincourt.

THINK THROUGH HISTORY
C. Recognizing Effects What were some of the consequences of the Hundred Years' War?

HISTORY MAKERS

JOAN OF ARC
1412?–1431

When Joan was just 13 she began to have visions and hear what she believed were voices of the saints urging her to help Charles VII drive the English from France. When helping to lift the English siege of Orléans, she said:

You, men of England, who have no right in the kingdom of France, the King of Heaven sends the order through me, Joan the Maid, to return to your own country.

In 1430, she was turned over to a Church court for trial. Because of her claim to hear voices, Joan was tried for witchcraft and heresy. In truth, her trial was more political than religious. The English were embarrassed that a teenage girl had defeated them.

Section 4 Assessment

1. TERMS & NAMES

Identify
- Avignon
- Great Schism
- John Wycliffe
- Jan Hus
- bubonic plague
- Hundred Years' War
- Joan of Arc

2. TAKING NOTES

Using a chart like the one below, identify the main cause and the long-term effect of the three events.

	Main Cause	Long-Term Effect
Split in Church		
Bubonic plague		
Hundred Years' War		

Which event had some positive economic effects? Explain.

3. IDENTIFYING PROBLEMS

What problems did survivors face after the bubonic plague swept through their town?

THINK ABOUT
- the number of dead
- the social, political, and economic chaos

4. ANALYZING THEMES

Religious and Ethical Systems Do you think John Wycliffe and Jan Hus posed a real threat to the Church? Why or why not?

THINK ABOUT
- the two men's ideas
- the condition of the Church at the time

The Formation of Western Europe **361**

TERMS & NAMES

Briefly explain the importance of each of the following to western Europe during the medieval period.

1. Crusade
2. Reconquista
3. Inquisition
4. three-field system
5. scholastics
6. Magna Carta
7. parliament
8. Great Schism
9. bubonic plague
10. Hundred Years' War

Interact *with* History

On page 340, you thought about whether or not you would join a Crusade before completely under-standing what the Crusades were and what sort of advantages and sacrifices they entailed. Now that you've read the chapter, reexamine whether or not you would join a Crusade. What might a Crusader bring home from his travels? What problems might a Crusader en-counter on his adventures? Discuss your opinions with a small group.

REVIEW QUESTIONS

SECTION 1 *(pages 341–346)*
Church Reform and the Crusades

11. What were the three main abuses that most distressed Church reformers? Explain the problem with each.
12. What was the main goal of the Crusades?

SECTION 2 *(pages 348–351)*
Trade, Towns, and Financial Revolution

13. Name a short-term and a longer-term effect of the switch to the three-field system.
14. How did the growth of towns hurt the feudal system?
15. What role did Jews and Muslims play in Christian Europe's financial revolution?

SECTION 3 *(pages 352–355)*
England and France Develop

16. How did William the Conqueror extend his rule over all of England after the Battle of Hastings?
17. What circumstances led King John to accept the Magna Carta?

SECTION 4 *(pages 356–361)*
A Century of Turmoil

18. Summarize the main ideas of John Wycliffe.
19. Why did the bubonic plague cause people to turn away from the Church?
20. How did the Hundred Years' War end European armies' reliance on mounted knights?

Visual Summary

The Church

The great Gothic cathedrals that soared heavenward were symbols of the Church's power. Yet this power did not go unchallenged. For decades, kings and popes engaged in power struggles.

Crusades

Although the First Crusade captured Jerusalem, later Crusades accomplished little.

Farming

Better farming methods—such as the three-field system and the use of horses—made it possible for farmers to grow more food. This brought a population increase in the Middle Ages.

The Bubonic Plague

The bubonic plague killed millions and weakened the manorial economy.

EUROPE IN THE MIDDLE AGES

Trade and Towns

As people moved from farms into towns, trade expanded, and guilds formed for both merchants and artisans.

Learning

Europe's first universities developed in the Middle Ages. Interest in learning grew in part as a result of the rediscovery of ancient Greek writings.

Government

England and France developed strong central governments in which arose the first stirrings of democracy in medieval Europe. This can be seen in Parliament and the Estates-General.

Hundred Years' War

The Hundred Years' War further weakened feudal power. The longbow doomed armored knights.

CRITICAL THINKING

1. EDUCATION AFTER THE CRUSADES

THEME **CULTURAL INTERACTION**   How might life have been different for Europeans if Muslims had not shared their knowledge and skills?

2. THE GREAT SCHISM

Using a problem-solution outline like the one below, summarize the Great Schism. Describe the problem, identify at least two attempted solutions, and note how the Church finally solved the problem.

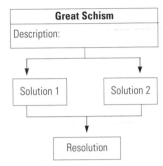

Great Schism

Description:

Solution 1   Solution 2

Resolution

3. JOAN OF ARC AND THE 15TH CENTURY

How does Joan of Arc's story reflect the violence and pessimism of the early 1400s?

4. ANALYZING PRIMARY SOURCES

In 1295, Edward I of England sent letters such as the following to sheriffs throughout the land, announcing a meeting of Parliament. Read the letter and answer the questions below it.

A VOICE FROM THE PAST

The king to the sheriff of Northampton, greeting. Whereas we wish to have a conference and discussion with the earls, barons, and other nobles of our realm concerning the provision of remedies for the dangers that in these days threaten the same kingdom . . . we command and firmly enjoin you that without delay you cause two knights, of the more discreet and more capable of labor, to be elected from the aforesaid county, and two citizens from each city of the aforesaid county, and two burgesses from each borough, and that you have them come to us . . . to do whatever in the aforesaid matters may be ordained by common counsel.

- Why is the king calling a meeting of Parliament?
- Who will represent the cities and boroughs, and how will they be chosen?

CHAPTER ACTIVITIES

1. LIVING HISTORY: Unit Portfolio Project

THEME **RELIGIOUS AND ETHICAL SYSTEMS**   Your unit portfolio project focuses on how religion affected life during the Middle Ages (see page 229). For Chapter 14, you might add one of the following ideas to your portfolio.

- Prepare the script for a newscast announcing the capture of Jerusalem by Crusaders and its impact on Christians and Muslims.
- Draw a cartoon about the clash between King Philip IV and Pope Boniface VIII. Try to show the conflict between religious and secular leaders.
- Write a speech that John Wycliffe might have given expressing his radical ideas about the Church.

2. CONNECT TO TODAY: Cooperative Learning

THEME **ECONOMICS**   The bubonic plague and the Hundred Years' War both had a major impact on the economy of medieval Europe. The plague, for example, meant that populations fell, trade declined, prices rose, farmland was abandoned, and workers were scarce and demanded higher wages. Even today, disease, natural catastrophes, and war can have a great impact on an economy. Work with a team to research and present to the class the effect of war, disease, or natural catastrophe on the economy of a country.

INTERNET   Use the Internet, magazines, or books to research the topic. You might choose a war such as the U.S. Civil War, World War II, or the Vietnam War. You might choose a disease such as heart disease or cancer. You might choose a natural disaster such as a hurricane or flood.

- As part of your presentation, make a graph that shows statistical information about the impact of the event you have chosen on the economy.
- Compare your team's event with those of other teams to determine their relative economic impacts.

3. INTERPRETING A TIME LINE

Revisit the unit time line on pages 228–229. Which events during the medieval period in Europe were triggered by a struggle for individual power?

FOCUS ON ART

The painting below shows Richard the Lion-Hearted (left) unhorsing Saladin during the Third Crusade. In fact the two men never met in personal combat. Notice the way the two leaders are depicted.

- What elements suggest that Richard is the hero of this painting?
- What elements suggest that Saladin is the villain?

Connect to History What evidence of the artist's bias is there in this painting about the confrontation between Islam and Christianity?

Societies and Empires of Africa, 800–1500

PREVIEWING THEMES

Religious and Ethical Systems

Beginning about 640, Islam spread into North Africa. Two groups of Muslim reformers—the Almoravids and the Almohads—built North African empires. Merchants and traders spread Islam into both West and East Africa, where it influenced rulers.

Interaction with Environment

In parts of Africa, hunter-gatherers used up an area's food supply and then moved on. In some Saharan villages, workers built houses of salt, the only available resource. The location of gold deposits determined where trade routes—and empires—were located.

Economics

Extensive trade networks developed in Africa because different regions had items—such as gold and salt—that other regions wanted. African city-states and empires that were able to control and tax such trade became wealthy and powerful.

INTERNET CONNECTION

Visit us at www.mcdougallittell.com to learn more about African civilizations, trade, and related topics.

AFRICA, 800–1500

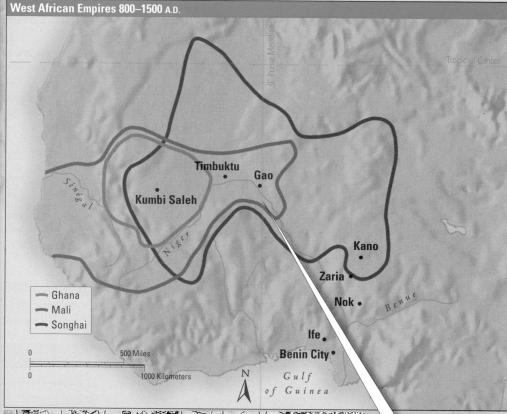

West African Empires 800–1500 A.D.

- Timbuktu
- Gao
- Kumbi Saleh
- Kano
- Zaria
- Nok
- Ife
- Benin City

Ghana
Mali
Songhai

0   500 Miles
0   1000 Kilometers

N

Gulf of Guinea

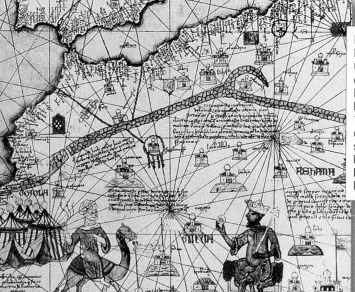

In **1324, Mansa Musa** left Mali for the hajj to Mecca. On the trip, he gave away enormous amounts of gold. Because of this, Europeans learned of Mali's wealth. In 1375, a Spanish mapmaker created an illustrated map showing Mansa Musa's kingdom in western Africa. Drawn on the map is Mansa Musa holding a gold nugget.

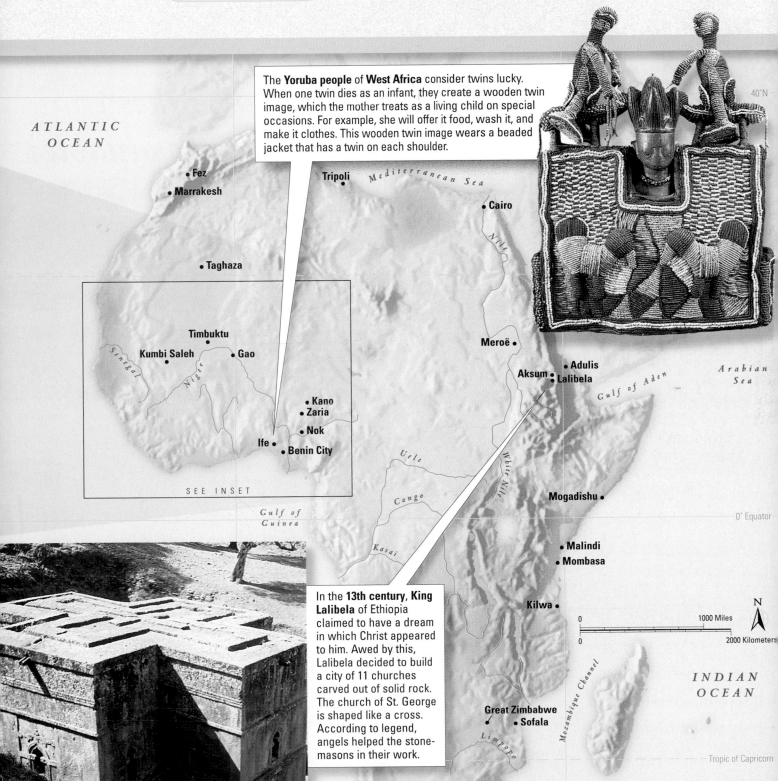

The **Yoruba people** of **West Africa** consider twins lucky. When one twin dies as an infant, they create a wooden twin image, which the mother treats as a living child on special occasions. For example, she will offer it food, wash it, and make it clothes. This wooden twin image wears a beaded jacket that has a twin on each shoulder.

In the **13th century**, **King Lalibela** of Ethiopia claimed to have a dream in which Christ appeared to him. Awed by this, Lalibela decided to build a city of 11 churches carved out of solid rock. The church of St. George is shaped like a cross. According to legend, angels helped the stone-masons in their work.

Interact *with* History

You are a trader who has traveled from a North African seaport south across the Sahara. You have arrived at the great trading center of Timbuktu. Among your trade items are manufactured goods and salt. In Timbuktu, you will meet with traders from the gold-mining regions to the south. You want to receive as much gold as possible for your trade items. The traders from the south want to receive as much salt and as many manufactured goods as they can in exchange for their gold. Together you must come to an agreement about what various trade items are worth.

What makes trade items valuable?

To survive the trip across the Sahara, traders stopped at oases for water. However, it was 500 miles to Timbuktu from the nearest oasis! The journey was very hard.

The camel was the only animal that could go without water long enough to cross the Sahara.

EXAMINING *the* ISSUES

- Does an item have to be a luxury to be extremely valuable?

- How do scarcity, usefulness, and transportation cost affect an item's value?

- Do all items have the same value to all people?

As you discuss these questions in class, think about what you have learned about other trading peoples, such as the Phoenicians and the Europeans.

As you read about trade in the various regions of Africa, notice what steps rulers took to control trade moving through their territory.

This cloth was shipped across the Mediterranean Sea to North Africa. Then it began the long journey to Timbuktu.

Workers in the Sahara endured hardship to mine this salt. In a hot climate, salt helps the human body to retain water. Salt was scarce in the gold-mining region.

The king often demanded these gold nuggets as taxes. The bag contained gold dust, which the trader used as money.

These beautiful cowrie shells came all the way from East Africa. They were used as money.

North and Central African Societies

TERMS & NAMES
- lineage
- stateless societies
- patrilineal
- matrilineal
- Maghrib
- Almoravids
- Almohads

MAIN IDEA

North and central Africa developed hunting-gathering societies, stateless societies, and Muslim states.

WHY IT MATTERS NOW

Modern African nations often must find ways to include these various peoples and traditions in one society.

SETTING THE STAGE Throughout history, different groups of Africans have found different ways to organize themselves to meet their political, economic, and social needs. In the varied regions of Africa, climate and topography, or landforms, influenced how each community developed. Some people built desert empires united by religion. Others near the coast created political systems based on extended family ties. Still others lived in the rain forest and formed close-knit family groups to support themselves by hunting and gathering. Section 1 examines these three types of African societies. In addition, many African groups developed kingdoms and city-states—which are discussed in Sections 2 and 3.

Hunting-Gathering Societies

Hunting-gathering societies—the oldest form of social organization in the world—began in Africa. Hunting-gathering societies still exist in Africa today, though they form an extremely small percentage of the population. Scattered throughout Africa, these groups speak their own languages and often use distinctive hunting techniques. However, they all rely on hunting and gathering for survival. By studying these groups, scholars learn clues about how hunter-gatherers may have lived in the past. However, no hunter-gatherers today live precisely as prehistoric peoples did.

Forest Dwellers The Efe (AY·fay) are just one of several hunting-gathering societies in Africa. They make their home in the Ituri Forest in the Democratic Republic of Congo (formerly Zaire). Like their ancestors, the modern-day Efe live in small groups of no more than 50 members, all of whom are related. Each family occupies its own grass-and-brush shelter within a camp, but their homes are rarely permanent. Their search for food causes them to be somewhat nomadic. As a result, the Efe collect few possessions and move to new camps as they use up the resources in the surrounding area.

In the Efe society, women are the gatherers. They walk through the forest searching for roots, yams, mushrooms, and wild seeds. Efe men and older boys do all the hunting. Sometimes they gather in groups to hunt small antelope called duikers. At other times, hunters go solo and use poison-tipped arrows to kill mammals such as monkeys. On some occasions, Efe men collect wild honey, a prized delicacy of the forest. Unlike prehistoric hunter-gatherers, the Efe add to their diet by trading honey, wild game, and other forest products for crops grown by farmers in nearby villages.

Social Structure A respected older male, such as a father, uncle, or father-in-law, typically serves as group leader.

THINK THROUGH HISTORY
A. Drawing Conclusions
Considering the way the Efe live, why might they need to limit their groups to 50 members or less?

CONNECT *to* TODAY

Hunter-Gatherers

The girl shown below is a member of the Efe people. Today the Efe and other hunter-gatherers live in tropical rain forests in several African nations. However, they make up less than 1 percent of the population of Africa.

Hunter-gatherers also exist on other continents. The Inuit of North America have traditionally fished and hunted. Today, some use modern equipment such as rifles and snowmobiles. However, many have abandoned hunting to look for wage-paying work.

Modern society has disrupted the hunting-gathering culture of the Aborigines of Australia. They suffer high rates of poverty, disease, and unemployment. Today, Aborigines make up less than 2 percent of Australia's population.

Although members of the group listen to and value this man's opinion, he does not give orders or act as chief. Each family within the band makes its own decisions and is free to come and go. Group members settle arguments through long discussions. If conflicts cannot be settled by talking, a group member may decide to move to a different hunting band. Daily life for the Efe is not governed by formal, written laws. However, they do have logical guidelines that determine how members share food and possessions.

Stateless Societies

As in other parts of the world, family organization is central to African society. In many African societies, families are organized in groups called lineages. The members of a **lineage** (LIHN·ee·ihj) believe they are descendants of a common ancestor. Besides its living members, a lineage includes past generations (spirits of ancestors) and future generations (children not yet born). Within a lineage, members feel strong loyalties to one another.

South of the Sahara, many African groups developed systems of governing based on lineages. In some African societies, lineage groups took the place of rulers. These societies, known as **stateless societies,** did not have a centralized system of power. Instead, authority in a stateless society was balanced among lineages of equal power so that no one family had too much control. Most often, members of a stateless society worked through their differences to cooperate and share power. The Igbo (IHG·boh) people—also called Ibo—of southern Nigeria lived in a stateless society as early as the ninth century. (Although the Igbo lived in West Africa, their political structure was similar to stateless societies found in central Africa.) If a dispute arose within an Igbo village, respected elders from

When a respected elder of the Tiv dies, his skull and thigh bone are made into an *imborirungu*, shown here. The living elders use the *imborirungu* to try to communicate with the dead leader's soul.

Selected African Societies, 800–1500

ASIA

AFRICA

Mediterranean Sea

Nile R.

SAHARA

Tropic of Cancer

Niger R.

Oran
Fez • Tlemcen
Marrakech
ALMORAVID EMPIRE
ALMOHAD EMPIRE

Tiv
Igbo
Nuer
Efe   Mbuti
Congo   L. Victoria
Pygmies
Luba

ATLANTIC
OCEAN

San

0°

N

0   1,500 Miles

0   3,000 Kilometers

INDIAN OCEAN

Tropic of Capricorn

0–500 feet
500–2,000 feet
Over 2,000 feet
— Stateless society
— Muslim state
— Hunter-gatherers

Hunter-Gatherers

The seminomadic hunter-gatherers lived by gathering wild foods and hunting animals. When they exhausted an area's resources, they moved on.

- The **Efe** lived in the Ituri Forest of what is now the Democratic Republic of Congo. They were hunter-gatherers who traded with farming villages.
- The **San** (also called the **Bushmen**) lived in most of southern Africa and part of East Africa.

Stateless Societies

Stateless societies did not have centralized power. Instead, power was balanced among lineage groups, usually within villages.

- The **Tiv**, in what is today Nigeria, had no formal government.
- The **Igbo** of southern Nigeria resolved disputes by having elders from different lineages meet.
- The **Nuer** of the southern Sudan organized over 250,000 people without an official ruler.

Muslim States

In North Africa, two groups of Muslim reformers founded empires.

- In the 11th century, the **Almoravid** Dynasty controlled Mauritania, Morocco, and part of Spain.
- Beginning in the mid-1100s, the **Almohad** Dynasty controlled Morocco, much of the Maghrib, and part of Spain.

GEOGRAPHY SKILLBUILDER: Interpreting Maps
1. **Location** *Where were the Muslim states located?*
2. **Region** *Why would hunter-gatherers be spread across such a large region?*

different lineages settled the problem. While this political structure served the Igbo well for many centuries, Igbos later encountered challenges from European colonizers who expected one single leader to rule over the whole society. (See Chapter 27.)

Background
British colonizers misspelled "Igbo" as "Ibo." That is why there are two spellings.

Tracing Family Descent In African societies, the way a society traces lineage decides inheritance rights and what groups individuals belong to. Members of a **patrilineal** society trace their ancestors through their fathers. Inheritance passes from father to son. When a son marries, then he, his wife, and their children remain part of his father's extended family.

In a **matrilineal** society, children trace their ancestors through their mothers. Young men from a matrilineal culture inherit land and wealth from their mother's family. Although group memberships and inheritance rights in a matrilineal society are based on descent from women, men usually hold the positions of authority.

Background
In matrilineal societies that are also kingdoms, the king's heir is his sister's son, not his own son.

Age-Set System In many African societies, young people form close ties to individuals outside their lineage through the age-set system. An age set consists of young people within a region who are born during a certain time period. Each age set passes together through clearly identified life stages, such as warrior or elder. Ceremonies mark the passage to each new stage.

Men and women have different life stages, and each stage has its own duties and importance. Responsibilities can include working on community building projects, herding cattle, or assisting in the raising of children. Societies like the Igbo use the age-set system to teach discipline, community service, and leadership skills to their young.

THINK THROUGH HISTORY
B. Making Inferences What advantages might an age-set system have for a society?

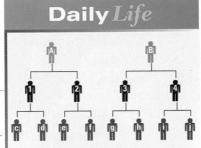

Daily Life

Negotiating Conflict

In a stateless society, the power to negotiate conflicts shifts from generation to generation as circumstances demand.

Look at the diagram of two lineages above. If **d** is in conflict with **f**, then **c** will side with his brother **d** and **e** will side with his brother **f**. Therefore, the parents—**1** and **2**—will meet to negotiate.

If **f** is in conflict with **g**, both entire lineages will take sides in the dispute. Therefore, the members of the oldest surviving generation—**A** and **B**—must meet to negotiate.

Muslim States

While stateless societies developed south of the Sahara, Islam played a vital role in the political history of North Africa. After Muhammad's death in 632, Muslims swept across the northwest part of the continent. They converted many by conquest and others peacefully. By 670, Muslims ruled Egypt and had entered the **Maghrib,** the part of North Africa that is today the Mediterranean coast of Morocco, Tunisia, and Algeria.

As Islam spread, some African rulers converted to Islam. These African Muslim rulers then based their government upon Islamic law. Muslims believe that God's law is a higher authority than any human law. Therefore, Muslim rulers often relied on religious scholars as government advisers.

Islamic Law In Islam, following the law is a religious obligation. Muslims do not separate their personal life from their religious life, and Islamic law regulates almost all areas of human life. Because of this, Islamic law helped to bring order to Muslim states. It provided the state with a set of values that shaped a common identity.

In addition to unifying individual states, law helped to unify the Muslim world. Even though various Muslim states might have ethnic or cultural differences, they lived under a common law. Islamic law has been such a significant force in African history that some states—especially in North Africa—are still politically and socially influenced by it today.

Among those who converted to Islam were the Berbers. Fiercely independent desert dwellers, the Berbers were the original inhabitants of North Africa. Until their conquest by the Muslim Arabs in the 600s, some of these nomadic African people were Christians and Jews. While they accepted Islam as their faith, many maintained their Berber identities and loyalties. Two Berber groups, the Almoravids and the Almohads, founded empires that united the Maghrib under Muslim rule.

Almoravid Reformers In the 11th century, Muslim reformers founded the Almoravid (AL·muh·RAHV·uhd) Dynasty. Its members came from a Berber group liv-

ing in the western Sahara in what is today Mauritania. The movement began after a devout Berber Muslim made a hajj, or pilgrimage, to Mecca. On his journey home, he convinced a Muslim scholar from Morocco named Abd Allah Ibn Yasin to return with him to teach his people about Islam. Ibn Yasin's teachings soon attracted followers, and he founded a strict religious brotherhood known as the **Almoravids.** According to one theory about the name's origin, the group lived in a *ribat*, or fortified monastery. They were therefore called the "people of the *ribat*"—*al-Murabitun*, which eventually became "Almoravid."

In the 1050s, Ibn Yasin led the Almoravids in an effort to spread Islam through conquest. Although Ibn Yasin died in battle in 1059, the Almoravids went on to take Morocco and found Marrakech. It became their capital. They overran the West African empire of Ghana by 1076. The Almoravids also captured parts of southern Spain, where they were called Moors.

Almohads Take Over In the mid-1100s, the **Almohads** (AL·moh·HADZ), another group of Berber Muslim reformers, wrested power from the Almoravids. The Almohads began as a militant religious movement in the Atlas Mountains of Morocco. (In Arabic, the Almohads are known as *al-Muwahhidun*, meaning "those who affirm the unity of God.")

The Almohads followed the teachings of Ibn Tumart. After a pilgrimage to Mecca, Ibn Tumart denounced the later Almoravid rulers for moving away from the traditional practice of Islam. He urged his followers to strictly obey the teachings of the Qur'an and Islamic law. The Almohads, led by Abd al-Mumin, fought to oust the Almoravids and remain true to traditional Islamic beliefs.

By 1148 the Almohads controlled most of Morocco and ended Almoravid rule. The new Muslim reformers kept Marrakech as their capital. By the end of the 12th century, they had conquered much of southern Spain. In Africa, their territory stretched from Marrakech to Tripoli and Tunis on the Mediterranean. The Almohad Dynasty gradually declined and broke up into individual Muslim dynasties. While the Almohad Dynasty lasted just over 100 years, it united the Maghrib under one rule for the first time.

Stronger empires were about to emerge to the south of the Almohad Empire. Societies in West Africa—discussed in Section 2—created magnificent empires that boasted tremendous economic and political power and strong links to international trade routes.

THINK THROUGH HISTORY
C. Recognizing Effects What was the main effect of Almohad rule on the Maghrib?

SPOTLIGHT ON

Marrakech

Located in west central Morocco, Marrakech was once the capital of both the Almoravid and the Almohad dynasties. During the height of its prosperity in the 1400s, the city's location on the edge of the Sahara made it an important trade center. It was filled with bustling markets like the present-day wool market shown above.

Marrakech also became an important Islamic religious center. It attracted scholars and thinkers from throughout the Islamic world. Today, with a population of over 600,000, Marrakech is Morocco's third largest city and once again a hub of trade. As in the past, Marrakech is famous for its fine leather work and carpets.

Section 1 Assessment

1. TERMS & NAMES

Identify
- lineage
- stateless societies
- patrilineal
- matrilineal
- Maghrib
- Almoravids
- Almohads

2. TAKING NOTES

Using a web diagram like the one below, list characteristics of stateless societies.

( ) ( )
(stateless societies)
( ) ( )

How might these characteristics have helped stateless societies to endure for many centuries?

3. COMPARING

In what ways are hunting-gathering societies and stateless societies similar?

THINK ABOUT
- family structures
- social structures
- methods of handling conflict

4. THEME ACTIVITY

Religious and Ethical Systems Working with a partner, prepare a time line showing the impact of Islam on North Africa. Include significant events for the period described in this section.

TERMS & NAMES
- Ghana
- Mali
- Sundiata
- Mansa Musa
- Ibn Battuta
- Songhai
- Hausa
- Yoruba
- Benin

2 West African Empires and Civilizations

MAIN IDEA	WHY IT MATTERS NOW
West Africa contained several powerful empires and states, including Ghana, Mali, and Songhai.	These empires demonstrate the richness of African culture before European colonization.

SETTING THE STAGE While the Almohads and Almoravids were building empires in North Africa, three powerful empires flourished in West Africa. These ancient African empires arose in the Sahel—the savanna region just south of the Sahara. They grew strong through the controlling of trade.

Ghana: Land of Gold

By A.D. 200, trade across the Sahara had existed for centuries. However, this trade remained infrequent and irregular because of the harsh desert conditions. Most pack animals—oxen, donkeys, and horses—could not travel very far in the hot, dry Sahara without rest or water. Then in the third century A.D., Berber nomads began using camels. The camel could plod steadily over much longer distances, covering as much as 60 miles in a day. In addition, it could travel up to ten days without water, twice as long as most pack animals. With the camel, nomads blazed new routes across the desert and trade increased.

The trade routes crossed the savanna through the region farmed by the Soninke (soh·NIHN·keh) people. The Soninke people called their ruler *ghana,* or war chief. Muslim traders began to use the word to refer to the Soninke region. By the 700s, Soninke rulers of the kingdom of **Ghana** were growing rich from taxing the goods that traders carried through their territory.

Gold-Salt Trade The two most important trade items were gold and salt. Gold came from a forest region south of the savanna between the Niger (NY·juhr) and Senegal (SEHN·ih·GAWL) rivers. Miners dug gold from shafts as deep as 100 feet or sifted it from fast-moving streams. Some sources estimate that until about 1350, at least two-thirds of the world's supply of gold came from West Africa. Although rich in gold, West Africa's savanna and forests lacked salt, a material essential to human life. The Sahara contained deposits of salt. In fact, in the Saharan village of Taghaza, workers built their houses from salt blocks because it was the only material available.

Arab and Berber traders crossed the desert with camel caravans loaded down with salt. They also carried cloth, weapons, and manufactured goods from ports on the Mediterranean. After a long journey, they reached the market towns of the savanna. Meanwhile, African traders brought gold north from the forest regions.

Merchants met in trading cities, where they exchanged goods under the watchful eye of the king's tax collector. In addition to taxing trade, royal officials made sure that all traders weighed goods fairly and did business according to law. Royal guards also provided protection from bandits.

Empire of Ghana In his royal palace, the king stored gold nuggets and slabs of salt (collected as taxes). Only the king had the right to own gold nuggets, although gold dust freely circulated in the marketplace. By this means, the king limited the supply of gold and kept its price from falling. Ghana's African ruler acted as a religious leader,

Background
Salt helps the human body retain water in hot weather. It also preserves food so that it does not spoil so quickly.

THINK THROUGH HISTORY
A. Recognizing Effects What were positive and negative effects of the king's control of trade?

Miners in a forest region of West Africa dug up gold nuggets like this. The king of Ghana passed a law that all nuggets should be given to him.

Societies and Empires of Africa **371**

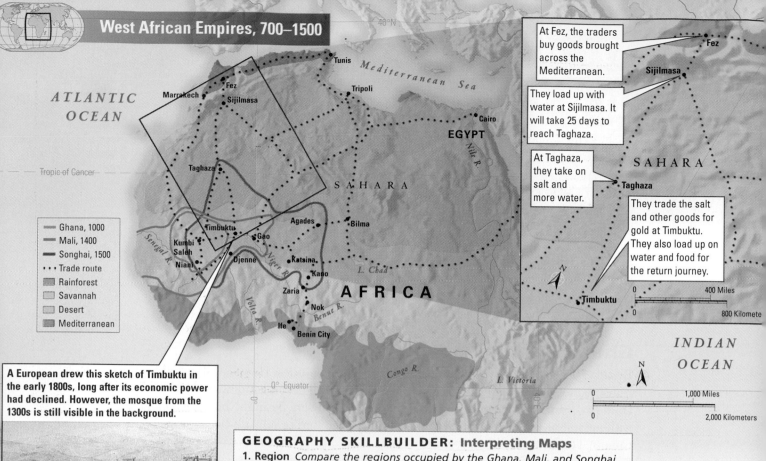

At Fez, the traders buy goods brought across the Mediterranean.

They load up with water at Sijilmasa. It will take 25 days to reach Taghaza.

At Taghaza, they take on salt and more water.

They trade the salt and other goods for gold at Timbuktu. They also load up on water and food for the return journey.

Ghana, 1000
Mali, 1400
Songhai, 1500
• • • Trade route
Rainforest
Savannah
Desert
Mediterranean

0 ____ 400 Miles
0 ____ 800 Kilometers

0 ____ 1,000 Miles
0 ____ 2,000 Kilometers

A European drew this sketch of Timbuktu in the early 1800s, long after its economic power had declined. However, the mosque from the 1300s is still visible in the background.

GEOGRAPHY SKILLBUILDER: Interpreting Maps

1. **Region** Compare the regions occupied by the Ghana, Mali, and Songhai empires in terms of size and location.
2. **Human-Environment Interaction** How did the environment both contribute resources to and cause problems for traders?

chief judge, and military commander. He headed a large bureaucracy and could call up a huge army. In 1067, a Muslim geographer and scholar named al-Bakri wrote a description of Ghana's royal court:

A VOICE FROM THE PAST

The king adorns himself . . . wearing necklaces and bracelets. . . . The court of appeal is held in a domed pavilion around which stand ten horses with gold embroidered trappings. Behind the king stand ten pages holding shields and swords decorated with gold, and on his right are the sons of the subordinate [lower] kings of his country, all wearing splendid garments and with their hair mixed with gold.

AL-BAKRI, quoted in *Africa in the Days of Exploration*

By the year 800, Ghana had become an empire. Because Ghana's king controlled trade and commanded a large army, he could demand taxes and gifts from the chiefs of surrounding lands. As long as the chiefs made their payments, the king left them in peace to rule their own people.

Islamic Influences While Islam spread through North Africa by conquest, south of the Sahara, Islam spread through trade. Muslim merchants and teachers settled in the states south of the Sahara and introduced their faith there.

Eventually, Ghana's rulers converted to Islam. By the 11th century, Muslim advisers were helping the king run his kingdom. While Ghana's African rulers and many members of the court accepted Islam, many people in the empire clung to their animistic beliefs and practices. Much of the population never converted. Those who did kept many of their former beliefs, which they observed along with Islam. Among the upper class, Islam's growth encouraged the spread of literacy. To study the Qur'an, converts to Islam had to learn to read and write Arabic.

Background
Al-Bakri claimed that Ghana's army was 200,000 strong. Some modern scholars believe that figure was exaggerated.

Background
Animism is the belief that spirits—residing in animals, plants, and natural forces—play an important role in regulating daily life.

In 1076 the Muslim Almoravids of North Africa completed their conquest of Ghana. Although the Almoravids eventually withdrew from Ghana, the war had badly disrupted the gold-salt trade. Ghana never regained its power.

Empire of Mali

By 1235 the kingdom of **Mali** had emerged. Its founders were Mande-speaking people, who lived south of Ghana. Like Ghana's, Mali's wealth was built on gold. As Ghana remained weak, people who had been under its control began to act independently. In addition, miners found new gold deposits farther east. This caused the most important trade routes to shift eastward, which made a new group of people—the people of Mali—wealthy. It also allowed them to seize power.

Sundiata Conquers an Empire
Mali's first great leader, **Sundiata** (sun·JAHT·ah), came to power by crushing a cruel, unpopular leader. Then, in the words of a Mande oral tradition, "the world knew no other master but Sundiata." Sundiata became Mali's *mansa*, or emperor. Through a series of military victories, he took over the kingdom of Ghana and the trading cities of Kumbi and Walata. A period of peace and prosperity followed.

Sundiata proved to be as great a leader in peace as he had been in war. He put able administrators in charge of Mali's finances, defense, and foreign affairs. From his new capital at Niani, he promoted agriculture and reestablished the gold-salt trade. Niani became an important center of commerce and trade. People began to call Sundiata's empire Mali, meaning "where the king lives."

Mansa Musa Expands Mali Sundiata died in 1255. Influenced by Arab traders, some of Mali's next rulers became Muslims. These African Muslim rulers built mosques, attended public prayers, and supported the preaching of Muslim holy men. The most famous of them was **Mansa Musa** (MAHN·sah moo·SAH), who may have been Sundiata's grandnephew.

Like Sundiata, Mansa Musa was a skilled military leader who exercised royal control over the gold-salt trade and put down every rebellion. His 100,000-man army kept order and protected Mali from attack. Under Mansa Musa, the empire expanded to roughly twice the size of the empire of Ghana. To govern his far-reaching empire, he divided it into provinces and appointed governors, who ruled fairly and efficiently.

A devout Muslim, Mansa Musa went on a hajj to Mecca from 1324 to 1325. When he returned, Mansa Musa ordered the building of new mosques at the trading cities of Timbuktu (TIHM·buhk·TOO) and Gao. Timbuktu became one of the most important cities of the empire. It attracted Muslim judges, doctors, religious leaders, and scholars from far and wide to its mosques and universities.

HISTORY MAKERS

Sundiata
?–1255

Sundiata came from the kingdom of Kangaba near the present-day Mali-Guinea border. According to oral tradition, he was one of 12 royal brothers who were heirs to the throne of Kangaba.

When Sumanguru, ruler of a neighboring state, overran Kangaba in the early 1200s, he wanted to eliminate rivals, so he murdered all of Sundiata's brothers. He spared Sundiata, who was sickly and seemed unlikely to survive. However, as Sundiata grew up, he gained strength and became a popular leader of many warriors. In 1235, Sundiata's army defeated Sumanguru and his troops.

Although a Muslim, Sundiata also performed traditional African religious ceremonies as emperor. This helped him unify his empire.

Mansa Musa
?–1332

The strongest of Sundiata's successors, Mansa Musa was a devout Muslim. On his hajj, Mansa Musa stopped in Cairo, Egypt. Five hundred slaves, each carrying a staff of gold, arrived first. They were followed by 80 camels, each carrying 300 pounds of gold dust. Hundreds of other camels brought supplies. Thousands of servants and officials completed the procession.

An Egyptian official wrote:

This man Mansa Musa spread upon Cairo the flood of his generosity: there was no person, officer of the court, or holder of any office of the Sultanate who did not receive a sum of gold from him.

Mansa Musa gave away so much gold that the value of this precious metal declined in Egypt for 12 years.

This is a Spanish mapmaker's idea of how Mansa Musa looked.

Travels of Ibn Battuta In 1352, one of Mansa Musa's successors prepared to receive a traveler and historian named **Ibn Battuta** (IHB·uhn ba·TOO·tah). A native of Tangier in North Africa, Ibn Battuta had traveled for 27 years, visiting most of the countries in the Islamic world.

After leaving the royal palace, Ibn Battuta visited Timbuktu and other cities in Mali. He found he could travel without fear of crime. As a devout Muslim, he praised the people for their study of the Qur'an, but criticized them for not strictly practicing Islam's moral code. However, Mali's justice system also impressed him:

> **A VOICE FROM THE PAST**
> They are seldom unjust, and have a greater abhorrence of injustice than any other people. Their sultan shows no mercy to anyone who is guilty of the least act of it. There is complete security in their country. Neither traveler nor inhabitant in it has anything to fear from robbers.
>
> **IBN BATTUTA,** quoted in *Africa in the Days of Exploration*

Ibn Battuta left Mali in 1353. Within 50 years, the once-powerful empire began to weaken. Most of Mansa Musa's successors lacked his ability to govern well. In addition, the gold trade that was one basis of Mali's wealth again shifted eastward as new goldfields were developed.

Empire of Songhai

As Mali declined in the 1400s, people who had been under its control began to break away. Among them were the **Songhai** (SAWNG·HY) to the east. They built up an army, extended their territory to the large bend in the Niger River near Gao, and gained control of the all-important trade routes. Gao was the capital of their empire.

THINK THROUGH HISTORY
C. Making Inferences Why might the people who had been conquered by Mali want to break away?

Sunni Ali, a Conquering Hero The Songhai had two extraordinary rulers. One was Sunni Ali, who built a vast empire by military conquest. Sunni Ali's rule began in 1464 and lasted almost 30 years.

Sunni Ali built a professional army that had a riverboat fleet of war canoes and a mobile fighting force on horseback. He forged the Songhai empire through his skill as a military commander and his aggressive leadership. In 1468, Sunni Ali achieved his first major military triumph. He captured the city of Timbuktu, which had been an important part of Mali's empire.

Five years later, he took Djenné, also a trade city that had a university. To take Djenné, Sunni Ali besieged the city for seven years before it fell in 1473. Sunni Ali sealed the takeover of Djenné by marrying its queen.

Askia Muhammad Governs Well After Sunni Ali's death in 1492, his son succeeded him as ruler. Almost at once, he faced a major revolt by Muslims who were angry that he did not practice their religion faithfully. The leader of the revolt was a devout Muslim named Askia Muhammad. He drove Sunni Ali's son from power and replaced him.

Daily *Life*

Islam in West Africa

South of the Sahara, many converts to Islam also kept their African beliefs. They found ways to include their traditional rituals and customs into their new religion.

The status of women in West African societies demonstrates how local custom altered Muslim practice. In many 15th-century Muslim societies, women seldom left their homes. When they did, they veiled their faces. Muslim women in West Africa, however, did not wear veils. They also mingled freely with men in public—which shocked visiting Muslim religious leaders.

Cultural blending also affected architecture. West Africans used local techniques to build the mosque at Kawara, shown below. They sculpted it beautifully from mud.

During his 35-year rule, Askia Muhammad proved to be an excellent administrator. He set up an efficient tax system and chose able officials. Adding to the centralized government created by Sunni Ali, he appointed officials to serve as ministers of the treasury, army, navy, and agriculture. Under his rule, the well-governed empire thrived.

Despite its wealth and learning, the Songhai Empire lacked modern weapons. In 1591, a Moroccan fighting force of several thousand men equipped with gunpowder and cannons crossed the Sahara and invaded Songhai. The Moroccan troops quickly defeated the Songhai warriors, who were armed only with swords and spears. The collapse of the Songhai Empire ended a 1,000-year period in which powerful kingdoms and empires ruled the central region of West Africa.

Background
The Chinese invented gunpowder in the 9th century. About 1304, Arabs developed the first gun, which shot arrows.

Other Peoples of West Africa

While empires rose and fell in some parts of West Africa, in other areas city-states developed. As in Ghana, Mali, and Songhai, Muslim traditions influenced some of these city-states. Other city-states held to their traditional African beliefs.

Hausa City-States Compete The **Hausa** (HOW·suh) were a group of people named after the language they spoke. The city-states of the Hausa people first emerged between the years 1000 and 1200 in the savanna area east of Mali and Songhai in what is today northern Nigeria. Songhai briefly ruled the Hausa city-states, but they soon regained their independence. In such city-states as Kano, Katsina, and Zazzau (later Zaria), local rulers built walled cities for their capitals. These cities had populations of 50,000 or more. From their capitals, Hausa rulers governed the farming villages outside the city walls.

Each ruler depended on the crops of the farmers and on a thriving trade in salt, grain, and cotton cloth made by urban weavers. Because they were located on trade routes that linked other West African states with the Mediterranean, Kano and Katsina became major trading states. They profited greatly from supplying the needs of caravans. Kano was noted for its woven and dyed cloth and for its leather goods.

Zazzau, the southernmost state, conducted a vigorous trade in enslaved persons. Zazzau's traders raided an area south of the city and sold their captives to traders in other Hausa states. These traders sold them to other North or West African societies in exchange for horses, harnesses, and guns. The Hausa kept some enslaved workers to build and repair city walls and grow food for the cities.

All the Hausa city-states had similar forms of government. Rulers held great power over their subjects, but ministers and other officials acted to check this power. For protection from outside enemies and from each other, each city-state raised an army of mounted horsemen. Although rulers often schemed and fought to gain control over their neighbors, none succeeded for long. The constant fighting among city-states prevented any one of them from building a Hausa empire.

THINK THROUGH HISTORY
D. Analyzing Causes In your own words, restate the main reason that the Hausa did not develop an empire.

Yoruba Kings and Artists Like the Hausa, the **Yoruba** (YAWR·uh·buh) people all spoke a common language. Originally the Yoruba-speaking people belonged to a number of small city-states in the forests on the southern edge of the savanna in what is today Benin and southwestern Nigeria. In these communities most people farmed. Over time, some of these smaller communities joined together under strong leaders. This led to the formation of several localized Yoruba kingdoms.

Considered divine, Yoruba kings served as the most important religious and political leaders in their kingdoms. All Yoruba chiefs traced their descent from the first ruler of Ife (EE·fay). According to legend,

SPOTLIGHT ON

Queen Amina's Reign

In the 1500s, the Hausa city-state of Zazzau (later called Zaria) was governed by Queen Amina. She was remembered as the "headdress among the turbans." Her rule was distinguished for its military conquests.

The *Kano Chronicle,* a history of the city-state of Kano, records:

At this time Zaria, under Queen Amina, conquered all the towns as far as Kawararafa and Nupe. Every town paid tribute to her. . . . Her conquests extended over 34 years.

Queen Amina's commitment to her Muslim faith also led her to encourage Muslim scholars, judges, and religious leaders from religious centers at Kano and Timbuktu to come to Zazzau.

This modern Hausa village in Nigeria has many traditionally constructed mud buildings.

Benin Sculpture

According to tradition, Yoruba artists taught their techniques to artists in nearby Benin. One of the primary functions of the artists of Benin was to please the ruler by recording his history or displaying his power. Adorning the palace walls were brass plaques commemorating the ruler's great achievements. Brass heads showed the ruler and his family as idealized figures.

Brass Leopard

This snarling leopard is a symbol of the king's royal power. It is also a water vessel used on ceremonial occasions. Water was poured into the hollow vessel through a hole on top of the head. When the vessel was tilted, water poured out through the nostrils.

Bronze Box

This box is shaped like a section of the palace. On the center tower are a bird, which symbolizes disaster, and a python. Standing on the ridge of the roof are two Portuguese soldiers holding guns.

Queen Mother

Benin is perhaps most famous for royal heads such as this one. In Benin, the queen mother held a great deal of power. To symbolize that, she wore a woven crown called a "chicken's beak."

Connect *to* History

Drawing Conclusions What does each of these sculptures reveal about who had power in Benin? What can you conclude about changes that might have been happening in Benin?

 SEE SKILLBUILDER HANDBOOK, PAGE 1006

Connect *to* Today

Comparing How do people today try to demonstrate their power to others—through art or through some other way? Explain.

the creator sent this first ruler down to earth at Ife, where he founded the first Yoruba state. His many sons became the heads of other Yoruba kingdoms. All Yoruba chiefs regarded the king of Ife as their highest spiritual authority. To demonstrate his power, each king surrounded himself with a large royal court and soldier-bodyguards. However, a secret society of religious and political leaders limited the king's rule by reviewing the decisions he made.

Ife and Oyo were the two largest Yoruba kingdoms. Ife, developed by 1100, was the most powerful Yoruba kingdom until the late 1600s, when Oyo became more prosperous. As large urban centers, both Ife and Oyo had high walls surrounding them. With fertile soil and ample rainfall, most rural farms in the surrounding areas produced surplus food, which was sent to the cities. This enabled city dwellers to become traders and craftspeople.

The Ife produced gifted artists who carved in wood and ivory. They produced terra cotta sculptures and cast in bronze, brass, and copper. Some scholars believe that the rulers supported artists, who may have lived at court. Many clay and metal casts portray Ife rulers in an idealistic way.

Vocabulary
terra cotta: a reddish-brown clay, hard ceramic.

Kingdom of Benin To the south and west of Ife, near the delta of the Niger River, lay the kingdom of **Benin** (buh·NIHN). Like the Yoruba people of Ife and Oyo, its people made their homes in the forest. The first kings of Benin date from the 1300s. Like the Yoruba kings, the oba, or ruler, of Benin based his right to rule on claims of descent from the first king of Ife.

In the 1400s, the oba named Ewuare made Benin into a major West African state. He did so by building a powerful army. He used it to control an area that by 1500 stretched from the Niger River delta in the east to what is today Lagos, Nigeria. Ewuare also strengthened Benin City by building walls around it. Inside the city, broad streets were lined by neat rows of houses.

The huge palace contained many courtyards and works of art. Artists working for the oba created magnificent brass heads of the royal family and copper figurines. Brass plaques on the walls and columns of the royal palace of the oba showed legends, historical scenes, and the great deeds of the oba and his nobles. According to tradition, Benin artists learned their craft from an Ife artist brought to Benin by the oba to teach them.

In the 1480s, Portuguese trading ships began to sail into Benin's port at Gwatto. The Portuguese traded with Benin merchants for pepper, leopard skins, ivory, and enslaved persons. This began several centuries of European interference in Africa—during which they enslaved Africans and seized African territory for colonies. Meanwhile, East Africans—discussed in Section 3—prospered from trade and developed thriving cities and empires.

Although carved sometime within the last two centuries, this mother and child is done in a traditional Yoruba style.

Section 2 Assessment

1. TERMS & NAMES

Identify
- Ghana
- Mali
- Sundiata
- Mansa Musa
- Ibn Battuta
- Songhai
- Hausa
- Yoruba
- Benin

2. TAKING NOTES

Compare the Mali Empire and the Songhai Empire using a Venn diagram like the one below.

Mali

both

Songhai

3. DRAWING CONCLUSIONS

Which of the two—the Yoruba people or the people of Benin—had more influence on the other? Explain.

THINK ABOUT
- when the kingdoms flourished
- political traditions of each
- artistic traditions of each

4. ANALYZING THEMES

Economics What do you think was the most effective method Ghana used to regulate its economy? Explain.

THINK ABOUT
- trade routes
- ownership of gold
- taxes

3 Eastern City-States and Southern Empires

MAIN IDEA

From 1000 to 1500, East African city-states and southern African empires gained wealth and power through trade.

WHY IT MATTERS NOW

The country of Zimbabwe and cities such as Mogadishu and Mombasa have their roots in this time period.

SETTING THE STAGE As early as the third century, the kingdom of Aksum had taken part in an extensive trade network. From its Red Sea port, Aksum traded with Arabia, Persia, India, and Rome. In the 600s, Muslim forces gained control of Arabia, the Red Sea, and North Africa. The Muslims cut off the Aksumites from their port. The Aksumites moved their capital south from Aksum to Roha (later called Lalibela) shortly before 1100. In the meantime, other cities on the east coast were thriving on Indian Ocean trade.

Global Impact

Swahili

Over the centuries, contacts between two peoples—Bantu speakers and Arabs—led to the creation of a new people and a new language. Many Arab traders married African women. In time, people of mixed Arab and African ancestry came to be called Swahili. The word comes from an Arabic term meaning "people of the coast" and refers to the East African coast.

Although Swahili peoples do not share a single culture, they do speak a common language. Swahili is a Bantu language with many words borrowed from Arabic. Today, Swahili is spoken by about 30 million people—about half of all people who speak a Bantu language. In Tanzania and Kenya, Swahili is the official language.

East Coast Trade Cities

By 1100, waves of Bantu-speaking people had migrated across central Africa to the east coast. There they established farming and fishing villages. At the same time, traders took advantage of the monsoons to make their way across the Indian Ocean to East Africa. Slowly, the existing coastal villages grew into bustling seaports, built on trade between East African merchants and traders from Arabia, Persia, and India. As trade increased, many Muslim Arab and Persian traders settled in these port cities. Arabic blended with the Bantu language to create the **Swahili** (swah·HEE·lee) language.

Persian traders moved south from the Horn of Africa—a triangular peninsula near Arabia. They brought Asian manufactured goods to Africa and African raw materials to Asia. In the coastal markets, Arab traders sold porcelain bowls from China and jewels and cotton cloth from India. They bought African ivory, gold, tortoiseshell, ambergris, leopard skins, and rhinoceros horns to carry to Arabia.

By 1300, more than 35 trading cities dotted the coast from Mogadishu in the north to Kilwa and Sofala in the south. Like the empires of West Africa, these seaports grew wealthy by controlling all incoming and outgoing trade. Some cities also manufactured trade goods for export. For example, weavers in Mogadishu and Sofala made cloth. Workers in Mombasa and Malindi made iron tools.

Background
More Bantu-speaking people moved south than east. Eventually, they settled much of southern Africa.

Vocabulary
ambergris: a grayish-white substance from the intestines of sperm whales, used to make perfume.

In some parts of Africa, cowrie shells were used for currency. The cowrie is a sea snail that lives in the Indian Ocean. Its shell is beautifully colored.

Trade Goods

Raw Materials	Point of Origin	Products Made
• leopard skins	• savanna region	• saddles
• tortoiseshell	• shells of hawksbill sea turtles	• combs
• gold	• mines in southern Africa	• coins, jewelry
• ivory	• tusks from elephants in savanna region	• carved chess pieces and sword hilts

SKILLBUILDER: Interpreting Charts
1. Which raw materials came from the savanna region?
2. Rank the raw materials in order of value, and explain your decision.

The City-State of Kilwa In 1331, Ibn Battuta visited Kilwa. He called it one of the most beautiful cities in the world. He admired the luxurious way that its Muslim rulers and merchants lived. The richest families lived in fine houses of coral and stone. They slept in beds inlaid with ivory and their meals were served on Chinese porcelain. Wealthy Muslim women wore silk robes and gold and silver bracelets.

Kilwa grew rich because it was as far south on the coast as a ship from India could sail in one monsoon season. Therefore, trade goods from southerly regions had to funnel into Kilwa, so Asian merchants could buy them.

In addition, in the late 1200s Kilwa had seized the port of Sofala, which was a trading center for gold mined inland. By controlling Sofala, Kilwa was able to control the overseas trade of gold from southern Africa. This made Kilwa the wealthiest, most powerful coastal city-state.

THINK THROUGH HISTORY
A. Analyzing Causes What were the two main reasons Kilwa became so wealthy?

East African Trade, 1000

GEOGRAPHY SKILLBUILDER: Interpreting Maps
1. **Movement** How far did a trader have to travel to make a round trip from Calicut in India to Kilwa in Africa and back again?
2. **Human-Environment Interaction** Which monsoon would a trader rely on to sail from India to Africa?

Portuguese Conquest In 1488, the first Portuguese ships rounded the southern tip of Africa and sailed north, looking for a sea route to India. They wanted to gain profits from the Asian trade in spices, perfumes, and silks. When the Portuguese saw the wealth of the East African city-states, they decided to conquer those cities and take over the trade themselves.

Using their heavy ships' guns, the Portuguese took Sofala, Kilwa, and Mombasa. They burned parts of Kilwa and built forts on the sites of Kilwa and Mombasa. The Portuguese remained a presence on the East African coast for the next two centuries.

Islamic Influences

As in West Africa, Muslim traders introduced Islam to the East African coast, and the growth of commerce caused it to spread. Even the smallest towns had a mosque for the faithful. A Muslim sultan, or ruler, governed most cities. In addition, most government officials and wealthy merchants were Muslims.

Islamic Law In 1331, Ibn Battuta visited the East African city of Mogadishu. He described how Muslim religious leaders and government officials decided legal matters:

THINK THROUGH HISTORY
B. Summarizing Name the four types of people who decided legal matters and what type of cases they judged.

A VOICE FROM THE PAST
The Shaikh [sultan] takes his place in his hall of audience and sends for the Qadi [judge]. He takes his place on the Shaikh's left and then the lawyers come in and the chief of them sit in front of the Shaikh. . . . Then food is brought and . . . those who are in the audience chamber eat in the presence of the Shaikh. . . . After this the Shaikh retires to his private apartments and the Qadi, the wazirs [government ministers] . . . and . . . chief amirs [military commanders] sit to hear causes and complaints. Questions of religious law are decided by the Qadi, other cases are judged by the . . . wazirs and amirs. If a case requires the views of the [Shaikh], it is put in writing for him. He sends back an immediate reply.
IBN BATTUTA, *Travels of Ibn Battuta*

Most rulers, government officials, and merchants were Muslim. However, the vast majority of people along the East African coast held on to their traditional religious beliefs. This was also true of the people who lived in inland villages.

Enslavement of Africans Along with luxury goods, Arab Muslim traders exported enslaved persons from the East African coast. Traders sent Africans acquired through kidnapping and raids to markets in Arabia, Persia, and Iraq. The wealthy in these countries often bought enslaved persons to do burdensome domestic tasks. Muslim traders shipped enslaved Africans across the Indian Ocean to India, where Indian rulers employed them as soldiers. Enslaved Africans also worked on docks and ships at Muslim-controlled ports and as household servants in China.

Although traders had been enslaving East Africans and selling them overseas since about the ninth century, the numbers remained small—perhaps about 1,000 a year. The trade in enslaved persons did not increase dramatically until the 1700s. At that time, Europeans started to buy captured Africans for their colonial plantations.

THINK THROUGH HISTORY
C. Drawing Conclusions How extensive was the trade in enslaved persons from East Africa before 1700?

Southern Africa and Great Zimbabwe

The gold and ivory that helped the coastal city-states grow rich came from the interior of southern Africa. In southeastern Africa the Shona people established a city called **Great Zimbabwe** (zihm·BAHB·way), which grew into an empire built on the gold trade.

Background
The Shona are a group of Bantu-speaking peoples.

Great Zimbabwe By 1000, the Shona people had claimed the fertile, well-watered plateau between the Zambezi and Limpopo rivers in modern Zimbabwe. The area was well suited to farming and cattle raising. Its location also had economic advantages. Great Zimbabwe stood near an important trade route linking the inland goldfields with the coastal trading city of Sofala. Sometime after 1000, Great Zimbabwe gained control of these trade routes. From the 1200s through the 1400s, it became the capital of a thriving state. Its leaders taxed the traders who traveled these routes. They also demanded payments from less powerful chiefs. The city of Great Zimbabwe was the economic, political, and religious center of its empire.

By 1450, the city of Great Zimbabwe was abandoned. No one knows for sure why it happened. According to one theory, cattle grazing had worn out the grasslands. In addition, farming had worn out the soil, and people had used up the salt and timber. The area could no longer support a large population.

Ruins of Zimbabwe Almost everything that is known about Great Zimbabwe comes from its impressive 60 acres of ruins. Portuguese explorers knew about the site in the

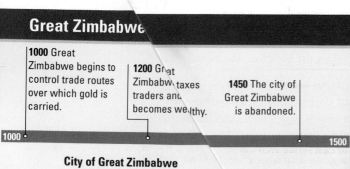

Great Zimbabwe

1000 Great Zimbabwe begins to control trade routes over which gold is carried.

1200 Great Zimbabwe taxes traders and becomes wealthy.

1450 The city of Great Zimbabwe is abandoned.

1000 — 1500

City of Great Zimbabwe
The Shona people built this impressive city to be the center of their empire.

- It covered more than 60 acres.
- Its population was more than 10,000.
- The walls contain approximately 900,000 stone blocks. They were so well built that the blocks hold together without mortar.

This photograph shows part of the Great Enclosure and the cone-shaped tower. ➤

This picture of a person standing next to the tower shows how very high both the tower and the enclosing walls are.

1500s. Karl Mauch, a German explorer, was one of the first Europeans to physically rediscover the remains of these stone dwellings in 1871.

The word *zimbabwe* comes from a Shona phrase meaning "stone enclosure." The ruins consist of two complexes of stone buildings that once housed the royal palace of Great Zimbabwe's rulers. The Great Enclosure is a massive curving wall up to 36 feet high and 15 feet thick. Because there was no way for soldiers to climb to the top of the walls, archaeologists theorize that they were not used primarily as defenses. The massive walls were probably built to impress visitors with the strength of Zimbabwe and its ruler. Inside the walls stands a cone-shaped tower. Among the ruins were found tall figures of birds, carved from soapstone. Archaeologists believe the construction of Great Zimbabwe may have taken 400 years.

Background
Most other walled cities were built so that soldiers could climb to the top of the walls and shoot arrows at attackers.

Mutapa Empire According to Shona oral tradition, a man named Mutota left Great Zimbabwe about 1420 to find a new source of salt. Traveling north, he settled in a valley with fertile soil, good rainfall, and ample wood. There he founded a new state to replace Great Zimbabwe. As the state grew, its leader Mutota used his army to dominate the northern Shona people living in the area. He forced them to make payments to him.

These conquered people called Mutota and his successors *mwene mutapa,* meaning conqueror or "master pillager." The Portuguese who arrived on the East African coast in the early 1500s believed *mwene mutapa* to be a title of respect for the ruler. The term is also the origin of the name of the **Mutapa** Empire. By the time of Mutota's death, the Mutapa Empire had conquered all of what is now Zimbabwe except the eastern portion. By 1480 Mutota's son Matope claimed control of the area along the Zambezi River to the Indian Ocean coast.

The Mutapa Empire was able to mine gold deposited in nearby rivers and streams. In addition, Mutapa rulers forced people in conquered areas to mine gold for them. The rulers sent gold to the coastal city-states in exchange for luxuries. Even before the death of Matope, the southern part of his empire broke away. However, the Mutapa Dynasty continued to remain in control of the smaller empire.

In the 1500s, the Portuguese tried to conquer the empire. When they failed to do so, they resorted to interfering in Mutapa politics. They helped to depose one ruler and put one they could control on the throne. This was a forerunner of increasing European interference in Africa in centuries to come.

This is a Portuguese portrait of one of the kings of the Mutapa Empire.

THINK THROUGH HISTORY
D. Making Inferences Why do you think the Portuguese wanted to conquer the Mutapa Empire?

Section **3** Assessment

1. TERMS & NAMES

Identify
- Swahili
- Great Zimbabwe
- Mutapa

2. TAKING NOTES

Use a chart like the one below to explain one example of cultural interaction brought about by trade on the coast of East Africa.

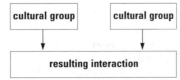

cultural group	cultural group

resulting interaction

Do you think this interaction had a positive or negative effect? Explain.

3. COMPARING

Compare the Portuguese who arrived in East Africa with the rulers of the Mutapa Empire.

THINK ABOUT
- how they treated other groups of people
- what motivated their actions

4. THEME ACTIVITY

Interaction with Environment Create a chart, sketch, or collage that demonstrates how the people of Great Zimbabwe interacted with their environment, both positively and negatively, over time.

Chapter 15 Assessment

TERMS & NAMES
Briefly explain the importance of each of the following to the societies and empires of Africa from 800 to 1500.

1. lineage
2. stateless societies
3. patrilineal
4. matrilineal
5. Ghana
6. Mali
7. Ibn Battuta
8. Songhai
9. Swahili
10. Great Zimbabwe

Interact with History

On page 366, you looked at a situation in which traders exchanged gold for salt. Now that you've read the chapter, reevaluate what makes trade items valuable. How did environmental conditions affect what items had value in Africa? Did government policies have any effect on value? Consider what you learned about trading states in both West and East Africa.

REVIEW QUESTIONS

SECTION 1 *(pages 367–370)*
North and Central African Societies

11. How is a dispute settled in Efe society?
12. What is an age-set system?
13. How were the beginnings of the Almoravid and Almohad empires similar?

SECTION 2 *(pages 371–377)*
West African Empires and Civilizations

14. What accounted for Ghana's financial success?
15. Name two ways Islam spread through Africa.
16. Describe the economy of the Hausa city-states.

SECTION 3 *(pages 378–381)*
Eastern City-States and Southern Empires

17. How did the Swahili language evolve?
18. Why was it important for Kilwa to control Sofala?
19. Who was most affected by the introduction of Islam to East Africa?
20. What was the relationship of Great Zimbabwe to the Mutapa Empire?

Visual Summary

Societies and Empires of Africa

	Organization & Time Periods	Significant Facts
Igbo people	• Existed as a stateless society from **9th through 19th centuries**	• Elders resolved conflicts
Almoravids	• Muslim state from **mid-1000s to mid-1100s**	• Founded city of Marrakech
Almohads	• Muslim state from **mid-1100s to mid-1200s**	• Unified the Maghrib under one authority for first time in history
Ghana	• West African empire from **700s to 1076**	• Grew wealthy and powerful by controlling gold-salt trade
Mali	• West African empire from **1235 to 1400s**	• Mansa Musa's hajj made Mali's wealth famous
Songhai	• West African empire that flourished in the **1400s and 1500s**	• Conquered Mali and gained control of trade routes
Benin	• West African trading kingdom strong in **1400s and 1500s**	• Famous for bronze and brass works of art
Kilwa	• East African city-state flourished from **1200s to 1400s**	• Grew wealthy from trade
Great Zimbabwe	• Capital of trade-based empire from **1200s until about 1450**	• City abandoned, perhaps because natural resources were used up
Mutapa Empire	• Founded **about 1420** by man from Great Zimbabwe	• Remained independent in spite of Portuguese attempts to conquer

CRITICAL THINKING

1. ADAPTING TO THE DESERT

THEME **INTERACTION WITH ENVIRONMENT** How did people adapt to the harsh conditions of the Sahara? Discuss both traders who crossed the Sahara and people who lived in the Saharan village of Taghaza.

2. AFRICAN LEADERS, 800–1500

Create a chart like the one below. For each leader, list what group of people he led and one of his significant achievements.

Leader	Group	Significant achievement
Ibn Yasin		
Ibn Tumart		
Mansa Musa		
Askia Muhammad		
Ewuare		
Mutota		

3. TRADE NETWORKS

Do you think that Africa in the year 1300 was connected to most of the world through trade, or was it relatively isolated from the rest of the world? Support your answer with evidence from the chapter.

4. ANALYZING PRIMARY SOURCES

The following quotation comes from a description of Timbuktu, written by Leo Africanus, a Muslim traveler. Read the paragraph and then answer the questions below it.

> **A VOICE FROM THE PAST**
> The rich king of Timbuktu hath many plates and scepters of gold, some whereof weigh 1,300 pounds: and he keeps a magnificent and well-furnished court. When he travelleth any whither he rideth upon a camel which is led by some of his noblemen; and so he doth likewise when he goeth forth to warfare, and all his soldiers ride upon horses. Whoever will speak unto this king must first fall down before his feet, and then taking up earth must first sprinkle it upon his own head and shoulders.
>
> **LEO AFRICANUS**, *A Geographical History of Africa*

- Do you think Leo Africanus was impressed by the ruler of Timbuktu or not? Explain your opinion.
- How did the king of Timbuktu demonstrate his royal status?

CHAPTER ACTIVITIES

1. LIVING HISTORY: Unit Portfolio Project

THEME **RELIGIOUS AND ETHICAL SYSTEMS** Your unit portfolio project focuses on the growth and influence of religious and ethical systems. For Chapter 15, you might use one of the following ideas to add to your portfolio:

- Write an interview with one Muslim ruler from this chapter. Discuss how Islam influenced his political decisions.
- With a small group, put on a skit enacting the story of how the creator caused the first Yoruba state to be established.
- Create a diagram showing which levels of East African society converted to Islam and which retained African beliefs.

2. CONNECT TO TODAY: Cooperative Learning

THEME **ECONOMICS** In this chapter, you read about how trade affected the economies of East African city-states. Today, much of eastern Africa still relies heavily on trade.

Work with a team to create a map that shows what goods present-day East African nations trade and who their trading partners are.

 Using the Internet or your library, research East African trade today.

- Find information on exports and imports, quantities shipped, where the goods are going, and how they are being transported.
- Look for examples of trade maps in this textbook, in historical atlases, and on the Internet.
- Create your own map showing East African trade today.

3. INTERPRETING A TIME LINE

Revisit the unit time line on pages 228–229. Use the Chapter 15 time line to find out when Great Zimbabwe was abandoned. Then use the other chapter time lines to name another event that was happening about the same time.

FOCUS ON GEOGRAPHY

Look at this map of western Africa in 1997. The map shows where some of the ethnic groups that you studied in this chapter live today. The groups are labeled in red.

- Which is the most widespread ethnic group? In what nations does that group live?
- Which groups live in modern Nigeria?

Connect to History
Compare this map to the map on page 368. Which groups are on both maps? Do they live in the same regions that they used to inhabit?

Western Africa, 1997

Connecting Hemispheres
900–1800

In this marine painting, Ludolf Backhuysen depicts a powerful Dutch fleet at sea. During this period, Europeans explored the world and interacted with the people of different lands for the first time.

Connecting Hemispheres

	600–900	1000	1100	1200	1300	1400

CHAPTER 16 900–1500

Peoples and Empires in the Americas

600 Central America Maya civilization thrives

600 Mexico Teotihuacan civilization grows

800 North America Anasazi civilization develops

1000 Mexico Toltec civilization dominates

1150 North America Cahokia settlement at peak (Mississippians)

1200s Mexico Aztecs begin civilization

1200s Peru Inca Empire begins

1325 Mexico Aztecs build Tenochtitlan

◀ **600 Mexico**

CHAPTER 17 1300–1600

European Renaissance and Reformation

1300 Italy Renaissance begins

1353 Italy Boccaccio finishes writing the *Decameron*

CHAPTER 18 1300–1700

The Muslim World Expands

1300s India ▶

1300 Anatolia Osman establishes Ottoman state

1361 Anatolia Ottoman Orkhan I captures Adrianople

1398 India Timur the Lame devastates India

CHAPTER 19 1400–1800

An Age of Exploration and Isolation

1368 China Hong Wu founds Ming Dynasty

1400s China ▶

CHAPTER 20 1492–1800

The Atlantic World

	600–900	1000	1100	1200	1300	1400

Living History
Unit 4 Portfolio Project

THEME Cultural Interaction

Your portfolio for Unit 4 will trace the ways cultures interact with one another and show the results of those influences. Types of interaction include conquest, trade, migration, and heritage. Results include the sharing of technology, religious concepts, political ideas, goods, crops, foods, diseases, and knowledge of all kinds.

Living History Project Choices

Each Chapter Assessment offers you choices of ways to show the cultural interaction in that chapter. Activities include the following:

Chapter **16** dialogue, poster, article

Chapter **17** magazine, letter, role-play

Chapter **18** speech, political cartoon, inscription

Chapter **19** letter, reply, editorial

Chapter **20** political cartoon, editorial, journal entry

1438 *Peru*
Pachacuti becomes ruler of Incas

1500s *Peru*
Inca Empire at height

1502 *Mexico*
Montezuma becomes Aztec ruler

▼ **1500s *England***

1455 *Germany*
Gutenberg Bible produced on printing press

1497 *Italy*
Leonardo da Vinci paints *The Last Supper*

1508 *Italy*
Michelangelo begins painting Sistine Chapel

1517 *Germany*
Martin Luther begins Reformation

1534 *England*
Henry VIII breaks from Church

1601 *England*
William Shakespeare writes *Hamlet*

1603 *England*
Queen Elizabeth I dies, ending Tudor rule

1453 *Europe*
Ottomans conquer Constantinople

1498 *Portugal*
Vasco da Gama sails to India

1501 *Persia*
Safavid Isma'il conquers Persia

1520 *Anatolia*
Suleiman the Magnificent rules Ottoman Empire

1526 *India*
Babur founds Mughal Empire

1631 *India* Shah Jahan builds Taj Mahal

1658 *India*
Aurangzeb rules Mughal Empire

1419 *Portugal*
Prince Henry starts navigation school

1433 *China* Last voyage of Zheng He

1494 *Spain and Portugal* Treaty of Tordesillas splits "New World"

1514 *China*
First Portuguese ships reach China

1522 *Spain*
Magellan's crew sails around world

1603 *Japan*
Tokugawa regime begins

1636 *China*
Manchus conquer Korea

1644 *China*
Manchus found Qing Dynasty

1721 *Japan*
Edo (Tokyo) becomes world's largest city

1793 *China*
British seek trade concessions with Chinese

▼ **1675 *North America***

1492 *Americas*
Columbus sails to Hispaniola

1502 *Africa*
First slaves exported for work in the Americas

1521 *Mexico*
Cortés conquers Aztecs

1533 *Peru* Pizarro conquers Inca

1607 *North America* English settle Jamestown

1608 *Canada*
Champlain founds Quebec

1675 *North America* Colonists and Indians clash in King Philip's War

1739 *North America*
South Carolina slaves lead Stono Rebellion

1754 *North America*
French and Indian War begins

People and Empires in the Americas, 900–1500

PREVIEWING THEMES

Cultural Interaction

Cultures in the Americas had frequent contact across miles and time. Both conquest and trade brought different cultures together. In Mesoamerica the cultures shared ideas about gods and even calendars.

Power and Authority

Societies in the Americas ranged from small tribal bands to immense empires. Some empires were ruled by priest-kings, and others by warrior-kings. In Peru, a welfare state took care of all the people within the empire.

Religious and Ethical Systems

In the Americas, religion was a powerful force. Many societies combined religious and state rule. To please the gods, people built huge temples and other structures. They built empires and captured slaves in the name of the gods. Much of their art was focused on the gods and the need to please them.

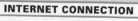
INTERNET CONNECTION

Visit us at www.mcdougallittell.com to learn more about people of the Americas.

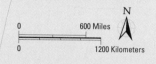
THE AMERICAS, 900–1500

0   600 Miles
0   1200 Kilometers

N

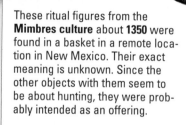

These ritual figures from the **Mimbres culture** about **1350** were found in a basket in a remote location in New Mexico. Their exact meaning is unknown. Since the other objects with them seem to be about hunting, they were probably intended as an offering.

This Eagle Knight shows how important warriors were to the **Aztec** society. It was found in the Eagle Knight House near the Great Temple of **Tenochtitlan**. The fierce-looking knight belonged to the Aztec nobility and dedicated himself to the service of the god Sol. The Aztecs ruled a large empire between **1200 and 1521**.

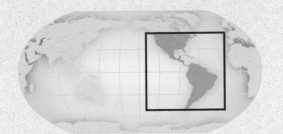

NORTH AMERICA

ANASAZI
and
HOHOKAM

ADENA

HOPEWELL
MISSISSIPPIAN

MESOAMERICA

AZTEC

MAYA

Chac, a rain god of the **Maya, 300–900,** reclines in front of the Temple of the Warriors. He holds a stone bowl, which was a receptacle for sacrifices, such as human hearts, made to the gods.

ATLANTIC
OCEAN

A painted wooden ceremonial cup, called a kero, was created in the form of a jaguar. It dates from the **Incan Empire, 1400–1532.** The Inca depicted jaguars in many different styles. Jaguars were Incan symbols of power and authority. They were also portrayed often on ceramic bowls.

0° Equator

SOUTH AMERICA

INCA

PACIFIC
OCEAN

30°S

389

Interact *with* History

These images are of ravens and a killer whale found in the Pacific Ocean.

As a historian studying a culture with no written language, you are forced to study the artifacts of that culture. In many ways you are like a detective. You look at the evidence and clues to draw conclusions about the culture. Imagine you have found the mask shown on this page. Study the clues and see how much you can learn about the Bella Coola.

What does this mask reveal about the society?

This mask, used by the Bella Coola during a ceremony, tells the legend of Ahlquntam II, the chief god in the land of creation.

Carved of red cedar and painted, the mask was moved by strings and mechanical devices across the rear house wall during a ceremony.

Legend says Ahlquntam II used the sun as a canoe to cross the sky. He wore a cloak lined with salmon.

EXAMINING *the* ISSUES

- What do the materials and images used reveal about the environment in which the Bella Coola lived?

- What do the images or figures tell you about what was important in the culture?

- Why might it be important to know by whom or when the mask might have been worn?

- How else might you find out information about this culture?

Discuss these questions with your classmates. Think about the kinds of information you have learned about other cultures that did not have a written language. You may recall ways historians learned about the very earliest cultures.

As you read this chapter, examine the masks made by different peoples of the Americas. Think about what those masks reveal about the various cultures.

Diverse Societies of North America

MAIN IDEA	WHY IT MATTERS NOW
Complex North American societies were linked to each other through culture and economics.	Traditions and ideas from these cultures became part of the cultures of North America.

SETTING THE STAGE Between 40,000 and 12,000 years ago, hunter-gatherers migrated across the Bering Strait land bridge from Asia and began to populate the Americas. Migrating southward, those first Americans reached the southern tip of South America by somewhere between 12,000 and 7000 B.C. At the same time, they spread out across North America. Over the centuries, early North American peoples adapted to their environment, creating a diverse set of cultures.

Complex Societies Build and Trade

In some ways, the early cultures north of the Rio Grande River were less developed than those of South America and Mesoamerica. The North American groups created no great empires. They left few ruins as spectacular as those of ancient Mexico or Peru. Nevertheless, the first peoples of North America did create complex societies. These societies were able to conduct long-distance trade and construct magnificent buildings.

Northwest Coast—Cultures of Abundance The Pacific Northwest—from Oregon to Alaska—was rich in resources and supported a sizable population. To the Kwakiutl, Nootka, and Haida peoples, the most important resource was the sea. They hunted whales in canoes. Some canoes were large enough to carry at least 15 people. In addition to the many resources of the sea, the coastal forest provided plentiful food. In this abundant environment, the Northwest Coast tribes developed societies in which differences in wealth created social classes. Families displayed their rank and prosperity in an elaborate ceremony called the **potlatch** (PAHT·LACH). In this ceremony, they gave food, drink, and gifts to the community.

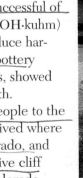

Cliff Palace, located at Mesa Verde, Colorado, was an Anasazi pueblo. It had 200 rooms.

Pueblo People Construct Complex Buildings The dry, desert lands of the Southwest were a much harsher environment than the temperate Pacific coast. However, as early as 3000 B.C. the peoples of the Southwest were beginning to farm the land. Among the most successful of these early farmers were the Hohokam (huh·HOH·kuhm) of central Arizona. They used irrigation to produce harvests of corn, beans, and squash. Their use of pottery rather than baskets, and certain religious rituals, showed contact with Mesoamerican peoples to the south.

The Hohokam were also influenced by a people to the north: the **Anasazi** (AH·nuh·SAH·zee). They lived where the present-day states of Utah, Arizona, Colorado, and New Mexico meet. The Anasazi built impressive cliff dwellings, such as the ones at Mesa Verde, Colorado. These houses were built in shallow caves in the sheer walls of deep canyons. By the A.D. 900s, the Anasazi were living in **pueblos** (PWEHB·lohs), villages of large, apartment-style compounds made of stone and sun-baked clay.

North American Culture Areas about 1400

Inuit

Kutchin

Inuit

Inuit

Hudson Bay

Inuit

Tlingit

Beaver

Cree

Bella Coola

Blackfoot

Ojibwa

Algonquin

Kwakiutl

Nez Percé

Mandan

Mississippi R.

Huron

Crow

Lakota

Iroquois

PACIFIC OCEAN

Coo

Shoshone

Cheyenne

Miami

Delaware

Pomo

Arapaho

Shawnee

Hopi

Osage

Apache

Cherokee

Navajo

Pueblo

Papago

Comanche

Natchez

Gulf of Mexico

ATLANTIC OCEAN

Caribbean Sea

40°N

40°W

Arctic Circle

N

0   1,000 Miles

0   2,000 Kilometers

Tropic of Cancer

Native American Cultures
- Arctic
- Subarctic
- Northwest Coast
- Plateau
- Great Basin
- California
- Southwest
- Great Plains
- Eastern Woodlands
- Southeast
- Mesoamerica

Osage Tribe name

GEOGRAPHY SKILLBUILDER: Interpreting Maps
1. **Region** *Which culture group had the largest number of tribes?*
2. **Human-Environment Interaction** *In which culture areas would movement of trade goods be made easier by river and lake connections?*

One of the largest pueblos, begun around A.D. 900, was Pueblo Bonito, a Spanish name meaning "beautiful village." Its construction required a high degree of social organization and inventiveness. Like other people of the Americas, the Anasazi did not have horses, mules, or the wheel. Instead, they relied on human labor to quarry sandstone from the canyon walls and move it to the site. Skilled builders then used a mud-like mortar to construct walls up to five stories high. Windows were small to keep out the burning sun. When completed, Pueblo Bonito probably housed about 1,000 people and contained more than 600 rooms. In addition, a number of underground ceremonial chambers called kivas (KEE·vuhs) were used for a variety of religious practices.

Many Anasazi pueblos were abandoned around 1200. Their descendants, the Pueblo peoples, continued many Anasazi customs. Pueblo groups like the Hopi and Zuni used kivas for religious ceremonies. They also created beautiful pottery and woven blankets. They traded these, along with corn and other farm products, with Plains Indians to the east, who supplied bison meat and hides. These nomadic Plains tribes eventually became known by such names as the Comanche, Kiowa, and Apache.

Mound Builders Forge Ties with Eastern Peoples Beyond the Great Plains, in the wooded lands east of the Mississippi River, other ancient peoples—the Mound Builders—were creating their own unique traditions. Beginning around 800 B.C., two cultures, known as Adena and Hopewell, built large burial mounds and filled them with finely crafted copper and stone objects. Some mounds, such as Ohio's Great Serpent Mound, had the shape of animals when seen from above.

This Anasazi pitcher dates from A.D. 1100. The black and white spirals form a traditional design.

Background
Tribes in the Plains are classified into groups based on one of six basic language families.

The last Mound Builder culture, the **Mississippian,** lasted from A.D. 800 until the arrival of Europeans in the 1500s. These people built giant earthen pyramids such as the one at Cahokia (kuh·HOH·kee·uh), Illinois. They created thriving villages based on farming and trade. Between 1000 and 1200, as many as 10,000 people lived at Cahokia, the leading site of Mississippian culture. Cahokia was led by priest-rulers, who regulated farming activities. The priest-rulers may have been influenced by the cultures of Mesoamerica. The heart of the community was a 100-foot-high, flat-topped pyramid, which was crowned by a wooden temple.

These Mississippian lands were located in a crossroads region between east and west. They enjoyed easy transportation on the Mississippi and Ohio rivers. They came into contact with many other peoples, including those of the Eastern Woodlands.

Woodlands Tribes Build Alliances The eastern tribes had much in common with the Mississippian peoples, including a similar environment. Despite the similar environment, woodlands groups developed a variety of cultures. They spoke distinct languages belonging to language families such as Algonquian, Iroquoian, and Muskogean. The woodlands peoples often clashed with each other over land. In some areas, tribes formed political alliances to ensure protection of tribal lands. The best example of a political alliance was the **Iroquois** (IHR·uh·KWOY), a group of tribes speaking related languages living in the eastern Great Lakes region. In the late 1500s, five of these tribes in upper New York—the Mohawk, Oneida, Onondaga, Cayuga, and Seneca—formed the Iroquois League. According to legend, Chief Hiawatha created this league. His goal was to promote joint defense and cooperation among the tribes. The confederacy lasted for almost 200 years.

THINK THROUGH HISTORY
A. Drawing Conclusions Of what value would a political alliance be to an individual tribe?

Cultural Connections

The Iroquois alliance was a notable example of a political link between early North American peoples. For the most part, however, the connections between native North Americans were economic and cultural. They traded, had similar religious beliefs, and shared social patterns.

Trading Networks Tie Tribes Together Trade was a major factor linking the peoples of North America. Trade centers and traveling merchants were found throughout North America. Along the Columbia River in Oregon, the Chinook people established a lively marketplace that brought together trade goods from all over the West. The Mississippians were also active traders. Their trade network stretched from the Rocky Mountains to the Atlantic coast and from the Great Lakes to the Gulf of Mexico. Sometimes goods traveled hundreds or even thousands of miles from their original source. This was especially true of exotic items such as colored feathers or copper jewelry.

Religion Shapes Views of Life Another practice early Americans shared was religion. Nearly all native North Americans believed that the world around them was filled with nature spirits. Most Native Americans recognized a number of sacred spirits. Some groups held up one supreme being, or "Great Spirit," above all others. North American peoples believed that the spirits gave them rituals and customs to guide them in their lives and to satisfy their basic needs. If people practiced these rituals, they would live in peace and harmony.

Native American religious beliefs also included great respect for the land as the source of life. Native Americans used the land but tried to alter it as little as possible. The land was sacred, not something that could be bought and sold. Later, when

Background
The belief that natural objects have a spirit is called animism.

Europeans arrived in North America, the issue of ownership of land became a problem. A Native American expressed his view of this dilemma:

A VOICE FROM THE PAST
Some of our chiefs make the claim that the land belongs to us. It is not what the Great Spirit told me. He told me that the land belongs to Him, that no people own the land, and that I was not to forget to tell this to the white people.

KANNEKUK, Kickapoo prophet, quoted in *Through Indian Eyes*

Harmony with nature was an important part of Native American life, and so was harmony in relationships with people.

Shared Social Patterns The family was the basis for social organization for Native Americans. Generally, the family unit was the extended family, including parents, children, grandparents, and other close relatives. Some tribes further organized families into clans: groups of families descended from a common ancestor. In some tribes, clan members lived together in large houses or groups of houses.

Common among American Indian clans was the use of **totems** (TOH·tuhmz). The term refers to a natural object that an individual, clan, or group identifies itself with. The totem was used as a symbol of the unity of a group or clan. It also helped define certain behaviors and the social relationships of a group. The term comes from an Ojibwa Indian language spoken in the Great Lakes area, but refers to a cultural practice found throughout the Americas. For example, Northwestern peoples displayed totem symbols on masks, boats, and huge poles set in front of their houses. Others used totem symbols in rituals or dances associated with important group events such as marriages, the naming of children, or the planting or harvesting of crops.

There were hundreds of different patterns of North American Indian life. Some societies were small and dealt with life in a limited region of the vast North American continent. Other groups were much larger, and were linked by trade and culture to other groups in North America and Mesoamerica. As you will learn in Section 2, peoples in Mesoamerica and South America also lived in societies that varied from simple to complex. Three of these cultures—the Maya, the Aztec, and the Inca—would develop sophisticated ways of life like those of highly developed cultures in other parts of the globe.

Totem poles marked important events such as the naming of a chief.

THINK THROUGH HISTORY
B. Making Inferences What artificial symbols are used by nations or organizations in a way similar to totems?

Section 1 Assessment

1. TERMS & NAMES

Identify
- potlatch
- Anasazi
- pueblos
- Mississippian
- Iroquois
- totems

2. TAKING NOTES

Draw a Venn diagram like the one below. Compare and contrast Native Americans of the Northwest Coast and the Southwest.

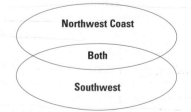

Northwest Coast

Both

Southwest

How did environment affect the development of these cultures?

3. COMPARING

In what ways did the peoples of North America share similar cultural patterns?

THINK ABOUT
- how the people viewed the environment
- the role of family in their lives
- religion

4. ANALYZING THEMES

Cultural Interaction What evidence is there that societies in North America interacted with each other?

THINK ABOUT
- how goods were obtained
- ways to defend against enemies
- what kinds of evidence historians find and consider valid

Mayan Kings and Cities

MAIN IDEA	WHY IT MATTERS NOW
The Maya developed a highly complex civilization based on city-states controlled by dynasties of kings.	Descendants of the Maya still occupy the same territory.

SETTING THE STAGE In the early centuries A.D., most North American peoples were beginning to develop complex societies. Further south, the peoples of Mexico and Central America were entering into the full flower of civilization. A prime example of this cultural flowering was the Maya, who built an extraordinary civilization in the heart of Mesoamerica.

Maya Create Urban Kingdoms

The homeland of the Maya stretched from southern Mexico into northern Central America. This area includes a highland region and a lowland region. The lowlands lie to the north. They include the dry scrub forest of the Yucatan (YOO·kuh·TAN) Peninsula and the dense, steamy jungles of southeastern Mexico and northern Guatemala. The highlands are further south—a range of cool, cloud-wreathed mountains that stretch from southern Mexico to El Salvador.

While the Olmec were building their civilization along the Gulf Coast in the period from 1200 B.C. to 400 B.C., the Maya were also evolving. They took on Olmec influences, blending these with local customs. By A.D. 250, Mayan culture had burst forth in a flourishing civilization.

Urban Centers The period from A.D. 250 to 900 is known as the Classic Period of Mayan civilization. During this time, the Maya built spectacular cities such as **Tikal** (tee·KAHL), a major center in northern Guatemala. Other important sites included Copan, Palenque, Uxmal, and Chichen Itza. Each of these was an independent city-state, ruled by a god-king and serving as a center for religious ceremonies and trade.

Mayan cities featured giant pyramids, temples, palaces, and elaborate stone carvings dedicated to the gods and to important rulers. Tens of thousands of people lived in residential areas surrounding the city center, which bustled with activity.

Mesoamerican Civilizations 200 B.C.–A.D. 1521

Legend:
- Teotihuacan Civilization, 200 B.C.–A.D. 700
- Toltec Heartland, A.D. 900–1100
- Aztec Civilization, A.D. 1200–1521
- Mayan Civilization, A.D. 250–900

Map labels: Tropic of Cancer, Gulf of Mexico, Lake Texcoco, Tula, Teotihuacan, Tenochtitlan, Uxmal, Chichen Itza, Yucatan Peninsula, Palenque, Piedras Negras, Tikal, Copan, 20°N, 100°W, 90°W, PACIFIC OCEAN

0 — 250 Miles
0 — 500 Kilometers

GEOGRAPHY SKILLBUILDER: Interpreting Maps
The map shows about 1,700 years of occupation of Mesoamerica. During this time cultures influenced each other through trade and the conquering of lands.
1. **Region** Which civilization occupied the Yucatan Peninsula?
2. **Region** What other civilization areas were eventually incorporated into the Aztec area?

Archaeologists have identified at least 50 major Mayan sites, all with monumental architecture. For example, Pyramid IV at Tikal stretched 212 feet into the jungle sky. In fact, the Tikal pyramids were the tallest structures in the Americas until 1903, when the Flatiron Building was built in New York City. In addition to temples and pyramids, each Mayan city featured a ball court. In this stone-sided playing field, the Maya played a game that had religious and political significance. The Maya believed the playing of this game would maintain the cycles of the sun and moon and bring life-giving rains.

THINK THROUGH HISTORY
A. Drawing Conclusions What does the ability to construct complex buildings reveal about a society?

Agriculture and Trade Support Cities Although the Mayan city-states were independent of each other, they were linked through alliances and trade. Cities exchanged the products of their local environment such as salt, flint, feathers, shells, and honey. Also traded were craft goods like cotton textiles and jade ornaments. While the Maya did not have a uniform currency, cacao (chocolate) beans sometimes served as one.

Background
Only the wealthy consumed chocolate as a drink. It was flavored with honey and vanilla.

As in the rest of Mesoamerica, agriculture—particularly the growing of maize, beans, and squash—provided the basis for Mayan life. For years, experts assumed that the Maya practiced slash-and-burn agriculture. This method involves farmers clearing the land by burning existing vegetation and planting crops in the ashes. Evidence now shows, however, that the Maya also developed more sophisticated methods, including planting on raised beds above swamps and on hillside terraces. These methods allowed Mayan farmers to produce large amounts of food to be traded in the cities.

Kingdoms Built on Dynasties Successful farming methods led to the accumulation of wealth and the development of social classes. The noble class, which included priests and the leading warriors, occupied the top rung of Mayan society. Below them came merchants and those with specialized knowledge, such as master artisans. Finally, at the bottom, came the peasant majority.

The Mayan king sat at the top of this class structure. He was regarded as a holy figure and his position was hereditary. When he died, he passed the throne on to his eldest son. Other sons of the ruler might expect to join the priesthood.

This is the death mask of a seventh-century ruler of Palenque, a Mayan city-state. The mask is a mosaic of jade with eyes of shell and obsidian.

Religion Shapes Mayan Life

Religion influenced most aspects of Mayan life. The Maya believed in many gods, who inhabited 13 layers of the sky and the 9 layers of the underworld. There were gods of corn, of death, of rain, and of war. Gods could be good or evil, and sometimes both. Gods also were associated with the four directions and with different colors: white for north, black for west, yellow for south, red for east, and green in the center. The Maya believed that each day was a living god whose behavior could be predicted with the help of an intricate system of calendars.

Religious Practices The Maya worshiped their gods in various ways. They prayed and made offerings of food, flowers, and incense. They also pierced their bodies with sharp needles and offered their blood, believing that this would nourish the gods. Sometimes the Maya even carried out human sacrifice, usually of captured enemies. At Chichen Itza (chee·CHEHN ee·TSAH), in the Yucatan, they threw captives into a deep sinkhole lake, called a *cenote* (say·NO·tay), along with gold, jade, and other offerings. The Maya believed that human sacrifice pleased the gods and kept the world in balance. Nevertheless, the Maya's use of sacrifice never reached the extremes of some other Mesoamerican peoples.

Math Develops to Support Religion Mayan religious beliefs also led to the development of the calendar, mathematics, and astronomy. Mayans believed that time was

Chichen Itza

Mayan cities feature very large structures that seem to be designed for ceremonial or religious purposes. Inscriptions on the buildings, the buildings' contents, chambers, and even the locations of the buildings reveal important information about the culture. Chichen Itza, a Mayan city located on the Yucatan Peninsula in Mexico, has huge buildings to honor rulers, warriors, and gods.

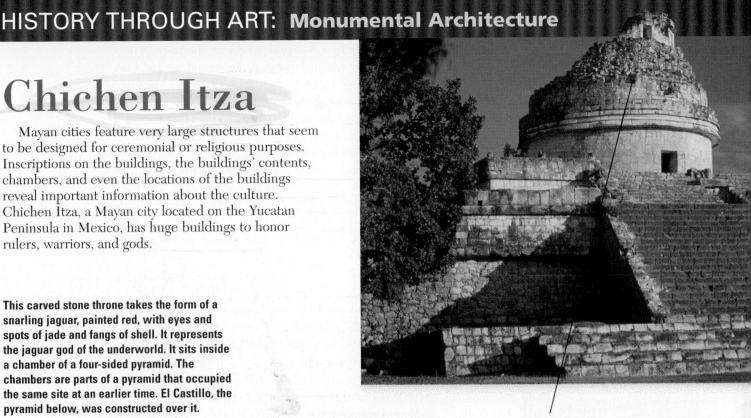

This carved stone throne takes the form of a snarling jaguar, painted red, with eyes and spots of jade and fangs of shell. It represents the jaguar god of the underworld. It sits inside a chamber of a four-sided pyramid. The chambers are parts of a pyramid that occupied the same site at an earlier time. El Castillo, the pyramid below, was constructed over it.

El Caracol—"The Snail"
Resembling a modern observatory, El Caracol shows the Mayans' knowledge of astronomy. Window-like openings in the tower align with the sunset during both spring and autumn equinoxes. The Maya studied the movements of the sun, moon, and stars because these movements related to the activities of the gods.

El Castillo—"The Castle"
This temple, also called the Pyramid of Kukulcan, sat at the top of four spectacular stairways. It was dedicated to the worship of Kukulcan, the feathered serpent god. The stairs to the temple were constructed so that at certain times of the day it looked as if a writhing serpent was crawling up them.

Connect to History

Analyzing Motives In what ways do the huge buildings at Chichen Itza show how the Mayan people felt about their gods?

SEE SKILLBUILDER HANDBOOK, PAGE 994

Connect to Today

Drawing Conclusions What conclusions might someone make about U.S. culture from viewing the heads of the presidents at Mount Rushmore?

a burden carried on the back of a god. At the end of a day, month, or year, one god would lay the burden down and another would pick it up. A day would be lucky or unlucky, depending on the nature of the god. Thus it was very important to have an accurate calendar to know which god was in charge of the day.

The Maya developed a 260-day religious calendar, which consisted of twenty 13-day months. A second 365-day solar calendar consisted of eighteen 20-day months, with a separate period of five days at the end. The two calendars were linked together like meshed gears so that any given day could be identified in both cycles. The calendar helped identify the best time to plant crops, attack enemies, or crown new rulers.

The Maya based their calendar on careful observation of the planets, sun, and moon. Highly skilled Mayan astronomers and mathematicians calculated the solar year at 365.2420 days. (Only .0002 of a day too short.) The Mayan astronomers were able to attain such great precision by using a math system that included the concept of zero. The Maya used a shell symbol for zero, dots for the numbers 1 to 4, and a bar for 5. The Mayan number system was a base 20 system. They used the numerical system primarily for calendar and astronomical work, not to count people or objects.

SPOTLIGHT ON

Calendar Glyph

The glyph shown above is the date "9 Zotz" on the 365-day calendar. The symbol stands for the name of the month. The number is represented by the bar, which equals 5, and dots, which together equal 4.

Pictured above is a group of Mayan hieroglyphs from Temple 18 at Palenque. They are undecoded. Like Egyptian hieroglyphics, the glyphs can be grouped into two categories: those that are word signs and those that are syllables. The way the glyphs are translated involves deciding if the sign sets are word pictures or syllables.

Many of the glyphs on stone monuments are records of kings and the history of their rule. Other glyphs provide information on the Mayan gods and religious activities.

Written Language Preserves History The Maya also developed the most advanced writing system in the ancient Americas. Mayan writing consisted of about 800 hieroglyphic symbols, or **glyphs** (glihfs). Some of these glyphs stand for whole words, while others represent syllables. The Maya used their writing system to record important historical events, carving their glyphs in stone or recording them in a bark-paper book known as a **codex** (KOH·DEHKS). Only three of these ancient books have survived.

Other original books telling of Mayan history and customs do exist, however. These were written down by Mayan peoples after the arrival of the Spanish. The most famous of these books, the ***Popol Vuh*** (POH·pohl VOO), recounts the Highland Maya's version of the story of creation. "Before the world was created, Calm and Silence were the great kings that ruled," reads the first sentence in the book. "Nothing existed, there was nothing."

THINK THROUGH HISTORY
B. Making Inferences How are math, astronomy, and calendars related?

Background
The codex was made of long strips of bark paper that were folded like a fan.

A VOICE FROM THE PAST

Then let the emptiness fill! they said. Let the water weave its way downward so the earth can show its face! Let the light break on the ridges, let the sky fill up with the yellow light of dawn! Let our glory be a man walking on a path through the trees! "Earth!" the Creators called. They called only once, and it was there, from a mist, from a cloud of dust, the mountains appeared instantly.

From the Popol Vuh

Mysterious Mayan Decline

The remarkable history of the Maya ended in mystery. In the late 800s, the Maya suddenly abandoned many of their cities. Some Mayan sites in the Yucatan, such as Chichen Itza and Uxmal, continued to thrive for several more centuries. Invaders from the north, the Toltec, moved into the lands occupied by the Maya. These warlike peoples from central Mexico changed the culture. The high civilization of Mayan cities like Tikal and Copan disappeared.

No one knows exactly why this happened, though experts offer several overlapping theories. By the 700s, warfare had broken out among the various Mayan city-states. This violence caused some Maya to flee their cities and take refuge in the jungle. Increased warfare disrupted trade and produced economic hardship. In addition, population growth and over-farming may have caused ecological damage, causing food shortages, famine, and disease. All these circumstances probably contributed to the fall of Mayan civilization. By the time the Spanish arrived in the early 1500s, the Maya were divided into small, weak city-states that gave little hint of their former glory.

As the Mayan civilization faded, other peoples of Mesoamerica were growing in strength and sophistication. Like the Maya, these peoples would trace some of their ancestry to the Olmec. Eventually, these people would dominate the Valley of Mexico and lands beyond it, as you will learn in Section 3.

THINK THROUGH HISTORY
C. Evaluating Which of the causes for the fall of the Maya do you think was most important? Explain.

Vocabulary
theocracy: combined state and religious rule

A trio of modern Mayan women sell textiles at the marketplace. The traditional designs on their clothing and the textiles have been used on Mayan fabrics for hundreds of years.

Maya

Traits of Civilization	Strength Leading to Power	Weakness Leading to Decline
Religious beliefs and theocracy	United culture Loyalty to the king	Many physical and human resources funneled into religious activities
Independent city-states	Wealthy and prosperous culture	Frequent warfare occurs between kingdoms
Intensive agriculture	Production of more food feeds a larger population	Soil depletion and population growth creates need for more land

SKILLBUILDER: Interpreting Charts
1. *Which trait aids in building a sense of loyalty to the ruler?*
2. *How can intensive agriculture be both a strength and a weakness?*

Section 2 Assessment

1. TERMS & NAMES

Identify
• Tikal
• glyph
• codex
• *Popol Vuh*

2. TAKING NOTES

Draw a diagram like the one below and fill in details that support the main idea in the center. You may want to review the characteristics of a civilization found in Chapter 1.

The Maya developed a highly complex civilization in Mesoamerica.

| Supporting detail | Supporting detail | Supporting detail |

3. DRAWING CONCLUSIONS

How important do you think the development of advanced mathematics was in the creation of the Mayan calendar?

THINK ABOUT
• how records are kept over long periods of time
• the need for numbers larger than 20
• the need for precision

4. THEME ACTIVITY

Religious and Ethical Systems Imagine that you are a reporter visiting Mayan city-states. Write a one-page article that describes various aspects of the Mayan religion.

3 The Aztecs Control Central Mexico

MAIN IDEA	WHY IT MATTERS NOW
Through alliances and conquest, the Aztecs created a powerful empire in Mexico.	This time period saw the origins of one of the 20th century's most populous cities, Mexico City.

SETTING THE STAGE While the Maya were developing their civilization to the south, other high cultures were evolving in central Mexico. Some of the most important developments took place in and around the Valley of Mexico. This valley, where modern Mexico City is located, eventually became the site of the greatest empire of Mesoamerica, the Aztec. The Aztecs were preceded by two other important civilizations who traced their ancestry to the Olmec and Zapotec.

The Valley of Mexico

The Valley of Mexico, a mountain basin 7,000 feet above sea level, served as the home base of several powerful cultures. The valley had several large, shallow lakes at its center, accessible resources, and fertile soil. These advantages attracted the people of Teotihuacan (TAY·oh·TEE·wah·KAHN) and the Toltecs. They settled in the valley and developed advanced civilizations that controlled much of the area. (See the map on page 395.)

Teotihuacan: An Early City-State The first major civilization of central Mexico was Teotihuacan, a city-state whose ruins lie just outside Mexico City. In the first century A.D., villagers at this site began to plan and construct a monumental city, even larger than Monte Albán, in Oaxaca.

At its peak in the sixth century, Teotihuacan had as many as 125,000 people, making it one of the largest cities in the world at the time. In the heart of the city was the giant Pyramid of the Sun. This 200-foot-tall pyramid was larger at its base than Egypt's Great Pyramid. The city also included numerous apartment compounds and artisan workshops.

Teotihuacan became the center of a thriving trade network that extended far into Central America. The city's most valuable trade item was **obsidian** (ahb·SIHD·ee·uhn),

below

Below is the Street of the Dead at Teotihuacan. Along the sides of the mile and a half long street are pyramid platforms that were originally topped with temples. The Pyramid of the Sun is visible in the distance.

below

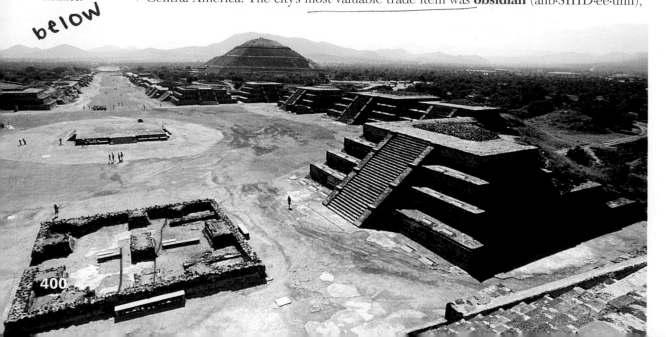

a hard, glassy green or black rock found in the Valley of Mexico and used to make razor sharp weapons. There is no evidence that Teotihuacan conquered its neighbors or tried to create an empire. However, evidence of art styles and religious beliefs from Teotihuacan have been found throughout Mesoamerica.

After centuries of growth, the city abruptly declined. By 750 it was virtually abandoned. The vast ruins astonished later settlers in the area, who named the site Teotihuacan, meaning "City of the Gods."

Toltecs Take Over After the fall of Teotihuacan, no single culture dominated central Mexico for decades. Then, around 900, a new people from the southwest, the Toltecs, rose to power. For the next three centuries, the Toltecs ruled over the heart of Mexico from their capital at Tula, just north of Mexico City. Like other Mesoamericans, they built pyramids and temples. They also carved tall pillars in the shape of armed warriors.

In fact, the Toltecs were an extremely warlike people whose empire was based on conquest. They worshiped a fierce war god who demanded blood and human sacrifice from his followers. According to legend, an early Toltec king, Topiltzin, tried to replace this war god with a god of peace. That god was named **Quetzalcoatl** (keht·SAHL·koh·AHT·uhl), the Feathered Serpent. Magically, Topiltzin and Quetzalcoatl merged, becoming a single god-king and ruling in peace. Followers of the war god rebelled, however, overthrowing Quetzalcoatl and returning the Toltecs to their warlike ways. Through trade and conquest, Toltec power spread as far as the Yucatan, where it influenced late-Mayan culture. By the early 1200s, however, the Toltec reign had ended.

The Quetzalcoatl legend lived on, though, taking on the power of myth. According to legend, after his exile from Tula, the god traveled east, crossing the sea on a raft of snakes. It was said that he would return one day, bringing a new reign of light and peace. That myth would come back to haunt the greatest empire of Mexico, the Aztecs.

Aztecs Build an Empire

The Aztecs arrived in the Valley of Mexico around A.D. 1200. It was home to a number of small city-states that had survived the collapse of Toltec rule. The Aztecs, who were then called the Mexica, were a poor, nomadic people from the harsh deserts of northern Mexico. Fierce and ambitious, they soon adapted to local ways, finding work as soldiers-for-hire to local rulers.

According to an Aztec legend, the Aztecs' sun god, Huitzilopochtli (wee·tsee·loh·POHCH·tlee), told them to found a city of their own. He said to look for a place where an eagle perched on a cactus, holding a snake in its mouth. Part of the legend is captured in these words:

A VOICE FROM THE PAST
The place where the eagle screams,
where he spreads his wings;
the place where he feeds,
where the fish jump,
where the serpents
coil up and hiss!
This shall be Mexico Tenochtitlan
and many things shall happen!

Cronica Mexicayotl

THINK THROUGH HISTORY
A. Making Inferences Why would the followers of the war god rebel against the king?

Background
The eagle on a cactus with the snake appears on the national flag of Mexico.

Quetzalcoatl: Feathered Serpent God
The story of Quetzalcoatl is found throughout Mesoamerican culture. This god, as seen above, was a combination of a snake and the brightly colored quetzal bird. He had his origins in Teotihuacan, where he represented the earth and rain.

He was later adopted by the Toltecs, who saw him as the god of the morning and evening star, Venus, and as a bringer of culture. The Maya also worshiped Quetzalcoatl, as did the Aztecs. They saw him as a god of learning and a symbol of death and rebirth.

The quetzal bird that represents the god is found throughout the forests of Central and South America. Its three-foot-long emerald green tail feathers were highly valued by the Maya and the Aztecs, who traded to obtain them.

Today, the quetzal bird appears on the coat of arms of the country of Guatemala. Also, the currency of that country is called the quetzal.

They found such a place on a small island in Lake Texcoco, at the center of the valley. There, in 1325, they founded their city, which they named Tenochtitlan (teh·NOCH·tee·TLAHN).

Aztecs Grow Stronger Over the years, the Aztecs gradually increased in strength and number. In 1428, they joined with two other city-states—Texcoco and Tlacopan—to form the **Triple Alliance.** This alliance became the leading power in the Valley of Mexico and soon gained control over neighboring regions. By the early 1500s, they controlled a vast Mesoamerican empire, which stretched from central Mexico to the Atlantic and Pacific coasts and south into Oaxaca. This empire was divided into 38 provinces. It had an estimated population of between 5 and 15 million people.

The Aztec state based its power on military conquest and the tribute it gained from conquered people. The Aztecs exercised loose control over much of their empire. They often let local rulers govern their own regions. The Aztecs did demand tribute, however, in the form of gold, maize, cacao beans, cotton, jade, and other products. If local rulers failed to pay tribute, or otherwise defied the Aztecs, the Aztec warriors would respond brutally. They would destroy villages and capture or slaughter the inhabitants.

Nobles Rule Aztec Society At the height of the Aztec Empire, military leaders held great power in Aztec society. Along with government officials and priests, these military leaders made up the noble class. Many nobles owned vast estates, which they ruled over like lords, living a life of great wealth and luxury.

The other two broad classes in Aztec society were the commoners and the slaves. Commoners included merchants, artisans, soldiers, and farmers who owned their own land. The merchants were a special type of elite. They often traveled widely, acting as spies for the emperor and gaining great wealth for themselves. The lowest class, the slaves, were captives who did many different jobs.

The emperor sat at the top of the Aztec social pyramid. Although he sometimes consulted with top generals or officials, his power was absolute. He lived in royal splendor in a magnificent palace, surrounded by servants and his wives. Visitors had to treat him like a god. They entered his presence in bare feet and cast their eyes down so as not to look at him.

THINK THROUGH HISTORY
B. Compare How are the Aztecs' methods of controlling the empire like those of other empires you have read about?

Background
The Aztec emperor's palace grounds included a zoo.

CONNECT *to* TODAY

Aztec Ruins Unearthed

On February 21, 1978, electric company workers broke through a thick layer of concrete on a street in Mexico City. Underneath the street was an enormous piece of carved rock. It was the statue of the Aztec moon goddess. The location of the accidental find proved to be the Great Temple of Tenochtitlan, the most sacred Aztec shrine.

The world's largest city, Mexico City, is built on the ruins of Tenochtitlan. Although the lake that surrounded the Aztec capital is gone, many of the ruins of Aztec civilization remain. Most of these ruins lie buried beneath city streets, but a few major sites such as the Great Temple have been excavated and rebuilt.

Trade Brings Wealth The Aztecs controlled an extensive trade network, which brought many products from faraway regions to the capital at Tenochtitlan. The economic heart of the city was the huge market of Tlatelolco (TLAH·tehl·AWL·koh). According to Hernando Cortés, the Spanish conqueror of Mexico, this market was larger than any in Spain.

A VOICE FROM THE PAST

Day after day 60,000 people congregate here to buy and sell. Every imaginable kind of merchandise is available from all parts of the Empire, foodstuffs and dress, . . . gold, silver, copper, . . . precious stones, leather, bone, mussels, coral, cotton, feathers. . . . Everything is sold by the piece or by measurement, never by weight. In the main market there is a law court in which there are always ten or twelve judges performing their office and taking decisions on all marketing controversies.

HERNANDO CORTÉS, *Letters of Information*

Much of the agricultural produce sold at the market was grown on *chinampas,* farm plots built on the marshy fringes of the lake. These plots, which spread out from Tenochtitlan in all directions, were extremely productive. They provided the food needed for a huge urban population.

Background
Chinampas, sometimes called "floating gardens," were an agricultural practice passed on from the earliest settlers thousands of years earlier.

Tenochtitlan: A Planned City By the early 1500s, Tenochtitlan had become an extraordinary urban center. With an estimated population of 200,000 people, it was larger than London or any other European capital of the time. Tenochtitlan remained on its original island site. To connect the island to the mainland, Aztec engineers built three raised roads called causeways over the water and marshland. Other cities ringed the lake, creating a dense concentration of people in the Valley of Mexico. One of Cortés's soldiers, Bernal Díaz, was amazed to find a bustling urban civilization in the heart of Mexico:

A VOICE FROM THE PAST

When we saw all those cities and villages built in the water, and other great towns on dry land, and that straight and level causeway leading to Mexico, we were astounded. These great towns and cues [pyramids] and buildings rising from the water, all made of stone, seemed like an enchanted vision. . . . Indeed, some of our soldiers asked whether it was not all a dream.

BERNAL DÍAZ, *The Conquest of New Spain*

In Tenochtitlan, palaces, temples, markets, and residential districts were connected by streets and avenues. Canals divided the city, allowing canoes to bring people and cargo directly into the city center. Aqueducts funneled fresh water in from the mainland.

At the center of the city was a huge, walled complex, filled with palaces, temples, and government buildings. The main structure in this complex was the Great Temple. It was a giant pyramid with twin temples at the top, the Aztec religious center.

Background
The twin temples were dedicated to the sun god and the rain god

Religion, the Center of Aztec Life

Religion played a major role in Aztec society. In Tenochtitlan there were hundreds of temples and religious structures dedicated to the gods. The Aztecs adopted many of their gods and religious beliefs from other Mesoamerican peoples, particularly the Toltecs.

Aztec religious practice centered on elaborate public ceremonies designed to communicate with the gods and win their favor. At these ceremonies, priests made offerings to the gods and presented ritual dramas, songs, and dances featuring masked performers. The Aztec ceremonial calendar was full of religious festivals, which varied according to the god being honored.

Sacrifices for the Sun God The most important rituals involved the sun god, Huitzilopochtli. According to Aztec belief, Huitzilopochtli made the sun rise every day, but only when he was nourished by human blood. Without regular offerings of blood, the sun would fall from the sky and all life would perish. For that reason, Aztec priests carried out human sacrifice on a massive scale. Thousands of victims, usually prisoners of war, were led to the altar atop the Great Temple, where priests carved out their hearts using obsidian knives.

To fulfill this sacred duty, the priests required a steady supply of war captives. This in turn pushed the Aztec military to carry out new conquests. The battle tactics of Aztec warriors were designed to provide live prisoners of war for the sacrifices.

THINK THROUGH HISTORY
C. Clarifying Why were so many war captives taken?

Men on a flying wheel and dancers entertain warriors on a festival day. Sacrificial offerings are carried to the top of the pyramid. The picture is a detail from a fresco at the National Palace in Mexico, painted by Diego Rivera in 1950.

403

Measuring Time

Personal experiences and changes in the environment force all humans to sense time. How that passage of time is measured is a cultural characteristic that reflects the needs of the society. For example, if the society needs to know when a yearly flood will take place, the measuring of time will provide an answer. The need to get many people to work together at an identical time requires a different measurement of time. Cultures have devised a variety of ways to measure time to meet their needs. As you compare and contrast the methods of measuring time on these pages, think about what needs each of these timepieces helps meet.

In 1884, nations around the world agreed to set standard time zones. They begin at the Prime Meridian. There are 24 standard zones that cover the earth's surface at intervals of 60 minutes.

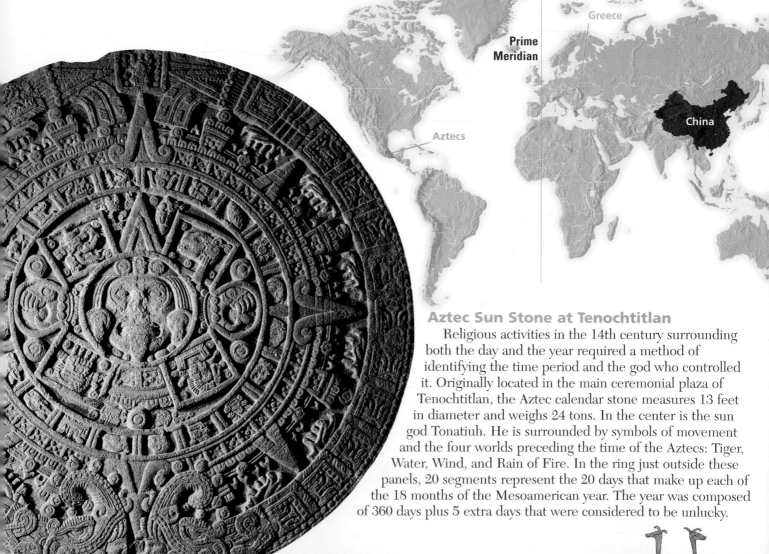

Greece

Prime Meridian

China

Aztecs

Aztec Sun Stone at Tenochtitlan

Religious activities in the 14th century surrounding both the day and the year required a method of identifying the time period and the god who controlled it. Originally located in the main ceremonial plaza of Tenochtitlan, the Aztec calendar stone measures 13 feet in diameter and weighs 24 tons. In the center is the sun god Tonatiuh. He is surrounded by symbols of movement and the four worlds preceding the time of the Aztecs: Tiger, Water, Wind, and Rain of Fire. In the ring just outside these panels, 20 segments represent the 20 days that make up each of the 18 months of the Mesoamerican year. The year was composed of 360 days plus 5 extra days that were considered to be unlucky.

a closer look AZTEC CALENDARS

The Aztec gods pictured here were closely associated with the calendar and the passage of time. Since gods ruled specific periods of time, it was important to know which gods controlled the day. During the time they ruled, offerings were made to them.

Sundial

The need to know which part of the day to pray or assemble created a need for a timepiece with more exactness. The earliest known sundial dates from about the eighth century B.C. The style pictured above was used by the astronomer Ptolemy in Alexandria in A.D. 125–141.

A sundial tells time by measuring the angles of a shadow cast by the sun. A flat triangular piece of metal is set in the center of the dial. The shadow it casts on the dial tells the time. The dial face is divided into hours, and sometimes half and quarter hours. Many sundials have faces numbered from 5 A.M. to 7 P.M. in Roman numerals.

Chinese Mechanical Clock

Built in A.D. 1090, during the Song Dynasty, this clock's movements were driven by water flowing into buckets on a waterwheel inside the clock tower. As each bucket filled, a lever tilted, the wheel turned, and a new bucket was filled. Every 15 minutes, bells and gongs rang. To chime the hours, revolving figures appeared at the clock windows. For accuracy, the mechanical movement was coordinated with the celestial globe at the top of the tower.

Wristwatch

Wristwatches became popular during World War I when soldiers and pilots needed both convenience and precision in measuring time. This modern navigator style chronograph shows the time, acts as a stop watch, and can calculate miles per hour.

Connect _to_ History

Contrasting For which need for measuring time were the majority of the clocks/calendars invented?

 SEE SKILLBUILDER
HANDBOOK, PAGE 992

Connect _to_ Today

Reporting Find out the reasons for the origin of daylight-savings time. Also try to find out what impact daylight-savings time has on the use of electricity in the United States. Write a brief report on your findings.

 INTERNET CONNECTION

Visit us at **www.mcdougallittell.com** to learn more about time measurement through history.

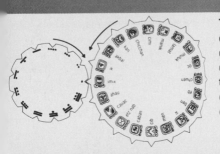

The Aztecs, like the Maya, used two calendars to calculate time—a 260-day religious calendar and a 365-day solar one. They meshed as if they were a pair of wheels. Once every 52 years both cycles started on the same day.

Masks such as this were sometimes placed on the head of a dead person. The mosaic pattern dates from the Teotihuacan era and was repeated in Aztec masks. The mosaic pieces are jade, coral, and shell on an obsidian base.

Problems in the Aztec Empire

Eventually, the Aztecs' need for an ever-expanding empire created problems for them. In 1502 a new ruler, **Montezuma II** (MAHN·tih·ZOO·muh), was crowned emperor. Under Montezuma, the Aztec empire began to weaken. For nearly a century, the Aztecs had been demanding tribute and sacrificial victims from the provinces under their control. Now, with the population of Tenochtitlan growing ever greater, the emperor called for even more tribute and sacrifice. A number of provinces rose up against Aztec oppression. This began a period of unrest and rebellion, which the military had to put down.

Montezuma tried to reduce pressure on the provinces caused by great demands for tribute payment. He froze and reduced the number of government officials. But resentment continued to grow. Then, as domestic problems simmered, another threat appeared: the arrival of the Spanish. To many Aztecs, the strangers from across the sea brought to mind the old legend regarding the return of Quetzalcoatl.

Further south in the high mountain valleys of the Andes, another empire was developing, one that would transcend the Aztec empire in land area, power, and wealth. The Inca, too, worshiped the sun and had large armies, but the society they built was much different from that of the Aztecs, as you will see in Section 4.

THINK THROUGH HISTORY
D. Making Inferences Why would freezing the number of government officials reduce the need for tribute money?

Aztec

Traits of Civilization	Strength Leading to Power	Weakness Leading to Decline
Religious beliefs and theocracy	United culture Loyalty to the king	Many physical and human resources funneled into religious activities
Powerful army	Adds land, power, and prisoners for religious sacrifice	Need for prisoners changes warfare style to less deadly and less aggressive
Empire of tribute states	Provides wealth and power and prisoners for religious sacrifice	Tribute states are rebellious and need to be controlled

SKILLBUILDER: Interpreting Charts
1. *How was the tribute system both a strength and a weakness?*
2. *How are the army and religious beliefs linked in the Aztec Empire?*

Section 3 Assessment

1. TERMS & NAMES
Identify
• obsidian
• Quetzalcoatl
• Triple Alliance
• Montezuma II

2. TAKING NOTES
Draw a chain of events diagram like the one below and fill in the main events that led to the establishment and growth of the Aztec Empire.

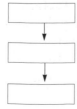

3. RECOGNIZING EFFECTS
How did the Aztec need for victims for sacrifice lead to problems controlling the empire?

THINK ABOUT
• reactions of the conquered peoples
• changes in army tactics

4. THEME ACTIVITY
Power and Authority With a small group of students, write a short play in which Montezuma discusses with his advisers how to gain control of rebellious provinces of the Aztec Empire. Be sure one adviser wants to keep peace at all costs.

4 The Inca Create a Mountain Empire

MAIN IDEA	WHY IT MATTERS NOW
The Inca built a vast empire supported by taxes, governed by a bureaucracy, and linked by extensive road systems.	The Inca system of government was similar to some socialist governments in the 20th century.

SETTING THE STAGE While the Aztecs were ruling in Mexico, another people—the Inca—were creating an equally powerful state in South America. From their capital in southern Peru, the Inca spread outward in all directions. They brought various Andean peoples under their control and built the largest empire ever seen in the Americas.

This gold mask is covered with cinnabar, a red ore. The eyes are formed of tree resin. The ear spools are marks of nobility. The mask is from the Siccan culture, which was conquered by the Chimu.

The Inca Come to Power

Like the Aztecs, the Inca built their empire on cultural foundations thousands of years old. Ancient civilizations such as Chavín, Moche, and Nazca had already established a tradition of high culture in Peru. They were followed by the Huari and Tiahuanaco cultures of southern Peru and Bolivia. The Chimu, an impressive civilization of the 1300s based in the northern coastal region once controlled by the Moche, came next. The Inca would create an even more powerful state, however, extending their rule over the entire Andean region.

Incan Beginnings The word *Inca* was originally the name of the ruling family of a group of people living in a high plateau of the Andes. After wandering the highlands for years, the Inca finally settled on fertile lands in the Valley of Cuzco. By the 1200s, the Inca had established their own small kingdom in the valley.

During this early period, the Inca developed traditions and beliefs that helped launch and unify their empire. One of these traditions was the belief that the Incan ruler was descended from the sun god, Inti, who would bring prosperity and greatness to the Incan state. Only men from one of 11 noble lineages believed to be descendants of the sun god could be selected as the Incan leader. These 11 families were called *orejones*, "Big Ears," because of the large plugs they wore in their earlobes.

Another tradition was the custom of worshiping dead rulers, who were preserved as sacred mummies. The mummies were brought to all important events and housed in special chambers. These royal mummies and their descendants retained rights to all the wealth and property accumulated during the king's lifetime. Succeeding rulers had to acquire their own wealth, which led them to conquer new territories.

Pachacuti Builds an Empire At first the Incan kingdom grew slowly. In 1438, however, a powerful and ambitious ruler, **Pachacuti** (PAH·chah·KOO·tee), took the throne. Under his leadership, the Inca expanded quickly, conquering all of Peru and then moving into neighboring lands. By 1500 the Inca ruled an empire that stretched 2,500 miles along the western coast of South America, from Ecuador in the north to Chile and Argentina in the south. The Inca called this

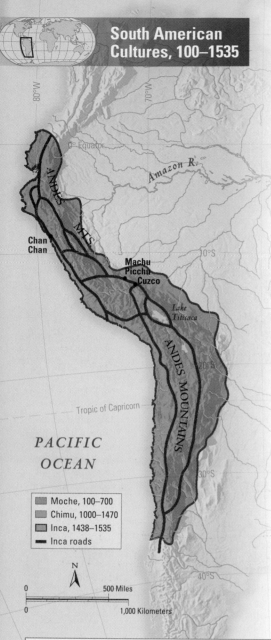

South American Cultures, 100–1535

Chan Chan

Machu Picchu
Cuzco

Lake Titicaca

ANDES MTS.

ANDES MOUNTAINS

Amazon R.

0° Equator

10°S

20°S

30°S

40°S

Tropic of Capricorn

PACIFIC OCEAN

Moche, 100–700
Chimu, 1000–1470
Inca, 1438–1535
— Inca roads

N

0   500 Miles
0   1,000 Kilometers

**GEOGRAPHY SKILLBUILDER:
Interpreting Maps**

1. **Place** *The lands of which earlier South American cultures were included in the Incan Empire?*
2. **Human-Environment Interaction** *Look at the shape and terrain of the Incan Empire. What problems related to geography might occur in controlling the land?*

empire Tihuantinsuya, or "Land of the Four Quarters." It included about 80 provinces and perhaps as many as 16 million people.

Pachacuti and his successors accomplished this feat of conquest through a combination of diplomacy and military force. The Inca had a powerful military but used force only when necessary. The Inca were clever diplomats. Before attacking, they typically offered enemy states an honorable surrender. They would allow them to keep their own customs and rulers in exchange for loyalty to the Incan state. Because of this kind treatment, many states gave up without resisting.

Once an area was defeated, the Inca would make every effort to gain the loyalty of the newly conquered people. According to a 16th-century Spanish observer:

> **A VOICE FROM THE PAST**
> The Inca always had the mastery, but when the enemies were vanquished, they were not destroyed; on the contrary, orders were given to release the captives and restore the spoils, and allow them to retain their estates. For the Inca desired to show them that they should not be so mad as to revolt against his royal person and reject his friendship; rather they should wish to be his friends, as were those in other provinces.
>
> **PEDRO DE CIEZA DE LEÓN,** *Chronicle of Peru*

Incan Government Creates Unity

The Inca were also extraordinary organizers and administrators. To control the huge empire, the rulers divided their territory and its people into manageable units, governed by a central bureaucracy. The Inca created an efficient economic system to support the empire and an extensive road system to tie it together. They also imposed a single official language, Quechua (KEHCH·wuh), and founded schools to teach Incan ways. Certain social groups were identified by officially dictated patterns on clothing. All of these actions were calculated to unify the variety of people controlled by the Inca.

Incan Cities Show Government Presence To exercise control over their empire, the Inca built many cities in conquered areas. The architecture of government buildings was the same all over the empire, making the presence of the government apparent. As in Rome, all roads led to the capital, Cuzco. The heart of the Incan Empire, Cuzco was a splendid city of temples, plazas, and palaces. "Cuzco was grand and stately," wrote Cieza de León. "It had fine streets, . . . and the houses were built of solid stones, beautifully joined." Like the Romans, the Inca were masterful engineers and stonemasons. Though they had no iron tools and did not use the wheel, Incan builders carved and transported huge blocks of stone, fitting them together perfectly without mortar. Many Incan walls still stand in Cuzco, undisturbed by the region's frequent earthquakes.

Incan Government Organizes Communities The Incan system of government was based on age-old patterns of community cooperation. Small groups of people known as **ayllu** (EYE·loo) worked together for the common good, building irrigation

THINK THROUGH HISTORY
A. Forming and Supporting an Opinion Of all the methods used to create unity, which do you think would be most successful? Why?

canals and agricultural terraces on steep hillsides. The ayllu also stored food and other supplies to distribute during hard times.

The Inca took this principle of community organization and welfare and applied it to their empire. They incorporated the ayllu structure into a governing system based on the decimal system. They divided families into groups of 10, 100, 1,000, and 10,000. Each group was led by a chief. He was part of a chain of command. That chain stretched from the community and regional levels all the way to Cuzco, where the Incan ruler and his council of state held court. In general, local administration was left in the hands of local rulers, and villages were allowed to continue their traditional ways. If a community resisted Incan control, however, the Inca might relocate the whole group to a different territory. The resisters would be placed under the control of rulers appointed by the high rulers.

THINK THROUGH HISTORY
B. Recognizing Effects How would relocating troublesome people help government control of an area?

The main demand the Incan state placed on its subjects was for tribute, mainly in the form of labor. The labor tribute was known as **mita** (MEE·tuh). It required all able-bodied citizens to work for the state a certain number of days every year. Mita workers might labor on state farmlands, produce craft goods for state warehouses, or help build public works, such as roads, palaces, or irrigation canals.

Roads Link the Empire The most spectacular public works project was the Incan road system. A marvel of engineering, this road system symbolized the power of the Incan state. The 14,000-mile-long network of roads and bridges spanned the empire, traversing rugged mountains and harsh deserts. The roads ranged from paved stone to simple paths. Along the roads, the Inca built guest houses to provide shelter for weary travelers. A system of runners, known as *chasquis* (SHAH·skeys), traveled these roads as a kind of postal service, carrying messages from one end of the empire to the other. The road system also allowed the easy movement of troops to bring control to zones where trouble might be brewing.

State Controls the Economy Incan power was also evident in economic life. The Incan state controlled most economic activity, regulating the production and distribution of goods. Land was organized into upper and lower geographical units, each producing goods the other could not. The units were linked together to create a total economy. Unlike the Maya and the Aztec, the Inca allowed little private commerce or trade.

Historians have compared the Incan system to a type of socialism or a modern welfare state. Citizens were expected to work for the state and were cared for in return. For example, the aged and disabled were often supported by the state. The state also held public feasts, distributing food and maize beer as a reward for citizens' labor.

Land ownership was divided in three ways: state lands, religious lands, and community lands. Farmers worked on all three types of land. Expanding on irrigation systems developed by earlier people, the Inca created a massive water management system that stored water for the dry season. They even straightened an entire river channel to better provide water for agriculture.

Background
The irrigation systems were originally built by the Moche, Chimu, and Tiwankans.

With a terracing system they produced crops such as maize and quinoa, a grain native to the Andes. The Inca developed a method for freeze-drying potatoes. They then stored the freeze-dried potatoes, called *chuño* in huge warehouses for times of shortages of food. The *chuño* could be kept indefinitely.

Government Keeps Records Despite the sophistication of many aspects of Incan life, the Inca never developed a writing system. History and literature were

A miniature silver llama illustrates how important the llama was in Incan society. It helped transport goods and food in the mountains, provided wool and meat, and was offered to the gods as a sacrifice.

SPOTLIGHT ON

Incan Relay Messengers
Communication in the Incan Empire was the task of runner-messengers called *chasquis*. The system worked like a modern relay race. A runner would "hand off" a memorized message or package to another runner waiting at a way station. That runner would sprint to the next station along the road.

The stations were placed about every mile or so along the main roads, which covered about 3,100 miles. In this way, a message could travel 140 miles a day. The distance from Cuzco to the coast could be covered in just three days. A century later, the same journey took the Spanish 12 days on horseback!

The *chasquis* who traveled the Inca roads served in 15-day shifts. This job was a part of their mita labor tax.

memorized as part of an oral tradition. For numerical information, the Inca created an accounting device known as the **quipu** (see "Spotlight" on page 18), a set of knotted strings that could be used to record data. The knots and their position on the cord indicated numbers. Additionally, the colors of the cords indicated categories of information important to the government. For example, red strings were used to count warriors.

The Inca also developed an elaborate calendar system with two types of calendars, one for night and one for day. They were used primarily for religious purposes. Like the calendars of the Maya and the Aztec, the two calendars provided information about the gods who, the Inca believed, ruled the day and time. Like the Maya, Incan mathematicians and astronomers used complicated methods to create calendars necessary for the proper worship of the gods.

One and one-half miles up a mountain, Machu Picchu could only be reached by a log bridge across a deep canyon. Although the details of its origin and its abandonment are unclear, some historians believe that it was a religious or ceremonial city.

Religion Supports the State

As in ancient Mexico, religion was important to the Inca and helped reinforce the power of the state. The Inca worshiped fewer gods than the Aztecs. The Inca focused on key nature spirits such as the moon, the stars, and thunder. In the balance of ANIMISM

nature, the Inca saw patterns for the way humans should relate to each other and to the earth. Chief of the Incan gods was a creator god called Viracocha. Next in importance was the sun god, Inti. Because the Incan ruler was considered a descendant of Inti, sun worship amounted to worship of the king.

Incan priests led the sun-worship services, assisted by young women known as *mamakuna*, or "virgins of the sun." These women, all unmarried, were drafted by the Inca for a lifetime of religious service. The young women were trained in religious activities, as teachers, spinners, weavers, and beer makers. Young men, known as *yamacuna*, also served as full-time workers for the state and in religious activities. Sacrifice of llamas and exchange of goods were a part of the religious activities. The goods were distributed by the priest to the people as gifts from the gods.

The Temple of the Sun in Cuzco

Background
Notice the similarity to the Egyptian ideas about the sun and the ruler.

was the most sacred of all Incan shrines. It was heavily decorated in gold, a metal the Inca referred to as "sweat of the sun." According to Garcilaso de la Vega, the son of an Inca princess, the temple even had a garden crafted entirely from precious metals.

A VOICE FROM THE PAST
Here could be seen all sorts of plants, flowers, trees, animals, both small and large, wild and tame, tiny crawling creatures such as snakes, lizards, and snails, as well as butterflies and birds of every size. . . . All of these valuable works were made by the goldsmiths attached to the Temple, from the tribute of gold and silver that arrived every year from all the provinces of the Empire.

GARCILASO DE LA VEGA, *The Incas*

In addition to producing beautiful gold and silver articles, Incan artisans even covered walls in Cuzco with shining sheets of gold.

Cuzco was the administrative and ceremonial capital of the Incan Empire. It included a sun temple and storage areas. Other Incan cities also had monumental architecture and seemed to have multiple purposes. For example, Machu Picchu, discovered by Hiram Bingham in 1912, was isolated and mysterious. Like Cuzco, Machu Picchu also had a sun temple, public buildings, a water system, and a central plaza. Some sources suggest it was an estate of Pachacuti. Others believe it was a retreat for Inca rulers or the elite. Its true function has not been determined.

Discord in the Empire

Vocabulary
litter: a chair that is carried by bearers

In the early 1500s, the Inca empire was at the height of its glory. King Huayna Capac toured the empire in a royal litter, covered with gold and surrounded by attendants. Trouble was on the way, however. Stopping in Quito, Ecuador, the king opened a gift box. Out flew butterflies and moths, considered an evil omen. About 1525, while still in Quito, Huayna Capac died of disease. Soon after his death, civil war broke out between Huayna Capac's sons, Atahualpa (ah·tah·WAHL·pah) and Huascar (WAHS·kahr), who both claimed the throne. Atahualpa won, but the war tore the empire apart. As you will learn in Chapter 20, within a few years, the Spanish arrived. Taking advantage of Incan weakness, they would soon divide and conquer the empire.

Inca		
Traits of Civilization	**Strength Leading to Power**	**Weakness Leading to Decline**
Religious beliefs and theocracy	United culture Loyalty to the emperor	Many physical and human resources funneled into religious activities
Major road systems	Connected entire empire and aided control	Enemy could also use roads to move troops
Type of welfare state with huge bureaucracy	Care for entire population during good and bad times	People unable to care for themselves with the elimination of the welfare state

SKILLBUILDER: Interpreting Charts
1. *In your opinion, which of the three traits leading to power was the most valuable? Briefly discuss your reasons.*
2. *Which trait did you find repeated in the Maya and Aztec Empires?*

Section 4 Assessment

1. TERMS & NAMES
Identify
- Pachacuti
- ayllu
- mita
- quipu

2. TAKING NOTES
Draw a diagram like the one below and fill in the methods the Inca used to achieve the idea in the center.

The Inca built a vast empire, which was largely unified under their control.

Which of these methods for unification were acceptable to the conquered people? Explain.

3. ANALYZING MOTIVES
Why do you think the Inca used the ayllu system as the basis for governing the people of the empire?

THINK ABOUT
- ways to control a large empire
- the ease of using a system that already existed

4. THEME ACTIVITY
Power and Authority Choose a partner to debate the value of the welfare state of the Inca. One partner should support the welfare state and the other should be against it. Focus the debate on the advantages and disadvantages of the Incan welfare state.

People and Empires in the Americas

North America
600–1600

- Government by a variety of small tribes to very complex societies
- Similar religious beliefs in the Great Spirit
- Economy influenced by the environment
- Trade links to other groups

Mesoamerica: Maya
250–900

- Government by city-state kings
- Religion plays a major role in society and rule
- Trade links between city-states and other Mesoamerican groups
- Math and astronomy develop to support religious beliefs
- Pyramid builders
- Written language using hieroglyphs

Mesoamerica: Aztec
1200–1521

- Government by warrior-kings
- Religion plays a major role in society and rule
- Trade links between tribute states and other Mesoamerican groups
- Human sacrifice practiced for religious offerings
- Pyramid builders
- Pictorial written language

South America: Inca
1400–1532

- Government by theocracy—sun-god king
- Religion plays a major role in society and rule
- Social welfare state cares for all people
- Extensive road system links the country together

TERMS & NAMES

Briefly explain the importance of each of the following to the development of Native American cultures in North America, Mesoamerica, or South America.

1. pueblos
2. Mississippian
3. Iroquois
4. Tikal
5. glyph
6. Quetzalcoatl
7. Triple Alliance
8. Montezuma II
9. Pachacuti
10. mita

REVIEW QUESTIONS

SECTION 1 (pages 391–394)
Diverse Societies of North America

11. Why were Native American societies in North America so diverse?
12. What were the three things that most Native Americans in North America had in common?

SECTION 2 (pages 395–399)
Mayan Kings and Cities

13. What role did religion play in Mayan life?
14. What were three major achievements of the Mayan civilization?

SECTION 3 (pages 400–406)
The Aztecs Control Central Mexico

15. How did the Aztecs build and control their empire?
16. What role did trade play in the Aztec Empire?
17. Why did the Aztecs sacrifice human beings to their gods?

SECTION 4 (pages 407–411)
The Inca Create a Mountain Empire

18. How did the Inca custom of worshiping dead rulers affect the conquest of new territories?
19. List three ways in which the Inca government involved itself in people's lives.
20. How did Inca religion reinforce the power of the state?

Interact *with* History

From the mask clues and detective thinking, you should have determined that the Bella Coola society was a salmon fishing society that lived in forests by the Pacific Ocean. They probably used the mask in a ceremony about the chief god bringing fish to the people. Using the guide questions on the Interact page, look back in the chapter at the masks in each section to see what you can determine about other cultures.

CRITICAL THINKING

1. NATIVE AMERICAN RELIGIOUS BELIEFS

THEME RELIGIOUS AND ETHICAL SYSTEMS Compare the religious beliefs of the Maya, the Aztecs, and the Inca. How were they similar? How were they different?

2. CONTROLLING THE VALLEY OF MEXICO

From the beginning of the first century A.D., the Valley of Mexico was controlled by three major cultural groups. Find two dates for each culture and place them on the time line below. Write a brief description of the importance of each date.

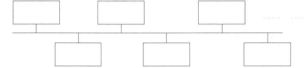

3. INCAN GOVERNMENT AND SOCIETY

What can you infer about the values of the Inca from the fact that the government provided care for citizens who were aged or unable to care for themselves?

4. ANALYZING PRIMARY SOURCES

The following quotation is an Iroquois prayer to the Great Spirit and to other spirits in nature. Read the prayer and answer the questions below it.

A VOICE FROM THE PAST

We return thanks to our mother, the earth, which sustains us. We return thanks to the rivers and streams, which supply us with water. . . . We return thanks to the corn, and to her sisters, the beans and squashes, which give us life. . . . We return thanks to the sun, that he has looked upon the earth with a beneficent eye. . . . We return thanks to the Great Spirit . . . who directs all things for the good of his children.

Quoted in *In the Trail of the Wind*

- How did the Iroquois feel about nature?
- What role did the Great Spirit play for the Iroquois?

CHAPTER ACTIVITIES

1. LIVING HISTORY: Unit Portfolio Project

THEME CULTURAL INTERACTION Your unit portfolio project focuses on showing cultural interaction through conquest, trade, migration, and heritage (see page 387). For Chapter 16, you might use one of the following ideas to add to your portfolio:

- Imagine you are a Chinook trader from the Northwest Coast heading for an intertribal marketplace on the Columbia River. Do research on the trade items of peoples of the Northwest and those of the interior plains. Write a dialogue between you as a Chinook trader and one or more traders from other areas discussing the goods you will trade.

- The Toltec culture influenced the religious ideas of both the Aztec and the Maya. Do research on the Toltec, Maya, and Aztec gods. Then make a poster that illustrates how some of the Toltec gods were portrayed in the Maya and Aztec cultures.

INTERNET Aztec cultural ruins have been excavated in Mexico City. Using the Internet, magazines, and books, research how the Plaza of the Three Cultures and the Great Temple have preserved the cultures of the people of Mexico. Then write a one-page news article that describes these places and shows the heritage of the Mexican people.

2. CONNECT TO TODAY: Cooperative Learning

THEME POWER AND AUTHORITY The Iroquois League, or Confederacy, originally formed over 400 years ago, in 1570, is still in operation today. Work with a team to prepare a six-page advertising brochure that discusses the founding of the confederacy, its history through the years, and how it is functioning today. Use the Internet, magazines, and books such as *White Roots of Peace: The Iroquois Book of Life* to research the topic.

3. INTERPRETING A TIME LINE

Revisit the unit time line on pages 386–387. Find the dates for Chapter 16. Look at the dates for other cultures in this unit. Which empires were in power in other parts of the world at about the same time as the Aztecs and the Inca?

FOCUS ON GEOGRAPHY

This Spanish map (1519?) is a bird's-eye view of the island city of Tenochtitlan. Notice the roadway connections to the mainland and the canals that connected parts of the city.

- How many direct links to the mainland are there?
- What appears to be in the center of the city?

Connect to History Why was this location selected for a city?

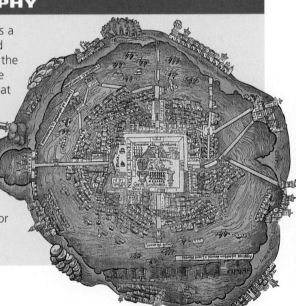

CHAPTER 17
European Renaissance and Reformation, 1300–1600

Cultural Interaction

Most medieval European art expressed either the values of Christianity or the code of chivalry. During the Renaissance, scholars and artists developed new cultural and artistic ideas based on the rediscovery of the literature of classical Greece and Rome.

Religious and Ethical Systems

For centuries, religious leaders had sought to reform the Catholic Church. They wanted to make it live up to its ideals. In the 1500s, Martin Luther began a reform movement called the Reformation. This led to the founding of Protestant churches.

Revolution

European scholars gained access to classical documents that they thought had been lost after the fall of Rome. This revolutionized their thinking. New ideas and values swept Europe. The invention of the printing press aided the spread of these revolutionary ideas. The printing press also spread ideas that called for a revolutionary rejection of the pope's authority.

↪ **INTERNET CONNECTION**

Visit us at **www.mcdougallittell.com** to learn more about Renaissance artists, the Reformation, and related topics.

EUROPE, 1500

ATLANTIC OCEAN

IRELAN

By **1527**, King Henry VIII of England was sure that his queen was too old to bear a son. **Anne Boleyn** caught his eye. Anne was pretty and young enough to have children. When the pope refused to end Henry's first marriage, Henry started his own church. An English archbishop ended Henry's marriage and Anne became Henry's second wife.

Bay Bisc

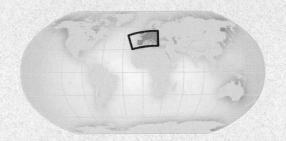

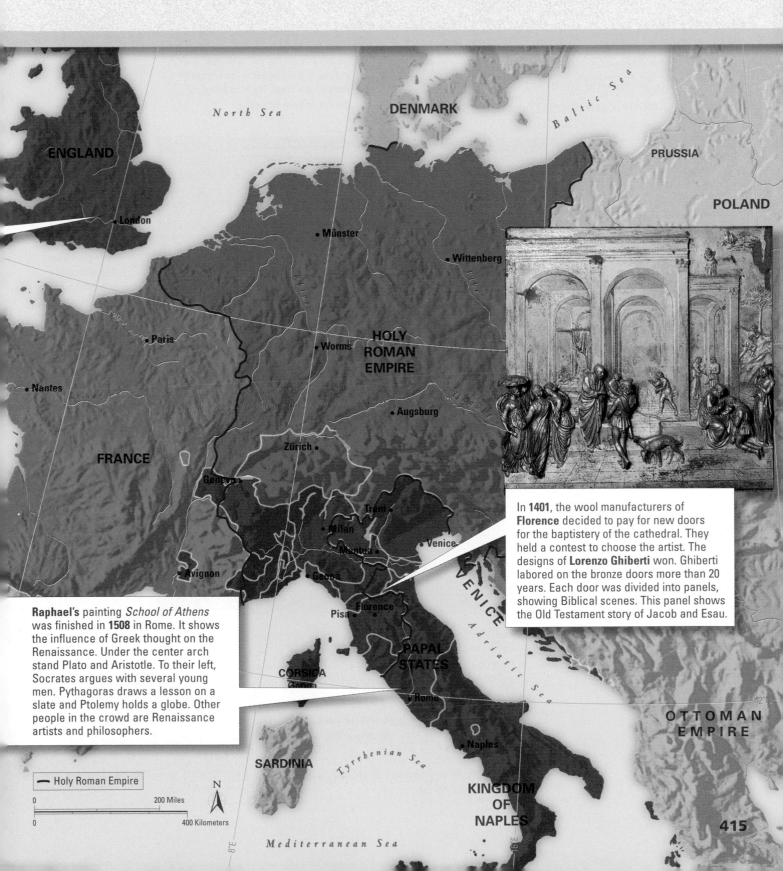

In **1401**, the wool manufacturers of **Florence** decided to pay for new doors for the baptistery of the cathedral. They held a contest to choose the artist. The designs of **Lorenzo Ghiberti** won. Ghiberti labored on the bronze doors more than 20 years. Each door was divided into panels, showing Biblical scenes. This panel shows the Old Testament story of Jacob and Esau.

Raphael's painting *School of Athens* was finished in **1508** in Rome. It shows the influence of Greek thought on the Renaissance. Under the center arch stand Plato and Aristotle. To their left, Socrates argues with several young men. Pythagoras draws a lesson on a slate and Ptolemy holds a globe. Other people in the crowd are Renaissance artists and philosophers.

— Holy Roman Empire

0   200 Miles

0   400 Kilometers

415

Interact *with* History

You are a historian looking at primary sources from the Renaissance. One of them is this painting by Jan van Eyck.

Chancellor Rolin, a powerful government official in Burgundy (later part of France), asked the artist to paint this portrait. You are analyzing it to discover Rolin's values and how he wanted to be viewed by others. You can also use the art to learn about the times.

What do we learn from art?

1 Van Eyck used a recently rediscovered technique called perspective, which makes distant objects look smaller than close ones. He also used oil paints, a new invention.

5 Renaissance artists were influenced by classical art. The columns and arches show classical influence.

2 This painting shows the infant Jesus and his mother Mary in 15th century Europe. By portraying biblical characters in their own time, Renaissance artists showed the importance of religion in their lives.

3 Van Eyck included many details simply for the sake of beauty. These include the fancy design on the floor, the folds of Mary's cloak, and the scenery outside the arches.

4 Renaissance artists portrayed the importance of individuals. Chancellor Rolin is kneeling to show respect, but he wears a fur-trimmed robe that shows his high status.

EXAMINING *the* ISSUES

- What does art tell us about the values and beliefs of the society that produced it?

- What does art show about how people of that society viewed themselves?

- How does art reflect a society's standards of beauty?

As a class, discuss these questions. In your discussion, review what you know about art in other places such as Egypt, India, China, and Benin.

As you read about the Renaissance, notice what the art of that time reveals about European society.

Italy: Birthplace of the Renaissance

TERMS & NAMES
- Renaissance
- humanism
- secular
- patron
- perspective
- vernacular

MAIN IDEA	WHY IT MATTERS NOW
The European Renaissance, a rebirth of learning and the arts, began in Italy in the 1300s.	Renaissance ideas about classical studies, art, and literature still influence modern thought.

SETTING THE STAGE During the late Middle Ages, Europeans suffered from both war and plague. Those who survived wanted to enjoy life. As a result, they questioned the Church, which taught Christians to endure suffering to get a heavenly reward. They also questioned the structures of medieval society, which blocked social advancement. Educated people gradually began to reject medieval values and look to the classical past for ideas.

Italy's Advantages

The years 1300 to 1600 saw an explosion of creativity in Europe. Historians call this period the **Renaissance** (REHN·ih·SAHNS). The term means rebirth—in this case a rebirth of art and learning. The Renaissance began in northern Italy around 1300 and later spread north. One reason northern Europe lagged behind is that France and England were locked in the Hundred Years' War. Italy also had three advantages that fostered the Renaissance: thriving cities, a wealthy merchant class, and the classical heritage of Greece and Rome.

Urban Centers Overseas trade, spurred by the Crusades, had led to the growth of large city-states in northern Italy. The region also had many sizable towns. Thus, northern Italy was urban while the rest of Europe was still mostly rural. Since cities are often places where people exchange new ideas, they were an ideal breeding ground for an intellectual revolution.

Background
Florence lost up to 55,000 out of a population of 85,000.

The bubonic plague struck these cities hard, killing up to 60 percent of the population. This brought economic changes. Because there were fewer laborers, survivors could demand higher wages. In addition, the reduced population shrank opportunities for business expansion. Wealthy merchants began to pursue other interests, such as art.

Merchants and the Medici Milan, Florence, and other Italian city-states ran their own affairs. Each collected taxes and had its own army. Because city-states were relatively small, a high percentage of citizens could be intensely involved in political life. Merchants were the wealthiest, most powerful class, and they dominated politics. Unlike nobles, merchants did not inherit social rank. Success in business depended mostly on their own wits. As a result, many successful merchants believed they deserved power and wealth because of their individual merit. Individual achievement was to become an important Renaissance theme.

THINK THROUGH HISTORY
A. Making Inferences Why do you suppose Cosimo de' Medici preferred to rule from behind the scenes rather than openly?

Florence came under the rule of one powerful family, the Medici (MEHD·ih·chee). They had made a fortune in trade and banking. Cosimo de' Medici was the wealthiest European of his time. In 1434, he won control of Florence's government. He did not seek political office for himself, but instead influenced members of the ruling council by giving them loans. For 30 years, he was virtually dictator of Florence.

SPOTLIGHT ON

Other Renaissances

A Renaissance can be a rebirth of the arts and learning at any time in history. For example, the Tang (618–907) and Song (960–1279) dynasties in China oversaw a period of great artistic and technological advances.

Like the Italian Renaissance, the achievements of the Tang and the Song had roots in an earlier time—the Han Dynasty (202 B.C. to A.D. 220). After the Han collapsed, China experienced turmoil.

When order was restored, Chinese culture flourished. The Chinese invented gunpowder and printing. The most famous Chinese poets of all time wrote literary masterpieces. Breakthroughs were made in architecture, painting, and pottery. In many ways, the Tang and Song period was a true Renaissance.

Medici Family

Giant banks with branches in many cities are nothing new. The Medici bank had branch offices not only throughout Italy but also in the major cities of Europe.

A rival family grew so jealous of the Medici that they plotted to kill Lorenzo (see bust below) and his brother Giuliano. As the Medici attended Mass, assassins murdered Giuliano at the altar. Drawing his sword, Lorenzo escaped to a small room and held off his attackers until help arrived. Then he had the killers brutally, publicly executed.

More positively, Lorenzo was a generous patron of the arts who collected many rare manuscripts. Eventually the Medici family made their library available to the public.

Cosimo de' Medici died in 1464, but his family retained control of Florence. His grandson, Lorenzo de' Medici, came into power in 1469. He became known as Lorenzo the Magnificent. Like his grandfather, Lorenzo ruled as a dictator yet kept up the appearance of having an elected government. Although the Medici did not foster true republican government, they aided the Renaissance by supporting the arts.

Classical Heritage Renaissance scholars looked down on the art and literature of the Middle Ages and wanted to return to the learning of the Greeks and Romans. One reason the Renaissance began in Italy is that artists and scholars drew inspiration from the ruins of Rome that surrounded them.

In the 1300s, scholars studied ancient Latin manuscripts, which had been preserved in monasteries. Then, when Constantinople fell to the Ottoman Turks in 1453, Byzantine scholars fled to Rome with ancient Greek manuscripts—which Italian scholars had assumed were lost forever.

Classical and Worldly Values

As scholars studied these Greek works, they became increasingly influenced by classical ideas. These ideas helped them to develop a new outlook on life, which had several characteristics.

Classics Lead to Humanism The study of classical texts led to **humanism,** which focused on human potential and achievements. Instead of trying to make classical texts agree with Christian teaching as medieval scholars had, humanists studied them to understand ancient Greek values. Humanists influenced artists and architects to carry on classical traditions. In addition, humanists popularized the study of subjects common to classical education, such as history, literature, and philosophy. These subjects are called the humanities.

Enjoyment of Worldly Pleasures In the Middle Ages, some religious people had proved their piety by wearing rough clothing and eating the plainest foods. However, humanists suggested that a person might enjoy life without offending God. In Renaissance Italy, the wealthy openly enjoyed material luxuries, fine music, and tasty foods.

Most people remained devout Catholics. However, the basic spirit of Renaissance society was **secular**—worldly and concerned with the here and now. Even church leaders became more worldly. They lived in beautiful mansions, threw lavish banquets, and wore expensive clothes.

Patrons of the Arts In addition to seeking pleasure, Renaissance popes beautified Rome by spending huge amounts of money for art. They became **patrons** of the arts by financially supporting artists. Renaissance merchants also were patrons of the arts. Wealthy families such as the Medici generously supported artists. By having their portraits painted or by donating public art to the city, the wealthy demonstrated their own importance.

The Renaissance Man Renaissance writers first introduced the idea that some people were artistic geniuses. Though genius was rare, all educated people were expected to create art. In fact, the ideal individual strove to master almost every area of study. A man who excelled in many fields was praised as a "universal man." Later ages called such people "Renaissance men."

A book called *The Courtier* (1528) by Baldassare Castiglione (KAHS·teel·YOH·nay) taught how to become such a person. A young man, said Castiglione, should be

THINK THROUGH HISTORY
B. Analyzing Causes What were the three advantages that caused the Renaissance to start in Italy?

Background
The words *humanist* and *humanities* come from the Latin word *humanitas,* which referred to the literary culture that every educated person should know.

charming, witty, and well educated in the classics. He should dance, sing, play music, and write poetry. In addition, he should be a skilled rider, wrestler, and swordsman. Above all, he should have self-control:

> **A VOICE FROM THE PAST**
> Let the man we are seeking be very bold, stern, and always among the first, where the enemy are to be seen; and in every other place, gentle, modest, reserved, above all things avoiding ostentation [showiness] and that impudent [bold] self-praise by which men ever excite hatred and disgust in all who hear them.
> **BALDASSARE CASTLIGLIONE,** *The Courtier*

The Renaissance Woman According to *The Courtier,* upper-class women also should know the classics and be charming. Yet they were not expected to seek fame. They were expected to inspire art but rarely to create it. Upper-class Renaissance women were far better educated than the women of the Middle Ages. However, most Renaissance women had less influence than medieval women had.

A few women, such as Isabella d'Este, did exercise power. Born into the ruling family of the city-state of Ferrara, she married the ruler of another city-state, Mantua. She brought many Renaissance artists to her court and acquired an art collection that was famous throughout Europe. She was also skilled in politics. When her husband was taken captive in war, she defended Mantua and won his release.

This is a 19th-century engraving of the Renaissance writer Baldassare Castiglione.

Renaissance Revolutionizes Art

Supported by patrons like Isabella d'Este, dozens of talented artists worked in northern Italy. As the Renaissance advanced, artistic styles changed. Medieval artists used religious subjects and tried to convey a spiritual ideal. Renaissance artists also often portrayed religious subjects, but they used a realistic style copied from classical models. Greek and Roman subjects also became popular.

Following the new emphasis on individuals, painters began to paint prominent citizens. These realistic portraits revealed what was distinctive about each person. In addition, artists such as the sculptor and painter Michelangelo (MY·kuhl·AN·juh·LOH) glorified the human body. (See page 420.)

THINK THROUGH HISTORY
C. Synthesizing
Merchants believed in their own individual merit. How did this belief affect artistic styles?

New Techniques Donatello (DAHN·uh·TEHL·oh) made sculpture more realistic by carving natural postures and expressions that reveal personality. He revived a classical form by carving the statue *David.* It was the first European sculpture of a large, free-standing nude since ancient times. Renaissance artists, such as the painter Masaccio (muh·SAH·chee·oh), also rediscovered the technique of **perspective,** which indicates three dimensions.

Marriage of the Virgin (1504), Raphael

Perspective in Paintings

Perspective is a technique that creates the appearance of three dimensions. Classical artists used perspective, but medieval artists abandoned the technique. In the 1400s, Italian artists rediscovered perspective. Since then, it has remained an important part of Western art.

Perspective is based on an optical illusion. As parallel lines stretch away from a viewer, they seem to draw together—until they meet at a spot on the horizon called the vanishing point.

vanishing point

horizon

Michelangelo–Renaissance Artist

Like Leonardo da Vinci, Michelangelo Buonarroti was a true Renaissance man. He excelled at almost every area of study. Michelangelo was a painter, a sculptor, an architect, and a poet.

Michelangelo is most famous for the way he portrayed the human body in painting and sculpture. Influenced by classical art, he created figures that are forceful and show heroic grandeur and power. By doing this, he explored the Renaissance theme of human potential.

St. Peter's Basilica

As an architect, he designed this dome to top St. Peter's Basilica [Church] in Rome. Michelangelo began working on the church in 1546. It still wasn't finished when he died in 1564. Another architect had to finish the dome.

Sistine Chapel

From 1508 to 1512, Michelangelo painted the ceiling of the Sistine Chapel in Rome. This detail shows the Biblical prophet Joel. Many of the panels show classical influences, such as the two youths who stand behind Joel instead of angels. Like many Renaissance artists, Michelangelo blended Christian and Greek ideals.

Connect *to* History

Clarifying How does the work of Michelangelo show that he was influenced by Renaissance values? Explain.

 SEE SKILLBUILDER HANDBOOK, PAGE 992

Connect *to* Today

Researching Look through books on 20th century art to find artists who work in more than one medium, such as painting and sculpture. Share your findings with the class.

David

Influenced by classical statues, Michelangelo sculpted *David* from 1501 to 1504. Michelangelo portrayed the Biblical hero in the moments just before battle. His posture is graceful, yet his figure also displays strength. The statue, which is 18 feet tall, towers over the viewer. This conveys a sense of power.

Leonardo, Renaissance Man

Leonardo da Vinci (LAY·uh·NAHR·doh duh·VIHN·chee) was a painter, sculptor, inventor, and scientist. A true "Renaissance man," he was deeply interested in how things worked. He studied how a muscle moves or how veins are arranged in a leaf. He filled his notebooks with observations and sketches of new inventions, and he incorporated his findings in his art.

Among his many masterpieces, Leonardo painted one of the best-known portraits in the world, the Mona Lisa. The woman in the portrait seems so real that many writers have tried to explain the thoughts behind her slight smile. Leonardo also produced a famous religious painting, *The Last Supper.* It shows the personalities of Jesus' disciples through facial expressions.

Raphael Advances Realism

Raphael (RAF·ee·uhl) was younger than Michelangelo and Leonardo. He learned from studying their works. One of Raphael's favorite subjects was the Madonna and child. Raphael often portrayed their expressions as gentle and calm.

In his greatest achievement, Raphael filled the walls of Pope Julius II's library with several paintings. One of these, *School of Athens* (page 414), conveys the classical influence of the Renaissance. It shows classical and Renaissance figures together. Listening to Greek philosophers are Raphael and Michelangelo, among others.

HISTORY MAKERS

Leonardo da Vinci
1452–1519

Leonardo da Vinci's notebooks—and life—are mysterious in many ways. Some 3,500 pages closely covered with writings and drawings survive, but these may be only one-fourth of what Leonardo produced.

His writing is clear and easy to read—but only if you look at it in a mirror. He wrote backwards in "mirror-writing." No one knows why he took the time to do this.

Leonardo planned scholarly works that he never wrote, and he planned great feats of engineering that were never built. Only 17 of his paintings survive, and several of those were unfinished. The drawing above is the only self-portrait known to exist. And yet the work that Leonardo did produce is so amazing that his reputation as one of the world's geniuses is secure.

Raphael
1483–1520

One of the artists influenced by Leonardo, Raphael began his career early. His father, Giovanni Santi, was a painter, and Raphael learned the basics of his art in his father's studio. At a young age, Raphael went to study with a painter named Perugino. He stayed there about ten years and then went to Florence.

In 1508, Raphael was asked by Pope Julius II to work for him in Rome. Raphael created a series of magnificent frescoes, paintings done on wet plaster, for the pope's private rooms in the Vatican.

Raphael, unlike many of his fellow artists, was easy to like. When he died on his 37th birthday after a short illness, many Romans—including the pope and his court—were stricken with grief and went into mourning.

Women Painters Although Renaissance society generally restricted women's roles, a few Italian women became painters. Sofonisba Anguissola (ahng·GWEES·soh·lah) was the first woman artist to gain an international reputation. She is known for portraits of her sisters and of prominent people such as King Phillip II of Spain. Artemisia Gentileschi (JAYN·tee·LEHS·kee) trained with her painter father and helped with his work. In her own paintings, Gentileschi painted pictures of strong, heroic women.

Renaissance Writers Change Literature

Renaissance writers produced works that not only reflected their time, but also used techniques that writers rely on today. Some followed the example of the medieval writer Dante. He wrote in the **vernacular,** his native language, instead of classical Latin. Dante's native language was Italian. In addition, Renaissance writers wrote either for self-expression or to portray the individuality of their subjects. In these ways, writers of the Renaissance began trends that modern writers still follow.

Petrarch and Boccaccio Francesco Petrarch (PEE·trahrk) was one of the earliest and most influential humanists. He was also a great poet. Petrarch wrote both in Italian and in Latin. In Italian, he wrote sonnets—14-line poems. They were about a mysterious woman named Laura, who was his ideal. (Little is known of Laura except that she died of the plague in 1348.) In classical Latin, he wrote letters to his many important friends.

The Italian writer Boccaccio (boh·KAH·chee·oh) is best known for the *Decameron*, a series of realistic, sometimes off-color stories. The stories are supposedly told by a group of worldly young people waiting in a villa to avoid the plague sweeping through Florence. The humor of the *Decameron* is cutting. Boccaccio presents the follies of his characters—and all humans—with some sarcasm.

Machiavelli Advises Rulers *The Prince* (1513), by Niccolò Machiavelli (MAK·ee·uh·VEHL·ee), also examines the imperfect conduct of human beings. He does so in the form of a political guidebook. In *The Prince*, Machiavelli examines how a ruler can gain power and keep it in spite of his enemies. In answering this question, he began with the idea that most people are selfish, fickle, and corrupt.

To succeed in such a wicked world, Machiavelli said, a prince must be strong as a lion and shrewd as a fox. He might have to trick his enemies and even his own people for the good of the state. In *The Prince*, Machiavelli was not concerned with what was morally right, but with what was politically effective:

A VOICE FROM THE PAST
Everyone admits how praiseworthy it is in a prince to keep faith, and to live with integrity and not with craft. Nevertheless our experience has been that those princes who have done great things have held good faith of little account, and have known how to circumvent the intellect of men by craft, and in the end have overcome those who have relied on their word.

NICCOLÒ MACHIAVELLI, *The Prince*

THINK THROUGH HISTORY
D. Supporting Opinions Do you think Machiavelli is right in his view that rulers must trick people and ignore morality? Explain.

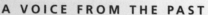

Niccolò Machiavelli, shown here with his hand on a book, was much more than just a cynical political thinker. He was also a patriot, a poet, and a historian.

Women Writers The women writers who gained fame in the Renaissance usually wrote about personal subjects, not politics. Yet, some of them had great influence. Vittoria Colonna exchanged sonnets with Michelangelo and helped Castiglione publish *The Courtier.* Her own poems are often very personal. For example, when her husband was away at war, she wrote to him, "Your uncertain enterprises do not hurt you; / but we who wait, mournfully grieving, / are wounded by doubt and fear."

Toward the end of the 15th century, Renaissance ideas began to spread north from Italy to countries such as France, Germany, and England. Northern artists and thinkers would adapt the Renaissance ideals in their own ways.

Section 1 Assessment

1. TERMS & NAMES
Identify
• Renaissance
• humanism
• secular
• patron
• perspective
• vernacular

2. TAKING NOTES
Using a big-idea outline like the one below, record the main ideas from the section about the Italian Renaissance.

Renaissance
I. Italy's advantages
  A.
  B.
  C.
II. Classical and worldly values

3. SUPPORTING OPINIONS
Name three people from this section whom you regard as a "Renaissance man" or a "Renaissance woman." Explain your choices.

THINK ABOUT
• the idea of the "universal man"
• Castiglione's description of such a person
• which people from this section seem to match that description

4. ANALYZING THEMES
Revolution How did the Renaissance revolutionize European art and thought?

THINK ABOUT
• changes in ideas since medieval times
• changes in artistic techniques
• changes in artistic subjects

The Northern Renaissance

MAIN IDEA	WHY IT MATTERS NOW
In the 1400s, northern Europeans began to adapt the ideas of the Renaissance.	Renaissance ideas such as the importance of the individual are a strong part of modern thought.

SETTING THE STAGE The work of such artists as Leonardo da Vinci, Michelangelo, and Raphael showed the Renaissance spirit. All three artists demonstrated an interest in classical culture, a curiosity about the world, and a belief in human potential. These ideas impressed scholars and students who visited Italy. Merchants also carried these ideas when they traveled out of Italy. By the late 1400s, Renaissance ideas had spread to northern Europe—especially England, France, Germany, and Flanders.

Background
Flanders was a region in northern Europe. It included part of France and part of the Netherlands. The people of Flanders are the Flemish.

The Northern Renaissance Begins

By 1450 the population of northern Europe, which had been shattered by the bubonic plague, was beginning to recover. In addition, the destructive Hundred Years' War between France and England ended in 1453. Many cities grew rapidly. Urban merchants became wealthy enough to sponsor artists. This happened first in Flanders, which was rich from long-distance trade and the cloth industry. Then it happened in other countries.

As Section 1 explained, Italy was divided into city-states. In contrast, England and France were unified under strong monarchs. These rulers often sponsored the arts. For example, Francis I of France purchased Renaissance paintings. He also invited Leonardo da Vinci to retire in France, and hired Italian artists and architects to rebuild his castle at Fontainebleau (FAHN·tihn·BLOH). When completed, Fontainebleau became a showcase of the French Renaissance. Because of monarchs like Francis, royal courts played a major role in introducing Renaissance styles to northern Europe.

As Renaissance ideas spread out of Italy, they mingled with northern traditions. As a result, the northern Renaissance developed its own character. Many humanists there were more interested in religious ideas than in the secular themes popular in Italy. The Renaissance ideal of human dignity inspired some northern humanists to develop plans for social reform based on Christian values.

Albrecht Dürer painted *Adoration of the Trinity* after returning from studying in Italy.

Artistic Ideas Spread

In 1494, a French king claimed the throne of Naples in southern Italy and launched an invasion through northern Italy. As the war dragged on, many Italian artists and writers left for a safer life in northern Europe. With them, they brought the styles and techniques of the Renaissance. In addition, artists who studied in Italy also carried Renaissance ideas north.

THINK THROUGH HISTORY
A. Analyzing Causes How did the war in Italy spread the Renaissance?

German Painters Perhaps the most famous person to do this was the German artist Albrecht Dürer (DYUR·uhr). The son of a goldsmith, Dürer decided to become a painter. After serving an apprenticeship, he traveled to Italy to study in 1494.

After returning to Germany, Dürer produced woodcuts and engravings that became influential. Many of his prints portray religious subjects such as the one on page 423. Others portray classical myths. He also painted realistic landscapes and a self-portrait in which he portrayed himself as a Renaissance man. The popularity of Dürer's work helped to spread Renaissance styles. His work inspired other German artists.

Dürer's emphasis upon realism influenced the work of another German artist, Hans Holbein (HOHL·byn) the Younger. Holbein specialized in painting portraits that are almost photographic in detail. He enjoyed great success in England, where he painted portraits of King Henry VIII and other members of the royal family.

Flemish Painters As in Italy, wealthy merchant families in Flanders were attracted to the Renaissance emphasis on individualism and worldly pleasures. Their patronage helped to make Flanders the artistic center of northern Europe.

As in Italy, the Renaissance in Flanders was marked by an interest in realism. The first great Flemish Renaissance painter was Jan van Eyck (yahn van YK). Van Eyck lived from sometime in the late 1300s to 1441 and worked at the height of the Italian Renaissance.

Oil-based paints had recently been developed. Van Eyck used them to develop techniques that painters still use. Because oil paint does not dry quickly, it can be blended more easily than other paints. By applying layer upon layer of paint, van Eyck was able to create a variety of subtle colors in clothing and jewels. Oil painting became popular and spread to Italy.

THINK THROUGH HISTORY
B. Contrasting
How was the development and spread of oil painting different from many other Renaissance developments?

Daily *Life*

Flemish Peasant Life

The Flemish painter Pieter Bruegel often portrayed peasants. Many of his paintings provide information about peasant life in the 1500s.

Peasant Wedding (1568), shown below, portrays a wedding feast in a rough but clean barn. The bride sits under the paper crown hanging on a piece of green cloth. Two young men who may be her brothers are pouring drinks and passing out plates.

Who, then, is the groom? Possibly the man sitting across the table from the bride and leaning back on a three-legged stool.

Children and at least one dog have come to the party. The couple to the right of the bride and the man on the far right with a sword are dressed more elegantly than the other guests. They may be wealthy townsfolk related to the groom.

In addition to new techniques, van Eyck's paintings display unusually realistic details and reveal the personality of their subjects. His work influenced later artists in northern Europe.

Flemish painting reached its peak after 1550 with the work of Pieter Bruegel (BROY-guhl) the Elder. Like van Eyck, Bruegel was interested in realistic details and individual people. He captured scenes from everyday peasant life such as weddings, dances, harvests, and the changing seasons. Bruegel also produced paintings that illustrated proverbs or taught a moral. Some of his paintings protested harsh Spanish rule over his country.

In all his work, Bruegel's rich colors, vivid details, and balanced use of space give a sense of life and feeling. He was also very skillful in portraying large numbers of people. Not only did Bruegel produce a large number of paintings, he inspired two sons and three grandsons to also became painters.

Northern Writers Try to Reform Society

Just as Italian art influenced northern European painters, so did Renaissance ideas influence the writers and philosophers of northern Europe. These writers adopted the ideal of humanism. However, some gave it a more religious slant. Because of this, some northern humanists are also called Christian humanists.

Christian Humanists The best known of the Christian humanists were Desiderius Erasmus (DEHZ-ih-DEER-ee-uhs ih-RAZ-muhs) of Holland and Thomas More of England. The two were close friends.

Born in Rotterdam, Erasmus received honors from princes, kings, and cardinals for his brilliant writings. In 1509, while he was a guest in More's house, Erasmus wrote his most famous work, *The Praise of Folly*. This book poked fun at greedy merchants, heartsick lovers, quarrelsome scholars, and pompous priests. Although some of Erasmus's most stinging barbs were aimed at the clergy, his work is strongly Christian. Erasmus believed in a Christianity of the heart, not one of ceremonies or rules. He thought that in order to improve society, all people should study the Bible.

THINK THROUGH HISTORY
C. Making Inferences What point do you think More was making about his own society?

Also concerned with society's flaws, Thomas More tried to show a better model. In 1516, he wrote the book *Utopia* about an imaginary land inhabited by a peace-loving people. In Greek, **Utopia** means "no place," but in English it has come to mean an ideal place because of More's book. In Utopia, greed, corruption, war, and crime had been weeded out. Because the Utopians weren't greedy, they had little use for money:

> Gold and silver, of which money is made, are so treated . . . that no one values them more highly than their true nature deserves. Who does not see that they are far inferior to iron in usefulness since without iron mortals cannot live any more than without fire and water?
>
> **THOMAS MORE**, *Utopia*

The French humanist François Rabelais (RAB-eh-LAY) provided a contrast to Erasmus and More in several ways. They wrote in Latin, while Rabelais wrote his comic adventure *Gargantua and Pantagruel* in vernacular French. More secular than either Erasmus or More, Rabelais believed that human beings were basically good. They should live by their instincts rather than religious rules. As he told of the wild adventures of the giants Gargantua and Pantagruel, he poked fun at his society. Rabelais's humor was uproarious and earthy, although he made many serious points about the nature of humanity, education, and government.

William Shakespeare William Shakespeare wrote in Renaissance England. Many people regard him as the greatest playwright of all time. Shakespeare was born in

The Christian humanist Thomas More wrote about a nearly perfect society called Utopia. He did this to show his own society how to improve.

CONNECT *to* TODAY

William Shakespeare

Shakespeare's plays were very popular in London in the 1600s. They are popular today as well, but they appear in many places besides London. Shakespearean festivals are regularly held in such places as Stratford-upon-Avon, England; Stratford, Ontario, Canada; and Austin, Texas.

Even though he has been dead for almost 400 years, Shakespeare is one of Hollywood's favorite writers. In the 1990s, two film versions of *Hamlet* hit the theaters, as did a version of *Romeo and Juliet*. The poster below is from the 1990 version of *Hamlet*, starring Mel Gibson and Glenn Close.

1564 in Stratford-upon-Avon, a small town about 90 miles northwest of London. By 1592 he was living in London and writing poems and plays.

His works display a masterful command of the English language and a deep understanding of human beings. He revealed the souls of men and women through scenes of dramatic conflict. His most famous plays include the tragedies *Macbeth, King Lear, Hamlet, Romeo and Juliet,* and the comedy *A Midsummer Night's Dream.* Many of these plays frankly examine human flaws. However, Shakespeare also had one of his characters deliver a speech that expresses the Renaissance's high view of human nature:

A VOICE FROM THE PAST

What a piece of work is a man, how noble in reason, how infinite in faculties, in form and moving, how express and admirable in action, how like an angel in apprehension [understanding], how like a god! the beauty of the world; the paragon of animals.

WILLIAM SHAKESPEARE, *Hamlet*

THINK THROUGH HISTORY
D. Summarizing
State at least two ways in which Shakespeare's work showed Renaissance influences.

Like many Renaissance writers, Shakespeare revered the classics and drew on them for inspiration and plots. One of his great tragedies, for example, tells the story of the assassination of Julius Caesar—the Roman general and statesman.

The Elizabethan Age The Renaissance in England is also called the Elizabethan Age, for Queen Elizabeth I. She reigned from 1558 to 1603. Elizabeth was well-educated and knew French, Italian, Latin, and Greek. In addition to running a kingdom (see page 432), she also wrote poetry. As queen, she patronized artists and writers. Poet Edmund Spenser dedicated his long poem *The Faerie Queene* (1590) to her with these words: "To the most high, mighty, and magnificent Empress, renowned for piety, virtue, and all gracious government, Elizabeth."

Printing Spreads Renaissance Ideas

One thing that helped spread Renaissance ideas throughout Europe was a new invention that adapted Chinese technology. The Chinese had invented block printing, in which a printer carved a word or letter on a wooden block, inked the block, and then used it to print on paper. Around 1045, Bi Sheng invented movable type, or a separate piece of type for each character in the language. However, since the Chinese writing system contained thousands of different characters, most Chinese printers found movable type impractical.

Gutenberg Invents the Printing Press During the 13th century, block-printed items reached Europe from China. European printers began to use block printing to create whole pages to bind into books. However, this process was too slow to satisfy the Renaissance demand for knowledge and books. Johann Gutenberg, a craftsman from Mainz, Germany, reinvented movable type around 1440. The method was practical for Europeans because their languages have a very small number of letters in their alphabets.

Gutenberg then invented the **printing press.** The printing press is a machine that presses paper against a tray full of inked movable type. Using this invention, Gutenberg printed a complete Bible, the **Gutenberg Bible,** in about 1455. It was the first full-size book printed with movable type.

History of Book Making

- 2700 B.C., Egyptians write books on papyrus scrolls.
- 1000 B.C., Chinese make books by writing on strips of bamboo.
- A.D. 300, Romans write on sheets of parchment (treated animal skin). These are sewn together into books.
- 800, Irish monks hand-write and hand-illustrate *The Book of Kells.*
- About 1455, Gutenberg prints the first complete book on a printing press—similar to the one shown at left.

Only 46 copies of the Gutenberg Bible still exist in the world. Because of this, each copy is considered priceless. A part of a page is shown above.

Printing Spreads Learning The printing press had a revolutionary impact on European society. It enabled a printer to produce hundreds of copies, all exactly alike, of a single work. For the first time, books were cheap enough that many people could buy them. Printing spread quickly to other cities in Europe. By 1500, presses in about 250 cities had printed between 9 and 10 million books.

New ideas spread more quickly than ever before. At first printers produced many religious works. Soon they began to provide books on other subjects such as travel guides and medical manuals. The availability of books encouraged people to learn to read and so caused a rise in literacy.

THINK THROUGH HISTORY
E. Recognizing Effects What were the major effects of the invention of the printing press?

Writing in vernacular languages also increased because even people who could not afford a classical education could now buy books. Printers produced the Bible in the vernacular, which allowed more people to read it. People began to interpret the Bible for themselves and to become more critical of priests and their behavior. This eventually led to demands for religious reform.

The End of the Renaissance In both Italy and northern Europe, the Renaissance had stirred a burst of creative activity. Artists in both regions studied classical culture, praised individual achievement, and produced works using new techniques. During the 1600s, new ideas and artistic styles appeared. Nonetheless, Renaissance ideals continued to influence European thought. For example, the Renaissance belief in the dignity of the individual played a key role in the gradual rise of democratic ideas.

Section 2 Assessment

1. TERMS & NAMES

Identify
- Utopia
- printing press
- Gutenberg Bible

2. TAKING NOTES

On a time line like the one below, show important events in the Northern Renaissance.

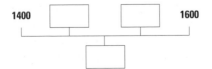

Which of the events do you think was most important? Explain.

3. RECOGNIZING EFFECTS

Choose one Northern Renaissance figure. Explain how he or she was influenced by Renaissance ideas.

THINK ABOUT
- the influence of humanism
- the use of new techniques
- the concept of the Renaissance man or woman

4. THEME ACTIVITY

Cultural Interaction Working in a small team, reproduce a map of Europe in 1500. On the map, use arrows, pictures, and captions to show the spread of Renaissance ideas and developments. Include not only the spread of ideas north from Italy, but also innovations that spread southward from northern Europe.

3 Luther Starts the Reformation

TERMS & NAMES
- indulgence
- Reformation
- Lutheran
- Protestant
- Peace of Augsburg
- annul
- Anglican

MAIN IDEA

Martin Luther's protest over abuses in the Catholic Church led to the founding of Protestant churches.

WHY IT MATTERS NOW

Nearly one-fourth of the Christians in today's world are Protestants.

SETTING THE STAGE By the tenth century, the church in Rome had come to dominate religious life in northern and western Europe. However, the Roman Catholic Church had not won universal approval. Over the centuries, rulers, scholars, and members of the clergy criticized church practices. Even though church leaders made several important reforms during the Middle Ages, the problems lingered.

Causes of the Reformation

By 1500, additional forces weakened the Church. The Renaissance emphasis on the secular and the individual challenged Church authority. The printing press spread these secular ideas. In addition, rulers resented the popes' attempts to control them. In Germany—divided into many competing states—it was difficult for the pope or the emperor to impose central authority. Finally, northern merchants resented paying church taxes to Rome. Spurred by political and social forces, a new movement for religious reform began in Germany. It then swept much of Europe.

Problems in the Catholic Church Critics of the Church claimed that its leaders were corrupt. The popes who ruled during the Renaissance patronized the arts, spent extravagantly on personal pleasure, and fought wars. Pope Pius II admitted, "If the truth be confessed, the luxury and pomp of our courts is too great." Another pope, Alexander VI, publicly admitted that he had several children. These popes were too busy pursuing worldly affairs to have much time for spiritual duties.

The lower clergy had problems as well. Many priests and monks were so poorly educated that they could scarcely read, let alone teach people. Others broke their priestly vows by marrying, or by gambling or drinking to excess.

Early Calls for Reform Influenced by reformers, people had come to expect higher standards of conduct from priests and church leaders. In the late 1300s and early 1400s, John Wycliffe of England and Jan Hus of Bohemia had advocated church reform. They denied that the pope had the right to worldly power. They also taught that the Bible had more authority than Church leaders. In the 1500s, Christian humanists like Desiderius Erasmus and Thomas More added their voices to the chorus of criticism.

In the 1490s, an Italian friar named Girolamo Savonarola (jih·RAHL·uh·MOH SAV·uh·nuh·ROH·luh) came to Florence. He preached fiery sermons calling for reform. In 1497, the people of Florence responded to Savonarola by burning their worldly possessions, such as gambling equipment, in a giant bonfire. Only a year later, the Florentines turned against Savonarola, and he was executed for heresy.

THINK THROUGH HISTORY
A. Analyzing Causes How did political, social, and economic forces weaken the Church?

As this portrait shows, the friar Girolamo Savonarola was a serious-minded man. Disapproving of the worldly values of his time, he urged the people of Florence to give up their luxuries.

Luther Challenges the Church

Although some reformers died for their beliefs, their calls for change lived on. In addition, many Europeans were reading religious works for themselves and forming their own opinions about the Church. The atmosphere in Europe was ripe for reform by the early 1500s.

Martin Luther The son of a miner, Martin Luther became a monk in 1505. From 1512 until his death he taught scripture at the University of Wittenberg in the German state of Saxony. All he wanted was to be a good Christian, not to lead a religious revolution.

In 1517 Luther decided to take a public stand against the actions of a friar named Johann Tetzel. Tetzel was raising money to rebuild St. Peter's Cathedral in Rome. He did this by selling indulgences. An **indulgence** was a pardon. It released a sinner from performing the penalty—such as saying certain prayers—that a priest imposed for sins. Indulgences were not supposed to affect God's right to judge. Unfortunately, Tetzel gave people the impression that by buying indulgences, they could buy their way into heaven.

Background
The door of the church served as a type of bulletin board for the University of Wittenberg. If scholars wanted to debate a subject, they would post their opinions on the door.

The 95 Theses Luther was troubled by Tetzel's tactics. He wrote 95 Theses, or formal statements, attacking the "pardon-merchants." On October 31, 1517, he posted his theses on the door of the castle church in Wittenberg and invited other scholars to debate him. Someone copied Luther's words and took them to a printer. Quickly, Luther's name became known all over Germany. His actions began the **Reformation,** a movement for religious reform. It led to the founding of Christian churches that did not accept the pope's authority.

Soon Luther went far beyond criticizing indulgences. He wanted a full reform of the Church. His teachings rested on three main ideas:

- People could win salvation only by faith in God's gift of forgiveness. The Church taught that faith and "good works" were needed for salvation.
- All Church teachings should be clearly based on the words of the Bible. The pope and church traditions were false authorities.
- All people with faith were equal. Therefore, people did not need priests to interpret the Bible for them.

HISTORY MAKERS

**Martin Luther
1483–1546**
Martin Luther was sometimes unhappy as a child. Like many parents of that time, his father and mother were very strict. Luther later told stories of their beating him.

In one way, fear led Luther to become a monk. His father wanted him to go to law school, but at the age of 21, Luther was caught in a terrible thunderstorm. Lightning struck close to him. Convinced he would die, he cried out, "Saint Anne, help me! I will become a monk."

Even as a monk, Luther felt sinful, lost, and rejected by God. He confessed his sins regularly, fasted, and did penance. However, by studying the Bible, Luther came to the conclusion that faith alone was the key to salvation. Only then did he experience peace.

The Response to Luther

Luther himself was astonished at how rapidly his ideas spread and attracted followers. Many rulers and merchants had been unhappy with the Church for political and economic reasons. They saw Luther's protests as an excuse to throw off Church control.

THINK THROUGH HISTORY
B. Synthesizing
Review the list of Luther's teachings above. Which of these points help you to understand why he felt it was all right to defy the pope?

The Pope's Threat Initially, the Church officials in Rome viewed Luther simply as a rebellious monk who needed to be punished by his superiors. However, as Luther's ideas became increasingly radical, the pope realized that the monk was a serious threat. In one angry reply to Church criticism, Luther actually suggested that Christians drive the pope from the Church by force.

In 1520, Pope Leo X issued a decree threatening Luther with excommunication unless he took back his statements. Luther did not take back a word. Instead, his students at Wittenberg gathered around a bonfire and cheered as he threw the pope's decree into the flames. Leo excommunicated Luther.

The Emperor's Opposition A devout Catholic, the Holy Roman emperor also opposed Luther's teaching. Although only 20 years old, Emperor Charles V controlled a vast empire, including Germany. He summoned Luther to the town of Worms in 1521 to stand trial. German princes and bishops crowded into the hall to witness the testimony. Told to recant, or take back his statements, Luther refused.

A VOICE FROM THE PAST
I am bound by the Scriptures I have quoted and my conscience is captive to the Word of God. I cannot and I will not retract anything, since it is neither safe nor right to go against conscience. I cannot do otherwise, here I stand, may God help me. Amen.

LUTHER, quoted in *The Protestant Reformation* by Lewis W. Spitz

A month after Luther made that speech, Charles issued an imperial order, the Edict of Worms. It declared Luther an outlaw and a heretic. According to this edict, no one in the empire was to give Luther food or shelter. All his books were to be burned. However, the ruler of the state where Luther lived disobeyed the emperor. For almost a year after the trial, Prince Frederick the Wise of Saxony sheltered Luther in one of his castles. While there, Luther translated the New Testament into German.

Luther returned to Wittenberg in 1522. There he discovered that many of his ideas were already being put into practice. Priests dressed in ordinary clothes and called themselves ministers. They led services in German instead of in Latin. Some ministers had married, because Luther taught that the clergy should be free to wed. Instead of continuing to seek reforms in the Catholic Church, Luther and his followers had become a separate religious group, called **Lutherans.**

The Peasants' Revolt Some people began to apply Luther's revolutionary ideas to society. In 1524, German peasants, excited by reformers' talk of Christian freedom, demanded an end to serfdom. Bands of angry peasants went about the countryside raiding monasteries, pillaging, and burning.

The revolt horrified Luther. He wrote a pamphlet urging the German princes to show the peasants no mercy. With brutal thoroughness, the princes' armies crushed the revolt. They massacred as many as 100,000 people. Feeling betrayed by Luther, many peasants rejected his religious leadership. However, through writings and lectures, Luther remained influential until the end of his life.

THINK THROUGH HISTORY
C. Drawing Conclusions Why would Luther and his followers want the Bible and sermons to be in German?

SPOTLIGHT ON

Witch Hunts
Soon after the Reformation began, the number of people executed for being witches rose dramatically. From 1561 to 1670 in Germany, 3,229 people accused of witchcraft were burned at the stake, as the engraving above shows. Between 1559 and 1736 in England, almost 1,000 witches were put to death. Eighty percent of the people accused of witchcraft were women.

Some historians think that people felt so frightened by the ongoing religious conflicts they blamed them on witches. Other historians believe that religious reformers stirred up negative feelings about women that had long been part of Western culture. All agree that those executed for witchcraft were innocent victims.

Germany at War In contrast to the bitter peasants, many northern German princes supported Lutheranism. While some princes genuinely shared Luther's beliefs, others liked Luther's ideas for selfish reasons. They saw his teachings as a good excuse to seize Church property and to assert their independence from Charles V.

In 1529, German princes who remained loyal to the pope agreed to join forces against Luther's ideas. Princes who supported Luther signed a protest against that agreement. These protesting princes came to be known as Protestants. Eventually, the term **Protestant** was applied to Christians who belonged to non-Catholic churches.

Still determined that his subjects remain Catholic, Holy Roman Emperor Charles V went to war against the Protestant princes of Germany. Even though he defeated them in 1547, he failed to force them back into the Catholic Church.

Weary of fighting, Charles ordered all German princes, both Protestant and Catholic, to assemble in the city of Augsburg. At that meeting, the princes agreed that the religion of each German state was to be decided by its ruler. This famous religious settlement, signed in 1555, was known as the **Peace of Augsburg.**

THINK THROUGH HISTORY
D. Analyzing Motives Explain the different motives that German princes had for becoming Lutheran.

England Becomes Protestant

The Catholic Church soon faced another great challenge to its authority. Unlike Luther, the man who broke England's ties to the Roman Catholic Church did so for political and personal, not religious, reasons.

Henry VIII Wants a Son When Henry became king of England, he was a devout Catholic. Political needs soon tested his religious loyalty. He needed a male heir. Henry's father had become king after a long civil war. Henry feared that a similar war would start if he died without a son as his heir. He and his wife, Catherine of Aragon, had one living child—a daughter, Mary—but no woman had ever successfully claimed the English throne.

By 1527, Henry was convinced that the 42-year-old Catherine would have no more children. He wanted to divorce her and take a younger queen. Church law did not allow divorce. However, the pope could **annul,** or set aside, Henry's marriage if he could find proof that it had never been legal in the first place. Excuses were frequently found to annul royal marriages if they produced no heirs. In 1527, King Henry asked the pope to annul his marriage, but the pope turned him down. The pope did not want to offend Catherine's powerful nephew, the Holy Roman Emperor Charles V.

Background
The pope had taken the losing side in a war against Emperor Charles V, who was now holding him prisoner. The pope did not dare annul Henry's marriage to Charles's aunt.

The Reformation Parliament Henry solved his marriage problem himself. In 1529, he called Parliament into session and asked it to pass a set of laws that ended the pope's power in England. This Parliament is known as the Reformation Parliament.

In 1533, Henry secretly married Anne Boleyn (BUL·ihn), who was in her twenties. Parliament legalized Henry's divorce from Catherine. In 1534, Henry's break with the pope was made complete when Parliament voted to approve the Act of Supremacy. This act made the English king, not the pope, the official head of England's Church.

Consequences of Henry's Changes Soon after making himself supreme head of the Church of England, Henry closed all English monasteries. He seized their wealth and lands. The monasteries had owned perhaps 20 percent of the land in England, so this act vastly increased royal power and enriched Henry's treasury.

Henry did not get the male heir he sought immediately. After Anne Boleyn gave birth to a girl, she fell out of Henry's favor. Eventually, he ordered her imprisoned in the Tower of London and later beheaded in 1536. Before his death, Henry married four more times. His third wife gave him a son named Edward.

HISTORY MAKERS

Henry VIII
1491–1547

When Henry became king in 1509, he was young, strong, handsome, and intelligent. He loved sports, literature, music, and food. He also loved his Roman Catholic faith.

In 1521, he wrote a pamphlet attacking Martin Luther and his teachings. Impressed by Henry's loyalty, the pope gave him a special title, "Defender of the Faith."

Even Henry's religious actions were driven by political ambition. One of his motives for defending Catholicism was to keep up with his fellow European monarchs. Earlier popes had granted Spanish monarchs the title "Catholic Sovereigns" and French monarchs the title "Most Christian." Although Henry was proud of his papal honor, eventually his political needs drove him to break with the Church.

Henry VIII's Family Causes Religious Turmoil

1509 Henry VIII becomes king.

1516 Daughter Mary is born.

1527 Henry asks the pope to end his first marriage; the pope refuses.

1529 Henry breaks with pope; begins Protestant Anglican church.

1533 Henry marries Anne Boleyn; daughter Elizabeth is born.

1536 Anne Boleyn is beheaded.

1537 Henry's third wife has son, Edward. She dies from complications.

1540-1542 Henry divorces fourth wife and beheads fifth wife.

1547 Henry dies; his sixth wife outlives him; Edward VI begins six-year rule; Protestants are strong.

1553 Catholic Mary I begins rule and kills Protestants.

1558 Elizabeth I begins rule; she restores Protestant church.

1500 — 1560

After Henry's death in 1547, each of his three children eventually ruled. This created religious turmoil. Edward VI became king at age nine and ruled only six years. During his reign, the Protestants gained power. Edward's half-sister Mary ruled next. She was a Catholic who returned the English Church to the rule of the pope. Mary had many Protestants killed. England's next ruler was Anne Boleyn's daughter, Elizabeth.

Elizabeth Restores Protestantism Inheriting the throne in 1558, Elizabeth I returned her kingdom to Protestantism. In 1559, Parliament followed Elizabeth's request and set up a national church much like the one under Henry VIII. This was to be the only legal church in England. People were required to attend its services or pay a fine. Parliament declared that Elizabeth was head of the Church of England, or **Anglican** Church.

Elizabeth decided to establish a state church that moderate Catholics and moderate Protestants might both accept. As a concession to Protestants, priests in the Church of England were allowed to marry. They could deliver sermons in English, not Latin. As a concession to Catholics, the Church of England kept some of the trappings of the Catholic service such as rich robes and golden crucifixes. Under Elizabeth, the Book of Common Prayer was revised to be somewhat more acceptable to Catholics.

The Spanish Armada While Elizabeth was able to restore religious peace to her country, she soon faced the threat of invasion from the king of Catholic Spain. Philip II planned to attack England for several reasons. One reason was that Elizabeth had supported Protestant subjects who rebelled against him. In 1588, Philip assembled an invasion force of 130 ships, 8,000 sailors, and 19,000 soldiers. This force—known as the Spanish Armada—reached the southwest coast of England on July 29. However, bad weather and the English fleet defeated the Spanish completely.

Although Elizabeth's reign was triumphant, she had some difficulties. Money was one problem. In the late 1500s, the English began to think about building an American empire as a new source of income. (See Chapter 19.) While colonies strengthened England economically, they did not enrich the queen directly. The queen's constant need for money would carry over into the next reign and lead to bitter conflict between the monarch and Parliament. In the meantime, other countries experienced bloody religious conflicts.

THINK THROUGH HISTORY
E. Recognizing Effects How did Henry VIII and his three children cause religious turmoil in England?

HISTORY MAKERS

Elizabeth I
1533–1603

Elizabeth I was the third of Henry VIII's children to rule England. Like her father, Elizabeth had a fierce temper and a robust nature. Athletic as a girl, she showed amazing energy and strength into her sixties.

When the Spanish Armada threatened England, Elizabeth rode into the camp of soldiers preparing to defend their country. For this occasion, she wore her brightest red wig adorned with two white plumes that were easy for all to see above the soldier's long pikes.

From her horse, Elizabeth gave encouragement to her soldiers:

I know I have the body of a weak and feeble woman, but I have the heart and stomach of a king, and a king of England, too, and I think foul scorn [of] . . . any prince of Europe [who] should dare invade the borders of my realm.

Section ❸ Assessment

1. TERMS & NAMES

Identify
• indulgence
• Reformation
• Lutheran
• Protestant
• Peace of Augsburg
• annul
• Anglican

2. TAKING NOTES

Using a cause-and-effect graphic like the one below, show the main cause and several effects of Luther's action in posting the 95 Theses.

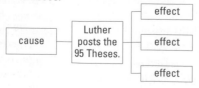

Which effect do you think had the most permanent impact? Explain.

3. SUPPORTING OPINIONS

Who do you think had a better reason to break with the Church, Luther or Henry VIII? Support your answer with details from the text.

THINK ABOUT
• why Luther criticized the Church
• what Henry asked the pope to do for him
• the Church's response to Luther
• the pope's response to Henry

4. ANALYZING THEMES

Revolution Which of Luther's ideas do you think might have motivated the peasants to revolt in 1524? Explain.

THINK ABOUT
• Luther's criticisms of the Church
• what change the peasants demanded
• the actions the peasants took

4 The Reformation Continues

TERMS & NAMES
- predestination
- Calvinism
- theocracy
- Presbyterian
- Anabaptist
- Catholic Reformation
- Jesuits
- Council of Trent

MAIN IDEA	WHY IT MATTERS NOW
John Calvin and other Reformation leaders began new Protestant churches. The Catholic Church also made reforms.	Many Protestant churches began during this period, and many Catholic schools are the result of Catholic reforms.

SETTING THE STAGE Under the leadership of Elizabeth I, the Church of England remained similar to the Catholic Church in many of its doctrines and ceremonies. Meanwhile, other forms of Protestantism were developing elsewhere in Europe.

Calvin Begins Another Protestant Church

In 1521, the year Luther stood trial at Worms, John Calvin was a 12-year-old boy. Born in France, Calvin grew up to have as much influence on Protestants as Luther did. Calvin would give order to the new faith that Luther had begun.

Calvin and His Teachings In 1536, Calvin published a book called *Institutes of the Christian Religion*. This work expressed Calvin's ideas about God, salvation, and human nature. It also created a system of Protestant theology.

Calvin taught that men and women are sinful by nature. Taking Luther's idea that humans cannot earn salvation, Calvin went on to say that God chooses a very few people to save. Calvin called these few the "elect." He believed that God has known since the beginning of time who will be saved. This doctrine is called **predestination.** The religion based on Calvin's teachings is called **Calvinism.**

Calvin Runs Geneva Calvin believed that the ideal government was a **theocracy,** a government controlled by religious leaders. In 1541, Protestants in Geneva, Switzerland, asked Calvin to lead their city. When Calvin arrived there in the 1540s, Geneva was a self-governing city of about 20,000 people.

Calvin and his followers ran the city according to strict rules. Everyone attended religion class. No one wore bright clothing or played card games. Authorities would imprison, excommunicate, or banish those who broke such rules. Anyone who preached different doctrines might be burned at the stake. Yet, to many Protestants, Calvin's Geneva was a model city of highly moral citizens.

Calvinism Spreads One of the admiring visitors to Geneva was a preacher from Scotland named John Knox. When he returned home in 1559, Knox put Calvin's ideas to work in Scottish towns. Each community church was governed by a small group of laymen called elders or presbyters (PREHZ·buh·tuhrs). Followers of Knox became known as **Presbyterians.** In the 1560s, Protestant nobles led by Knox succeeded in making Calvinism Scotland's official religion. They also deposed their Catholic queen in favor of her infant son.

Elsewhere, Swiss, Dutch, and French reformers adopted the Calvinist form of church organization. One reason Calvin is considered so influential is that many Protestant churches today

Background
The deposed queen was Mary, Queen of Scots—Elizabeth I's cousin and heir. Many English Catholics wanted Mary to rule. Eventually, Elizabeth had Mary executed for taking part in plots against her.

HISTORY MAKERS

John Calvin
1509–1564

Unlike Luther, Calvin wrote little about his personal life. A quiet boy, he grew up to study law and philosophy at the University of Paris. Early in the 1530s, he came under the influence of French followers of Luther. When King Francis I ordered these Protestants arrested, Calvin fled. Eventually, he made his way to Geneva, Switzerland.

Calvin and his followers rigidly regulated morality in Geneva. Perhaps because of this, Calvinism is often described as strict and grim. However, Calvin taught that people should enjoy God's gifts. He wrote that it was not

anywhere forbidden to laugh, or to enjoy food, or to add new possessions to old . . . or to be delighted with musical harmonies, or to drink wine.

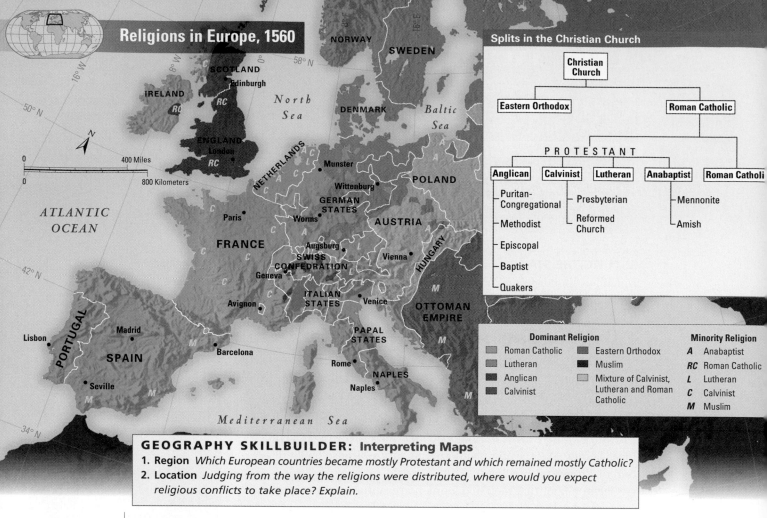

Religions in Europe, 1560

Splits in the Christian Church

Christian Church
- Eastern Orthodox
- Roman Catholic
  - PROTESTANT
    - Anglican
      - Puritan-Congregational
      - Methodist
      - Episcopal
      - Baptist
      - Quakers
    - Calvinist
      - Presbyterian
      - Reformed Church
    - Lutheran
    - Anabaptist
      - Mennonite
      - Amish
    - Roman Catholic

Dominant Religion
- Roman Catholic
- Lutheran
- Anglican
- Calvinist
- Eastern Orthodox
- Muslim
- Mixture of Calvinist, Lutheran and Roman Catholic

Minority Religion
- *A* Anabaptist
- *RC* Roman Catholic
- *L* Lutheran
- *C* Calvinist
- *M* Muslim

GEOGRAPHY SKILLBUILDER: Interpreting Maps
1. **Region** *Which European countries became mostly Protestant and which remained mostly Catholic?*
2. **Location** *Judging from the way the religions were distributed, where would you expect religious conflicts to take place? Explain.*

trace their roots to Calvin. Over the years, however, many of them have softened Calvin's strict teachings.

In France, Calvin's followers were called Huguenots. Hatred between Catholics and Huguenots frequently led to violence. The worst outbreak of fury occurred in Paris on August 24, 1572—the Catholic feast of St. Bartholomew's Day. At dawn, Catholic mobs began hunting for Protestants and brutally murdering them. The massacres spread to other cities and lasted six months. Thousands, perhaps up to 12,000, Huguenots were killed.

Although Catholic, Marguerite of Navarre held unorthodox, mystical personal beliefs. She supported the call for reform in the Church.

Other Reformers

Protestants taught that the Bible is the source of all truth about religion and that all people should read it to discover those truths. As Christians began to interpret the Bible for themselves, new Protestant groups formed over differences in belief.

THINK THROUGH HISTORY
A. Analyzing Causes How did Protestant teaching cause further divisions in the Christian church?

The Anabaptists One such group baptized only those persons who were old enough to decide to be Christian. They said that people who had been baptized as children should be rebaptized as adults. These believers were called **Anabaptists** from the Greek for "baptize again." Anabaptists also taught that church and state should be separate, and they refused to fight in wars. They shared their possessions. Viewing Anabaptists as radicals who threatened society, both Catholics and Protestants persecuted them. Yet, the Anabaptists survived and became the forerunners of the Mennonites and the Amish. Their teaching influenced the later Quakers and Baptists, who split from the Anglican church.

Women of the Reformation Many women played prominent roles in the Reformation, especially from 1519 to 1580. For example, Marguerite of Navarre, the sister of King Francis I, protected John Calvin from being executed for his beliefs while he lived in France. Other noblewomen played similar roles in protecting reformers.

Several wives of reformers also achieved fame. Katherina Zell, married to prominent reformer Matthew Zell of Strasbourg, once scolded a minister for speaking harshly of another. The minister responded by saying that she had "disturbed the peace." Katherina Zell answered his criticism sharply:

A VOICE FROM THE PAST
Do you call this disturbing the peace that instead of spending my time in frivolous amusements I have visited the plague infested and carried out the dead? I have visited those in prison and under sentence of death. Often for three days and three nights I have neither eaten nor slept. I have never mounted the pulpit, but I have done more than any minister in visiting those in misery.

KATHERINA ZELL, quoted in *Women of the Reformation*

Luther's wife Katherina von Bora played a more typical, behind-the-scenes role. However, her young life was unusual. Sent to a convent at about age 10, Katherina had taken the vows of a nun by 16. Inspired by Luther's teaching, she escaped from her convent. Some stories claim she escaped by hiding in an empty barrel that had contained smoked herring.

After marrying Luther, Katherina had six children. She managed the family finances, fed all who visited their house, and supported her husband's work. She submitted respectfully to Luther but also argued with him about woman's equal role in marriage. Their well-run household became a model for others to follow.

As Protestant religions became more firmly established, their organization became more formal. Male religious leaders narrowly limited women's activities to the home and discouraged them from being leaders.

THINK THROUGH HISTORY
B. Making Inferences Why was it easier for women to take part in the earlier stages of the Reformation than the later stages?

The Catholic Reformation

While Protestant churches won many followers, millions remained true to Catholicism. Helping Catholics to remain loyal was a movement within the Catholic Church to reform itself. This movement is now known as the **Catholic Reformation.** One great Catholic reformer was Ignatius (ihg·NAY·shuhs) of Loyola.

Ignatius of Loyola Ignatius grew up in his father's castle in Loyola, Spain. The great turning point in his life came in 1521 when he was injured in a war. During his recovery, Ignatius thought about his past sins and about the life of Jesus. His daily devotions, he believed, cleansed his soul. In 1522, he began writing a book called *Spiritual Exercises* that laid out a day-by-day plan of meditation, prayer, and study. Ignatius compared spiritual and physical exercise:

A VOICE FROM THE PAST
Just as walking, traveling, and running are bodily exercises, preparing the soul to remove ill-ordered affections, and after their removal seeking and finding the will of God with respect to the ordering of one's own life and the salvation of one's soul, are Spiritual Exercises.

IGNATIUS OF LOYOLA, *Spiritual Exercises*

For the next 18 years, Ignatius gathered followers. In 1540, the pope made Ignatius's followers a religious order called the Society of Jesus. Members of the order were commonly called **Jesuits** (JEHZH·u·ihts).

The Jesuits concentrated on three activities. First, they founded superb schools throughout Europe. Jesuit teachers were rigorously trained in both classical studies and theology. The Jesuits' second mission was to convert non-Christians to Catholicism, so they sent out missionaries. Their third goal was to stop Protestantism from

Global Impact

Jesuit Missionaries
The work of Jesuit missionaries has had a lasting impact around the globe. By the time Ignatius died in 1556, about a thousand Jesuits were working in Europe, Africa, Asia, and the Americas. Two of the most famous Jesuit missionaries of the 1500s were Francis Xavier, who worked in India, and Matteo Ricci, who worked in China.

One reason the Jesuits had such a permanent impact is that they founded schools, colleges, and universities throughout the world. For example, the Jesuits today run about 45 high schools and 28 colleges and universities in the United States. Two of these are Boston College and Marquette University.

spreading. The zeal of the Jesuits overcame the drift toward Protestantism in Poland and southern Germany.

Reforming Popes Two popes of the 1500s took the lead in reforming the Catholic Church. Paul III, who was pope from 1534 to 1549, took four important steps toward reform. First, he directed a council of cardinals to investigate indulgence selling and other abuses within the Church. Second, he approved the Jesuit order. Third, he used the Inquisition to seek out and punish heresy in papal territory. Fourth, and most important, he

Background
This Inquisition was called the Roman Inquisition. It generally was more moderate than the Spanish Inquisition described in Chapter 14.

This Italian painting of the Council of Trent shows the large number of church leaders who met to discuss Catholic reforms.

decided to call a great council of Church leaders to meet in Trent, in northern Italy. In the years between 1545 and 1563, at the **Council of Trent,** Catholic bishops and cardinals agreed on several doctrines:

- The church's interpretation of the Bible was final. Any Christian who substituted his or her own interpretation was a heretic.
- Christians need faith and good works for salvation. They were not saved by faith alone, as Luther argued.
- The Bible and Church tradition were equally powerful authorities for guiding Christian life.
- Indulgences were valid expressions of faith. (But the false selling of indulgences was banned.)

Another reforming pope, Paul IV, vigorously carried out the council's decrees. In 1559, he had officials draw up a list of books considered dangerous to the Catholic faith. This list was known as the Index of Forbidden Books. Catholic bishops throughout Europe were ordered to gather up the offensive books (including Protestant Bibles) and burn them in bonfires. In Venice alone, 10,000 books were burned in one day.

Legacy of the Reformation The Reformation had enduring effects. Protestant churches flourished, despite religious wars and persecutions. Because of the Reformation, religion no longer united Europe. As the Church's power declined, individual monarchs and states gained power. This paved the way for modern nation-states. In addition, the reformers' successful revolt against Church authority laid the groundwork for a rejection of Christian belief that occurred in Western culture in later centuries. Therefore, through its political and social effects, the Reformation helped to set the stage for the modern world.

Section 4 Assessment

1. TERMS & NAMES

Identify
- predestination
- Calvinism
- theocracy
- Presbyterian
- Anabaptist
- Catholic Reformation
- Jesuits
- Council of Trent

2. TAKING NOTES

Using a chart like the one below, compare the ideas of the reformers who came after Luther.

Reformers	Ideas
John Calvin	
Anabaptists	
Catholic Reformers	

3. EVALUATING DECISIONS

Which of the steps taken by Popes Paul III and Paul IV to reform the Catholic Church do you think were wise? Which were unwise? Explain.

THINK ABOUT
- the goals of the reforming popes
- whether the steps clearly addressed those goals
- possible effects of each step

4. THEME ACTIVITY

Religious and Ethical Systems In a group of three, hold a debate on whether Calvin was right to establish such a strict theocracy in Geneva. Debate such points as whether church leaders should be political rulers and whether government should try to control personal morality. One team member should support Calvin's policy, one should oppose it, and one should act as moderator.

The Reformation

Martin Luther's criticisms of the Catholic church grew sharper over time. Some Catholics, in turn, responded with personal attacks on Luther. In recent times, historians have focused less on the theological and personal issues connected with the Reformation. Instead, many modern scholars analyze political, social, and economic conditions that contributed to the Reformation.

LETTER
Martin Luther

Although Luther began by criticizing the practice of selling indulgences, he soon began to attack the whole system of church government. In 1520, he sent the pope the following criticism of the Church leaders who served under him in Rome.

The Roman Church has become the most licentious [sinful] den of thieves. . . . They err who ascribe to thee the right of interpreting Scripture, for under cover of thy name they seek to set up their own wickedness in the Church, and, alas, through them Satan has already made much headway under thy predecessors. In short, believe none who exalt thee, believe those who humble thee.

ENGRAVING
Anonymous

In the early 1500s, an anonymous Catholic author published an engraving attacking Luther's "game of heresy." The following lines are part of a poem that appeared on the engraving.

I have in my simple way foreseen
What Luther's teaching promises
to bring:
Great rebellion and bloodletting,
Much hatred and strife.
The fear of God will vanish forever,
Together with the whole of Scripture,
And authority will everywhere
be despised.

HISTORIAN'S COMMENTARY
Steven Ozment

In 1992, historian Steven Ozment published *Protestants: The Birth of a Revolution*. Here he comments on some of the political aspects of the Reformation.

Beginning as a protest against arbitrary, self-aggrandizing, hierarchical authority in the person of the pope, the Reformation came to be closely identified in the minds of contemporaries with what we today might call states' rights or local control. To many townspeople and villagers, Luther seemed a godsend for their struggle to remain politically free and independent; they embraced his Reformation as a conserving political force, even though they knew it threatened to undo traditional religious beliefs and practices.

HISTORIAN'S COMMENTARY
G. R. Elton

In *Reformation Europe*, published in 1963, G. R. Elton notes the role of geography and trade in the spread of Reformation ideas.

Could the Reformation have spread so far and so fast if it had started anywhere but in Germany? At any rate, the fact that it had its beginnings in the middle of Europe made possible a very rapid radiation in all directions; the whole circle of countries surrounding the Empire came one after the other under its influence. Germany's position at the center of European trade also helped greatly. German merchants carried not only goods but Lutheran ideas and books to Venice and France; the north German Hanse [a trade league] transported the Reformation to the Scandinavian countries, parceled up with bales of cloth and cargoes of grain; trading links with Germany did much to encourage the growth of Lutheranism in the eastern lands.

Connect *to* History

Analyzing Causes How did politics and economics help spread the Reformation?

Comparing Compare Luther's attitude toward Church leaders with the Catholic attitudes toward him.

SEE SKILLBUILDER HANDBOOK, PAGES 995 and 996

Connect *to* Today

Comparing How do religious leaders spread their ideas today?

 CD-ROM For another perspective on the Reformation, see the World History: Electronic Library of Primary Sources.

TERMS & NAMES

Briefly explain the importance of each of the following to European history from 1300 to 1600.

1. Renaissance
2. humanism
3. secular
4. printing press
5. indulgence
6. Reformation
7. Protestant
8. Peace of Augsburg
9. Catholic Reformation
10. Council of Trent

Interact *with* History

On page 416, you looked at a painting and discussed what you learned about Renaissance society from that painting. Now choose one other piece of art from the chapter. Explain what you learn about Renaissance or Reformation society from that piece of art.

REVIEW QUESTIONS

SECTION 1 *(pages 417-422)*

Italy: Birthplace of the Renaissance

11. How did the merchant class in northern Italy influence the Renaissance?

12. How did art change during the Renaissance?

SECTION 2 *(pages 423-427)*

The Northern Renaissance

13. How did northern European rulers encourage the spread of Renaissance ideas?

14. How does Albrecht Dürer's work reflect Renaissance ideas?

15. What did Christian humanists set out to do, and what method did they use?

SECTION 3 *(pages 428-432)*

Luther Starts the Reformation

16. What act by Martin Luther set off the Reformation?

17. Why did the Holy Roman Emperor go to war against Protestant German princes?

18. How did England establish a state church apart from the Catholic Church?

SECTION 4 *(pages 433-436)*

The Reformation Continues

19. What were the main teachings of John Calvin?

20. What role did the Jesuits play in the Catholic Reformation?

Visual Summary

European Renaissance and Reformation

Effect in Renaissance	Social Change	Effect in Reformation
• Art celebrates individual and personal expression.	• Growing emphasis on individual	• Individuals interpret Bible for themselves.
• Merchants sponsor artists and pay to beautify city.	• Growing prosperity of merchants	• German merchants resent flow of money to Church in Rome.
• Rulers sponsor artists and philosophers.	• Decline of feudalism and growing power of princes and kings	• Rulers defy pope and become Protestant.
• Political, social, and artistic theories spread.	• Printing press and spread of learning	• Luther's 95 Theses spread; Bible printed in vernacular languages, so more people have access.

CRITICAL THINKING

1. POWER OF THE WRITTEN WORD

THEME REVOLUTION Beginning in the 1300s, Europeans overturned many of the structures and ideas of the Middle Ages. How did the printing press contribute to this revolution? Explain.

2. REFORMING THE REFORMER

Choose one of the Protestant groups who came after Luther, such as Calvinists or Anabaptists. Do you think they thought Luther went too far in reforming Catholic Church practices or not far enough? Explain your answer by citing differences in their beliefs.

3. RENAISSANCE AND REFORMATION TODAY

Go back through the chapter and take note of Renaissance and Reformation developments that still influence modern life. Record your findings on a chart like the one shown.

Legacy of the Renaissance and Reformation in Modern Life	
Artistic	Political
Religious	Social

4. ANALYZING PRIMARY SOURCES

In the following excerpt from *The Prince*, Niccolò Machiavelli discusses what a ruler should do to win a good reputation among his subjects. Read the paragraph and answer the questions below it.

> **A VOICE FROM THE PAST**
> A prince must also show himself a lover of merit [excellence], give preferment [promotion] to the able, and honour those who excel in every art. Moreover he must encourage his citizens to follow their callings [professions] quietly, whether in commerce, or agriculture, or any other trade that men follow. . . . [The prince] should offer rewards to whoever does these things, and to whoever seeks in any way to improve his city or state.

- How was Machiavelli's description of a prince's duties influenced by Renaissance values?

- Do you agree with Machiavelli that a prince should do these things? Explain the effect you think such behavior would have on the prince's subjects.

CHAPTER ACTIVITIES

1. LIVING HISTORY: Unit Portfolio Project

THEME CULTURAL INTERACTION Your unit portfolio project focuses on the spread of ideas among cultures (see page 387). For Chapter 17, you might use one of the following ideas to add to your portfolio.

- Design the cover and prepare the table of contents for a 15th-century magazine devoted to Europe's classical heritage. The table of contents should include article titles and a brief summary of each article.

- As Francis I, write a letter to Leonardo da Vinci asking him to retire in France. Explain why you want Italian artists to come to your country.

- With a partner, role-play the reunion of two art students in 1500. One has returned from Italy; the other studied in Flanders. They should compare their techniques and views about art. Audiotape the role-play.

2. CONNECT TO TODAY: Cooperative Learning

THEME RELIGIOUS AND ETHICAL SYSTEMS During the late 20th century, both Protestants and Catholics made delayed responses to the Reformation. In the 1960s, the Catholic Church held a council called Vatican II to promote additional reforms. In 1997, several U.S. Protestant denominations signed a document agreeing to form closer ties with one another.

Work with a team to create a poster that explains one of these developments and how it is a response to the Reformation.

 Use the Internet, news magazines, encyclopedias, or books to research the topic. Look for specific information about what was decided during Vatican II or in the Protestant agreement.

- In your group, decide what are the most important points about Vatican II or the Protestant agreement. Discuss how these points either carry on or undo the work of the Reformation.

- Display your information on a poster. You may convey the information in either a written or an illustrated form, as long as it is clear and accurate.

3. INTERPRETING A TIME LINE

Revisit the Unit Time Line on pages 386–387. On the Chapter 17 time line, identify important writers of the period. Did they write before or after the invention of the printing press?

FOCUS ON ART

Look carefully at this drawing of a machine from the notebooks of Leonardo da Vinci. Notice the blade that curves around the center shaft and the round mechanism at the bottom of the shaft.

- What might happen if the shaft started to turn?

- What do you think Leonardo was trying to invent when he drew this machine?

- What modern machine does this drawing remind you of?

Connect to History A ruler paid Leonardo for some of his ideas for machines. How might a ruler use a machine like the one shown here?

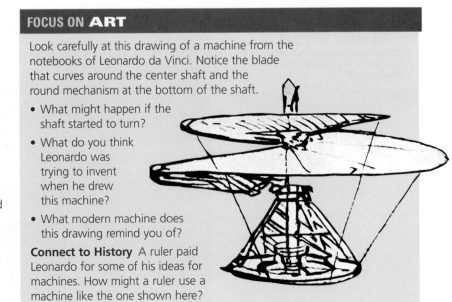

CHAPTER 18

The Muslim World Expands, 1300–1700

PREVIEWING THEMES

Cultural Interaction

As powerful societies moved to expand their empires, Turkish, Mongol, Persian, and Arab ways of life came face to face. The result was a flowering of Islamic culture, which peaked in the 16th century.

Empire Building

Many conquerors emerged in the Muslim world between the 12th and 16th centuries. From their conquests arose three of the great empires of history—the Ottomans in Turkey, the Safavids in Iran, and the Mughals in India.

Power and Authority

The rulers of all three great Muslim empires of this era based their authority on the Islamic religion. Advanced technology and effective artillery supported this authority on the battlefield.

INTERNET CONNECTION

Visit us at **www.mcdougallittell.com** to learn more about the Ottoman, the Safavid, and the Mughal empires.

EMPIRE BUILDERS, 1700

Constantinople was one of the most influential cities of the 15th-century world and seemed invulnerable. Its legend lasted far into the next century when Italian Jacopo Palma Giovane recreated the clamor and chaos of its fall to the **Ottomans** in his painting *The First Attack on Constantinople by the Turks in 1453.* This 51-day Ottoman siege by 125 ships, 100,000 men, and cannons that launched half-ton boulders turned the city into a Muslim outpost.

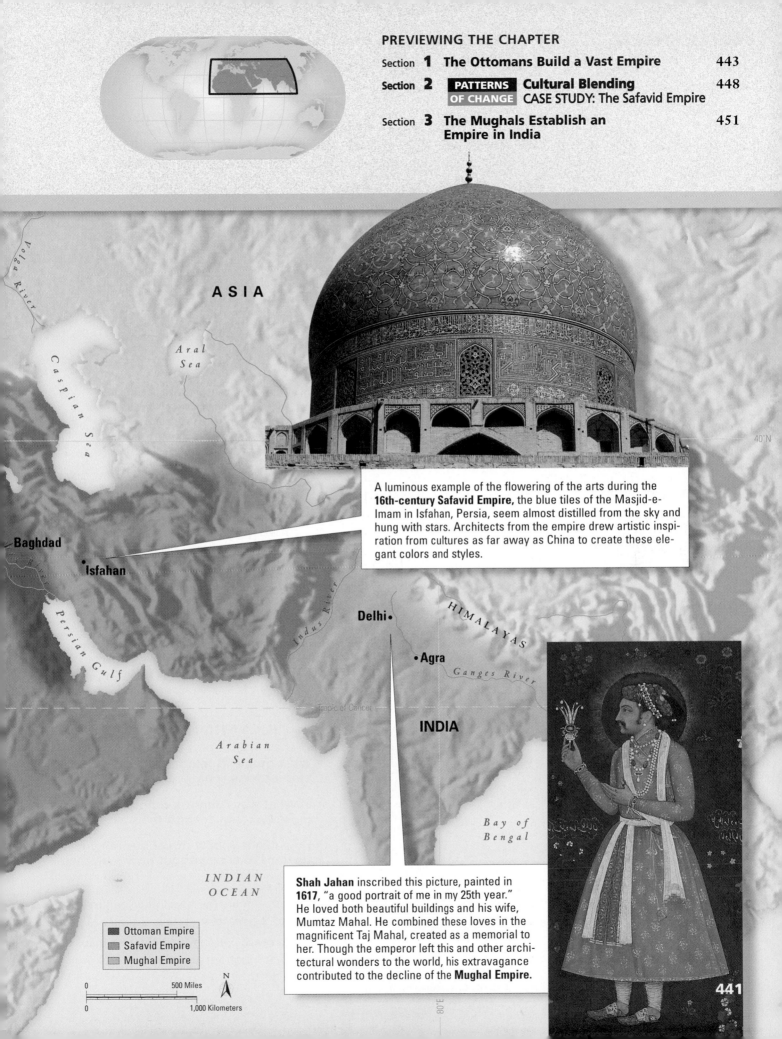

ASIA

A luminous example of the flowering of the arts during the **16th-century Safavid Empire,** the blue tiles of the Masjid-e-Imam in Isfahan, Persia, seem almost distilled from the sky and hung with stars. Architects from the empire drew artistic inspiration from cultures as far away as China to create these elegant colors and styles.

Shah Jahan inscribed this picture, painted in **1617,** "a good portrait of me in my 25th year." He loved both beautiful buildings and his wife, Mumtaz Mahal. He combined these loves in the magnificent Taj Mahal, created as a memorial to her. Though the emperor left this and other architectural wonders to the world, his extravagance contributed to the decline of the **Mughal Empire.**

Ottoman Empire
Safavid Empire
Mughal Empire

0   500 Miles
0   1,000 Kilometers

441

Interact *with* History

You are a 15th-century Ottoman sultan, the ruler of a growing empire. To increase your power and control over the area, you go to war against your neighbors. With a well-trained army and modern weapons, you conquer most of them easily. They do not share your religion and way of life, however, and if you allow them too much freedom, they might rebel. On the other hand, enslaving them and keeping them under strict control might sap your empire's resources.

This Ottoman sultan sees conquered people as an asset to his empire and integrates them into his court.

How will you treat the people you conquer?

The Ottomans force young Christian boys from conquered territories to become soldiers and convert to Islam. Many miss their old way of life terribly and resent serving as slaves to the sultan. Others see this as a way to improve their lives.

Once a slave himself, this man has been rewarded for his competence and good leadership. He kneels and swears allegiance to the sultan, who has appointed him leader of the elite military corps and adviser to the throne.

Military chiefs (left) and scholars (right) wear distinctive headgear to identify their rank. Drawn from all segments of Ottoman society, they are united in their loyal service to the sultan.

EXAMINING *the* ISSUES

- What problems might conquered people present for a conqueror?

- In what ways might a conqueror integrate those he conquers into the society?

- How might people of various religions and customs coexist without giving up their ways of life?

As a class, discuss the ways other empires, such as Rome or Egypt, treated their conquered peoples.

As you read, consider why the Ottomans developed their unique system of slavery. Do you think it was effective?

1 The Ottomans Build a Vast Empire

TERMS & NAMES
- ghazi
- Osman
- Timur the Lame
- Mehmet II
- Suleiman the Lawgiver
- janissary
- *devshirme*

MAIN IDEA

The Ottomans established a Muslim empire that combined many cultures and lasted for more than 600 years.

WHY IT MATTERS NOW

Many modern societies—from Algeria to the Balkan countries—had their origins under Ottoman rule.

SETTING THE STAGE In 1300, the Byzantine Empire had begun to shrink, and the Mongols had destroyed the Turkish Seljuk sultanate, or kingdom, of Rum. Anatolia was inhabited mostly by the descendants of nomadic Turks. They were a militaristic people who had a long history of invading other countries. They were loyal to their own groups and were not united by a strong central power.

Turks Settle in Christian Byzantium

Many Anatolian Turks saw themselves as **ghazis** (GAH·zees), or warriors for Islam. The ghazis were similar to the Christian knights in Europe during the Middle Ages. However, they formed military societies under the leadership of an emir and followed a strict Islamic code of conduct. They raided the territories of the "infidels," or people who didn't believe in Islam. These "infidels" lived on the frontiers of the Byzantine Empire.

Vocabulary
emir: a prince or chief (derived from the Arabic *'amir,* meaning "commander").

Osman Establishes a State The most successful ghazi was **Osman.** People in the West called him Othman, however, and named his followers Ottomans. Osman built a small state in Anatolia between 1300 and 1326. His successors expanded it by buying land, forming alliances with other emirs, and conquering everyone they could.

The Ottomans' military success was largely based on the use of gunpowder. They replaced their archers on horseback with musket-carrying foot soldiers. They also were among the first people to use cannons as offensive weapons. Even heavily walled cities fell to an all-out attack by the Turks.

The second Ottoman leader, Orkhan I, felt strong enough to declare himself sultan, meaning "overlord" or "one with power." And in 1361, the Ottomans captured Adrianople (ay·dree·uh·NOH·puhl), the second most important city in the Byzantine Empire. A new Turkish Empire was on the rise.

The Ottomans acted kindly toward the people they conquered, however. They ruled through local officials appointed by the sultan and often improved the lives of the peasants. Most Muslims were required to serve in Turkish armies but did not have to pay a personal tax to the state. Non-Muslims did not have to serve in the army but had to pay the tax.

Timur the Lame Rebels Most of the conquered peoples seem to have adjusted to this somewhat lenient rule. The rise of the Ottoman Empire was briefly interrupted in the early 1400s, though, by a rebellious warrior and conqueror from Samarkand in central Asia. He was called Timur-i-Lang, or **Timur the Lame,** in his homeland. Europeans called him Tamerlane. Timur claimed to be descended

HISTORY MAKERS

Osman
1258–1326?

Osman I was just one of many ghazi princes who operated along the Byzantine frontier until 1301. At that time he gained sudden fame by defeating a 2,000-man Byzantine army with a much smaller force. This victory drew people eager for adventure, and enabled Osman to undertake larger conquests.

Osman's greatest success came in the last year of his life. That year his forces conquered the city of Bursa in northwest Turkey. Osman himself was too old and weak to lead the battle. Therefore, his son, Orkhan, commanded the troops. When Osman died, he probably had no idea that this conquest marked the birth of one of history's largest and longest-lived empires.

from the Mongol conqueror, Genghis Khan. Although historians doubt the truth of this claim, Timur was certainly as ferocious as Genghis Khan. He was also physically impressive. Tall and with a large head, he had a dark, rosy complexion. This was set off by white hair, which he had had since he was a child.

Timur conquered both Russia and Persia. He also burned the powerful city of Baghdad in present-day Iraq to the ground. In 1398, he swept through northern India, leaving destruction and decaying corpses in his wake. He butchered the inhabitants of Delhi and made a pyramid of their skulls. Moving back west into Anatolia, he crushed the Ottoman forces at the Battle of Ankara in 1402. This defeat halted the expansion of their empire. Timur then took their sultan back to Samarkand in an iron cage. The sultan died in captivity.

Timur himself died three years later on his way to conquer China. His body was returned to Samarkand, where he was buried in a magnificent tomb. That tomb remains a glorious sight today.

Timur the Lame's steely strength blazes from his eyes in this painting by an unknown 14th-century Italian artist.

THINK THROUGH HISTORY
A. Recognizing Effects What were Timur the Lame's accomplishments?

Powerful Sultans Spur Dramatic Expansion

As soon as Timur moved out of Anatolia on the way to China, war broke out among the four sons of the Ottoman sultan. Mehmet I defeated his brothers and took the throne. His son, Murad II, restored the Ottoman military to its former power. Murad defeated the Venetians, invaded Hungary, and overcame an army of Italian crusaders in the Balkans. He was the first of four powerful sultans who kept the Ottoman Empire expanding through 1566.

Mehmet II Conquers Constantinople Murad's son **Mehmet II,** or Mehmet the Conqueror, achieved the most dramatic feat in Ottoman history. By the time Mehmet took power in 1451, the ancient city of Constantinople had shrunk from a population of a million to a mere 50,000. Although it controlled no territory outside its walls, it still dominated the Bosporus Strait. Controlling this waterway meant that it could choke off traffic between the Ottomans' territories in Asia and in the Balkans.

Mehmet II decided to face this situation head-on. "Give me Constantinople!" he thundered, shortly after taking power at age 21. He spent two years building a force of 125 ships and 100,000 foot soldiers. Then, in April 1453, he launched his attack. The Byzantine emperor in Constantinople sent desperate appeals to the Christian West, but only 700 volunteers from Italy responded.

THINK THROUGH HISTORY
B. Analyzing Motives Why was taking Constantinople so important to Mehmet II?

Mehmet's forces began firing on the city walls with mighty cannons. One of these was a 26-foot gun that fired 1,200-pound boulders. Constantinople's 7,000 defenders could barely man all the walls. A chain across the Golden Horn between the Bosporus Strait and the Sea of Marmara kept the Turkish fleet out of the city's harbor. But beginning on the night of April 21, Mehmet's army advanced. They dragged 70 ships over a hill on greased runners from the Bosporus to the harbor. Constantinople was thus under attack from two sides. The city held out for five weeks, but the Turks finally found a break in the wall and gained entry to the city. The Muslim historian Oruc reported:

A VOICE FROM THE PAST

The ghazis, entering by force on every side, found a way in through the breaches in the fortress made by the guns. . . . Mounting on the tower they destroyed the infidels who were inside and entered the city. They looted and plundered. They seized their money and possessions and made their sons and daughters slaves. . . . They plundered for three days, and after three days plunder was forbidden.

ORUC, quoted in *The Muslim Discovery of Europe*

Background
Conquerors did not usually limit the plundering of the cities they captured. Mehmet stopped the sacking of Constantinople after three days to protect the treasures he had won.

Mehmet then proceeded to the Hagia Sophia on the Bosporus. This was the most important church in the Eastern Christian world. Reportedly, he found a soldier hacking at the marble floors. The church now belonged to the Muslim sultan. Therefore, Mehmet insisted that it be treated with respect. He had the soldier put to death. He then declared the Hagia Sophia a mosque. Muslim prayers were held there the first Friday the Ottomans occupied the city.

Mehmet the Conqueror, as he was now called, proved to be an able ruler as well as a magnificent warrior. He opened Constantinople to new citizens of many religions and backgrounds. Jews, Christians, and Muslims, Turks and non-Turks all flowed in. They helped rebuild the city that was now called Istanbul.

Background
Between the reigns of Mehmet II and Selim the Grim, Bayazid II oversaw the internal development and economic growth of the Ottoman Empire.

Selim the Grim Takes Islam's Holy Cities The next important sultan came to power in 1512. He did so by overthrowing his father and murdering his brothers. To protect his position, he also executed his nephews and all but one of his sons. It is small wonder that he is known as Selim the Grim. For all his brutality, Selim was an effective sultan and a great general. In 1514, he defeated the Safavids (suh·FAH·vihdz) of Persia at the Battle of Chaldiran. Then he swept south through Syria and Palestine and into North Africa. At the same time that Cortez was toppling the Aztec Empire in the Americas, Selim captured Mecca and Medina, the holiest cities of Islam. Finally he took Cairo, the intellectual center of the Muslim world. This conquest ended the Egyptian Mameluke Dynasty. The once-great civilization of Egypt had become just another province in the growing Ottoman Empire.

Suleiman the Lawgiver

Mehmet the Conqueror and Selim the Grim had achieved impressive military successes. However, the Ottoman Empire didn't reach its peak size and grandeur until the reign of Selim's son, Suleiman I (SOO·lay·mahn). Suleiman came to the throne in

Ottoman Empire, 1451–1566

- Ottoman Empire, 1451
- Acquisitions to 1481
- Acquisitions to 1521
- Acquisitions to 1566
- ★ Battles

GEOGRAPHY SKILLBUILDER:
Interpreting Maps
1. **Region** By what year did the Ottoman Empire reach its farthest westward extent?
2. **Movement** What landforms might have prevented the Ottomans from expanding farther east?

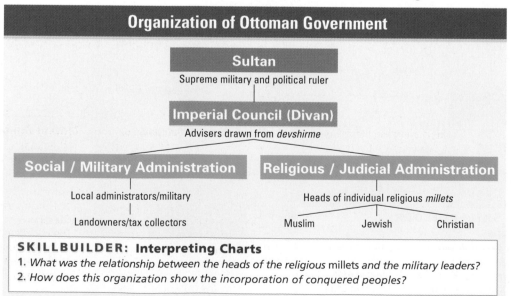

1520 and ruled for 46 years. His own people called him **Suleiman the Lawgiver.** He was known in the West, though, as Suleiman the Magnificent. This title was a tribute to the splendor of his court and to his cultural achievements.

The Empire Reaches Its Limits Suleiman was above all a military leader. He conquered the important city of Belgrade in 1521. The next year, Turkish forces captured the island of Rhodes in the Mediterranean. With that conquest, the Ottomans dominated the whole eastern Mediterranean.

Applying their immense naval power, the Ottomans captured Tripoli. They then continued conquering peoples along the North African coastline. Finally, they reached the Moroccan border. Although the Ottomans occupied only the coastal cities of Africa, they managed to control trade routes to the interior of the continent.

In 1525, Suleiman advanced into Hungary and Austria, throwing central Europe into a panic. Suleiman's armies then pushed to the outskirts of Vienna, Austria. But there the Ottoman expansion ended. When the 1529 siege of Vienna failed, Suleiman devoted himself to domestic affairs for two years. He then moved his forces east to deal with border uprisings with Safavid Persia. Reigning from Istanbul, Suleiman had waged war with central Europeans, North Africans, and central Asians. He had become the most powerful monarch on earth. Only Charles V, head of the Hapsburg Empire in Europe, came close to rivaling his power.

Highly Structured Social Organization Suleiman's massive Ottoman Empire required an efficient government structure and social organization. The empire was a complex military state. The Ottoman family—a dynasty that ruled for 600 years—held the power. Surrounding the family was the palace bureaucracy. It was staffed by the sultan's 20,000 personal slaves.

Among the sultan's slaves were the **janissaries.** This elite force of 30,000 was drawn from the peoples of conquered Christian territories as part of a policy called **devshirme** (dehv·SHEER·meh). Under the *devshirme* system, the sultan's army took boys from their families, educated them, converted them to Islam, and trained them as soldiers. Their superb discipline made them the heart of the Ottoman war machine. In fact, Christian families sometimes bribed officials to take their children into the janissary corps, because the brightest ones could rise to high government posts. The Ottomans also took non-Muslim girls from their families to become slaves to the wealthy.

In accordance with Islamic law, the Ottomans granted freedom of worship to other religious communities—particularly to Christians and Jews. They treated these communities as *millets*, or nations. They allowed each to follow its own religious laws and

Suleiman the Lawgiver's magnificent turban marked him as an influential man. But it was his outstanding contributions to Ottoman territory and culture that made his mark in history.

THINK THROUGH HISTORY
C. Making Inferences What were the advantages and disadvantages of the *devshirme* system to the recruited slaves?

Organization of Ottoman Government

Sultan
Supreme military and political ruler

Imperial Council (Divan)
Advisers drawn from *devshirme*

Social / Military Administration
Local administrators/military
Landowners/tax collectors

Religious / Judicial Administration
Heads of individual religious *millets*
Muslim   Jewish   Christian

SKILLBUILDER: Interpreting Charts
1. *What was the relationship between the heads of the religious* millets *and the military leaders?*
2. *How does this organization show the incorporation of conquered peoples?*

practices. The head of the *millets* reported to the sultan and his staff. This patchwork system kept conflict among people of the various religions to a minimum. But it may have sowed the seeds of modern ethnic conflicts in the area.

Cultural Achievements Binding the Ottoman Empire together in a workable social structure was surely Suleiman's crowning achievement. Suleiman was required to follow Islamic law, which covered most social matters. He did, however, simplify the system of taxation and reduce the government bureaucracy. These two changes bettered the daily life of almost every citizen. These reforms helped earn him the title of Lawgiver.

Suleiman had broad interests, which contributed to the cultural achievements of the empire. Even amid his many military campaigns, he found time to study poetry, history, geography, astronomy, mathematics, and architecture. He employed one of the world's finest architects, Sinan, who was probably from Albania. Sinan's masterpiece, the Mosque of Suleiman, is an immense complex topped with domes and half domes. It includes four schools, a college, a library, a bath, and a hospital.

Art and literature also flourished under Suleiman's rule. Both painters and poets looked to Persia and Arabia for models. The works that they produced used these foreign influences to express original Ottoman ideas in the Turkish style.

Despite Suleiman's magnificent social and cultural achievements and his splendid city of Istanbul, though, the Ottoman Empire was losing ground. Its decline had already begun.

THINK THROUGH HISTORY
D. Summarizing
What were the major cultural achievements of Suleiman's reign?

Suleiman's artistic nature was reflected in everything he did, including his signature (above).

The Empire Declines Slowly

Suleiman himself set the stage for this decline. Perhaps fearing for his position, he killed his ablest son and drove another into exile. His third son, the incompetent Selim II, inherited the throne. In 1571, Spain and Italy destroyed Selim's Turkish fleet at the Battle of Lepanto. This was a rare defeat for the Ottomans' superior sea power.

At the same time, corruption was eating away at the government. As each sultan grew older, his possible heirs began jockeying for power. It became customary for each new sultan to have his brothers strangled with the silk string of a bow. The sultan would then keep his sons prisoner in the harem, cutting them off from education or contact with the world. This practice produced a long line of weak, ignorant sultans who eventually brought ruin on the empire.

The great Ottoman Empire crumbled slowly. It continued to influence the world into the early 20th century. It was finally dissolved with the creation of the nation of Turkey after World War I. But throughout its long life, other Muslim empires were on the rise.

Section 1 Assessment

1. TERMS & NAMES

Identify
- ghazi
- Osman
- Timur the Lame
- Mehmet II
- Suleiman the Lawgiver
- janissary
- *devshirme*

2. TAKING NOTES

Using a chart like the one below, list the main rulers of the Ottoman Empire and their chief accomplishments.

Ottoman Ruler	Major Accomplishment

Rank these leaders in order of their impact on the Ottoman Empire.

3. EVALUATING DECISIONS

Do you think that the Ottomans were wise in staffing their military and government with slaves? Why or why not?

THINK ABOUT
- the loyalty of slaves to the sultan
- the training slaves received
- others who might have served in the government

4. ANALYZING THEMES

Empire Building Do you think that Suleiman's religious tolerance helped or hurt the Ottoman Empire? Explain.

THINK ABOUT
- Suleiman's treatment of non-Muslims
- the effect on the individual religious groups
- the long-term effect on the empire as a whole

Cultural Blending

2

CASE STUDY: The Safavid Empire

TERMS & NAMES
- Safavid
- Isma'il
- Shah Abbas
- Isfahan

MAIN IDEA	WHY IT MATTERS NOW
Many world cultures incorporate influences from various peoples and traditions.	Modern Iran, which plays a key role in global politics, is descended from the culturally diverse Safavid Empire.

SETTING THE STAGE The Ottoman Empire provides a striking example of how interaction among peoples can produce a blending of cultures. This mixture often combines the best of contributing cultures in new and exciting ways.

Patterns of Cultural Blending

As the 17th-century British poet John Donne observed, "No man is an island." But no group of people, or culture, is an island, either. Throughout history, peoples have mingled and interacted, giving rise to new cultural blends.

Causes of Cultural Blending Cultural blending usually occurs in places where two or more cultures interact. This interaction most often is prompted by one or a combination of the following four activities: migration, trade, conquest, and pursuit of religious converts or religious freedom. Societies that are able to benefit from cultural blending are open to new ways and willing to adapt and change.

The blending that contributed to the culture of the Ottomans, for example, depended on all of these activities except migration. Surrounded by the peoples of Christian Byzantium, the Turks were motivated to win both territory for their empire and converts to their Muslim religion. Suleiman's interest in learning and culture prompted him to bring the best foreign artists and scholars to his court.

THINK THROUGH HISTORY
A. Summarizing
What four activities often contribute to cultural blending?

Cultural Blending Through History Similar patterns of blending have occurred throughout the world and across the ages. A few examples are shown below.

PATTERNS OF CHANGE: Cultural Blending

Location	Interacting Cultures	Reason for Interaction	Some Results of Interaction
India—1000 B.C.	Aryan and Dravidian Indian	Migration	Vedic culture, forerunner of Hinduism
East Africa—A.D. 700	Arab, African, Indian, Islamic, Christian	Trade, religious converts	New trade language, Swahili
Russia—A.D. 1000	Christian and Slavic	Religious converts	Eastern Christianity, Russian identity
Mexico—A.D. 1500	Spanish and Aztec Indian	Conquest	Mestizo culture, Mexican Catholicism
United States—A.D. 1900	European, Asian, Caribbean	Migration, religious freedom	Cultural diversity

SKILLBUILDER: Interpreting Charts
1. *What aspects of culture, such as language and religion, did these cultural blendings affect?*
2. *What evidence of cultural blending do you see in the United States today?*

The Safavids Build a Shi'i Empire

Conquest and ongoing cultural interaction also fueled the development of another empire—the **Safavids.** Originally, the Safavids were members of an Islamic religious brotherhood. They were named after their founder, Safi al-Din, who died in 1334. Although the Safavids were of Iranian origin, they claimed that they were descended from the prophet Muhammad. In the 15th century, the Safavids aligned themselves with the Shi'i branch of Islam.

The Shi'i Safavids were persecuted on religious grounds by the Ottoman Sunni Muslims. This treatment was a departure from the Sunni's traditional religious tolerance. The Safavids were also squeezed geographically between the Ottomans and Uzbek tribespeople. (See the map on page 450.) To protect themselves from these potential enemies, the Safavids concentrated on building a powerful army.

Isma'il Conquers Persia The Safavid military became a force to reckon with. They wore unique red headgear with 12 folds, and so became known as the "redheads." In 1499, the leader of the redheads was a 14-year-old named **Isma'il** (is·MAH·eel). Despite his youth, he was a brilliant warrior. Within two years, he had seized most of what is now Iran. To celebrate his achievement, he took the ancient Persian title of shah, or king. He also established Shi'i Islam as the state religion:

A VOICE FROM THE PAST

[Isma'il] is loved and revered by his people as a god, and especially by his soldiers, many of whom enter into battle without armour, expecting their master . . . to watch over them in the fight. . . . The name of God is forgotten throughout Persia and only that of Isma'il is remembered.

A 16TH-CENTURY VENETIAN TRAVELER, quoted in *Encyclopedia of Islam*

Despite the reverence of his people, however, Isma'il became a religious tyrant. Any citizen who did not convert to Shi'ism was put to death. Isma'il destroyed the Sunni population of Baghdad in his confrontation with the Ottomans. Their leader, Selim the Grim, later ordered the execution of all Shi'a in the Ottoman empire. As many as 40,000 died. Their final faceoff was at the Battle of Chaldiran in 1514. But the confrontation between the cultures did not end then. In fact, it still continues today.

Isma'il's son Tahmasp took up the struggle. He expanded the Safavid Empire up to the Caucasus Mountains northeast of Turkey and brought Christians under Safavid rule. In adding this territory to the empire, Tahmasp laid the groundwork for the golden age of the Safavids.

Cultural Blending During the Reign of Shah Abbas This golden age came under **Shah Abbas,** or Abbas the Great. He took the throne in 1587. During his reign, he helped create a Safavid culture that drew from the best of the Ottoman, Persian, and Arab worlds.

Shah Abbas reformed both military and civilian aspects of life. He limited the power of the military redheads. He then created two new armies that would be loyal to him alone. One of these was an army of Persians. The other was a force like the Ottoman janissaries, which Abbas recruited from the Christian north. He equipped both of these armies with modern artillery. Abbas also reformed his government. He punished corruption severely and promoted only officials who proved their competence and loyalty.

Shah Abbas established relations with Europe. As a result, industry and art flourished. He also brought Chinese artisans to the

THINK THROUGH HISTORY
B. Making Inferences Which of Isma'il's traits do you think made him such a successful conqueror?

HISTORY MAKERS

**Shah Abbas
1571–1629**

Shah Abbas had a rocky road to the Safavid throne. When Abbas was only two, Uzbek tribespeople killed his mother and brother, and Abbas was taken into hiding. He reclaimed his kingdom at age 14.

As shah, he was committed to his nation's welfare. Legends say that he disguised himself and mingled with the common people to learn about and serve them better.

Abbas's greatest legacy, however, was probably his capital city, Isfahan. Its broad boulevards, extensive gardens, and magnificent buildings prompted a popular Persian saying of the time, "Isfahan is half the world."

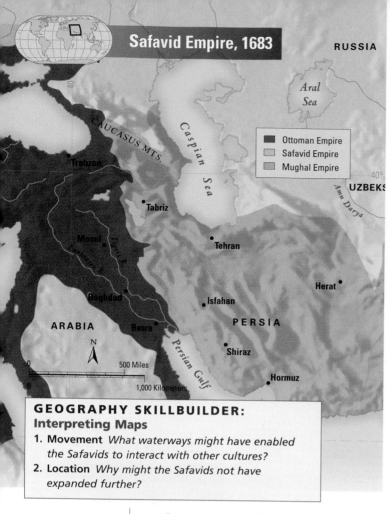

Safavid Empire, 1683

RUSSIA

Aral Sea

Caspian Sea

CAUCASUS MTS.

Trabzon

Tabriz

Mosul

Tehran

Baghdad

Isfahan

Herat

ARABIA

Basra

PERSIA

Shiraz

Hormuz

Persian Gulf

500 Miles

1,000 Kilometers

UZBEKS

40°

Legend:
- Ottoman Empire
- Safavid Empire
- Mughal Empire

GEOGRAPHY SKILLBUILDER:
Interpreting Maps
1. **Movement** *What waterways might have enabled the Safavids to interact with other cultures?*
2. **Location** *Why might the Safavids not have expanded further?*

Safavid Empire. This collaboration gave rise to gorgeous artwork. These decorations beautified the many mosques, palaces, and marketplaces of Abbas's rebuilt capital city of **Isfahan.**

The most important result of Western influence on the Safavids, however, may have been the demand for Persian carpets. This demand helped change carpet weaving from a local craft to a national industry.

The Dynasty Declines Quickly Shah Abbas unfortunately made the same mistake the Ottoman monarch Suleiman made. He killed or blinded his ablest sons. Abbas was succeeded by his incompetent grandson, Safi. This pampered young prince led the Safavids down the same road to decline that the Ottomans had taken, only more quickly.

By 1722, tribal armies from Afghanistan were taking over the eastern portions of the Safavid realm. Ottoman forces were attacking from the west. Some historians claim that these attacks marked the downfall of the Safavids.

In 1736, however, a ruler from a Sunni family—Nadir Shah Afshar—took command. He conquered all the way to India and created a new Persian empire. But Nadir Shah was a cruel man as well as an inspired military leader. One of his own troops assassinated him. With Nadir Shah's death in 1747, his empire also fell apart.

THINK THROUGH HISTORY
C. Comparing In what ways were Shah Abbas and Suleiman the Lawgiver similar?

The Safavid Legacy Although the Safavid Empire died out as a political power, the culture that it produced endured. In this culture, the worldly and artistic features of Persian civilization mingled with the religious elements of Shi'ism. The Safavids also borrowed many ways from their enemies, the Ottomans. They based their government on the Ottoman model, welcomed foreigners into their empire, and created a slave army similar to the janissaries.

At the same time that the Safavids flourished, cultural blending and conquest led to the growth of a new empire in India, as you will learn in Section 3.

Section ❷ Assessment

1. TERMS & NAMES
Identify
• Safavid
• Isma'il
• Shah Abbas
• Isfahan

2. TAKING NOTES
Using a cause-and-effect diagram like the one below, indicate the events that enabled the Safavids to build a powerful empire.

Events   Effect

⟶ Powerful Safavid Empire

3. ANALYZING MOTIVES
Within a century after the Safavids adopted Shi'i Islam, their leader, Isma'il, became a religious tyrant. Why might he have become so intolerant?
THINK ABOUT
• the persecution of Safavids by Ottoman Sunni Muslims
• the role of religion in Safavid life
• the geographic location of the Safavid Empire

4. THEME ACTIVITY
Cultural Interaction Write a letter from Shah Abbas to a Chinese artist persuading him to come teach and work in the Safavid Empire. In the letter, explain why the Safavids are interested in Chinese art and how they treat people from other cultures.

The Mughals Establish an Empire in India

TERMS & NAMES
- Mughal
- Babur
- Akbar
- Jahangir
- Nur Jahan
- Sikh
- Shah Jahan
- Taj Mahal
- Aurangzeb

MAIN IDEA

The Mughal Empire brought Turks, Persians, and Indians together in a vast empire.

WHY IT MATTERS NOW

The legacy of great art and deep social division left by the Mughal Empire still influences southern Asia.

SETTING THE STAGE In the late 15th century, India included lush lands studded with cities and temples. The Hindu lower classes labored in the service of their Muslim or Hindu masters. At the same time, nomadic warriors roamed the highlands to the northwest, eager for battle.

Early History of the Mughal Empire

The people who invaded India called themselves **Mughals,** which means "Mongols." The land they invaded had been through a long period of turmoil. The Gupta Empire crumbled in the 600s. First, Arabs invaded. Then, warlike Muslim tribes from central Asia carved northwestern India into many small kingdoms. Those kingdoms were ruled by leaders called Rajputs, or "sons of kings."

Ongoing Conflicts The 8th century began with a long, bloody clash between Hindus and Muslims in this fragmented land. For almost 300 years, though, the Hindus held off the Arab Muslims. They were able to advance only as far as the Indus River valley. Starting around the year 1000, however, well-trained Turkish armies swept into India. Led by Sultan Mahmud (muh·MOOD) of Ghazni, they devastated Indian cities and temples in 17 brutal campaigns. These attacks left the region weakened and vulnerable to other conquerors. Delhi eventually became the capital of a loose empire of Turkish warlords called the Delhi Sultanate. These sultans treated the Hindus as conquered people.

Between the 13th and 16th centuries, 33 different sultans ruled this divided territory from its seat in Delhi. In 1398, Timur the Lame destroyed Delhi so completely that, according to one witness, "for two whole months, not a bird moved in

Growth of the Mughal Empire, 1526–1707

- Mughal Empire, 1526—Babur
- Added by 1605—Akbar
- Added by 1707—Aurangzeb

Kabul
KASHMIR
PUNJAB
Lahore
Indus R.
HIMALAYAS
Brahmaputra R.
Delhi
Agra
Ganges R.
Benares
Patna
BENGAL
Dacca
Tropic of Cancer
Calcutta
Surat
Arabian Sea
Bombay
DECCAN PLATEAU
Bay of Bengal
Madras
Calicut
Pondicherry
Cochin
CEYLON

0   300 Miles
0   600 Kilometers

GEOGRAPHY SKILLBUILDER: Interpreting Maps

1. **Movement** *During which time period was the most territory added to the Mughal Empire?*
2. **Location** *What landform might have prevented the empire from expanding farther east?*

451

the city." Delhi eventually was rebuilt. But it was not until the 16th century that a leader arose who would unify the empire.

Babur Founds an Empire In 1494, an 11-year-old boy named **Babur** inherited a kingdom in the area that is now Uzbekistan and Tajikistan. It was only a tiny kingdom, and his elders soon took it away and drove him south. But the boy built up an army. In the years that followed, he swept down into India and laid the groundwork for the vast Mughal Empire.

Babur was a strong, sensitive leader. According to legend, he could leap a wall holding a man under each arm. But he also wrote poetry and loved art and gardens. He was a brilliant general as well. In 1526, for example, Babur led 12,000 troops to victory against an army of 100,000 commanded by a sultan of Delhi. Perhaps it was his sensitivity to his soldiers that made him such an effective leader:

> **A VOICE FROM THE PAST**
> Some in the army were very anxious and full of fear. Nothing recommends anxiety and fear. . . . Why? Because what God has fixed in eternity cannot be changed. But . . . it was no reproach to be afraid and anxious. . . . Why? Because those thus anxious and afraid were there with a two or three months' journey between them and their homes; our affair was with a foreign tribe and people; none knew their tongue, nor did they know ours.
>
> **BABUR,** *The Babur-Nama (Memoirs of Babur)*

A year later, Babur also defeated a massive Rajput army. After Babur's death, his incompetent son, Humayun, lost most of the territory Babur had gained. Babur's 13-year-old grandson took over the throne after Humayun's death.

Background
One of the secrets of Babur's success is that he lashed cannons together to fire massive volleys against troops mounted on elephants.

HISTORY MAKERS

Akbar
1542–1605
Akbar was brilliant and curious, especially about religion. He even invented a religion of his own—the "Divine Faith"—which combined elements of Hinduism, Jainism, Christianity, and Sufism. The religion attracted few followers, however, and offended Muslims so much that they attempted a brief revolt against Akbar in 1581. When he died, so did the "Divine Faith."

Surprisingly, despite his wisdom and his achievements, Akbar could not read. He hired others to read to him from his library of 24,000 books.

The Golden Age of Akbar

Babur's grandson was called **Akbar,** which means "Great One." Akbar certainly lived up to his name by ruling India with wisdom and tolerance from 1556 to 1605.

A Liberal Ruler Akbar was a Muslim, and he firmly defended religious freedom. He proved his tolerance by marrying, among others, two Hindus, a Christian, and a Muslim. He allowed his wives to practice their religious rituals in the palace. He proved his tolerance again by abolishing both the tax on Hindu pilgrims and the hated *jizya*, or tax on non-Muslims. He even appointed a Spanish Jesuit to tutor his second son. Akbar was a genius at cultural blending.

Akbar governed through a bureaucracy of officials. Natives and foreigners, Hindus and Muslims, could all rise to high office. This approach contributed to the quality of his government. Akbar's chief finance minister, Todar Mal, for example, created a clever—and effective—taxation policy. He calculated the tax as a percent of the value of the peasants' crops, similar to the present-day U.S. graduated income tax. Because this tax was fair and affordable, the number of peasants who paid it increased. This payment brought in much needed money for the empire.

Akbar's land policies had more mixed results. He gave generous land grants to his bureaucrats. After they died, however, he reclaimed the lands and distributed them as he saw fit. On the positive side, this policy prevented the growth of feudal aristocracies. On the other hand, it did not encourage dedication and hard work by the Mughal officials. Their children would not inherit the land or benefit from their parents' work. So the officials apparently saw no point in devoting themselves to their property.

THINK THROUGH HISTORY
A. Comparing In what ways were Akbar's attitudes toward religion similar to those of Suleiman the Lawgiver?

A Military Conqueror For all his humanity, however, Akbar recognized military power as the root of his strength. He believed in war for its own sake. "A monarch should ever be intent on conquest," he said, "otherwise his neighbors rise in arms against him." Like the Safavids and the Ottomans, Akbar equipped his armies with heavy artillery. Cannons enabled him to crack into walled cities and extend his rule into much of the Deccan plateau. In a brilliant move, he appointed some Rajputs as officers. In this way he turned potential enemies into allies. This combination of military power and political wisdom enabled Akbar to unify a land of at least 100 million people—more than all of Europe put together.

A Flowering of Culture As Akbar extended the Mughal Empire, he welcomed influences from the many cultures it included. This cultural mingling affected art, education, politics, and the language as well. Persian was the language of Akbar's court and of high culture. The common people, however, spoke Hindi, a mixture of Persian and a local language. Hindi remains one of the most widely spoken languages in India today. Out of the Mughal armies, where soldiers of many backgrounds rubbed shoulders, came yet another new language. This language was Urdu, which means "from the soldier's camp." A blend of Arabic, Persian, and Hindi, Urdu is today the official language of Pakistan.

The arts flourished at the Mughal court, especially in the form of book illustrations. These small, highly detailed and colorful paintings were called miniatures. They were brought to a peak of perfection in the Safavid Empire. Babur's son, Humayun, brought two masters of this art to his court to teach it to the Mughals. Some of the most famous Mughal miniatures adorned the *Akbarnamah* ("Book of Akbar"), the story of the great emperor's campaigns and deeds. Indian art drew from Western traditions as well. After Akbar's time, for example, portraits of the Mughal emperors showed them wearing halos like Western saints.

Literature and Architecture Hindu literature also enjoyed a revival in Akbar's time. Akbar established a large library. The poet Tulsi Das, for example, was a contemporary of Akbar's. He retold the epic love story of Rama and Sita from the 4th-century B.C. Indian poem *Ramayana* (rah·MAH·yuh·nuh) in Hindi. This retelling, the *Ramcaritmanas,* is now even more popular than the original.

Akbar devoted himself to architecture, too. The style developed under his reign is still known as Akbar period architecture. Its massive, but graceful, structures are decorated with intricate stonework that depicts Hindu themes. The capital city of Fatehpur Sikri is one of the most important examples of this type of architecture. Akbar had this red-sandstone city built to thank a holy man who had predicted the birth of his first son. It included a great mosque, many palaces and other houses, as well as official and religious buildings. This magnificent city was abandoned after only 15 years because its water supply ran out. Ironically, the son whose birth it honored eventually rebelled against his father. He may even have plotted to cause his father's death.

Akbar's Successors

With Akbar's death in 1605, the Mughal court changed to deal with the changing times. The next three emperors were powerful men, and each left his mark on the Mughal Empire.

Background
In Hindu myth, Rama was the perfect king, one of the personalities of the protector god, Vishnu.

Headgear had symbolic importance in the society of Hindus in India. An important person's turban might include 50 yards of cloth wound around and held together with a jeweled pin such as this one.

Since World War II, India has seen the rise of several powerful women. Unlike Nur Jahan, however, they achieved power on their own—not through their husbands.

Indira Gandhi headed the Congress-I Party and dominated Indian politics for almost 30 years. She was elected prime minister in 1966 and again in 1980. Gandhi was assassinated in 1984 by Sikh terrorists.

In neighboring Pakistan, Benazir Bhutto (shown below), took charge of the Pakistan People's Party after her father was executed by his political enemies. She won election as her country's prime minister in 1988—the first woman to run a modern Muslim state. Pakistan's president unseated her, but she was reelected in 1993. In 1996, however, the president again ousted her from office. The supreme court ruled that her government was corrupt. Ironically, that was partially because her husband had made corrupt business deals.

Jahangir and Nur Jahan Akbar's son called himself **Jahangir** (juh·hahn·GEER)—"Grasper of the World." And he certainly did hold India in a powerful grasp. It was not his own hand in the iron glove, though, since Jahangir was an extremely weak ruler. For most of his reign, he left the affairs of state to his wife.

Jahangir's wife was the Persian princess **Nur Jahan.** She was a remarkably talented women with a variety of interests. Tiger hunting was among her favorite pastimes, and she rode horses with legendary skill. She composed poetry whenever the mood struck her. She also designed clothes that still influence Indian fashions. Above all, she was a brilliant politician who perfectly understood the use of power. As the real ruler of India from 1611 to 1622, she installed her father as prime minister in the Mughal court. She saw Jahangir's son Khusrau as her ticket to future power. But when Khusrau rebelled against his father, Nur Jahan ousted him. She then shifted her favor to another son, the future emperor, Shah Jahan.

This rejection of Khusrau affected more than the political future of the empire. It was also the basis of a long and bitter religious conflict. Both Nur Jahan and Jahangir rejected Akbar's religious tolerance and tried to promote only Islam in the Mughal state. When Khusrau rebelled against his father, he turned to the **Sikhs.** This was a nonviolent religious group whose doctrines blended Buddhism, Hinduism, and Sufism (Islamic mysticism). Their leader, Guru Arjun, sheltered Khusrau and defended him. In response, the Mughal rulers had Arjun arrested and tortured to death. The Sikhs thus became the target of the Mughals' particular hatred.

THINK THROUGH HISTORY
B. Analyzing Causes How did the Mughals' dislike of the Sikhs develop?

Shah Jahan Like his grandfather, **Shah Jahan** was a cultured man. He could not tolerate competition, however, and secured his throne by assassinating all his possible rivals. But he did have a great passion for two things: beautiful buildings and his wife Mumtaz Mahal (moom·TAHZ mah·HAHL). Nur Jahan had arranged this marriage between Jahangir's son and her niece for political reasons. Shah Jahan, however, fell genuinely in love with his Persian princess.

In 1631, Mumtaz Mahal died at age 38 giving birth to her 14th child. "Empire has no sweetness," the heartbroken Shah Jahan lamented, "life has no relish for me now." To enshrine his wife's memory, he ordered that a tomb be built "as beautiful as she was beautiful." Fine white marble and fabulous jewels were gathered from many parts of Asia. Some 20,000 workers labored for 22 years to build the famous tomb now known as the **Taj Mahal.** This memorial has been called one of the most beautiful buildings in the world. Its towering marble dome and slender towers look like lace and seem to change color as the sun moves across the sky. The inside of the building is as magnificent as the exterior. It is a glittering garden of thousands of carved marble flowers inlaid with tiny precious stones.

Shah Jahan also built the Red Fort at Delhi and completed the Peacock Throne, a priceless seat of gold encrusted with diamonds, rubies, emeralds, and pearls. The throne has a canopy that displays the figure of a peacock lined with blue sapphires. This magnificent throne was lost to the conqueror Nadir Shah in 1739.

Background
Shortly after Shah Jahan spent huge sums of money on the Taj Mahal, King Louis XIV began building his elaborate palace at Versailles. Both rulers heavily taxed their people to pay for their extravagance.

The People Suffer But while Shah Jahan was building lovely things, his country was suffering. A Dutch merchant who was in India during a famine at that time reported that ". . . men abandoned towns and villages and wandered helplessly . . . eyes sunk deep in head, lips pale and covered with slime, the skin hard, the bones showing through. . . ." Farmers needed tools, roads, and ways of irrigating their crops and dealing with India's harsh environment. What they got instead were taxes and more taxes to support the building of monuments, their rulers' extravagant living, and war.

THINK THROUGH HISTORY
C. Making Inferences Do you think Shah Jahan's policies helped or harmed the Mughal Empire?

All was not well in the royal court either. When Shah Jahan became ill in 1657, his four sons scrambled for the throne. The third son, **Aurangzeb** (AWR·uhng·zehb), moved first and most decisively. In a bitter civil war, he executed his older brother, who was his most serious rival. Then he arrested his father and put him in prison. When Shah Jahan died several years later, a mirror was found in his room, angled so that he could gaze from his cell at the reflection of the Taj Mahal. Aurangzeb, however, had his eyes on the empire.

Aurangzeb Aurangzeb ruled from 1658 to 1707. He was a master at military strategy and an aggressive empire builder. Although he expanded the Mughal holdings to their greatest size, the power of the empire weakened during his reign.

This loss of power was due largely to Aurangzeb's oppression of the people. He rigidly enforced Islamic laws, outlawing drinking, gambling, and other vices. He also appointed censors to police his subjects' morals and make sure they prayed at the appointed times. He also tried to erase all the gains Hindus had made under Akbar. For example, he brought back the hated tax on non-Muslims and dismissed Hindus from high positions in his government. He banned the construction of new temples and had Hindu monuments destroyed. Not surprisingly, these actions outraged the Hindus.

The Hindu Rajputs, whom Akbar had converted from potential enemies to allies, rebelled. Aurangzeb defeated them repeatedly, but never completely. In the southwest, militant Hindus called Marathas founded their own breakaway state. Aurangzeb captured their leader, but the Marathas turned to guerrilla warfare. Aurangzeb could never conquer them. Meanwhile, the Sikhs had transformed themselves into a militant brotherhood. They began to build a state in the Punjab, an area in northwest India.

Set in a formal garden and mirrored in a reflecting pool, the Taj Mahal draws tourists to Agra, southeast of New Delhi in India. It remains a monument to both love and the Mughal Empire.

The Muslim World Expands **455**

Mughal Society News

Nur Jahan is the power behind the throne and even designs the royal wardrobe.

Diet News

A person who does a good deed for the Mughal emperor may be rewarded with his weight in rupees (a unit of money). In fact, both the emperor's flute player and his astrologer recently received this generous prize. Sources said that the stout astrologer pocketed 200 rupees more than the musician.

The Doctor Is In

When a woman of the Mughal court gets sick, she must not be seen by a male doctor. The doctor first wraps his head in a cashmere shawl, which serves as a blindfold. He follows a servant into the women's quarters, where the patient lies hidden behind a curtain. If she needs to have a wound treated, the patient sticks her arm or leg out through the curtain. The doctor then examines the patient from his side of the curtain.

Woman of the Week

Naming Nur Jahan, the monarch's favorite queen "Woman of the Week" is a king-size understatement. Woman of the century is more like it. But people in the know go even further and call her "Light of the World"—and for good reason. In addition to being the true power behind Jahangir's throne, she excels in the arts, business, and sports.

Nur Jahan's bold, original designs for cloth, dresses with long trains, and even carpets dominate India's fashion scene. From her harem, Nur Jahan runs a bustling trade in indigo and cloth. She's also an accomplished huntress, and last week killed four tigers.

The Shopping Corner

If you're trying to impress the emperor, bring him a unique gift. This is how he voted on recent offerings:

Thumbs Up	Thumbs Down
• walnut-sized ruby	• faded velvet
• portraits of English royal family	• mirror with loose frame
• unusual fish	• map showing a compressed view of India

Moving Day

Relocating the Mughal royal court requires as much effort as moving a small city. Simply transporting the royal tents requires 100 elephants, 500 camels, 400 carts, and 100 human bearers. When the procession stops for the night, it spans a length of 20 miles.

Connect *to* History

Making Inferences What can you conclude about the lives of women in the Mughal court?

SEE SKILLBUILDER HANDBOOK, PAGE 1005

Connect *to* Today

Women's Studies Using information from the "Connect to Today" feature on page 454 and the library or the Internet, research the public role of women in several Muslim cultures today. How has the role of women changed since Mughal times?

Aurangzeb had to levy oppressive taxes to pay for the wars against these increasing numbers of enemies. He had done away with all taxes not authorized by Islamic law, so he doubled the taxes on Hindu merchants. This increased tax burden deepened the Hindus' bitterness and led to further rebellion. As a result, Aurangzeb needed to raise more money to increase his army. The more territory he conquered, the more desperate his situation became.

The Empire's Decline and Decay

By the end of Aurangzeb's reign, he had drained the empire of its resources. Most of his subjects felt little or no loyalty to him. According to a Dutch observer, "The condition of the common people in India is very miserable. . . . Their huts are low, built generally of mud . . . their bedding is scanty and thin . . . of little use when the weather is bitterly cold. . . . The nobles live in indescribable luxury and extravagance, caring only to indulge themselves whilst they can in every kind of pleasure." Over two million people died in a famine while Aurangzeb was away waging war.

THINK THROUGH HISTORY
D. Recognizing Effects How did Aurangzeb's personal qualities and political policies affect the Mughal Empire?

As the power of the central state weakened, the power of local lords grew. After Aurangzeb's death, his sons fought a war of succession. Bahadur, who won the war, was over 60 when he gained the throne. This exhausted emperor did not last long. In fact, three emperors reigned in the 12 years after Aurengzeb died. By the end of this period, the Mughal emperor was nothing but a wealthy figurehead. He ruled not a united empire but a patchwork of independent states.

As the Mughal Empire was rising and falling and creating its cultural legacy, Western traders were slowly building their own power. The Portuguese were the first Europeans to reach India. In fact, they arrived just before Babur did. But they were ousted by the Dutch, who, in turn, gave way to the French and the English. The great Mughal emperors did not feel threatened by the European traders. Shah Jahan let the English build a fortified trading post at Madras. In 1661, Aurangzeb casually handed them the port of Bombay. Aurangzeb had no idea that he had given India's next conquerors their first foothold in a future empire.

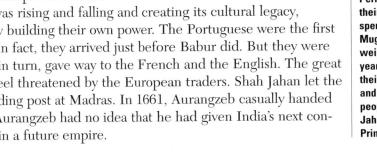

Perhaps to offset their excessive spending, the Mughal rulers were weighed once a year. They donated their weight in gold and silver to the people. Here, Jahangir weighs Prince Khurran.

Section ③ Assessment

1. TERMS & NAMES

Identify
- Mughal
- Babur
- Akbar
- Jahangir
- Nur Jahan
- Sikh
- Shah Jahan
- Taj Mahal
- Aurangzeb

2. TAKING NOTES

Using a time line like the one below, indicate the effects each leader had on the Mughal Empire. Write positive effects above the line and negative effects below the line.

Effects on Mughal Empire

3. COMPARING AND CONTRASTING

In what ways was the golden age of Akbar similar to and different from the flowering of the Safavid Empire under Shah Abbas and of the Ottoman Empire under Suleiman I?

THINK ABOUT
- the rulers' cultural and military achievements
- their tolerance of other cultures
- their successors

4. ANALYZING THEMES

Power and Authority Do you think Shah Jahan made good use of his power and authority? Why or why not?

THINK ABOUT
- how Shah Jahan came to power
- the beautiful buildings he built
- conditions in India during his reign

TERMS & NAMES

Briefly explain the importance of each of the following to the Ottoman, Safavid, or Mughal empires.

1. Timur the Lame
2. Mehmet II
3. Suleiman the Lawgiver
4. *devshirme*
5. Isma'il
6. Shah Abbas
7. Babur
8. Akbar
9. Nur Jahan
10. Aurangzeb

Interact *with* History

On page 442, you considered how you might treat the people you conquered. Now that you have learned more about three Muslim empires, in what ways do you think you would change your policies? In what ways would you follow and differ from the Ottomans' example? Discuss your thoughts with a small group of classmates.

REVIEW QUESTIONS

SECTION 1 (*pages 443–447*)
The Ottomans Build a Vast Empire

11. Why were the Ottomans such successful conquerors?
12. How did Mehmet the Conqueror show his tolerance of other cultures?
13. Why was Selim the Grim's capture of Mecca, Medina, and Cairo so significant?
14. What role did slaves play in Ottoman society?

SECTION 2 (*pages 448–450*)
Cultural Blending
Case Study: The Safavid Empire

15. According to the 16th-century Voice from the Past on page 449, "The name of God is forgotten throughout Persia and only that of Isma'il is remembered." What deeds—both positive and negative—contributed to Isma'il's fame?
16. What ideas did Shah Abbas borrow from his enemies, the Ottomans?
17. In what other ways did the Safavids interweave foreign ideas into their culture?

SECTION 3 (*pages 451–457*)
The Mughals Establish an Empire in India

18. What opposition did the Mughals face when they invaded India?
19. In what ways did Akbar defend religious freedom during his reign?
20. How did Akbar's successors promote religious conflict in the empire?

Visual Summary

The Muslim World Expands

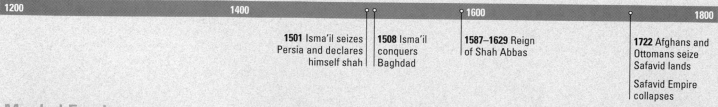

Ottoman Empire

| 1200 | 1400 | 1600 | 1800 |

1280–1326 Reign of Osman I
1361 Ottomans capture Adrianople
1451–1481 Reign of Mehmet II
1453 Turks take Constantinople
1520–1566 Reign of Suleiman I
1571 Defeat at Battle of Lepanto begins decline of Ottoman Empire

Safavid Empire

| 1200 | 1400 | 1600 | 1800 |

1501 Isma'il seizes Persia and declares himself shah
1508 Isma'il conquers Baghdad
1587–1629 Reign of Shah Abbas
1722 Afghans and Ottomans seize Safavid lands

Safavid Empire collapses

Mughal Empire

| 1200 | 1400 | 1600 | 1800 |

1494 Babur begins his rise to power
1526 Babur seizes Delhi
1556–1605 Reign of Akbar
1628–1658 Reign of Shah Jahan
1658–1707 Reign of Aurangzeb
1719 Mughal Empire declines

CRITICAL THINKING

1. CONSTANTINOPLE'S LAST STAND

Why do you think that so few European countries helped defend Constantinople from the Ottomans? In considering your answer, review what you learned about the results of the Crusades in the Holy Roman Empire in Chapter 14.

2. GROWTH OF AN EMPIRE

THEME **EMPIRE BUILDING** Conquest of new territories certainly contributed to the growth of the Muslim empires you read about. How might it have also hindered this growth?

3. MUSLIM MIRROR ON THE WALL

Using a Venn diagram like the one below, compare the personal traits and policies of Suleiman I and Akbar.

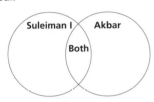

4. ANALYZING PRIMARY SOURCES

The Greek historian Kritovoulos was appointed a governor in the court of Mehmet II after his conquest of Constantinople. In the following quotation, Kritovoulos gives his view of Mehmet's actions. Read the paragraph and answer the questions below it.

A VOICE FROM THE PAST
When the Sultan [Mehmet] had captured the City of Constantinople, almost his very first care was to have the City repopulated. He also undertook the further care and repairs of it. He sent an order in the form of an imperial command to every part of his realm, that as many inhabitants as possible be transferred to the City, not only Christians but also his own people and many of the Hebrews.

KRITOVOULOS, *History of Mehmet the Conqueror*

- Does the tone of this statement indicate that Kritovoulos thought Mehmet dealt fairly with Constantinople? Why or why not?
- Why do you think Mehmet wanted to open the city to Christians and Hebrews as well as Muslims? Support your answer with information from the chapter.

CHAPTER ACTIVITIES

1. LIVING HISTORY: Unit Portfolio Project

THEME **CULTURAL INTERACTION** Your unit portfolio project focuses on the cultural interaction that resulted from the expansion of the Muslim world (see page 387). For Chapter 18 you might use one of the following ideas to add to your portfolio.

- Expand your ideas for the Interact with History activity on the previous page into a speech to your people. Explain your policies and ask for your people's support.
- Draw a political cartoon showing that the Safavids borrowed ideas from their enemies, the Ottomans.
- Write an inscription for Akbar's tombstone, focusing on his religious tolerance and on the mix of cultures in his government bureaucracy.

2. CONNECT TO TODAY: Cooperative Learning

THEME **POWER AND AUTHORITY** The Muslim empires you have studied based their rule on the Islamic religion. Islam remains an important social and political force in modern Turkey, Iran, India, and Pakistan.

Work with a team to find out the status of Muslims in one of these countries today. Then collaborate with the other teams to create a summary chart of these modern Muslim countries.

 Using the Internet or other reference sources, determine the status of Muslims in your team's country.

- What role do Muslims play in the government?
- Do the country's leaders promote religious tolerance? Explain.
- What is the overall economic status of Muslims?

3. INTERPRETING A TIME LINE

Look at the time lines on the facing page. Which empire lasted longest? Which was the shortest lived?

FOCUS ON GRAPHS

Compare the territory and population of the following seven empires at their height.

- Which four empires had about the same territory?
- Which of those empires had the fewest people per square mile?

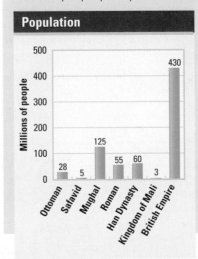

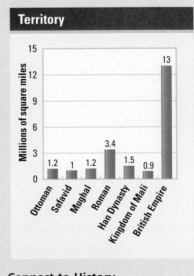

Connect to History
Why might the Safavid Empire have remained so relatively small?

An Age of Exploration and Isolation, 1400–1800

PREVIEWING THEMES

Cultural Interaction

European exploration of Asia resulted in a meeting of different cultures. While this cultural interaction spurred the exchange of many goods and ideas, the people of Asia also resisted European influence.

Economics

The desire for wealth was a driving force behind European exploration of the East. Europeans sought control over the trade of popular goods from Asian countries; European merchants and sailors took to the seas in search of these lands.

Science & Technology

Europeans were able to explore faraway lands only after they improved their sailing technology. Innovations in shipbuilding and navigational techniques allowed Europeans to expand far beyond their borders.

INTERNET CONNECTION

Visit us at **www.mcdougallittell.com** to learn more about this age of exploration and isolation.

EUROPE AND ASIA, AROUND 1500

Norwegian Sea

North Sea

Baltic Sea

Moscow •

ENGLAND

London •   Amsterdam •

NETHERLANDS

Paris •

FRANCE

E U R O P E

OTTOMAN EMPIRE

SPAIN

Rome •

Lisbon •

PORTUGAL

Mediterranean Sea

Tripoli •

Arabian Sea

INDIAN OCEAN

By the **early 1400s, Europeans** were improving their navigational techniques in an effort to explore the lands beyond their shores. Here, for example, a French mapmaker uses an instrument to determine his position on the globe.

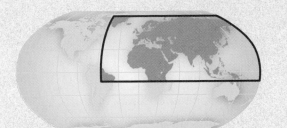

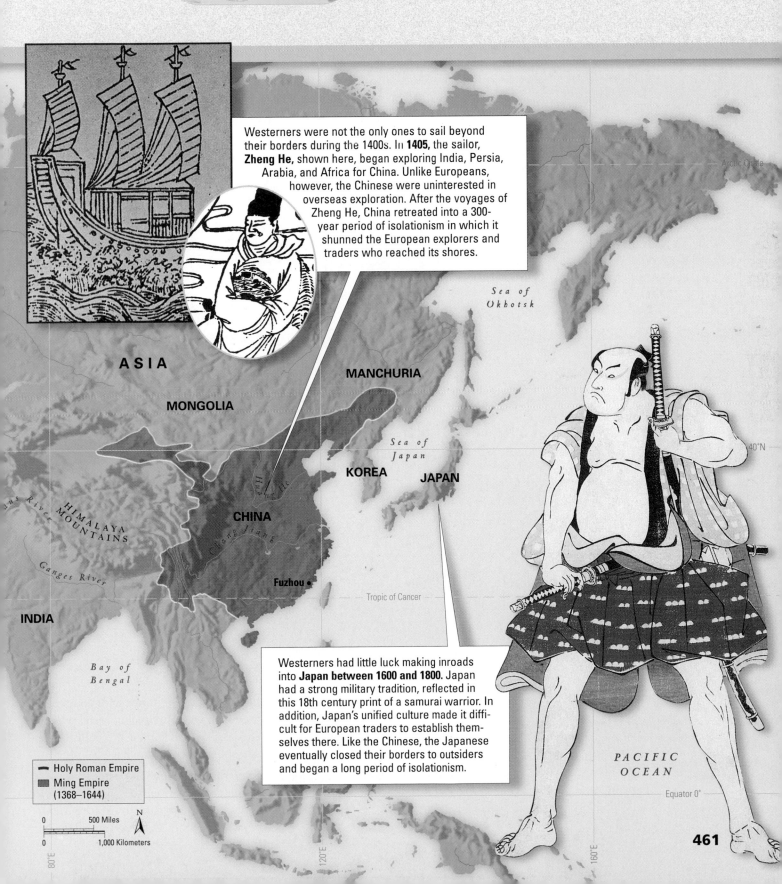

Westerners were not the only ones to sail beyond their borders during the 1400s. In **1405,** the sailor, **Zheng He,** shown here, began exploring India, Persia, Arabia, and Africa for China. Unlike Europeans, however, the Chinese were uninterested in overseas exploration. After the voyages of Zheng He, China retreated into a 300-year period of isolationism in which it shunned the European explorers and traders who reached its shores.

Westerners had little luck making inroads into **Japan between 1600 and 1800.** Japan had a strong military tradition, reflected in this 18th century print of a samurai warrior. In addition, Japan's unified culture made it difficult for European traders to establish themselves there. Like the Chinese, the Japanese eventually closed their borders to outsiders and began a long period of isolationism.

— Holy Roman Empire

▨ Ming Empire
(1368–1644)

0   500 Miles

0   1,000 Kilometers

461

Interact *with* History

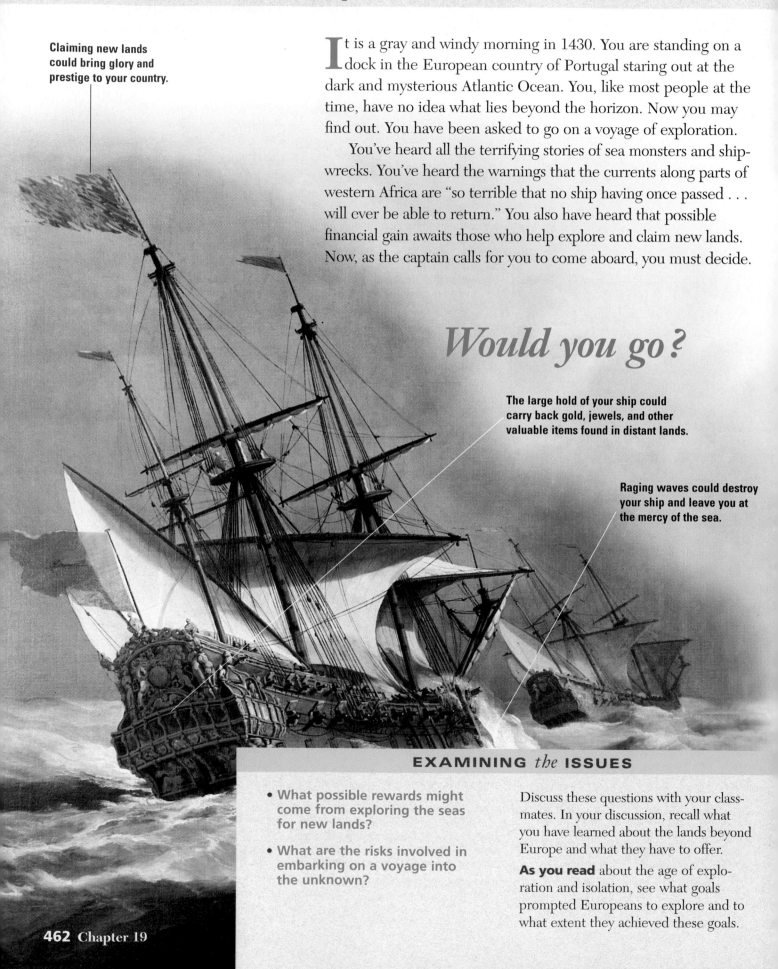

Claiming new lands could bring glory and prestige to your country.

It is a gray and windy morning in 1430. You are standing on a dock in the European country of Portugal staring out at the dark and mysterious Atlantic Ocean. You, like most people at the time, have no idea what lies beyond the horizon. Now you may find out. You have been asked to go on a voyage of exploration.

You've heard all the terrifying stories of sea monsters and shipwrecks. You've heard the warnings that the currents along parts of western Africa are "so terrible that no ship having once passed . . . will ever be able to return." You also have heard that possible financial gain awaits those who help explore and claim new lands. Now, as the captain calls for you to come aboard, you must decide.

Would you go?

The large hold of your ship could carry back gold, jewels, and other valuable items found in distant lands.

Raging waves could destroy your ship and leave you at the mercy of the sea.

EXAMINING *the* ISSUES

- What possible rewards might come from exploring the seas for new lands?

- What are the risks involved in embarking on a voyage into the unknown?

Discuss these questions with your classmates. In your discussion, recall what you have learned about the lands beyond Europe and what they have to offer.

As you read about the age of exploration and isolation, see what goals prompted Europeans to explore and to what extent they achieved these goals.

Europeans Explore the East

TERMS & NAMES
- Bartolomeu Dias
- Prince Henry
- Vasco da Gama
- Treaty of Tordesillas
- Dutch East India Company

MAIN IDEA	WHY IT MATTERS NOW
Driven by the desire for wealth and Christian converts, Europeans began an age of exploration.	European exploration was an important step toward the global interaction that characterizes the world today.

SETTING THE STAGE By the early 1400s, Europeans were ready to venture beyond their borders. As Chapter 17 explained, the Renaissance encouraged, among other things, a new spirit of adventure and curiosity. This spirit of adventure—along with several other important factors—prompted Europeans to explore the world around them. This chapter and the next one describe how these explorations began a long process that would bring together the peoples of many different lands and permanently change the world.

This globe depicts the Europeans' view of the world around 1492. Europe and Africa, shown here, were the lands Europeans had explored most by that time.

Many Factors Encourage Exploration

Europeans had not been completely isolated from the rest of the world before the 1400s. Beginning around 1100, European crusaders battled Muslims for control of the Holy Lands in Southwest Asia. In 1275, the Italian trader Marco Polo reached the court of Kublai Khan in China. For the most part, however, Europeans had neither the interest nor the ability to explore foreign lands. That changed by the early 1400s. The desire to grow rich and to spread Christianity, coupled with advances in sailing technology, spurred an age of European exploration.

Europeans Seek Greater Wealth The desire for new sources of wealth was the main reason for European exploration. Through overseas exploration, merchants and traders hoped ultimately to benefit from what had become a profitable business in Europe: the trade of spices and other luxury goods from Asia. The people of Europe had been introduced to these items during the Crusades, the wars fought between Christians and Muslims from 1096 to 1270 (see Chapter 14). After the Crusades ended, Europeans continued to demand such spices as nutmeg, ginger, cinnamon, and pepper—all of which added flavor to the bland foods of Europe. Because demand for these goods was greater than the supply, merchants could charge high prices and thus make great profits.

The Muslims and Italians controlled the trade of goods from East to West. Muslims sold Asian goods to Italian merchants, who controlled trade across the land routes of the Mediterranean region. The Italian merchants resold the items at increased prices to merchants throughout Europe. Other European traders did not like this arrangement. Paying such high prices to the Italians severely cut into their own profits. By the 1400s, European merchants—as well as the new monarchs of England, Spain, Portugal, and France—sought to bypass the Italian merchants. This meant finding a sea route directly to Asia.

THINK THROUGH HISTORY
A. Analyzing Issues
Why did many European merchants dislike the way goods were traded from East to West?

The Spread of Christianity The desire to spread Christianity also fueled European exploration. Aside from leaving Europeans with a taste for spices, the Crusades left feelings of hostility between Christians and Muslims. European nations believed that they had a sacred duty not only to continue fighting

Muslims, but also to convert non-Christians throughout the world.

Europeans hoped to obtain popular goods directly from the peoples of Asia. They also hoped to Christianize them. **Bartolomeu Dias,** an early Portuguese explorer, explained his motives: "to serve God and His Majesty, to give light to those who were in darkness and to grow rich as all men desire to do."

Technological Advances While "God, glory, and gold" were the primary motives for exploration, advances in technology made the voyages of discovery possible. During the 1200s, it would have been nearly impossible for a European sea captain to cross 3,000 miles of ocean and return again. The main problem was that European ships could not sail against the wind. In the 1400s, shipbuilders designed a new vessel—the caravel. The caravel was sturdier than earlier vessels. In addition, its triangular sails allowed it to sail effectively against the wind.

Europeans also improved their navigational techniques. To better determine their location on the sea, sailors used the astrolabe, which the Muslims had perfected. The astrolabe was a brass circle with carefully adjusted rings marked off in degrees. Using the rings to sight the stars, a sea captain could tell how far north or south of the equator he was. Explorers were also able to more accurately track their direction by using a magnetic compass invented by the Chinese.

THINK THROUGH HISTORY
B. Summarizing
How does the phrase, "God, glory, and gold" summarize the Europeans' motives for exploration?

HISTORY MAKERS

**Prince Henry
1394–1460**

For his role in promoting Portuguese exploration, Prince Henry is often called Henry the Navigator. Historians paint Henry as a quiet and extremely driven man. So consumed was he by the quest to find new lands, that he reportedly shunned female companionship.

Throughout his life, Henry supposedly showed little emotion. It was said that no one ever saw him lose his temper. When angry with someone, Henry allegedly just waved them from his presence, uttering, "I commend you to God, may you be fortunate." While some considered him to be cold and distant, others insisted that the prince had a sensitive side. One writer claimed that upon learning of the death of a friend, Henry wept nonstop for several days.

Portugal Leads the Way

The leader in developing and applying these sailing innovations was Portugal. Located on the Atlantic Ocean at the southwest corner of Europe, Portugal first established trading outposts along the west coast of Africa. Eventually, Portuguese explorers pushed farther east into the Indian Ocean.

The Portuguese Explore Africa Portugal took the lead in overseas exploration in part due to strong government support. The nation's most enthusiastic supporter of exploration was **Prince Henry,** the son of Portugal's king. Henry's dreams of overseas exploration began in 1415 when he helped conquer the Muslim city of Ceuta in North Africa. There, he had his first glimpse of the dazzling wealth that lay beyond Europe. Throughout Ceuta, the Portuguese invaders found exotic stores filled with pepper, cinnamon, cloves, and other spices. In addition, they encountered large supplies of gold, silver, and jewels.

Henry returned to Portugal determined to reach the source of these treasures in the East. The prince also wished to spread the Christian faith. In 1419, Henry founded a navigation school on the southwestern coast of Portugal. Map makers, instrument makers, shipbuilders, scientists, and sea captains gathered there to perfect their trade.

Within several years, Portuguese ships began creeping down the western coast of Africa. By the time Henry died in 1460, the Portuguese had established a series of trading posts along the shores of Africa. There, they traded with Africans for such profitable items as gold and ivory. Eventually, they traded for African captives to be used as slaves. Having established their presence along Africa's western coast, Portuguese explorers plotted their next daring move. They would find a sea route to Asia.

Portuguese Sailors Reach Asia The Portuguese believed that to reach Asia by sea, they would have to sail around the southern tip of Africa. In 1488, Portuguese captain Bartolomeu Dias ventured

The Tools of Exploration

Out on the open seas, winds easily blew ships off course. With only the sun, moon, and stars to guide them, few sailors willingly ventured beyond the sight of land. In order to travel to distant parts of the world, European inventors and sailors experimented with new tools for navigation and new designs for sailing ships.

The triangular sails allowed the caravel to sail effectively against the wind. With these sails the ship could tack (sail on a zigzag course) more directly into the wind than could a square-rigged ship.

Here, a naval officer uses a sextant, which replaced the astrolabe in measuring the height of the stars above the horizon.

The improved rudder allowed the caravel to turn more easily.

The large cargo area was capable of carrying the numerous supplies needed for long voyages.

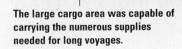

This 16th century Italian compass (with its lid beside it) is typical of those taken by navigators on the great voyages of exploration. The compass was invented by the Chinese.

Connect _to_ History

Analyzing Motives Why did inventors and sailors develop better tools for navigation?

SEE SKILLBUILDER HANDBOOK, PAGE 994

Connect _to_ Today

Modern Sailing Investigate what types of navigational or other tools modern sailors use. Choose one tool and write a brief explanation of what it does. Be prepared to present your report to the class.

Background
Dias named Africa's southern tip the Cape of Storms. However, Portugal's ruler was so pleased with the explorer's journey, that he renamed it the Cape of Good Hope.

farther down the coast of Africa until he reached the tip. As he arrived, a huge storm rose and battered his fleet for days. When the storm ended, Dias realized his ships had been blown around the tip to the other side of the continent. Dias explored the southeast coast of Africa and then considered sailing to India. However, his crew was exhausted and food supplies were low. As a result, the captain returned home.

With the southern tip of Africa finally rounded, the Portuguese continued pushing east. In 1498, the Portuguese explorer **Vasco da Gama** reached the port of Calicut, on the southwestern coast of India. Da Gama and his crew were amazed by the spices, as well as the rare silks and precious gems, that filled Calicut's shops. The Portuguese sailors filled their ships with such spices as pepper and cinnamon and returned to Portugal in 1499. The Portuguese gave da Gama a hero's welcome. His remarkable voyage of 27,000 miles had given Portugal a direct sea route to India.

Spanish Claims Before da Gama's historic voyage, as the Portuguese established trading posts along the west coast of Africa, Spain watched with increasing envy. The Spanish monarchs also desired a direct sea route to the treasures of Asia.

In 1492, an Italian sea captain, Christopher Columbus, convinced Spain to finance what was at that time a bold plan: finding a route to Asia by sailing west across the Atlantic Ocean. In October of that year, Columbus reached the shores of an island in the Caribbean. Columbus's voyage would open the way for European colonization of the American continents—a process that would forever change the world. The immediate impact of Columbus's voyage, however, was to increase tensions between Spain and Portugal.

Columbus thought that he had indeed reached Asia. Believing him to be right, Portugal suspected that Columbus had claimed for Spain lands that Portuguese sailors might have reached first. The rivalry between Spain and Portugal grew more tense. In 1493, Pope Alexander VI stepped in to keep peace between the two nations. He suggested an imaginary dividing line, drawn north to south, through the Atlantic Ocean. All lands to the west of the line, known as the Line of Demarcation, would be Spain's. All lands to the east of the line would belong to Portugal.

Portugal complained that the line gave too much to Spain. So it was moved farther west to include parts of modern-day Brazil for the Portuguese. In 1494, Spain and Portugal signed the **Treaty of Tordesillas,** in which they agreed to honor the line. The era of exploration and colonization was about to begin in earnest.

THINK THROUGH HISTORY
C. Analyzing Issues How did the Treaty of Tordesillas ease tensions between Spain and Portugal?

Trading Empires in the Indian Ocean

With da Gama's voyage, Europeans had finally opened direct sea trade with Asia. They also opened an era of violent conflict in the East. European nations scrambled to establish profitable trading outposts along the shores of South and Southeast Asia. And all the while they battled the region's inhabitants, as well as each other.

Portugal's Trading Empire In the years following da Gama's voyage, Portugal built a bustling trading empire throughout the Indian Ocean. As they moved into the region, they took control of the spice trade from Muslim merchants. In 1509, Portugal extended its control over the area when it defeated a Muslim fleet off the coast of India.

The following year, the Portuguese captured Goa, a port city on India's west coast. They made it the capital of their trading empire. They then sailed farther east to Indonesia, also known as the East Indies. In 1511, a Portuguese fleet attacked the city of Malacca on the west coast of the Malay peninsula. In capturing the town, the

Background
Indonesia is the fourth most populous country in the world. It consists of some 13,670 islands, but only about 7,000 are inhabited.

Portuguese seized control of the Strait of Malacca. Seizing this waterway gave them control of the Moluccas. These were islands so rich in spices that they became known as the Spice Islands.

In convincing his crew to attack Malacca, Portuguese sea captain Afonso de Albuquerque stressed his country's intense desire to crush the Muslim-Italian domination over Asian trade:

A VOICE FROM THE PAST

. . . If we deprive them [Muslims] of this their ancient market there, there does not remain for them a single port in the whole of these parts, where they can carry on their trade in these things. . . . I hold it as very certain that if we take this trade of Malacca away out of their hands, Cairo and Mecca are entirely ruined, and to Venice will no spiceries . . . [be] . . . conveyed except that which her merchants go and buy in Portugal.

AFONSO DE ALBUQUERQUE, from *The Commentaries of the Great Afonso Dalbuquerque*

Portugal did indeed break the old trade network from the East—much to the delight of European consumers. Portuguese merchants brought back goods from Asia at about a fifth of what they cost when purchased through the Arabs and Italians. As a result, more Europeans could afford these items.

In time, Portugal's success in Asia attracted the attention of other European nations. As early as 1521, a Spanish expedition led by Ferdinand Magellan arrived in the Philippines. Spain claimed the islands and began settling them in 1565. By the early 1600s, the rest of Europe had begun descending upon Asia. They were looking to establish their own trade empires in the East.

Other Nations Drive Out the Portuguese Beginning around 1600, the English and Dutch began to challenge Portugal's dominance over the Indian Ocean trade. The Dutch Republic is also known as the Netherlands. It is a small country situated along

THINK THROUGH HISTORY
D. Recognizing Effects How did the European domination of the Indian Ocean trade eventually impact Europeans back home?

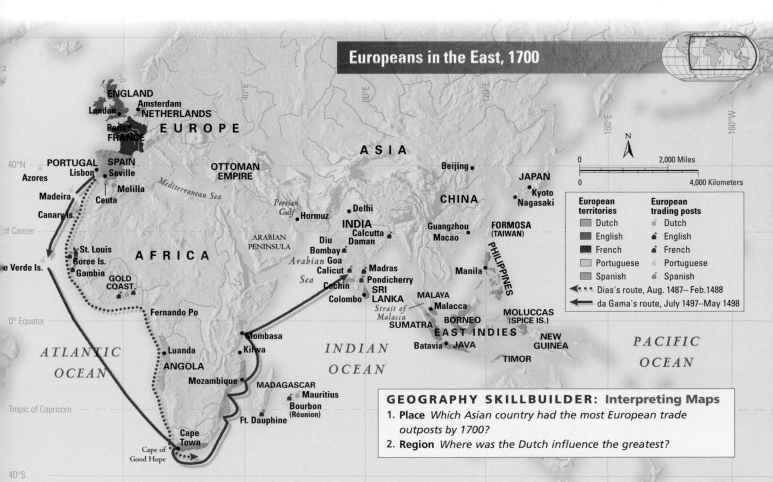

Europeans in the East, 1700

GEOGRAPHY SKILLBUILDER: Interpreting Maps
1. **Place** Which Asian country had the most European trade outposts by 1700?
2. **Region** Where was the Dutch influence the greatest?

467

the North Sea in northwestern Europe. Since the early 1500s, Spain had ruled this area. In 1581, the people of the region declared their independence from Spain and established the Dutch Republic.

In a short time, the Netherlands became a leading sea power. By 1600, the Dutch owned the largest fleet of ships in the world—20,000 vessels. Together, the English and Dutch broke Portuguese control of the Asian region. The two nations then battled one another for dominance of the area. Each nation had formed an East India Company to establish and direct trade throughout Asia. These companies had the power to mint money, make treaties, and even raise their own armies. The **Dutch East India Company** was richer and more powerful than England's company. As a result, the Dutch eventually drove out the English and established their dominance over the region.

THINK THROUGH HISTORY
E. Analyzing Issues
How were the Dutch able to dominate the Indian Ocean trade?

CONNECT *to* TODAY

The Dutch in South Africa
Since colonizing the Cape of Good Hope, the Dutch have retained a powerful and controversial presence in South Africa. Dutch settlers, known as Boers, continually battled the British after Great Britain seized the region in 1806.

The Boers, who now call themselves Afrikaners, gained some control in 1924. They began restricting the rights of the nation's mostly nonwhite population. In 1948, the Afrikaners took control of the government. They established apartheid, a legal system of severe discrimination.

During the 1990s, the government began repealing its apartheid laws, as it finally agreed to share power with the Africans.

European Trade Outposts In 1619, the Dutch established their trading headquarters at Batavia on the island of Java. From there they expanded west to conquer several nearby islands. In addition, the Dutch seized both the port of Malacca and the valuable Spice Islands from Portugal. Throughout the 1600s, the Netherlands increased its control over the Indian Ocean trade. With so many goods from the East traveling to the Netherlands, the nation's capital, Amsterdam, became a leading commercial center. By 1700, the Dutch ruled much of Indonesia and had trading posts in numerous Asian countries. They also controlled the Cape of Good Hope on the southern tip of Africa.

By this time, however, Britain and France had gained a foothold in the region. Having failed to gain control of the larger area, the English East India Company focused much of its energy on establishing outposts in India. There, the English built up a successful business trading fine cloth on the European market. In 1664, France also entered the Asia trade with its own East India Company. The company struggled at first, as it faced continual attacks by the Dutch. The French company finally established an outpost in India in the 1720s. However, it never showed a strong profit.

As the Europeans battled for a share of the profitable Indian Ocean trade, their influence in inland Southeast Asia remained relatively limited. European traders did gain control of numerous port cities throughout the region. However, their influence rarely spread beyond the ports into the countries' interiors. From 1500 to about 1800—when Europeans began to conquer much of the region—the peoples of Asia remained largely unaffected by European contact. As the next two sections explain, European traders who sailed farther east to seek riches in China and Japan had even less success in spreading Western culture.

THINK THROUGH HISTORY
F. Recognizing Effects How did the arrival of Europeans affect the peoples of the East in general?

Section ❶ Assessment

1. TERMS & NAMES
Identify
• Bartolomeu Dias
• Prince Henry
• Vasco da Gama
• Treaty of Tordesillas
• Dutch East India Company

2. TAKING NOTES
Trace the establishment of Portugal's trading empire in the Indian Ocean by supplying the significant event for each date shown on the time line below.

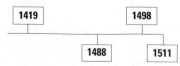

1419		1498
	1488	1511

Write the lead paragraph for a news story about one of the time line events.

3. MAKING INFERENCES
What did the Treaty of Tordesillas reveal about Europeans' attitudes toward non-European lands and peoples?

THINK ABOUT
• the dispute between the Portuguese and Spanish
• how the treaty settled the dispute

4. ANALYZING THEMES
Science and Technology In what ways did Europeans owe some of their sailing technology to other peoples of the world?

THINK ABOUT
• the astrolabe
• the compass

China Rejects European Outreach

TERMS & NAMES
- Ming Dynasty
- Hongwu
- Yonglo
- Zheng He
- Manchus
- Qing Dynasty
- Kangxi

MAIN IDEA	WHY IT MATTERS NOW
Advances under the Ming and Qing dynasties left China self-contained and uninterested in European contact.	China's independence from the West continues today, even as it forges new economic ties with the outside world.

SETTING THE STAGE Europeans made healthy profits in the Indian Ocean trade. Looking for additional sources of wealth, they sought a trading relationship with China. By the time westerners arrived in the 1500s, China had driven out its Mongol rulers and had united under the Ming Dynasty.

The Ming Dynasty

By the time the first Portuguese ships dropped anchor off the Chinese coast in 1514, China had become the dominant power in the region under the rule of the **Ming Dynasty** (1368–1644). In recognition of China's power, vassal states from Korea to Southeast Asia paid their Ming overlords regular tribute, a payment by one nation to another to acknowledge its submission. China expected the Europeans to do the same. The Ming rulers would not allow outsiders from distant lands to threaten the peace and prosperity they had brought to China following the end of Mongol rule.

The Rise of the Ming Hongwu, the son of a peasant, commanded the rebel army that drove the Mongols out of China in 1368. That same year he became the first emperor of the Ming Dynasty. Hongwu continued to rule from the former Yuan capital of Nanjing in the south. He began reforms designed to restore agricultural lands devastated by war, erase all traces of the Mongol past, and promote China's power and prosperity. Hongwu's agricultural reforms increased rice production and improved irrigation. He also encouraged the introduction of fish farming and the growing of commercial crops, such as cotton and sugar cane.

The first Ming emperor used respected traditions and institutions to bring stability to China. For example, he encouraged a return to Confucian moral standards. He improved imperial administration by restoring the merit-based civil service examination system. Later in his rule, however, when problems began to develop, Hongwu became a ruthless tyrant. Suspecting plots against his rule everywhere, he conducted purges in which many thousands of government officials were killed.

Hongwu's death in 1398 led to a power struggle. His son **Yonglo** (yung·lu) emerged victorious from this struggle. Yonglo continued many of his father's policies, although he moved the royal court to Beijing. In addition, Yonglo had a far-ranging curiosity about the outside world. In 1405—before Europeans began to sail beyond their borders—he launched the first of seven voyages of exploration. All were led by a Chinese Muslim admiral named **Zheng He** (jung huh).

The Voyages of Zheng He Zheng He's expeditions were remarkable for their magnitude. Everything about them was large—distances traveled, size of the fleet, and measurements of the ships themselves. The earliest voyages were to Southeast Asia and India. Later expeditions roamed as far as Arabia and eastern Africa.

Vocabulary
vassal states: countries that recognize the overlordship, or domination, of another country.

Background
Confucianism stressed social order, harmony, and good government through education, strong family relationships, and respect for elders.

Vocabulary
purges: ways of ridding a nation, or political party, of people considered undesirable.

This blue and white porcelain vase, with its finely detailed pattern, is from the Ming Dynasty. Ming porcelain is considered to be one of the culture's most famous achievements.

An Age of Exploration and Isolation **469**

Yonglo hoped to impress the world with the power and splendor of Ming China and also hoped to expand China's tribute system. Zheng He's voyages accomplished these goals. From about 40 to 300 ships sailed in each expedition. Among them were fighting ships, storage vessels, and huge "treasure" ships up to 440 feet long. The fleet's crews numbered over 27,000 on some voyages. They included sailors, soldiers, carpenters, interpreters, accountants, doctors, and religious leaders. Like some huge floating city, the fleet sailed from port to port along the Indian Ocean.

Everywhere Zheng He went, he distributed gifts, such as gold, silver, silk, and scented oils, to show Chinese superiority. As a result, more than 16 countries sent tribute to the Ming court. Many envoys traveled to China. Still, Chinese scholar-officials complained that these voyages wasted valuable resources. After the seventh voyage ended in 1433, there were no more. China withdrew into its self-sufficient isolation.

Ming Relations with Foreign Countries China's official trade policies in the 1500s reflected its isolation. To keep the influence of outsiders to a minimum, only the government was to conduct foreign trade, through three coastal ports. In reality, trade flourished up and down the coast. Profit-minded Chinese merchants smuggled cargoes of silk, porcelain, and other valuable goods out of the country into the eager hands of European merchants. Usually, Europeans paid for their purchases with silver—much of it from mines in the Americas.

Demand for Chinese goods had a ripple effect on the economy. Industries such as silk making and ceramics grew rapidly. Manufacturing and commerce increased. However, China did not become highly industrialized for two main reasons. First, the whole idea of commerce offended China's Confucian beliefs. Merchants, it was said, made their money "supporting foreigners and robbery." Second, Chinese economic policies traditionally favored agriculture. Taxes on agriculture stayed low. Taxes on manufacturing and trade skyrocketed.

Accompanying European traders into China were Christian missionaries. The missionaries brought Christianity as well as a variety of European inventions, including the clock and the prism. The first missionary to have an impact was an Italian Jesuit, Matteo Ricci. He gained special favor at the Ming court through his intelligence and his ability to speak and write Chinese. However, many educated Chinese opposed Christianity.

Vocabulary
envoys: government representatives sent to a foreign country.

THINK THROUGH HISTORY
A. Making Inferences What do you think the people of other countries thought about China when they were visited on one of Zheng He's voyages?

SPOTLIGHT ON

The Forbidden City

A stunning monument to China's isolationism was an extravagant palace complex at the capital city, Beijing. It was built by emperor Yonglo between 1404 and 1420. The palace was known as the Forbidden City because all commoners and foreigners were forbidden to enter without special permission. Inside the complex's 35-foot-tall red walls, the emperors of China conducted the business of state and lived in luxury and isolation.

Only the emperor, his family, and his court lived in the palace—which contained 9,000 rooms. Maintaining such a splendid palace city was expensive. For example, every day some 6,000 cooks made meals for 10,000 to 15,000 people. In 1949, the palace complex was converted into a museum and opened to the public.

The Qing Dynasty

By 1600, the Ming had ruled for more than 200 years, and the dynasty was weakening. Its problems grew—ineffective rulers, corrupt officials, and a government out of money. Higher taxes and bad harvests pushed millions of peasants toward starvation. Civil strife and rebellion followed.

Beyond the northeast end of the Great Wall lay Manchuria. In 1644, the **Manchus** (MAN·chooz), the people of that region, invaded China. The Ming could not repel the invasion, and the dynasty collapsed. The Manchus took over Beijing, and the Manchu leader became China's new emperor. As the Mongols had done, the Manchus took a Chinese name for their dynasty, the **Qing** (chihng) **Dynasty.** They would rule China for more than 260 years and bring Taiwan, Chinese Central Asia, Mongolia, and Tibet into China.

China Under the Qing Dynasty Many Chinese resisted rule by the non-Chinese Manchus. Rebellions flared up periodically for decades. The Manchus forced Chinese men to wear their hair in a pigtail as a sign of submission to their rule. The Manchus, however, slowly earned the people's respect. They upheld China's traditional Confucian beliefs and social structures. They made the country's frontiers safe and restored China's prosperity. Two powerful Manchu rulers contributed greatly to the acceptance of the new dynasty.

The first, **Kangxi** (kahng·shee), became emperor in 1661 and ruled for some 60 years. Kangxi reduced government expenses and lowered taxes. A scholar and patron of the arts, Kangxi gained the support of Chinese intellectuals by offering them government positions. He also enjoyed the company of the Jesuits at court. They informed him of the latest developments in science, medicine, and mathematics in Europe.

Under Kangxi's grandson Qian-long (chyahn·lung), who ruled from 1736 to 1795, China reached its greatest size and prosperity. An industrious emperor like his grandfather, Qian-long often rose at dawn to work on the problems of the empire. Those problems included armed nomads on its borders, Christian missionaries, and European merchants.

Manchus Continue a Policy of Isolation To the Chinese, their country—the Middle Kingdom—had been the cultural center of the universe for two thousand years. If foreign states wished to trade with China, they would have to follow Chinese rules. These included trading only at special ports and paying tribute.

The Dutch, masters of the Indian Ocean trade by the time of Qian-long, accepted these restrictions. Their diplomats paid tribute to China's emperor through gifts and by performing the required "kowtow" ritual. This ritual involved their kneeling in front of the emperor and touching their heads to the ground nine times. As a result, the Chinese accepted the Dutch as trading partners. The Dutch returned home with traditional porcelains and silk, as well as China's highly prized new trade item—tea. By 1800, tea would make up 80 percent of shipments to Europe.

Great Britain also wanted to increase trade with China. However, the British did not like China's trade restrictions. In 1793, a British mission led by Lord George Macartney delivered a letter from King George III to Qian-long. The letter asked for a better trade arrangement, including Chinese acceptance of British manufactured goods. Macartney refused to kowtow to the emperor, although he reportedly bowed

THINK THROUGH HISTORY
B. Summarizing
How did the Manchus earn the respect of the Chinese?

Background
Tea was first known in China around 2700 B.C. as a medicine. It did not become a daily drink until the third century A.D.

HISTORY MAKERS

**Kangxi
1654–1722**

The emperor Kangxi had too much curiosity to remain isolated in the Forbidden City. To calm the Chinese in areas devastated by the Manchu conquest, Kangxi set out on a series of "tours."

On tours I learned about the common people's grievances by talking with them. . . . I asked peasants about their officials, looked at their houses, and discussed their crops.

In 1696, with Mongols threatening the northern border, Kangxi exhibited the kind of leadership unheard of in later Ming times. Instead of waiting in the palace for news from the front, he personally led 80,000 troops to victory over the Mongols.

on one knee. Qian-long denied Britain's request. As Qian-long made clear in a letter to the British king, China was self-sufficient:

THINK THROUGH HISTORY
C. Making Inferences Why do you think the kowtow ritual was so important to the Chinese emperor?

> **A VOICE FROM THE PAST**
> . . . There is nothing we lack, as your principal envoy and others have themselves observed. We have never set much store on strange or ingenious objects, nor do we need any more of your country's manufactures.
>
> **QIAN-LONG,** from a letter to King George III of Great Britain

In the 1800s, the British, Dutch, and others would attempt to chip away at China's trade restrictions until the empire itself began to crack, as Chapter 28 will describe.

CONNECT *to* TODAY

North Korea: The Hermit Kingdom

In the 17th and 18th centuries, Korea's strict isolation from the outside world caused it to be described as "the hermit kingdom." In the 1990s, this description can still be applied to communist North Korea. Closed to outsiders, North Korea has very little contact with other nations, even South Korea. China is still its only real ally.

Korea Under the Manchus In 1636, even before they came to power in China, the Manchus conquered nearby Korea and made it a vassal state. As a member of the Chinese tribute system, Korea had long existed in China's shadow. Koreans organized their government according to Confucian principles. They adopted China's technology, its culture, and especially its policy of isolation.

When the Manchus established the Qing Dynasty, Korea's political relationship with China did not change. If anything, it grew stronger. Under the Manchus, Korea was China's "little brother." Below the surface, however, Korea did change. The Manchu invasion, combined with a Japanese attack in the 1590s, provoked strong feelings of nationalism in the Korean people. This sentiment was most evident in their art. Instead of traditional Chinese subjects, many artists chose to explore popular Korean themes. Painters, for example, depicted Korean wrestling matches. They painted Korean peasants tending their fields and landscapes of the Korean countryside.

Daily Life in Ming and Qing China

The Chinese devotion to agriculture began to pay off during the late Ming and early Qing dynasties. Greater rice production, along with the general peace and prosperity of the 1600s and 1700s, ushered in a better life for most Chinese. During this period, the population also doubled. It reached more than 300 million in 1800.

The Growth of Early Modern China

A Population Boom

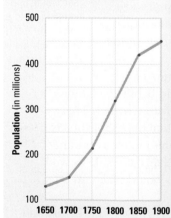

This detail from Zhang Zeduan's painting, *Going Up-River at the Qing Ming Festival*, reflects the growth of urban life under the Ming and Qing.

SKILLBUILDER: Interpreting Graphs
1. *By roughly what percentage did China's population increase between 1650 and 1900?*
2. *How might the growth of population, towns, and culture be related?*

Family and the Role of Women Most Chinese families farmed the land. They farmed in much the same way as their ancestors had for thousands of years. During the Qing Dynasty, irrigation and the use of fertilizer increased. Farmers began to grow new crops. These crops, such as corn and sweet potatoes, had been brought by the Europeans from the Americas. With increased food production, nutrition and diet improved. Such changes encouraged families to expand, and a population explosion followed.

These expanded Chinese families favored sons over daughters. Only a son was allowed to carry on vital religious rituals. A son would raise his own family under his parents' roof, assuring aging parents of help with the farming. Because of this, females were not valued, and many female infants were killed as a result. Men dominated the household and their wives, but women did have some significant responsibilities. Besides working in the fields, they supervised the children's education and managed the family's finances. Although most women were forced to remain secluded in their homes, some found outside jobs as midwives or textile workers, for example.

Still, women generally suffered as a result of their inferior status in Chinese society. One glaring example was the continuation of the traditional practice of foot-binding. One-half to two-thirds of all Chinese women in this period may have undergone this painful procedure, which left them barely able to walk. The practice continued into the 20th century.

Cultural Developments The culture of early modern China was based mainly on traditional forms. It was a conservative reaction to changes in Chinese life. These changes included the Manchu conquest, the coming of the Europeans, and the population growth. The great masterpiece of traditional Chinese fiction was written during this period. *Dream of the Red Chamber* by Cao Zhan examines upper-class Manchu society in the 1700s. It has been praised for the sensitive portrayal of its female characters.

Most artists of the time painted in traditional styles, which valued technique over creativity. In pottery, technical skill as well as experimentation led to the production of high-quality ceramics, including porcelain.

Drama was a popular entertainment, especially in rural China, where literacy rates were low. Plays that presented Chinese history and portrayed cultural heroes served two purposes. They entertained people, and they also helped unify Chinese society by creating a kind of national culture.

While China was attempting to preserve its traditions and its isolation, another civilization that developed in relative seclusion—the Japanese—was in conflict. As you will learn in Section 3, it faced problems caused both by internal power struggles and by the arrival of foreigners.

Under the Ming and Qing, the arts, including painting, flourished. This detail, from one of two paintings entitled *Occupations of the Court Ladies,* shows society's privileged women relaxing.

THINK THROUGH HISTORY
D. Recognizing Effects What were the consequences of the emphasis on tradition in the culture of early modern China?

Section ❷ Assessment

1. TERMS & NAMES

Identify
• Ming Dynasty
• Hongwu
• Yonglo
• Zheng He
• Manchus
• Qing Dynasty
• Kangxi

2. TAKING NOTES

Complete a chart like the one below, listing five relevant facts about each emperor.

Emperor	Relevant Facts
Hongwu	
Yonglo	
Kangxi	
Qian-long	

Choose one emperor and write a one-paragraph biography using the information listed in the chart and text.

3. MAKING DECISIONS

When Qian-long expected Lord George Macartney to kowtow, what do you think Macartney should have done? Why?

THINK ABOUT
• cultural differences
• effect on trading
• the kowtow ritual
• political correctness

4. THEME ACTIVITY

Cultural Interaction Work in small groups to draw, paint, or sketch a mural of a Zheng He expedition. Include the figures, objects, maps, and symbols necessary to convey relevant information from the text. Use the pictures and maps in this chapter for additional ideas. Present the mural to your class.

TERMS & NAMES
- daimyo
- Oda Nobunaga
- Toyotomi Hideyoshi
- Tokugawa Shogunate
- kabuki
- haiku

3 Japan Limits Western Contacts

MAIN IDEA	WHY IT MATTERS NOW
The Tokugawa regime unified Japan and began a 200-year period of isolation, autocracy, and economic growth.	Even now, Japan continues to limit and control dealings with foreigners, especially in the area of trade.

SETTING THE STAGE In the 1300s, the unity that had been achieved in Japan in the previous century broke down. Shoguns, or military leaders, in the north and south fought for power. Although these two rival courts came back together at the end of the century, a series of politically weak shoguns let control of the country slip from their grasp.

Strong Leaders Take Control

In 1467, civil war shattered Japan's feudal system. The country collapsed into chaos. Centralized rule ended. Power drained away from the shogun to territorial lords in hundreds of separate domains.

Vocabulary
domains: the lands belonging to a single lord.

This samurai armor consists of leather and iron plates. It was made in 1714 for the Lord of Akita, a region in northwest Japan.

Local Lords Rule A violent era of disorder followed. This time in Japanese history, which lasted from 1467 to 1568, is known as the *Sengoku*, or "Warring States," period. Powerful samurai seized control of old feudal estates. They offered peasants and others protection in return for their loyalty. These warrior-chieftains, called **daimyo** (DYE·mee·oh), became lords in a new kind of Japanese feudalism. Under this system, security came from this group of powerful warlords. The emperor at Kyoto became a figurehead.

The new Japanese feudalism resembled European feudalism in many ways. The daimyo built fortified castles and created small armies of samurai on horses. Later they added foot soldiers with muskets (guns) to their ranks. Rival daimyo often fought each other for territory. This led to endless disorder throughout the land.

Vocabulary
figurehead: a person holding a position of seeming leadership but having no real power.

New Leaders Restore Order A number of ambitious daimyo hoped to gather enough power to take control of the entire country. One of them, the brutal and ambitious **Oda Nobunaga** (oh·dah noh·boo·nah·gah), defeated his rivals and seized the imperial capital Kyoto in 1568.

Following his own motto, "Rule the empire by force," Nobunaga sought to eliminate his remaining enemies. These included rival daimyo as well as wealthy Buddhist monasteries aligned with them. In 1575, Nobunaga's 3,000 musketeers crushed an enemy force of samurai cavalry. This was the first time firearms had been used effectively in battle in Japan. However, Nobunaga was not able to unify Japan. He committed seppuku, the ritual suicide of a samurai, in 1582, when one of his own generals turned on him.

Nobunaga's best general, **Toyotomi Hideyoshi** (toh·you·toh·mee hee·deh·yoh·shee), continued his fallen leader's mission. Hideyoshi set out to destroy the daimyos that remained hostile. By 1590, by combining brute force with shrewd political alliances, he controlled most of the country. Hideyoshi did not stop with Japan. With the idea of eventually conquering China, he invaded Korea in 1592 and began a long campaign against the Koreans and their Ming Chinese allies. When Hideyoshi died in 1598, his troops withdrew from Korea.

Vocabulary
musketeers: soldiers armed with muskets.

Tokugawa Shogunate Unites Japan

One of Hideyoshi's strongest daimyo allies, Tokugawa Ieyasu (toh·koo·gah·wah ee·yeh·yah·soo), completed the unification of Japan. In 1600, Ieyasu defeated his rivals at the Battle of Sekigahara. His victory earned him the loyalty of daimyo throughout Japan. Three years later, Ieyasu became the sole ruler, or shogun. He then moved Japan's capital to his power base at Edo, a small fishing village that would later become the city of Tokyo.

Japan was unified, but the daimyo still governed at the local level. To keep them from rebelling, Ieyasu required that they spend every other year in the capital. Even when they returned to their lands, they had to leave their families behind as hostages in Edo. Through this "alternate attendance policy" and other restrictions, Ieyasu tamed the daimyo. This was a major step toward restoring centralized government to Japan. As a result, the rule of law overcame the rule of the sword.

Ieyasu founded the **Tokugawa Shogunate,** which would continue until 1867. On his deathbed in 1616, Ieyasu advised his son and successor, Hidetada, "Take care of the people. Strive to be virtuous. Never neglect to protect the country." Most of the Tokugawa shoguns followed that advice, and their rule brought a welcome stability to Japan.

THINK THROUGH HISTORY
A. Drawing Conclusions How would the "alternate attendance policy" restrict the daimyo?

Vocabulary
shogunate: the administration or rule of a shogun.

Japanese Society

Emperor
Held highest rank in society but had no political power

Daimyo
Large landowners

Shogun
Actual ruler

Samurai Warriors
Loyal to daimyo and shogun

Peasants
Four-fifths of the population

Merchants
Low status but gradually gained influence

Artisans
Craftspeople such as artists and blacksmiths

Tokugawa Society and Culture

Japan enjoyed more than two centuries of stability, prosperity, and isolation under the Tokugawa shoguns. The farming community produced more food, and the population rose. Still, the vast majority of peasants, weighed down by heavy taxes, led lives filled with misery. The people who prospered in Tokugawa society were the merchant class and the rich. However, everyone, rich and poor alike, benefited from a flowering of Japanese culture during this era.

Social History In Japan, as in China, Confucian values influenced ideas about society. According to Confucius, the ideal society depended on agriculture, not urban commerce. Farmers, not merchants, made ideal citizens. In the real world of Tokugawa Japan, however, peasant farmers bore the main tax burden and faced more difficulties than any other class. Many of them abandoned farm life and headed for the expanding towns and cities. There they mixed with samurai, artisans, and merchants—the other main classes of Tokugawa society.

By the mid-1700s, Japan began to shift from a rural to an urban society. Edo had grown by that time from a small town in 1600 to perhaps the largest city in the world. Its population was more than one million. The rise of large commercial centers increased employment opportunities for women. Women found jobs in entertainment, textile manufacturing, and publishing. Still, the typical Japanese woman led a sheltered and restricted life as a peasant wife. She worked in the fields, managed the household, cared for the children, and obeyed her husband without question.

Culture Under the Tokugawa Shogunate Traditional culture continued to thrive. Samurai attended ceremonial noh dramas based on tragic themes. They read tales of

Chapter ❶❾ Assessment

TERMS & NAMES

Briefly explain the importance of the following to European exploration and the growth of China and Japan.

1. Bartolomeu Dias
2. Vasco da Gama
3. Treaty of Tordesillas
4. Dutch East India Company
5. Ming Dynasty
6. Manchus
7. Qing Dynasty
8. Oda Nobunaga
9. Toyotomi Hideyoshi
10. Tokugawa Shogunate

Interact *with* History

On page 462, you decided whether or not to go on a voyage of exploration. Now that you have read the chapter, reevaluate your decision. If you decided to go, did what you read reaffirm your decision? Why or why not? If you chose not to go, explain what your feelings are now. Discuss your answers within a small group.

REVIEW QUESTIONS

SECTION 1 *(pages 463–468)*
Europeans Explore the East

11. What factors helped spur European exploration?
12. What role did Portugal's Prince Henry play in overseas exploration?
13. What was the significance of Bartolomeu Dias's voyage? Vasco da Gama's?
14. Why were the Dutch so successful in establishing a trading empire in the Indian Ocean?

SECTION 2 *(pages 469–473)*
China Rejects European Outreach

15. Why didn't China undergo widespread industrialization?
16. Name two technological advancements the missionaries brought to China.
17. List five reasons why the Ming Dynasty fell to civil disorder.

SECTION 3 *(pages 474–477)*
Japan Limits Western Contacts

18. Why was the period between 1467 and 1568 called the Age of the Warring States?
19. What was the difference between the Confucian ideal of society and the real society of Japan?
20. Briefly describe the new drama, literature, and art found in Japanese cities.

Visual Summary

An Age of Exploration and Isolation

EXPLORATION

- In 1405, Zheng He of China launches voyages of exploration to southeast Asia, India, Arabia, and eastern Africa.
- Beginning in the early 1500s, the Portuguese establish trading outposts throughout Asia and gain control of the spice trade.
- The Dutch drive out the Portuguese by the early 1600s and establish their own trading empire in the East.
- Europeans sail farther east to China and Japan in search of more trade; both nations ultimately reject European advances.

ISOLATION

- China abandons its voyages of exploration in 1433.
- Beginning in the 1500s, the Chinese severely restrict trade with foreigners.
- Japan outlaws Christianity in 1612 and drives out Christian missionaries.
- Beginning in the mid 1600s, the Japanese institute a "closed country policy" and remain isolated from Europe for 200 years.

CRITICAL THINKING

1. SAILING INNOVATIONS

THEME SCIENCE AND TECHNOLOGY Of all the technological advances that helped prompt European exploration, which do you think was the the most important? Why?

2. EMPERORS OF THE FORBIDDEN CITY

How might an emperor's attitude toward living in the Forbidden City affect his leadership? Consider how he might view his country, its people, and the outside world. Also think about the role of leaders and the values you think they should hold.

3. MISSIONARIES IN JAPAN

In a time line like the one below, trace the developments which led to Japan's expulsion of Christianity.

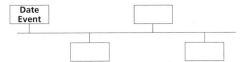

4. ANALYZING PRIMARY SOURCES

Emperor Kangxi invited Christian missionaries to his court, where they shared ideas about science, religion, government, and trade. In the following personal account, Kangxi reflects on what he has learned from the Europeans.

> **A VOICE FROM THE PAST**
> But I was careful not to refer to these Westerners as "Great Officials," and corrected Governor Liu Yin-shu when he referred to the Jesuits Regis and Fridelli . . . as if they were honored imperial commissioners. For even though some of the Western methods are different from our own, and may even be an improvement, there is little about them that is new. The principles of mathematics all derive from the Book of Changes, and the Western methods are Chinese in origin: this algebra—"A-erh-chu-pa-erh"—springs from an Eastern word. And though it was indeed the Westerners who showed us something our ancient calendar experts did not know—namely how to calculate the angles of the northern pole—this but shows the truth of what Chu Hsi arrived at through his investigation of things: the earth is like the yolk within an egg.
>
> **KANGXI**, quoted in *Emperor of China: Self-portrait of K'ang-hsi*

- What do you think is Kangxi's attitude toward Westerners?
- Do you think Kangxi is a true scholar?

CHAPTER ACTIVITIES

1. LIVING HISTORY: Unit Portfolio Project

THEME CULTURAL INTERACTION Your Unit Portfolio project focuses on the ways in which different cultures interact (see page 387). For Chapter 19, you might use one of the following ideas to add to your portfolio.

- Imagine you are the Jesuit missionary, Matteo Ricci. Write a letter home describing your impressions of Chinese rule and culture.
- Draft a reply for King George III to the letter written by China's emperor, Qian-long, on page 472. Convince the emperor to open China by explaining the benefits of economic and cultural interaction.
- Imagine you are a Malaccan newspaper editor. Write an editorial about the arrival of Europeans, as well as their motives for being there.

2. CONNECT TO TODAY: Cooperative Learning

THEME ECONOMICS The primary force behind overseas exploration was economic, as Europeans sailed beyond their borders in search of new sources of wealth. Today the West retains strong economic ties with Asia. In recent years, maintaining those ties with China has been a hotly debated topic in the United States.

Work with a small team and prepare to debate another team over the issue of U.S. trade with China.

Using the Internet, magazines, and other library sources, research the issues involved in the debate over U.S. trade with China.

- After being assigned one or the other position on the issue, work together to gather information that supports your side's position.
- In front of the class, debate a group that has taken the opposite position.

3. INTERPRETING A TIME LINE

Reexamine the unit time line on pages 386–387. Convert the Chapter 19 time line into a cartoon strip that conveys the same information.

FOCUS ON GEOGRAPHY

This map, produced by the German cartographer Henricus Martellus in about 1490, is believed to be the first world map to incorporate the discoveries made by Bartolomeu Dias.

- Where is Europe on the map?
- What is the continent in the lower left corner of the map?

Connect to History Obtain a modern-day world map and compare it with this one. How do you rate Martellus's assumptions of how the world to the east of Africa looked?

Interact *with* History

The year is 1520. You are a Native American living in central Mexico, and you are suddenly faced with a decision that may change your life forever. A group of white invaders, known as the Spanish, are engaged in fierce battle with the nearby Aztecs. You and many others have long hated the powerful Aztecs, who rule the land with a harsh and cruel hand. However, you are frightened of these newcomers who ride on large beasts and fire loud weapons.

Many of your friends are joining different sides of the fight. You can choose not to fight at all. However, if you do decide to fight, you must choose a side.

Which side would you choose?

The Aztecs are more familiar with the land and can easily outmaneuver the Spaniards.

Some of your friends, embittered by years of mistreatment by the Aztecs, have chosen to fight on the side of the Spanish.

The Spaniards' advantages include superior weapons, armor, dogs, and horses.

You know very little about the invading Spanish and what they have in mind for you.

EXAMINING *the* ISSUES

- What risks are involved in supporting the invaders, whom you know almost nothing about?

- Does the fact that the Aztecs share a similar culture and heritage with you make a difference in your decision?

- What are the advantages and disadvantages of not fighting at all?

Discuss these questions with your classmates. In your discussion, examine whether invading armies throughout history have made life better or worse for people in the areas they conquer.

As you read about colonization in the Americas, see what course many natives took and learn the outcome of the battle between the Aztecs and Spanish.

Spanish Conquests in the Americas

TERMS & NAMES
- **Christopher Columbus**
- **colony**
- **Hernando Cortés**
- **conquistadors**
- **Montezuma II**
- **Francisco Pizarro**
- **mestizo**
- *encomienda*

MAIN IDEA	**WHY IT MATTERS NOW**
The voyages of Columbus prompted the Spanish to carve out the first European colonies in the Americas.	Throughout the Americas, Spanish culture, language, and descendants are the legacy of this period.

SETTING THE STAGE As you read in the previous chapter, competition for wealth in the East among European nations was fierce. This competition prompted sea captain **Christopher Columbus** to make a daring voyage for Spain in 1492. Instead of sailing east, Columbus sailed west across the Atlantic in search of an alternate trade route to Asia and its riches. Columbus never reached Asia. Instead he stepped onto an island in the Caribbean. That event set in motion a process that would bring together the peoples of Europe, Africa, and the Americas. And the world would change forever.

Columbus's Voyage Paves the Way

No one paid much attention as the *Niña*, *Pinta*, and *Santa María* slid out of a Spanish port around dawn on August 3, 1492. In a matter of months, however, Columbus's fleet would make history. It would reach the shores of what was to Europeans an astonishing new world.

First Encounters In the early hours of October 12, 1492, the long-awaited cry came. A lookout aboard the *Pinta* caught sight of a shoreline in the distance. *"Tierra! Tierra!"* he shouted. "Land! Land!" By dawn, Columbus and his crew were ashore. Thinking he had successfully reached the East Indies, Columbus called the surprised inhabitants who greeted him, *los indios*. The term translated into "Indian," a word mistakenly applied to all the native peoples of the Americas. In his memoirs, Columbus recounted his first meeting with the native peoples:

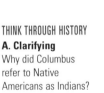

THINK THROUGH HISTORY
A. Clarifying
Why did Columbus refer to Native Americans as Indians?

> **A VOICE FROM THE PAST**
> I presented them with some red caps, and strings of glass beads to wear upon the neck, and many other trifles of small value, wherewith they were much delighted, and became wonderfully attached to us. Afterwards they came swimming to the boats where we were, bringing parrots, balls of cotton thread, javelins, and many other things which they exchanged for the articles we gave them . . . in fact they accepted anything and gave what they had with the utmost good will.
> **CHRISTOPHER COLUMBUS,** *Journal of Columbus*

Columbus, however, had miscalculated where he was. He had not reached the East Indies. Scholars believe he landed instead on an island in the Bahamas in the Caribbean Sea. The natives there were not Indians, but a group who called themselves the Taino. Nonetheless, Columbus claimed the island for Spain. He named it San Salvador, or "Holy Savior."

Columbus, like other explorers, was interested in gold. Finding none on San Salvador, he explored other islands throughout the Caribbean, staking his claim to each one. "It was my wish to bypass no island without taking possession," he wrote.

In early 1493, Columbus returned to Spain. The reports he relayed about his journey delighted the Spanish monarchs. Spain's rulers, who had funded his first voyage, agreed

This portrait of Christopher Columbus was painted by the Spanish artist Pedro Berruguete, who lived at the same time. It is believed to be the most accurate depiction of the Italian sea captain.

The Atlantic World **483**

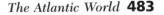

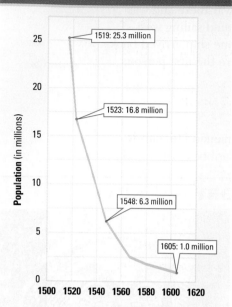

Native Population of Central Mexico

Population (in millions)

- 1519: 25.3 million
- 1523: 16.8 million
- 1548: 6.3 million
- 1605: 1.0 million

1500 1520 1540 1560 1580 1600 1620

Source: *The Population of Latin America*

SKILLBUILDER:
Interpreting Graphs

1. *By what percentage did the native population decrease between 1519 and 1605?*
2. *How did the sharp decline in the native population—due greatly to disease—affect the Spaniards' attempts to conquer the region?*

stunning victory. First, the Spanish had the advantage of superior weaponry. Aztec arrows were no match for the Spaniards' muskets and cannons.

Second, Cortés was able to enlist the help of various native groups. With the aid of a native woman translator named Malinche, Cortés learned that some natives resented the Aztecs. They hated their harsh practices, including human sacrifice. Through Malinche, Cortés convinced these natives to fight on his side.

Finally, and most important, the natives could do little to stop the invisible warrior that marched alongside the Spaniards—disease. Measles, mumps, smallpox, and typhus were just some of the diseases Europeans had brought with them to the Americas. Native Americans had never been exposed to these diseases. Thus, they had developed no natural immunity to them. As a result, they died by the hundreds of thousands. By the time Cortés launched his counterattack, the Aztec population had been greatly reduced by smallpox and measles. In time, European disease would truly devastate the natives of central Mexico.

Pizarro Subdues the Inca In 1532, another conquistador, **Francisco Pizarro,** marched an even smaller force into South America. He conquered the mighty Inca Empire. (See Chapter 16.) Pizarro and his army of about 200 met the Inca ruler, Atahualpa (Ah·tuh·WAHL·puh), near the city of Cajamarca. Atahualpa, who commanded a force of about 30,000, brought several thousand mostly unarmed men for the meeting. The Spaniards crushed the Inca force and kidnapped Atahualpa.

Atahualpa offered to fill a room once with gold and twice with silver in exchange for his release. However, after receiving the ransom, the Spanish strangled the Inca king. Demoralized by their leader's death, the remaining Inca force retreated from Cajamarca. Pizarro then marched on the Inca capital, Cuzco. He captured it without a struggle.

As Cortés and Pizarro conquered the once mighty civilizations of the Americas, fellow conquistadors defeated other native peoples. Spanish explorers also conquered the Maya in Yucatan and Guatemala. By the middle of the 16th century, Spain had created a wide-reaching American empire. It included New Spain (Mexico and parts of Guatemala), as well as other lands in Central and South America and the Caribbean.

Spain's Pattern of Conquest In building their new American empire, the Spaniards drew from techniques used during the *reconquista* of Spain. When conquering the Muslims, the Spanish lived among them and imposed upon them their Spanish culture. The Spanish settlers to the Americas, known as *peninsulares,* were mostly men. As a result, marriage between Spanish settlers and native women was common. These marriages created a large **mestizo**—or mixed Spanish and Native American—population. Their descendants live today in Mexico, other Latin American countries, and the United States.

Although the Spanish conquerors lived among and intermarried with the native people, they also oppressed them. In their effort to exploit the land for its precious resources, the Spanish forced Native Americans to labor within a system known as **encomienda.** Under this system, natives farmed, ranched, or mined for Spanish landlords. These landlords had received the rights to the natives' labor from Spanish authorities. The holders of *encomiendas* promised the Spanish rulers that they would act fairly and respect the workers. However, many abused the natives and worked many laborers to death, especially inside dangerous mines. The Spanish employed the same system in the Caribbean.

Background
The Aztecs practice of human sacrifice was based on the belief that if they did not feed human blood to the sun, it would fail to rise.

THINK THROUGH HISTORY
C. Analyzing Issues
What factors enabled the Spanish to defeat the Aztecs?

Background
Beginning around 1100, the *reconquista* was a centuries-long effort to drive the Muslims out of Spain.

Background
In 1494, the Treaty of Tordesillas between Spain and Portugal gave the Portuguese the rights to Brazil.

The Portuguese in Brazil One area of South America that remained outside of Spanish control was Brazil. In 1500, Cabral claimed the land for Portugal. During the 1530s, colonists began settling Brazil's coastal region. Finding little gold or silver, the settlers began growing sugar. Clearing out huge swaths of forest land, the Portuguese built giant sugar plantations. The demand for sugar in Europe was great, and the colony soon enriched Portugal. In time, the colonists pushed further west into Brazil. They settled even more land for the production of sugar.

Along the way, the Portuguese—like the Spanish—conquered Native Americans and inflicted thousands of them with disease. Also like the Spanish, the Portuguese enslaved a great number of the land's original inhabitants.

Spain Expands Its Influence

Spain's American colonies helped make it the richest, most powerful nation in the world during much of the 16th century. Ships filled with treasures from the Americas continually sailed into Spanish harbors. This newfound wealth helped usher in a golden age of art and culture in Spain. (See Chapter 21.)

Throughout the 16th century, Spain also increased its military might. To protect its treasure-filled ships, Spain built a powerful navy. The Spanish also strengthened their other military forces, creating a skillful and determined army. For a century and a half, Spain's army never lost a battle. Meanwhile, Spain enlarged its American empire by settling in parts of what is now the United States.

Conquistadors Push North Dreams of new conquests prompted Spain to back a series of expeditions into the southwestern United States. The Spanish actually had settled in parts of the United States before they even dreamed of building an empire on the American mainland. In 1513, Spanish explorer Juan Ponce de León wandered through modern-day Florida and claimed it for Spain.

In this 19th-century illustration, Coronado leads his army back to Mexico after failing to find wealth in the southwest United States. During his return, Coronado fell from his horse and had to travel part of the way on a stretcher.

By 1540, after building an empire that stretched from Mexico to Peru, the Spanish once again looked to the land that is now the United States. That year, Francisco Vásquez de Coronado led an expedition throughout much of present-day Arizona, New Mexico, Texas, Oklahoma, and Kansas. He was searching for another wealthy empire to conquer. Coronado found little gold amidst the dry deserts of the Southwest. As a result, the Spanish monarchy assigned mostly priests to explore and colonize the future United States.

Catholic priests had accompanied conquistadors from the very beginning of American colonization. The conquistadors had come in search of wealth. The priests who accompanied them had come in search of converts. In the winter of 1609–1610, Pedro de Peralta, governor of Spain's northern holdings—called New Mexico—led settlers to a tributary on the upper Rio Grande. Together they built a capital called Santa Fe, or "Holy Faith." In the next two decades, a string of Christian missions arose among the Pueblo, the native inhabitants of the region. Scattered missions, forts, and small ranches dotted the lands of New Mexico. These became the headquarters for advancing the Catholic religion.

THINK THROUGH HISTORY
D. Contrasting How did Spain's colony in New Mexico differ from its colonies in New Spain?

Opposition to Spanish Rule Spanish priests worked to spread Christianity in the Americas. They also pushed for better treatment of Native Americans. Priests spoke out against the cruel treatment of natives. In particular, they criticized the harsh pattern of labor that emerged under the *encomienda* system. "There is nothing more detestable or cruel," Dominican monk Bartolomé de Las Casas wrote, "than the tyranny which the Spaniards use toward the Indians for the getting of pearl [riches]."

Largely in response to the writings of Las Casas and others, the Spanish government abolished the *encomienda* system in 1542. To meet the colonies' desperate need for labor, Las Casas suggested the use of Africans. "The labor of one . . . [African] . . . [is] more valuable than that of four Indians," Las Casas declared. The priest later changed his view and denounced African slavery. However, many others promoted it. The Spanish, as well as the other nations that colonized the Americas, would soon enslave Africans to meet their growing labor needs.

Native Resistance Opposition to the Spanish method of colonization came not only from Spanish priests, but from the natives themselves. Resistance to Spain's attempt at domination began shortly after the Spanish arrived in the Caribbean. In November of 1493, Columbus encountered resistance in his attempt to conquer the present-day island of St. Croix. Before finally surrendering, the inhabitants defended themselves by firing poison arrows. Efforts to control the Taino on Hispaniola were even more difficult. After several rebellions, the Taino submitted to Columbus for several years. They revolted yet again in 1495.

As late as the end of the 17th century, natives in New Mexico fought against Spanish rule. While there were no silver mines to work in the region, the natives there still felt the weight of Spanish force. In converting the natives to Christianity, Spanish priests and soldiers often burned their sacred objects and prohibited many native rituals. The Spanish also forced natives to work for them and sometimes abused them physically. Native Americans who practiced their own religion were beaten.

In 1680, Popé, a Pueblo ruler, led a well-organized uprising against the Spanish. The rebellion involved some 17,000 warriors from villages all over New Mexico. The native fighters drove the Spanish back into New Spain. For the next 12 years—until the Spanish regained control of the area— the southwest region of the future United States once again belonged to its original inhabitants. By this time, however, the rulers of Spain had far greater concerns. Nearly 80 years before Popé ran the Spanish out of New Mexico, the other nations of Europe had begun to establish their own colonies in the Americas.

This European drawing of the 1600s depicts Indians taking revenge on a Spanish colonist— by pouring gold down his throat.

THINK THROUGH HISTORY
E. Analyzing Causes
Why did the natives of New Mexico revolt against Spanish settlers?

Section 1 Assessment

1. TERMS & NAMES

Identify
- Christopher Columbus
- colony
- Hernando Cortés
- conquistadors
- Montezuma II
- Francisco Pizarro
- mestizo
- *encomienda*

2. TAKING NOTES

Using a diagram like the one below, trace the major events in the establishment of Spain's empire in the Americas beginning with Columbus's arrival.

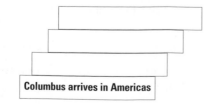

Columbus arrives in Americas

3. RECOGNIZING BIAS

Reread "A Voice from the Past" on page 483. How might Columbus's view of the Taino Indians have led the Spanish to think they could take advantage of and impose their will on the natives?

THINK ABOUT
- the Taino's desire for Spanish items even of "small value"
- the Taino's willingness to give whatever they had to the Spanish
- the Taino's appearance as a peaceful people

4. THEME ACTIVITY

Empire Building Working in small groups, debate the merits of Spain's colonization of the Americas. Have one half of the group take the position of conquistadors, and the other take the position of Native Americans.

THINK ABOUT
- how colonization of the Americas affected Spain
- what effect colonization had on the Native Americans

The Legacy of Columbus

In the years and centuries since his historic journeys, people still debate the legacy of Christopher Columbus's voyages. Some argue they were the heroic first steps in the creation of great and democratic societies. Others claim they were the beginnings of an era of widespread cruelty and bloodshed.

HISTORIAN'S COMMENTARY
Samuel Eliot Morison

Morison, a strong supporter of Columbus, laments that the sea captain died without realizing the true greatness of his deeds.

One only wishes that the Admiral might have been afforded the sense of fulfillment that would have come from foreseeing all that flowed from his discoveries; that would have turned all the sorrows of his last years to joy. The whole history of the Americas stems from the Four Voyages of Columbus; and as the Greek city-states looked back to the deathless gods as their founders, so today a score of independent nations and dominions unite in homage to Christopher, the stout-hearted son of Genoa, who carried Christian civilization across the Ocean Sea.

ESSAY
Alphonse Lamartine

Lamartine, a French writer and politician, praises Columbus for bringing the virtues of civil society to the Americas.

All of the characteristics of a truly great man are united in Columbus. Genius, labor, patience, obscurity of origin, overcome by energy of will; mild but persisting firmness . . . fearlessness of death in civil strife; confidence in the destiny—not of an individual but of the human race. . . . He was worthy to represent the ancient world before that unknown continent on which he was the first to set foot, and carry to these men of a new race all the virtues, without any of the vices, of the elder hemisphere. So great was his influence on the destiny of the earth, that none more than he ever deserved the name of Civilizer.

EYEWITNESS ACCOUNT
Bartolomé de Las Casas

Las Casas was an early Spanish missionary who watched fellow Spaniards unleash attack dogs on Native Americans. He predicted that Columbus's legacy would be one of disaster for America's original inhabitants.

. . . Their other frightening weapon after the horses: twenty hunting greyhounds. They were unleashed and fell on the Indians at the cry of *Tómalo!* ["Get them!"] Within an hour they had preyed on one hundred of them. As the Indians were used to going completely naked, it is easy to imagine what the fierce greyhounds did, urged to bite naked bodies and skin much more delicate than that of the wild boars they were used to. . . . This tactic, begun here and invented by the devil, spread throughout these Indies and will end when there is no more land nor people to subjugate and destroy in this part of the world.

ESSAY
Suzan Shown Harjo

Harjo, a Native American, disputes the so-called benefits that resulted from Columbus's voyages and the European colonization of the Americas that followed.

"We will be asked to buy into the thinking that . . . genocide and ecocide are offset by the benefits of horses, cut-glass beads, pickup trucks, and microwave ovens."

Connect *to* History

Contrasting What opposing ideas are presented on this page?

 SEE SKILLBUILDER HANDBOOK, PAGE 996

Connect *to* Today

Supporting an Opinion
Find several opinions about Columbus in 1992—the 500th anniversary of his discovery of America. Choose the opinion you agree with most and write a brief paper explaining why.

 For another perspective on the legacy of Columbus, see World History: Electronic Library of Primary Sources.

TERMS & NAMES
• **New France**
• **Jamestown**
• **Pilgrims**
• **Puritans**
• **New Netherland**
• **French and Indian War**
• **Metacom**

2 Competing Claims in North America

MAIN IDEA	WHY IT MATTERS NOW
Several European nations fought for control of North America, and England eventually emerged victorious.	The English settlers in North America left a legacy of law and government that guides the United States today.

SETTING THE STAGE Spain's successful colonization efforts in the Americas did not go unnoticed. Other European nations soon became interested in obtaining their own valuable colonies across the Atlantic. The Treaty of Tordesillas had divided the newly discovered lands between Spain and Portugal. However, other European countries ignored the treaty. They set out to build their own empires in the Americas.

European Nations Settle North America

Magellan's voyage showed that ships could reach Asia by way of the Pacific Ocean. Spain claimed the route around the southern tip of South America. Other European countries hoped to find an easier and more direct route to the Pacific. If it existed, a northwest route through North America to Asia would become a highly profitable trade route. Not finding the route, the French, English, and Dutch instead established colonies in North America.

CONNECT *to* TODAY

Cajun Culture

French culture still thrives in Louisiana due in large part to the influence of people known as Cajuns. Cajuns are the descendants of French colonists who in 1604 settled the region known as Acadia in eastern Canada. Battles with the British led thousands of Acadians to move to French settlements in Louisiana, where their legacy lives on.

Today, more than 1 million Louisianans speak French. In addition, Cajun food, such as a spicy, thick soup called gumbo, is popular not only in the Bayou region but also throughout the United States. Also popular around the nation are the fast-paced sounds of Cajun zydeco music.

Explorers Establish New France Just as Columbus had before them, the early French explorers sailed west with dreams of reaching the East Indies. One such explorer was Giovanni da Verrazzano (VEHR·uh·ZAHN·noh), an Italian in the service of France. In 1524, he sailed to North America in search of a possible sea route to the Pacific. While he did not find the route, Verrazzano did discover what is today New York Harbor. Ten years later, the Frenchman Jacques Cartier (kahr·TYAY) reached a gulf off the eastern coast of Canada that led to a broad river. Cartier named the river the St. Lawrence. He followed it inward until he reached a large island dominated by a hill. He named the island Mont Royal, which later became known as Montreal. In 1608, another French explorer, Samuel de Champlain, sailed up the St. Lawrence. He laid claim to a region he called Quebec. The settlement grew. It eventually became the base of France's colonial empire in North America, known as **New France.**

After establishing Quebec, the French penetrated the heart of the North American continent. In 1673, French priest Jacques Marquette and trader Louis Joliet explored the Great Lakes and the upper Mississippi River. Nearly 10 years later, Sieur de La Salle explored the lower Mississippi. He claimed the entire river valley for France. He named it Louisiana in honor of the French king, Louis XIV. By the early 1700s, New France covered much of what is now the midwest United States and eastern Canada. (See the map on page 493.)

A Trading Empire France's North American empire was immense. But it was sparsely populated. By 1760, the European population of New France had grown to only about 65,000. A large number of French colonists had no desire to build towns or raise families. These settlers included Catholic priests who sought to convert

Native Americans. They also included young, single men engaged in what had become New France's main economic activity: fur trade.

By the late 1500s, one of the hottest fashion trends in Europe was hats made of beaver skin. Beavers were almost extinct in Europe but plentiful in North America. This led to a thriving trade in furs. Unlike the English, the French were less interested in occupying territories than they were in making money off the land.

THINK THROUGH HISTORY
A. Summarizing
Why were France's North American holdings so sparsely populated?

The English Settle at Jamestown The explorations of the Spanish and French fired the imagination of the English. In 1606, a company of London investors obtained from King James a charter to found a colony in North America. In 1607, the company's three ships—and more than 100 settlers—pushed out of an English harbor. Four months later, the North American shore rose along the horizon. After reaching the coast of Virginia, the vessels slipped into a broad coastal river. They sailed inland until they reached a small peninsula. There, the colonists climbed off their ships and claimed the land as theirs. They named the settlement **Jamestown** in honor of their king.

The colony's start was disastrous. The settlers were more interested in finding gold than planting crops. They soon fell victim to their harsh surroundings. During the first few years, seven out of every ten people died of hunger, disease, or fighting with the Native Americans. After several months in this hostile environment, one settler described the terrible situation:

A VOICE FROM THE PAST
Thus we lived for the space of five months in this miserable distress . . . our men night and day groaning in every corner of the fort, most pitiful to hear. If there were any conscience in men, it would make their hearts to bleed to hear the pitiful murmuring and outcries of our sick men for relief, every night and day for the space of six weeks: some departing out of the World, many times three or four in a night; in the morning their bodies trailed out of their cabins like dogs, to be buried.

A JAMESTOWN COLONIST, quoted in *A New World*

The first English colonists arrive at Jamestown in 1607, as depicted in this 19th-century engraving.

Despite their nightmarish start, the colonists eventually gained a foothold in their new land. Jamestown became England's first permanent settlement in North America. The colony's outlook improved greatly after farmers there discovered tobacco. High demand in England for tobacco turned it into a profitable cash crop, or a crop grown primarily for sale. The colony, however, continued to struggle financially. Jamestown's investors finally let King James take over the colony. As a royal colony, Jamestown slowly grew and prospered.

Background
Puritans took their name from their desire to "purify" the English church.

Puritans Create a "New England" In 1620, as the colonists at Jamestown were struggling to survive, a group known as **Pilgrims** founded a second English colony, Plymouth, in Massachusetts. Persecuted for their religious beliefs in England, these colonists sought religious freedom. Eight years later, a group known as **Puritans** also sought religious freedom from England's Anglican Church. They established a larger colony at nearby Massachusetts Bay.

THINK THROUGH HISTORY
B. Contrasting
In what ways did the colonies at Jamestown and Massachusetts Bay differ?

The Puritans wanted to build a model community that would set an example for other Christians to follow. Although the colony experienced early difficulties, it gradually took hold. This was due in large part to the numerous families in the colony, unlike the mostly single, male population in Jamestown. Family life created a sense of order among the settlers. It also ensured that the population would reproduce itself.

The Dutch Found New Netherland Following the English and French into North America were the Dutch. The Dutch had established the Dutch East India Company in 1602 to compete for trade in the Indian Ocean. Several years later, they turned their attention to the Americas. In 1609, Henry Hudson, an Englishman in the service of the Netherlands, sailed west. He was searching for a northwest sea route to Asia. Hudson did not find a route. He did, however, explore three waterways near present-day New York that were later named for him—the Hudson River, Hudson Bay, and Hudson Strait.

The Dutch claimed the region along these waterways. They established a fur trade with the Iroquois Indians. They also built trading posts along the Hudson River at Fort Orange (now Albany) and on Manhattan Island, at the mouth of the river. Dutch merchants quickly formed the Dutch West India Company. In 1621, the Dutch government granted the company permission to colonize the region and expand the thriving fur trade. The Dutch holdings in North America became known as **New Netherland.**

Although the Dutch company profited from its fur trade, it was slow to attract Dutch colonists. To encourage settlers to come and stay, the colony opened its doors to a variety of peoples. Gradually, more Dutch, as well as Germans, French, Scandinavians, and other Europeans settled the area. The colony's population was so ethnically diverse that one visitor called it a great "confusion of tongues." The Dutch reputation for religious tolerance also drew people of many faiths, including Protestants, Catholics, Muslims, and Jews.

THINK THROUGH HISTORY
C. Contrasting
How were the Dutch and French colonies different from the English colonies in North America?

Colonizing the Caribbean During the 1600s, the nations of Europe also colonized the Caribbean. The French seized control of several Caribbean islands, including present-day Haiti, Guadeloupe, and Martinique. The English settled Barbados and Jamaica. In 1634, the Dutch captured what are now the Netherlands Antilles and Aruba from Spain.

On these islands, the Europeans built huge tobacco and sugar plantations. These products, although profitable, demanded a large and steady supply of free labor. Enslaved Africans eventually would supply this labor.

The Fight for North America

SPOTLIGHT ON

Pirates

The battle for colonial supremacy occurred not only on land, but also on the sea. Acting on behalf of their government, privately owned armed ships, known as privateers, attacked merchant ships of enemy nations and sank or robbed them.

Also patrolling the high seas were pirates. Unlike privateers, pirates were not licensed by any country. They attacked ships for their gold and did not care what nation the vessels represented. Pirates were ruthless men who did not hesitate to kill for treasure.

One of the most well-known pirates was Edward B. Teach, whose prominent beard earned him the nickname Blackbeard (above). According to one account, Blackbeard attempted to frighten his victims by sticking "lighted matches under his hat, which appeared on both sides of his face and eyes, naturally fierce and wild. . . ."

As they expanded their settlements in North America, the nations of France, England, and the Netherlands battled each other for colonial supremacy. After years of skirmishes and war, the English gained control of much of the continent.

The English Oust the Dutch To the English, New Netherland had become a "Dutch wedge" separating its northern and southern colonies. In 1664, the English king, Charles II, granted his brother, the Duke of York, permission to drive out the Dutch. When the duke's fleet arrived at New Netherland, the Dutch surrendered without firing a shot. The Duke of York claimed the colony for England and renamed it New York.

With the Dutch gone, the English continued to colonize the Atlantic coast of North America. By 1750, about 1.3 million English settlers lived in 13 colonies stretching from New Hampshire to Georgia.

England Battles France The English soon became hungry for more land to suit their growing colonial population. So they pushed further west into the continent. By doing so, however, they collided with France's North American holdings. France and England, long-time enemies, had brought their dislike for one another with them to North America. As their colonies expanded, they began to interfere with each other. It seemed that a major conflict was on the horizon.

That conflict began in 1754. That year a dispute over land claims in the Ohio Valley led to a war between the British and French on the North American continent. The conflict became known as

Background
In 1707, England united with Scotland to become the United Kingdom of Great Britain.

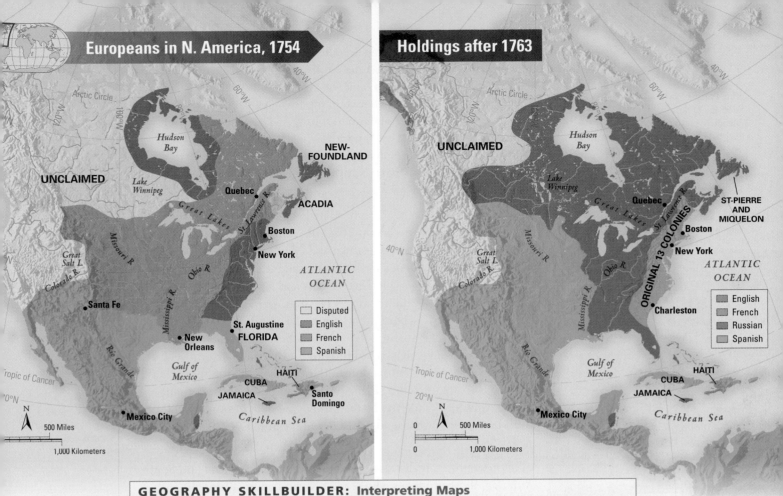

Europeans in N. America, 1754

Arctic Circle

Hudson
Bay

UNCLAIMED

NEW-
FOUNDLAND

Lake
Winnipeg

Quebec

ACADIA

Great Lakes

St. Lawrence R.

Boston

New York

ATLANTIC
OCEAN

Missouri R.

Great
Salt L.

Colorado R.

Ohio R.

Santa Fe

Mississippi R.

St. Augustine
FLORIDA

Disputed
English
French
Spanish

New
Orleans

Rio Grande

Gulf of
Mexico

HAITI

CUBA

Tropic of Cancer

JAMAICA

Santo
Domingo

Mexico City

Caribbean Sea

N

500 Miles

1,000 Kilometers

Holdings after 1763

Arctic Circle

Hudson
Bay

UNCLAIMED

Lake
Winnipeg

Quebec

ST-PIERRE
AND
MIQUELON

Great Lakes

St. Lawrence R.

Boston

ORIGINAL 13 COLONIES

New York

ATLANTIC
OCEAN

40°N

Missouri R.

Great
Salt L.

Colorado R.

Ohio R.

English
French
Russian
Spanish

Charleston

Mississippi R.

Tropic of Cancer

20°N

Rio Grande

Gulf of
Mexico

HAITI

CUBA

JAMAICA

Mexico City

Caribbean Sea

N

0   500 Miles

0   1,000 Kilometers

GEOGRAPHY SKILLBUILDER: Interpreting Maps

1. **Region** *Which nation claimed the largest area of the present-day United States in 1754?*
2. **Place** *How did Britain's North American empire change after 1763?*

Background
The name French and Indian War was the colonists' name for the war. The French and many Indians were allied against the British and the colonists.

the **French and Indian War.** The war became part of a larger conflict known as the Seven Years' War. Britain and France—along with their European allies—also battled for territorial and colonial supremacy in Europe and the West Indies.

In North America, the British colonists, with the help of the British Army, defeated the French in 1763. The French surrendered most of their colonial holdings on the continent. As a result of the French and Indian War, the British seized control of nearly the entire eastern half of North America.

Native American Reaction

As in Mexico and South America, the arrival of Europeans in the present-day United States had a great impact on Native Americans. European colonization brought mostly disaster for the lands' original inhabitants, as many fell to disease and warfare.

A Strained Relationship French and Dutch settlers developed a mostly cooperative relationship with the Native Americans. This was due mainly to the mutual benefits of the fur trade. Native Americans did most of the trapping and then traded the furs to the French for such items as guns, hatchets, mirrors, and beads. The Dutch also cooperated with Native Americans in an effort to establish a fur-trading enterprise.

The groups, however, did not live together in complete harmony. Dutch settlers engaged in fighting with various Native American groups over land claims and trading rights. In 1643, for example, the Dutch and Wappinger tribe fought a bloody battle in which hundreds died. For the most part, however, the French and Dutch colonists lived together peacefully with their North American hosts.

THINK THROUGH HISTORY
D. Analyzing Issues
Why were the Dutch and French able to coexist in relative peace with the Native Americans?

The same could not be said of the English. Early relations between English settlers and Native Americans were cooperative. However, they quickly worsened—mostly over

King Philip's War was one of the bloodiest battles fought between English colonists and Native Americans. About 600 colonists and 3,000 Indians were killed during the fighting.

the issues of land and religion. Unlike the French and Dutch, the English sought to populate their colonies in North America. This meant pushing the natives off their land. The English colonists seized more and more land for their swelling population—and to grow more tobacco. As a result, tensions between the two groups rose.

Misunderstandings over religion also heightened tensions. The English settlers, particularly the Puritans, considered Native Americans heathens—people without a faith. Over time, many Puritans viewed Native Americans as agents of the devil and as a threat to their godly society. For their part, Native Americans developed a similarly hard view toward the white invaders.

THINK THROUGH HISTORY
E. Identifying Problems Why did the issues of land and religion cause such strife between the Native Americans and English settlers?

Settlers and Native Americans Battle The hostility between the English settlers and Native Americans led to warfare. As early as 1622, the Powhatan tribe attacked colonial villages around Jamestown and killed about 350 settlers. The colonists eventually struck back and massacred hundreds of Powhatan.

One of the bloodiest battles colonists and Native Americans waged was known as King Philip's War. It began in 1675 when the Native American ruler **Metacom** (also known as King Philip) led an attack on 52 colonial villages throughout Massachusetts. In the months that followed, both sides massacred hundreds of victims. After a year of fierce fighting, the colonists defeated the natives. Throughout the 17th century, many more smaller skirmishes erupted throughout North America. While the Native Americans fought fiercely, they were no match for the colonists' rifles and cannons.

Natives Fall to Disease More destructive than the Europeans' weapons were their diseases. Like the Spanish in Central and South America, the Europeans who settled North America brought with them several diseases. And just as had happened in Mexico and Peru, the diseases devastated the native population in North America.

In 1616, for example, an epidemic of smallpox ravaged Native Americans living along the New England coast. The population of one tribe, the Massachusett, dropped from 24,000 to 750 by 1631. Thousands of other natives throughout the region also perished.

Background
To celebrate their victory over Metacom, the Puritans cut off his head and displayed it at Plymouth for many years.

"They died on heapes, as they lay in their houses," observed one eyewitness. From South Carolina to Missouri, nearly whole tribes fell to smallpox, measles, and other diseases.

Throughout the Americas, the loss of native life due to disease was incredible. One of the effects of this loss was a severe shortage of labor in the colonies. In order to meet their growing labor needs, European colonists from South America to North America soon turned to another group: Africans, whom they would enslave by the millions.

Section 2 Assessment

1. TERMS & NAMES

Identify
- New France
- Jamestown
- Pilgrims
- Puritans
- New Netherland
- French and Indian War
- Metacom

2. TAKING NOTES

Copy this chart and fill in the location of each settlement and the main reasons for its establishment.

Name of Settlement	General Location	Reasons for Establishment
New France		
New Netherland		
Massachusetts Bay		

Write a letter convincing someone to settle in one of the settlements.

3. MAKING INFERENCES

What may have been one reason the English eventually beat the French in North America?

THINK ABOUT
- how England's colonies differed from those of the French
- English and French colonial populations on the eve of the French and Indian War

4. ANALYZING THEMES

Cultural Interaction
Imagine that you have been asked to settle a dispute between a group of English colonists and Native Americans. Summarize each side's grievances and offer possible solutions.

The Atlantic Slave Trade

MAIN IDEA	WHY IT MATTERS NOW
To meet their growing labor needs, Europeans enslaved millions of Africans in forced labor in the Americas.	Descendants of enslaved Africans represent a significant part of the Americas' population today.

SETTING THE STAGE Sugar plantations and tobacco farms required a large supply of workers to make them profitable for their owners. European owners had planned to use Native Americans as a source of cheap labor. But millions of Native Americans died from disease and warfare. Therefore, the Europeans in Brazil, the Caribbean, and the southern colonies of North America soon turned to Africa for workers.

The Evolution of African Slavery

Beginning around 1500, European colonists began enslaving Africans in the Americas in order to meet their great demand for large numbers of people to work as cheap labor.

Slavery in Africa As it had in other parts of the world, slavery had existed in Africa for many years. In most regions, however, it was a relatively minor institution. The spread of Islam into Africa during the seventh century, however, ushered in an increase in slavery and the slave trade. African rulers justified enslavement with the Muslim belief that non-Muslim prisoners of war could be bought and sold as slaves. As a result, between 650 and 1600, black as well as white Muslims transported as many as 4.8 million Africans—mostly prisoners of war and criminals—to the Muslim lands of Southwest Asia. Once there, these enslaved Africans worked primarily as domestic servants.

In most African and Muslim societies, slaves had some legal rights and opportunity for social mobility. In the Muslim world, slaves even occupied positions of influence and power. Some served as generals in the army. Others bought large estates and even owned slaves of their own. In African societies, slaves could escape their bondage in numerous ways, including marrying into the family they served. Furthermore, slavery in Africa was not hereditary. Thus the sons and daughters of slaves were considered free.

THINK THROUGH HISTORY
A. Summarizing
What were some characteristics of Muslim and African slavery?

The Desire for Africans The first Europeans to explore Africa were the Portuguese during the 1400s. Initially, Portuguese traders were more interested in trading for gold than for captured Africans. That changed, however, with the colonization of the Americas. At first, European colonists in the Americas forced Native Americans to work their profitable mines and plantations. As natives began dying by the millions from disease, Europeans became desperate for new workers.

To resupply their labor force, colonists in the Americas soon looked to Africa. Europeans saw several advantages in using Africans. First, many Africans had been exposed to various European diseases and had built up some immunity to them. Second, many Africans had experience in farming and thus could be taught large-scale plantation work. Third, Africans—strangers to the Americas—had little knowledge of

SPOTLIGHT ON

Slavery

The enslavement of human beings by others is believed to be as old as civilization itself. Slavery probably began with the development of farming about 10,000 years ago. Farming gave people the need to force prisoners of war to work for them.

Slavery has existed in numerous societies around the world. People were enslaved in civilizations from Egypt to China to India, as well as among Indians in America, and in Greece and Rome.

Race was not always a factor in slavery. Often, slaves were captured prisoners of war, or people of a different nationality or religion. In ancient Rome, for example, both owners and slaves were white.

However, the slavery that developed in the Americas was based largely on race. Europeans viewed black people as naturally inferior. Because of this, slavery in the Americas was hereditary—children of slaves were also slaves.

the land and had no familiar tribes in which to hide. As a result, they were less likely to try to escape.

In time, the buying and selling of Africans for work in the Americas—known as the **Atlantic slave trade**—became a massive enterprise. Between 1500 and 1600, nearly 300,000 Africans were transported to the Americas. During the next century, that number climbed to almost 1.5 million. By the time the Atlantic slave trade ended around 1870, Europeans had imported about 9.5 million Africans to the Americas.

Spain and Portugal Lead the Way The Spanish took an early lead in importing Africans to the Americas. As early as 1511, a small number of Africans were working in the copper mines on Hispaniola. In time, Spain moved on from the Caribbean and began to colonize the American mainland. As a result, the Spanish imported and enslaved thousands more Africans. By 1650, nearly 300,000 Africans labored throughout Spanish America on plantations and in gold and silver mines.

By this time, however, the Portuguese had surpassed the Spanish in the importation of Africans to the Americas. During the 1600s, Brazil dominated the European sugar market. As the colony's sugar industry grew, so too did European colonists' demand for slaves. During the 17th century, more than 40 percent of all Africans brought to the Americas went to Brazil. By the time the slave trade ended, Brazil had received more than 3.6 million Africans. That was nearly 10 times the number of Africans who would arrive in North America.

The development of sugar, shown here in its cane form, helped spur the growth of slavery in the Americas.

Slavery Spreads Throughout the Americas As the other European nations established colonies in the Americas, their demand for cheap labor grew. Thus, they also began to import and enslave large numbers of Africans. A majority of these slaves labored on sugar, tobacco, and coffee plantations in the Dutch, French, and English colonies in the Caribbean.

As England's presence in the Americas grew, it came to dominate the Atlantic slave trade. From 1690 until the nation abolished the slave trade in 1807, England was the leading carrier of enslaved Africans. By the time the slave trade ended, the English had transported nearly 1.7 million Africans to their colonies in the West Indies.

A much smaller number of enslaved Africans eventually arrived in what is now the United States. In all, nearly 400,000 Africans were imported to Britain's North American colonies. Once in North America, however, the slave population steadily grew. By 1830, roughly 2 million slaves toiled in the United States.

African Cooperation and Resistance Many African rulers and merchants played a willing role in the Atlantic slave trade. Those African leaders who had been selling Africans as slaves to Muslims and other African rulers saw little difference in selling them to Westerners. Most European traders, rather than travel inland, waited in ports along the western and eastern coasts of Africa. African merchants, with the help of local rulers, captured Africans to be enslaved. They then delivered them to the Europeans in exchange for gold, guns, and other goods.

As the slave trade grew, some African rulers voiced their opposition to the practice. One such ruler was King Nzinga Mbemba of Congo in west-central Africa. Mbemba, also known as Affonso, had originally participated in the slave trade. However, he soon realized its devastating effect on African societies. In 1526, he wrote a letter to the king of Portugal in which he protested the taking of Africans for enslavement:

A VOICE FROM THE PAST

And we cannot reckon how great the damage is, since . . . merchants are taking every day our natives, sons of the land and the sons of our noblemen and vassals and our relatives, because the thieves and men of bad conscience grab them . . . they grab them and get them to be sold; and so great, Sir, is the corruption . . . that our country is being completely depopulated, and Your Highness should not agree with this nor accept it. . . . *it is our will that in these Kingdoms there should not be any trade of slaves nor outlet for them.*

KING AFFONSO, quoted in *African Civilization Revisited*

Background
The total number of Arricans taken from Africa during the Atlantic slave trade is thought to be even higher. Scholars believe that many Africans perished during the voyage to the Americas. Thus, they were unaccounted for.

Background
By 1690, the slave population on the British island of Barbados was 60,000—three times that of the white population.

Despite Affonso's plea, the slave trade continued and steadily grew. Lured by its profits, many African rulers continued to participate. As for African merchants, they simply developed new trade routes to avoid rulers who refused to cooperate.

A Forced Journey

After being captured, African men and women were shipped to the Americas as part of a profitable trade network. Along the way, millions of captured Africans endured a dehumanizing voyage across the Atlantic. Many died on the way.

The Triangular Trade Africans transported to the Americas were part of a transatlantic trading network known as the **triangular trade.** Over one trade route, Europeans transported manufactured goods to the west coast of Africa. There, traders exchanged these goods for captured Africans. The Africans were then transported across the Atlantic Ocean and sold in the West Indies. Merchants then bought sugar, coffee, and tobacco in the West Indies and sailed back to Europe to sell these products.

On another triangular route, merchants carried rum and other goods from the New England colonies to Africa. There they exchanged their merchandise for Africans. The traders then transported the Africans to the West Indies and sold them for sugar and molasses. They then sold these goods to rum producers in New England.

Various other transatlantic routes existed. In fact, the "triangular" trade encompassed a network of trade routes crisscrossing the Northern and Southern colonies, the West Indies, England, Europe, and Africa. The network carried a variety of traded goods. These included furs, fruit, tar, and tobacco, as well as millions of African people.

The Middle Passage The voyage that brought captured Africans to the West Indies and later to North and South America was known as the **middle passage.** It was so named because it was considered the middle leg of the transatlantic trade triangle.

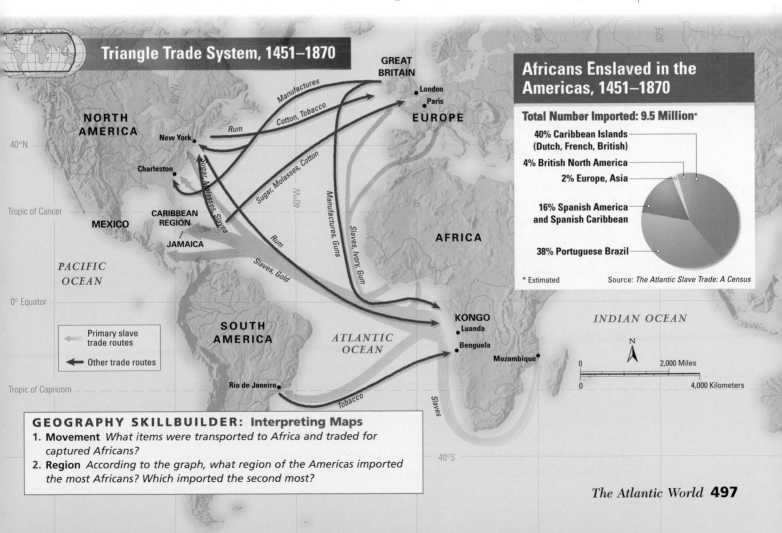

Triangle Trade System, 1451–1870

Africans Enslaved in the Americas, 1451–1870

Total Number Imported: 9.5 Million*

- 40% Caribbean Islands (Dutch, French, British)
- 4% British North America
- 2% Europe, Asia
- 16% Spanish America and Spanish Caribbean
- 38% Portuguese Brazil

* Estimated   Source: *The Atlantic Slave Trade: A Census*

Primary slave trade routes
Other trade routes

GEOGRAPHY SKILLBUILDER: Interpreting Maps
1. **Movement** What items were transported to Africa and traded for captured Africans?
2. **Region** According to the graph, what region of the Americas imported the most Africans? Which imported the second most?

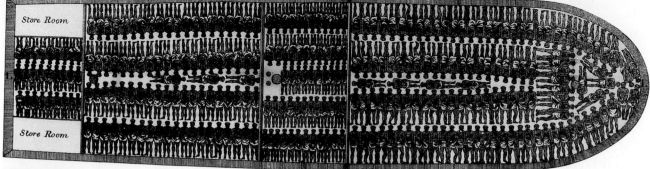

This design of a British slave ship offers a glimpse of what life was like for enslaved Africans during their trip to the Americas.

Olaudah Equiano

Sickening cruelty characterized this journey. In the bustling ports along the African coasts, European traders packed Africans into the dark holds of large ships. On board a slave ship, Africans fell victim to whippings and beatings from merchants, as well as diseases that swept through the vessel. The smell of blood, sweat, and excrement filled the hold. African captives often lived in their own vomit and waste. One African, Olaudah Equiano, recalled the inhumane conditions on his trip from West Africa to the West Indies at age 11 in 1756:

> I was soon put down under the decks, and there I received such a salutation [greeting] in my nostrils as I never experienced in my life; so that, with the loathsomeness of the stench, and crying together, I became so sick and low that I was not able to eat . . . but soon, to my grief, two of the white men offered me eatables; and on my refusing to eat, one of them held me fast by the hands, and laid me across . . . the windlass, and tied my feet, while the other flogged me severely.
>
> **OLAUDAH EQUIANO,** quoted in *Eyewitness: The Negro in American History*

Background
After working for some time in the West Indies, Equiano was freed. He eventually went to England, where he crusaded against slavery.

Numerous Africans died aboard the slave ships from disease or from cruel treatment by merchants. Many others committed suicide by plunging into the ocean rather than be enslaved. Scholars estimate that roughly 20 percent of the Africans aboard each slave ship perished during the brutal trip to the Americas.

Slavery in the Americas

Africans who survived their ocean voyage entered a difficult life of bondage in the Americas. Forced to work in a strange land, enslaved Africans coped in a variety of ways. Many embraced their African culture, while others rebelled against their enslavers.

A Harsh Life Upon arriving in the Americas, captured Africans usually were auctioned off to the highest bidder. A British minister who visited a slave market in Brazil commented on the process: "When a customer comes in, they [the slaves] are turned before him; such as he wishes are handled by the purchaser in different parts, exactly as I have seen butchers feeling a calf."

After being sold, slaves worked in mines or fields or as domestic servants. Whatever their task, slaves lived a grueling existence. Many lived on little food in small, dreary huts. They worked long days and often suffered whippings and beatings. In much of the Americas, slavery was a lifelong condition, as well as a hereditary one. This meant that the sons and daughters of slaves were born into a lifetime of bondage.

Resistance and Rebellion To cope with the horrors of slavery, Africans developed a way of life based strongly on their cultural heritage. They kept alive such things as their musical traditions as well as the stories of their ancestors.

Enslaved Africans also found ways to resist their bondage. They made themselves less productive by breaking hoes, uprooting plants, and working slowly. This resistance hurt their owners' profit. Although they were unfamiliar with the land, thousands of slaves also ran away.

Some slaves pushed their resistance to open revolt. As early as 1522, about 20 slaves on Hispaniola attacked and killed several Spanish colonists. Larger revolts occurred throughout Spanish settlements during the 16th century. In Colombia, for example, enslaved Africans destroyed the town of Santa Marta in 1530.

Occasional uprisings also occurred throughout Brazil, the West Indies, and North America. In 1739, a group of slaves in South Carolina led an uprising known as the Stono Rebellion. They killed several colonists and then engaged the local militia in battle. Many slaves died during the fighting. Those who were captured were executed. Despite the ultimate failure of slave revolts, uprisings continued into the 1800s.

THINK THROUGH HISTORY
D. Summarizing In what ways did enslaved Africans resist their bondage?

Consequences of the Atlantic Slave Trade

The Atlantic slave trade had a profound impact on both Africa and the Americas. In Africa, numerous cultures lost generations of their fittest members—their young and able—to European traders and plantation owners. In addition, countless African families were torn apart. Many of them were never reunited. The slave trade devastated African societies in another way: by introducing guns into the continent. More effective than spears, guns were in great demand by African rulers seeking to conquer new territory. Firearms, which African chiefs and kings traded for potential slaves, helped spread war and conflict throughout Africa.

While they were unwilling participants in the growth of the colonies, African slaves contributed greatly to the economic and cultural development of the Americas. Their greatest contribution was their labor. Without their back-breaking work, colonies such as those on Haiti and Barbados may not have survived. In addition to their muscle, enslaved Africans also brought their expertise, especially in agriculture. Africans from the Upper Guinea region in West Africa, for example, brought their rice-growing techniques to South Carolina. There, they helped make that colony a profitable rice producer. Africans also brought with them their culture. Aspects of their culture—including art, music, and food—continue to influence American societies.

THINK THROUGH HISTORY
E. Recognizing Effects What are some of the contributions that Africans have made to the Americas?

The influx of so many Africans to the Americas also has left its mark on the very population itself. From the United States to Brazil, many of the nations of the Western Hemisphere today have substantial African-American populations. Furthermore, many Latin American countries—where intermarriage between slaves and colonists was much more common than in North America—have sizable mixed-race populations.

As the next section explains, Africans were not the only cargo transported across the Atlantic during the colonization of the Americas. The settlement of the Americas brought many different items from Europe, Asia, and Africa to North and South America. It also introduced items from the Americas to the rest of the world.

CONNECT *to* TODAY

Gullah

One legacy of African slaves lives in the quick-paced words of Gullah. Gullah is a combination of English and colonial speech and the languages from several West African societies. Nearly 6,000 African words have been identified in Gullah. The American descendants of slaves still speak Gullah on the Sea Islands of South Carolina and Georgia and on the mainland nearby.

Gullah speakers live in relatively isolated communities. Over the years they have contributed words to the language spoken in the United States. The words include goober (peanut), juke (as in jukebox), and voodoo (witchcraft).

Section ③ Assessment

1. TERMS & NAMES

Identify
• Atlantic slave trade
• triangular trade
• middle passage

2. TAKING NOTES

Using a diagram like the one below, list the ways in which the Atlantic slave trade affected both Africa and the Americas.

Consequences of the Slave Trade	
In Africa	**In the Americas**
1.	1.
2.	2.
3.	3.

3. CONTRASTING

How was slavery in the Americas different from slavery in Africa and Muslim lands?

THINK ABOUT
• the length of bondage
• the children of slaves
• opportunities for slaves within each society
• racial basis

4. THEME ACTIVITY

Cultural Interaction

Reread the excerpt from King Affonso's letter on page 496. Imagine you are an African ruler. Write your own letter to a European leader in which you try to convince him or her to stop participating in the slave trade. Include in your letter the various aspects of slavery and the slave trade you learned about in this section.

The Columbian Exchange and Global Trade

TERMS & NAMES
- Columbian Exchange
- Commercial Revolution
- capitalism
- joint-stock company
- mercantilism
- favorable balance of trade

MAIN IDEA	WHY IT MATTERS NOW
The colonization of the Americas introduced new and different items into the Eastern and Western hemispheres.	This global exchange of goods permanently changed Europe, Asia, Africa, and the Americas.

SETTING THE STAGE The colonization of the Americas dramatically changed the world. It prompted both voluntary and forced migration of millions of people. It also led to the establishment of new and powerful societies. European settlement of the Americas also changed the world in less noticeable but equally important ways. It led to the exchange of new items that greatly affected the lives of people throughout the world.

The Columbian Exchange

The global transfer of foods, plants, and animals during the colonization of the Americas was known as the **Columbian Exchange**. Ships from the Americas brought back a wide array of items that Europeans, Asians, and Africans had never before seen. They included such plants as tomatoes, squash, pineapples, tobacco, and cacao beans (for chocolate).

Perhaps the most important items to travel from the Americas to the rest of the world were corn and potatoes. Corn and potatoes were inexpensive to grow and highly nutritious. Over time, both crops became an important and steady part of diets throughout the world. These foods helped people live healthier and longer lives. Thus they played a significant role in boosting the world's population. The planting of the first white potato in Ireland and the first sweet potato in China probably changed more lives than the deeds of 100 kings.

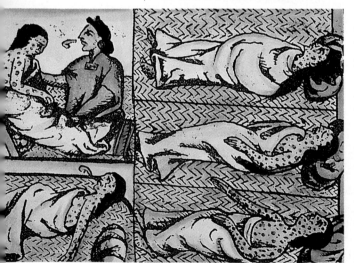

In this Spanish illustration, a medicine man tends to an Aztec with smallpox.

Traffic across the Atlantic did not flow in just one direction, however. Europeans introduced various livestock animals into the Americas. These included horses, cattle, and pigs. Foods from Africa (including some that originated in Asia) migrated west in European ships. They included bananas, black-eyed peas, and yams.

Some aspects of the Columbian Exchange had a tragic impact on many Native Americans. Disease was just as much a part of the Columbian Exchange as goods and food. The diseases Europeans brought with them, which included smallpox and measles, led to the death of millions of Native Americans.

THINK THROUGH HISTORY
A. Making Inferences Why is the Columbian Exchange considered a significant event?

A Commercial Revolution

The establishment of colonial empires in the Americas influenced the nations of Europe in still other ways. New wealth from the Americas was coupled with a dramatic growth in overseas trade. These together prompted a wave of new business and trade practices in Europe during the 16th and 17th centuries. These practices—many of which served as the root of today's financial dealings—dramatically changed the economic atmosphere of Europe. Together they became known as the **Commercial Revolution**.

The Columbian Exchange

Few events transformed the world like the Columbian Exchange. This global transfer of plants, animals, disease, and especially food, brought together the Eastern and Western hemispheres and touched, in some way, nearly all the peoples of the world.

Frightening Foods

Several foods from the Americas that we now take for granted at first amazed and terrified Europeans.

Early on, people thought the tomato was harmful to eat. "If I should eat this fruit," explained one Italian man, "it would be injurious and harmful to me." One German official warned that the tomato "should not be taken internally."

In 1619, officials in Burgundy, France, banned the potato, explaining that "too frequent use of them caused the leprosy." In 1774, starving peasants in Prussia refused to eat the spud.

The culinary life we owe Columbus is a progressive dinner in which the whole human race takes part but no one need leave home to sample all the courses.

Raymond Sokolov

The Columbian Exchange

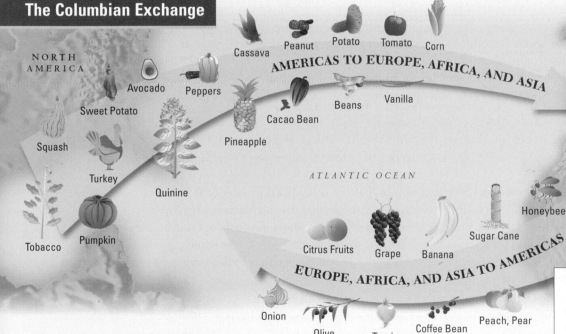

AMERICAS TO EUROPE, AFRICA, AND ASIA

NORTH AMERICA

Cassava · Peanut · Potato · Tomato · Corn

Avocado · Peppers

Sweet Potato

Squash

Turkey

Quinine

Pineapple · Cacao Bean · Beans · Vanilla

Tobacco · Pumpkin

ATLANTIC OCEAN

Citrus Fruits · Grape · Banana · Sugar Cane · Honeybee

EUROPE, AFRICA, AND ASIA TO AMERICAS

Onion · Olive · Turnip · Coffee Bean · Peach, Pear

EUROPE

Disease
• Smallpox
• Influenza
• Typhus
• Measles
• Malaria
• Diphtheria
• Whooping Cough

Livestock
• Cattle
• Sheep
• Pig
• Horse

Grains
• Wheat
• Rice
• Barley
• Oats

AFRICA

Patterns of Interaction

Think about your favorite foods. Chances are that at least one originated in a distant land. Throughout history, the introduction of new foods into a region has dramatically changed lives—for better and worse. Dependence on the potato, for example, led to a famine in Ireland. This prompted a massive migration of Irish people to other countries. In the Americas, the introduction of sugar led to riches for some and enslavement for many others.

▶ VIDEO *The Geography of Food: The Impact of Potatoes and Sugar*

Connect to History

Forming Opinions What were the most beneficial and harmful aspects of the Columbian Exchange? Why?

 SEE SKILLBUILDER HANDBOOK, PAGE 1004

Connect to Today

Researching Find out what are the major items exchanged or traded between the United States and either Asia, Africa, or Europe. Report your findings to the class.

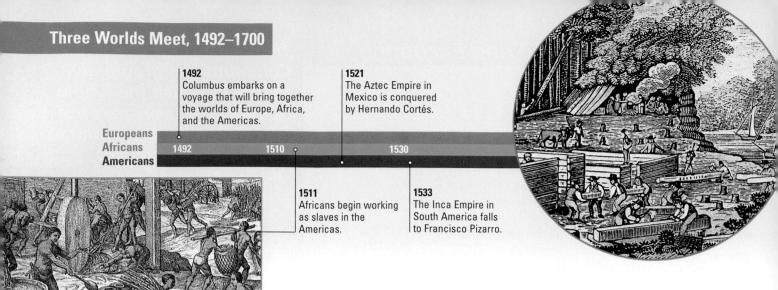

1492
Columbus embarks on a voyage that will bring together the worlds of Europe, Africa, and the Americas.

1521
The Aztec Empire in Mexico is conquered by Hernando Cortés.

Europeans
Africans
Americans

1492   1510   1530

1511
Africans begin working as slaves in the Americas.

1533
The Inca Empire in South America falls to Francisco Pizarro.

The Rise of Capitalism One aspect of the European Commercial Revolution was the growth of **capitalism.** Capitalism is an economic system based on private ownership and the investment of wealth for profit. No longer were governments the sole owners of great wealth. Due to overseas colonization and trade, numerous merchants had obtained great wealth. These merchants continued to invest their money in trade and overseas exploration. Profits from these investments enabled merchants and traders to reinvest even more money in other enterprises. As a result, businesses across Europe grew and flourished.

The increase in economic activity in Europe led to an overall increase in many nations' money supply. This in turn brought on inflation, or the steady rise in the price of goods. Inflation occurs when people have more money to spend and thus demand more goods and services. Because the supply of goods is less than the demand requires, the goods become both scarce and more valuable. Prices, then, rise. At this time in Europe, the costs of many goods rose. Spain, for example, endured a crushing bout of inflation during the 1600s, as boatloads of gold and silver from the Americas greatly increased the nation's money supply.

Joint-Stock Companies Another business venture developed during this period was the **joint-stock company.** The joint-stock company worked much like the modern-day corporation. It involved a number of people pooling their wealth for a common purpose.

In Europe during the 1500s and 1600s, that common purpose was American colonization. It took large amounts of money to establish overseas colonies. Moreover, while profits may have been great, so were risks. Many ships, for instance, never completed the long and dangerous ocean voyage. Because joint-stock companies involved numerous investors, the individual members paid only a fraction of the total colonization cost. If the colony failed, investors lost only their small share. If the colony thrived, the investors shared in the profits. It was a joint-stock company that was responsible for establishing Jamestown, England's first North American colony.

The Growth of Mercantilism During this time, the nations of Europe adopted a new economic policy known as **mercantilism.** The theory of mercantilism held that a country's power depended mainly on its wealth. It was wealth, after all, that allowed nations to build strong navies and purchase vital goods. As a result, the goal of every nation became the attainment of as much wealth as possible.

According to the theory of mercantilism, a nation could increase its wealth and power in two ways. First, it could obtain as much gold and silver as possible. Second, it could establish a **favorable balance of trade,** in which it sold more goods than it bought. A nation's ultimate goal under mercantilism was to become self-sufficient, not

Vocabulary
invest: to spend time, money, or effort for future advantage or benefit.

THINK THROUGH HISTORY
B. Making Inferences Why would a joint-stock company be popular with investors in overseas colonies?

1607	1628		1700
Colonists found Jamestown, first permanent English settlement in North America.	Puritans establish the Massachusetts Bay Colony in North America.		The number of enslaved Africans imported to the Americas reaches almost 1.5 million. It will climb to nearly 6 million by the end of the century.

1610	1630		1670	1690

1650
The number of Africans toiling in Spanish America reaches 300,000.

1675
Native Americans battle colonists in King Philip's War.

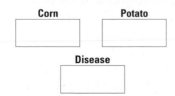

dependent on other countries for goods. An English author of the time wrote about the new economic idea of mercantilism:

A VOICE FROM THE PAST
Although a Kingdom may be enriched by gifts received, or by purchases taken from some other Nations. . . . these are things uncertain and of small consideration when they happen. The ordinary means therefore to increase our wealth and treasure is by Foreign Trade, wherein we must ever observe this rule: to sell more to strangers yearly than we consume of theirs in value.

THOMAS MUN, quoted in *World Civilizations*

THINK THROUGH HISTORY
C. Summarizing
What role did colonies play in the policy of mercantilism?

Mercantilism went hand in hand with colonization, for colonies played a vital role in this new economic practice. Aside from providing silver and gold, colonies provided raw materials that could not be found in the home country, such as wood or furs. In addition to playing the role of supplier, the colonies under mercantilism also provided a market. The home country could sell its goods to their colonies.

Changes in European Society The economic changes that swept through much of Europe during the age of American colonization also led to changes in European society. The Commercial Revolution spurred the growth of towns and the rise of the merchant class. Merchants—because they controlled great wealth—rose in status.

The changes in European society, however, only went so far. While towns and cities grew in size, much of Europe's population continued to live in rural areas. And although merchants and traders enjoyed a period of social mobility, a majority of Europeans remained poor. More than anything else, the Commercial Revolution increased the wealth of European nations. Also, as Chapter 21 will describe, the new economic practices helped to expand the power of European rulers.

Section 4 Assessment

1. TERMS & NAMES

Identify
• Columbian Exchange
• Commercial Revolution
• capitalism
• joint-stock company
• mercantilism
• favorable balance of trade

2. TAKING NOTES

For each Columbian Exchange item or aspect below, write where it originated and explain its significance.

Corn	Potato

Disease

Write an explanation of one of the items to someone who has never encountered it.

3. MAKING INFERENCES

Why were colonies considered so important to the nations of Europe?

THINK ABOUT
• the philosophy of mercantilism
• the notion of a favorable balance of trade

4. ANALYZING THEMES

Economics Do you think the economic changes in Europe during the era of American colonization qualify as a revolution? Why or why not?

THINK ABOUT
• the legacy of the new business and trade practices
• how the economic changes affected European society as a whole

The Atlantic World **503**

TERMS & NAMES

Briefly explain the importance of each of the following in the European colonization of the Americas.

1. conquistadors
2. Montezuma II
3. *encomienda*
4. Jamestown
5. French and Indian War
6. Atlantic slave trade
7. triangular trade
8. Columbian Exchange
9. Commercial Revolution
10. mercantilism

Interact *with* History

On page 482 you examined the choices some Native Americans faced during the invasion by Spanish conquistadors. Now that you have read the chapter, rethink the choice you made. If you chose to side with the Spaniards, would you now change your mind? Why or why not? If you decided to fight with the Aztecs, what are your feelings now? Discuss your opinions with a small group.

REVIEW QUESTIONS

SECTION 1 *(pages 483–488)*
Spanish Conquests in the Americas

11. Why did Columbus set sail on the Atlantic?
12. List three goals of the Spanish in the Americas.
13. Why did Popé lead a rebellion against the Spanish?

SECTION 2 *(pages 490–494)*
Competing Claims in North America

14. What did the Europeans mostly grow in their Caribbean colonies?
15. What was the result of the French and Indian War?

SECTION 3 *(pages 495–499)*
The Atlantic Slave Trade

16. What factors led European colonists to use Africans to resupply their labor force?
17. Describe the conditions on board a slave ship.
18. Name several ways in which enslaved Africans resisted their position in the Americas.

SECTION 4 *(pages 500–503)*
The Columbian Exchange and Global Trade

19. Why was the introduction of corn and potatoes to Europe and Asia so significant?
20. Explain the economic policy of mercantilism.

Visual Summary

The Atlantic World

Europeans

- Beginning around 1500, the Spanish and Portuguese colonize Central and South America and establish prosperous overseas empires.
- Throughout the 1600s and 1700s, the English, French, and Dutch battle for control of North America, with the English emerging victorious.
- Over time, Europeans take control of nearly all of the Americas and create new societies.

GLOBAL INTERACTION

Africans

- Beginning around 1500, millions of Africans are taken from their homeland and forced to labor as slaves for Europeans in the Americas.
- Numerous Africans perish during the brutal ocean voyage to the Americas, known as the middle passage.
- Africans eventually become an important part of the Americas, as they populate the various regions and lend aspects of their culture to American societies.

Native Americans

- Between 1520 and 1533, the once mighty Aztec and Inca empires fall to the invading Spanish.
- Throughout the Americas, the native population is devastated by European conquests and diseases.
- In Central and South America, many Spanish settlers and Native Americans intermarry, creating a large mestizo population that thrives today.

CRITICAL THINKING

1. THE TOOLS OF CONQUEST

THEME EMPIRE BUILDING In conquering much of the Americas, Europeans were aided by several things. What were they? Which do you consider to be the most important? Why?

2. EXPLORERS OF THE WEST

Copy the chart below on your paper. For each explorer named, write which nation sponsored him and the regions he explored.

Explorer	Nation	Regions
Pedro Álvares Cabral		
Ferdinand Magellan		
Francisco Vásquez de Coronado		
Jacques Cartier		
Samuel de Champlain		
Henry Hudson		

3. A HISTORIC VOYAGE

It has been said that Columbus's voyage began a process that changed the world forever. Explain the meaning of this statement. In your explanation, consider all the peoples and places American colonization impacted and what effects it had on them.

4. ANALYZING PRIMARY SOURCES

In 1630, a Puritan minister, John Cotton, delivered a sermon to fellow Puritans as they embarked on their journey to America. In it, Cotton tried to reassure the future colonists that they could legitimately claim a new land.

> **A VOICE FROM THE PAST**
> Where there is a vacant place, there is liberty for . . . [Christians] . . . to come and inhabit, though they neither buy it nor ask their leaves. . . . Indeed, no nation is to drive out another without special commission from Heaven . . . unless the natives do unjustly wrong them, and will not recompense the wrongs done in a peaceable fort [way]. And then they may right themselves by lawful war and subdue the country unto themselves.
>
> **JOHN COTTON,** quoted in *The Annals of America*

- What do you think Native Americans might have said about Cotton's statement that America was a "vacant place"?

- How might the last part of Cotton's statement have helped the Puritans to justify taking land from the Native Americans?

- How is this passage an example of a biased statement?

CHAPTER ACTIVITIES

1. LIVING HISTORY: Unit Portfolio Project

THEME CULTURAL INTERACTION Your unit portfolio project focuses on showing how different cultures have interacted in history. (See page 387.) For Chapter 20, you might use one of the following ideas to add to your portfolio:

- Draw a political cartoon that contrasts the Europeans' and Native Americans' view of American colonization.

- Write a newspaper editorial explaining how Africans helped create the societies that grew in the Americas.

- Imagine you are a Native American entering an English colony for the first time. Write a journal entry describing your encounter with the culture.

2. CONNECT TO TODAY: Cooperative Learning

THEME ECONOMICS The Columbian Exchange marked the beginning of worldwide trade. The plants, foods, and animals that traveled across hemispheres during the Columbian Exchange are now just some of the many foods and items that are traded around the globe today.

Work with a team to chart the global trade of a chosen food or item.

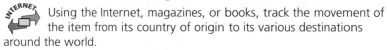 Using the Internet, magazines, or books, track the movement of the item from its country of origin to its various destinations around the world.

- Determine how much of the item the various countries import. Compare the cost of the item in these countries.

- Compare your team's item with those of the other teams to determine which is the most popular.

3. INTERPRETING A TIME LINE

Revisit the time line on pages 386–387. Examine the Chapter 20 time line. Which two events do you think had the most lasting effects on the Americas? Explain why.

FOCUS ON ART

This Aztec drawing depicts natives attacking several Spaniards, who after killing Indian nobles, took refuge in a nearby palace.

- How does the image depict the clash of cultures in the Americas?

- What is the drawing's point of view regarding the Aztec warriors? The Spanish?

Connect to History Of the factors that enabled the Spanish to defeat the Aztecs, which one is visible in this drawing?

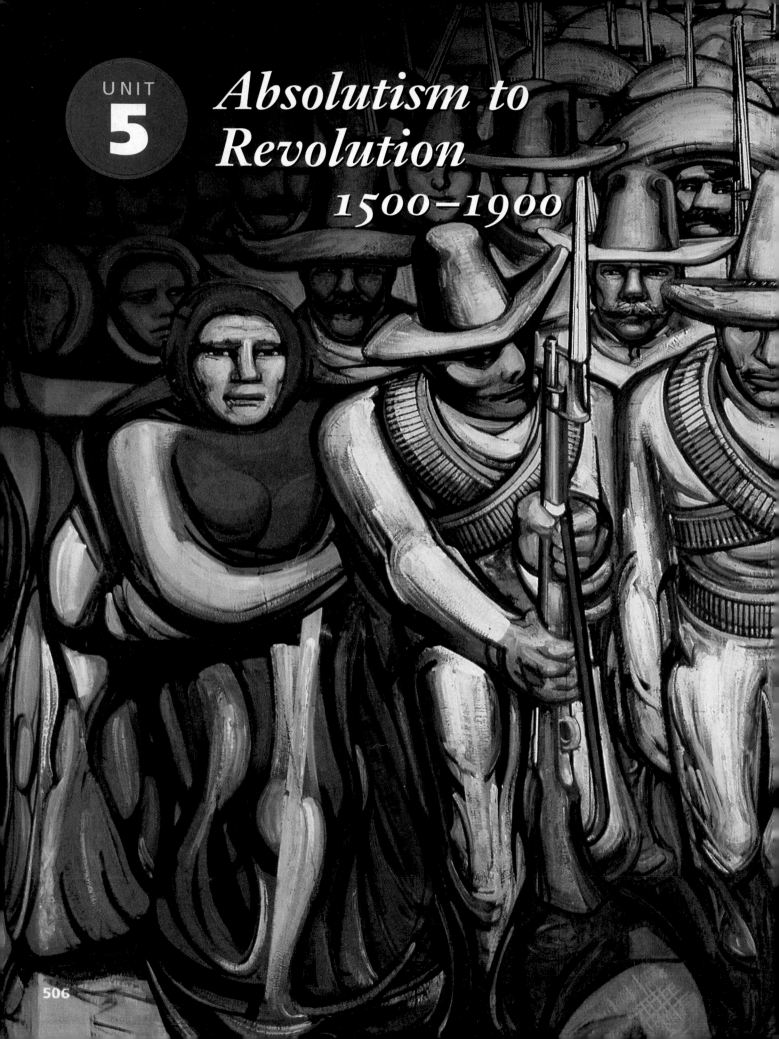

Absolutism to Revolution
1500–1900

This scene is from a mural entitled *From Porfirio's Dictatorship to the Revolution*, by the Mexican artist David Alfaro Siqueiros. During this time, revolution swept the globe as people from Europe to Latin America overthrew old institutions.

	1500	1550	1600	1650	1700

CHAPTER 21 1500–1800
Absolute Monarchs in Europe

1520–1566 *Ottoman Empire* Suleiman I reigns as sultan

1533 *Russia* Ivan the Terrible assumes throne at age three

1581 *Russia* Czar Ivan the Terrible kills his son and heir

1588 *England* English navy defeats Spanish Armada

1611 *England* First King James Bible is printed

1618 *Bohemia* Thirty Years' War begins

1643 *France* Louis XIV begins 72-year reign

1649 *England* Oliver Cromwell and Puritans execute English king

1661 *France* Louis XIV begins 40-year building of palace at Versailles

1689 *England* William of Orange becomes king

CHAPTER 22 1550–1789
Enlightenment and Revolution

1543 *Poland* Copernicus presents heliocentric theory

1590 *Holland* Zacharias Janssen develops microscope

1572 *Denmark* Tycho Brahe discovers nova in space

1609 *Italy* Galileo uses telescope to study moon

1633 *Italy* Inquisition condemns Galileo

1660 *Britain* Navigation Acts restrict trade in American colonies

1687 *Britain* Newton presents the law of gravity

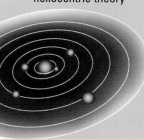

▲ **1500s**

CHAPTER 23 1789–1815
The French Revolution and Napoleon

1700s *France* ▶

CHAPTER 24 1789–1900
Nationalist Revolutions Sweep the West

1500	1550	1600	1650	1700

1703 *Russia*
Peter the Great orders St. Petersburg to be built

1740 *Austria*
Maria Theresa inherits throne

1756 *Prussia*
Frederick the Great starts Seven Years' War

◄ **1700s** *Prussia*

1740 *Britain*
Samuel Richardson publishes novel *Pamela*

1748 *France*
Montesquieu publishes *Spirit of the Laws*

1759 *France*
Voltaire writes *Candide*

1751 *France* Diderot begins publishing *Encyclopedia*

1762 *Russia*
Catherine the Great becomes empress

1776 *America* Colonies declare independence from Britain

1788 *United States*
Constitution ratified

1789 *France*
French Revolution begins

1793 *France*
King Louis XVI executed by guillotine

1793-1794 *France*
Robespierre conducts Reign of Terror

1804 *France* Napoleon becomes emperor

1805-1812 *France*
Napoleon conquers most countries in Europe

1815 *France* Napoleon defeated at Waterloo

1815 *Austria* Congress of Vienna restores old European boundaries

1804 *Haiti* gains independence from France

1821 *Mexico* declares independence

1830 *Greece* wins full independence

1848 *Europe* Revolutions sweep Europe

◄ **1800s** *Greece*

1861 *Russia*
Alexander II frees the serfs

1870 *Italy*
Italy is unified

1871 *Germany* Franco-Prussian War ends; Germany is unified

Living History
Unit 5 Portfolio Project

THEME Revolution

Your portfolio for Unit 5 will compare and contrast the different kinds of revolutions that take place during this time period. While some groups overthrow governments, others overthrow long-held ideas about science, economy, religion, and even art. You can compare and contrast the causes of these revolutions, how they occur, and their results.

Living History Project Choices
Each Chapter Assessment offers you choices of ways to show the revolutionary changes that take place in that chapter. Activities include the following:

Chapter 21 poster, editorial, HistoryMaker

Chapter 22 magazine cover, news report, song lyrics

Chapter 23 interviews, cartoons, dialogue

Chapter 24 newspaper report, speech, how-to book

Absolute Monarchs in Europe, 1500–1800

PREVIEWING THEMES

Power and Authority

Because of the Reformation and the Age of Exploration, Europe experienced religious, economic, and political turmoil. To deal with these crises, European rulers increased their power. They claimed God gave them the authority to do so.

Revolution

When the Spanish king tried to wipe out Protestantism, the Spanish Netherlands revolted. When English kings tried to increase their power at the expense of Parliament, they lost their thrones. England had two revolutions—one bloody and one bloodless.

Economics

When Spain imported tons of silver from the Americas, it experienced severe inflation. Spain spent much money to buy goods from the Spanish Netherlands, which had a thriving commercial empire. France used the practice of mercantilism to improve its economy.

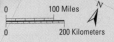

INTERNET CONNECTION

Visit us at www.mcdougallittell.com to learn more about European monarchs.

- ▨ French Bourbon lands
- ▨ Spanish Bourbon lands
- ▨ Austrian Hapsburg lands
- ▨ Prussian lands
- ▨ British Stuart lands
- ▨ Russian lands
- — Boundary of Holy Roman Empire

0   100 Miles
0   200 Kilometers

EUROPE, 1650

Oliver Cromwell overthrew the English king in **1649** and set up a republican government. However, he eventually seized as much power as any monarch. He waged war, doubled the late king's budget, and regulated the economy. He also banned newspapers, hired spies to keep track of his enemies, and executed his opponents.

SCOTLAND

IRELAND

North Sea

ENGLAND

London

UNITED NETHERLAND
Amsterdam •
Utrecht •

• Paris

• Nantes

FRANCE

SWITZERLA

Bay of Biscay

SAVOY

MIL

GEN

TUSCA

PORTUGAL
Lisbon •

• Madrid

CORSI
Geno

SPAIN

MINORCA
Gr. Br.

SARDIN
Austri

• Gibraltar

Mediterranean Sea

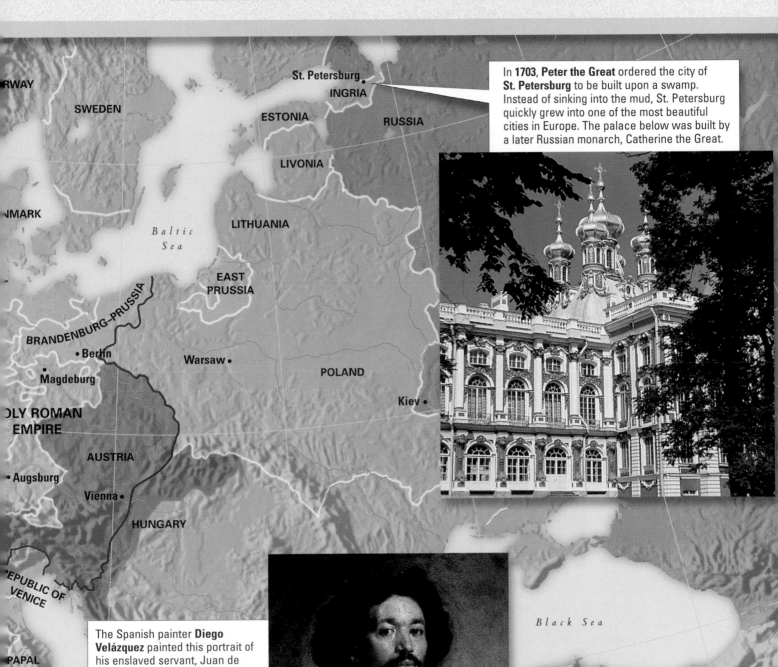

In **1703**, **Peter the Great** ordered the city of **St. Petersburg** to be built upon a swamp. Instead of sinking into the mud, St. Petersburg quickly grew into one of the most beautiful cities in Europe. The palace below was built by a later Russian monarch, Catherine the Great.

The Spanish painter **Diego Velázquez** painted this portrait of his enslaved servant, Juan de Pareja, in **1650**. Velázquez taught Pareja to be a painter and granted him his freedom, also in **1650**. The painting is notable for the human dignity it gives to its subject.

511

Interact *with* History

You are the monarch of a European nation. After a long struggle—during which your life was in danger—you have come into power. Now that you have the throne, you want to make sure that no one ever threatens you again. In addition, you want everyone to believe that you are the greatest ruler in all of Europe. You decide to build a palace that will impress both your subjects and visitors to your kingdom.

How will you design your palace?

The workers in this painting are building a 2,000-room palace for Louis XIV of France. The royal court will live there.

Instead of defensive walls and moats, elegant gardens and lawns will surround the palace. This is to impress visitors, especially rival monarchs and statesmen.

In the foreground, workers move champagne-colored stones for the palace walls. The king chose these stones for their beauty.

The Building of Versailles, Adam François van der Meulen, 1632-1690, The Royal Collection © Her Majesty Queen Elizabeth II

EXAMINING *the* ISSUES

- What will be your palace's main function: as a fortress, the seat of government, housing for the court, or a place to entertain visitors?

- What qualities do you want people to associate with your rule: military strength, wealth, political power, cultural brilliance?

- How can a palace demonstrate the qualities that you have decided are important? What features should the palace have?

As a class, discuss these questions. You may want to refer back to other royal building projects that you have studied. Some examples are the hanging gardens in Babylon, the castles in feudal Europe, and Great Zimbabwe in Africa.

As you read about absolute monarchs in Europe, notice their building projects. Especially note the projects of Philip II of Spain, Louis XIV of France, and Peter the Great of Russia.

1 Spain's Empire and European Absolutism

MAIN IDEA	WHY IT MATTERS NOW
During a time of religious and economic instability, Philip II ruled Spain with a strong hand.	When faced with crises, many heads of government take on additional economic or political powers.

SETTING THE STAGE From 1520 to 1566, Suleiman I exercised great power as sultan of the Ottoman Empire. A European monarch of the same period—Charles V—came close to matching Suleiman's power. As the Hapsburg king, Charles inherited Spain, Spain's American colonies, parts of Italy, and lands in Austria and the Netherlands. As the elected Holy Roman emperor, he ruled much of Germany. It was the first time since Charlemagne that a European ruler controlled so much territory.

Spain's Powerful Empire

A devout Catholic, Charles not only fought Muslims but also opposed Lutherans. In 1555, he unwillingly agreed to the Peace of Augsburg. It allowed German princes to choose the religion for their territory. The following year, Charles V divided his immense empire and retired to a monastery. To his brother Ferdinand, he left Austria and the Holy Roman Empire. His son, **Philip II,** inherited Spain, the Spanish Netherlands, and the American colonies.

Philip II's Empire Philip was shy, serious, and—like his father—deeply religious. However, he could be aggressive for the sake of his empire. In 1580, the king of Portugal died without an heir. Because Philip was the king's nephew, he seized the Portuguese kingdom. Counting Portuguese strongholds in Africa, India, and the East Indies, he now had an empire that circled the globe.

Philip's empire provided him with incredible wealth. By 1600, American mines had supplied Spain with an estimated 339,000 pounds of gold. Between 1550 and 1650, roughly 16,000 tons of silver bullion were unloaded from Spanish galleons. The king of Spain claimed between a fourth and a fifth of every shipload of treasure as his royal share. With this wealth, Spain was able to support a large standing army of 50,000 soldiers.

Vocabulary
bullion: gold or silver in the form of solid bars.

Defender of Catholicism When Philip took power, Europe was experiencing religious wars, caused by the Reformation. However, religious conflict was not new to Spain. The Reconquista—the campaign to drive Muslims from Spain—had been completed only 64 years before. In addition, Philip's great-grandparents Isabella and Ferdinand had used the Inquisition to investigate suspected heretics.

Philip saw himself as part of this tradition. He believed it was his duty to defend Catholicism against the Muslims of the Ottoman Empire and the Protestants of Europe. In 1571 the pope called on all Catholic princes to take up arms against the mounting power of the Ottoman Empire. Philip responded like a true crusader. Two hundred and fifty Spanish and Venetian ships defeated a large Ottoman fleet in

HISTORY MAKERS

**Philip II of Spain
1527–1598**

The most powerful ruler in Europe, Philip was also the hardest working. He demanded reports, reports, and more reports from his advisers. Then, in his tiny office, he would agonize over decisions. Often he could not bring himself to choose one policy over another. Then the government of Spain would grind to a halt.

Yet Philip would not allow anyone to help him. When his father was still emperor, he told Philip not to trust his advisers completely. Perhaps Philip followed his father's advice too closely. Deeply suspicious, he trusted no one for long. As his own court historian wrote, "His smile and his dagger were very close."

a fierce battle near Lepanto. In 1588, Philip launched the Spanish Armada in an attempt to punish Protestant England. However, his fleet was defeated.

Although this setback weakened Spain seriously, its wealth gave it the appearance of strength for a while longer. Philip's gray granite palace, the Escorial, had massive walls and huge gates that demonstrated his power. The Escorial also reflected Philip's faith. Within its walls stood a monastery as well as a palace.

THINK THROUGH HISTORY
A. Making Inferences What did Philip want his palace to demonstrate about his monarchy?

Golden Age of Spanish Art Spain's great wealth did more than support navies and build palaces. It also allowed monarchs and nobles to become patrons of artists. During the 16th and 17th centuries, Spain experienced a golden age in the arts. The works of two great painters show both the faith and the pride of Spain during this period.

Born in Crete, El Greco (GREHK·oh) spent much of his adult life in Spain. His real name was Domenikos Theotokopoulos, but Spaniards called him El Greco, meaning "the Greek." El Greco's art often puzzled the people of his time. He chose brilliant, sometimes clashing colors, distorted the human figure, and expressed emotion symbolically in his paintings. Although unusual, El Greco's techniques showed the deep Catholic faith of Spain. He painted saints and martyrs as huge, long-limbed figures that have a supernatural air.

The paintings of Diego Velázquez (vuh·LAHS·kehs), on the other hand, showed the pride of Spain's monarchy. Velázquez, who painted 50 years after El Greco, was the court painter to Philip IV of Spain. He is best known for his portraits of the royal family and scenes of court life. Like El Greco, he was noted for using rich colors. (See his painting of Juan de Pareja on page 511.)

Don Quixote The publication of *Don Quixote de la Mancha* in 1605 is often called the birth of the modern European novel. In this book, Miguel de Cervantes (suhr·VAN·teez) wrote about a poor Spanish nobleman. This nobleman went a little crazy after reading too many books about heroic knights. Hoping to "right every manner of wrong," Don Quixote rode forth in a rusty suit of armor, mounted on a feeble nag. At one point he mistook some windmills for giants:

SPOTLIGHT On

The Defeat of the Spanish Armada

The Spanish Navy reigned supreme on the Atlantic until 1588. That year, the Spanish Armada—the naval fleet assembled to invade England—went down to defeat.

After a series of raids on his treasure ships, King Philip II of Spain dispatched about 130 ships. They carried 19,000 soldiers to the English Channel in the summer of 1588. England, however, was ready. English warships outmaneuvered the Spanish vessels and bombarded the Armada with their heavier long-range cannons. (See picture above.) Stormy weather further damaged the Armada.

The defeat of the Armada was a significant event. It dealt a crippling blow to Spain's dominance on the high seas. It also opened the way for the rest of Europe to venture into the Americas.

> **A VOICE FROM THE PAST**
> He rushed with [his horse's] utmost speed upon the first windmill he could come at, and, running his lance into the sail, the wind whirled about with such swiftness, that the rapidity of such motion presently broke the lance into shivers, and hurled away both knight and horse along with it, till down he fell, rolling a good way off into the field.
> **MIGUEL DE CERVANTES**, *Don Quixote de la Mancha*

Some critics believe that Cervantes was mocking chivalry, the knightly code of the Middle Ages. Others maintain that the book is about an idealistic person who longs for the romantic past because he is frustrated with his materialistic world.

Problems Weaken the Spanish Empire

Certainly, the age in which Cervantes wrote was a materialistic one. The gold and silver coming from the Americas made Spain temporarily wealthy. However, such treasure helped to cause long-term economic problems.

Inflation and Taxes One of these problems was severe inflation, which had two causes. First, Spain's population had been growing. As more people demanded food and other goods, merchants were able to raise prices. Second, as silver bullion flooded the market, its value dropped. It took increased amounts of silver to buy things.

Spain's economic decline also had other causes. When Spain expelled the Jews and Moors (Muslims) around 1500, it lost many valuable artisans and businesspeople. In addition, Spain's nobles did not have to pay taxes. The tax burden fell on the lower classes. That burden prevented them from accumulating enough wealth to start their own businesses. Therefore, Spain never developed a middle class.

Making Spain's Enemies Rich Guilds that had emerged in the Middle Ages still dominated business in Spain. Such guilds used old-fashioned methods. This made Spanish cloth and manufactured goods more expensive than those made elsewhere. As a result, Spaniards bought much of what they needed from France, England, and the Netherlands. Spain's great wealth flowed into the pockets of foreigners, who were mostly Spain's enemies.

THINK THROUGH HISTORY
B. Identifying Problems Explain why Spain's economy did not really benefit from the gold and silver from the Americas.

To finance their wars, Spanish kings borrowed money from German and Italian bankers. When shiploads of silver came in, the money was sent abroad to repay debts. The economy was so feeble that Philip had to declare the Spanish state bankrupt three times.

The Dutch Revolt In the Spanish Netherlands, Philip had to maintain an army to keep his subjects under control. The Dutch had little in common with their Spanish rulers. While Spain was Catholic, the Netherlands had many Calvinist congregations. Also, Spain had a sluggish economy, while the Dutch were involved in trade and had a prosperous middle class.

Philip raised taxes in the Netherlands and took steps to crush Protestantism. In response, in 1566, angry Protestant mobs swept through Catholic churches. They destroyed religious paintings and statues. Philip then sent an army under the Spanish duke of Alva to punish them. On a single day in 1568, the duke executed 1,500 Protestants and suspected rebels.

In the struggle against the Spanish, William of Orange emerged as a great leader. William's motives for fighting the Spaniards were political, not religious. He wanted to free the Netherlands from Spain. At first, William lost battle after battle. Then, in 1574, when the Spaniards had the city of Leiden under seige, the Dutch took a desperate step. Their lands were called the Low Countries, because much of the land was actually below sea level. Only great dikes kept the seawater from flooding over the fields. The Dutch opened the floodgates, flooding the land with water. The floods drove the Spanish troops from their camp outside Leiden.

Background
William was a prince of the House of Orange, a dynasty that originated in Orange, France.

Finally, in 1579, the seven northern provinces of the Netherlands, which were largely Protestant, united and declared their independence from Spain. They became the United Provinces of the Netherlands. The ten southern provinces (present-day Belgium) were Catholic and remained under Spanish control.

The Independent Dutch Prosper

The United Provinces of the Netherlands was different from other European states of the time. For one thing, religious toleration was practiced there. In addition, the United Provinces was not a kingdom but a republic. Each province had an elected governor, whose power depended on the support of merchants and landholders.

Global Impact

Tulip Mania

Tulips came to Europe from Turkey around 1550. People went wild over the flowers' delicate beauty and exotic colors and began to buy rare varieties.

The supply of tulips could not meet the demand, and prices began to rise. One man even traded his mansion for three bulbs! Soon people were spending all their savings on bulbs and taking out loans to buy more.

Tulip mania reached a peak between 1633 and 1637. Then people began to doubt whether prices could continue to rise. In fact, tulip prices sank rapidly. Many Dutch families lost property and were left with bulbs that were nearly worthless.

Even so, tulips remained popular in the Netherlands—which is one of the world's biggest exporters of tulip bulbs today.

This painting by Rembrandt is called *The Syndics*. A syndic was a city official. Such art shows that city leaders and the middle class played a major role in Dutch society.

Dutch Trading Empire The stability of the government allowed the Dutch people to concentrate on economic growth. The merchants of Amsterdam bought surplus grain in Poland and crammed it into their warehouses. When they heard about poor harvests in southern Europe, they shipped the grain south while prices were highest. Western Europe was also short of timber, a fact that Dutch merchants were quick to use for their benefit. They shipped Scandinavian lumber to Spain, France, Italy, and England, all in ships owned by Dutch capitalists. The Dutch had the largest fleet of ships in the world—perhaps 4,800 ships in 1636. Gradually, the Dutch replaced the Italians as the bankers of Europe. One reason for this is that the trade routes of the Atlantic became more important than those of the Mediterranean.

Dutch Art During the 1600s, the Netherlands became what Florence had been during the 1400s. It boasted not only the best banks but also many of the best artists in Europe. As in Florence, wealthy merchants sponsored many of these artists.

The greatest Dutch artist of the period was Rembrandt van Rijn (REHM·BRANT vahn RYN). Rembrandt painted portraits of wealthy middle-class merchants. He also produced group portraits. In *The Syndics* (shown above), he portrayed a group of city officials. Rembrandt showed the individuality of each man by capturing his distinctive facial expression and posture. Rembrandt also used sharp contrasts of light and shadow to draw attention to his focus.

Another artist fascinated with the effects of light was Jan Vermeer (YAHN vuhr·MEER). Like many other Dutch artists, he chose domestic, indoor settings for his portraits. He often painted women doing such familiar activities as pouring milk from a jug or reading a letter. Unlike Rembrandt, who was famous in his time, Vermeer did not become widely admired until the late 19th century. The work of both Rembrandt and Vermeer reveals how important merchants, civic leaders, and the middle class in general were in 17th-century Netherlands.

Absolutism in Europe

Even though Philip II lost his Dutch possessions, he was a forceful ruler in many ways. He tried to control every aspect of his empire's affairs. During the next few centuries, many European monarchs would also claim the authority to rule without limits.

Background
The large fleet helped the Dutch East India Company to dominate the Asian spice trade and the Indian Ocean trade. This added to Dutch prosperity.

THINK THROUGH HISTORY
C. Drawing Conclusions How was Philip II typical of an absolute monarch?

The Theory of Absolutism These rulers wanted to be **absolute monarchs,** kings or queens who believed that all power within their state's boundaries rested in their hands. Their goal was to control every aspect of society. Absolute monarchs believed in **divine right,** the idea that God created the monarchy and that the monarch acted as God's representative on earth. An absolute monarch answered only to God, not to his or her subjects.

These ideas were not new to the 16th century. Absolute rulers from ancient times included Darius in Persia, Shi Huangdi in China, and the Roman Caesars. After the decline of the Roman Empire, however, European monarchs had been weak. The feudal nobility, the Church, and other rulers had limited the power that any one monarch could wield.

Growing Power of Europe's Monarchs As Europe emerged from the Middle Ages, monarchs grew increasingly powerful. The decline of feudalism, the rise of cities, and the growth of national kingdoms all helped to centralize authority. In addition, the growing middle class usually backed monarchs, because they promised a peaceful, supportive climate for business. Monarchs used the wealth of colonies to pay for their ambitions. Church authority also broke down during the late Middle Ages and the Reformation. That opened the way for monarchs to assume even greater control. In 1576, Jean Bodin, an influential French writer, defined absolute rule:

> **A VOICE FROM THE PAST**
> The first characteristic of the sovereign prince is the power to make general and special laws, but—and this qualification is important—without the consent of superiors, equals, or inferiors. If the prince requires the consent of superiors, then he is a subject himself; if that of equals, he shares his authority with others; if that of his subjects, senate or people, he is not sovereign.
>
> **JEAN BODIN,** *Six Books on the State*

Crises Lead to Absolutism The 17th century was a period of great upheaval in Europe. Religious and territorial conflicts between states led to almost continuous warfare. This caused governments to build huge armies and to levy even heavier taxes on an already suffering population. These pressures in turn would bring on widespread unrest. Sometimes peasants revolted. In response to these crises, monarchs tried to impose order by increasing their own power. As absolute rulers, they regulated everything from religious worship to social gatherings. To seem more powerful, they increased the size of their courts. They created new government bureaucracies to control their countries' economic life. Their goal was to free themselves from the limitations imposed by the nobility and by representative bodies such as Parliament. Only with such freedom could they rule absolutely, as did the most famous monarch of his time, Louis XIV of France.

Section 1 Assessment

1. TERMS & NAMES

Identify
• Philip II
• absolute monarch
• divine right

2. TAKING NOTES

On a chart like the one shown, list the conditions that allowed European monarchs to gain power. Then list the ways they exercised their increased power.

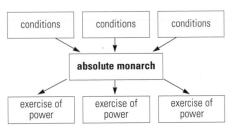

3. DRAWING CONCLUSIONS

What does the art described in this section reveal about the cultures of Spain and the Netherlands?

THINK ABOUT
• what the art of Velázquez and El Greco reveals about Spain
• what the art of Rembrandt and Vermeer reveals about the Netherlands

4. THEME ACTIVITY

Economics With a partner, create an illustrated poster contrasting the economies of Spain and the Netherlands around 1600. Compare such characteristics as

• sources of wealth
• existence of a middle class
• trends such as inflation or high taxes
• who controlled financial services

TERMS & NAMES
• **Edict of Nantes**
• **Cardinal Richelieu**
• **skepticism**
• **Louis XIV**
• **intendant**
• **Jean Baptiste Colbert**
• **War of the Spanish Succession**

2 France's Ultimate Monarch

MAIN IDEA	WHY IT MATTERS NOW
After a century of war and riots, France was ruled by Louis XIV, the most powerful monarch of his time.	Louis used his power to build a great palace and sponsor art that is part of France's cultural legacy.

SETTING THE STAGE In 1559, King Henry II of France died, leaving four young sons. Three of them ruled, one after the other, but all proved incompetent. The real power behind the throne during this period was their mother, Catherine de Médicis. Catherine tried to preserve royal authority, but growing conflicts between Catholics and Huguenots—French Protestants—rocked the country.

Background
Catherine was descended from the Renaissance de' Medici family. She spelled her name the French way.

Religious Wars Create a Crisis

Between 1562 and 1598, Huguenots and Catholics fought eight religious wars. Chaos spread through France. For example, in 1572 the St. Bartholomew's Day Massacre in Paris sparked a six-week, nationwide slaughter of Huguenots.

Henry of Navarre The massacre occurred when many Huguenot nobles were in Paris. They were attending the marriage of Catherine's daughter to a Huguenot prince, Henry of Navarre. Most of these nobles died, but Henry survived. Descended from the popular medieval king Louis IX, Henry was robust, athletic, and handsome. In 1589, when both Catherine and her last son died, Prince Henry inherited the throne. He became Henry IV, the first king of the Bourbon dynasty in France. As king, he showed himself to be decisive, fearless in battle, and a clever politician.

Background
The Bourbon dynasty took its name from a French town.

Many Catholics, including the people of Paris, opposed Henry. For the sake of his war-weary country, Henry chose to give up Protestantism and become a Catholic. Explaining his conversion, Henry declared, "Paris is well worth a Mass."

In 1598, Henry took another step toward healing France's wounds. He declared that the Huguenots could live in peace in France and set up their own houses of worship in some cities. This declaration of religious toleration was called the **Edict of Nantes.**

Phillipe de Champaigne painted many portraits of the powerful Cardinal Richelieu. This triple portrait shows his front view and two profiles.

Aided by an adviser who enacted wise financial policies, Henry devoted his reign to rebuilding France and its prosperity. He restored the French monarchy to a strong position. After a generation of war, most French people welcomed peace. Some people, however, hated Henry for his religious compromises. In 1610, a fanatic leaped into the royal carriage and stabbed Henry to death.

THINK THROUGH HISTORY
A. Recognizing Effects What were the effects of Henry's conversion to Catholicism and of the Edict of Nantes?

Louis XIII and Cardinal Richelieu
After Henry IV's death, his son Louis XIII reigned. Louis was a weak king, but in 1624 he appointed a strong minister who made up for all of Louis's weaknesses.

Cardinal Richelieu (RIHSH·uh·LOO) became, in effect, the ruler of France. For several years, he had been a hard-working leader of the Catholic church in France. Although he tried sincerely to lead according to moral principles, he was also ambitious and enjoyed exercising authority. As Louis XIII's minister, he was able to pursue his ambitions in the political arena.

This lean-faced, hawk-nosed cardinal took two steps to increase the power of the Bourbon monarchy. First, he moved against Huguenots. He believed that Protestantism often served as an excuse for political conspiracies against the Catholic king. Although Richelieu did not end the Huguenots' right to worship, he forbade Protestant cities from having walls. He did not want them to be able to defy the king and then withdraw behind strong defenses.

Second, he sought to weaken the nobles' power. Richelieu ordered nobles to take down their fortified castles. He increased the power of government agents who came from the middle class. This action ended the need for the king to use noble officials.

Richelieu also wanted to make France the strongest state in Europe. The greatest obstacle to this, he believed, was the Hapsburg rulers whose lands surrounded France. Hapsburgs ruled Spain, Austria, the Netherlands, and parts of Germany. To limit Hapsburg power, Richelieu involved France in the Thirty Years' War.

THINK THROUGH HISTORY
B. Making Inferences How did Richelieu's actions toward Huguenots and the nobility strengthen the monarchy?

Background
Skepticism goes back to the Greek philosophers who lived as early as the 200s B.C. Like the French skeptics, Greek skeptics argued against strongly held beliefs.

Writers Express Skepticism As France regained political power, a new French intellectual movement developed. French thinkers had witnessed the religious wars with horror. What they saw turned them toward **skepticism,** the idea that nothing can ever be known for certain. These thinkers expressed an attitude of doubt toward churches that claimed to have the only correct set of doctrines. To doubt old ideas, skeptics thought, was the first step toward finding truth.

Michel de Montaigne lived during the worst years of the French religious wars. After the death of a dear friend, Montaigne retired to his library and thought deeply about life's meaning. To communicate his ideas, Montaigne developed a new form of literature, the essay. An essay is a brief work that expresses a person's thoughts and opinions.

In one essay, Montaigne pointed out that whenever a new belief arose, it replaced an old belief that people once accepted as truth. In the same way, he went on, the new belief would also probably be replaced by some different idea in the future. For these reasons, Montaigne believed that humans could never have absolute knowledge of what is true. To remind himself of this, he had the beams of his study painted with the sentence "All that is certain is that nothing is certain."

Another French writer of the time, René Descartes, was a brilliant thinker. In his *Meditations of First Philosophy*, Descartes examined the skeptical argument that one could never be certain of anything. Descartes used his observations and his reason to answer such arguments. In doing so, he created a philosophy that influenced modern thinkers and helped to develop the scientific method. Because of this, he became an important figure in the Enlightenment. (See Chapter 22.)

Louis XIV Rules Absolutely

The efforts of Henry IV and Richelieu to strengthen the French monarchy paved the way for the most powerful ruler in French history—**Louis XIV.** In Louis's view, he and the state were one and the same. He reportedly boasted, *"L'état, c'est moi,"* meaning "I am the state." Although Louis XIV became the strongest king of his time, when he began his reign he was only a five-year-old boy.

Louis, the Boy King When Louis became king in 1643, the true ruler of France was Richelieu's successor, Cardinal Mazarin (MAZ·uh·RAN). Mazarin's greatest triumph

SPOTLIGHT ON

The Three Musketeers
The uneasy relationship between Louis XIII and Cardinal Richelieu provides the background for a lively work of historical fiction—*The Three Musketeers.*

It was written by Alexandre Dumas *père* (the father) in 1844. The novel is based on actual events involving the intrigues at Louis XIII's royal court. The main characters, the musketeers, are members of Louis's guard. They often become involved in sword fights, using weapons like the one shown below. From this novel comes the famous slogan "All for one and one for all." Hollywood has produced at least six film versions of this classic, a sign of its lasting popularity.

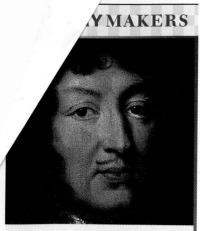

Louis XIV
1638–1715

Although Louis XIV stood only 5 feet 5 inches tall, his erect and dignified posture made him appear much taller. (It also helped that he wore high-heeled shoes.)

Louis had very strong likes and dislikes. He hated cities and loved to travel through France's countryside. The people who traveled with him were at his mercy, however, for he allowed no stopping except for his own comfort.

Louis liked to be informed of every detail in his government. He explained to his son the secrets of his success:

Two things without doubt were absolutely necessary: very hard work on my part, and a wise choice of persons capable of seconding it.

It is small wonder that the vain Louis XIV liked to be called the Sun King. He believed that, as with the sun, all power radiated from him.

came in 1648, with the ending of the Thirty Years' War. The peace treaty made France the most powerful country in Europe.

Many people in France, particularly the nobles, hated Mazarin because he increased taxes and strengthened the central government. From 1648 to 1653, violent anti-Mazarin riots tore France apart. At times, the nobles who led the riots threatened the young king's life. Even after the violence was over, Louis never forgot his fear or his anger at the nobility. He determined to become so strong that they could never threaten him again.

In the end, the rebellion failed for three reasons. Its leaders distrusted one another even more than they distrusted Mazarin. In addition, the government used violent repression. Finally, peasants and townspeople grew weary of disorder and fighting. For many years afterward, the people of France accepted the oppressive laws of an absolute king. They were convinced that the alternative—rebellion—was even worse.

Louis Takes Control When Cardinal Mazarin died in 1661, the 23-year-old Louis took control of the government himself. A courtier remembered coming into the king's apartments that morning with the chancellor and hearing Louis announce, "The scene has changed. In the government of my realm . . . I shall have other principles than those of the late cardinal. You know my wishes, gentlemen; it now remains for you to execute them."

Louis weakened the power of the nobles by excluding them from his councils. In contrast, he increased the power of the government agents called **intendants,** who collected taxes and administered justice. To keep power under central control, he made sure that local officials communicated regularly with him.

Economic Growth Louis devoted himself to helping France attain economic, political, and cultural brilliance. No one assisted him more in achieving these goals than his minister of finance, **Jean Baptiste Colbert** (kawl·BEHR). Colbert believed in the theory of mercantilism. To prevent wealth from leaving the country, Colbert tried to make France self-sufficient. He wanted it to be able to manufacture everything it needed instead of relying on imports.

To expand manufacturing, Colbert gave government funds and tax benefits to French companies. To protect France's industries, he placed a high tariff on goods from other countries. Colbert also recognized the importance of colonies, which provided raw materials and a market for manufactured goods. The French government encouraged people to migrate to France's colony in Canada. There the fur trade added to French commerce.

After Colbert's death, Louis announced a policy that slowed France's economic progress. In 1685 he cancelled the Edict of Nantes, which protected the religious freedom of Huguenots. In response, thousands of Huguenot artisans and business people fled the country. Louis's policy thus robbed France of many skilled workers.

Louis's Grand Style

In his personal finances, Louis spent a fortune to surround himself with luxury. For example, each meal was a feast. An observer claimed that the king once devoured four plates of soup, a whole pheasant, a partridge in garlic sauce, two slices of ham, a salad, a plate of pastries, fruit, and hard-boiled eggs in a single sitting! Nearly 500 cooks, waiters, and other servants worked to satisfy his tastes.

THINK THROUGH HISTORY
C. Recognizing Effects What effects did the years of riots have on Louis XIV? on his subjects?

Vocabulary
mercantilism: the economic theory that nations should protect their home industries and export more than they import.

Louis Controls the Nobility Every morning, the chief valet woke Louis at 7:30. Outside the curtains of Louis's canopy bed stood at least 100 of the most privileged nobles at court. They were waiting to help the great king dress. Only four would be allowed the honor of handing Louis his slippers or holding his sleeves for him.

Meanwhile, outside the bedchamber, lesser nobles waited in the palace halls and hoped Louis would notice them. A kingly nod, a glance of approval, a kind word—these marks of royal attention determined whether a noble succeeded or failed. A duke recorded how Louis turned against nobles who did not come to court to flatter him:

A VOICE FROM THE PAST

He looked to the right and to the left, not only upon rising but upon going to bed, at his meals, in passing through his apartments, or his gardens. . . . He marked well all absentees from the Court, found out the reason of their absence, and never lost an opportunity of acting toward them as the occasion might seem to justify. . . . When their names were in any way mentioned, "I do not know them," the King would reply haughtily.

DUKE OF SAINT-SIMON, *Memoirs of Louis XIV and the Regency*

THINK THROUGH HISTORY
D. Making Inferences How did Louis's treatment of the nobles reflect his belief in his absolute authority?

Having the nobles at the palace increased royal authority in two ways. It made the nobility totally dependent on Louis. It also took them from their homes, thereby giving more power to the intendants. Louis required hundreds of nobles to live with him at the splendid palace he built at Versailles, 11 miles southwest of Paris.

The Splendor of Versailles Everything about the Versailles palace was immense. It faced a huge royal courtyard dominated by a statue of Louis XIV. The palace itself stretched for a distance of about 500 yards.

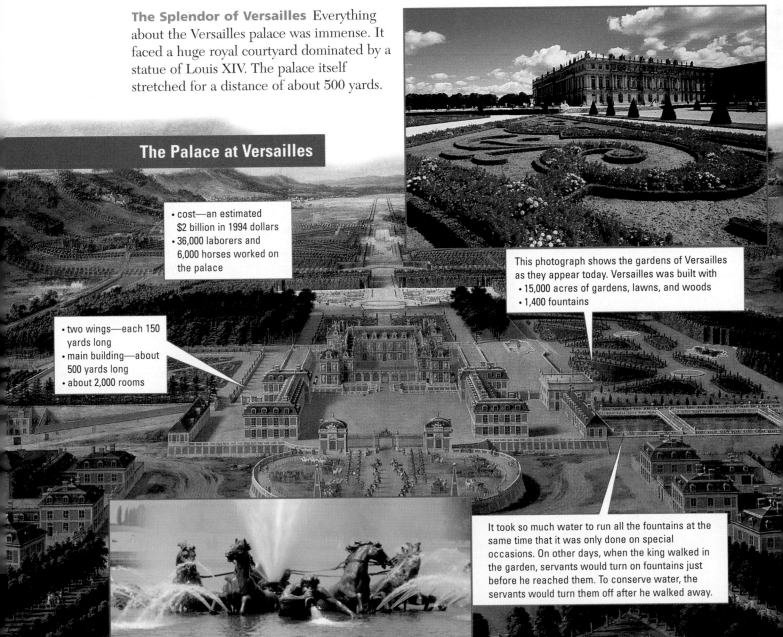

The Palace at Versailles

- cost—an estimated $2 billion in 1994 dollars
- 36,000 laborers and 6,000 horses worked on the palace

- two wings—each 150 yards long
- main building—about 500 yards long
- about 2,000 rooms

This photograph shows the gardens of Versailles as they appear today. Versailles was built with
- 15,000 acres of gardens, lawns, and woods
- 1,400 fountains

It took so much water to run all the fountains at the same time that it was only done on special occasions. On other days, when the king walked in the garden, servants would turn on fountains just before he reached them. To conserve water, the servants would turn them off after he walked away.

In fact, the palace was so long that food from the kitchens was often cold by the time servants reached Louis's chambers.

Because of its great size, Versailles was like a small royal city. Its rich decoration and furnishings clearly showed Louis's wealth and power to everyone who came to the palace. The elaborate ceremonies there impressed the king's subjects and aroused the admiration and envy of all other European monarchs.

Patronage of the Arts Versailles was a center of the arts during Louis's reign. Louis made opera and ballet more popular. He even danced the title role in the ballet *The Sun King*. One of his favorite writers was Molière (mohl·YAIR), who wrote some of the funniest plays in French literature. Molière's comedies include *Tartuffe*, which mocks religious hypocrisy. *The Would-be Gentleman* mocks the newly rich, and *The Imaginary Invalid* mocks hypochondriacs.

Not since Augustus of Rome had there been a monarch who aided the arts as much as Louis. Under Louis, the chief purpose of art was no longer to glorify God, as it had been in the Middle Ages. Nor was its purpose to glorify human potential, as it had been in the Renaissance. Now the purpose of art was to glorify the king and promote values that supported Louis's absolute rule.

Louis Fights Disastrous Wars

Under Louis, France was the most powerful country in Europe. In 1660, France had about 20 million people. This was four times as many as England and 10 times as many as the Dutch republic. The French army, numbering 100,000 in peacetime and 400,000 in wartime, was far ahead of other states' armies in size, training, and weaponry.

Attempts to Expand France's Boundaries In 1667, just six years after Mazarin's death, Louis invaded the Spanish Netherlands. Through this campaign, he gained 12 towns. Encouraged by his success, he personally led an army into the Dutch Netherlands in 1672. The Dutch saved their country by opening the dikes and flooding the countryside. This was the same tactic they had used in their revolt against Spain a century earlier. The war ended in 1678 with the Treaty of Nijmegen. France gained several towns and a region called Franche-Comté.

Louis decided to fight additional wars, but his luck had run out. By the end of the 1680s, a European-wide alliance had formed to stop France. By joining together, weaker countries could match France's strength. This defensive strategy was meant to achieve a balance of power, in which no single country or group of countries could dominate others.

In 1689, the Dutch prince William of Orange became the king of England. He joined the League of Augsburg, which consisted of the Hapsburg emperor, the kings of Sweden and Spain, and the leaders of several smaller European states. Joined together, these countries equaled France's strength.

The painting below shows the Siege of Namur, which took place during Louis XIV's war with the League of Augsburg.

France at this time had been weakened by a series of poor harvests. That, added to the constant warfare, brought great suffering to the French people. So, too, did new taxes, which Louis imposed to finance his wars.

War of the Spanish Succession Tired of hardship, the French people longed for peace. What they got was another war. In 1700, the childless king of Spain, Charles II, died after promising his throne to Louis XIV's 17-year-old grandson, Philip of Anjou. The two greatest powers in Europe, enemies for so long, were now both ruled by Bourbons.

Other countries felt threatened by this increase in the Bourbon dynasty's power. In 1701, England, Austria, the Dutch republic, Portugal, and several German and Italian states joined together against France and Spain. The long struggle that followed is known as the **War of the Spanish Succession.**

The costly war dragged on until 1713. The Treaty of Utrecht was signed in that year. Under its terms, Louis's grandson was allowed to remain king of Spain so long as the thrones of France and Spain were not united.

The big winner in the war was Great Britain. From Spain, Britain took Gibraltar, a fortress that controlled the entrance to the Mediterranean. Spain also granted a British company an *asiento*—permission to send enslaved Africans to Spain's American colonies. This increased Britain's involvement in trading enslaved Africans. In addition, France gave Britain the North American territories of Nova Scotia and Newfoundland, and abandoned claims to the Hudson Bay region. The Austrian Hapsburgs took the Spanish Netherlands and other Spanish lands in Italy. Prussia and Savoy were recognized as kingdoms.

Background
Louis XIV lived so long that he outlived his son and two grandsons. His great-grandson succeeded him as Louis XV.

Louis's Death and Legacy Louis's last years were more sad than glorious. Realizing that his wars had ruined France, he regretted the suffering he had brought to his people. He died in bed in 1715. News of his death prompted rejoicing throughout France. The people had had enough of the Sun King.

Louis left a mixed legacy to his country. France was certainly a power to be reckoned with in Europe. But the staggering debts and resentment over the royal abuse of power would plague Louis XIV's heirs. Eventually, this resentment led to revolution. In the meantime, Louis's enemies in Prussia and Austria had been experimenting with their own forms of absolute monarchy, as you will learn in Section 3.

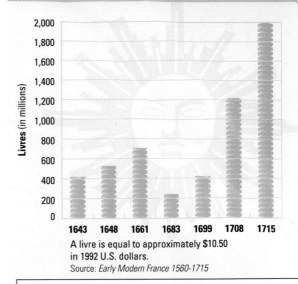

Debt of the Royal Family, 1643–1715

Livres (in millions)

| 1643 | 1648 | 1661 | 1683 | 1699 | 1708 | 1715 |

A livre is equal to approximately $10.50 in 1992 U.S. dollars.
Source: *Early Modern France 1560-1715*

SKILLBUILDER: Interpreting Charts
1. *How many times greater was the royal debt in 1715 than in 1643?*
2. *What was the royal debt of 1715 equal to in 1992 dollars?*

Section 2 Assessment

1. TERMS & NAMES

Identify
• Edict of Nantes
• Cardinal Richelieu
• skepticism
• Louis XIV
• intendant
• Jean Baptiste Colbert
• War of the Spanish Succession

2. TAKING NOTES

On a time line like the one shown, list the major events of Louis XIV's reign.

1643   1715

Identify which events on your time line strengthened the French monarchy and which weakened it.

3. SUPPORTING OPINIONS

Many historians think of Louis XIV as the perfect example of an absolute monarch. Do you agree? Explain why or why not.

THINK ABOUT
• the description of an absolute monarch at the end of Section 1
• the ways in which Louis XIV fits that description
• any ways in which Louis XIV does not fit the description

4. ANALYZING THEMES

Economics How did the policies of Colbert and Louis XIV affect the French economy? Explain both positive and negative effects.

THINK ABOUT
• Colbert's attempts to make France self-sufficient
• what happened when Louis cancelled the Edict of Nantes
• the cost of Versailles and wars

Absolute Monarchs in Europe **523**

Power Clothes

Traditionally, rulers have used clothing to show their status as monarchs. Past rulers frequently wore symbols that only rulers were allowed to wear. In addition, they often chose clothing that indicated wealth or military strength. For example, in one portrait Louis XIV of France wears the uniform of a Roman general to show his military might. As you study the following pictures, notice whether the rulers conveyed power through royal symbols, wealth, or military strength.

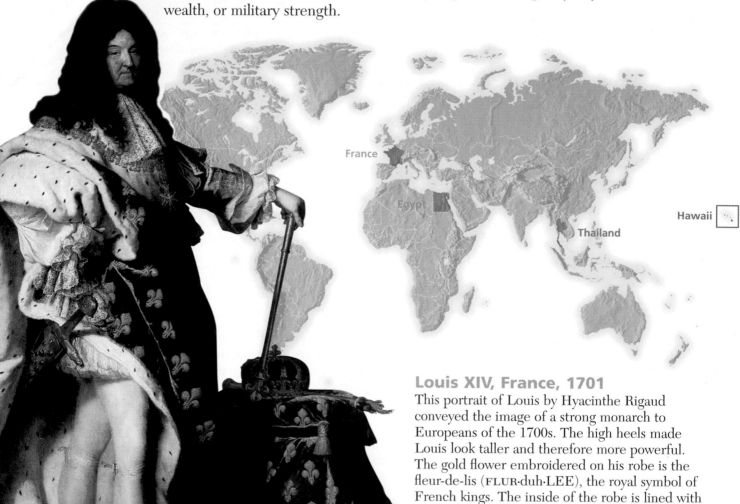

France

Egypt

Hawaii

Thailand

Louis XIV, France, 1701

This portrait of Louis by Hyacinthe Rigaud conveyed the image of a strong monarch to Europeans of the 1700s. The high heels made Louis look taller and therefore more powerful. The gold flower embroidered on his robe is the fleur-de-lis (FLUR·duh·LEE), the royal symbol of French kings. The inside of the robe is lined with ermine, a type of fur that only nobles wore. The sword, scepter, and crown are additional symbols of royal power.

a closer look LOUIS XIV

Ostrich plumes were very expensive, so usually only royalty or the nobility wore them. This plumed hat belonged to Louis.

Queen Hatshepsut, Egypt, 1490 B.C.

Although a woman, Hatshepsut ruled as pharaoh. This red granite statue shows her wearing two symbols of royal power—the false beard and the headdress with the asp (snake), both worn only by pharaohs.

High Chief Boki and his wife, Liliha; Hawaii, about 1824

In Hawaii, only male chiefs of high rank could wear feather garments, such as the cloak and helmets shown here. The red and yellow feathers came from birds native to the islands. Each cloak required about a half million feathers.

King Bhumibol Adulyadej, Thailand, 1990

Just as Louis XIV liked to dress as a Roman general, many modern rulers portray themselves as military leaders. Here King Bhumibol Adulyadej prays while wearing a white military uniform and rows of medals.

Connect *to* History

Clarifying Which of the rulers on this page wear clothing that displays wealth? military power? symbols that only rulers were allowed to wear?

SEE SKILLBUILDER HANDBOOK, PAGE 992.

Connect *to* Today

Clarifying In today's world, many books and articles tell businesspeople how to dress to convey a sense of power. Find at least one of these books or articles and read to discover the main points of advice. List the main points and share them with the class.

This is a copy of a diamond cross that Louis XIV had. The stones in the middle are set in the design of a dove. The dove's beak is a ruby.

This bust shows the elaborate wigs that French monarchs and nobles wore.

3 Central European Monarchs Clash

MAIN IDEA	WHY IT MATTERS NOW
After a period of turmoil, absolute monarchs ruled Austria and the Germanic state of Prussia.	Prussia built a strong military tradition in Germany that contributed in part to world wars in the 20th century.

SETTING THE STAGE For a brief while, it appeared that the German rulers had settled their religious differences through the Peace of Augsburg (1555). They had agreed that the faith of each prince would determine the religion of his subjects. Churches in Germany could be either Lutheran or Catholic, but not Calvinist.

The Thirty Years' War

The peace was short-lived—soon to be replaced by a long war. After the Peace of Augsburg, the Catholic and Lutheran princes of Germany watched each other suspiciously. Each religion tried to gain followers. In addition, both sides felt threatened by Calvinism, which was spreading in Germany and gaining many followers. As tension mounted, the Lutherans joined together in the Protestant Union in 1608. The following year, the Catholic princes formed the Catholic League. Now, only a spark would set off a war.

Bohemian Protestants Revolt That spark came in 1618. The future Holy Roman emperor, Ferdinand II, was head of the Hapsburg family. As such, he ruled the Czech kingdom of Bohemia. The Protestants in Bohemia did not trust Ferdinand, who was a foreigner and a Catholic. When he closed some Protestant churches, the Protestants revolted. Ferdinand sent an army into Bohemia to crush the revolt. Several German Protestant princes took this chance to challenge their Catholic emperor.

This engraving shows the siege of the German city of Magdeburg in 1631. The city was destroyed during the Thirty Years' War.

Thus began the **Thirty Years' War**—a conflict over religion, over territory, and for power among European ruling families. Historians think of it as having two main phases: the phase of Hapsburg triumphs and the phase of Hapsburg defeats.

Hapsburg Triumphs The Thirty Years' War lasted from 1618 to 1648. During the first 12 years, Hapsburg armies from Austria and Spain crushed the troops hired by the Protestant princes. They succeeded in putting down the Czech uprising. They also defeated the German Protestants who had supported the Czechs.

Ferdinand II paid his army of 125,000 men by allowing them to plunder, or rob, German villages. This huge army destroyed everything in

THINK THROUGH HISTORY
A. Analyzing Motives Why did Ferdinand attack northern Germany?

its path. The mayor of Magdeburg in northern Germany described the horrible destruction of his city:

A VOICE FROM THE PAST
In this frenzied rage, the great and splendid city that had stood like a fair princess in the land was now . . . given over to the flames, and thousands of innocent men, women, and children, in the midst of a horrible din of heartrending shrieks and cries, were tortured and put to death in so cruel and shameful a manner that no words would suffice to describe it nor no tears to bewail it.

OTTO VON GUERICKE, quoted in *Readings in European History*

THINK THROUGH HISTORY
B. Drawing Conclusions
Judging from their actions, do you think the two French cardinals were motivated more by religion or politics? Why?

Hapsburg Defeats The Protestant Gustavus Adolphus of Sweden and his disciplined army of 13,000 shifted the tide of war in 1630. They drove the Hapsburg armies out of northern Germany. However, Gustavus Adolphus was killed in battle in 1632.

Cardinal Richelieu and Cardinal Mazarin of France dominated the remaining years of the war. Although Catholic, these two cardinals feared the Hapsburgs more than the Protestants. They did not want other European rulers to have as much power as the French king. Therefore, in 1635, Richelieu sent French troops to join the German and Swedish Protestants in their struggle against the Hapsburg armies.

Peace of Westphalia The war did great damage to Germany. Its population dropped from 20 million to about 16 million. Both trade and agriculture were disrupted, and Germany's economy was ruined. Germany had a long, difficult recovery from this devastation. That is a major reason that it did not become a unified state until the 1800s.

The Peace of Westphalia (1648) ended the war and had important consequences. First, it weakened the Hapsburg states of Spain and Austria. Second, it strengthened France by awarding it German territory. Third, it made German princes independent of the Holy Roman emperor. Fourth, it ended religious wars in Europe. Fifth, it introduced a new method of peace negotiation. In that method, still used today, all participants meet to settle the problems of a war and decide the terms of peace.

Background
The Holy Roman Empire was a loose union of states that shared a common emperor. The Peace of Westphalia weakened the empire but did not end it.

Europe After the Thirty Years' War, 1648

Population Losses During the War

Up to 15% | 33–66%
15–33% | Over 66%
— The Holy Roman Empire

GEOGRAPHY SKILLBUILDER: Interpreting Maps
1. **Place** *Name at least five modern European countries that existed at the end of the Thirty Years' War.*
2. **Region** *Refer to the inset map. Which regions lost the most population in the Thirty Years' War?*

Beginning of Modern States The treaty thus abandoned the idea of a Catholic empire that would rule most of Europe. It recognized Europe as a group of independent states that could negotiate for themselves. Each independent state was seen as essentially equal to the others. This marked the beginning of the modern state system and was the most important result of the Thirty Years' War.

Central Europe Differs from the West

The formation of strong states occurred more slowly in central Europe. The major powers of this region were the kingdom of Poland, the Holy Roman Empire, and the Ottoman Empire. None of them was well-organized in the mid-1600s.

Economic Contrasts One reason for this is that the economy of central Europe developed differently from that of western Europe. During the late Middle Ages, serfs in western Europe slowly won freedom and moved to towns. There, they joined middle-class townspeople, who gained economic power because of the commercial revolution and the development of capitalism. In turn, western European monarchs taxed the towns. They used the tax money to raise armies and reduce the influence of the nobility.

By contrast, the landowning aristocracy in central Europe passed laws restricting the ability of serfs to gain freedom and move to cities. These nobles wanted to keep the serfs on the land, where they could produce large harvests. The nobles could then sell the surplus crops to western European cities at great profit. To increase productivity, the aristocracy increased their control over their serfs. By 1700, Polish landowners could demand that their serfs work as much as six days a week. This left the serfs only one day a week to grow their own food.

Several Weak Empires The landowning nobles in central Europe not only held down the serfs but also blocked the development of strong kings. For example, the Polish nobility elected the Polish king and sharply limited his power. They allowed the king little income, no law courts, and no standing army.

The two empires of central Europe were also weak. Although Suleiman the Magnificent had conquered Hungary and threatened Vienna in 1529, the Ottoman Empire could not take its European conquest any farther. From then on the Ottoman Empire declined from its peak of power.

In addition, the Holy Roman Empire was seriously weakened by the Thirty Years' War. No longer able to command the obedience of the German states, the Holy Roman Empire had no real power. These old, weakened empires and kingdoms left a power vacuum in central Europe. In the late 1600s, two German-speaking families decided to try to fill this vacuum by becoming absolute rulers themselves.

This is the imperial crest of the Hapsburgs. It shows a double-headed eagle with a crown.

Austria Grows Stronger One of these families was the Hapsburgs of Austria. Even after the terrible losses in the Thirty Years' War, Austria remained the most powerful and important state within the Holy Roman Empire. The Austrian Hapsburgs took several steps to become absolute monarchs. First, during the Thirty Years' War, they reconquered Bohemia. The Hapsburgs wiped out Protestantism there and created a new Czech nobility that pledged loyalty to them. Second, after the war, the Hapsburg ruler centralized the government and created a standing army. Third, by 1699, the Hapsburgs had retaken Hungary from the Ottomans.

In 1711, Charles VI became the Hapsburg ruler. Charles's empire was a difficult one to rule. Within its borders lived a diverse assortment of people—Czechs, Hungarians, Italians, Croatians, and Germans. Only the fact that one Hapsburg ruler wore the Austrian, Hungarian, and Bohemian crowns kept the empire together.

Background
Western Europe included such countries as England, France, and the Netherlands.

THINK THROUGH HISTORY
C. Contrasting How did the economies of central and western Europe differ?

Background
Bohemia was a kingdom. The Czechs were the people who lived there.

Maria Theresa Inherits the Austrian Throne How could the Hapsburgs make sure that they continued to rule all those lands? Charles VI spent his entire reign working out an answer to this problem. By endless arm-twisting, he persuaded other leaders of Europe to sign an agreement that declared they would recognize Charles's eldest daughter as the heir to all his Hapsburg territories. That heir was a young woman named **Maria Theresa.** In theory, this agreement guaranteed Maria Theresa a peaceful reign. Instead, she faced years of war. Her main enemy was Prussia, a new state to the north of Austria.

Prussia and Austria Clash

Like Austria, Prussia rose to power in the late 1600s. Like the Hapsburgs of Austria, Prussia's ruling family, the Hohenzollerns, also had ambitions. Those ambitions threatened to upset central Europe's delicate balance of power.

The Rise of Prussia and Frederick the Great The Hohenzollerns built up their state from a number of small holdings—beginning with the German states of Brandenburg and Prussia. In 1640, a 20-year-old Hohenzollern named Frederick William inherited the title of elector of Brandenburg. After seeing the destruction of the Thirty Years' War, Frederick William, later known as the Great Elector, decided that having a strong army was the only way to ensure safety.

To protect their lands, the Great Elector and his descendants moved toward absolute monarchy. They created a standing army—the best in Europe. They built it to a force of 80,000 men. To pay for the army, they introduced permanent taxation. Beginning with the Great Elector's son, they called themselves kings. They also weakened the representative assemblies of their territories.

Prussia's landowning nobility, the Junkers (YUNG·kuhrz), resisted the king's growing power. However, in the early 1700s, King Frederick William I bought their cooperation. He gave the Junkers the exclusive right to be officers in his army. Prussia became a rigidly controlled, military society.

Frederick William worried that his son, Frederick, was not military enough to rule. The prince loved music, philosophy, and poetry. In 1730, when he and a friend tried to run away, they were caught. To punish Frederick, the king ordered him to witness his friend's beheading. Despite such bitter memories, Frederick II, known as **Frederick the Great,** followed his father's military policies when he came to

HISTORY MAKERS

Maria Theresa
1717–1780

An able ruler, Maria Theresa also devoted herself to her family. Unlike many monarchs, she married for love. She gave birth to 16 children, 10 of whom reached adulthood.

Maria Theresa continued to advise her children even after they were grown. Perhaps her most famous child was Marie Antoinette, wife of Louis XVI of France. Maria Theresa often scolded Marie for spending too much money and making the French people angry.

As empress, Maria Theresa decreased the power of the nobility. Very religious, she cared more for the peasants' well-being than most rulers. She limited the amount of labor that nobles could force peasants to do. She argued: "The peasantry must be able to sustain itself."

Frederick the Great
1712–1786

Although they reigned during the same time, Frederick the Great and Maria Theresa were very different. Where Maria was religious, Frederick was practical and atheistic. Maria Theresa had a happy home life; Frederick married a woman whom he never cared for and neglected. Maria Theresa had a huge family; Frederick died without a son to succeed him.

An aggressor in foreign affairs, Frederick once wrote that "the fundamental role of governments is the principle of extending their territories." With regard to domestic affairs, he encouraged religious toleration and legal reform. Frederick earned the title "the Great" by achieving his goals for Prussia, in both domestic and foreign affairs.

power. However, he also softened some of his father's laws, because he believed that a ruler should be like a father to his people:

A VOICE FROM THE PAST
A prince . . . is only the first servant of the state, who is obliged to act with probity [honesty] and prudence. . . . As the sovereign is properly the head of a family of citizens, the father of his people, he ought on all occasions to be the last refuge of the unfortunate.
FREDERICK II, *Essay on Forms of Government*

CONNECT *to* TODAY

Quebec Separatists

In North America, the Seven Years' War was called the French and Indian War. As a result of this war, the British took over France's American colonies. Today Canada has a large French-speaking population, many of whom believe that they should be independent from Canada. A demonstration for independence is shown above.

In 1995, Quebec voters narrowly rejected a vote for independence. Before the vote was taken, Jacques Parizeau, then Quebec's premier and leader of the secessionist movement, said, "We, the people of Quebec, through our National Assembly, proclaim: Quebec is a sovereign [independent] country." Although the vote did not make Parizeau's declaration come true, separation continues to be an important issue in Quebec.

War of the Austrian Succession In 1740, Maria Theresa succeeded her father, just five months after Frederick II became king of Prussia. Frederick wanted the Austrian land of Silesia, which bordered Prussia. Silesia produced iron ore, textiles, and food products. Frederick assumed that because Maria Theresa was a woman, she would not be forceful enough to defend her lands. In 1740, he sent his army to occupy Silesia, beginning the War of the Austrian Succession.

Even though Maria Theresa had recently given birth, she journeyed to Hungary. There she held her infant in her arms as she asked the Hungarian nobles for aid. Even though the nobles resented their Hapsburg rulers, they pledged to give Maria Theresa an army. Great Britain also joined Austria to fight its longtime enemy France, which was Prussia's ally. Although Maria Theresa did stop Prussia's aggression, she lost Silesia at the Treaty of Aix-la-Chapelle in 1748.

The Seven Years' War Maria Theresa decided that the French kings were no longer Austria's chief enemies. She made an alliance with them. The result was a diplomatic revolution. When Frederick heard of her actions, he signed a treaty with Britain—Austria's former ally. Now, Austria, France, Russia, and others were allied against Britain and Prussia. Not only had Austria and Prussia switched allies, but for the first time Russia was playing a role in European affairs.

In 1756, Frederick attacked Saxony, an Austrian ally. Soon every great European power was involved in the war. Fought in Europe, India, and North America, the war lasted until 1763. It was called the **Seven Years' War.** The war did not change the territorial situation in Europe.

It was a different story on other continents. Both France and Britain had colonies in North America and the West Indies. Both were competing economically in India. The British emerged as the real victors in the Seven Years' War. France lost its colonies in North America, and Britain gained sole economic domination of India. This set the stage for further British expansion in India in the 1800s, as you will see in Chapter 27.

THINK THROUGH HISTORY
E. Making Inferences Why would iron ore, agriculture, and textiles be helpful acquisitions for Frederick the Great?

Section ③ Assessment

1. TERMS & NAMES
Identify
• Thirty Years' War
• Maria Theresa
• Frederick the Great
• Seven Years' War

2. TAKING NOTES
On a chart like the one shown, compare Maria Theresa and Frederick the Great.

Points of Comparison	Maria Theresa	Frederick the Great
years of reign		
foreign policy		
success in war		
their policies as monarchs		

3. RECOGNIZING EFFECTS
Name several ways that the Peace of Westphalia laid the foundations of modern Europe.

THINK ABOUT
• religious effects
• diplomatic effects
• political effects

4. THEME ACTIVITY
Power and Authority Write an outline for a lecture on "How to Increase Royal Power and Become an Absolute Monarch." In your outline, jot down examples that support your main points. The examples should be of Hapsburg and Hohenzollern actions that increased the power of those ruling families.

Russian Czars Increase Power

MAIN IDEA	WHY IT MATTERS NOW
Peter the Great made many changes in Russia to try to make it more like western Europe.	Many Russians today debate whether to model themselves on the West or to focus on traditional Russian culture.

SETTING THE STAGE Ivan III of Moscow, who ruled Russia from 1462 to 1505, accomplished several things. First, he conquered much of the territory around Moscow. Second, he liberated Russia from the Mongols. Third, he began to centralize the Russian government. This laid the foundation for the absolute monarchy that would come later.

From Ivan to the Romanovs

Ivan III was succeeded by his son, Vasily, who ruled for 28 years. Vasily continued his father's work of adding territory to the growing Russian state. He also increased the power of the central government, a trend that would continue under his son, Ivan IV.

The First Czar Ivan IV, called **Ivan the Terrible,** came to the throne in 1533 when he was only three years old. His young life was disrupted by struggles for power among Russia's landowning nobles, known as **boyars.** The boyars fought to control young Ivan. When he was 16, Ivan seized power and had himself crowned czar. This title meant "caesar," and Ivan was the first Russian ruler to use it officially. He also married the beautiful Anastasia, related to an old boyar family, the Romanovs.

The years from 1547 to 1560 are often called Ivan's "good period." He won great victories, added lands to Russia, gave Russia a code of laws, and ruled justly.

Rule by Terror Ivan's "bad period" began in 1560 after Anastasia died. Accusing the boyars of poisoning his wife, Ivan turned against them. He organized his own police force, whose chief duty was to hunt down and murder people Ivan considered traitors. The members of this police force dressed in black and rode black horses.

Using these secret police, Ivan executed many boyars, their families, and the peasants who worked their lands. Thousands of people died. Ivan seized the boyars' estates and gave them to a new class of nobles, who had to remain loyal to him or lose their land. One noble, Prince Kurbsky, described the suffering Ivan caused him:

Background
Prince Kurbsky was an adviser to Ivan and also won many battles for him. When Ivan turned against him, Kurbsky fled to Lithuania.

A VOICE FROM THE PAST
In front of your army have I marched—and marched again; and no dishonor have I brought upon you, but only brilliant victories. . . . But to you, O czar, was all this as naught; rather do you show us your intolerable wrath and bitterest hatred, and furthermore, burning stoves [a means of torture].

PRINCE ANDREW KURBSKY, letter to Czar Ivan IV

This portrait of Ivan IV is painted in the style of Russian icons. Perhaps this style was chosen to encourage deep respect for Ivan— who believed in his divine right to rule.

Absolute Monarchs in Europe **531**

Eventually, Ivan committed an act that was both a personal tragedy and a national disaster. In 1581, during a violent quarrel, he killed his oldest son and heir. When Ivan died three years later, only his weak second son was left to rule.

Rise of the Romanovs Ivan's son proved to be physically and mentally incapable of ruling. After he died without an heir, Russia experienced a period of turmoil known as the Time of Troubles. Boyars struggled for power, and heirs of czars died under mysterious conditions. Several imposters tried to claim the throne.

Finally, in 1613, representatives from many Russian cities met to choose the next czar. Their choice was Michael Romanov, grandnephew of Ivan the Terrible's wife Anastasia. Thus began the Romanov dynasty, which ruled Russia for 300 years (1613–1917).

THINK THROUGH HISTORY
A. Recognizing Effects What were the long-term effects of Ivan's murder of his oldest son?

Peter the Great Takes the Throne

Over time, the Romanovs restored order to Russia. They strengthened government by passing a law code and putting down a revolt. This paved the way for the absolute rule of Czar Peter I. At first, Peter shared the throne with a feeble-minded half-brother. However, in 1696, Peter became sole ruler of Russia. He is known to history as **Peter the Great,** because he was one of Russia's greatest reformers. He also continued the trend of increasing the czar's power.

HISTORY MAKERS

**Peter the Great
1672–1725**

Peter the Great had the mind of a genius, the body of a giant, and the ferocious temper of a bear. One could not help but look up to Peter, who stood about 6 feet 8 inches tall. He was so strong that he was known to take a heavy silver plate and roll it up as if it were a piece of paper.

Peter had a good, if crude, sense of humor and loved to make practical jokes. But heaven help the person who crossed his path. If someone annoyed him, he would take his massive fist and knock the offender unconscious. If he were angrier, he would have the person's nostrils torn out with iron pincers.

Although Peter saw himself as a father to his people, he was cruel to his own family. When his oldest son opposed him, he had him imprisoned and killed.

Russia's Differences from Europe When Peter I came to power, Russia was still a land of boyars and serfs. Serfdom in Russia lasted much longer than it did in western Europe. Serfdom continued in Russia into the mid-1800s. When a Russian landowner sold a piece of land, he sold the serfs with it. Landowners could give serfs away as presents or to pay debts. It was also against the law for serfs to run away from their owners.

Most boyars knew little of western Europe. In the Middle Ages, Russia had looked to Constantinople, not to Rome, for leadership. Then Mongol rule had cut Russia off from the Renaissance and the Age of Exploration. Geographic barriers also isolated Russia. Its only seaport, Archangel, was choked with ice much of the year. The few travelers who reached Moscow were usually Dutch or German, and they had to stay in a separate part of the city.

Religious differences widened the gap between western Europe and Russia. The Russians had adopted the Eastern Orthodox branch of Christianity. Western Europeans were mostly Catholics or Protestants, and the Russians viewed them as heretics and avoided them.

THINK THROUGH HISTORY
B. Summarizing Restate the main reasons that Russia was culturally different from western Europe.

Peter Visits the West In the 1680s, people in the German quarter of Moscow were accustomed to seeing the young Peter striding through their neighborhood on his long legs. (Peter was more than six and a half feet tall.) He was fascinated by the modern tools and machines in the foreigners' shops. Above all, he had a passion for ships and the sea. The young czar believed that Russia's future depended on having a warm-water port. Only then could Russia compete with the more modern states of western Europe.

Peter was 24 years old when he became sole ruler of Russia. In 1697, just one year later, he embarked on the "Grand Embassy," a long visit to western Europe. Peter's goal was to learn about European customs and industrial techniques. With him were 200 servants and 55 boyars. Never before had a czar traveled among Western "heretics."

On his journey, Peter insisted on keeping his identity a secret. He went to the Netherlands in the plain clothes of an ordinary worker and labored as a ship's carpenter for four months. However, a Russian giant in a Dutch seaport attracted attention. Word of his identity soon spread. Yet if a fellow worker addressed him as "Your Majesty" or "Sire," he would not answer. After all, he was just plain "Carpenter Peter." Peter also visited England and Austria before returning home.

Peter Rules Absolutely

Inspired by his trip to the West, Peter resolved that Russia would compete with Europe on both military and commercial terms. Peter's goal of **westernization**, of using western Europe as a model for change, was not an end in itself. Peter saw it as a way to make Russia stronger.

THINK THROUGH HISTORY
C. Recognizing Bias Judging from this remark, what was Peter's view of his people?

Peter's Reforms Although Peter believed Russia needed to change, he knew that many of his people disagreed. As he said to one official, "For you know yourself that, though a thing be good and necessary, our people will not do it unless forced to." To force change upon his state, Peter increased his powers as an absolute ruler.

Peter brought the Russian Orthodox church under state control. He abolished the office of patriarch, head of the church. He set up a group called the Holy Synod to run the church—under his direction.

Like Ivan the Terrible, Peter reduced the power of the great landowners. He recruited able men from lower-ranking families. He then promoted them to positions of authority and rewarded them with grants of land. Because these men owed everything to the czar, they were loyal to him alone.

To modernize his army, Peter hired European officers, who drilled his soldiers in European tactics with European weapons. Being a soldier became a lifetime job. By the time of Peter's death, the Russian army numbered 200,000 men. To pay for this huge army, Peter imposed heavy taxes.

CONNECT *to* TODAY

Russia: East vs. West
Peter's reforms sparked the beginning of a debate in Russia that continues today—whether to westernize or to focus on Russian culture. The breakup of the Soviet Union in 1991 has led to developments in both directions.

Many ethnic groups have established individual republics or are striving to do so. On the other hand, Russia and other former Soviet countries are experimenting with democracy and a market economy. These are distinctly Western traditions.

Because Russia straddles two continents—Asia and Europe—the tension between East and West will probably be an enduring part of its culture.

1462 | **Acquisitions to 1682**
Acquisitions to 1505 | **Acquisitions to 1725**
Acquisitions to 1584 | **Acquisitions to 1796**

The Expansion of Russia, 1500–1800

GEOGRAPHY SKILLBUILDER: Interpreting Maps
1. **Location** Locate the territories that Peter added to Russia during his reign, from 1682 to 1725. What bodies of water did Russia gain access to because of these acquisitions?
2. **Region** Who added a larger amount of territory to Russia—Ivan III, who ruled from 1462 to 1505, or Peter the Great?

New Russian News

Your Money or Your Beard

About a year ago, as part of his attempt to westernize Russia, Peter the Great decided that the Russian custom of wearing beards showed too much Mongol influence. Our modernizing czar offered most men a hard choice: shave their beards, or plunk down money to keep their whiskers. Those who paid the beard tax received a token (shown below) to prove that they had the right to have hairy faces.

Peter's beard tax ranged from a sixth of a kopeck for a peasant to one hundred rubles a year for a wealthy merchant. The rich had to pay 60,000 times as much as the poor!

Now that the policy has been in effect for a year, the results are in. Most peasants and merchants and all priests and monks chose to pay rather than shave. All soldiers, officers, and court officials are clean-shaven for a good reason: Peter didn't give them a choice.

Winter Happenings: Moscow

It takes more than sub-zero temperatures to keep hardy Russians home. While some people brave the frigid air to sell their wares or to shop, others find delight at the fair.

Yesterday's outdoor market featured the rock-hard frozen carcasses of cows, sheep, pigs, and chickens piled into pyramidlike heaps. On hand-pulled sleds, shoppers carted home their purchases of meat, butter, eggs, and fish.

This winter scene shows bustling activity in Ivan the Great Square in Moscow.

Clowns, magicians, jugglers, and musicians entertained at the outdoor fair. For the athletic, there was an ice-skating rink, as well as a 35-foot ice hill to delight sledders. Dizzy visitors swung back and forth in boats suspended from a wooden frame.

Happy New Year!

Forward-looking Russians are celebrating the new year with festivities in January—instead of waiting until September, as their grandparents would have done. Just last month, Peter the Great decreed that Russia would adopt the calendar used by western Europe. He ushered in the calendar change with a fireworks display and a week of public feasting.

Build It Today, Move in Tomorrow

Need a new house or a replacement part for your current dwelling? Check out the carpenter's market at the end of any major street. There you'll find logs cut in a variety of lengths and widths and marked for easy assembly. In addition, ready-made beams, roof shingles, and door and window frames are also offered for sale.

With a little help from your friends, you can move into your new house in almost no time at all. Some tips for keeping that new house cozy in the winter:

- Buy windows with double glass.
- Keep ceilings low.
- Stuff the spaces between the logs with moss.
- Make a steep roof so that snow will slide off.

Connect *to* History

Synthesizing How have Russians adapted to their cold climate? Discuss transportation, housing, and activities.

 SEE SKILLBUILDER HANDBOOK, PAGE 1007

Connect *to* Today

Researching At the library, research the records of the winter Olympics for the last 20 years to learn what events Russians (or Soviets) participated in and how many they won. What winter sports do modern Russians like and excel at?

Westernizing Russia As part of his attempts to westernize Russia, Peter

- introduced potatoes, which became a staple of the Russian diet
- started Russia's first newspaper and edited its first issue himself
- raised women's status by having them attend social gatherings
- ordered the nobles to give up their traditional clothes for Western fashions

Peter also believed education was a key to Russia's progress. In his journal, Peter (referring to himself as "the Czar") described his efforts to advance learning:

A VOICE FROM THE PAST
A school of marine [navigation] was opened, and schools for the other arts and sciences began to be introduced gradually. . . . At the same time the Czar permitted his subjects to leave the country in order to study the sciences in foreign lands. This was forbidden in former times under pain of death, but now not only was permission given for it but many were forced to undertake it.

CZAR PETER I, quoted in *Peter the Great,* edited by L. Jay Oliva

A New Capital To promote education and growth, Peter wanted a seaport that would make it easier to travel to the West. Therefore, Peter fought Sweden to gain a piece of the Baltic coast. After 21 long years of war, Russia finally won the "window on the sea" that Peter wanted.

Actually, Peter had secured that window many years before Sweden officially surrendered it. In 1703 he began building a new city on Swedish lands occupied by Russian troops. Although the swampy site was unhealthful, it seemed ideal to Peter. Ships could sail down the Neva River into the Baltic Sea and on to western Europe. Peter called the city St. Petersburg, after his patron saint.

To build a city on a desolate swamp was no easy matter. Every summer, the army forced thousands of luckless serfs to leave home and work at St. Petersburg. An estimated 25,000 to 100,000 people died from the terrible working conditions and widespread diseases. When St. Petersburg was finished, Peter ordered many Russian nobles to leave the comforts of Moscow and settle in his new capital.

For better or for worse, Peter the Great had tried to reform the culture and government of Russia. To an amazing extent he had succeeded. By the time of his death in 1725, Russia was a power to be reckoned with in Europe. Meanwhile, another great European power, England, had been developing a form of government that limited the power of absolute monarchs, as you will see in Section 5.

THINK THROUGH HISTORY
D. Synthesizing
Which of Peter's actions in the building of St. Petersburg demonstrate his power as an absolute monarch?

This 1753 painting shows a view of St. Petersburg from the water. The ships indicate that it did become a booming port, as Peter had wanted.

Section 4 Assessment

1. TERMS & NAMES

Identify
- Ivan the Terrible
- boyars
- Peter the Great
- westernization

2. TAKING NOTES

On a cluster diagram like the one shown, list the important events of Peter the Great's reign.

Peter the Great

3. SUPPORTING OPINIONS

Do you think Ivan the Terrible or Peter the Great was more of an absolute monarch? Explain the standards by which you made your decision.

THINK ABOUT
- ways that each increased the power of the Russian czar
- long term effects of each one's rule

4. ANALYZING THEMES

Power and Authority Which of Peter the Great's actions reveal that he saw himself as the highest authority in Russia? Explain.

THINK ABOUT
- steps he took to reduce the authority of others
- actions that overturned traditional sources of authority in Russia

Absolute Monarchs in Europe **535**

TERMS & NAMES
- Charles I
- English Civil War
- Oliver Cromwell
- Restoration
- habeas corpus
- Glorious Revolution
- constitutional monarchy
- cabinet

5 Parliament Limits the English Monarchy

MAIN IDEA

Absolute rulers in England were overthrown, and Parliament gained power.

WHY IT MATTERS NOW

Many of the government reforms of this period contributed to the democratic tradition of the United States.

SETTING THE STAGE During her reign, Queen Elizabeth I of England had frequent conflicts with Parliament. Many of the arguments were over money, because the treasury did not have enough funds to pay the queen's expenses. By the time Elizabeth died in 1603, she left a huge debt for her successor to deal with. Parliament's financial power was one obstacle to English rulers' becoming absolute monarchs.

Monarchs Clash with Parliament

Elizabeth had no child, and her nearest relative was her cousin, James Stuart. Already king of Scotland, James Stuart became King James I of England in 1603. Although England and Scotland were not united until 1707, they now shared a ruler.

James's Problems James inherited the unsettled issues of Elizabeth's reign. The key question was how much power Parliament would have in governing. James believed he had absolute authority to rule. He said in a speech, "Kings are justly called gods, for that they exercise a manner or resemblance of divine power upon earth."

Elizabeth had also believed in her divine right to rule, but she was more tactful than James. She flattered Parliament to get her way. James thought it was beneath him to try to win Parliament's favor. His worst struggles with Parliament were over money. Parliament was reluctant to pay for James's expensive court and foreign wars.

In addition, James offended the Puritan members of Parliament. Because James was a Calvinist, the Puritans hoped he would enact reforms to purify the English church of Catholic practices. However, James resented being told what to do. Except for agreeing to a new translation of the Bible, he refused to make Puritan reforms.

Charles I Fights Parliament In 1625, James I died. **Charles I,** his son, took the throne. Charles always needed money—in part because he was at war with both Spain and France. Several times when Parliament refused to give him funds, he dissolved it.

By 1628, Charles was forced to call Parliament again. This time it refused to grant him any money until he signed a document that is known as the Petition of Right. In this petition, the king agreed to four points:

- He would not imprison subjects without due cause.
- He would not levy taxes without Parliament's consent.
- He would not house soldiers in private homes.
- He would not impose martial law in peacetime.

After agreeing to the petition, Charles ignored it. Even so, the petition was important. It set forth the idea that the law was higher

Background
James was the son of Mary, Queen of Scots—whom Elizabeth had executed for plotting against her.

SPOTLIGHT ON

King James Bible

James I was very interested in religion and scholarship. It bothered him that although there were many English translations of the Bible, none was as well-written as he wanted. Therefore, he sponsored a committee of Bible scholars to create a new, royally approved translation.

The new version of the Bible was first printed in 1611. The King James Bible is noted for the elegance and power of its language. It is still read by millions of English-speaking Protestants throughout the world.

THINK THROUGH HISTORY
A. Making Inferences Explain how the Petition of Right contradicted the idea of absolute monarchy.

than the king. This contradicted theories of absolute monarchy. In 1629, Charles dissolved Parliament and refused to call it back into session. To get money, he imposed all kinds of fees and fines on the English people. His popularity decreased year by year.

English Civil War

Charles offended Puritans by upholding church ritual and a formal prayer book. In addition, in 1637, Charles tried to force the Presbyterian Scots to accept a version of the Anglican prayer book. He wanted both his kingdoms to follow one religion. The Scots rebelled, assembled a huge army, and threatened to invade England. To meet this danger, Charles needed money—money he could get only by calling Parliament into session. This gave Parliament a chance to oppose him.

War Topples a King During the autumn of 1641, Parliament passed laws to limit royal power. Furious, Charles tried to arrest Parliament's leaders in January 1642, but they escaped. Equally furious, a mob of Londoners raged outside the palace. Charles fled London and raised an army in the north of England, where people were loyal to him.

From 1642 to 1649, supporters and opponents of King Charles fought the **English Civil War.** Those who remained loyal to Charles were called Royalists or Cavaliers. On the other side were Puritan supporters of Parliament. Because these men wore their hair short over their ears, Cavaliers mockingly called them Roundheads.

At first neither side could gain a lasting advantage. However, by 1644 the Puritans found a general who could win—**Oliver Cromwell.** In 1646, Cromwell's New Model Army defeated the Cavaliers. By the following year, the Puritans held the king prisoner.

In 1649, Cromwell and the Puritans brought Charles to trial for treason. They found him guilty and sentenced him to death. The execution of Charles was revolutionary. Kings had often been overthrown, killed in battle, or put to death in secret. Never before had a reigning monarch faced a public trial and execution.

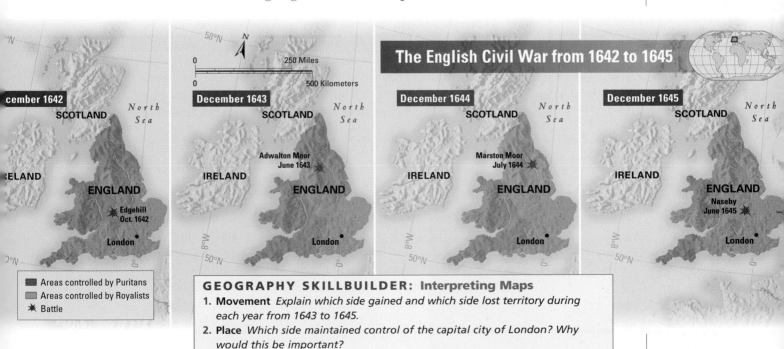

The English Civil War from 1642 to 1645

December 1642 — SCOTLAND, North Sea, IRELAND, ENGLAND, Edgehill Oct. 1642, London

December 1643 — 58°N, 0 250 Miles, 0 500 Kilometers, SCOTLAND, North Sea, Adwalton Moor June 1643, IRELAND, ENGLAND, London, 8°W, 50°N

December 1644 — SCOTLAND, North Sea, Marston Moor July 1644, IRELAND, ENGLAND, London, 8°W, 50°N

December 1645 — SCOTLAND, North Sea, IRELAND, ENGLAND, Naseby June 1645, London, 8°W, 50°N

■ Areas controlled by Puritans
■ Areas controlled by Royalists
✳ Battle

GEOGRAPHY SKILLBUILDER: Interpreting Maps
1. **Movement** Explain which side gained and which side lost territory during each year from 1643 to 1645.
2. **Place** Which side maintained control of the capital city of London? Why would this be important?

THINK THROUGH HISTORY
B. Comparing What did Cromwell's rule have in common with an absolute monarchy?

Cromwell's Rule Cromwell now held the reins of power. In 1649, he abolished the monarchy and the House of Lords. He established a commonwealth—a republican form of government. In 1653, Cromwell sent the remaining members of Parliament home. Cromwell's associate John Lambert drafted a constitution, the first written constitution of any modern European state. However, Cromwell eventually tore up the document and ruled as a military dictator.

Absolute Monarchs in Europe **537**

Cromwell almost immediately had to put down a rebellion in Ireland. Henry VIII and his children had brought that country under English rule. In 1649 Cromwell landed on Irish shores with an army and crushed the uprising. The lands and homes of the Irish were taken from them and given to English soldiers. Fighting, plague, and famine killed an estimated 616,000 Irish.

Puritan Morality In England, Cromwell and the Puritans sought to reform society. They made laws that promoted Puritan morality and abolished activities they found sinful, such as going to the theater. In a speech, Cromwell explained his reasons for this:

> **A VOICE FROM THE PAST**
> I did hint to you my thoughts about the reformation of manners; and those abuses that are in this nation through disorder . . . should be much in your hearts. . . . I am confident our liberty and prosperity depends upon—reformation. To make it a shame to see men to be bold in sin and profaneness—and God will bless you. You will be a blessing to the nation.
> **OLIVER CROMWELL**, speech of September 17, 1656

SPOTLIGHT ON

The London Fire
A disastrous fire broke out in London on September 2, 1666. It began in the house of the king's baker, near London Bridge. The flames, stirred by a strong east wind, leaped from building to building. People desperately tried to escape. The Thames River was crawling with boats filled with survivors and their belongings.

Samuel Pepys, a public official, wrote an eyewitness account of the fire in his diary:

> It made me weep to see it. The churches, houses, and all on fire and flaming at once; and a horrid noise the flames made, and the cracking of houses at their ruin.

In the end, the fire destroyed St. Paul's Cathedral, 87 parish churches, and around 13,000 houses. It was the worst fire in London's history.

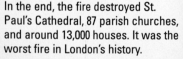

Although a strict Puritan, Cromwell favored religious toleration for all Christians except Catholics. He even welcomed back Jews, who had been expelled from England in 1290.

Restoration and Revolution

Oliver Cromwell ruled until his death in 1658. Shortly afterward, the government he had established collapsed, and a new Parliament was selected. The English people were sick of military rule. In 1659, Parliament voted to ask the older son of Charles I to rule England.

Charles II Reigns When Prince Charles entered London in 1660, crowds shouted joyfully and bells rang. On this note of celebration, the reign of Charles II began. Because he restored the monarchy, the period of his rule is called the **Restoration.**

Charles also restored the theater, sporting events, and dancing, which the Puritans had banned. Theater, especially comedy, and the other arts flourished during the Restoration. For the first time, women appeared on the English stage to play female roles.

During Charles II's reign, Parliament passed an important guarantee of freedom, **habeas corpus.** This 1679 law gave every prisoner the right to obtain a writ or document ordering that the prisoner be brought before a judge. The judge would decide whether the prisoner should be tried or set free. Because of the Habeas Corpus Act, a monarch could not put someone in jail simply for opposing the ruler. Also, prisoners could not be held indefinitely without trials.

In addition, Parliament debated who should inherit Charles's throne. Because Charles had no legitimate child, his heir was his brother James, who was Catholic. A group called the Whigs opposed James, and a group called the Tories supported him. These two groups were the ancestors of England's first political parties.

Background
Habeas corpus comes from Latin words meaning "to have the body."

James II and the Glorious Revolution In 1685, Charles II died, and James II became king. James soon offended his subjects by flaunting his Catholicism. Violating English law, he appointed several Catholics to high office. When Parliament protested, James dissolved it. In 1688, James's second wife gave birth to a son. English Protestants became terrified at the prospect of a line of Catholic kings.

THINK THROUGH HISTORY
C. Contrasting How was the overthrow of James II different from the overthrow of Charles I?

James had an older daughter, Mary, who was Protestant. She was also the wife of William of Orange, a prince of the Netherlands. Seven members of Parliament invited William and Mary to overthrow James for the sake of Protestantism. When William led his army to London in 1688, James fled to France. This bloodless overthrow of King James II is called the **Glorious Revolution.**

Political Changes

At their coronation, William and Mary vowed "to govern the people of this kingdom of England . . . according to the statutes in Parliament agreed on and the laws and customs of the same." By doing so, William and Mary recognized Parliament as their partner in governing. England had become not an absolute monarchy but a **constitutional monarchy,** where laws limited the ruler's power.

Bill of Rights To make clear the limits of royal power, Parliament drafted a Bill of Rights in 1689. This document listed many things that a ruler could not do:

- No suspending of Parliament's laws
- No levying of taxes without a specific grant from Parliament
- No interfering with freedom of speech in Parliament
- No penalty for a citizen who petitions the king about grievances

William and Mary officially consented to these and other limits on their royal power.

Cabinet System Develops After 1688, no British monarch could rule without consent of Parliament. At the same time, Parliament could not rule without the consent of the monarch. If the two disagreed, government came to a standstill.

Background
Although the power of Parliament increased, England was still not democratic. Parliament represented the upper classes, not the majority of the English people.

During the 1700s, this potential problem was remedied by the development of a group of government ministers called the **cabinet.** These ministers acted in the ruler's name but in reality represented the major party of Parliament. Therefore, they became the link between the monarch and the majority in Parliament.

Over time, the cabinet became the center of power and policymaking. Under the cabinet system, the leader of the majority party in Parliament heads the cabinet and is called the prime minister. This system of English government continues today.

CONNECT *to* TODAY

U.S. Democracy
The United States adopted many of the government reforms and institutions that the English developed during this period. These include the following:

- the right to obtain habeas corpus—a document that prevents authorities from holding a person in jail without being charged
- a Bill of Rights, guaranteeing such rights as freedom of speech and freedom of worship
- a strong legislature and strong executive, which act as checks on each other
- a cabinet, made up of heads of executive departments, such as the Department of State
- two dominant political parties

Section 5 Assessment

1. TERMS & NAMES

Identify
- Charles I
- English Civil War
- Oliver Cromwell
- Restoration
- habeas corpus
- Glorious Revolution
- constitutional monarchy
- cabinet

2. TAKING NOTES

On a chart like the one shown, list the causes of each monarch's conflicts with Parliament.

Monarch	Conflicts with Parliament
James I	
Charles I	
James II	

What patterns do you see in the causes of these conflicts?

3. EVALUATING DECISIONS

In your opinion, which decisions of Charles I made his conflict with Parliament worse? Explain.

THINK ABOUT
- decisions that lost him the support of Parliament
- decisions that lost him the support of his people

4. THEME ACTIVITY

Revolution Using a dictionary, encyclopedia, or your textbook for reference, write a definition of revolution. Then write a paragraph explaining how the English Civil War and the Glorious Revolution are examples of revolution.

Absolute Monarchs in Europe

Long-Term Causes

- decline of feudalism
- rise of cities and growth of middle class
- growth of national kingdoms
- loss of Church authority

Immediate Causes

- religious and territorial conflicts
- buildup of armies
- need for increased taxes
- revolts by peasants or nobles

European Monarchs Claim Divine Right to Rule Absolutely

Immediate Effects

- regulation of religion and society
- larger courts
- huge building projects
- new government bureaucracies
- loss of power by nobility and legislatures

Long-Term Effects

- revolution in France
- western European influence on Russia
- English political reforms that influence U.S. democracy

TERMS & NAMES

Briefly explain the importance of each of the following during the age of absolute monarchs in Europe.

1. absolute monarch
2. divine right
3. Louis XIV
4. War of the Spanish Succession
5. Thirty Years' War
6. Seven Years' War
7. Peter the Great
8. English Civil War
9. Glorious Revolution
10. constitutional monarchy

REVIEW QUESTIONS

SECTION 1 *(pages 513–517)*

Spain's Empire and European Absolutism

11. Name three actions that demonstrate that Philip II of Spain saw himself as a defender of Catholicism.
12. According to French writer Jean Bodin, should a prince share power with anyone else? Explain why or why not.

SECTION 2 *(pages 518–525)*

France's Ultimate Monarch

13. Name two ways that Louis XIV controlled the French nobility.
14. In what ways did Louis XIV cause suffering to the French people?

SECTION 3 *(pages 526–530)*

Central European Monarchs Clash

15. What were six results of the Peace of Westphalia?
16. What was the reason that Maria Theresa and Frederick the Great fought two wars against each other?

SECTION 4 *(pages 531–535)*

Russia Czars Increase Power

17. List three differences between Russia and western Europe.
18. What were Peter the Great's goals for Russia?

SECTION 5 *(pages 536–539)*

Parliament Limits the English Monarchy

19. Describe the causes, participants, and outcome of the English Civil War.
20. List at least three ways that Parliament tried to limit the power of the English monarchy.

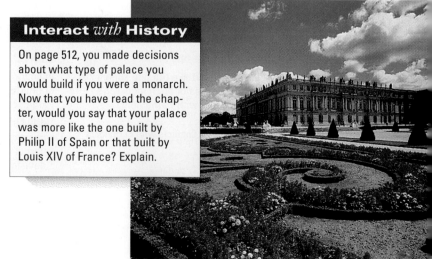

Interact *with* History

On page 512, you made decisions about what type of palace you would build if you were a monarch. Now that you have read the chapter, would you say that your palace was more like the one built by Philip II of Spain or that built by Louis XIV of France? Explain.

CRITICAL THINKING

1. IMPROVING THE ECONOMY

THEME ECONOMICS Of all the monarchs that you studied in this chapter, which one do you think helped his or her country's economy the most? Explain your answer by citing evidence from the chapter.

2. MONARCHS RULE ABSOLUTELY

Create a chart like the one shown. In the left-hand column of your chart, list actions that absolute monarchs often took to increase their power. Then for each action, name at least one monarch who actually did that. Use at least five different monarchs in your chart as examples.

Actions of absolute monarchs	Example of a monarch who did this

3. LAND GRABBERS

Many of the monarchs that you studied in this chapter tried to increase their countries' territory. Why might an absolute monarch want to gain territory? Explain what benefits these monarchs hoped to gain.

4. ANALYZING PRIMARY SOURCES

After the Glorious Revolution of 1688, Parliament passed the Bill of Rights in 1689. The following is an excerpt from that document. Read it and then answer the questions that follow.

> **A VOICE FROM THE PAST**
>
> That the pretended power of suspending [canceling] of laws or the execution [carrying out] of laws by regal authority without consent of Parliament is illegal; . . .
>
> That it is the right of the subjects to petition [make requests of] the king, and all commitments [imprisonments] and prosecutions for such petitioning are illegal;
>
> That the raising or keeping a standing army within the kingdom in time of peace, unless it be with consent of Parliament, is against the law; . . .
>
> That election of members of Parliament ought to be free [not restricted].
>
> Bill of Rights

- In what ways did Parliament limit the power of the monarch?
- How did the Parliament try to protect itself?

CHAPTER ACTIVITIES

1. LIVING HISTORY: Unit Portfolio Project

THEME REVOLUTION Your unit portfolio project focuses on showing the causes and results of various revolutions (see page 509). For Chapter 21, you might use one of the following ideas to add to your portfolio.

- Peter the Great tried to revolutionize Russian culture and society. Create an educational poster that Peter could have used to explain one practice he wanted his people to give up and what he wanted to replace it with.
- Write an editorial stating whether you think the English Civil War or the Glorious Revolution was more revolutionary. To support your opinion, examine both short-term and long-term effects.
- Write a HistoryMaker, like the ones you've read throughout this textbook, focusing on Oliver Cromwell as a leader of a revolution.

2. CONNECT TO TODAY: Cooperative Learning

THEME POWER AND AUTHORITY One of the ideas that came out of this time period is that Parliament should prevent the English monarch from exercising too much power. In the United States, the legislative body also limits the power of the head of government. At the same time, in the United States the head of government—or chief executive—also limits the power of the legislature. Create a diagram that shows how these two branches of government limit each other's power.

- Use the Internet, the library, or other sources to research the various branches of the U.S. national government.
- Identify the legislative and executive branches of government and the powers of each. Especially note how each branch acts to limit the power of the other.
- Display this information on a diagram. Some of the diagrams in this textbook might provide ideas for how to use visual elements such as arrows to demonstrate relationships.

3. INTERPRETING A TIME LINE

Revisit the unit time line on pages 508–509. Use the Chapter 21 time line to find out when Louis XIV began his reign. What happened in England shortly after Louis took the throne? How might that have affected his views on monarchy?

FOCUS ON GEOGRAPHY

On the map, notice which modern European nations are still ruled by royal monarchs.

- Of the countries that you studied in this chapter, which have monarchs today?

Connect to History
- Which of those countries was a republic during the period of this chapter?
- Did the countries whose rulers exercised the most power retain the monarchy? Explain.

Modern European Monarchs

0 500 Miles
0 1,000 Kilometers

■ Nations with monarchs today

NORWAY
SWEDEN
DENMARK
UNITED KINGDOM
NETHERLANDS
ATLANTIC OCEAN
BELGIUM
LUXEMBOURG
LIECHTENSTEIN
MONACO
SPAIN
ANDORRA

CHAPTER 22

Enlightenment and Revolution, 1550–1789

Revolution

Between the 16th and 18th centuries, a series of revolutions helped usher in the modern era in Western history. First was a revolution in understanding, called the Scientific Revolution. Second was a revolution of ideas, called the Enlightenment. Third was a revolution in action—the American Revolution.

Science and Technology

The Scientific Revolution began when some astronomers questioned the old understanding of how the universe operates—one that was deeply tied to people's religious beliefs. By shattering this view, the astronomers opened a new universe of scientific discovery.

Power and Authority

Like their counterparts in science, the political thinkers of the Enlightenment challenged established ideas about power and authority. A ruler does not own authority by divine right, the thinkers said. Rather, a ruler receives authority by the consent of the people. Such ideas led to the political upheaval of the American Revolution.

INTERNET CONNECTION

Visit us at **www.mcdougallittell.com** to learn more about the Scientific Revolution, the Enlightenment, and the American Revolution.

CENTERS OF ENLIGHTENMENT, 1750

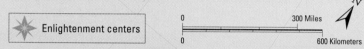

✦ Enlightenment centers

0 _____ 300 Miles
0 _____ 600 Kilometers

Eastern North America

Boston

Philadelphia

Williamsburg

40°N
70°W
30°N
80°W

0 _____ 250 Miles
0 _____ 500 Kilometers

SPAIN

ATLANTIC OCEAN

34°N

In **1775**, the brilliant orator **Patrick Henry** delivered his now famous speech to the Second Virginia Convention. In this speech he declared, "Give me liberty, or give me death!" In this 19th-century painting by artist Peter Rothermel, Henry speaks before the Virginia House of Burgesses. He repeatedly spoke against British laws that restricted the colonists' rights.

24°W
26°W
16°W

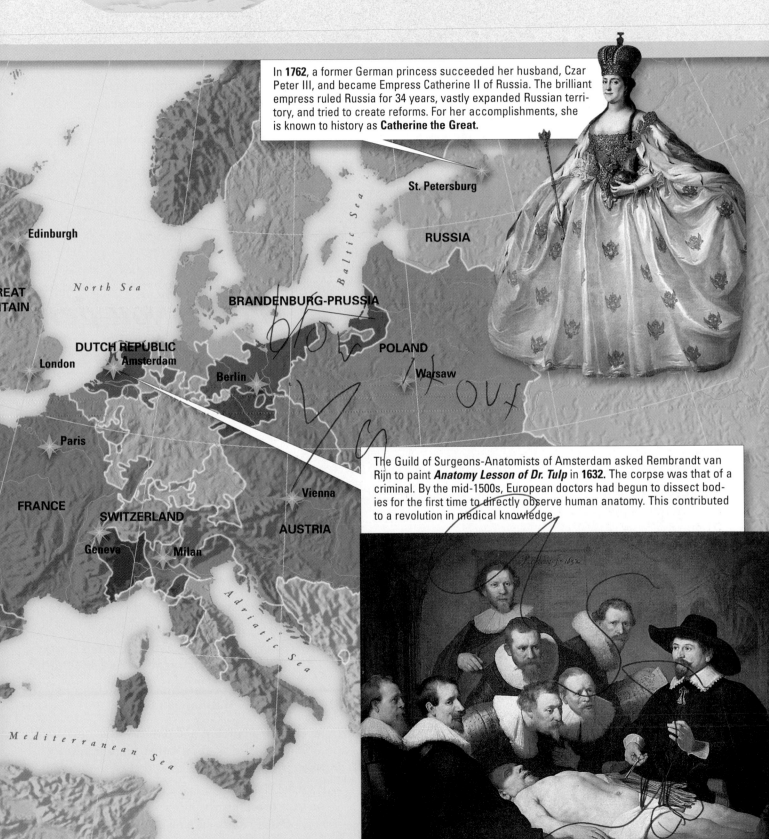

In **1762**, a former German princess succeeded her husband, Czar Peter III, and became Empress Catherine II of Russia. The brilliant empress ruled Russia for 34 years, vastly expanded Russian territory, and tried to create reforms. For her accomplishments, she is known to history as **Catherine the Great.**

The Guild of Surgeons-Anatomists of Amsterdam asked Rembrandt van Rijn to paint *Anatomy Lesson of Dr. Tulp* in **1632**. The corpse was that of a criminal. By the mid-1500s, European doctors had begun to dissect bodies for the first time to directly observe human anatomy. This contributed to a revolution in medical knowledge.

Interact *with* History

It is the year 1633, and the Italian scientist Galileo Galilei faces a life-or-death dilemma. The Roman Inquisition, a court of the Catholic Church, has condemned him for holding an idea—that the earth revolves around the sun. The court has asked Galileo to publicly deny this idea. If he agrees, the court will show leniency. If he refuses, Galileo will likely face torture or a painful death.

The idea that the earth revolves around the sun had been put forth almost a century before by the Polish astronomer Copernicus. Galileo is firmly convinced that Copernicus was right. Galileo has been looking through a telescope at the planets and stars. What he has seen with his own eyes is proof enough of Copernicus's theory.

The church has denounced Copernicus's theory as dangerous to the faith. The idea that the earth is the center of the universe is part of church teachings. Church leaders have warned Galileo to stop defending the new theory. But Galileo has written a book that explains why Copernicus's ideas make sense. Now he is on trial.

Put yourself in the place of Galileo as he weighs the choice the Inquisition has given him.

Galileo tries to defend himself before the Inquisition. The court, however, demands that he recant.

Would you deny an idea you know to be true?

EXAMINING *the* ISSUES

- By silencing Galileo, the church wanted to suppress an idea. Do you think this was an effective strategy? Can an idea have a life of its own?

- Are there any cases in which an idea is too dangerous to be openly discussed or taught?

- Galileo faced persecution for teaching new ideas. Could this happen today?

Meet in small groups and discuss these questions. As you share ideas, recall other times in history when people expressed ideas that were different from accepted ones.

As you read this chapter, watch for the effects revolutionary ideas have on others.

The Scientific Revolution

TERMS & NAMES
• Scientific Revolution
• Nicolaus Copernicus
• heliocentric theory
• Johannes Kepler
• Galileo Galilei
• scientific method
• Francis Bacon
• René Descartes
• Isaac Newton

MAIN IDEA

In the mid-1500s, scientists began to question accepted beliefs and make new theories based on experimentation.

WHY IT MATTERS NOW

Scientists' questioning led to the development of the scientific method still in use today.

SETTING THE STAGE The Renaissance inspired a spirit of curiosity in many fields. Scholars began to question ideas that had been accepted for hundreds of years. During the Reformation, religious leaders challenged accepted ways of thinking about God and salvation. While the Reformation was taking place, another revolution in European thought was also occurring. It challenged how people viewed their place in the universe.

The Roots of Modern Science

Before 1500, scholars generally decided what was true or false by referring to an ancient Greek or Roman author or to the Bible. Whatever Aristotle said about the material world was true unless the Bible said otherwise. Few European scholars questioned the scientific ideas of the ancient thinkers or the church by carefully observing nature for themselves.

The Medieval View During the Middle Ages, most scholars believed that the earth was an unmoving object located at the center of the universe. According to that belief, the moon, the sun, and the planets all moved in perfectly circular paths around the earth. Beyond the planets lay a sphere of fixed stars, with heaven still farther beyond. Common sense seemed to support this view. After all, the sun appeared to be moving around the earth as it rose in the morning and set in the evening.

This earth-centered view of the universe, called the geocentric theory, was supported by more than just common sense. The idea came from Aristotle, the Greek philosopher of the fourth century B.C. The Greek astronomer Ptolemy expanded the theory in the second century A.D. In addition, Christianity taught that God had deliberately placed earth at the center of the universe. Earth was thus a special place on which the great drama of life took place.

This drawing from an astrology text of 1531 shows the signs of the zodiac moving around the earth. It is based on Ptolemy's system, with the earth at the center.

THINK THROUGH HISTORY
A. Analyzing Issues
Why did most people believe the geocentric theory?

A New Way of Thinking Beginning in the mid-1500s, a few scholars published works that challenged the ideas of the ancient thinkers and the church. As these scholars replaced old assumptions with new theories, they launched a change in European thought that historians call the Scientific Revolution. The **Scientific Revolution** was a new way of thinking about the natural world. That way was based upon careful observation and a willingness to question accepted beliefs.

A combination of discoveries and circumstances led to the Scientific Revolution and helped spread its impact. By the late Middle Ages, European scholars had translated many works by Muslim scholars. These scholars had compiled a storehouse of ancient and current scientific knowledge. Based on this knowledge, medieval universities added scientific courses in astronomy, physics, and mathematics.

During the Renaissance, scholars uncovered many classical manuscripts. They found that the ancient authorities often did not agree with each other. Moreover,

European explorers traveled to Africa, Asia, and the Americas. Such lands were inhabited by peoples and animals previously unknown in Europe. These discoveries opened Europeans to the possibility that there were new truths to be found. The invention of the printing press during this period helped spread challenging ideas—both old and new—more widely among Europe's thinkers.

The age of European exploration also fueled a great deal of scientific research, especially in astronomy and mathematics. Navigators needed better instruments and geographic measurements, for example, to determine their location in the open sea. As scientists began to look more closely at the world around them, they made observations that did not match the ancient beliefs. They found they had reached the limit of the classical world's knowledge. Yet, they still needed to know more.

A Revolutionary Model of the Universe

The first major challenge to accepted scientific thinking came in the field of astronomy. The Scientific Revolution started when a small group of scholars began to question the geocentric theory.

This model shows how Copernicus saw the planets revolving around the sun—in perfect circles.

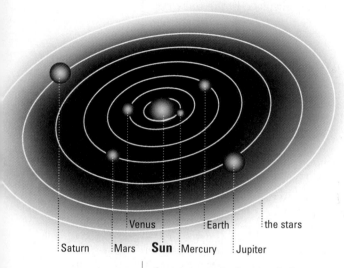

Saturn : Mars : **Sun** : Mercury : Jupiter

Venus : Earth : the stars

The Heliocentric Theory Although backed by authority and common sense, the geocentric theory did not accurately explain the movements of the sun, moon, and planets. This problem troubled a Polish cleric and astronomer named **Nicolaus Copernicus** (koh·PUR·nuh·kuhs). In the early 1500s, Copernicus became interested in an old Greek idea that the sun stood at the center of the universe. After studying planetary movements for more than 25 years, Copernicus reasoned that indeed, the stars, the earth, and the other planets revolved around the sun.

Copernicus's **heliocentric,** or sun-centered, **theory** still did not completely explain why the planets orbited the way they did. He also knew that most scholars and clergy would reject his theory because it contradicted their religious views. Fearing ridicule or persecution, Copernicus did not publish his findings until 1543, the last year of his life. He received a copy of his book, *On the Revolutions of the Heavenly Bodies,* on his deathbed.

THINK THROUGH HISTORY
B. Clarifying How did Copernicus arrive at the heliocentric theory?

While revolutionary, Copernicus's book caused little stir at first. Over the next century and a half, other scientists built on the foundations he had laid. A Danish astronomer, Tycho Brahe (TEE·koh brah), carefully recorded the movements of the planets for many years. Brahe produced mountains of accurate data based on his observations. However, it was left to his followers to make mathematical sense of them.

After Brahe's death in 1601, his assistant, a brilliant mathematician named **Johannes Kepler,** continued his work. After studying Brahe's data, Kepler concluded that certain mathematical laws govern planetary motion. One of these laws showed that the planets revolve around the sun in elliptical orbits instead of circles, as was previously thought. Kepler's laws showed that Copernicus's basic ideas were true. They demonstrated mathematically that the planets revolve around the sun.

THINK THROUGH HISTORY
C. Recognizing Effects How did Kepler's findings support the heliocentric theory?

Galileo's Discoveries In 1581, a 17-year-old Italian student named **Galileo Galilei** sat in a cathedral closely watching a chandelier swing on its chain. Aristotle had said that a pendulum swings at a slower rhythm as it approaches its resting place. Using his beating pulse, Galileo carefully timed the chandelier's swings. Aristotle's idea was wrong. Instead, each swing of the pendulum took exactly the same amount of time. Galileo had discovered the law of the pendulum.

In another study, Galileo found that a falling object accelerates at a fixed and predictable rate. Galileo also tested Aristotle's theory that heavy objects fall faster than lighter ones. According to legend, he dropped stones of different weights from the Leaning Tower of Pisa. He then calculated how fast each fell. Contrary to Aristotle's assumption, the objects fell at the same speed.

Later, Galileo learned that a Dutch lens maker had built an instrument that could enlarge far-off objects. Without seeing this device, Galileo successfully built his own telescope. After making some improvements, Galileo used his telescope to study the heavens in 1609.

Then in 1610, he published a series of newsletters called *Starry Messenger,* which described his astonishing observations. Galileo announced that Jupiter had four moons and that the sun had dark spots. He also noted that the earth's moon had a rough, uneven surface. His description of the moon's surface shattered Aristotle's theory that the moon and stars were made of a pure, perfect substance. Galileo's observations, as well as his laws of motion, also clearly supported the theories of Copernicus.

Conflict with the Church Galileo's findings frightened both Catholic and Protestant leaders because they went against church teaching and authority. If people believed the church could be wrong about this, they could question other church teachings as well.

In 1616, the Catholic Church warned Galileo not to defend the ideas of Copernicus. Although Galileo remained publicly silent, he continued his studies. Then, in 1632, he published *Dialogue Concerning the Two Chief World Systems.* This book presented the ideas of both Copernicus and Ptolemy, but it clearly showed that Galileo supported the Copernican theory. The pope angrily summoned Galileo to Rome to stand trial before the Inquisition.

Galileo stood before the court in 1633. Under the threat of torture, he knelt before the cardinals and read aloud a signed confession. In it, he agreed that the ideas of Copernicus were false.

> **A VOICE FROM THE PAST**
> With sincere heart and unpretended faith I abjure, curse, and detest the aforesaid errors and heresies [of Copernicus] and also every other error . . . contrary to the Holy Church, and I swear that in the future I will never again say or assert . . . anything that might cause a similar suspicion toward me.
>
> **GALILEO GALILEI,** quoted in *The Discoverers*

Galileo used this telescope to observe the moon. He saw that the moon's surface is rough, not smooth as others thought.

CONNECT *to* TODAY

The Vatican Clears Galileo
In 1992, Pope John Paul II officially acknowledged that Galileo was correct in asserting that the earth revolves around the sun. His pronouncement came after a 13-year study of Galileo's case by a Vatican science panel.

The panel concluded that church leaders were clearly wrong to condemn Galileo but that they had acted in good faith. They were working within the knowledge of their time, the panel said. Therefore, they could not see how Galileo's discoveries could go along with their interpretation of the Bible.

Galileo was never again a free man. He lived under house arrest and died in 1642 at his villa near Florence. However, his books and ideas still spread all over Europe.

The Scientific Method

The revolution in scientific thinking that Copernicus, Kepler, and Galileo began eventually developed into a new approach to science called the scientific method. The **scientific method** is a logical procedure for gathering and testing ideas. It begins with a problem or question arising from an observation. Scientists next form a hypothesis, or unproved assumption. The hypothesis is then tested in an experiment or on the basis of data. In the final step, scientists analyze and interpret their data to reach a new conclusion. That conclusion either confirms or disproves the hypothesis.

The scientific method did not develop overnight. The work of two important thinkers of the 1600s, Francis Bacon and René Descartes, helped to advance the new approach.

Francis Bacon, an English politician and writer, had a passionate interest in science. He believed that by better understanding the world, scientists would generate practical knowledge that would improve people's lives. In his writings, Bacon attacked medieval

1572 Brahe discovers nova, or bright new star, which contradicts Aristotle's idea that universe is unchanging.

1609 Kepler publishes first two laws of planetary motion.

1610 Galileo publishes *Starry Messenger.*

1520   1570   1620

1543 Copernicus publishes heliocentric theory.

Vesalius publishes human anatomy textbook.

1590 Janssen invents microscope.

1620 Bacon's book *Novum Organum (New Instrument)* encourages experimental method.

Nicolaus Copernicus began the Scientific Revolution with his heliocentric theory.

This microscope dates from the 17th century.

scholars for relying too heavily on the conclusions of Aristotle and other ancient thinkers. He also criticized the way in which both Aristotle and medieval scholars arrived at their conclusions. They had reasoned from abstract theories. Instead, he urged scientists to experiment. Scientists, he wrote, should observe the world and gather information about it first. Then they should draw conclusions from that information. This approach is called empiricism, or the experimental method.

In France, **René Descartes** (day·KAHRT) also took a keen interest in science. He developed analytical geometry, which linked algebra and geometry. This provided an important new tool for scientific research.

Like Bacon, Descartes believed that scientists needed to reject old assumptions and teachings. As a mathematician, however, his approach to gaining knowledge differed from Bacon's. Rather than using experimentation, Descartes relied on mathematics and logic. He believed that everything should be doubted until proved by reason. The only thing he knew for certain was that he existed—because, as he wrote, "I think, therefore I am." From this starting point, he followed a train of strict reasoning to arrive at other basic truths.

Modern scientific methods are based on the ideas of Bacon and Descartes. Scientists have shown that observation and experimentation, together with general laws that can be expressed mathematically, can lead people to a better understanding of the natural world.

THINK THROUGH HISTORY
D. Contrasting How did Descartes's approach to science differ from Bacon's?

Changing Idea: Scientific Method

Old Science
Scholars generally relied on ancient authorities, church teachings, common sense and reasoning to explain the physical world.

New Science
In time, scholars began to use observation, experimentation, and scientific reasoning to gather knowledge and draw conclusions about the physical world.

Newton Explains the Law of Gravity

By the mid-1600s, the accomplishments of Copernicus, Kepler, and Galileo had shattered the old views of astronomy and physics. Later, the great English scientist **Isaac Newton** helped to bring together their breakthroughs under a single theory of motion.

Newton studied mathematics and physics at Cambridge University. By the time he was 24, Newton was certain that all physical objects were affected equally by the same forces. Kepler had worked out laws for a planet's motion around the sun. Galileo had studied the motion of pendulums. Newton's great discovery was that the same force ruled the motions of the planets, the pendulum, and all matter on earth and in space.

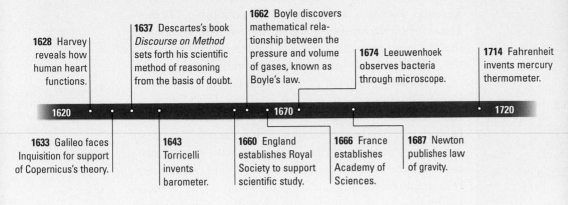

1628 Harvey reveals how human heart functions.

1637 Descartes's book *Discourse on Method* sets forth his scientific method of reasoning from the basis of doubt.

1662 Boyle discovers mathematical relationship between the pressure and volume of gases, known as Boyle's law.

1674 Leeuwenhoek observes bacteria through microscope.

1714 Fahrenheit invents mercury thermometer.

1620 • • • • • • 1670 • • 1720

1633 Galileo faces Inquisition for support of Copernicus's theory.

1643 Torricelli invents barometer.

1660 England establishes Royal Society to support scientific study.

1666 France establishes Academy of Sciences.

1687 Newton publishes law of gravity.

Isaac Newton's law of gravity explained how the same physical laws governed motion both on the earth and in the heavens.

He disproved the idea of Aristotle that one set of physical laws governed earth and another set governed the rest of the universe.

THINK THROUGH HISTORY
E. Clarifying Why was the law of gravitation important?

The key idea that linked motion in the heavens with motion on the earth was the law of universal gravitation. According to this law, every object in the universe attracts every other object. The degree of attraction depends on the mass of the objects and the distance between them.

In 1687, Newton published his ideas in a work called *Mathematical Principles of Natural Philosophy*—one of the most important scientific books ever written. The universe he described was like a giant clock. Its parts all worked together perfectly in ways that could be expressed mathematically. Newton believed that God was the creator of this orderly universe, the clockmaker who had set everything in motion.

The Scientific Revolution Spreads

After astronomers explored the secrets of the universe, other scientists began to study the secrets of nature on earth. Careful observation and the use of the scientific method eventually became important in many different fields.

Scientific Instruments Scientists developed new tools and instruments to make the precise observations that the scientific method demanded. The first microscope was invented by a Dutch maker of eyeglasses, Zacharias Janssen (YAHN·suhn), in 1590. In the 1670s, a Dutch drapery merchant and amateur scientist named Anton van Leeuwenhoek (LAY·vuhn·HUK) used a microscope to observe bacteria swimming in tooth scrapings. He also saw red blood cells for the first time. His examination of grubs, maggots, and other such organisms showed that they did not come to life spontaneously, as was previously thought. Rather, they were immature insects.

In 1643, one of Galileo's students, Evangelista Torricelli (TAWR·uh·CHEHL·ee), developed the first mercury barometer, a tool for measuring atmospheric pressure and predicting weather. In 1714, the Dutch physicist Gabriel Fahrenheit (FAR·uhn·HYT) made the first thermometer to use mercury in glass. Fahrenheit's thermometer showed water freezing at 32°. A Swedish astronomer, Anders Celsius (SEHL·see·uhs), created another scale for the mercury thermometer in 1742. Celsius's scale showed freezing at 0°.

Medicine and the Human Body During the Middle Ages, European doctors had accepted as fact the writings of an ancient Greek physician named Galen. However, Galen had never dissected the body of a human being. Instead, he had studied the anatomy of pigs and other animals. Galen assumed that human anatomy was much the same. Galen's assumptions were proved wrong by Andreas Vesalius, a Flemish physician. Vesalius dissected human corpses (despite disapproval of this practice) and published his observations. His book, *On the Fabric of the Human Body* (1543), was filled with detailed drawings of human organs, bones, and muscle.

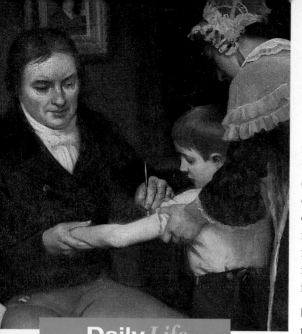

An English doctor named William Harvey continued Vesalius's work in anatomy. In 1628, he published *On the Motion of the Heart and Blood in Animals,* which showed that the heart acted as a pump to circulate blood throughout the body. He also described the function of blood vessels.

In the late 1700s, British physician Edward Jenner introduced a vaccine to prevent smallpox. Inoculation using live smallpox germs had been practiced in Asia for centuries. While beneficial, this technique was also dangerous. Jenner discovered that inoculation with germs from a cattle disease called cowpox gave permanent protection from smallpox for humans. Because cowpox was a much milder disease, the risks for this form of inoculation were much lower. Jenner used cowpox to produce the world's first vaccination.

Vocabulary
inoculation: injecting a germ into a person's body so as to create an immunity to the disease.

Discoveries in Chemistry Robert Boyle pioneered the use of the scientific method in chemistry. He is considered the founder of modern chemistry. In a book called *The Sceptical Chymist* (1661), Boyle challenged Aristotle's idea that the physical world consisted of four elements—earth, air, fire, and water. Instead, Boyle proposed that matter was made up of smaller primary particles that joined together in different ways. Boyle's most famous contribution to chemistry is Boyle's law. This law explains how the volume, temperature, and pressure of gas affect each other.

Another chemist, Joseph Priestley, separated one pure gas from air in 1774. He noticed how good he felt after breathing this special air and watched how alert two mice were while breathing it. Wrote Priestley, "Who can tell but that, in time, this pure air may become a fashionable article of luxury? Hitherto only two mice and I have had the privilege of breathing it." Meanwhile, in France, Antoine Lavoisier (lah·vwah·ZYAY) was performing similar experiments. In 1779, Lavoisier named the newly discovered gas oxygen.

Other scholars and philosophers applied a scientific approach to other areas of life. Believing themselves to be orderly, rational, and industrious, they thought of themselves as enlightened. They would become the leaders of a new intellectual and social movement called the Enlightenment.

Daily *Life*

Smallpox Inoculations

In the 1600s and 1700s, few words raised as much dread as *smallpox.* This contagious disease killed many infants and young children and left others horribly scarred.

In the early 1700s, an English writer named Lady Mary Wortley Montagu observed women in Turkey deliberately inoculating their young children against smallpox. They did this by breaking the skin and applying some liquid taken from the sore of a victim.

Children who were inoculated caught smallpox, but they had a good chance of getting only a mild case. This protected them from ever having the disease again.

Lady Montagu bravely had her son inoculated. She brought the procedure back to Britain, and from there it spread all over Europe.

Section ❶ Assessment

1. TERMS & NAMES

Identify
- Scientific Revolution
- Nicolaus Copernicus
- heliocentric theory
- Johannes Kepler
- Galileo Galilei
- scientific method
- Francis Bacon
- René Descartes
- Isaac Newton

2. TAKING NOTES

Use a web diagram such as the one below to show the events and circumstances that led to the Scientific Revolution.

Causes of the Scientific Revolution

3. DRAWING CONCLUSIONS

"If I have seen farther than others," said Newton, "it is because I have stood on the shoulders of giants." Who were the giants to whom Newton was referring? Could this be said of any scientific accomplishment? Explain.

4. THEME ACTIVITY

Science & Technology Working in groups of three or four, create a Scientific Revolution Discovery Board. Use these categories: Astronomy, Science, Medicine, Chemistry, Biology. Include important people, ideas, accomplishments.

The Enlightenment in Europe

TERMS & NAMES
- Enlightenment
- social contract
- John Locke
- natural rights
- philosophe
- Voltaire
- Montesquieu
- separation of powers
- Jean Jacques Rousseau
- Mary Wollstonecraft

MAIN IDEA

A revolution in intellectual activity changed Europeans' view of government and society.

WHY IT MATTERS NOW

Freedoms and some forms of government in many countries today are a result of Enlightenment thinking.

SETTING THE STAGE The influence of the Scientific Revolution soon spread beyond the world of science. Philosophers admired Newton because he had used reason to explain the laws governing nature. People began to look for laws governing human behavior as well. They hoped to apply reason and the scientific method to all aspects of society—government, religion, economics, and education. In this way, the ideas of the Scientific Revolution paved the way for a new movement called the **Enlightenment,** or the Age of Reason. This movement reached its height in the mid-1700s.

Two Views on Government

The Enlightenment started from some key ideas put forth by two English political thinkers of the 1600s, Thomas Hobbes and John Locke. Both men experienced the political turmoil of England early in that century. However, they came to very different conclusions about government and human nature.

Hobbes's Social Contract Thomas Hobbes expressed his views in a work called *Leviathan* (1651). The horrors of the English Civil War convinced him that all humans were naturally selfish and wicked. Without governments to keep order, Hobbes said, there would be "war of every man against every man." In this state of nature, as Hobbes called it, life would be "solitary, poor, nasty, brutish, and short."

Hobbes argued that to escape such a bleak life, people gave up their rights to a strong ruler. In exchange, they gained law and order. Hobbes called this agreement, by which people created government, the **social contract.** Because people acted in their own self-interest, Hobbes said, the ruler needed total power to keep citizens under control. The best government was one that had the awesome power of a leviathan (sea monster). In Hobbes's view, such a government was an absolute monarchy, which could impose order and demand obedience.

This engraving depicts the beheading of Charles I. Hobbes developed his political ideas out of the violent events in England in the early 1600s.

THINK THROUGH HISTORY
A. Clarifying
According to Hobbes, why would people want to live under the rule of an absolute monarch?

Locke's Natural Rights The philosopher **John Locke** held a different, more positive, view of human nature. He believed that people could learn from experience and improve themselves. As reasonable beings, they had the natural ability to govern their own affairs and to look after the welfare of society. Locke criticized absolute monarchy and favored the idea of self-government.

According to Locke, all people are born free and equal, with three **natural rights**—life, liberty, and property. The purpose of government, said Locke, is to protect these rights. If a government fails to do so, citizens have a right to overthrow it. Locke

THINK THROUGH HISTORY
B. Contrasting How does Locke's view of human nature differ from that of Hobbes?

Changing Idea: The Right to Govern

Old Idea		New Idea
A monarch's rule is justified by divine right.		A government's power comes from the consent of the governed.

published his ideas in 1690, two years after the Glorious Revolution. His book, *Two Treatises on Government,* served to justify the overthrow of James II.

Locke's theory had a deep influence on modern political thinking. His statement that a government's power comes from the consent of the people is the foundation of modern democracy. The ideas of government by popular consent and the right to rebel against unjust rulers helped inspire struggles for liberty in Europe and the Americas.

HISTORY MAKERS

Voltaire
1694–1778

Voltaire corresponded with several European monarchs and nobles. Among them was the Prussian king Frederick II. At the king's invitation, Voltaire spent three years at Frederick's palace. At first, the two men seemed like ideal companions. Both were witty. Both cared nothing for appearances and dressed in shabby, rumpled clothes. Each friend paid the other elegant compliments.

Before long, however, the king and the philosophe got on each other's nerves. Voltaire disliked editing Frederick's mediocre poetry. Frederick suspected Voltaire of some shady business dealings. Eventually, Voltaire tried to sneak away, but Prussian soldiers captured him and made him spend the night in jail.

After returning to France, Voltaire described the Prussian king as "a nasty monkey, perfidious friend, [and] wretched poet." Frederick returned the abuse, calling Voltaire a "miser, dirty rogue, [and] coward."

The Philosophes Advocate Reason

The Enlightenment reached its height in France in the mid-1700s. Paris became the meeting place for people who wanted to discuss politics and ideas. The social critics of this period in France were known as **philosophes** (FIHL·uh·SAHFS), the French word for philosophers. The philosophes believed that people could apply reason to all aspects of life—just as Isaac Newton had applied reason to science. Five important concepts formed the core of their philosophy:

1. **Reason** Enlightened thinkers believed truth could be discovered through reason or logical thinking. Reason, they said, was the absence of intolerance, bigotry, or prejudice in one's thinking.

2. **Nature** The philosophes referred to nature frequently. To them, what was natural was also good and reasonable. They believed that there were natural laws of economics and politics just as there were natural laws of motion.

3. **Happiness** A person who lived by nature's laws would find happiness, the philosophes said. They were impatient with the medieval notion that people should accept misery in this world to find joy in the hereafter. The philosophes wanted well-being on earth, and they believed it was possible.

4. **Progress** The philosophes were the first Europeans to believe in progress for society. Now that people used a scientific approach, they believed, society and humankind could be perfected.

5. **Liberty** The philosophes envied the liberties that the English people had won in their Glorious Revolution and Bill of Rights. In France, there were many restrictions on speech, religion, trade, and personal travel. Through reason, the philosophes believed, society could be set free.

Voltaire Combats Intolerance Probably the most brilliant and influential of the philosophes was François Marie Arouet. Using the pen name **Voltaire,** he published more than 70 books of political essays, philosophy, history, fiction, and drama.

Voltaire often used satire against his opponents. He made frequent targets of the clergy, the aristocracy, and the government. His sharp tongue made him enemies at the French court, and twice he was sent to prison. After his second jail term, Voltaire was exiled to England for two years. There, Voltaire came to admire the English government much more than his own. After he returned to Paris,

THINK THROUGH HISTORY
C. Comparing How were the philosophes' views similar to Locke's?

Vocabulary
satire: irony, sarcasm, or wit used to attack folly, vice, or stupidity.

much of his work mocked the laws and customs of France. He even dared to raise doubts about the Christian religion. The French king and France's Catholic bishops were outraged. In 1734, fearing another unpleasant jail term, Voltaire fled Paris.

Although he made powerful enemies, Voltaire never stopped fighting for tolerance, reason, freedom of religious belief, and freedom of speech. He used his quill pen as if it were a deadly weapon in a thinker's war against humanity's worst enemies—intolerance, prejudice, and superstition. Such attitudes were, he said, *l'infâme*—infamous or evil things. He often ended his letters with a fighting slogan, *"Écrasez l'infâme!"* (ay·crah·ZAY lahn·FAM). The phrase meant "Crush the evil thing!"

Montesquieu and the Separation of Powers Another influential French writer, the Baron de **Montesquieu** (MAHN·tuh·SKYOO), devoted himself to the study of political liberty. An aristocrat and lawyer, Montesquieu studied the history of ancient Rome. He concluded that Rome's collapse was directly related to its loss of political liberties.

Like Voltaire, Montesquieu believed that Britain was the best-governed country of his own day. Here was a government, he thought, in which power was balanced among three groups of officials. The British king and his ministers held executive power. They carried out the laws of the state. The members of Parliament held legislative, or lawmaking, power. The judges of the English courts held judicial power. They interpreted the laws to see how each applied to a specific case. Montesquieu called this division of power among different branches **separation of powers.**

THINK THROUGH HISTORY
D. Analyzing Issues
What advantages did Montesquieu see in the separation of powers?

Montesquieu oversimplified the British system (it did not actually separate powers this way). His idea, however, became a part of his most famous book, *On the Spirit of Laws* (1748). In his book, Montesquieu proposed that separation of powers would keep any individual or group from gaining total control of the government. "Power," he wrote, "should be a check to power." Each branch of government would serve as a check on the other two. This idea later would be called "checks and balances."

Montesquieu's book was admired by political leaders in the British colonies of North America. His ideas about separation of powers and checks and balances became the basis for the United States Constitution.

> **"Power should be a check to power."**
> Baron de Montesquieu

Changing Idea: Government Powers

Old Idea
Monarch rules with absolute authority.

New Idea
Separation of government powers among executive, legislative, and judicial branches.

Rousseau: Champion of Freedom A third great philosophe, **Jean Jacques Rousseau** (roo·SOH), was passionately committed to individual freedom. The son of a poor Swiss watchmaker, Rousseau worked as an engraver, music teacher, tutor, and secretary. Eventually, Rousseau made his way to Paris and won recognition as a writer of essays. There he met and befriended other philosophes, although he felt out of place in the circles of Paris high society in which they traveled.

A strange, brilliant, and controversial figure, Rousseau strongly disagreed with other Enlightenment thinkers on many matters. Most philosophes believed that reason, science, and art would improve life for all people. Rousseau, however, argued that civilization corrupted people's natural goodness. "Man is born free, and everywhere he is in chains," he wrote. In the earliest times, according to Rousseau, people had lived as free and equal individuals in a primitive "state of nature." As people became civilized, however, the strongest among them forced everyone else to obey unjust laws. Thus, freedom and equality were destroyed.

> **"Man is born free, and everywhere he is in chains."**
> Jean Jacques Rousseau

Enlightenment and Revolution **553**

Attitudes Toward Children

Before the mid-1700s, people commonly believed that children were naturally sinful. Parents raised their children with a harsh hand and treated them like miniature adults.

During the Enlightenment, such attitudes changed. People believed children should be better educated and could be allowed to mature into adulthood. Parents lessened the use of corporal punishment and increased play time.

By 1780, there was a new market for rocking horses, jigsaw puzzles, and baby clothes. In Britain, the first Mother Goose book of nursery rhymes appeared. Books like *The Newtonian System of the Universe Digested for Young Minds* by Tom Telescope appeared in print. Children even began to get discount tickets to museums and curiosity shows.

Belief in Progress The first effect was a belief in progress. Pioneers such as Galileo and Newton had discovered the key for unlocking the mysteries of nature in the 1500s and 1600s. With the door thus opened, the growth of scientific knowledge seemed to quicken in the 1700s. Scientists made key new discoveries in chemistry, physics, biology, and mechanics. The successes of the Scientific Revolution gave people the confidence that human reason could solve social problems. Philosophes and reformers urged an end to the practice of slavery. They also argued for more social equality and improvements in education. Through reason, a better society was possible.

A More Secular Outlook A second outcome was the rise of a more secular, or worldly, outlook. During the Enlightenment, people began to openly question their religious beliefs and the teachings of the church. Before the Scientific Revolution, people accepted the mysteries of the universe as the mysteries of God. One by one, scientists discovered that these mysteries could be explained mathematically. Newton himself was a deeply religious man, and he sought to reveal God's majesty through his work. However, his findings caused some people to change the way they thought about God.

Voltaire and other critics attacked some of the beliefs and practices of organized Christianity. They wanted to rid religious faith of superstition and fear and promote tolerance of all religions.

Importance of the Individual Faith in science and in progress produced a third outcome—the rise of individualism. As people began to turn away from the church and royalty for guidance, they looked to themselves instead.

The philosophes encouraged people to use their own ability to reason in order to judge what is right or wrong. They also emphasized the importance of the individual in society. Government, they argued, was formed by individuals to promote their welfare. The British thinker Adam Smith extended the emphasis on the individual to economic thinking. He believed that individuals acting in their own self-interest created economic progress. Smith's theory is discussed in detail in Chapter 25.

During the Enlightenment, reason took center stage. The greatest minds of Europe followed each other's work with interest and often met to discuss their ideas. Some of the kings and queens of Europe were also very interested. As you will learn in Section 3, they sought to apply some of the philosophes' ideas to create progress in their countries.

Section **2** Assessment

1. TERMS & NAMES

Identify
- Enlightenment
- social contract
- John Locke
- natural rights
- philosophe
- Voltaire
- Montesquieu
- separation of powers
- Jean Jacques Rousseau
- Mary Wollstonecraft

2. TAKING NOTES

In a chart like the one below, list the important ideas of Hobbes, Locke, Voltaire, Montesquieu, Rousseau, Beccaria, and Wollstonecraft.

Thinker	Key Idea

Choose one of these thinkers and write a paragraph on how his or her ideas are influential today.

3. SYNTHESIZING

For each of the statements below, identify who said it and explain what it means. Then say how each viewpoint reflects Enlightenment ideas.

- "Power should be a check to power."
- "Man is born free, and everywhere he is in chains."
- "Let women share the rights and she will emulate the virtues of men."

4. ANALYZING THEMES

Power and Authority

Compare the views of Hobbes, Locke, and Rousseau on government. How do their differing ideas reflect their understanding of human behavior?

THINK ABOUT
- how each philosopher viewed the "state of nature"
- what each considered the source of a government's authority

European Values

Writers and artists of the Enlightenment often used satire to comment on European values. Using wit and humor, they ridiculed ideas and customs for the purpose of improving society. Satire allowed artists to explore human faults and failings in a way that is powerful but not preachy. In the two literary excerpts and the drawing below, notice how the writer or artist makes his point.

LITERATURE
Voltaire

Voltaire wrote *Candide* (1759) to attack a philosophy called Optimism, which held that all is right with the world. The hero of the story, a young man named Candide, encounters the most awful disasters and human evils as he travels far and wide. In this passage, Candide has met a slave in Surinam, a Dutch colony in South America. The slave explains why he is missing a leg and a hand.

"When we're working at the sugar mill and catch our finger in the grinding-wheel, they cut off our hand. When we try to run away, they cut off a leg. I have been in both of these situations. This is the price you pay for the sugar you eat in Europe. . . .

"The Dutch fetishes [i.e., missionaries] who converted me [to Christianity] tell me every Sunday that we are all the sons of Adam, Whites and Blacks alike. I'm no genealogist, but if these preachers are right, we are all cousins born of first cousins. Well, you will grant me that you can't treat a relative much worse than this."

LITERATURE
Jonathan Swift

The narrator of *Gulliver's Travels* (1726), an English doctor named Lemuel Gulliver, takes four disastrous voyages that leave him stranded in strange lands. In the following passage, Gulliver tries to win points with the king of Brobdingnag—a land of giants—by offering to show him how to make guns and cannons. The reaction of the king, who is above such things, shows how Swift felt about the inhuman side of the human race.

[I told the king that] a proper quantity of this powder [gunpowder] rammed into a hollow tube of brass or iron . . . would drive a ball of iron or lead with such violence and speed, as nothing was able to sustain its force. That, the largest balls thus discharged, would not only destroy whole ranks of an army at once; but batter the strongest walls to the ground; sink down ships with a thousand men in each, to the bottom of the sea; and when linked together by a chain, would cut through masts and rigging; divide hundreds of bodies in the middle, and lay all waste before them. . . .

The king was struck with horror at the description I had given of those terrible engines. . . . He was amazed how so impotent and grovelling an insect as I (these were his expressions) could entertain such inhuman ideas, and in so familiar a manner as to appear wholly unmoved at all the scenes of blood and desolation, which I had painted as the common effects of those destructive machines; whereof, he said, some evil genius, enemy to mankind, must have been the first contriver [inventor].

ENGRAVING
Francisco Goya

The Spanish artist Francisco Goya issued a series of 80 engravings called *Los Caprichos* (*Caprices*) in 1797. In them, he criticized a range of "human errors and evils" and also satirized Spanish politics and society. In the image shown here, titled "Out Hunting for Teeth," Goya attacks superstition. He wrote this caption for the image:

The teeth of a man who has been hung are indispensable for casting a spell. Without this ingredient, nothing succeeds. A pity that people believe such nonsense.

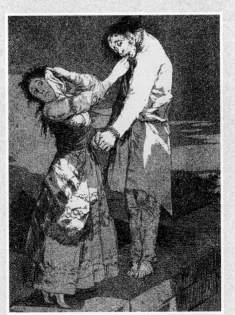

Connect *to* History

Clarifying Write a statement that summarizes the main point each writer and artist is making. What techniques do they use to reinforce their messages?

SEE SKILLBUILDER HANDBOOK, PAGE 992

Connect *to* Today

Writing Both Voltaire and Swift used a fictional travel narrative as a type of satire. Imagine you are an alien visitor to your school or community. Write a letter or a narrative that describes how the people you see think and behave.

 For another perspective on the Enlightenment, see World History: Electronic Library of Primary Sources.

The Spread of Enlightenment Ideas

TERMS & NAMES
- salon
- baroque
- neoclassical
- enlightened despot
- Catherine the Great

MAIN IDEA

Enlightenment ideas spread through the Western world and profoundly influenced the arts and government.

WHY IT MATTERS NOW

An "enlightened" problem-solving approach to government and society prevails in modern civilization today.

SETTING THE STAGE The philosophes' views often got them in trouble. In France it was illegal to criticize either the Catholic Church or the government. Many philosophes landed in jail or were exiled. Voltaire, for example, experienced both punishments. Nevertheless, Enlightenment ideas spread throughout Europe.

A World of Ideas

In the 1700s, Paris was the cultural and intellectual capital of Europe. Young people from around Europe—and also from the Americas—came to study, philosophize, and enjoy fine culture. The brightest minds of the age gathered there. From their circles radiated the ideas of the Enlightenment.

The Paris Salons The buzz of Enlightenment ideas was most intense in the mansions of several wealthy women of Paris. There, in their large drawing rooms, these hostesses held regular social gatherings called **salons.** At these events, philosophers, writers, artists, scientists, and other great intellects met to discuss ideas and enjoy artistic performances.

The most influential of the salon hostesses in Voltaire's time was Marie-Thérèse Geoffrin (zhuh·frehn). Self-educated and from the well-to-do middle class, Madame Geoffrin was friends with both philosophes and heads of state. She corresponded with the king of Sweden and Catherine the Great of Russia.

This painting by Anicet Charles Lemonnier shows a salon in the home of Madame Geoffrin (inset, and seated third from right). The guests are listening to an actor reading aloud from a new play.

Diderot's *Encyclopedia* Madame Geoffrin also helped finance the project of a leading philosophe named Denis Diderot (DEE·duh·ROH). Diderot imagined a large set of books to which all the leading scholars of Europe would contribute articles and essays. This *Encyclopedia*, as he called it, would bring together all the most current and enlightened thinking about science, technology, art, government, and more. Diderot began publishing the first volumes in 1751.

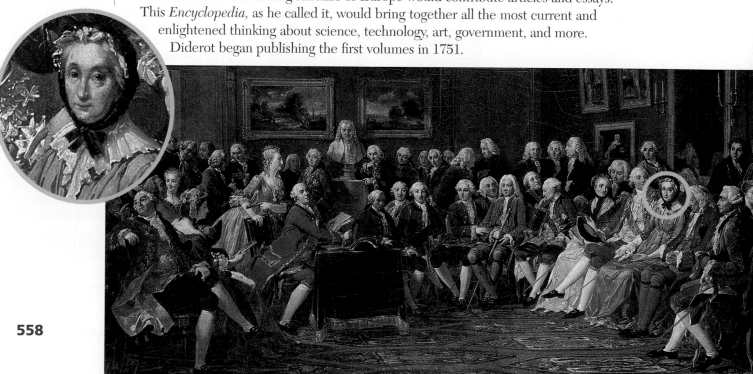

THINK THROUGH HISTORY
A. Making Inferences In what ways did the *Encyclopedia* project reflect the Age of Enlightenment?

The Enlightenment views expressed in the articles soon angered both the French government and the Catholic Church. Their censors banned the work. They said it undermined royal authority, encouraged a spirit of revolt, and fostered "moral corruption, irreligion, and unbelief." Fearing arrest, some leading philosophes withdrew from the project and urged Diderot to quit. Diderot pressed on, however, and finally won permission to continue publishing the *Encyclopedia.* New volumes came out regularly under his editorship until 1772.

New Ideas Circulate The salons and the *Encyclopedia* helped spread Enlightenment ideas to educated people all over Europe. The enlightened thinkers of Europe considered themselves part of an intellectual community. They shared their ideas through books, personal letters, visits back and forth, and magazine articles. As one writer of the day described the flurry of communication, "Never have new ideas had such rapid circulation at such long distance."

Enlightenment ideas also eventually reached middle-class people through newspapers, pamphlets, and even political songs. Enlightenment ideas about government and equality attracted the attention of a growing literate middle class. This group had money but limited status and political power. With their money, middle-class people could afford to buy many books and support the work of artists. Through its purchasing power, this group had growing influence over European culture in the 1700s.

This detail of *Seated Woman with Book,* by French artist Jean-Baptiste Chardin, shows a middle-class woman whose interests include reading. In the 1700s, the middle class had more leisure time for such pursuits.

Art and Literature in the Age of Reason

The Enlightenment ideals of order and reason were reflected in the arts—music, literature, painting, and architecture. European art of the 1600s and early 1700s had been dominated by the style called **baroque**—a grand, ornate style. Monarchs had built elaborate palaces such as Versailles (see page 521). Musicians like the German composer Johann Sebastian Bach and the English composer George Frederick Handel had written dramatic organ and choral music. Artists had created paintings rich in color, detail, and ornate imagery.

THINK THROUGH HISTORY
B. Contrasting How does the art of the baroque and classical periods differ in style?

Under the influence of the Enlightenment, styles began to change. The arts began to reflect the new emphasis on order and balance. Artists and architects worked in a simple and elegant style that borrowed ideas and themes from classical Greece and Rome. The style of the late 1700s is therefore called **neoclassical** ("new classical"). In music, the style of this period is called classical.

Classical Music Three composers in Vienna, Austria, rank among the greatest figures of the classical period in music. They were Franz Joseph Haydn, Wolfgang Amadeus Mozart, and Ludwig van Beethoven.

Haydn was particularly important in developing new musical forms, such as the sonata and symphony. Mozart was a gifted child who began composing music at the age of five and gave concerts throughout Europe as a youth. At 12, he wrote his first opera. Mozart's great operas—*The Marriage of Figaro, Don Giovanni,* and *The Magic Flute*—set a new standard for elegance and originality. Although he lived only to age 35, he wrote more than 600 musical works.

Beethoven showed enormous range in his work. He wrote beautiful piano music, string quartets, and stirring symphonies. Beethoven's earlier works were in the same classical style as Mozart's. However, his later compositions began new trends, which carried music into the Age of Romanticism.

Popularity of the Novel Writers in the 18th century also developed new styles and forms of literature. A number of European authors began writing novels—lengthy works of prose fiction. These books were popular with a wide middle-class audience,

Art in the Age of Enlightenment

The Enlightenment influenced many European painters of the middle and late 1700s. Increasingly, artists looked for inspiration in the material world—in nature and human nature. Some artists showed an Enlightenment interest in science and social issues in their work. Others emphasized a new sensitivity toward individuals.

The Individual

The French painter Elisabeth-Louise Vigée-Le Brun was one of the most celebrated portrait artists of the late 1700s. She was the favorite painter of Queen Marie Antoinette of France. Her portraits bring out the personalities of her subjects. Her own energy, success, and independence also reflected the Enlightenment spirit. These qualities shine through this detail of a self-portrait with her daughter.

The Promise of Science

The English artist Joseph Wright of Derby was fascinated by science and its impact on people's lives. The painting below, *Philosopher Giving a Lecture on the Orrery*, shows children and adults gazing into a miniature planetarium. The way Wright uses light in this picture makes a point about how science can educate and enlighten people.

Politics and Society

The English artist William Hogarth often used satire in his paintings. In the painting above, *Canvassing for Votes—The Election*, he comments on political corruption. While the candidate flirts with the ladies on the balcony, his supporters offer a man money for his vote. Hogarth's detailed, realistic style and moralistic topics were meant—like the popular novels of his day—to appeal to a wide middle-class audience.

Connect *to* History

Analyzing Issues Imagine you are a philosophe who moonlights as an art critic. For each of these paintings, write a brief statement about how it reflects Enlightenment ideas.

SEE SKILLBUILDER HANDBOOK, PAGE 1001

Connect *to* Today

Updating a Picture Choose one of the paintings on this page and think about how you might change it to depict politics, science, or people today. You might describe the modern version in words or using a sketch or other kind of artwork.

who liked the entertaining stories written in everyday language. Writers—including many women—turned out a flood of popular novels in the 1700s.

English novelists such as Samuel Richardson and Henry Fielding developed many of the features of the modern novel. Their works had carefully crafted plots, used suspense and climax, and explored their characters' thoughts and feelings. Richardson's *Pamela* is often considered the first true English novel. It told the story of a young servant girl who refused the advances of her master. In Fielding's comic masterpiece *Tom Jones*, the hero of the book is an orphan who has been kicked out of his adopted home. He travels all over England and overcomes numerous obstacles to win the hand of his lady.

A third popular English novelist was Daniel Defoe, author of the adventure *Robinson Crusoe*. Crusoe is a sailor stranded on a tropical island. Through his wits and the help of a native he calls Friday, Crusoe learns how to survive on the island and is eventually rescued.

Enlightenment and Monarchy

From the salons, artists' studios, and concert halls of Europe, the Enlightenment spirit also swept through Europe's royal courts. Many philosophes, including Voltaire, believed that the best form of government was a monarchy in which the ruler respected the people's rights. The philosophes tried to convince monarchs to rule justly. Some monarchs embraced the new ideas and made reforms that reflected the Enlightenment spirit. They became known as **enlightened despots.** *Despot* means absolute ruler.

THINK THROUGH HISTORY
C. Analyzing Motives Why did the enlightened despots undertake reforms?

The enlightened despots supported the philosophes' ideas. But they also had no intention of giving up any power. The changes they made were motivated by two desires: they wanted to make their countries stronger and their own rule more effective. The foremost of Europe's enlightened despots were Frederick II of Prussia, Holy Roman Emperor Joseph II of Austria, and Catherine the Great of Russia.

Frederick the Great Frederick II, the king of Prussia from 1740 to 1786, once wrote to Voltaire: "I must enlighten my people, cultivate their manners and morals, and make them as happy as human beings can be, or as happy as the means at my disposal permit." Frederick indeed committed himself to reforming Prussia. He granted many religious freedoms, reduced censorship, and improved education. He also reformed the justice system and abolished the use of torture. However, Frederick's changes only went so far. For example, he believed that serfdom was wrong, but he did nothing to end it. This was because he needed the support of wealthy landowners. As a result, he never challenged the power of the Junkers or tried to change the existing social order.

Perhaps Frederick's most important contribution was his attitude toward being king. He called himself "the first servant of the state." From the beginning of his reign, he made it clear that his goal was to serve and strengthen his country. This attitude was clearly one that appealed to the philosophes.

Changing Idea: Relationship Between Ruler and State

Old Idea
The state and its citizens exist to serve the monarch—as Louis XIV reportedly said, "I am the state."

New Idea
The monarch exists to serve the state and support citizens' welfare—as Frederick the Great said, a ruler is only "the first servant of the state."

Joseph II The most radical royal reformer was Joseph II of Austria. The son and successor of Maria Theresa, Joseph II ruled Austria from 1780 to 1790. He introduced legal reforms and freedom of the press. He also supported freedom of worship—even for Protestants, Orthodox Christians, and Jews. In his most radical reform, Joseph abolished serfdom and ordered that peasants be paid for their labor with cash. Not

Catherine the Great
1729–1796

Catherine was the daughter of a minor German prince. At age 15, she was summoned to the distant Russian court at St. Petersburg. She was to marry the Grand Duke Peter, heir to the Russian throne.

The marriage between Catherine and Peter was a disaster. Peter was mentally unstable. His chief pleasure was playing with toy soldiers. More than once he tormented his own dogs.

Catherine soon saw that Peter's weakness gave her a chance to seize power. She made important friends among Russia's army officers, and she became known as the most intelligent and best-informed person at court. In 1762, only months after her husband became czar as Peter III, Catherine had him arrested and confined. Soon afterward, Peter conveniently died, probably by murder.

surprisingly, the nobles firmly resisted this change. Like many of Joseph's reforms, it was undone after his death.

Catherine the Great The ruler most admired by the philosophes was Catherine II, known as **Catherine the Great.** She ruled Russia from 1762 to 1796. The well-educated empress read the works of philosophes, and she exchanged many letters with Voltaire. She ruled with absolute authority, but she also took steps to modernize and reform Russia.

In 1767, Catherine formed a commission to review Russia's laws. She presented it with a brilliant proposal for reforms based on the ideas of Montesquieu and Beccaria. Among other changes, she recommended allowing religious toleration and abolishing torture and capital punishment. Her commission, however, accomplished none of these lofty goals.

Catherine eventually put in place limited reforms, but she did little to improve the life of the Russian peasants. Her thinking about enlightened ideas changed after a massive uprising of serfs in 1773. With great brutality, Catherine's army crushed the rebellion. Catherine had previously favored an end to serfdom. However, the revolt convinced her that she needed the nobles' support to keep her throne. Therefore, she gave the nobles absolute power over the serfs. As a result, Russian serfs lost their last traces of freedom.

Catherine Expands Russia Peter the Great had fought for years to win a port on the Baltic Sea. Likewise, Catherine sought access to the Black Sea. In two wars with the Ottoman Turks, her armies finally won control of the northern shore of the Black Sea. Russia also gained the right to send ships through Ottoman-controlled straits leading from the Black Sea to the Mediterranean Sea.

Catherine also expanded her empire westward into Poland. In Poland, the king was relatively weak, and independent nobles held the most power. The three neighboring powers—Russia, Prussia, and Austria—each tried to assert their influence over the country. In 1772, these land-hungry neighbors each took a piece of Poland in what is called the First Partition of Poland. In further partitions in 1793 and 1795, they grabbed up the rest of Poland's territory. With these partitions, Poland disappeared from the map of Europe. It did not reappear as an independent country until after World War I.

By the end of her remarkable reign, Catherine had vastly enlarged the Russian empire. Meanwhile, as Russia was becoming an international power, another great power, Britain, faced a challenge in its 13 American colonies. Inspired by Enlightenment ideas, colonial leaders decided to cast off British rule and found an independent republic.

THINK THROUGH HISTORY
D. Synthesizing
How accurately does the term *enlightened despot* describe Catherine the Great? Explain.

Section 3 Assessment

1. TERMS & NAMES

Identify
• salon
• baroque
• neoclassical
• enlightened despot
• Catherine the Great

2. TAKING NOTES

Copy the concept web shown below and add to it examples that illustrate the concepts.

Write two generalizations about the spread of Enlightenment ideas.

3. DRAWING CONCLUSIONS

What advantages do you think salons had over earlier forms of communication in spreading new ideas? Justify your response with specific references to the text.

THINK ABOUT
• who hosted the salons and where they were held
• who was invited to the salons
• church and state influence on publishing and education

4. THEME ACTIVITY

Power and Authority
Imagine you are a public relations consultant for Frederick the Great, Joseph II, or Catherine the Great. The monarch you represent wants to be named "Most Enlightened Despot of the 1700s." Write a press release or design a poster or flyer that presents reasons why your client should be given this honor.

TERMS & NAMES
- Declaration of Independence
- Thomas Jefferson
- checks and balances
- federal system
- Bill of Rights

4 American Revolution: The Birth of a Republic

MAIN IDEA	WHY IT MATTERS NOW
Enlightenment ideas helped spur the American colonies to create a new nation.	The revolution created a republic, the United States of America, that became a model for many nations of the world.

SETTING THE STAGE Philosophes such as Voltaire considered England's government the most progressive in Europe. England's ruler was no despot, not even an enlightened one. His power had been limited by law. The Glorious Revolution of 1688 had given England a constitutional monarchy. However, while the English monarch's power was being limited at home, the power of the English nation was spreading overseas.

Britain and Its American Colonies

When George III became king of Great Britain in 1760, his Atlantic coastal colonies were growing by leaps and bounds. Their combined population went from about 250,000 in 1700 to 2,150,000 in 1770, an eightfold increase. Economically, the colonies thrived on trade with the nations of Europe.

Along with increasing population and prosperity, a new sense of identity was growing in the colonists' minds. By the mid-1700s, colonists had been living in America for nearly 150 years. Each of the 13 colonies had its own government, and people were used to a great degree of independence. Colonists saw themselves less as British and more as Virginians or Pennsylvanians. However, they were still British subjects and were expected to obey British law.

In the 1660s, Parliament had passed trade laws called the Navigation Acts. These laws prevented colonists from selling their most valuable products to any country except Britain. In addition, colonists had to pay high taxes on imported French and Dutch goods. However, colonists found ways to get around these laws. Some merchants smuggled in goods to avoid paying British taxes. Smugglers could sneak in and out of the many small harbors all along the lengthy Atlantic coastline. British customs agents found it difficult to enforce the Navigation Acts.

For many years, Britain felt no need to tighten its hold on the colonies. Despite the smuggling, Britain's mercantilist policies had made colonial trade very profitable. Britain bought American raw materials for low prices and sold manufactured goods to the colonists. And despite British trade restrictions, colonial merchants also thrived. However, after the French and Indian War ended in 1763, Britain toughened its trade laws. These changes sparked growing anger in the colonies.

Americans Win Independence

In 1760, when George III took the throne, most Americans had no thoughts of either revolution or independence. They still thought of themselves as loyal subjects of the British king. Yet by 1776, many Americans were willing to risk their lives to break free of Britain.

During the French and Indian War, Great Britain had run up a huge debt in the war against France. Because American colonists benefited from Britain's victory, Britain expected the colonists to help pay the costs of the war. In 1765, Parliament passed the Stamp Act. According

THINK THROUGH HISTORY
A. Recognizing Effects How did some colonists respond to the Navigation Acts?

Background
The French and Indian War was the part of the Seven Years' War fought in North America.

Many educated colonists were influenced by Enlightenment thought. This French snuff box pictures (left to right) Voltaire, Rousseau, and colonial statesman Benjamin Franklin.

to this law, colonists had to pay a tax to have an official stamp put on wills, deeds, newspapers, and other printed material.

American colonists were outraged. They had never paid taxes directly to the British government before. Colonial lawyers argued that the stamp tax violated colonists' natural rights. In Britain, citizens consented to taxes through their representatives in Parliament. Because the colonists had no such representatives, Parliament could not tax them. The colonists demonstrated their defiance of this tax with angry protests and a boycott of British manufactured goods. The boycott proved so effective that Parliament gave up and repealed the Stamp Act in 1766.

Growing Hostility Leads to War Over the next decade, further events steadily led to war. Some colonial leaders, such as Boston's Samuel Adams, favored independence from Britain. They encouraged conflict with British authorities. At the same time, George III and his ministers made enemies of many moderate colonists by their harsh stands. In 1773, to protest an import tax on tea, Adams organized a raid against three British ships in Boston Harbor. The raiders dumped 342 chests of tea into the water. George III, infuriated by the "Boston Tea Party," as it was called, ordered the British navy to close the port of Boston. British troops occupied the city.

In September 1774, representatives from every colony except Georgia gathered in Philadelphia to form the First Continental Congress. This group protested the treatment of Boston. When the king paid little attention to their complaints, all 13 colonies decided to form the Second Continental Congress to debate their next move.

On April 19, 1775, British soldiers and American militiamen exchanged gunfire on the village green in Lexington, Massachusetts. The fighting spread to nearby Concord. When news of the fighting reached the Second Continental Congress, its members voted to raise an army under the command of a Virginian named George Washington. The American Revolution had begun.

Enlightenment Ideas Influence American Colonists Although a war had begun, the American colonists still debated their attachment to Great Britain. Many colonists wanted to remain part of Britain. A growing number, however, favored independence. They heard the persuasive arguments of colonial leaders such as Patrick Henry, John Adams, and Benjamin Franklin. These leaders used Enlightenment ideas to justify independence. The colonists had asked for the same political rights as people in Britain, they said, but the king had stubbornly refused. Therefore, the colonists were justified in rebelling against a tyrant who had broken the social contract.

In July 1776, the Second Continental Congress issued the **Declaration of Independence.** This document, written by **Thomas Jefferson,** was firmly based on the ideas of John Locke and the Enlightenment. The Declaration reflected these ideas in its eloquent argument for natural rights.

> **A VOICE FROM THE PAST**
> We hold these Truths to be self-evident, that all Men are created equal, that they are endowed by their Creator with certain unalienable Rights, that among these are Life, Liberty, and the Pursuit of Happiness; that to secure these Rights, Governments are instituted among Men, deriving their just Powers from the Consent of the Governed.
>
> Declaration of Independence

Since Locke had asserted that people had the right to rebel against an unjust ruler, the Declaration of Independence included a long list

Vocabulary
boycott: refusal to buy goods produced in a certain place or by a certain group.

HISTORY MAKERS

**Thomas Jefferson
1743–1826**

The author of the Declaration of Independence, Thomas Jefferson of Virginia was a true figure of the Enlightenment. As a writer and statesman, he supported free speech, religious freedom, and other civil liberties. At the same time, he was also a slave owner.

Outside of politics, Jefferson was accomplished in many fields, including law, science, agriculture, and languages. He invented many practical devices, including an improved type of plow. One of the great architects of early America, he designed his magnificent home, Monticello. He also designed the Virginia state capitol building in Richmond and many buildings for the University of Virginia.

Of all his many achievements, Jefferson wanted to be most remembered for three: author of the Declaration of Independence, author of the Statute of Virginia for Religious Freedom, and founder of the University of Virginia.

THINK THROUGH HISTORY
C. Comparing How do Jefferson's "unalienable rights" compare with the natural rights expressed by Locke?

of George III's abuses. The document ended by breaking the ties between the colonies and Britain. The colonies, the Declaration said, "are absolved from all allegiance to the British crown."

Success for the Colonists When war was first declared, the odds seemed heavily weighted against the Americans. Washington's ragtag, poorly trained army faced the well-trained forces of the most powerful country in the world. In the end, however, the Americans won their war for independence.

Several reasons explain their success. First, the Americans' motivation for fighting was much stronger than that of the British, since their army was defending their homeland. Second, the overconfident British generals made several mistakes. Third, time itself was on the side of the Americans. The British could win battle after battle, as they did, and still lose the war. Fighting an overseas war, 3,000 miles from London, was terribly expensive. After a few years, tax-weary British citizens clamored for peace.

Finally, the Americans did not fight alone. Louis XVI of France had little sympathy for the ideals of the American Revolution, but he was eager to weaken France's rival, Britain. French entry into the war in 1778 was decisive. In 1781, combined forces of about 9,500 Americans and 7,800 French trapped a British army commanded by Lord Cornwallis near Yorktown, Virginia. Unable to escape, Cornwallis surrendered. The Americans were victorious.

North America, 1783

Legend:
- ■ British territory
- ■ French territory
- ■ Russian territory
- ■ Spanish territory
- ■ Claimed by U.S. and Great Britain
- ■ Claimed by U.S. and Spain

Map labels: 160°E, 160°W, 80°N, 40°W, 120°W, 90°W, 40°N, Arctic Circle, ALASKA, UNCLAIMED, Hudson Bay, PACIFIC OCEAN, CANADA, Quebec, Boston, New York, UNITED STATES, Missouri R., Ohio R., ATLANTIC OCEAN, LOUISIANA TERRITORY, Colorado R., Mississippi R., Charleston, FLORIDA, New Orleans, BAHAMAS, PUERTO RICO, Rio Grande, Gulf of Mexico, NEW SPAIN, Tropic of Cancer, CUBA, JAMAICA, Mexico City, HONDURAS, HISPANIOLA, Caribbean Sea, SOUTH AMERICA

0 500 Miles
0 1,000 Kilometers

GEOGRAPHY SKILLBUILDER: Interpreting Maps
1. **Region** What feature formed the western border of the United States?
2. **Human-Environment Interaction** What European countries had claims on the North American continent in 1783?

Changing Idea: Colonial Attachment to Britain

Old Idea
American colonists considered themselves as subjects of the British king.

New Idea
After a long train of perceived abuses by the king, the colonists asserted their right to declare independence.

Americans Create a Republic

Shortly after declaring their independence, the 13 individual states recognized the need for a national government. As victory became certain, in 1781 all 13 states ratified a constitution. This plan of government was known as the Articles of Confederation. The Articles established the United States as a republic—a government in which citizens rule through elected representatives.

The Articles Create a Weak National Government To protect their authority, the 13 states created a loose confederation in which they held most of the power. Thus, the Articles of Confederation deliberately created a weak national government.

There were no executive or judicial branches. Instead, the Articles established only one body of government, the Congress. Each state, regardless of size, had one vote in Congress. Congress could declare war, enter into treaties, and coin money. It had no power, however, to collect taxes or regulate trade. Passing new laws was difficult because laws needed the approval of 9 of the 13 states.

These limits on the national government soon produced many problems. Although the new national government needed money in order to operate, it could only request contributions from the states. Angry Revolutionary War veterans bitterly complained that Congress still owed them back pay. Meanwhile, several states issued their own money. Some states even put tariffs on goods from neighboring states.

The nation's growing financial problems sparked a violent protest in Massachusetts. Debt-ridden farmers, led by a war veteran named Daniel Shays, demanded that the state lower taxes and issue paper money so that they could repay their debts. When the state refused, the rebels attacked several courthouses. Massachusetts authorities quickly crushed Shays's Rebellion.

THINK THROUGH HISTORY
D. Making Inferences What was the fundamental cause of the nation's problems under the Articles of Confederation?

A New Constitution Concerned leaders such as George Washington and James Madison believed that Shays's Rebellion underscored the need for a strong national government. In February 1787, Congress approved a Constitutional Convention to revise the Articles of Confederation. The Constitutional Convention held its first session on May 25, 1787. The 55 delegates were experienced statesmen who were familiar with the political theories of Locke, Montesquieu, and Rousseau.

Although the delegates shared basic ideas on government, they sometimes disagreed on how to put them into practice. For almost four months the delegates argued over important questions. Who should be represented in Congress? How many votes should each state have? The delegates' deliberations produced not only compromises but also new approaches to governing. Using the political ideas of the Enlightenment, the delegates created a new system of government.

The Federal System Like Montesquieu, the delegates distrusted a powerful central government controlled by one person or group. They therefore established three separate branches—legislative, executive, and judicial. This provided a built-in system of **checks**

U.S. Constitution: An Enlightenment Document

Enlightenment Idea	U.S. Constitution
Locke A government's power comes from the consent of the people	• Preamble begins "We the people of the United States" to establish legitimacy. • Creates representative government • Limits government powers
Montesquieu Separation of powers	• Federal system of government • Powers divided among three branches • System of checks and balances
Rousseau Direct democracy	• Public election of president and Congress
Voltaire Free speech, religious toleration	• Bill of Rights provides for freedom of speech and religion.
Beccaria Accused have rights, no torture	• Bill of Rights protects rights of accused and prohibits cruel and unusual punishment.

SKILLBUILDER: Interpreting Charts
1. *From whose idea stems the system of checks and balances?*
2. *Which of the Enlightenment ideas are reflected in the Bill of Rights?*

and **balances,** with each branch checking the actions of the other two. For example, the president received the power to veto legislation passed by Congress. However, the Congress could override a presidential veto with the approval of two-thirds of its members.

Although the Constitution created a strong central government, it did not eliminate local governments. Instead, the Constitution set up a **federal system** in which power was divided between national and state governments.

The delegates agreed with Locke and Rousseau that governments draw their authority from the consent of the governed. The Constitution's preamble sums up this principle:

A VOICE FROM THE PAST
We the People of the United States, in order to form a more perfect Union, establish Justice, insure domestic Tranquillity, provide for the common defense, promote the general Welfare, and secure the Blessings of Liberty to ourselves and our Posterity, do ordain and establish this Constitution for the United States of America.
CONSTITUTION OF THE UNITED STATES OF AMERICA

The Bill of Rights The delegates signed the new Constitution on September 17, 1787. In order to become law, however, the Constitution required approval by conventions in at least 9 of the 13 states. These conventions were marked by sharp debate. Supporters of the Constitution, called the Federalists, argued that the new government would provide a better balance between national and state powers. Their opponents, the Antifederalists, feared that the Constitution gave the central government too much power. They also wanted a bill of rights to protect the rights of individual citizens.

THINK THROUGH HISTORY
E. Analyzing Issues
Explain the controversy over ratifying the Constitution. What did each side believe?

In order to gain support, the Federalists promised to add a bill of rights to the Constitution. This promise cleared the way for approval. Congress formally added to the Constitution the ten amendments known as the **Bill of Rights.** These amendments protected such basic rights as freedom of speech, press, assembly, and religion. Many of these rights had been advocated by Voltaire, Rousseau, and Locke.

The Constitution and Bill of Rights marked a turning point in people's ideas about government. Both documents put Enlightenment ideas into practice. They expressed an optimistic view that reason and reform could prevail and that progress was inevitable. Such optimism swept across the Atlantic. However, the monarchies and the privileged classes didn't give up power and position easily. As Chapter 23 explains, the struggle to attain the principles of the Enlightenment continued in France.

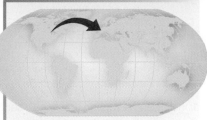

Global Impact

The French Revolution
The American Revolution inspired the growing number of French people who were seeking reform in their own country. They saw the new government of the United States as a step toward realizing the ideals of the Enlightenment. They hoped the next step would be reform in France.

The Declaration of Independence was widely circulated and admired in France. French officers like the Marquis de Lafayette, who fought for American independence, returned to France with stories of the war. Such personal accounts intrigued many a reader.

When the French bishop Charles-Maurice de Talleyrand wrote about this time period years later, he would say, "We talked of nothing but America."

Section 4 Assessment

1. TERMS & NAMES

Identify
• Declaration of Independence
• Thomas Jefferson
• checks and balances
• federal system
• Bill of Rights

2. TAKING NOTES

Create a chart like the one below. On the left, list problems faced by the Americans as colonists and in shaping their republic. On the right, record their actions and decisions to solve those problems.

Problem	Solution
	·

Which of the solutions that you recorded represented a compromise?

3. ANALYZING ISSUES

How does the opening statement from the Declaration of Independence (page 564) reflect enlightened thinking?

4. ANALYZING THEMES

Revolution Do you think the American Revolution would have happened if there had not been an Age of Enlightenment? Explain.

THINK ABOUT
• John Locke's impact on government
• other British colonies
• Enlightenment ideas

TERMS & NAMES

Briefly explain the importance of each of the following to the Scientific Revolution, the Enlightenment, or the American Revolution (1550–1789).

1. heliocentric theory
2. Galileo Galilei
3. Isaac Newton
4. social contract
5. natural rights
6. separation of powers
7. salon
8. enlightened despot
9. Declaration of Independence
10. federal system

Interact *with* History

On page 544, you put yourself in the dilemma of Galileo. As you have read, Galileo did recant, but the idea he supported eventually became widely accepted. Think about the decisions of both Galileo and the church. Did the choices they made advance their goals? Discuss your opinions with a small group.

REVIEW QUESTIONS

SECTION 1 *(pages 545–550)*
The Scientific Revolution

11. According to Ptolemy, what was earth's position in the universe? How did Copernicus's view differ? Which did Kepler's observations support?

12. What are four steps in the scientific method?

13. List four new instruments that came into use during the Scientific Revolution. Identify the purpose of each one.

SECTION 2 *(pages 551–556)*
The Enlightenment in Europe

14. How did the ideas of Hobbes and Locke differ?

15. What did Montesquieu believe led to the fall of Rome? What did he admire about the government of Britain?

16. How did the Enlightenment lead to a more secular outlook?

SECTION 3 *(pages 558–562)*
The Spread of Enlightenment Ideas

17. Name three developments in the arts during the Enlightenment.

18. What sorts of reforms did the enlightened despots make? In what respects did their reforms fail?

SECTION 4 *(pages 563–567)*
American Revolution: The Birth of a Republic

19. Why did the Articles of Confederation result in a weak national government?

20. How did the writers of the U.S. Constitution put into practice the idea of separation of powers? A system of checks and balances?

Visual Summary

Enlightenment and Revolution, 1550–1789

Scientific Revolution
- Heliocentric theory challenges geocentric theory.
- Mathematics and observation support heliocentric theory.
- Scientific method develops.
- Scientists make discoveries in many fields.

A new way of thinking about the world develops—based on observation and a willingness to question assumptions.

Enlightenment
- People try to apply the scientific approach to all aspects of society.
- Political scientists propose new ideas about government.
- Philosophes advocate the use of reason to discover truths.
- Philosophes address social issues through reason.

Enlightenment writers challenge many accepted ideas about government and society.

Spread of Enlightenment Ideas
- Enlightenment ideas appeal to thinkers and artists across Europe.
- Salons help spread Enlightenment thinking.
- Ideas spread to literate middle class.
- Enlightened despots attempt reforms.

Enlightenment ideas sweep through European society and also to colonial America.

American Revolution
- Enlightenment ideas influence colonists.
- Britain taxes colonies after French and Indian War.
- Colonists denounce taxation without representation.
- War begins in Lexington and Concord.

Colonists declare independence, defeat Britain, and establish republic.

CRITICAL THINKING

1. ROLE OF TECHNOLOGY

What role did new technology play in the Scientific Revolution?

2. THE U.S. CONSTITUTION

THEME POWER AND AUTHORITY What was the source of the Constitution's authority? How did this reflect Enlightenment ideas?

3. REVOLUTIONARY IDEAS

Create a two-column table like the one below. In the left column, list important new ideas that arose during the Scientific Revolution and Enlightenment. In the right column, briefly explain why the idea was revolutionary.

New Idea	Why Revolutionary

4. ANALYZING PRIMARY SOURCES

One of Voltaire's most passionate causes was religious toleration. The following excerpt comes from his *Treatise on Toleration* (1763). Voltaire wrote the essay in response to the case of a French Protestant who was falsely accused of murdering his Catholic son. The man was tortured and executed by French authorities. Read the passage and answer the questions that follow.

> **A VOICE FROM THE PAST**
> No great . . . eloquence is needed to prove that Christians should tolerate one another. I go even further and declare that we must look upon all men as our brothers. . . . Are we not all the children of one father and creatures of the same God? . . .
> This little globe, nothing more than a point, rolls in space like so many other globes; we are lost in this immensity. Man, some five feet tall, is surely a very small part of the universe. One of these imperceptible [virtually invisible] beings says to some of his neighbors in Arabia or Africa: "Listen to me, for the God of all these worlds has enlightened me: there are nine hundred million little ants like us on earth, but only my anthill is beloved of God; he will hold all others in horror through all eternity; only mine will be blessed, the others will be eternally wretched."

- Summarize the main point conveyed in this passage. How does Voltaire illustrate his point?
- Do you think Voltaire is directing his message to one religion in particular or to all organized religions? Explain your response.

CHAPTER ACTIVITIES

1. LIVING HISTORY: Unit Portfolio Project

THEME REVOLUTION Your unit portfolio project focuses on showing the similarities and differences among revolutions (see page 509). For Chapter 22, you might use one of the following ideas to add to your portfolio:

- Design the cover for a special magazine issue that spotlights the most revolutionary thinker of the Scientific Revolution or Enlightenment. Indicate the focus of the articles that might appear inside the magazine by writing the table of contents page.
- Present a live or taped news report covering a major event of the American Revolution or early republic.
- Write song lyrics for a Revolutionary War ballad or march that explain why the Americans are fighting for independence.

2. CONNECT TO TODAY: Cooperative Learning

THEME SCIENCE AND TECHNOLOGY The Scientific Revolution produced ideas that profoundly changed how people viewed the natural world. In today's world, scientific discoveries have become commonplace. Yet often they are as revolutionary as those of the 16th century.

Work with a team to create a visual presentation highlighting a recent breakthrough in science or medicine. Focus on how the new knowledge changed what scientists previously thought about the topic.

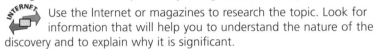 Use the Internet or magazines to research the topic. Look for information that will help you to understand the nature of the discovery and to explain why it is significant.

- Write two brief sentences that summarize the difference in scientific understanding before and after the breakthrough. For an example of such a summary, look at the box on page 548.
- Use text, charts, and other illustrations to explain the discovery's impact.

3. INTERPRETING A TIME LINE

Revisit the unit time line on pages 508–509. What events in Chapters 23 and 24 were probably influenced by the Enlightenment? Why?

FOCUS ON FINE ART

The Spanish artist Francisco Goya produced this engraving, titled *The Sleep of Reason Produces Monsters,* in 1797. Here is his caption: "Imagination abandoned by reason produces impossible monsters; united with her, she is the mother of the arts and the source of their wonders."

- What do you think the monsters represent?
- What is the artist saying will happen when a person lets his or her reason go to sleep?

Connect to History How does the engraving reflect the ideas of Enlightenment thinkers?

CHAPTER 23

The French Revolution and Napoleon, 1789–1815

PREVIEWING THEMES

Power and Authority

With absolute rulers dominating Europe, Enlightenment thinkers began questioning why so few held so much power. The French Revolution was an attempt to put power in the hands of the many. Power changed hands several times in this short period of history.

Revolution

The success of the American Revolution inspired the French, some of whom even participated in it. The French people were deeply affected by the colonists' overthrow of the British and, in turn, revolted against their own repressive rulers.

Economics

The gap between the rich and the poor widened when France's economy weakened. Hungry peasants and city dwellers were outraged by what they felt was unjust treatment. The economy of France became a major cause of the Revolution.

INTERNET CONNECTION

Visit us at **www.mcdougallittell.com** to learn more about the French Revolution, Napoleon, and related topics.

EUROPE, 1789

At Versailles, **Queen Marie Antoinette** spent so much money on clothes that in **1785** her enemies falsely accused her of buying a necklace with 647 diamonds. The rumor increased her unpopularity.

— Holy Roman Empire

0   200 Miles

0   400 Kilometers

N

ATLANTIC OCEAN

SPAIN

⊙ **Madrid**

In Paris, a mob stormed the **Bastille**, the fortress looming in the background, and seized the weapons stored there. This **1789** event ignited the French Revolution.

• Cádiz
• Gibraltar

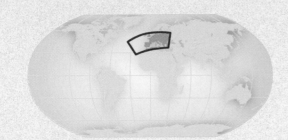

GREAT BRITAIN

NETHERLANDS

● London

Brussels ●

Amiens ●

Versailles ● Paris

FRANCE

Loire River

SWITZERLAND

● Milan

Po River

COMTAT VENAISSIN
Papal States

SARDINIA

GENOA

TUSCANY

PAPAL STATES

VENICE

● Rome

Naples ●

KINGDOM OF THE TWO SICILIES

Mediterranean Sea

● Berlin

Elbe River

PRUSSIA

Warsaw ●

POLAND

HOLY ROMAN EMPIRE

Danube River

Vienna ●

AUSTRIA

After an alliance of nations defeated the French emperor Napoleon, the **Congress of Vienna** met in **1815** to decide who would rule in Europe. Aristocrats at the congress celebrated the victory with balls and banquets.

Napoleon led a French army into Italy and defeated France's enemy, Austria, in **1796**. This detail of *Napoleon Crossing the St. Bernard Pass* by Jacques Louis David presents a heroic Napoleon astride a magnificent stallion. Actually, Napoleon crossed the Alps on a mule, not a horse.

The mob waves the severed heads of palace guards on poles.

City people shout demands for bread and equality.

Angry peasants carry shovels, rakes, and any other weapons they can find.

Some women carry branches that symbolize the liberty tree.

Y ou are returning home from a bakery that is out of bread—again. You have no food to take to your starving children. You are desperate.

Suddenly you turn a corner and come upon the king's palace. King Louis and his wife are living there in luxury while your children and most of your fellow citizens are starving. You see a mob surrounding the palace, demanding food and relief from heavy taxes. They have turned violent.

Would you join the mob?

EXAMINING *the* ISSUES

- **How could such a situation develop in one of the most advanced countries in the world?**

- **What could make people angry enough to behead others and then carry their heads on poles?**

- **How successful could a revolution of peasants be?**

Discuss these questions with your class-mates. In your discussion, remember what you've learned about other revolutionary conflicts, such as the American Revolution and the English Civil War.

As you read about the French Revolution in this chapter, see how events turn out for the peasants.

Revolution Threatens the French King

TERMS & NAMES
- Old Regime
- estate
- Louis XVI
- Marie Antoinette
- Estates-General
- National Assembly
- Tennis Court Oath
- Great Fear

MAIN IDEA	WHY IT MATTERS NOW
Economic and social inequalities in the Old Regime helped cause the French Revolution.	Throughout history, economic and social inequalities have at times led peoples to revolt against their governments.

SETTING THE STAGE In the 1700s, France was considered the most advanced country of Europe. It was the center of the Enlightenment. It had a large population and a prosperous foreign trade. France's culture was widely praised and emulated by the rest of the world. However, the appearance of success was deceiving. There was great unrest in France, caused by high prices, high taxes, and disturbing questions raised by the Enlightenment ideas of Rousseau and Voltaire.

The Old Regime

In the 1770s, the system of feudalism left over from the Middle Ages—called the **Old Regime**—remained in place. The people of France were still divided into three large social classes, or **estates.**

The Privileged Estates Two of the estates had privileges, including access to high offices and exemptions from paying taxes, that were not granted to the members of the third.

The Roman Catholic Church, whose clergy formed the First Estate, owned 10 percent of the land in France. It provided education and relief services to the poor and contributed about 2 percent of its income to the government.

The Second Estate was made up of rich nobles, much of whose wealth was in land. Although they made up only 2 percent of the population, the nobles owned 20 percent of the land and paid almost no taxes. The majority of the clergy and the nobility scorned Enlightenment ideas as radical notions that threatened their status and power as privileged persons.

This medallion bears the image of King Louis XVI of France.

The Third Estate About 98 percent of the people belonged to the Third Estate. The three groups that made up this estate differed greatly in their economic conditions.

The first group—the bourgeoisie (BUR·zhwah·ZEE)—were merchants and artisans. They were well-educated and believed strongly in the Enlightenment ideals of liberty and equality. Although some of the bourgeoisie were as rich as nobles, they paid high taxes and lacked privileges like the other members of the Third Estate. Many felt that their wealth entitled them to a greater degree of social status and political power.

The workers of France's cities—cooks, servants, and others—formed the second group within the Third Estate, a group poorer than the bourgeoisie. Paid low wages and frequently out of work, they often went hungry. If the cost of bread rose, mobs of these workers might attack carts of grain and bread to steal what they needed.

Peasants formed the largest group within the Third Estate—more than 80 percent of France's 26 million people. Peasants paid about half their income in dues to nobles, tithes to the church, and taxes to the king's agents. They even paid taxes on such basic staples as salt. Peasants joined the urban poor in resenting the clergy and the nobles for their privileges and special treatment. The heavily taxed and discontented Third Estate was eager for change.

Vocabulary
bourgeoisie: the middle class. (The term derives from the walled cities, or *bourgs,* in which the middle class began to develop in the 1200s.)

The French Revolution and Napoleon **573**

■ First Estate
- made up of clergy of Roman Catholic Church
- scorned Enlightenment ideas

■ Second Estate
- made up of rich nobles
- held highest offices in government
- disagreed about Enlightenment ideas

■ Third Estate
- included bourgeoisie, urban lower class, and peasant farmers
- had no power to influence government
- embraced Enlightenment ideas

Population of France, 1787

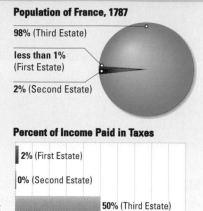

98% (Third Estate)

less than 1% (First Estate)

2% (Second Estate)

Percent of Income Paid in Taxes

2% (First Estate)

0% (Second Estate)

50% (Third Estate)

0%   20%   40%   60%   80%   100%

> **SKILLBUILDER: Interpreting Charts and Political Cartoons**
> *The Third Estate intensely resented the wealthy First and Second Estates.*
> 1. *How do the chart and the graphs help explain the political cartoon?*
> 2. *Why might the First and Second Estates be opposed to change?*

The Forces of Change

In addition to the growing resentment of the lower classes, other factors were contributing to the revolutionary mood in France.

Enlightenment Ideas New views about power and authority in government were spreading among the Third Estate. The people began questioning long-standing notions about the structure of society and using words like *equality, liberty,* and *democracy.* The success of the American Revolution inspired them, and they discussed the radical ideas of Rousseau and Voltaire. Many shared the beliefs of the Comte d'Antraigues, a friend of Rousseau's:

> **A VOICE FROM THE PAST**
> The Third Estate is the People and the People is the foundation of the State; it is in fact the State itself; the other orders are merely political categories while by the *immutable laws of nature* the People is everything. Everything should be subordinated to it. . . . It is in the People that all national power resides and for the People that all states exist.
> **COMTE D'ANTRAIGUES,** quoted in *Citizens: A Chronicle of the French Revolution*

Economic Woes France's once prosperous economy was failing. The population was expanding rapidly, as were trade and production. However, the heavy burden of taxes made it impossible to conduct business profitably within France. The cost of living rose for everyone. In addition, bad weather in the 1780s caused widespread crop failures, resulting in a severe shortage of grain. The price of bread doubled in 1789, and many people faced starvation.

During this period, France's government sank deeply into debt. Extravagant spending by the king and queen was part of the problem. **Louis XVI,** who became king in 1774, inherited part of the debt from his predecessors. He also borrowed heavily in order to help the American revolutionaries in their war against Great Britain—France's chief rival—thereby nearly doubling the government's debt. When bankers, in 1786, refused to lend the government any more money, Louis faced serious problems.

A Weak Leader Strong leadership might have prevented the coming crisis, but Louis XVI was indecisive and allowed matters to drift. He paid little attention to his government advisers, preferring to spend his time hunting or tinkering with locks rather than attending to the details of governing.

Louis had married his wife, **Marie Antoinette,** when he was 15 and she was 14. Because Marie was a member of the royal family of Austria, France's long-time enemy, she became unpopular as soon as she set foot in France. As queen, Marie spent so much money on gowns, jewels, and gifts that she became known as Madame Deficit.

Rather than cutting expenses and increasing taxes, Louis put off dealing with the emergency until France faced bankruptcy. Then, when he tried to tax aristocrats, the Second Estate forced him to call a meeting of the **Estates-General**—an assembly of representatives from all three estates—to get approval for the tax reform. He had the meeting—the first in 175 years—on May 5, 1789, at Versailles.

Revolution Dawns

The clergy and the nobles had dominated the Estates-General throughout the Middle Ages and expected to do so in the 1789 meeting. Under the assembly's medieval rules, each estate's delegates met in a separate hall to vote, and each estate had one vote. The two privileged estates could always outvote the Third Estate.

The National Assembly The Third Estate delegates, mostly members of the bourgeoisie whose views had been shaped by the Enlightenment, were eager to make changes in the government. They insisted that all three estates meet together and that each delegate have a vote. This would give the advantage to the Third Estate, which had as many delegates as the other two estates combined.

Siding with the nobles, the king ordered the Estates-General to follow the medieval rules. The delegates of the Third Estate, however, became more and more determined to wield power. A leading spokesperson for their viewpoint was a clergyman sympathetic to their cause, the Abbé Sieyès (AB·AY syay·YEHS), who argued, "What is the Third Estate? Everything. What has it been up to now in the political order? Nothing. What does it demand? To become something herein." In a dramatic speech, he suggested that the Third Estate delegates name themselves the **National Assembly** and pass laws and reforms in the name of the French people.

HISTORY MAKERS

Marie Antoinette
1755–1793

Marie Antoinette was a pretty, lighthearted, charming woman. However, she was unpopular with the French because of her spending and her involvement in controversial court affairs. She referred to Louis as "the poor man" and sometimes set the clock forward an hour to be rid of his presence.

Marie refused to wear the tight-fitting clothing styles of the day and introduced a loose cotton dress for women. The elderly, who viewed the dress as an undergarment, thought that Marie's clothing was scandalous. The French silk industry was equally angry.

In constant need of entertainment, Marie often spent her time playing cards. One year she lost the equivalent of $1.5 million by gambling in card games.

HISTORY THROUGH ART: Fine Art

A Woman of the Revolution [La maraîchère] (1795), Jacques Louis David

The gap between rich and poor in 18th-century France is clear in these portraits. David, painter of the Revolution, depicted a common woman (*left*) whose appearance displays none of the luxury of the French court (*right*).

Connect *to* History

Comparing What details of the women's expressions and clothing most clearly show the contrasts in lives?

 SEE SKILLBUILDER HANDBOOK, PAGE 996.

Connect *to* Today

Contrasting How would you visually convey the gap between rich and poor in your country?

Marie Antoinette, Jacques Gautier d'Agoty

After a long night of excited debate, the delegates of the Third Estate agreed to Sieyès's idea by an overwhelming majority. On June 17, 1789, they voted to establish the National Assembly, in effect proclaiming the end of absolute monarchy and the beginning of representative government. This vote was the first deliberate act of revolution.

Three days later, the Third Estate delegates found themselves locked out of their meeting room. They broke down a door to an indoor tennis court, pledging to stay until they had drawn up a new constitution. Their pledge was called the **Tennis Court Oath.**

Storming the Bastille In response, Louis tried to make peace with the Third Estate by yielding to the National Assembly's demands. He ordered the nobles and the clergy to join the Third Estate in the National Assembly. At the same time, sensing trouble, the king stationed his mercenary army of Swiss guards in Paris, since he no longer trusted the loyalty of the French soldiers.

In Paris, rumors flew that foreign troops were coming to massacre French citizens. People gathered weapons in order to defend Paris against the king's foreign troops. On July 14, a mob tried to get gunpowder from the Bastille, a Paris prison. The angry crowd overwhelmed the king's soldiers, and the Bastille fell into the control of the citizens. The fall of the Bastille became a great symbolic act of revolution to the French people. Ever since, July 14 has been a French national holiday, similar to the U.S. Fourth of July.

Vocabulary
mercenary army: a group of soldiers who will work for any country or employer that will pay them.

Daily *Life*

The Women's March

When the women of Paris marched 12 miles in the rain to the luxurious palace at Versailles, they were infuriated. They deeply resented the extravagances of Louis and Marie Antoinette at a time when their own children were starving.

After forcing the king and queen out of the palace, the women followed Louis's family and entourage of almost 60,000 persons to Paris—another 12-mile march.

During their return, they sang that they were bringing "the baker, the baker's wife, and the baker's lad" to Paris. (They expected the "baker" to provide bread to alleviate the terrible hunger in the city.) Revolutionary leaders would later honor the women as heroes of the Revolution.

A Great Fear Sweeps France

Before long, rebellion spread from Paris into the countryside. From one village to the next, wild rumors circulated that the nobles were hiring outlaws to terrorize the peasants.

A wave of senseless panic called the **Great Fear** rolled through France. When the peasants met no enemy bandits, they became outlaws themselves. Waving pitchforks and torches, they broke into nobles' manor houses, tore up the old legal papers that bound them to pay feudal dues, and in some cases burned the manor houses as well.

In October 1789, approximately 6,000 Parisian women rioted over the rising price of bread. Their anger quickly turned against the king and queen. Seizing knives and axes, the women and a great many men marched on Versailles. They broke into the palace and killed two guards. The women demanded that Louis and Marie Antoinette come to Paris. Finally, the king agreed to take his wife and children to Paris.

Three hours later the king, his family, and servants left Versailles, never again to see their magnificent palace. Their exit signaled the change of power and radical reforms about to overtake France.

THINK THROUGH HISTORY
B. Recognizing Effects How did the women's march mark a turning point in the relationship between the king and the people?

Section ❶ Assessment

1. TERMS & NAMES
Identify
• Old Regime
• estate
• Louis XVI
• Marie Antoinette
• Estates-General
• National Assembly
• Tennis Court Oath
• Great Fear

2. TAKING NOTES
Use a web diagram like the one below to show the causes of the French Revolution.

Causes of Revolution

3. FORMING OPINIONS
Do you think that changes in the French government were inevitable?

THINK ABOUT
• the leadership of Louis XVI
• the French national debt
• Enlightenment ideas
• other world revolutions

4. ANALYZING THEMES
Economics How were the economic conditions in France similar to or different from those in England and the American colonies before their revolutions?

THINK ABOUT
• France's three estates
• the role of taxation
• France's national debt
• conditions in England before the Civil War
• conditions in the colonies before the American Revolution

Revolution Brings Reform and Terror

TERMS & NAMES
- **Declaration of the Rights of Man**
- **Legislative Assembly**
- **émigrés**
- **sans-culottes**
- **guillotine**
- **Maximilien Robespierre**
- **Committee of Public Safety**
- **Reign of Terror**

MAIN IDEA	**WHY IT MATTERS NOW**
The revolutionary government of France made reforms but also used terror and violence to retain power.	Some governments that lack the support of a majority of their people still use terrorism to control their citizens.

SETTING THE STAGE Peasants were not the only members of French society to feel the Great Fear; nobles and clergymen were equally afraid. Throughout France, bands of angry peasants struck out against members of the upper classes. In the summer of 1789, a few months before the women's march to Versailles, some nobles and clergymen in the National Assembly responded to the uprisings in an emotional late-night meeting.

The Assembly Reforms France

Throughout the night of August 4, 1789, noblemen made grand speeches, declaring their love of liberty and equality. Although motivated more by fear than by idealism, they joined other members of the National Assembly in sweeping away the feudal privileges of the First Estate and the Second Estate, thus making commoners and peasants equal to the nobles and the clergy. By morning, the Old Regime was dead.

The Rights of Man Three weeks later, on August 27, the National Assembly adopted a statement of revolutionary ideals called "A Declaration of the Rights of Man and of the Citizen," commonly known as the **Declaration of the Rights of Man.** Reflecting the influence of Enlightenment ideas and of the Declaration of Independence, the document stated that "men are born and remain free and equal in rights" and that "the aim of all political association is the preservation of the natural . . . rights of man. These rights are liberty, property, security, and resistance to oppression." Other articles of the famous document guaranteed citizens equal justice, freedom of speech, and freedom of religion. As the French people embraced the principles of the declaration, the expression "Liberty, Equality, Fraternity" became the slogan of the Revolution.

However, the Declaration of the Rights of Man did not apply to women. When Olympe de Gouges (aw·LAMP duh GOOZH) wrote a declaration of the rights of women, not only were her ideas rejected, but she eventually lost her head as an enemy of the Revolution.

A State-Controlled Church During 1790, many of the National Assembly's reforms focused on the relationship between church and state. The assembly took over church lands and declared that church officials and priests were to be elected by property owners and paid as state officials. Thus, the Catholic Church lost both its lands and its political independence. The reasons for the assembly's actions were economic. The delegates hesitated to further tax the bourgeoisie, who were strong supporters of the Revolution. However, the delegates were willing to sell church lands to help pay off France's large debt.

THINK THROUGH HISTORY
A. Synthesizing
How did the slogan "Liberty, Equality, Fraternity" sum up the goals of the Revolution?

HISTORY MAKERS

Olympe de Gouges
1748–1793

Olympe de Gouges was a playwright and journalist whose feminist writings reached a large audience. In 1791 this strong supporter of democracy demanded the same rights for French women that French men were demanding for themselves. In her "Declaration of the Rights of Woman and the Female Citizen," she challenged the oppression of male authority and the notion of male-female inequality:

Male and female citizens, being equal in the eyes of the law, must be equally admitted to all honors, positions, and public employment according to their capacity and without other distinctions besides those of their virtues and talents.

The French Revolution and Napoleon **577**

The assembly's actions alarmed millions of devout French peasants, who rallied to the support of their parish priests. Many French peasants, like their priests, were conservative Catholics. Although the assembly's move to make the church a part of the state was in accord with Enlightenment philosophy, it offended such Catholics, who believed that the pope should rule over a church independent of the state.

These changes in the church drove a wedge between the peasants and the bourgeoisie. From this time on, the peasants often opposed further revolutionary changes.

Louis Tries to Escape As the National Assembly restructured the relationship between church and state, Louis XVI pondered his fate as a monarch. Some of the king's advisers warned Louis that he and his family were in danger. Many supporters of the monarchy thought France unsafe and left the country. Then, in June 1791, Louis and his family tried to escape from France to the Austrian Netherlands. As they neared the French border, however, a postmaster recognized the king from his portrait on some paper money. The royal family was returned to Paris under guard. By his attempted escape, Louis XVI had increased the influence of his radical enemies and sealed his own doom.

Conflicting Goals Cause Divisions

For two years, the National Assembly argued over a new constitution for France. By 1791, the delegates had made significant changes in France's government and society.

A Limited Monarchy The National Assembly created a limited constitutional monarchy. The new constitution stripped the king of much of his authority and gave the Legislative Assembly the power to create French law. Although the king and his ministers would still hold the executive power to enforce laws, France's assemblymen would be the lawmakers in the country.

In September 1791, the National Assembly completed its new constitution, which Louis reluctantly approved, and then handed over its power to a new assembly—the **Legislative Assembly.** This assembly had the power to create laws and to approve or prevent any war the king declared on other nations.

Factions Split France Despite the new government, old problems, such as food shortages and government debt, remained. Angry cries for more liberty, more equality, and more bread soon caused the Revolution's leaders to turn against one another. The Legislative Assembly split into three general groups, each of which sat in a different part of the meeting hall. (The three divisions are summarized below.)

THINK THROUGH HISTORY
B. Identifying Problems What problems were not solved by the new government?

The Legislative Assembly

Radicals	Moderates	Conservatives
• sat on the left side of the hall; were called left-wing and said to be on the left	• sat in the center of the hall and were called centrists	• sat on the right side of the hall; were called right-wing and said to be on the right
• opposed the king and the idea of a monarchy	• wanted some changes in government, but not as many as the radicals	• upheld the idea of a limited monarchy
• wanted sweeping changes in government and proposed that common people have full power in a republic		• wanted few changes in government

SKILLBUILDER: Interpreting Charts
1. *What do the divisions in the Legislative Assembly say about the differences in French society?*
2. *What similarities and differences do you see between the political factions in the Legislative Assembly and those in the U.S. government today?*

Although these groups disagreed, there were groups in France that were far more extreme. **Émigrés** (EHM·ih·GRAYZ)—nobles and others who had fled France during the peasant uprisings—were on the extreme right. They hoped to undo the Revolution and restore the Old Regime.

On the extreme left, the most radical group was the **sans-culottes** (SANZ kyoo·LAHTS), "those without knee breeches." Unlike the upper classes, who wore fancy knee-length pants, sans-culottes wore regular trousers. They were Parisian wage-earners and small shopkeepers who wanted a greater voice in government, lower food prices, and an end to food shortages. Although they did not have a role in the assembly, they soon discovered other ways to exert their power as a group, especially by influencing one of the political clubs that developed later.

War and Extreme Measures

In 1792, the French were faced not only with reforms at home but also with a disastrous foreign war. Monarchs and nobles in many European countries feared the changes that were taking place in France. They worried that peasant revolts similar to the ones in France could break out in their own countries.

War with Austria French radicals hoped to spread their revolution to all the peoples of Europe. When Austria and Prussia proposed that France put Louis back on the throne, the Legislative Assembly responded by declaring war on Austria in April 1792. Prussia later joined Austria in the war against the French. By going to war with France, the European leaders believed, they would be helping Louis XVI to regain his position as an absolute monarch, as well as preserving their own positions as monarchs.

The war began badly for the poorly equipped French forces. By the summer of 1792, enemy armies were advancing toward Paris. On July 25, the Prussian commander threatened to destroy Paris if the revolutionaries harmed any member of the royal family. This rash statement infuriated the Parisians. On August 10, about 20,000 men and women invaded the Tuileries, the royal palace where Louis and his family were staying. The king's Swiss guard of 900 men fought desperately to defend Louis. The mob brutally massacred them and imprisoned Louis, Marie Antoinette, and their children in a stone tower. A witness in the palace recalled the scene:

In June 1792, rioters invaded the Tuileries—Louis's palace in Paris. They shouted at Louis and waved swords in his face for hours before being persuaded to leave peacefully.

A VOICE FROM THE PAST
I ran from place to place, and finding the apartments and staircases already strewed with dead bodies, I . . . ran away to the Dauphin's garden gate where some Marseillais [citizen soldiers from Marseille], who had just butchered several of the Swiss, were stripping them. One of them came up to me with a bloody sword in his hand, saying, "Hello, citizen! Without arms! Here, take this and help us to kill." But luckily . . . I managed to make my escape. Some of the Swiss who were persued took refuge in an adjoining stable. I concealed myself in the same place. They were soon cut to pieces close to me. . . .

UNNAMED ROYAL SERVANT, quoted in *The Days of the French Revolution*

France's war with Austria and Prussia also affected daily life in Paris. During the summer of 1792, Parisians learned that French troops were failing to hold back the approaching Prussian forces. Just as bands of volunteer soldiers were preparing to leave Paris and reinforce the French soldiers in the field, they heard rumors that the royalists imprisoned in Paris would seize control of the city in their absence. Angry citizens responded by taking the law into their own hands. For several days in early September, Parisians raided the prisons and murdered over 1,000 prisoners. Many royalists, nobles, and clergymen fell victim to the angry mobs in these so-called September massacres.

THINK THROUGH HISTORY
C. Recognizing Causes What did the September massacres show about the mood of the people?

Faced with the threat of the Parisian radicals, the members of the Legislative Assembly gave up the idea of a limited monarchy. They set aside the Constitution of 1791, declared the king deposed, and dissolved their assembly, calling for the election of a new legislature.

The new governing body, elected in September, called itself the National Convention. Just as the new government took office, France had a stroke of luck. A French army won a battle against the Austrians and Prussians. For the moment, France was out of danger from abroad.

Radicals Execute the King During the frenzied summer of 1792, the leaders of the mobs on the streets had more real power than any government assembly. Although the mobs were made up of the poor, their leaders came from the bourgeoisie.

Both men and women of the middle class joined political clubs. The most radical club in 1792 was the Jacobin (JAK·uh·bihn) Club, where violent speech-making was the order of the day. The Jacobins wanted to remove the king and establish a republic.

One of the prominent radical leaders was Jean Paul Marat (mah·RAH). During the Revolution, he edited a radical newspaper. His fiery editorials called for "five or six hundred heads cut off" to rid France of the enemies of the Revolution. Georges Danton (zhawrzh dahn·TAWN), a revolutionary leader who was devoted to the rights of Paris's poor people, joined the club as a talented speaker.

The National Convention, meeting in Paris on September 21, quickly abolished the monarchy and declared France a republic. Adult male citizens were granted the right to vote and hold office. Despite the important part they had already played in the Revolution, women were not given the right to vote. The delegates reduced Louis XVI's role from that of a king to that of a common citizen and prisoner. Then, guided by radical Jacobins, they tried Louis for treason and found him guilty. By a very close vote, they sentenced him to death.

In this engraving, titled *Execution of Louis XVI*, a revolutionary presents Louis's head to the crowd after the king's execution in Paris.

On January 21, 1793, the ex-king walked with calm dignity up the steps of the scaffold to be beheaded by a machine called the **guillotine** (GIHL·uh·TEEN). Thousands died by the guillotine during the French Revolution.

France's Citizen Army The new republic's first problem was the continuing war with Austria and Prussia. Early in 1793, Great Britain, Holland, and Spain joined Prussia and Austria in an alliance known as the First Coalition. Forced to contend with so many enemies, France suffered a string of defeats.

The Jacobin leaders took extreme steps to meet the new danger. In February 1793, the National Convention decreed a draft into the army of 300,000 French citizens between the ages of 18 and 40. By 1794, the army had grown to 800,000 and included women.

Vocabulary
coalition: a temporary alliance between groups for some specific purpose.

The Guillotine

If you think the guillotine was a cruel form of capital punishment, think again. Dr. Joseph Ignace Guillotin proposed a machine that satisfied many needs—it was efficient, humane, and democratic. A physician and member of the National Assembly, Guillotin claimed that those executed with the device "wouldn't even feel the slightest pain."

Prior to the guillotine's introduction in 1792, many French criminals had suffered through horrible punishments in public places. Although public punishments continued to attract large crowds, not all spectators were pleased with the new machine. Some witnesses felt that death by the guillotine occurred much too quickly to be enjoyed by an audience.

Some doctors believed that a victim's head retained its hearing and eyesight for up to 15 minutes after the blade's deadly blow. All remains were eventually gathered and buried in simple graves.

Earlier Forms of Punishment

Criminals in 17th- and 18th-century France sometimes faced one or more of the following fatal penalties:

- Burning
- Strangulation
- Being broken on a wheel
- Hanging
- Dismemberment
- Beheading
- Being pulled apart by horses

Once the executioner cranked the blade to the top, a mechanism released it. The sharp weighted blade fell, severing the victim's head from his or her body.

Woman knitters, or *tricoteuses*, were regular spectators at executions and knitted stockings for soldiers as they sat near the base of the scaffold.

Connect *to* History

Synthesizing In what ways was the guillotine an efficient means of execution?

SEE SKILLBUILDER HANDBOOK, PAGE 1007.

Connect *to* Today

Comparing France continued to use the guillotine until the late 1970s. Compare this instrument of capital punishment with the ones used in the United States today, and present your findings in an oral report. Speculate on what the goals of capital punishment are and whether they have been achieved—in the French Revolution or in today's world.

INTERNET CONNECTION

Visit us at **www.mcdougallittell.com** to learn more about the French Revolution and Napoleon.

Beheading by Class

More than 2,100 people were executed during the last 132 days of the Reign of Terror. The pie graph below displays the breakdown of beheadings by class.

- First Estate
- Second Estate
- Third Estate

Before each execution, bound victims traveled from the prison to the scaffold in horse-drawn carts during a 1½ hour procession through city streets.

On this late-18th-century French inkwell, the liberty cap worn by revolutionaries crushes a clergyman of the Old Regime.

The Terror Grips France

Foreign armies were not the only enemies of the French republic. The Jacobins had thousands of enemies within France itself—peasants who were horrified by the beheading of the king, priests who would not accept government control, and rival leaders who were stirring up rebellion in the provinces. How to contain and control these enemies became a central issue.

Robespierre Assumes Control As dozens of leaders struggled for power, **Maximilien Robespierre** (ROHBZ·peer) slowly gathered control into his own hands. Robespierre and his supporters set out to build a "republic of virtue." They tried to wipe out every trace of France's past monarchy and nobility. Many families named Leroy ("king"), for instance, changed their names to something less political. No household item was too small to escape the influence of Robespierre—even the kings, queens, and jacks in decks of cards were changed to figures that represented revolutionary ideals.

Firm believers in reason, the radicals changed the calendar to be more scientific. They divided the year into 12 months of 30 days and renamed each month. The new calendar had no Sundays because the radicals considered religion old-fashioned and dangerous. They even closed all churches in Paris, and towns all over France soon did the same.

In the summer of 1793, Robespierre became the leader of the **Committee of Public Safety.** As head of the committee, he decided who should be considered enemies of the republic. The committee often had people tried in the morning and guillotined the same afternoon. From July 1793 to July 1794, Robespierre governed France nearly as a dictator, and the period of his rule became known as the **Reign of Terror.** In his speeches, Robespierre justified the Reign of Terror, explaining that it enabled French citizens to remain true to the ideals of the Revolution. In this speech excerpt, Robespierre makes a connection between virtue and terror:

A VOICE FROM THE PAST
The first maxim of our politics ought to be to lead the people by means of reason and the enemies of the people by terror. If the basis of popular government in time of peace is virtue, the basis of popular government in time of revolution is both virtue and terror: virtue without which terror is murderous, terror without which virtue is powerless. Terror is nothing else than swift, severe, indomitable justice; it flows, then, from virtue.

MAXIMILIEN ROBESPIERRE, quoted in *Problems of Western Civilization: The Challenge of History*

THINK THROUGH HISTORY
D. Summarizing
How did Robespierre justify his use of terror?

The most famous victim of the Terror was the widowed queen, Marie Antoinette. Calm and dignified, she rode in the death cart past jeering crowds. On the scaffold, she accidentally stepped on her executioner's foot. "Monsieur," she apologized, "I beg your pardon. I did not do it on purpose." Those were her last words.

The "enemies of the republic" who troubled Robespierre the most were fellow revolutionaries who challenged his leadership. In October 1793, revolutionary courts pronounced death sentences on many of the leaders who had first helped set up the republic. Their only crime was that they were less radical than Robespierre.

By the beginning of 1794, even Georges Danton found himself in danger. (Marat had already been stabbed to death by a young woman.) Danton's friends in the

National Convention, afraid to defend him, joined in condemning him to death. On the scaffold, he told the executioner, "Don't forget to show my head to the people. It's well worth seeing."

Besides leading political figures, thousands of unknown people were sent to death on the flimsiest of charges. A revolutionary court sentenced an 18-year-old youth to die by the guillotine for sawing down a tree that had been planted as a symbol of liberty. A tavern keeper was executed because he sold sour wine "to the defenders of the country."

During the Terror, approximately 3,000 people were executed in Paris. Some historians believe that as many as 40,000 were killed all together. About 85 percent were peasants or members of the urban poor or middle class—common people for whose benefit the Revolution had supposedly been carried out.

End of the Terror

Vocabulary
conspirators:
people involved in
a secret plot.

By July 1794, the members of the National Convention knew that none of them were safe from Robespierre. To save themselves, they turned on him. A group of conspirators demanded his arrest, shouting, "Down with the tyrant!" The next day the Revolution's last powerful leader went to the guillotine. The Reign of Terror, the radical phase of the French Revolution, ended when Maximilien Robespierre lost his head on July 28, 1794.

French public opinion shifted dramatically to the right after Robespierre's death. People of all classes had grown weary of the Terror. They were also tired of the skyrocketing prices of bread, salt, and other necessities of life after the Terror.

In 1795, moderate leaders in the National Convention drafted a new plan of government. The third since 1789, the new constitution placed power firmly in the hands of the upper middle class and called for a two-house legislature and an executive body of five men, known as the Directory. The five directors were moderates, not revolutionary idealists. Some of them freely enriched themselves at the public's expense. Despite their corruption, however, they gave their troubled country a period of order.

The Directory also found the right general to command France's armies. This supremely talented young man was named Napoleon Bonaparte.

Section 2 Assessment

1. TERMS & NAMES

Identify
- Declaration of the Rights of Man
- Legislative Assembly
- émigrés
- sans-culottes
- guillotine
- Maximilien Robespierre
- Committee of Public Safety
- Reign of Terror

2. TAKING NOTES

Recreate the cause-and-effect graphic below on your paper. Fill in the main events that occurred after the creation of the Constitution of 1791.

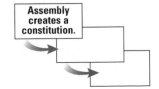

3. RECOGNIZING CAUSES

After the French rejected the king's absolute control, they struggled to create a more democratic government. However, in 1793, Robespierre became a dictator. What caused this to happen?

THINK ABOUT
- the political climate prior to Robespierre's rule
- the need for a leader
- Robespierre's personality

4. THEME ACTIVITY

Revolution Create a revolutionaries' "Wall of Fame." Working in small teams, write short biographies of revolutionary figures mentioned in this section (including pictures if possible). Then add biographies of other revolutionary figures—from England and the Americas— mentioned in the unit.

Napoleon Forges an Empire

TERMS & NAMES
• Napoleon Bonaparte
• coup d'état
• plebiscite
• lycée
• concordat
• Napoleonic Code
• Battle of Trafalgar

MAIN IDEA	WHY IT MATTERS NOW
A military genius, Napoleon Bonaparte, seized power in France and made himself emperor.	In times of political turmoil, military dictators often seize control of nations, as in Haiti in 1991.

SETTING THE STAGE Napoleon was a short man (five feet three inches tall) who cast a long shadow over the history of modern times. He would come to be recognized as one of the world's greatest military geniuses, along with Alexander the Great of Macedonia, Hannibal of Carthage, and Julius Caesar of Rome. In only four years (1795–1799), Napoleon rose from relative obscurity to become master of France.

Napoleon Grasps the Power

HISTORY MAKERS

**Napoleon Bonaparte
1769–1821**

Napoleon Bonaparte had a magnetism that attracted the admiration of his men. His speeches were designed to inspire his troops to valorous feats. In one speech, he told soldiers,"If the victory is for a moment uncertain, you shall see your Emperor place himself on the front line."

Bonaparte was generous in his rewards to the troops. Many received the Legion of Honor—a medal for bravery. Sometimes Napoleon would take the medal from his own chest to present it to a soldier. (He kept a few spares in his pocket for these occasions.)
A cavalry commander, Auguste de Colbert, wrote, "He awakened in my soul the desire for glory."

Napoleon Bonaparte was born in 1769 on the Mediterranean island of Corsica. When he was nine years old, his parents sent him to a military school in northern France. In 1785, at the age of 16, he finished school and became a lieutenant in the artillery. When the Revolution broke out, Napoleon joined the army of the new government.

Hero of the Hour In October 1795, fate handed the young officer a chance for glory. When royalist rebels marched on the National Convention, a government official told Napoleon to defend the delegates. Napoleon and his gunners greeted the thousands of royalists with a cannonade. Within minutes, the attackers fled in panic and confusion. Napoleon Bonaparte became the hero of the hour and was hailed throughout Paris as the savior of the French republic.

In 1796, the Directory appointed Napoleon to lead a French army against the forces of Austria and the Kingdom of Sardinia. Crossing the Alps, the young general swept into Italy and won a series of remarkable victories, which crushed the Austrian troops' threat to France. Next, in an attempt to protect French trade interests and to disrupt British trade with India, Napoleon led an expedition to Egypt. Unfortunately, his luck did not hold. His army was pinned down in Egypt, and his naval forces were defeated by the British admiral Horatio Nelson. However, he managed to keep the reports of his defeat out of the press, so that by 1799 the words "the general" could mean only one man to the French—Napoleon.

Coup d'État By 1799, the Directory had lost control of the political situation and the confidence of the French people. Only the directors' control of the army kept them in power. Upon Napoleon's return from Egypt, the Abbé Sieyès urged him to seize political power. Napoleon and Josephine, his lovely socialite wife, set a plan in motion. Napoleon met with influential persons to discuss his role in the Directory, while Josephine used her connections with the wealthy directors to influence their decisions. The action began on November 9, 1799, when Napoleon was put in charge of the military. It ended the next day when his troops drove out the members of one chamber of the

Vocabulary
cannonade: a bombardment with heavy artillery fire.

THINK THROUGH HISTORY
A. Analyzing
Causes For what
reasons was
Napoleon able to
become a dictator?

national legislature. The legislature voted to dissolve the Directory. In its place, the legislature established a group of three consuls, one of whom was Napoleon. Napoleon quickly assumed dictatorial powers as the first consul of the French republic. A sudden seizure of power like Napoleon's is known as a coup—from the French phrase **coup d'état** (KOO day·TAH), or "blow of state."

At the time of Napoleon's coup, France was still at war. In 1799, British diplomats assembled the Second Coalition of anti-French powers—Britain, Austria, and Russia— with the goal of driving Napoleon from power. Once again, Napoleon rode from Paris at the head of his troops. Eventually, as a result of war and diplomacy, all three nations signed peace agreements with France. By 1802, Europe was at peace for the first time in ten years. Napoleon was free to focus his energies on restoring order in France.

Napoleon Rules France

At first, Napoleon pretended to be the constitutionally chosen leader of a free republic. In 1800, a **plebiscite** (PLEHB·ih·SYT), or vote of the people, was held to approve a new constitution, the fourth in eight years. Desperate for strong leadership, the people voted overwhelmingly in favor of the constitution, which gave all real power to Napoleon as first consul.

Restoring Order at Home Under Napoleon, France would have order and stability. He did not try to return the nation to the days of Louis XVI; instead, he kept many of the changes that had come with the Revolution. He supported laws that would both strengthen the central government and achieve some of the goals of the Revolution, such as a stable economy and more equality in taxation.

The first order of business was to get the economy on a solid footing. Napoleon set up an efficient tax-collection system and established a national bank. In addition to assuring the government a steady supply of tax money, these actions promoted sound financial management and better control of the economy.

Napoleon also needed to reduce government corruption and improve the delivery of government services. He dismissed corrupt officials and, in order to provide his government with trained officials, set up **lycées,** or government-run public schools. The students at the lycées included children of ordinary citizens as well as children of

Napoleon Brings Order After the Revolution

	The Economy	Government & Society	Religion
Goals of the Revolution	• Equal taxation • Lower inflation	• Less government corruption • Equal opportunity in government	• Less powerful Catholic Church • Religious tolerance
Napoleon's Actions	• Set up fairer tax code • Set up national bank • Stabilized currency • Gave state loans to businesses	• Appointed officials by merit • Fired corrupt officials • Created lycées • Created code of laws	• Recognized Catholicism as "faith of Frenchmen" • Signed concordat with pope • Retained seized church lands
Results	• Equal taxation • Stable economy	• Honest, competent officials • Equal opportunity in government • Public education	• Religious tolerance • Government control of church lands • Government recognition of church influence

SKILLBUILDER: Interpreting Charts
Napoleon's changes brought France closer to achieving the Revolution's goals.
1. *Which goals of the Revolution did Napoleon achieve?*
2. *If you had been a member of the bourgeoisie in Napoleon's France, would you have been satisfied with the results of Napoleon's actions? Why or why not?*

the wealthy. The trained candidates could then be appointed to public office on the basis of merit rather than family connections.

Both the clergy and the peasants wanted to restore the position of the church in France. Napoleon signed a **concordat** (agreement) with Pope Pius VII, spelling out a new relationship between church and state. The government recognized the influence of the church but rejected church control in national affairs. Specifically the French government would appoint bishops, but the bishops would appoint parish priests. The concordat gained Napoleon the support of the organized church as well as the majority of the French people.

Napoleon thought that his greatest work was his comprehensive system of laws, known as the **Napoleonic Code.** Although the code gave the country a uniform set of laws and eliminated many injustices, it actually limited liberty and promoted order and authority over individual rights. The code took away some rights that women had won during the Revolution, such as the right to sell their property. Freedom of speech and of the press, also established during the Revolution, were restricted rather than expanded. The new laws also restored slavery in the French colonies of the Caribbean, which the revolutionary government had abolished.

The emperor Napoleon appears almost godlike in this 1806 portrait by Jean Auguste Dominique Ingres, entitled *Napoleon on His Imperial Throne.*

Napoleon Crowned as Emperor In 1804, Napoleon decided to make himself emperor, and the French voters supported him. On December 2, 1804, dressed in a splendid robe of purple velvet, Napoleon walked down the long aisle of Notre Dame Cathedral in Paris. The pope waited for him with a glittering crown. As thousands watched, the new emperor took the crown from the pope and placed it on his own head. With this arrogant gesture, Napoleon signaled that he was more powerful than the church, which had traditionally crowned the rulers of France.

Napoleon Creates an Empire

Napoleon was not content simply to be master of France. He wanted to control the rest of Europe and to reassert French power in the New World. He envisioned his western empire to include Louisiana, Florida, French Guiana, and the French West Indies. He knew that the key to this area was the sugar-producing French colony of Saint Domingue on the island of Hispaniola.

New World Territories In 1789, when the ideas of the Revolution had reached the planters in Saint Domingue, they had demanded that the National Assembly give them the same privileges as the people of France. Eventually, the slaves in the colony had demanded their freedom. A civil war had erupted, and slaves under the leadership of Toussaint L'Ouverture had seized control of the productive colony. In 1801, Napoleon decided to regain French control of the war-torn island and restore its productive sugar industry. Although he sent 23,000 soldiers to accomplish the task, the former slaves proved to be difficult to defeat, and thousands of soldiers died of yellow fever.

When the expedition to Saint Domingue was unsuccessful and the U.S. government showed interest in buying the port of New Orleans, Napoleon recognized an opportunity to make some money and cut his losses in the Americas. He offered to sell all of the Louisiana Territory to the United States, and in 1803 President

THINK THROUGH HISTORY
B. Analyzing Motives Why would Napoleon crown himself?

Jefferson's administration agreed to purchase the land for $15 million. Napoleon was delighted. He saw a twofold benefit to the sale: he would gain money to finance operations in Europe, and he would further punish his British enemies. He exulted,"The sale assures forever the power of the United States, and I have given England a rival who, sooner or later, will humble her pride."

Conquering Europe Napoleon abandoned his imperial ambitions in the New World and turned his attention to Europe. He had already annexed the Austrian Netherlands and parts of Italy to France and set up a puppet government in Switzerland. Now he looked to expand his influence further. Fearful of his ambitions, Britain persuaded Russia, Austria, and Sweden to join in a third coalition against France.

Napoleon met this challenge with his usual boldness. He rallied the troops and rode out to defeat the Third Coalition, exclaiming, "My army is formidable. . . . Once we had an Army of the Rhine, an Army of Italy, an Army of Holland; there has never been a French Army—but now it exists, and we shall soon see it in action." In a series of brilliant battles, Napoleon crushed the opposition. (See the map on page 588.) The commanders of the enemy armies could never predict his next move and took heavy losses. After the Battle of Austerlitz, Napoleon issued a proclamation expressing his pride in his troops:

A VOICE FROM THE PAST

Soldiers! I am pleased with you. On the day of Austerlitz, you justified everything that I was expecting of your intrepidity. . . . In less than four hours, an army of 100,000 men, commanded by the emperors of Russia and Austria, was cut up and dispersed. . . . 120 pieces of artillery, 20 generals, and more than 30,000 men taken prisoner—such are the results of this day which will forever be famous. . . . My nation will be overjoyed to see you again. And it will be enough for you to say, "I was at Austerlitz," to hear the reply: "There is a brave man!"

NAPOLEON, quoted in *Napoleon* by André Castelot

Eventually, the rulers of Austria, Prussia, and Russia all signed peace treaties with Napoleon, whose proud and patriotic army had enabled him to build the largest European empire since the Romans'. The only major enemy left undefeated was Britain, whose power lay in its navy. In 1805, Napoleon tried to remove the threat of that navy.

The Battle of Trafalgar In his war against the Third Coalition, Napoleon lost only one major battle, the **Battle of Trafalgar** (truh·FAL·guhr)—but that naval defeat was more important than all of Napoleon's victories on land. The battle took place in 1805 off the southern coast of Spain. The commander of the British fleet, Horatio Nelson—the admiral who had defeated Napoleon's fleet near Egypt in 1798—outmaneuvered the larger French-Spanish fleet, showing as much brilliance in warfare at sea as Napoleon had in warfare on land. (See map inset on page 588.) During the furious battle, Nelson was mortally wounded by a French sharpshooter. As he lay dying aboard his flagship, Nelson heard the welcome news of British victory. "Now I am satisfied," murmured the admiral. "Thank God, I have done my duty."

The destruction of the French fleet had two major results. First, it assured the supremacy of the British navy for the next hundred years. Second, it forced Napoleon to give up his plans of invading Britain. He had to look for another way to control his powerful enemy across the English Channel. Eventually, Napoleon's extravagant efforts to crush Britain would lead to his own undoing.

The French Empire During the first decade of the 1800s, Napoleon's victories had given him mastery over most of Europe. By 1812, the only major European countries free from Napoleon's control were Britain, the Ottoman Empire, Portugal, and Sweden.

As the map on page 588 shows, Napoleon controlled numerous supposedly independent lands in addition to those that were formally part of the French Empire. These included

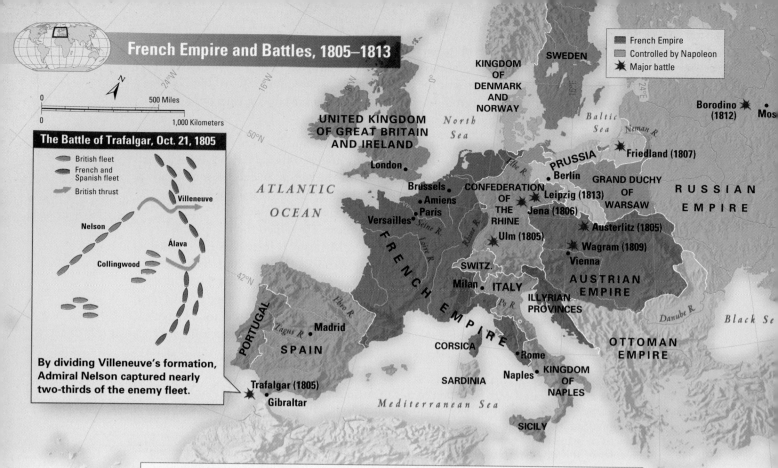

French Empire and Battles, 1805–1813

Legend:
- French Empire
- Controlled by Napoleon
- ✴ Major battle

0 — 500 Miles
0 — 1,000 Kilometers

The Battle of Trafalgar, Oct. 21, 1805

- British fleet
- French and Spanish fleet
- → British thrust

Villeneuve
Nelson
Álava
Collingwood

By dividing Villeneuve's formation, Admiral Nelson captured nearly two-thirds of the enemy fleet.

Map labels: SWEDEN, KINGDOM OF DENMARK AND NORWAY, North Sea, Baltic Sea, Neman R., Borodino (1812), Mos..., UNITED KINGDOM OF GREAT BRITAIN AND IRELAND, London, PRUSSIA, Friedland (1807), Berlin, GRAND DUCHY OF WARSAW, RUSSIAN EMPIRE, Brussels, CONFEDERATION OF THE RHINE, Leipzig (1813), Amiens, Jena (1806), Paris, Versailles, Seine R., Ulm (1805), Austerlitz (1805), Wagram (1809), Vienna, ATLANTIC OCEAN, FRENCH EMPIRE, SWITZ., Milan, ITALY, ILLYRIAN PROVINCES, AUSTRIAN EMPIRE, Danube R., Black Se..., PORTUGAL, Madrid, SPAIN, CORSICA, Rome, OTTOMAN EMPIRE, Naples, KINGDOM OF NAPLES, Trafalgar (1805), Gibraltar, SARDINIA, Mediterranean Sea, SICILY

GEOGRAPHY SKILLBUILDER: Interpreting Maps

1. **Region** What was the extent (north to south, east to west) of Napoleon's empire in 1812?
2. **Location** Where was the Battle of Trafalgar fought? What tactic did Nelson use, and why was it successful?

Spain, the Grand Duchy of Warsaw, and a number of German kingdoms in central Europe. The rulers of these countries were Napoleon's puppets; some, in fact, were his brothers and in-laws. Furthermore, the powerful countries of Russia, Prussia, and Austria were loosely attached to Napoleon's empire through alliances. Not totally under Napoleon's control, they were easily manipulated by threats of military action.

Ironically, Napoleon's power and military threats actually made the conquered peoples more conscious of their loyalty to their own nations. The French empire was huge but unstable. Napoleon was able to maintain it at its greatest extent for only five years (1807–1812). Then it quickly fell to pieces. Its sudden collapse was caused in part by Napoleon himself.

Section 3 Assessment

1. TERMS & NAMES
Identify
- Napoleon Bonaparte
- coup d'état
- plebiscite
- lycée
- concordat
- Napoleonic Code
- Battle of Trafalgar

2. TAKING NOTES
Create a time line showing events leading to the crowning of Napoleon as emperor of France.

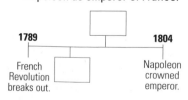

1789 — French Revolution breaks out.
1804 — Napoleon crowned emperor.

Which of these events did Napoleon cause?

3. FORMING AN OPINION
There is an old question: "Do the times make the man, or does the man make the times?" In your opinion, was Napoleon the creator of or the creation of his times?

THINK ABOUT
- the government after the Terror
- Napoleon's defense of France
- Napoleon's popularity

4. ANALYZING THEMES
Power and Authority To keep his empire together, Napoleon had to deal with forces both inside and outside the French Empire. In your judgment, which area was more crucial to control?

THINK ABOUT
- the length of the period of civil unrest in France
- the power and activities of the other European nations

Napoleon's Empire Collapses

TERMS & NAMES
- blockade
- Continental System
- guerrilla
- Peninsular War
- scorched-earth policy
- Waterloo
- Hundred Days

MAIN IDEA	WHY IT MATTERS NOW
Napoleon's conquests aroused nationalistic feelings across Europe and contributed to his downfall.	In the 1990s, nationalistic feelings contributed to the breakup of nations such as Yugoslavia.

SETTING THE STAGE Napoleon worried that his vast empire would fall apart unless he had an heir whose right to succeed him was undisputed, so he decided that he needed a son. Consequently, he divorced Josephine, who had failed to bear him a child, and formed an alliance with the Austrian royal family by marrying Marie Louise, the grand-niece of Marie Antoinette. In 1811, Marie Louise gave birth to a son, Napoleon II, whom his father named king of Rome.

Napoleon's Three Costly Mistakes

Napoleon's own personality proved to be the greatest danger to the future of his empire. "I love power," he once said, "as a musician loves his violin." It was the drive for power that had raised Napoleon to great heights, and the same love of power led to his doom. In his efforts to extend the French Empire and crush Britain, Napoleon made three disastrous misjudgments.

The Continental System In November 1806, Napoleon signed a decree ordering a **blockade**—a forcible closing of ports—to prevent all trade and communication between Great Britain and other European nations. Napoleon called this policy the **Continental System** because it was supposed to make continental Europe more self-sufficient. It was also intended to destroy Britain's commercial and industrial economy.

A STOPPAGE to a STRIDE over the GLOBE

"Little Johnny Bull"—Great Britain—waves a sword at Napoleon as the emperor straddles the globe.

Unfortunately for Napoleon, his blockade was not nearly tight enough. Aided by the British, smugglers managed to bring cargo from Britain into Europe. At times, Napoleon's allies disregarded his order—in fact, Napoleon's own brother Louis, whom Napoleon had made king of Holland, defied the policy. For these reasons, the blockade weakened British trade but did not destroy it.

In addition, Britain responded with its own blockade. The British navy stopped neutral ships bound for the continent and forced them to sail to a British port to be searched and taxed. Because the British had a stronger navy, they were better able than the French to make their blockade work.

Background
England's navy had been the strongest in Europe ever since its defeat of the Spanish Armada in 1588.

American ships were among those stopped by the British navy. Angered, the U.S. Congress declared war on Britain in 1812. The War of 1812 ended in a draw, however, and was only a minor inconvenience to Britain in its struggle with Napoleon.

In effect, the Continental System hurt Napoleon more than it hurt his enemies. It weakened the economies of France and the other lands under Napoleon's control more than it damaged Britain.

The Peninsular War In 1808, Napoleon made a second costly mistake. Because Portugal was ignoring the Continental System, he sent an army through Spain to invade Portugal. When Spanish towns rioted in protest, Napoleon deposed the Spanish king and put his brother Joseph on the throne. This move outraged the Spanish people and enflamed their nationalistic feelings, since they remained fiercely loyal to their former monarch.

The French Revolution and Napoleon **589**

In addition, Spain was a devoutly Catholic nation with a long history of persecuting those who deviated from the faith. Because the French Revolution had weakened the Catholic Church in France, many Spanish Catholics feared that their French conquerors would undermine the church in Spain. In fact, the French did attack church power by outlawing the Spanish Inquisition, which was still prosecuting people accused of heresy.

For five years (1808–1813), bands of Spanish peasant fighters, known as **guerrillas,** struck at French armies in Spain. The guerrillas were not an army that Napoleon could defeat in open battle; they were ordinary people who ambushed French troops and then fled into hiding. The British added to the French troubles in Spain by sending troops to aid the rebels. Napoleon lost about 300,000 men during this **Peninsular War** (so called because Spain lies on the Iberian Peninsula). These losses weakened the French Empire.

In Spain and elsewhere, nationalism, or loyalty to one's own country, was becoming a powerful weapon against Napoleon. People who had at first welcomed the French as their liberators now felt abused by a foreign conqueror. Like the Spanish guerrillas, Germans and Italians and other conquered peoples turned against the French.

The Invasion of Russia In 1812, Napoleon's thirst for power led to his most disastrous mistake of all. Even though Alexander I had become Napoleon's ally, the Russian czar refused to stop selling grain to Britain. In addition, the French and Russian rulers suspected each other of having competing designs on Poland. Because of this breakdown in their alliance, Napoleon decided to invade Russia.

In June 1812, Napoleon and his Grand Army marched into Russia. Many of his troops were not French. They had been drafted from all over Europe, and they felt little loyalty to Napoleon.

As Napoleon's army entered Russia, Alexander pulled back his troops, refusing to be lured into an unequal battle. As the Russians retreated toward Moscow, they practiced a **scorched-earth policy,** burning grain fields and slaughtering livestock so as to leave nothing that the enemy could eat. Desperate soldiers deserted the French army to search for scraps of food.

On September 7, 1812, the two armies finally clashed in the Battle of Borodino. During the morning, the advantage swung back and forth between the Russians and the French. After several more hours of indecisive fighting, the Russians retreated— giving Napoleon a narrow victory that allowed him to take Moscow.

When Napoleon finally entered Moscow on September 14, he soon found it in flames. Rather than surrender Russia's "holy city" to the French, Alexander had set fire to it. Napoleon stayed in the ruined city for five weeks, expecting the czar to make a peace offer, but no offer ever came. By then, it was the middle of October, too late to advance farther and perhaps too late even to retreat.

Grimly, Napoleon ordered his starving army to turn back. As the snows began to fall in early November, Russian raiders mercilessly attacked Napoleon's ragged, retreating army. One French sergeant recorded, "Many of the survivors were walking barefoot, using pieces of wood as canes, but their feet were frozen so hard that the sound they made on the road was like that of wooden clogs."

As the soldiers staggered through the snow, many dropped in their tracks from wounds, exhaustion, hunger, and cold. The temperature fell to about 30 degrees below zero, so cold that birds fell dead from the sky. Finally, in the middle of December, the last survivors straggled out of Russia. Of his Grand Army, Napoleon had only 10,000 soldiers who were left fit to fight.

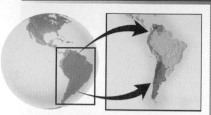

GlobalImpact

Latin American Revolutions

Class conflict had begun in Spain's American colonies long before the Peninsular War. *Peninsulares,* colonists who had been born in Spain, dominated colonial society. Creoles, those born in the colonies themselves, were denied power.

When Napoleon forced the Spanish king to abdicate, Creole leaders in the colonies saw the collapse of the Spanish government as an opportunity to take over colonial governments and gain independence from Spain.

Among the leaders who worked for independence were Simón Bolívar of Venezuela and José de San Martín of Argentina. Both Venezuela and Argentina had to struggle long and hard to defeat the Spanish, but they did prevail.

THINK THROUGH HISTORY
A. Recognizing Effects How could the growing feelings of nationalism in European countries hurt Napoleon?

Background
Napoleon wanted to capture Moscow because it is located near three rivers and thus provides easy access to most of European Russia.

Napoleon's Russian Campaign, 1812

Legend:
- Advancing troops
- Retreating troops
- = 10,000 soldiers
- = 10,000 lost troops

422,000 — June 1812
Napoleon and his troops march across the Neman River and into Russia.

50,000
Napoleon sends troops to Polotsk to protect his left flank.

175,000
Reduced by desertion, disease, starvation, and capture, an army of 175,000 arrives in Smolensk. Another 30,000 die there.

130,000 — Sept. 7, 1812
Napoleon's army fights the Battle of Borodino and suffers 30,000 casualties.

Sept. 14, 1812 Napoleon enters Moscow to find it in ashes, torched by the czar. He waits, hoping to induce the czar to surrender.

Oct. 18, 1812 Frustrated and starving, having waited too long for the czar, the 100,000 survivors of the Grand Army begin their hellish retreat through the cruel Russian winter.

November 1812 — 37,000
The army returns to Smolensk and finds famine. The remaining 24,000 march on, abandoning their wounded.

Dec. 6, 1812 — 28,000
Troops march for the Neman River. Only 10,000 make it out of Russia.

50,000
The 30,000 in Polotsk join the 20,000 survivors. Thousands drown while trying to cross the Berezina River.

Map labels: Western Dvina River, RUSSIA, PRUSSIA, GRAND DUCHY OF WARSAW, Kovno, Vilna, Glubokoye, Polotsk, Vitebsk, Smolensk, Vyazma, Borodino, Moscow, Maloyaroslavets, Moscow R., Oka R., Dnieper R., Berezina River, Neman River, Molodechno, Borisov, Minsk

0 100 Miles
0 200 Kilometers

Source: Chart by Charles Joseph Minard, 1861

SKILLBUILDER: Interpreting Maps and Graphs

1. How many troops did Napoleon start the Russian campaign with? How many survived?
2. Review the graph on the right. Why was Napoleon's decision to stay in Moscow until mid-October a tactical blunder?

Retreat from Russia, 1812

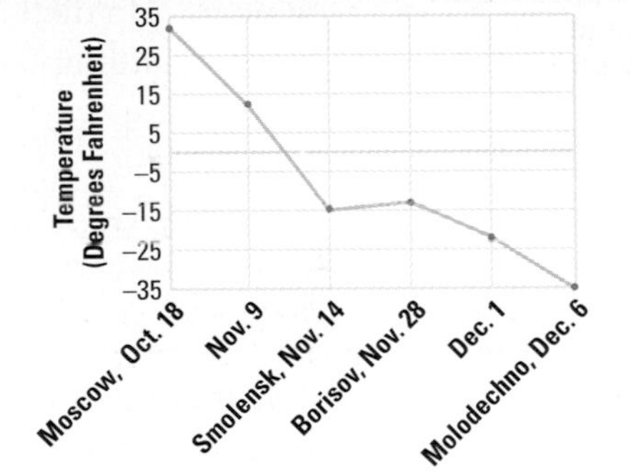

(Graph: Temperature (Degrees Fahrenheit) vs. locations)

Moscow, Oct. 18; Nov. 9; Smolensk, Nov. 14; Borisov, Nov. 28; Dec. 1; Molodechno, Dec. 6

Napoleon's Downfall

Napoleon's enemies were quick to take advantage of his weakness. Britain, Russia, Prussia, and Sweden joined forces against him in the Fourth Coalition. Napoleon had hoped that his marriage to Marie Louise would keep at least Austria on his side, but Austria also joined the coalition. All of the main powers of Europe were now at war with France.

The Coalition Defeats Napoleon In only a few months, Napoleon managed to raise another army. He faced his enemies outside the German city of Leipzig (LYP·sihg) in October 1813. At this crucial point, Napoleon's army no longer consisted of trained veterans. In the Battle of Leipzig, the allies cut his inexperienced army to pieces.

Napoleon's empire crumbled quickly. By January 1814, armies of Austrians, Russians, and Prussians were pushing steadily toward Paris. In March, the Russian czar and the Prussian king led their troops in a triumphant parade through the French capital. Napoleon wanted to fight on, but his generals refused.

In April 1814, the defeated emperor gave up his throne and accepted the terms of surrender drawn up by Alexander I. The victors gave Napoleon a small pension and exiled, or banished, him to Elba, a tiny island off the Italian coast. Although the allies expected no further trouble from Napoleon, they were wrong. Napoleon was a man of action who, at age 45, would find it difficult to retire.

A Comeback Fails As Napoleon arrived on Elba, a Bourbon king arrived in Paris to rule France—Louis XVIII, brother of the guillotined king. (Louis XVI's son and heir had died in prison in 1795.) However, the new king quickly became unpopular among

Background
Royalists had called Louis XVI's son Louis XVII after his father was guillotined.

This portrait by Paul Delaroche, entitled *Napoleon I After His Abdication*, shows Napoleon's depression after he abdicated his throne.

his subjects—especially the peasants, who suspected him of wanting to undo the Revolution's land reforms.

The news that the French king was in trouble was all the incentive Napoleon needed to try to regain power. He escaped from Elba and, on March 1, 1815, landed in France. In a proclamation, he urged the French to rally to his cause. "Victory will march at full speed," he said. "You will be the liberators of your country." Thousands of French people welcomed Napoleon back. The ranks of his army swelled with volunteers as it approached Paris. Within days, Napoleon was again emperor of France. Louis XVIII fled to the border.

In response, the European allies quickly marshaled their armies. The British army, led by the Duke of Wellington, prepared for battle near the village of **Waterloo** in Belgium. On June 18, 1815, Napoleon attacked. The British army defended its ground all day. Late in the afternoon, the Prussian army arrived. Together, the British and the Prussian forces attacked the French. Two days later, Napoleon's exhausted troops gave way, and the British and Prussian forces chased them from the field.

This defeat ended Napoleon's last bid for power, called the **Hundred Days.** Taking no chances this time, the British shipped Napoleon to St. Helena, a remote island in the South Atlantic. There, he lived in lonely exile for six years, writing his memoirs. He died in 1821 of a stomach ailment, perhaps cancer. Shortly before his death, he attempted to justify all he had done during his life:

Background
Napoleon was emperor for 10 years; he was exiled to Elba for 1 year; he ruled again for 100 days; then he was exiled to St. Helena for 6 years.

> **A VOICE FROM THE PAST**
> Such work as mine is not done twice in a century. . . . I have saved the Revolution as it lay dying. I have cleansed it of its crimes, and have held it up to the people shining with fame. I have inspired France and Europe with new ideas that will never be forgotten.
>
> **NAPOLEON,** quoted in *Napoleon at St. Helena*

Without doubt, Napoleon was a military genius and a brilliant administrator. Yet all his victories must be measured against the millions of lives that were lost in his wars. Of his many achievements, only his law code and some of his reforms in France's government proved lasting—and they were not won on the battlefield. A later French statesman and writer, Alexis de Tocqueville, summed up Napoleon's character by saying, "He was as great as a man can be without virtue." Napoleon's defeat opened the door for the freed European countries to establish a new order.

Section 4 Assessment

1. TERMS & NAMES

Identify
- blockade
- Continental System
- guerrilla
- Peninsular War
- scorched-earth policy
- Waterloo
- Hundred Days

2. TAKING NOTES

Create a two-column chart like the one below, listing Napoleon's three disastrous mistakes and the effects that each one had on his empire.

Napoleon's Mistakes	Effect on Empire

Which mistake was most serious? Why?

3. ANALYZING MOTIVES

What were the main reasons people in other European countries resisted Napoleon?

THINK ABOUT
- why some of his own allies refused to abide by the Continental System
- why the Spanish fought a guerrilla war for several years
- why the Russians destroyed their own crops and cities

4. THEME ACTIVITY

Power and Authority Using information from Sections 3 and 4, create a chart, sketch, or drawing to show what positive and negative effects Napoleon's rule had on France. Then judge Napoleon's use of power, showing your judgment in a visual way. Be prepared to defend your opinion.

The Congress of Vienna Convenes

TERMS & NAMES
- **Congress of Vienna**
- **Klemens von Metternich**
- **balance of power**
- **legitimacy**
- **Holy Alliance**
- **Concert of Europe**

MAIN IDEA	WHY IT MATTERS NOW
After exiling Napoleon, European leaders at the Congress of Vienna tried to restore order and reestablish peace.	International bodies such as the United Nations play an active role in trying to maintain world peace and stability today.

SETTING THE STAGE European heads of government were looking to establish long-lasting peace and stability on the continent after the defeat of Napoleon. They had a goal of a new European order—one of collective security and stability for the entire continent. A series of meetings in Vienna, known as the **Congress of Vienna,** were called to set up policies to achieve this goal. Originally, the Congress of Vienna was scheduled to last for four weeks. Instead, it went on for eight months.

Metternich Restores Stability

Most of the decisions made in Vienna during the winter of 1814–1815 were made in secret among representatives of the five "great powers." The rulers of three of these countries—King Frederick William III of Prussia, Czar Alexander I of Russia, and Emperor Francis I of Austria—were themselves in Vienna. Britain and France were represented by their foreign ministers. However, none of these men were as influential as the foreign minister of Austria, Prince **Klemens von Metternich** (MEHT·uhr·nihk).

Metternich distrusted the democratic ideals of the French Revolution. Like most other European aristocrats, he maintained that Napoleon's expansionist dictatorship had been a natural outcome of experiments with democracy. Metternich wanted to keep things as they were and remarked, "The first and greatest concern for the immense majority of every nation is the stability of laws—never their change."

Metternich had three goals at the Congress of Vienna. First, he wanted to prevent future French aggression by surrounding France with strong countries. Second, he wanted to restore a **balance of power,** so that no country would be a threat to others. Third, he wanted to restore Europe's royal families to the thrones they had held before Napoleon's conquests.

The Containment of France The congress made the weaker countries around France stronger:

- The former Austrian Netherlands and Dutch Republic were united to form the Kingdom of the Netherlands.
- A group of 39 German states were loosely joined as the newly created German Confederation, dominated by Austria.
- Switzerland was recognized as an independent nation.
- The Kingdom of Sardinia in Italy was strengthened by the addition of Genoa.

These changes allowed the countries of Europe to contain France and prevent it from overpowering weaker nations. (See the map on page 596.)

HISTORY MAKERS

**Klemens von Metternich
1773–1859**

Klemens von Metternich was a tall, handsome man whose charm worked equally well on his fellow diplomats and on the elegant ladies of Vienna. He spoke five languages fluently and thought of himself as a European, not as a citizen of any single country. "Europe has for a long time held for me the significance of a fatherland," he once said.

Early in his career, Metternich linked himself to the Hapsburgs, the rulers of Austria. In 1809, he became Austria's foreign minister, and he held that office for the next 39 years. Because of his immense influence on European politics, these years are often called the Age of Metternich.

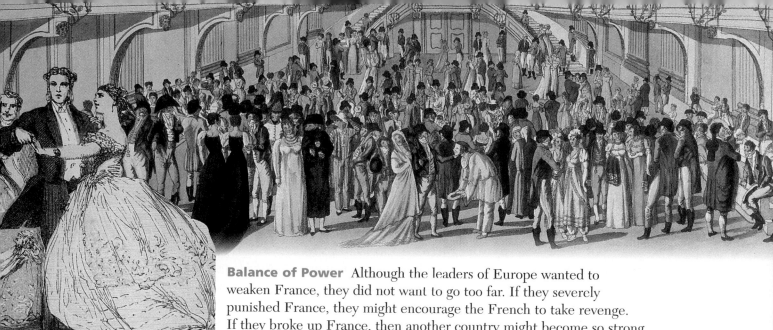

Balance of Power Although the leaders of Europe wanted to weaken France, they did not want to go too far. If they severely punished France, they might encourage the French to take revenge. If they broke up France, then another country might become so strong that it would threaten them all. Thus, the victorious powers were surprisingly easy on the defeated nation. Although the French were required to give up all the territories Napoleon had taken, France remained intact, with roughly the same boundaries it had had in 1790. France also kept some of its overseas possessions, its army, and an independent government. As a result, France remained a major but diminished European power, and no country in Europe could easily overpower another.

During the Congress of Vienna, diplomats exchanged secrets and made deals during the endless rounds of parties. Much of the congress's work was accomplished by means of such "diplomacy through entertainment."

Legitimacy The great powers affirmed the principle of **legitimacy**—agreeing that as many as possible of the rulers whom Napoleon had driven from their thrones should be restored to power. In France, the brother of Louis XVI returned to power as King Louis XVIII. He wisely adopted a constitution and ruled as a constitutional monarch. The congress also restored the Bourbon rulers of Spain and the Kingdom of the Two Sicilies. Hapsburg princes came back to rule several states in northern Italy. Many (though not all) of the former rulers of the German states of central Europe also regained their thrones. The participants in the Congress of Vienna believed that the return of the former monarchs would stabilize political relations among the nations.

The Congress of Vienna was a political triumph in many ways. Because its settlements were fair enough for no country to be left bearing a grudge, it did not sow the seeds of future wars. In that sense, it was more successful than many other peace meetings in history. For the first time, the nations of an entire continent were cooperating to control political affairs. On June 13, 1815, four days after the signing of the document that ended the congress, an observer wrote down his impressions:

A VOICE FROM THE PAST
It is contended that, on the whole, the Congress in its eight months of meetings has performed a tremendous task and never has a congress achieved more meaningful or grander results. . . . The majority of people now are saying: "The minister of foreign affairs [Metternich] has reaped honor from his work, from the conception and execution of the idea of the Congress of Vienna, and from the meeting of the sovereigns in consequence thereof."

CONFIDENTIAL AGENT, quoted in *The Congress of Vienna: An Eyewitness Account*

How lasting was the peace? None of the five great powers waged war on one another until 1853, in the Crimean War. By agreeing to come to one another's aid in case of threats to peace, the European nations had temporarily assured that there would be a balance of power on the continent and that no nation would be able to expand at the expense of others. The Congress of Vienna had created a time of peace in Europe.

Political Changes Beyond Vienna

Background
Conservatives wanted the political situation to return to what it had been before the French Revolution.

The Congress of Vienna was a victory for conservatives. Kings and princes were restored in country after country, in keeping with Metternich's goals. Nevertheless, there were important differences from one country to another. Louis XVIII's decision to rule France as a constitutional monarch meant that both Britain and France now had constitutional monarchies. Generally speaking, however, the governments in eastern Europe were more conservative than these. The rulers of Russia, Prussia, and Austria were absolute monarchs.

Conservative Europe The rulers of Europe were very jittery about the legacy of the French Revolution, especially the threatening revolutionary ideals of liberty, equality, and fraternity. Late in 1815, Czar Alexander, Emperor Francis I of Austria, and King Frederick William III of Prussia entered a league called the **Holy Alliance.** That agreement loosely bound them together. Finally, a series of alliances devised by Metternich, called the **Concert of Europe,** assured that nations would help one another if any revolutions broke out.

Across Europe, conservatives held firm control of the governments, but they could not contain the ideas that had emerged during the French Revolution. France after 1815 was deeply divided politically. Conservatives were happy with the monarchy of Louis XVIII and were determined to make it last. Liberals wanted the king to share more power with the Chamber of Deputies and to grant the middle class the right to vote. Many people in the lower class remained committed to the ideals of liberty, equality, and fraternity even though women and many poor men could not vote. In other countries as well, like Austria, Prussia, and the small German states, there was an explosive mixture of ideas and factions that would contribute directly to revolutions in 1830 and again in 1848.

Despite their efforts to undo the French Revolution, the leaders at the Congress of Vienna could not turn back the clock. The Revolution had given Europe its first experiment in democratic government. Although the experiment had failed, it had set new political ideas in motion. The major political divisions of the early 1800s had their roots in the French Revolution.

> **CONNECT *to* TODAY**
>
> **Congress of Vienna— United Nations**
>
> The work of the Congress of Vienna and the Concert of Europe was intended to keep the world safe from war. The modern equivalent is the United Nations, an international organization established in 1945 and continuing today, whose purpose is to promote world peace.
>
> Like the Congress of Vienna, the United Nations was formed by major powers after a war (World War II). They agreed to cooperate to reduce tensions and bring greater harmony to international relations. Although not always successful, both the Concert of Europe and the United Nations used diplomacy to keep peace.

THINK THROUGH HISTORY
B. Identifying Effects What seeds of democracy had been sown by the French Revolution?

Revolution in Latin America The actions of the Congress of Vienna had consequences beyond Europe. When the congress restored Ferdinand VII to the Spanish throne, the reasons for the Spanish colonial revolts against Napoleon's puppet king, Joseph Bonaparte, should have disappeared. However, clashes among conservatives, liberals, and radicals erupted quickly.

In the colonies, the royalist *peninsulares* wanted to restore their power and control over the land, and the liberal Creoles saw their chance to retain and expand the powers they had seized. Revolts against the king broke out in many parts of Spanish America, with only Mexico remaining loyal to Ferdinand. In 1820, a liberalist revolt in Spain prompted the Spanish king to tighten control over both Spain and its American colonies. This action angered the Mexicans, who rose in revolt and successfully threw off Spain's control. A liberalist revolt in Portugal at about the same time created an opportunity for Brazilians to declare independence as well.

Long-Term Legacy The Congress of Vienna left a legacy that would influence world politics for the next 100 years. The continent-wide efforts to establish and maintain a balance of power diminished the size and the power of France, while the power of Britain and Prussia increased. Nationalism began to grow in Italy, Germany, Greece, and other areas that the congress had put under foreign control. Eventually, the nationalistic feelings would explode into revolutions, and new nations would be

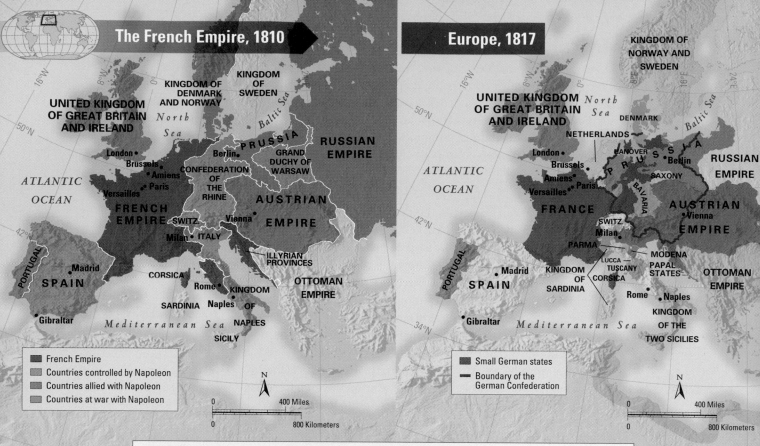

The French Empire, 1810

KINGDOM OF DENMARK AND NORWAY
KINGDOM OF SWEDEN
UNITED KINGDOM OF GREAT BRITAIN AND IRELAND
North Sea
Baltic Sea
PRUSSIA
London
Brussels
Berlin
GRAND DUCHY OF WARSAW
CONFEDERATION OF THE RHINE
Amiens
Paris
Versailles
ATLANTIC OCEAN
FRENCH EMPIRE
SWITZ.
Vienna
AUSTRIAN EMPIRE
RUSSIAN EMPIRE
Milan
ITALY
ILLYRIAN PROVINCES
PORTUGAL
Madrid
CORSICA
Rome
KINGDOM OF NAPLES
OTTOMAN EMPIRE
SPAIN
SARDINIA
Naples
Gibraltar
Mediterranean Sea
SICILY

- French Empire
- Countries controlled by Napoleon
- Countries allied with Napoleon
- Countries at war with Napoleon

0   400 Miles
0   800 Kilometers

Europe, 1817

KINGDOM OF NORWAY AND SWEDEN
UNITED KINGDOM OF GREAT BRITAIN AND IRELAND
North Sea
DENMARK
Baltic Sea
NETHERLANDS
London
Brussels
HANOVER
Berlin
P R U S S I A
Amiens
Paris
SAXONY
Versailles
ATLANTIC OCEAN
FRANCE
BAVARIA
SWITZ.
Milan
Vienna
AUSTRIAN EMPIRE
RUSSIAN EMPIRE
PARMA
PORTUGAL
Madrid
KINGDOM OF SARDINIA
LUCCA
TUSCANY
CORSICA
MODENA
PAPAL STATES
Rome
Naples
OTTOMAN EMPIRE
SPAIN
Gibraltar
Mediterranean Sea
KINGDOM OF THE TWO SICILIES

- Small German states
- Boundary of the German Confederation

0   400 Miles
0   800 Kilometers

GEOGRAPHY SKILLBUILDER: Interpreting Maps
1. **Region** *What parts of Napoleon's French Empire did France lose as a result of the Congress of Vienna agreements?*
2. **Region** *In what sense did the territorial changes of 1815 reflect a restoration of order and balance?*

formed. European colonies also responded to the power shift. Spanish colonies took advantage of the events in Europe to declare their independence and break away from their European rulers.

On the other hand, ideas about the basis of power and authority had changed permanently as a result of the French Revolution. Old ideas about who should control governments were discarded. More and more, the principles of democracy were seen as the best way for equity and justice to prevail for all people. Europeans challenged old economic patterns of taxation and property ownership and began to adopt more equal treatment for all. The French Revolution changed the "business as usual" attitude that had dominated Europe for centuries. A new era had begun.

THINK THROUGH HISTORY
C. Summarizing
How did the French Revolution affect not only Europe but also other areas of the world?

Section 5 Assessment

1. TERMS & NAMES
Identify
- Congress of Vienna
- Klemens von Metternich
- balance of power
- legitimacy
- Holy Alliance
- Concert of Europe

2. TAKING NOTES
Think about the ways in which the three main goals of Metternich's plan at the Congress of Vienna solved a political problem. Fill in the chart below.

Metternich's Plan	
Problem	Solution

What was the overall effect of Metternich's plan on France?

3. EVALUATING
From France's point of view, were the decisions made at the Congress of Vienna fair?

THINK ABOUT
- Metternich's three goals
- France's loss of territory
- the fears of the rest of Europe

4. ANALYZING THEMES
Power and Authority Why do you think liberals and conservatives differed over who should have power?

THINK ABOUT
- Old Regime privileges
- attitudes toward change
- Enlightenment ideas

The French Revolution

Even today, historians have a wide variety of opinions about what caused the French Revolution and whether it was a good thing. The following excerpts, dating from the 1790s to 1859, show a variety of opinions about the Revolution.

SPEECH
Maximilien Robespierre

On February 5, 1794, the revolutionary leader Robespierre delivered a speech justifying the Revolution.

What is the goal for which we strive? A peaceful enjoyment of liberty and equality, the rule of that eternal justice whose laws are engraved, not upon marble or stone, but in the hearts of all men.

We wish an order of things where all low and cruel passions are enchained by the laws, all beneficent and generous feelings aroused; . . . where the citizen is subject to the magistrate, the magistrate to the people, the people to justice; where the nation safeguards the welfare of each individual, and each individual proudly enjoys the prosperity and glory of his fatherland.

LETTER
Thomas Paine

In 1790, Paine—a strong supporter of the American Revolution—defended the French Revolution against its critics.

It is no longer the paltry cause of kings or of this or of that individual, that calls France and her armies into action. It is the great cause of all. It is the establishment of a new era, that shall blot despotism from the earth, and fix, on the lasting principles of peace and citizenship, the great Republic of Man.

The scene that now opens itself to France extends far beyond the boundaries of her own dominions. Every nation is becoming her ally, and every court has become her enemy. It is now the cause of all nations, against the cause of all courts.

LITERATURE
Charles Dickens

In 1859, the English writer Dickens wrote *A Tale of Two Cities*, a novel about the French Revolution for which he did much research. In the following scene, Charles Darnay—an aristocrat who gave up his title because he hated the injustices done to the people—has returned to France and been put on trial.

His judges sat upon the bench in feathered hats; but the rough red cap and tricolored cockade was the headdress otherwise prevailing. Looking at the jury and the turbulent audience, he might have thought that the usual order of things was reversed, and that the felons were trying the honest men. The lowest, cruelest, and worst populace of a city, never without its quantity of low, cruel, and bad, were the directing spirits of the scene. . . .

Charles Evrémonde, called Darnay, was accused by the public prosecutor as an emigrant, whose life was forfeit to the Republic, under the decree which banished all emigrants on pain of Death. It was nothing that the decree bore date since his return to France. There he was, and there was the decree; he had been taken in France, and his head was demanded.

"Take off his head!" cried the audience. "An enemy to the Republic!"

ESSAY
Edmund Burke

A British statesman, Burke was one of the earliest and most severe critics of the French Revolution. In October 1793, he expressed this opinion.

"The Jacobin Revolution is carried on by men of no rank, of no consideration, of wild, savage minds, full of levity, arrogance, and presumption, without morals."

Connect *to* **History**

Summarizing In your own words, summarize the attitude toward the French Revolution expressed in each of these excerpts.

SEE SKILLBUILDER HANDBOOK, PAGE 992.

Connect *to* **Today**

Research Find a modern view of the French Revolution and bring it to class. It may be a historian's analysis or an artistic portrayal, such as a novel or film.

CD-ROM For another perspective on the French Revolution, see World History Electronic Library of Primary Sources.

The French Revolution and Napoleon

Long-Term Causes

- Enlightenment ideas—liberty and equality
- Example furnished by the American Revolution
- Social and economic injustices of the Old Regime

Immediate Causes

- Economic crisis—famine and government debt
- Weak leadership
- Discontent of the Third Estate

Revolution

- Fall of the Bastille
- National Assembly
- Declaration of the Rights of Man and a new constitution

Immediate Effects

- End of the Old Regime
- Execution of monarchs
- War with the First Coalition
- Reign of Terror
- Rise of Napoleon

Long-Term Effects

- Conservative reaction
- Decline in French power
- Spread of Enlightenment ideas
- Growth of nationalism
- Rise of international organizations (Congress of Vienna)
- Revolutions in Latin America

TERMS & NAMES

Briefly explain the importance of each of the following during the French Revolution or the rise and fall of Napoleon's rule.

1. estate
2. Great Fear
3. Declaration of the Rights of Man
4. guillotine
5. Maximilien Robespierre
6. coup d'état
7. Napoleonic Code
8. Continental System
9. Waterloo
10. Congress of Vienna

REVIEW QUESTIONS

SECTION 1 *(pages 573–576)*

Revolution Threatens the French King

11. Why were the members of the Third Estate dissatisfied with their way of life under the Old Regime?
12. Why was the fall of the Bastille important to the French people?

SECTION 2 *(pages 577–583)*

Revolution Brings Reform and Terror

13. Name three political reforms that resulted from the French Revolution.
14. What was the Reign of Terror, and how did it end?

SECTION 3 *(pages 584–588)*

Napoleon Forges an Empire

15. Summarize Napoleon's reforms in France.
16. What steps did Napoleon take to create an empire in Europe?

SECTION 4 *(pages 589–592)*

Napoleon's Empire Collapses

17. What factors led to Napoleon's defeat in Russia?
18. Summarize the reasons that the European allies were able to defeat Napoleon in 1814 and again in 1815.

SECTION 5 *(pages 593–597)*

The Congress of Vienna Convenes

19. What were Metternich's three goals at the Congress of Vienna?
20. How did the Congress of Vienna assure peace in Europe for the next 38 years?

Interact *with* History

On page 572, you looked at a French mob's actions before completely knowing why they occurred. Now that you've read the chapter, reevaluate your decision about joining the mob. Were the mob's actions justified? effective? Would you have advised different actions? Discuss your opinions with a small group.

CRITICAL THINKING

1. CONGRESS OF VIENNA

THEME POWER AND AUTHORITY How did the Congress of Vienna affect power and authority in European countries after Napoleon's defeat? Consider both who held power in the countries and the power of the countries themselves.

2. NAPOLEON'S CAREER

Below is a chart of dates and events in Napoleon's career. Copy the chart on your paper. For each event, draw an arrow up or down to show whether Napoleon gained or lost power because of it.

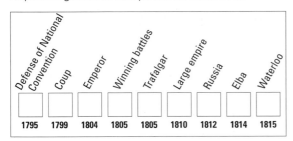

Defense of National Convention	Coup	Emperor	Winning battles	Trafalgar	Large empire	Russia	Elba	Waterloo
1795	1799	1804	1805	1805	1810	1812	1814	1815

3. EFFECTS OF REVOLUTION

There is a saying: "Revolutions devour their own children." What evidence from this chapter supports that statement? Why might revolutions generally be dangerous to their participants?

4. ANALYZING PRIMARY SOURCES

The following quotation from the South American liberator Simón Bolívar shows what he thought would happen if Napoleon came to the New World after his defeat at Waterloo. Read the paragraph and answer the questions below it.

> **A VOICE FROM THE PAST**
> If South America is struck by the thunderbolt of Bonaparte's arrival, misfortune will ever be ours if our country accords him a friendly reception. His thirst for conquest is insatiable [cannot be satisfied]; he has mowed down the flower of European youth . . . in order to carry out his ambitious projects. The same designs will bring him to the New World.

- What was Bolívar's judgment of Napoleon? What words convey it to you?

- Do you agree with Bolívar, or do you think Napoleon had less selfish motives for his actions? Support your opinion with details from the text.

CHAPTER ACTIVITIES

1. LIVING HISTORY: Unit Portfolio Project

THEME REVOLUTION Your unit portfolio project focuses on showing the similarities and differences among revolutions (see page 509). For Chapter 23, you might use one of the following ideas to add to your portfolio:

- Ask classmates to role-play French people from different estates as you interview them about their feelings toward the Revolution. Tape-record your interviews and add a commentary to create an "objective" newscast.
- Draw cartoons that compare and contrast a member of France's Third Estate with an American colonist.
- Write a dialogue between King George III of England and King Louis XVI of France, in which they discuss their problems with rebelling subjects.

2. CONNECT TO TODAY: Cooperative Learning

THEME ECONOMICS One major cause of the French Revolution was the extreme contrast between the lives of the few rich and the many poor in France. Some people feel that the gap between the rich and poor in the United States today is similar.

Work with a team to create a graph showing the distribution of wealth in the United States today.

INTERNET Use the Internet or magazines to research the topic. Look for statistics that answer such questions as, What percentages of the population own various proportions of the country's wealth? What percentage of individuals live at or below the poverty line? How much is the wealthiest person in the United States worth?

- Look for parallel statistics. Figure out how to present them visually. You may use any type of graphic as long as it is labeled clearly.
- Make comparisons between the distribution of wealth in France before the Revolution and the distribution of wealth in the United States today.

3. INTERPRETING A TIME LINE

Revisit the unit time line on pages 508–509. Which three events entered for the period 1780–1815 do you think were most significant? Why?

FOCUS ON GEOGRAPHY

Notice the locations of Britain and France in this map.

- How far away from France is Britain?
- What geographical barrier protected Britain from becoming part of Napoleon's empire?

Connect to History What would Napoleon have needed to do to overcome that geographical barrier? Did he? What happened?

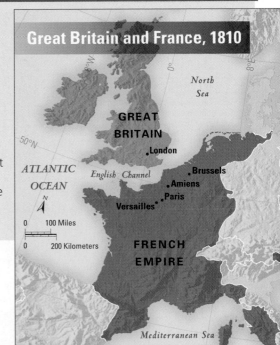

Great Britain and France, 1810

North Sea

GREAT BRITAIN

London

ATLANTIC OCEAN

English Channel

Brussels

Amiens

Paris

Versailles

FRENCH EMPIRE

Mediterranean Sea

50°N

0 100 Miles

0 200 Kilometers

Nationalist Revolutions Sweep the West 1789–1900

PREVIEWING THEMES

Revolution

The 19th century was a time of revolutions around the Western world, as people under foreign rule established their own nation-states. The 1800s were also a time of revolutionary changes in literature, music, and art.

Power and Authority

In country after country, governments controlled by aristocrats came crashing down. In their place, revolutionaries set up republics and nation-states. With mixed success at first, members of the middle class increased their influence in government.

Cultural Interaction

The ideas of nationalism and democracy swept out over Europe from France, finally reaching across the Atlantic to the Americas. Likewise, the ideas of the Romantic movement and later the Realist movement revolutionized art, music, and literature.

INTERNET CONNECTION

Visit us at **www.mcdougallittell.com** to learn more about nationalism, romanticism, realism, and related topics.

REGIONS OF NATIONALIST REVOLUTIONS 1789–1900

Central and South America

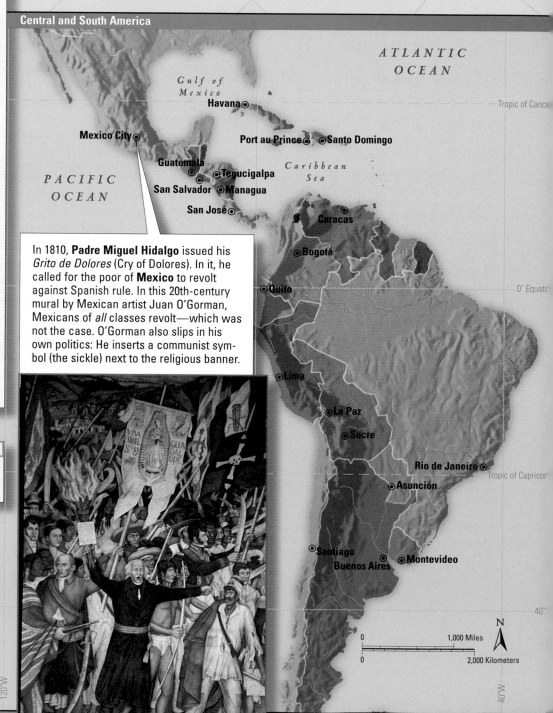

In 1810, **Padre Miguel Hidalgo** issued his *Grito de Dolores* (Cry of Dolores). In it, he called for the poor of **Mexico** to revolt against Spanish rule. In this 20th-century mural by Mexican artist Juan O'Gorman, Mexicans of *all* classes revolt—which was not the case. O'Gorman also slips in his own politics: He inserts a communist symbol (the sickle) next to the religious banner.

ATLANTIC OCEAN

Gulf of Mexico

Tropic of Cancer

Havana

Mexico City

Port au Prince   Santo Domingo

Guatemala
Tegucigalpa
San Salvador   Managua

PACIFIC OCEAN

Caribbean Sea

San José

Caracas

Bogotá

Quito   0° Equator

Lima

La Paz

Sucre

Rio de Janeiro   Tropic of Capricorn

Asunción

Santiago   Montevideo
Buenos Aires

40°

0   1,000 Miles

0   2,000 Kilometers

N

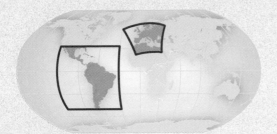

In **November 1860**, colorful Italian revolutionary **Giuseppe Garibaldi** met on a bridge in **Naples** with **Victor Emmanuel**, the king of Piedmont-Sardinia. To assure Italy's unity, Garibaldi made a grand gesture. During the Naples meeting, he handed over his southern conquests to Victor Emmanuel. By Garibaldi's generous act, north and south were joined. The Kingdom of Italy was born. This 19th-century fresco recalls the event.

In 1806, **Napoleon** began construction of the **Arc de Triomphe** in **Paris**. It was not completed until 1836—15 years after the emperor died. The heroic sculptures celebrate the victories of Napoleon's armies. Even today, the Arc de Triomphe is the largest triumphal arch in the world. It is also one of the symbols of France's capital city.

601

Y ou are an artist in a nation that has just freed itself from foreign rule. The new government is asking you to design a symbol that will show what your country stands for. It's up to you to design the symbol that best suits the spirit of your people. Will your symbol be peaceful or warlike, dignified or joyful? Or will it be a combination of these and other qualities?

UNITED STATES

The olive branch and arrows symbolize a desire for peace but a readiness for war. The Latin phrase *E pluribus unum* means "Out of many, one," expressing unity in diversity.

Your country is free. What kind of national symbol will you design?

AUSTRIA

The hammer and sickle symbolize agriculture and industry. The broken chains celebrate Austria's liberation from Germany at the end of World War II.

BOTSWANA

Industry and livestock are connected by water, the key to the country's prosperity. *Pula* in the Setswana language means "rain," "water," "wealth."

PERU

The country's wealth is shown by the vicuña (with its silky fur), the quinine tree (which helps to cure malaria), and a horn of plenty.

URUGUAY

The shield features symbols of justice, strength, freedom, and prosperity.

EXAMINING *the* ISSUES

- **What values and goals of your new country do you want to show?**

- **What symbol will you use?**

- **Will your symbol represent your country's past or future? Its land? Its goals?**

- **Will your design have words that also express values?**

As a class, discuss these questions. During the discussion, think of the role played by symbols in expressing a country's view of itself and the world.

As you read about the rise of new nations in Latin America and Europe, think of how artists encourage national pride.

Latin American Peoples Win Independence

TERMS & NAMES
• *peninsulares*
• creoles
• mulattos
• Simón Bolívar
• José de San Martín
• Miguel Hidalgo
• José Morelos

MAIN IDEA

Spurred by discontent and Enlightenment ideas, peoples in Latin America fought colonial rule.

WHY IT MATTERS NOW

Sixteen of today's Latin American nations gained their independence at this time.

SETTING THE STAGE By the late 1700s, the Americas, already troubled by Enlightenment ideas, were electrified by the news of the French Revolution. The French ideals of liberty, equality, and fraternity inspired many Latin Americans to rise up against their French, Spanish, and Portuguese masters.

Revolution in Haiti

The French colony called Saint Domingue was the first Latin American territory to free itself from European rule. Saint Domingue, now known as Haiti, occupied the western third of the island of Hispaniola in the Caribbean Sea.

Background
About 35,000 Europeans stood at the top of the social ladder in Haiti in the late 1700s. They were mainly French.

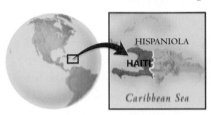

Nearly 500,000 enslaved Africans—the vast majority of Saint Domingue's population—lived at the bottom of the social system. Most slaves worked on plantations, and they outnumbered their masters dramatically. White masters thus used brutal methods to terrorize slaves and keep them powerless.

The Fight for Freedom The slaves soon showed that, in fact, they were not powerless. In August 1791, an African priest named Boukman raised a call for revolution. Within a few days, 100,000 slaves rose in revolt. A leader soon emerged, Toussaint L'Ouverture (too·SAN loo·vair·TOOR), an ex-slave. Toussaint was untrained in the military and in diplomacy. Even so, he rose to become a skilled general and diplomat. It is said that he got the name L'Ouverture ("opening" in French) because he was so skilled at finding openings in the enemy lines. By 1801, Toussaint had moved into Spanish Santo Domingo (the eastern two-thirds of Hispaniola). He took control of the territory and freed the slaves.

In January 1802, 16,000 French troops landed in Saint Domingue to depose Toussaint. In May, Toussaint agreed to halt the revolution if the French would end slavery. Despite the agreement, the French soon accused him of planning another uprising. They seized him and sent him to a prison in the French Alps. In that cold mountain jail, he died 10 months later, in April 1803.

Haiti's Independence Toussaint's general, Jean-Jacques Dessalines (zhahn·ZHAHK day·sah·LEEN), took up the fight for freedom where Toussaint had left off. On January 1, 1804, General Dessalines declared the colony an independent country. It was the first black colony to free itself from European control. He called the country Haiti, which meant "mountainous land" in the language of the native Arawak inhabitants of the island.

Background
By 1600, almost the entire Arawak population had disappeared because of European conquest, warfare, disease, or slavery.

This statue, called *The Unknown Maroon of Saint Domingue,* stands in front of Haiti's National Palace. *Maroon* was a name for runaway slaves. Using a shell as a trumpet, the maroon is sounding the call to freedom.

Latin America Sweeps to Freedom

Latin American colonial society was sharply divided into classes based on birth. At the top of Spanish American society were the ***peninsulares*** (peh·neen·soo·LAH·rehs), men who had been born in Spain. Only peninsulares could hold high office in Spanish colonial government. In this way, Spain kept the loyalty of its colonial leaders. **Creoles**, Spaniards born in Latin America, ranked after the *peninsulares.* Creoles could not hold high-level political office. But they could rise as officers in Spanish colonial armies. Together these two minority groups controlled wealth and power in the Spanish colonies.

Below the *peninsulares* and creoles came the mestizos (persons of mixed European and Indian ancestry) Next were the **mulattos** (persons of mixed European and African ancestry) and Africans. At the bottom of the social ladder stood Indians. Unlike enslaved Africans, Indians were of little economic value to the Spaniards. As a result, they were more severely oppressed than any other group.

This 18th-century painting shows a lower-class mestizo family in Mexico. Like many of the poor, this is a family of vendors. They are setting up their stand for market day.

Background
The *peninsulares* got their name because they came from the Iberian Peninsula, where Spain is located.

THINK THROUGH HISTORY
A. Recognizing Effects How might creole officers serving in colonial armies become a threat to Spanish rule?

Creoles Spearhead Independence Even though they could not hold high public office, creoles were the least oppressed of those born in Latin America. They were also the best educated. In fact, many wealthy young creoles traveled to Europe for their education. In Europe, they read about and adopted Enlightenment ideas. When they returned to Latin America, they brought ideas of revolution with them.

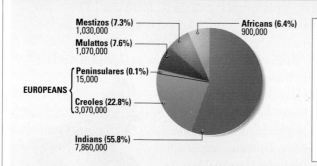

The Divisions in Spanish Colonial Society in 1789

Mestizos (7.3%) 1,030,000
Africans (6.4%) 900,000
Mulattos (7.6%) 1,070,000
Peninsulares (0.1%) 15,000
EUROPEANS
Creoles (22.8%) 3,070,000
Indians (55.8%) 7,860,000

SKILLBUILDER: Interpreting Charts

1. *Which two groups made up the vast majority of the population in Spanish America?*
2. *Looking at the chart, what was one possible reason that creoles felt resentful of the privileges of the* peninsulares*?*

Creoles not only held revolutionary ideas. They also felt that Spain had inflicted serious injustices on them. A creole aristocrat wrote this complaint to the king of Spain:

A VOICE FROM THE PAST

[T]he Viceroys here and their retainers . . . mock, humiliate and oppress us. . . . The more distinguished the unhappy Americans are, the more they suffer. . . . Their honor and reputations are attacked, insulting them by depriving them of any honorific office of consequence.

MARQUÉS DE SAN JORGE, quoted in *Americas: The Changing Face of Latin America and the Caribbean*

Background
Of the 170 Spanish viceroys (colonial governors) between 1492 and 1810, 166 were *peninsulares;* only four were creoles.

Spanish royal officials suppressed actions and ideas that might fuel creole discontent. For example, Colombian patriot Antonio Nariño published a translation of the French *Declaration of the Rights of Man.* He was quickly sentenced to exile in Africa.

Events in Europe Trigger Latin American Revolutions Napoleon's conquest of Spain in 1808 finally triggered revolts in the Spanish colonies. After he had removed Spain's King Ferdinand VII, Napoleon made his brother Joseph king of Spain. Many creoles might have supported a Spanish king. However, they felt no loyalty to a king imposed by the French. Creoles argued that when the real king was removed, power shifted to the people.

In 1810, rebellion broke out in several parts of Latin America. In 1814, with the defeat of Napoleon, King Ferdinand VII returned to Spain. But the creoles had already begun their drive for independence. And they would continue until victory.

THINK THROUGH HISTORY
B. Summarizing
What factors caused the revolutions in Spanish America?

The *Libertadores* End Spanish Rule

The South American wars of independence produced two brilliant generals. Their leadership largely achieved victory for the rebels. One was **Simón Bolívar** (see·MAWN boh·LEE·vahr), a wealthy Venezuelan creole. Called *Libertador* (Liberator), Bolívar was at the same time romantic and practical, a writer and a fighter.

The other great liberator was **José de San Martín** (hoh·SAY day san mahr·TEEN). Unlike the dashing Bolívar, San Martín was a simple, modest man. But he too displayed great courage in battle. Though born in Argentina, he spent much of his youth in Spain as a career military officer. San Martín believed in strict military discipline. However, he also showed concern for the well-being of his troops.

Bolívar's Route to Victory Simón Bolívar's native Venezuela declared its independence from Spain in 1811. But the struggle for independence had only begun. Bolívar's volunteer army of revolutionaries suffered numerous defeats. Twice he had to go into exile. A turning point came in August 1819. Bolívar led over 2,000 soldiers on a daring march through the Andes into what is now Colombia. (See the 1830 map on page 608.) Coming from this direction, Bolívar took the Spanish army in Bogotá completely by surprise. There he won a decisive victory.

By 1821, Bolívar had won Venezuela's independence. He then marched south into Ecuador. In Ecuador, Bolívar would finally meet with José de San Martín. Together they would decide the future of the Latin American revolutionary movement.

Educated in Spain from the age of six, José de San Martín returned to Latin America as a man in his early 30s. Fighting for 10 years, he became the liberator of Argentina, Chile, and Peru.

San Martín Triumphs and Withdraws San Martín's Argentina had declared its independence in 1816. However, Spanish forces in nearby Chile and Peru still posed a threat. In 1817, San Martín led his army on a grueling march across the Andes to Chile. He was joined there by forces led by Bernardo O'Higgins, son of a former viceroy of Peru. With O'Higgins's help, San Martín finally freed Chile.

Next, in 1821 San Martín took his army north by sea to Lima, Peru. His plan was to drive out the remaining Spanish forces there. However, he needed a much larger force to accomplish this. This was the problem that faced both San Martín and Bolívar as they met at Guayaquil, Ecuador, in 1822.

No one knows how the two men reached an agreement. But San Martín left his army for Bolívar to command. Soon after, San Martín sailed for Europe. He died, almost forgotten, on French soil in 1850.

With unified revolutionary forces, Bolívar's army went on to defeat the Spanish at the Battle of Ayacucho (Peru) on December 9, 1824. In this last major battle of the war for independence, the Spanish colonies in Latin America won their freedom.

Cavour Looks South As Cavour was uniting the north of Italy, he began to consider the possibility of controlling the south. He secretly started helping nationalist rebels in southern Italy. In May 1860, a small army of Italian nationalists led by a bold and romantic soldier, **Giuseppe Garibaldi** (GAR·uh·BAWL·dee), captured Sicily. In battle, Garibaldi always wore a bright red shirt, as did his followers. As a result, they became known as the **Red Shirts.**

From Sicily, Garibaldi crossed to the Italian mainland and marched north. Volunteers flocked to his banner. In an election, voters gave Garibaldi permission to unite the southern areas he conquered with the Kingdom of Piedmont-Sardinia. Cavour arranged for King Victor Emmanuel II to meet Garibaldi in Naples. "The Red One" willingly agreed to step aside and let the Sardinian king rule.

Challenges After Unification In 1866, the Austrian province of Venetia, which included the city of Venice, became part of Italy. In 1870, Italian forces took over the last part of a territory known as the Papal States. The Roman Catholic popes had governed the territory as both its spiritual and earthly rulers. With this victory, the city of Rome came under Italian control. Soon after, Rome became the capital of the united Kingdom of Italy. The pope, however, would continue to govern a section of Rome known as Vatican City.

Despite unification, Italy suffered from many unsolved problems. Centuries of separation had bred fierce rivalries among the different Italian provinces. The greatest tension arose between the industrialized north and the agricultural south. The people of these two regions had very different ways of life, and they scarcely understood each other's versions of the Italian language. In the Italian parliament, disorganized parties with vague policies constantly squabbled. As a result, prime ministers and cabinets changed frequently.

In addition to its political instability, Italy also faced severe economic problems. Bloody peasant revolts broke out in the south. At the same time, strikes and riots troubled the northern cities. Meanwhile, the Italian government could not deal with the country's economic problems. As a result, Italy entered the 20th century as a poor country.

THINK THROUGH HISTORY
B. Analyzing Causes Besides their old rivalries, what is another reason why the Italian provinces might have a hard time cooperating?

HISTORY MAKERS

Giuseppe Garibaldi
1807–1882

Giuseppe Garibaldi might have been a character out of a romantic novel. Fisherman, trader, naval commander, guerrilla fighter, poet, rancher, teacher, idealistic revolutionary in Europe and South America— Garibaldi captured the imagination of Europe. The red shirts of his soldiers helped spread his fame, but they started out simply as the cheapest way to clothe his soldiers.

The independence of Italy was Garibaldi's great dream. The French writer Alexandre Dumas wrote of him: "Once mention the word independence, or that of Italy, and he becomes a volcano in eruption."

Garibaldi's bravery attracted the attention of U.S. President Abraham Lincoln. In 1861, Lincoln offered him a command in the Civil War. Garibaldi declined for two reasons: he felt Lincoln did not condemn slavery strongly enough, and he told Lincoln that he wanted to command the entire Union Army!

CASE STUDY: Germany

The Rise of Prussia

Like Italy, Germany also achieved national unity in the mid-1800s. Since 1815, 39 German states had formed a loose grouping called the German Confederation. The two largest states, the Austro-Hungarian Empire and Prussia, dominated the confederation.

Prussia enjoyed several advantages that would eventually help it forge a strong German state. First of all, unlike the Austro-Hungarian Empire, Prussia had a mainly German population. As a result, nationalism actually unified Prussia, while ethnic groups in Austria-Hungary tore it apart. Moreover, Prussia's army was by far the most powerful in central Europe. Finally, Prussia industrialized more quickly than other German states.

Prussia Leads German Unification Like many other European powers, Prussia experienced the disorder of the revolutions of 1848. In that year, Berlin rioters forced the frightened and unstable Prussian king, Frederick William IV, to call a constitutional convention. The convention then drew up a liberal constitution for the kingdom.

In 1861, Wilhelm I succeeded Frederick William to the throne. The strong-minded Wilhelm first moved to reform the army and double the already powerful Prussian military. However, his liberal parliament refused him the money for his reforms.

Wilhelm saw the parliament's refusal as a major challenge to his authority. He was supported in his view by the Junkers (YUNG-kuhrz), members of Prussia's wealthy landowning class. The Junkers were strongly conservative and opposed liberal ideas. For that reason, Wilhelm drew all his ministers and army officers from the Junker class. In 1862, to help solve his problem with parliament, Wilhelm chose a conservative Junker named **Otto von Bismarck** as his prime minister. Bismarck was a master of what came to be known as **realpolitik.** This German term means "the politics of reality." The word described tough power politics with no room for idealism. With realpolitik as his style, Bismarck would become one of the commanding figures of German history.

Unable to persuade parliament to grant Wilhelm's desires, Bismarck took a dramatic step. With the king's approval, he declared that he would rule without the consent of parliament and without a legal budget. Those actions were in direct violation of the constitution. In his first speech as prime minister, he defiantly told members of the Prussian parliament, "The great questions of the day will not be settled by speeches or by majority decisions—that was the great mistake of 1848 and 1849—but by blood and iron."

THINK THROUGH HISTORY
C. Drawing Conclusions
Bismarck succeeded in ignoring both the parliament and constitution of Prussia. How do you think his success would affect Prussian government?

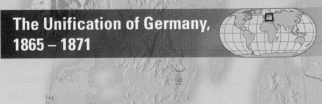

The Unification of Germany, 1865 – 1871

GEOGRAPHY SKILLBUILDER: Interpreting Maps

1. **Location** What was unusual about the territory of Prussia as it existed in 1865?
2. **Regions** After 1865, what year saw the biggest expansion of Prussian territory?

Germany Expands Though he was devoted to country and king, Bismarck was also ambitious. One contemporary described him as a man "who is striving after supreme power, including military power." By working to expand Prussia, he could satisfy both his patriotism and his desire for power. In 1864, Bismarck took the first step toward molding an empire. He formed an alliance between Prussia and Austria. They then went to war against Denmark to win two border provinces, Schleswig and Holstein.

A quick victory increased national pride among Prussians. It also won new respect from other Germans and lent support for Prussia as head of a unified Germany. After the victory, Prussia governed Schleswig, while Austria controlled Holstein. Bismarck suspected that this arrangement would soon lead to friction between the two powers. And such tensions would suit his plans perfectly.

Bismarck Eliminates Austria To disable his powerful rival, Bismarck purposely stirred up border conflicts with Austria over Schleswig and Holstein. The tensions provoked Austria into declaring war on Prussia in 1866. This conflict became known as the Seven Weeks' War. As the name suggests, the war was over quickly. The Prussians used their superior training and equipment to win a smashing victory. They humiliated Austria. The Austrians lost the region of Venetia, which was given to Italy. They also had to accept Prussian annexation of yet more German territory.

With its victory in the Seven Weeks' War, Prussia took control of northern Germany. For the first time, the eastern and western parts of the Prussian kingdom were joined. In 1867, the remaining states of the north joined a North German Confederation, which Prussia dominated completely.

Background
Many Germans looked on Austria as their natural leader. Vienna had been capital of the Holy Roman Empire and was a center of German music, art, and literature.

**Otto von Bismarck
1815–1898**

Germans have still not decided how to judge Otto von Bismarck. To some Germans, he was the greatest and noblest of Germany's statesmen. They say he almost single-handedly unified the nation and raised it to greatness. To others, he was a devious politician who abused his powers and led Germany into dictatorship.

Bismarck's complex personality has also fascinated historians. By 1895, 650 books had already been written about his life. His speeches, letters, and his memoirs do not help to simplify him. They show him to be both cunning and deeply religious. At one moment, he could declare "It is the destiny of the weak to be devoured by the strong." At another moment he could claim "We Germans shall never wage aggressive war, ambitious war, a war of conquest."

The Franco-Prussian War By 1867, a few southern German states remained independent of Prussia. The majority of southern Germans were Catholics. So, many in the region resisted domination by a Protestant Prussia. However, Bismarck felt he could win the support of southerners if they faced a threat from outside. He reasoned that a war with France would rally the south.

Bismarck was an expert at manufacturing "incidents" to gain his ends. And he was successful with France. He published an altered version of a diplomatic telegram he had received. The telegram gave a false description of a meeting between Wilhelm I and the French ambassador. In the description, Wilhelm seemed to insult the French. Reacting to the insult, France declared war on Prussia on July 19, 1870.

At once, the Prussian army poured into northern France. In September 1870, the Prussian army surrounded the main French force at Sedan. Among the 80,000 French prisoners taken was Napoleon III himself—a beaten and broken man. Only Paris held out against the Germans. For four months, Parisians withstood a German siege. Finally, hunger forced them to surrender.

The Franco-Prussian War was the final stage in German unification. Now the nationalistic fever also seized people in southern Germany. They finally accepted Prussian leadership.

On January 18, 1871, at the captured French palace of Versailles, King Wilhelm I of Prussia was crowned **kaiser** (KY·zuhr), or emperor. Germans called their empire the Second Reich. (The Holy Roman Empire was the first.) Bismarck had achieved Prussian dominance over Germany and Europe "by blood and iron," as he had set out to do.

Background
Food became so scarce during the siege of Paris that people ate sawdust, leather, and rats. Parisians even slaughtered animals in the zoo for food.

The Balance of Power Shifts

The 1815 Congress of Vienna established five Great Powers in Europe—Britain, France, Austria, Prussia, and Russia. The wars of the mid-1800s greatly strengthened one of the Great Powers, as Prussia became Germany. In 1815, the Great Powers were nearly equal in strength. By 1871, however, Britain and Germany were clearly the most powerful—both militarily and economically. Austria, Russia, and Italy lagged far behind. France struggled along somewhere in the middle. The European balance of power had broken down. This shift also found expression in the art of the period. In fact, during that century, artists, composers, and writers pointed to paths that European society should follow.

Section 3 Assessment

1. TERMS & NAMES
Identify
- Camillo di Cavour
- Giuseppe Garibaldi
- Red Shirts
- Otto von Bismarck
- realpolitik
- kaiser

2. TAKING NOTES
On your own paper, make a time line like the one below. On it, show the development of independent nation-states in Europe.

Congress of
Vienna 1815

1800 1820 1840 1860 1880 1900

3. ANALYZING ISSUES
Look at the quotation from Bismarck's "blood and iron" speech (page 617). How would you say his approach to settling political issues differed from the approach of liberals?

THINK ABOUT
- the goals of liberals
- the meaning of the phrase "blood and iron"
- Bismarck's goals and how he attained them

4. ANALYZING THEMES
Revolution How might Cavour and Garibaldi have criticized each other as contributors to Italian unity?

THINK ABOUT
- the personalities of the two men
- methods used by Cavour and Garibaldi to win Italian unity

Revolutions in the Arts

MAIN IDEA	WHY IT MATTERS NOW
Artistic and intellectual movements both reflected and fueled changes in Europe during the 1800s.	Romanticism and realism continue to dominate the novels, dramas, and films produced today.

SETTING THE STAGE European countries passed through severe political troubles during the 1800s. At the same time, two separate artistic and intellectual movements divided the century in half. Thinkers and artists focused on ideas of freedom, the rights of individuals, and an idealistic view of history during the first half of the century. After the great revolutions of 1848, political focus shifted to men who practiced realpolitik. Similarly, intellectuals and artists expressed a "realistic" view of the world. In their view of the world, the rich pursued their selfish interests while ordinary people struggled and suffered.

The Romantic Movement

At the beginning of the 19th century, the Enlightenment idea of reason gradually gave way to another major movement: romanticism. **Romanticism** was a movement in art and ideas. It showed deep interest both in nature and in the thoughts and feelings of the individual. In many ways, romantic thinkers and writers reacted against the ideals of the Enlightenment. Romantics rejected the rigidly ordered world of the middle-class. They turned from reason to emotion, from society to nature. Nationalism also fired the romantic imagination. For example, a fighter for freedom in Greece, Lord Byron also ranked as one of the leading romantic poets of the time.

The Ideas of Romanticism Emotion, sometimes wild emotion, was a key element of romanticism. Nevertheless, romanticism went beyond feelings. Romantics expressed a wide range of ideas and attitudes. In general, romantic thinkers and artists

- emphasized inner feelings, emotions, imagination
- focused on the mysterious and the supernatural; also, on the odd, exotic, and grotesque or horrifying
- loved the beauties of untamed nature
- idealized the past as a simpler and nobler time
- glorified heroes and heroic actions
- cherished folk traditions, music, and stories
- valued the common people and the individual
- promoted radical change and democracy

Not all romantics gave the same emphasis to these features. The brothers Jakob and Wilhelm Grimm, for example, concentrated on history and the sense of national pride it fostered. During the first half of the 19th century, they collected German fairy tales. They also created a dictionary and grammar of the German language. Both the tales and the dictionary of the Grimm brothers celebrated the spirit of

THINK THROUGH HISTORY
A. Analyzing Causes
Which ideas of romanticism would encourage nationalism?

Background
The Grimm brothers also collected tales from other countries: England, Scotland, Ireland, Spain, the Netherlands, Scandinavia, and Serbia.

Though created in the early 20th century, this watercolor of British artist Arthur Rackham is full of romantic fantasy. It illustrates the tale "The Old Woman in the Wood" by Jakob and Wilhelm Grimm.

being German. And they celebrated the German spirit long before Germans had united into a single country.

Other writers and artists focused on strong individuals. They glorified real or mythical rebels and leaders, such as Napoleon or the legendary King Arthur. Still others celebrated the beauty and mystery of unspoiled nature. For example, one of France's leading romantic novelists, Amandine Aurore Dupin (better known as George Sand), lovingly described the French countryside and country life. British writer Emily Brontë set her powerful romantic novel, *Wuthering Heights*, in the windswept moors of northern England. The British poet William Blake believed he could "see a World in a Grain of Sand/And a Heaven in a Wild Flower." In painting, English romantic artist Joseph Turner captured the raging of the sea. Another English artist, John Constable, celebrated the peaceful English countryside. Whatever their particular emphasis, romantic writers and artists affected all the arts.

Background
Dupin used the pen name George Sand because she knew that critics would not take a woman writer seriously.

Romanticism in Literature Germany produced one of the earliest and greatest romantic writers. In 1774, Johann Wolfgang von Goethe (YO·hahn VUHLF·gahng fuhn GER·tuh) published *The Sorrows of Young Werther.* Goethe's novel told of a sensitive young man whose hopeless love for a virtuous married woman drives him to suicide.

Victor Hugo led the French romantics. Hugo's huge output of poems, plays, and novels expressed romanticism's revolutionary spirit. His works also reflect the romantic fascination with history and support for the individual. His novels *Les Misérables* and *The Hunchback of Notre Dame* both show the struggles of individuals against a hostile society.

Background
Victor Hugo championed the cause of freedom in France. When Napoleon III overthrew the Second Republic, Hugo left France in protest.

The British romantic poets William Wordsworth and Samuel Taylor Coleridge both honored nature as the source of truth and beauty. To Wordsworth, nature was richly alive. Coleridge, on the other hand, put the accent on horror and the supernatural in his poem "The Rime of the Ancient Mariner." Later English romantic poets, such as Byron, Shelley, and Keats, wrote poems celebrating rebellious heroes, passionate love, and the mystery and beauty of nature. Like many romantics, many of these British poets lived stormy lives and died young. Byron, for example, died at the age of 36, while Shelley died at 29.

SPOTLIGHT ON

Frankenstein

In *Frankenstein,* a rational scientist, Dr. Frankenstein, oversteps the limits of humanity by creating life itself. Since his goal is unnatural, he succeeds only in creating a physical monster who cannot live with humans because of his ugliness.

In addition to Gothic horror, the novel embodies a number of major romantic themes. Mary Shelley warns of the danger of humans meddling with nature. Also, despite his horrible appearance, the creature is sensitive and gentle. Like many romantics of Shelley's day, the creature feels lost in an unsympathetic and alien world. Finally, his solitude drives him to madness.

The story of Frankenstein, originally published in 1818, still enjoys an enormous readership. The book has inspired many films—some serious, such as *Frankenstein* with actor Boris Karloff, and some satirical, such as producer Mel Brooks's *Young Frankenstein.*

The Gothic Novel The Gothic horror story was a form that became hugely popular. These novels often took place in medieval Gothic castles. They were also filled with fearful, violent, sometimes supernatural events. Mary Shelley, wife of the poet Percy Shelley, wrote one of the earliest and most successful Gothic horror novels, *Frankenstein.* The novel told the story of a monster created from the body parts of dead human beings. The following passage shows Mary Shelley's romantic imagination at work. She describes how the idea for the monster took shape. After an evening telling ghost stories with her husband and Lord Byron, the following vision appeared to her:

A VOICE FROM THE PAST

Night waned upon this talk, and even the witching hour had gone by, before we retired to rest. When I placed my head on my pillow, I did not sleep, nor could I be said to think. My imagination, unbidden, possessed and guided me. . . . I saw—with shut eyes, but acute mental vision—I saw the pale student of [unholy] arts kneeling beside the thing he had put together. I saw the hideous phantasm of a man stretched out, and then, on the working of some powerful engine, show signs of life, and stir with an uneasy, half-vital motion.

MARY SHELLEY, Introduction to *Frankenstein*

THINK THROUGH HISTORY
B. Summarizing
What are some of the feelings that are key to romantic literature and art?

Romantic Composers Emphasize Emotion Emotion dominated the music produced by romantic composers. Romantic composers moved away from the tightly controlled, formal compositions of the Enlightenment period. Instead, they celebrated heroism and villainy, tragedy and joy, with a new power of expression.

One of romanticism's first composers rose to become its greatest: Ludwig van Beethoven (LOOD·vihg vahn BAY·toh·vuhn). In his early years, Beethoven wrote the classical music of the Enlightenment. But in later years, he turned to romantic compositions. His Ninth Symphony soars, celebrating freedom, dignity, and triumph.

While they never matched Beethoven's greatness, later romantic composers also appealed to the hearts and souls of their listeners. Robert Schumann's compositions sparkle with merriment. Like many romantic composers, Felix Mendelssohn drew on literature, such as Shakespeare's *A Midsummer Night's Dream*, as the inspiration for his music. Polish composer and concert pianist Frederic Chopin (SHOH·pan) was popular both with other musicians and with the public. Chopin's compositions, such as his first and second piano concertos, contain melodies that are still familiar today.

Romanticism made music a popular art form. As music became part of middle-class life, musicians and composers became popular heroes of romanticism. Composer and pianist Franz Liszt (lihst), for example, achieved earnings and popularity equal to that of today's rock stars.

The Shift to Realism

By the middle of the 19th century, rapid industrialization had a deep effect on everyday life in Europe. And this change began to make the dreams of the romantics seem pointless. In literature and the visual arts, **realism** tried to show life as it is, not as it should be. Realist painting reflected the increasing political importance of the working class in the 1850s. The growing class of industrial workers lived grim lives in dirty, crowded cities. Along with paintings, novels proved especially suited to describing workers' suffering. The interest in science and the scientific method during this period encouraged this "realistic" approach to art and literature. Science operated through objective observation and the reporting of facts. That new invention, the camera, also recorded objective and precise images. In the same way, realist authors observed and reported as precisely and objectively as they could.

Writers Study Society Realism in literature flourished in France with writers such as Honoré de Balzac and Emile Zola. Balzac wrote a massive series of almost one hundred novels entitled *The Human Comedy*. These stories detail the lives of over 2,000 people from all levels of French society following the Revolution. They also describe in detail the brutal struggle for wealth and power among France's business class. Zola's explosive novels scandalized France at the end of the 1800s. He exposed the miseries of French workers in small shops, factories, and coal mines. His revelations shocked readers. His work spurred reforms of labor laws and working conditions in France.

The famous English realist novelist, Charles Dickens, created unforgettable characters and scenes. Many were humorous, but others showed the despair of London's

HISTORY MAKERS

Ludwig van Beethoven
1770–1827

A genius of European music, Beethoven suffered the most tragic disability a composer can endure. At the age of 30, he began to go deaf. His deafness grew worse for 19 years. By 1819, it was total.

At first, Beethoven's handicap barely affected his career. His composing and concerts went on as before. By 1802, however, he knew that his hearing would only worsen. He suffered then from bouts of depression. The depressions would bring him to the brink of suicide. Nonetheless, he would rebound:

> . . . It seemed unthinkable for me to leave the world forever before I had produced all that I felt called upon to produce. . . .

After 1819, Beethoven's friends had to write their questions to him in notebooks. He continued to compose, however, and left many "sketchbooks" of musical ideas he would never hear.

Artistic Movements

In the 19th century, as always, artistic movements reflected the social conditions of the time. During the first half of the century, common people began to fight for political power. During that same period, romanticism was the dominant artistic style. By mid-century, political realism had taken over. At the same time, art began to celebrate working, sweating, everyday people. But the romantic ideal did not die. By the end of the century, a new movement called impressionism portrayed the life of middle-class people as a beautiful dream.

Romanticism

Romantic landscape artists idealized nature. Some emphasized the harmony between humans and nature. Others showed nature's power and mystery, as in this painting, *Moonrise Over the Sea,* by German artist Caspar David Friedrich. Still other romantic artists focused on heroes and scenes from history, legend, or literature.

Realism

Realist artists reacted against the dreams of the romantics. These artists believed that their art should portray people as they really were, not as they should be. *The Winnowers,* by Gustave Courbet, the most famous realist, shows the world of everyday work. The winnowers are removing hulls from newly harvested grain. Courbet does not romanticize the work. He records it.

Impressionism

Impressionists aimed at capturing their immediate "impression" of a brief moment. They used bright colors and loose brushwork to catch the fleeting light that sparkles and shimmers. As a result, *Poppies at Argenteuil* by Claude Monet shows less attention to exact "realistic" detail than does *The Winnowers.* It also does not express the sense of serene mystery of *Moonrise Over the Sea.*

Connect *to* History

Synthesizing Artists choose specific elements for their paintings to create the world they want to show. Compare the settings, use of color and light, sharpness of line, and atmosphere of these paintings.

SEE SKILLBUILDER HANDBOOK, PAGE 1007

Connect *to* Today

Comparing Look for examples of modern art in books and magazines. Show examples of paintings where artists still use techniques that could be called romantic or realist or impressionist.

working poor. In this passage, Dickens describes the gloom of working-class life:

Photographers Capture the Passing Moment As realist painters and writers detailed the lives of actual people, photographers could record an instant in time with scientific precision. The first practical photographs were called daguerreotypes (duh·GEHR·uh·TYPS). They were named after their French inventor, Louis Daguerre. Daguerre was an artist who created scenery for theaters. To improve the realism of his scenery, Daguerre developed his photographic invention. The images produced in his daguerrotypes were startlingly real and won him worldwide fame.

Daguerrotype prints were made on metal. However, the British inventor William Talbot invented a light-sensitive paper that he used to produce photographic negatives. The advantage of paper was that many prints could be made from one negative. The Talbot process also allowed photos to be reproduced in books and newspapers. Mass distribution gained a wide audience for the realism of photography. With its scientific, mechanical, and mass-produced features, photography was the art of the new industrial age.

"Ships at Low Tide," an early photograph taken in 1844 by William Talbot.

Impressionists React Against Realism Beginning in the 1860s, a group of painters in Paris reacted against the realistic style. Instead of showing life "as it really is," they tried giving their impression of a subject or a moment in time. For this reason, this style of art came to be known as **impressionism.** Fascinated by light, impressionist artists used pure, shimmering colors to capture a moment seen at a glance.

Artists like Edouard Manet (mah·NAY), Claude Monet (moh·NAY), Edgar Degas (duh·GAH), and Pierre-Auguste Renoir (ruhn·WHAR) also found new subjects for their art. Unlike the realists, impressionists showed a more positive view of the new urban society in western Europe. Instead of abused workers, they showed shop clerks and dock workers enjoying themselves in dance halls and cafés. They painted performers in the theater and circuses. And they glorified the delights of the life of the rising middle class.

Section 4 Assessment

1. TERMS & NAMES

Identify
• romanticism
• realism
• impressionism

2. TAKING NOTES

Using a chart like the one below, contrast romanticism, realism, and impressionism. For each movement, provide a brief description, the social conditions that each reflects, and representative artists.

Movement	Description	Social Conditions	Artists
Romanticism			
Realism			
Impressionism			

3. ANALYZING CAUSES

How might a realist novel bring about changes in society? Describe the steps by which this might happen.

THINK ABOUT
• the conditions described in realist novels
• who reads realist novels
• how political change takes place

4. THEME ACTIVITY

Revolution Listen to a symphony or concerto by Beethoven. Imagine that you are a music critic who has previously heard only formal classical compositions. Write a review of Beethoven's piece. Make the theme of your review the revolutionary quality of Beethoven's music—which you may admire or dislike.

TERMS & NAMES

Briefly explain the importance of each of the following to the revolutions in Latin America or Europe.

1. creoles
2. Simón Bolívar
3. conservatives
4. liberals
5. nationalism
6. Camillo di Cavour
7. Otto von Bismarck
8. realpolitik
9. romanticism
10. realism

Interact *with* History

On page 602, you were asked to create a symbol for your newly independent country. Show your symbol to the class. Explain the elements of your design and what they are intended to express. With your classmates' comments in mind, what might you change in your design?

REVIEW QUESTIONS

SECTION 1 *(pages 603–608)*
Latin American Peoples Win Independence

11. What caused the creoles in South America to rebel against Spain?

12. What role did Agustín de Iturbide play in the independence of Mexico and of the countries of Central America?

13. Who was Dom Pedro, and what role did he play in Brazil's move to independence?

SECTION 2 *(pages 609–612)*
Revolutions Disrupt Europe

14. Why did so many people in Europe and North America support the revolution of Greek nationalists against the Ottoman Empire?

15. How successful were the revolts of 1848? Explain.

SECTION 3 *(pages 613–618)*
Nationalism
Case Studies: Italy and Germany

16. How did nationalism in the 1800s work as a force both for disunity and for unity?

17. What approaches did Camillo di Cavour use to try to acquire more territory for Piedmont-Sardinia?

18. What strategy did Otto von Bismarck use to try to make Prussia the leader of a united Germany?

SECTION 4 *(pages 619–623)*
Revolutions in the Arts

19. Name two ideas or attitudes of the romantic movement that reflected the ideals of nationalism.

20. What new conditions caused a change in the arts from romanticism to realism?

Visual Summary

Nationalist Revolutions Sweep the West

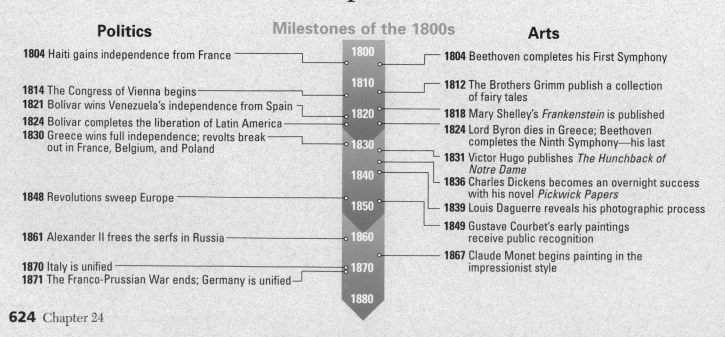

Politics

Milestones of the 1800s

Arts

1804 Haiti gains independence from France

1814 The Congress of Vienna begins
1821 Bolívar wins Venezuela's independence from Spain
1824 Bolívar completes the liberation of Latin America
1830 Greece wins full independence; revolts break out in France, Belgium, and Poland

1848 Revolutions sweep Europe

1861 Alexander II frees the serfs in Russia

1870 Italy is unified
1871 The Franco-Prussian War ends; Germany is unified

1800
1810
1820
1830
1840
1850
1860
1870
1880

1804 Beethoven completes his First Symphony

1812 The Brothers Grimm publish a collection of fairy tales

1818 Mary Shelley's *Frankenstein* is published

1824 Lord Byron dies in Greece; Beethoven completes the Ninth Symphony—his last

1831 Victor Hugo publishes *The Hunchback of Notre Dame*

1836 Charles Dickens becomes an overnight success with his novel *Pickwick Papers*

1839 Louis Daguerre reveals his photographic process

1849 Gustave Courbet's early paintings receive public recognition

1867 Claude Monet begins painting in the impressionist style

CRITICAL THINKING

1. GARIBALDI'S CHOICE

THEME **POWER AND AUTHORITY** Giuseppe Garibaldi stepped aside to let Victor Emmanuel II rule areas that Garibaldi had conquered in southern Italy. Why do you think he made that choice?

2. NATIONALISM

Using a chart like the one below, describe the nationalist movement in each of the following countries and the results of those movements.

Country	Nationalism and its Results
Mexico	
Greece	
Italy	
Germany	

3. THE MEANS TO VICTORY

In the 1800s, revolutionaries often fought with inferior weapons and scarce supplies. How do you think nationalism might help revolutionaries overcome the disadvantages of old weapons and poor supplies to win a war for national independence? Explain.

4. ANALYZING PRIMARY SOURCES

In a speech to the German parliament in 1888, Otto von Bismarck called for further expansion of the army. In the following quote from that speech, "the Iron Chancellor" explains why Germany must always be prepared for war.

> **A VOICE FROM THE PAST**
> When I say that we must strive continually to be ready for all emergencies, I advance the proposition that, on account of our geographical position, we must make greater efforts than other powers would be obliged to make in view of the same ends. We lie in the middle of Europe. We have at least three fronts on which we can be attacked. France has only an eastern boundary; Russia only its western, exposed to assault. . . . So we are spurred forward on both sides to endeavors which perhaps we would not make otherwise.
> **OTTO VON BISMARCK,** speech to the German parliament on February 6, 1888.

- According to Bismarck, what key factor makes Germany a potential target for invasion? Why?
- Do you think Bismarck might have been overstating the threat to Germany? Explain.

CHAPTER ACTIVITIES

1. LIVING HISTORY: Unit Portfolio Project

THEME **REVOLUTION** Your unit portfolio project focuses on showing the similarities and differences among revolutions (see page 509). For Chapter 24, you might use one of the following ideas to add to your portfolio.

- Ask classmates to role-play bystanders present at Padre Hidalgo's *grito de Dolores*. Ask them to express their feelings about what they have witnessed. Audiotape their comments and use them to write a newspaper report about Mexicans' reactions to the event.
- Write a speech that might have been delivered to a rally somewhere in Europe. Urge the country's leaders to help the Greeks in their struggle for independence from the Ottoman Empire.
- Create a "How-to Booklet for Nationalists," based on the strategies used either by Cavour or by Bismarck.

2. CONNECT TO TODAY: Research Project

THEME **CULTURAL INTERACTION** Romanticism and realism in the arts reflected social and political conditions. In various forms, these two artistic movements still exist today. Create a chart comparing romantic and realistic aspects of modern films.

INTERNET Use the Internet, newspapers, magazines, or your own personal experience to search for romantic and realistic portrayals of social and political conditions in movies today.

- For your chart, make two lists—one for examples of modern films that are romantic and one for films that are realistic. Include still shots from movies that support your findings.
- In your search, consider movies from at least three countries.

3. INTERPRETING A TIME LINE

Revisit the unit time line on pages 508–509. If you were shown only the period from 1820 to 1848, what fate would you predict for Europe's old order? Why?

FOCUS ON **POLITICAL CARTOONS**

The 19th-century French cartoonist Charles Philipon was testing a law to see how far away an artist could get from the true features of Louis-Philippe before being condemned to prison and a fine. Since the French word *poire* ("pear") also means "fool,"

- how does the cartoonist show King Louis-Philippe developing as a monarch?
- what do you think was the legal fate of the cartoonist?

Connect to History What right was Charles Philipon standing up for by drawing his cartoon and testing the law?

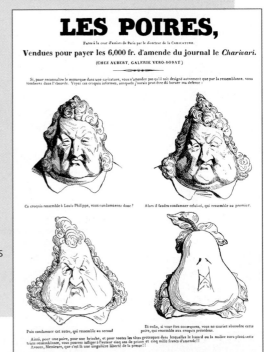

LES POIRES,

Faites à la cour d'assises de Paris par le directeur de la CARICATURE.

Vendues pour payer les 6,000 fr. d'amende du journal le *Charivari.*

(CHEZ AUBERT, GALERIE VÉRO-DODAT.)

626

Industrialism and the Race for Empire

1800	1815	1830	1845	1860

CHAPTER 25 1700–1900
The Industrial Revolution

1700–1815

1701 Britain Jethro Tull invents seed drill

1733 Britain John Kay invents flying shuttle

1764 Britain James Hargreaves invents spinning jenny

1776 Britain Adam Smith publishes *The Wealth of Nations*

1793 U.S. Eli Whitney invents cotton gin

1807 U.S. Robert Fulton launches steamboat, the *Clermont*

1811 Britain Luddites attack factories

1813 U.S. Lowell textile factories open

1830 Britain Rail line between Liverpool and Manchester opened

1848 Germany Marx and Engels publish *The Communist Manifesto*

1850 Britain Population of city of Manchester reaches 300,000

CHAPTER 26 1815–1914
An Age of Democracy and Progress

1800s *United States* ▶

1832 Britain First Reform Bill passes

1837 Britain Victoria becomes queen

1838 Britain Chartist movement presents demands on People's Charter

1840 New Zealand Maoris sign treaty to accept British rule

1845 Ireland Great potato famine begins

1847 Mexico U.S. wins Mexican-American War

1848 U.S. Woman suffragists hold Seneca Falls Convention

1859 Britain Charles Darwin presents theory of evolution

CHAPTER 27 1850–1914
The Age of Imperialism

1800s *India* ▶

1853 Ottoman Empire Crimean War with Russia breaks out

1857 India Sepoy Mutiny

CHAPTER 28 1800–1914
Transformations Around the Globe

1823 U.S. President Monroe issues Monroe Doctrine

1833 Mexico Santa Anna becomes president

1839 China China and Britain fight first Opium War

1840s Mexico Benito Juárez begins liberal reform movement

1848 U.S. Treaty of Guadalupe Hidalgo adds California and other southwestern states to U.S.

1853 China Taiping rebels capture Nanjing and declare it new capital

1854 Japan Treaty of Kanagawa gives U.S. access to two ports

1800	1815	1830	1845	1860

1863 *France*
Martin brothers develop open-hearth steel furnace

1866 *Sweden*
Alfred Nobel invents dynamite

1875 *Britain*
Labor unions win right to strike

1886 *U.S.*
Forerunner of AFL labor union forms

1896 *U.S.*
Henry Ford builds his first automobile

◀ **1800s *Germany*** ▶

Living History
Unit 6 Portfolio Project

THEME Empire Building

Your portfolio for Unit 6 will follow the growth of nations as they build empires and dominate other cultures. You will record not only the effects on the empire-building nations, but also the effects of their colonizing on the lands and peoples whom they take over.

Living History Project Choices
Each Chapter Assessment offers you choices of ways to show the building of empires in that chapter. Activities include the following:

Chapter 25 debate, letter, poster

Chapter 26 handbill, editorial, political cartoon

Chapter 27 script, diary, display

Chapter 28 debate, advertisement, action figure

1860s *France* Louis Pasteur develops process of pasteurization

1865 *U.S.*
Civil War ends

1867 *Canada*
Dominion of Canada is formed

1871 *France*
Paris Commune takes control of Paris

1875 *France*
Third Republic begins

1879 *U.S.*
Thomas Edison invents light bulb

1894 *France*
Captain Alfred Dreyfus found guilty of espionage

1901 *Britain*
Queen Victoria dies

1903 *Britain*
Emmeline Pankhurst forms Women's Social and Political Union

1908 *U.S.*
Henry Ford introduces the Model T

1869 *Egypt*
Suez Canal completed

1871 *Congo*
Stanley finds Dr. Livingstone in central Africa

1884-85 *Germany*
Berlin Conference divides Africa among European nations

1885 *India*
Formation of the Indian National Congress

1889 *Ethiopia* Menelik II leads Ethiopia

1893 *Vietnam* France takes over Indochina

1898 *Hawaii*
U.S. annexes Hawaii

1898 *Philippines*
U.S. acquires Philippine Islands

1902 *South Africa* Boer War ends

1905 *East Africa*
Maji Maji rebellion

1907 *Persia* Russia and Britain divide Persia into spheres of influence

1908 *Persia*
Oil discovered

1861 *China* Empress Cixi begins reign

1867 *Japan* Meiji era begins a period of modernization

1867 Mexico Juárez reelected president after France defeated

1868 *Cuba* Ten-year struggle for independence from Spain begins

1876 *Mexico*
Porfirio Díaz comes to power

1894 *Korea* Sino-Japanese War begins

1898 *Cuba* Spanish-American War begins

1900 *China* Boxer Rebellion protests foreign influence in China

1904 *Manchuria*
Russo-Japanese War for possession of Manchuria

1910 *Korea*
Japan annexes Korea

1910 *Mexico* Mexican Revolution begins

1912 *China*
Qing Dynasty falls; Sun Yixian elected president

1914 *Panama*
Panama Canal opens

◀ **1800s *Japan***

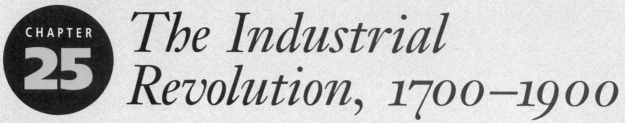

The Industrial Revolution, 1700–1900

PREVIEWING THEMES

Science & Technology
From the spinning jenny to the locomotive train, there was an explosion of inventions and technological advances. These improvements paved the way for the Industrial Revolution.

Empire Building
The global power balance shifted after the Industrial Revolution. This shift occurred because industrialized nations dominated the rest of the world.

Economics
The Industrial Revolution transformed economic systems. In part, this was because nations dramatically changed the way they produced and distributed goods.

INTERNET CONNECTION

Visit us at **www.mcdougallittell.com** to learn more about the Industrial Revolution.

EUROPE AND THE U.S. IN THE 1800s

— U.S. Railroads 1840

0   1,000 Miles

0   2,000 Kilometers

N

Hudson Bay

CANADA

New York

Washington, D.C.

St Louis

UNITED STATES OF AMERICA

New Orleans

Gulf of Mexico

PACIFIC OCEAN

Caribbean Sea

Locomotives began to crisscross the eastern **United States** in the **1840s.** At that time, train tracks started to connect some American cities. Railroads enabled raw materials and finished goods to move back and forth between mines, factories, cities, and ports.

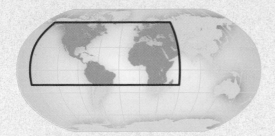

As industrialization swept across the countries of Western Europe in the **19th century,** workers began to organize. They did so in order to defend their interests against those of the factory owners. Here workers in **Germany** meet before a strike in order to plan their strategy.

British workers are shown here laboring in terrible smoke and heat. They are "drawing the retorts"—that is, releasing heat from the furnaces. The place shown is the Great Gas Light Establishment in Brick Lane in **London** in the early **1800s.**

You are a 15-year-old living in England where the Industrial
Revolution has spurred the growth of thousands of factories.
Cheap labor is in great demand. Like millions of other teenagers, you
do not go to school. Instead you work in a factory six days a week, 14
hours a day. The small pay you receive is needed to help support your
family. You trudge to work before dawn every day and work until after
sundown. The dangerous machines injure your fellow workers.
Minding the machines is exhausting, dirty, and dangerous. Inside the
factory the air is foul, and it is so dark it is hard to see.

What would you do to change your situation?

Children had to work
around dangerous
machinery in which a
small hand could easily
be caught and injured.

Adult overseers sometimes
whipped exhausted children in
order to keep them awake
during their long, 14-hour days.

Children were expected to
carry heavy loads as part
of their job in the factory.

EXAMINING *the* ISSUES

- **What factory conditions concern you the most?**

- **Would you attempt to change conditions in the factory?**

- **Would you join a union, go to school, or run away?**

In small groups, discuss these questions; then
share your conclusions with your class. In your
discussions, think about how children live in
pre-industrial and industrial societies all over
the world.

As you read about the changes caused
by industrialization, note how reform movements eventually improve conditions for all
laborers, including children.

632

The Beginnings of Industrialization

TERMS & NAMES
• Industrial Revolution
• enclosure
• crop rotation
• industrialization
• factors of production
• factory
• entrepreneur

MAIN IDEA	WHY IT MATTERS NOW
The Industrial Revolution started in England and soon spread elsewhere.	The changes that began in Britain paved the way for modern industrial societies.

SETTING THE STAGE In the United States, France, and Latin America, political revolutions brought in new governments. A different type of revolution now transformed the way people did work. The **Industrial Revolution** refers to the greatly increased output of machine-made goods that began in England during the 18th century. Before the Industrial Revolution, people wove textiles by hand. Beginning in the middle 1700s, machines did this and other jobs as well. The Industrial Revolution started in England and soon spread to Continental Europe and North America.

The Industrial Revolution Begins

By 1700, small farms covered England's landscape. Wealthy landowners, however, bought up much of the land that village farmers had once worked. Beginning in the early 1700s, large landowners dramatically improved farming methods. These agricultural changes amounted to an agricultural revolution. They eventually paved the way for the Industrial Revolution.

The Agricultural Revolution After buying up the land of village farmers, wealthy landowners enclosed their land with fences or hedges. The increase in their landholdings enabled them to cultivate larger fields, using new seeding and harvesting methods. Within these larger fields, called **enclosures,** landowners experimented to discover more productive farming methods to boost crop yields. The enclosure movement had two important results. First, landowners experimented with new agricultural methods. Second, large landowners forced small farmers to become tenant farmers or to give up farming and move to the cities.

Jethro Tull was one of the first of these scientific farmers. He saw that the usual way of sowing seed by scattering it across the ground was wasteful. Many of the seeds failed to take root. He solved this problem with an invention called the seed drill in about 1701. The seed drill allowed farmers to sow seeds in well-spaced rows at specific depths. A larger share of the seed germinated, boosting crop yields.

Crop Rotation The process of **crop rotation** proved to be one of the best developments of the scientific farmers. The process improved upon older methods of crop rotation, such as the medieval three-field system. One year, for example, a farmer might plant a field with wheat, which exhausted soil nutrients. The next year he planted a root crop, such as turnips, to restore nutrients. This might be followed in turn by barley, then clover.

Livestock breeders improved their methods, too. In the 1700s, for example, Robert Bakewell increased his mutton output by allowing only his best sheep to breed. Other farmers followed Bakewell's lead. Between 1700 and 1786 the average weight for lambs climbed from 18 to 50 pounds.

THINK THROUGH HISTORY
A. Recognizing Effects What were some of the effects of enclosure and crop rotation?

Agricultural Revolution

Jethro Tull's Seed Drill

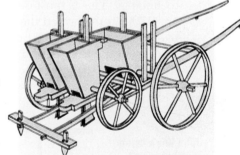

The seed drill enabled farmers to plant methodically. They abandoned the wasteful broadcast method of scattering handfuls of seed across the fields.

These improvements in farming that began in the early 1700s made up an agricultural revolution. As food supplies increased and living conditions improved, England's population mushroomed. An increasing population boosted the demand for food and goods. As farmers lost their land to large enclosed farms, many became factory workers.

Britain's Advantages Why did the Industrial Revolution begin in England? In addition to a large population of workers, the small island country had extensive natural resources. And **industrialization**—the process of developing machine production of goods—required such resources. These natural resources included 1) water power and coal to fuel the new machines; 2) iron ore to construct machines, tools, and buildings; 3) rivers for inland transportation; 4) harbors from which its merchant ships set sail.

Economic Strength and Political Stability In addition to its natural resources, Britain had an expanding economy to support industrialization. Businesspeople invested in the manufacture of new inventions. Britain's highly developed banking system also contributed to the country's industrialization. People were encouraged by the availability of bank loans to invest in new machinery and expand their operations. Growing overseas trade, economic prosperity, and a climate of progress contributed to the increased demand for goods.

Britain's political stability gave the country a tremendous advantage over its neighbors. Though Britain took part in many wars during the 1700s, none of these struggles occurred on British soil. Furthermore, their military and political successes gave the British a positive attitude. Parliament also passed laws that protected business and helped expansion. Other countries had some of these advantages. However, Britain had all the **factors of production.** These were the resources needed to produce goods and services that the Industrial Revolution required. They included land, labor, and capital (or wealth).

THINK THROUGH HISTORY
B. Recognizing Effects How did population growth spur the Industrial Revolution?

THINK THROUGH HISTORY
C. Making Inferences How might Britain's advantages and early industrialization have affected its prosperity in the 19th century?

GlobalImpact : Revolutions in Technology

Technology in the Textile Industry

The Industrial Revolution that began in Britain was spurred by a revolution in technology. This is most obvious in the textile industry where inventions in the late 1700s transformed the manufacture of cloth. These developments, in turn, had an impact on the rest of the world. For example, England's cotton came from plantations in the American South, where cotton production skyrocketed from 1790 to 1810 in response to demand from the textile mills of England.

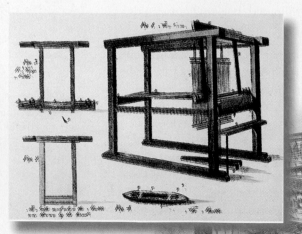

John Kay's flying shuttle speedily carried threads of yarn back and forth when the weaver pulled a handle. The flying shuttle greatly increased the productivity of weavers.

James Hargreaves's spinning jenny dramatically increased the output of spinners. It helped them to keep pace with the weavers.

Inventions Spur Technological Advances

In an explosion of creativity, inventions now revolutionized industry. Britain's textile industry clothed the world in wool, linen, and cotton. This industry was the first to be transformed. Cloth merchants boosted their profits by speeding up the process by which spinners and weavers made cloth.

Major Inventions in the Textile Industry By 1800, several major inventions had modernized the cotton industry. One invention led to another. In 1733, a machinist named John Kay made a shuttle that sped back and forth on wheels. This flying shuttle, a boat-shaped piece of wood to which yarn was attached, doubled the work a weaver could do in a day.

Because spinners could not keep up with these speedy weavers, a cash prize attracted contestants to produce a better spinning machine. Around 1764, a textile worker named James Hargreaves invented a spinning wheel he named after his daughter. Hargreaves's spinning jenny allowed one spinner to work eight threads at a time.

At first, textile workers operated the flying shuttle and the spinning jenny by hand. Richard Arkwright invented the water frame in 1769. The machine used the water-power from rapid streams to drive spinning wheels.

In 1779, Samuel Crompton combined features of the spinning jenny and the water frame to produce the spinning mule. The spinning mule made thread that was stronger, finer, and more consistent than earlier spinning machines. Run by water-power, Edmund Cartwright's power loom sped up weaving after its invention in 1787.

The water frame, the spinning mule, and the power loom were bulky and expensive machines. They took the work of spinning and weaving out of the house. Wealthy textile merchants set up the machines in large buildings called **factories.** At first,

Background
The spinning mule was so named because, just as a mule is the off-spring of a horse and donkey, this machine was the offspring of two inventions.

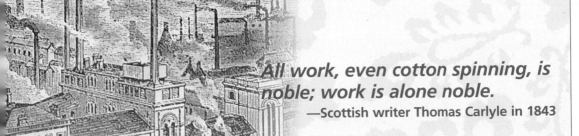

All work, even cotton spinning, is noble; work is alone noble.
—Scottish writer Thomas Carlyle in 1843

The first factories were built to house spinning and weaving machines in the textile industry and to keep the processes secret. Such factories were built close to rivers and streams, which provided a source of energy.

Connect *to* History

Synthesizing Technological innovation and industrialization took place in the textile industry during the Industrial Revolution. How might these forces have provided a model for other industries?

SEE SKILLBUILDER HANDBOOK, PAGE 1007

Connect *to* Today

Hypothesizing How might the textile industry be affected by new technology, including the computer?

Patterns of Interaction

Inventions in the textile industry started in Britain and brought about the Industrial Revolution. This revolution soon spread to other countries in Europe and the United States. The process of industrialization is still spreading around the world, especially in Third World countries. A similar technological revolution is occurring in today's world of electronics. The telephone, television, and (more recently) the computer and the Internet are transforming the spread of information around the world.

 VIDEO *Technology Transforms An Age: The Industrial and Electronic Revolutions*

The Industrial Revolution **635**

the new factories needed waterpower, so they were built near sources of water such as rivers and streams:

THINK THROUGH HISTORY
D. Summarizing
What were the major inventions in the textile industry?

A VOICE FROM THE PAST

. . . A great number of streams . . . furnish water-power adequate to turn many hundred mills: they afford the element of water, indispensable for scouring, bleaching, printing, dyeing, and other processes of manufacture: and when collected in their larger channels, or employed to feed canals, they supply a superior inland navigation, so important for the transit of raw materials and merchandise.

EDWARD BAINS, *The History of Cotton Manufacture in Great Britain* (1835)

British Cotton Consumption

New inventions led to a big increase in the production and consumption of textiles, including cotton. The consumption of cotton rose dramatically in Britain during the 1800s. The following chart shows the increase in cotton consumption as measured in thousands of metric tons for each decade of the century.

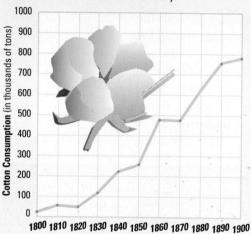

Cotton Consumption (in thousands of tons)

1800 1810 1820 1830 1840 1850 1860 1870 1880 1890 1900

Source: *Historical Statistics of the United States*

SKILLBUILDER: Interpreting Graphs
1. *In what decade did the steepest increase in cotton consumption in Britain take place?*
2. *In what two decades did the consumption of cotton level off or slightly decrease?*

England's cotton came from plantations in the American South in the 1790s. Removing seeds from the raw cotton by hand was hard work. In 1793, an American inventor named Eli Whitney invented a machine to speed the chore. His cotton gin multiplied the amount of cotton that could be cleaned. American cotton production skyrocketed from 1.5 million pounds in 1790 to 85 million pounds in 1810.

Improvements in Transportation Progress in the textile industry spurred other industrial improvements. The first such development, the steam engine, stemmed from the search for a cheap, convenient source of power. The earliest steam engine was used in mining as early as 1705. But this early model gobbled great quantities of fuel, making it expensive to run.

James Watt, a mathematical instrument maker at the University of Glasgow in Scotland, thought about the problem for two years. In 1765, Watt figured out a way to make the steam engine work faster and more efficiently while burning less fuel. In 1774, Watt joined with a businessman named Matthew Boulton. This **entrepreneur** (AHN·truh·pruh·NUR)—a person who organizes, manages, and takes on the risks of a business—paid Watt a salary and encouraged him to build better engines.

Water Transportation Steam could also be used to propel boats. An American inventor named Robert Fulton ordered a steam engine from Boulton and Watt. After its first successful trip in 1807, Fulton's steamboat, the *Clermont*, ferried passengers up and down New York's Hudson River.

In England, water transportation improved with the creation of a network of canals, or human-made waterways. By the mid-1800s, 4,250 miles of inland channels slashed the cost of transporting raw materials.

Road Transportation British roads improved, too, thanks largely to the efforts of John McAdam, a Scottish engineer. Working in the early 1800s, McAdam equipped roadbeds with a layer of large stones for drainage. On top, he placed a carefully smoothed layer of crushed rock. Even in rainy weather heavy wagons could travel over the new "macadam" roads without sinking in mud.

Private investors formed companies that built roads and then operated them for profit. People called the new roads turnpikes because travelers had to stop at tollgates (turnstiles or turnpikes) to pay a toll before traveling farther.

The Railway Age Begins Steam-driven machinery propelled English factories in the late 1700s. A steam engine on wheels—the railroad locomotive—drove English industry after 1820.

In 1804, an English engineer named Richard Trevithick won a bet of several thousand dollars. He did this by hauling ten tons of iron over nearly ten miles of track in a steam-driven locomotive. Other British engineers soon built improved versions of Trevithick's locomotive. One of these early railroad engineers was George Stephenson. He had gained a solid reputation by building some 20 engines for mine operators in northern England. In 1821, Stephenson began work on the world's first railroad line. It was to run 27 miles from the Yorkshire coalfields to the port of Stockton on the North Sea. In 1825, the railroad opened. It used four locomotives that Stephenson had designed and built.

The Liverpool-Manchester Railroad News of this success quickly spread throughout Britain. The entrepreneurs of northern England wanted a railroad line to connect the port of Liverpool with the inland city of Manchester. The track was laid. In 1829 trials were held to choose the best locomotive for use on the new line. Five engines entered the competition. None could compare with the *Rocket*, designed by Stephenson and his son. Smoke poured from its tall smokestack and its two pistons pumped to and fro as they drove the front wheels. The *Rocket* hauled a 13-ton load at an unheard-of speed—more than 24 miles per hour. The Liverpool-Manchester Railway opened officially in 1830. It was an immediate success.

Railroads Revolutionize Life in Britain
First, railroads spurred industrial growth by giving manufacturers a cheap way to transport materials and finished products. Second, the railroad boom created hundreds of thousands of new jobs for both railroad workers and miners. These miners provided iron for the tracks and coal for the steam engines. Third, the railroads boosted England's agricultural and fishing industries, which could transport their products to distant cities. Finally, by making travel easier, railroads encouraged country people to take distant city jobs. Also, railroads lured city dwellers to resorts in the countryside. Like a locomotive racing across the country, the Industrial Revolution brought rapid and unsettling changes to people's lives.

THINK THROUGH HISTORY
E. Synthesizing
How did improvements in transportation promote industrialization in Britain?

SPOTLIGHT ON

Inventions in America
Across the Atlantic in the United States, American inventors worked at making railroad travel more comfortable. They invented, for example, adjustable upholstered seats that converted into couches so that everyone could travel first class.

American inventors also revolutionized agriculture, manufacturing, and communications:

• Cyrus McCormick's reaper, invented in 1831, boosted American wheat production.

• In 1837, a New England painter named Samuel F. B. Morse first sent electrical signals over a telegraph.

• In 1851, I. M. Singer improved the sewing machine by inventing a foot treadle.

• Scottish-born inventor Alexander Graham Bell patented the telephone in 1876.

Section 1 Assessment

1. TERMS & NAMES

Identify
• Industrial Revolution
• enclosure
• crop rotation
• industrialization
• factors of production
• factory
• entrepreneur

2. TAKING NOTES

Create a two-column chart like the one below that lists four natural resources needed for industrialization and how each is used.

Natural Resource	Use
1. coal	
2.	
3.	
4.	

3. MAKING INFERENCES

What effect did entrepreneurs have upon the Industrial Revolution?

THINK ABOUT
• new technological developments
• business opportunities
• increase in prosperity

4. THEME ACTIVITY

Science and Technology
Write a letter as a British government official during the Industrial Revolution. Write to a government official in a non-industrial nation about how the railroad has changed Britain.

2 Industrialization

PATTERNS OF CHANGE

CASE STUDY: Manchester

MAIN IDEA

The factory system changed the way people lived and worked, introducing a variety of problems.

WHY IT MATTERS NOW

The difficult process of industrialization is being repeated in many less-developed countries today.

SETTING THE STAGE The Industrial Revolution eventually led to a better quality of life for most people. Yet the change to machine production also caused immense human suffering. In Britain, the Industrial Revolution proved to be a mixed blessing.

Industrialization Changes Ways of Life

The pace of industrialization quickened in Britain. By the 1800s more people could afford to heat their homes with coal from Wales and to dine on Scottish beef. They wore better clothing, too, woven on power looms in England's industrial cities. These cities soon swelled with workers. However, other people suffered from industrialization.

Growth of Industrial Cities For centuries, most Europeans had lived in rural areas. After 1800, the balance shifted toward cities. The growth of the factory system—manufacturing goods in a central location—brought waves of jobseekers to cities and towns. Between 1800 and 1850, the number of European cities boasting more than 100,000 inhabitants rose from 22 to 47. Most of Europe's urban areas at least doubled in population. This period was one of **urbanization**—city building and the movement of people to cities. Some cities, such as Glasgow and Berlin, tripled or even quadrupled in size.

Factories developed in clusters because entrepreneurs built them near sources of energy. Major new industrial centers sprang up between the coal-rich area of southern Wales and the Clyde River valley in Scotland. The biggest of these centers developed in England.

Britain's capital, London, was the country's most important city. Containing twice as many people as its closest rival (Paris), London became Europe's largest city. It had a population of about 1 million people by 1800. During the 1800s London's population exploded, providing a vast labor pool and market for new industry.

Newer cities challenged London's industrial leadership. Birmingham and Sheffield became iron-smelting centers. Leeds and Manchester dominated textile manufacturing. Along with the port of Liverpool, Manchester formed the center of Britain's bustling cotton industry. During the 1800s, Manchester experienced rapid growth. In 1760, the population of this market town was around 45,000. By 1850, it had swelled to 300,000 people.

As cities grew all over Europe, people crowded into tenements and row houses such as these in London.

Living Conditions No plans, no sanitary codes, and no building codes controlled the growth of England's cities. They lacked adequate housing, education, and police protection for the people who poured in from the countryside seeking jobs. Most of the unpaved streets had no drains and collected heaps of garbage. Workers lived in dark, dirty shelters, whole families crowding into one bedroom.

Vocabulary
cholera: a deadly
disease caused by
bacteria that usually
occur in contaminated
drinking water.

Not surprisingly, sickness was widespread. Cholera epidemics regularly swept through the slums of Great Britain's industrial cities. In 1842, a British government study showed an average life span to be 17 years for working-class people in one large city, compared with 38 years in a nearby rural area.

Elizabeth Gaskell's *Mary Barton* (1848) is a work of fiction. Nonetheless, its realistic description of the dank cellar dwelling place of one family in a Manchester slum presents a startlingly accurate portrayal of urban life at the time:

A VOICE FROM THE PAST
You went down one step even from the foul area into the cellar in which a family of human beings lived. It was very dark inside. The window-panes many of them were broken and stuffed with rags . . . . the smell was so fetid [foul] as almost to knock the two men down . . . . they began to penetrate the thick darkness of the place, and to see three or four little children rolling on the damp, nay wet brick floor, through which the stagnant, filthy moisture of the street oozed up. . . .

ELIZABETH GASKELL, *Mary Barton*

Working Conditions Factory owners wanted to keep their machines running for as many hours a day as possible. As a result, the average worker spent 14 hours a day at the job, 6 days a week. Instead of changing with the seasons, the work was the same week after week, year after year. Workers had to keep up with the machines.

Industry also posed new dangers in work. Factories were seldom well-lit or clean. Machines injured workers in countless ways. A boiler might explode or a drive belt might catch the worker's arm. And there was no government program to provide aid in case of injury. The most dangerous conditions of all were found in the coal mines. Frequent accidents, damp conditions, and the constant breathing of coal dust made the average miner's life span ten years shorter than that of other workers.

THINK THROUGH HISTORY
**A. Drawing
Conclusions** What
was the impact of
living and working con-
ditions on workers?

Class Tensions Not everyone in the new cities lived miserably. Well-to-do merchants and factory owners built fancy homes in the suburbs. In addition, a new class began to emerge.

Though poverty gripped Britain's working classes, the Industrial Revolution created enormous amounts of money in the country. Most of this wealth lined the pockets of factory owners, shippers, and merchants. These wealthy people made up a growing **middle class**—a social class of skilled workers, professionals, businesspeople, and wealthy farmers.

The new middle class transformed the social structure of Great Britain. In the past, landowners and aristocrats occupied the top position in British society. With most of the wealth, they wielded the power. Now some factory owners, merchants, and investment bankers grew wealthier than the landowners and aristocrats.

Yet important social distinctions divided the two wealthy classes. Landowners looked down on those who had made their fortunes in the "vulgar" business world. Not until late in the 1800s were rich entrepreneurs considered the social equals of the lords of the countryside.

Gradually, a larger middle class—neither rich nor poor—emerged. This group included an upper middle class of government employees, doctors, lawyers, and managers of factories, mines, and shops. A lower middle class consisted of factory overseers and such skilled workers as toolmakers, mechanical drafters, and printers. These people enjoyed a comfortable standard of living.

THINK THROUGH HISTORY
B. Summarizing
Describe the social
classes in Britain.

During the years 1800 to 1850, however, poor workers saw little improvement in their own living and working conditions. Frustrated workers watched their livelihoods disappear as machines replaced them. In response, they smashed the machines they thought were putting them out of work. One group of such workers was called the Luddites. They were named after Ned Ludd. Ludd, probably a mythical English

Elizabeth Gaskell
(1810–1865) was a
British writer whose
novels such as
Mary Barton (1848)
and *North and South*
(1855) show a
sympathy for the
working class.
Cranford (1853)
deals with the life
of a peaceful
English village.

laborer, was said to have destroyed weaving machinery around 1779. The Luddites attacked whole factories in northern England beginning in 1811, destroying labor-saving machinery. Outside the factories, mob disorder took the form of riots, mainly because of the poor living and working conditions of the workers.

Positive Effects of the Industrial Revolution Despite the problems that followed industrialization, the Industrial Revolution eventually had a number of positive effects. It created jobs for workers. It contributed to the wealth of the nation. It fostered technological progress and invention. It greatly increased the production of goods and raised the standard of living. Perhaps most important, it provided the hope of improvement in people's lives.

The Industrial Revolution produced a number of other benefits as well. These included healthier diets; better housing; and cheaper, mass-produced clothing. Because the Industrial Revolution created a demand for engineers as well as clerical and professional workers, it expanded educational opportunities.

The middle and upper classes prospered immediately from the Industrial Revolution. For the workers it took longer, but their lives gradually improved during the 1800s. Labor eventually won higher wages, shorter hours, and better working conditions.

PATTERNS OF CHANGE: Industrialization

Effects of Industrialization

Size of Cities	• Growth of factories, bringing job seekers to cities • Urban areas doubling, tripling, or quadrupling in size • Factories developing near sources of energy • Many new industrial cities specializing in certain industries
Living Conditions	• No sanitary codes or building controls • Lack of adequate housing, education, and police protection • Lack of running water and indoor plumbing • Frequent epidemics sweeping through slums • Eventually, better housing, healthier diets, and cheaper clothing
Working Conditions	• Industrialization creating new jobs for workers • Workers trying to keep pace with machines • Factories dirty and unsanitary • Workers running dangerous machines for long hours in unsafe conditions • Harsh and severe factory discipline • Eventually, higher wages, shorter hours, and better working conditions
Emerging Social Classes	• Growing middle class of factory owners, shippers, and merchants • Upper class of landowners and aristocrats resentful of rich middle class • Lower middle class of factory overseers and skilled workers • Workers overworked and underpaid • In general, a rising standard of living, with some groups excluded

SKILLBUILDER: Interpreting Charts
1. *Which social class benefited most and which suffered most from industrialization?*
2. *What were some of the advantages and disadvantages of industrialization?*

The long-term effects of the Industrial Revolution are still evident. Most people today in the industrialized countries can afford consumer goods that would have been considered luxuries fifty or a hundred years ago. Further, their living and working conditions are much improved over those of workers in the 19th century.

As the Industrial Revolution in Manchester demonstrated, economic success can unleash a variety of problems. Even today, the economic pressures of industrialization frequently lead to the overuse of natural resources and the abuse of the environment. The profits derived from industrialization, however, permit thoughtful governments to invest in urban improvements.

The Mills of Manchester

Manchester's unique advantages made it a leading example of the new industrial city. This northern English town had ready access to water power. It also had available labor from the nearby countryside and an outlet to the sea at Liverpool.

"From this filthy sewer pure gold flows," wrote Alexis de Tocqueville (ah·lehk·SEE duh TOHK·vihl), the French writer, after he visited Manchester in 1835. Indeed, the industrial giant showed the best and worst of the Industrial Revolution. Manchester's rapid, unplanned growth made it a filthy sewer for the poor people who worked there. But gold certainly flowed toward the mill owners and the new middle class. Eventually, although not immediately, the working class saw their standard of living rise as well.

Manchester's businesspeople took pride in mastering each detail of the manufacturing process, working many hours and risking their own money. For their efforts, they pocketed high profits and erected gracious homes on the outskirts of town.

To provide the mill owners with their high profits, workers labored under terrible conditions. Children as young as six joined their parents in the factories. There, for six days a week, they toiled from 6 A.M. to 7 or 8 P.M., with only a half an hour for lunch and an hour for dinner. To keep the children awake, mill supervisors beat them. Tiny hands repaired broken threads in Manchester's spinning machines, replaced thread in the bobbins, or swept up cotton fluff. The dangerous machinery injured many children. The fluff filled their lungs and made them cough.

THINK THROUGH HISTORY
C. Drawing Conclusions
Whose interests did child labor serve?

Until the first Factory Act passed in 1819, the British government exerted little control over child labor in Manchester and other factory cities. The act restricted working age and hours. For years after the act passed, young children still did heavy, dangerous work in Manchester's factories.

Putting so much industry into one place polluted the natural environment. The coal that powered factories and warmed houses blackened the air. Textile dyes and

An English engraving of 1876 shows a bird's-eye view of the city of Manchester during the Industrial Revolution.

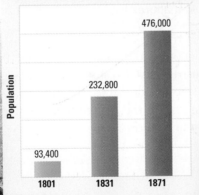

Manchester's Growth

Population

476,000 (1871)

232,800 (1831)

93,400 (1801)

1801   1831   1871

SKILLBUILDER: Interpreting Graphs

1. How many people did the city of Manchester gain between 1801 and 1831? How many did it gain between 1831 and 1871?
2. What does the engraving show were the effects of such rapid growth?

641

William Cooper began working in a textile factory at the age of ten. He had a sister who worked upstairs in the same factory. In 1832, Cooper was called to testify before a parliamentary committee about the conditions among child laborers in the textile industry. The following sketch of his day is based upon his testimony.

5 A.M.—The workday began. Cooper and his sister rose as early as 4:00 or 4:30 in the morning in order to get to the factory for the start of their workday at 5:00. Children usually grabbed their breakfast on the run.

12 noon—The children were given a 40-minute break for lunch. This was the only break they received during the whole course of the day.

3 P.M.—The children often became drowsy during the afternoon or evening hours. In order to keep them awake, adult overseers sometimes whipped the children.

11 P.M.—Cooper's sister worked another two hours even though she had to be back at work at 5:00 the next morning.

9 P.M.—William Cooper's day ended after an exhausting 16-hour shift at work.

6 P.M.—There was no break allowed for an evening meal. Children ate on the run. From 12:40 until 9:00 at night, the children worked without a break.

CONNECT *to* TODAY

Child Labor

To save on labor costs in the 1990s, many corporations have moved their manufacturing operations overseas to poor countries. In sweatshops in these developing countries, young children work long hours under wretched conditions. They are unprotected by child labor laws. For mere pennies per hour, children sort vegetables, stitch soccer balls, or assemble expensive basketball shoes.

In the United States each year $178 billion worth of clothing is sold. Some studies estimate more than half of that clothing is manufactured in sweatshops where children work. Like the children who toiled in Manchester's factories in the 1800s, children labor to help support their families.

other wastes poisoned Manchester's Irwell River. The following description of the river was written by an eyewitness observer in 1862:

A VOICE FROM THE PAST

Steam boilers discharge into it their seething contents, and drains and sewers their fetid impurities; till at length it rolls on—here between tall dingy walls, there under precipices of red sandstone—considerably less a river than a flood of liquid manure.

HUGH MILLER, "Old Red Sandstone"

Manchester produced consumer goods and created wealth on a grand scale. Yet this unplanned industrial city also stood as a reminder of industrialization's dark side. In the 1800s, the industrialization that began in Great Britain spread to the United States and to continental Europe, as you will learn in Section 3.

Section **2** Assessment

1. TERMS & NAMES
Identify
• urbanization
• middle class

2. TAKING NOTES
Create a pyramid like the one below listing the social classes in industrial England. List the types of laborers and professionals included in each group.

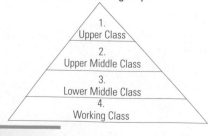

1. Upper Class
2. Upper Middle Class
3. Lower Middle Class
4. Working Class

3. ANALYZING ISSUES
How did industrialization contribute to city growth?

THINK ABOUT
• growth of industry
• creation of jobs
• the economic advantages of centralization

4. ANALYZING THEMES
Economics How might a factory owner have justified the harsh conditions in his factory?

THINK ABOUT
• class distinctions
• the spread of factories
• financial gains

3 Industrialization Spreads

MAIN IDEA	WHY IT MATTERS NOW
The industrialization that began in Great Britain spread to other parts of the world.	The Industrial Revolution set the stage for the growth of modern cities.

SETTING THE STAGE Britain's favorable location, geography, financial systems, political stability, and natural resources sparked its industrialization. British power-driven machinery began to mass-produce textiles and other goods at the end of the 1700s. Paying low wages to many workers, British merchants built the world's first factories. When these factories prospered, wealthy business leaders invented more labor-saving machines. They also built more factories, and eventually industrialized the country. The Industrial Revolution that began in Britain soon spread to other countries. They had similar conditions that made them ripe for industrialization.

Industrial Development in the United States

The United States possessed the same resources that allowed Britain to mechanize its industries and develop large-scale factories. America also had rushing rivers, rich deposits of coal and iron ore, and a supply of immigrant laborers. During the War of 1812, Britain blockaded the United States in an attempt to keep it from engaging in international trade. This blockade forced the young country to use its own resources to develop independent industries. Those industries would manufacture the goods the United States could no longer import.

Background
The War of 1812 began over British interference with America's merchant ships. It ended in a draw between Britain and the United States.

Industrialization in the United States As in Britain, industrialization in the United States began in the textile industry. Eager to keep the secrets of industrialization to itself, Britain had forbidden engineers, mechanics, and toolmakers to leave the country. In 1789, however, a young British mill worker named Samuel Slater emigrated to the United States. There Slater built a spinning machine from memory and a partial design. The following year, Moses Brown opened the first factory in the United States to house Slater's machines in Pawtucket, Rhode Island. But the Pawtucket factory mass-produced only one part of finished cloth, the thread.

In 1813, Francis Cabot Lowell and four other investors revolutionized the American textile industry. They mechanized every stage in the manufacture of cloth. Their weaving factory in Waltham, Massachusetts, earned the partners enough money to fund a larger operation in another Massachusetts town. When Francis Lowell died, the remaining partners named the town after him. By the late 1820s, Lowell, Massachusetts, had become a booming manufacturing center and a model for other such towns.

Thousands of workers, mostly young single women, flocked from their rural homes to work as mill girls in factory towns like Lowell. To ensure proper behavior, the young women were watched closely inside and outside the factory. The mill girls toiled over 12 hours a day, six days a week, for

These Massachusetts women of the mid-19th century are shown holding shuttles that were used during weaving.

decent wages. For some young women, the mill job meant a welcome alternative to becoming a servant, often the only other job open to them:

A VOICE FROM THE PAST
Country girls were naturally independent, and the feeling that at this new work the few hours they had of everyday leisure were entirely their own was a satisfaction to them. They preferred it to going out as "hired help." It was like a young man's pleasure in entering upon business for himself. Girls had never tried that experiment before, and they liked it.

LUCY LARCOM, *A New England Girlhood*

THINK THROUGH HISTORY
A. Forming and Supporting Opinions
Why did Lucy Larcom think mill work benefited young women?

Textiles led the way, but clothing manufacture and shoemaking also underwent mechanization. Especially in the Northeast, skilled workers and farmers had formerly worked at home. Now they labored in factories in towns and cities such as Waltham, Lowell, and Lawrence, Massachusetts.

Later Expansion of U.S. Industry There was a great deal of industrial growth in the Northeast in the early 1800s. Nonetheless, the United States remained primarily an agricultural nation until the Civil War ended in 1865. During the last third of the 1800s, however, the country experienced a technological boom. As in Britain, a number of causes contributed to this boom. These included a wealth of natural resources, among them oil, coal, and iron; a burst of inventions, such as the electric light bulb and the telephone; and a swelling urban population that consumed the new manufactured goods.

Also as in Britain, railroads played a major role in America's industrialization. Cities like Chicago and Minneapolis expanded rapidly during the late 1800s. This was due to their location along the nation's expanding railroad lines. Chicago's stockyards and Minneapolis's grain industries prospered by selling their products to the rest of the country.

Indeed, the railroads themselves proved to be a profitable business. By the end of the 1800s, a limited number of large, powerful companies controlled over two-thirds of the nation's railroad tracks. Businesses of all kinds began to merge as the railroads had. Smaller companies joined together to form a larger one.

Building large businesses like railroads required a great deal of money. To raise the money, entrepreneurs sold shares of stock. People who bought stock became

Vocabulary
stock: a share in certain rights of ownership of a business.

The Growth of the United States

Railroad System, 1840

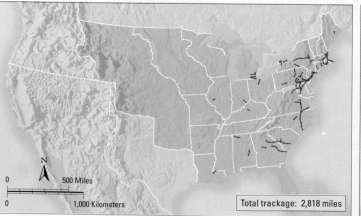

0   500 Miles
0   1,000 Kilometers

Total trackage: 2,818 miles

Railroad System, 1890

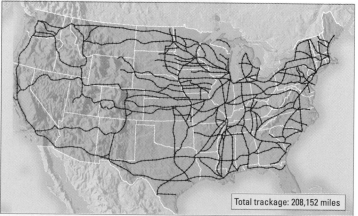

Total trackage: 208,152 miles

SKILLBUILDER: Interpreting Maps
1. **Region** *In what part of the country were the first railroads built?*
   By 1890, what other part of the country was densely covered by railroad tracks?
2. **Movement** *In what direction did the railroads help people move across the country?*

part-owners of these businesses called corporations. A **corporation** is a business owned by stockholders who share in its profits but are not personally responsible for its debts. In the late 1800s large corporations such as Standard Oil (founded by John D. Rockefeller) and the Carnegie Steel Company (founded by Andrew Carnegie) sprang up. They sought to control every aspect of their own industries in order to make big profits.

Big business—the giants that controlled entire industries—also made big profits by cutting the cost of producing goods. While workers earned small wages for long hours at hard labor, stockholders earned high profits and corporate leaders made fortunes.

Industrialization Reaches Continental Europe

European businesses yearned to adopt the "British miracle," the result of Britain's profitable new methods of manufacturing goods. Yet the troubles sparked by the French Revolution and the Napoleonic wars had halted trade, interrupted communication, and caused inflation in some parts of the continent. European countries were absorbed in the French Revolution and the Napoleonic wars between 1789 and 1815. They watched the gap widen between themselves and Britain. Nonetheless, industrialization eventually reached continental Europe.

Beginnings in Belgium Belgium led Europe in adopting Britain's new technology. Belgium had rich deposits of iron and coal as well as fine waterways for transportation.

Samuel Slater had smuggled to the United States the design of a spinning machine. Like him, British skilled workers played a key role in carrying industrialization to Belgium. A Lancashire carpenter named William Cockerill made his way to Belgium in 1799. He carried secret plans for building spinning machinery. Cockerill's son John eventually built an enormous industrial enterprise in eastern Belgium. It produced machinery, steam engines, and railway locomotives. Carrying the latest British advances, more British workers came to work with Cockerill. Several then founded their own companies in Europe.

Germany Industrializes Germany was a politically divided empire. Economic isolation and scattered resources hampered countrywide industrialization in the early 1800s. Instead, pockets of industrialization appeared, as in the coal-rich Ruhr Valley of west-central Germany. Beginning around 1835, Germany began to copy the British model. Germany imported British equipment and engineers. German manufacturers also sent their children to England to learn industrial management.

Most important, Germany built railroads that linked its growing manufacturing cities, such as Frankfurt, with the Ruhr Valley's coal and iron deposits. In 1858, a German economist wrote, "Railroads and machine shops, coal mines and iron foundries, spinneries and rolling mills seem to spring up out of the ground, and smokestacks sprout from the earth like mushrooms."

Germany's economic strength spurred its ability to develop as a military power. By the late 19th century, Germany had become both an industrial and a military giant.

Expansion Throughout Europe In the rest of Europe, as in Germany, industrialization during the early 1800s proceeded by region rather than by country. Even in countries where agriculture dominated, pockets of industrialization arose. For example, Bohemia developed its spinning industry. Spain's Catalonia processed more cotton than Belgium. Northern Italy mechanized its textile production, specializing in silk spinning. Serf labor ran factories in regions around Moscow and St. Petersburg.

In France, continual industrial growth occurred only after 1850, when the central government constructed railroads. These railroads created a thriving national market for new French products.

German workers labor in a steel mill in this 1875 painting by Adolph von Menzel.

THINK THROUGH HISTORY
B. Analyzing Causes What factors slowed industrialization in Germany?

For a variety of reasons, many European countries did not industrialize. In some nations, the social structure delayed the adoption of new methods of production. The accidents of geography held back others. In Austria-Hungary and Spain, transportation posed great obstacles. Austria-Hungary's mountains defeated railroad builders. Spain lacked both good roads and waterways for canals.

Worldwide Impact of Industrialization

The Industrial Revolution shifted the world balance of power. It promoted competition between industrialized nations and increased poverty in less developed nations.

GlobalImpact

Industrialism Spreads to Egypt

When an Ottoman officer named Muhammad Ali (1769–1849) took power in Egypt, the new ruler sought to propel his country into the industrialized world. Muhammad Ali reformed Egypt's government and improved communications. He also established cotton mills, a glass factory, and a sugar refinery.

To earn the money required to purchase European goods and services, Muhammad Ali also advanced the development of commercial agriculture. During his rule, landlords forced peasants to become tenant farmers and grow cash crops for European markets. The modernizing and industrializing of Egypt were often done at the expense of the peasants.

Rise of Global Inequality Industrialization widened the gap between industrialized and non-industrialized countries, even while it strengthened their economic ties. To keep factories running and workers fed, industrialized countries required a steady supply of raw materials from less developed lands. In turn, industrialized countries viewed poor countries as markets for their manufactured products. A large inequality developed between the industrialized West and the rest of the world.

Britain led in exploiting its overseas colonies for resources and markets. Soon other European countries, the United States, Russia, and Japan followed Britain's lead, seizing colonies for their economic resources. Imperialism, the policy of extending one country's rule over many other lands, gave even more power and wealth to these already wealthy nations. Imperialism was born out of the cycle of industrialization, the development of new markets around the world, and the need for resources to supply the factories of Europe. (See Chapter 27.)

Transformation of Society Between 1700 and 1900, revolutions in agriculture, production, transportation, and communication changed the lives of people in Western Europe and the United States. Industrialization gave Europe tremendous economic power. Much of Europe was gaining the capability to produce many goods faster and more cheaply. In contrast, the economies of Asia and Africa were still based on agriculture and small workshops.

The industrialization that took place in the 1700s and 1800s revolutionized every aspect of society, from daily life to life expectancy. Despite the hardships early urban workers suffered, population, health, and wealth eventually rose dramatically in all industrialized countries. The development of a middle class created great opportunities for education and democratic participation. Greater democratic participation, in turn, fueled a powerful movement for social reform.

THINK THROUGH HISTORY
C. Clarifying Why did imperialism grow out of industrialization?

Section **3** Assessment

1. TERMS & NAMES

Identify
• corporation

2. TAKING NOTES

Using a web diagram like the one below, show the effects of industrialization on the world.

Worldwide Effects

3. RECOGNIZING BIAS

Go back to the quote from Lucy Larcom on page 644. Do you think her feelings about working in the mill are typical? Why or why not?

THINK ABOUT
• her experiences in a mill
• her possible bias

4. THEME ACTIVITY

Empire Building Draw a political cartoon that could have been used by the British government. It should show their sense of their own superiority over non-industrialized nations that they planned to colonize.

TERMS & NAMES
- laissez faire
- Adam Smith
- capitalism
- utilitarianism
- socialism
- Karl Marx
- communism
- union
- collective bargaining
- strike

4 An Age of Reforms

MAIN IDEA	WHY IT MATTERS NOW
The Industrial Revolution led to economic, social, and political reforms.	Many modern social welfare programs developed during this period.

SETTING THE STAGE In industrialized countries in the 1800s, many business leaders believed that progress opened a gap between rich and poor. These leaders cautioned governments to stay out of business and economic affairs. Reformers, however, felt that governments should play an active role in bettering conditions for the poor.

The Philosophers of Industrialization

The term **laissez faire** (LEHS·ay·FAIR) refers to the economic policy of letting owners of industry and business set working conditions without interference. That policy favors a free market unregulated by the government. The term comes from a French phrase that means "let do " and by extension, "let people do as they please."

Laissez-faire Economics Laissez faire stemmed from French economic philosophers of the 18th-century Enlightenment. They criticized the idea that nations grow wealthy by placing heavy tariffs on foreign goods. In fact, they argued, government regulations only interfered with the production of wealth. These philosophers believed that if the government allowed free trade—the flow of commerce in the world market without government regulation—the economy would prosper.

Adam Smith, a professor at the University of Glasgow, Scotland, defended the idea of a free economy, or free markets, in his 1776 book *The Wealth of Nations*. According to Smith, economic liberty guaranteed economic progress. Smith claimed that government need not interfere in the economy.

The Ideas of Malthus and Ricardo Economists Thomas Malthus and David Ricardo supported Smith's basic ideas. Like Smith, they believed that natural laws governed economic life. Their important ideas were the foundation of laissez-faire capitalism. **Capitalism** is an economic system in which money is invested in business ventures with the goal of making a profit. These ideas helped bring about the Industrial Revolution.

In *An Essay on the Principle of Population*, written in 1798, Thomas Malthus argued that population tended to increase more rapidly than the food supply. Without wars and epidemics to kill off the extra people, most were destined to be poor and miserable. The predictions of Malthus seemed to be coming true in the 1840s.

David Ricardo, a wealthy stockbroker, took Malthus's theory one step further in his book, *Principles of Political Economy and Taxation* (1817). Like Malthus, Ricardo believed that a permanent underclass would always be poor. In a market system, if there are many workers and abundant resources, then labor and resources are cheap. If there

Background
Ricardo stated the "iron law of wages." He argued that because of population growth wages would be just high enough to keep workers from starving.

HISTORY MAKERS

Adam Smith
1723–1790

In his book *The Wealth of Nations*, Smith argued that if individuals freely followed their own self-interest, the world would be an orderly and progressive place. After all, sellers made money by producing things that other people wanted to buy. Buyers spent money for the things they wanted most. In such a marketplace, Smith thought, social harmony would result without any government direction, "as if by an invisible hand." Smith's ideas were central to the development of capitalism.

Smith applied an invisible hand of his own. When the economist died, people discovered that he had secretly donated large chunks of his income to charities.

Capitalism vs. Marxism

Capitalist Ideas	Marxist Ideas
• Progress results when individuals follow their own self-interest.	• All great movements in history are the result of an economic class struggle.
• Businesses follow their own self-interest when they compete with one another for the consumer's money.	• The "haves" take advantage of the "have-nots."
• Each producer tries to provide goods and services that are better and less expensive than those of competitors.	• The Industrial Revolution intensified the class struggle.
• Consumers compete with one another to purchase the best goods at the lowest prices.	• Workers are exploited by employers.
• Market economy aims to produce the best products and the lowest prices.	• The labor of workers creates profit for employers.
Adam Smith	• The capitalist system will eventually destroy itself. The state will wither away as a classless society develops. **Karl Marx**
• Government should not interfere in the economy.	

SKILLBUILDER: Interpreting Charts

1. Which ideas of Marxism seem to be a direct reaction to the Industrial Revolution?
2. Which system of ideas seems dominant in the world today? Support your opinion.

They believed that economic forces alone dominated society. Time has shown, however, that religion, nationalism, ethnic loyalties, and a desire for democratic reforms may be as strong influences on history as economic forces. In addition, the gap between the rich and poor within the industrialized countries failed to widen in the way that Marx and Engels predicted, mostly because of the following types of reform.

Unionization and Legislative Reform

Factory workers faced long hours, dirty and dangerous working conditions, and the threat of being laid off. By the 1800s, working people became more active in politics. To press for reforms, workers joined together in voluntary associations called **unions.**

The Union Movement A union spoke for all the workers in a particular trade. Unions engaged in **collective bargaining**—negotiations between workers and their employers. They bargained for better working conditions and higher pay. If factory owners refused these demands, union members could **strike,** or refuse to work.

Skilled workers led the way in forming unions because their special skills gave them extra bargaining power. Management would have trouble replacing such skilled workers as carpenters, printers, and spinners. Thus the earliest unions helped the lower middle class more than they helped the poorest workers.

The union movement underwent slow, painful growth in both Great Britain and the United States. For years, the British government denied workers the right to form unions. The government saw unions as a threat to social order and stability. Indeed, the Combination Acts of 1799 and 1800 outlawed unions and strikes. Bravely ignoring the threat of jail or job loss, factory workers joined unions anyway. Parliament finally repealed the Combination Acts in 1824. After 1825, the British government unhappily tolerated unions.

British unions had shared goals of raising wages and improving working conditions. By 1875, British trade unions had won the right to strike and picket peacefully. They had also built up a membership of about 1 million people.

In the United States, skilled workers had belonged to unions since the early 1800s. In 1886, several unions joined together to form the organization that would become the

American Federation of Labor (AFL). A series of successful strikes won AFL members higher wages and shorter hours.

Reform Laws In both Great Britain and the United States, new laws reformed some of the worst abuses of industrialization. In 1832, for example, Parliament set up a committee to investigate child labor. As a result of this committee's findings, Parliament passed the Factory Act of 1833. The new law made it illegal to hire children under 9 years old. Children from the ages of 9 to 12 could not work more than 8 hours a day. Young people from 13 to 17 could not work more than 12 hours. In 1842 the Mines Act prevented women and children from working underground.

In 1847, the Parliament passed a bill that helped working women as well as their children. The Ten Hours Act of 1847 limited the workday to ten hours for women and children who worked in factories.

Reformers in the United States also passed legislation to protect child workers. In 1904, a group of progressive reformers organized the National Child Labor Committee to end child labor. Arguing that child labor lowered wages for all workers, labor union members joined the reformers. Together these groups pressured national and state politicians to ban child labor and set maximum working hours. The Supreme Court in 1919 had objected to a federal child labor law. However, it did allow individual states to legally limit the working hours of women and, later, of men.

This print shows an attack on the work-house, a prison in which limited sentences at manual labor are served. The attack took place in Stockport, England, during demonstrations by workers in the 1830s. The workers are shown distri-buting bread from the workhouse.

THINK THROUGH HISTORY
D. Summarizing
What were some of the important reform bills passed in Britain during this period?

Other Reform Movements

Almost from the beginning, reform movements sprang up in response to the negative impact of industrialization. These reforms included improving the workplace and extending the right to vote to working-class men. The same impulse toward reform, along with the ideals of the French Revolution, also helped to end slavery and promote new rights for women and children.

Abolition of Slavery William Wilberforce, a highly religious man, was a member of Parliament who led the fight for abolition—the end of the slave trade and slavery in the British Empire. Parliament passed a bill to end the slave trade in the British West Indies in 1807. After he retired from Parliament in 1825, Wilberforce continued his fight to free the slaves. Britain finally abolished slavery in its empire in 1833.

British antislavery activists had mixed motives. Some were morally against slavery, such as the abolitionist William Wilberforce. Others viewed slave labor as an economic threat. Furthermore, a new class of industrialists developed who supported cheap labor rather than slave labor. They soon gained power in Parliament.

THINK THROUGH HISTORY
E. Summarizing
What were some of the motives of British abolitionists?

In the United States the movement to fulfill the promise of the Declaration of Independence by ending slavery grew in the early 1800s. The enslavement of African people finally ended in the United States when the Union won the Civil War in 1865.

With the end of the U.S. Civil War, enslavement persisted in the Americas only in Puerto Rico, Cuba, and Brazil. In Puerto Rico, slavery was ended in 1873. Spain finally abolished slavery in its Cuban colony in 1886. Not until 1888 did Brazil's huge enslaved population win freedom.

**Jane Addams
1860–1935**

After graduating from college, Jane Addams wondered what to do with her life.

I gradually became convinced that it would be a good thing to rent a house in a part of the city where many primitive and actual needs are found, in which young women who had been given over too exclusively to study, might . . . learn of life from life itself.

Addams and her friend Ellen Starr set up Hull House in a working-class district in Chicago. Eventually the facilities included a nursery, a gym, a kitchen, and a boarding house for working women. Hull House not only served the immigrant population of the neighborhood, it also trained social workers.

Women Fight for Change The Industrial Revolution proved a mixed blessing for women. On the one hand, factory work offered higher wages than work done at home. Women spinners in Manchester, for example, earned much more money than women who stayed home to spin cotton thread. On the other hand, women factory workers usually made only one-third as much money as men.

Women led reform movements to address this and other pressing social issues. During the mid-1800s, for example, women formed unions in the trades where they dominated. In Britain, some women served as safety inspectors in factories where other women worked. In the United States, college-educated women like Jane Addams ran settlement houses. These community centers served the poor residents of slum neighborhoods.

In both the United States and Britain, women who had rallied for the abolition of slavery began to wonder why their own rights should be denied on the basis of gender. The movement for women's rights began in the United States as early as 1848. Women activists around the world joined to found the International Council for Women in 1888. Delegates and observers from 27 countries attended the council's 1899 meeting.

**THINK THROUGH HISTORY
F. Making Inferences** Why might women abolitionists have headed the movement for women's rights?

Reforms Spread to Many Areas of Life In the United States and Western Europe, reformers tried to correct the problems troubling the newly industrialized nations. Public education and prison reform ranked high on the reformers' lists.

One of the most prominent U.S. reformers, Horace Mann of Massachusetts, favored free public education for all children. Mann, who spent his own childhood working at hard labor, warned, "If we do not prepare children to become good citizens . . . if we do not enrich their minds with knowledge, then our republic must go down to destruction." By the 1850s many states were starting to establish a system of public schools. In Western Europe, free public schooling became available in the late 1800s.

In 1831, French writer Alexis de Tocqueville had contrasted the brutal conditions in American prisons to the "extended liberty" of American society. Reformers took on the challenge of prison reform, emphasizing the goal of restoring prisoners to useful lives.

During the 1800s, democracy grew in the industrialized countries even as foreign expansion increased. The industrialized western democracies faced new challenges both at home and abroad. You will learn about these challenges in Chapter 26.

Section 4 Assessment

1. TERMS & NAMES

Identify
• laissez faire
• Adam Smith
• capitalism
• utilitarianism
• socialism
• Karl Marx
• communism
• union
• collective bargaining
• strike

2. TAKING NOTES

Compare capitalism with Marxism using a Venn diagram such as the one below.

Capitalism only

Both

Marxism only

Write a paragraph comparing and contrasting capitalism and Marxism.

3. IDENTIFYING PROBLEMS

What were the main problems faced by the unions during the 1800s? How did the unions overcome these problems?

THINK ABOUT
• government restrictions
• labor reforms
• skilled workers vs. unskilled workers

4. ANALYZING THEMES

Economics According to Marx and Engels, economic forces alone dominate society. How important do you think such forces are? Support your opinion using evidence from this and previous chapters.

THINK ABOUT
• other forces, like ethnic loyalties, desire for democracy
• causes of the Industrial Revolution
• the class structure

Industrialization

Industrialization eventually lifted the standard of living for many people in Europe and North America in the 1800s. Yet the process also brought suffering to countless workers who crowded into filthy cities to toil for starvation wages. The following excerpts reveal a variety of perspectives on this major historical event.

TESTIMONY
Ellison Jack

An 11-year-old girl who worked in the mines testified before a Parliamentary commission on child labor in 1842.

I have been working below three years on my father's account; he takes me down at two in the morning, and I come up at one and two next afternoon. I go to bed at six at night to be ready for work next morning. . . . I have to bear my burthen [burden] up four traps, or ladders, before I get to the main road which leads to the pit bottom. My task is four or five tubs. . . . I fill five tubs in twenty journeys.

I have had the strap [beating] when I did not do my bidding. Am very glad when my task is wrought, as it sore fatigues.

LETTER

Mary Paul

Mary Paul worked in a textile factory in Lowell, Massachusetts. In an 1846 letter to her father in New Hampshire, the 16-year-old expressed her satisfaction with her situation at Lowell.

I am at work in a spinning room tending four sides of warp which is one girl's work. The overseer tells me that he never had a girl get along better than I do. . . . I have a very good boarding place, have enough to eat. . . . The girls are all kind and obliging. . . . I think that the factory is the best place for me and if any girl wants employment, I advise them to come to Lowell.

BOOK
Andrew Carnegie

In his autobiography, published in 1920, the multimillionaire industrialist views with optimism the growth of American industry.

America is soon to change from being the dearest steel manufacturing country to the cheapest. Already the shipyards of Belfast are our customers. This is but the beginning. Under present conditions America can produce steel as cheaply as any other land, notwithstanding its higher-priced labor. There is no other labor so cheap as the dearest in the mechanical field, provided it is free, contented, zealous, and reaping reward as it renders service. And here America leads.

One great advantage which America will have in competing in the markets of the world is that her manufacturers will have the best home market. Upon this they can depend for a return upon capital, and the surplus product can be exported with advantage, even when the prices received for it do no more than cover actual cost, provided the exports be charged with their proportion of all expenses. The nation that has the best home market, especially if products are standardized, as ours are, can soon outsell the foreign producer.

BOOK
Friedrich Engels

Friedrich Engels, who managed a textile factory in Manchester, England, spent his nights wandering the city's slums.

Nobody troubles about the poor as they struggle helplessly in the whirlpool of modern industrial life. The working man may be lucky enough to find employment, if by his labor he can enrich some member of the middle classes. But his wages are so low that they hardly keep body and soul together. If he cannot find work, he can steal, unless he is afraid of the police; or he can go hungry and then the police will see to it that he will die of hunger in such a way as not to disturb the equanimity of the middle classes.

Connect *to* History

Contrasting Contrast two different points of view on the Industrial Revolution. Why do you think the viewpoints differ?

SEE SKILLBUILDER HANDBOOK, PAGE 996

Connect *to* Today

Researching Find a modern view of industrialization in an editorial cartoon, a poem, an excerpt from a novel, or a photograph. Bring it to class and explain its point of view.

 CD-ROM For another perspective on the Industrial Revolution, see World History: Electronic Library of Primary Sources.

Chapter **25** Assessment

TERMS & NAMES

Briefly explain the importance of each of the following to industrialization.

1. Industrial Revolution
2. enclosure
3. factory
4. urbanization
5. middle class
6. corporation
7. laissez faire
8. socialism
9. Karl Marx
10. collective bargaining

Interact *with* History

On page 632, you looked at working conditions in an English factory in the 19th century before reading about the Industrial Revolution. Now that you've read the chapter, rethink your decision about what you would do to change your situation. What factory working conditions would you like to see change? What benefits might a union bring? What disadvantages might result if workers organize? Discuss your opinions with a small group.

REVIEW QUESTIONS

SECTION 1 *(pages 633–637)*
The Beginnings of Industrialization

11. What were the four natural resources needed for British industrialization?
12. How did the enclosure movement change agriculture in England?
13. Name two inventions that were created during the Industrial Revolution. Describe their impact.

SECTION 2 *(pages 638–642)*
Patterns of Change: Industrialization

14. Describe the living conditions in Britain during industrialization.
15. How did the new middle class transform the social structure of Great Britain during industrialization?
16. How did industrialization affect Manchester's natural environment?

SECTION 3 *(pages 643–646)*
Industrialization Spreads

17. Why were other European countries slower to industrialize than Britain?
18. What helps to explain the rise of global inequality during the Industrial Revolution?

SECTION 4 *(pages 647–652)*
An Age of Reforms

19. What were the two warring classes that Marx and Engels outlined in *The Communist Manifesto*?
20. Name two ways women fought for change during the Industrial Revolution.

Visual Summary

The Industrial Revolution

Economic Effects

- New inventions and development of factories
- Rapidly growing industry in the 1800s
- Increased production and higher demand for raw materials
- Growth of worldwide trade
- Population explosion and a large labor force
- Exploitation of mineral resources
- Highly developed banking and investment system
- Advances in transportation, agriculture, and communication

Social Effects

- Long hours worked by children in factories
- Increase in population of cities
- Poor city planning
- Loss of family stability
- Expansion of middle class
- Harsh conditions for laborers
- Workers' progress vs. laissez-faire economic attitudes
- Improved standard of living
- Creation of new jobs
- Encouragement of technological progress

Political Effects

- Child labor laws to end abuses
- Reformers urging equal distribution of wealth
- Trade unions
- Social reform movements, such as utilitarianism, utopianism, socialism, and Marxism
- Reform bills in Parliament

CRITICAL THINKING

1. INDUSTRIAL REVOLUTION BRINGS CHANGE

How significant were the changes the Industrial Revolution brought to the world? How enduring were they? Explain your conclusion. Think about economic, social, and political changes.

2. TECHNOLOGICAL ADVANCES

THEME SCIENCE & TECHNOLOGY Create a chart like the one below that lists some of the major technological advances and their effects on industrial society.

Technological Advance	Effect(s)

3. MILITARY POWER

How did the Industrial Revolution help to increase Germany's military power?

4. ANALYZING PRIMARY SOURCES

The following quotation comes from Charles Dickens's *Hard Times,* first published in book form in 1854. In *Hard Times,* as well as in several of his other novels, Dickens exposes such evils of industrialization as child labor, polluted cities, and corrupt factory owners. The following excerpt begins the chapter "No Way Out." Read the paragraph and answer the questions that follow.

> **A VOICE FROM THE PAST**
> The Fairy Palaces burst into illumination before pale morning showed the monstrous serpents of smoke trailing themselves over Coketown. A clattering of clogs upon the pavement, a rapid ringing of bells, and all the melancholy mad elephants, polished and oiled up for the day's monotony, were at their heavy exercise again.

- What is Dickens's opinion of the factory town? What words give you that impression?

- Why do you think Dickens called the chapter "No Way Out"?

CHAPTER ACTIVITIES

1. LIVING HISTORY: Unit Portfolio Project

THEME EMPIRE BUILDING Your unit portfolio project focuses on how different nations built empires (see page 629). For Chapter 25, you might use one of the following ideas to add to your portfolio:

- Would a non-industrialized or an industrialized nation more likely be an empire builder in the 19th and 20th centuries? Stage a debate to discuss this question. Videotape the session.

- You are an artisan in a non-industrialized nation threatened by a flood of cheap European goods into your marketplace. Write a letter to the editor of a local paper describing your situation, with any suggestions for improvement.

- Work with a partner to create British posters advertising their manufactured goods in overseas, less-developed markets.

2. CONNECT TO TODAY: Cooperative Learning

THEME ECONOMICS You read about harsh child labor practices during the Industrial Revolution. Today, child labor still exists in many developing nations, with many of the same unsanitary, unsafe, and grueling conditions. Work with a team to find out what the various child labor situations are in different places.

 Using the Internet or your library, research organizations that are fighting child labor.

- Write a letter, or in some other manner voice your concern and support to these organizations.

3. INTERPRETING A TIME LINE

Revisit the unit time line on pages 628–629. Look at events for Chapter 25. Write two more entries that could be added to the time line from Chapter 25. Support your answer with evidence from the text.

FOCUS ON **GRAPHS**

The graph to the right shows population growth in four European cities from 1700 to 1900, that is, before and after the Industrial Revolution.

- Which city had the smallest population in 1700? How many people had it gained by 1900?

- Which city gained the most people in this period? How many people did it gain between 1700 and 1900?

Connect to History
Why did cities grow so rapidly in this period? What lured people to the cities?

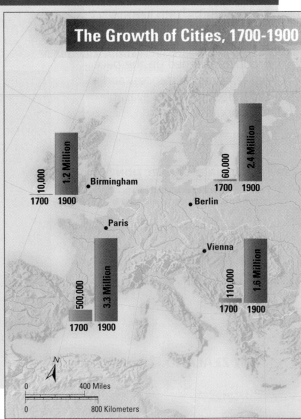

The Growth of Cities, 1700-1900

Birmingham — 10,000 (1700), 1.2 Million (1900)
Berlin — 60,000 (1700), 2.4 Million (1900)
Paris — 500,000 (1700), 3.3 Million (1900)
Vienna — 110,000 (1700), 1.5 Million (1900)

0 — 400 Miles
0 — 800 Kilometers

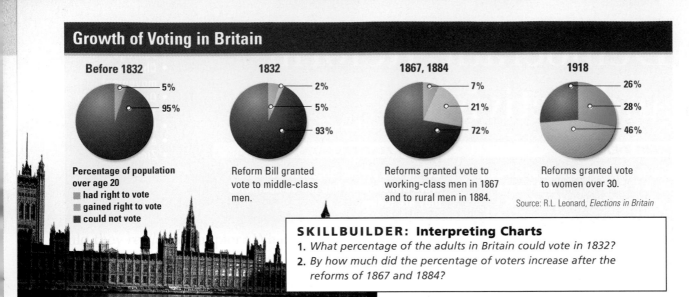

Growth of Voting in Britain

Before 1832

5%

95%

Percentage of population over age 20
- ■ had right to vote
- ■ gained right to vote
- ■ could not vote

1832

2%

5%

93%

Reform Bill granted vote to middle-class men.

1867, 1884

7%

21%

72%

Reforms granted vote to working-class men in 1867 and to rural men in 1884.

1918

26%

28%

46%

Reforms granted vote to women over 30.

Source: R.L. Leonard, *Elections in Britain*

> **SKILLBUILDER: Interpreting Charts**
> 1. *What percentage of the adults in Britain could vote in 1832?*
> 2. *By how much did the percentage of voters increase after the reforms of 1867 and 1884?*

The modern Parliament building was completed in 1867.

vote. The passage of the bill, however, encouraged reformers. Among the workers and other groups who still could not vote, a popular movement arose to press for more rights. It was called the **Chartist movement** because the group first presented its demands to Parliament on a petition called The People's Charter of 1838.

The People's Charter called for suffrage for all men and annual Parliamentary elections. It also proposed to reform Parliament in other ways. In Britain at the time, eligible men voted openly by voice. Since their vote was not secret, they could feel pressure to vote in a certain way. Moreover, members of Parliament had to own land and received no salary, so they needed to be independently wealthy. The Chartists wanted to make Parliament more responsive to the interests of the lower classes. To achieve this, they demanded a secret ballot, an end to the property requirements for serving in Parliament, and pay for members of Parliament.

Parliament rejected the Chartists' demands. However, their protests convinced many people that workers had sound complaints. Over the years, workers continued to press for political reform, and Parliament eventually responded. It gave the vote to working-class men in 1867 and to male rural workers in 1884. After 1884, therefore, most adult males in Britain had the right to vote. By the early 1900s, all the demands of the Chartists, except for annual elections, became law.

The Victorian Age The figure who presided over all this historic change was **Queen Victoria.** Victoria came to the throne in 1837 at the age of 18. She was queen for 64 years, one of the longest reigns in history. During the Victorian Age, the British empire reached the height of its wealth and power. Victoria was popular with her subjects, and she performed her duties wisely and capably. However, she was forced to accept a new, virtually powerless role for the British monarchy.

The kings who preceded Victoria in the 1700s and 1800s had exercised great influence over Parliament. The spread of democracy in the 1800s shifted political power almost completely to Parliament, and especially to the elected House of Commons. Now the government was completely run by the prime minister and the cabinet. Thus, ever since Queen Victoria, British monarchs have been mainly symbolic rulers with no political power.

Women Demand the Vote

By 1890, several industrial countries had universal male suffrage (the right of all men to vote). No country, however, allowed women to vote. As more men gained suffrage, more women demanded the same.

HISTORY MAKERS

**Queen Victoria
1819–1901**

Three years after her coronation, Queen Victoria fell in love with her cousin Albert, a German prince. She proposed to him and they were married in 1840. Together they had nine children. The strait-laced Prince Albert established a tone of polite propriety at court, and the royal couple presented a picture of loving family life that became a British ideal.

After Albert died in 1861, the Queen wore black silk for the rest of her life in mourning. She once said of Albert, "Without him everything loses its interest."

**THINK THROUGH HISTORY
B. Making Inferences** Why do you think the Chartists demanded a secret ballot rather than public voting?

**THINK THROUGH HISTORY
C. Making Inferences** Why might Queen Victoria have accepted a powerless new role for the British monarchy? Think about other monarchies in Europe in the 1800s.

Victorian Ladies' News

Mind Your Tea and Cakes

Taking afternoon tea at about 5:00 P.M. has become as English as London fog, but tea drinkers should be careful to buy supplies only from reputable sources. Some so-called tea merchants add coloring to convert blackthorn leaves into something that looks like tea. In London, several factories dye recycled tea leaves for dishonest merchants to sell as new tea.

Be careful, too, about those cakes you serve with your tea. To get the brightest colors to decorate cakes, some dishonest bakers use dangerous chemicals: copper and zinc to get gold and silver; iron for blue and lead for red; and even arsenic for green.

Cholera Comes from Bad Water

London: This fall, Dr. John Snow published a revised edition of his 1849 pamphlet entitled "On the Mode of Communication of Cholera." In his pamphlet, Dr. Snow uses case examples to show that contaminated drinking water caused the cholera epidemics that killed thousands of poor Londoners in 1831–1832, 1848–1849, and 1854. Dr. Snow's critics scorn his theory, maintaining that cholera spreads from the air that surrounds rubbish heaps.

CHOLERA.

THE

DUDLEY BOARD OF HEALTH,

HEREBY GIVE NOTICE, THAT IN CONSEQUENCE OF THE

Church-yards at Dudley

Being so full, no one who has died of the CHOLERA will be permitted to be buried after *SUNDAY* next, (To-morrow) in either of the Burial Grounds of *St. Thomas's,* or *St. Edmund's,* in this Town.

All Persons who die from CHOLERA, must for the future be buried in the Church-yard at Netherton.

BOARD of HEALTH, DUDLEY.
September 1st, 1832.

W. MAURICE, PRINTER, HIGH STREET, DUDLEY.

Riding the Rails

If you want to travel quickly and cheaply, you can't beat the new and improved British railways. Regular trains will speed you to your destination at 20 miles an hour; on express routes, you'll whiz along at nearly 40. Here are some tips for happier traveling:

- Bring your own candles if you intend to read at night.
- Prepare to rent a metal foot warmer if you're taking a winter journey.
- Bring your own food or prepare to brave the crowds at station restaurants.
- For long journeys, tote a chamber pot in a basket.

London's Paddington Station bustles with passengers in this painting.

Victorian Manners

The proper gentleman

- lets a lady walk or ride along the wall
- never speaks to a lady unless she speaks to him first
- precedes a lady walking upstairs and follows one walking downstairs
- takes the backward-facing seat in a carriage and gets out first to help a lady dismount
- never smokes in a lady's presence

The proper lady

- never walks alone or never walks unchaperoned if she is unmarried and under 30
- does not go alone to make a social call on a man
- never wears pearls or diamonds in the morning
- never dances more than three dances with the same partner

Connect *to* History

Synthesizing List examples from this page to demonstrate that popular culture in Victorian England admired both tradition and change.

 SEE SKILLBUILDER HANDBOOK, PAGE 1007

Connect *to* Today

Researching Using the library or Internet, research some aspect of American culture that shows an example of either tradition or dramatic change. As possible subjects, consider transportation, communications, entertainment, or fashion.

Organization and Resistance During the 1800s, women in both Great Britain and the United States worked to gain the right to vote. In the United States, women such as Lucretia Mott and Elizabeth Cady Stanton organized a campaign for women's rights as early as 1848. From a convention in Seneca Falls, New York, they issued a declaration of women's rights modeled on the Declaration of Independence. "We hold these truths to be self-evident," the declaration stated, "that all men and women are created equal."

A VOICE FROM THE PAST

The history of mankind is a history of repeated injuries and usurpations on the part of man toward woman, having in direct object the establishment of an absolute tyranny over her. To prove this, let facts be submitted to a candid world.

He has never permitted her to exercise her inalienable right to the elective franchise. He has compelled her to submit to laws in the formation of which she has no voice.

THE SENECA FALLS CONVENTION, "Declaration of Sentiments"

THINK THROUGH HISTORY
D. Clarifying In your own words, summarize the main issue expressed in this passage.

British women, too, organized reform societies and protested unfair laws and customs. As women became more vocal, however, resistance to their demands grew. Many people, both men and women, thought that women's suffrage was too radical a break with tradition. Some claimed that women lacked the ability to take part in politics.

Militant Protests After decades of peaceful efforts to win the right to vote, some women took more drastic steps. In Britain, Emmeline Pankhurst formed the Women's Social and Political Union (WSPU) in 1903. The WSPU became the most militant organization for women's rights. Besides peaceful demonstrations and parades, its members heckled government speakers, cut telegraph wires, and committed arson. Their goal was to draw attention to the cause of women's suffrage.

Emmeline Pankhurst, her daughters Christabel and Sylvia, and other WSPU members were arrested and imprisoned many times. When they were jailed, the Pankhursts led hunger strikes to keep their cause in the public eye. British officials force-fed Sylvia and other activists to keep them alive. One WSPU member, Emily Davison, did give her life for the women's movement. As a protest, she threw herself in front of the king's horse at the English Derby.

Though the women's suffrage movement commanded wide attention between 1880 and 1914, its successes were gradual. Women did not win the right to vote in national elections in Great Britain and the United States until after World War I.

GlobalImpact

The Women's Movement

By the 1880s, women were working internationally to win more rights. In 1888, women activists from the United States, Canada, and Europe met in Washington, D.C., for the International Council of Women. In 1893, delegates and observers from 27 countries attended a large congress of women in Chicago. They came from lands as far apart as New Zealand, Argentina, Iceland, Persia, and China.

The first countries to grant women's suffrage were New Zealand (1893) and Australia (1902). Only in two European countries—Finland (1906, then part of the Russian Empire) and Norway (1913)—did women gain voting rights before World War I. In the United States, the territory of Wyoming allowed women to vote in 1869. Several other Western states followed suit.

Democracy in France

While Great Britain moved toward true democracy in the late 1800s, democracy finally took permanent hold in France. However, France's road to democracy was rocky.

The Third Republic In the aftermath of the Franco-Prussian War, France went through a series of crises. After being released by Prussia, Napoleon III spent his last years in exile in Britain. France's National Assembly met to decide on a new government.

Meanwhile, in March 1871, a radical government called the Paris Commune took control of Paris. In May, troops loyal to the National Assembly marched into the city. Parisian workers threw up barricades in the streets and fought the army block by block. After a week of fighting, the army stamped out the Communards, as supporters of the Commune were called. About 20,000 Parisians were massacred, and much of the city burned.

Not until 1875 could the National Assembly agree on a new government. Eventually, the members voted to set up a republic. In the words of a leading French politician, it

Background
During the Franco-Prussian War, the Germans captured Napoleon III and held Paris under siege for four months. The siege ended in late January 1871.

was "the system of government that divides us least." The **Third Republic,** as this new system was called, lasted over 60 years. However, France remained bitterly divided. A dozen political parties competed for power. Between 1871 and 1914, France averaged a change of government every ten months.

The Dreyfus Affair During the 1880s and 1890s, the unsteady Third Republic was threatened by monarchists, aristocrats, clergy, and army leaders. These groups wanted to return France to a monarchy or to have military rule. A controversy known as the **Dreyfus affair** became a battleground for these opposing forces. Widespread feelings of **anti-Semitism,** or prejudice against Jews, also played a role in this scandal.

In 1894, Captain Alfred Dreyfus, one of the few Jewish officers in the French army, was accused of selling military secrets to Germany. A court found him guilty, based on false evidence, and sentenced him to life in prison. In a few years, new evidence showed that Dreyfus had been framed by other army officers.

Public opinion was sharply divided over the scandal. Many army leaders, nationalists, leaders in the clergy, and anti-Jewish groups refused to let the case be reopened. They feared sudden action would cast doubt on the honor of the army. Dreyfus's defenders insisted that justice was more important and that he should be freed. In 1898, the writer Émile Zola published an open letter titled *J'accuse!* (I Accuse) in a popular French newspaper. In the letter, Zola denounced the army for covering up a scandal. Zola was given a year in prison for his views, but his letter gave strength to Dreyfus's cause. Eventually, the French government officially declared his innocence.

The Rise of Zionism The Dreyfus case showed the strength of anti-Semitism in France and other parts of Western Europe. However, persecution of Jews was even more severe in Eastern Europe. Russian officials, for example, permitted and even encouraged pogroms (puh·GRAHMS)—organized campaigns of violence against Jewish communities. From the late 1880s on, thousands of Jews fled Eastern Europe. Many headed for the United States.

For many Jews, the long history of exile and persecution convinced them that they should work for a separate homeland in Palestine. In the 1890s, a movement known as **Zionism** developed to pursue this goal. Its leader was Theodor Herzl (HEHRT·suhl), a writer in Vienna. It took many years, however, before the state of Israel was established, making the dream a reality.

THINK THROUGH HISTORY
E. Analyzing Issues
Explain the controversy over the Dreyfus affair.

Background
Zion is another name for Israel, the Jewish homeland.

Communards lie massacred in this painting titled *A Street in Paris in May 1871, or the Commune* by Maximilien Luce.

Section ❶ Assessment

1. TERMS & NAMES

Identify
• suffrage
• Chartist movement
• Queen Victoria
• Third Republic
• Dreyfus affair
• anti-Semitism
• Zionism

2. TAKING NOTES

List and evaluate five significant events from this section, using a table like the one shown. Next to each event, put a "+" if it expanded democracy, a "−" if it negatively affected democracy, and a "0" if it had a mixed impact.

Event	Evaluation

3. ANALYZING ISSUES

Look again at the excerpt from the Seneca Falls "Declaration of Sentiments" on page 662. Why do you think the members of the Seneca Falls Convention chose to model their demands on the Declaration of Independence? (It may be helpful to locate the similar section in a copy of the Declaration of Independence and compare the two passages.)

4. THEME ACTIVITY

Economics Among the Chartists' demands was pay for members of Parliament. Often when a U.S. legislature raises the pay for its own members, it creates controversy. Imagine such a raise is being considered. Write a "letter to the editor" that supports or criticizes the raise. Be sure to refer to the historical reasons for giving pay to legislators.

TERMS & NAMES
- dominion
- Maori
- Aborigine
- penal colony
- home rule

2 Self-Rule for British Colonies

MAIN IDEA	WHY IT MATTERS NOW
Britain allowed self-rule in Canada, Australia, and New Zealand but delayed independence for Ireland.	Canada, Australia, and New Zealand are strong democracies today, while Ireland is divided and troubled.

SETTING THE STAGE By 1800, Great Britain had colonies around the world. These included small outposts in Africa and Asia. In these areas, thc British managed trade with the local peoples, but they had little influence over the population at large. In the colonies of Canada, Australia, and New Zealand, on the other hand, European colonists had overrun and replaced the native populations. As Britain industrialized and prospered in the 1800s, so did these colonies. Like the United States, which had already broken away from British rule, some of these colonies were becoming strong enough to stand on their own.

Canada Struggles for Self-Rule

Canada was originally home to many Native American peoples, including the Algonquin, Huron, Cree, Blackfoot, and Inuit. The first European country to colonize Canada was France. Great Britain took possession of the country in 1763, following the French and Indian War. The thousands of French who remained there lived mostly in the lower St. Lawrence Valley. Many English-speaking colonists arrived in Canada after it came under British rule. Some came from Great Britain, and others were Americans who had stayed loyal to Britain after the American Revolution. They settled separately from the French—mostly along the Atlantic seaboard and north of the Great Lakes.

The earliest French colonists had included many fur trappers and missionaries. They tended to live among the Native Americans rather than displace them. Some French intermarried with Native Americans. As more French and British settlers arrived, they took over much of eastern and southern Canada. Native groups in the north and west, however, remained largely undisturbed until later in the 1800s.

French and English Canada Religious and cultural differences between the mostly Roman Catholic French and the mainly Protestant English-speaking colonists caused conflict in Canada. Both groups also pressed Britain for a greater voice in governing their own affairs. In 1791 the British Parliament tried to resolve both issues by creating two new Canadian provinces. Upper Canada (now Ontario) had an English-speaking majority. Lower Canada (now Quebec) had a French-speaking majority. Each province had its own elected assembly with limited powers.

The Durham Report The division of Upper and Lower Canada eased colonial tensions only temporarily. In both colonies, the royal governor and a small group of wealthy British held most of the power. During the early 1800s, the people in both colonies, led by middle-class professionals, began to demand political and economic reforms. In Lower Canada, these demands were also fueled by French resentment toward British rule. In the late 1830s, rebellions broke out in both

THINK THROUGH HISTORY
A. Clarifying Why did Britain create Upper Canada and Lower Canada? Who lived in each colony?

Upper and Lower Canada. The British Parliament remembered the events that had led to the American Revolution. So, it sent a reform-minded statesman, Lord Durham, to investigate Canadians' demands for self-rule.

Durham's report, issued in 1839, urged two major reforms. First, Upper and Lower Canada should be reunited as the Province of Canada, and British immigration should be encouraged. In this way, Durham said, the French would slowly become part of the dominant English culture. Second, colonists in the provinces of Canada should be allowed to govern themselves in domestic matters. Parliament should regulate only in matters of foreign policy. Within ten years, both proposals had been carried out.

THINK THROUGH HISTORY
B. Recognizing Effects How do you think Durham's recommendations affected French-speaking Canadians?

The Dominion of Canada By the mid-1800s, many Canadians believed that Canada needed a central government. A central government would be better able to protect the interests of Canadians against the United States, whose territory now extended from the Atlantic to the Pacific oceans. In 1867, Nova Scotia and New Brunswick joined with the Province of Canada to form the Dominion of Canada. As a **dominion,** Canada was self-governing in domestic affairs but remained part of the British Empire.

Canada's Westward Expansion Canada's first prime minister, John MacDonald, quickly expanded Canada westward by purchasing lands and persuading frontier territories to join the Canadian union. Canada stretched to the Pacific Ocean by 1871. MacDonald also began the construction of a transcontinental railroad to unite distant parts of the dominion. It was completed in 1885.

The dominion government also took other steps to strengthen Canada. It encouraged foreign investment to develop Canada's rich supply of natural resources. It also encouraged immigration to provide a labor force for Canada's farms and factories.

CONNECT *to* TODAY

The Nunavut Territory

While Canada expanded westward in the 1870s, it also gained vast lands in the Arctic north. Most of the inhabitants of this sparsely populated region were Inuit. This native people had developed a way of life in the harsh Arctic climate over a period of thousands of years.

During the 20th century, the northern region became important to Canada for its rich natural resources and as a location for military bases. At the same time, the Inuit wanted more control over the resources of their native lands and a greater voice in their own affairs.

In the early 1990s, the Inuit and the Canadian government agreed to create a new self-governing territory called Nunavut in 1999. The name is an Inuit word meaning "Our Land." Nunavut includes the eastern two-thirds of the Northwest Territories—an area of land one-fifth the size of Canada.

Australia and New Zealand

The British sea captain James Cook claimed New Zealand in 1769 and Australia in 1770 for Great Britain. Both lands were already inhabited. On New Zealand, Cook was greeted by the **Maoris,** a Polynesian people who had settled on New Zealand's two main islands around A.D. 800. Maori culture was based on farming, hunting, and fishing. Although the Maoris had driven away Dutch explorers in the 1640s, they made peace with Cook. As British colonization began, however, they stood ready to defend their land.

When Cook reached Australia, he considered the land uninhabited. In fact, Australia was sparsely populated by **Aborigines,** as Europeans later called the native peoples. These nomadic peoples fished, hunted, and gathered food. As they did not practice warfare among themselves, they at first raised little resistance to the flood of British immigrants who settled their country.

Britain's Penal Colony Britain began colonizing Australia in 1788—not with ordinary settlers, but with convicted criminals. The prisons in England were severely overcrowded. To solve this problem, the British government established a penal colony in Australia. A **penal colony** is a place where convicts were sent to serve their sentences as an alternative to prison. Many European nations used penal colonies as a way to prevent overcrowding of their prisons. After their release, the freed convicts could buy land and settle as free men and women.

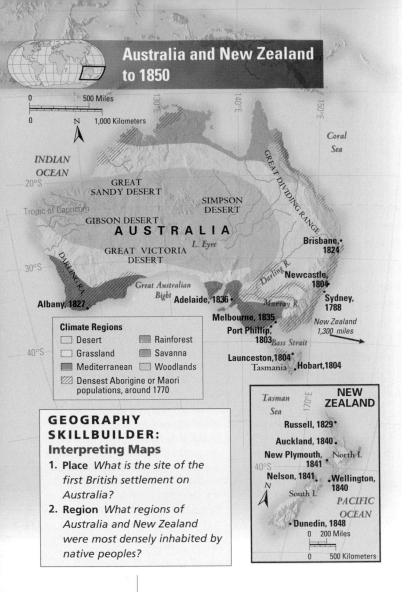

Australia and New Zealand to 1850

Climate Regions
- Desert
- Grassland
- Mediterranean
- Rainforest
- Savanna
- Woodlands
- Densest Aborigine or Maori populations, around 1770

GEOGRAPHY SKILLBUILDER: Interpreting Maps
1. **Place** What is the site of the first British settlement on Australia?
2. **Region** What regions of Australia and New Zealand were most densely inhabited by native peoples?

Free Settlers Arrive In time, the former convicts in both Australia and New Zealand were joined by other British settlers who came of their own free will. In the early 1800s, an Australian settler named John MacArthur experimented with breeds of sheep until he found one that produced high quality wool and thrived in the country's warm dry weather. Although sheep are not native to Australia, the raising and export of wool became its biggest business. Australians say that their country "rode to prosperity on the back of a sheep."

To encourage immigration, the government offered settlers cheap land. It used the money from land sales to lure laborers from Britain by paying the costs of the long voyage. The population grew steadily in the early 1800s and then skyrocketed after a gold rush in 1851.

The scattered settlements on Australia's east coast grew into separate colonies. Meanwhile, a few pioneers pushed westward across the vast dry interior and established outposts in western Australia. In the 1860s, settlers finally pressured the British to stop sending convicts to Australia.

Settling New Zealand European settlement of New Zealand grew more slowly. This was because the British did not claim ownership of New Zealand, as it did Australia. Rather, it recognized the land rights of the Maoris. Among the first British settlers in New Zealand were convicts who had escaped from Australia. In 1814, missionary groups began arriving from Australia seeking to convert the Maoris to Christianity.

The arrival of more foreigners stirred conflicts between the Maoris and the European settlers over land. Responding to the settlers' pleas, the British decided to annex New Zealand in 1838 and appointed a governor to negotiate with the Maoris. In a treaty signed in 1840, the Maoris accepted British rule in exchange for recognition of their land rights. Britain quickly established colonies around New Zealand. Many colonists successfully turned to producing wool and other agricultural products for export.

THINK THROUGH HISTORY
C. Contrasting How did the colonial settlement of Australia and New Zealand differ?

Self-Government Like many Canadians, the colonists of Australia and New Zealand wanted to rule themselves yet remain in the British Empire. During the 1850s, the colonies in both Australia and New Zealand became self-governing and created parliamentary forms of government. In 1901, the Australian colonies were united under a federal constitution as the Commonwealth of Australia. During the early 1900s, both Australia and New Zealand became dominions.

The people of Australia and New Zealand pioneered a number of political reforms. For example, the secret ballot, sometimes called the Australian ballot, was first used in Australia in the 1850s. In 1893, New Zealand became the first nation in the world to give full voting rights to women. These rights were granted only to white women of European descent.

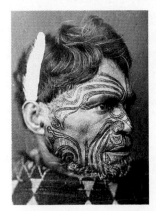

This photo from the early 20th century shows a Maori man with traditional dress and face markings.

Status of Native Peoples Native peoples and other non-Europeans were generally excluded from democracy and prosperity. As in the Americas, diseases brought by the Europeans killed a great number of both Aborigines and Maoris. As Australian settlement grew, the colonists displaced or killed many Aborigines. Sheep ranchers in particular took possession of vast tracts of land for grazing. Both the loss of open land and the spread of diseases contributed to the destruction of the Aborigines' way of life.

In New Zealand, tensions between settlers and Maoris continued to grow after it became a British colony. Between 1845 and 1872, the colonial government fought the Maoris in a series of wars. Reduced by disease and outgunned by British weapons, the Maoris were finally driven into a remote part of the country.

The Irish Fight for Home Rule

English expansion into Ireland had begun in the 1100s, when the pope granted control of Ireland to the English king. English knights invaded Ireland, and many settled there to form a new aristocracy. The Irish, who had their own ancestry, culture, and language, bitterly resented the English presence.

This resentment grew stronger after English King Henry VIII tried to tighten England's hold on Ireland. In hopes of planting a pro-English population in Ireland, Henry VIII and some later English leaders (including Elizabeth I and Oliver Cromwell) encouraged English and Scottish subjects to move there. Large numbers did, mostly to the north. Religious differences between the native Irish, who were Catholic, and these Protestant settlers caused conflicts.

Laws imposed in the 1500s and 1600s limited the rights of Catholics. For example, Catholics could no longer hold public office. They had to pay taxes to support the Church of Ireland, which was Protestant. In addition, English was made Ireland's official language.

Many Irish hated British rule. However, the British government was determined to preserve its control over Ireland. It formally joined Ireland to Britain in 1801. Though a setback for Irish nationalism, this move did give Ireland representation in the British Parliament. One brilliant Irish leader, Daniel O'Connell, persuaded Parliament to pass the Catholic Emancipation Act in 1829. This law restored many rights to Catholics.

Background
The act that joined Ireland to Britain created the United Kingdom of Great Britain and Ireland. The 1707 Act of Union had created Great Britain out of England, Scotland, and Wales.

Background
Before the famine, the average Irish adult ate an estimated 9 to 14 pounds of potatoes a day.

The Great Famine In the 1840s, Ireland experienced one of the worst famines of modern history. For many years, Irish peasants had depended on potatoes as virtually their sole source of food. From 1845 to 1848, a plant fungus ruined nearly all of Ireland's potato crop. Out of a population of 8 million, about a million people died from starvation and disease over the next few years. A traveler described what he saw on a journey through Ireland in 1847:

A VOICE FROM THE PAST
We entered a cabin. Stretched in one dark corner, scarcely visible, from the smoke and rags that covered them, were three children huddled together, lying there *because they were too weak to rise*, pale and ghastly, their little limbs—on removing a portion of the filthy covering—perfectly emaciated, eyes sunk, voice gone, and evidently in the last stage of actual starvation.

WILLIAM BENNETT, quoted in *The Peoples of Ireland*

The Great Famine, 1845–1851

Fate of the Irish during the famine

- 70% remained in Ireland, though millions more Irish emigrated after 1851
- 12% died
- 18% emigrated

Where they emigrated to (1851)

Australia, 2.5%
Canada, 11.5%
Britain, 36%
United States, 50%

Sources: R.F. Foster, *Modern Ireland, 1600–1972;* D. Fitzpatrick, *Irish Emigration, 1804–1921*

SKILLBUILDER:
Interpreting Graphs
1. *What percentage of Ireland's population died during the great famine?*
2. *Which country received the most Irish emigrants?*

During the famine years, about a million-and-a-half people fled from Ireland. Most went to the United States; others went to Britain, Canada, and Australia. At home, in Ireland, the British government enforced the demands of the English landowners that the Irish peasants pay their rent. Many Irish lost their land and fell hopelessly in debt, while large landowners profited from higher food prices. This situation fueled even greater Irish resentment toward their British overlords.

Demands for Home Rule During the second half of the 1800s, opposition to British rule over Ireland took two forms. Some people wanted Ireland to be completely independent. A greater number of Irish preferred **home rule**—local control over internal matters only. The British refused, however, to consider home rule for many decades.

One reason for Britain's opposition to home rule was concern for Ireland's Protestants. Protestants made up a small minority of the population. Most lived in the northern part of Ireland, known as Ulster. Irish Protestants feared being a minority in a country dominated by Catholics. Finally, in 1914, Parliament enacted a home rule bill for southern Ireland. Just one month before the plan was to take effect, World War I broke out in Europe. The issue of Irish independence was put on hold.

Rebellion and Division Frustrated over the delay in independence, a small group of Irish nationalists rebelled in Dublin in Easter week, 1916. British troops quickly put down the Easter Rising and executed its leaders. Their fate, however, aroused wider popular support for the nationalist movement.

After World War I ended, the Irish nationalists won a major victory in the elections for the British Parliament. To protest delays in home rule, the nationalist members decided not to attend Parliament. Instead, they formed an underground Irish government and led a series of violent attacks against British officials in Ireland. The attacks sparked war between the nationalists and the British government.

In 1921, Britain tried to end the violence by dividing Ireland and granting home rule to southern Ireland. Ulster, or Northern Ireland, remained a part of Great Britain. The south became a dominion called the Irish Free State. However, many Irish nationalists, led by Eamon De Valera, continued to seek total independence from Britain. In 1949, the Irish Free State declared itself the independent Republic of Ireland.

NO HOME RULE
LET OUR FLAG RUN OUT STRAIGHT IN THE WIND, THE OLD RED SHALL BE FLOATED AGAIN
WHEN THE RANKS THAT THINNED SHALL BE THINNED, WHEN THE NAMES THAT ARE TWENTY ARE TEN.
ULSTER !

This poster urges Protestant Northern Ireland to reject home rule. The militant tone foreshadows the continuing political troubles in Northern Ireland today.

THINK THROUGH HISTORY
D. Evaluating Decisions Was Britain's policy in dividing Ireland successful? Why or why not?

CONNECT to TODAY

"Troubles" in Northern Ireland

When Northern Ireland decided to stay united with Great Britain, many Catholics there refused to accept the partition, or division. Catholics also resented that the Protestant majority controlled Northern Ireland's government and economy.

In the late 1960s, Catholic groups began to demonstrate for more civil rights. Their protests touched off violent rioting and fighting between Catholics and Protestants. Militant groups on both sides engaged in terrorism. This violent period, called the "troubles," continued into the 1990s.

In 1999, on the heels of a historic peace accord, Catholics and Protestants began sharing power in a new home-rule government. Nonetheless, tensions between the two sides remain.

Section 2 Assessment

1. TERMS & NAMES

Identify
- dominion
- Maori
- Aborigine
- penal colony
- home rule

2. TAKING NOTES

Using a chart like the one below, compare progress toward self-rule by recording significant political events in Canada, Australia, New Zealand, and Ireland during the period.

Country	Political Events
Canada	
Australia	
New Zealand	
Ireland	

3. COMPARING

How was Great Britain's policy towards Canada beginning in the late 1700s similar to its policy towards Ireland in the 1900s?

THINK ABOUT
- the creation of Upper and Lower Canada
- the division of Ireland into Northern Ireland and the Irish Free State

4. ANALYZING THEMES

Empire Building At various times, England encouraged emigration to each of the colonies covered in this section. What effects did this policy have on these areas?

THINK ABOUT
- cultural divisions in Canada
- native peoples in Canada, Australia, and New Zealand
- political divisions in Ireland

Expansion and Crisis in the United States

TERMS & NAMES
- manifest destiny
- Abraham Lincoln
- secede
- U.S. Civil War
- Emancipation Proclamation
- segregation

MAIN IDEA

The United States expanded across North America and fought a bloody civil war.

WHY IT MATTERS NOW

The 20th-century movements to ensure civil rights for African Americans and Hispanics are a legacy of this period.

SETTING THE STAGE The United States had won its independence from Britain in 1783. At the end of the Revolutionary War, the Mississippi River marked the western boundary of the new republic. As the original United States filled with settlers, land-hungry newcomers pushed beyond the Mississippi, looking for opportunity. The government helped them by acquiring new territory for settlement.

Americans Move Westward

Piece by piece, the United States added new territory. In 1803, President Thomas Jefferson bought the Louisiana Territory from France. The Louisiana Purchase nearly doubled the size of the new republic and extended its boundary to the Rocky Mountains. In 1819, Spain gave up Florida to the United States. In 1846, a treaty with Great Britain gave the United States part of the Oregon Territory. In the north, the nation now stretched from the Atlantic Ocean to the Pacific Ocean.

War with Mexico Meanwhile, the United States had entered a war with Mexico over Texas. When Mexico had gained its independence from Spain in 1821, it included the lands west of the Louisiana Purchase—from Texas to California. Many American settlers moved into these areas, with Mexico's acceptance. Some settlers were unhappy with Mexico's rule.

The largest number of American settlers were in the Mexican territory of Texas. In 1836, Texans revolted against Mexican rule. For nine-and-a-half years, Texas was an independent country. Then, in 1845, the United States annexed Texas. Mexico responded angrily to what it believed was an act of aggression.

Between May 1846 and September 1847, war flared between the two countries. In bitter fighting, U.S. troops captured Mexico City and forced Mexico to surrender. As part of the settlement of the Mexican-American War, Mexico ceded, or gave up possession of, territory to the United States. The Mexican Cession included California and a huge amount of territory in the Southwest. A few years later, in 1853, the Gadsden Purchase from Mexico brought the lower continental United States to its present boundaries.

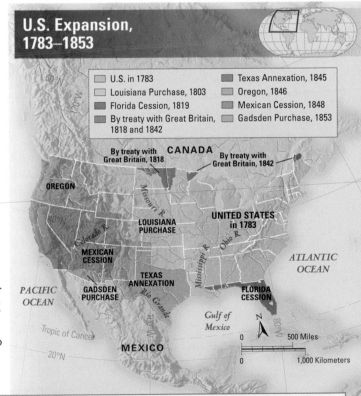

U.S. Expansion, 1783–1853

- U.S. in 1783
- Louisiana Purchase, 1803
- Florida Cession, 1819
- By treaty with Great Britain, 1818 and 1842
- Texas Annexation, 1845
- Oregon, 1846
- Mexican Cession, 1848
- Gadsden Purchase, 1853

GEOGRAPHY SKILLBUILDER: Interpreting Maps
1. **Movement** What was the first territory to be added to the United States after 1783?
2. **Region** What present-day states were part of the Mexican Cession?

Manifest Destiny Many Americans eagerly supported their country's westward expansion. These people believed in **manifest destiny**—the idea that the United States had the right and duty to rule North America from the Atlantic Ocean to the Pacific Ocean. Government leaders used manifest destiny as a way of justifying any action that helped white settlers occupy new land. This included evicting Native Americans from their tribal lands.

Vocabulary
manifest: clearly apparent or obvious.

The Indian Removal Act of 1830 made such actions official policy. This law enabled the federal government to force Native Americans living in the East to move to the West. Georgia's Cherokee tribe challenged the law before the Supreme Court. The Court, however, ruled the suit was invalid. Like many other Native American tribes, the Cherokees had to move. They traveled 800 miles to Oklahoma, mostly on foot, on a journey later called the Trail of Tears. About a quarter of the Cherokees died on the trip. A survivor recalled how the journey began:

A VOICE FROM THE PAST
The day was bright and beautiful, but a gloomy thoughtfulness was depicted in the lineaments of every face. . . . At this very moment a low sound of distant thunder fell on my ear . . . and sent forth a murmur, I almost thought a voice of divine indignation for the wrong of my poor and unhappy countrymen, driven by brutal power from all they loved and cherished in the land of their fathers.

WILLIAM SHOREY COODEY, quoted in *The Trail of Tears*

When the Cherokees reached their destination, they ended up on land far inferior to that which they had been forced to leave. Nor did the trail end there. As whites moved west during the second half of the 19th century, the government continued to push Native Americans off their land to make room for the new settlers. Eventually, the government demanded that Native Americans abandon most of their lands and move to reservations.

Civil War Tests Democracy

America's westward expansion raised questions about what laws and customs should be followed in the West. Ever since the nation's early days, the northern and southern parts of the United States had followed different ways of life. Each section wanted to extend its own way of life to the new territories and states in the West.

North and South The North had a diversified economy with both farms and industry. For both its factories and farms, the North depended on free workers. The South's economy, on the other hand, was based on just a few cash crops, mainly cotton. Southern planters relied on slave labor.

THINK THROUGH HISTORY
A. Contrasting
What were the main economic differences between the Northern and Southern states?

The economic differences between the two regions led to a conflict over slavery. Many Northerners considered slavery morally wrong. They wanted to outlaw slavery in the new western states. Some wanted to abolish slavery altogether. Most white Southerners believed slavery was necessary for their economy. They wanted laws to protect slavery in the West so that they could continue to raise cotton on the fertile soil there.

The disagreement over slavery fueled a debate about the rights of the individual states against those of the federal government. Southern politicians argued that the states had freely joined the Union, and so they could freely leave. Most Northerners felt that the Constitution of the United States had established the Union once and for all—it could not be broken.

Civil War Breaks Out Conflict between the North and South reached a climax in 1860, when **Abraham Lincoln** was elected President. Southerners fiercely opposed Lincoln, who had promised to stop the spread of slavery. One by one, Southern states began to **secede,** or withdraw, from the Union. These states came together as the Confederate States of America.

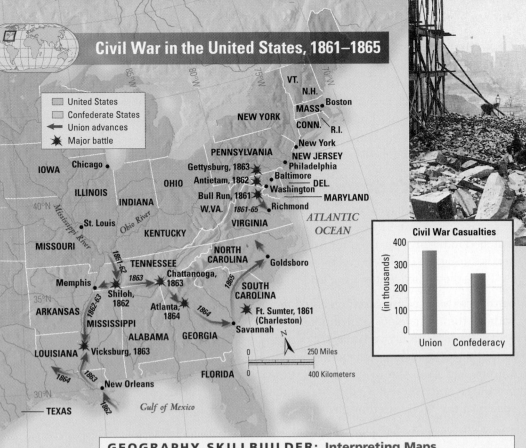

Civil War in the United States, 1861–1865

Legend:
- United States
- Confederate States
- → Union advances
- ✳ Major battle

Map labels: IOWA, Chicago, ILLINOIS, INDIANA, OHIO, St. Louis, MISSOURI, Ohio River, KENTUCKY, Mississippi River, Memphis, TENNESSEE, Chattanooga 1863, Shiloh 1862, ARKANSAS, MISSISSIPPI, ALABAMA, Atlanta 1864, GEORGIA, LOUISIANA, Vicksburg 1863, New Orleans, TEXAS, Gulf of Mexico, FLORIDA, Savannah, SOUTH CAROLINA, Ft. Sumter 1861 (Charleston), NORTH CAROLINA, Goldsboro, VIRGINIA, Richmond, W.VA. 1861–65, Bull Run 1861, Washington, MARYLAND, DEL., Baltimore, Antietam 1862, Philadelphia, Gettysburg 1863, NEW JERSEY, New York, PENNSYLVANIA, NEW YORK, CONN., R.I., MASS., Boston, N.H., VT., ATLANTIC OCEAN

Scale: 250 Miles / 400 Kilometers

Civil War Casualties (in thousands): Union (approx. 360), Confederacy (approx. 260)

Like many other cities in the South, Richmond, Virginia, lay in ruins after the Civil War.

GEOGRAPHY SKILLBUILDER: Interpreting Maps

1. **Place** *Where and when was the northernmost battle fought in the war?*
2. **Human-Environment Interaction** *Which side do you think suffered the most devastation? Why?*

HISTORY MAKERS

Abraham Lincoln
1809–1865

Lincoln passionately believed in preserving the Union. His upbringing might help explain why. The son of rural, illiterate parents, he educated himself. After working as rail splitter, boatman, storekeeper, and surveyor, he taught himself to be a lawyer. This led to careers in law and politics—and eventually to the White House.

In Europe, people were more or less fixed in the level of society into which they had been born. Yet the United States had been founded on the belief that all men were created equal. Therefore, Lincoln was free to achieve whatever he could. Small wonder that he fought to preserve the democracy he described as the "last best hope of earth."

On April 12, 1861, Confederate forces fired on Fort Sumter, a federal fort in Charleston, South Carolina. Lincoln ordered the army to bring the rebel states back into the Union. The **U.S. Civil War** had begun. Four years of fighting followed, most of it in the South. Although the South had superior military leadership, the North had a larger population, better transportation, greater resources, and more factories to turn out weapons and supplies. These advantages proved too much for the South to overcome. In April 1865, the South surrendered. The United States had survived the toughest test of its democracy.

THINK THROUGH HISTORY
B. Analyzing Issues
Did the Emancipation Proclamation reflect a change in Lincoln's main goal for the war?

Abolition of Slavery From the beginning of the war, Lincoln declared that it was being fought to save the Union and not to end slavery. Lincoln eventually decided that ending slavery would help to save the Union. Early in 1863, he issued the **Emancipation Proclamation,** declaring that all slaves in the Confederate states were free.

At first, the proclamation freed no slaves, because the Confederate states did not accept it as law. As Union armies advanced into the South, however, they freed slaves in the lands they conquered. The Emancipation Proclamation also showed people in Europe that the war was being fought against slavery. The proclamation made many Europeans, especially the British, less sympathetic to the South. They did not send the money and supplies that the South had hoped they would.

In the aftermath of the war, the U.S. Congress passed the Thirteenth Amendment to the Constitution, which forever abolished slavery in all parts of the United States. Soon after, the Fourteenth and Fifteenth Amendments extended the rights of citizenship to all Americans, black or white, and guaranteed former slaves the right to vote.

An Age of Democracy and Progress **671**

Reconstruction From 1865 to 1877, Union troops occupied the South and enforced the constitutional protections. This period is called Reconstruction. After federal troops left the South, white Southerners passed laws that limited African Americans' rights and made it difficult for them to vote. Such laws also encouraged **segregation,** or separation, of blacks and whites in the South. African Americans continued to face discrimination in Northern states as well. Decades passed before African Americans made significant progress towards equality with other citizens.

Postwar Economic Expansion

While the South struggled to rebuild its shattered economy, the United States as a whole experienced a period of industrial expansion unmatched in history. The need for mass production and distribution of goods during the Civil War greatly speeded America's industrialization. By 1914, the United States was a leading industrial power in the world.

Immigration Industrialization could not have occurred so rapidly without the tremendous contribution of immigrants. During the 1870s, immigrants arrived at a rate of nearly 2,000 a day. By 1914, more than 20 million people had moved to the United States from Europe and Asia. Many settled in the growing industrial cities of the Northeast and Midwest. Others staked their claims in the open spaces of the West, lured by government offers of free land.

The Railroads As settlers moved west, so did the nation's rail system. In 1862, Congress had authorized money to build a transcontinental railroad. For seven years, Chinese and Irish immigrants, Mexican Americans, African Americans, and others did the backbreaking labor. They dug tunnels, built bridges, and hammered down the heavy steel tracks and wooden ties. When the transcontinental railroad was completed in 1869, railroads linked California with the Midwest and Eastern United States.

By 1900, nearly 200,000 miles of track spiderwebbed the nation. This massive system linked farm to city and boosted trade and industry. For one thing, the railroads bought huge quantities of steel. Also, trains brought materials such as coal and iron ore to factories and moved the finished goods quickly to market. They carried corn, wheat, and cattle from the Great Plains to processing plants in St. Louis, Chicago, and Minneapolis. These developments helped to make the United States a world leader in the great explosion of technological progress that marked the late nineteenth century.

THINK THROUGH HISTORY
C. Recognizing Effects How did railroads affect the growth of the United States?

Section 3 Assessment

1. TERMS & NAMES

Identify
• manifest destiny
• Abraham Lincoln
• secede
• U.S Civil War
• Emancipation Proclamation
• segregation

2. TAKING NOTES

Following the example below, create a time line showing the major events of the United States in the 19th century.

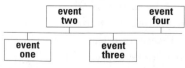

Indicate which events contributed to U.S. expansion and which events involved a war or other crisis. Label your time line "Expansion and Crisis in the United States."

3. DISTINGUISHING FACT FROM OPINION

Reread the quotation from William Shorey Coodey on page 670. What facts are conveyed in his statement? What opinions—judgment, beliefs, or feelings—does he express about the Trail of Tears? How does he use his description of events to help justify his opinions?

4. ANALYZING THEMES

Economics Imagine that circumstances had forced the North to surrender to the South in the Civil War. Therefore, two countries shared the region now occupied by the United States. What economic effects might this have had on the North? the South? the region as a whole?

THINK ABOUT
• the issue of slavery
• the impact of the Civil War
• postwar economic expansion of the United States

TERMS & NAMES
- assembly line
- mass culture
- Charles Darwin
- theory of evolution
- radioactivity
- psychology

4 Nineteenth-Century Progress

MAIN IDEA	WHY IT MATTERS NOW
Breakthroughs in science and technology transformed daily life and entertainment.	Electric lights, telephones, cars, and many other conveniences of modern life were invented during this period.

SETTING THE STAGE The Industrial Revolution happened because of inventions like the spinning jenny and the steam engine. In turn, the demands of growing industries spurred even greater advances in technology. By the late 1800s, advances in both industry and technology were occurring faster than ever before. In industrialized countries, economic growth produced many social changes. At the same time, a surge of scientific discovery pushed the frontiers of knowledge forward.

Inventions Change Ways of Life

In the early 1800s, coal and steam drove the machines of industry. By the late 1800s, new kinds of energy were coming into use. One was gasoline, which powered a new type of engine called an internal combustion engine. Small, light, and efficient, this engine would eventually make the automobile possible. Another kind of energy was the mysterious force called electricity. In the 1870s, the electric generator was developed, which produced a current that could power machines. This invention made it possible to bring the magic of electricity into daily life.

Edison the Inventor If electricity seemed like magic to people in the 19th century, Thomas Edison was perhaps the century's greatest magician. Over his career, Edison patented more than 1,000 inventions, including the light bulb and the phonograph.

Early in his career, Edison started a research laboratory in Menlo Park, New Jersey. Most of his important inventions were developed there, with help from the researchers he employed. Indeed, the idea of a laboratory for industrial research and development may have been Edison's most important invention.

Bell and Marconi Revolutionize Communication Other inventors helped harness electricity to transmit sounds over great distances. Alexander Graham Bell was a teacher of deaf students who invented the telephone in his spare time. He displayed his device at the Philadelphia Exposition of 1876. The emperor of Brazil used it to speak to his aide in another room. When he heard the reply he exclaimed, "My word! It speaks Portuguese!"

The Italian inventor Guglielmo Marconi used theoretical discoveries about electromagnetic waves to create the first radio in 1895. This device was important because it sent messages (using Morse Code) through the air, without the use of wires. Primitive radios soon became standard equipment for ships at sea. Not until later could radios transmit human voices.

Ford Sparks the Automobile Industry In the 1880s, German inventors used a gasoline engine to power a vehicle—the automobile.

An Age of Inventions

Light Bulb
Edison and his team invented the first practical electric light bulb in 1879. Within a few years, Edison had perfected a longer-lasting bulb and begun installing electric lighting in New York City.

Telephone
Alexander Graham Bell demonstrated the first telephone in 1876. It quickly became an essential of modern life. By 1900, there were nearly 2 million telephones in the United States. By 1912, there were 8.7 million.

Automobile Assembly Line
Ford's major innovation was to improve efficiency in his factory. By introducing the assembly line, he reduced the time it took to build a car from 12.5 to 1.5 worker-hours.

Airplane
Through trial and error, the Wright brothers designed wings that provided lift and balance in flight. Their design is based on principles that are still used in every aircraft.

Automobile technology developed quickly, but since early cars were built by hand, they were expensive to buy and repair.

An American mechanic named Henry Ford decided to make cars that were affordable for most people. "The way to make automobiles is to make them all alike," he said, "just as one pin is like another when it comes from the pin factory." To build his cars alike, Ford used standardized, interchangeable parts. He also built them on an **assembly line**—a line of workers who each put a single piece on unfinished cars as they passed on a moving belt.

Assembly line workers could put together an entire Model T Ford in less than two hours. When Ford introduced this plain, black, reliable car in 1908, it sold for $850. As his production costs fell, Ford lowered the price. Eventually it dropped to less than $300—well within the reach of the middle class. Other factories adopted Ford's ideas. By 1914, more than 600,000 cars were traveling around on the world's roads.

The Wright Brothers Fly Two bicycle mechanics from Dayton, Ohio, named Wilbur and Orville Wright solved the age-old riddle of flight. On December 17, 1903, they flew a gasoline-powered flying machine at Kitty Hawk, North Carolina. The longest flight that day lasted only 59 seconds, but it was enough to begin a whole new industry—aircraft.

THINK THROUGH HISTORY
A. Making Inferences Why do you think Ford reduced the price of the Model T?

The Rise of Mass Culture

In earlier periods, art, music, and most theater had been largely the concern of the wealthy. This group had the money, leisure time, and education to enjoy high culture. It was not until about 1900 that people could speak of **mass culture**—the appeal of art, writing, music, and other forms of entertainment to a much larger audience.

French artist Henri de Toulouse-Lautrec designed this bicycle poster in 1896.

Changes Produce Mass Culture There were several causes for the rise of mass culture around the turn of the century. First, the spread of public education increased literacy in both Europe and North America. This, in turn, provided a mass market for books, newspapers, and magazines. Improvements in communications made it possible to meet the broad demand for information and entertainment. For example, new high-speed presses duplicated thousands of pages in a few hours. They made publications cheaper and easier to produce. The invention of the phonograph and records brought music directly into people's homes.

Working folks now had more time for leisure pursuits. By 1900, most industrial countries had limited the working day to ten hours. Most people worked Monday through Friday and a half-day on Saturday. This five-and-a-half day work week created the "weekend," a special time for relaxation. More leisure time in evenings and on weekends allowed workers to take part in activities that their grandparents never had time to enjoy.

THINK THROUGH HISTORY
B. Analyzing Causes What changes led to the rise of mass culture around 1900?

Music Halls and Vaudeville A popular leisure activity was a trip to the local music hall. On a typical evening, a music hall might offer a dozen or more different acts. It might feature singers, dancers, comedians, jugglers, magicians, acrobats, and even trained parakeets. In the United States, musical variety shows were called vaudeville.

Vaudeville acts traveled from town to town, appearing at theaters with names such as the Gaiety, the Grand, and the Orpheum.

Movies Are Born During the 1880s, several inventors worked at trying to record and project moving images. One successful design came from France. Another came from Thomas Edison's laboratory. The earliest motion pictures caused a sensation only because of their novelty. They were black and white, lasted less than a minute, and had no plot. One of Edison's first films, for example, showed nothing but a man sneezing.

By the early 1900s, filmmakers were producing the first feature films (see Something in Common, page 676). Movies quickly became big business. By 1910, five million Americans attended some 10,000 theaters each day to watch silent movies. The European movie industry experienced similar growth.

Sports Entertain Millions With new time at their disposal, ordinary people began to enjoy all kinds of sports and outdoor activities. For every person who played sports, even more enjoyed watching them. Spectator sports now became entertainment for many. In the United States, football and baseball soared in popularity. In Europe, the first professional soccer clubs formed and drew big crowds—120,000 fans turned out to watch a 1913 match in England. Favorite English sports such as cricket spread to the British colonies of Australia, India, and South Africa.

As a result of the growing interest in sports, the international Olympic Games began in 1896. They revived the ancient Greek tradition of holding an athletic competition among countries every four years. Fittingly, the first modern Olympics took place in Athens.

Fans pack a stadium to watch an English soccer championship in 1911.

New Ideas in Medicine and Science

Earlier centuries had established the scientific method as a road to knowledge. Now this method brought powerful new insights into nature as well as many practical results.

The Germ Theory of Disease An important breakthrough in the history of medicine was the germ theory of disease. It was developed by French chemist Louis Pasteur in the mid-1800s. While examining the fermentation process of alcohol, Pasteur discovered that it was caused by microscopic organisms he called bacteria. He also learned that heat killed bacteria. This led him to develop the process of *pasteurization* to kill germs in liquids such as milk. Soon, it became clear to Pasteur and others that bacteria also caused diseases.

A British surgeon named Joseph Lister read about Pasteur's work. He thought germs might explain why half of all surgical patients died of infections. In 1865, he ordered that his surgical wards be kept spotlessly clean. He insisted that wounds be washed in antiseptics, or germ-killing liquids. As a result, 85 percent of Lister's patients survived. Soon, other hospitals began to follow Lister's standards of cleanliness.

Public officials, too, began to understand that cleanliness helped prevent the spread of disease. Cities built plumbing and sewer systems and took other steps to improve public health. Meanwhile, medical researchers developed vaccines or cures for such deadly diseases as typhus, typhoid fever, diphtheria, and yellow fever. These advances helped people live longer, healthier lives.

THINK THROUGH HISTORY
C. Recognizing Effects What impact did the germ theory of disease have on public health?

An Age of Democracy and Progress **675**

Mass Entertainment

In 1903, an American filmmaker named Edwin S. Porter presented the first feature film, *The Great Train Robbery.* Audiences packed theaters on both sides of the Atlantic to see it. Movies soon became one of the most popular forms of mass entertainment around the world. Today, billions of people still flock to movie theaters, despite newer forms of entertainment such as television and videos. One reason that going to the movies remains popular is the pleasure of shared experience—seeing a movie, a play, a circus, or sporting event as part of a large audience.

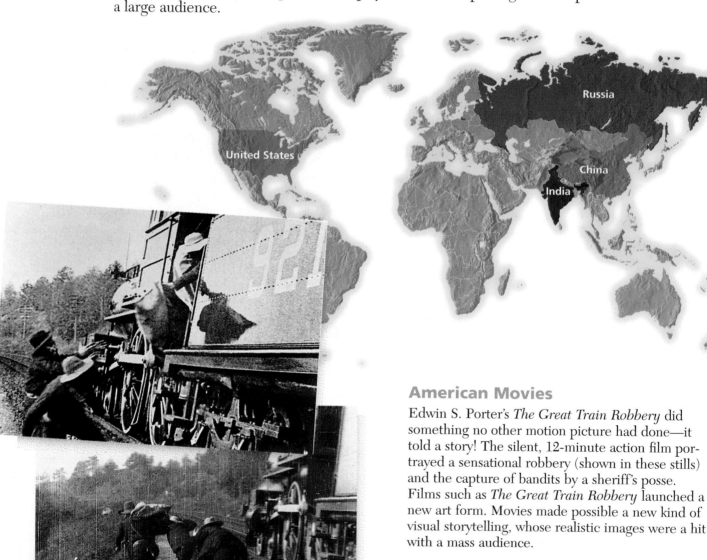

American Movies

Edwin S. Porter's *The Great Train Robbery* did something no other motion picture had done—it told a story! The silent, 12-minute action film portrayed a sensational robbery (shown in these stills) and the capture of bandits by a sheriff's posse. Films such as *The Great Train Robbery* launched a new art form. Movies made possible a new kind of visual storytelling, whose realistic images were a hit with a mass audience.

a closer look MOVIE STARS

"Little Mary" Pickford, as she was affectionately known, is best remembered for portraying sweet, innocent roles.

Francis X. Bushman was a popular leading man. He is shown here in *Ben Hur* (1926).

Russian Circus

The Russian circus began when an English showman sent a troupe of stunt horse riders to Empress Catherine the Great in the 1790s. Russia has been famous for the popularity and quality of its circuses ever since. Most Russian circuses, like this one with animal trainer Vyacheslav Zolkin, feature trained bears. Russian circuses usually use a single ring so that audiences can sit close to the performers.

Chinese Opera

The performing arts have a long history in China. Characters in Chinese drama, such as this troupe from the Beijing Opera, wear elaborate silk costumes and stylized facial makeup or masks. The character of the actors is expressed in part through the symbolic use of color. This scene is from *The Story of the White Snake,* a tragic love story about a white snake that is transformed into a human being and marries a young man.

Camel Races in India

Seasonal festivals provide entertainment in areas throughout the world. Thousands of people from all over India, as well as foreign tourists, flock to the town of Pushkar in November for its annual fair. Although the main business is camel trading, the Pushkar fair is enlivened with dramas, food stalls, magic shows—and the races. Shown here is a camel rider racing at these annual festivities. These races are as eagerly anticipated as the Kentucky Derby is in the United States.

Theda Bara, the silent screen's "vamp," became an overnight sensation after her first starring role in 1915.

Connect *to* History

Analyzing Causes How does each type of entertainment reflect its country's culture?

SEE SKILLBUILDER HANDBOOK, PAGE 995

Connect *to* Today

Making a Chart List at least three other forms of entertainment that you enjoy during your leisure. Combine them in a class chart. Identify which ones are individual experiences and which are pop culture events.

INTERNET CONNECTION

Visit us at www.mcdougallittell.com to learn more about popular entertainment.

**Charles Darwin
1809–1882**

The key event in Charles Darwin's life was his five-year journey as a naturalist aboard the *H.M.S. Beagle.* The ship was on an expedition to survey the western and southern coast of South America and some Pacific islands. Darwin kept notebooks of the plants and animals he saw in various environments. After he came home, he used the data in these notebooks to develop his theory of evolution.

Darwin's Theory of Evolution No scientific idea of modern times aroused more controversy than the work of English biologist **Charles Darwin.** The cause of the controversy was Darwin's answer to the question that faced biologists: How can we explain the tremendous variety of plants and animals on earth? A widely accepted answer in the 1800s was the idea of special creation. According to this view, every kind of plant and animal had been created by God at the beginning of the world and had remained the same since then.

Darwin challenged the idea of special creation. Based on his research, he developed a theory that all forms of life, including human beings, evolved from earlier living forms that had existed millions of years ago.

In 1859, Darwin published his thinking in a book titled *The Origin of Species by Means of Natural Selection.* According to the idea of natural selection, populations tend to grow faster than the food supply and so must compete for food. The members of a species that survive are those that are fittest, or best adapted to their environment. These surviving members of a species produce offspring that share their advantages. Gradually, over many generations, the species may change. In this way, new species evolve. Darwin's idea of change through natural selection came to be called the **theory of evolution.**

The Origin of Species caused great excitement among scientists. At the same time, Darwin's ideas roused a storm of debate outside the scientific community. Many people believed that the idea of evolution directly contradicted the account of creation in the Bible. Even today, well over 100 years after *The Origin of Species* was first published, Darwin's ideas are controversial.

**THINK THROUGH HISTORY
D. Clarifying**
According to Darwin, how does natural selection affect evolution?

Mendel and Genetics Although Darwin said that living things passed on their variations from one generation to the next, he did not know how they did so. In the 1850s and 1860s, an Austrian monk named Gregor Mendel discovered that there is a pattern to the way that certain traits are inherited. Although his work was not widely known until 1900, Mendel's work began the science of genetics. Later, biologists discovered genes, the units of living matter that carry traits from parents to offspring.

This photograph shows Marie Curie in her laboratory.

Advances in Chemistry and Physics In 1803, the British chemist John Dalton theorized that all matter is made of tiny particles called atoms. Dalton showed that elements contain only one kind of atom, which has a specific weight. Compounds, on the other hand, contain more than one kind of atom.

In 1869, Dmitri Mendeleev (MEHN·duh·LAY·uhf), a Russian chemist, organized a chart on which all the known elements were arranged in order of weight, from lightest to heaviest. He left gaps where he predicted that new elements would be discovered. Later, his predictions proved correct. Mendeleev's chart, called the Periodic Table, is still used by scientists today.

A husband and wife team working in Paris discovered two of the missing elements. Marie and Pierre Curie found that a mineral called pitchblende released a powerful form of energy. In 1898, Marie Curie gave this energy the name **radioactivity.** The Curies discovered two new elements that they named radium and polonium. Both were highly radioactive. In 1903, the Curies shared the Nobel Prize for physics for their work on radioactivity. In 1911, Marie won the Nobel Prize for chemistry for the discovery of radium and polonium.

Physicists around 1900 tried to unravel the secrets of the atom. Earlier scientists believed that the atom was the smallest particle that existed. A British physicist named Ernest Rutherford suggested that atoms were made up of yet smaller particles. Each atom, he said, had a nucleus surrounded by one or more particles called electrons. Soon other physicists such as Max Planck, Neils Bohr, and Albert Einstein were studying the structure and energy of atoms. Their discoveries, discussed in Chapter 31, were fully as revolutionary as Newton's or Darwin's ideas.

The Social Sciences

The scientific theories of the 1800s prompted scholars to study human society and behavior in a scientific way. Interest in these fields grew enormously during that century, as global expeditions produced a flood of new discoveries about ancient civilizations and world cultures. This interest led to the development of modern social sciences such as archaeology, anthropology, and sociology.

An important new social science was **psychology,** the study of the human mind and behavior. The Russian biologist Ivan Pavlov broke new ground in psychology with a famous experiment in the early 1900s. Ordinarily, a dog's mouth waters at the smell of food. Pavlov began ringing a bell each time he gave food to a dog. Eventually, the dog learned to associate the bell with food. Each time the bell rang, the dog salivated, even if no food was present.

Pavlov concluded that an animal's reflexes could be changed, or conditioned, through training. He also applied these findings to humans. He believed that human actions were often unconscious reactions to experiences and could be changed by training.

Another pioneer in psychology, the Austrian doctor Sigmund Freud, also believed that the unconscious mind drives how people think and act. In Freud's view, unconscious forces such as suppressed memories, desires, and impulses help shape behavior. He created a type of therapy called psychoanalysis to help people deal with the psychological conflicts created by these forces.

As Chapter 31 explains, Freud's theories became very influential. However, his idea that the mind was beyond conscious control also shocked many people. The ideas of Freud and Pavlov challenged the fundamental idea of the Enlightenment—that reason was supreme. The new ideas about psychology began to shake the 19th-century faith that humans could perfect themselves and society through reason.

THINK THROUGH HISTORY
E. Clarifying Why was the work of Pavlov and Freud groundbreaking?

SPOTLIGHT ON

Social Darwinism

Charles Darwin was a biologist, but a number of 19th-century thinkers tried to apply his ideas about plants and animals to economics and politics. The leader in this movement was Herbert Spencer, an English philosopher.

Free economic competition, Spencer argued, was natural selection in action. The best companies make profits, while inefficient ones go bankrupt. Spencer applied the same rules to individuals. Those who were fittest for survival enjoyed wealth and success, while the poor remained poor because they were unfit. This idea became known as Social Darwinism.

Some Social Darwinists expanded these ideas into racist thinking. They claimed that certain groups of people were "fitter"—brighter, stronger, and more advanced—than others. These "superior races," they said, were intended by nature to dominate "lesser peoples." Many Europeans used such arguments to justify the spread of imperialism, which is described in Chapter 27.

Section 4 Assessment

1. TERMS & NAMES

Identify
- assembly line
- mass culture
- Charles Darwin
- theory of evolution
- radioactivity
- psychology

2. TAKING NOTES

Using a web diagram like the one below, connect the inventors, scientists, and thinkers with the invention, discovery, or new idea for which they were responsible.

People and Progress

Which breakthrough do you think helped people the most? Why?

3. COMPARING AND CONTRASTING

How is the mass culture that rose at the end of the 19th century similar to mass culture today? How is it different? Explain your response.

THINK ABOUT
- the role of technology
- increase in leisure time
- new forms of entertainment

4. THEME ACTIVITY

Science and Technology
Choose one of the inventions, discoveries, or new ideas that occurred in this period and plan a museum exhibit of that breakthrough. Decide how to display the invention or discovery. Write a description of it, who was responsible for it, and how it has affected peoples' lives.

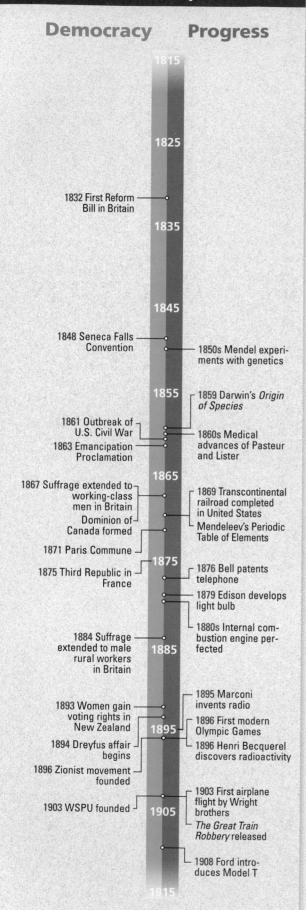

Democracy   **Progress**

1815

1825

1832 First Reform Bill in Britain

1835

1845

1848 Seneca Falls Convention

1850s Mendel experiments with genetics

1855

1859 Darwin's *Origin of Species*

1861 Outbreak of U.S. Civil War

1863 Emancipation Proclamation

1860s Medical advances of Pasteur and Lister

1865

1867 Suffrage extended to working-class men in Britain

Dominion of Canada formed

1871 Paris Commune

1869 Transcontinental railroad completed in United States

Mendeleev's Periodic Table of Elements

1875 Third Republic in France

1875

1876 Bell patents telephone

1879 Edison develops light bulb

1880s Internal combustion engine perfected

1884 Suffrage extended to male rural workers in Britain

1885

1893 Women gain voting rights in New Zealand

1894 Dreyfus affair begins

1896 Zionist movement founded

1895 Marconi invents radio

1895

1896 First modern Olympic Games

1896 Henri Becquerel discovers radioactivity

1903 WSPU founded

1903 First airplane flight by Wright brothers

The Great Train Robbery released

1905

1908 Ford introduces Model T

1915

TERMS & NAMES

Briefly explain the importance of each of the following to the reforms, crises, or advances of Western nations from 1815 to 1914.

1. suffrage
2. anti-Semitism
3. dominion
4. penal colony
5. home rule
6. manifest destiny
7. Emancipation Proclamation
8. segregation
9. assembly line
10. theory of evolution

REVIEW QUESTIONS

SECTION 1 *(pages 659–663)*
Democratic Reform and Activism

11. What political reforms had the effect of expanding democracy for men in Britain?
12. How did the Women's Social and Political Union call attention to its cause?

SECTION 2 *(pages 664–668)*
Self-Rule for British Colonies

13. What cultural conflict caused problems for Canada?
14. How did Australia's early history differ from that of other British colonies?
15. Why did the British government pass a home rule bill for southern Ireland only?

SECTION 3 *(pages 669–672)*
Expansion and Crisis in the United States

16. In what different ways did the United States gain territory in the 1800s?
17. How did the North and South differ economically? Why was the issue of slavery so divisive?

SECTION 4 *(pages 673–679)*
Nineteenth-Century Progress

18. What was Darwin's principle of natural selection? Why did many people oppose his theory of evolution?
19. What contributions did each of the following scientists make?
   (a) Mendel (b) Dalton (c) Mendeleev (d) Marie Curie (e) Rutherford
20. How did Pavlov and Freud contribute to the study of psychology?

1906 Ford 6 Cylinder Touring Car
Price **$2,500**

6 cylinders—40 h. p. 4 to 50 miles per hour on high gear. *Perfected* magneto ignition—mechanical oiler, 114 inch wheel base, luxurious body for 5 passengers, weight 2000 pounds.

1906 Ford Runabout, as advanced as our touring car in design and even more surprising in price—will be fully illustrated and described in our next advertisement.

Both these Cars on exhibition at the New York Automobile Show.

Ford Motor Company
Detroit, Mich.

Members American Motor Car Manufacturers Association, Chicago   Canadian Trade supplied by the Ford Motor Co. of Canada, Ltd., Walkerville, Ont.

Interact *with* History

On page 658, you considered the benefits and drawbacks of technological progress. Now consider the inventions you read about in this chapter. Write a paragraph explaining which you think was most significant. State the reasons for your choice. Consider

- Which affected the most people?
- Which changed daily life the most?
- Which changed industry the most?
- Which produced the greatest benefit with the fewest drawbacks?

Share your paragraph with the class.

CRITICAL THINKING

1. ASSEMBLY LINE WORK

THEME ECONOMICS Using the quotation from Henry Ford on page 674, explain how his attitude on making goods might have differed from those of a traditional craftsperson. From a worker's point of view, what would be the advantages and disadvantages of an assembly line?

2. AN ERA OF CHANGE

Create a web diagram of the major political, economic, social and cultural, and scientific and technological changes of the 1800s and early 1900s.

3. SOCIAL DARWINISM

Charles Darwin did not fully agree with the Social Darwinists. How do natural selection and economic competition differ?

4. ANALYZING PRIMARY SOURCES

On January 11, 1898, Major Esterhazy, the army officer who had actually committed the crimes of which Alfred Dreyfus was accused, was judged innocent by a court martial, or military court. Two days later, Émile Zola published an open letter about the Dreyfus affair. Part of that letter appears below.

A VOICE FROM THE PAST

It is only now that the Affair is beginning, because only now are men assuming clear positions: on the one hand, the guilty, who do not wish justice to be done; on the other, the followers of justice, who will give their lives so that justice may triumph.

I accuse the War Office of having carried on in the press an abominable campaign in order to screen their mistake and mislead the public.

I accuse the first Court Martial of having violated the law by condemning an accused man on the basis of a secret document and I accuse the second Court Martial of having, in obedience to orders, screened that illegal act by knowingly acquitting a guilty man.

As to the men I accuse, I do not know them. I have never seen them, I have no resentment or hatred toward them. I have but one passion—that of light.

- Of what crimes did Zola accuse the French War Office and the Courts Martial?
- What did Zola claim to be his motive for making these accusations?

CHAPTER ACTIVITIES

1. LIVING HISTORY: Unit Portfolio Project

THEME EMPIRE BUILDING Your unit portfolio project focuses on the effects of empire building on all the lands and peoples involved (see page 629). For Chapter 26 you might use one of the following ideas to add to your portfolio.

- Design and produce a handbill that might have been distributed by English-speaking Canadians demanding a representative government.
- Write an editorial that might have appeared in a newspaper in 19th-century New Zealand. In the editorial, address the issue of British settlers' taking land from the Maori, and the Maori response.
- Draw a political cartoon that reflects how Britain treated Ireland during the Great Famine.

2. CONNECT TO TODAY: Cooperative Learning

THEME SCIENCE AND TECHNOLOGY Breakthroughs in science, technology, and medicine transformed daily life in the 1800s. Many of those inventions and discoveries still affect us today. Work with a partner to make a collage of 19th-century breakthroughs as they are reflected in modern life.

- Begin by noting all the inventions and discoveries presented in the chapter. Then brainstorm ways that they might be represented visually.
- In magazines or newspapers, look for the pictures you need. If you cannot find a particular picture, try drawing it.
- Determine a creative way to identify the pictures and link them with the 19th-century breakthroughs.

3. INTERPRETING A TIME LINE

Revisit the time line on pages 628–629, and study the segment for Chapter 26. Which event do you think was the most significant? Why?

FOCUS ON **POLITICAL CARTOONS**

This 1852 English cartoon titled "A Court for King Cholera" depicts a poor section of the city. Notice the children playing with a dead rat and the woman picking through the rubbish heap. At the time, some health experts believed that the epidemic disease cholera spread from the air around rubbish heaps.

- What does the artist say about the unhealthy living conditions of the poor?
- Do you think the artist is sympathetic to the urban poor? Why or why not?

Connect to History What changes took place in the 19th century that helped eliminate the spread of diseases like cholera in Western cities?

CHAPTER 27

The Age of Imperialism, 1850–1914

PREVIEWING THEMES

Empire Building

The Industrial Revolution gave European nations the necessary technology to dominate other peoples. During the 1800s, the European powers competed with one another to claim parts of Africa, Southeast Asia, India, and the Pacific. Toward the end of the century, the United States established its own overseas colonies in the Pacific.

Economics

The imperialists regarded their colonies as captive markets as well as sources of raw materials and trade goods. The colonizers demanded production of cash crops at the expense of the peasants' own subsistence agriculture. In tropical areas, plantation agriculture increased the need for laborers and spurred immigration.

Power and Authority

Colonizers were divided on the best method of rule. Britain and the United States ruled indirectly, using local leaders and institutions where possible. The French and others ruled the colonies directly from a central authority. Often the two methods were blended.

INTERNET CONNECTION

Visit us at **www.mcdougallittell.com** to learn more about imperialism.

EUROPEAN COLONIES, 1850–1914

Territory Controlled By:
- Belgium
- France
- German Empire
- Great Britain
- Italy
- The Netherlands
- Portugal
- Russian Empire
- Spain
- United States
- Independent States

0   500 Miles
0   1,000 Kilometers

N

ATLANTIC OCEAN

This sculptured brass weight was used by the **Asante** people of Africa. The elaborate nature of the weight may indicate that trade was especially important to the Asante. The British traded with the Asante on the west coast of **Africa,** also known as the Gold Coast.

Queen Victoria of **England** ruled during most of the Age of Imperialism. During her reign, the saying, "The sun never sets on the British Empire" was true of the colonial holdings of Britain.

Ethiopian ruler **Menelik II** defeated the Italians at the Battle of Adowa in **1896**. The Ethiopians' defeat of the Italians was one of the few successful resistances to the European imperialists.

PACIFIC OCEAN

INDIAN OCEAN

Arctic Circle

40°N

Tropic of Cancer

Equator 0°

Tropic of Capricorn

683

Interact *with* History

The 19th-century Europeans have access to steam engines and medical advances. They have the technical know-how to develop the resources of the land they control. They want to develop these resources to make themselves great profits. Many believe that they also have both the right and the responsibility to develop the lands and cultures of less advanced areas of the world.

You wonder about the Europeans' thinking. What rights and responsibilities do they really have? How much should they try to change other peoples and other cultures?

Railroads will bring the products grown or mined to market and carry people to different parts of the conquered country.

What impact might these Europeans have on the land and people they conquer?

Wireless radio will allow communication to wide areas of the country.

Mining gold and diamonds will destroy the land that has been taken away from the local inhabitants.

Local rule might be eliminated or replaced with rule by European monarchs and their representatives.

EXAMINING *the* ISSUES

- Does a technologically advanced nation have a responsibility to share its advances with less developed areas?

- Is it acceptable to impose your culture on another culture group?

- Who should benefit from the resources of a place?

- Is there such a thing as having too much power over others?

Discuss these questions with your classmates. In your discussion, remember what you have already learned about conquests and cultural changes.

As you read about imperialists in this chapter, look for their effects on both the colonizers and the colonized.

① Imperialists Divide Africa

TERMS & NAMES
- imperialism
- racism
- Social Darwinism
- Berlin Conference 1884–85
- Shaka
- Boer
- Great Trek
- Boer War

MAIN IDEA

Ignoring the claims of African ethnic groups, kingdoms, and city-states, Europeans established colonial claims.

WHY IT MATTERS NOW

African nations continue to feel the effects of the colonial presence of 100 years ago.

SETTING THE STAGE Industrialization stirred ambitions in many European nations. They wanted more resources to fuel their industrial production. They competed for new markets for their goods. They looked to Africa and Asia as sources of the raw materials and as markets for cloth, plows, guns, and other industrial products.

Africa Before Imperialism

In the mid-1800s, on the eve of the European domination of Africa, African peoples were divided into hundreds of ethnic and linguistic groups. Most continued to follow traditional beliefs, while others converted to Islam or Christianity. These groups spoke more than 1,000 different languages. Politically, they ranged from large empires that united many ethnic groups to independent villages. The largest empire in West Africa at its peak had a population of about 10 million people.

Although Europeans had established contacts with Africans as early as the 1450s, they actually controlled very little land. Powerful African armies were able to keep the Europeans out of most of Africa for 400 years. As late as 1880, Europeans controlled only 10 percent of the continent's land, mainly on the coast.

Furthermore, European travel into the interior on a large-scale basis was virtually impossible. Europeans could not navigate African rivers that had so many rapids and cataracts and drastically changing flows. Until the introduction of steam-powered riverboats, Europeans would not be able to conduct major expeditions into the interior of Africa.

THINK THROUGH HISTORY
A. Analyzing Causes Why did the Europeans control such a small portion of Africa in the 1800s?

Finally, large networks of Africans conducted trade. These trade networks kept Europeans from controlling the sources of trade items such as gold and ivory. These trade networks were specialized. The Chokwe, for example, devoted themselves to collecting ivory and beeswax in the Angola highlands. Others such as the Yao carried their goods to merchants on the coast.

Nations Compete for Overseas Empires

Those Europeans who did penetrate the interior of Africa tended to be explorers, missionaries, or humanitarians who opposed the slave trade. Europeans and Americans learned about Africa through travel books and newspapers. These publications competed for readers by hiring reporters to search the globe for stories of adventure, mystery, or excitement.

The Congo Sparks Interest In the late 1860s, David Livingstone, a minister from Scotland, traveled with a group of Africans deep into central Africa. They were searching for the source of the Nile. When several years passed with no word from him or his party, many people feared he was dead. An American newspaper hired reporter Henry Stanley to find Livingstone. In 1871, he found Dr. Livingstone on the shores of Lake Tanganyika. Stanley's account of the meeting made headlines around the world.

This highly valued ivory mask is one of four taken from the King of Benin in 1897. It was worn with several others on the belt of a ceremonial costume of the king.

"Dr. Livingstone, I presume?" was the greeting of American reporter Henry Stanley in their famous meeting in 1871 at Lake Tanganyika. This picture is from a drawing based on Dr. Livingstone's own material.

In 1879, Stanley returned to Africa, and in 1882 he signed treaties with local chiefs of the Congo River valley. The treaties gave King Leopold II of Belgium personal control of these lands.

Leopold claimed that his primary motive in establishing the colony was to abolish the slave trade. However, he licensed companies that brutally exploited Africans, by forcing them to collect sap from rubber plants. The time required to do this interfered with the care of their own food crops. So severe were the forced labor, excessive taxation, and abuses of the native Congolese that humanitarians from around the world demanded changes. In 1908, the Belgian government took over the colony. The Belgian Congo, as the colony later became known, was 80 times larger than Belgium. Leopold's seizure of the Congo alarmed France. Earlier, in 1882, the French had approved a treaty that gave France the north bank of the Congo River. Soon Britain, Germany, Italy, Portugal, and Spain were also claiming parts of Africa.

Motives Driving Imperialism Economic, political, and social forces accelerated the drive to take over land in all parts of the globe. The takeover of a country or territory by a stronger nation with the intent of dominating the political, economic, and social life of the people of that nation is called **imperialism.** The Industrial Revolution provided European countries with a need to add lands to their control. As European nations industrialized, they searched for new markets and raw materials to improve their economies.

The race for colonies grew out of a strong sense of national pride as well as from economic competition. Europeans viewed an empire as a measure of national greatness. "All great nations in the fullness of their strength have desired to set their mark upon barbarian lands," wrote the German historian Heinrich von Treitschke, "and those who fail to participate in this great rivalry will play a pitiable role in time to come." As the competition for colonies intensified, each country was determined to plant its flag on as much of the world as possible.

Because of their advanced technology, many Europeans basically believed that they were better than other peoples. This belief was **racism,** the idea that one race is superior to others. The attitude was a reflection of a social theory of the time, called **Social Darwinism.** In this theory, Charles Darwin's ideas about evolution and "survival of the fittest" were applied to social change. Those who were fittest for survival enjoyed wealth and success and were considered superior to others. According to the theory, non-Europeans were considered to be on a lower scale of cultural and physical development because they did not have the technology that Europeans had. Europeans believed that they had the right and the duty to bring the results of their progress to other countries. Cecil Rhodes, a successful businessman and one of the major supporters of British expansion, clearly stated this position:

A VOICE FROM THE PAST

I contend that we [Britons] are the first race in the world, and the more of the world we inhabit, the better it is for the human race. . . . It is our duty to seize every opportunity of acquiring more territory and we should keep this one idea steadily before our eyes that more territory simply means more of the Anglo-Saxon race, more of the best, the most human, most honourable race the world possesses.

CECIL RHODES, *Confession of Faith* 1877

THINK THROUGH HISTORY
B. Making Inferences What attitude about the British does Rhodes's statement display?

The push for expansion also came from missionaries who worked to Christianize the peoples of Asia, Africa, and the Pacific Islands. Many missionaries believed that European rule was the best way to end evil practices such as the slave trade. They also wanted to "civilize," that is, to "westernize," the peoples of the foreign land.

Forces Enabling Imperialism External and internal forces contributed to the Europeans' conquest of Africa. The overwhelming advantage was the Europeans' technological superiority. The Maxim gun, invented in 1889, was the world's first automatic machine gun. European countries quickly acquired the Maxim, while the resisting Africans were forced to rely on outdated weapons.

European countries also had the means to control their empire. The invention of the steam engine allowed Europeans to easily travel upstream to establish bases of control deep in the African continent. Railroads, cables, and steamers allowed close communications within a colony and between the colony and its controlling nation. All these made control easier.

Even with superior arms and steam engines to transport them, Europeans might still have stayed confined to the coast. Europeans were highly susceptible to malaria. One discovery changed that—the drug quinine. Regular doses of quinine protected Europeans from attacks of this disease caused by mosquitoes.

Internal factors also made the European sweep through Africa easier. Africans' huge variety of languages and cultures discouraged unity among them. Wars fought between ethnic groups over land, water, and trade rights also prevented a unified stand. Europeans soon learned to play rival groups against each other. Finally, Africans fought at a tremendous disadvantage because they did not have the weapons and technology the Europeans had.

THINK THROUGH HISTORY
C. Analyzing Issues
Which external factor was most likely to have caused the downfall of African cultures?

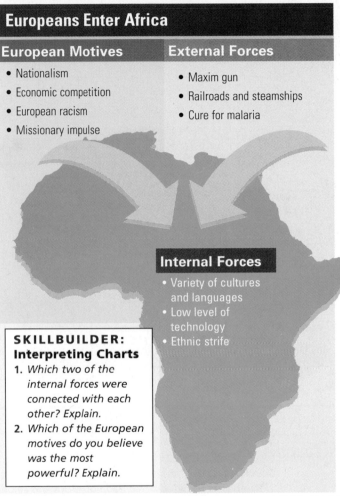

Europeans Enter Africa

European Motives	External Forces
• Nationalism	• Maxim gun
• Economic competition	• Railroads and steamships
• European racism	• Cure for malaria
• Missionary impulse	

Internal Forces
• Variety of cultures and languages
• Low level of technology
• Ethnic strife

SKILLBUILDER: Interpreting Charts
1. *Which two of the internal forces were connected with each other? Explain.*
2. *Which of the European motives do you believe was the most powerful? Explain.*

African Lands Become European Colonies

The scramble for African territory began in earnest about 1880. At that time, the French began to expand from the West African coast toward western Sudan. The discoveries of diamonds in 1867 and gold in 1886 in South Africa increased European interest in colonizing the land. No European power wanted to be left out of the race.

Berlin Conference Divides Africa The competition was so fierce that European countries feared war among themselves. To prevent fighting, 14 European nations met at the **Berlin Conference** in **1884–85** to lay down rules for the division of Africa. They agreed that any European country could claim land in Africa by notifying other nations of their claims and showing they could control the area. The European nations

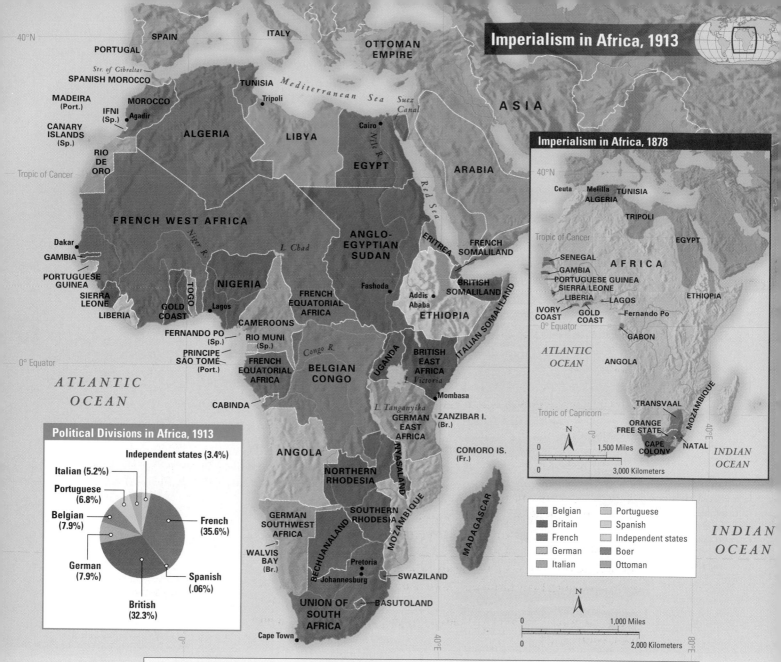

Imperialism in Africa, 1913

40°N
SPAIN
ITALY
OTTOMAN EMPIRE
PORTUGAL
Str. of Gibraltar
SPANISH MOROCCO
TUNISIA
Mediterranean Sea Suez Canal
MADEIRA (Port.)
MOROCCO
Tripoli
ASIA
IFNI (Sp.) Agadir
CANARY ISLANDS (Sp.)
ALGERIA
LIBYA
Cairo
RIO DE ORO
Tropic of Cancer
ARABIA
FRENCH WEST AFRICA
Niger R.
L. Chad
EGYPT
Red Sea
ANGLO-EGYPTIAN SUDAN
Dakar
ERITREA
FRENCH SOMALILAND
GAMBIA
Fashoda
PORTUGUESE GUINEA
NIGERIA
FRENCH EQUATORIAL AFRICA
Addis Ababa
BRITISH SOMALILAND
SIERRA LEONE
TOGO
GOLD COAST
Lagos
CAMEROONS
ETHIOPIA
ITALIAN SOMALILAND
LIBERIA
FERNANDO PO (Sp.)
RIO MUNI (Sp.)
Congo R.
UGANDA
0° Equator
PRINCIPE SÃO TOME (Port.)
FRENCH EQUATORIAL AFRICA
BELGIAN CONGO
BRITISH EAST AFRICA
L. Victoria
ATLANTIC OCEAN
CABINDA
Mombasa
L. Tanganyika
GERMAN EAST AFRICA
ZANZIBAR I. (Br.)
ANGOLA
NYASALAND
COMORO IS. (Fr.)
NORTHERN RHODESIA
MOZAMBIQUE
MADAGASCAR
GERMAN SOUTHWEST AFRICA
SOUTHERN RHODESIA
INDIAN OCEAN
WALVIS BAY (Br.)
BECHUANALAND
SWAZILAND
Pretoria
Johannesburg
UNION OF SOUTH AFRICA
BASUTOLAND
Cape Town

Imperialism in Africa, 1878

40°N
Ceuta Melilla TUNISIA
ALGERIA
TRIPOLI
Tropic of Cancer
EGYPT
SENEGAL
AFRICA
GAMBIA
PORTUGUESE GUINEA
SIERRA LEONE
LIBERIA LAGOS
ETHIOPIA
IVORY COAST GOLD COAST
Fernando Po
0° Equator
GABON
ATLANTIC OCEAN
ANGOLA
Tropic of Capricorn
TRANSVAAL
MOZAMBIQUE
N
ORANGE FREE STATE
0   1,500 Miles
CAPE COLONY
NATAL
INDIAN OCEAN
0   3,000 Kilometers

Political Divisions in Africa, 1913

Independent states (3.4%)
Italian (5.2%)
Portuguese (6.8%)
Belgian (7.9%)
French (35.6%)
German (7.9%)
Spanish (.06%)
British (32.3%)

Legend:
- Belgian
- Britain
- French
- German
- Italian
- Portuguese
- Spanish
- Independent states
- Boer
- Ottoman

N

0   1,000 Miles
0   2,000 Kilometers

GEOGRAPHY SKILLBUILDER: Interpreting Maps and Charts

1. **Region** *About what percentage of Africa was colonized by Europeans in 1878? How much by 1913?*
2. **Region** *According to the map of 1913, which two imperial powers held the most land? According to the chart, what percentage of land in Africa was held by the two powers?*

---

divided the rest of the continent with little thought to how African ethnic or linguistic groups were distributed. No African ruler attended these meetings, yet the conference sealed Africa's fate. By 1914, only Liberia and Ethiopia remained free from European control.

Demand for Product Shapes Colonies When European countries began colonizing, many believed that Africans would soon be buying European goods in great quantities. They were wrong; European goods were not bought. However, European businesses still needed raw materials from Africa. Businesses eventually developed cash-crop plantations to grow peanuts, palm oil, cocoa, and rubber. These products displaced the food crops grown by farmers to feed their families.

The major source of great wealth in Africa proved to be the continent's rich mineral resources. The Belgian Congo contained untold wealth in copper and tin. Even these riches seemed small compared to the gold and diamonds in South Africa.

THINK THROUGH HISTORY
D. Recognizing Effects What sort of problems might result from combining or splitting groups of people?

Three Groups Clash over South Africa

The history of South Africa is a history of Africans, Dutch, and British clashing over land and resources. Although the African lands seemed empty to the Europeans, there were huge areas claimed by various ethnic groups. The local control of these lands, especially in the east, had been in dispute for about 100 years.

Zulu Expansion From the late 1700s to the late 1800s, a series of local wars shook southern Africa. Around 1816, a Zulu chief, **Shaka,** used highly disciplined warriors and good military organization to create a large centralized state. Shaka's successors, however, were unable to keep the kingdom intact against the superior arms of the British invaders. The Zulu land became a part of British-controlled land in 1887.

Boers and British Settle in the Cape The Dutch first came to the Cape of Good Hope in 1652 to establish a way station for their ships sailing between the Dutch East Indies and home. Dutch settlers known as **Boers** (Dutch for "farmers") gradually took over native Africans' land and established large farms. When the British took over the Cape Colony in the 1800s, the two groups of settlers clashed over British policy regarding land and slaves.

In the 1830s, to escape the British, several thousand Boers began to move north. This movement has become known as the **Great Trek.** The Boers soon found themselves fighting fiercely with Zulu and other African groups whose land they were taking.

The Boer War Diamonds and gold were discovered in southern Africa in the 1860s and 1880s. Suddenly, "outsiders" from all parts of the world rushed in to make their fortunes. The Boers tried to keep the outsiders from gaining political rights. An attempt to start a rebellion against the Boers failed. The Boers blamed the British. In 1899, the Boers took up arms against the British.

In many ways the **Boer War** between the British and the Boers was the first modern "total" war. The Boers launched commando raids and used guerrilla tactics against the British. The British countered by burning Boer farms and imprisoning women and children in disease-ridden concentration camps. Britain won the war. In 1902, the Boer republics were joined into a self-governing Union of South Africa, controlled by the British.

The establishing of colonies signaled a change in the way of life of the Africans. The Europeans made efforts to change the political, social, and economic lives of the peoples they conquered. You will learn about these changes in Section 2.

THINK THROUGH HISTORY
E. Contrasting How was the struggle for land in the Boer War different from other takeovers in Africa?

GlobalImpact

Americans in the Boer War

Americans as well as nationals from other countries volunteered to fight in the Boer War (1899–1902). Although they joined both sides, most fought for the Boers. They believed the Boers were fighting for freedom against British tyrants.

One group of 46 Irish Americans from Chicago and Massachusetts caused an international scandal when they deserted their Red Cross unit and took up arms for the Boers.

Some Irish who fought for the Boers became leaders in the Irish rebellion when they returned home. John MacBride, a leader of a Boer unit that included many Irish Americans, later took part in the 1916 Easter Rising in Dublin. He was executed by the British.

Section ❶ Assessment

1. TERMS & NAMES

Identify
- imperialism
- racism
- Social Darwinism
- Berlin Conference 1884–85
- Shaka
- Boer
- Great Trek
- Boer War

2. TAKING NOTES

Copy the spider map below and fill in the four motives that caused the growth of imperialism during the late 1800s.

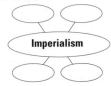

How did Europeans use Social Darwinism to justify empire-building?

3. MAKING INFERENCES

What can you infer about the Europeans' attitude toward Africans from the Berlin Conference?

THINK ABOUT
- who attended the conference
- the outcome of the conference

4. THEME ACTIVITY

Empire Building Create a time line that includes events that occurred in South Africa between 1800 and 1914. What motives caused most of these events?

2 Imperialism

CASE STUDY: Nigeria

TERMS & NAMES
- paternalism
- assimilation
- Menelik II

MAIN IDEA	WHY IT MATTERS NOW
Europeans embarked on a new phase of empire-building that affected both Africa and the rest of the world.	Many former colonies have political problems that are the result of colonial rule.

SETTING THE STAGE The Berlin Conference of 1884–85 was a Europeans' conference, and the Boer War was a Europeans' war. Europeans argued and fought among themselves over the lands of Africa. In carving up Africa, the European countries paid little or no attention to historical political divisions such as kingdoms or caliphates, or to ethnic and language groupings. Uppermost in the minds of the Europeans was the ability to control the land, its people, and their resources.

Colonial Control Takes Many Forms

The imperialism of the 18th and 19th centuries was conducted differently than the empire-building of the 15th and 16th centuries. In the earlier period, imperial powers often did not penetrate far into the conquered areas in Asia and Africa. Nor did they always have a substantial influence on the lives of the people. During this new period of imperialism, the Europeans demanded more influence over the economic, political, and social lives of the people. They were determined to shape the economies of the lands to benefit European economies. They also wanted the people to adopt European customs.

Forms of Colonial Control Each European nation had certain policies and goals for establishing colonies. To establish control of an area, Europeans used different techniques. Over time, four forms of colonial control emerged: colony, protectorate, sphere of influence, and economic imperialism. In practice, gaining control of an area might involve the use of several of these forms.

PATTERNS OF CHANGE: Imperialism

Forms of Imperialism	Characteristics	Example
Colony	A country or a region governed internally by a foreign power	Somaliland in East Africa was a French colony.
Protectorate	A country or territory with its own internal government but under the control of an outside power	Britain established a protectorate over the Niger River delta.
Sphere of Influence	An area in which an outside power claims exclusive investment or trading privileges	Liberia was under the sphere of influence of the United States.
Economic Imperialism	Independent but less developed nations controlled by private business interests rather than by other governments	The Dole Fruit company controlled pineapple trade in Hawaii.

SKILLBUILDER: Interpreting Charts
1. *Which two forms are guided by interests in business or trade?*
2. *What is the difference between a protectorate and a colony?*

Patterns of Imperialist Management

In addition to the external form of control preferred by the colonizing country, European rulers also needed to develop methods of day-to-day management of the colony. Two basic methods of internal management emerged. Britain and other nations such as the United States in its Pacific Island colonies preferred indirect control. France and most other European nations wielded a more direct control. Later, when colonies gained independence, the management method used had an influence on the type of government chosen in the new nation.

Indirect Control Indirect control relied on existing political rulers. In some areas, the British asked a local ruler to accept British authority to rule. These local officials handled much of the daily management of the colony. In addition, each colony had a legislative council that included colonial officials as well as local merchants and professionals nominated by the colonial governor.

The assumption was that the councils would train local leaders in the British method of government and that a time would come when the local population would govern itself. This happened earlier in the British colonies of South Africa and Canada. In the 1890s, the United States began to colonize. It chose the indirect method of control for its colonies.

Direct Control The French and other European powers preferred a more direct control of their colonies. They viewed the Africans as children unable to handle the complex business of running a country. Based on this attitude, the Europeans developed a policy called **paternalism.** Using that policy, Europeans governed people in a fatherly way by providing for their needs but not giving them rights. To accomplish this, the Europeans brought in their own bureaucrats and did not train local people in European methods of governing.

The French also supported a policy of **assimilation.** That policy was based on the idea that in time, the local populations would become absorbed into French culture. To aid in the transition, all local schools, courts, and businesses were patterned after French institutions. In practice, the French abandoned the ideal of assimilation for all but a few places and settled for a policy of "association." They recognized African institutions and culture but regarded them as inferior to French culture. Other European nations used this style of rule but made changes to suit their European culture.

THINK THROUGH HISTORY
A. Comparing How was the policy of paternalism like Social Darwinism?

Management Methods

Indirect Control	Direct Control
• Local government officials were used	• Foreign officials brought in to rule
• Limited self-rule	• No self-rule
• Goal: to develop future leaders	• Goal: assimilation
• Government institutions are based on European styles but may have local rules	• Government institutions are based only on European styles
Examples • British colonies such as Nigeria, India, Burma • U.S. colonies on Pacific Islands	Examples • French colonies such as Somaliland, Vietnam • German colonies such as Tanganyika • Portuguese colonies such as Angola

SKILLBUILDER: Interpreting Charts
1. *In which management method are the people less empowered to rule themselves? Explain.*
2. *In what ways are the two management methods different?*

African Weaving

When Europeans began colonizing Africa, they found a variety of cultures, many with distinctive textiles. Just as the colonizers learned to identify peoples from the textiles they wore, so historians also learn from these fabrics. For example, the materials used in the fabrics reveal clues about the environment of the weavers. The designs and patterns often used traditional symbols or myths of the culture. When and how the fabrics were used also provide information about the culture's celebrations and social roles. Many of these fabrics, such as the ones below, continue to be produced in modern times.

A modern-day Ivory Coast chief wears kente cloth. *Kente* is a general term for silk cloth. Only royalty are allowed to wear kente cloth.

Adinkra Cloth

Gyaman people of the Ivory Coast produced this hand-printed and embroidered cloth. Stamp patterns were made from a gourd and dipped in a dye made of bark paste. The cloth was stamped with symbols. The name of each symbol represented a proverb, an event, or a human, animal, or plant. The symbol shown (rams' horns) is a sign of strength and humility.

Kuba Cloth

Made by Kuba people of Congo, this cloth was made of raffia, a palm-leaf fiber. The cloth design was based on traditional geometric styles. The cloth was worn at ceremonial events, was used as currency, and may have been offered for part of a dowry.

Kente Cloth

This cloth was produced by the Asante people of Ghana. The word *kente* is not used by the Asante. It comes from a Fante (another society) word for basket. The Asante called the cloth *asasia*. Asasia production was a monopoly of the king of the Asante.

Connect *to* History

Contrasting Each of these textiles reflects a specific group. Identify characteristics that make the textiles different from each other.

 SEE SKILLBUILDER HANDBOOK, PAGE 996

Connect *to* Today

Comparing To show their roots, some African Americans wear clothing with a kente cloth pattern. What other ethnic groups have specific clothing that connects them to their roots?

Nigeria, 1914

Hausa-Fulani
Igbo
Yoruba
British-imposed border

0   250 Miles
0   500 Kilometers

FRENCH WEST AFRICA

Niger R.

Lake Chad

1851, British annex Lagos

NIGERIA

Benue R.

Lagos

After 1884–85 Berlin Conference, Britain declares a protectorate over Niger Delta

Niger R.

The Royal Niger Company controls the palm-oil trade

CAMEROONS

Gulf of Guinea

A British Colony

A close look at Britain's rule of Nigeria illustrates the forms of imperialism used by European powers to gain control of an area, and also shows management methods used to continue the control of the economic and political life of the area.

In 1807, Britain outlawed the slave trade. The British freed some slaves on the West African coast, who then helped the British in overtaking other groups. To get a group's land, the British swayed that group's enemies to help fight them. The winning African groups might then bow to British control.

Later, the Royal Niger Company gained control of the palm-oil trade along the Niger River. In 1884–85, the Berlin Conference gave Britain a protectorate in lands along the Niger River. In 1914, the British claimed the entire area of Nigeria as a colony. But in this new age of imperialism, it was necessary to not only claim the territory but also to govern the people living there.

THINK THROUGH HISTORY
B. Summarizing
Which forms of imperialistic control did Britain use in Nigeria?

GEOGRAPHY SKILLBUILDER: Interpreting Maps
1. **Region** *How many major culture regions are found within the colony of Nigeria? What sort of problems might result from combining or splitting groups of people?*
2. **Movement** *Why might the British want to be able to control the Niger River?*

Nigeria is one of the most culturally diverse areas in Africa. About 250 different ethnic groups lived there. The three largest groups were the Hausa-Fulani in the north, the Yoruba in the southwest, and the Igbo in the southeast. The groups in the area claimed by Britain were different from each other in many ways including language, culture, and religion. The Hausa-Fulani people of the north were Muslim and were accustomed to a strong central government. The Igbo and Yoruba peoples relied on local chiefs or governing councils for control. The Hausa-Fulani and Yoruba were traditional enemies.

THINK THROUGH HISTORY
C. Analyzing Motives Why was using local governments to control a colony a logical solution for the British?

Britain did not have enough troops to govern such a wide and complex area. So it turned to indirect rule of the land. The British relied on local administrations and chiefs to keep order, avoid rebellion, and collect taxes.

Ruling indirectly through local officials functioned well in northern Nigeria. There the traditional government was most like the British style of government. The process did not work as well in eastern or southwestern Nigeria, where the chiefdoms and councils had trouble with British indirect rule. One reason was that the British appointed chiefs where there had been no chiefs before. Then the British restricted their powers. This left the chiefs with little real status and led to problems governing the area.

African Resistance

Across Africa, European attempts to colonize the lands were met with resistance. The contest between African states and European powers was never equal due to the Europeans' superior arms. Sometimes African societies tried to form alliances with the Europeans. They hoped the agreement would allow them to remain independent. In some cases the Europeans did help defeat the rivals, but they then turned on their African allies. Other times Africans resisted the Europeans with whatever forces they could raise. With the single exception of Ethiopia, all these attempts at resistance ultimately failed. Edward Morel, a British journalist who lived for a time in the Congo, made an observation about the Africans' fate:

> **A VOICE FROM THE PAST**
> Nor is violent physical opposition to abuse and injustice henceforth possible for the African in any part of Africa. His chances of effective resistance have been steadily dwindling with the increasing perfectibility in the killing power of modern armament.
> Thus the African is really helpless against the material gods of the white man, as embodied in the trinity of imperialism, capitalistic exploitation, and militarism.
> **EDWARD MOREL,** *The Black Man's Burden*

THINK THROUGH HISTORY
D. Clarifying What does Morel believe is the fate of Africa?

Unsuccessful Movements The unsuccessful resistance attempts included active resistance and religious movements. Algeria's almost 50-year resistance to French rule was one outstanding example of active resistance. In West Africa, Samori Touré led resistance against the French for 16 years.

Africans in German East Africa put their faith in a spiritual defense. African villagers resisted the Germans' insistence that they plant cotton, a cash crop for export, rather than attend to their own food crops. In 1905, the belief suddenly arose that a magic water (*maji-maji*) sprinkled on their bodies would turn the Germans' bullets into water. The uprising became known as the Maji Maji rebellion. When resistance fighters armed with spears and protected by the magic water attacked a German machine-gun post, they were mowed down by the thousands. Officially, Germans recorded 26,000 resisters dead. But almost twice that number perished in the famine that followed.

Resistance Movements in Africa, 1881–1914

Algerian Berbers and Arabs 1830–1884
TUNISIA
Mediterranean Sea
ALGERIA
LIBYA
Arabi Pasha 1881–1882
EGYPT
Tropic of Cancer
Rabih 1897–1900
ANGLO-EGYPTIAN SUDAN
Mahdist State 1881–1898
Mande 1884–1898
FRENCH WEST AFRICA
L. Chad
Khartoum
BRITISH SOMALILAND
Daboya
GOLD COAST
Fashoda
ETHIOPIA
Menelik II 1893–1896
CAMEROONS
ITALIAN SOMALILAND
0° Equator
Asante 1900
BELGIAN CONGO
UGANDA
BRITISH EAST AFRICA
INDIAN OCEAN
ATLANTIC OCEAN
N
GERMAN EAST AFRICA
Maji Maji 1905–1906
Mashona 1896
MADAGASCAR
0   1,000 Miles
ANGOLA
0   2,000 Kilometers
GERMAN SOUTHWEST AFRICA
SOUTHERN RHODESIA
Tropic of Capricorn
Ndebele, 1896
Menalamba 1898–1904
Area of resistance
Herero and Hottentot 1904–1906
SOUTH AFRICA
ZULULAND

GEOGRAPHY SKILLBUILDER: Interpreting Maps
1. **Region** *Which region had the largest area affected by resistance?*
2. **Region** *Was any region unaffected by resistance movements?*

Ethiopia: A Successful Resistance

Ethiopia was the only African nation to successfully resist the Europeans. Its victory was due to one man—**Menelik II.** He became emperor of Ethiopia in 1889. He successfully played Italians, French, and British against each other, all of whom were striving to bring Ethiopia into their spheres of influence. In the meantime he built up a large arsenal of modern weapons purchased from France and Russia. About to sign a treaty with Italy, Menelik discovered differences between the wording of the treaty in Amharic—the Ethiopian language—and in Italian. Menelik believed he was giving up a tiny portion of Ethiopia. However, the Italians claimed all of Ethiopia as a protectorate. Meanwhile, Italian forces were advancing into northern Ethiopia. Menelik declared war. In 1896, in one of the greatest battles in the history of Africa—the Battle of Adowa—Ethiopian forces successfully defeated the Italians and maintained their nation's independence.

THINK THROUGH HISTORY
E. Analyzing Causes Why would the French and Russians sell arms to Ethiopia?

Impact of Colonial Rule

European colonial rule forever altered Africans' lives. For the most part, the effects were negative, but in some cases the Europeans brought benefits.

On the positive side, colonialism reduced local warfare. Now, under the control of the European military, raids between rival tribes were reduced. Humanitarian efforts in some colonies improved sanitation and brought hospitals and schools. As a result, life spans increased and literacy rates improved. Also positive was the economic expansion. African products came to be valued on the international market. To aid the economic growth, African colonies gained railroads, dams, and telephone and telegraph lines. But for the most part, these only benefited European business interests, not Africans' lives.

On the negative side, Africans lost control of their land and their independence. Many died of new diseases such as smallpox. They also lost thousands of their people in resisting the Europeans. Famines resulted from the change to cash crops in place of subsistence agriculture.

Africans also suffered from a breakdown of their traditional cultures. Traditional authority figures were replaced. Homes and property were transferred with little regard to their importance to the people. Men were forced to leave villages to find ways to support themselves and their families. They had to work in mines, on European-owned farms, or on government projects such as railroad building. Contempt for the traditional culture and admiration of European life undermined stable societies and caused identity problems for Africans.

The most troublesome political legacy from the colonial period was the dividing of the African continent. Long-term rival chiefdoms were sometimes united, while at other times, kinship groups were split between colonies. The artificial boundaries that combined or unnaturally divided groups created problems that plagued African colonies during European occupation. These boundaries continue to create problems for the nations that evolved from the former colonies.

The patterns of behavior of imperialist powers were similar, no matter where their colonies were located. Dealing with local traditions and peoples continued to cause problems in other areas of the world dominated by Europeans. Resistance to the European imperialists also continued, as you will see in Section 3.

THINK THROUGH HISTORY
F. Recognizing Effects Why might the problems caused by artificial boundaries continue after the Europeans left?

HISTORY MAKERS

Samori Touré
about 1830–1900

Samori Touré is a hero of the Mandinka people. His empire is often compared to the great Mali Empire of the 1300s.

Touré was a nationalist who built a powerful Mandinkan kingdom by conquering neighboring states. His kingdom became the third largest empire in West Africa.

For 16 years, Touré opposed the French imperialists in West Africa. The well-armed Mandinkas were France's greatest foe in West Africa, and the two armies clashed several times. The Mandinkan Empire was finally brought down, not in battle, but by a famine.

Sekou Touré, the first president of the nation of Guinea in 1958, claimed to be the grandson of Samori Touré.

Section 2 Assessment

1. TERMS & NAMES

Identify
- paternalism
- assimilation
- Menelik II

2. TAKING NOTES

Re-create the chart below on your paper. Fill in the information on how Europeans controlled and managed other areas of the world.

European Imperialism	
Forms of Control	
Management Methods	

3. FORMING OPINIONS

Do you think Europeans could have conquered Africa if the Industrial Revolution had never occurred? Explain your answer.

THINK ABOUT
- the limited role of Europeans in Africa until the late 1800s
- what inventions changed Europeans' ability to enter Africa

4. THEME ACTIVITY

Power and Authority With a small group of students, divide into two teams, one representing the Europeans and one representing the Africans. Debate the following statement: "The negative effects of imperialism outweighed its positive results."

Views of Imperialism

European imperialism extended to the continents beyond Africa. As imperialism spread, the colonizer and the colonized viewed the experience of imperialism in very different ways. Some Europeans were outspoken about the superiority they felt toward the peoples they conquered. Others thought imperialism was very wrong. Even the conquered had mixed feelings about their encounter with the Europeans.

ESSAY
J. A. Hobson

A journalist and essayist, Hobson was an outspoken critic of imperialism. His 1902 book, *Imperialism,* made a great impression on his fellow Britons.

For Europe to rule Asia by force for purposes of gain, and to justify that rule by the pretence that she is civilizing Asia and raising her to a higher level of spiritual life, will be adjudged by history, perhaps, to be the crowning wrong and folly of Imperialism. What Asia has to give, her priceless stores of wisdom garnered from her experience of ages, we refuse to take; the much or little which we could give we spoil by the brutal manner of our giving. This is what Imperialism has done, and is doing, for Asia.

SPEECH
Jules Ferry

In a speech before the French National Assembly on July 28,1883, Jules Ferry summarized reasons for supporting French imperialism.

Nations are great in our times only by means of the activities which they develop; it is not simply 'by the peaceful shining forth of institutions . . .' that they are great at this hour. . . . Something else is needed for France: . . . that she must also be a great country exercising all of her rightful influence over the destiny of Europe, that she ought to propagate this influence throughout the world and carry everywhere that she can her language, her customs, her flag, her arms, and her genius.

SPEECH
Dadabhai Naoroji

Dadabhai Naoroji was the first Indian elected to the British Parliament. He was also a part of the founding of the Indian National Congress. In 1871, he delivered a speech answering a question about the impact of Great Britain on India. In the speech he listed positives and negatives about the rule of the British. The conclusion of the speech is printed below.

To sum up the whole, the British rule has been—morally, a great blessing; politically peace and order on one hand, blunders on the other, materially, impoverishment. . . . The natives call the British system "Sakar ki Churi," the knife of sugar. That is to say there is no oppression, it is all smooth and sweet, but it is the knife, notwithstanding. I mention this that you should know these feelings. Our great misfortune is that you do not know our wants. When you will know our real wishes, I have not the least doubt that you would do justice. The genius and spirit of the British people is fair play and justice.

POLITICAL CARTOON
Devilfish in Egyptian Waters

Notice that Egypt is not yet one of the areas controlled by the British.

THE DEVILFISH IN EGYPTIAN WATERS.

Connect *to* History

Analyzing Effects For each excerpt, list the positive and negative effects of imperialism mentioned by the speaker.

 SEE SKILLBUILDER
HANDBOOK, PAGE 995.

Connect *to* Today

Research List the countries controlled by England as shown in the political cartoon. Research to find out what year each of them became independent. Make a chart showing the countries in order by the year they were freed from colonial status. Next to each one also write its current name.

 CD-ROM   For another perspective on imperialism, see *World History: Electronic Library of Primary Sources.*

Muslim Lands Fall to Imperialist Demands

MAIN IDEA	**WHY IT MATTERS NOW**
European nations expanded their empires by seizing territories from Muslim states.	Political events in this vital resource area are still influenced by actions from the imperialistic period.

SETTING THE STAGE The European powers who carved up Africa among themselves also looked elsewhere to see what other lands they could control. The Muslim lands that rimmed the Mediterranean had largely been claimed as a result of Arab and Ottoman conquests. Now the Muslim power in those areas was weakening. Europeans competed with each other to gain control of this strategically important area.

Ottoman Empire Loses Power

The Ottoman Empire at its peak stretched from Hungary in the north, through Greece, around the Black Sea, south through Syria, and across Egypt all the way west to the borders of Morocco. But during the empire's last 300 years, it steadily declined in power. The declining empire had difficulties trying to fit into the modern world. However, the Ottomans made attempts to change before they finally were unable to hold back the European imperialist powers.

Reforms Fail When Suleiman I, the last great Ottoman sultan, died in 1566, he was followed by a succession of weak sultans. The ruling party broke up into a number of quarreling, often corrupt factions. Along with weakening power came other problems. Corruption and theft had caused financial losses. Coinage was devalued, causing inflation. Unemployed ex-soldiers and students caused trouble. Once a leader in scientific, mechanical, and administrative achievements, the Ottoman Empire fell further and further behind Europe.

When Selim III came into power in 1789, he attempted to modernize the army. The older janissary corps resisted his efforts. Selim III was overthrown and reform movements were temporarily abandoned. Meanwhile, nationalist feelings began to stir among the Ottoman's subject peoples. In 1830, Greece gained its independence, and Serbia gained self-rule. The Ottomans' weakness was becoming apparent to European powers, who were expanding their territories. They began to look for ways to take the lands away from the Ottomans.

Ottoman Empire, 1699–1914

- Ottoman Empire at its greatest extent in 1699
- Ottoman Empire in 1914
- Territory becomes part of

GEOGRAPHY SKILLBUILDER: Interpreting Maps
1. **Region** Approximately how much of the Ottoman Empire was lost by 1914?
2. **Region** How many European nations claimed parts of the Ottoman Empire? Which areas became independent?

The Age of Imperialism **697**

This 1897 lithograph shows the British forces at the Battle of Balaklava in the Crimean War. This battle was the inspiration for a famous poem by Alfred, Lord Tennyson, "The Charge of the Light Brigade."

Europeans Grab Territory

Geopolitics—an interest in or taking of land for its strategic location or products—played an important role in the fate of the Ottoman Empire. World powers were attracted to its strategic location. The Ottomans controlled access to the Mediterranean and the Atlantic sea trade. Merchants in landlocked countries that lay beyond the Black Sea had to go through Ottoman lands. Russia, for example, desperately wanted passage for its grain exports across the Black Sea and into the Mediterranean Sea. This desire strongly influenced Russia's relations with the Ottoman Empire. Russia attempted to win Ottoman favor, formed alliances with Ottoman enemies, and finally waged war against the Ottomans. Discovery of oil in Persia and the Arabian Peninsula around 1900 focused even more attention on the area.

Russia and the Crimean War Each generation of Russian czars launched a war on the Ottomans to try to gain land on the Black Sea. In 1853, war broke out between the Russians and the Ottomans. The war was called the **Crimean War,** after a peninsula in the Black Sea where most of the war was fought. Britain and France wanted to prevent the Russians from gaining control of additional Ottoman lands. So they entered the war on the side of the Ottoman Empire. The combined forces of the Ottomans, Britain, and France defeated Russia. The Crimean War was the first war in which women, led by Florence Nightingale, established their position as army nurses. It was also the first war to be covered by newspaper correspondents.

The Crimean War revealed the Ottoman Empire's military weakness. Despite the help of Britain and France, the Ottoman Empire continued to lose lands. The Russians came to the aid of Slavic people in the Balkans who rebelled against the Ottomans. The Ottomans lost control of Romania, Montenegro, Cyprus, Bosnia, Herzegovina, and an area that became Bulgaria. The Ottomans lost land in Africa, too. By the beginning of World War I, the Ottoman Empire was reduced to a small portion of its former size.

Observing the slow decline of the Ottoman Empire, some Muslim leaders decided that their countries would either have to adjust to the modern world or be consumed by it. Egypt and Persia both initiated political and social reforms, in part to block European domination of their lands.

Egypt Tries Reform Modernization came to Egypt as a result of the interest in the area created by the French Revolution. Egypt's strategic location at the head of the Red Sea appeared valuable to France and Britain. After Napoleon failed to win Egypt, a new leader emerged: Muhammad Ali. The Ottomans sent him to govern

THINK THROUGH HISTORY
A. Analyzing Causes Why would the decline of the Ottoman Empire make other Muslim countries try to change?

Egypt, but he soon broke away from Ottoman control. In 1841, he fought a series of battles in which he gained control of Syria and Arabia. Through the combined efforts of European powers, he and his heirs were recognized as hereditary rulers of Egypt.

Muhammad Ali began a series of reforms in the military and in the economy. He personally directed a shift of Egyptian agriculture to a plantation cash crop—cotton. This brought Egypt into the international marketplace, but at a cost to the peasants. They lost the use of lands they traditionally farmed. They were forced to grow cash crops in place of food crops.

Muhammad Ali's efforts to modernize Egypt were continued by his grandson, Isma'il. Isma'il supported the construction of the **Suez Canal.** The canal was a man-made waterway that cut through the Isthmus of Suez. It connected the Red Sea to the Mediterranean. It was built mainly with French money and Egyptian labor. The Suez Canal was opened in 1869 with a huge international celebration. However, Isma'il's modernization efforts, such as irrigation projects and communication networks, were enormously expensive. Egypt soon found that it could not pay its European bankers even the interest on its $450 million debt. The British insisted on overseeing financial control of the canal, and in 1882 the British occupied Egypt.

British control of the Suez Canal remained an important part of British imperial policy. The canal was viewed as the "Lifeline of the Empire" because it allowed the British quicker access to its colonies in Asia and Africa. A British imperialist, Joseph Chamberlain, presented a speech to Parliament. In it he supported the continued control of the canal:

THINK THOUGH HISTORY
**B. Recognizing
Effects** What two
effects did raising cot-
ton have on Egyptian
agriculture?

A VOICE FROM THE PAST
I approve of the continued occupation of Egypt; and for the same reasons I have urged upon this Government, . . . the necessity for using every legitimate opportunity to extend our influence and control in that great African continent which is now being opened up to civilization and to commerce. . . .
JOSEPH CHAMBERLAIN, in a speech, January 22, 1894

Persia Pressured to Change Elsewhere in southwest Asia, Russia and Britain competed to exploit Persia commercially and to bring that country under their own spheres of influence. Russia was especially interested in gaining access to the Persian Gulf and the Indian Ocean. Twice Persia gave up territories to Russia after military defeats in 1813 and 1828. Britain was interested in using Afghanistan as a buffer between India and Russia.

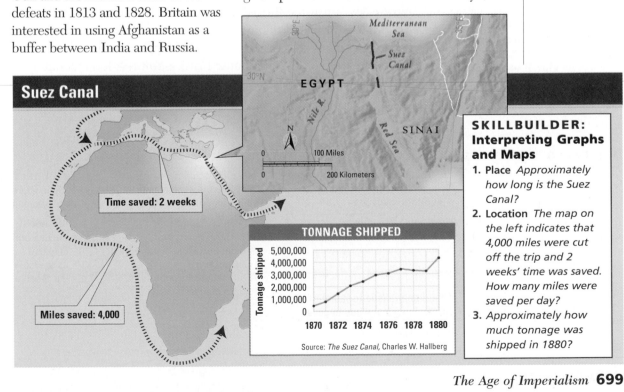

Suez Canal

Time saved: 2 weeks

Miles saved: 4,000

TONNAGE SHIPPED

Tonnage shipped: 5,000,000 / 4,000,000 / 3,000,000 / 2,000,000 / 1,000,000 / 0

1870 1872 1874 1876 1878 1880

Source: *The Suez Canal,* Charles W. Hallberg

EGYPT — Mediterranean Sea — Suez Canal — Nile R. — Red Sea — SINAI

0   100 Miles
0   200 Kilometers

**SKILLBUILDER:
Interpreting Graphs
and Maps**

1. **Place** *Approximately how long is the Suez Canal?*

2. **Location** *The map on the left indicates that 4,000 miles were cut off the trip and 2 weeks' time was saved. How many miles were saved per day?*

3. *Approximately how much tonnage was shipped in 1880?*

In 1857, Persia resisted British demands but was forced to give up all claims to Afghanistan. Britain's interest in Persia increased greatly after the discovery of oil there in 1908.

Persia lacked the capital to develop its own resources. To raise money and to gain economic prestige, the Persian ruler began granting concessions to Western businesses. Businesses bought the right to operate in a certain area or develop a certain product. For example, a British corporation, the Anglo-Persian Oil Company, began to develop Persia's rich oil fields in the early 1900s.

Tension arose between the often corrupt rulers, who wanted to sell concessions to Europeans, and the people. The people were often backed by religious leaders who feared change or disliked Western influence in their nation. In 1891, Nasir al-Din attempted to sell the rights to export and distribute Persian tobacco to a British company. This action outraged Sayyid Jamal al-Din al-Afghani, a modernist leader, who helped set up a tobacco boycott by the heavy-smoking Persians. In the following quote, he expresses his contempt for the Persian ruler:

Background
Britain needed oil for its ships, which now ran on oil rather than coal. Thus, they needed greater supplies of petroleum.

A VOICE FROM THE PAST
. . . He has sold to the foes of our Faith the greater part of the Persian lands and the profits derived from them, for example . . . tobacco, with the chief centers of its cultivation, the lands on which it is grown and the warehouses, carriers, and sellers, wherever these are found. . . .

In short, this criminal has offered the provinces of Persia to auction among the Powers, and is selling the realms of Islam and the abodes of Muhammad and his household to foreigners.

SAYYID JAMAL AL-DIN AL-AFGHANI, in a letter to Hasan Shirazi, April 1891

THINK THROUGH HISTORY
C. Clarifying Why did al-Afghani condemn the actions of the Persian ruler?

The tobacco boycott worked. Riots broke out and the ruler was compelled to cancel the concession. As unrest continued in Persia, the government was unable to control the situation. In 1906, a group of revolutionaries forced the ruler to establish a constitution. In 1907, Russia and Britain took over the country and divided it into spheres of influence.

In the Muslim lands, the European imperialists gained control by using economic imperialism and creating spheres of influence. Although some governments made attempts at modernization, in most cases it was too little too late. In other areas of the globe, imperialists provided the modernization. India, for example, became a colony that experienced massive change as a result of the occupation of the imperialist British. You will learn about India in Section 4.

CONNECT *to* TODAY

Tobacco and Politics

Tobacco production is a huge industry in the world. It is estimated that about 7 million metric tons of tobacco are consumed each year. (That is about 6 trillion cigarettes per year.)

In some countries, production of tobacco is a major part of the economy. Taxes on tobacco products generate much revenue in countries across the world. Since the tobacco industry creates huge profits, it often has an impact on the politics of a country as well.

Health concerns about tobacco consumption have also found their way into politics. Worldwide, countries are looking at government control of tobacco products as a way to deal with health problems.

Since the 1980s the World Health Organization has promoted a World No-Tobacco Day, which occurs on May 31 each year.

Section ❸ Assessment

1. TERMS & NAMES
Identify
- geopolitics
- Crimean War
- Suez Canal

2. TAKING NOTES
Re-create the diagram below and fill in at least three details that support the main idea.

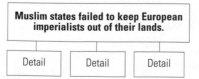

Muslim states failed to keep European imperialists out of their lands.

| Detail | Detail | Detail |

What imperialistic forms of control did the Europeans use to govern these lands?

3. COMPARING AND CONTRASTING
How were the reactions of African and Muslim rulers to imperialism similar? How were they different?

THINK ABOUT
- African and Muslim patterns of resistance
- African and Muslim efforts toward modernization

4. ANALYZING THEMES
Economics Why did European imperialist powers want to take over Ottoman Empire lands?

THINK ABOUT
- the location of the Ottoman Empire
- its special resources
- European ambitions

4 British Imperialism in India

MAIN IDEA	WHY IT MATTERS NOW
As the Mughal Empire declined, Britain seized Indian territory until it controlled almost the whole subcontinent.	India, the second most populated nation in the world, has its political roots in this colony.

SETTING THE STAGE British economic interest in India began in the 1600s, when the British East India Company set up trading posts at Bombay, Madras, and Calcutta. At first, India's ruling Mughal Dynasty kept European traders under control. By 1707, however, the Mughal Empire was collapsing. Dozens of small states, each headed by a ruler or maharajah, broke away from Mughal control.

British Expand Control Over India

The East India Company quickly took advantage of the growing weakness of the Mughals. In 1757, Robert Clive led company troops in a decisive victory over Indian forces at the Battle of Plassey. From that time on, the East India Company was the leading power in India. The area controlled by the company grew over time. Eventually, it governed directly or indirectly an area that included modern Bangladesh, most of southern India, and nearly all the territory along the Ganges River in the north.

East India Company Dominates Officially, the British government regulated the East India Company's efforts both in London and in India. Until the beginning of the 19th century, the company ruled India with little interference from the British government. The company even had its own army, led by British officers and staffed by **sepoys,** or Indian soldiers. The governor of Bombay, Mountstuart Elphinstone, referred to the sepoy army as "a delicate and dangerous machine, which a little mismanagement may easily turn against us."

"Jewel in the Crown" Produces Trade Products At first, India was treasured by the British more for its potential than its actual profit. The Industrial Revolution had turned Britain into the world's workshop, and India was a major supplier of raw materials for that workshop. Its 300 million people were also a large potential market for British-made goods. It is not surprising, then, that the British considered India the brightest **"jewel in the crown"** — the most valuable of all of Britain's colonies.

The British set up restrictions that prevented the Indian economy from operating on its own. British policies called for India to produce raw materials for British manufacturing and to buy British finished goods. In addition,

Tea from the Lipton plantation in Darjeeling is loaded onto an elephant for transport to Calcutta.

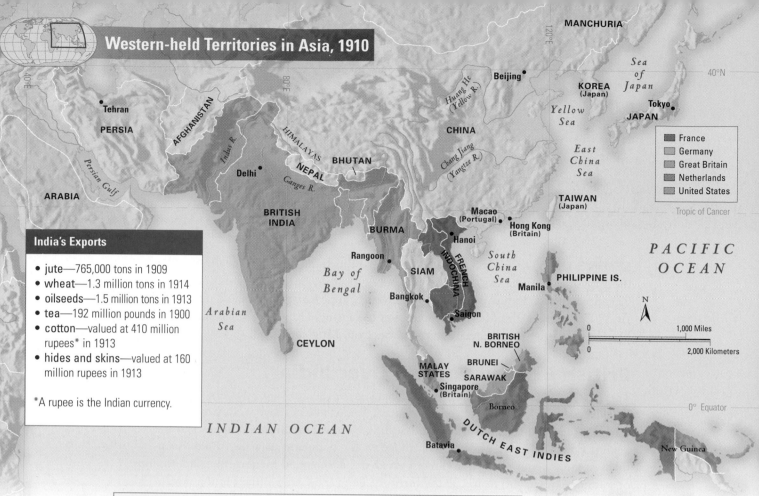

Western-held Territories in Asia, 1910

India's Exports

- jute—765,000 tons in 1909
- wheat—1.3 million tons in 1914
- oilseeds—1.5 million tons in 1913
- tea—192 million pounds in 1900
- cotton—valued at 410 million rupees* in 1913
- hides and skins—valued at 160 million rupees in 1913

*A rupee is the Indian currency.

Map labels: MANCHURIA, Beijing, KOREA (Japan), Sea of Japan, Tokyo, JAPAN, Yellow Sea, CHINA, East China Sea, TAIWAN (Japan), Macao (Portugal), Hong Kong (Britain), Hanoi, South China Sea, PHILIPPINE IS., Manila, PACIFIC OCEAN, Saigon, BRITISH N. BORNEO, BRUNEI, SARAWAK, Borneo, New Guinea, DUTCH EAST INDIES, Batavia, Singapore (Britain), MALAY STATES, Bangkok, SIAM, Rangoon, BURMA, BRITISH INDIA, Delhi, NEPAL, BHUTAN, HIMALAYAS, Ganges R., Indus R., AFGHANISTAN, Tehran, PERSIA, ARABIA, Persian Gulf, Arabian Sea, Bay of Bengal, CEYLON, INDIAN OCEAN, FRENCH INDOCHINA, Huang He (Yellow R.), Chang Jiang (Yangtze R.)

Legend: France, Germany, Great Britain, Netherlands, United States. Tropic of Cancer. 0° Equator. 40°N. 120°E. 80°E. 40°E.

Scale: 0 — 1,000 Miles; 0 — 2,000 Kilometers

GEOGRAPHY SKILLBUILDER: Interpreting Maps

1. **Region** Which nation in 1900 held the most land in colonies?
2. **Location** How is the location of India a great advantage for trade?

Indian competition with British finished goods was prohibited. For example, India's own handloom textile industry was almost put out of business by imported British textiles. Cheap cloth and ready-made clothes from England flooded the Indian market and drove out local producers.

India became economically valuable only after the British established a railroad network. Railroads transported raw products from the interior to the ports and manufactured goods back again. The majority of the raw materials were agricultural products produced on plantations. Plantation crops included tea, indigo, coffee, cotton, and jute. Another crop was opium. The British shipped opium to China and exchanged it for tea, which they then sold in England.

Trading these crops was closely tied to international events. For example, the Crimean War in the 1850s cut off the supply of Russian jute to Scottish jute mills. This boosted the export of raw jute from Bengal, a province in India. Likewise, cotton production in India increased when the Civil War in the United States cut off supplies of cotton for British textile mills.

Impact of Colonialism India both benefited from and was oppressed by British colonialism. On the positive side, the laying of the world's third largest railroad network was a major British achievement. When completed, the railroads enabled India to develop a modern economy and brought unity to the connected regions. Along with the railroads, a modern road network, telephone and telegraph lines, dams, bridges, and irrigation canals enabled India to modernize. Sanitation and public health improved. Schools and colleges were founded, and literacy increased. Also, British troops cleared central India of bandits and put an end to local warfare among competing local rulers.

Vocabulary
jute: a fiber used for sacks and cord.

THINK THROUGH HISTORY
A. Summarizing On which continents are Indian goods being traded?

On the negative side, the British held much of the political and economic power. The British restricted Indian-owned industries such as cotton textiles. The emphasis on cash crops resulted in a loss of self-sufficiency for many villagers. The conversion to cash crops reduced food production, causing famines in the late 1800s. The British officially adopted a hands-off policy regarding Indian religious and social customs. Even so, the increased presence of missionaries and the outspoken racist attitude of most British officials threatened Indian traditional life.

Indians Rebel

By 1850, the British controlled most of the Indian subcontinent. However, there were many pockets of discontent. Many Indians believed that in addition to controlling their land the British were trying to convert them to Christianity. The Indian people also resented the constant racism that the British expressed toward them.

Sepoy Rebellion As economic problems increased for Indians, so did their feelings of resentment and nationalism. In 1857, gossip spread among the sepoys, the Indian soldiers, that the cartridges of their new Enfield rifles were sealed with beef and pork fat. To use the cartridges, soldiers had to bite off the seal. Both Hindus, who consider the cow sacred, and Muslims, who do not eat pork, were outraged by the news.

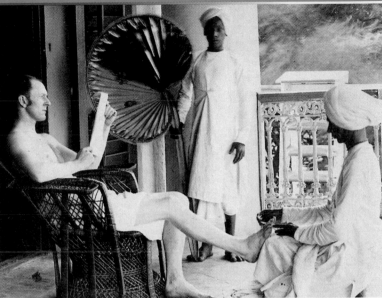

Daily Life

British Army

Social class determined the way of life for the British Army in India. Upper-class men served as officers. Lower-class British served at lesser rank and did not advance past the rank of sergeant. Only men with the rank of sergeant and above were allowed to bring their wives to India.

Each English officer's wife attempted to re-create England in the home setting. Like a general, she directed an army of 20 to 30 servants.

Officers and enlisted men spent much of each day involved in sports such as cricket, polo, and rugby. Athletics were encouraged to keep the men from "drink and idleness." The upper-class officers also spent time socializing at fancy-dress dances, concerts, and after-polo events.

Indian Servants

Caste determined Indian occupations. Jobs were strictly divided by caste. Castes were divided into four broad categories called varna. Indian civil servants were of the third varna. House and personal servants were of the fourth varna.

Even within the varna, jobs were strictly regulated, which is why such large servant staffs were required. For example, in the picture above, although both were of the same varna, the person washing the man's feet was of a different caste than the person doing the fanning.

The social life of the servants centered around religious festivals and ceremonies marking important life passages. These included a child's first haircut, religious initiation, engagement, marriage, or childbirth.

A garrison commander was shocked when 85 of the 90 sepoys refused to accept the cartridges. The British handled the crisis badly. The soldiers who had disobeyed were jailed. The next day, on May 10, 1857, the sepoys rebelled. They marched to Delhi, where they were joined by Indian soldiers stationed there. They captured the city of Delhi. From Delhi, the rebellion spread to northern and central India.

Some historians have called this outbreak the **Sepoy Mutiny.** The uprising spread over much of northern India. Fierce fighting took place. Both British and sepoys tried to slaughter each other's armies. The East India Company took more than a year to regain control of the country. The British government sent troops to help them.

The Indians could not unite against the British due to weak leadership and serious splits between Hindus and Muslims. Hindus did not want the Muslim Mughal Empire restored. Indeed, many Hindus preferred British rule to Muslim rule. Most

THINK THROUGH HISTORY
B. Recognizing Effects Look back at Elphinstone's comment on page 701. Did the Sepoy Mutiny prove him correct? Explain your answer.

The Age of Imperialism **703**

This English engraving shows the British troops defending the Royal Residency at Lucknow against a sepoy attack on July 30, 1857.

of the princes and maharajahs who had made alliances with the East India Company did not take part in the rebellion. The Sikhs, a religious group that had been hostile to the Mughals, also remained loyal to the British. Indeed, from then on, the bearded and turbaned Sikhs became the mainstay of Britain's army in India.

Turning Point The mutiny marked a turning point in Indian history. As a result of the mutiny, in 1858, the British government took direct command of India. The part of India that was under direct British rule was called the Raj. The term **Raj** referred to British rule over India from 1757 until 1947. India was divided into 11 provinces and some 250 districts. Sometimes a handful of officials were the only British among the million or so people in a district. A cabinet minister in London directed policy, and a British governor-general in India carried out the government's orders. After 1877, this official held the title of viceroy. To reward the many princes who had remained loyal to Britain, the British promised to respect all treaties the East India Company had made with them. They also promised that the Indian states that were still free would remain independent. Unofficially, however, Britain won greater and greater control of those states.

The Sepoy Mutiny fueled the racist attitudes of the English. The English attitude is illustrated in the following quote by Lord Kitchener, British commander in chief of the army in India:

A VOICE FROM THE PAST
It is this consciousness of the inherent superiority of the European which has won for us India. However well educated and clever a native may be, and however brave he may prove himself, I believe that no rank we can bestow on him would cause him to be considered an equal of the British officer.

LORD KITCHENER, quoted in K. M. Panikkar, *Asia and Western Dominance*

The mutiny increased distrust between the British and the Indians. A political pamphlet suggested that both Hindus and Muslims "are being ruined under the tyranny and oppression of the . . . treacherous English."

THINK THROUGH HISTORY
C. Recognizing Effects In what ways did the Sepoy Mutiny change the political climate of India?

Indian Nationalist Movements Begin

In the early 1800s, some Indians began demanding more modernization and a greater role in governing themselves. Ram Mohun Roy, a modern-thinking, well-educated Indian, began a campaign to move India away from traditional practices and ideas. Sometimes called the "Father of Modern India," Ram Mohun Roy called for an end to widow suicide, which he believed was a murderous act. He saw child marriages and the rigid caste separation as parts of religious life that needed to be changed to bring India into a more modern frame of mind. He believed that if the practices were not changed, India would continue to be controlled by outsiders. Roy's writings inspired other Indian reformers to call for adoption of Western ways. Roy also founded a social reform movement that worked for change in India.

Besides modernization and westernization, nationalist feelings started to surface in India. Indians resented a system that made them second-class citizens in their own country. Even Indians with a European education faced discrimination. They were barred from top posts in the Indian Civil Service. Those who managed to get middle-level jobs were paid less than Europeans. A British engineer on the East India Railway, for example, made nearly 20 times as much money as an Indian engineer.

A spirit of Indian nationalism led to the founding of two nationalist groups, the Indian National Congress in 1885 and the Muslim League in 1906. At first, such groups concentrated on specific concerns for Indians. Gradually their demands broadened. By the early 1900s, they were calling for self-government.

The nationalists were further inflamed in 1905 by the partition of Bengal. The province, which had a population of 85 million, was too large for administrative purposes. So the British divided it into a Hindu section and a Muslim section. Acts of terrorism broke out. The province was on the edge of open rebellion. In 1911, yielding to the pressure, the British took back the order and divided the province in a different way.

Conflict over the control of India continued to develop between the Indians and the British in the following years. Elsewhere in Southeast Asia, the same struggles for control of land took place between local groups and the major European powers that dominated them. You will learn about them in Section 5.

Background
Hindu tradition known as *suttee* called for a widow to be burned alive on the funeral pyre of her husband.

THINK THROUGH HISTORY
D. Analyzing Motives Why would the British think that dividing the Hindus and Muslims into separate sections would be good?

HISTORY MAKERS

Ram Mohun Roy 1772–1833

An extremely bright student, Ram Mohun Roy learned Persian, Sanskrit, and Arabic as a child. He spent many hours studying the religions of the world to understand people. He also studied the social and political ideas of the American and French revolutions.

Roy watched his sister-in-law burned alive on the funeral pyre of her husband. After that, he resolved to end practices that rooted India to the past. He challenged traditional Hindu culture and called for modernization of Hindu society.

The Hindu reform society he organized, Brahmo Samaj, shaped the thinking of the 19th-century Indian reformers. The society was the forerunner of the Indian nationalist movements.

Section 4 Assessment

1. TERMS & NAMES
Identify
• sepoy
• "jewel in the crown"
• Sepoy Mutiny
• Raj

2. TAKING NOTES
Re-create on your paper the cause-and-effect diagram below and fill in the effects of the three causes listed.

Cause	Effect
1. Decline of the Mughal Empire	
2. Colonial policies	
3. Sepoy Mutiny	

Which of the effects you listed later became causes?

3. ANALYZING
How did imperialism contribute to unity and the growth of nationalism in India?

THINK ABOUT
• the benefits of imperialism
• the negative effects of imperialism

4. ANALYZING THEMES
Empire Building How did economic imperialism lead to India's becoming a British colony?

THINK ABOUT
• the role of the British East India Company
• the Sepoy Mutiny

Interact *with* History

Life is good for you as a member of the local government in 19th-century China, but it could be even better. People from the West are eager to trade with your country. China, however, produces all that its people need, and government officials discourage contact with foreigners. Many foreign products, such as ceramics, are inferior to Chinese goods. The foreigners, however, do offer items that can improve your life, including rifles, cameras, and small sticks called matches that can be scraped against a rock to start a fire. You are curious about these inventions. But you wonder why the foreigners are so eager to trade with China and what they hope to gain.

Would you trade with the foreigners?

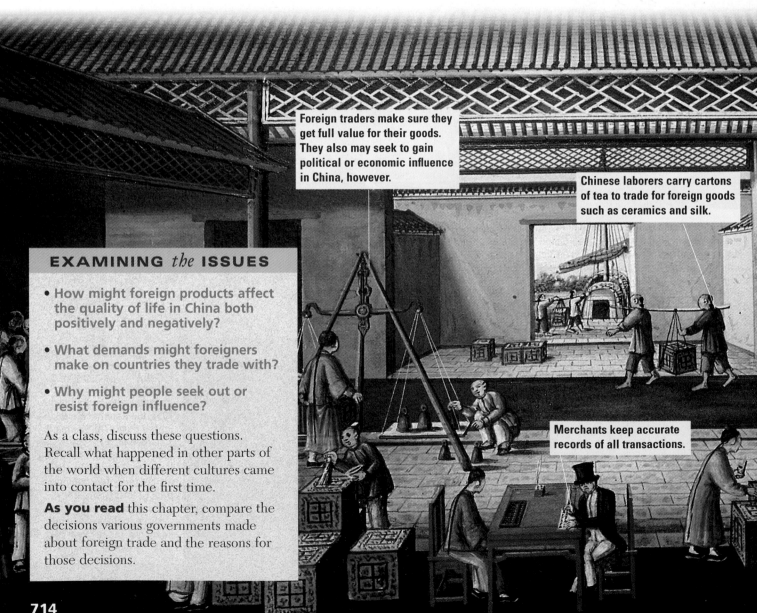

Foreign traders make sure they get full value for their goods. They also may seek to gain political or economic influence in China, however.

Chinese laborers carry cartons of tea to trade for foreign goods such as ceramics and silk.

Merchants keep accurate records of all transactions.

EXAMINING *the* ISSUES

- How might foreign products affect the quality of life in China both positively and negatively?

- What demands might foreigners make on countries they trade with?

- Why might people seek out or resist foreign influence?

As a class, discuss these questions. Recall what happened in other parts of the world when different cultures came into contact for the first time.

As you read this chapter, compare the decisions various governments made about foreign trade and the reasons for those decisions.

TERMS & NAMES
- Opium War
- extraterritorial rights
- Taiping Rebellion
- sphere of influence
- Open Door Policy
- Boxer Rebellion

1 China Responds to Pressure from the West

MAIN IDEA

Western economic pressure forced China to open to foreign trade and influence.

WHY IT MATTERS NOW

China has become an increasingly important member of the global community.

SETTING THE STAGE In the late 18th century, China had more people than any other empire in the world. Under the Manchus of the Qing Dynasty, the empire was stable and secure. The people lived by traditions that were thousands of years old.

China Resists Foreign Influence

Out of pride in their ancient culture, the Chinese looked down on all foreigners. In 1793, however, the Qing emperor agreed to receive an ambassador from England. The Englishman brought gifts of the West's most advanced technology—clocks, globes, musical instruments, and even a hot-air balloon. The emperor was not impressed. In a letter to England's King George III, he stated that the Chinese already had everything they needed. They were not interested in the "strange objects" and gadgets that the West was offering them.

China Remains Self-Sufficient The basis of Qing China's wealth was its healthy agricultural economy. During the 11th century, China had acquired a quick-growing strain of rice from Southeast Asia. By the time of the Qing Dynasty, the rice was being grown throughout the southern part of the country. Around the same time—the 17th and 18th centuries—Spanish and Portuguese traders brought maize, sweet potatoes, and peanuts from the Americas. These crops helped China increase the productivity of its land and more effectively feed its 300 million people. Better nutrition, in turn, led to a population boom.

China also had extensive mining and manufacturing industries. Rich salt, tin, silver, and iron mines produced great quantities of ore. The mines provided work for tens of thousands of people. The Chinese also produced beautiful silks, high-quality cottons, and fine porcelain. The Chinese people were essentially self-sufficient.

This 18th-century painted fan depicts Guangzhou in southern China as a cosmopolitan port, flying the flags of its many foreign traders. The rest of China, however, remained firmly isolated until the mid-19th century.

The Tea-Opium Connection Because of their self-sufficiency, the Chinese had little interest in trading with the West. For decades, the only place they would allow foreigners to do business was at the southern port of Guangzhou (gwahng·joh). And the balance of trade at Guangzhou was clearly in China's favor. This means that China earned much more for its exports than it spent on imports. The British imported millions of pounds of tea from China every year and exported goods worth much less. They made up for the difference in silver. This imbalance drained Britain's silver supply.

European merchants were determined to find a product the Chinese would buy in large quantities. Eventually they found one—opium. Opium is a habit-forming narcotic made from the poppy plant. Chinese doctors had been using it to relieve pain for hundreds of years. In the late 18th century, however, British merchants smuggled opium into China for nonmedical use. It took a few decades for opium smoking to catch on, but by 1835, as many as 12 million Chinese people were addicted to the drug.

War Breaks Out This growing supply of opium caused great social, moral, and monetary problems for the country. The Qing emperor was angry. In 1839, one of the emperor's highest advisers wrote a letter to England's Queen Victoria about the problem:

A VOICE FROM THE PAST
By what right do they [British merchants] . . . use the poisonous drug [opium] to injure the Chinese people? . . . I have heard that the smoking of opium is very strictly forbidden by your country; that is because the harm caused by opium is clearly understood. Since it is not permitted to do harm to your own country, then even less should you let it be passed on to the harm of other countries.

LIN ZEXU, quoted in *China's Response to the West*

The pleas went unanswered, and Britain refused to stop trading opium. The result was an open clash between the British and the Chinese—the **Opium War** of 1839. The battles took place mostly at sea. China's outdated ships were no match for Britain's steam-powered gunboats and sophisticated cannons. As a result, the Chinese suffered a humiliating defeat. In 1842, they signed a peace treaty, the Treaty of Nanjing.

This treaty gave Britain the island of Hong Kong. After signing another treaty in 1844, U.S. and other foreign citizens also gained **extraterritorial rights.** These rights provided exemption from Chinese law at four Chinese ports besides Guangzhou. Many Chinese greatly resented these privileges and the foreigners among them. And a bustling trade in opium continued.

THINK THROUGH HISTORY
A. Analyzing Issues
What conflicting British and Chinese positions led to the Opium War?

CONNECT *to* TODAY

Hong Kong
The Treaty of Nanjing gave the island of Hong Kong to the British. After another conflict in 1899, China leased that territory and parts of the mainland to Britain for 99 years. On July 1, 1997, Hong Kong returned to Chinese control.

Although the name *Hong Kong* means "fragrant harbor," this bustling economic center is one of the most crowded places on earth. About 15,000 people occupy each square mile.

Nearly all the residents of Hong Kong are Chinese. Most of them are emigrants from Communist mainland China. The major cities, Hong Kong City and Kowloon, are bustling centers of banking, manufacturing, tourism, and trade. High-rise buildings and gaudy neon signs rub shoulders with open-air markets and traditional shops on the cities' winding, narrow streets.

There has been almost a century of exposure to capitalism and British rule in Hong Kong. Integration of the former colony into Chinese society probably will be difficult for everyone.

Internal Problems Increase

Foreigners were not the greatest of China's problems in the mid-19th century, however. Its own population provided an overwhelming challenge. That population had grown to 430 million by 1850—a 30-percent gain in only 60 years. Yet food production had barely increased. As a result, hunger was widespread, even in good years. In the frequent bad years, the Huang He (Yellow River) broke through its dikes and flooded vast farming areas. Millions starved.

The Chinese government itself was riddled with corruption and could do little to ease its people's suffering. Dikes that might have held back the river had fallen into disrepair. Public granaries were empty. Talented people who were unable or unwilling to bribe state examiners often were denied government jobs. The people became discouraged, and opium addiction rose steadily. As their problems mounted, the Chinese actively began to rebel against the Qing Dynasty.

The Taiping Rebellion The rebellion that was to become China's largest was led by Hong Xiuquan (hung shee·oo·choo·ahn). The Treaty of Nanjing had granted Christian missionaries increased privileges in China. The missionaries greatly influenced this sensitive young man. Hong had mystical visions and wanted to save the world, beginning with China. He dreamed of a "Heavenly Kingdom of Great Peace." In this kingdom, all Chinese people would share China's vast wealth and no one would live in poverty. Hong's revolt was called the **Taiping Rebellion,** from the Chinese expression *taiping,* meaning "great peace."

Beginning in the late 1840s, Hong organized an army made up mainly of peasants—both men and women—from southern China. By 1853, 1 million people had joined his rebel forces. That year, Hong captured the city of Nanjing and declared it his capital. The Taiping government controlled large areas of southeastern China.

Over the next ten years, however, the Qing regained control of the country. Imperial troops, local militias, and British and French forces all fought against the Taiping. By 1864, they crushed the 14-year rebellion. But China paid a terrible price. Huge, hungry armies had destroyed fertile farmland in their search for food. At least 20 million—and possibly twice that many—people died.

THINK THROUGH HISTORY
B. Recognizing Effects What were the results of the Taiping Rebellion?

HISTORY MAKERS

Hong Xiuquan 1814–1864

Hong Xiuquan came from a rural family. As a young man, he tried to move up in Chinese society by seeking a government post. However, he kept failing the civil service exam. In his early twenties, Hong had a dream that ordered him to fight evil. From then on, he worked to overthrow the "evil" Qing dynasty and the same Qing system that he had tried so hard to enter. To destroy evil, Hong and his rebel followers destroyed Qing artworks and outlawed such Qing symbols as the pigtail.

Hong slowly developed his own personal vision of Christianity. That vision led him to forbid opium, tobacco, alcohol, and gambling. Under Hong, men and women were treated as equals. Women, for example, could fight for Hong's cause just as men could. However, men and women were divided into separate divisions, and even husbands and wives were not allowed contact.

After winning Nanjing, Hong withdrew into his mystical visions. After years of bloody feuding among his lieutenants, Hong's Taiping government fell. After that defeat, thousands of his followers burned themselves to death rather than surrender to the emperor.

China Wrestles with Reform

The Taiping Rebellion and other smaller uprisings put tremendous internal pressure on the Chinese government. And, despite the Treaty of Nanjing, external pressure from foreign powers was increasing. At the Qing court, stormy debates raged about how best to deal with these pressures. Some government leaders called for reforms patterned on Western ways. Others insisted on honoring Chinese traditions. The Chinese Empire was conservative overall, though. Clinging to traditional ways and resisting change started at the top.

Background
The Dowager Empress Cixi first served as ruler for two emperors who took the throne as children. When she gained the throne herself she was known as "dowager," or endowed empress.

The Dowager Empress Cixi Resists Change During the last half of the 19th century, there was only one person at the top in the Qing imperial palace. The Dowager Empress Cixi (tsoo·shee) ruled China, with only one brief gap, from 1861 until 1908.

Although she was committed to traditional values, the Dowager Empress did support certain reforms. In the 1860s, for example, she backed the self-strengthening movement. That program aimed to update China's educational system, diplomatic service,

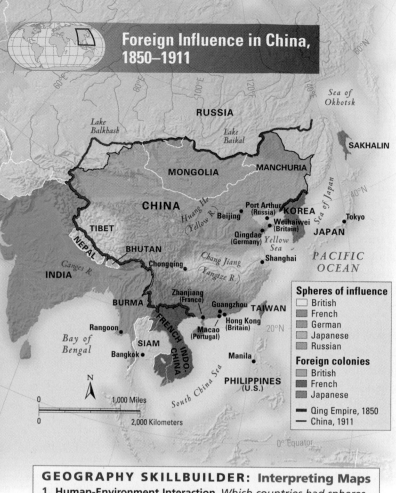

RUSSIA

Lake Balkhash

Lake Baikal

Sea of Okhotsk

SAKHALIN

MONGOLIA

MANCHURIA

CHINA

Port Arthur (Russia)

Beijing

KOREA

Weihaiwei (Britain)

Tokyo

TIBET

Huang He (Yellow R.)

Qingdao (Germany)

Yellow Sea

JAPAN

Sea of Japan

NEPAL

BHUTAN

Chang Jiang (Yangtze R.)

Chongqing

Shanghai

PACIFIC OCEAN

Ganges R.

INDIA

BURMA

Zhanjiang (France)

Guangzhou

TAIWAN

Rangoon

Macao (Portugal)

Hong Kong (Britain)

20°N

Bay of Bengal

SIAM

Bangkok

Manila

Bangkok

FRENCH INDO-CHINA

PHILIPPINES (U.S.)

South China Sea

N

0   1,000 Miles

0   2,000 Kilometers

0° Equator

Spheres of influence
- British
- French
- German
- Japanese
- Russian

Foreign colonies
- British
- French
- Japanese

— Qing Empire, 1850
— China, 1911

GEOGRAPHY SKILLBUILDER: Interpreting Maps

1. **Human-Environment Interaction** *Which countries had spheres of influence in China?*
2. **Location** *What foreign power shown on the map had access to inland China? What geographic feature made this possible?*

and military. Under this program, China set up arsenals to manufacture steam-powered gunboats, rifles, and ammunition. By 1875, these ammunition supply and storage facilities were among the largest in the world.

The self-strengthening movement had mixed results, however. The ability to produce its own warships and ammunition was undoubtedly good for China's morale. But the Chinese hired foreigners to run many of its arsenals. These outsiders often didn't feel comfortable working with Chinese resources. So they imported both raw materials and factory machinery from abroad. This practice contributed to both an imbalance in trade for China and a lack of quality control. In addition, the movement lacked support from the Chinese people as a whole.

Other Nations Step In China's weak military technology and its economic and political problems were not a secret from the rest of the world. Throughout the late 19th century, many foreign nations took advantage of this weakness and attacked China. Treaty negotiations after each conflict gave the West increasing control over China's economy. As shown in the map, many of Europe's main political powers and Japan gained a strong foothold in China. This foothold, or **sphere of influence,** was a region in which the foreign nation controlled trade and investment.

THINK THROUGH HISTORY
C. Making Inferences What importance did spheres of influence have for China and for the nations involved?

The United States was a long-time trading partner with China. Americans worried that other nations would soon divide China into formal colonies and shut out American traders. To prevent this occurrence, in 1899 the United States declared the **Open Door Policy.** This policy proposed that China's "doors" be open to merchants of all nations. Britain and the other European nations agreed. The policy thus protected both American trading rights in China and China's freedom from colonization. But the country was still at the mercy of foreign powers.

Chinese Nationalism Grows

Humiliated by their loss of power, many Chinese pressed for strong reforms. Among them was China's young emperor, Guangxu (gwahng·shoo). In June 1898, Guangxu's aunt, the Dowager Empress Cixi, was relaxing at the summer palace. Assuming that he had her support, Guangxu introduced measures to modernize China. These measures called for overhauling China's educational system, strengthening the economy, modernizing the military, and streamlining the government. Guangxu asked progressive, creative advisers to help carry out his programs.

Most Qing officials saw these innovations as threats to their power. They reacted with alarm. In September 1899, they called the Dowager Empress back to the imperial court. Guangxu realized too late that he had misjudged her. Striking with the same speed as her nephew, the Dowager Empress Cixi placed him under arrest at the palace. She then took back her own power. She reversed his reforms and executed a number of the movement's leaders. Guangxu's Hundred Days of Reform ended without a single long-term change. The Chinese people's frustration with their situation did change, however. It grew.

The Boxer Rebellion This widespread frustration finally erupted. Poor peasants and workers particularly resented the special privileges granted to foreigners. They also resented Chinese Christians, who were protected by foreign missionaries. To demonstrate their discontent, they formed a secret organization called the Society of Harmonious Fists. They soon came to be known as the Boxers. Their campaign against the Dowager Empress's rule and foreigner privilege was called the **Boxer Rebellion.**

In the spring of 1900, the Boxers descended on Beijing. Shouting "Death to the foreign devils," the Boxers surrounded the European section of the city. They kept it under siege for several months. The Dowager Empress expressed support for the Boxers but did not back her words with military aid. In August, a multinational force of 20,000 troops marched toward Beijing. Soldiers from Britain, France, Germany, Austria, Italy, Russia, Japan, and the United States quickly defeated the Boxers.

Despite the failure of the Boxer Rebellion, a strong sense of nationalism had emerged in China. The Chinese people realized that their country must resist more foreign intervention. Most important, however, the government must become responsive to their needs.

The Beginnings of Reform At this point, even the Qing court realized that China needed to make profound changes to survive. In 1905, the Dowager Empress sent a select group of Chinese officials on a world tour to study the operation of different governments. The group traveled to Japan, the United States, Britain, France, Germany, Russia, and Italy. On its return in the spring of 1906, the officials recommended that China restructure its government. They based their suggestions on the constitutional monarchy of Japan. The empress accepted this recommendation and began making reforms. Although she convened a national assembly within a year, change was slow. In 1908, the court announced that it would establish a full constitutional government by 1917.

Unfortunately, however, the turmoil in China did not end with these progressive steps. Unrest would continue for the next four decades as the Chinese faced internal and external threats. But as wholeheartedly as China had struggled to remain isolated from the outside world, its neighbor Japan responded to Western influence in a much different way.

THINK THROUGH HISTORY
D. Analyzing Causes Why did the Boxer Rebellion fail?

Boxer rebels like this one drawn by a 20th-century artist were driven by a fierce hatred of foreigners. They used their fists, swords, and guns in an unsuccessful attempt to oust the "foreign devils" from China.

Section 1 Assessment

1. TERMS & NAMES

Identify
• Opium War
• extraterritorial rights
• Taiping Rebellion
• sphere of influence
• Open Door Policy
• Boxer Rebellion

2. TAKING NOTES

In a flow chart like the one below, list the major events in China's dealings with foreign nations between 1830 and 1900. Include both policies and actual confrontations.

1830   1839   1900

Opium
War

3. RECOGNIZING EFFECTS

Do you think the opium trade was finally more harmful or beneficial to China? Explain.

THINK ABOUT
• the effects of the Opium War
• other Chinese responses to foreign influence
• the aftermath of the Boxer Rebellion

4. THEME ACTIVITY

Cultural Interaction Under the long rule of the Dowager Empress Cixi, China fiercely resisted foreign influence. As a class or in a small group, role-play a debate among the Dowager Empress's advisers. Some should argue for continued isolation, and others for openness to foreign influence and trade.

2 Japan Modernizes

TERMS & NAMES
- Treaty of Kanagawa
- Meiji era
- Russo-Japanese War
- annexation

MAIN IDEA

Japan followed the model of Western powers by industrializing and expanding its foreign influence.

WHY IT MATTERS NOW

Japan's continued development of its own way of life has made it a leading world power.

SETTING THE STAGE In the early 17th century, Japan had shut itself off from almost all contact with other nations. Under the rule of the Tokugawa shoguns, the society was tightly ordered. The shogun parceled out land to the lords. The peasants worked for and lived under the protection of their lord and his samurai. This rigid system kept Japan free of civil war. Peace and relative prosperity reigned for two centuries.

Daily *Life*

Japanese Women

Japan not only restricted its citizens' contact with the outside world but it also severely confined its own women. The supreme duty of a woman was to honor the men in her life. Her restrictive dress and footwear helped ensure that she did not stray far from her place in the home.

As a child, she was expected to be obedient to her father, and as a wife, to her husband. Even as a widow, she was expected to submit to her son or sons.

In Japan today, increasing numbers of women work outside the home, most of them as "office ladies" or "OLs." These secretarial workers have no opportunity to advance, and are arguably no better off than their grandmothers were.

The number of women managers is increasing today, however, and Japanese women are becoming more vocal about playing an active role in their society.

Japan Ends Its Isolation

The Japanese had almost no contact with the industrialized world during this time of isolation. They continued, however, to trade with China and with Dutch traders from Indonesia. They also had diplomatic contact with Korea. However, trade was growing in importance, both inside and outside Japan.

Facing the Demand for Foreign Trade In the early 19th century, Westerners began trying to convince the Japanese to open their ports to trade. British, French, Russian, and American officials occasionally anchored off the Japanese coast. Like China, however, Japan repeatedly refused to receive them. Then, in 1853, U.S. Commodore Matthew Perry took four ships into what is now Tokyo Harbor. The Japanese were astounded by these massive black wooden ships that were powered by steam. They were also shocked by the cannons and rifles. These weapons could have wiped out hundreds of the fiercest samurai in a matter of seconds. The Tokugawa shogun realized he had no choice but to receive the letter Perry had brought from U.S. President Millard Fillmore:

A VOICE FROM THE PAST

It seems to be wise from time to time to make new laws. . . . If your Imperial Majesty were so far to change the ancient laws as to allow a free trade between the two countries [the U.S. and Japan], it would be extremely beneficial to both. . . . Our steamships, in crossing the great ocean, burn a great deal of coal, and it is not convenient to bring it all the way from America. We wish that our steamships and other vessels should be allowed to stop in Japan and supply themselves with coal, provisions, and water. They will pay for them, in money, or anything else your Imperial Majesty's subjects may prefer.

MILLARD FILLMORE, quoted in *Millard Fillmore Papers*

Polite as President Fillmore's letter was, Perry delivered it with a threat. He would come back with a larger fleet in a year to receive Japan's reply. That reply was the **Treaty of Kanagawa**, which was signed in 1854. Under the terms of the treaty, Japan opened two ports at which American ships could take on supplies. The treaty

THINK THROUGH HISTORY
A. Recognizing Effects How did the Treaty of Kanagawa affect Japan?

also allowed the United States to set up an embassy in Japan. Once the United States had a foot in Japan's door, other Western powers soon followed. By 1860, Japan, like China, had granted foreigners permission to trade at treaty ports. It had also extended extraterritorial rights to many foreign nations.

Reform and Modernization Under the Meiji Reign The Japanese, however, were angry that the shogun had given in to the foreigners' demands. They feared that he was losing control over the country. The people rallied around Japan's young emperor, Mutsuhito (moot·soo·HEE·toh), who appealed to Japan's strong sense of pride and nationalism. In 1867, the Tokugawa shogun stepped down. He thus ended the military dictatorships that had lasted since the 12th century. Mutsuhito established a new government. He chose the name *Meiji* for his reign, which means "enlightened rule." Only 15 when he took over, Mutsuhito reigned for 45 years. This period of Japanese history—from 1867 to 1912—is called the **Meiji era.**

As part of this new enlightenment, the Meiji emperor realized that the best way to oppose Western imperialism was to adopt new ways. The feudal lords, for example, realized that private ownership of land prevented the entire country from benefiting from it. In one of the first acts of the Meiji era, they gave their land to the emperor.

Another way the Meiji government attempted to modernize Japan was by sending its statesmen to Europe and North America to study foreign ways. The Japanese chose what they believed to be the best Western civilization had to offer and adapted it to their own country. They admired Germany's strong centralized government, for example. And they used its constitution as a model for their own. As in Germany, a small group of men held political power in Japan. They were determined to build a mighty nation.

The Japanese also admired the discipline of the German army and the skill of the British navy. They attempted to imitate these European powers as they modernized their military. Japan adopted the American system of universal public education and required that all Japanese children attend school. Their teachers often included foreign experts. Students could go abroad to study as well.

China and Japan Confront the West

The Dowager Empress Cixi
(1862–1908)

China
- Remains committed to traditional values
- Loses numerous territorial conflicts
- Grants other nations spheres of influence within China
- Finally accepts necessity for reform

Both
- Have well-established traditional values
- Initially resist change
- Oppose Western imperialism

Japan
- Considers modernization to be necessary
- Borrows and adapts Western ways
- Strengthens its economic and military power
- Becomes an empire builder

The Meiji Emperor Mutsuhito
(1867–1912)

SKILLBUILDER: Interpreting Charts
1. *According to this Venn diagram, in what ways did China and Japan deal differently with Western influence?*
2. *What similar responses did each country share despite the different paths they followed?*

The emperor also energetically supported following the Western path of industrialization. By the early 20th century, the Japanese economy had become as modern as any in the world. The country built its first railroad line in 1872. The track connected Tokyo, the nation's capital, with the port of Yokohama, 20 miles to the south. By 1914, Japan had more than 7,000 miles of rails. Coal production grew from half a million tons in 1875 to more than 21 million tons in 1913. Meanwhile, large, state-supported companies built thousands of factories. Traditional Japanese industries, such as tea processing and silk production, expanded to give the country unique products to trade. Developing modern industries, such as shipbuilding and weapons production, made Japan competitive with the West.

Japanese Imperialism Grows

Japan's race to modernize paid off. By 1890, the country had several dozen warships and 500,000 well-trained, well-armed soldiers. It had become the strongest military power in Asia.

Japan had gained military, political, and economic strength. It then sought to eliminate the extraterritorial rights of foreigners. The Japanese foreign minister assured foreigners that they could rely on fair treatment in Japan. This was because its constitution and legal codes were similar to those of European nations, he explained. His reasoning was convincing, and in 1894, Britain and the other foreign powers abolished the extraterritorial rights of their citizens living in Japan. Japan's feeling of strength and equality with the Western nations rose.

As Japan's sense of power grew, the nation also became more imperialistic. Like many European nations, Japan saw empire building as a way of protecting its security and meeting economic needs. As in Europe, national pride also played a large part in this policy. The Japanese were determined to show the world that they were a powerful nation.

THINK THROUGH HISTORY
B. Making Inferences Why did Japan become imperialistic?

Japan Attacks China The Japanese first turned their sights to their Asian neighbors. Japan's neighbor, Korea, is not far from southern Japan (see the map on page 718). In 1876, Japan forced Korea to open three ports to Japanese trade. But China also considered Korea to be important as both a trading partner and a military outpost. Recognizing their similar interests in Korea, Japan and China signed a hands-off agreement. In 1885, both countries pledged that they would not send their armies into Korea.

In June 1894, however, China broke that agreement. Rebellions had broken out against Korea's king. He asked China for military help in putting them down. Chinese troops marched into Korea. Japan protested and sent its troops to Korea to fight the Chinese. The Sino-Japanese War had begun. Within a few months, Japan had driven the Chinese out of Korea, had destroyed the Chinese navy, and had begun taking over Manchuria. In 1895, China and Japan signed a peace treaty. This treaty gave Japan its first colonies—Taiwan and the Pescadores Islands.

Vocabulary
Sino: a prefix meaning "Chinese."

Russo-Japanese War Most Western nations had expected China to win the showdown with Japan fairly easily. The Japanese victory surprised them. It also changed the world's balance of power. Russia and Japan emerged as the major powers—and enemies—in East Asia.

Russia and Japan soon went to war over Manchuria. This was a region north of Korea that was under Chinese rule. In 1903, Japan offered to recognize Russia's rights in Manchuria if the Russians would agree to stay out of Korea. But the Russians refused. So, in February 1904, Japan launched a surprise attack. It struck at the

Background
Russia began expanding into Asia in the 1580s. It became a world power in the late 1700s under Catherine the Great.

Global Impact

Changing Image of the East
The Japanese victory over the Russians in 1905 exploded a strong Western myth. Many Westerners believed that white people were a superior race. The overwhelming success of European colonialism and imperialism in the Americas, Africa, and Asia had reinforced this belief. But the Japanese had shown Europeans that people of other races were their equals in modern warfare.

Unfortunately, Japan's military victory led to a different form of Western racism. Influenced by the ideas of Germany's emperor Wilhelm II, the West imagined the Japanese uniting with the Chinese and conquering Europe. The resulting racist Western fear of what it called the "yellow peril" influenced world politics for many decades.

Russian navy, which was anchored off the coast of Manchuria. In the resulting **Russo-Japanese War,** Japan drove Russian troops out of Korea. Japan won brutal land battles and captured most of Russia's Pacific fleet. It also destroyed Russia's Baltic fleet, which had sailed all the way around Africa to participate in the war.

In 1905, Japan and Russia began peace negotiations. U.S. president Theodore Roosevelt helped draft the treaty, which the two nations signed on a ship off Portsmouth, New Hampshire. This agreement, the Treaty of Portsmouth, gave Japan the captured territories. It also forced Russia to withdraw from Manchuria and to stay out of Korea.

Korea Under Japanese Occupation After defeating Russia, Japan attacked Korea with a vengeance. In 1905, it made Korea a protectorate. Japan sent in "advisers," who grabbed more and more power from the Korean government. The Korean king was unable to rally international support for his regime. In 1907, he gave up control of the country. Within two years the Korean Imperial Army was disbanded. In 1910, Japan officially imposed **annexation** in Korea, or brought that country under Japan's control.

The Japanese were harsh rulers. For the next 35 years, they forbade public protest. They shut down Korean newspapers and took over Korean schools. There they replaced the study of Korean language and history with that of Japan. They took land away from Korean farmers and gave it to Japanese settlers. They encouraged Japanese businessmen to start industries in Korea, but forbade Koreans from going into business in their own country. Resentment of the Japanese led to nonviolent protests and to a growing Korean nationalist movement. The Japanese did modernize Korean factories and transportation and communications systems, however. Despite this technological progress, Japan's repressive rule in Korea was an example of imperialism at its worst.

The rest of the world clearly saw the brutal results of Japan's imperialism in Korea. Nevertheless, the United States and other European countries moved ahead with their own imperialistic aims, as you will learn in Section 3.

Vocabulary
protectorate: a country under the partial control and protection of another nation.

THINK THROUGH HISTORY
C. Clarifying How did Japan treat the Koreans after it annexed the country?

L'HOMME DU JOUR : LE MIKADO

ENCORE UN QUI VEND LA PEAU DE L'OURS
Dessin de LÉANDRE.

SKILLBUILDER:
Interpreting Political Cartoons
1. *In this cartoon of the Russo-Japanese War, which animal represents Russia and which represents Japan?*
2. *Whom do you think the Japanese and the Russians are crushing?*

Section 2 Assessment

1. TERMS & NAMES

Identify
• Treaty of Kanagawa
• Meiji era
• Russo-Japanese War
• annexation

2. TAKING NOTES

In a chart like the one below, list the steps that Japan took toward modernization and the events that contributed to its growth as an imperialistic power.

Modernization	Imperialism

Do you think that Japan could have become an imperialistic power if it had not modernized? Why or why not?

3. FORMING AN OPINION

In your view, was Japan's aggressive imperialism justified? Support your answer with examples from the text.

THINK ABOUT
• reasons for Japan's early isolation
• what Japan could gain from imperialism
• Japan's treatment of conquered peoples

4. ANALYZING THEMES

Empire Building What influences do you think were most important in provoking Japan to build its empire?

THINK ABOUT
• Japan's size and geographical features
• Japan's relations with China and Russia
• the interest of countries such as Britain and the United States in Japan

Transformations Around the Globe **723**

TERMS & NAMES
- caudillo
- Monroe Doctrine
- José Martí
- Spanish-American War
- Panama Canal
- Roosevelt Corollary

3 U.S. Economic Imperialism in Latin America

MAIN IDEA	WHY IT MATTERS NOW
The United States put increasing economic and political pressure on Latin America during the 19th century.	This policy set the stage for 20th-century relations between Latin America and the United States.

SETTING THE STAGE Latin America's long struggle to gain independence from colonial domination between the late 18th and the mid-19th centuries left the new nations in shambles. Weeds choked off farm fields. Cities and towns collapsed. The new nations faced a struggle for recovery as difficult as their struggle for independence had been.

Latin America After Independence

Political independence meant little for most citizens of the new Latin American nations. The majority remained poor, illiterate laborers caught up in a cycle of poverty.

Colonial Legacy During colonial times, most Latin Americans worked for large landowners. The employers paid their workers with vouchers that could be used only at their own supply stores. Since wages were low and prices were high, workers went into debt. Their debt accumulated and passed from one generation to the next. These "free" workers were almost like slaves in a system known as peonage.

The landowners, on the other hand, only got wealthier after independence. Many new Latin American governments took over the lands owned by native peoples and by the Catholic Church. They then put those lands up for sale. Wealthy landowners were the only people able to afford to buy them, and they snapped them up. But as one Argentinean newspaper reported, "Their greed for land does not equal their ability to use it intelligently." The unequal distribution of land and its poor use combined to prevent social and economic development in Latin America.

The land—and its rich resources—was and is Latin America's major asset. The peasants worked all of their lives in the fields and remained poor and propertyless, as many still are today.

Political Instability Political instability also was a widespread problem in 19th-century Latin America. Many Latin American army leaders had gained fame and power during their long struggle for independence. They often continued to assert their power. They controlled the new nations as dictators, or **caudillos.** By 1830, nearly all the countries of Latin America were ruled by caudillos. One typical caudillo was Juan Vicente Gómez. He was a ruthless man who ruled Venezuela for nearly 30 years after seizing power in 1908. "All Venezuela is my cattle ranch," he once boasted.

There were some exceptions, however. Reform-minded presidents, such as Argentina's Domingo Sarmiento, made strong commitments to improving education. During Sarmiento's presidency, between 1868 and 1874, the number of students in Argentina doubled. But such reformers usually didn't stay in office long. Eventually a caudillo would return to power, forcing the reformer out at the point of a bayonet or gun.

The caudillos found little opposition. The upper classes usually supported them because they opposed giving power to the lower classes. In addition, Latin Americans had gained little experience with democracy under European colonial rule. So the dictatorship of a caudillo did not seem unusual to them. But even when caudillos

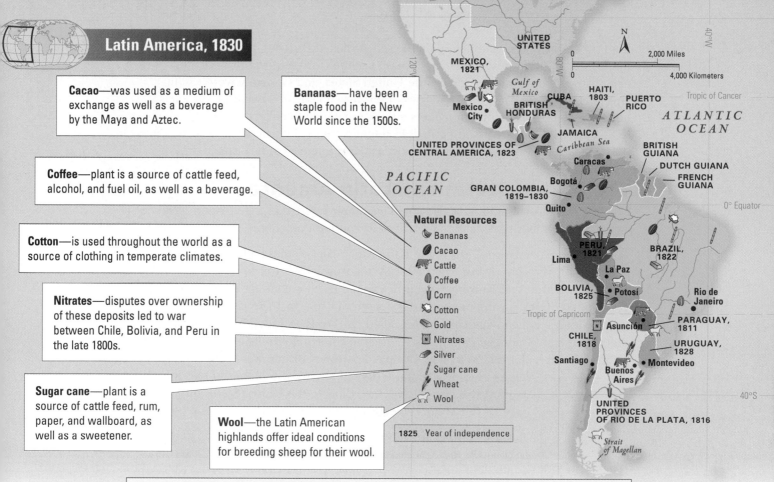

Latin America, 1830

Cacao—was used as a medium of exchange as well as a beverage by the Maya and Aztec.

Bananas—have been a staple food in the New World since the 1500s.

Coffee—plant is a source of cattle feed, alcohol, and fuel oil, as well as a beverage.

Cotton—is used throughout the world as a source of clothing in temperate climates.

Nitrates—disputes over ownership of these deposits led to war between Chile, Bolivia, and Peru in the late 1800s.

Sugar cane—plant is a source of cattle feed, rum, paper, and wallboard, as well as a sweetener.

Wool—the Latin American highlands offer ideal conditions for breeding sheep for their wool.

Natural Resources
- Bananas
- Cacao
- Cattle
- Coffee
- Corn
- Cotton
- Gold
- Nitrates
- Silver
- Sugar cane
- Wheat
- Wool

1825 Year of independence

GEOGRAPHY SKILLBUILDER: Interpreting Maps
1. **Region** *Which Latin American countries remained under colonial rule in 1830?*
2. **Human-Environment Interaction** *Which country had the most different types of natural resources?*

THINK THROUGH HISTORY
A. Identifying Problems What difficulties did lower-class Latin Americans continue to face after independence?

weren't in power, most Latin Americans still lacked a voice in the government. Voting rights—and so, political power—were restricted to the relatively few members of the upper and middle classes who owned property or could read.

Economies Grow Under Foreign Influence

When colonial rule ended in Latin America in the early 1800s, the new nations were no longer restricted to trading with colonial powers. Britain and, later, the United States became Latin America's main trading partners.

Old Products and New Markets No matter with whom the new Latin American nations were trading, their economies continued to depend on exports. As during the colonial era, each country concentrated on one or two products. With advances in technology, however, Latin America's exports grew. The development of the steamship and the building of railroads in the 19th century, for example, greatly increased Latin American trade. Toward the end of the century, the invention of refrigeration helped increase Latin America's exports. The sale of beef, fruits and vegetables, and other perishable goods soared.

But foreign nations benefited far more from the increased trade than Latin America did. In exchange for their exports, Latin Americans imported European and North American manufactured goods. They therefore had little reason to develop their own manufacturing industries. And as long as Latin America remained unindustrialized, it could not play a leading role on the world stage.

Outside Investment and Interference Furthermore, Latin American countries used little of their export income to build roads, schools, or hospitals. Nor did they

Transformations Around the Globe **725**

fund programs that would help them be self-sufficient. Instead, they often borrowed money—at high interest rates—to develop facilities for their export industries. Countries such as Britain, France, the United States, and Germany were willing lenders. The Latin American countries often were unable to pay back their loans, however. In response, foreign lenders either threatened to collect the debt by force or to take over the facility it had funded. Foreigners thus gained control of many industries in Latin America. Thus began a new age of economic colonialism.

The United States and Latin America

Long before the United States had a real economic interest in Latin America, it was aware that its security depended on that of its southern neighbors.

The Monroe Doctrine Most of the Latin American colonies had gained their independence by the early 1800s. But their position was not secure. Many Latin Americans feared that European countries would try to reconquer the new republics. The United States, a young nation itself, feared this too. In 1823, therefore, President James Monroe issued what came to be called the **Monroe Doctrine.** This document stated that "the American continents . . . are henceforth not to be considered as subjects for future colonization by any European powers." Britain was Latin America's largest trading partner. It agreed to back the Monroe Doctrine with its powerful navy. Until 1898, though, the United States did little to enforce the Monroe Doctrine. Cuba provided a real testing ground.

Cuba Declares Independence Cuba was one of Spain's last colonies in the Americas. In 1868, Cuba declared its independence and fought a ten-year war against Spain. In 1878, with the island in ruins, the Cubans gave up the fight.

But some Cubans continued to seek independence. In 1895, **José Martí,** a writer who had been exiled, returned to fight for Cuban independence. Martí was killed early in the war, but the Cubans battled on.

By that time, the United States had developed substantial business holdings in Cuba. Therefore it had an economic stake in the fate of the country. In addition, the Spanish had forced many Cuban civilians into concentration camps. Americans objected to the Spanish brutality. In 1898, the United States joined the Cuban war for independence. This conflict, which came to be known as the **Spanish-American War,** lasted about four months. Years of fighting had exhausted the Spanish soldiers, and they gave up easily.

In 1901, Cuba became an independent nation, at least in name. But the Cubans resented U.S. intervention, the military government the United States had installed, and its preventing Cuba from becoming truly independent. The split that began to develop between the United States and Cuba continues to keep those close neighbors miles apart a century later.

After its defeat in the Spanish-American War, Spain turned over the last of its colonies. Puerto Rico, Guam, and the Philippines became U.S. territories. Having become the dominant imperial power in Latin America, the United States next set its sights on Panama.

The Panama Canal Connects the Oceans Latin Americans were beginning to regard the United States as the political and economic "Colossus of the North." It was also a huge country geographically. By the 1870s, the transcontinental railroad connected its east and west coasts. Land travel was long and difficult, however. And sea travel involved a trip around the tip of South America. This was a

HISTORY MAKERS

**José Martí
1853–1895**

José Martí was only 15 in 1868 when he first began speaking out for Cuban independence. In 1871, the Spanish colonial government punished Martí's open opposition with exile to Spain.

With only a brief return to his homeland in 1878, Martí remained in exile for about 20 years. He lived most of his life in New York City. There he continued his career as a writer and a revolutionary. "Life on earth is a hand-to-hand combat . . . between the law of love and the law of hate," he proclaimed.

While in New York, Martí helped raise an army to fight for Cuban independence. He died on the battlefield only a month after the war began. But Martí's cry for freedom echoes in his essays and poems and in folk songs that are still sung throughout the world.

THINK THROUGH HISTORY
B. Analyzing Motives Why did the United States join the Cuban war for independence?

journey of about 13,000 miles. If a canal could be dug across a narrow section of Central America, the coast-to-coast journey would be cut in half. The United States had been thinking about such a project since the early 19th century. In the 1880s, a French company tried—but failed—to build a canal across Panama.

Despite the French failure, Americans remained enthusiastic about the canal. And no one was more enthusiastic than President Theodore Roosevelt, who led the nation from 1901 to 1909. In 1903, Panama was a province of Colombia. Roosevelt offered that country $10 million plus a yearly payment for the right to build a canal. When the Colombian government demanded more money, the United States responded by encouraging a revolution in Panama. The Panamanians had been trying to break away from Colombia for almost a century. In 1903, with help from the U.S. navy, they won their country's independence. In gratitude, Panama gave the United States a ten-mile-wide zone in which to build a canal.

THINK THROUGH HISTORY
C. Making Inferences Why was the United States so interested in building the Panama Canal?

For the next ten years, American engineers battled floods, heat, and disease-carrying insects to build the massive waterway. The United States began a campaign to destroy the mosquitoes that carried yellow fever and malaria, and the rats that carried bubonic plague. The effort to control these diseases was eventually successful. But thousands of workers died during construction of the canal. The **Panama Canal** finally opened in 1914. Ships from both hemispheres soon began to use it. Latin America had become a crossroads of world trade. And the United States controlled the tollgate.

Roosevelt Corollary The building of the Panama Canal was only one way that the United States expanded its influence in Latin America in the early 20th century. Its presence in Cuba and large investments in many Central and South American countries strengthened its foothold. To protect those economic interests, in 1904, President Roosevelt issued a corollary, or extension, to the Monroe Doctrine. The **Roosevelt Corollary** gave the United States the right to be "an international police power" in the Western Hemisphere.

The United States used the Roosevelt Corollary many times in the following years to justify American intervention in Latin America. The troops occupied some countries for decades. Many Latin Americans protested this intervention by the United States. But they were powerless to stop their giant neighbor to the north.

The U.S. government turned a deaf ear to these protests. It could not ignore the rumblings of revolution just over its border with Mexico, however. You will learn about this revolution in Section 4.

In the view of this political cartoonist, the Roosevelt Corollary gave the U.S. president so much power, the Caribbean became his wading pool.

THE BIG STICK IN THE CARIBBEAN SEA
From the *Herald* (New York)

Section 3 Assessment

1. TERMS & NAMES

Identify
• caudillo
• Monroe Doctrine
• José Martí
• Spanish-American War
• Panama Canal
• Roosevelt Corollary

2. TAKING NOTES

Using a time line like the one below, list the major events of U.S. involvement in Latin America.

1823   1898   1903 1904   1914

Which event do you think was most beneficial to Latin America? Why?

3. FORMING OPINIONS

Do you think that U.S. imperialism was more beneficial or harmful to Latin American people? Explain.

THINK ABOUT
• the benefits provided by U.S.-owned companies
• the harmful effects of foreign economic and political influence

4. THEME ACTIVITY

Revolution It is 1898 and you have been fighting for the independence of your country, Cuba, for three years. The United States has just joined the war against Spain. Design a political poster that shows your feelings about U.S. participation in this war.

Panama Canal

The Panama Canal is considered one of the world's greatest engineering accomplishments. Its completion changed the course of history by opening a worldwide trade route between the Atlantic and Pacific oceans. As shown in the 1914 map below, ships are raised and lowered a total of 170 feet during the 51-mile trip through the canal. It usually takes 15 to 20 hours.

The canal also had a lasting effect on other technologies. Ships are now built to dimensions that will allow them to pass through its locks.

This 1910 engraving shows the excavation of the Gaillard, or Culebra, Cut, at the narrowest part of the canal. Completion of this nine-mile cut took seven years because of frequent landslides. By the time the entire canal was finished, workers had dug up about 211 million cubic yards of earth.

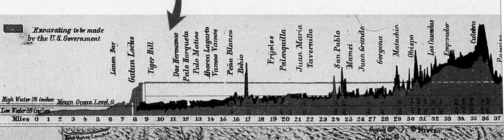

The Gatun Locks include three levels of water-filled chambers that raise or lower ships 85 feet. Electric locomotives called mules help guide ships through the locks.

Canal Facts

- The canal took ten years to build (1904–1914) and cost $380 million.
- Thousands of workers died from diseases while building it.
- The trip from San Francisco to New York City via the Panama Canal is about 7,800 miles shorter than the trip around South America.
- The canal now handles more than 13,000 ships a year from around 70 nations carrying 168 million short tons of cargo.
- The United States collected about $340 million a year in tolls.
- Panama took control of the canal on December 31, 1999.

Connect to History

Identifying Problems What difficulties did workers face in constructing the canal?

SEE SKILLBUILDER HANDBOOK, PAGE 993

Connect to Today

Evaluating Decisions In the more than 80 years since it was built, do you think that the benefits of the Panama Canal to world trade have outweighed the costs in time, money, and human life? Explain your answer.

The Mexican Revolution

TERMS & NAMES
- Antonio López de Santa Anna
- Benito Juárez
- *La Reforma*
- Porfirio Díaz
- Francisco Madero
- Francisco "Pancho" Villa
- Emiliano Zapata

MAIN IDEA	WHY IT MATTERS NOW
Political, economic, and social inequalities in Mexico triggered a period of revolution and reform.	Mexico has moved toward political democracy and is a strong economic force in the Americas.

SETTING THE STAGE The legacy of Spanish colonialism and long-term political instability that plagued the newly emerging Latin American nations in the 19th century caused problems for Mexico as well. Only Mexico, however, shared a border with the United States. The "Colossus of the North" wanted to extend its territory to the Pacific Ocean. But most of the lands in the American Southwest belonged to Mexico.

Santa Anna and the Mexican War

During the early 19th century, no one dominated Mexican political life more than **Antonio López de Santa Anna.** Santa Anna played a leading role in Mexico's fight for independence from Spain in 1821. In 1829, he fought against Spain again, as the colonial power tried to reconquer Mexico. Then, in 1833, Santa Anna became Mexico's president.

One of Latin America's most powerful caudillos, Santa Anna was a clever politician. He would support a measure one year and oppose it the next if he thought that would keep him in power. His policy apparently worked. Between 1833 and 1855, Santa Anna was Mexico's president four times. He gave up the presidency twice, however, to serve Mexico in a more urgent cause—retaining the territory of Texas.

Mexicans and Americans fought in a blazing, bloody battle at the Alamo, from February 23 to March 6, 1836. Santa Anna's forces had one of their few victories in the attempt to hold the Texas territory.

The Texas Revolt In the 1820s, Mexico encouraged American citizens to move to the Mexican territory of Texas to help populate the country. Thousands of English-speaking colonists, or Anglos, did. In return for inexpensive land, they pledged to follow the laws of Mexico. As the Anglo population grew, though, tensions developed between the colonists and Mexico over several issues, including slavery and religion. As a result, many Texas colonists wanted greater self-government. But when Mexico refused to grant this, Stephen Austin encouraged a revolt against Mexico in 1835.

Santa Anna led Mexican forces north to try to hold the rebellious territory. He won a few early battles, including a bitter fight at the Alamo. However, he was unsuccessful at the Battle of San Jacinto. His troops were defeated, and he was captured. Sam Houston released Santa Anna after he promised to respect the independence of Texas. When he returned to Mexico in 1836, Santa Anna was quickly ousted from power.

War and the Fall of Santa Anna Santa Anna regained power, though, and fought against the United States again. In 1845, the United States annexed Texas.

Outraged Mexicans considered this a U.S. act of aggression. In a dispute over the border, the United States invaded Mexico. Santa Anna's army fought valiantly. But U.S. troops defeated them after two years of war. In 1848, the two nations signed the Treaty of Guadalupe Hidalgo. The United States received the northern third of what was then Mexico, including California and the American Southwest. Santa Anna went into exile. He returned as dictator one final time, however, in 1853. After his final fall, in 1855, he remained in exile for almost 20 years. When he returned to Mexico in 1874, he was poor, blind, powerless, and essentially forgotten.

Juárez and *La Reforma*

During the mid-19th century, as Santa Anna's power rose and fell, a liberal reformer, **Benito Juárez,** strongly influenced the politics of Mexico. Juárez was Santa Anna's complete opposite in background as well as in goals. Santa Anna came from a well-off Creole family. Juárez was a poor, orphaned Zapotec Indian. While Santa Anna put his own personal power first, Juárez worked primarily to serve his country.

THINK THROUGH HISTORY
A. Contrasting In what ways did Benito Juárez differ from Santa Anna?

Benito Juárez Rises to Power Ancestry and racial background were important elements of political power and economic success in 19th-century Mexico. For that reason, the rise of Benito Juárez was clearly due to his personal leadership qualities. Juárez was raised on a small farm in the Mexican state of Oaxaca. When he was 12, he moved to the city of Oaxaca. He started going to school at age 15, and in 1829, he entered a newly opened state-run university. He received his law degree in 1831.

He then returned to the city of Oaxaca, where he opened a law office. Most of his clients were poor people who could not otherwise have afforded legal assistance. Juárez gained a reputation for honesty, integrity, hard work, and good judgment. He was elected to the city legislature and then rose steadily in power. Beginning in 1847, he served as governor of the state of Oaxaca.

Juárez Works for Reform Throughout the late 1840s and early 1850s, Juárez worked to start a liberal reform movement. He called this movement *La Reforma.* Redistribution of land, separation of church and state, and increased educational opportunities were among its goals. In 1853, however, Santa Anna returned to power for the last time. He sent Juárez and other liberals into exile.

Just two years later, rebellion against Santa Anna brought down his government. Benito Juárez and other liberal leaders returned to Mexico to deal with their country's tremendous problems. As in other Latin American nations, rich landowners kept most other Mexicans in a cycle of debt and poverty. Liberal leader Ponciano Arriaga described how these circumstances led to great problems for both poor farmers and the government:

A VOICE FROM THE PAST

There are Mexican landowners who occupy . . . an extent of land greater than the areas of some of our sovereign states, greater even than that of one of several European states. In this vast area, much of which lies idle, deserted, abandoned . . . live four or five million Mexicans who know no other industry than agriculture, yet are without land or the means to work it, and who cannot emigrate in the hope of bettering their fortunes. . . . How can a hungry, naked, miserable people practice popular government? How can we proclaim the equal rights of men and leave the majority of the nation in [this condition]?

PONCIANO ARRIAGA, speech to the Constitutional Convention, 1856–1857

THINK THROUGH HISTORY
B. Identifying Problems What does Ponciano Arriaga think is Mexico's greatest problem?

The French Invade Mexico Not surprisingly, Arriaga's ideas and those of the other liberals in government threatened most conservative upper-class Mexicans. To express their dissatisfaction, these conservative rebels fought against the liberal government. The civil war lasted for three years before the government defeated the rebels. Juárez took over the presidency in 1858. He was officially elected president in 1861.

The end of the civil war did not end Mexico's troubles, though. The country was deeply in debt. Exiled conservatives plotted with some Europeans to reconquer Mexico. In 1862, France was ruled by Napoleon III, who sent a large army to Mexico. Within 18 months, France had taken over the country. Napoleon appointed Austrian archduke Maximilian to rule Mexico as emperor. Juárez and other Mexicans fought against French rule. After five years under siege, the French decided that the struggle was too costly. They ordered the army to withdraw from Mexico in 1867. Maximilian was captured and executed.

Juárez was reelected Mexico's president in 1867. He returned to the reforms he had proposed more than ten years earlier. He began rebuilding the country, which had been shattered during decades of war. He promoted trade with foreign countries, the opening of new roads, the building of railroads, and the establishment of a telegraph service. He set up a national education system, separate from that run by the Catholic Church. In 1872, Juárez died of a heart attack. But after half a century of civil strife and chaos, he left his country a legacy of relative peace, progress, and reform.

HISTORY THROUGH ART: Political Art

A century after Mexico's long struggle for independence, artist José Clemente Orozco made many paintings dealing with the burdens that prevent people from being free, happy, and creative. Here he depicts the starving, suffering masses protesting their oppression by those in power *(right)*. Benito Juárez emerges as a product of and symbol of hope for his people *(below)*.

Fresco detail at University of Guadalajara (1936–1939), José Clemente Orozco

Fresco detail at Hospicio Cabañas (1948), José Clemente Orozco

Connect *to* History

Making Inferences What conclusions can you draw about Orozco's feeling for his people from these two murals?

 SEE SKILLBUILDER HANDBOOK, PAGE 1005

Connect *to* Today

Comparing What modern countries or peoples face problems similar to those of the 19th-century Mexico that Orozco portrayed?

Porfirio Díaz and "Order and Progress"

Juárez's era of reform didn't last long, however. In the mid-1870s, a new caudillo, **Porfirio Díaz,** came to power. Like Juárez, Díaz was an Indian from Oaxaca. He rose through the army and became a noted general in the fight against the French. In 1876, Díaz took control of Mexico by ousting the president. He had the support of the military, whose power had been reduced during and after the Juárez years. Indians and small landholders also supported him, because they thought he would work for land reforms.

During the Díaz years, elections became meaningless. Díaz offered land, power, or political favors to anyone who supported him. He terrorized many who didn't support him, ordering them to be beaten or put in jail. As a political slogan, Díaz adapted a rallying cry from the Juárez era. Juárez's "Liberty, Order, and Progress" became merely "Order and Progress." With this motto and his strong-arm methods, Díaz remained in power until 1911.

Order and progress did come to Mexico under Díaz, in spite of his methods. Railroads expanded, banks were built, the currency stabilized, and foreign investment grew. Mexico seemed to be a stable, prospering country. But appearances were deceiving. The wealthy owned more and more land, which they didn't put to good use. As a result, food costs rose steadily. Most Mexicans remained poor farmers and workers, and they continued to grow poorer.

THINK THROUGH HISTORY
C. Recognizing Effects What effects did Díaz's rule have on Mexico?

Revolution and Civil War

In the early 1900s, Mexicans from many walks of life began to protest Díaz's harsh rule. Idealistic liberals hungered for liberty. Farm laborers hungered for land. Workers hungered for fairer wages and better working conditions. Even some of Díaz's hand-picked political allies spoke out for reform. A variety of political parties began to form. Among the most powerful was a party led by Francisco Madero.

Madero Begins the Revolution Born into one of Mexico's ten richest families, **Francisco Madero** was educated in the United States and France. He believed in democracy and wanted to strengthen its hold in Mexico. Madero announced his candidacy for president of Mexico early in 1910. Soon afterward, Díaz had him arrested. From exile in the United States, Madero called for an armed revolution against Díaz.

The Mexican Revolution began slowly. Leaders arose in different parts of Mexico and gathered their own armies. In the north, cowboy **Francisco "Pancho" Villa** became immensely popular. He had a bold Robin-Hood policy of taking money from the rich and giving it to the poor. South of Mexico City, another strong, popular leader, **Emiliano Zapata,** raised a powerful revolutionary army. Like Villa, Zapata came from a poor family. He was determined to see that land was returned to peasants and small farmers. He wanted the laws reformed to protect their rights. "*Tierra y Libertad* [Land and Liberty]" was his battle cry. Villa, Zapata, and other armed revolutionaries won important victories against Díaz's army. By the spring of 1911, Díaz agreed to step down. He called for new elections.

Mexican Leaders Struggle for Power Madero was elected president in November 1911. But he had a difficult time holding on to power. He resigned and was murdered shortly afterward. The military leader General Victoriano Huerta then took over the presidency.

HISTORY MAKERS

**Francisco "Pancho" Villa
1877?–1923**

Pancho Villa was famous in Mexico, but infamous in the United States. In 1916, the United States permitted revolutionary politician Venustiano Carranza to use U.S. trains to transport troops who were fighting Villa in northern Mexico. In retaliation, Villa raided the town of Columbus, New Mexico, and killed 16 Americans traveling on a train in northern Mexico.

President Wilson was furious and ordered the U.S. Army to capture Villa. Villa hid out in the desert country he knew so well. The Americans never did find him.

Meanwhile, the Mexican government considered the American pursuit of Villa to be an invasion of its country. The United States and Mexico might well have gone to war over Villa. However, the United States entered World War I in 1917, forcing the withdrawal of its troops from Mexico.

Huerta was unpopular with many people, including Villa and Zapata. These revolutionary leaders allied themselves with another politician who also wanted to overthrow Huerta. His name was Venustiano Carranza. Their three armies advanced, seizing the Mexican countryside from Huerta's forces and approaching the capital, Mexico City. They overthrew Huerta only 15 months after he took power.

Carranza took over the government. He then turned his army on his former revolutionary allies. Both Villa and Zapata continued to fight. In 1919, however, Carranza lured Zapata into a trap and murdered him. With Zapata's death, the civil war also came to an end. More than a million Mexicans had lost their lives.

The New Mexican Constitution Carranza began a revision of Mexico's constitution. It was adopted in 1917. A revolutionary document, that constitution is still in effect today. As shown in the chart below, it promoted education, land reforms, and workers' rights. Carranza didn't support the final version of the constitution, however, and in 1920, he was overthrown by his former general, Alvaro Obregón.

Reforms of Mexican Constitution of 1917

Land	Religion	Labor	Social Issues
• Breakup of large estates • Restrictions on foreign ownership of land • Government control of resources (oil)	• State takeover of land owned by the Church	• Minimum wage for workers • Right to strike • Institution of labor unions	• Equal pay for equal work • Limited legal rights for women (spending money and bringing lawsuits)

SKILLBUILDER: Interpreting Charts
1. *Which reforms do you think landowners resented?*
2. *Which reforms benefited workers?*

Although Obregón seized power violently, he did not remain a dictator. Instead, he supported the reforms the constitution called for. He also promoted public education. Mexican public schools taught a common language—Spanish—and stressed nationalism. In this way, his policies helped unite the various regions and peoples of the country. Nevertheless, Obregón was assassinated in 1928.

The next year, a new political party that attempted to address the interests of all sectors of the society arose. Although the Institutional Revolutionary Party (PRI) did not tolerate opposition, it initiated an ongoing period of peace and political stability in Mexico. While Mexico was struggling toward peace, however, the rest of the world was on the brink of war.

THINK THROUGH HISTORY
D. Summarizing
What were Obregón's accomplishments?

Section 4 Assessment

1. TERMS & NAMES

Identify
• Antonio López de Santa Anna
• Benito Juárez
• *La Reforma*
• Porfirio Díaz
• Francisco Madero
• Francisco "Pancho" Villa
• Emiliano Zapata

2. TAKING NOTES

In a chart like the one below, list the major accomplishment of each Mexican leader.

Leader	Major Accomplishment

Which leader do you think benefited his country most? Why?

3. ANALYZING ISSUES

Why did Juárez have trouble putting his liberal program *La Reforma* into action?

THINK ABOUT
• the types of reforms Juárez wanted
• how those reforms would affect Mexicans of the upper and lower classes
• the political climate of the country

4. ANALYZING THEMES

Revolution Juárez's motto for change in Mexico was "Liberty, Order, and Progress." Díaz's slogan was "Order and Progress." What did this difference in goals mean for the country?

THINK ABOUT
• Juárez's accomplishments
• Díaz's accomplishments
• the value of order and progress without liberty

TERMS & NAMES

Briefly explain the importance of each of the following to the changes in global power between 1800 and 1914.

1. Opium War
2. Taiping Rebellion
3. Boxer Rebellion
4. Meiji era
5. Russo-Japanese War
6. Monroe Doctrine
7. Spanish-American War
8. Antonio López de Santa Anna
9. Benito Juárez
10. Francisco "Pancho" Villa

Interact *with* History

On page 714, you considered whether or not you would urge your country to trade with foreigners. Now that you've learned how several countries dealt with foreign influence and what the results were, would you change your recommendation? Discuss your ideas in a small group.

REVIEW QUESTIONS

SECTION 1 *(pages 715–719)*

China Responds to Pressure from the West

11. Why was China traditionally not interested in trading with the West?
12. What conditions during the Qing Dynasty gave rise to the Taiping Rebellion?
13. Although Guangxu's Hundred Days of Reform failed, what changes did it finally set in motion?

SECTION 2 *(pages 720–723)*

Japan Modernizes

14. What events caused Japan to end its isolation and begin to westernize?
15. What were the results of Japan's growing imperialism at the end of the 19th century?

SECTION 3 *(pages 724–727)*

U.S. Economic Imperialism in Latin America

16. How were Latin American caudillos able to achieve power and hold on to it?
17. What effects did the Monroe Doctrine and the Roosevelt Corollary have on Latin America?
18. Why was the United States so intent on building the Panama Canal?

SECTION 4 *(pages 729–733)*

The Mexican Revolution

19. What were the major causes of tension between the Mexicans and the American colonists who settled in Texas?
20. What roles did Francisco "Pancho" Villa and Emiliano Zapata play in the Mexican Revolution?

Visual Summary

Transformations Around the Globe

China

- Fails to prevent Britain from pursuing illegal opium trade in 1839 **Opium War**
- Deals with internal unrest during almost two decades of Hong Xiuquan's **Taiping Rebellion**
- Attempts to build self-sufficiency during 1860s in **self-strengthening movement**
- Violently opposes foreigners in 1900 **Boxer Rebellion**
- Begins to establish **constitutional government** in 1908

Japan

- Signs 1854 **Treaty of Kanagawa,** opening Japanese ports to foreign trade
- Modernizes based on Western models during **Meiji era** (1867–1912)
- Fights 1894 **Sino-Japanese War** seeking control of Korea
- Wages 1904 **Russo-Japanese War** seeking control of Manchuria
- Annexes **Korea** in 1910

Foreign Influence

Latin America

- Depends on **exports** to fuel economy
- Receives much **foreign investment**
- Gains U.S. military support in 1898 **Spanish-American War**
- Becomes crossroads of world trade when U.S. completes **Panama Canal** in 1914

Mexico

- Fights to hold **Texas territory** from U.S. colonialism (1835–1845)
- Tries to establish a national identity in the early 1850s under Benito Juárez's *La Reforma*
- Overcomes **French occupation** in 1867
- Stages the **Mexican Revolution** in 1910

CRITICAL THINKING

1. BYPASSING THE EMPRESS

Do you think that Emperor Guangxu would have been able to put his reforms into practice if the Dowager Empress Cixi had not intervened? Why or why not? Think about China's government, its attitude toward foreign influence, and Guangxu's power.

2. THE SWORD VS. THE PEN

THEME REVOLUTION Consider what you have learned in this and other chapters about Latin American colonial history and about how countries undergo change. What are the pros and cons of both military strategies and peaceful political means of improving a country's economic, social, and political conditions?

3. CHARTING SANTA ANNA'S CAREER

On a time line like the one below, indicate the major events of Santa Anna's military and political career in Mexico. Why do you think he was able to remain in power for so long?

Fights for independence
from Spain

1820s

4. ANALYZING PRIMARY SOURCES

In 1877, the Meiji era of modernization in Japan had been underway for about a decade. The following excerpt from an article in one of Japan's major newspapers, the *Tokyo Times,* comments on the changes that had taken place. Read the selection and answer the questions that follow.

A VOICE FROM THE PAST

In the second and third years of Meiji, the demand for foreign goods remarkably increased. Those who formerly looked upon them with contempt changed their minds and even dressed in foreign clothes. Our males adopted the European style. They put on fine tall hats instead of wearing large [queues] on their heads, and took to carrying sticks after discarding their swords. They dressed in coats of the English fashion and trousers of the American. They would only eat from tables and nothing would satisfy them but French cookery.

- Do you think this newswriter sees the adoption of foreign ways as a good or a bad thing for Japan? What specific words in the article make you feel that way?
- What dangers might a nation face when its people uncritically take on the behaviors and ways of life of another culture?

CHAPTER ACTIVITIES

1. LIVING HISTORY: Unit Portfolio Project

THEME EMPIRE BUILDING Your unit portfolio project focuses on empire building and colonialism. For Chapter 28, you might use one of the ideas suggested below:

- Stage a debate between a conservative member of the Dowager Empress Cixi's court and an official in Emperor Mutsuhito's Meiji government. Each should defend the leader's position on dealing with foreign intervention.
- Create a poster that dramatically illustrates one of the challenges that Mexico faced from the 1840s to the 1920s.
- Design an action figure based on one of the reformers or leaders you studied in this chapter. Draw a picture of the figure or construct a simple model. Then write a paragraph describing the reformer.

2. CONNECT TO TODAY: Cooperative Learning

THEME CULTURAL INTERACTION On May 5, 1862, badly outnumbered Mexican forces defeated the French at the Battle of Puebla. Mexicans still celebrate their country's triumph on the holiday Cinco de Mayo.

Working with a team, honor Cinco de Mayo by presenting a report to the class about some aspect of Mexican culture.

 Use the Internet, books, interviews, and other resources to gather information about topics such as Mexican customs and traditions, music, dance, holidays, food, or art.

- Collect pictures or samples, or decide how you will demonstrate your Mexican custom to make it come alive for the class.
- Consider staging a cultural fair and inviting other students, administrators, parents, and community members to participate.

3. INTERPRETING A TIME LINE

Study the unit time line on pages 628–629. Which events on the Chapter 28 segment were the result of U.S. imperialism? of European imperialism? of Japanese imperialism?

FOCUS ON GEOGRAPHY

The United States wanted the Panama Canal so badly that it both supported a revolution and suffered the deaths of thousands of workers to get it built.

- How many miles did the canal cut from a trip between San Francisco and New Orleans?
- Would a trip from Rio de Janeiro to Valparaíso be shorter via the Panama Canal or the Strait of Magellan?

Connect to History How might the canal have forced Latin American countries to change?

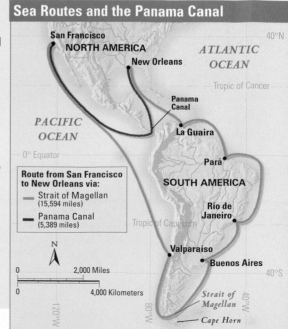

Sea Routes and the Panama Canal

The World
at War
1900–1945

This painting, entitled *The Menin Road*, depicts the desolate, bombed-out landscape of World War I through the eyes of artist Paul Nash. Sadly, the war was merely the opening act of a half-century of global violence and bloodshed.

	1905	1910	1915	1920	1925

CHAPTER 29 1914–1918
The Great War

1915–1919

1914 *The Balkans* Austria-Hungary's Archduke Franz Ferdinand and his wife are assassinated

1914 *Europe* World War I begins; Russia, France, and Britain against Germany and Austria-Hungary

1915 *Southwest Asia* Allies and Central Powers clash at Gallipoli in the Ottoman Empire

1916 *France* French suffer massive losses at the Battles of Verdun and Somme

1917 *U.S.* U.S. enters the war on the side of the Allies

1918 *Russia* Russia withdraws from the war and signs a peace treaty with Germany

1918 *Europe* The Allies defeat the Central Powers, ending World War I

1919 *France* The Allies and Germany sign the Treaty of Versailles

CHAPTER 30 1900–1939
Revolution and Nationalism

1905 *Russia* Workers revolt in St. Petersburg

1912 *China* Qing Dynasty topples

1917 *Russia* Russian Revolution ushers in a communist government

1918-20 *Russia* Civil war between Bolshevik Red Army and White Army

1919 *India* Gandhi becomes leader of the independence movement

1921 *China* Communist party forms

1922 *Russia* Union of Soviet Socialist Republics (USSR) is formed

1923 *Turkey* Kemal becomes president of the Turkish republic

CHAPTER 31 1919–1939
Years of Crisis

1919 *Germany* Weimar Republic is set up as democratic government

1920 *U.S.* First radio station broadcasts in Pittsburgh

1922 *Italy* Benito Mussolini comes to power

1923 *Germany* Hitler writes *Mein Kampf* while in jail

CHAPTER 32 1939–1945
World War II

◄ *1930s Germany*

	1905	1910	1915	1920	1925

Living History
Unit 7 Portfolio Project

1915 Germany ▶

THEME Science and Technology

Your portfolio for Unit 7 will record some of the many innovations in science and technology that occur during and between the First and Second World Wars. From military technology to civilian scientific gains, the rate of technical and scientific growth in this period was incredibly fast.

Living History Project Choices

Each Chapter Assessment offers you choices of ways to show the advances in science and technology in that chapter. Activities include the following:

Chapter 29 historical fiction, report, display diagram

Chapter 30 travel poster, science fiction story, diagrams

Chapter 31 artistic work, demonstration speech, fictional account

Chapter 32 invention cards, questions, time line

1925 China
Sun Yixian dies; Jiang Jieshi heads Kuomintang

1928 U.S.S.R.
Stalin becomes dictator

1930 China
Civil war between Nationalists and Communists erupts

1930 India
Gandhi organizes the Salt March

1934 China
Mao Zedong leads the Long March

1937 China
Japan invades China; Chinese civil war suspended

1930s India ▶

1927 U.S.
Charles Lindbergh flies solo from New York to Paris

1929 U.S.
Stock market crashes

1931 China
Japan invades Manchuria

1933 Germany
Adolf Hitler appointed chancellor

1935–1939

1935 Ethiopia
Italy attacks Ethiopia

1936 Spain Civil war erupts

1937 China Japan invades China

1938 Germany Nazis destroy Jewish businesses on *Kristallnacht*

1938 Austria Germany annexes Austria

1939 Czechoslovakia Germany seizes Czechoslovakia

1939 Soviet Union Nazi-Soviet nonaggression pact signed

1939 Central Europe
Germany invades Poland; World War II begins

1940–1945

1940 France, Britain
France surrenders; Battle of Britain begins

1941 Eastern Europe
Germany invades Soviet Union

1941 U.S. Japan bombs Pearl Harbor; U.S. declares war on Japan

1943 Soviet Union Germans surrender at Stalingrad

1944 France Allies invade Europe on D-Day

1945 Germany
Germany surrenders to Allies

1945 Japan
U.S. drops atomic bombs; Japan surrenders

CHAPTER 29

The Great War, 1914–1918

PREVIEWING THEMES

Science & Technology

Advances in weaponry, from improvements to the machine gun and airplane, to the invention of the tank, led to mass devastation during World War I.

Economics

The war greatly affected many European economies. The warring governments—desperate for resources—converted many industries to munitions factories. They also took greater control of the production of goods. In addition, they put thousands of unemployed people to work.

Power and Authority

The quest among European nations for greater power played a role in causing World War I. By the turn of the 20th century, the nations of Europe—driven by intense feelings of superiority—competed with each other on many fronts. They also built large armies to display their might.

INTERNET CONNECTION

Visit us at **www.mcdougallittell.com** to learn more about World War I.

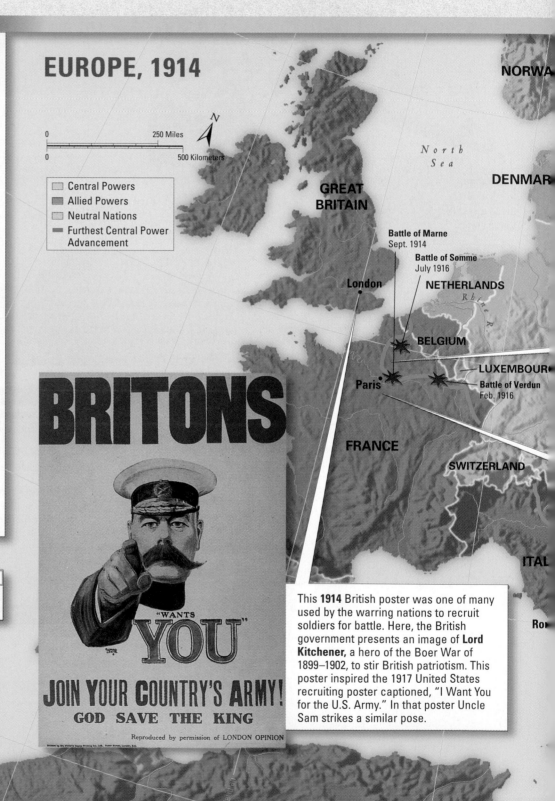

EUROPE, 1914

0   250 Miles
0   500 Kilometers

☐ Central Powers
■ Allied Powers
☐ Neutral Nations
▬ Furthest Central Power Advancement

NORWAY

North Sea

DENMARK

GREAT BRITAIN

London

Battle of Marne Sept. 1914
Battle of Somme July 1916
NETHERLANDS
Rhine R.
BELGIUM

Paris

LUXEMBOURG
Battle of Verdun Feb. 1916

FRANCE

SWITZERLAND

ITAL

Ro

ATLANTIC OCEAN

This **1914** British poster was one of many used by the warring nations to recruit soldiers for battle. Here, the British government presents an image of **Lord Kitchener,** a hero of the Boer War of 1899–1902, to stir British patriotism. This poster inspired the 1917 United States recruiting poster captioned, "I Want You for the U.S. Army." In that poster Uncle Sam strikes a similar pose.

BRITONS

"WANTS"
YOU

JOIN YOUR COUNTRY'S ARMY!
GOD SAVE THE KING

Reproduced by permission of LONDON OPINION

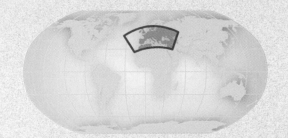

SWEDEN

Baltic Sea

Battle of Masurian Lakes
Sept. 1914

Battle of Tannenburg
Aug. 1914

GERMAN EMPIRE

Vistula R.

• Berlin

Petrograd •

RUSSIA

A German machine-gun team engages the enemy along the **Western Front**. The invention of new weapons and the improvement of others led to the killing of people on a scale the world had never before seen. The terrible destruction throughout Europe prompted one French soldier to write, "Humanity is mad! It must be mad to do what it is doing! . . . Hell cannot be so terrible."

Danube

Vienna •

AUSTRIA-HUNGARY

BOSNIA AND HERZEGOVINA

• Sarajevo

SERBIA

ALBANIA

GREECE

Mediterranean Sea

This painting by John Christen Johansen depicts the signing of the **Treaty of Versailles** in **1919**. The treaty, failing to resolve many issues that caused the war, left many nations unsatisfied. Particularly bitter was Germany, which was forced to accept full responsibility for the war. "We are required to admit that we alone are war guilty," declared a senior German delegate. "Such an admission on my lips would be a lie."

Interact *with* History

It is the summer of 1914 in Europe and tensions are high. The continent has been divided into two rival camps. The countries in each camp have pledged to fight alongside one another in case of war. Suddenly the unthinkable happens. The leader of a country you are allied with is assassinated. The dead leader's country blames a rival nation and declares war. The country calls on you to keep your word and join the war on its side.

As a member of your country's government, you are called to an emergency meeting to discuss your nation's response. On one hand, you have promised to support your ally. However, if you declare war, it probably will set off a chain reaction of war declarations throughout the two camps. As a result, all of Europe could find itself locked in a large, destructive war.

The leader of an allied nation is murdered. His country declares war and asks for your support.

If all nations keep their pledges to go to war, it will force millions of Europeans to fight and die.

Would you support your ally?

Your rival countries also have agreed to help each other in case one goes to war.

EXAMINING *the* ISSUES

- Should you always support a friend, no matter what he or she does?

- What might be the risks of refusing to help an ally?

- What might be the consequences of a war involving all of Europe?

As a class, discuss these questions. In your discussion, consider the various reasons why countries go to war.

As you read about World War I in this chapter, see how the nations reacted to this situation and what factors influenced their decisions.

The Stage
Is Set for War

MAIN IDEA	**WHY IT MATTERS NOW**
In Europe, military buildup, nationalistic feelings, and rival alliances set the stage for a continental war.	Ethnic conflict in the Balkan region, which helped start the war, continued to erupt in that area in the 1990s.

SETTING THE STAGE At the turn of the 20th century, the nations of Europe had been at peace with one another for nearly 30 years. An entire generation had grown up ignorant of the horrors of war. Some Europeans believed that progress had made war a thing of the past. Yet in little more than a decade, a massive war would engulf Europe and spread across the globe.

An Uneasy Peace Grips Europe

Efforts to outlaw war and achieve a permanent peace had been gaining momentum in Europe since the middle of the 19th century. By 1900, hundreds of peace organizations were active. In addition, peace congresses convened regularly between 1843 and 1907. However, below this surface of peace and goodwill, several forces were at work that would help propel Europe into war.

The Steady Rise of Nationalism One such force was nationalism, or a deep devotion to one's nation. Nationalism can serve as a unifying force within a country. However, it also can cause intense competition between nations, with each seeking to overpower the other. By the turn of the 20th century, a fierce rivalry indeed had developed among Europe's Great Powers. Those nations were Germany, Austria-Hungary, Great Britain, Russia, Italy, and France.

This increasing rivalry among European nations stemmed from several sources. Competition for materials and markets was one. Great Britain, home of the Industrial Revolution, had long been Europe's leader in industry, finance, and shipping. After 1850, however, other nations began to challenge Britain's power. One such nation was Germany. Germany's many new industries made its economy the fastest-growing one on the continent. As a result, Germany competed with Great Britain for industrial dominance.

Nationalistic rivalries also grew out of territorial disputes. France, for example, had never gotten over the loss of Alsace-Lorraine to Germany in the Franco-Prussian War (1870). Austria-Hungary and Russia both tried to dominate in the Balkans, a region in southeast Europe. Within the Balkans, the intense nationalism of Serbs, Bulgarians, Romanians, and other ethnic groups led to demands for independence.

THINK THROUGH HISTORY
A. Analyzing Issues
What helped fuel nationalistic rivalries among the countries of Europe?

Imperialism Another force that helped set the stage for war in Europe was imperialism. As Chapter 27 explained, the nations of Europe competed fiercely for colonies in Africa and Asia. The quest for colonies sometimes pushed European nations to the brink of war. In 1905 and again in 1911, Germany and France nearly fought over who would control Morocco, in northern Africa. With most of Europe supporting France, Germany eventually backed down. As European countries continued to compete for overseas empires, their sense of rivalry and mistrust of one another deepened.

German chancellor Otto von Bismarck led his nation to victory over France in the Franco-Prussian War in 1870. The war, which earned Germany some French territory, increased tensions between the two nations.

The Great War **743**

The Growth of Militarism Beginning in the 1890s, increasing nationalism led to a dangerous European arms race. The nations of Europe believed that to be truly great, they needed to have a powerful military. By 1914, all the Great Powers except Britain had large standing armies. In addition, military experts stressed the importance of being able to quickly mobilize, or organize and move troops in case of a war. Generals in each country developed highly detailed plans for such a mobilization.

The policy of glorifying military power and keeping an army prepared for war was known as **militarism.** Having a large and strong standing army made citizens feel patriotic. However, it also frightened some people. As early as 1895, Frédéric Passy, a peace activist and future Nobel Peace Prize winner, expressed a concern that many shared:

A VOICE FROM THE PAST

The entire able-bodied population are preparing to massacre one another; though no one, it is true, wants to attack, and everybody protests his love of peace and determination to maintain it, yet the whole world feels that it only requires some unforeseen incident, some unpreventable accident, for the spark to fall in a flash . . . and blow all Europe sky-high.

FRÉDÉRIC PASSY, quoted in *Nobel: The Man and His Prizes*

Background
The Nobel Peace Prize is named after Alfred Nobel, a Swedish inventor and industrialist. He established a fund to award prizes annually for strides made in several categories, including the advancement of peace. Ironically, Nobel's most noteworthy invention was dynamite.

HISTORY MAKERS

**Kaiser Wilhelm II
1859–1941**

Wilhelm II was related to the leaders of two nations he eventually would engage in war. Wilhelm, George V of Great Britain, and Nicholas II of Russia were all cousins.

The Kaiser thought a great deal of himself and his place in history. Once, when a doctor told him he had a small cold, Wilhelm reportedly responded, "No, it is a big cold. Everything about me must be big."

The Kaiser also could be sly and deceitful. After he forced the popular Bismarck to resign, Wilhelm pretended to be upset. "I feel as sorrowful as though I had lost my grandfather all over again," he announced publicly. Most people, however, including Bismarck, were not fooled. In his retirement, the former chancellor grumbled that Wilhelm "thinks he knows better than anyone. He recognizes no authority but himself."

Tangled Alliances

The growing international rivalries had led to the creation of several military alliances among the Great Powers as early as the 1870s. This alliance system had been designed to keep peace in Europe. But it would instead help push the continent into war.

Bismarck Forges Early Pacts Between 1864 and 1871, Prussia's blood-and-iron chancellor, Otto von Bismarck, freely used war to unify Germany. After 1871, however, Bismarck declared Germany to be a "satisfied power." He then turned his energies to maintaining peace in Europe.

Bismarck saw France as the greatest threat to peace. He believed that France still wanted revenge for its defeat in the Franco-Prussian War. Bismarck's first goal, therefore, was to isolate France. "As long as it is without allies," Bismarck stressed, "France poses no danger to us." In 1879, Bismarck formed the Dual Alliance between Germany and Austria-Hungary. Three years later, Italy joined the two countries, forming the **Triple Alliance**. In 1887, Bismarck took yet another possible ally away from France by making a treaty with Russia.

Bismarck knew that his network of alliances was unstable. Two of Germany's allies, Russia and Austria, were bitter rivals for the Balkans. The slightest shift in diplomatic winds could blow apart the fragile web of treaties.

Shifting Alliances Threaten Peace In 1890, Germany's foreign policy changed dramatically. That year, **Kaiser Wilhelm II**—who two years earlier had become ruler of Germany—forced Bismarck to resign. A proud and stubborn man, Wilhelm II did not wish to share power with anyone. Besides wanting to assert his own power, the new Kaiser was eager to show the world just how mighty Germany had become. The army was his greatest pride. "I and the army were born for one another," Wilhelm declared shortly after taking power.

Wilhelm set Germany on a new course. He let his nation's treaty with Russia lapse in 1890. Russia responded by forming a defensive military alliance with France in 1892 and 1894. Such an alliance had been Bismarck's fear. War with either Russia or France would

Vocabulary
chancellor: the chief minister of state in many European countries.

Vocabulary
impulsive: inclined to
act on a sudden feeling
rather than thought.

make Germany the enemy of both. Germany would then be forced to fight a two-front war, or a war on both its eastern and western borders.

Next, the impulsive Kaiser, envious of Britain's large empire and mighty navy, decided to challenge Britain. During the 1890s, Germany built its own small colonial empire. At the same time, Wilhelm started a tremendous shipbuilding program in an effort to make the German navy equal to Britain's.

Alarmed, Great Britain began to enlarge its own fleet. In 1904, Britain formed an entente, or alliance, with France. In 1907, Britain made another entente, this time with both France and Russia. The **Triple Entente,** as it was called, did not bind Britain to fight with France and Russia. However, it did almost certainly ensure that Britain would not fight against them.

By 1907, two rival camps existed in Europe. On one side was the Triple Alliance—Germany, Austria-Hungary, and Italy. On the other side was the

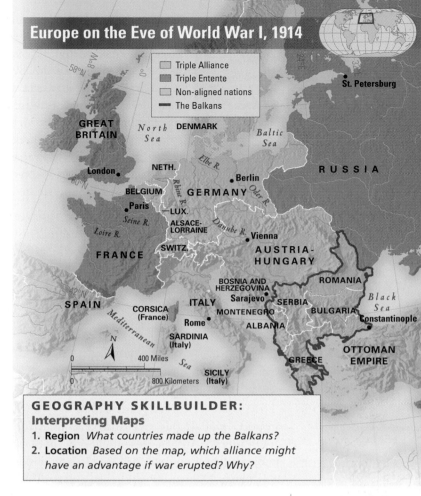

Europe on the Eve of World War I, 1914

Triple Alliance
Triple Entente
Non-aligned nations
The Balkans

GEOGRAPHY SKILLBUILDER:
Interpreting Maps
1. **Region** *What countries made up the Balkans?*
2. **Location** *Based on the map, which alliance might have an advantage if war erupted? Why?*

THINK THROUGH HISTORY
B. Summarizing
Which countries made
up the Triple Alliance?
the Triple Entente?

Triple Entente—Great Britain, France, and Russia. A dispute between two rival powers could draw the entire continent into war.

Crisis in the Balkans

Nowhere was that dispute more likely to occur than on the Balkan Peninsula. This mountainous peninsula in the southeastern corner of Europe was home to an assortment of ethnic groups. With a long history of nationalist uprisings and ethnic clashes, the Balkans were known as the "powder keg" of Europe.

Europe's Powder Keg By the early 1900s, the Ottoman Empire— which included the Balkan region—was in rapid decline. While some Balkan groups struggled to free themselves from Ottoman rule, others already had succeeded in breaking away from their Turkish rulers. These peoples had formed new nations, including Bulgaria, Greece, Montenegro, Romania, and Serbia.

Nationalism was a powerful force in these countries. Each group longed to extend its borders. Serbia, for example, had a large Slavic population. Serbia hoped to absorb all the Slavs on the Balkan Peninsula. On this issue of Serbian nationalism, Russia and Austria-Hungary were in direct conflict. Russia, itself a mostly Slavic nation, supported Serbian nationalism. Austria, which feared rebellion among its small Slavic population, felt threatened by Serbia's growth. In addition, both Russia and Austria-Hungary had hoped to fill the power vacuum created by the Ottoman decline in the Balkans.

In 1908, Austria annexed, or took over, Bosnia and Herzegovina.

SPOTLIGHT ON

The Armenian Massacre
One group that suffered greatly for its independence efforts was the Armenians. By the 1880s, the roughly 2.5 million Christian Armenians in the Ottoman Empire had begun to demand their freedom. As a result, relations between the group and its Turkish rulers grew strained.

Throughout the 1890s, Turkish troops killed tens of thousands of Armenians. When World War I erupted in 1914, the Armenians pledged their support to the Turks' enemies. In response, the Turkish government deported nearly 2 million Armenians. Along the way, more than 600,000 died of starvation or were killed by Turkish soldiers.

CONNECT *to* TODAY

The War in Bosnia

Intense nationalism in the Balkans led to bloodshed once again in the 1990s. Beginning in 1991, the different ethnic groups living in the country of Yugoslavia declared their independence. As the Yugoslavian republics of Slovenia, Croatia, and Bosnia and Herzegovina all broke away, the country dissolved into civil war. Serbia—Yugoslavia's largest and most influential republic—fought the independence efforts of other groups.

Eventually, the war took a terrible turn—particularly in Bosnia. With the support of the Serbian republic, Serbs living in Bosnia began a murderous campaign of "ethnic cleansing" to rid Bosnia of its non-Serb peoples. Although a United Nations-enforced agreement ended the fighting in 1996, anger and ethnic hatreds still simmer.

These were two Balkan areas with large Slavic populations. Serbian leaders, who had sought to rule these provinces, were outraged. The possibility of war arose. Russia offered Serbia full support, but the offer meant little. Russia was totally unprepared for war. When Germany stood firmly behind Austria, Russia and Serbia had to back down.

By 1914, tensions in the Balkan region were once again on the rise. Serbia had emerged victorious from several local conflicts. As a result, the nation had gained additional territory and a new confidence. It was more eager than ever to take Bosnia and Herzegovina away from Austria. In response, Austria-Hungary vowed to crush any Serbian effort to undermine its authority in the Balkans.

A Shot Rings Throughout Europe Into this poisoned atmosphere of mutual dislike and mistrust stepped the heir to the Austro-Hungarian throne, Archduke Franz Ferdinand, and his wife, Sophie. On June 28, 1914, the couple paid a state visit to Sarajevo, the capital of Bosnia. It was to be their last. The royal pair were shot at point-blank range as they rode through the streets of Sarajevo in an open car. The killer was Gavrilo Princip, a 19-year-old member of the Black Hand. The Black Hand was a secret society committed to ridding Bosnia of Austrian rule.

Because the assassin was a Serbian, Austria decided to use the murders as an excuse to punish Serbia. An angry Kaiser Wilhelm II urged Austria to be aggressive, and he offered Germany's unconditional support. In effect this gave Austria license to do what it wanted with Serbia.

On July 23, Austria presented Serbia with an ultimatum. An ultimatum is a list of demands that if not met, will lead to serious consequences. The ultimatum was deliberately harsh. Demands included an end to all anti-Austrian activity. In addition, Serbian leaders would have had to allow Austrian officials into their country to conduct an investigation into the assassinations. Serbia knew that refusing the ultimatum would lead to war against the more powerful Austria. Therefore, Serbian leaders agreed to most of Austria's demands. They offered to have several others settled by an international conference.

Austria, however, was in no mood to negotiate. The nation's leaders, it seemed, had already settled on war. On July 28, Austria rejected Serbia's offer and declared war. That same day, Serbia's ally, Russia, took action. Russian leaders ordered the mobilization of troops toward the Austrian border.

Leaders all over Europe suddenly took alarm. The fragile European stability seemed about to collapse. The British foreign minister, the Italian government, and even Kaiser Wilhelm himself urged Austria and Russia to negotiate. But it was too late. The machinery of war had been set in motion.

THINK THROUGH HISTORY
C. Analyzing Issues
Explain the reasons for the hostility between Austria-Hungary and Serbia.

Section ❶ Assessment

1. TERMS & NAMES

Identify
- militarism
- Triple Alliance
- Kaiser Wilhelm II
- Triple Entente

2. TAKING NOTES

Create a time line of major events that led to World War I.

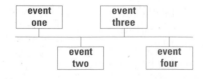

Write the lead paragraph of a news story about one event.

3. ANALYZING ISSUES

Why might the "machinery of war," set in motion by the assassination of Archduke Ferdinand, have been difficult to stop?

THINK ABOUT
- nationalism
- militarism
- the alliance system

4. ANALYZING THEMES

Power & Authority With another student, play the roles of Bismarck and Kaiser Wilhelm. In front of the class, debate each other over Germany's foreign policy goals.

THINK ABOUT
- the extent of Germany's "satisfaction" as a world power
- keeping Russia as an ally
- peace in Europe

TERMS & NAMES
• Schlieffen Plan
• Central Powers
• Allies
• Western Front
• trench warfare
• Eastern Front

2 War Consumes Europe

MAIN IDEA	WHY IT MATTERS NOW
One European nation after another was drawn into a large and industrialized war that resulted in many casualties.	Much of the technology of modern warfare, such as fighter planes and tanks, was introduced in World War I.

SETTING THE STAGE The assassination of Archduke Franz Ferdinand on June 28, 1914, was the spark that ignited a giant blaze. This single terrorist act set off a chain reaction within the alliance system that would result in the largest war Europe—and the world—had ever seen.

The Alliance System Collapses

By 1914, Europe was divided into two rival camps. One alliance, the Triple Entente, included Great Britain, France, and Russia. The other, known as the Triple Alliance, included Germany, Austria-Hungary, and Italy.

Austria-Hungary's declaration of war against Serbia set off a chain reaction within the alliance system. The countries of Europe followed through on their numerous and complex pledges to support one another. As a result, nearly all the nations of Europe soon were drawn into the war.

A Chain Reaction In response to Austria's declaration of war, Russia, Serbia's ally, began moving its army toward the Russian-Austrian border. Expecting Germany to join Austria, Russia also mobilized along the German border. Czar Nicholas II of Russia told the Kaiser that the maneuvers were just a precaution. Yet to Germany, Russia's mobilization amounted to a declaration of war. On August 1, the German government declared war on Russia.

Russia looked to its ally France for help. Germany, however, did not even wait for France to react. Two days after declaring war on Russia, Germany also declared war on France. Much of Europe was now locked in battle.

The Schlieffen Plan Germany quickly put its military plan into effect. The plan was named after its designer, General Alfred Graf von Schlieffen (SHLEE·fuhn). In the event of a two-front war, Schlieffen had called for attacking France and then Russia. The general had reasoned that Russia—with its lack of railroads—would have difficulty mobilizing its troops. Under the **Schlieffen Plan,** a large part of the German army would race west, to defeat France, and then return to fight Russia in the east.

Speed was vital to the German plan. The French had troops all along their border with Germany. Thus, the Germans knew that breaking through would be slow work. There was another route, however: France's northern border with Belgium was unprotected.

Germany demanded that its troops be allowed to pass through Belgium on their way to France. Belgium, a neutral country, refused. Germany then invaded Belgium. This brought Great Britain into the conflict. The British had close

THINK THROUGH HISTORY
A. Making Inferences Why was speed so important to the Schlieffen Plan?

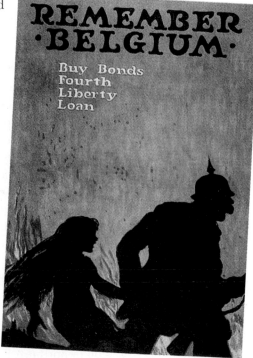

This war poster shows a German soldier dragging off a woman during the invasion of Belgium. The image was intended to stir public outrage over the attack.

REMEMBER BELGIUM

Buy Bonds
Fourth
Liberty
Loan

World War I in Europe, 1914–1918

Legend:
- Allied countries
- Central Powers
- Neutral countries
- Central Powers advance
- Allied advances
- Farthest Central Powers advance
- Farthest Allied advance
- Central powers victory
- Allied victory
- Armistice Line, Nov. 1918

GEOGRAPHY SKILLBUILDER: Interpreting Maps

1. **Location** *In which country was almost all of the war in the West fought?*
2. **Location** *What geographic disadvantage did Germany and Austria-Hungary face in fighting the war? How might this have affected their war strategy?*

ties with Belgium, one of their nearest neighbors on the continent. Outraged over the violation of Belgian neutrality, Britain declared war on Germany on August 4.

European Nations Take Sides By mid-August 1914, the battle lines were clearly drawn. On one side were Germany and Austria-Hungary. They were known as the **Central Powers,** because of their location in the heart of Europe. Bulgaria and the Ottoman Empire would later join the Central Powers in the hopes of regaining lost territories.

On the other side were Great Britain, France, and Russia. Together, they were known as the Allied Powers or the **Allies.** Japan joined the Allies within weeks. Italy, which at first was neutral, joined the Allies nine months into the war. Italy claimed that its membership in the Triple Alliance had been a defensive strategy. The Italians felt that the Germans had made an unprovoked attack on Belgium. Therefore, the Italians argued, they were not obligated to stand by their old ally.

In the late summer of 1914, millions of soldiers marched happily off to battle, convinced that the war would be short. Only a few people foresaw the horror ahead. One of them was Britain's foreign minister, Sir Edward Grey. Staring out over London at nightfall, Grey said sadly to a friend, "The lamps are going out all over Europe. We shall not see them lit again in our lifetime."

Background
Before the war, the Central Powers were part of the Triple Alliance, and the Allies were known as the Triple Entente.

A Bloody Stalemate Along the Western Front

It did not take long for Sir Edward Grey's prediction to ring true. As the summer of 1914 turned to fall, Germany's lightning-quick strike instead turned into a long and bloody stalemate, or deadlock, along the battlefields of France. This deadlocked region in northern France became known as the **Western Front.**

The Conflict Grinds to a Halt Early on, Germany's Schlieffen Plan worked brilliantly. By the end of August, the Germans had overrun Belgium and swept into France. By September 3, German units were on the edge of Paris. A major German victory appeared just days away. The French military then came into possession of intelligence that told them the exact direction the German army was about to take.

On September 5, the Allies attacked the Germans northeast of Paris, in the valley of the Marne River. Every available soldier was hurled into the struggle. When reinforcements were needed, more than 600 taxicabs rushed soldiers from Paris to the front. After four days of fighting, the German generals gave the order to retreat. "It was an inspiring thought," a British officer later wrote, "that the time had now come to chase the German." By September 13, the Germans had been driven back nearly 60 miles.

Although it was only the first major clash on the Western Front, the First Battle of the Marne was perhaps the single most important event of the war. The defeat of the Germans left the Schlieffen Plan in ruins. A quick victory in the west no longer seemed possible. In the east, Russian forces had already invaded Germany. Germany was going to have to fight a long war on two fronts. Realizing this, the German high command sent thousands of troops from France to aid its forces in the east. Meanwhile, the war on the Western Front settled into a stalemate.

War in the Trenches By early 1915, opposing armies on the Western Front had dug miles of parallel trenches to protect themselves from enemy fire. This set the stage for what became known as **trench warfare.** In this type of warfare, soldiers fought each other from trenches. And armies traded huge losses for pitifully small land gains.

Life in the trenches was pure misery. "The men slept in mud, washed in mud, ate mud, and dreamed mud," wrote one soldier. The trenches swarmed with rats. Fresh food was nonexistent. Sleep was nearly impossible.

The space between the opposing trenches won the grim name "no man's land." When the officers ordered an attack, their men went "over the top" of their trenches into this bombed-out landscape. There, they usually met murderous rounds of machine-gun fire. Staying put in the trench, however, did not ensure one's safety. Artillery fire brought death right into the trenches. "Shells of all calibers kept raining on our sector," wrote one French soldier. "The trenches disappeared, filled with earth

Along the Western Front, soldiers battled one another from trenches dug out of the earth. Here, a British soldier peers out of the trench at "no man's land."

749

Poison Gas
Soldiers wore masks to protect themselves from a horrible new weapon—poison gas. Gas was introduced by the Germans but used by both sides. While some gases caused blinding or severe blisters, others caused death by choking.

Tank
The tank was an armored combat vehicle that moved on chain tracks. It was introduced by the British in 1916 at the Battle of the Somme. The early tanks were slow and clumsy. They eventually improved, and thus aided the Allies in their war effort.

Machine Gun
The machine gun, which fires ammunition automatically, was much improved by the time of World War I. As a result, it saw wide use in combat. Because the gun could wipe out waves of attackers and make it difficult for forces to advance, it helped create a stalemate.

. . . the air was unbreathable. Our blinded, wounded, crawling, and shouting soldiers kept falling on top of us and died splashing us with blood. It was living hell."

The Western Front had become a "terrain of death." It stretched nearly 500 miles from the North Sea to the Swiss border. A British officer described it in a letter:

A VOICE FROM THE PAST
Imagine a broad belt, ten miles or so in width, stretching from the Channel to the German frontier near Basle, which is positively littered with the bodies of men and scarified with their rude graves; in which farms, villages and cottages are shapeless heaps of blackened masonry; in which fields, roads and trees are pitted and torn and twisted by shells and disfigured by dead horses, cattle, sheep and goats, scattered in every attitude of repulsive distortion and dismemberment.

VALENTINE FLEMING, quoted in *The First World War*

Military strategists were at a loss. New tools of war—machine guns, poison gas, armored tanks, larger artillery—had not delivered the fast-moving war they had expected. All this new technology did was kill huge numbers of people more effectively.

The slaughter reached a peak in 1916. In February, the Germans launched a massive attack against the French near Verdun. Each side lost more than 300,000 men.

In July of 1916, the British army tried to relieve the pressure on the French. British forces attacked the Germans northwest of Verdun, in the valley of the Somme River. In the first day of battle alone, more than 20,000 British soldiers were killed. By the time the Battle of the Somme ended in November, each side had suffered over half a million casualties.

What did the warring sides gain? Near Verdun, the Germans advanced about four miles. In the Somme valley, the British gained about five miles.

Background
In war, a casualty is anyone killed, injured, captured, or considered missing in action.

The Battle on the Eastern Front

Even as the war on the Western Front claimed thousands of lives, both sides were sending millions more men to fight on the **Eastern Front.** This area was a stretch of battlefield along the German and Russian border. Here, Russians and Serbs battled Germans, Austrians, and Turks. The war in the east was a more mobile war than that in the west. Here too, however, slaughter and stalemate were common.

Central Powers Gain the Advantage At the very beginning of the war, Russian forces had launched an attack into both Austria and Germany. At the end of August 1914, Germany counterattacked near the town of Tannenberg. During the four-day battle that followed, the Germans crushed the invading Russian army and drove it into full retreat. Germany regained East Prussia and seized numerous guns and horses from the enemy. More than 30,000 Russian soldiers were killed.

Airplane
World War I signaled the first time in history that planes were used in a combat role. At first, nations used planes for taking photographs of enemy lines. Soon, both sides used them to drop bombs. Guns soon were attached to the planes, and pilots fought each other in the air.

Submarine
In 1914, the Germans introduced the submarine as an effective warship. German submarines, known as U-boats, eventually waged unrestricted warfare on Allied ships. The submarine's primary weapon was the torpedo, a self-propelled underwater missile.

Russia fared somewhat better against the Austrians. Russian forces defeated the Austrians twice in September 1914, driving them deep into Austria. Not until December of that year did the Austrian army—with German assistance—manage to turn the tide. In a 17-day battle near Limanowa, Austria defeated the Russians and drove them eastward. Two weeks later, the Austrian army pushed the Russians out of Austria-Hungary.

Russia's War Effort Weakens By 1916, Russia's war effort was near collapse. Unlike the nations of western Europe, Russia had yet to become industrialized. As a result, the Russian army was continually short on food, guns, ammunition, clothes, boots, and blankets. Moreover, the Allies were unable to ship supplies to Russia's ports. In the north, a German naval fleet blocked the Baltic Sea. In the south, the Ottomans still controlled the straits leading from the Mediterranean to the Black Sea.

The Russian army had only one asset—its numbers. Throughout the war the Russian army suffered enormous battlefield losses. More than 2 million Russian soldiers were killed, wounded, or captured in 1915 alone. And yet the army continually rebuilt its ranks from the country's enormous population. For more than three years, the battered Russian army managed to tie up hundreds of thousands of German troops in the east. Thus, Germany could not hurl its full fighting force at the west.

Germany and her allies, however, were concerned with more than just the Eastern or Western Fronts. As the war raged on, fighting spread beyond Europe to Africa, as well as to Southwest and Southeast Asia. In the years after it began, the massive European conflict indeed became a world war.

THINK THROUGH HISTORY
C. Synthesizing
Why was Russia's involvement in the war so important to the other Allies?

Section ❷ Assessment

1. TERMS & NAMES
Identify
- Schlieffen Plan
- Central Powers
- Allies
- Western Front
- trench warfare
- Eastern Front

2. TAKING NOTES
Using a chart like the one below, write the immediate reason why each nation declared war on the other.

War Declaration	Reason for Declaration
Germany on Russia	
Germany on France	
Britain on Germany	

3. COMPARING AND CONTRASTING
How was war on the Western Front and Eastern Front different? How was it the same?

THINK ABOUT
- trench warfare
- which nations fought on each front
- war casualties

4. THEME ACTIVITY
Science & Technology
Draw a political cartoon showing the effects of the new technology on warfare. Include a caption that expresses the point of the cartoon.

Aviation

World War I introduced plane warfare. And with it came daring dogfights and legendary pilots. Two such pilots were America's Eddie Rickenbacker and Germany's Baron Manfred von Richthofen, better known as the Red Baron. In a larger sense, however, the war ushered in an era of great progress in the field of aviation. In the warring nations' quest to dominate the skies, they produced thousands of planes and continually worked to improve engine designs. After the war, these nations converted their war planes to commercial use. They also began designing larger, stronger planes for civilian transport. The age of air travel had begun.

By 1926, passenger airlines were operating in Europe, Africa, Australia, and North and South America. Built in 1928, the Ford Tri-motor model, shown below, was one of the better-known American passenger planes of the time.

On the eve of World War I, planes were still considered a novelty. Here, an early plane races an automobile at a track in Columbus, Ohio, in 1914. The finish was so close that no one knew who won.

Designers of the early passenger planes made sure to devote plenty of space for luggage.

The three-motor system gave the plane greater power. It became the prototype for many later models.

The Tri-motor carried about 10 passengers. Temperature control, however, was still many years away. Passengers often bundled up in coats to keep warm.

Annual Ridership

Riders (in billions)

- 1930 — Less than 3 million*
- 1960 — 100 million*
- 1990s — 1.25 billion*

*estimated
Source: *The World Book Encyclopedia*

Connect *to* History

Clarifying What role did World War I play in the advancement of aviation technology?

SEE SKILLBUILDER HANDBOOK, PAGE 992.

Connect *to* Today

Investigating Find out about any one of today's more advanced aircraft, such as the Concorde, or the latest military jet or commercial airplane. Write a brief report about the craft's most advanced and interesting features. Present your report to the class.

TERMS & NAMES
• unrestricted submarine warfare
• total war
• rationing
• propaganda
• armistice

3 War Affects the World

MAIN IDEA

World War I spread to several continents and required the full resources of many governments.

WHY IT MATTERS NOW

The war propelled the United States to a new position of international power, which it retains today.

SETTING THE STAGE By early 1915, it was apparent to all the warring nations that swift victory had eluded them. As war on both European fronts promised to be a grim, drawn-out affair, all the Great Powers looked for new allies to tip the balance. They also sought new war fronts on which to achieve victory.

A Truly Global Conflict

Geographical widening of the war actually had begun soon after the conflict started. Japan entered the war on the Allies' side. The Ottoman Turks and later Bulgaria allied themselves with Germany and the Central Powers. That widened the conflict further. By early 1915, the only major neutral power left besides the United States was Italy. And Italy joined the Allies in April. None of these alliances gave an advantage to either side. But they did give military leaders more war zones in which to try to secure victory.

Fighting Rages Beyond Europe As the war dragged on, the Allies desperately searched for a way to end the stalemate. A promising strategy seemed to be to attack a region in the Ottoman Empire known as the Dardanelles. This narrow sea strait was the gateway to the Ottoman capital, Constantinople. By securing the Dardanelles, the

Allies believed that they could take Constantinople, defeat the Turks, and establish a supply line to Russia. They might even be able to mount an offensive into the Austrian heartland by way of the Danube River.

The effort to take the Dardanelles strait began in February 1915. It was known as the Gallipoli campaign. British, Australian, New Zealand, and French troops made repeated assaults on the Gallipoli Peninsula on the western side of the strait. Turkish troops, some commanded by German officers, vigorously defended the region. By May, Gallipoli had turned into another bloody stalemate. Both sides dug trenches, from which they battled for the rest of the year. In December, the Allies gave up the campaign and began to evacuate. They had suffered about 250,000 casualties.

Despite the Allies' failure at Gallipoli, they remained determined to topple the Ottoman Empire. In Southwest Asia, the British helped Arab nationalists rise up against their Turkish rulers. Particularly devoted to the Arab cause was a British soldier named T. E. Lawrence. Better known as Lawrence of Arabia, he helped lead daring guerrilla raids against the Turks. With the help of the Arabs, Allied armies took control of Baghdad, Jerusalem, and Damascus.

Background

Although the Ottoman Empire had greatly declined by World War I, it still ruled Arab lands in Southwest Asia.

In various parts of Asia and Africa, Germany's colonial possessions came under assault. The Japanese quickly overran German outposts in China. They also captured Germany's Pacific island colonies.

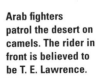

Arab fighters patrol the desert on camels. The rider in front is believed to be T. E. Lawrence.

753

English and French troops attacked Germany's four African possessions. They seized control of three.

Elsewhere in Asia and Africa, the British and French recruited subjects in their colonies for the struggle. Fighting troops as well as laborers came from India, South Africa, Senegal, Egypt, Algeria, and Indochina. Many fought and died on the battle-field. Others worked to keep the frontlines supplied. Some colonial subjects wanted nothing to do with their European rulers' conflicts. Others volunteered in the hope that service would lead to their independence. This was the view of Indian political leader Mohandas Gandhi, who supported Indian participation in the war. "If we would improve our status through the help and cooperation of the British," he wrote, "it was our duty to win their help by standing by them in their hour of need."

THINK THROUGH HISTORY
A. Summarizing
How did Europe's colonial subjects help in the war effort?

The United States Enters the War In 1917, the focus of the war shifted to the high seas. That year, the Germans intensified the submarine warfare that had raged in the Atlantic Ocean since shortly after the war began. By 1917, failed crops, as well as a British naval blockade, caused severe food shortages in Germany. Desperate to strike back, Germany decided to establish its own naval blockade around Britain. In January 1917, the Germans announced that their submarines would sink without warning any ship in the waters around Britain. This policy was called **unrestricted submarine warfare.**

Vocabulary
blockade: the forced closing off of a city or other area to traffic and communication through the use of ships or land forces.

The Germans had tried this policy before. On May 7, 1915, a German submarine, or U-boat, had sunk the British passenger ship *Lusitania*. The attack left 1,198 people dead, including 128 U.S. citizens. Germany claimed that the ship had been carrying ammuni-tion—which turned out to be true. Nevertheless, the American public was outraged. President Woodrow Wilson sent a strong protest to Germany. After two further attacks, the Germans finally agreed to stop attacking neutral and passenger ships.

However, the Germans returned to unrestricted submarine warfare in 1917. They knew it might lead to war with the United States. They gambled that their naval

The World at War, 1914–1918

War rages in Southwest Asia as Arab nationalists battle their Turkish rulers.

Main fighting of the war occurs on Western and Eastern Fronts.

Japan declares war on Germany in 1914; seizes German colonies in China and the Pacific.

The United States enters the war on the side of the Allies in 1917.

Brazil is the only South American country to enter the war. It supports the Allies with warships and personnel.

The European colonies throughout Africa become a battlefield as the warring parties strike at one another's colonial possessions.

India provides about 1.3 million men to fight and labor alongside their British rulers throughout Europe.

Both countries fight on the side of the Allies and contribute many troops to the Gallipoli campaign of 1915, in Southwest Asia.

GEOGRAPHY SKILLBUILDER: Interpreting Maps
1. **Region** Which countries were aligned with the European Allies?
2. **Location** Outside of Europe, where was World War I fought?

blockade would starve Britain into defeat before the United States could mobilize. Ignoring warnings by President Wilson, German U-boats sank three American ships.

In February 1917, another German action pushed the United States closer to war. The British intercepted a telegram from Germany's foreign secretary, Arthur Zimmermann, to the German ambassador in Mexico. The message said that Germany would help Mexico "reconquer" the land it had lost to the United States if Mexico would ally itself with Germany. The British decoded the message and gave it to the U.S. government.

Background
Land Mexico considered "lost" to the United States included New Mexico, Texas, and Arizona.

When the Zimmermann note was made public, Americans called for war against Germany. Even before news of the note, many Americans had sided with the Allies. A large part of the American population felt a bond with England. The two nations shared a common ancestry and language, as well as similar democratic institutions and legal systems. In addition, reports—some true and others not—of German war atrocities stirred anti-German sentiment in the United States. More important, America's economic ties with the Allies were far stronger than those with the Central Powers. America traded with Great Britain and France more than twice as much as with Germany.

Vocabulary
atrocity: an act of extreme cruelty or violence.

The Zimmermann note simply proved to be the last straw. On April 2, 1917, President Wilson asked Congress to declare war. The United States entered the war on the side of the Allies.

War Affects the Home Front

By the time the United States joined the Allies, the war had been going on for nearly three years. In those three years, Europe had lost more men in battle than in all the wars of the previous three centuries. The war had claimed the lives of millions and had changed countless lives forever. The Great War, as the conflict came to be known, affected everyone. It touched not only the soldiers in the trenches, but civilians as well. It affected not just military institutions, but also political, economic, and social institutions.

Governments Wage Total War World War I soon became a **total war.** This meant that countries devoted all their resources to the war effort. In Britain, Germany, Austria, Russia, and France, the entire force of government was dedicated to winning the conflict.

In each country, the wartime government took control of the economy. Governments told factories what to produce and how much. Numerous facilities were converted to munitions factories. Nearly every able-bodied civilian was put to work. Unemployment in many European countries nearly disappeared. European governments even enlisted the help of foreign workers. For example, thousands of civilians were deported from German-occupied Belgium and France to work in Germany as farm and factory laborers. Britain and France recruited Chinese, West Indian, Algerian, and Egyptian laborers to work behind their lines at the front.

So many goods were in short supply that governments turned to **rationing.** Under this system, people could buy only small amounts of those items that were also needed for the war effort. Eventually, rationing covered a wide range of goods, from butter to shoe leather.

Governments also suppressed antiwar activity—sometimes forcibly. In addition, they censored news about the war. Many leaders feared

GlobalImpact

Influenza Epidemic

In the spring of 1918, a powerful new enemy emerged, threatening nations on each side of World War I. This "enemy" was a deadly strain of influenza. The Spanish flu, as it was popularly known, hit England and India in May. By the fall, it had spread through Europe, Russia, Asia, and to the United States.

The influenza epidemic killed soldiers and civilians alike. In India, at least 12 million people died of influenza. In Berlin, on a single day in October, 1,500 people died. In the end, this global epidemic was more destructive than the war itself, killing 20 million people worldwide.

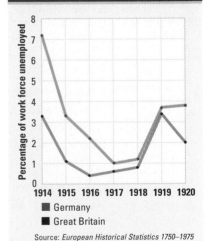

Unemployment in Germany and Britain

Percentage of work force unemployed

■ Germany
■ Great Britain

Source: *European Historical Statistics 1750–1975*

**SKILLBUILDER:
Interpreting Graphs**
1. *During which year did each country see its lowest unemployment rate?*
2. *Why might unemployment have been lowest during the war years?*

that honest reporting of the war would turn people against it. Governments also used **propaganda**—one-sided information designed to persuade—to keep up morale and support for the war. One of the main instruments of propaganda was the war poster. In nations throughout Europe, striking, colorful posters urged support for the war by painting the enemy as monsters and allies as heroes. (See poster on page 747.)

The War's Impact on Women Total war meant that governments turned to help from women as never before. Thousands of women replaced men in factories, offices, and shops. Women built tanks and munitions, plowed fields, paved streets, and ran hospitals. They also kept troops supplied with food, clothing, and weapons. Although most women left the work force when the war ended, they changed many people's views of what women were capable of doing.

THINK THROUGH HISTORY
B. Summarizing
Describe how the governments of the warring nations fought a total war.

The Allies Win the War

With the United States finally in the war, the balance, it seemed, was about to tip in the Allies' favor. Before that happened, however, events in Russia gave Germany a victory on the Eastern Front.

Russia Withdraws from the War By March 1917, civil unrest in Russia—due in part to war-related shortages of food and fuel—had brought the czar's government to the brink of collapse. Czar Nicholas, faced with the

In total war all citizens were called on to help in the war effort. Thus women were offered new employment opportunities. Pictured here are women workers at a French munitions factory.

prospect of revolution, abdicated his throne on March 15. In his place a provisional government was established. The new government pledged to continue fighting the war. However, by 1917, nearly 5.5 million Russian soldiers had been wounded, killed, or taken prisoner. The war-weary Russian army refused to fight any longer.

Vocabulary
abdicate: to formally give up a high office or responsibility.

Eight months later, a second revolution shook Russia (see Chapter 30). In November 1917, Communist leader Vladimir Ilyich Lenin seized power. Lenin insisted on ending his country's involvement in the war. One of his first acts was to offer Germany a truce. In March 1918, Germany and Russia signed the Treaty of Brest-Litovsk, which ended the war between them.

The treaty was extremely hard on Russia. It required the Russian government to surrender lands to Germany that now include Finland, Poland, Ukraine, Estonia, Latvia, and Lithuania. (See map on page 762.) Even though the treaty became invalid after the war, these nations still gained their independence.

A Failed Final Push Russia's withdrawal from the war at last allowed Germany to send nearly all its forces to the Western Front. In March 1918, the Germans mounted one final, massive attack on the Allies in France. More than 6,000 German cannons opened the offensive with the largest artillery attack of the entire war.

As in the opening weeks of the war, the German forces crushed everything in their path. By late May 1918, the Germans had again reached the Marne River. Paris was less than 40 miles away. Victory seemed within reach.

By this time, however, the German military had weakened. The effort to reach the Marne had exhausted men and supplies alike. Sensing this weakness, the Allies—with the aid of nearly 140,000 fresh American troops—launched a counterattack. Marshal Ferdinand Foch, the French commander of the Allied forces, used Americans to fill the gaps in his ranks. The U.S. soldiers were inexperienced but courageous and eager to

July 1918
Allies defeat Germany
at Second Battle of
the Marne.

November 1918
Warring nations
sign armistice
ending the war.

1914

June 1914
Archduke
Ferdinand and
his wife are
assassinated.

July 1914
Austria-
Hungary
declares war
on Serbia.

July–August 1914
Russia, France, and
Britain go to war
against Germany
and Austria-Hungary.

1916

1916
Combatants
suffer devas-
tating losses
at battles of
Verdun and
the Somme.

1917

1917
United
States enters
the war.

1918

March 1918
Russia withdraws
from the war.

fight. A British nurse, Vera Brittain, later recalled her joy in seeing the American reinforcements:

A VOICE FROM THE PAST

They were swinging rapidly toward Camiers, and though the sight of soldiers marching was now too familiar to arouse curiosity, an unusual quality of bold vigor in their swift stride caused me to stare at them with puzzled interest. They looked larger than ordinary men; their tall, straight figures were in vivid contrast to the undersized armies of pale recruits to which we had grown accustomed. . . . Then I heard an excited exclamation from a group of Sisters behind me. "Look! Look! Here are the Americans!"

VERA BRITTAIN, *Testament of Youth*

British and German soldiers help one another during a break in the fighting.

THINK THROUGH HISTORY
C. Comparing How was the Second Battle of the Marne similar to the first?

In July 1918, the Allies and Germans clashed at the Second Battle of the Marne. Leading the Allied attack were some 350 tanks that rumbled slowly forward, smashing through the German lines. With the arrival of 2 million more American troops, the Allied forces began to advance steadily toward Germany.

Soon, the Central Powers began to crumble. First the Bulgarians and then the Ottoman Turks surrendered. In October, a revolution in Austria-Hungary brought that empire to an end. In Germany, soldiers mutinied, and the public turned on the Kaiser.

On November 9, 1918, Kaiser Wilhelm II was forced to step down. Germany declared itself a republic. A representative of the new German government met with Marshal Foch. In a railway car in a forest near Paris, the two signed an **armistice,** or an agreement to stop fighting. On November 11, World War I came to an end.

After four years of slaughter and destruction, the time had come to forge a peace settlement. Leaders of the victorious nations gathered outside Paris to work out the terms of peace. While these leaders had come with high hopes, the peace settlement they crafted left many feeling bitter and betrayed.

Section 3 Assessment

1. TERMS & NAMES
Identify
• unrestricted submarine warfare
• total war
• rationing
• propaganda
• armistice

2. TAKING NOTES
Using a chart like the one below, list the reasons why the United States entered World War I.

Reasons for U.S. Entry
1.
2.
3.
4.

3. ANALYZING ISSUES
In what ways was World War I truly a global conflict?

THINK ABOUT
• where the war was fought
• who participated in the war effort

4. ANALYZING THEMES
Economics How did the concept of total war affect the warring nations' economies?

THINK ABOUT
• the governments' new role in their economies
• the scarcity of food and other products
• the role of women
• unemployment rates during the war years

The Great War **757**

Honoring War Heroes

Throughout history, people around the world have shared in a somber, healing ritual: honoring their country's soldiers killed in battle. In many nations, people come together to honor those citizens who have fought and died for their country. After World War I, France built a ceremonial grave to honor all of its soldiers killed in the great conflict. From early times to today, other nations have paid their respects to their dead soldiers with medals, monuments, and parades.

Tomb of the Unknown Soldier

A woman pays her quiet respects at the Tomb of the Unknown Soldier in Paris. On top of the memorial rests an eternal flame in honor of France's dead soldiers. Each year on Armistice Day, the president of France lays a wreath at the site. Following World War I, similar memorials to unknown dead soldiers were created in the United States, Great Britain, Belgium, and Italy.

a closer look WORLD WAR I MONUMENTS

This German war memorial was built in 1926 and placed in the courtyard of the Technical University in Berlin.

The Wall

A man pays tribute at the Vietnam Veterans Memorial in Washington, D.C. The monument, known as the Wall, is a memorial to the men and women who fought and died in the Vietnam War in the 1960s and 1970s. The monument consists of two adjoining black granite walls inscribed with the names of all Americans who either died in the war or were listed as missing in action.

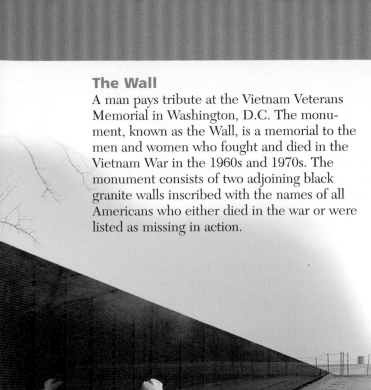

Trajan's Column

The Romans relied greatly on their powerful military to oversee a huge empire. Consequently, they glorified war and soldiers with numerous statues and monuments. Shown here is a detail from Trajan's Column, in Rome. The 100-foot-high column was dedicated in A.D. 113 to the emperor Trajan after he conquered Dacia. The column is a continuous spiral carving of soldiers and battle scenes.

"The People's Heroes"

This monument is a tribute to the Chinese armed forces, officially known as the People's Liberation Army. The monument, which sits in Beijing, is called the Memorial to the People's Heroes. It is a tribute to the soldiers, past and present, who have taken part in the struggle to forge a Communist China, which began around 1946.

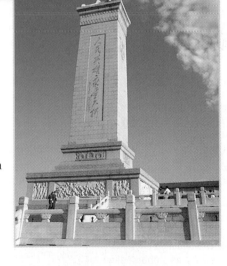

Great Britain built its own Tomb of the Unknown Warrior in London to honor those who lost their lives in World War I.

Connect *to* History

Analyzing Motives Why do you think nations honor their dead soldiers?

  SEE SKILLBUILDER HANDBOOK, PAGE 994

Connect *to* Today

Designing Working with one or more students, design a memorial to your country's dead soldiers. Include any words or images that you feel convey your message. Present the memorial to the class.

A Flawed Peace

TERMS & NAMES
- **Woodrow Wilson**
- **Georges Clemenceau**
- **David Lloyd George**
- **Fourteen Points**
- **self-determination**
- **Treaty of Versailles**
- **League of Nations**

MAIN IDEA

After winning the war, the Allies dictated a harsh peace settlement that left many nations feeling betrayed.

WHY IT MATTERS NOW

Hard feelings left by the peace settlement helped cause World War II.

SETTING THE STAGE World War I was over. The killing had stopped. The terms of peace, however, still had to be worked out. On January 18, 1919, a conference to establish those terms began at the Palace of Versailles, outside Paris. For one year this conference would be the scene of vigorous, often bitter debate. The Allied powers struggled to solve their conflicting aims in various peace treaties.

The Allies Meet at Versailles

Attending the talks, known as the Paris Peace Conference, were delegates representing 32 countries. However, the meeting's major decisions were hammered out by a group known as the Big Four: **Woodrow Wilson** of the United States, **Georges Clemenceau** of France, **David Lloyd George** of Great Britain, and Vittorio Orlando of Italy. Russia, in the grip of civil war, was not represented. Neither were Germany and its allies.

Wilson's Plan for Peace In January 1918, while the war was still raging, President Wilson had drawn up a series of proposals. Known as the **Fourteen Points,** they outlined a plan for achieving a just and lasting peace. The first five points included an end to secret treaties, freedom of the seas, free trade, and reduced national armies and navies. The fifth goal was the adjustment of colonial claims with fairness toward colonial peoples. The sixth through thirteenth points were specific suggestions for changing borders and creating new nations. The guiding idea behind these points was **self-determination.** This meant allowing people to decide for themselves under what government they wished to live.

Finally, the fourteenth point proposed a "general association of nations" that would protect "great and small states alike." This reflected Wilson's hope for an organization that could peacefully negotiate solutions to world conflicts.

HISTORY MAKERS

Georges Clemenceau
1841–1929

Woodrow Wilson
1856–1924

The most hostile relationship at the Paris Peace Conference was that between two allies: Wilson and Clemenceau. These two highly intelligent and committed leaders brought very different visions of peace to the negotiating table.

Woodrow Wilson was the son of a Presbyterian minister. He had been a history scholar, professor, and president of Princeton University before becoming president. A morally upright man, he was guided by a deep inner religious faith.

Clemenceau, by contrast, had been a physician, journalist, and

sometime playwright before becoming premier of France.

In Paris, the two men clashed. Wilson's idealism, as embodied in the Fourteen Points, stood in stark contrast to Clemenceau's desire to punish Germany.

The stubborn personalities of the two men made reaching agreement even harder. Lloyd George of Britain summed it up nicely when he was asked how he did at the Paris Peace Conference. "Not badly," he replied, "considering I was seated between Jesus Christ and Napoleon."

THINK THROUGH HISTORY
A. Summarizing
What were Wilson's general goals for the postwar world?

THINK THROUGH HISTORY
B. Contrasting
How did Britain and France's aims at Versailles differ from Wilson's?

The Allies Dictate a Harsh Peace As the Paris Peace Conference opened, Britain and France showed little sign of agreeing to Wilson's vision of peace. Both nations were concerned with national security. They also wanted to strip Germany of its war-making power. The French, in particular, were determined to punish Germany. France was where much of the fighting had occurred. The nation had lost more than a million soldiers and had seen large amounts of its land destroyed. Clemenceau wanted Germany to pay for the suffering the war had caused.

The differences between French, British, and U.S. aims led to heated arguments among the nations' leaders. Finally a compromise was reached. The **Treaty of Versailles** between Germany and the Allied powers was signed on June 28, 1919— five years to the day after Franz Ferdinand's assassination in Sarajevo.

Adopting Wilson's fourteenth point, the treaty created a **League of Nations.** The league was to be an international association whose goal would be to keep peace among nations. The five Allied powers—the United States, Great Britain, France, Italy, and Japan—were to be permanent members of the league's Executive Council. Its General Assembly would consist of representatives of 32 Allied and neutral nations. Germany was deliberately excluded. Also left out was Russia. Russia's early withdrawal from the war and its revolutionary leadership had made it an outcast in the eyes of the other Allies.

The treaty also punished Germany. The defeated nation lost substantial territory and had severe restrictions placed on its military operations. As punishing as these provisions were, the harshest was Article 231. It was also known as the "war guilt" clause. It placed sole responsibility for the war on Germany's shoulders. As a result, Germany had to pay reparations to the Allies.

All of Germany's territories in Africa and the Pacific were declared mandates, or territories to be administered by the League of Nations. Under the peace agreement, the Allies would govern the mandates until they were judged ready for independence.

Vocabulary
reparations: money paid by a defeated nation to compensate for damage or injury during a war.

The Treaty of Versailles: Major Provisions

League of Nations	Territorial Losses	Military Restrictions	War Guilt
• International peace organization; membership to include Allied war powers and 32 Allied and neutral nations • Germany and Russia excluded	• Germany returns Alsace-Lorraine to France; French border extended to the west bank of the Rhine River • Germany surrenders all of its overseas colonies in Africa and the Pacific	• Limits set on the size of the German army • Germany prohibited from importing or manufacturing weapons or war materiel • Germany forbidden to build or buy submarines or have an air force	• Sole responsibility for the war placed on Germany's shoulders • Germany forced to pay the Allies $33 billion in reparations over 30 years

SKILLBUILDER: Interpreting Charts
1. In what ways did the treaty punish Germany?
2. What two provinces were returned to France as a result of the treaty?

The Creation of New Nations The Versailles treaty with Germany was just one of five treaties negotiated by the Allies. The Western powers signed separate peace treaties in 1919 and 1920 with each of the other defeated nations: Austria, Hungary, Bulgaria, and the Ottoman Empire.

These treaties, too, led to huge land losses for the Central Powers. Several new countries were created out of the Austro-Hungarian Empire. Austria, Hungary, Czechoslovakia, and Yugoslavia were all recognized as independent nations.

The Great War

Long-Term Causes

- Nationalism spurs competition among European nations.
- Imperialism deepens national rivalries.
- Militarism leads to large standing armies.
- The alliance system divides Europe into two rival camps.

Immediate Causes

- The assassination of Archduke Franz Ferdinand in June 1914 prompts Austria to declare war on Serbia.
- The alliance system requires nations to support their allies. European countries declare war on one another.

WORLD WAR I

Immediate Effects

- A generation of Europeans are killed or wounded.
- Dynasties fall in Germany, Austria-Hungary, and Russia.
- New countries are created.
- The League of Nations is established to help promote peace.

Long-Term Effects

- Many nations feel bitter and betrayed by the peace settlements.
- Problems that helped cause the war—nationalism, competition—remain.

TERMS & NAMES

Briefly explain the importance of each of the following regarding World War I.

1. Triple Alliance
2. Triple Entente
3. Central Powers
4. Allies
5. trench warfare
6. total war
7. armistice
8. Fourteen Points
9. Treaty of Versailles
10. League of Nations

REVIEW QUESTIONS

SECTION 1 *(pages 743–746)*
The Stage Is Set for War

11. How did nationalism, imperialism, and militarism help set the stage for World War I?
12. Why were the Balkans known as "the powder keg of Europe"?

SECTION 2 *(pages 747–751)*
War Consumes Europe

13. Why was the first Battle of the Marne considered so significant?
14. Where was the Western Front? the Eastern Front?
15. What were the characteristics of trench warfare?

SECTION 3 *(pages 753–757)*
War Affects the World

16. What was the purpose of the Gallipoli campaign?
17. What factors prompted the United States to enter the war?
18. In what ways was World War I a total war?

SECTION 4 *(pages 760–763)*
A Flawed Peace

19. What was the purpose of the League of Nations?
20. What was the mandate system, and why did it leave many groups feeling betrayed?

Interact *with* History

On page 742, you examined whether you would keep your word and follow your ally into war. Now that you have read the chapter, reevaluate your decision.

If you chose to support your ally, do you still feel it was the right thing to do? Why or why not?

If you decided to break your pledge and stay out of war, what are your feelings now? Discuss your opinions with a small group.

CRITICAL THINKING

1. ALLIED LEADERS

THEME **POWER AND AUTHORITY** Often, it is the people in power who determine events and make history. How did the Treaty of Versailles reflect the different personalities and agendas of the men in power at the .end of World War I?

2. THE ALLIANCE SYSTEM

Trace the formation of the two major alliance systems that dominated Europe on the eve of World War I by providing the event that corresponds with each date on the chart.

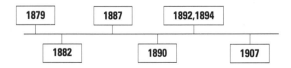

3. A HOLLOW VICTORY

Winston Churchill, Great Britain's prime minister in the 1940s and 1950s, was under-secretary of the British navy during World War I. He said that the Allied victory in World War I had been "bought so dear [high in price] as to be indistinguishable from defeat." What did he mean by this statement? Use examples from the text to support your answer.

4. ANALYZING PRIMARY SOURCES

The following quotation is from an editorial in the German newspaper *Vossische Zeitung* on May 18, 1915. It is in response to President Wilson's protest to the German government after the sinking of the British passenger ship *Lusitania*. The writer believes that Americans were aboard the ship to deter a possible attack against the ship—and its war cargo.

A VOICE FROM THE PAST
The responsibility for the death of so many American citizens, which is deeply regretted by everyone in Germany, in a large measure falls upon the American government. It could not admit that Americans were being used as shields for English contraband [smuggled goods]. In this regard America had permitted herself to be misused in a disgraceful manner by England. And now, instead of calling England to account, she sends a note to the German government.

- Why does the writer hold the American government responsible for the deaths of the Americans on board?

- How does this paragraph reinforce the idea that history can be based on different points of view?

CHAPTER ACTIVITIES

1. LIVING HISTORY: Unit Portfolio Project

THEME **SCIENCE AND TECHNOLOGY** Your unit portfolio project focuses on how science and technology have influenced history. (See page 739.) For Chapter 29, you might use one of the following ideas to add to your portfolio:

- Write a piece of historical fiction describing a World War I airplane battle.

- After doing further research, write a brief report describing what life was like aboard a German U-boat.

- Using images from magazines and books, create a display to show how technology affects warfare.

2. CONNECT TO TODAY: Cooperative Learning

THEME **ECONOMICS** While World War I was extremely costly, staying prepared for the possibility of war today is also expensive.

Work with a small team to present the military and defense budgets of several of the world's nations.

Use the Internet and other resources to research the topic. Have each group member be responsible for one country.

- Examine how much money each country spends on military and defense, as well as what percentage of the overall budget it represents.

- Combine your research on a large chart and present it to the class.

- Discuss whether the amounts spent for military and defense are justified.

3. INTERPRETING A TIME LINE

Revisit the unit time line on pages 738–739. Examine the Chapter 29 time line. For each event, draw an image or symbol that represents that event.

FOCUS ON **GRAPHS**

This graph provides the total number of troops mobilized, as well as the number of military deaths each major nation suffered in World War I.

- Which nation suffered the most deaths? Which one suffered the least?

- Which nations had more than a million soldiers killed?

Connect to History

Based on the number of troops each side mobilized, what may be one reason the Allies won?

World War I Battlefield Deaths

Total Number of Troops Mobilized

Allied Powers: 42 million

Central Powers: 23 million

Battlefield Deaths of Major Combatants

USA 116,000
Ottoman Empire 325,000
Italy 650,000
*British Empire 908,000
Austria-Hungary 1.2 million
France 1.3 million
Russia 1.7 million
Germany 1.8 million

*Includes troops from Britain, Canada, Australia, New Zealand, India, and South Africa   Source: *Encyclopaedia Britannica*

You are living in a country in which the government benefits a small, wealthy class and ignores the demands of the vast majority. Thousands of poor peasants and workers have few rights.

The government has failed to tackle economic, social, and political problems. Various revolutionary groups are all clamoring for change. Some groups call for a violent overthrow of the government. Others believe in battling injustice and achieving change through nonviolent methods, such as peaceful strikes and protests.

In 1920, Mohandas K. Gandhi became the leader of the independence movement to free India of British rule.

In the late 1920s, Communist leader Mao Zedong believed revolution would solve China's problems.

How do you resist oppressive rule— with violent or nonviolent action?

"[Nonviolent] resistance . . . is superior to the force of arms . . . One who is free from hatred requires no sword."

"A revolution is not a dinner party . . . A revolution is an insurrection, an act of violence by which one class overthrows another."

EXAMINING *the* ISSUES

- **What situations might provoke some people to take violent steps to achieve change?**

- **What strengths would a person need to remain nonviolent in the face of violent attacks?**

- **How might armed and powerful opponents respond to groups committed to nonviolent action?**

- **Which strategy—violence or nonviolence—would prove more successful and bring more long-lasting consequences? Why?**

As a class, discuss these questions. In your discussion, consider what you have learned about the strategies revolutionaries used to accomplish change in other countries, such as France, the United States, Brazil, Mexico, Haiti, and so on.

As you read about the revolutions in Russia and China and the independence movement in India, see which strategy was used and rate its effectiveness for achieving change.

TERMS & NAMES
- pogrom
- Trans-Siberian Railway
- Bolsheviks
- V. I. Lenin
- Duma
- Rasputin
- provisional government
- soviet

Revolutions in Russia

1

MAIN IDEA	WHY IT MATTERS NOW
Long-term social unrest in Russia erupted in revolution, ushering in the first Communist government.	The Communist Party controlled the Soviet Union until the country's breakup in 1991.

SETTING THE STAGE The Russian Revolution was like a firecracker with a very long fuse. The explosion came in 1917. Yet the fuse had been burning for nearly a century. The cruel, oppressive rule of most 19th-century czars caused widespread social unrest for decades. Anger over social inequalities and the ruthless treatment of peasants grew. The czars' unfair governing sparked many violent reactions. Army officers revolted in 1825. Hundreds of peasants rioted. Secret revolutionary groups formed and plotted to overthrow the government. In 1881, student revolutionaries were angry over the slow pace of political change. They assassinated the reform-minded czar, Alexander II. Russia was heading toward a full-scale revolution.

Alexander III Upholds the Autocracy

In 1881, Alexander III succeeded his father, Alexander II, to the throne and halted all reforms in Russia. Like his grandfather, Nicholas I, Alexander III clung to the principles of autocracy, a government in which he had total power. Alexander III was determined to strengthen "autocracy, orthodoxy, and nationality." Anyone who questioned the absolute authority of the czar, worshiped outside the Russian Orthodox Church, or spoke a language other than Russian was tagged as dangerous.

To wipe out revolutionaries, Alexander III used harsh measures. He imposed strict censorship codes on published materials and written documents, including private letters. His secret police carefully watched both secondary schools and universities. Teachers had to send detailed reports on every student. Political prisoners were exiled to Siberia, a region of eastern and central Russia.

To establish a uniform Russian culture, Alexander III oppressed other national groups within Russia. He made Russian the official language of the empire and forbade the use of minority languages, such as Polish, in schools. Alexander made Jews the target of persecution. He subjected them to new laws that encouraged prejudice. Jews could not buy land or live among other Russians. Universities set strict quotas for Jewish students. A wave of **pogroms**—organized violence against Jews—broke out in many parts of Russia. Police and soldiers stood by and watched Russian citizens loot and destroy Jewish homes, stores, and synagogues.

THINK THROUGH HISTORY
A. Summarizing
What methods did Alexander III use to maintain his authority over the Russian people?

Alexander III turned Russia into a police state, teeming with spies and informers.

Nicholas II Resists Change

When Nicholas II became czar in 1894, he announced, "The principle of autocracy will be maintained by me as firmly and unswervingly as by my lamented father [Alexander III]." Nicholas stubbornly refused to surrender any of his power. His trust in the tradition of Russian autocracy blinded him to the changing conditions of his times. Yet the sweeping forces of change would override his pledge to preserve the czarist rule of Russia's past.

Revolution and Nationalism **769**

The Trans-Siberian Railway

The Trans-Siberian Railway ran about 5,800 miles across the vast area of Siberia, from Moscow to the city of Vladivostok on the Sea of Japan. Like the transcontinental railroad in the United States (built from 1863 to 1869), the Trans-Siberian Railway was constructed over difficult terrain and completed in sections.

To celebrate the opening of the Trans-Siberian Railway, Czar Nicholas II had the jewelry firm of Fabergé create a golden Easter egg (shown below) for Czarina Alexandra. The inscription on the silver band encircling the egg reads, "Great Siberian Railway, 1900." Hidden inside the egg is a wonderful surprise—a miniature replica of a train studded with precious gems. The tiny engine is actually a wind-up toy that can pull the cars attached to it.

Economic Growth and Its Impact The number of factories more than doubled between 1863 and 1900. In spite of this, at the beginning of Nicholas II's reign, Russia lagged behind the industrial nations of western Europe. In the 1890s, Sergey Witte (VYEET·tyih), the czar's most capable minister, launched a program to move the country forward. Through higher taxes and foreign investments, Witte helped finance the buildup of Russian industries. Witte's steps also boosted the growth of heavy industry, particularly steel. By around 1900, Russia had become the world's fourth-ranking producer of steel. Only the United States, Germany, and Great Britain produced more steel.

Witte also pushed for the building of the great **Trans-Siberian Railway**—the world's longest continuous rail line. With the help of British and French investors, work began in 1891. The Trans-Siberian Railway was completed in 1904. It connected European Russia in the west with Russian ports on the Pacific Ocean in the east.

The Revolutionary Movement Grows Rapid industrialization also stirred discontent among the people of Russia. The growth of factories brought new problems. Among these problems were grueling working conditions, miserably low wages, and child labor. Trade unions were outlawed. Still, exploited laborers who worked in factories and built the railway lines organized strikes. Workers were unhappy with their low standard of living and lack of political power. The gap between rich and poor was enormous.

Amid the widespread unrest of workers and other members of Russian society, various revolutionary movements began to grow. They also competed for power. The group that would eventually succeed in establishing a new government in Russia followed the views of Karl Marx. These revolutionaries believed that the industrial class of workers would overthrow the czar. The industrial class would then form "a dictatorship of the proletariat." In such a state, the workers would rule.

In 1903, Russian Marxists split into two groups over revolutionary tactics. The Mensheviks (MEHN·shuh·vihks) wanted a broad base of popular support for the revolution. The **Bolsheviks** (BOHL·shuh·vihks) supported a small number of committed revolutionaries willing to sacrifice everything for radical change.

The major leader of the Bolsheviks was Vladimir Ilyich Ulyanov (ool·YAH·nuhf). He adopted the name of **Lenin.** He had an engaging personality and was an excellent organizer. He was also ruthless. These traits would ultimately help him gain command of the Bolsheviks. In the early 1900s, Lenin fled to western Europe to avoid arrest by the czarist regime. He maintained contact with other Bolsheviks. Lenin then waited until he could safely return to Russia.

Crises at Home and Abroad

The revolutionaries would not have to wait long to realize their visions. Between 1904 and 1917, Russia faced a series of crises. These events showed the czar's weakness and paved the way for revolution.

The Russo-Japanese War In the late 1800s, Russia and Japan were imperialist powers. They both competed for control of Korea and Manchuria. The two nations signed a series of agreements over the territories, but Russia broke them. In retaliation, Japan attacked the Russians at Port Arthur, Manchuria, in February 1904.

Though Russian soldiers and sailors went confidently to war, the Japanese defeated them. News of repeated losses sparked unrest at home and led to revolt in the midst of the war.

Vocabulary
minister: person in charge of an area of government, such as finance.

THINK THROUGH HISTORY
B. Analyzing Causes Why did industrialization in Russia lead to unrest?

Background
Karl Marx, a 19th-century German philosopher, argued that the workers of the world would one day overthrow the ruling class and share equally in society's wealth.

Bloody Sunday: The Revolution of 1905 On January 22, 1905, about 200,000 workers and their families approached the czar's Winter Palace in St. Petersburg. They carried a petition asking for better working conditions, more personal freedom, and an elected national legislature. Nicholas II was not at the palace. His generals and police chiefs were. They ordered the soldiers to fire on the crowd. Between 500 and 1,000 unarmed people were killed. Russians quickly named the event "Bloody Sunday." Lenin called the incident a "dress rehearsal" for the later revolution that would usher in a Communist regime.

Bloody Sunday provoked a wave of strikes and violence that spread across the country. Though Nicholas still opposed reform, in October 1905 he reluctantly promised more freedom. He approved the creation of the **Duma** (DOO·muh)—Russia's first parliament. The first Duma met in May 1906. Its leaders were moderates who wanted Russia to become a constitutional monarchy similar to Britain. Hesitant to share his power, the czar dissolved the Duma after ten weeks. Other Dumas would meet later. Yet none would have real power to make sweeping reforms.

World War I: The Final Blow In 1914, Nicholas II made the fateful decision to drag Russia into World War I. Russia, though, was unprepared to handle the military and economic costs. Russia's weak generals and poorly equipped troops were no match for the German army. Before a year had passed, more than 4 million Russian soldiers had been killed, wounded, or taken prisoner. German machine guns mowed down advancing Russians by the thousands. Defeat followed defeat. As in the Russo-Japanese War, Russia's involvement in World War I revealed the weaknesses of czarist rule and military leadership.

In 1915, Nicholas moved his headquarters to the war front. From there, he hoped to rally his discouraged troops to victory. His wife, Czarina Alexandra, ran the government while he was away. She ignored the czar's chief advisers. Instead, she continued to fall under the influence of the mysterious **Rasputin** (ras·PYOO·tihn)—a self-described "holy man." He claimed to have magical healing powers.

Alexis, Nicholas and Alexandra's son, suffered from hemophilia, a life-threatening disease. Rasputin seemed to ease the boy's symptoms. To show her gratitude, Alexandra allowed Rasputin to make key political decisions. He opposed reform measures and obtained powerful positions for his friends. He spread corruption throughout the royal court. In 1916, a group of nobles murdered Rasputin. They feared his increasing role in government affairs.

Meanwhile, the war was destroying the morale of Russian troops. Soldiers mutinied, deserted, or ignored orders. On the homefront, food and fuel supplies were dwindling. Prices were wildly inflated. People from all classes were clamoring for change and an end to the war. Neither Nicholas nor Alexandra proved capable of tackling these enormous problems.

HISTORY MAKERS

Rasputin
1872–1916

Born a peasant in Siberia, Rasputin became a religious teacher, although he was never ordained as a priest. The sinister monk seemed to cast a hypnotic spell on people, especially Czarina Alexandra and her ailing son. Rasputin's reputation for having mysterious powers followed him to his grave.

In December 1916, a small group of young aristocrats plotted his assassination because he was reportedly taking control of the government. They lured him to a mansion and fed him poisoned cakes. The poison apparently had no effect on Rasputin's extraordinary strength. The conspirators then shot him several times. Assuming he was finally dead, they threw him in the Neva River. When his body was discovered three days later, doctors confirmed the cause of his death—drowning.

Rasputin's death threw the czarina into shock. His prediction haunted her: "If I die or you desert me, in six months you will lose your son and your throne."

The March Revolution

In March 1917, women textile workers in Petrograd led a citywide strike. Soon afterward, riots flared up over shortages of bread and fuel. Nearly 200,000 workers swarmed the streets. At first the soldiers obeyed orders to shoot the rioters but later sided with them. The soldiers fired at their commanding officers and joined the rebellion. Large crowds gathered, shouting "Down with the autocracy!" and "Down with the war!"

The Czar Steps Down The local protest exploded into a general uprising—the March Revolution. It forced Czar Nicholas II to abdicate his throne. A year later revolutionaries executed Nicholas and his family. The czarist rule of the Romanovs, which spanned over three centuries, had finally collapsed. The March Revolution succeeded in bringing down the czar. Yet it failed to set up a strong government to replace his regime.

Leaders of the Duma established a **provisional government**, or temporary government. It was eventually headed by Alexander Kerensky. His decision to continue fighting the war cost him the support of both soldiers and civilians. As the war dragged on, conditions inside Russia worsened. Angry peasants demanded land. City workers grew more radical. Social revolutionaries, competing for power, formed soviets. **Soviets** were local councils consisting of workers, peasants, and soldiers. In many cities, especially Petrograd, the soviets had more influence than the provisional government.

Lenin Returns to Russia The Germans launched their own "secret weapon" that would erode the provisional government's authority. They arranged Lenin's return to Russia after many years of exile. The Germans believed that Lenin and his Bolshevik supporters would stir unrest in Russia and hurt the Russian war effort. Traveling in a sealed railway boxcar, Lenin reached Petrograd in April 1917.

The Bolshevik Revolution

Lenin and the Bolsheviks recognized their opportunity to seize power. They soon gained control of the Petrograd soviet, as well as the soviets in other major Russian cities. By the fall of 1917, people in the cities were rallying to the call, "All power to the soviets." Lenin's slogan—"Peace, Land, and Bread"—was gaining widespread appeal. Lenin decided to take action.

The Provisional Government Topples In November 1917, without warning, Bolshevik Red Guards made up of armed factory workers stormed the Winter Palace in Petrograd. They took over government offices and arrested the leaders of the provisional government. The Bolshevik Revolution was over in a matter of hours. Kerensky and his colleagues disappeared almost as quickly as the czarist regime they had replaced.

THINK THROUGH HISTORY
C. Making Inferences Why did Kerensky's decision to continue fighting the war cost him the support of the Russian people?

Causes and Effects of Two Russian Revolutions

Causes	Russian Revolutions of 1917	Effects
• Widespread discontent among all classes of Russian society	• Abdication of Czar Nicholas	• Civil war (1918–1920)
• Agitation from revolutionaries	• Failure of provisional government	• Czar and his family killed—end of czarist rule
• Weak leadership of Czar Nicholas II	• Growing power of soviets	• Peace with Germany under Treaty of Brest-Litovsk (1918)
• Defeat in Russo-Japanese War (1905)	• Lenin's return to Russia	• Bolshevik control of government
• Bloody Sunday (1905)	• Bolshevik takeover under Lenin	• Russian economy in ruins
• Losses in World War I		
• Strikes and riots		

SKILLBUILDER: Interpreting Charts
1. *Based on the chart, form a generalization about why the Russian Revolutions occurred.*
2. *What similarities exist between the causes of the Revolution and the effects?*

Russian Revolution and Civil War, 1905–1922

- ▬ Western boundaries of Russia, 1905–1917
- ★ Bolshevik uprisings, 1917–1918
- ▮ Bolshevik territory, Oct. 1919
- ▫ Territories lost (Treaty of Brest-Litovsk, 1918)
- ◀ White Russian and Allied attacks, 1918–1920
- ◀ Bolshevik counterattacks, 1918–1920
- ✸ Major civil war battle areas, 1918–1920
- ▬ Boundaries of Russia, 1922

Romanov family executed, 1918

Ukraine lost in Treaty of Brest-Litovsk; regained in 1922

GEOGRAPHY SKILLBUILDER: Interpreting Maps

1. **Region** *What was the extent (north to south, east to west) of the Bolshevik territory in 1919?*
2. **Region** *What European countries were no longer within Russian boundaries by 1922 because of the Brest-Litovsk treaty?*

Bolsheviks in Power Lenin's next step was tackling the problems he inherited from czarist rule. Within days after the Bolshevik takeover, Lenin ordered that all farmland be distributed among the peasants. Lenin and the Bolsheviks gave control of factories to the workers. The Bolshevik government also signed a truce with Germany to stop all fighting on the eastern war front and began peace talks.

In March 1918, Russia and Germany signed the Treaty of Brest-Litovsk. The price of peace was costly. Russia surrendered a large chunk of its territory to Germany and its allies. The humiliating terms of this treaty triggered widespread anger among many Russians. They objected to the Bolsheviks and their policies.

During the Bolshevik Revolution of 1917, these Petrograd workers seized an armored car from the provisional government's forces.

Civil War Rages in Russia Still recovering from their painful losses of land to Germany, the Bolsheviks now faced a new challenge—stamping out their enemies at home. Their opponents formed the White Army. The revolutionary leader Leon Trotsky, who helped negotiate the Treaty of Brest-Litovsk, expertly commanded the Bolshevik Red Army. From 1918 to 1920, civil war raged in Russia. Several Western nations, including the United States, sent military aid and forces to Russia to help the White Army.

THINK THROUGH HISTORY
D. Identifying Problems What problems did Lenin and the Bolsheviks face after the revolution?

Russia's civil war proved far more deadly than the earlier revolutions. Around 15 million Russians died in the three-year struggle and in the famine that followed. The destruction and loss of life from fighting, hunger, and a worldwide flu epidemic left Russia in chaos.

In the end the Red Army triumphed and finally crushed all opposition to Bolshevik rule. The victory showed that the Bolsheviks were able both to seize power and to maintain it. Yet in the aftermath of the civil war, Lenin and the Bolsheviks faced overwhelming problems.

1984

George Orwell wrote the chilling novel *1984* in response to the threat of two totalitarian regimes. They were Communist Russia under Stalin and Nazi Germany under Adolf Hitler. The novel depicts a frightening world in which personal freedom and privacy have vanished. The sinister slogan "Big Brother Is Watching You" appears everywhere. Even citizens' homes have television cameras that constantly survey their behavior.

Orwell intended his novel, published in 1949, as a warning, not as a prophecy. He sounded an alarm about a world that a totalitarian state could create through modern technology. For millions of people in the Soviet Union and Nazi Germany, the world of totalitarianism was not fiction. It was terrifying fact.

themselves were not above suspicion, especially if they did not meet their quotas of "criminals" arrested. Every family came to fear the knock on the door in the early hours of the morning. Such a surprise visit from the secret police usually meant the arrest of a family member.

When the Great Purge ended in 1939, Stalin had gained total control of both the Soviet government and the Communist Party. Historians estimate that Stalin was responsible for the deaths of 8 million to 13 million people.

Indoctrination and Propaganda Totalitarian states rely on indoctrination—instruction in the government's set of beliefs—to mold people's minds. Party leaders in the Soviet Union lectured workers and peasants on the ideals of communism. They also stressed the importance of sacrifice and hard work to build the Communist state. State-supported youth groups served as training grounds for future party members.

Totalitarian states also spread propaganda. Propaganda is biased or incomplete information used to sway people to accept certain beliefs or actions. Soviet newspapers and radio broadcasts glorified the achievements of communism, Stalin, and his economic programs.

Under Stalin, art also became a method of propaganda. In 1930, an editorial in the Communist Party newspaper *Pravda* explained the purpose of art: "Literature, the cinema, the arts are levers in the hands of the proletariat which must be used to show the masses positive models of initiative and heroic labor." **Socialist realism** was an artistic style that praised Soviet life and Communist values. It became a vehicle to rally the workers. Yevgeny Yevtushenko, a Russian poet, described this form of artistic expression:

A VOICE FROM THE PAST

Blankly smiling workers and collective farmers looked out from the covers of books. Almost every novel and short story had a happy ending. Painters more and more often took as their subjects state banquets, weddings, solemn public meetings, and parades.

Poets visited factories and construction sites but wrote more about machines than about the men who worked them. If machines could read, they might have found such poems interesting. Human beings did not.

YEVGENY YEVTUSHENKO, *A Precocious Autobiography*

THINK THROUGH HISTORY
B. Making Inferences What forms of art did Stalin encourage?

Censorship Many Soviet writers, composers, and other artists also fell victim to official censorship. Stalin would not tolerate individual creativity that threatened the conformity and obedience required of citizens in a totalitarian state. The government also controlled all newspapers, motion pictures, radio, and other sources of information.

Religious Persecution Communists aimed to replace religious teachings with the ideals of communism. Under Stalin, the government and the League of the Militant Godless, an officially sponsored group of atheists, spread propaganda attacking religion. "Museums of atheism" displayed exhibits to show that religious beliefs were mere superstitions. Yet many people in the Soviet Union still clung to their faiths.

Vocabulary
atheists: people who do not think there is a god.

The Russian Orthodox Church was the main target of persecution. Other religious groups, including Roman Catholics and Jews, also suffered greatly under Stalin's totalitarian rule. The police destroyed magnificent churches and synagogues. Many religious leaders of all faiths were killed or sent to labor camps.

Propaganda Through Art

Low-cost printing techniques made socialist realism posters an important form of propaganda in the Soviet Union. People might not listen to the radio or go to propaganda films. However, if they left their houses, they could not avoid viewing the posters plastered on buildings and walls in every town.

Images of energetic laborers, such as the special groups called "shock brigades," urged Soviets to work harder. Portraits glorifying Stalin were also popular subjects of Soviet posters.

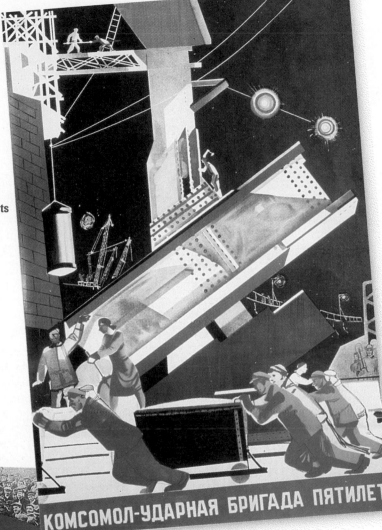

The slogan on this poster reads, "Young Communists [are] the Shock Brigade of the Five-Year Plan."

The slogan on the above poster reads, "Day Laborers and Young Communists—Join the Tractor Shock Brigades for Spring Sowing."

This profile of Stalin is imposed on a shadowy image of Lenin. Miniature portraits of other Communist leaders trail off in the background.

Connect *to* History

Analyzing Issues What messages do you think these posters communicate?

SEE SKILLBUILDER HANDBOOK, PAGE 1001

Connect *to* Today

Comparing How do the Soviet posters portraying workers resemble the billboards that modern-day advertisers use to sell products? Support your answer with examples.

Daily Life Under Stalin

Stalin's totalitarian rule revolutionized Soviet society. Women's roles greatly expanded. People became better educated and mastered new technical skills. The dramatic changes in people's lives had a downside, though. As servants of a totalitarian state, they would make great sacrifices in exchange for progress.

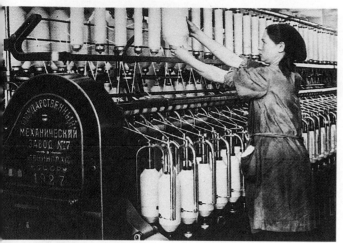

This Soviet woman worked in a textile factory during Stalin's regime.

Soviet Women With the Bolshevik Revolution of 1917, women won equal rights. After Stalin became dictator, women helped the state-controlled economy prosper. Under his Five-Year Plans, they had no choice but to join the labor force in increasing numbers. Young women performed the same jobs as men. Millions of women worked in factories and built dams and roads.

Given new educational opportunities, women prepared for careers in engineering and science. Medicine, in particular, attracted many women. By 1950, they made up 75 percent of Soviet doctors.

Soviet women paid a heavy price for their rising status in society. Besides their full-time jobs, they were responsible for housework and child care. Motherhood was also considered a patriotic duty in totalitarian regimes. Soviet women were expected to provide the state with future generations of loyal, obedient citizens.

THINK THROUGH HISTORY
C. Evaluating What were the pros and cons of women's new roles in Soviet society under Stalin?

Education Under Stalin, the government controlled all education—from nursery schools through the universities. Schoolchildren learned the virtues of the Communist Party. College professors and students who questioned the Communist Party's interpretations of history or science risked losing their jobs or faced imprisonment.

Education was not merely indoctrination. Stalin's economic plans created a high demand for many skilled workers. University and technical training became the key to a better life. As one young man explained, "If a person does not want to become a collective farmer or just a cleaning woman, the only means you have to get something is through education."

By the mid-1930s, Stalin had forcibly transformed the Soviet Union into a totalitarian regime, as well as an industrial and a political power. He stood unopposed as dictator and maintained his authority over the Communist Party. Stalin also ushered in a period of total social control and rule by terror. His network of laws and regulations guided every aspect of individual behavior.

Like Russia, China would fall under the influence of Karl Marx's theories and Communist beliefs. The dynamic leader Mao Zedong would pave the way for transforming China into a totalitarian Communist state, as you will read in Section 3.

Section 2 Assessment

1. TERMS & NAMES

Identify
- Joseph Stalin
- totalitarianism
- command economy
- collective farm
- kulak
- Great Purge
- socialist realism

2. TAKING NOTES

Create a chart like the one below listing the weapons of totalitarianism. Cite examples from Stalinist Russia for each method shown.

Weapons	Examples
Police Terror	
Propaganda	
Censorship	
Religious Persecution	

Which method do you think was most influential in maintaining Stalin's totalitarian rule? Why?

3. SYNTHESIZING

What kind of person would be considered an ideal citizen under Stalin's totalitarian regime? Support your answer with reasons.

THINK ABOUT
- the chart explaining the key traits of totalitarianism
- personal qualities that are prized under totalitarianism
- people who were persecuted or punished under Stalin

4. THEME ACTIVITY

Economics Role-play an industrial worker in a steel mill, a peasant on a collective farm, or a student at a technical school. Write a secret journal entry describing what your life is like under Stalin's economic plans.

Collapse of Chinese Imperial Rule

TERMS & NAMES
• Kuomintang
• Sun Yixian
• Mao Zedong
• May Fourth Movement
• Long March

MAIN IDEA

After the fall of the Qing dynasty, nationalist and Communist movements struggled for power.

WHY IT MATTERS NOW

The seeds of China's late-20th-century political thought, communism, were planted at this time.

SETTING THE STAGE In the early 1900s, China was ripe for revolution. China had faced years of humiliation at the hands of outsiders. Foreign countries controlled China's trade and economic resources. Many Chinese believed that modernization and nationalism held the country's keys for survival. They wanted to build up the army and navy, to construct modern factories, and to reform education. Yet others feared change. They believed that China's greatness lay in its traditional ways.

Nationalists Overthrow Qing Dynasty

Among the groups pushing for modernization and nationalization was the **Kuomintang** (KWOH·mihn·TANG), or the Nationalist Party. Its first great leader, **Sun Yixian** (soon yee·shyahn), was a physician who had spent many years in the United States. In 1912, Sun's Revolutionary Alliance, a forerunner of the Kuomintang, succeeded in overthrowing the last emperor of the Qing dynasty. The Qing had ruled China since 1644.

Shaky Start for the New Republic In 1912, Sun became president of the new Republic of China. He held the post for just six weeks. Sun hoped to establish a modern government based on the "Three Principles of the People": (1) nationalism—an end to foreign control, (2) people's rights—democracy, and (3) people's livelihood—economic security for all Chinese. Sun Yixian considered nationalism vital. He said, "The Chinese people . . . do not have national spirit. Therefore even though we have four hundred million people gathered together in one China, in reality, they are just a heap of loose sand." Despite his lasting influence as a revolutionary leader, Sun lacked the authority and the military support to secure national unity.

Sun turned over the presidency to Yuan Shikai (yoo·ahn shee·ky), a powerful general. Yuan quickly betrayed the democratic ideals of the revolution. By 1913, he was ruling as a military dictator. His actions sparked local revolts. Even Yuan's own generals refused to fight the rebels. After Yuan died in 1916, chaos reigned. China remained divided and Sun's Kuomintang powerless. Civil war broke out as one rival group battled another. Sun tried to reorganize his Kuomintang. Real authority, though, fell into the hands of provincial warlords. They ruled territories as large as their armies could conquer.

As always during times of unrest, the Chinese peasants suffered most. Warlord armies terrorized the countryside. They pillaged and looted everywhere. Roads and bridges fell into disrepair, and crops were destroyed. Famine took the lives of millions. This was the situation in China as World War I was being waged in Europe.

Vocabulary
warlord: powerful military leader.

HISTORY MAKERS

Sun Yixian
1866–1925

A traditional Chinese proverb says that knowing what to do is easier than doing it. Sun Yixian disagreed. "Knowledge is difficult," he said. "Action is easy."

Sun led an action-filled life. He traveled, organized, and plotted tirelessly to bring down the Qing dynasty. Aware of Sun's activity and influence, Qing officials tracked him down in London. They kidnapped him and held him prisoner. They planned to ship him back to China, where he faced probable execution.

Sun would meet his death, he said, by "first having my ankles crushed in a vise and broken by a hammer, my eyelids cut off, and finally being chopped up into small fragments so that none could claim my mortal remains." Sun's British friends helped him escape his captors. The episode made him world-famous as a leader of the revolution in China. Sun Yixian is still known as the "father of modern China."

On a spring evening in the early 1930s during the Great Depression, you are one of thousands of Germans gathered at an outdoor stadium in Munich. You are unemployed; your country is suffering. Like everyone else, you have come to this mass meeting to hear two politicians campaigning for office. Huge speakers blare out patriotic music, while you and the rest of the crowd wait impatiently for the speeches to begin.

Before long you will have to cast your ballot.

First candidate's platform:

- Remember Germany's long and glorious past.
- Our present leadership is indecisive; we need a strong, effective leader.
- Rebuild the army to protect against enemies.
- Regain the lands taken unfairly from us.
- Make sacrifices to return to economic health.
- Put the welfare of the state above all, and our country will be a great power again.

Second candidate's platform:

- There are no simple or quick solutions to problems.
- Put people back to work, but economic recovery will be slow.
- Provide for the poor, elderly, and sick.
- Avoid reckless military spending.
- Act responsibly to safeguard democracy.
- Be a good neighbor country; honor our debts and treaty commitments.

Which candidate will you choose?

EXAMINING *the* ISSUES

- **What strategy does each candidate have for solving the nation's problems?**

- **How does each candidate view the role of the citizen in meeting the challenges facing the nation?**

- **Which candidate makes the strongest appeal to the listener's emotions?**

As a class, discuss these questions. In your discussion, remember what you have read about the defeated nations' bitterness toward the Versailles Treaty following World War I. How might this influence which candidate voters favor?

As you read this chapter, see how dictators were voted into power as people lost faith in democratic government in the 1920s and 1930s. Examine the factors that influenced political decisions in this troubled time.

An Age of Uncertainty

TERMS & NAMES
- **Albert Einstein**
- **theory of relativity**
- **Sigmund Freud**
- **existentialism**
- **Friedrich Nietzsche**
- **surrealism**
- **jazz**
- **Charles Lindbergh**

MAIN IDEA

The postwar period was one of loss and uncertainty but also one of invention, creativity, and new ideas.

WHY IT MATTERS NOW

Postwar trends in physics, psychiatry, art, literature, communication, music, and transportation still affect our lives.

SETTING THE STAGE The horrors of World War I shattered the Enlightenment belief that progress would continue and reason would prevail. New ideas and patterns of life developed in the 1920s that changed the way people looked at the world.

Science Challenges Old Ideas

The ideas of two remarkable thinkers became widely known during this "age of uncertainty." They were Albert Einstein and Sigmund Freud. Both had an enormous impact on the 20th century. Einstein and Freud challenged some of the most deeply rooted ideas that people held about themselves and their world. They were part of a scientific revolution as important as that brought about centuries earlier by Copernicus and Galileo.

Impact of Einstein's Theory of Relativity A German-born physicist, **Albert Einstein,** offered startling new ideas on space, time, energy, and matter. He began by tackling a problem that baffled physicists. Scientists had found that light travels at exactly the same speed no matter what direction it moves in relation to earth. Earth moves through space, yet its movement did not affect the speed at which light seemed to travel. This finding seemed to break the laws of motion and gravity discovered by Isaac Newton.

In 1905, Einstein theorized that while the speed of light is constant, other things that seem constant, such as space and time, are not. Space and time can change when measured relative to an object moving near the speed of light—about 186,000 miles per second. Since relative motion is the key to Einstein's idea, it is called the **theory of relativity.** Einstein's ideas had implications not only for science but for how people viewed the world. Now uncertainty and relativity replaced Newton's comforting belief of a world operating according to absolute laws of motion and gravity.

Influence of Freudian Psychology The ideas of **Sigmund Freud,** an Austrian physician, were as revolutionary as Einstein's. Freud treated patients with psychological problems. From his experiences, he constructed a theory about the human mind. He believed that much of human behavior is irrational, or beyond reason. He called the irrational part of the mind the unconscious. In the unconscious, a number of drives existed, especially pleasure-seeking drives, of which the conscious mind was unaware. Freud's theories, first published in *The Interpretation of Dreams* (1900), met with opposition, especially his ideas about the unconscious. His ideas weakened faith in reason. All the same, by the 1920s, Freud's theories had developed widespread influence.

HISTORY MAKERS

Albert Einstein
1879–1955

Albert Einstein was the greatest scientific genius since Isaac Newton. He was thought to be a slow learner as a child because he did not talk at the same age as other children. Later in life, he recalled that at age two or three he wanted to speak in sentences. But he did not want to say sentences aloud until he was sure he had them right.

As a child, Einstein was quiet, serious, and solitary. He was also a daydreamer who did not impress his teachers. In this, he was unlike many geniuses who showed exceptional ability at an early age.

However, it was at this time that Einstein developed a desire to stay with a question until it was answered. He later called this his "flight from wonder."

THINK THROUGH HISTORY
A. Recognizing Effects Why were the ideas of Einstein and Freud revolutionary?

Literature in an Age of Doubt

The brutality of World War I caused philosophers and writers to question accepted ideas about reason and progress. Disillusioned by the war, many people also feared the future and expressed doubts about traditional religious beliefs. Some artists and writers expressed their anxieties by creating unsettling visions of the present and the future.

In 1922, T. S. Eliot, an American poet living in England, wrote that Western society had lost its spiritual values. He described the postwar world as a barren "waste land," drained of hope and faith. In 1924, the Irish poet William Butler Yeats conveyed a sense of dark times ahead in the poem "The Second Coming:" "Things fall apart; the centre cannot hold; / Mere anarchy is loosed upon the world . . ."

Thinkers React to Uncertainties In their search for meaning in an uncertain world, some thinkers turned to the philosophy known as **existentialism.** Leaders of this movement included the philosophers Jean Paul Sartre (SAHR·truh) of France and Karl Jaspers of Germany. Existentialists believed that there is no universal meaning to life. Each person gives his or her own meaning to life through choices made and actions taken. The existentialists would have their greatest influence after World War II.

The existentialists had been influenced by the German philosopher **Friedrich Nietzsche** (NEE·chuh). In the 1880s, Nietzsche wrote that Western society had put too much stress on such ideas as reason, democracy, and progress. This stifled actions based on emotion and instinct. As a result, individuality and creativity suffered. Nietzsche urged a return to the ancient heroic values of pride, assertiveness, and strength. He wrote that through willpower and courage, some humans could become supermen. They could rise above and control the common herd. His ideas attracted growing attention in the 20th century and had a great impact on politics in Italy and Germany in the 1920s and 1930s.

Writers Reflect Society's Concerns New attitudes also appeared in literature. The French poet Paul Valéry spoke for many writers of the 1920s when he described how he felt restless and uneasy:

A VOICE FROM THE PAST
We think of what has disappeared, and we are almost destroyed by what has been destroyed; we do not know what will be born, and we fear the future. . . . Doubt and disorder are in us and with us. There is no thinking man, however shrewd or learned he may be, who can hope to dominate this anxiety, to escape from this impression of darkness.

PAUL VALÉRY, *Variété*

The horror of war made a deep impression on many writers. The Czech-born author Franz Kafka wrote eerie novels like *The Trial* (1925) and *The Castle* (1926). His books featured people crushed in threatening situations they could neither understand nor escape. He started writing before the war, but much of his work was published after his death in 1924. It struck a chord among readers in the uneasy postwar years.

Many novels showed the influence of Freud's theories on the unconscious. The Irish-born author James Joyce caused a stir with his stream-of-consciousness novel *Ulysses* (1922). This lengthy book focused on a single day in the lives of three Dubliners. Joyce broke with normal sentence structure and vocabulary, trying to mirror the workings of the human mind.

The Lost Generation

During the 1920s, many American writers, musicians, and painters left the United States to live in Europe. Among them were writers Ernest Hemingway, John Dos Passos, and F. Scott Fitzgerald.

These expatriates, people who left their native country to live elsewhere, often settled in Paris. They gathered at the home of American writer Gertrude Stein. There they mixed with Europe's leading artists and intellectuals.

Stein called these expatriates the "Lost Generation." She remarked, "All of you young people who served in the war [World War I], you are the lost generation."

In his first major novel, *The Sun Also Rises* (1926), Hemingway captured the desperation of the young expatriate crowd. They moved frantically from one European city to another, trying to find meaning in life. Life empty of meaning is the theme of Fitzgerald's *The Great Gatsby* (1925).

The GREAT GATSBY

F·SCOTT·FITZGERALD

Vocabulary
stream of consciousness: a literary technique a writer uses to present a character's thoughts and feelings as they develop.

Rebellion in the Arts

Although many of the new directions in painting, architecture, and music began in the prewar period, they evolved after the war.

Painters Break Away from Tradition Artists rebelled against earlier realistic styles of painting. They wanted to depict the inner world of emotion and imagination rather than show realistic representations of objects. Expressionist painters like Paul Klee and Wassily Kandinsky used bold colors and distorted or exaggerated shapes and forms.

Inspired by traditional African art, Georges Braque of France and Pablo Picasso of Spain founded Cubism in 1907. Cubism transformed natural shapes into geometric forms. Objects were broken down into different parts with sharp angles and edges. Often several views were depicted at the same time.

The Dada movement (1916–1924) was as much a protest as an art movement. Its message was that established values had been made meaningless by the savagery of World War I. The term *Dada*, French for "hobbyhorse," was reportedly picked at random. Sounding like a nonsense word, it fit the spirit of the movement. Dadaist works were meant to be absurd, nonsensical, and meaningless.

Surrealism followed Dada. Inspired by Freud's ideas, **surrealism** was an art movement that sought to link the world of dreams with real life. The term *surreal* means "beyond or above reality."

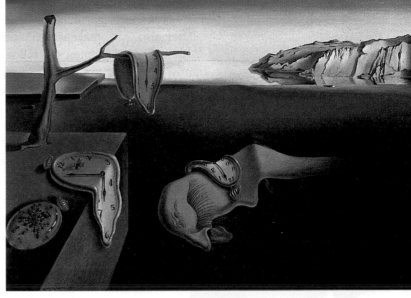

The Persistence of Memory, a surrealist work by Spanish artist Salvador Dali, 1931, shows watches melting in a desert landscape. Insects feed on the clockwork.

Surrealists tried to call on the unconscious part of their minds. Their paintings frequently had a dream-like quality and depicted objects in unrealistic ways.

Architects Move in New Directions An architectural revolution occurred when architects rejected traditional building styles for completely new forms. Instead of highly ornamented structures, they constructed buildings in which the design reflected the building's function or use. The American architect Frank Lloyd Wright pioneered this new style, known as functionalism. He designed houses featuring clean, low lines and open interiors that blended with the surrounding landscape. Walter Gropius led the functionalist movement in Germany. After the war, he started an art and design school in Weimar called the Bauhaus.

Composers Try New Styles In both classical and popular music, composers moved away from traditional styles. In his ballet masterpiece, *The Rite of Spring*, the Russian composer Igor Stravinsky used irregular rhythms and dissonances, or harsh combinations of sound. The audience booed and walked out of its opening performance. The Austrian composer Arnold Schoenberg rejected traditional harmonies and musical scales. He created his own 12-tone scale in which the notes were unrelated except as mathematical patterns.

A new popular musical style called **jazz** came out of the United States. It was developed by musicians, mainly African Americans, in New Orleans, Memphis, and Chicago. It swept the United States and Europe. The lively, loose beat of jazz seemed to capture the new freedom of the age. Uninhibited, energetic jazz dances, such as the Charleston and the Black Bottom, at first shocked respectable society before becoming widely accepted.

1920s. At first only the rich were able to afford air travel. Still, everyone enjoyed the exploits of the aviation pioneers, including Amelia Earhart. She was an American who, in 1932, became the first woman to fly solo across the Atlantic.

Radio Reaches Millions Guglielmo Marconi conducted his first successful experiments with radio in 1895. However, the real push for radio development came during World War I. The advantages of wireless communication in battle were so great that all countries gave radio research a high priority. Armies developed a wide range of radio equipment that would also have uses in peacetime.

In 1920, the world's first commercial radio station—KDKA in Pittsburgh, Pennsylvania—began broadcasting. Almost overnight, radio mania swept the United States. Soon every major city had stations broadcasting news, plays, and even live sporting events. In many European nations, unlike the United States, radio broadcasting was controlled by the government. In Great Britain, radio was a public monopoly run solely by the British Broadcasting Company, or BBC. Like Americans, however, Europeans eagerly listened to a variety of radio broadcasts. Soon most families owned a radio.

Movies Revolutionize Popular Entertainment In the 1920s, motion pictures were a major industry. Many countries, from Cuba to Japan, produced movies. In Europe, film was a serious art form. Directors like Sergei Eisenstein in Russia and Fritz Lang in Germany created films that explored psychological or political themes. However, in the Los Angeles suburb of Hollywood, where 90 percent of all films were made, movies were entertainment.

From Hollywood in the 1920s came the zany, slapstick comedies of Mack Sennett and his Keystone Kops, and dramas that starred Mary Pickford or Rudolph Valentino. But the king of the silent screen was the English-born Charlie Chaplin, a comic genius best known for his portrayal of the lonely little tramp bewildered by life. In the late 1920s, the addition of sound transformed movies. By the mid-1930s, nearly 90 million Americans escaped from the hardships of life by attending movies each week.

The advances in transportation and communication that followed the war had brought the world in closer touch. Countries had become more interdependent economically. Global prosperity came to depend on the economic well-being of all major nations, especially the United States.

Section ❶ Assessment

1. TERMS & NAMES

Identify
- Albert Einstein
- theory of relativity
- Sigmund Freud
- existentialism
- Friedrich Nietzsche
- surrealism
- jazz
- Charles Lindbergh

2. TAKING NOTES

Draw a chart like the one below. For each category shown, name two people you read about who contributed to that field.

FIELD	CONTRIBUTORS
philosophy	
literature	
art	
architecture	
music	

Write one or two sentences about their beliefs or contributions.

3. FORMING AN OPINION

In your opinion, whose ideas had a bigger impact on the world—Einstein's or Freud's? Give reasons to support your position.

THINK ABOUT
- the state of knowledge before their contributions
- the field in which they worked
- how life would be different without their contributions

4. THEME ACTIVITY

Science and Technology As a class, hold a media event. In small groups, choose a topic from the scientific and technological contributions of the 1920s. Collect pictures, audio tapes, biographies, or literature that represent the people or ideas you have chosen. Present your topic to the class and use your collection to help create a multimedia effect.

TERMS & NAMES
- coalition government
- Weimar Republic
- Great Depression
- Franklin D. Roosevelt
- New Deal

2 A Global Depression

MAIN IDEA	WHY IT MATTERS NOW
An economic depression in the United States spread throughout the world and lasted for a decade.	Many social and economic programs introduced worldwide to combat the Great Depression are still operating.

SETTING THE STAGE By the late 1920s, European nations were rebuilding war-torn economies. They were aided by loans from the more prosperous United States. In the United States, Americans seemed confident that the country would continue on the road to even greater economic prosperity. One sign of this was the booming stock market. Yet the American economy had serious weaknesses that were soon to bring about the most severe economic downturn the world had yet known.

Europe After the War

In both human suffering and economic terms, the cost of World War I was immense. The Great War left every major European country nearly bankrupt. Only the United States and Japan came out of the war in better financial shape than before. Neither had been a wartime battlefield. In fact, both had expanded their trade during the war. In addition, Europe's domination in world affairs had declined since the war. The long and brutal fight had drained the continent's resources.

THINK THROUGH HISTORY
A. Drawing Conclusions How did World War I change the balance of economic power in the world?

Demonstrators flee gunfire in the streets of Petrograd in 1917 as the Russian Provisional Government tries to fight off Bolshevik (Communist) revolutionaries.

New Democracies Are Unstable War's end saw the sudden rise of new democracies. From 1914 to 1918, Europe's last absolute rulers had been overthrown. The dynasties of the Hohenzollerns in Germany, the Hapsburgs in Austria-Hungary, the Romanovs in Russia, and the Ottomans in Turkey all ended. The first of the new governments was formed in Russia in 1917. The Provisional Government, as it was called, hoped to establish constitutional and democratic rule. However, within months it had fallen to a Communist dictatorship. Even so, for the first time, most European nations had democratic governments.

Many citizens of the new democracies had little experience with representative government. For generations, kings and emperors had ruled Germany and the new nations formed from Austria-Hungary. Even in France and Italy, whose parliaments had existed before World War I, the large number of political parties made effective government difficult. Some countries had a dozen or more political groups. In these countries, it was almost impossible for one party to win enough support to govern effectively. When no single party won a majority, a **coalition government,** or temporary alliance of several parties, was needed to form a parliamentary majority. Because the parties disagreed on so many policies, coalitions seldom lasted very long. France,

for example, endured some 40 changes of government from 1919 to 1939.

Frequent changes in government made it hard for democratic countries to develop strong leadership and move toward long-term goals. In peaceful times, a country could get by with weak leadership. However, the weaknesses of a coalition government became a major problem in times of crisis. Voters in several countries were then willing to sacrifice democracy for strong, totalitarian leadership.

Weimar Republic Is Weak Germany's new democratic government was set up in 1919. Known as the **Weimar** (WY·MAHR) **Republic,** it was named after the city where the national assembly met. The Weimar Republic had serious weaknesses from the start. First, Germany lacked a strong democratic tradition. Furthermore, postwar Germany had several major political parties and many minor ones. Worst of all, millions of Germans blamed the Weimar government, not their wartime leaders, for the country's defeat and postwar humiliation. It was, after all, the Weimar government that had signed the Treaty of Versailles.

"Money to burn"—this German woman uses millions of marks made worthless by inflation as heating fuel in the early 1920s.

THINK THROUGH HISTORY
B. Identifying Problems What political problems did the Weimar Republic face?

Inflation Causes Crisis in Germany Germany also faced enormous economic problems that began during the war. Unlike Britain and France, Germany did not greatly increase its wartime taxes. To pay the expenses of the war, the Germans simply printed money. After Germany's defeat, this paper money steadily lost its value. Burdened with heavy reparations payments to the Allies and with other economic problems, Germany printed even more money. The result was the value of the mark, as Germany's currency was called, fell sharply. Severe inflation set in. Germans needed more and more money to buy even the most basic goods. For example, in Berlin a loaf of bread cost less than a mark in 1918, more than 160 marks in 1922, and some 200 billion marks by late 1923. People took wheelbarrows full of money to buy food. The mark had become worthless.

Consequently, people with fixed incomes saw their life savings become worthless. The money people had saved to buy a house now barely covered the cost of a table. Many Germans also questioned the value of their new democratic government.

Background
Germany's reparations payments for damages caused during World War I totaled $33 billion.

Attempts at Economic Stability Germany recovered from the 1923 inflation thanks largely to the work of an international committee. The committee was headed by Charles Dawes, an American banker. The Dawes Plan provided for a $200 million loan from American banks to stabilize German currency and strengthen its economy. The plan also set a more realistic schedule for Germany's reparations payments.

Put into effect in 1924, the Dawes Plan helped slow inflation. As the German economy began to recover, it attracted more loans and investments from the United States. By 1929, German factories were producing as much as they had before the war.

Efforts at a Lasting Peace As prosperity returned, Germany's foreign minister, Gustav Stresemann (STRAY·zuh·MAHN), and France's foreign minister, Aristide Briand (bree·AHND), tried to improve relations between their countries. In 1925, they met in Locarno, Switzerland, with officials from Belgium, Italy, and Britain. They signed a treaty promising that France and Germany would never again make war against each other. Germany also agreed to respect the existing borders of France and Belgium. It then was admitted to the League of Nations.

In 1928, the hopes raised by the "spirit of Locarno" led to the Kellogg-Briand peace pact. Frank Kellogg, the U.S. Secretary of State, arranged this agreement with France's Briand. Almost every country in the world, including the Soviet Union, signed. They pledged "to renounce war as an instrument of national policy."

Unfortunately, the treaty had no means to enforce its provisions. The League of Nations, the obvious choice as enforcer, had no armed forces. The refusal of the United States to join the League also weakened it. Nonetheless, the peace agreements seemed a good start. In addition, Europeans were enjoying an economic boom based largely on massive American investment.

The Great Depression

In the late 1920s, the world economy was like a delicately balanced house of cards. The key card that held up the rest was American economic prosperity. If the United States economy weakened, the whole world's economic system might collapse. In 1929, it did.

A Flawed U.S. Economy Despite prosperity, three weaknesses in the U.S. economy caused serious problems. These were uneven distribution of wealth, overproduction by business and agriculture, and lessening demand for consumer goods.

By 1929, American factories were turning out nearly half of the world's industrial goods. The rising productivity led to enormous profits. However, this new wealth was not evenly distributed. The richest 5 percent of the population received 33 percent of all personal income in 1929. Yet 60 percent of all American families earned less than $2,000 a year. Thus, most families were too poor to buy the goods being produced. Unable to sell all their goods, store owners eventually cut back their orders from factories. Factories in turn reduced production and laid off workers. A downward economic spiral began. As more workers lost their jobs, families bought even fewer goods. In turn, factories made further cuts in production and laid off more workers.

During the 1920s, overproduction affected American farmers as well. Scientific farming methods and new farm machinery had dramatically increased crop yields. American farmers were producing more food. Meanwhile they faced new competition from farmers in Australia, Latin America, and Europe. As a result, a worldwide surplus of agricultural products drove prices and profits down.

THINK THROUGH HISTORY
C. Identifying Problems What major weaknesses had appeared in the American economy by 1929?

Unable to sell their crops at a profit, many farmers could not pay off the bank loans that kept them in business. Their unpaid debts weakened banks and forced some to close. The danger signs of overproduction by factories and farms should have warned people against gambling on the stock market. Yet no one heeded the warning.

The Stock Market Crashes In 1929, Wall Street, in New York City, was the financial capital of the world. Banks and investment companies lined its sidewalks. At Wall Street's New York Stock Exchange, optimism about the booming U.S. economy showed in soaring prices for stocks. To get in on the boom, many middle-income people began buying stocks on margin. This meant that they paid a small percentage of a stock's price as a down payment and borrowed the rest from a stockbroker. The

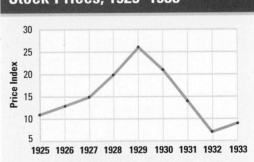

Stock Prices, 1925–1933

Price Index

Graph-Source: *Historical Statistics of the United States*

SKILLBUILDER: Interpreting Graphs
1. *What year did stock prices fall lowest before beginning to rise again?*
2. *What was the average stock price in 1929? in 1932?*

Daily *Life*

Life in the Depression

During the Great Depression of 1929 to 1939, millions of people world-wide lost their jobs or their farms. They faced a future without hope.

At first the unemployed had to depend on the charity of others to survive. Here unemployed workers in Paris wait in line for free bread. Many jobless and their families begged for food, clothing, and shelter. Some lost their homes and had to live in shanties, or shacks. Others turned to thievery or abandoned their families.

Local governments and charities opened soup kitchens to provide free food. There were long lines of applicants for what work was available, and these jobs usually paid low wages.

Conditions improved when national governments established programs for relief. However, recovery came slowly. The Depression ended only when nations began gearing up for war.

system worked well as long as stock prices were rising. However, if they fell, investors had no money to pay off the loan.

In September 1929, some investors began to feel that stock prices were unnaturally high. They started selling their stocks, believing the rates would soon go down. By Thursday, October 24, the gradual lowering of stock prices had became an all-out slide downward. A panic resulted. Everyone wanted to sell stocks, and no one wanted to buy. Prices sank quickly. The wild shouting of 1,000 brokers and their assistants at the Stock Exchange became what one observer called a "weird roar." Prices plunged to a new low on Tuesday, October 29. A record 16 million stocks were sold. Then the market collapsed.

In the stock market crash, billions of dollars in "paper wealth" simply vanished. People could not pay the money they owed on margin purchases. Stocks they had bought at high prices were now worthless. Within months of the crash, unemployment rates began to rise as industrial production, prices, and wages declined. A long business slump, or depression, followed. The **Great Depression,** as it came to be called, touched every corner of the American economy. By 1932, factory production had been cut in half. Thousands of businesses failed, and banks closed. Around 9 million people lost the money in their savings accounts when banks had no money to pay them. Many farmers lost their lands when they could not make mortgage payments. By 1933 one-fourth of all American workers had no jobs.

A Global Depression The collapse of the American economy sent shock waves around the world. Worried American bankers demanded repayment of their overseas loans, and American investors withdrew their money from Europe. The American market for European goods dropped sharply as the U.S. Congress placed high tariffs on imported goods so that American dollars would stay in the United States and support American workers. The government was trying to force Americans to buy American goods. This policy backfired. Conditions worsened for the United States. Many countries who depended on exporting goods to the United States also suffered. Moreover, when the United States raised tariffs, it set off a chain reaction. Other nations imposed their own higher tariffs. World trade dropped

Background
The day of the stock market crash, Tuesday, October 29, 1929, is called "Black Tuesday."

Vocabulary
tariffs: taxes charged by a government on imported or exported goods.

Unemployment Rate, 1928–1938

Unemployment Rate, 1928–1938

- Hitler comes to power
- Roosevelt begins New Deal
- Stock market crashes

Great Britain ■ Germany ■ United States

Sources: *European Historical Statistics: 1750–1970;*
Historical Statistics of the United States: Colonial Times to 1970.

SKILLBUILDER: Interpreting Graphs

1. *What nation had the highest rate of unemployment? How high did it reach?*
2. *When did unemployment begin to decrease in the United States? Germany? Great Britain?*

THINK THROUGH HISTORY
D. Synthesizing
What problems did the collapse of the American economy cause in other countries?

by 65 percent. This contributed further to the economic downturn. Unemployment rates soared.

Because of war debts and dependence on American loans and investments, Germany and Austria were particularly hard hit. In 1931, Austria's largest bank failed. This started a financial panic in central European countries and sent their economies plunging.

In Asia, the Japanese economy also slumped. Japanese farmers suffered greatly during the Depression. In the rice-growing areas of the northeast, crop failures in 1931 led to famine. Starving families ate tree bark and the roots of wild plants. City workers suffered, too, as the value of exports fell by half between 1929 and 1931. As many as 3 million workers lost their jobs, forcing many to go back to their rural villages.

The economic crisis fell heavily in Latin America as well. Many of its nations were tied to the global economy by trade in such cash crops or raw materials as sugar, beef, copper, and tin. During the 1920s, world prices and market demand for these products were already dropping. As European and U.S. demand for Latin American products dried up in the 1930s, prices for these goods collapsed. At the same time, the cost of imported goods rose, pushed up by high tariffs. Latin American nations that had borrowed heavily from other nations could not repay their debts. The worldwide crisis spread rapidly.

The World Responds to the Crisis

The Depression confronted democracies with a serious challenge to their economic and political systems. Each country met the crisis in its own way.

Britain Takes Steps to Improve Its Economy Because its economy depended on foreign trade, the Depression hit Britain severely. To meet the emergency, British voters elected a multi-party coalition known as the National Government. This government's policies were designed to rescue the nation from economic calamity. It passed high protective tariffs, increased taxes, and regulated the currency. It also lowered interest rates to encourage industrial growth. These measures brought about a slow but steady recovery. By 1937, unemployment had been cut in half, and production had risen above 1929 levels. Britain avoided political extremes and preserved democracy.

France Responds to Economic Crisis Unlike Britain, France had a more self-sufficient economy. In 1930, it was still heavily agricultural and less dependent on foreign trade. Thus, France was somewhat cushioned against the Depression. Nevertheless, by 1935, one million French workers were unemployed.

The economic crisis contributed to political instability. In 1933, five coalition governments formed and fell. Many political leaders were frightened by the growth of anti-democratic forces both in France and in other parts of Europe. So in 1936, moderates, Socialists, and Communists formed a coalition. The Popular Front, as it was called, passed a series of reforms to help the workers. These reforms included pay increases, holidays with pay, and a 40-hour work week. Unfortunately, price increases quickly offset wage gains. Unemployment remained high. Yet France also preserved democratic government.

Background
Scandinavia, in northern Europe, includes Sweden, Norway, and Denmark. Finland and Iceland are often also included in the region.

Socialist Governments Find Solutions The Socialist governments in the Scandinavian countries of Denmark, Sweden, and Norway also met the challenge of economic crisis successfully. They built their recovery programs on an existing

economy and rebuilding its armed forces. He vowed to give Italy strong leadership. Mussolini had founded the Fascist Party in 1919. At first, he failed to win widespread support. As economic conditions worsened, however, his popularity rapidly increased. Finally, Mussolini publicly criticized Italy's government. Groups of Fascists wearing black shirts attacked Communists and Socialists on the streets. This campaign of terror weakened his opponents. Because Mussolini played on the fear of a workers' revolt, he began to win support from the middle classes, the aristocracy, and industrial leaders.

In October 1922, about 30,000 Fascists marched on Rome. They demanded that King Victor Emmanuel III put Mussolini in charge of the government. The king decided that Mussolini was the best hope for his dynasty to survive, so he let Mussolini form a government. Thus, after widespread violence and a threat of armed uprising, Mussolini took power "legally." At the time, a foreign diplomat described him as "an actor, a dangerous rascal, and possibly slightly off his head."

Il Duce's Leadership Mussolini was now Il Duce (ihl DOO·chay), or the leader. He abolished democracy and outlawed all political parties except the Fascists. Secret police jailed his opponents. Government censors forced radio stations and publications to broadcast or publish only Fascist doctrines. Mussolini outlawed strikes. He sought to control the economy by allying the Fascists with the industrialists and large landowners.

Under his leadership, Italy became the model for Fascists in other countries. However, Mussolini never had the total control achieved by Joseph Stalin in the Soviet Union or Adolf Hitler in Germany.

Hitler Takes Control in Germany

When Mussolini became dictator of Italy in the mid-1920s, **Adolf Hitler** was a little-known political leader whose early life had been marked by disappointment. Born in a small town in Austria in 1889, he dropped out of high school and failed as an artist. When World War I broke out, Hitler found a new beginning. He would fight to defend Germany and crush its opponents. He volunteered for the German army and was twice awarded the Iron Cross, a medal for bravery.

The Rise of the Nazis At the end of the war, Hitler settled in Munich. In early 1920, he joined a tiny right-wing political group. This group shared his belief that Germany had to overturn the Treaty of Versailles and combat communism. The group later named itself the National Socialist German Workers' Party, called Nazi for short. Its policies, supported by people in the middle and lower middle classes, formed the German brand of fascism known as **Nazism.** The party adopted the swastika, or hooked cross, as its symbol. The Nazis also set up a private militia called the storm troopers or Brownshirts.

Within a short time, Hitler's success as an organizer and speaker led him to be chosen *der Führer* (duhr FYUR·uhr), or the leader, of the Nazi

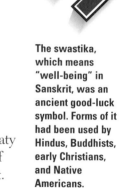

The swastika, which means "well-being" in Sanskrit, was an ancient good-luck symbol. Forms of it had been used by Hindus, Buddhists, early Christians, and Native Americans.

"Heil Hitler!" Hitler Youth members salute their Führer at a rally in the 1930s. Hitler skillfully used mass rallies to generate enthusiasm.

party. These skills also helped make the Nazis a growing political force. Inspired by Mussolini's march on Rome, Hitler and the Nazis plotted to seize power in Munich in 1923. The attempt failed, and Hitler was arrested. He was tried for treason, but sympathetic judges sentenced him to only five years in prison. He served less than nine months.

While in jail, Hitler wrote **Mein Kampf** (*My Struggle*). This book set forth his beliefs and his goals for Germany. It became the blueprint, or plan of action, for the Nazis. Hitler asserted that the Germans, especially those who were blond and blue-eyed—whom he incorrectly called "Aryans"—were a "master race." He declared that non-Aryan "races"—such as Jews, Slavs, and Gypsies—were inferior or subhuman. He called the Versailles Treaty an outrage and vowed to regain the lands taken from Germany. Hitler also declared that Germany was overcrowded and needed more **lebensraum,** or living space. He promised to get that space by conquering eastern Europe and Russia.

After leaving prison in 1924, Hitler revived the Nazi party. Most Germans ignored him and his angry message until the Depression ended the nation's brief postwar recovery. When American loans stopped, the German economy collapsed. Factories ground to a halt and banks closed. Nearly six million people, about 30 percent of Germany's work force, were unemployed in 1932. Civil unrest broke out. Frightened and confused, Germans now turned to Hitler, hoping for security and firm leadership.

Hitler Becomes Chancellor The Nazis had become the largest political party by 1932. Conservative leaders mistakenly believed they could control Hitler and use him for their purposes. In January 1933, they advised President Paul von Hindenburg to name Hitler chancellor. Only Hitler, they said, could stand up to the strong Communist party in Germany. Thus Hitler came to power legally. Soon after, General Erich Ludendorff, a former Hitler ally, wrote to Hindenburg:

> **A VOICE FROM THE PAST**
> By naming Hitler as *Reichschancellor,* you have delivered up our holy Fatherland to one of the greatest [rabblerousers] of all time. I solemnly [predict] that this accursed man will plunge our Reich into the abyss and bring our nation into inconceivable misery.
> **ERICH LUDENDORFF,** from a letter to President Hindenburg, February 1, 1933

Once in office, Hitler acted quickly to strengthen his position. He called for new elections, hoping to win a parliamentary majority. Six days before the election, a fire destroyed the Reichstag building where parliament met. The Nazis blamed the Communists. By stirring up fear of the Communists, the Nazis and their allies won a slim majority.

With majority control, Hitler demanded dictatorial, or absolute, power for four years. Only one deputy dared to speak against the resulting Enabling Act. Hitler used his new power to turn Germany into a totalitarian state. He banned all other political parties and had opponents arrested. Meanwhile, an elite, black-uniformed unit called the SS (*Schutzstaffel,* or protection squad) was created. It was loyal only to Hitler. In 1934, the SS arrested and murdered hundreds of Hitler's enemies. This brutal action and the terror applied by the Gestapo, the Nazi secret police, shocked most Germans into total obedience.

The Nazis quickly took command of the economy. New laws banned strikes, dissolved independent labor unions, and gave the government authority over business and labor. Hitler put millions of Germans to work. They constructed factories, built highways, manufactured weapons, and served in the military. As a result, unemployment dropped from about 6 to 1.5 million in 1936.

The Führer Is Supreme Hitler wanted more than just economic and political power—he wanted control over every aspect of German life. To shape public opinion and to win

THINK THROUGH HISTORY
B. Summarizing What were the key ideas and goals that Hitler presented in *Mein Kampf?*

Vocabulary
chancellor: the prime minister in certain countries

THINK THROUGH HISTORY
C. Making Inferences Why did Germans at first support Hitler?

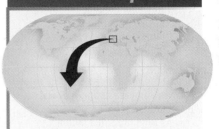

Global Impact

Fascism to Argentina
Juan Perón served as Argentina's president from 1946 to 1955 and again in 1973 and 1974. The two years he spent in Europe before World War II greatly influenced his strong-man rule.

A career army officer, Perón went to Italy in 1939 for military training. He then served at the Argentine embassy in Rome. A visit to Berlin gave Perón a chance to see Nazi Germany. The ability of Hitler and Mussolini to manipulate their citizens impressed Perón.

When Perón himself gained power, he patterned his military dictatorship on that of the European Fascists. Like them, he restrained his opponents through press censorship and suppression of civil rights. But he never achieved the same total control as his fascist role models.

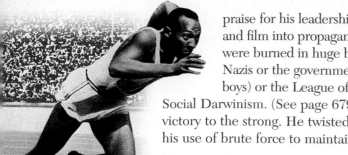

praise for his leadership, Hitler turned the press, radio, literature, painting, and film into propaganda tools. Books that did not conform to Nazi beliefs were burned in huge bonfires. Churches were forbidden to criticize the Nazis or the government. Schoolchildren had to join the Hitler Youth (for boys) or the League of German Girls. Hitler was greatly influenced by Social Darwinism. (See page 679.) He believed that a continuous struggle brought victory to the strong. He twisted the philosophy of Friedrich Nietzsche to support his use of brute force to maintain power and his glorification of war.

Hitler Makes War on the Jews Hatred of Jews, or anti-Semitism, was a key part of Nazi ideology. Although Jews were less than one percent of the population, the Nazis used them as scapegoats for all Germany's troubles since the war. This led to a wave of anti-Semitism across Germany. Beginning in 1933, the Nazis passed laws depriving Jews of most of their rights. Violence against Jews mounted. On the night of November 9, 1938, Nazi mobs attacked Jews in their homes and on the streets and destroyed thousands of Jewish-owned buildings. This rampage, called *Kristallnacht* (Night of the Broken Glass), signaled the real start of the process of eliminating the Jews from German life. (See Chapter 32.)

Background
The term *anti-Semitism* is derived from the fact that the earliest Jews were Semites (people who spoke a Semitic language).

Other Countries Fall to Dictators

While Fascists took power in Italy and Germany, the nations formed in eastern Europe after World War I also were falling to dictators. The parliamentary governments that had been set up in these countries rarely lasted. In Hungary in 1919, after a brief Communist regime, military forces and wealthy landowners joined to make Admiral Miklós Horthy the first European postwar dictator. In Poland, Marshal Joseph Pilsudski (pihl·SOOT·skee) seized power in 1926. In Yugoslavia, Albania, Bulgaria, and Romania, kings turned to strong-man rule. They suspended constitutions and silenced foes. In 1935, one democracy, Czechoslovakia, remained in eastern Europe.

Elsewhere in Europe, only in nations with strong democratic traditions—Britain, France, and the Scandinavian countries—did democracy survive. With no democratic experience and severe economic problems, many Europeans saw dictatorship as the only way to prevent instability. Although all of these dictatorships restricted civil rights, none asserted control with the brutality of the Russian Communists or the Nazis.

By the mid-1930s, the powerful nations of the world were split into two antagonistic camps—democratic and totalitarian. And to gain their ends, the Fascist dictatorships had indicated a willingness to use military aggression.

Section 3 Assessment

1. TERMS & NAMES

Identify
• fascism
• Benito Mussolini
• Adolf Hitler
• Nazism
• *Mein Kampf*
• *lebensraum*

2. TAKING NOTES

Draw a chart like the one below. Compare Mussolini and Hitler by completing the chart.

	Hitler	Mussolini
Method of taking power		
Style of leadership		
Handling of economic crisis		
Goals		

Were the two more alike or different? Explain why.

3. DRAWING CONCLUSIONS

Why did a movement like fascism and leaders like Mussolini and Hitler come to power during a period of crisis?

THINK ABOUT
• what problems Italy and Germany faced
• political traditions in each country
• the state of the world at the time

4. THEME ACTIVITY

Power and Authority
Imagine you live in Italy and it is 1933, ten years since Benito Mussolini became dictator. In Germany, President Paul von Hindenburg is considering appointing Adolf Hitler, a Fascist like Mussolini, chancellor of Germany. What would you advise Hindenburg to do? Write him a letter telling him what has happened in your country under a fascist dictatorship.

TERMS & NAMES
• appeasement
• Axis Powers
• Francisco Franco
• isolationism
• Third Reich
• Munich Conference

4 Aggressors on the March

MAIN IDEA

As Germany, Italy, and Japan conquered other countries, the rest of the world did nothing to stop them.

WHY IT MATTERS NOW

Many nations today take a more active and collective role in world affairs, as in the United Nations.

SETTING THE STAGE By the mid-1930s, Germany and Italy seemed bent on military conquest. The major democracies—Britain, France, and the United States—were distracted by economic problems at home and longed to remain at peace. The Soviet Union was not committed to either camp. With the world moving toward war, many people pinned their hopes for peace on the League of Nations.

World Drifts Toward War

As fascism spread in Europe, a powerful nation in Asia moved toward a similar system. Following a period of reform and progress in the 1920s, Japan fell under military rule.

Democracy Struggles in Japan During the 1920s, the Japanese government became more democratic. In 1922, Japan signed an international treaty agreeing to respect China's borders. In 1928, it signed the Kellogg-Briand Pact renouncing war. Japan's parliamentary system had several weaknesses, however. Its constitution put strict limits on the powers of the prime minister and the cabinet. Most importantly, civilian leaders had little control over the armed forces. Military leaders reported only to the emperor.

Militarists Take Control of Japan As long as Japan remained prosperous, the civilian government kept power. When the Great Depression struck in 1930, the government was blamed. Military leaders gained support and soon won control of the country. Unlike the Fascists in Europe, the militarists did not try to establish a new system of government. They wanted to restore traditional control of the government to the military. Instead of a forceful leader like Mussolini or Hitler, the militarists made the emperor the symbol of state power.

Keeping Emperor Hirohito as head of state won popular support for the army leaders who ruled in his name. Like Hitler and Mussolini, Japan's militarists were extreme nationalists. They wanted to solve the country's economic problems by foreign expansion. They planned a Pacific empire that included a conquered China. The empire would provide Japan with raw materials and markets for its goods. It would also give Japan room for its rising population.

Japan Invades Manchuria Japanese businesses had invested heavily in China's northeast province, Manchuria. It was an area rich in iron and coal. In 1931, the Japanese army seized Manchuria, despite objections from the Japanese parliament. The army then set up a puppet government. Japanese engineers and technicians began arriving in large numbers to build mines and factories.

Victorious Japanese troops march through the streets after occupying Manchuria in 1931.

Background
The control of the government by the military had centuries-old roots in Japanese history. The shoguns had been military leaders.

THINK THROUGH HISTORY
A. Comparing
Compare the militarists in Japan with the European Fascists.

The Japanese attack on Manchuria was the first direct challenge to the League of Nations. In the early 1930s, the League's members included all major democracies except the United States. Also members were the three countries that posed the greatest threat to peace—Germany, Japan, and Italy. When Japan seized Manchuria, many League members vigorously protested. The League condemned Japanese aggression, but it had no power to enforce its decisions. Japan ignored the protests and withdrew from the League in 1933.

THINK THROUGH HISTORY
B. Making Inferences What was the major weakness of the League of Nations? Why?

Japan Invades China Four years later, a border incident touched off a full-scale war between Japan and China. On July 7, 1937, the Japanese and the Chinese exchanged shots at a railroad bridge near Beijing. Japanese forces then swept into northern China. Despite having a million soldiers, China's army led by Jiang Jieshi was no match for the better equipped and trained Japanese.

Beijing and other northern cities as well as the capital, Nanjing, fell to the Japanese in 1937. Japanese troops killed tens of thousands of captured soldiers and civilians in Nanjing. Forced to retreat westward, Jiang Jieshi set up a new capital at Chongqing. At the same time, Chinese guerrillas led by China's Communist leader, Mao Zedong, continued to fight in the conquered area.

Mussolini Attacks Ethiopia The League's failure to stop the Japanese encouraged Mussolini to plan aggression of his own. Mussolini dreamed of building a colonial empire in Africa like that of Britain and France. He bitterly complained that Britain and France had left only "a collection of deserts" from which to choose.

Ethiopia was one of Africa's four remaining independent nations. The Ethiopians had successfully resisted an Italian attempt at conquest during the 1890s. To avenge that defeat, Mussolini ordered a massive invasion of Ethiopia in October 1935. The spears and swords of the Ethiopians were no match for Italian airplanes, tanks, guns, and poison gas. In May 1936, Mussolini told a cheering crowd that "Italy has at last her empire . . . a Fascist empire."

The Ethiopian emperor Haile Selassie urgently appealed to the League for help. Although the League condemned the attack, its members did nothing. Britain continued to let Italian troops and supplies pass through the British-controlled Suez Canal on their way to Ethiopia. By giving in to Mussolini in Africa, Britain and France hoped to keep peace in Europe.

Hitler Defies Versailles Treaty Hitler had long pledged to undo the Versailles Treaty. Among its provisions, the treaty limited the size of Germany's army. In March 1935, the Führer announced that Germany would not obey these restrictions. In fact, Germany had already begun rebuilding its armed forces. The League issued only a mild condemnation. Banners throughout Germany announced, "Today Germany! Tomorrow the World!"

HISTORY MAKERS

HAILE SELASSIE
1892–1975

Haile Selassie, the emperor of Ethiopia, belonged to a dynasty that traced its roots back to King Solomon and the Queen of Sheba. When he became emperor in 1930, he was hailed as the 111th descendant of Solomon and Sheba to rule.

Five years after he took the throne, his country was invaded by Italy. Selassie was forced into exile. On June 30, 1936, he appeared before the League of Nations to plead for its help.

He warned League members that if they failed to impose military sanctions on Italy, "God and history will remember your judgment. . . . It is us today. It will be you tomorrow." The League did not heed his warning.

Aggression in Europe and Asia, 1930–1939

September 1931 Japan invades Manchuria.

October 1935 Italy attacks Ethiopia.

March 1938 Germany annexes Austria.

September 1938 Germany takes Sudetenland.

1930   1935   1939

March 1936 Germany occupies Rhineland.

July 1937 Japan invades China.

March 1939 Germany seizes Czechoslovakia.

April 1939 Italy conquers Albania

The League's failure to stop Germany from rearming convinced Hitler to take even greater risks. The treaty had forbidden German troops to enter a 30-mile-wide zone on either side of the Rhine River. Known as the Rhineland, it formed a buffer zone between Germany and France. It was also an important industrial area. On March 7, 1936, German troops moved into the Rhineland. Stunned, the French were unwilling to risk war. The British urged **appeasement,** giving in to an aggressor to keep peace.

Hitler later admitted that he would have backed down if the French and British had challenged him. The German reoccupation of the Rhineland marked a turning point in the march toward war. First, it strengthened Hitler's power and prestige within Germany. Cautious generals who had urged restraint now agreed to follow him. Second, the balance of power changed in Germany's favor. France and Belgium were now open to attack from German troops. Finally, the weak response by France and Britain encouraged Hitler to speed up his military and territorial expansion.

Hitler's growing strength convinced Mussolini that he should seek an alliance with Germany. In October 1936, the two dictators reached an agreement that became known as the Rome-Berlin Axis. A month later, Germany also made an agreement with Japan. Germany, Italy, and Japan came to be called the **Axis Powers.**

Civil War Erupts in Spain Hitler and Mussolini again tested the will of the democracies of Europe in the Spanish civil war. Spain had been a monarchy until 1931, when a republic was declared. The government, run by liberals and socialists, held office amid many crises. In July 1936, army leaders, favoring a Fascist-style government, joined General **Francisco Franco** in a revolt. Thus began a civil war that dragged on for three years.

Hitler and Mussolini sent troops, tanks, and airplanes to help Franco's forces, which were called the Nationalists. The armed forces of

Vocabulary
axis: a straight line around which an object rotates. Hitler and Mussolini expected their alliance to become the axis around which Europe would rotate.

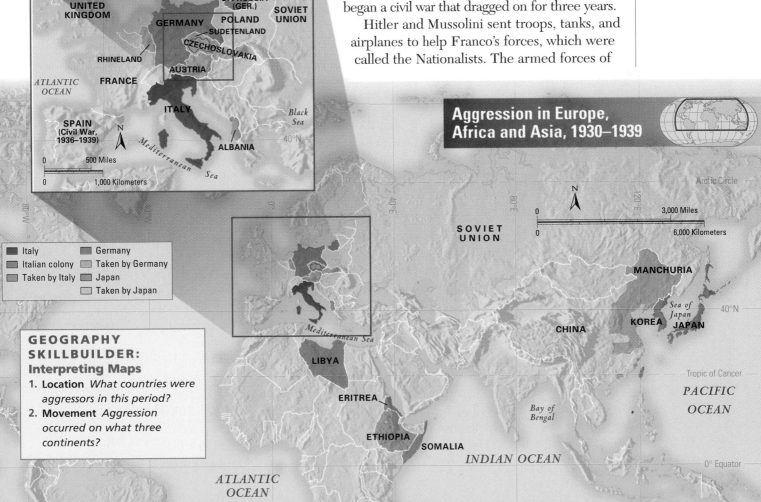

GEOGRAPHY SKILLBUILDER: Interpreting Maps
1. **Location** What countries were aggressors in this period?
2. **Movement** Aggression occurred on what three continents?

Aggression in Europe, Africa and Asia, 1930–1939

Connect *to* History

Analyzing Visuals How does Picasso's use of image and color depict the horrors of the Spanish Civil War?

SEE SKILLBUILDER HANDBOOK, PAGE 1007

Connect *to* Today

Research Research the civil war in Bosnia. Collect different types of visuals that show the horror of that war. Describe your selections.

The Spanish artist Pablo Picasso painted *Guernica* shortly after Nazi planes destroyed the ancient Basque city of Guernica in 1937. The air attacks killed a thousand people, one out of every eight residents. At left, a mother cries over her dead child. In the center, a horse screams and a soldier lies dead. At right, a woman falls from a burning house. The canvas is huge—11 feet high and 25 feet long.

the Republicans, as supporters of Spain's elected government were known, received little help from abroad. The Western democracies remained neutral. Only the Soviet Union sent equipment and advisers. An International Brigade of volunteers fought on the Republican side but had little chance against a professional army. Early in 1939, Republican resistance collapsed. Franco became Spain's Fascist dictator.

THINK THROUGH HISTORY
C. Summarizing What foreign countries were involved in the Spanish Civil War?

Western Democracies Fail to Halt Aggression

Instead of taking a stand against Fascist aggression in the 1930s, Britain and France repeatedly made concessions, hoping to keep peace. Both nations were dealing with serious economic problems as a result of the Great Depression. In addition, the horrors of World War I had created a deep desire to avoid war. Allowing Hitler and Mussolini small territorial gains seemed a small price to pay for peace.

United States Follows an Isolationist Policy Many Americans resisted accepting the nation's new position as a world leader. **Isolationism**—the belief that political ties to other countries should be avoided—won wide support. Isolationists argued that entry into World War I had been a costly error. They were determined to prevent a repeat of this mistake. Beginning in 1935, Congress passed three Neutrality Acts. These laws banned loans and the sale of arms to nations at war. The isolationists believed this action would keep the United States out of another foreign war.

The German Reich Expands On November 5, 1937, Hitler announced to his advisers his plans to absorb Austria and Czechoslovakia into the **Third Reich** (ryk), or German Empire. The Germans would then expand into Poland and Russia. Hitler's first target was Austria. The Treaty of Versailles prohibited Anschluss (AHN·SHLUS), or a union between Austria and Germany. However, many Austrians supported unity with Germany. In March 1938, Hitler sent his army into Austria and annexed it. France and Britain ignored their pledge to protect Austrian independence.

Hitler next turned to Czechoslovakia. After World War I, Czechoslovakia had developed into a prosperous democracy with a strong army and a defense treaty with France. About 3 million German-speaking people lived in the western border regions of Czechoslovakia called the Sudetenland. (See map, page 813.) This heavily fortified area formed the Czechs' main defense against Germany. The Anschluss raised pro-Nazi feelings among Sudeten Germans. In September 1938, Hitler demanded that the Sudetenland be given to Germany. The Czechs refused and asked France for help.

Background
According to Hitler, there were three great German empires. They were the Holy Roman Empire; the German Empire of 1871–1918; and the Third Reich, ruled by the Nazis. The Third Reich, Hitler believed, would last 1,000 years.

Britain and France Again Choose Appeasement France and Britain were preparing for war when Mussolini proposed a meeting of Germany, France, Britain, and Italy in Munich, Germany. The **Munich Conference** was held on September 29, 1938. The Czechs were not invited. British Prime Minister Neville Chamberlain believed that he could preserve peace by giving in to Hitler's demand. The next morning, a tense world learned that the crisis was over. Britain and France agreed that Hitler could take the Sudetenland. In exchange, Hitler pledged to respect Czechoslovakia's new borders.

Chamberlain's policy of appeasement seemed to have prevented war. When he returned to London, Chamberlain told cheering crowds, "I believe it is peace for our time." Winston Churchill, then a member of the British Parliament, strongly disagreed. He opposed the appeasement policy and gloomily warned of its consequences.

A VOICE FROM THE PAST
We are in the presence of a disaster of the first magnitude. . . . we have sustained a defeat without a war. . . . And do not suppose that this is the end. . . . This is only the first sip, the first foretaste of a bitter cup which will be proffered to us year by year unless, by a supreme recovery of moral health and martial vigor, we arise again and take our stand for freedom as in the olden time.

WINSTON CHURCHILL, speech before the House of Commons, October 5, 1938

THINK THROUGH HISTORY
D. Recognizing Effects What were the effects of isolationism and appeasement?

Less than six months after the Munich meeting, Hitler's troops took Czechoslovakia. Soon after, Mussolini seized nearby Albania. Then Hitler demanded that Poland return the former German port of Danzig. The Poles refused and turned to Britain and France for aid. Both countries said they would guarantee Polish independence. But appeasement had convinced Hitler that neither nation would risk war.

Nazis and Soviets Sign Nonaggression Pact Britain and France asked the Soviet Union to join them in stopping Hitler's aggression. Negotiations proceeded slowly. The two democracies distrusted the Communist government, and Stalin resented having been left out of the Munich Conference. As the Soviet leader talked with Britain and France, he also bargained with Hitler. The two dictators reached an agreement. Once bitter enemies, fascist Germany and communist Russia now publicly committed never to attack one another. On August 23, 1939, a nonaggression pact was signed. As the Axis Powers moved unchecked at the end of the decade, the whole world waited to see what would happen next. War appeared inevitable.

CONNECT to TODAY

Aggression in the Persian Gulf
After World War II, the Munich Conference of 1938 became a symbol for surrender. Leaders of democracies vowed never again to appease a ruthless dictator. U.S. President George Bush used Munich as an example when responding to aggression in the Persian Gulf in 1990.

When troops of Iraqi dictator Saddam Hussein invaded nearby Kuwait, the United States responded to Kuwait's call for help by forming a coalition of forces to fight the Persian Gulf War. In explaining why, Bush noted how Britain's Neville Chamberlain failed to help Czechoslovakia after Hitler claimed the Sudetenland. Bush said:

The world cannot turn a blind eye to aggression. You know the tragic consequences when nations, confronted with aggression, choose to tell themselves it is no concern of theirs, "just a quarrel [as Chamberlain said] in a faraway country between people of whom we know nothing."

Section ❹ Assessment

1. TERMS & NAMES

Identify
- appeasement
- Axis Powers
- Francisco Franco
- isolationism
- Third Reich
- Munich Conference

2. TAKING NOTES

Trace the movement of Japan from democratic reform in the 1920s to military aggression in the 1930s by supplying the events following the dates shown on the time line below.

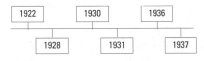

What event was the most significant? Why?

3. DRAWING CONCLUSIONS

Review Germany's aggressive actions after Hitler defied the Versailles Treaty by rebuilding Germany's armed forces. At what point do you think Hitler concluded that he could take any territory without being stopped? Why?

THINK ABOUT
- Hitler's goals
- responses of the democracies to his statements and actions
- the role of the League of Nations

4. ANALYZING THEMES

Power and Authority After World War I, many Americans became isolationists. Do you recommend that America practice isolationism today? Why or why not?

THINK ABOUT
- America's role as world leader
- the global economy
- America's domestic problems
- the economic and political goals of other countries

The Great Depression

Long-Term Causes

- World economies are connected.
- Some countries have huge war debts from World War I.
- Europe relies on American loans and investments.
- Prosperity is built on borrowed money.
- Wealth is unequally distributed.

Immediate Causes

- U.S. stock market crashes.
- Banks demand repayment of loans.
- Farms fail and factories close.
- Americans reduce foreign trade to protect economy.
- Americans stop loans to foreign countries.
- American banking system collapses.

Worldwide Economic Depression

Immediate Effects

- Millions become unemployed worldwide.
- Businesses go bankrupt.
- Governments take emergency measures to protect economies.
- Citizens lose faith in capitalism and democracy.
- Nations turn toward authoritarian leaders.

Long-Term Effects

- Nazis take control in Germany.
- Fascists come to power in other countries.
- Democracies try social welfare programs.
- Japan expands in East Asia.
- World War II breaks out.

TERMS & NAMES

Briefly explain the importance of each of the following during the years 1919 to 1939.

1. Albert Einstein
2. Sigmund Freud
3. Weimar Republic
4. New Deal
5. fascism
6. Benito Mussolini
7. Adolf Hitler
8. appeasement
9. Francisco Franco
10. Munich Conference

REVIEW QUESTIONS

SECTION 1 (pages 795–800)
An Age of Uncertainty

11. What effect did Einstein's theory of relativity and Freud's theory of the unconscious have on the public?

12. What advances were made in transportation and communication in the 1920s and 1930s?

SECTION 2 (pages 801–806)
A Global Depression

13. List three reasons the Weimar Republic was considered weak.

14. What was the Dawes Plan? How did it affect the German economy?

15. What caused the stock market crash of 1929?

SECTION 3 (pages 807–810)
Fascism Rises in Europe

16. List three political and economic reasons the Italians turned to Mussolini.

17. List three of Hitler's beliefs and goals presented in *Mein Kampf*.

SECTION 4 (pages 811–815)
Aggressors on the March

18. Explain how Japan planned to solve its economic problems.

19. Why was Germany's reoccupation of the Rhineland a significant turning point toward war?

20. Briefly describe the Spanish Civil War. Include when it occurred, who fought, and who won.

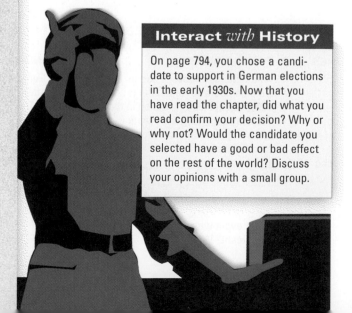

Interact *with* History

On page 794, you chose a candidate to support in German elections in the early 1930s. Now that you have read the chapter, did what you read confirm your decision? Why or why not? Would the candidate you selected have a good or bad effect on the rest of the world? Discuss your opinions with a small group.

CRITICAL THINKING

1. THE STOCK MARKET CRASH

THEME ECONOMICS Your text says that the economy in 1929 was "like a delicately balanced house of cards." Use a sequence graphic like the one below to identify the events that led to the stock market collapse.

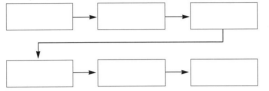

2. SUPPORT FOR FASCISM

Millions of people were attracted to fascist principles and leaders following World War I. What conditions made them give their support to these authoritarian doctrines? What were the advantages and disadvantages of being under fascist rule?

3. THE LEAGUE OF NATIONS

What weaknesses made the League of Nations an ineffective force for peace in the 1920s and 1930s? Give specific examples to prove your point.

4. ANALYZING PRIMARY SOURCES

In 1938, France, Britain, Italy, and Germany met to discuss Hitler's demand for the Sudetenland. Columbia Broadcasting System transmitted the following live report on radios around the world.

A VOICE FROM THE PAST

Prague—6:30 p.m.   September 29
WILLIAM SHIRER: It took the Big Four just five hours and twenty-five minutes here in Munich today to dispel the clouds of war and come to an agreement over the partition of Czechoslovakia. There is to be no European war. . . the price of that peace is, roughly, the ceding by Czechoslovakia of the Sudeten territory to Herr Hitler's Germany. The German Führer gets what he wanted, only he has to wait a little longer for it. . . .

His waiting ten short days has saved Europe from a world war. . . most of the peoples of Europe are happy that they won't have to be marching off to war on Saturday. Probably only the Czechs. . . are not too happy. But there seems very little that they can do about it in face of all the might and power represented here. . .

WILLIAM SHIRER, quoted in *The Strenuous Decade*

- Summarize the news Shirer is reporting.
- What do you think is Shirer's opinion about it? Give specific examples to support your opinion.

CHAPTER ACTIVITIES

1. LIVING HISTORY: Unit Portfolio Project

THEME SCIENCE AND TECHNOLOGY Your unit portfolio project focuses on the impact of scientific and technological innovation on history. For chapter 31, you might select one of the following ideas to add to your portfolio.

- Study the style of an architect, artist, author, or musician in this chapter. Compose or create your own work imitating this person's style. For example, design a functional building like Wright or a cubist painting like Picasso.
- Give a demonstration speech on an invention, tool, or other device from this time period. While showing the class how it works, explain its social, political, or economic effects.
- With a small group, invent a weapon to be used for peaceful purposes by the League of Nations, and rewrite history. Choose an incident of aggression that you read about and write a fictional account headlined *League's New Weapon Halts Fascists*. Read your version of history to the class.

2. CONNECT TO TODAY: Cooperative Learning

THEME POWER AND AUTHORITY After World War I, authoritarian leaders came to power in many countries during times of crisis. Could a Hitler or Mussolini come to power now in any country? Work with a small group. Select a country to research.

 Using the Internet and library sources, investigate your chosen country's political and economic condition today. Review its history.

- Use information from your research to prepare a scenario, or situation, where a dictator could take power in that country. Present your results.

3. INTERPRETING A TIME LINE

Review the unit time line on page 739. Which three events most seriously defied the peace treaties of this time period? In a short paragraph, explain why. Share your paragraph with another student.

FOCUS ON CHARTS

Comparing Fascism/Nazism and Communism Fascism/Nazism and Communism are two different totalitarian political systems with some common characteristics.

	Fascism/Nazism	Communism
Basic principles	Authoritarian; action-oriented; charismatic leader; state more important than individual	Marxist-Leninist ideas; dictatorship of proletariat; state more important than individual
Political	Nationalist; racist (Nazism); one-party rule; supreme leader	Internationalist; one-party rule; supreme leader
Social	Supported by middle class, industrialists, and military	Supported by workers and peasants
Cultural	Censorship; indoctrination; secret police	Censorship; indoctrination; secret police
Economic	Private property control by state corporations or state	Collective ownership; centralized state planning
Examples	Italy, Spain, Germany	U.S.S.R.

- What characteristics do they have in common? How do they differ?

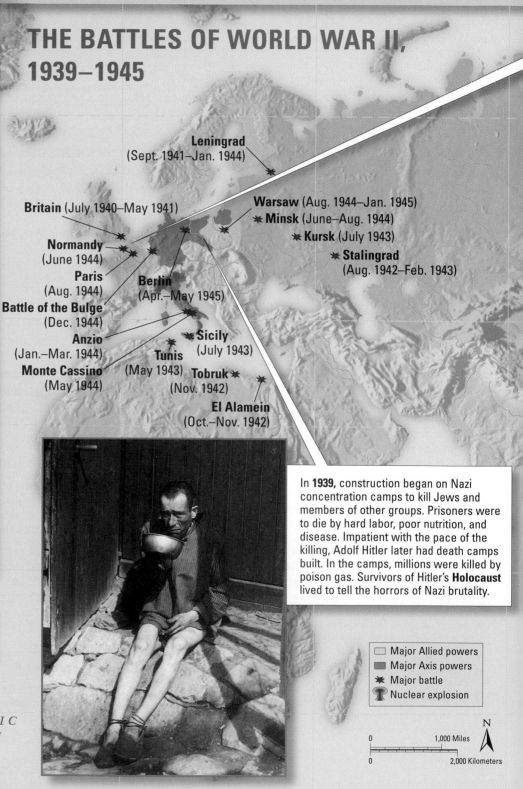

CHAPTER 32

World War II, 1939–1945

PREVIEWING THEMES

Science and Technology
Far-reaching developments in science and technology changed the course of World War II. Important improvements in aircraft, tanks, and submarines had occurred since World War I. The invention of radar, aircraft carriers, and especially the atomic bomb changed how war was fought.

Empire Building
Germany, Italy, and Japan tried to build empires. They began expanding their own territories by conquering other nations and dominating them politically and economically.

Economics
Fighting the Nazi terror weakened the economies of Great Britain, the Soviet Union, and most other European allies. When the United States entered the war, its economy actually grew sharply after years of depression. With the strength of its economy, the United States strengthened the Allied effort with its resources and products.

INTERNET CONNECTION

Visit us at **www.mcdougallittell.com** to learn more about World War II.

THE BATTLES OF WORLD WAR II, 1939–1945

Leningrad (Sept. 1941–Jan. 1944)

Britain (July 1940–May 1941)

Warsaw (Aug. 1944–Jan. 1945)
✹ Minsk (June–Aug. 1944)
✹ Kursk (July 1943)

Normandy (June 1944)

✹ Stalingrad (Aug. 1942–Feb. 1943)

Paris (Aug. 1944)

Berlin (Apr.–May 1945)

Battle of the Bulge (Dec. 1944)

Anzio (Jan.–Mar. 1944)

✹ Sicily (July 1943)

Tunis (May 1943)

Monte Cassino (May 1944)

Tobruk ✹ (Nov. 1942)

El Alamein (Oct.–Nov. 1942)

In **1939,** construction began on Nazi concentration camps to kill Jews and members of other groups. Prisoners were to die by hard labor, poor nutrition, and disease. Impatient with the pace of the killing, Adolf Hitler later had death camps built. In the camps, millions were killed by poison gas. Survivors of Hitler's **Holocaust** lived to tell the horrors of Nazi brutality.

☐ Major Allied powers
■ Major Axis powers
✹ Major battle
⚛ Nuclear explosion

ATLANTIC OCEAN

N

| 0 | 1,000 Miles |
| 0 | 2,000 Kilometers |

On **June 6, 1944,** the Allies launched the greatest naval and land campaign in history against Nazi forces in **Normandy.** Supreme Commander U.S. General Dwight David Eisenhower led the attack against the Nazis with massive air and ground forces. Despite huge losses, the Allies' invasion of Europe spelled the beginning of the end of Adolf Hitler's regime.

Hiroshima (Aug. 6, 1945)

Nagasaki
(Aug. 9, 1945)

Midway (June 1942)

Okinawa (Apr.–June 1945)

Iwo Jima (Feb.–March 1945)

Tropic of Cancer

Pearl Harbor (Dec. 1941)

Philippine Sea (June 1944)   **Wake Island** (Dec. 1941)

Bataan   **Saipan** (June–July 1944)
              Guam (July–Aug. 1944)

*PACIFIC
OCEAN*

Leyte Gulf
(Oct. 1944)

Singapore (Feb. 1942)

0° Equator

Hollandia (Apr. 1944)

On **April 9, 1942,** the Bataan Peninsula in the Philippines fell to Japan. After their victory, the Japanese led 70,000 American and Filipino prisoners of war on a 60-mile forced march north—the **Bataan Death March.** The prisoners marched under a blazing sun. They were also starved and brutally beaten. Prisoners who showed signs of weakening were often buried alive.

Guadalcanal (Aug. 1942–Feb. 1943)

*DIAN
CEAN*

120° E

Interact *with* History

World War II has been going on for several years—at great cost in lives to your side and the enemy's. You are an air force commander who has just received a report from military intelligence. The report identifies a city in enemy territory that is a major weapons manufacturing center. You and other officers know that by destroying the arms factories in the city, the war could be shortened. Thousands of lives could be saved. On the other hand, the bombing will kill hundreds, maybe thousands, of civilians living near the enemy factories. How do you weigh the lives that will be saved against the lives that will be lost?

Would you bomb this city?

One plane-load of bombs will wipe out a vital enemy weapons factory, along with hundreds of civilian homes around it.

This is a bomb factory in the middle of a residential area.

Radar tells the pilot where to drop the bombs, but at 10,000 feet, he cannot see the casualties they will cause.

This raid will probably shorten the war by at least two months.

EXAMINING *the* ISSUES

- Does shortening a war to save lives justify killing civilians?

- How are civilians sometimes as much a part of a war effort as soldiers?

- What percentage of lives saved would justify the deaths caused in the bombing?

As a class, discuss these questions. In your discussion, weigh the arguments for and against both choices.

As you read about World War II, think about the role that civilians play in a situation of total war. Think also about the hard moral choices that people often face in times of war.

Hitler's Lightning War

TERMS & NAMES
- nonaggression pact
- blitzkrieg
- Charles de Gaulle
- Winston Churchill
- Battle of Britain
- Atlantic Charter

MAIN IDEA

Using the sudden, mass attack called the blitzkrieg, Germany overran much of Europe and North Africa.

WHY IT MATTERS NOW

Hitler's actions set off World War II. The results of the war still affect the politics and economics of today's world.

SETTING THE STAGE During the 1930s, Hitler played on the hopes and fears of the Western democracies. Each time the Nazi dictator grabbed new territory, he would declare an end to his demands. Peace seemed guaranteed—until Hitler started expanding again.

Germany Sparks a New War in Europe

After his moves into the Rhineland (March 1936), Austria (March 1938), and Czechoslovakia (September 1938 and March 1939), the Führer turned his eyes to Poland. On April 28, 1939, Hitler spoke before the Reichstag. He demanded that the Polish Corridor, along with its port city of Danzig, be returned to Germany. After World War I, the Allies had cut out the Polish Corridor from German territory to give Poland access to the sea.

This time, Great Britain and France decided to resist this threat of aggression. At this point, as was mentioned in Chapter 31, Soviet dictator Joseph Stalin signed a 10-year **nonaggression pact** with Hitler on August 23. After being excluded from the Munich Conference, Stalin was not eager to join with the West. Also, Hitler was promising him territory. In the public part of the pact, Germany and the Soviet Union promised not to attack each other. Secretly, however, they agreed that they would divide Poland between them. They also secretly agreed that the USSR could take over Finland and the Baltic countries (Lithuania, Latvia, and Estonia).

Background
Hitler hated communism, as Stalin despised fascism. Nonetheless, Hitler did not want to fight both the Allies *and* the Soviet Union. And Stalin wanted to keep his country out of a costly European war.

Germany's Lightning Attack on Poland The new nonaggression pact removed the threat to Germany of a Soviet attack from the east. Hitler then quickly moved ahead with plans to conquer Poland. His surprise attack took place at dawn on September 1, 1939. German warplanes invaded Polish airspace, raining bombs and terror on the Poles. At the same time, German tanks and troop trucks rumbled across the Polish border. The trucks carried more than 1.5 million soldiers into the assault. German aircraft and artillery then began a merciless bombing of Poland's capital, Warsaw. The city crumbled under the assault. A stunned world looked on. No one yet realized that the Polish invasion had unleashed World War II.

France and Great Britain declared war on Germany on September 3. But Poland fell three weeks before those nations could make any military response. After his victory, Hitler annexed the western half of Poland. That region had a large German population.

A propaganda poster proclaims to the German nation: "One People, One Reich, One Führer!"

World War II: German Advances, 1939–1941

Axis nations, 1938
Axis-controlled, 1941
Allies
Neutral nations
→ German advances

GEOGRAPHY SKILLBUILDER:
Interpreting Maps
1. **Region** *Which countries did Germany invade?*
2. **Location** *In what way was Germany's geographic location an advantage when it was on the offensive in the war?*

The German invasion of Poland was the first test of Germany's newest military strategy—the **blitzkrieg** (BLIHTS·kreeg), or "lightning war." It involved using fast-moving airplanes and tanks, followed by massive infantry forces, to take the enemy by surprise. Then, blitzkrieg forces swiftly crushed all opposition with overwhelming force. In the case of Poland, the strategy worked.

The Soviets Make Their Move On September 17, after his secret agreement with Hitler, Stalin sent Soviet troops to occupy the eastern half of Poland. Stalin then began annexing the regions in the second part of the agreement. Lithuania, Latvia, and Estonia fell without a struggle, but Finland resisted.

In November 1939, Stalin sent nearly 1 million Soviet troops into Finland. He thought that his soldiers would win a quick victory. So, Stalin did not worry about the Finnish winter. This was a crucial mistake. The Finns were outnumbered and outgunned, but they fiercely defended their country. In the freezing weather, they attacked on swift skis. Meanwhile, the Soviets struggled through deep snow, crippled by frostbite. Despite their losses, the Soviet invaders finally won through sheer force of numbers. By March 1940, Stalin had forced the Finns to accept his surrender terms.

THINK THROUGH HISTORY
A. Analyzing Motives What would you say were the political reasons behind Stalin's actions in Europe at the beginning of World War II?

The Phony War For almost seven months after the fall of Poland, there was a strange calm in the land fighting in Europe. After their declaration of war, the French and British had mobilized their armies. They stationed their troops along the Maginot (MAZH·uh·NOH) Line, a system of fortifications along France's border with Germany. There they waited for Germans to attack—but nothing happened. With little to do, the bored Allied soldiers stared eastward toward the enemy. Equally bored, German soldiers stared back from their Siegfried Line a few miles away. Germans jokingly called it the *sitzkrieg,* or "sitting war." Some newspapers referred to it simply as "the phony war."

Suddenly, on April 9, 1940, the phony war ended. Hitler launched a surprise invasion of Denmark and Norway. He planned to build bases along the Norwegian and Danish coasts to strike at Great Britain. In just four hours after the attack, Denmark fell. Two months later, Norway surrendered as well.

The Battle for France and Great Britain

In May of 1940, Hitler began a dramatic sweep through Holland, Belgium, and Luxembourg. This was part of a strategy to strike at France. Keeping the Allies' attention on those countries, Hitler then sent an even larger force of tanks and troop trucks to slice through the Ardennes (ahr·DEHN). This was a heavily wooded area in northeastern France and Luxembourg. Moving through the forest, the

Germans "squeezed between" the Maginot Line. From there, they moved across France and reached France's northern coast in 10 days.

France Battles Back When the Germans reached the French coast, they swung north again and joined forces with German troops in Belgium. By May 26, 1940, the Germans had trapped the Allied forces around the northern French city of Lille (leel). With a German victory inevitable, Belgium surrendered. Outnumbered, outgunned, and pounded from the air, the Allies escaped to the beaches of Dunkirk, a French port city on the English Channel. They were trapped with their backs to the sea.

In one of the most heroic acts of the war, Great Britain set out to rescue the army. It sent a fleet of some 850 ships across the English Channel to Dunkirk. Along with Royal Navy ships, civilian craft—yachts, lifeboats, motorboats, paddle steamers, and fishing boats—joined the rescue effort. From May 26 to June 4, this amateur armada, under heavy fire from German bombers, sailed back and forth from Britain to Dunkirk. The boats carried an incredible 338,000 battle-weary soldiers to safety.

Hundreds of British soldiers crowd aboard ship during the mass evacuation at Dunkirk.

France Falls Following Dunkirk, France seemed doomed to defeat. On June 10, sensing a quick victory, Italy's Benito Mussolini joined forces with Hitler and declared war on both Great Britain and France. Italy then attacked France from the south. By June 14, Paris had fallen to the Germans. Nazi troops marched triumphantly down the city's main boulevard.

Two days later, seeing defeat approaching, the French parliament asked Marshal Henri Pétain (pay·TAN), an aging hero from World War I, to become prime minister. On June 22, 1940, France surrendered. The Germans took control of the northern part of the country. They left the southern part to a puppet government headed by Pétain. The headquarters of this government was in the city of Vichy (VEESH·ee).

After France fell, a French general named **Charles de Gaulle** (duh GOHL) fled to London. There, he set up a government-in-exile committed to reconquering France. On June 18, 1940, he delivered a broadcast from England. He called on the people of France to resist:

Background
Hitler demanded that the surrender take place in the same railroad car where the French had dictated terms to the Germans in World War I.

> **A VOICE FROM THE PAST**
> It is the bounden [obligatory] duty of all Frenchmen who still bear arms to continue the struggle. For them to lay down their arms, to evacuate any position of military importance, or agree to hand over any part of French territory, however small, to enemy control would be a crime against our country. . . .
> **GENERAL CHARLES DE GAULLE,** quoted in *Charles de Gaulle: A Biography*

De Gaulle went on to organize the Free French military forces that battled the Nazis until France was liberated in 1944.

Germany Attacks Great Britain With the fall of France, Great Britain stood alone against the Nazis. **Winston Churchill,** the new British prime minister, had already declared that his nation would never give in. In a speech, he said, "We shall fight on the beaches, we shall fight on the landing grounds, we shall fight in the fields and in the streets . . . we shall never surrender."

**Winston Churchill
1874–1965**

Probably the greatest weapon the British had as they stood alone against Hitler's Germany was the nation's prime minister—Winston Churchill. "Big Winnie," Londoners boasted, "was the lad for us. . . ."

Although as a youngster Churchill had a speech defect, he grew to become one of the greatest orators of all time. He used all his gifts as a speaker to rally the people behind the effort to crush Germany. He declared that Britain would

. . . wage war, by sea, land, and air, with all our might and with all the strength that God can give us . . . against monstrous tyranny.

Hitler now turned his mind to an invasion of Great Britain. His plan—*Operation Sea Lion*—was first to knock out the Royal Air Force (RAF) and then to land 250,000 soldiers on England's shores. In the summer of 1940, the Luftwaffe (LOOFT·VAHF·uh), Germany's air force, began bombing Great Britain. Badly outnumbered, the RAF had 2,900 planes to the Luftwaffe's 4,500. At first, the Germans targeted British airfields and aircraft factories. Then, on September 7, 1940, they began focusing on the cities, especially London—to break British morale. Bombs exploded daily in city streets. They killed civilians and set buildings ablaze. However, despite the destruction and loss of life, the British fought on.

Background
Luftwaffe in German means "air weapon."

Vocabulary
morale: state of mind.

With the pressure off the airfields, the RAF hit back hard. Two secret weapons helped turn the tide in their favor. One was an electronic tracking system known as radar. Developed in the late 1930s, radar could tell the number, speed, and direction of incoming warplanes. The other was a German code-making machine named Enigma. A complete Enigma machine was smuggled to Great Britain in 1938. With Enigma in their possession, the British had German secret messages open to them. With information gathered by these devices, RAF fliers could quickly get to their airplanes and inflict deadly harm on the enemy.

To avoid the RAF's attacks, the Germans gave up daylight raids in October 1940 in favor of night bombing. At sunset, the wail of sirens filled the air as Londoners flocked to the subways. There they spent the night in air-raid shelters. Some rode out the blasts at home in basements or in smaller air-raid shelters.

The **Battle of Britain** continued until May 10, 1941. Stunned by British resistance, Hitler decided to call off his attacks. Instead, he focused his attention on Eastern Europe and the Mediterranean. The Battle of Britain had ended. And, from it, the Allies had learned a crucial lesson: Hitler's advances could be blocked.

The Eastern Front and the Mediterranean

The stubborn resistance of the British in the Battle of Britain caused a shift in Hitler's strategy in Europe. Although the resistance surprised Hitler, it did not defeat him. He would deal with Great Britain later. Instead, he turned his attention east to the Balkans and the Mediterranean area—and to the ultimate prize, the Soviet Union.

Germany and Italy Attack North Africa Germany's first objective in the Mediterranean region was North Africa—mainly because of Hitler's partner Mussolini. Despite Italy's alliance with Germany, the country had remained neutral at the beginning of the war. With Hitler's conquest of France, however, Mussolini knew he had to take action. Otherwise, Italy would not share in Germany's victories. "I need a few thousand dead," he told a member of his staff. After declaring war on France and Great Britain, Italy became Germany's most important Axis ally. Then, Mussolini moved into France along with the Nazis.

**THINK THROUGH HISTORY
B. Drawing Conclusions** How could "a few thousand dead" have helped Mussolini's position in the Axis powers?

Mussolini took his next step in September 1940. While the Battle of Britain was raging, he ordered Italy's North African army to move east from Libya. His goal was to seize British-controlled Egypt. Egypt's Suez Canal was key to reaching the oil fields of the Middle East. Within a week, Italian troops had pushed 60 miles inside Egypt, forcing British units back. Then both sides dug in and waited.

Background
The Middle East is an area that includes the countries of Southwest Asia and northeast Africa.

Great Britain Strikes Back Finally, in December, the British decided to strike back. The result was a disaster for the Italians. By February 1941, the British had swept 500 miles across North Africa. They had taken 130,000 Italian prisoners.

Hitler had to step in to save his Axis partner. In February 1941, he sent General Erwin Rommel, later known as the "Desert Fox," to Libya. His mission was to command a newly formed tank corps, the Afrika Korps. Determined to take control of Egypt and the Suez Canal, Rommel attacked the British at Agheila (uh·GAY·luh) on March 24. Caught by surprise, British forces retreated 500 miles east to Tobruk.

However, by mid-January 1942, after fierce fighting for Tobruk, the British drove Rommel back to where he had started. By June, the tide of battle turned again. Rommel regrouped, pushed the British back across the desert, and seized Tobruk. This was a shattering loss for the Allies. Rommel later wrote, "To every man of us, Tobruk was a symbol of British resistance, and we were now going to finish with it for good."

Background
The Balkan countries include Albania, Bulgaria, Greece, parts of Romania and Turkey, and most of the former Yugoslavia.

The War in the Balkans While Rommel campaigned in North Africa, Hitler was active in the Balkans. As early as the summer of 1940, Hitler had begun planning to attack his ally, the USSR, by the following spring. The Balkan countries of southeastern Europe were key to Hitler's invasion plan. Hitler wanted to build bases in southeastern Europe for the attack on the Soviet Union. He also wanted to make sure that the British did not interfere.

To prepare for his invasion, Hitler moved to expand his influence in the Balkans. In the face of overwhelming German strength, Bulgaria, Romania, and Hungary cooperated by joining the Axis powers in early 1941. Yugoslavia and Greece, which had pro-British governments, resisted. On Sunday, April 6, 1941, Hitler invaded both countries. Yugoslavia fell in 11 days. Greece surrendered in 17. In Athens, the Nazis celebrated their victory by raising swastikas on the Acropolis.

Hitler Invades the Soviet Union With the Balkans firmly in control, Hitler could move ahead with his plan to invade the Soviet Union. He called that plan *Operation Barbarossa.* Early on Sunday morning, June 22, 1941, the roar of German tanks and aircraft announced the beginning of the blitzkrieg invasion. The Soviet Union was not prepared for this attack. With its 5 million men, the Red Army was the largest in the world. But it was neither well equipped nor well trained.

The invasion rolled on week after week until the Germans had pushed 500 miles inside the Soviet Union. As the Russians retreated, they burned and destroyed everything in the enemy's path. Russians had used this same strategy against Napoleon.

By September 8, Germans had surrounded Leningrad and isolated the city from the rest of the world. If necessary, Hitler would starve the city's 2.5 million inhabitants. German bombs destroyed warehouses where food was stored. Desperately hungry, people began eating cattle and horse feed, as well as cats and dogs and, finally, crows and rats. More than 1 million people died in Leningrad that terrible winter. Yet the city refused to fall.

Seeing that Leningrad would not surrender, Hitler looked to Moscow, the capital and heart of the Soviet Union. A Nazi drive on the capital began on October 2, 1941.

A Soviet photo taken in 1942 shows the horrors of the war in the Soviet Union. Civilians in the Crimea search over a barren field for their dead loved ones.

By December, the Germans had advanced to the outskirts of Moscow. Soviet General Georgi Zhukov (ZHOO·kuhf) counterattacked. He had 100 fresh Siberian divisions and the harsh Soviet winter on his side.

As temperatures fell, the Germans, in summer uniforms, retreated. Their fuel and oil froze. Tanks, trucks, and weapons became useless. Ignoring Napoleon's winter defeat 130 years before, the Führer sent his generals a stunning order: "No retreat!" German troops dug in about 125 miles west of the capital. They held the line against the Soviets until March 1943. Nonetheless, Moscow had been saved and had cost the Germans 500,000 lives.

THINK THROUGH HISTORY
C. Making Inferences What does the fact that German armies were not prepared for the Russian winter indicate about Hitler's expectations for the campaign in the Soviet Union?

The United States Aids Its Allies

As disturbing as these events were to Americans, bitter memories of World War I convinced most people in the United States that their country should not get involved. Between 1935 and 1937, Congress passed a series of Neutrality Acts. The laws made it illegal to sell arms or lend money to nations at war. But President Roosevelt knew that if the Allies fell, the United States would be drawn into the war. In September 1939, he persuaded Congress to allow the Allies to buy American arms. According to his plan, they would pay cash and then carry the goods on their own ships.

U.S. industry achieved amazing rates of speed when it began to produce for the war effort. This ship, for example, was produced in a U.S. shipyard in only 10 days.

Under the Lend-Lease Act, passed in March 1941, the president could lend or lease arms and other supplies to any country vital to the United States. By the summer of 1941, the U.S. Navy was escorting British ships carrying U.S. arms. In response, Hitler ordered his submarines to sink any cargo ships they met.

Although the United States had not yet entered the war, Roosevelt and Churchill met secretly on a battleship off Newfoundland on August 9. The two leaders issued a joint declaration called the **Atlantic Charter.** It upheld free trade among nations and the right of people to choose their own government. The charter later served as the Allies' peace plan at the end of World War II.

On September 4, a German U-boat suddenly fired on a U.S. destroyer in the Atlantic. Roosevelt ordered navy commanders to respond. They were to shoot German submarines on sight. The United States was now involved in an undeclared naval war with Hitler. To almost everyone's surprise, however, the attack that actually drew the United States into the war did not come from Germany. It came from Japan.

Background
Newfoundland is a province of Canada.

Section 1 Assessment

1. TERMS & NAMES

Identify
• nonaggression pact
• blitzkrieg
• Charles de Gaulle
• Winston Churchill
• Battle of Britain
• Atlantic Charter

2. TAKING NOTES

Create a chart like the one below. Identify the effects of each of these early events of World War II.

Cause	Effect
First blitzkrieg	
Allies stranded at Dunkirk	
British radar detects German aircraft	
Lend-Lease Act	

3. MAKING INFERENCES

Great Britain and the Soviet city of Leningrad each fought off a German invasion. Other countries gave in to the Germans without much resistance. What factors do you think a country's leaders consider when deciding whether to surrender or to fight?

THINK ABOUT
• the country's ability to fight
• the costs of resisting
• the costs of surrendering

4. THEME ACTIVITY

Economics In groups of 3 or 4, prepare a dramatic scene for a play or film that focuses on an economic problem that might have been suffered by Europeans during World War II.

Japan Strikes in the Pacific

TERMS & NAMES
- Isoroku Yamamoto
- Pearl Harbor
- Battle of Midway
- Douglas MacArthur
- Battle of Guadalcanal

MAIN IDEA	**WHY IT MATTERS NOW**
Carving out an empire, Japan attacked Pearl Harbor in Hawaii and brought the United States into World War II.	World War II established the role of the United States as a leading player in international affairs.

SETTING THE STAGE Like Hitler, Japan's military leaders also had dreams of empire. Japan was overcrowded and faced shortages of raw materials. To solve these problems— and to encourage nationalism—the Japanese began a program of empire building that would lead to war.

Japan Seeks a Pacific Empire

Japan's expansion began in 1931. In that year, Japanese troops took over Manchuria in northeastern China. Six years later, Japanese armies swept into the heartland of China. They expected quick victory. Chinese resistance, however, caused the war to drag on. This caused a strain on Japan's economy. To increase their resources, Japanese leaders looked toward the rich European colonies of Southeast Asia.

The Surprise Attack on Pearl Harbor By August 1940, Americans had cracked a Japanese secret code. They were well aware of Japanese plans for Southeast Asia. If Japan conquered European colonies there, it could also threaten the American-controlled Philippine Islands and Guam. To stop the Japanese advance, the U.S. government sent aid to strengthen Chinese resistance. And when the Japanese overran French Indochina in July 1941, Roosevelt cut off oil shipments to Japan.

Background
French Indochina was an area now made up by Vietnam, Cambodia, and Laos.

Despite an oil shortage, the Japanese continued their conquests. They hoped to catch the United States by surprise. So they planned massive attacks in Southeast Asia and in the Pacific—both at the same time. Japan's greatest naval strategist, Admiral **Isoroku Yamamoto** (ih·soh·ROO·koo YAH·muh·MOH·toh), also argued that the U.S. fleet in Hawaii was "a dagger pointed at our throat" and must be destroyed.

Early in the morning of December 7, 1941, American sailors at **Pearl Harbor** in Hawaii awoke to the roar of explosives. A Japanese attack was underway! The United States had known from a coded Japanese message that an attack might come. But they did not know when or where it would occur. Within two hours, the Japanese had sunk or damaged 18 ships, including 8 battleships—nearly the whole U.S. Pacific fleet. Some 2,400 Americans were killed— with more than 1,000 wounded. News of the attack stunned the American people. The next day, Congress declared war on Japan. In his speech to Congress, President Roosevelt described December 7 as "a date which will live in infamy."

The *U.S.S. West Virginia* in flames after taking a direct hit during the Japanese attack on Pearl Harbor.

The Tide of Japanese Victories The Japanese had planned a series of strikes at the United States in the Pacific. After the bombing at Pearl Harbor, the Japanese seized Guam and Wake Island in the western Pacific. They then launched an attack on the Philippines. In January 1942, the Japanese marched into the Philippine capital of Manila. They overwhelmed American and Filipino defenders on the Bataan Peninsula (buh·TAN) in April—and in May, on the island of Corregidor.

The Japanese also hit the British, seizing Hong Kong and invading Malaya. By February 1942, the Japanese had reached Singapore. After a fierce pounding, the colony surrendered. By March, the Japanese had conquered the resource-rich Dutch East Indies (now Indonesia), including the islands of Java, Sumatra, Borneo, and Celebes (SEHL·uh·BEEZ). After Malaya, the Japanese took Burma, between China and India. China received supplies by way of the Burma Road. The Japanese could now close off the road. Now they might force the Chinese to surrender.

By the time Burma fell, Japan had conquered more than 1 million square miles of land with about 150 million people. Before these conquests, the Japanese had tried to win the support of Asians with the anticolonialist idea of "Asia for the Asians." After victory, however, the Japanese quickly made it clear that they had come as conquerors.

Native peoples often received the same brutal treatment as the 150,000 prisoners of war. On what is called the Bataan Death March, the Japanese subjected prisoners to terrible cruelties. One American soldier reported:

A VOICE FROM THE PAST

I was questioned by a Japanese officer who found out that I had been in a Philippine Scout Battalion. The [Japanese] hated the Scouts. . . . Anyway, they took me outside and I was forced to watch as they buried six of my Scouts alive. They made the men dig their own graves, and then had them kneel down in a pit. The guards hit them over the head with shovels to stun them and piled earth on top.

LIEUTENANT JOHN SPAINHOWER, quoted in *War Diary 1939–1945*

Background
According to the centuries-old warrior code called *Bushido,* a Japanese soldier must commit suicide, or hari-kari, rather than surrender. So Japanese soldiers had contempt for Allied prisoners of war.

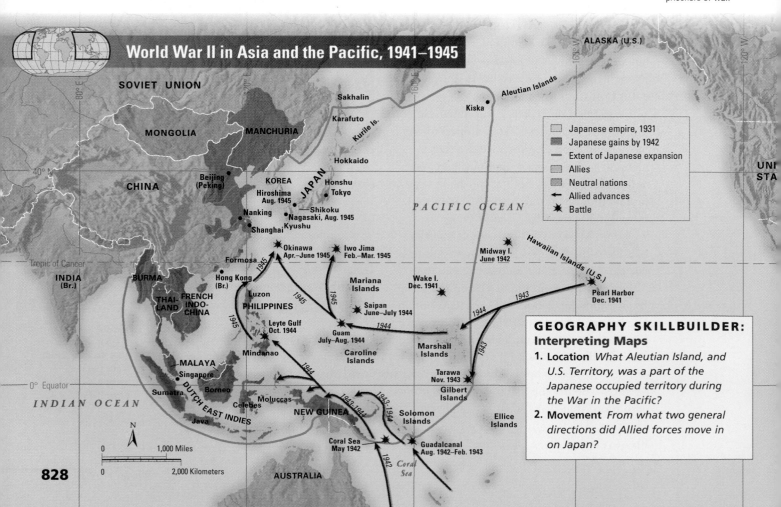

World War II in Asia and the Pacific, 1941–1945

Legend:
- Japanese empire, 1931
- Japanese gains by 1942
- Extent of Japanese expansion
- Allies
- Neutral nations
- Allied advances
- Battle

GEOGRAPHY SKILLBUILDER: Interpreting Maps

1. **Location** *What Aleutian Island, and U.S. Territory, was a part of the Japanese occupied territory during the War in the Pacific?*
2. **Movement** *From what two general directions did Allied forces move in on Japan?*

The Allies Strike Back

After a string of victories, the Japanese seemed unbeatable. Nonetheless, the Allies—mainly Americans and Australians—were anxious to strike back in the Pacific. In April 1942, the United States wanted revenge for Pearl Harbor. So the United States sent 16 B-25 bombers under the command of Lieutenant Colonel James H. Doolittle to bomb Tokyo and other major Japanese cities. The bombs did little damage. The attack, however, made an important psychological point: the Japanese could be attacked.

The Allies Turn the Tide of War Doolittle's raid on Japan raised American morale and shook the confidence of some Japanese. As one Japanese citizen described it, "We started to doubt that we were invincible." In addition, Japan had won a vast empire that was becoming difficult to defend and control.

Vocabulary
invincible:
unconquerable.

Slowly, the Allies began to turn the tide of war. Early in May 1942, an American fleet with Australian support intercepted a Japanese strike force. The force had been about to attack Port Moresby. The city housed a critical Allied air base in southeastern New Guinea (GIHN·ee). From this base, the Japanese could have easily invaded Australia.

In the battle that followed—the Battle of the Coral Sea—both fleets fought using a new kind of naval warfare. The opposing ships did not fire a single shot. In fact, they often could not see one other. Instead, airplanes taking off from huge aircraft carriers did all the fighting. In the end, the battle was something of a draw. The Allies lost more ships than the Japanese, who claimed victory. But the Allies had stopped Japan's southward expansion for the first time.

The Battle of Midway Japan next targeted Midway Island, west of Hawaii. The island was home to a key American airfield. However, by June 1942, yet another Japanese code had been broken. As a result, the new commander in chief of the U.S. Pacific Fleet, Admiral Chester Nimitz, knew that a force of over 150 ships was heading toward Midway. The Japanese fleet was the largest naval force ever assembled. It could also boast the world's largest battleship, carrying Admiral Yamamoto himself. Yamamoto hoped not only to seize Midway but also to finish off the U.S. Pacific fleet. He hoped the American force would come from Pearl Harbor to defend the island.

THINK THROUGH HISTORY
A. Analyzing Motives What reasons might Admiral Yamamoto have had for thinking the Americans would send their entire Pacific fleet to defend Midway Island?

As happened in other battles of the Pacific war, U.S. Marines destroy a cave connected to a Japanese fort on the island of Iwo Jima.

Nimitz was outnumbered four to one in ships and planes. Even so, he was preparing an ambush for the Japanese at Midway. On June 4, with American forces hidden beyond the horizon, Nimitz allowed the enemy to launch the first strike. As Japanese planes roared over Midway Island, American carrier planes swooped in to attack Japanese ships. Many Japanese planes were still on the decks of the ships. The strategy was a success. American pilots destroyed 332 Japanese planes, all four aircraft carriers, and one support ship. Yamamoto ordered his crippled fleet to withdraw. By June 6, 1942, the battle was over. One Japanese official commented, "The Americans had avenged Pearl Harbor." The **Battle of Midway** had also turned the tide of war in the Pacific against the Japanese.

The Allies Go on the Offensive With morale high after their Midway victory, the Allies took the offensive. The Pacific war was one of vast distances. Japanese troops had dug in on hundreds of islands across the ocean. General **Douglas MacArthur** was

Young M.I. Libau was only 14 years old when Nazis attacked his family's home. Libau described what the Nazis did:

A VOICE FROM THE PAST
All the things for which my parents had worked for eighteen long years were destroyed in less than ten minutes. Piles of valuable glasses, expensive furniture, linens—in short, everything was destroyed. . . . The Nazis left us, yelling, "Don't try to leave this house! We'll soon be back again and take you to a concentration camp to be shot."

M.I. LIBAU, quoted in *Never to Forget: The Jews of the Holocaust*

Kristallnacht marked a major step-up in the Nazi policy of Jewish persecution. The future for Jews in Germany looked grim.

The Flood of Refugees After Kristallnacht, some Jews realized that violence against them was bound to increase. By the end of 1939, a number of Jews in Germany had fled for safety to other countries. Many of them, however, remained in Germany. Later, there would be millions more in territories conquered by Hitler. At first, Hitler favored emigration as a solution to what he called "the Jewish problem." The Nazis sped up the process. They forced Jews who did not want to leave into emigrating.

Getting other countries to continue admitting Germany's Jews became a problem. France had admitted 25,000 Jewish refugees and wanted no more. The British, who had accepted 80,000 Jews, worried about fueling anti-Semitism if that number increased. Some 40,000 Jews found homes in Latin America, but that region had closed its doors by the end of 1938. The United States took in around 100,000 refugees (including German scientist Albert Einstein). Many Americans, however, wanted U.S. doors closed. Germany's foreign minister observed: "We all want to get rid of our Jews. The difficulty is that no country wishes to receive them."

Isolating the Jews Hitler found that he could not get rid of Jews through emigration. So he put another part of his plan into effect. Hitler ordered Jews in all countries under his control to be moved into certain cities in Poland. In those cities, they were herded into dismal, overcrowded **ghettos,** or segregated Jewish areas. The Nazis then sealed off the ghettos with barbed wire and stone walls. They wanted the Jews inside to starve or die from disease. One survivor wrote, "One sees people dying, lying with arms and legs outstretched in the middle of the road. Their legs are bloated, often frostbitten, and their faces distorted with pain."

This pile of shoes taken from Nazi victims represents the murder of thousands of Jews. The inset shows the living inmates at Auschwitz trying to salvage shoes left by the dead.

THINK THROUGH HISTORY
B. Analyzing Causes Why might Hitler have chosen Poland to put his ghetto policy for "the Jewish problem" into effect?

Even under these horrible conditions, the Jews hung on. Some formed resistance organizations within the ghettos. They smuggled in food and other needed items. In the midst of chaos, Jews also struggled to keep their traditions. Ghetto theaters produced plays and concerts. Teachers taught lessons in secret schools. Scholars kept records so that one day people would find out the truth.

Hitler's "Final Solution"

Hitler soon grew impatient waiting for Jews to die from starvation or disease in the ghettos. He decided to take more direct action. His plan was called the **"Final Solution."** It was actually a program of **genocide,** the systematic killing of an entire people.

Hitler believed that his plan of conquest depended on the purity of the Aryan race. To protect racial purity, the Nazis not only had to eliminate the Jews, but also other races, nationalities, or groups they viewed as inferior—as "subhumans." They included gypsies, Poles, Russians, homosexuals, the insane, the disabled, and the incurably ill. But the Nazis focused especially on the Jews.

The Mass Killings Begin After Hitler invaded Poland in 1939, it was still not clear that the Führer meant to eliminate Jews totally. As Nazi armies swept across Eastern Europe, Hitler sent SS units from town to town to hunt Jews down. The SS (Hitler's elite security force) and some thousands of collaborators rounded up Jews—men, women, young children, and even babies—and took them to isolated spots. They then shot their prisoners in pits that became the prisoners' grave.

Jews in communities not reached by the killing squads were rounded up and taken to concentration camps, or slave-labor prisons. These camps were located mainly in Germany and Poland. Later, Nazis built camps in other countries they occupied. (See the map on page 847.) Hitler hoped that the horrible conditions in the camps would speed the total elimination of the Jews.

The prisoners worked seven days a week as slaves for the SS or for German businesses. Guards severely beat or killed their prisoners for not working fast enough. With meals of thin soup, a scrap of bread, and potato peelings, most prisoners lost 50 pounds the first month. "Hunger was so intense," recalled one survivor, "that if a bit of soup spilled over, prisoners would . . . dig their spoons into the mud and stuff the mess into their mouths."

The Final Stage: Mass Extermination The "Final Solution" officially reached its final stage in early 1942. At that time, the Nazis built extermination camps equipped with gas chambers for mass murder. The Nazis built the first six death camps in Poland. The first, Chelmno, actually began operating in late 1941. (See the map on

Vocabulary
collaborators: people who assist an occupying enemy force.

Background
Nazis also slaughtered 5 million Poles, Soviets, and others they considered as "undesirables."

SPOTLIGHT ON

Nazi Medicine

Nazi doctors, such as the notorious Josef Mengele, used many concentration camp prisoners as guinea pigs for their experiments. To promote "racial purity," doctors tested sterilization methods on some prisoners. Doctors infected other prisoners with typhus and other deadly diseases to see how long they could survive. To practice surgery, student doctors would operate on prisoners without anesthesia. In the hands of the Nazis, even medicine became an instrument of pain and destruction.

Slave workers in the Buchenwald concentration camp in Germany. They were among the lucky to have survived to the end of the war. The prisoner highlighted with a circle is Nobel Prize winning author Elie Wiesel. (See "A Voice from the Past," page 834.)

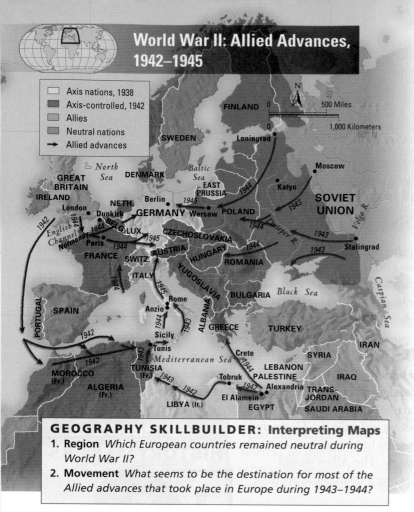

World War II: Allied Advances, 1942–1945

- ☐ Axis nations, 1938
- ■ Axis-controlled, 1942
- ☐ Allies
- ■ Neutral nations
- → Allied advances

GEOGRAPHY SKILLBUILDER: Interpreting Maps
1. **Region** *Which European countries remained neutral during World War II?*
2. **Movement** *What seems to be the destination for most of the Allied advances that took place in Europe during 1943–1944?*

Turning Point at Stalingrad As Rommel suffered defeats in North Africa, German armies also met their match in the Soviet Union. They had stalled at Leningrad and Moscow. Germans suffered heavy losses in battle because of the Russian winter. When the summer of 1942 arrived, German tanks were again ready to roll. Hitler sent his Sixth Army south to seize the rich oil fields in the Caucasus Mountains. The army was also to capture Stalingrad (now Volgograd) on the Volga River. With its 500,000 people, Stalingrad was a major industrial center.

The **Battle of Stalingrad** began on August 23, 1942. The Luftwaffe went on nightly bombing raids that set much of the city ablaze and reduced the rest to rubble. The situation looked desperate. Nonetheless, Stalin had already told his commanders to defend the city named after him at all costs. "Not one step backward," he ordered.

By early November 1942, Germans controlled 90 percent of the ruined city. Stalingrad was an "enormous cloud of burning, blinding smoke," as one German officer wrote. Then, another Russian winter set in. On November 19, Soviet troops outside the city launched a counterattack. Closing in around Stalingrad, they trapped the Germans inside and cut off their supplies. Hitler's commander, General Friedrich von Paulus, begged him to order a retreat. But Hitler refused, saying the city was "to be held at all costs."

On February 2, 1943, some 90,000 frostbitten, half-starved German troops surrendered to the Soviets. These pitiful survivors were all that remained of an army of 330,000. Stalingrad's defense had cost the Soviets over 1 million soldiers. The city they defended was 99 percent destroyed. After Stalingrad, however, the Germans were on the defensive, with the Soviets pushing them steadily westward.

The Invasion of Italy As the Battle of Stalingrad raged, Stalin continued to urge the British and the Americans to invade France. In January 1943, Roosevelt and Churchill met at Casablanca, Morocco, and decided to attack Italy first. On July 10, 1943, Allied forces of 180,000 soldiers landed on Sicily and captured it from Italian and German troops by August.

THINK THROUGH HISTORY
A. Making Inferences What advantages might a weaker army fighting on its home soil have over a stronger invading army?

These dazed, freezing, and starved German prisoners were actually lucky to be alive. About 240,000 Germans died during the battle for the city of Stalingrad.

The conquest of Sicily toppled Mussolini from power. On July 25, King Victor Emmanuel III fired the dictator and had him arrested. On September 3, Italy surrendered. But the Germans seized control of northern Italy and put Mussolini back in charge. Finally, the Germans retreated northward, and the victorious Allies entered Rome on June 4, 1944. Fighting in Italy, however, continued until Germany fell in May 1945. On April 28, 1945, as the Germans were retreating from northern Italy, the Italian resistance ambushed some trucks. Inside one of them, resistance fighters found Mussolini disguised as a German soldier. The following day, he was shot, and his body was hanged in the Milan town square.

Life on Allied Home Fronts

Wherever Allied forces fought, people on the home fronts rallied to support them. In war-torn countries like the Soviet Union or Great Britain, civilians lost their lives and endured extreme hardships. Except for a few of its territories, such as Hawaii, the United States did not suffer invasion or bombing. Nonetheless, Americans at home made a crucial contribution to the Allied war effort. Americans produced the weapons and equipment that would help win the war.

In a practice drill in Great Britain, a mock Nazi infiltrator disguised as a nanny "opens fire" on a sentry of the Home Guard after he asked her for identification.

Mobilizing for Total War Defeating the Axis powers required mobilizing for total war. In the United States, factories converted their peacetime operations to wartime production and made everything from machine guns to boots. Automobile factories produced tanks. A U.S. typewriter company made armor-piercing shells. By 1944, almost 18 million U.S. workers—many of them women—were working in war industries.

With factories turning out products for the war, a shortage of consumer goods hit the United States. From meat and sugar to tires and gasoline, from nylon stockings to laundry soap, the American government rationed scarce items. Setting the speed limit at 35 miles per hour also helped to save on gasoline and rubber. In European countries directly affected by the war, rationing was even more drastic.

To inspire their people to greater efforts, Allied governments conducted highly effective propaganda campaigns. In the Soviet Union, a Moscow youngster collected enough scrap metal to produce 14,000 artillery shells. Another Russian family, the Shirmanovs, used their life savings to buy a tank for the Red Army. In the United States, youngsters saved their pennies and bought government war stamps and bonds to help finance the war.

Civil Rights Curtailed by the War Government propaganda also had a negative effect. After Pearl Harbor, a wave of prejudice arose in the United States against the 127,000 Japanese Americans. Most lived in Hawaii and on the West Coast. The bombing of Pearl Harbor frightened Americans. This fear, encouraged by government propaganda, was turned against Japanese Americans. They were suddenly seen as "the enemy." On February 19, 1942, President Roosevelt set up a program of internment and loss of property, since Japanese Americans were considered a threat to the country.

In March, the military began rounding up "aliens" and shipping them to relocation camps. Two-thirds of those interned were Nisei, or Japanese Americans who were native-born American citizens. The camps were restricted military areas located away from the coast. With such a location, it was thought that the Nisei could not participate in an invasion. From 1941 until 1946, the United States imprisoned some 31,275 people it wrongly considered "enemy aliens (foreigners)." Most of those prisoners were American citizens of Japanese descent.

HISTORY MAKERS

General Dwight Eisenhower
1890–1969

In his career, U.S. General Dwight Eisenhower had shown an uncommon ability to work with all kinds of people—even competitive Allies. His Chief of Staff said of Eisenhower, "The sun rises and sets on him for me." He was also wildly popular with the troops, who affectionately called him "Uncle Ike."

So, it was not a surprise when in December 1943, U.S. Army Chief of Staff George Marshall named Eisenhower as supreme commander of the Allied forces in Europe. The new commander's "people skills" enabled him to join American and British forces together to put a permanent end to Nazi aggression.

Allied Victory in Europe

While the Allies were dealing with issues on the home front, they were preparing to push toward victory in Europe. By the end of 1942, the war had begun to turn in favor of the Allies. By 1943, the Allies began secretly building a force in Great Britain. Their plan was to attack the Germans across the English Channel.

The D-Day Invasion By May 1944, the invasion force was ready. Thousands of planes, ships, tanks, landing craft, and 3.5 million troops awaited orders to attack. American General Dwight D. Eisenhower, the commander of this enormous force, planned to strike on the coast of Normandy, in northwestern France. The Germans knew that an attack was coming. But they did not know where it would be launched. To keep Hitler guessing, the Allies set up a huge dummy army with its own headquarters and equipment. They ordered the make-believe army to attack at the French seaport of Calais (ka·LAY).

Code-named *Operation Overlord*, the invasion of Normandy was the greatest land and sea attack in history. The day chosen for the invasion to begin—called **D-Day**—was June 6, 1944.

At dawn on June 6, British, American, French, and Canadian troops fought their way onto a 60-mile stretch of beach in Normandy. The Germans had dug in with machine guns, rocket launchers, and cannons. They protected themselves behind concrete walls three feet thick. Among the Americans alone, 3,000 soldiers died on the beach that day. Captain Joseph Dawson said, "The beach was a total chaos, with men's bodies everywhere, with wounded men crying both in the water and on the shingle [coarse gravel]."

Despite heavy casualties, the Allies held the beachheads. A month later, more than 1 million additional troops had landed. On July 25, the Allies punched a hole in the German defenses near Saint-Lô (san·LOH), and General George Patton's Third Army raced through.

Background
The name *D-Day* came from the words *designated + day.*

Vocabulary
beachheads: enemy shoreline captured just before invading forces move inland.

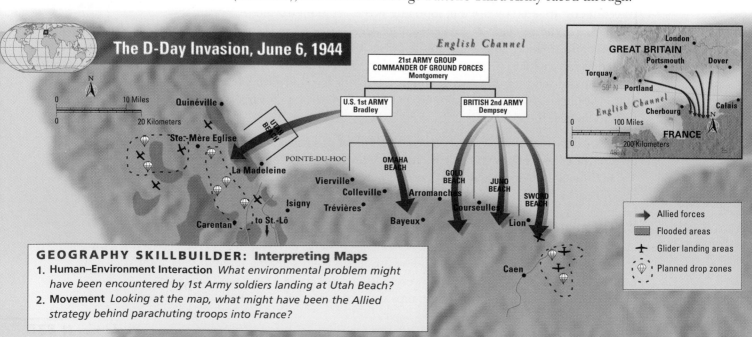

The D-Day Invasion, June 6, 1944

English Channel

21st ARMY GROUP COMMANDER OF GROUND FORCES Montgomery

U.S. 1st ARMY Bradley

BRITISH 2nd ARMY Dempsey

Quinéville
Ste.-Mère Eglise
POINTE-DU-HOC
La Madeleine
UTAH BEACH
Vierville
Colleville
OMAHA BEACH
GOLD BEACH
Arromanches
JUNO BEACH
SWORD BEACH
Isigny
Trévières
Courseulles
Carentan
to St.-Lô
Bayeux
Lion
Caen

0   10 Miles
0   20 Kilometers

GREAT BRITAIN
London
Portsmouth
Dover
Torquay
Portland
Cherbourg
Calais
English Channel
FRANCE

0   100 Miles
0   200 Kilometers

→ Allied forces
▨ Flooded areas
✛ Glider landing areas
⬗ Planned drop zones

GEOGRAPHY SKILLBUILDER: Interpreting Maps

1. **Human–Environment Interaction** *What environmental problem might have been encountered by 1st Army soldiers landing at Utah Beach?*
2. **Movement** *Looking at the map, what might have been the Allied strategy behind parachuting troops into France?*

Soon, the Germans were retreating. On August 25, the Allies marched triumphantly into Paris. By September, they had liberated France, Belgium, Luxembourg, and much of the Netherlands. They then set their sights on Germany.

The Battle of the Bulge As Allied forces moved toward Germany from the west, the Soviet army was advancing toward Germany from the east. Hitler now faced a war on two fronts. In a desperate gamble, the Führer decided to counterattack in the west. The Führer hoped a victory would split American and British forces and break up Allied supply lines. Explaining the reasoning behind his plan, Hitler said, "This battle is to decide whether we shall live or die. . . . All resistance must be broken in a wave of terror."

On December 16, German tanks broke through weak American defenses along an 85-mile front in the Ardennes. The push into the Allied lines gave the campaign its name—the **Battle of the Bulge.** Although caught off guard, the Allies eventually pushed the Germans back and won. The Nazis could do little but retreat, since Hitler had lost men that he could no longer replace.

Germany's Unconditional Surrender After the Battle of the Bulge, the war in Europe neared its end. In late March 1945, the Allies rolled across the Rhine River into Germany. By the middle of April, a noose was closing around Berlin. Three million Allied soldiers approached Berlin from the southwest. Six million Soviet troops approached from the east—some of them just 40 miles from the capital. By April 25, 1945, the Soviets had surrounded the capital, as their artillery pounded the city.

Vocabulary
capitulation: surrender.

While Soviet shells burst over Berlin, Hitler prepared for his end in an underground headquarters beneath the crumbling city. On April 29, he married his long-time companion, Eva Braun. He also wrote his final address to the German people. In it, he blamed Jews for starting the war and his generals for losing it. "I myself and my wife choose to die in order to escape the disgrace of . . . capitulation," he said. "I die with a happy heart aware of the immeasurable deeds of our soldiers at the front." Two days later, Hitler shot himself after taking poison. His new wife simply swallowed poison. The bodies were then carried outside and burned.

On May 7, 1945, General Eisenhower accepted the unconditional surrender of the Third Reich from the German military. President Roosevelt, however, did not live to witness the long-awaited victory. He had died suddenly on April 12, as Allied armies were advancing toward Berlin. Roosevelt's successor, Harry Truman, received the news of the Nazi surrender. On May 8, the surrender was officially signed in Berlin. The United States and other Allied powers celebrated V-E Day—Victory in Europe Day. The war in Europe had ended at last.

Victory in the Pacific

Although the war in Europe was over, the Allies were still fighting the Japanese in the Pacific. With the Allied victory at Guadalcanal, however, the Japanese advances in the Pacific had been stopped. For the rest of the war, the Japanese retreated before the counterattack of the Allied powers.

The Japanese Retreat By the fall of 1944, the Allies were moving in on Japan. In October, Allied forces landed on the island of Leyte (LAY·tee) in the Philippines. General MacArthur, who had been forced to surrender the islands in February 1942, waded ashore. He then declared, "People of the Philippines, I have returned."

Actually, the takeover would not be quite that easy. The Japanese had decided to destroy the American fleet. The Allies could not then resupply their ground troops. To

SPOTLIGHT ON

Dresden

On the night of February 13, 1945, 800 British and American bombers launched a massive air attack on Dresden, a German city southeast of Berlin. During the bombing, some 4,000 tons of explosives were dropped, creating raging firestorms. One author described the city as a "furnace fueled by people," as its citizens—mostly women, children, and the elderly—burned to death. Estimates of those killed vary from 35,000 to 135,000.

The firestorm reduced Dresden to rubble, accomplishing no important military goals but killing many civilians. Dresden has come to symbolize the strategy of "total war": massive attacks on both military and civilian targets to break a country's fighting spirit.

The Atomic Bomb

On the eve of World War II, scientists in Germany succeeded in splitting the nucleus of a uranium atom, releasing a huge amount of energy. Albert Einstein wrote to President Franklin Roosevelt and warned him that Nazi Germany might be working to develop atomic weapons. Roosevelt responded by giving his approval for an American program, later code-named the Manhattan Project, to develop an atomic bomb. Roosevelt's decision set off a race to assure that the United States would be the first to develop the bomb.

My body seemed all black, everything seemed dark, dark all over. . . . Then I thought, "The world is ending."
An Atomic Bomb Survivor

A boy carries his brother through the leveled city of Nagasaki. This is one of a series of photos taken by Japanese photographer Yosuke Yamahata soon after the atomic bomb devastated the city on August 9, 1945.

On the morning of August 6, 1945, the B-29 bomber *Enola Gay,* flown by commander Colonel Paul W. Tibbets, Jr., took off from Tinian Island in the Mariana Islands. At precisely 8:16 A.M., the atomic bomb exploded above Hiroshima, a city on the Japanese island of Honshu.

Hiroshima: Day of Fire

Effects of the bombing

Ground temperatures	7,000°F
Hurricane force winds	980 miles per hour
Energy released	20,000 tons of TNT
Buildings destroyed	62,000 buildings
Killed immediately	70,000 people
Dead by the end of 1945	140,000 people
Total deaths related to A-bomb	200,000 people

The overwhelming destructive power of the Hiroshima bomb, and of the bomb dropped on Nagasaki three days later, changed the nature of war forever. Nuclear destruction also led to questions about the ethics of scientists and politicians who chose to use the bomb.

Patterns of Interaction

Just as in World War I, the conflicts of World War II spurred the development of ever more powerful weapons. Mightier tanks, more elusive submarines, faster fighter planes—all emerged from this period. From ancient times to the present day, the pattern remains the same: Every new weapon causes other countries to develop others of similar or greater force. This pattern results in a deadly race for an ultimate weapon: for example, the atomic bomb.

VIDEO *Arming for War: Modern and Medieval Weapons*

Connect *to* History

Making Inferences What advantages did the United States have over Germany in the race to develop the atomic bomb?

SEE SKILLBUILDER HANDBOOK, PAGE 1005

Connect *to* Today

Contrast If you had to design a memorial to the victims of the Hiroshima and Nagasaki bombings, what symbol would you use? Make a sketch of your memorial.

Nagasaki citizens trudge through the still smoldering ruins of their city in another photo by Yosuke Yamahata.

carry out this strategy, the Japanese had to risk almost their entire fleet. They gambled everything on October 23, in the Battle of Leyte Gulf. Within three days, the Japanese navy had lost disastrously—eliminating it as a fighting force in the war. Now, only the Japanese army and the feared kamikaze stood between the Allies and Japan. The **kamikaze** were Japanese suicide pilots. They would sink Allied ships by crash-diving into them in their bomb-filled planes.

In March 1945, after a month of bitter fighting and heavy losses, American Marines took Iwo Jima (EE·wuh JEE·muh), an island 660 miles from Tokyo. On April 1, U.S. troops moved to the island of Okinawa, only about 350 miles from southern Japan. The Japanese put up a desperate fight. Nevertheless, on June 22, the bloodiest land battle of the war ended. The Japanese lost 110,000 troops, and the Americans, 12,500.

The Atomic Bomb Brings Japanese Surrender After Okinawa, the next stop had to be Japan. President Truman's advisers had informed him that an invasion of the Japanese homeland might cost the Allies half a million lives. Truman had to make a decision whether to use a powerful new weapon called the atomic bomb, or A-bomb. The A-bomb would bring the war to the quickest possible end. It had been developed by the top-secret Manhattan Project, headed by General Leslie Groves and chief scientist J. Robert Oppenheimer. The Manhattan Project became a major spending item in U.S. military budgets. Truman only learned of the new bomb's existence when he became president.

THINK THROUGH HISTORY
C. Forming an Opinion Was it necessary to drop the second atomic bomb on Nagasaki?

The first atomic bomb was exploded in a desert in New Mexico on July 16, 1945. President Truman then warned the Japanese. He told them that unless they surrendered, they could expect a "rain of ruin from the air." The Japanese did not reply. So, on August 6, 1945, the United States dropped an atomic bomb on Hiroshima, a Japanese city of 365,000 people. Almost 73,000 people died in the attack. Three days later, on August 9, a second bomb was dropped on Nagasaki, a city of 200,000. It killed about 37,500 people. Radiation killed many more. A Japanese journalist described the horror in Hiroshima:

A VOICE FROM THE PAST
Within a few seconds the thousands of people in the streets and the gardens in the center of the town were scorched by a wave of searing heat. Many were killed instantly, others lay writhing on the ground, screaming in agony from the intolerable pain of their burns. Everything standing upright in the way of the blast, walls, houses, factories, and other buildings, was annihilated.

JAPANESE JOURNALIST, quoted in *The American Heritage Picture History of World War II*

The Japanese surrendered to General Douglas MacArthur on September 2. The surrender took place aboard the United States battleship *Missouri* in Tokyo Bay. With Japan's surrender, the war had ended. Now, countries faced the task of rebuilding a war-torn world.

Section 4 Assessment

1. TERMS & NAMES

Identify
- Erwin Rommel
- Bernard Montgomery
- Dwight Eisenhower
- Battle of Stalingrad
- D-Day
- Battle of the Bulge
- kamikaze

2. TAKING NOTES

Create a chart like the one below, listing outcomes of the following World War II battles.

Battle	Outcome
Battle of El Alamein	
Battle of Stalingrad	
D-Day Invasion	
Battle of the Bulge	

Which battle do you think was most important in turning the war in favor of the Allies? Why?

3. SUMMARIZING

Based on what you have read in this section, how do governments gather support for a war effort on the home front?

THINK ABOUT
- the economy
- forms of propaganda
- individual participation in the war effort

4. ANALYZING THEMES

Science and Technology Do you think President Truman made the correct decision by ordering the atomic bomb dropped on Hiroshima and Nagasaki? Why or why not?

THINK ABOUT
- the likely consequences if the atomic bomb had not been dropped
- the destruction caused by the atomic bomb
- World War II after the dropping of the atomic bomb

The Devastation of Europe and Japan

MAIN IDEA	WHY IT MATTERS NOW
World War II cost millions of human lives and billions of dollars in damages. It left Europe and Japan in ruins.	The United States survived World War II undamaged, allowing it to become a world leader.

SETTING THE STAGE Allied victory in the war had been achieved at a high price. World War II had caused more death and destruction than any other conflict in history. It left 60 million dead, 50 million uprooted from their homes, and property damage that ran into billions of U.S. dollars.

Europe in Ruins

By the end of World War II, Europe lay in ruins. Close to 40 million Europeans had died—two-thirds of them civilians. Constant bombing and shelling had reduced hundreds of cities to rubble. The ground war had destroyed much of the countryside. Displaced persons from many nations were struggling to get home.

Background
Two-thirds of the deaths in the war occurred in Europe, making the war there far bloodier than in Asia.

A Harvest of Destruction A few of the great cities of Europe—Paris, Rome, Brussels—remained undamaged by war. Many, however, had suffered terrible destruction. The Blitz left blackened ruins in London. Over five years, 60,595 London civilians had died in the German bombings. Eastern Europe and Germany were far worse off. Warsaw, the capital of Poland, was almost wiped from the face of the earth. In 1939, Warsaw had a population of 1,289,000 people. When the Soviets entered the city in January 1945, only 153,000 people remained. In Berlin, 25,000 tons of Allied bombs had demolished 95 percent of the central city. One U.S. officer stationed in Berlin reported, "Wherever we looked we saw desolation. It was like a city of the dead."

Winston Churchill looks at Nazi firebomb damage to the British House of Commons.

After the bombings, many civilians stayed where they were and tried to get on with their lives. Some lived in partially destroyed homes or apartments. Others huddled in caves and cellars beneath the rubble. They had no water, no electricity, and very little food. Hunger was a constant companion. With factories destroyed or damaged, most people had no earnings to buy the food that was available.

Although many remained in the cities, a large number of city dwellers fled. They joined the army of displaced persons wandering Europe following the war. These displaced persons included the survivors of concentration camps, prisoners of war, and refugees fleeing the Soviet army. Millions found themselves in the wrong country when the postwar treaties changed national borders. They jammed the roads trying to get home, hoping to find their families or to find a safe place.

Simon Weisenthal described the search made by survivors of the Holocaust:

A VOICE FROM THE PAST
Across Europe a wild tide of frantic survivors was flowing. . . . Many of them didn't really know where to go. . . . And yet the survivors continued their pilgrimage of despair, sleeping on highways or in railroad stations, waiting for another train, another horse-drawn cart to come along, always driven to hope. "Perhaps someone is still alive. . . ." Someone might tell where to find a wife, a mother, children, a brother—or whether they were dead. . . . The desire to find one's people was stronger than hunger, thirst, fatigue.
SIMON WEISENTHAL, quoted in *Never to Forget: The Jews of the Holocaust*

Misery Continues After the War Although the war had ended, misery in Europe continued for years. Europe lay ravaged by the fighting. Agriculture was disrupted. Most able-bodied men had served in the military and the women had worked in war production. Few remained to plant the fields. With the transportation system destroyed, the meager harvests often did not reach the cities. Thousands died as famine and disease spread through the bombed-out cities. In August 1945, 4,000 citizens of Berlin died every day. To get a few potatoes, people would barter any valuable items they had left. The first post-war winter brought more suffering as people went without shoes and coats.

Vocabulary
barter: to trade goods and services without money.

Postwar Governments and Politics

Despairing Europeans often blamed their leaders for the war and its aftermath. Once the Germans had lost, some prewar governments—like those in Belgium, Holland, Denmark, and Norway—returned quickly. In countries like Germany, Italy, and France, however, a return to the old leadership was not so simple. Hitler's Nazi government had brought Germany to ruins. Mussolini had led Italy to defeat. The Vichy government had collaborated with the Nazis. Much of the old leadership was in disgrace. Besides, in Italy and France, many resistance fighters were Communists.

THINK THROUGH HISTORY
A. Identifying Problems Why might it have been difficult to find democratic government leaders in post-Nazi Germany?

After the war, the Communist Party promised change, and millions were ready to listen. In both France and Italy, Communist Party membership skyrocketed. The Communists made huge gains in the first postwar elections. Anxious to speed up a political takeover, the Communists staged a series of violent strikes. Alarmed French and Italians reacted by voting for anti-Communist parties. Communist membership and influence then began to decline. And they declined even more so as the economies of France and Italy began to recover.

An Attempt at Justice: The Nuremberg Trials While nations were struggling to recover politically and economically, they also were trying to deal with Germany's guilt in the Holocaust. To make sure that such crimes would never happen again, the Allies put Nazis on trial. In 1946, an International Military Tribunal representing 23 nations put Nazi war criminals on trial in Nuremberg, Germany. In the first of the **Nuremberg Trials,** 22 Nazi leaders were charged with waging a war of aggression. They were also accused of violating the laws of war and of committing "crimes against humanity"—the murder of 11 million people.

Führer Adolf Hitler, SS chief Heinrich Himmler, and Minister of Propaganda Joseph Goebbels had escaped trial by committing suicide. However, Marshal Hermann Göring, Deputy Führer Rudolf Hess, and other high ranking Nazi leaders had to face the charges.

Of the 22 defendants, 12 were sentenced to death. Göring cheated the executioner by killing himself. The rest were hanged on October 16, 1946. Hans Frank, the "Slayer of Poles," was the only convicted Nazi to express remorse: "A thousand years will pass," he said, "and still this guilt of Germany

CONNECT *to* TODAY

Genocide in Rwanda
Genocide is a crime that human beings have committed against one another throughout history. In April 1994, the president of the East African nation of Rwanda died in a suspicious plane crash. The president was a member of the Hutu tribe. In Rwanda, the Hutu and Tutsi tribes have long hated and fought each other.

After the president's death, about 1 million Tutsis were slaughtered by the majority Hutus. In the end, Tutsi rebels ended the worst of the genocide.

The United Nations has set up an international war crimes tribunal to judge the worst acts of genocide. Yet, many criminals are still at large, and ethnic conflict in Rwanda continues.

will not have been erased." The bodies of those executed were burned at the concentration camp of Dachau (DAHK·ow). They were cremated in the same ovens that had burned so many of their victims.

The Effects of Defeat in Japan

The defeat suffered by Japan in World War II left the country in ruins. Two million lives had been lost in the war. The country's major cities had been largely destroyed by Allied bombing raids, including the capital, Tokyo. The atomic bomb had left Hiroshima and Nagasaki as blackened wastelands. The Allies had stripped Japan of its colonial empire. They even took away areas that had belonged to the Japanese for centuries.

The United States Occupies Japan Even after these disasters, some Japanese military leaders wanted to continue the fight. In a radio broadcast on August 15, 1945, Emperor Hirohito urged the Japanese people to lay down their arms and work together to rebuild Japan. "Should we continue to fight," he declared, "it would only result in an ultimate collapse . . . of the Japanese nation." Two weeks after that broadcast, General Douglas MacArthur, now supreme commander for the Allied powers, accepted the Japanese surrender. He took charge of the U.S. occupation.

Emperor Hirohito and U.S. General Douglas MacArthur look distant and uncomfortable as they pose for a photo. The photo was taken in the American Embassy in Tokyo on September 27, 1945.

Demilitarization in Japan MacArthur was determined to be fair and not to plant the seeds for a future war. Nevertheless, to ensure that fighting would end, he began a process of **demilitarization**—disbanding the Japanese armed forces. He achieved this quickly, leaving the Japanese with only a small police force. MacArthur also began bringing war criminals to trial. Out of 25 surviving defendants, former Premier Hideki Tojo and six others were condemned to hang.

The general then turned his attention to democratization—the process of creating a government elected by the people. In February 1946, MacArthur and his American political advisers drew up a new constitution. It changed the empire into a parliamentary democracy like that of Great Britain. The Japanese accepted the constitution. It went into effect on May 3, 1947.

MacArthur was not told to revive the Japanese economy. However, he was instructed to broaden land ownership and increase the participation of workers and farmers in the new democracy. Absentee landlords with huge estates had to sell land to tenant farmers at reasonable prices. Workers could now create independent labor unions. Still bitter over Pearl Harbor, Americans did not provide much aid for rebuilding Japan. The United States did send 2 billion dollars in emergency relief. This was a small amount, however, considering the task that lay ahead.

THINK THROUGH HISTORY
B. Making Inferences How would demilitarization and a revived economy help Japan achieve democracy?

U.S. Occupation Brings Deep Changes

The new constitution was the most important achievement of the occupation. It brought deep changes to Japanese society. In 1945, the Japanese had agreed to surrender. They insisted, however, that "the supreme power of the emperor not be compromised." The Allies agreed, but now things had changed. A long Japanese tradition had viewed the emperor as a god. He was also an absolute ruler whose divine will was law. The emperor now had to declare that he was not a god. That admission was as

Costs of World War II: Allies and Axis

	Direct War Costs	Military Killed/Missing	Civilians Killed
United States	$288.0 billion*	292,131**	—
Great Britain	$117.0 billion	271,311	60,595
France	$111.3 billion	205,707***	173,260†
USSR	$93.0 billion	13,600,000	7,720,000
Germany	$212.3 billion	3,300,000	2,893,000††
Japan	$41.3 billion	1,140,429	953,000

*In 1994 dollars.
**An additional 115,187 servicemen died from non-battle causes.
***Before surrender to Nazis.
†Includes 65,000 murdered Jews.
††Includes about 170,000 murdered Jews and 56,000 foreign civilians in Germany.

SKILLBUILDER: Interpreting Charts
1. Which of the nations listed in the chart suffered the greatest human costs?
2. How does U.S. spending on the war compare with the spending of Germany and Japan?

shocking to the Japanese as defeat. His power was also dramatically reduced as he became a constitutional monarch. Like the ruler of Great Britain, the emperor became largely a figurehead—a symbol of Japan.

The new constitution guaranteed that real political power in Japan rested with the people. The people elected a two-house parliament, called the Diet. All citizens over the age of 20, including women, had the right to vote. The government was led by a prime minister chosen by a majority of the Diet. A constitutional bill of rights protected basic freedoms. One more key provision—Article 9—stated that the Japanese could no longer make war. They could only fight if attacked.

In September 1951, the United States and 48 other nations signed a formal peace treaty with Japan. The treaty officially ended the war. With no armed forces, the Japanese also agreed to continuing U.S. military protection for their country. Six months later, the U.S. occupation of Japan was over. Relieved of the burden of paying for the occupation, Japan's economy recovered more quickly. With the official end of the war, the United States and Japan became allies.

In the postwar world, however, enemies not only became allies. Allies also became enemies. World War II had changed the political landscape of Europe. It weakened some nations and strengthened others. The Soviet Union and the United States had come out of the war as allies. Nevertheless, once the fighting was over, the differences in their postwar goals emerged. These differences stirred up conflicts that would shape the modern world for decades.

THINK THROUGH HISTORY
C. Analyzing Causes Why did the Americans choose the British system of government for the Japanese, instead of the American system?

Section 5 Assessment

1. TERMS & NAMES
Identify
• Nuremberg Trials
• demilitarization

2. TAKING NOTES
Using a Venn diagram like the one below, compare and contrast the aftermath of World War II in Europe and Japan.

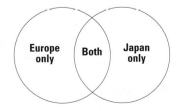

Europe only | Both | Japan only

3. ANALYZING CAUSES
Why do you think that many Europeans favored communism directly following World War II?

THINK ABOUT
• World War II destruction
• pre-World War II governments
• economic concerns

4. THEME ACTIVITY
Economics Draw a political cartoon from a Japanese absentee landlord's or industrialist's point of view on MacArthur's postwar economic reforms. Remember that MacArthur is an American making important changes in a country that is not his own.

Events of World War II

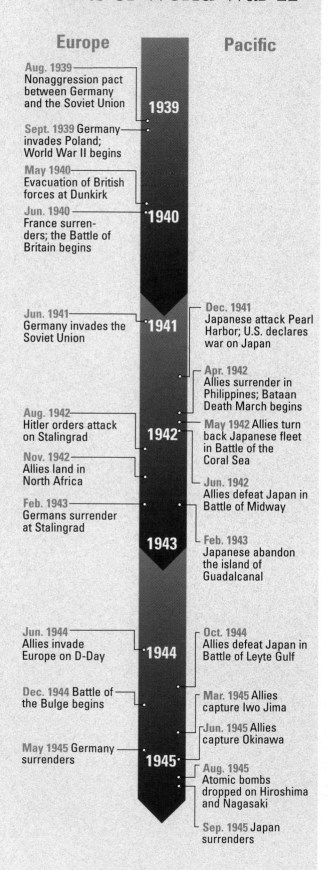

Europe   **Pacific**

1939

Aug. 1939 Nonaggression pact between Germany and the Soviet Union

Sept. 1939 Germany invades Poland; World War II begins

May 1940 Evacuation of British forces at Dunkirk

1940

Jun. 1940 France surrenders; the Battle of Britain begins

1941

Jun. 1941 Germany invades the Soviet Union

Dec. 1941 Japanese attack Pearl Harbor; U.S. declares war on Japan

Apr. 1942 Allies surrender in Philippines; Bataan Death March begins

Aug. 1942 Hitler orders attack on Stalingrad

1942

May 1942 Allies turn back Japanese fleet in Battle of the Coral Sea

Nov. 1942 Allies land in North Africa

Jun. 1942 Allies defeat Japan in Battle of Midway

Feb. 1943 Germans surrender at Stalingrad

1943

Feb. 1943 Japanese abandon the island of Guadalcanal

Jun. 1944 Allies invade Europe on D-Day

1944

Oct. 1944 Allies defeat Japan in Battle of Leyte Gulf

Dec. 1944 Battle of the Bulge begins

Mar. 1945 Allies capture Iwo Jima

Jun. 1945 Allies capture Okinawa

May 1945 Germany surrenders

1945

Aug. 1945 Atomic bombs dropped on Hiroshima and Nagasaki

Sep. 1945 Japan surrenders

TERMS & NAMES

Briefly explain the importance of each of the following during and after World War II.

1. blitzkrieg
2. Atlantic Charter
3. Isoroku Yamamoto
4. Battle of Midway
5. Holocaust
6. Final Solution
7. genocide
8. D-Day
9. Nuremberg Trials
10. demilitarization

REVIEW QUESTIONS

SECTION 1 *(pages 821–826)*

Hitler's Lightning War

11. What event finally unleashed World War II?
12. Why was capturing Egypt's Suez Canal so important to the Axis powers?

SECTION 2 *(pages 827–830)*

Japan Strikes in the Pacific

13. What was Yamamoto's objective at Pearl Harbor?
14. How did Japan try to win support from other Asian countries?

SECTION 3 *(pages 831–834)*

The Holocaust

15. Name two tactics that Hitler used to rid Germany of Jews before creating his "Final Solution."
16. What tactics did Hitler use during the "Final Solution"?

SECTION 4 *(pages 835–841)*

The Allies Are Victorious

17. Why were items rationed during the war?
18. What was *Operation Overlord?*

SECTION 5 *(pages 842–845)*

The Devastation of Europe and Japan

19. Why did Europeans leave their homes following the war?
20. What were two of the most important steps that MacArthur took in Japan following the war?

Interact *with* History

On page 820, you had to decide whether to bomb the civilian population in an enemy city to shorten a war. Now that you have read the chapter, what bombing incidents in World War II seem to reflect a decision to bomb civilians to speed victory? Remember to consider bombings carried out by both sides in the war.

CRITICAL THINKING

1. WAR LEADERS

Consider the personalities, tactics, and policies of Hitler, Rommel, MacArthur, and Churchill. What qualities do you think make a successful leader in war? Explain your answer.

2. WORLD WAR II BATTLES

Below is a list of World War II battles/conflicts. Copy the chart on your paper and specify for each whether the Axis powers or the Allied powers gained an advantage over their enemies.

Battle/Conflict	Allied or Axis Powers?
Battle of Britain	
War in the Balkans	
Pearl Harbor	
Battle of the Coral Sea	
Battle of Midway	
Battle of Stalingrad	

3. WAR GOALS

THEME **EMPIRE BUILDING** Compare and contrast Japan's and Germany's goals in World War II.

4. ANALYZING PRIMARY SOURCES

The following quotation comes from the August 29, 1945 edition of *The Christian Century*, a prominent Protestant journal. In this passage, the writer raises questions about the American use of the atomic bomb on the Japanese.

A VOICE FROM THE PAST

Perhaps it was inevitable that the bomb would ultimately be employed to bring Japan to the point of surrender. . . . But there was no military advantage in hurling the bomb upon Japan without warning. The least we might have done was to announce to our foe that we possessed the atomic bomb; that its destructive power was beyond anything known in warfare; and that its terrible effectiveness had been experimentally demonstrated in this country. . . . If she [Japan] doubted the good faith of our representations, it would have been a simple matter to select a demonstration target in the enemy's own country at a place where the loss of human life would be at a minimum. If, despite such warning, Japan had still held out, we would have been in a far less questionable position had we then dropped the bombs on Hiroshima and Nagasaki.

- Does *The Christian Century* oppose all use of the atomic bomb as a weapon of war? Explain.

- What advantages might the alternative proposed by *The Christian Century* have had in ending World War II?

CHAPTER ACTIVITIES

1. LIVING HISTORY: Unit Portfolio Project

THEME **SCIENCE AND TECHNOLOGY** Your unit portfolio project focuses on how science and technology influence history. For Chapter 32, you might use one of the following ideas to add to your portfolio:

- Do research and create a set of science and technology cards for important inventions developed or perfected during World War II. Include the following categories on your cards: *Name of Invention, Country, Year, Use in the War, Use Today.*

- Write a list of five questions that you would ask Robert Oppenheimer if you were on a committee deciding whether to develop an atomic bomb.

- Do research and create a science and technology time line for 1935–1945. Include major events of the war and five scientific and technological developments.

2. CONNECT TO TODAY: Cooperative Learning

THEME **ECONOMICS** During World War II, many nations, including the United States, converted their consumer-goods factories to produce vital products for the war effort. Today many of those factories still exist but are back to producing consumer goods.

Work with a team to prepare a short "company history."

Using the Internet, library, magazines, or Chamber of Commerce, do research on a consumer-goods company. (A consumer-goods company makes products for personal use or enjoyment—for example, cars, radios, clothing.) Look for a company that was around before 1945. (Several of today's important car and appliance manufacturers, as well as manufacturers of steel, tires, detergents, etc., existed before 1945.)

As you come up with ideas, try to find answers to questions such as: What products did the company make before World War II? During the war? After? What were working conditions like during the war? After the war? In a two- to three-page paper, write your company history. Include copies of any articles, photographs, or pictures that you find about the company.

3. INTERPRETING A TIME LINE

Revisit the unit time line on pages 738–739. Which two leaders do you think had the largest impact on events between 1939 and 1945? Why?

FOCUS ON **GEOGRAPHY**

Notice the locations in Europe of German death camps and labor camps.

- Which country had the most labor camps?

- Which country had the most death camps?

Connect to History
In what year did most of the death camps begin to operate? Why?

●	Labor camp
◆	Death camp
1942	Date founded
—	Border, 1933

LATVIA
Jungernhof 1942 ◆
Baltic Sea
EAST PRUSSIA
Stutthof, 1939
Neuengamme, 1940
Bergen-Belsen 1943
Ravensbrück, 1936
Sachsenhausen, 1936
NETH.
Vught, 1943
GERMANY
Chelmno 1941 ◆
Treblinka ◆ 1942
Sobibor 1942
POLAND
Mittelbau-Dora, 1943
Buchenwald 1937
Gross-Rosen 1941
BELG.
Theresienstadt 1941
Majdanek 1942 ◆
LUX.
Flossenbürg 1938
CZECH.
Auschwitz 1940 ◆
Plasow 1942 ◆
Belzec 1942 ◆
Natzweiler 1941
FRANCE
Dachau 1933
Mauthausen, 1941
SWITZ.
AUSTRIA
Jasenovac, 1941
Jadovno, 1941
YUGOSLAVIA
Sajmiste, 1941
Adriatic Sea
200 Miles
400 Kilometers

Black South Africans wait to vote during the nation's first "all-races" election in April 1994. While the present era has been one of struggle and strife, it also has produced events that show people's continuing desire to achieve democracy and justice.

	1945	1955	1965	1975

CHAPTER 33 1945–PRESENT
Restructuring the Postwar World

1945 *Yalta* Allied leaders meet to plan postwar world

1946 *Soviet Union, U.S.* Cold War begins

1946 *China* Civil war between Nationalists and Communists resumes

1950–53 *Korea* Korean War between North and South Korea

1953 *Iran* U.S. restores ousted shah to power

1958 *China* Mao Zedong begins Great Leap Forward

1959 *Cuba* Fidel Castro overthrows Batista

1960 *Soviet Union* Soviets catch U.S. spy plane in U-2 incident

1961 *Cuba* Castro routs U.S.-supported invasion of Bay of Pigs

1965 *Vietnam* U.S. sends troops to Vietnam

1966 *China* Red Guards begin Cultural Revolution in China

1969 *Vietnam* Nixon begins withdrawal of U.S. troops from Vietnam

CHAPTER 34 1945–PRESENT
The Colonies Become New Nations

1946 *Philippines* Philippines gains independence from U.S.

1947 *India* Independent India becomes partitioned into India and Pakistan

1948 *Middle East* Israel becomes a nation

1948 *India* Gandhi is assassinated

1957 *Ghana* Ghana achieves independence from Great Britain

1962 *Algeria* Algeria achieves independence from France

1964 *Kenya* Jomo Kenyatta becomes president

1965 *Malaysia* Singapore becomes independent

1967 *Indonesia* Suharto becomes president

1971 *East Pakistan* East Pakistan becomes independent Bangladesh

1973 *Middle East* Arab forces attack Israel in the Yom Kippur War

CHAPTER 35 1945–PRESENT
Struggles for Democracy

1946 *Argentina* Juan Perón is elected president and becomes a dictator

1948 *South Africa* National Party sets up apartheid

1960 *South Africa* Police kill 69 demonstrators in Sharpeville Massacre

1964 *Brazil* A military government seizes power

1966 *China* Mao Zedong launches Cultural Revolution

1967 *Nigeria* Biafra secedes and civil war erupts

CHAPTER 36 1960–PRESENT
Global Interdependence

◄1990s *Afghanistan*

	1945	1955	1965	1975

1979 *Iran* Shah flees Iran; Muslims take over government

1979 *Nicaragua* U.S. and Soviets support Marxist rebels

1979 *Afghanistan* Soviets invade Afghanistan

1981 *Iran* Islamic revolutionaries free U.S. hostages

1950s *China* ▶

1979 *Middle East* Camp David Accords signed by Egypt's Sadat and Israel's Begin ends war between Egypt and Israel

1981 *Egypt* Anwar Sadat is assassinated

1984 *India* Indira Gandhi is assassinated

1987 *Middle East* Palestinians begin intifada

1993 *Israel* Israel grants Palestinians self-rule in Gaza Strip and West Bank

1995 *Israel* Prime Minister Yitzhak Rabin is assassinated

1997 *Congo* Laurent Kabila becomes president of Democratic Republic of the Congo

1978 *China* Deng Xiaoping begins Four Modernizations

1982 *Argentina* Britain defeats Argentina in war over Falkland Islands

1989 *Germany* Berlin Wall is knocked down

1989 *China* Student demonstrators killed in Tiananmen Square

1991 *Soviet Union* Soviet Union breaks up into 15 republics

1992 *Bosnia-Herzegovina* Serbs begin war against Muslims and Croats

1994 *South Africa* First all-race election; Nelson Mandela becomes president

1997 *Mexico* Mexico elects multi-party congress

1997 *Hong Kong* Britain returns Hong Kong to China

▲1990s *South Africa*

1975 *Space* U.S. *Apollo* docks with Soviet *Soyuz* spacecraft

1975 *Finland* Helsinki Accords on Human Rights established

1986 *Space* Soviet space station *Mir* established in space

1990 *Middle East* Iraq occupies part of Kuwait, provoking Persian Gulf War

1992 *Brazil* Earth Summit Environmental Conference held in Rio de Janeiro

1995 *China* International Conference on Women held in Beijing

1995 *Worldwide* World Trade Organization established

Living History
Unit 8 Portfolio Project

THEME Economics

Your portfolio for Unit 8 will show the economic changes within and among nations from World War II to the present. You will trace the growing global interdependence of the economies of all nations of the world.

Living History Project Choices
Each Chapter Assessment offers you choices of ways to show how the economies of the nations grew or shrank and became tied to the economies of others. Activities include the following:

Chapter 33 newscast, poster, skit

Chapter 34 list, chart, magazine article

Chapter 35 action list, poster, interview

Chapter 36 poem or song, map, graphs or charts

Restructuring the Postwar World, 1945–present

Economics
After World War II, two conflicting economic systems—capitalism and communism—competed for influence and power. The major players in this struggle, the United States and the Soviet Union, each tried to win other nations to its side.

Revolution
In Asia, Latin America, and Eastern Europe, people revolted against repressive governments or rule by foreign powers. These revolutions often became the arenas for conflicts between the United States and the Soviet Union.

Empire Building
The United States and the Soviet Union used military, economic, and humanitarian aid to extend their control over other countries. They also sought to prevent the other superpower from gaining influence.

INTERNET CONNECTION

Visit us at **www.mcdougallittell.com** to learn more about the Cold War and the wars in Korea and Vietnam.

COLD WAR ENEMIES, 1946

UNITED
STATES

Beginning in the **late 1940s**, the **United States** and the **Soviet Union** faced off in a deadly arms race. Luckily for the world, each side merely stockpiled its weapons, afraid to make the first move.

ATLANTIC
OCEAN

During the **late 1970s, Nicaragua** became the arena for a U.S. stand against communism. These Communist Nicaraguan rebels fought to end the dictatorship of their country's U.S.-supported regime. But they also supported leftist rebels in El Salvador. In response, the United States backed anti-Communist guerrillas in Nicaragua called Contras.

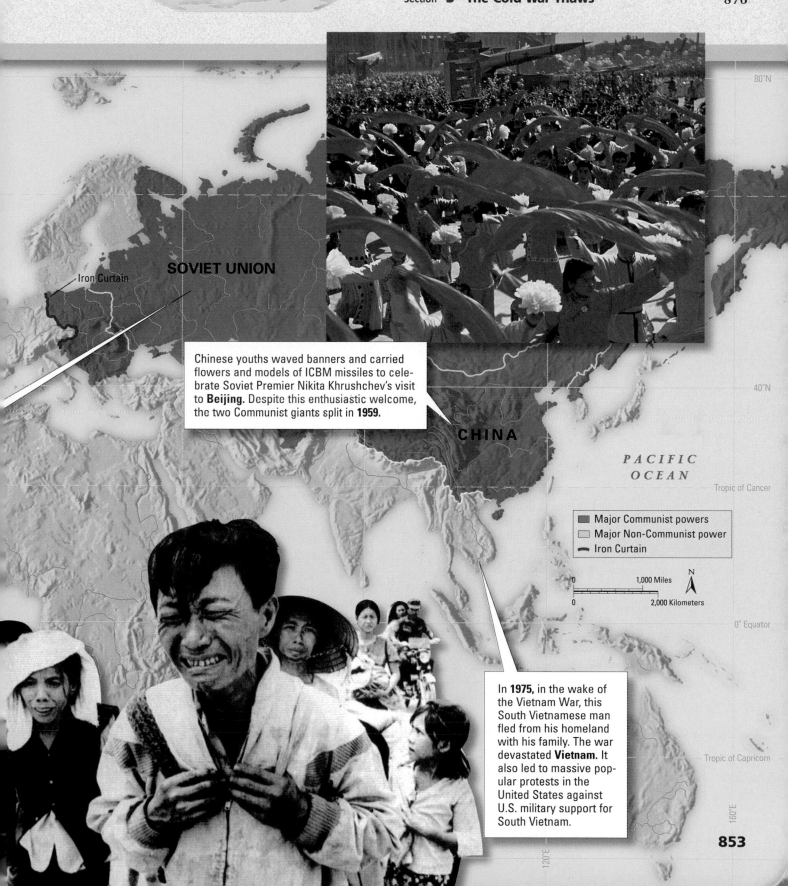

SOVIET UNION

Iron Curtain

CHINA

PACIFIC
OCEAN

Chinese youths waved banners and carried
flowers and models of ICBM missiles to celebrate Soviet Premier Nikita Khrushchev's visit
to **Beijing**. Despite this enthusiastic welcome,
the two Communist giants split in **1959**.

■ Major Communist powers
□ Major Non-Communist power
—・ Iron Curtain

0   1,000 Miles
0   2,000 Kilometers

In **1975**, in the wake of
the Vietnam War, this
South Vietnamese man
fled from his homeland
with his family. The war
devastated **Vietnam**. It
also led to massive pop-
ular protests in the
United States against
U.S. military support for
South Vietnam.

853

Worcester War II has ended and two superpowers—the United States and the Soviet Union—dominate the world. You are the leader of one of those superpowers. Civil war has broken out in a developing country that supplies you with essential raw materials.

For that reason, it is important for you to help restore peace. The ruler of that country is a brutal dictator who makes life miserable for his people. Rebels are fighting to topple him, but they are backed by your superpower enemy.

Would you support the country's ruler or the rebels?

Rebel forces are skilled at guerrilla warfare. With weapons supplied by your superpower enemy and their knowledge of the land, they are powerful military opponents.

The developing country has rich natural resources that both superpowers need.

Life is difficult for the country's people. They suffer even more as the civil war continues.

EXAMINING *the* ISSUES

- What is most important to you—aiding the people of the developing nation or preventing your enemy from gaining influence there?

- How might competing superpowers use weaker countries in their competition?

- How might being caught in a struggle between superpowers affect a developing nation?

As a class, discuss the effects of the conflict between superpowers on the rest of the world. Think about the experiences of Latin American and other countries under colonialism and how those lessons might be useful.

As you read about how the two superpowers divided up the world, notice the part weaker countries played in their conflict.

Two Superpowers Face Off

TERMS & NAMES
- United Nations
- iron curtain
- containment
- Truman Doctrine
- Marshall Plan
- Cold War
- NATO
- Warsaw Pact
- brinkmanship
- U-2 incident

MAIN IDEA	WHY IT MATTERS NOW
The conflicting aims between the United States and the Soviet Union led to global competition.	The conflicts between these two superpowers played a major role in reshaping the modern world.

SETTING THE STAGE During World War II, the United States and the Soviet Union joined forces to fight against the Germans. The Soviet army marched west. The Americans marched east to meet them in a defeated Germany. When the Allied soldiers met at the Elbe River, they embraced each other warmly. Their leaders, however, regarded each other much more coolly.

Former Allies Diverge

Even before World War II ended, the U.S. alliance with the Soviet Union had begun to unravel. The United States was upset that Joseph Stalin, the Soviet Union's leader, had signed a nonaggression pact with Adolf Hitler, Germany's leader, in 1939. Later, Stalin blamed the Allies for delaying their invasion of German-occupied Europe until 1944. Driven by these and other conflicts, the two allies began to pursue opposing goals.

A Joint Postwar Plan In February 1945, the war was not yet over. But the leaders of the three Allied nations—the United States, Britain, and the Soviet Union—met in the Soviet Black Sea resort city of Yalta. There, they agreed to divide Germany into zones of occupation controlled by the Allied military forces. Germany also would have to pay the Soviet Union to compensate for its loss of life and property. Stalin promised that Eastern Europeans would have free elections. Skeptical Winston Churchill recognized this as an empty promise. And he predicted that Stalin would keep his pledge only if the Eastern Europeans followed "a policy friendly to Russia." In return, Stalin agreed to join the war against Japan, an ally of Germany.

Creation of the United Nations In June 1945, the United States and the Soviet Union temporarily set aside their differences. They joined 48 other countries in forming the **United Nations.** This international organization was intended to protect the members against aggression. It was to be based in New York. The 50 nations that signed the UN charter pledged "to save succeeding generations from the scourge of war."

The charter for the new peacekeeping organization established a large body called the General Assembly. This was like an international town meeting. Each UN member nation could cast its vote on a broad range of issues, including membership. An 11-member body called the Security Council had the real power to investigate and settle disputes, though. The five permanent members of the Security Council were Britain, China,

France, the United States, and the Soviet Union. Each could veto any Security Council action. This provision was intended to prevent any members of the Council from voting as a bloc to override the others.

Differing U.S. and Soviet Goals Despite their agreement at Yalta and their mutual presence on the UN Security Council, the United States and the Soviet Union split sharply after the war ended. The war had affected these two superpowers very differently. The United States, the world's richest and most powerful country at that time, suffered 400,000 deaths. Its cities and factories remained intact, however. The Soviet Union experienced at least 50 times as many fatalities. One in four Soviets was wounded or killed. In addition, many Soviet cities were demolished. These contrasting situations, as well as striking political and economic differences, affected the two countries' postwar goals. As the following chart shows, their aims in postwar Europe were contradictory.

Superpower Aims in Europe	
United States	**Soviet Union**
• Encourage democracy in other countries to help prevent the rise of Communist governments	• Encourage communism in other countries as part of a worldwide workers' revolution
• Gain access to raw materials and markets to fuel booming industries	• Rebuild its war-ravaged economy using Eastern Europe's industrial equipment and raw materials
• Rebuild European governments to promote stability and create new markets for American goods	• Control Eastern Europe to protect Soviet borders and balance the U.S. influence in Western Europe
• Reunite Germany to stabilize it and increase the security of Europe	• Keep Germany divided to prevent its waging war again

SKILLBUILDER: Interpreting Charts
1. *Which Soviet aims involved self-protection?*
2. *Which U.S. and Soviet aims in Europe conflicted?*

THINK THROUGH HISTORY
A. Summarizing
Why did the United States and the Soviet Union split after the war?

The Soviet Union Corrals Eastern Europe

With the end of World War II, a major goal of the Soviet Union was to shield itself from another invasion from the west. Even before the devastation of World War II, centuries of history had taught the Soviets to fear invasion. Because it lacked natural western borders, Russia fell victim to each of its neighbors in turn. In the 17th century, the Poles captured the Kremlin. During the next century, the Swedes attacked. Napoleon overran Moscow in 1812. The Germans invaded Russia during World War I.

Soviets Build a Wall of Satellite Nations As the war drew to a close, the Soviet Union pushed the Nazis back across Eastern Europe. By the end of the war, Soviet troops occupied a strip of countries along the Soviet Union's own western border. The Soviet Union regarded these countries as a necessary buffer, or wall of protection. Stalin ignored the agreement made in Yalta to allow free elections in Eastern Europe. He installed or secured Communist governments in Albania, Bulgaria, Hungary, Czechoslovakia, Romania, Poland, and Yugoslavia.

The Soviet leader's American partner at Yalta, President Franklin D. Roosevelt, had died on April 12, 1945. Roosevelt's successor, President Harry S. Truman, was a tougher adversary for Stalin. To the new president, Stalin's reluctance to allow free elections in Poland and other Eastern European nations represented a clear violation of those countries' rights. Truman, Stalin, and Churchill met at Potsdam, Germany, in July 1945. There, President Truman pressed Stalin to permit free elections in Eastern Europe. The Soviet leader refused. In a speech in early 1946, Stalin declared that

Communist countries
Non-Communist countries

0   500 Miles
0   1,000 Kilometers

FINLAND
NORWAY
SWEDEN
North Sea
DENMARK
Baltic Sea
IRELAND
GREAT BRITAIN
NETH.
E. GER.
POLAND
SOVIET UNION
BELG.
WEST GERMANY
LUX.
CZECHOSLOVAKIA
ATLANTIC OCEAN
FRANCE
SWITZ.
AUSTRIA
HUNGARY
ROMANIA
ITALY
YUGOSLAVIA
BULGARIA
Black Sea
PORTUGAL
SPAIN
ALBANIA
GREECE
TURKEY
Mediterranean Sea
Aral Sea
Caspian Sea
Circle
LAND

DENMARK
Iron curtain
NETH.
British Zone
Berlin
POLAND
EAST GERMANY
WEST GERMANY
French Zone
CZECHOSLOVAKIA
50° N
FRANCE
American Zone
AUSTRIA
SWITZ.
0   200 Miles
0   400 Kilometers
ITALY

GEOGRAPHY SKILLBUILDER: Interpreting Maps

1. **Location** *In which part of Germany was Berlin located?*
2. **Place** *Which countries separated the Soviet Union from Western Europe?*

communism and capitalism could not exist in the same world. He said that war between the United States and the Soviet Union was certain.

The Iron Curtain Divides East and West Europe now lay divided between East and West. Germany's postwar fate, which had been decided at Yalta, left the country split into two sections. The Soviets controlled the eastern part, including half of Germany's capital, Berlin. Under a Communist government, East Germany was named the German Democratic Republic. The western zones became the Federal Republic of Germany in 1949. Winston Churchill described the division of Europe:

A VOICE FROM THE PAST

From Stettin in the Baltic to Trieste in the Adriatic, an iron curtain has descended across the continent. Behind that line lie all the capitals of the ancient states of Central and Eastern Europe. . . . All these famous cities and the populations around them lie in the Soviet sphere and all are subject in one form or another, not only to Soviet influence but to a very high and increasing measure of control from Moscow.

WINSTON CHURCHILL, "Iron Curtain" speech, March 5, 1946

THINK THROUGH HISTORY
B. Analyzing Causes What events led to the division of Europe?

Churchill's phrase **"iron curtain"** came to represent Europe's division between a mostly democratic Western Europe and a Communist Eastern Europe. From behind the iron curtain, Stalin termed Churchill's words a "call to war."

United States Counters Soviet Expansion

Soviet-American relations continued to worsen in 1946 and 1947. An increasingly worried United States sought to offset the growing Soviet threat in Eastern Europe. President Truman declared that it was time to stop "babying the Soviets." He adopted a foreign policy called **containment.** Containment was a policy directed at blocking Soviet influence and preventing the expansion of communism. Containment policies included creating alliances and helping weak countries resist Soviet advances.

The Truman Doctrine In a speech asking Congress for foreign aid for Turkey and Greece, President Truman contrasted democracy with communism:

> **A VOICE FROM THE PAST**
> One way of life is based upon the will of the majority, and is distinguished by free institutions . . . free elections . . . and freedom from political oppression. The second way of life is based upon the will of a minority forcibly imposed upon the majority. It relies upon terror and oppression . . . fixed elections, and the suppression of personal freedoms. I believe it must be the policy of the United States to support free people who are resisting attempted subjugation by armed minorities or by outside pressures.
> **HARRY S. TRUMAN,** speech to Congress, March 12, 1947

Truman's support for countries that rejected communism was called the **Truman Doctrine.** It caused great controversy. Some opponents objected to American interference in other nations' affairs. Others argued that the United States lacked the resources to carry on a global crusade against communism. Still others pointed out that some U.S. support would go to dictators. Congress, however, immediately authorized over $400 million in aid to Turkey and Greece.

The Marshall Plan Much of Western Europe lay in ruins after the war. Europe's problems included record-breaking cold and snow, postwar unemployment, lack of food, and economic turmoil. In June 1947, U.S. Secretary of State George Marshall proposed that America give aid to any European country that needed it. This assistance program, called the **Marshall Plan,** would provide food, machines, and other materials. As Congress debated the $12.5 billion program in February 1948, the Communists seized power in Czechoslovakia. Congress immediately approved the Marshall Plan. The plan achieved spectacular success in Western Europe and in Yugoslavia.

THINK THROUGH HISTORY
C. Making Inferences What was President Truman's major reason for offering aid to other countries?

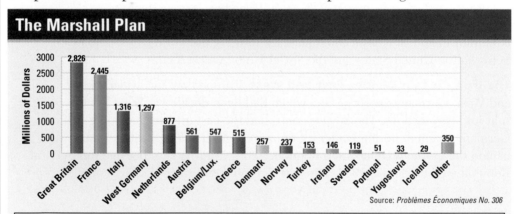

The Marshall Plan

Source: *Problèmes Économiques No. 306*

SKILLBUILDER: Interpreting Charts
1. *Which country received the most aid from the United States?*
2. *Why do you think Great Britain and France received so much aid?*

The Berlin Airlift While Europe began rebuilding, the United States and its allies clashed with the Soviet Union over Germany. The Soviets meant to keep their former enemy weak and divided. In 1948, France, Britain, and the United States decided to withdraw their forces from Germany. They would allow their three occupation zones to form one nation. The Soviet Union responded by holding West Berlin hostage.

Although Berlin lay well within the Soviet occupation zone of Germany, it too had been divided into four zones. The Soviet Union cut off highway, water, and rail traffic into Berlin's western zones. Since no supplies could get in, the city faced starvation. Stalin gambled that the threat would frighten Western countries. He hoped it would force them to surrender West Berlin or give up their idea of reunifying Germany.

The Soviet leader lost his gamble. To break the blockade, American and British officials flew food and supplies into West Berlin. For nearly 11 months, planes took

Children in West
Berlin in 1948
welcome planes
that landed every
few minutes with
supplies to break
the Soviet blockade
of the city.

THINK THROUGH HISTORY
D. Analyzing Issues
What Soviet actions
were the Truman
Doctrine, the Marshall
Plan, and the Berlin
airlift responses to?

off and landed every three minutes. In 277,000 flights, pilots brought in 2.3 million tons of supplies—food, fuel, medicine, and even Christmas presents. The Soviet Union, admitting defeat, lifted the Berlin blockade in May 1949.

The Cold War and a Divided World

These increasing conflicts were the beginnings of the **Cold War.** This was a state of diplomatic hostility that developed between the two superpowers. Beginning in 1949, the superpowers used spying, propaganda, diplomacy, and secret operations in their dealings with each other. Much of the world allied with one side or the other. In fact, until the Soviet Union finally broke up in 1991, the Cold War dictated not only U.S. and Soviet foreign policy. It influenced world alliances as well.

Rival Alliances The Berlin blockade heightened Western Europe's fears of Soviet aggression. As a result, in 1949, ten Western European nations joined with the United States and Canada to form a defensive military alliance. This alliance was called the North Atlantic Treaty Organization **(NATO).** These nations promised to meet an attack on any NATO member with armed force. For the United States, NATO membership marked the country's first peacetime military commitment.

The Soviet Union viewed NATO as a threat. In response, the Soviets developed an alliance system in 1955 as part of their own containment policy. It was known as the **Warsaw Pact.** This alliance included the Soviet Union, Poland, East Germany, Czechoslovakia, Hungary, Romania, Bulgaria, and Albania.

Not every country joined the new alliances, however. India, for example, chose to remain unallied with either side. And China, the world's largest communist country, came to distrust the Soviet Union. Like India, it remained unallied.

Nuclear Threat As these alliances were forming, the Cold War threatened to heat up enough to destroy the world. The United States already had atomic bombs. As early as 1949, the Soviet Union exploded its own atomic weapon. The superpowers had both become nuclear powers.

President Truman was determined to develop an even more deadly weapon before the Soviets did. He authorized work on a thermonuclear weapon in January 1950. This hydrogen or H-bomb would be thousands of times more powerful than the A -bomb.

Background
The East Germans
built a wall in 1961
to separate East and
West Berlin. This
Berlin Wall symbol-
ized the division of
the world into rival
camps.

Its power came from the fusion, or joining together, of atoms, rather than from the splitting of atoms, as in the A-bomb. In November 1952, the United States successfully tested the first H-bomb. By August of the following year, the Soviets had exploded their own thermonuclear weapon.

Dwight D. Eisenhower became the U.S. president in 1953. He appointed the firmly anti-Communist John Foster Dulles as his secretary of state. If the Soviet Union or its supporters attacked U.S. interests, Dulles threatened, the United States would "retaliate instantly, by means and at places of our own choosing." This willingness to go to the brink, or edge, of war became known as **brinkmanship.**

Brinkmanship required a reliable source of nuclear weapons and airplanes to deliver them. So the United States strengthened its air force and began producing stockpiles of nuclear weapons. In response, the Soviet Union made its own collection of nuclear bombs. This arms race would go on for four decades.

THINK THROUGH HISTORY
E. Recognizing Effects How did the U.S. policy of brinkmanship contribute to the arms race?

The Cold War in the Skies The Cold War also affected the science and education programs of the two countries. In August 1957, the Soviets announced the development of a rocket that could travel great distances. This was a true intercontinental ballistic missile, or ICBM. On October 4, the Soviets used an ICBM to push the first unmanned satellite above the earth's atmosphere.

The Cold War took to the skies as the United States and the Soviet Union raced to produce ICBMs. Missiles like this one were capable of inflicting destruction from great distances.

The launching of this Soviet satellite, *Sputnik I*, made Americans feel as if they had fallen behind in science and technology. In response, the U.S. government poured huge amounts of money into education, especially in science, mathematics, and foreign languages. Within months, by January 1958, the United States had successfully launched its own satellite.

In 1960, the skies provided the arena for an even more serious showdown between the superpowers. Five years earlier, President Eisenhower proposed an "open skies" policy. This policy stated that the United States and the Soviet Union could fly freely over each other's territory to guard against surprise nuclear attacks. The Soviet Union rejected Eisenhower's proposal. In response, the U.S. Central Intelligence Agency (CIA) authorized secret high-altitude spy flights over Soviet territory in planes called U-2s. In May 1960, the Soviets shot down a U-2 plane, and its pilot, Francis Gary Powers, was captured. The Soviets sentenced him to ten years in prison but released him after 19 months. This **U-2 incident** brought mistrust and tensions between the superpowers to a new height.

While Soviet Communists were squaring off against the United States, Communists in China were fighting an internal battle for control of that country.

Section 1 Assessment

1. TERMS & NAMES

Identify
• United Nations
• iron curtain
• containment
• Truman Doctrine
• Marshall Plan
• Cold War
• NATO
• Warsaw Pact
• brinkmanship
• U-2 incident

2. TAKING NOTES

Using a web diagram like the one below, list the causes of the Cold War between the United States and the Soviet Union.

Cold War

Which cause was a direct result of World War II? Explain.

3. ANALYZING MOTIVES

What were Stalin's objectives in supporting Communist governments in Eastern Europe?

THINK ABOUT
• the effects of World War II
• the location of the Soviet Union
• U.S. aims in Europe

4. THEME ACTIVITY

Economics Draw a cartoon that shows either capitalism from the Soviet point of view or communism from the U.S. point of view.

The Space Race

Beginning in the late 1950s, the United States and the Soviet Union competed for influence not only among the nations of the world, but in the skies as well. Once the superpowers had ICBMs to deliver nuclear warheads and aircraft for spying missions, they both began to develop technology that could be used to explore—and ultimately control—space.

The Soviet Union launched *Sputnik*, the first successful artificial space satellite, on October 4, 1957. As it circled the earth every 96 minutes, Premier Nikita Khrushchev boasted that his country would soon be "turning out long-range missiles like sausages." Unable to let this challenge go unanswered, the United States began beefing up its own space program. Its first attempts failed, however, and became known as "Stayputnik" or "Flopnik."

In a major technological triumph, the United States put human beings on the moon on July 20, 1969. In this historic "giant leap for mankind," astronaut Buzz Aldrin plants the U.S. flag and leaves his footprints on the lunar surface.

United States

1961 First American in space (Alan Shepard)

1962 First American orbits the earth (John Glenn, Jr.)

1969 First manned lunar landing

1976 *Viking 1* lands on Mars

1977 *Voyager 2* launched to Jupiter, Saturn, Uranus, and Neptune

1981 Space shuttle *Columbia* launched

1992 *Mars Observer* launched

1997 *Mars Pathfinder* explores surface of Mars

1960   1970   1980   1990

1975 U.S. and Soviet Union launch first joint space mission

1995 U.S. shuttle *Discovery* links up with Soviet Space Station *Mir*

1960   1980   1990

1970 *Venera 7* lands on Venus

1971 First manned space station *(Salyut 1)*

1988 Cosmonauts spend 366 days on space station *Mir*

1963 First woman in space (Valentina Tereshkova)

1961 First human orbits the earth (Yuri Gagarin)

1959 *Luna 2* probe reaches the moon

1997 Two spacecraft land on Mars

Soviet Union

This view of the Soviet spacecraft *Soyuz* taken from the window of the U.S. *Apollo* in 1975 shows the curve of the earth beneath them. It symbolizes the superpowers' realization that they would have to coexist in space as well as on earth.

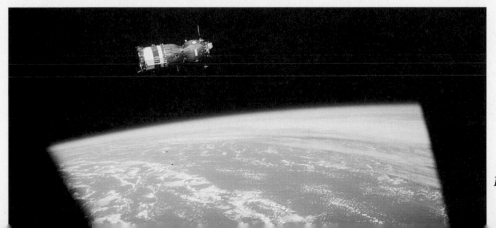

Connect *to* History

Comparing Which destinations in space did both the United States and the Soviet Union explore?

 SEE SKILLBUILDER HANDBOOK, PAGE 996

Connect *to* Today

Making Inferences What role might space continue to play in achieving world peace?

Communists Triumph in China

TERMS & NAMES
• Mao Zedong
• Jiang Jieshi
• commune
• Red Guards
• Cultural Revolution

MAIN IDEA

After World War II, Chinese Communists defeated Nationalist forces and two separate Chinas emerged.

WHY IT MATTERS NOW

China remains a Communist country and a major player on the world stage.

SETTING THE STAGE In World War II, China fought on the side of the victorious Allies. During the war, however, Japan's occupation armies devastated China's major cities. China's civilian death toll alone was in the millions. This vast country suffered casualties second only to those of the Soviet Union.

Civil War in China

When the Japanese invaded China in 1937, a bitter civil war was raging between the Nationalists and the Communists. During World War II, the political opponents temporarily united to fight the Japanese. With the war's end, however, they resumed their fight for control of the country.

Background
The Japanese had controlled Manchuria in northeast China since 1931. In 1937, they launched an all-out attack.

Internal Struggles Under their leader, **Mao Zedong** (mow dzuh·dahng), the Communists held a stronghold in northwestern China. From there, they mobilized Chinese peasants for guerrilla war against the Japanese in the northeast. Thanks to their efforts to teach literacy and improve food production, the Communists won the peasants' loyalty. By 1945, Mao's Red Army controlled much of northern China.

Meanwhile, the Nationalist forces under **Jiang Jieshi** (jee·ahng jee·shee), whose name was formerly spelled Chiang Kai-shek, dominated southwestern China. Protected from the Japanese by rugged mountain ranges, Jiang gathered an army of 2.5 million men. Between 1942 and 1945, the United States sent the Nationalist army at least $1.5 billion in aid to fight the Japanese. Instead of benefiting the army, however, these supplies and money often ended up in the hands of a few corrupt officers. In addition, Jiang's army actually fought few battles against the Japanese. Instead, the Nationalist army saved its strength for the coming battle against Mao's Red Army. As soon as the Japanese surrendered, the Nationalists and Communists resumed their civil war.

Background
The English spelling of Chinese words has been changed to make the pronunciation as close to Chinese as possible and to standardize it throughout the world.

Chinese peasants performed the backbreaking labor that supported the country. After World War II, the Communists worked hard to win their support.

Involvement of the United States That renewed civil war lasted from 1946 to 1949. At first, the Nationalists enjoyed a considerable advantage. Their army outnumbered the Communists' army by as much as three to one. And the United States provided nearly $2 billion more in aid.

The Nationalist forces, however, did little to win popular support. With China's economy collapsing, thousands of Nationalist soldiers deserted to the Communists. In spring 1949, China's major cities fell to the Red forces one by one. Mao's troops were well trained in guerrilla warfare. But they were also enthusiastic about his promised return of land to the peasants. The remnants of Jiang's shattered army fled south. In October 1949, Mao Zedong gained control of the country. He proclaimed it the

Chinese Political Opponents—1945

Nationalists		Communists
Jiang Jieshi	**LEADER**	Mao Zedong
Southern China	**AREA RULED**	Northern China
United States	**FOREIGN SUPPORT**	Soviet Union
Defeat of Communists	**DOMESTIC POLICY**	National liberation
Weak due to inflation and failing economy	**PUBLIC SUPPORT**	Strong due to promised land reform
Ineffective, corrupt leadership and poor morale	**MILITARY ORGANIZATION**	Experienced, motivated guerrilla army

SKILLBUILDER: Interpreting Charts
1. *Which party's domestic policy appealed more to Chinese peasants?*
2. *Which aspect of the Communist approach do you think was most responsible for Mao's victory?*

THINK THROUGH HISTORY
A. Recognizing Effects How did the outcome of the Chinese civil war contribute to Cold War tensions?

People's Republic of China. Jiang and other Nationalist leaders retreated to the island of Taiwan, which westerners called Formosa.

Mao Zedong's victory fueled U.S. anti-Communist feelings. Those feelings only grew after the Chinese and Soviets signed a treaty of friendship in February 1950. Many people in the United States viewed the takeover of China as another step in a Communist campaign to conquer the world.

Two Chinas and the Cold War

China had split into two nations. One was the island of Taiwan, or Nationalist China, with an area of 13,000 square miles. The mainland, or People's Republic of China, had an area of more than 3.5 million square miles. The existence of two Chinas, and the conflicting international loyalties they inspired, intensified the Cold War.

The Superpowers React After Jiang Jieshi fled to Taiwan, the United States helped him set up a Nationalist government on that small island. They called it the Republic of China. The Soviets gave financial, military, and technical aid to the Communist People's Republic of China. In addition, the Chinese and the Soviets pledged to come to each other's defense if either country were attacked.

The United States responded by attempting to enlarge its own sphere of influence in Asia. For example, the United States limited the Soviet Union's occupation of Japan to only the few small islands it had gained at the Yalta talks. The two superpowers divided up Korea into a Soviet-supported Communist north and a U.S.-supported south.

Communist China Continues to Expand In the early years of Mao's reign, Chinese troops expanded into southern, or Inner, Mongolia, Tibet, and India. Northern, or Outer, Mongolia, which bordered the Soviet Union, remained in the Soviet sphere. After declaring Inner Mongolia an "Autonomous Area," China challenged that autonomy. It took control of the country.

In a brutal assault in 1950 and 1951, China also took control of Tibet. This was another so-called Autonomous Area. The Chinese promised autonomy to Tibetans, who followed the religious leader, the Dalai Lama. When China's control over Tibet tightened in the late 1950s, however, the Dalai Lama fled to India. Tibetans responded by rioting.

Vocabulary
autonomous: self-governing.

India welcomed the Dalai Lama and other Tibetan refugees after Tibet's failed revolt in 1959. As a result, resentment between India and China grew. In 1962, when India trespassed across the two countries' unclear border into China's territory, Mao unleashed his forces. China held its border, but resentment continued.

Transformation and Revolution

For decades China had been either at war with or occupied by Japan. Mao and the Communists moved rapidly to strengthen their rule over China's 550 million people. The Communists claimed to have a new "Mandate of Heaven." And they aimed to restore China as a powerful nation.

Transformation Under Mao Zedong After taking power, the Chinese Communists began to tighten their hold on the country. The party's 4.5 million members made up just one percent of the Chinese population. But they were a highly disciplined group. Like the Soviets, the Chinese Communists set up two parallel organizations. These were the Communist party and the national government. Until 1959, Mao ruled as both chairman of the Communist party and head of state.

Mao's Marxist Socialism Mao determined to reshape China's economy based on Marxist socialism. Eighty percent of the population still lived in rural areas. But most Chinese farmers owned no land. Instead, ten percent of the rural population controlled 70 percent of the farmland. Under the Agrarian Reform Law of 1950, Mao seized the holdings of these landlords. He then divided them among the peasants. His forces killed more than a million landlords who resisted this policy.

To further his socialist principles, between 1953 and 1957, Mao's government forced the peasants to join collective farms. These farms each consisted of 200 to 300 households. The Chinese Communists also eagerly embraced Marxist ideas about women and the family. They made women fully equal in the home and in the workplace. They also instituted state-sponsored child care.

Mao's changes also transformed industry and business. Gradually, the government nationalized all private companies, or brought them under government ownership. In 1953, Mao launched a Soviet-style five-year plan that set high production targets for industry. The plan succeeded. By 1957, China's output of coal, cement, and electricity had doubled. Steel production had quadrupled.

Mao's Communes To expand the success of the first five-year plan in industry, Chinese leaders planned another ambitious program. Early in 1958, Mao proclaimed the "Great Leap Forward." This plan called for still larger collective farms, or **communes.** By the end of 1958, the government had created about 26,000 communes. The average commune sprawled over 15,000 acres and supported over 25,000 people.

In the strictly controlled life of the communes, peasants organized into "production battalions." Under the leadership of company and squad leaders, they worked the land together. They ate in communal dining rooms, slept in communal dormitories, and raised children in communal nurseries. And they owned nothing. The peasants had no incentive to work hard when only the state profited from their labor. Most of them hated living in the huge, impersonal communes.

The Great Leap Forward proved to be a great leap backward for China. Poor planning and inefficient "backyard" industries hampered growth. Worst of all, crop failures between 1958 and 1961 unleashed a famine that killed approximately 20 million people. The government officially discontinued the program in 1961.

HISTORY MAKERS

Mao Zedong
1893–1976

Born to a poor, but increasingly wealthy peasant family, Mao embraced Marxist socialism as a young man. Though he began as an urban labor organizer, Mao quickly realized the revolutionary potential of China's peasants. In a 1927 report, Mao predicted:

The force of the peasantry is like that of the raging winds and driving rain. . . . They will bury beneath them all forces of imperialism, militarism, corrupt officialdom, village bosses and evil gentry.

Mao's first attempt to lead the peasants in revolt failed in 1927. But during the Japanese occupation, Mao and his followers won the widespread support of the peasants by reducing rents and promising to redistribute land.

THINK THROUGH HISTORY
B. Analyzing Issues
What aspects of Marxist socialism did Mao try to bring to China?

New Policies and Mao's Response China was facing external problems as well as internal ones in the late 1950s. The spirit of cooperation that had bound the Soviet Union and China began to fade. Each sought to lead the worldwide Communist movement. They also shared the longest border in the world. And they faced numerous territorial disputes. In 1960, the Soviets halted economic aid to China.

After the failure of the Great Leap Forward and the split with the Soviet Union, Mao reduced his role in the government. Other leaders moved away from Mao's strict socialist ideas. Under the new leaders, for example, farm families could live in their own homes. They also could sell crops they grew on small private plots. Factory workers could compete for wage increases, bonuses, and promotions.

Mao disapproved of China's new economic policies, believing that they weakened the Communist goal of social equality. Determined to revive the revolution, Mao launched a new campaign in 1966. He urged China's young people to "learn revolution by making revolution." Millions of high school and college students responded to Mao's call. They left their classrooms and formed militia units called **Red Guards.**

The Cultural Revolution The Red Guards led a major uprising known as the **Cultural Revolution.** The goal of the Cultural Revolution was to establish a society of peasants and workers in which all were equal. The new hero was the peasant who worked with his hands. The life of the mind—intellectual and artistic activity—was considered useless and dangerous. To help stamp out this threat, the Red Guards shut down colleges and schools. They lashed out at professors, government officials, factory managers, and even their own parents. They targeted anyone who seemed to have special privileges or who resisted the regime. Exiled intellectuals had to "purify" themselves by doing hard labor in remote villages. Thousands of people were executed or died in jail.

The resulting widespread chaos closed down factories and threatened farm production. Civil war seemed possible. By 1976, even Mao admitted that the Cultural Revolution had to stop. With Mao's approval, the army dissolved the Red Guards. Zhou Enlai (joh ehn·leye), one of the founders of the Chinese Communist party and premier since 1949, began to restore order.

While China was struggling to become stable, the Cold War continued to rage. Between the 1950s and the 1970s, two full-scale wars broke out—in Korea and in Vietnam.

THINK THROUGH HISTORY
C. Making Inferences Why did the Cultural Revolution fail?

Daily *Life*

The Cultural Revolution
The Cultural Revolution started in 1966, when Chihua Wen was eight years old. For the next decade, his world, and that of every other Chinese child, was turned inside out.

Wen's neighbors were well-known revolutionary writers and loyal members of the Communist Party. Their loyalty became meaningless, however, the night the Red Guards (shown above) stormed into their apartment. There was the sound of breaking glass and a child's scream. Then the teenaged Guards carried a sack of books out to the yard and set them on fire.

They returned to the apartment and emerged carrying two heavy sacks. As they raced off with the sacks in the back of the truck, Wen heard sounds of gagging. "No one ever saw the couple or their child again," he said. And Wen never forgot what he had seen.

Section **2** Assessment

1. TERMS & NAMES

Identify
• Mao Zedong
• Jiang Jieshi
• commune
• Red Guards
• Cultural Revolution

2. TAKING NOTES

Using a chart like the one below, summarize the reforms Mao Zedong proposed for China.

Mao Zedong's Reforms

Aspect of Life	Reform
Agriculture	
Industry	
Family	

Create a propaganda poster supporting one of these reforms.

3. IDENTIFYING PROBLEMS

What circumstances prevented Mao's Great Leap Forward from bringing economic prosperity to China?

THINK ABOUT
• Mao's strict socialism
• life in a commune
• environmental problems

4. ANALYZING THEMES

Revolution What policies or actions enabled the Communists to defeat the Nationalists in their long civil war?

THINK ABOUT
• the goals of each group
• the leaders of the Communists and the Nationalists
• foreign support

TERMS & NAMES
• 38th parallel
• Douglas
  MacArthur
• Ho Chi Minh
• domino theory
• Ngo Dinh Diem
• Vietcong
• Vietnamization
• Khmer Rouge

3 War in Korea and Vietnam

MAIN IDEA	WHY IT MATTERS NOW
In Asia, the Cold War flared into actual wars supported mainly by the superpowers.	Today, Vietnam is a Communist country and Korea is split into Communist and non-Communist nations.

SETTING THE STAGE When World War II ended, Korea became a divided nation. North of the **38th parallel,** a line that crosses Korea at 38 degrees north latitude, Japanese troops surrendered to the Soviets. South of this line, the Japanese surrendered to the Americans. As in Germany, two nations developed. One was the Communist industrial north. The other was the non-Communist rural south.

War in Korea

By 1949, both the United States and the Soviet Union had withdrawn most of their troops from Korea. The Soviets gambled that the United States would not defend South Korea. So they supplied North Korea with tanks, airplanes, and money in an attempt to take over the peninsula.

Standoff at the 38th Parallel On June 25, 1950, the North Koreans swept across the 38th parallel in a surprise attack on South Korea. Within days, North Korean troops had penetrated deep into the south.

President Truman was convinced that the North Korean aggressors were repeating what Hitler, Mussolini, and the Japanese had done in the 1930s. His policy of containment was being put to the test. And Truman resolved to help South Korea resist Communist influence.

South Korea also asked the United Nations to intervene. When the matter came to a vote in the Security Council, the Soviets were absent. They had boycotted the council to protest the seating of Nationalist China (Taiwan) rather than mainland China. The Soviet Union thus forfeited its chance to veto the UN's plan of action. This plan was to send an international force to Korea to stop the invasion. A total of 15 nations, including Britain and Canada, participated under the leadership of General **Douglas MacArthur.**

Meanwhile, the North Koreans continued to advance. By September 1950, they controlled the entire Korean peninsula except for a tiny area around Pusan in the far southeast. That month, however, MacArthur launched a surprise attack. Troops moving north from Pusan met up with forces that had made an amphibious landing at Inchon. Caught in this pincer action, about half of the North Koreans surrendered. The rest retreated.

The Fighting Continues The UN army pursued the retreating North Korean troops across the 38th parallel into North Korea. By late November, UN troops had pushed the North Koreans almost to the Yalu River at the border with China. These troops were mostly from the United States.

Vocabulary
boycotted: refused to take part in.

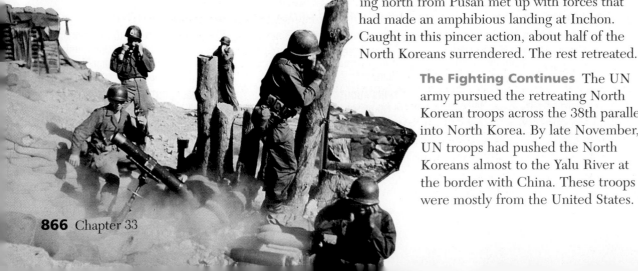

U.S. infantry troops fire heavy mortar shells at Communist strongholds in North Korea in 1950.

Then, in October 1950, the Chinese felt threatened by the American fleet off their coast. They sent 300,000 troops to aid North Korea. The fight between North and South Korea had grown into a war between the Chinese and the Americans.

Greatly outnumbering the UN forces, the Chinese drove them southward. By early January 1951, they had pushed all UN and South Korean troops out of North Korea. The Chinese then moved south. They finally captured the South Korean capital, Seoul.

"We face an entirely new war," declared General MacArthur. And he called for a nuclear attack against Chinese cities. President Truman disagreed, viewing MacArthur's proposals as reckless. "We are trying to prevent a world war, not start one," the president explained. MacArthur tried to go over the president's head by taking his case to Congress and to the press. In response, Truman fired him.

Over the next two years, UN forces continued to fight to drive the North Koreans back to the 38th parallel. By 1952, UN troops had recaptured Seoul and regained control of South Korea. Finally, in July 1953, the UN forces and North Korea signed a cease-fire agreement. After three years of fighting, the border between the two Koreas was set near the 38th parallel. This was almost where it had been before the war started. But approximately 5 million soldiers and civilians had died.

THINK THROUGH HISTORY
A. Recognizing Effects What effects did the Korean war have on the Korean people and nation?

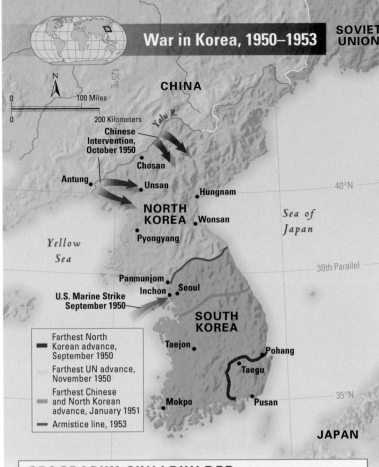

GEOGRAPHY SKILLBUILDER:
Interpreting Maps
1. **Movement** *What was the northernmost Korean city UN troops had reached by November 1950?*
2. **Movement** *Did North or South Korean forces advance further into the other's territory?*

Aftermath and Legacy of the War After the war, Korea remained divided into two countries. In North Korea, the Communist dictator Kim Il Sung established collective farms, developed heavy industry, and built up the country's military power. At Kim's death in 1994, his son Kim Jong Il ascended to power. Under Kim Jong Il's rule, Communist North Korea developed nuclear weapons. Although the country is well-armed, it has serious economic problems. It continues to struggle with shortages of energy and food.

On the other hand, South Korea prospered, thanks to massive aid from the United States and other countries. In the 1960s, South Korea concentrated on developing its industry and boosting foreign trade. A succession of dictatorships ruled the rapidly developing country. With the 1987 adoption of a democratic constitution, however, South Korea established free elections. During the 1980s and early 1990s, South Korea claimed one of the highest economic growth rates in the world.

Political differences keep the two Koreas apart, despite periodic discussions of reuniting the country. In a show of force in 1996, for example, North Korea sent troops into the demilitarized zone that separates the two nations. And the United States still maintains 37,000 troops in South Korea. In 1997, however, South Korea joined several other countries in sending food to North Korea. Although talks continue, the Communist North Koreans remain firmly opposed to reunification.

War in Vietnam

Like America's involvement in the Korean War, its involvement in Vietnam stemmed from its Cold War policy of containment. Beginning after World War II, many Americans and their leaders had one foreign policy goal. They were committed to halting the spread of communism.

By the 1950s, the United States had begun providing financial aid, advisers, and finally, half a million soldiers to a former French colony, Vietnam. America's aim was to keep Southeast Asia from embracing communism as China had done.

The Road to War In the early 1900s, France controlled most of resource-rich Southeast Asia. Nationalist independence movements, however, had begun to develop in the part of French Indochina that is now Vietnam. A young Vietnamese nationalist, **Ho Chi Minh,** turned to the Communists for help in his struggle. During the 1930s, Ho's Indochinese Communist party led revolts and strikes against the French. The French responded by jailing Vietnamese protesters. They also sentenced Ho, the party's leader, to death. Ho fled his death sentence but continued to inspire Vietnam's growing nationalist movement from exile. Ho returned to Vietnam in 1941, a year after the Japanese seized control of his country. He and other nationalists founded the Vietminh (Independence) League.

The Japanese left Vietnam in 1945, after their defeat in World War II. Ho Chi Minh believed that independence would surely follow. France, however, intended to regain its former colony.

War Breaks Out Vietnamese Nationalists and Communists joined to fight the French armies. While the French held most of the major cities, they remained powerless in the countryside. There the Vietminh had widespread peasant support. The Vietminh used hit-and-run tactics to confine the French to the cities.

The French people began to doubt that maintaining their colony in Vietnam was worth the lives and money the struggle cost. In 1954, the French suffered a major military defeat at Dien Bien Phu. They surrendered to Ho.

The United States had supported the French in Vietnam. With the defeat of the French, the United States saw a rising threat to the rest of Asia. U.S. President Eisenhower described this threat in terms of the **domino theory.** The Southeast Asian nations were like a row of dominos, he said. The fall of one to communism would lead to the fall of its neighbors. This theory became a major justification for U.S. foreign policy during the Cold War era.

After France's defeat, an international peace conference met in Geneva to discuss the future of Indochina. Based on these talks, Vietnam was divided at 17° north latitude. North of that line, Ho Chi Minh's Communist forces governed. To the south, the United States and France set up an anti-Communist government under the leadership of **Ngo Dinh Diem** (NOH dihn D'YEM).

HISTORY MAKERS

Ho Chi Minh
1890–1969

When he was young, the poor Vietnamese Nguyen That (uhng·wihn thaht) Thanh worked as a cook on a French steamship. In visiting American cities where the boat docked, such as Boston and New York, he learned about both American culture and ideals.

He later took a new name—Ho Chi Minh, meaning "He who enlightens." But he held onto those American ideals. Though a Communist, in announcing Vietnam's independence from France in 1945, he declared, "All men are created equal."

His people revered him and fondly called him Uncle Ho. However, Ho Chi Minh did not put his democratic ideals into practice. From 1954 to 1969, he ruled North Vietnam by crushing all opposition.

THINK THROUGH HISTORY
B. Making Inferences What actions might the United States have justified by the domino theory?

Vietnam—A Divided Country Diem, an unpopular leader, ruled the south as a dictator. In contrast, Ho Chi Minh began a popular program of land redistribution in the north. The United States sensed that an election might lead to victory for the Communists. So it supported Diem's cancellation of the elections.

Vietnamese opposition to Diem's corrupt government grew. Communist guerrillas, called **Vietcong,** began to gain strength in the south. While some of the Vietcong were trained soldiers from North Vietnam, most were South Vietnamese who hated Diem. Gradually, the Vietcong won control of large areas of the countryside.

In 1963, backed by the United States, a group of South Vietnamese generals planned a coup. Meeting almost no resistance, they overthrew and assassinated Diem. The new leaders, however, were no more popular than Diem had been. A takeover by the Communist Vietcong with the backing of North Vietnam seemed inevitable.

The United States Gets Involved

Faced with this possibility, the United States decided to escalate, or increase, its involvement. Americans had been serving as advisers to the South Vietnamese since the late 1950s. But their numbers steadily grew. The United States also sent increasing numbers of planes, tanks, and other military equipment to South Vietnam.

In August 1964, U.S. President Lyndon Johnson told Congress that North Vietnamese patrol boats had attacked two American destroyers in the Gulf of Tonkin. As a result, Congress authorized the president to send American troops into Vietnam. By late 1965, more than 185,000 American soldiers were fighting on Vietnamese soil, although war had not officially been declared. American planes had also begun to bomb North Vietnam. By 1968, more than half a million American soldiers were in combat there.

Background
The Chinese sent more than 300,000 troops to support the North Vietnamese during the war. Soviet pilots joined the Chinese in shooting down U.S. planes.

Background
Guerrilla warfare is carried out by small bands of local fighters, often in harsh terrain. It is characterized by surprise attacks, ambushes, and hit-and-run tactics.

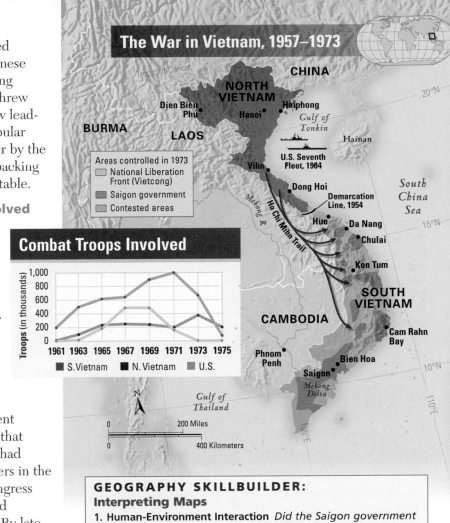

The War in Vietnam, 1957–1973

Areas controlled in 1973
- National Liberation Front (Vietcong)
- Saigon government
- Contested areas

Combat Troops Involved

Troops (in thousands)

1,000 / 800 / 600 / 400 / 200 / 0

1961 1963 1965 1967 1969 1971 1973 1975

■ S. Vietnam ■ N. Vietnam ■ U.S.

GEOGRAPHY SKILLBUILDER:
Interpreting Maps
1. **Human-Environment Interaction** *Did the Saigon government or the Vietcong control more of South Vietnam in 1973?*
2. **Movement** *Which country committed the most troops to the war in Vietnam?*

The United States boasted the best-equipped, most advanced army in the world. Yet the Americans faced two major difficulties. First, they were fighting a guerrilla war in unfamiliar jungle terrain. Second, the South Vietnamese government they were defending was becoming steadily more unpopular. At the same time, popular support for the Vietcong grew. Ho Chi Minh also strongly supported the Vietcong with troops and munitions, as did the Soviet Union and China.

Unable to win a decisive victory on the ground, the United States turned to air power. American forces bombed millions of acres of farmland and forest in an attempt to destroy enemy hideouts. This bombing strengthened peasants' opposition to the South Vietnamese government.

The United States Withdraws

During the late 1960s, the war grew increasingly unpopular in the United States. Dissatisfied youth began to protest the tremendous loss of life in an unpopular conflict on the other side of the world. Bowing to intense public pressure, President Richard Nixon began withdrawing U.S. troops from Vietnam in 1969. Nixon's plan was called **Vietnamization.** It allowed for U.S. troops to gradually pull out, while the South Vietnamese increased their combat role. Nixon wanted to pursue Vietnamization while preserving the South Vietnamese government. So he authorized a massive bombing campaign against North Vietnamese bases and supply routes. The president also authorized bombings in neighboring Laos and Cambodia to wipe out Vietcong hiding places.

The skulls of Cambodian citizens form a haunting memorial to the brutality of the Khmer Rouge during the 1970s.

Under continued popular protest and political pressure at home, President Nixon kept withdrawing U.S. troops. The last forces left in 1973. The North Vietnamese overran South Vietnam two years later because the South Vietnamese could not fend off the North Vietnamese on their own. The Communists renamed Saigon, the former capital of the South, Ho Chi Minh City to honor their dead leader. But more than 1.5 million Vietnamese and 58,000 Americans had also died during the war.

THINK THROUGH HISTORY
C. Recognizing Effects Why did Vietnamization fail?

Ongoing Turmoil in Cambodia The end of the war did not put an end to bloodshed and chaos in Southeast Asia, however. Cambodia (also known as Kampuchea) had suffered U.S. bombing during the war. And it remained unstable for years. In 1975, Communist rebels known as the **Khmer Rouge** set up a brutal Communist government under the leadership of Pol Pot. In a ruthless attempt to transform Cambodia into a rural society, Pol Pot's followers slaughtered 2 million people. This was almost one quarter of the nation's population. A Vietnamese invasion in 1978 overthrew the Khmer Rouge. The Vietnamese finally withdrew in 1989. In 1993, under the supervision of UN peacekeepers, Cambodia adopted a democratic constitution and held a free election. Pol Pot was captured and detained in 1997 for the war crimes he had committed.

Postwar Vietnam After 1975, the victorious North Vietnamese imposed strict controls over the South. Officials sent thousands of people to "reeducation camps" for training in Communist thought. They nationalized industries and strictly controlled businesses.

Communist oppression also caused 1.5 million people to flee from Vietnam. Most refugees escaped in dangerously overcrowded ships. More than 200,000 of these "boat people" died at sea. The survivors often spent long months in crowded refugee camps scattered across Southeast Asia. About 70,000 Vietnamese refugees eventually settled in the United States or in Canada.

Though Communists still govern Vietnam, the country now welcomes foreign investment. Much of that investment comes from Vietnam's old enemy, the United States. America lifted its trade embargo against Vietnam in 1994 and is moving toward official recognition of the country.

While the Cold War superpowers were struggling for power in the Korean and Vietnam wars, they also were using economic and diplomatic means to bring other countries under their control.

CONNECT *to* TODAY

Capitalism in Vietnam

Vietnam is now a Communist country. But its economy is modeled more on that of the Soviets' Cold War enemy, the United States. In 1997, a travel magazine claimed that Hanoi, the capital of Vietnam, "jumps with vitality, its streets and shops jammed with locals and handfuls of Western tourists and businesspeople."

Along Hanoi's shaded boulevards, billboards advertise American and Japanese copiers, motorcycles, video recorders, and soft drinks. On the streets, enterprising Vietnamese businesspeople offer more traditional services. These include bicycle repair, a haircut, a shave, or a tasty snack.

Section **3** Assessment

1. TERMS & NAMES

Identify
- 38th parallel
- Douglas MacArthur
- Ho Chi Minh
- domino theory
- Ngo Dinh Diem
- Vietcong
- Vietnamization
- Khmer Rouge

2. TAKING NOTES

Using a Venn diagram like the one below, compare and contrast the causes and effects of the wars in Vietnam and Korea.

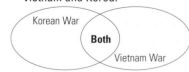

Do you think the similarities or the differences between the two wars are more striking? Why?

3. FORMING OPINIONS

Do you think U.S. involvement in Vietnam was justified? Why or why not?

THINK ABOUT
- the U.S. policy of containment
- the domino theory
- U.S. public opinion

4. THEME ACTIVITY

Empire Building Create a propaganda poster for either the United States or the Soviet Union supporting its involvement in Asia.

Cold War Around the World

TERMS & NAMES
- Third World
- nonaligned nations
- Fidel Castro
- Anastasio Somoza
- Daniel Ortega
- Shah Mohammed Reza Pahlavi
- Ayatollah Ruholla Khomeini

MAIN IDEA	WHY IT MATTERS NOW
The Cold War superpowers supported opposing sides in Latin American and Middle Eastern conflicts.	Many of these areas today are troubled by political, economic, and military conflict and crisis.

SETTING THE STAGE Vietnam was just one of many countries that attempted to shake off colonial rule after World War II. Local battles for independence provided yet another arena for competition between the Cold War superpowers.

Confrontations over Developing Nations

Background
In the 1970s, the three worlds were redefined in economic terms. The small but prosperous First World was at the top of a pyramid and the large, poverty-stricken Third World was at the bottom.

Following World War II, the world's nations were grouped politically into three "worlds." The First World was the United States and its allies. The Second World included the Soviet Union and its allies. The **Third World** consisted of developing nations, often newly independent, who were not aligned with either superpower.

These Third World countries in Latin America, Asia, and Africa experienced terrible poverty and political instability. This was largely due to a long history of imperialism. They also suffered from ethnic conflicts and lack of technology and education. Each desperately needed a political and economic system around which to build its society. Soviet-style communism and U.S.-style free-market democracy were the countries' main choices.

Cold War Strategies The United States, the Soviet Union, and, in some cases, China, used a variety of techniques to gain influence in the Third World. These competing superpowers sponsored or backed wars of revolution, liberation, or counterrevolution. The U.S. and Soviet spy agencies—the CIA and the KGB—engaged in a variety of covert, or secret, activities. These activities ranged from spying to assassination attempts. The United States also provided military aid, built schools, set up programs to combat poverty, and sent volunteer workers to developing nations in Latin America, Asia, and Africa. The Soviets offered military and technical assistance, mainly to India and Egypt.

Association of Nonaligned Nations Other developing nations also had pressing needs for assistance. They became important players in the Cold War competition between the United States, the Soviet Union, and also China.

THINK THROUGH HISTORY
A. Making Inferences What advantages and disadvantages might being nonaligned have offered a developing nation?

Not all Third World countries wished to play such a role, however. India, for example, vowed to remain neutral in the Cold War. Indonesia, a populous island nation in Southeast Asia, also struggled to stay uninvolved. In 1955, Indonesia hosted the leaders of Asian and African countries in the Bandung Conference. They met to form what they called a "third force" of such independent countries, or **nonaligned nations.**

Nations such as India and Indonesia remained neutral. But other countries took sides with the superpowers or played the competing sides off against each other.

The flour provided by U.S. aid helped keep these Colombian children alive. They also learned to make the flour sacks into clothing in a school run by missionaries.

Postwar Face-off in Latin America

After World War II, rapid industrialization, population growth, and a lingering gap between the rich and the poor led Latin American nations to seek aid from both

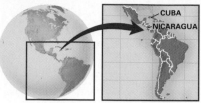

superpowers. During this period, many Latin American countries alternated between short-lived democracy and harsh military rule.

As described in Chapter 28, U.S. involvement in Latin America began long before World War II. American businesses backed leaders who often oppressed their people, but who protected U.S. interests. After the war, communism and nationalistic feelings inspired a wave of revolutionary movements. These found enthusiastic Soviet support. In response, the United States provided military support and economic assistance to anti-Communist dictators.

Cuban Revolution Throughout the 1950s, U.S. support maintained Cuba's unpopular dictator, Fulgencio Batista. Cuban resentment led to a popular revolution, which overthrew Batista in January 1959. A young lawyer named **Fidel Castro** led that revolution.

At first, many people praised Castro for bringing reforms to Cuba and improving the economy, literacy, health care, and conditions for women. Yet Castro was a harsh dictator. He suspended elections, jailed or executed his opponents, and strangled the press with tight government controls.

When Castro nationalized the Cuban economy, he took over U.S.-owned sugar mills and refineries. In response, President Eisenhower ordered an embargo on all trade with Cuba. As relations with the United States deteriorated, Castro turned to the Soviets for the economic and military aid he needed.

In 1960, the CIA planned an invasion of Cuba and began to train anti-Castro Cuban exiles to carry it out. In April 1961 these exiles landed at the Bay of Pigs in Cuba. The new president, Kennedy, approved the invasion but refused to send U.S. planes to support it. Castro's forces defeated the invaders, humiliating the United States.

The Cuban Missile Crisis The failed Bay of Pigs invasion convinced the Soviet leader, Nikita Khrushchev, that the United States would not resist Soviet expansion in Latin America. Consequently, in July 1962, Khrushchev secretly began to build 42 missile sites in Cuba. In October, an American spy plane discovered the sites. The U.S. President, John F. Kennedy, declared that missiles so close to the U.S. mainland were a threat. He demanded that the Soviets remove the missiles. Kennedy also announced a quarantine, or blockade, of Cuba to prevent the Soviets installing more missiles. Castro protested his country's being used as a tool in the Cold War:

> ## A VOICE FROM THE PAST
> Cuba did not and does not intend to be in the middle of a conflict between the East and the West. Our problem is above all one of national sovereignty. Cuba does not mean to get involved in the Cold War.
>
> **FIDEL CASTRO,** quoted in an interview October 27, 1962

Nevertheless, Cuba was deeply involved. Kennedy's demand for the removal of Soviet missiles put the United States and the Soviet Union on a collision course. U.S. troops assembled in Florida, ready to invade Cuba. People around the world began to fear that

HISTORY MAKERS

Fidel Castro
1927–

The son of a wealthy Spanish-Cuban farmer, Fidel Castro became involved in politics while enrolled at the University of Havana. He first attempted to overthrow the Cuban dictator, Batista, in 1953. He was imprisoned, but vowed not to give up the struggle for independence:

Personally, I am not interested in power nor do I envisage assuming it at any time. All that I will do is to make sure that the sacrifices of so many compatriots should not be in vain. . . .

Despite this declaration, Castro became a staunch Soviet ally and has been dictator of Cuba for over 30 years.

THINK THROUGH HISTORY
B. Contrasting
What differing U.S. and Soviet aims led to the Cuban missile crisis?

this standoff would lead to World War III and a nuclear disaster. Fortunately, Khrushchev agreed to remove the missiles in return for a U.S. promise not to invade Cuba.

The resolution of the Cuban missile crisis left Castro completely dependent on Soviet support. In exchange for this support, Castro backed Communist revolutions in Latin America and Africa. Approximately 36,000 Cubans fought in Angola's war against colonialism in the 1970s. Soviet aid to Cuba, however, ended abruptly with the breakup of the Soviet Union in 1991. This loss dealt a crippling blow to the Cuban economy. The country still suffers a scarcity of vital supplies. But the aging Castro refuses to adopt economic reforms or to give up power. An equally stubborn United States refuses to lift its trade embargo.

Civil War in Nicaragua Just as the United States had supported the unpopular Batista in Cuba, it had funded the Nicaraguan dictatorship of **Anastasio Somoza** and his family since 1933. In 1979, Communist Sandinista rebels toppled the dictatorship of Somoza's son. Both the United States and the Soviet Union initially gave aid to the Sandinistas and their leader, **Daniel Ortega** (awr·TAY·guh).

THINK THROUGH HISTORY
C. Analyzing Motives Why did the U.S. switch its support from the Sandinistas to the Contras?

The Sandinistas, however, had aided other socialist rebels in nearby El Salvador. To help the El Salvadoran government fight those rebels, the United States supported Nicaraguan anti-Communist rebel forces. These rebels were called Contras or *contrarevolucionarios.*

The civil war in Nicaragua lasted over a decade and seriously weakened the country's economy. Finally, in 1990, President Ortega agreed to hold free elections. He was defeated by Violeta Chamorro. In 1997, José Lacayo was elected president.

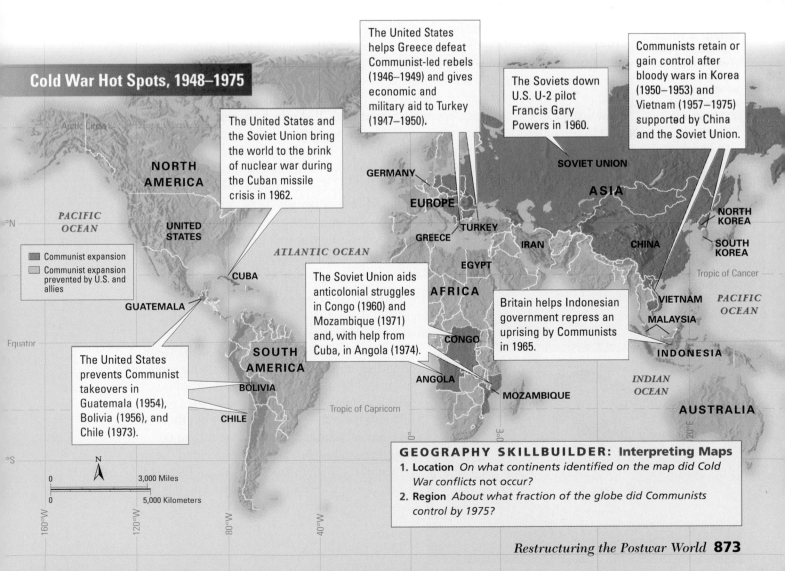

Cold War Hot Spots, 1948–1975

The United States helps Greece defeat Communist-led rebels (1946–1949) and gives economic and military aid to Turkey (1947–1950).

The Soviets down U.S. U-2 pilot Francis Gary Powers in 1960.

Communists retain or gain control after bloody wars in Korea (1950–1953) and Vietnam (1957–1975) supported by China and the Soviet Union.

The United States and the Soviet Union bring the world to the brink of nuclear war during the Cuban missile crisis in 1962.

The Soviet Union aids anticolonial struggles in Congo (1960) and Mozambique (1971) and, with help from Cuba, in Angola (1974).

Britain helps Indonesian government repress an uprising by Communists in 1965.

The United States prevents Communist takeovers in Guatemala (1954), Bolivia (1956), and Chile (1973).

■ Communist expansion
□ Communist expansion prevented by U.S. and allies

NORTH AMERICA, PACIFIC OCEAN, UNITED STATES, ATLANTIC OCEAN, CUBA, GUATEMALA, SOUTH AMERICA, BOLIVIA, CHILE, Equator, Tropic of Capricorn, GERMANY, EUROPE, TURKEY, GREECE, IRAN, EGYPT, AFRICA, CONGO, ANGOLA, MOZAMBIQUE, SOVIET UNION, ASIA, CHINA, NORTH KOREA, SOUTH KOREA, Tropic of Cancer, VIETNAM, MALAYSIA, INDONESIA, PACIFIC OCEAN, INDIAN OCEAN, AUSTRALIA, Arctic Circle

0 3,000 Miles
0 5,000 Kilometers

GEOGRAPHY SKILLBUILDER: Interpreting Maps
1. **Location** *On what continents identified on the map did Cold War conflicts not occur?*
2. **Region** *About what fraction of the globe did Communists control by 1975?*

Confrontations in the Middle East

As the map on the previous page shows, Cold War confrontations continued to erupt around the globe. (For more information about African conflicts, see Chapter 34.) With its rich supplies of oil, the Middle East lured both the United States and the Soviet Union.

Religious and Secular Values Clash in Iran Throughout the Middle East, wealth from the oil industry fueled a growing conflict between traditional Islamic values and

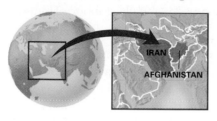

modern Western materialism. In no country did the clash between cultures erupt more dramatically than in the former Persia, or Iran.

After World War II, Iran's leader, **Shah Mohammed Reza Pahlavi** (PAH·luh·vee), embraced Western governments and wealthy Western oil companies. Angry Iranian nationalists resented these foreign alliances. They united under the leadership of Prime Minister Muhammad Mossaddeq (moh·sah·DEHK). They seized and nationalized a British-owned oil company and, in 1953, forced the shah to flee. Fearing that Mossaddeq might turn to the Soviets for support, the United States had him arrested. It then restored the shah to power.

THINK THROUGH HISTORY
D. Analyzing Motives Why did the United States support the Shah of Iran?

The United States Supports Secular Rule With U.S. support, the shah westernized his country. By the end of the 1950s, Iran's capital, Tehran, featured gleaming skyscrapers, foreign banks, and modern factories. Millions of Iranians, however, still lived in extreme poverty. And the shah's secret police brutally punished anyone who dared to oppose him. The shah also tried to weaken the political influence of religion in the country by limiting the role of Islamic legal and academic experts. Iran's conservative Muslim leaders, known as ayatollahs (eye·uh·TOH·luhz), bitterly opposed this move. They also opposed what they saw as socially and morally corrupting Western influences. They wanted Iran to become a republic ruled strictly by Islamic law.

The leader of this religious opposition, **Ayatollah Ruholla Khomeini** (koh·MAY·nee), was living in exile. Spurred by his tape-recorded messages, Iranian

Ayatollah Khomeini (top) supported the taking of U.S. hostages in Tehran in 1979. During their 14-month captivity, the hostages were blindfolded and paraded through the city streets (bottom).

workers went on strike. "Death to the shah!" and "Down with America!" they vowed. In late 1978, riots erupted in every major city in Iran. Faced with overwhelming opposition, the shah fled Iran in January 1979. A triumphant Khomeini returned from exile to establish an Islamic state. He banned the Western influences that the shah had brought to Iran and reinstated traditional Muslim values. Islamic law became the legal code for the country.

Khomeini's Anti-U.S. Policies Adherence to Islam ruled Khomeini's domestic policies. But hatred of the United States was at the heart of his politics. The Americans had long supported the shah. Their admitting him into the United States for medical treatment in 1979, however, was the final insult. That year, with the ayatollah's blessing, a group of young Islamic revolutionaries seized the U.S. embassy in Tehran. They took more than 60 Americans hostage. They also demanded the return of the shah to face trial. Most of the U.S. hostages remained prisoners for 444 days before they were released on January 20, 1981.

Background
The Shi'i and Sunni Muslims had been in conflict since they split over religious practice and beliefs in the 7th century A.D. (see Chapter 10).

Khomeini also encouraged Muslim fundamentalists, or strict believers, in other countries to overthrow their secular governments. Intended to be a means of unifying Muslims, this policy only heightened tensions between Iran and its neighbor, Iraq. While the Iranians were Shi'a, the Iraqis belonged to the rival Sunni Muslim sect. In addition, a military leader, Saddam Hussein (hoo·SAYN), governed Iraq as a secular state.

War broke out between the two countries in 1980. For eight years, Muslim killed Muslim in a territorial struggle. Caught in the middle, the United States secretly sold weapons to Iran in an effort to get their hostages released. A million Iranians and Iraqis died before a UN ceasefire ended the hostilities in 1988.

The Superpowers Face Off in Afghanistan Iran was not the only country in the Middle East in which Cold War tensions erupted. For several years following World War II, Afghanistan maintained its independence from both the neighboring Soviet Union and the United States. In the 1950s, however, Soviet influence in the country began to increase. In the late 1970s, a Muslim revolt threatened to topple Afghanistan's Communist regime. This revolt triggered a Soviet invasion in December 1979.

The Soviets expected to prop up the Afghan Communists quickly and withdraw. Instead, just as the United States had gotten mired in Vietnam in the 1960s, the Soviets found themselves stuck in Afghanistan. And like the Vietcong in Vietnam, determined Afghan rebel forces outmaneuvered and overpowered a military superpower. Soviet helicopter rocket attacks secured the cities. They failed to dislodge the rebels, called *mujahideen*, from their mountain strongholds, however. Supplied with American weapons, the *mujahideen* fought on.

THINK THROUGH HISTORY
E. Comparing In what ways were U.S. involvement in Vietnam and Soviet involvement in Afghanistan similar?

The United States had armed the rebels because they considered the Soviet invasion a threat to the rich Middle Eastern oil supplies. U.S. President Jimmy Carter sternly warned the Soviets that any attempt to gain control of the Persian Gulf would be "repelled by any means necessary, including military force." No threat developed, though. Therefore, the United States limited its response to an embargo of grain shipments to the Soviet Union. It also boycotted the 1980 summer Olympic games in Moscow.

In the 1980s, a new Soviet regime acknowledged the war's devastating costs to both Afghanistan and the Soviet Union. After a ten-year occupation—as long as U.S. involvement in Vietnam—President Mikhail Gorbachev ordered his forces to withdraw. The last Soviet troops left Afghanistan in February 1989. By then, internal unrest and economic problems were tearing the Soviet Union itself apart.

SPOTLIGHT ON

Boycott of 1980 Olympics

Sixty-two nations, including Japan, West Germany, and Canada, joined the U.S. boycott of the 1980 Moscow Olympics. In sympathy, 16 of the 81 teams who did participate refused to carry their national flags in the opening ceremony.

U.S. athletes had trained for years to compete in the Olympics. They received Congressional Olympic medals as a consolation for their dashed hopes and disappointment.

Disappointed athletes and other critics suggested that future games should be played in a neutral location. This move would help separate international sports competition from politics.

Section 4 Assessment

1. TERMS & NAMES

Identify
- Third World
- nonaligned nations
- Fidel Castro
- Anastasio Somoza
- Daniel Ortega
- Shah Mohammed Reza Pahlavi
- Ayatollah Ruholla Khomeini

2. TAKING NOTES

Using a flow chart like the one below, fill in the main events of U.S. involvement in Cuba.

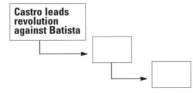

Castro leads revolution against Batista

Write a newspaper headline for one of the events you listed.

3. COMPARING

What similarities do you see among U.S. actions in Nicaragua, Cuba, and Iran?

THINK ABOUT
- the type of leader the United States supported in each country
- U.S. interests in these countries

4. ANALYZING THEMES

Economics Today, Cuba suffers a severe shortage of vital supplies, largely due to the U.S. trade embargo that has lasted for almost 40 years. Do you think the United States should lift that embargo? Why or why not?

THINK ABOUT
- Castro's leadership
- prior U.S. conflicts with Cuba
- human suffering

5 The Cold War Thaws

TERMS & NAMES
• Nikita Khrushchev
• destalinization
• Leonid Brezhnev
• John F. Kennedy
• Lyndon Johnson
• détente
• Richard M. Nixon
• SALT
• Ronald Reagan
• Star Wars

MAIN IDEA	WHY IT MATTERS NOW
The Cold War began to thaw as the superpowers entered an era of uneasy diplomacy.	The United States and the countries of the former Soviet Union continue to cooperate and maintain a cautious peace.

SETTING THE STAGE In the postwar years, the Soviet Union kept a firm grip on its satellite countries in Eastern Europe. These countries were Poland, Czechoslovakia, Hungary, Romania, Yugoslavia, Bulgaria, Albania, and East Germany. It did not allow them to direct and develop their own economies. Instead, it insisted that they develop industries to meet Soviet needs. These policies greatly hampered Eastern Europe's economic recovery.

The Soviets Dominate Eastern Europe

After Stalin died, a new, more moderate group of Soviet leaders came to power. These new leaders allowed their satellite countries a taste of independence, as long as they remained firmly Communist and allied with the Soviet Union. During the 1950s and 1960s, however, growing protest movements in Eastern Europe threatened the Soviet Union's grip over the region. Increasing tensions with Communist China also diverted Soviet attention and forces.

Destalinization and Rumblings of Protest Joseph Stalin died on March 5, 1953. Shortly after his death, a loyal member of the Communist party named **Nikita Khrushchev** became the dominant Soviet leader. The shrewd, tough Khrushchev publicly denounced Stalin for jailing and killing loyal Soviet citizens. His speech signaled the beginning of a policy called **destalinization,** or purging the country of Stalin's memory. Workers destroyed monuments of the former dictator and reburied his body outside the Kremlin wall. Khrushchev also called for "peaceful competition" with the capitalist states.

A toppled statue of Stalin lies in Moscow, a stark symbol of Khrushchev's policy of destalinization.

This new Soviet outlook did not change life in the satellite countries, however. Their resentment occasionally turned into active protest. In October 1956, for example, the Hungarian army joined with protesters to overthrow Hungary's Soviet-controlled government. Storming through the capital, Budapest, angry mobs waved Hungarian flags with the Communist hammer-and-sickle emblem cut out. "From the youngest child to the oldest man," one protester declared, "no one wants communism."

A popular and liberal Hungarian Communist leader named Imre Nagy (IHM·ray nahj) formed a new government. Nagy promised free elections and demanded that Soviet troops leave Hungary. In response, in early November, Soviet tanks rolled into Budapest. They were backed by infantry units. Thousands of Hungarian freedom fighters armed themselves with pistols and bottles. The Soviets overpowered them, however. The invaders replaced the Hungarian government with pro-Soviet leaders and eventually executed Nagy.

THINK THROUGH HISTORY
A. Recognizing Effects What effects did destalinization have on Soviet satellite countries?

The Victim

HUNGARY

Faces of Protest

Soviet tanks move into Prague in 1968
to stamp out Czech reforms.

The Survivor

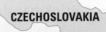

CZECHOSLOVAKIA

Imre Nagy (1896–1958)

Of peasant background, Imre Nagy was captured by the Soviets during World War I and recruited into their army. He became a Communist and lived in Moscow until 1944, when he returned to Soviet-occupied Hungary.

Although he held several posts in his country's Communist government, his loyalty remained with the peasants. Because of his independent approach, he fell in and out of favor with the Soviet regime. He led the anti-Soviet revolt in October 1956.

The Soviets forcefully put down the uprising and deported Nagy. They then brought him back to Hungary, where they tried and executed him. He remained in disgrace until the Hungarian Supreme Court cleared his name in 1989.

Alexander Dubček (1921–1992)

Alexander Dubček was the son of a member of the Czech Communist Party and moved rapidly up through the Communist ranks in Czechoslovakia.

In response to the spirit of change in the 1960s, Dubček instituted broad reforms in the 1968 Prague Spring. Not surprisingly, Soviet officials reacted negatively. Tanks rolled into Prague to suppress a feared revolt.

The Soviets expelled Dubček from the Communist Party in 1970. He survived, though. He regained political prominence in 1989, when the Communists agreed to share power in a coalition government. When the new nation of Slovakia was formed in 1992, Dubček became head of its Social Democratic Party.

Brezhnev and the Revolt in Czechoslovakia Despite this show of force in Hungary, Khrushchev lost prestige in his country as a result of the Cuban missile crisis. In 1964, Communist party leaders voted to remove him from power. His replacement, **Leonid Brezhnev,** quickly adopted repressive domestic policies. The Communist party strictly enforced laws to limit such basic human rights as freedom of speech and worship. Government censors carefully controlled what writers could publish. And Brezhnev clamped down on those who dared to protest his government's policies. For example, the secret police arrested many dissidents, including Aleksandr Solzhenitsyn, winner of the 1970 Nobel Prize for literature. They then expelled him from the Soviet Union.

Brezhnev made it clear that he would not tolerate dissent in Eastern Europe either. His policy was put to the test in early 1968. At that time, Czech Communist leader Alexander Dubček (DOOB·chehk) loosened controls on censorship to offer his country socialism with "a human face." This period of reform, when Czechoslovakia's capital bloomed with new ideas, became known as Prague Spring.

Prague Spring, however, did not survive the summer. On August 20, armed forces from the Warsaw Pact nations invaded Czechoslovakia. Brezhnev justified this invasion by claiming the Soviet right to prevent its satellites from rejecting communism.

Split with China While many of the Soviet satellite countries resisted Communist rule, China seemed firmly committed to communism. In fact, to cement the ties between their Communist powers, Mao and Stalin had signed a 30-year treaty of friendship in 1950. Their spirit of cooperation, however, ran out before the treaty did.

Background
Nikita Khrushchev was the first Soviet leader to leave office alive.

TERMS & NAMES

Briefly explain the importance of each of the following in reconstructing the postwar world since 1945.

1. containment
2. Cold War
3. Mao Zedong
4. Cultural Revolution
5. 38th parallel
6. Vietnamization
7. Fidel Castro
8. Nikita Khrushchev
9. détente
10. SALT

Interact *with* History

On page 854, you considered what action you would take in a civil war in a developing country that both the United States and the Soviet Union were interested in. Now that you have learned more about the Cold War, would your decision change? Discuss your ideas with a small group.

Visual Summary

REVIEW QUESTIONS

SECTION 1 *(pages 855–861)*
Two Superpowers Face Off

11. Why did some Americans oppose the Truman Doctrine?
12. How did the Soviet Union respond to the U.S. policy of brinkmanship?

SECTION 2 *(pages 862–865)*
Communists Triumph in China

13. Which sides did the superpowers support in the Chinese internal struggle for control of the country?
14. What were the results of Mao Zedong's Great Leap Forward and Cultural Revolution?

SECTION 3 *(pages 866–870)*
War in Korea and Vietnam

15. What effects did the Korean War have on Korea's land and people?
16. What major difficulties did the U.S. Army face in fighting the war in Vietnam?

SECTION 4 *(pages 871–875)*
Cold War Around the World

17. Why did developing nations often align themselves with one or the other superpower?
18. How did the Soviet Union respond to the U.S.-supported Bay of Pigs invasion?

SECTION 5 *(pages 876–879)*
The Cold War Thaws

19. In what ways did Soviet actions hamper Eastern Europe's economic recovery after World War II?
20. What policies characterized realpolitik and how did they affect the course of the Cold War?

Cold War, 1946–1980

United States

1946 Institutes containment policy to block Soviet influence

1948 Gives massive foreign aid to Europe under Marshall Plan

1952 Tests first H-bomb

1953 Adopts brinkmanship policy, which escalates Cold War

1965 Sends troops to Vietnam

1948 U.S. and Britain break Soviet blockade of Berlin with airlift

1950 Communist North Korea attacks South Korea

1960 U-2 incident reignites tension between super-powers

1962 U.S. blockades Cuba in response to buildup of Soviet missiles

1972 Nixon and Brezhnev sign SALT I treaty

1980 U.S. boycotts Moscow Summer Olympics to protest invasion of Afghanistan

1950 Signs friendship treaty with China

1953 Tests first H-bomb

1957 Launches Sputnik, starting space race

1956 Puts down revolt in Hungary and later executes Imre Nagy

1968 Violently brings Prague Spring to an end

1979 Invades Afghanistan

Soviet Union

CRITICAL THINKING

1. COLD WAR MANEUVERS

Using a web like the one below, indicate various tactics the Soviet Union and the United States used during the Cold War.

Cold War Tactics

2. RECOGNIZING THE ENEMY

American cartoonist Walt Kelly once said, "We have met the enemy, and he is us." In what sense do you think this saying applies to the Cold War superpowers? In what specific ways were the United States and the Soviet Union more similar than they were different?

3. FROM WORLD WAR TO COLD WAR

THEME EMPIRE BUILDING The Soviet Union emerged from World War II economically and physically devastated. How do you think the development of the Cold War would have proceeded if the United States had been in that position?

4. ANALYZING PRIMARY SOURCES

The following poem by Ho Chi Minh was broadcast over Hanoi Radio on January 1, 1968. Read the poem and answer the questions that follow.

A VOICE FROM THE PAST
This Spring far outshines the previous Springs,
Of victories throughout the land come happy tidings.
South and North, rushing heroically together, shall
smite the American invaders!
Go Forward!
Total victory shall be ours.

HO CHI MINH, quoted in *America and Vietnam*

- In Ho's opinion, who was the enemy in the Vietnam War?

- What purpose might the North Vietnamese have had in broadcasting this poem?

CHAPTER ACTIVITIES

1. LIVING HISTORY: Unit Portfolio Project

THEME ECONOMICS Your unit portfolio project focuses on the ways economic factors influence history. For Chapter 33, you might use one of the following ideas to add to your portfolio.

- Ask classmates to think about what life would be like for peasants in a Communist satellite country. Then stage an interview in which you ask them to discuss their feelings about communism and capitalism. Audiotape your interviews and add a commentary to create an "objective" newscast.

- Create a poster to teach elementary school students about the differences between capitalism and communism.

- Working in a small group, develop and perform a five- to ten-minute skit that pokes fun at communism or capitalism.

2. CONNECT TO TODAY: Cooperative Learning

THEME REVOLUTION During the Cold War, the superpowers played a part in many revolutions or upheavals in developing nations. This unrest continues today as countries struggle to develop suitable political and economic systems.

Working with a team, create an oral presentation about a current political struggle or revolution.

INTERNET Using the Internet or magazines, research a current political conflict. Investigate the beliefs, programs, tactics, and popular support of the rival factions. Determine which side is in power and what the outcome of the struggle appears to be.

- Collect photographs, charts, artifacts, or other visual aids to illustrate the issues involved in the struggle.

- If possible, interview people from that country who have immigrated to the United States and include their viewpoints in your presentation.

3. INTERPRETING A TIME LINE

Look back at the unit time line on pages 850–851. Which two events during the Cold War do you think had the greatest impact on the U.S. decision to pursue a policy of détente?

FOCUS ON GEOGRAPHY

Cold War tensions between the United States and the Soviet Union were fed by the fear of nuclear war.

- What does this map projection suggest about the distance between the countries?

- Which country had more ICBM bases?

Connect to History
How did the United States and the Soviet Union avoid a nuclear confrontation?

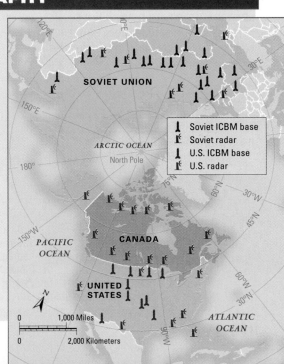

Soviet ICBM base
Soviet radar
U.S. ICBM base
U.S. radar

SOVIET UNION
ARCTIC OCEAN
North Pole
CANADA
PACIFIC OCEAN
UNITED STATES
ATLANTIC OCEAN

0 1,000 Miles
0 2,000 Kilometers

Interact *with* History

Independence has come to a former British colony, which has been divided into the new nations of India and Pakistan. Serious conflict occurs among the various factions within each country. The Hindu majority in India attacks Muslims, and the Muslim majority in Pakistan attacks Hindus. Some Hindus in Pakistan are choosing to stay in their homeland; others are choosing to flee to India to join the Hindu majority there. Either alternative involves risk.

You are a Hindu whose homeland is Pakistan. Trains are leaving that will carry you through hostile territory to a new homeland, where you will no longer be in a minority. What will you do? Will you leave your homeland behind in order to move to a new land to live among people who share your religious beliefs? Or will you stay where you are and take your chances?

After the passenger cars have been filled, refugees clamber on to every available surface. Hindus are desperate to escape from Pakistan.

Would you leave your homeland?

Hindu refugees are boarding a train in Pakistan. You could go to India, where your fellow Hindus are in the majority. The trip is dangerous, however, since you will be traveling through hostile territory.

EXAMINING *the* ISSUES

- **What might be the reasons to stay in your homeland?**

- **What might be the reasons to flee?**

- **Some members of your family flee and some stay. What will be the effects on your family over the long term?**

- **How might the problems of religious and ethnic conflict within a newly independent nation be resolved? What policies would you recommend to try to achieve unity?**

As a class, discuss these questions. In your discussion, remember what you've learned about what makes for a unified nation.

As you read in this chapter about the demands of Asians and Africans for self-rule and national identity, see how leaders try to unify newly independent countries made up of different groups.

Later, this train will be attacked by Muslims. Many of your fellow Hindus on the train will be killed or wounded. Similar attacks are launched by Hindus in India against Muslims.

The Indian Subcontinent Gains Independence

TERMS & NAMES
- Congress Party
- Muslim League
- Muhammad Ali Jinnah
- Lord Mountbatten
- partition
- Jawaharlal Nehru
- Indira Gandhi
- Rajiv Gandhi
- Benazir Bhutto

MAIN IDEA	WHY IT MATTERS NOW
New nations emerged from the British colony of India.	India today is the largest democracy in the world.

SETTING THE STAGE Britain had ruled India for many years. During this time, some Indians had been pressing for self-rule. In 1939, India was stunned when Britain committed India's armed forces to World War II without first consulting the colony's elected representatives. Indian nationalists felt humiliated. In 1942, the Congress Party launched a "Quit India" campaign. It was intended to drive Great Britain out of India. The end of World War II, in 1945, brought changes to the Indian subcontinent as dramatic as those anywhere in the world.

A Movement Toward Independence

The story was similar throughout the colonial world. When World War II broke out, Africans and Asians answered their colonial rulers' cries for help. These Africans and Asians fought on distant battlefields. They also guarded strategic bases and resources at home. The war brought soldiers from widely separated colonies into contact with one another. Soldiers from the colonies shared their frustrations, dreams for independence, and strategies for achieving it.

"Asia for Asians" During World War II, the Japanese "Asia for Asians" campaign helped to generate nationalism throughout the region. It also sparked independence movements in the various countries Japan occupied in Southeast Asia. The Japanese defeat of European forces was a sign to the nationalists that the Europeans were not as strong as they had thought them to be. Asian nationalists came to realize that their colonial masters were not unbeatable. Sometimes the Europeans suffered defeat at the hands of others—such as the Japanese—who were nonwhite and non-Western, like the nationalists.

THINK THROUGH HISTORY
A. Recognizing Effects What was the effect on Asians of Japanese victories over Europeans?

The Colonial Response Britain was recovering from the enormous costs of the war. It began to rethink the expense of maintaining and governing distant colonies. The new government in Britain also called into question the very basis of imperialism. Was it acceptable to take by force the land and resources of another nation in order to enrich the imperial nation?

Independence Brings Partition to India

In 1919, the British massacred unarmed Indians at Amritsar. (See Chapter 30.) This incident, more than any other single event, had marked the beginning of the end of British rule in India. The incident had caused millions of Indians to become strong nationalists overnight. A year later, in 1920, Mohandas Gandhi launched his first nonviolent

This photo shows British soldiers held in a Japanese prisoner-of-war camp at the end of World War II.

Wedding Rituals

In cultures throughout the world, people get married. They do so for a variety of reasons: to share life with a loved one, to raise a family, to gain social position, to gain independence, to carry on values and customs. In India, an elaborate wedding ritual has evolved within the Hindu tradition. That ritual expresses Hindus' deepest beliefs about the relationship between men and women, the importance of the family, and the role of the spiritual in the significant moments of life. Other cultures have different rituals with which they surround the wedding ceremony.

Hindu Wedding in India

Hindus traditionally bestow jewelry on brides. This bride is from West Bengal. She is bedecked with gold, silver, and enamel jewelry inlaid with precious stones. Her sari is from Benares and is made of fine silk and gold brocade. The colors of red and gold symbolize life and good luck. The design on the bride's hands is painted in henna. This traditional pattern is believed to keep away evil spirits.

a closer look HINDU RITUALS

A gold necklace called a thali is placed around the bride's neck. This necklace contains a medallion with the three symbols of the Hindu trinity—a conch shell, a trident, and a ring.

Orthodox Wedding in Russia

The Church of the Transfiguration in St. Petersburg, Russia, is the site of this Russian Orthodox wedding ceremony. Crowns are placed on the heads of the bride and groom, who hold candles. Orthodox churches make lavish use of gold and rich decoration to display religious works of art such as icons.

A Bridal Fair in Morocco

The bridal fair is part of the marriage ritual of some Berbers of Morocco. Marriageable young men and women attend the fair of Imilchil in the Atlas Mountains of North Africa in search of spouses. The women wear capes, headdresses, and veils as they survey the eligible prospects during the fair. Court-ship, engagement, and marriage all take place during the three days of the fair. The couples shown are waiting to enter the wedding tent.

Wedding in Guatemala

The Indians shown to the left are of Mayan descent. They live in the highlands of Guatemala. Villagers in Guatemala combine suit jackets and Indian clothing in a wedding ceremony. The clothes worn by the Indians identify their home villages.

Connect *to* History

Comparing What are some elements of the wedding ceremony that seem common from one culture to another?

 SEE SKILLBUILDER HANDBOOK, PAGE 996.

Connect *to* Today

Researching Read about wedding rituals in other cultures, and then write a couple of paragraphs describing the ritual that most appeals to you.

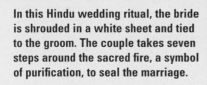

In this Hindu wedding ritual, the bride is shrouded in a white sheet and tied to the groom. The couple takes seven steps around the sacred fire, a symbol of purification, to seal the marriage.

The Colonies Become New Nations **891**

TERMS & NAMES
- Ferdinand Marcos
- Corazón Aquino
- Aung San
- Aung San Suu Kyi
- Sukarno
- Suharto

2 Southeast Asian Nations Gain Independence

MAIN IDEA	WHY IT MATTERS NOW
The European colonies in Southeast Asia became independent countries in the postwar period.	The power and influence of the Pacific Rim nations are likely to expand during the next century.

SETTING THE STAGE At the end of World War II, colonized people all over the world agitated for independence. As it had in India, Britain gave up control of its Southeast Asian colonies; it gave up Burma quickly and Malaysia after some delay. Some imperialists, the Dutch among them, were reluctant to give up their Southeast Asian possessions. They waged bitter and losing battles to retain control. The United States gave up its Asian colony in the Philippines soon after World War II.

The United States and the Philippines

The Philippines became the first of the world's colonies to achieve independence following World War II. The United States granted the Philippines independence in 1946, on the anniversary of its own Declaration of Independence, the Fourth of July.

The Philippines Achieves Independence The Filipinos' immediate goals were to rebuild the economy and to restore the capital of Manila. The city had been badly damaged in World War II. The United States had promised the Philippines $600 million in war damages. However, the U.S. government insisted that Filipinos approve the Bell Act in order to get the money. This act would establish free trade between the United States and the Philippines for eight years, to be followed by gradually increasing tariffs. Filipinos were worried that American businesses would exploit the resources and environment of the Philippines. In spite of this concern, Filipinos approved the Bell Act and received their money.

The United States wanted to maintain its military presence in the Philippines. With the onset of the Cold War (see Chapter 33), the United States needed to be able to protect its interests in Asia. Both China and the Soviet Union were opponents of the United States at the time. Both were Pacific powers with bases close to allies of the United States as well as to raw materials and resources vital to U.S. interests. Therefore, the United States demanded a 99-year lease on its military and naval bases in the Philippines. The bases—Clark Air Force Base and Subic Bay Naval Base near Manila—proved to be critical to the United States later, in the staging of the Korean and Vietnam wars.

These military bases also became the single greatest source of conflict between the United States and the Philippines. Many Filipinos regarded the bases as proof of American imperialism. Later agreements shortened the terms of the lease, and the United States gave up both bases in 1991.

Vocabulary
Filipino: an inhabitant of the Philippines.

Ships of the U.S. Navy docked at Subic Bay in the Philippines from 1901 to 1991.

THINK THROUGH HISTORY
A. Making Inferences Why might the United States have been interested in maintaining military bases in the Philippines?

BHUTAN

INDIA

CHINA

BURMA
1948

BANGLADESH

Hanoi

NORTH
VIETNAM
1954

LAOS
1953

Vientiane

Rangoon

THAILAND

PHILIPPINES
1946

Manila

South
China
Sea

Bangkok

CAMBODIA
1953

SOUTH
VIETNAM
1954

INDIAN
OCEAN

Phnom Penh

Saigon

PACIFIC
OCEAN

BRUNEI
(Br.)

MALAYSIA
1957

N

Kuala Lumpur

Singapore
1965

BORNEO

0° Equator

I N D O N E S I A
1949

0   500 Miles

0   1,000 Kilometers

Jakarta

Former French colony
Former British colony
Former Dutch colony
Former U.S. colony
Continuously independent
1945 Date of independence

GEOGRAPHY SKILLBUILDER: Interpreting Maps

1. **Region** *Which former Dutch colony is made up of a series of islands spread out from the Indian Ocean to the Pacific Ocean?*
2. **Region** *From what European country did the most colonies shown above gain their independence?*

After World War II, the Philippine government was still almost completely dependent on the United States economically and politically. The Philippine government looked for ways to lessen this dependency. It welcomed Japanese investments. It also broadened its contacts with Southeast Asian neighbors and with nonaligned nations.

The Marcos Regime and Corazón Aquino **Ferdinand Marcos** was elected president of the Philippines in 1965. The country suffered under his rule from 1966 to 1986. Marcos imposed an authoritarian regime and stole millions of dollars from the public treasury. Although the constitution limited Marcos to eight years in office, he got around this restriction by imposing martial law from 1972 to 1981. Two years later, his chief opponent, Benigno Aquino, Jr., was shot when he returned from the United States to the Philippines, lured by the promise of coming elections.

In the elections of 1986, Marcos ran against Aquino's widow, **Corazón Aquino**. Aquino won decisively, but Marcos refused to acknowledge her victory. When he declared himself the official winner, a public outcry resulted. He was forced into exile in Hawaii, where he later died. In 1995, the Philippines succeeded in recovering $475 million Marcos had stolen from his country and deposited in Swiss banks.

During Aquino's presidency, the Philippine government ratified a new constitution. It also negotiated successfully with the United States to end the lease on the U.S. military bases. In 1992, Fidel V. Ramos succeeded Aquino as president. Ramos is restricted by the constitution to a single six-year term. The single-term limit is intended to prevent the abuse of power that occurred during Marcos's 20-year rule.

Background
Before the Philippines belonged to the United States, it was a Spanish colony. This is why many Filipinos, who are mostly Asian, have Spanish names.

HISTORY MAKERS

Aung San Suu Kyi
1945–

Aung San Suu Kyi won the Nobel Peace Prize in 1991 for her efforts to establish democracy in Burma. She could not accept the award in person, however, because she was still under house arrest. The Nobel Prize committee said that in awarding her the peace prize, it intended

. . . to show its support for the many people throughout the world who are striving to attain democracy, human rights, and ethnic conciliation by peaceful means. Suu Kyi's struggle is one of the most extraordinary examples of civil courage in Asia in recent decades.

The military government had offered to free her if she would leave the country. However, she refused, insisting she would not leave until a civilian government was restored to Burma and all political prisoners were freed.

British Colonies Gain Independence

Britain's timetable for giving its colonies independence depended on local circumstances. Burma had been pressing for independence from Britain for decades. It became a sovereign republic in 1948 and chose not to join the British Commonwealth. In 1989, Burma was officially named Myanmar (myahn·MAH), its name in the Burmese language.

Burma Experiences Turmoil In the postwar years, Burma suffered one political upheaval after another. Its people struggled between repressive military governments and pro-democracy forces. When the Japanese occupied Burma during World War II, they had declared Burma a sovereign state. In fact, the Japanese were in control. Their demands for forced labor were particularly unpopular. The Burmese nationalists' army, led by **Aung San** (owng sahn), at first cooperated with the Japanese in order to drive the British out of Burma. Then the army linked up with British forces to defeat the Japanese. They succeeded in driving out the Japanese and were about to become independent. Then Aung San and most of his cabinet were gunned down on orders of Burmese political rivals.

Conflict among Communists and ethnic minorities disrupted the nation. In 1962, General Ne Win set up a repressive military government, with the goal of making Burma a socialist state. Although Ne Win stepped down in 1988, the military continued to rule Burma repressively. Also in 1988, **Aung San Suu Kyi** (owng sahn soo chee), the daughter of Aung San, returned to Burma after many years abroad. She became active in the newly formed National League for Democracy. For her pro-democracy activities, she was placed under house arrest for six years by the government. In the 1990 election—the country's first multiparty election in 30 years—the National League for Democracy won 80 percent of the seats. The military government refused to recognize the election, and it kept Aung San Suu Kyi under house arrest. She was finally released in 1995 though still kept under surveillance.

Malaysia and Singapore During World War II, the Japanese conquered the Malay Peninsula, formerly ruled by the British. The British returned to the peninsula after the Japanese defeat in 1945. They tried, unsuccessfully, to organize Malaya into one state. They also struggled to put down a Communist uprising. Ethnic groups resisted British efforts to unite their colonies on the peninsula and in the northern part of the island of Borneo. Malays were a slight majority on the peninsula, while Chinese were the largest group in Singapore. In 1957, the Federation of Malaya was created from Singapore, Malaya, Sarawak, and Sabah. The two regions—on the Malay Peninsula and on northern Borneo—were separated by 400 miles of ocean. In 1965, Singapore separated from the federation and became an independent city-state. The Federation of Malaysia—consisting of Malaya, Sarawak, and Sabah—was created. A coalition of many ethnic groups maintained steady economic progress in Malaysia.

Singapore, extremely prosperous, was one of the busiest ports in the world. Lee Kuan Yew ruled Singapore as prime minister from 1959 to 1990. Under his guidance, Singapore emerged as a banking center as well as a trade center. It had a standard of living far higher than any of its Southeast Asian neighbors. In early 1997, the Geneva World Economic Forum listed the world's most competitive economies. Singapore topped the list. It was followed, in order, by Hong Kong, the United States, Canada, New Zealand, Switzerland, and Great Britain.

Vocabulary
repressive government: a government that puts down opposition by force.

Vocabulary
house arrest: confinement to one's quarters, or house, rather than to prison.

THINK THROUGH HISTORY
B. Making Inferences What do these competitive economies all have in common?

Indonesia Gains Independence from the Dutch

The Japanese occupation of Indonesia during World War II destroyed the Dutch colonial order. Waiting in the wings to lead Indonesia was **Sukarno** (soo·KAHR·noh), known only by his one name. He was a leader of the Indonesian independence movement. In August 1945, two days after the Japanese surrendered, Sukarno proclaimed Indonesia's independence and named himself president. The Dutch, however, backed up initially by the British and the United States, attempted to regain control of Indonesia.

The Dutch in Indonesia Unlike British colonialists, who served their term in India and then returned to England, the pre-war Dutch looked upon the East Indies as their permanent home. To keep it that way, the Dutch resisted native Indonesians' attempts to enter the civil service or to acquire higher education. After the war, Indonesians were unwilling to return to their condition of servitude under the Dutch. They therefore put together a successful guerrilla army. After losing the support of the United Nations and the United States, the Dutch agreed to grant Indonesia its independence in 1949.

A Variety of People, Islands, and Religions The new Indonesia became the world's fourth most populous nation. It consisted of more than 13,600 islands, with 300 different ethnic groups, 250 languages, and most of the world's major religions. It contained the world's largest Islamic population. Sukarno, who took the official title of "life-time president," attempted to guide this diverse nation in a parliamentary democracy. Unfortunately, this attempt failed.

In 1965, a group of junior army officers attempted a coup, which was suppressed by a general named **Suharto** (suh·HAHR·toh). He then seized power for himself, and began a bloodbath in which 500,000 to 1 million Indonesians were killed.

Suharto, officially named president in 1967, turned Indonesia into a police state and imposed frequent periods of martial law. Outside observers heavily criticized him for his annexation of East Timor in 1976 and for human rights violations there. (East Timor freed itself from Indonesian rule in 1999.) The Chinese living in Indonesia met with discrimination but were tolerated because of their financial contributions to the state. Christians were persecuted. Bribery and corruption became commonplace. Growing unrest over both government repression and a crippling economic crisis moved Suharto to step down in 1998. In a sign of hope for the future, the nation in 1999 elected a new leader, Abdurrahman Wahid, in its first-ever democratic transfer of power.

THINK THROUGH HISTORY
C. Contrasting How did the British and the Dutch differ in their attitudes toward their colonies?

Vocabulary
coup: the sudden overthrow of a government by a small group of people.

Comparing Economies

Gross Domestic Product is the dollar value of all goods and services produced within a country during one year. In this graph, the GDP is divided by the number of productive workers in each country. This results in the GDP per capita, or per person.

■ Philippines
■ Singapore
■ United States

Sources: *World Statistics in Brief* (1978) and *World Statistics Pocketbook* (1995), published by the United Nations.

SKILLBUILDER:
Interpreting Graphs
1. Which country had the highest GDP per capita in both 1965 and 1991? Which had the lowest?
2. Which country showed the biggest increase in GDP per capita from 1985 to 1991?

Section ❷ Assessment

1. TERMS & NAMES

Identify
- Ferdinand Marcos
- Corazón Aquino
- Aung San
- Aung San Suu Kyi
- Sukarno
- Suharto

2. TAKING NOTES

Using a chart like the one below, summarize the major challenges the countries faced following independence.

Nation	Colonizer	Challenges Following Independence
The Philippines		
Burma		
Indonesia		

3. MAKING INFERENCES

Why do you think that the United States demanded a 99-year lease on military and naval bases in the Philippines?

THINK ABOUT
- U.S. economic interests in the Philippines
- geographical location
- reasons for military presence

4. THEME ACTIVITY

Power and Authority
Write a two-paragraph essay contrasting a peaceful transfer of authority from a colonial power to a newly independent nation with a transfer that was violent.

Israeli Independent News

Life on a Kibbutz

On this communal farm, women work right along with men in the fields. Children receive care from trained teachers and nurses. One young girl being raised on a kibbutz wrote her American friend about the freedom and responsibility of kibbutz life: "Among us the children's opinion is very important. We decide when and how to work and when to do a project. I study six hours a day and I work one and a half hours. I am also taking lessons in music and crafts."

A tractor driver carries a rifle slung across his back as he works to develop the land on his kibbutz.

Population Doubles in Three Years

Israel's Jewish population has doubled from 700,000 in May 1948 to 1,400,000 on the country's third birthday, thanks to a huge influx of immigrants. The new Israelis hail from 70 different countries, including Poland, Romania, Germany, Italy, Austria, Bulgaria, Libya, and Iraq. At a cost of about $1,600 per immigrant, the Jewish Agency sees to all the immigrants' needs when they first arrive, from housing to health care.

Chart: Population (in thousands), with bars for 1948 and 1951. Y-axis values: 0, 300, 600, 900, 1200, 1500.

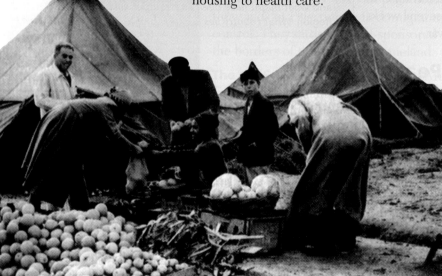

From Culture to Agriculture

Many of Israel's eager immigrants are former lawyers, professors, or physicians. They find themselves drawn to the hard work of clearing Israel's swamps and making her deserts bloom. At one collective farm, the professors who work as farmers could probably open their own college. Now, instead of teaching math, philosophy, or psychology, they eagerly pore over the latest publications on scientific farming from the U.S. Department of Agriculture.

Connect *to* History

Synthesizing From the articles in the newsletter, what problems did new immigrants to Israel face in 1951?

SEE SKILLBUILDER HANDBOOK, PAGE 1007.

Connect *to* Today

Researching In the library or on the Internet, research a facet of life in modern-day Israel. You might choose the kibbutzim, Palestinian-Israeli relations, or the current status of Jerusalem.

Tent cities have sprung up throughout Israel to house new immigrants. Within ten years, these temporary shelters will be replaced by permanent housing.

Temporary Housing Springs Up

Near the large towns and farming areas that offer employment, transit camps called *ma'abarot* offer shelter and food for Israel's refugees. Workers quickly raise tents and canvas huts to house the refugees. Then they build wooden huts to hold kindergartens, nurseries, clinics, and employment centers. Workers can erect a *ma'abarot* within a few weeks. These camps provide welcome shelter for hundreds of thousands of needy immigrants.

The Palestinians Demand Independence

Peace agreements between Israelis and Palestinians were harder to achieve. Unwilling to give up territories they had seized for security, the Israelis began to build settlements on the West Bank and the Gaza Strip.

The Intifada Palestinians living in Israel resented Israeli rule. As their anger mounted, they turned increasingly to the Palestine Liberation Organization, or **PLO,** led by Yasir Arafat (YAH·sur AR·uh·FAT). During the 1970s and 1980s, the military wing of the PLO conducted a campaign of armed struggle against Israel. Israel turned to strong measures, bombing suspected bases in Palestinian towns. In 1982, the Israeli army invaded Lebanon in an attempt to destroy strongholds in Palestinian villages. The Israelis soon became involved in Lebanon's civil war and were forced to withdraw.

In 1987, Palestinians began to express their frustrations in a widespread campaign of civil disobedience called the intifada, or "uprising." The intifada took the form of boycotts, demonstrations, attacks on Israeli soldiers, and rock throwing by unarmed teenagers. The intifada continued into the 1990s, with little progress made towards a solution. However, the civil disobedience affected world opinion, which, in turn, put pressure on Israel. Finally, in October 1991, Israeli and Palestinian delegates met for the first time in a series of peace talks.

The Declaration of Principles The status of the Israeli-occupied territories proved to be a bitterly divisive issue. In 1993, however, secret talks held in Oslo, Norway, produced a surprise agreement. In a document called the Declaration of Principles, Israel, under the leadership of Prime Minister Yitzhak Rabin (YIHTS·hahk rah·BEEN), agreed to grant the Palestinians self-rule in the Gaza Strip and the West Bank, beginning with the town of Jericho. Rabin and Arafat signed the agreement on September 13, 1993.

The difficulty of making an agreement work was demonstrated by the assassination of Rabin in 1995. He was killed by a right-wing Jewish extremist who opposed concessions to the Palestinians. Rabin was succeeded as prime minister by Benjamin Netanyahu (neh·tan·YAH·hoo), who had opposed the plan. Still, Netanyahu made efforts to keep to the agreement. In January 1997, he met with Arafat to work out plans for a partial Israeli withdrawal from Hebron, on the West Bank. In 1999, Ehud Barak won election as prime minister. While Barak voiced support for the peace plan, the two sides entered the new century still unable to craft a final agreement.

THINK THROUGH HISTORY
E. Forming an Opinion Political commentators have said that the Arab-Israeli conflict represents the struggle not of right against wrong, but of right against right. Do you agree or disagree? Explain.

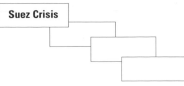

SPOTLIGHT ON

Oslo Peace Agreement

In 1993, the PLO and Israel conducted highly secret talks in an isolated farmhouse near Oslo, Norway. The Palestinian and Israeli leaders showed courage in working out a peace agreement sure to be unpopular with many of their followers. Their achievement was recognized in 1994. That year, the Nobel Peace Prize was awarded jointly to PLO Chairman Yasir Arafat, Israeli Prime Minister Yitzhak Rabin, and Israeli Foreign Minister Shimon Peres.

In making the award, the Nobel committee said the prize was intended to "serve as an encouragement to all the Israelis and Palestinians who are endeavoring to establish lasting peace in the region."

Section 4 Assessment

1. TERMS & NAMES

Identify
- Balfour Declaration
- Suez Crisis
- Six-Day War
- Anwar Sadat
- Golda Meir
- Menachem Begin
- Camp David Accords
- Hosni Mubarak
- PLO

2. TAKING NOTES

Draw a cause-and-effect graphic and fill in some important political and military events that occurred following the Suez Crisis.

> Suez Crisis

Write a paragraph explaining which event is most important.

3. ANALYZING ISSUES

Explain the conflict between Jews and Arabs over a Palestinian homeland. What does each side believe? What other factors influence this issue?

THINK ABOUT
- the Balfour Declaration
- the ancient history of the Middle East
- the economics of oil

4. THEME ACTIVITY

Power and Authority In groups of three or four, come up with a list of ten interview questions for Gamal Abdel Nasser, Anwar Sadat, Yasir Arafat, or Yitzhak Rabin.

Krenz's dramatic gamble to save communism did not work. When the public discovered evidence of widespread corruption among party leaders, Krenz and other top officials were forced to resign in disgrace. By the end of 1989, the East German Communist Party had ceased to exist.

Germany Is Reunified With the fall of Communism in East Germany, many Germans began to speak of **reunification**—the merging of the two Germanys. However, the movement for reunification worried many people. They feared that a united Germany would once again try to dominate Europe.

West German Chancellor Helmut Kohl assured world leaders that Germans had learned from the past. They were now committed to democracy and human rights. Kohl's assurances helped persuade other European nations to accept German reunification. Forty-five years after its crushing defeat in World War II, Germany was officially reunited on October 3, 1990.

Germany's Challenges The newly united Germany faced serious problems. More than 40 years of Communist rule had left eastern Germany in ruins. Its railroads, highways, and telephone system had not been modernized since World War II. Many East German industries produced shoddy goods that could not compete in the global market.

Rebuilding eastern Germany's bankrupt economy was going to be a difficult, costly process. To pay these costs, Kohl raised taxes. As taxpayers tightened their belts, workers in eastern Germany faced a second problem—unemployment. Inefficient factories closed, depriving millions of workers of their jobs.

THINK THROUGH HISTORY
D. Clarifying Why would Europeans fear the reunification of Germany?

In spite of these difficulties, German voters returned the ruling coalition of political parties to power in 1994. Kohl was re-elected chancellor. But the economic troubles continued, so in 1998, voters turned Kohl out of office and elected a new president, Gerhard Schroeder of the Socialist Democratic Party (SPD).

Reunification forced Germany to rethink its role in international affairs. As central Europe's largest country, Germany gained important global responsibilities. As Germany's global responsibilities grew, German leaders began to argue that the country deserved a permanent seat on the UN Security Council. The Security Council is a group of 15 nations with the authority to decide UN actions. As of 2000, however, Germany had not gained membership to the body.

Democracy Spreads

Changes in the Soviet Union, Poland, and Hungary had helped inspire reforms in East Germany. In the same way, changes in East Germany affected other Eastern European countries, including Czechoslovakia and Romania. In those countries, however, repressive governments delayed the movement toward democracy.

Czechoslovakia Reforms While huge crowds were demanding democracy in East Germany, neighboring Czechoslovakia remained quiet. Vivid memories of the violent crackdown against the reforms of 1968 made the Czechs cautious. A conservative government led by Milos Jakes resisted all change. In October 1989, the police arrested several dissidents. Among these was the Czech playwright Vaclav Havel (VAH·tslahv HAH·vehl), a popular critic of the government.

On October 28, 1989, 10,000 people gathered in Wenceslas Square in the center of Prague. They demanded democracy and freedom. Hundreds were arrested. Three weeks later, 25,000 students inspired by the fall of the Berlin Wall gathered in Prague to demand reform. Following orders from the government, the police brutally attacked the demonstrators and injured hundreds.

The government crackdown angered the Czech people. On each of the next eight days, huge crowds gathered in Wenceslas Square. They demanded an end to Communist rule. On November 24, 500,000 protesters crowded into downtown Prague. Within hours, Milos Jakes and his entire Politburo resigned. One month later, a new parliament elected Vaclav Havel president of Czechoslovakia.

Overthrow in Romania By late 1989, only Romania seemed unmoved by the calls of reform. Romania's ruthless Communist dictator Nicolae Ceausescu (chow·SHES·koo) maintained a firm grip on power. His secret police enforced his orders brutally. Nevertheless, Romanians were aware of the reforms in other countries. They began a protest movement of their own. One student explained their anger at the government:

A VOICE FROM THE PAST
We were raised on a mountain of lies. There was a fantastical difference between the things they told us and the things we saw. They published incredible statistics on agricultural production, and in the shops there was nothing to eat. On paper, we had freedom of expression, but anytime anyone said anything, members of the Communist Party told us to keep our mouths shut.

STEFAN GHENCEA, Romanian student

In December, Ceausescu ordered the army to fire on demonstrators in the city of Timisoara (tee·mee·SHWAH·rah). The army killed and wounded scores of people. The massacre in Timisoara ignited a popular uprising against Ceausescu. Within days, the army joined the people. They fought to defeat the secret police and overthrow their ruler. Shocked by the sudden collapse of his power, Ceausescu and his wife attempted to flee. They were captured, however, then hastily tried and executed on Christmas Day, 1989.

Romania held general elections in 1990 and in 1992. The government also made economic reforms to introduce elements of capitalism. At the same time, the slow pace of Gorbachev's economic reforms began to cause unrest in the Soviet Union.

THINK THROUGH HISTORY
E. Contrasting
Contrast the democratic revolutions in Czechoslovakia and Romania.

SPOTLIGHT ON

Television's Influence
Television played a key role in the movements for democracy. Mikhail Gorbachev used television to spread news of reform programs and bolster his image. In East Germany, people viewed Western programs and saw the contrast between affluence in the West and their own lower standard of living.

In Romania the role of television was more direct. Revolutionaries captured the state television station in Bucharest and broadcast their own views of the struggle. They used television to coordinate revolutionary actions in different parts of the country. When Nicolae Ceausescu and his wife were tried and executed, television carried the news throughout the country—along with pictures of their dead bodies. Ceausescu is shown below.

Section ❸ Assessment

1. TERMS & NAMES

Identify
- Politburo
- Mikhail Gorbachev
- glasnost
- perestroika
- Solidarity
- Lech Walesa
- reunification

2. TAKING NOTES

Use a time line like the one below to record significant events in the Soviet Union and Eastern Europe.

During which year did most of Eastern Europe turn toward democracy?

3. SYNTHESIZING

Explain how Gorbachev's reforms helped to move the Soviet Union closer toward democracy.

THINK ABOUT
- the democratic practices and conditions listed on the chart on page 911
- how Gorbachev's policies promoted those practices and conditions

4. THEME ACTIVITY

Cultural Interaction With a partner, create a cause-and-effect diagram to show how democratic reform spread through Eastern Europe. The diagram should show the order in which reform happened and which countries influenced others. You may want to look through this textbook for model diagrams.

4 Collapse of the Soviet Union

MAIN IDEA	WHY IT MATTERS NOW
In the early 1990s, the Soviet Union, Yugoslavia, and Czechoslovakia all broke apart.	Many of the new nations created after those breakups continue to struggle to establish democracy.

SETTING THE STAGE The reforms of the late 1980s brought high hopes to the people of the Soviet Union and Eastern Europe. For the first time in decades, they were free to make choices about the economic and political systems governing their lives. They soon discovered that increased freedom sometimes challenges the social order.

HISTORY MAKERS

Boris Yeltsin
1931–

Boris Yeltsin was raised in poverty. For 10 years, his family lived in a single room and slept on the floor next to their goat for warmth.

As a youth, Yeltsin earned good grades but behaved badly. Mikhail Gorbachev named him party boss and mayor of Moscow in 1985. Yeltsin's outspokenness got him into trouble. At one meeting, he launched into a bitter speech criticizing conservatives for working against perestroika. Gorbachev fired him for the sake of party unity.

Yeltsin made a dramatic comeback and won a seat in parliament in 1989. Parliament elected him president of Russia in 1990, and voters re-elected him in 1991. Due at least in part to his failing health—heart problems—Yeltsin resigned in 1999.

Unrest in the Soviet Union

As Eastern Europe gained freedom from Soviet control, various nationalities in the Soviet Union began to call for their own freedom. More than 100 ethnic groups lived in the Soviet Union. Russians were the largest, most powerful group. However, non-Russians formed a majority in the 14 Soviet republics other than Russia.

Ethnic tensions brewed beneath the surface of Soviet society. As reforms loosened central controls, unrest spread across the country. Nationalist groups in Georgia, Ukraine, and Moldavia (now Moldova) demanded self-rule. The Muslim peoples of Soviet Central Asia called for religious freedom.

Lithuania Defies Gorbachev The first challenge came from the Baltic nations of Lithuania, Estonia, and Latvia. These republics had been independent states between the two world wars—until the Soviets annexed them in 1940. Fifty years later, in March 1990, Lithuania declared its independence. To try to force it back into the Soviet Union, Gorbachev ordered a blockade of the republic.

Although Gorbachev was reluctant to use stronger measures, he feared that Lithuania's example might encourage other republics to secede. In January 1991 Soviet troops attacked unarmed civilians in Lithuania's capital. The army killed 14 and wounded more than 150.

Yeltsin Denounces Gorbachev The bloody assault in Lithuania and the lack of real economic progress in the Soviet Union damaged Gorbachev's popularity. More and more people looked for leadership to **Boris Yeltsin.** He was a member of parliament and the former mayor of Moscow. Yeltsin criticized the crackdown in Lithuania and the slow pace of reforms. In June 1991, voters overwhelmingly chose Yeltsin to become the Russian Republic's first directly elected president.

Yeltsin and Gorbachev were now on a collision course. In spite of their rivalry, they faced a common enemy in the old guard of Communist officials. Hard-liners—conservatives who opposed reform—were furious at Gorbachev. They were angry that he had given up the Soviet Union's role as the dominant force in Eastern Europe. They also feared losing their power and privileges. These officials vowed to overthrow Gorbachev and undo his reforms.

Background
About three-fourths of the Soviet population were Slavic peoples such as Russians or Ukrainians. Turkic peoples, such as Uzbeks or Azerbaijani, were the second largest group. Most of these were Muslim. Other groups included Georgians and Armenians.

Background
As part of government reform, Gorbachev became president of the Soviet Union—a new office modeled on the U.S. presidency. Each of the 15 republics was also allowed to have a president. For example, Yeltsin was the president of Russia.

Distribution of Territory, 1991

Other Republics
(23.3%)

Russian
Republic
(76.7%)

ARCTIC OCEAN

RUSSIA

Arctic Circle

Ob R.

Irtysh R.

Yenisey R.

Lena R.

Amur R.

Sea
of
Okhotsk

Tallinn • ESTONIA

Riga • LATVIA

• Moscow

Vilnius • Minsk

•SSIA • BELARUS

•ITHUANIA • Kiev

UKRAINE

• Chisinau

•OLDOVA

GEORGIA

Tbilisi •

ARMENIA •

Yerevan

• Baku

AZERBAIJAN

TURKMENISTAN

Ashgabat •

Black Sea

Caspian Sea

Volga R.

Aral
Sea

KAZAKHSTAN

Lake
Balkhash

Almaty •

Tashkent •

• Bishkek

KYRGYZSTAN

Dushanbe •

TAJIKISTAN

UZBEKISTAN

Lake
Baikal

editerranean Sea

Mediterranean Sea

Sea
of
Japan

PACIFIC
OCEAN

N

0   1,000 Miles

0   2,000 Kilometers

— Border of the Soviet Union

PACIFIC
OCEAN

40°N

GEOGRAPHY SKILLBUILDER: Interpreting Maps
1. **Place** *Name the 15 republics of the former Soviet Union.*
2. **Region** *Which republic received the largest percentage of the former Soviet Union's territory?*

The August Coup On August 18, 1991, the hard-liners detained Gorbachev at his vacation home on the Black Sea. They demanded his resignation as Soviet president. Early the next day, hundreds of tanks and armored vehicles rolled into Moscow. The hard-liners—who called themselves the State Committee—assumed that a show of force would ensure obedience. However, the Soviet people had lost their fear of the party. They were willing to defend their freedoms. Protesters gathered at the Russian parliament building, where Yeltsin had his office.

Around midday, Yeltsin emerged and climbed atop one of the tanks. As his supporters cheered, Yeltsin declared, "We proclaim all decisions and decrees of this committee to be illegal. . . . We appeal to the citizens of Russia to . . . demand a return of the country to normal constitutional developments."

On August 20, the State Committee ordered troops to attack the parliament, but they refused. Their refusal turned the tide. On August 21, the military withdrew its forces from Moscow. That night, Gorbachev returned to Moscow.

End of the Soviet Union The coup attempt sparked anger against the Communist party. Gorbachev resigned as general secretary of the party. The Soviet parliament voted to stop all party activities. Having first seized power in 1917 in a coup that succeeded, the all-powerful Communist Party now collapsed because of a coup that failed.

The coup also played a decisive role in accelerating the breakup of the Soviet Union. Estonia and Latvia quickly declared their independence. Other republics soon followed. Although Gorbachev pleaded for unity, no one was listening. By early December, all 15 republics had declared independence.

THINK THROUGH HISTORY
A. Analyzing Motives Why do you think the Soviet troops refused the order to attack the parliament?

Crowds of citizens surround the tanks in Moscow during the August coup attempt. The soldiers' refusal to fight doomed the coup.

Cuba

The Soviet collapse harmed Cuba. Since becoming a Communist state in the early 1960s, Cuba had depended on Soviet assistance. By the late 1980s, Cuba relied on the Soviet Union for more than three-fourths of its imports and all of its oil.

As reform swept the Soviet Union and Eastern Europe, Cuba's leader, Fidel Castro, criticized the reformers. He also vowed that Cuba would remain Communist.

After the August Coup of 1991, Soviet support of Cuba's economy came to an abrupt end. Cut off from Soviet aid and deeply affected by an American trade embargo, Cuba went into severe economic decline. During the 1990s, Cuba struggled to form new trade relationships and mend its tattered economy.

Yeltsin met with the leaders of other republics to chart a new course. They agreed to form the Commonwealth of Independent States, or **CIS,** a loose federation of former Soviet territories. Only the Baltic republics and Georgia refused to join. The formation of the CIS meant the death of the Soviet Union. On Christmas Day 1991, Gorbachev announced his resignation as president of the Soviet Union, a country that by then had ceased to exist.

Background
Georgia did join the CIS later, in 1993, but the Baltic states remained separate.

The Yeltsin Era

As president of the large Russian Republic, Boris Yeltsin was now the most powerful figure in the CIS. He would face many problems—an ailing economy, tough political opposition, and an unpopular war.

Yeltsin Faces Problems One of Yeltsin's goals was to reform the Russian economy. He adopted a bold plan known as **"shock therapy,"** an abrupt shift to free-market economics. To eliminate government involvement in the economy, Yeltsin lowered trade barriers, removed price controls, and ended subsidies to state-owned industries.

Initially, the plan produced more shock than therapy. Prices soared; from 1992 to 1994, the inflation rate averaged 800 percent. Many factories dependent on government money had to cut production or shut down entirely. This forced thousands of people out of work. By 1993, most Russians were suffering severe economic hardship:

Vocabulary
subsidies: government funds given to support industries.

A VOICE FROM THE PAST

A visitor to Moscow cannot escape the feeling of a society in collapse. Child beggars accost foreigners on the street. . . . Children ask why they should stay in school when educated professionals do not make enough money to survive. . . . A garment worker complains that now her wages do not cover even the food bills, while fear of growing crime makes her dread leaving home.

DAVID M. KOTZ, "The Cure That Could Kill"

**THINK THROUGH HISTORY
B. Evaluating Decisions** Compare Yeltsin's action here to his actions during the August Coup. Which actions were more supportive of democracy?

Economic problems fueled a political crisis. In October 1993, legislators opposed to Yeltsin's policies shut themselves inside the parliament building. Yeltsin ordered troops to bombard the building, forcing hundreds of rebel legislators to surrender. Many were killed. Opponents accused Yeltsin of acting like a dictator.

Chechnya Rebels Yeltsin's troubles included war in Chechnya (CHEHCH·nee·uh), a largely Muslim area in southwestern Russia. In 1991, Chechnya declared its independence, but Yeltsin denied the region's right to secede. In 1994, he ordered 40,000 Russian troops into the breakaway republic. Russian forces reduced the capital city of Grozny (GROHZ·nee) to rubble. News of the death and destruction sparked anger throughout Russia. With an election coming, Yeltsin sought to end the war. In August 1996, the two sides signed a peace treaty. That year, Yeltsin won re-election.

War soon broke out again between Russia and Chechnya. In 1999, as the fighting raged, Yeltsin resigned and named Russian Premier Vladimir Putin as acting president. Putin forcefully quashed the rebellion in Chechyna—a popular move that helped him win the presidential election in 2000. The nation's economic woes continue, however, and some observers wonder whether Russian democracy can survive.

Yugoslavia Falls Apart

Ethnic conflict also plagued Yugoslavia. This country, formed after World War I, had six major groups of people—Serbs, Croats, Muslims, Slovenes, Macedonians, and Montenegrins. Ethnic and religious differences dating back centuries caused these groups to view each other with suspicion. After World War II, Yugoslavia became a federation of six republics. Each republic had a mixed population.

A Bloody Breakup Josip Tito, who led Yugoslavia from 1945 to 1980, held the country together. After Tito's death, however, long-simmering ethnic resentments boiled over. Serbian leader Slobodan Milosevic (mee·LOH·sheh·vihch) asserted Serbian leadership over Yugoslavia. Two republics—Slovenia and Croatia—then declared independence. In June 1991, the Serbian-led Yugoslav army invaded both republics. After months of bloody fighting, both republics freed themselves from Serbian rule. In February 1992, Bosnia-Herzegovina joined Slovenia and Croatia in declaring independence. (In April, Serbia and Montenegro formed a new Yugoslavia. See the map below.) Bosnia's ethnically mixed population included Muslims (44 percent), Serbs (31 percent), and Croats (17 percent). While Bosnia's Muslims and Croats backed independence, Bosnian Serbs strongly opposed it. Supported by Serbia, the Bosnian Serbs launched a brutal war in March 1992.

During the war, the Serbs used murder and other forms of brutality against Bosnian Muslims living in Serb-held lands. Called **ethnic cleansing**, this policy was intended to rid Bosnia of its Muslim population. By 1995, the Serbs controlled 70 percent of Bosnia In December of that year, the leaders of the three factions involved in the war signed a UN and U.S.-brokered peace treaty. In September 1996, Bosnians elected a three-person presidency—one leader from each ethnic group. However, the nation continues to experience unrest.

Rebellion in Kosovo The Balkan region descended into violence and bloodshed again in 1998—this time in Kosovo, a province in southern Serbia made up almost entirely of ethnic Albanians. As an indepence movement in Kosovo grew increasingly violent, Serb forces invaded the province and fought back with a harsh hand. In response to growing reports of Serb atrocities—and the failure of diplomacy to bring peace—NATO began a bombing campaign against Yugoslavia in the spring of 1999. After enduring more than two months of sustained bombing, Yugoslav leaders finally withdrew their troops from Kosovo. However, the atmosphere in the region remains tense—and the future status of the province remains uncertain.

These two women stand in front of a building that has been heavily damaged in the war. The building is in Sarajevo, Bosnia.

GEOGRAPHY SKILLBUILDER: Interpreting Maps
1. **Region** *Which nations now make up what used to be Yugoslavia in 1989?*
2. **Location** *Where is Serbia located relative to the republics that declared independence from Yugoslavia?*

Eastern Europe Faces Problems

Compared with Yugoslavia, the nations of Eastern Europe were relatively stable in the 1990s and did not experience widespread violence. Nevertheless, countries like Poland faced ongoing challenges.

Poland Votes Out Walesa After becoming president in 1991, Lech Walesa tried to revive Poland's bankrupt economy. Like Boris Yeltsin, he adopted a strategy of shock therapy to move Poland toward a free market economy. As in Russia, inflation and unemployment shot up. By the mid-1990s, however, the economy was improving.

Nevertheless, many Poles remained unhappy with the pace of economic progress. In the elections of 1995, they turned Walesa out of office in favor of a former Communist, Aleksandr Kwasniewski (kfahs·N'YEHF·skee). Kwasniewski vowed to combine free market policies with greater social benefits. Despite his Communist background, it appeared that he was committed to democratic rule.

Czechoslovakia Breaks Up In Czechoslovakia, reformers also launched an economic program based on shock therapy. The program caused a sharp rise in unemployment. It especially hurt Slovakia, the republic occupying the eastern third of Czechoslovakia.

Unable to agree on economic policy, the country's two parts—Slovakia and the Czech Republic—drifted apart. In spite of President Havel's pleas for unity, a movement to split the nation gained support. Havel resigned because of this. Czechoslovakia split into two countries on January 1, 1993. Havel was elected president of the Czech Republic. He won re-election in 1998.

The nations of the former Soviet bloc had made many gains. Even so, they continued to face serious obstacles to democracy. Resolving ethnic conflicts remained crucial, as did economic progress:

THINK THROUGH HISTORY
D. Contrasting
Contrast the breakups of Yugoslavia and Czechoslovakia.

A VOICE FROM THE PAST

The clear lesson . . . is that opening up the political process without a corresponding opening up and success in the economy merely gives people more opportunity to gripe about more things. People can handle political processes. You can proclaim a free election and hold it relatively easily. You cannot propose economic success and obtain it easily.

U.S. SENATOR GEORGE MITCHELL, quoted in "Neophyte Democracies Present a Challenge to U.S."

If the nations of Eastern Europe and the former Soviet Union can improve their standard of living, democracy might have a better chance to grow. In the meantime, economic reforms in Communist China sparked demands for democratic reforms.

Section 4 Assessment

1. TERMS & NAMES

Identify
- Boris Yeltsin
- CIS
- "shock therapy"
- ethnic cleansing

2. TAKING NOTES

Use a chart like the one below to record the main reason or reasons that the Soviet Union, Yugoslavia, and Czechoslovakia each broke apart.

Former nations	Reasons for breakup
Soviet Union	
Yugoslavia	
Czechoslovakia	

3. ANALYZING CAUSES

Why did ethnic tension become such a severe problem in the Soviet Union and Yugoslavia in the early 1990s?

THINK ABOUT
- the role that past Communist leaders had played in holding those countries together
- the democratic reforms demanded by various ethnic groups
- how those demands affected national unity

4. ANALYZING THEMES

Revolution It has been said that Gorbachev's reforms led to a second Russian Revolution. What did this revolution overthrow?

THINK ABOUT
- changes in the Soviet government and in the political process
- who lost and who gained power

China Follows Its Own Path

TERMS & NAMES
- Zhou Enlai
- Deng Xiaoping
- Four Modernizations
- Tiananmen Square
- Hong Kong

MAIN IDEA

In recent years, China's government has experimented with capitalism but has rejected calls for democracy.

WHY IT MATTERS NOW

After the 1997 death of Chinese leader Deng Xiaoping, President Jiang Zemin seemed to be continuing those policies.

SETTING THE STAGE The trend toward democracy around the world also affected China to a limited degree. A political reform movement arose in the late 1980s. It built on economic reforms begun earlier in the decade. China's Communist government clamped down on the reformers, however, and maintained a firm grip on power.

Mao's Unexpected Legacy

After the Communists came to power in China in 1949, Mao Zedong set out to transform China. Mao believed that peasant equality, revolutionary spirit, and hard work were all that was needed to improve the Chinese economy. For example, intensive labor could make up for the lack of tractors on the huge agricultural cooperatives that the government had created.

However, lack of modern technology damaged Chinese efforts to increase agricultural and industrial output. In addition, Mao's policies stifled economic growth. He eliminated incentives for higher production. He tried to replace family life with life in the communes. These policies took away the peasants' motive to work for the good of themselves and their families.

Facing economic disaster, some Chinese Communists talked of modernizing the economy. Accusing them of "taking the capitalist road," Mao began the Cultural Revolution to cleanse China of anti-revolutionary influences. The

Mao's Attempts to Change China

Mao's Programs	Program's Results
First Five-Year Plan 1953–1957	• Industry grew 15 percent a year. • Agricultural output grew very slowly.
Great Leap Forward 1958–1962	• China suffered economic disaster—industrial declines and food shortages. • Mao lost influence.
Cultural Revolution 1966–1976	• Mao regained influence by backing radicals. • Purges and conflicts among leaders created economic, social, and political chaos. • Moderates increasingly opposed radicals in Communist Party.

SKILLBUILDER: Interpreting Charts
1. *Which had more successful results, the first five-year plan or the Great Leap Forward? Explain.*
2. *Did conditions improve or grow worse during the Cultural Revolution? Explain.*

THINK THROUGH HISTORY
A. Recognizing Effects What was the ultimate result of Mao's radical Communist policies? Why?

movement proved so destructive, however, that it caused many Chinese to distrust party leadership. Instead of saving radical communism, the Cultural Revolution turned many people against it. In the early 1970s, China entered another moderate period under **Zhou Enlai** (joh ehn·ly). Zhou had been premiere since 1949. During the Cultural Revolution, he had tried to restrain the radicals.

China and the West

Throughout the Cultural Revolution, China played almost no role in world affairs. In the early 1960s, China had split with the Soviet Union over the leadership of world communism. In addition, China displayed hostility toward the United States because of U.S. support for the government on Taiwan and memories of the Korean War.

China Opened Its Doors China's isolation worried Zhou. He began to send out signals that he was willing to form ties to the West. In 1971, Zhou startled the world by inviting an American table tennis team to tour China. It was the first visit by an American group to China since 1949.

The visit began a new era in Chinese-American relations. In 1971, the United States reversed its policy and endorsed UN membership for the People's Republic of China. The next year President Nixon made a state visit to China. He met with Mao and Zhou. The three leaders agreed to begin cultural exchanges and a limited amount of trade. In 1979, the United States and China established formal diplomatic relations.

Economic Reform Both Mao and Zhou died in 1976. Shortly afterward, moderates took control of the Communist Party. They jailed several of the radicals who had led the Cultural Revolution. By 1980, **Deng Xiaoping** (duhng show-pihng) had emerged as the most powerful leader in China. Like Mao and Zhou, Deng had survived the Long March. He was the last of the "old revolutionaries" who had ruled China since 1949.

Although a lifelong Communist, Deng boldly supported moderate economic policies. Unlike Mao, he was willing to use capitalist ideas to help China's economy. He embraced a set of goals known as the **Four Modernizations.** These called for progress in agriculture, industry, defense, and science and technology. Deng launched an ambitious program of economic reforms, which he called the "Second Revolution."

First, Deng eliminated Mao's unpopular communes and leased the land to individual farmers. The farmers paid rent by delivering a fixed quota of food to the government. They could then grow any crops they wished and sell them for a profit. Under this system, food production increased by 50 percent in the years 1978 to 1984.

Deng then extended his program to industry. The government permitted small private businesses to operate. It gave the managers of large state-owned industries more freedom to set production goals. Deng also welcomed some foreign technology and investment.

Deng's economic policies produced striking changes in Chinese life. As incomes increased, people began to buy appliances and televisions. Chinese youths now wore stylish clothes and listened to Western music. Gleaming hotels filled with foreign tourists symbolized China's new policy of openness.

Tiananmen Square

Deng's economic reforms produced a number of unexpected problems. As living standards improved, the gap between the rich and poor widened. Increasingly, the public believed that party officials took advantage of their positions by accepting bribes and enjoying privileges denied to others.

Furthermore, the new policies admitted not only Western investments and tourists but also Western political ideas. Increasing numbers of Chinese students studied abroad and learned about the West. Warned by hard-line officials that Communist values were at risk, Deng replied, "If you open the window, some flies naturally get in." In his view, the benefits of opening the economy exceeded the risks. Nevertheless, as Chinese students learned more about democracy, they began to question China's lack of political freedom.

Students Demand Democracy In 1989, students sparked a popular uprising that stunned China's leaders. Beginning in April of that year, more than 100,000 students occupied **Tiananmen** (tyahn-ahn-mehn) **Square.** This square is a huge public space in the heart of Beijing. The students mounted a protest for democracy by chanting, "Down with corruption!" "Down with dictatorship!" and "Long live democracy!"

The student protest won widespread popular support. When several thousand students began a hunger strike to highlight their cause, perhaps a million people poured into Tiananmen Square to support them. Many students now boldly called for Deng Xiaoping to resign.

Deng Orders a Crackdown Instead of considering political reform, Deng declared martial law. He ordered more than 250,000 troops to surround Beijing. One student recalled the mood at the time:

> **A VOICE FROM THE PAST**
> It would be a lie to say that we were not afraid, but we were mentally prepared and very determined. Some students could not believe that the army really would use deadly force. But most of all, we were motivated by a powerful sense of purpose. We believed that it would be worth sacrificing our lives for the sake of progress and democracy in China.
> **ANONYMOUS STUDENT,** *San Francisco Examiner*

Although many students left the square after martial law was declared, about 3,000 chose to remain and continue their protest. The students revived their spirits by defiantly erecting a 33-foot statue that they named the "Goddess of Democracy." It resembled the American Statue of Liberty.

On June 4, 1989, the standoff came to an end. Thousands of heavily armed soldiers stormed Tiananmen Square. Tanks smashed through barricades and crushed the Goddess of Democracy. Soldiers sprayed gunfire into crowds of frightened students. They also attacked protesters elsewhere in Beijing. The assault killed hundreds and wounded thousands.

The attack on Tiananmen Square marked the beginning of a massive government campaign to stamp out protest. Police arrested an estimated 10,000 people. The state used the media to announce that reports of a massacre were untrue. Officials claimed that a small group of criminals had plotted against the government. After showing great restraint, officials said, the army was forced to crush a riot. Television news, however, had already broadcast the truth to the world.

China in the 1990s

The brutal repression of the pro-democracy movement left Deng firmly in control of China. During the final years of his life, Deng continued his program of economic reforms. By the mid-1990s, China's booming economy was producing extraordinary changes:

> **A VOICE FROM THE PAST**
> The country today is an endless series of jolting surprises. Streets are clogged with traffic. There is construction everywhere. Indoor malls with glittering new department stores surge with customers for whom shopping is rapidly becoming the recreational pastime of choice. At night, restaurants are packed with China's new urban middle class, raucously eating, drinking, and chain-smoking until the air inside turns gray.
> **ORVILLE SCHELL,** "China—the End of an Era"

Although Deng moved out of the limelight in 1995, he remained China's unquestioned leader. In February 1997, after a long illness, Deng died. Communist Party General Secretary Jiang Zemin (jee·ahng zeh·meen) assumed the presidency.

China After Deng Many questions arose after Deng's death. What kind of leader would Jiang be? Would he be able to hold onto power and ensure political stability? A highly intelligent and educated man, Jiang had served as mayor of Shanghai. He was considered skilled, flexible, and practical. However, he had no military experience.

Daily *Life*

Training the Chinese Army
Xiao Ye is a former Chinese soldier living in the United States. After Tiananmen Square, he explained how Chinese soldiers are trained to obey orders without complaint:

We usually developed bleeding blisters on our feet after a few days of . . . hiking. Our feet were a mass of soggy peeling flesh and blood, and the pain was almost unbearable. . . . We considered the physical challenge a means of tempering [hardening] ourselves for the sake of the Party. . . . No one wanted to look bad. . . .

And during the days in Tiananmen, once again the soldiers did not complain. They obediently drove forward, aimed, and opened fire on command. In light of their training, how could it have been otherwise?

TERMS & NAMES

Briefly explain the importance of each of the following to the democratic movements that took place from 1945 to the present.

1. PRI
2. apartheid
3. Nelson Mandela
4. Mikhail Gorbachev
5. glasnost
6. perestroika
7. Lech Walesa
8. Boris Yeltsin
9. Deng Xiaoping
10. Tiananmen Square

Interact *with* History

On page 910, you considered what you might tell a foreign exchange student about how U.S. democracy works. Now that you've read the chapter, would your explanation be different? Would you add anything to what you said before? Would you change anything you said before?

REVIEW QUESTIONS

SECTION 1 (*pages 911–915*)
Patterns of Change: Democracy
Case Study: Latin American Democracies

11. Name four common democratic practices.
12. What group held up democratic progress in both Brazil and Argentina until the 1980s?

SECTION 2 (*pages 916–920*)
Democratic Challenges in African Nations

13. What brought about the civil war in Nigeria?
14. Name three significant steps toward democracy taken by South Africa in the 1990s.

SECTION 3 (*pages 921–925*)
Gorbachev Moves Toward Democracy

15. What were the main reforms promoted by Soviet leader Mikhail Gorbachev?
16. Which Eastern European nations overthrew Communist governments in 1989?

SECTION 4 (*pages 926–930*)
Collapse of the Soviet Union

17. What was the August Coup and how did it end?
18. What led to the breakup of Yugoslavia?

SECTION 5 (*pages 931–935*)
China Follows Its Own Path

19. What changes took place in China during the 1970s?
20. How did the Chinese government react to demands for democratic reform?

Visual Summary

18 Years of Democratic Struggles

1983 Argentina Holds first free election in 37 years

1983 Nigeria Military overthrows civilian rule

1985 Brazil Elects civilian government

1986 Soviet Union Begins economic and political reforms

1989 Poland Legalizes Solidarity trade union; agrees to free elections
Germany Opens Berlin Wall and starts reunification process
Hungary Disbands Communist Party
Czechoslovakia Holds free elections
Romania Overthrows a dictator

1989 China Government massacres protesters calling for democracy

1991 Soviet Union Breaks up peacefully into 15 republics

1991 Yugoslavia Ethnic conflicts lead to break-up of country; years of war follow

1993 Russia Yeltsin orders troops to attack opponents in parliament building

Progress toward Democracy

Setbacks to Democracy

2000 Mexico Ends 71 years of PRI rule

1999 Nigeria Free elections held

1996 South Africa Adopts new constitution

1983 — 1990 — 2000

CRITICAL THINKING

1. ROADBLOCKS TO DEMOCRACY

THEME CULTURAL INTERACTION Name some examples from this chapter in which the negative impact of one culture on another blocked democratic progress.

2. DEMOCRATIC LEADERSHIP

Create a chart like the one below. List several leaders who you think helped their nations make democratic progress. For each leader, cite one example of an action that made a positive difference.

Leader	Nation	Positive Action

3. LESSONS OF DEMOCRACY

Think about the democratic movements you have studied in this chapter. Especially consider what conditions helped those movements succeed and what conditions caused difficulties for them. What do you think were the hardest challenges facing democratic movements?

4. ANALYZING PRIMARY SOURCES

The following excerpt comes from an article written about changes in the culture of Hong Kong in the months before it was returned to China. Read the paragraph and then answer the questions below it.

A VOICE FROM THE PAST
Whatever else you can say about the new Hong Kong, it will be more Chinese. Liu Heung-shing, the editor of the new Hong Kong magazine *The Chinese*, says that "for any meaningful art and culture to take off here, Hong Kong must find somewhere to anchor itself. To find that anchor, people will have to go north [to mainland China]." . . . Increasing numbers of Hong Kong's Cantonese speakers are studying mainland Mandarin. . . . At the same time that [Hong Kong] must resist China to retain Britain's legacy of rule of law, it knows that the most logical place for it to turn for commerce and culture is China.

ORVILLE SCHELL, "The Coming of Mao Zedong Chic"

- What is the main change that is taking place in Hong Kong's culture?
- What point of view might a business person have about this change?
- What point of view might a politician have about this change?

CHAPTER ACTIVITIES

1. LIVING HISTORY: Unit Portfolio Project

THEME ECONOMICS Your unit portfolio project focuses on economic changes within nations. For Chapter 35, you might use one of the following ideas to add to your portfolio.

- A government official has asked you for suggestions on how to move a Communist economy to a free market economy. Go through the chapter and compile a "Things to Do" list based on actions that other governments have taken.
- Create a poster with two contrasting lists: "Signs of a Healthy Economy" and "Signs of an Unhealthy Economy."
- Write an interview in which Deng Xiaoping discusses his economic reforms. Have him explain his goals for China.

2. CONNECT TO TODAY: Cooperative Learning

THEME REVOLUTION In this chapter, you read about how the democratic reforms initiated by Gorbachev led to an overturn of the Communist Soviet government. In effect, this was a second Russian Revolution.

Work with a team to create time lines of the first Russian Revolution in 1917 and the revolutionary events of 1985 to 1991. Then write a paragraph about the impact of the second revolution on Russia today.

INTERNET Using the Internet or a library, research Russian politics today. Is there still a Communist party? Is the Communist party still trying to undo the democratic reforms?

- Use this textbook, encyclopedias, or history books to find events for your time lines.
- Illustrate your time lines with photographs, drawings, or political cartoons.
- In your paragraph, evaluate how successful you think the second Russian Revolution was. Do you think the change will be long-lasting? Explain.

3. INTERPRETING A TIME LINE

Revisit the unit time line on pages 850-851. Use the Chapter 35 time line to learn what happened in Argentina in 1946.

FOCUS ON **POLITICAL CARTOONS**

Look carefully at this political cartoon, dated June 7, 1989.
- Do you recognize any world leaders in this cartoon? If so, who?
- What is the cartoon saying about the state of communism in Poland, China, and the Soviet Union?
- What is the cartoon's point of view—for or against communism? Explain.

Connect to History Judging from what you have read in the chapter, was the cartoon correct in its assessment of the state of communism? Explain your answer by citing specific events for each nation.

Global Interdependence, 1960–present

PREVIEWING THEMES

Science and Technology

Advances in science and technology have changed the lives of people around the globe. People today eat better, and live longer, healthier, and more comfortable lives. Improved communication and transportation have allowed goods and ideas to move rapidly. Science has even reached out to new horizons in space.

Cultural Interaction

New inventions and innovations have brought the nations of the world closer and exposed people to the ideas and habits of other cultures. Cultures are now blending ideas, customs, and habits. The people of the world have developed a greater sense of being part of a larger global culture.

Economics

Since World War II, nations have worked to expand trade and commerce in world markets. Changes in transportation and technology along with the establishing of multi-national companies have blurred national boundaries and created a global market.

INTERNET CONNECTION

Visit us at **www.mcdougallittell.com** to learn more about global interdependence in the modern world.

THE WORLD TODAY

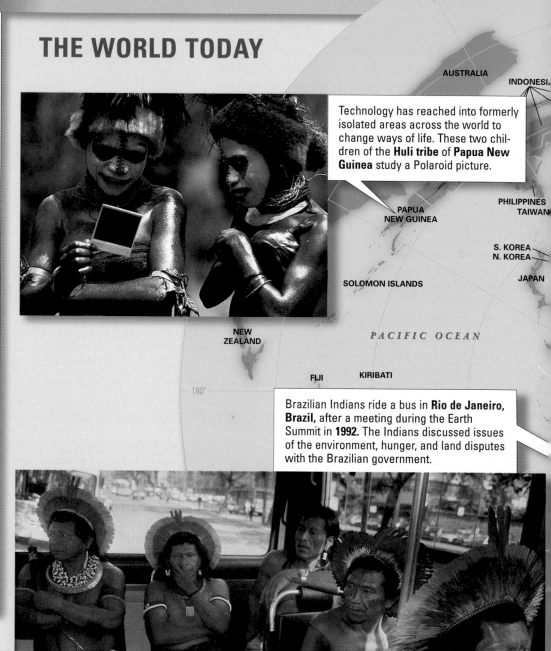

Technology has reached into formerly isolated areas across the world to change ways of life. These two children of the **Huli tribe** of **Papua New Guinea** study a Polaroid picture.

Brazilian Indians ride a bus in **Rio de Janeiro, Brazil,** after a meeting during the Earth Summit in **1992.** The Indians discussed issues of the environment, hunger, and land disputes with the Brazilian government.

AUSTRALIA
INDONESIA
PHILIPPINES
TAIWAN
PAPUA NEW GUINEA
S. KOREA
N. KOREA
JAPAN
SOLOMON ISLANDS
NEW ZEALAND
PACIFIC OCEAN
FIJI
KIRIBATI

Tibetan women demonstrate against human rights violations at the Forum on Women in **Huairou, China,** in September **1995.**

New technologies allow an Arab man in **Yemen** using a radio phone to conduct business or contact family and friends.

You are walking down a street of our nation's capital on a cloudy summer day. All of a sudden, the sky gets very dark and within minutes a heavy rain begins pouring down. You run for the closest shelter and find yourself at an international newsstand. As you wait for the rain to let up, you scan the headlines of dozens of newspapers from all over the world. They all focus on different events.

What impact do events in different countries have on your life?

Mir Cosmonauts Prepare for U.S. Crew Member

Southeast Asian Common Market Suggested

U.S., Israel, Palestinians to Work on Security

India Flash Floods Kill at Least 110

Brazil's Forests Fading Fastest, Tree Study Says

EXAMINING *the* ISSUES

- What evidence do the headlines give of economic interdependence in today's world?

- How do the headlines illustrate the political interdependence of different nations?

- What do the stories in the newspapers tell you about scientific and cultural interdependence among nations?

As a class, discuss these questions. Remember what you've learned about the recent history of nations in different regions of the world. Try to think of reasons why nations are becoming increasingly dependent on one another.

As you read this chapter, look for more examples of economic, political, and cultural interdependence among the nations of the world.

Science and Technology Shape Human Outlook

TERMS & NAMES
- Hubble Space Telescope
- Internet
- genetic engineering
- cloning
- green revolution

MAIN IDEA

Advances in technology after World War II led to increased global inter-action and improved quality of life.

WHY IT MATTERS NOW

The lives of all people around the world are affected by advances in science and technology.

SETTING THE STAGE Beginning in the late 1950s, the United States and the Soviet Union competed in the exploration of space. The Soviets launched Earth's first artificial satellite, *Sputnik I,* and put the first human in orbit around the planet. By the late 1960s, however, the United States had surpassed the Soviets. U.S. astronauts landed on the moon in 1969. The heavy emphasis on science and technology spilled over into developing products that improved the ways of life of human beings across the globe.

Probing the Solar System and Beyond

The space race of the 1950s, 1960s, and early 1970s was intensely competitive. Both the United States and the Soviet Union competed to reach the moon and beyond.

Both nations developed manned and unmanned space programs. Although the space race was competitive, it carried the seeds of global cooperation. Orbiting spacecraft beamed back images of a small blue planet, Earth, floating like a jewel in the black void of space. People around the world who saw this view of Earth received a stirring reminder that though they lived in different countries, they all shared the planet. Eventually, space exploration became one of the world's first and most successful arenas for coopera-tion between U.S. and Soviet scientists.

Four U.S. astronauts and one Russian cosmonaut worked together in the Shuttle *Atlantis* cargo bay. They linked with the *Mir* space station.

Space Race Becomes Cooperative In 1972, more than 15 years before the end of the Cold War, the United States and the Soviet Union signed an agreement. Their goal was to work toward docking *Apollo* and *Soyuz* spacecraft in space. Not only did the American and Soviet staffs have to work out engineering problems, they also had to learn each other's language. On July 17, 1975, an American *Apollo* spacecraft docked with the Soviet *Soyuz 19* spacecraft 140 miles above Earth. As the astronauts opened the hatch connecting the space vehicles, TV viewers across the globe watched the crews from Earth's fiercest rival countries greet each other.

This first cooperative venture in space between the United States and the USSR was an isolated event. Over the next 15 years, American and Soviet space programs separately developed space shuttles. Unlike the *Apollo* spacecraft, these shuttles were reusable and could return to Earth under their own power. During the 1980s, shuttle missions put crews in orbit around Earth. The missions were designed to accomplish a variety of scientific and technological experiments. Colonel Frederick Gregory, a

SPOTLIGHT ON

Space Junk

Since the late 1950s, thousands of objects have been sent into orbit. Some of these objects have crashed to Earth. For instance, in 1962, a small piece of metal that was part of the Russian satellite *Sputnik IV* fell from the sky and landed on a street in a small town in Wisconsin.

Larger, more dangerous objects have fallen to Earth. Space hazards have included a one-ton tank from the U.S. space station *Skylab* and a nuclear reactor from a failed Soviet satellite.

Space junk is a hazard in space as well. For example, a floating paint chip cracked the outer window of a space shuttle. Scientists try to combat the dangers posed by space junk by tracking debris and designing their spacecraft carefully.

Spacelab 3 astronaut, observed, "I think that science is the stuff that pays for itself on these missions. It's going to improve the quality of life down here [Earth]."

Beginning in the 1970s and increasing in the 1980s, people from different countries worked together to explore space. The Soviets were the first to send an international crew into space. In 1978, they invited Czech astronaut Vladimir Remek to orbit Earth in *Soyuz 28*. In the mid-1980s, the U.S. space agency invited people from Saudi Arabia, France, Germany, and Mexico to fly on the space shuttle.

Both the Soviets and the Americans had launched and lived in space stations since the early 1970s. Since 1986, the Soviet-launched *Mir* space station has been orbiting over 200 miles above Earth. In the mid-1990s, the Russians invited a number of U.S. astronauts to spend time on board *Mir*. Back on Earth, American and Russian scientists worked with scientists from 13 other nations to design and construct the first International Space Station.

Exploring the Universe Helping to study planets of the solar system, unmanned space probes such as *Voyager 2* sent dazzling pictures of Jupiter, Saturn, Uranus, and Neptune back to Earth. The Soviet *Venera* and *Vega* spacecraft and the U.S. *Magellan* spacecraft gathered in-depth information about Venus. In 1997, the U.S. space agency landed the *Pathfinder* probe on Mars. The public was fascinated with pictures sent back to Earth that included the activities of a mechanical rover named *Sojourner*.

In 1986, several nations, including Japan and the Soviet Union, sent spacecraft to study Halley's Comet as it swung by Earth. The U.S. space agency, NASA, and the European space agency, ESA, worked together to make and launch the **Hubble Space Telescope** in 1990. This advanced tool is today observing objects in the most remote regions of the universe.

Space Goes Commercial Meanwhile, private companies have become increasingly involved in space. One company has even contracted to take over much of the U.S. space shuttle program. Some companies launch rockets and satellites that help search for minerals and other resources on Earth. Satellites also follow the weather, aid long-distance learning programs, and even guide cars through cities. In the future, companies may use the zero-gravity environment of space to manufacture perfect crystals. They may eventually send solar collectors into orbit to help generate electricity for Earth. However, the most common commercial use of space today and in the near future will probably remain in the field of communications.

Expanding Global Communications

Since the 1960s, artificial satellites launched into orbit around Earth have aided worldwide communications. With satellite communication, the world was gradually transformed into a global village. Today, political and cultural events occurring in one part of the world often are witnessed live by people in other places. For example, in 1997, more than 2 billion television viewers across the world watched the funeral of Diana, the Princess of Wales. The linking of the globe through worldwide communications was made possible by the miniaturization of the computer.

Smaller, More Powerful Computers In the 1940s, when computers first came into use, they took up a huge room. The computer required fans or an elaborate air-conditioning system to cool the vacuum tubes that powered its operations. In the years since then, however, the circuitry that runs the computer had been miniaturized and made more powerful. This was due in part to the space program, where

THINK THROUGH HISTORY

A. Hypothesizing
Why might rival nations cooperate in space activities but not on Earth?

Background
Before 1986, Halley's Comet was last seen in 1910. It reappears once every 76 years.

equipment had to be downsized to fit in tiny space capsules. Silicon chips replaced the bulky vacuum tubes used earlier. Smaller than contact lenses, silicon chips hold millions of microscopic circuits.

Following this development, industries began to use computers and silicon chips to run assembly lines. A variety of consumer products such as microwave ovens, telephones, keyboard instruments, and cars today use computers and chips. Personal computers have become essential in most offices, and millions of people around the globe use personal computers in their homes.

Communications Networks Starting in the 1990s, businesses and individuals began using the Internet. The **Internet** is the voluntary linkage of computer networks around the world. It began in the late 1960s as a method of linking scientists so they could exchange information about research. Through telephone-line links, business and personal computers can be hooked up with computer networks. These networks allow users to communicate with people across the nation and around the world. Between 1994 and mid-1999, the number of worldwide Internet users soared from 3 million to 200 million.

Conducting business on the Internet has become a way of life for many. The Internet, along with fax machines, transmits information electronically to remote locations. Both paved the way for home offices and "telecommuting." Once again, as it has many times in the past, technology has changed how and where people work.

THINK THROUGH HISTORY
B. Summarizing
What types of technology have recently changed the workplace?

Transforming Human Life

Advances with computers and communications networks have transformed not only the ways people work but lifestyles as well. Technological progress in the sciences, medicine, and agriculture has changed the quality of the lives of millions of people.

Health and Medicine Before World War II, surgeons seldom performed operations on sensitive areas such as the eye, the inner ear, or the brain. Beginning in the 1950s, new technologies employed in advanced surgical techniques developed. More powerful microscopes and innovations such as the laser and ultrasound were among the improvements. For example, by the late 1970s, laser surgery to remove damaged lenses of the eye, such as lenses clouded with cataracts, was common. Such techniques made surgery safer and more accurate and improved patients' chances for quick recovery.

Advances in medical imaging also helped to improve health care. The use of CAT scans and MRI techniques gave doctors three-dimensional views of different organs or regions of the body. Using CAT scans and MRIs, doctors diagnose injuries, detect tumors, or collect other information needed to identify medical conditions.

In the 1980s, genetics, the study of heredity through research on genes, became a fast-growing field of science. Found in the cells of all organisms, genes are hereditary units that cause specific traits, such as eye color, in every living organism. Technology allowed scientists to isolate and examine individual genes that are responsible for different traits. Through **genetic engineering,** scientists were able to introduce new

Background
CAT scans use X-rays to make pictures of internal organs. MRIs use a magnetic field to do the same thing.

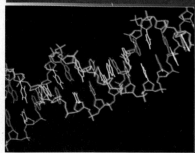

The Human Genome Project

Human genetic material (DNA) contains approximately 50,000 to 100,000 genes. Researchers established the Human Genome Project to map out the thousands of genes contained in DNA—a feat they achieved in 2000.

The information has led to the development of a new field of medicine called "molecular medicine." This field focuses on how genetic diseases develop and progress. It has resulted in early detection of disease. Eventually, it may lead to individualized treatment based on a person's genetic makeup.

Misuse of this information could drastically alter society. Therefore, a part of the project includes investigation of the ethical, legal, and social issues raised by genetic engineering.

genes into an organism to give that organism new traits. For example, with genetic engineering, scientists removed a gene from an Arctic fish and placed it in a plant. The resulting genetically engineered plant is better able to withstand frost.

Another aspect of genetic engineering is **cloning,** the creation of identical copies of DNA, the chemical chains of genes that determine heredity. Cloning actually allows scientists to reproduce both plants and animals that are identical to existing plants and animals. The applications of genetics research have led to many advances, especially in agriculture.

The Green Revolution In the 1950s, agricultural scientists around the world started a campaign known as the **green revolution.** It was an attempt to increase available food sources worldwide. Scientists promoted the use of fertilizers, pesticides, and high-yield, disease-resistant strains of a variety of crops. The green revolution helped avert famine in Asia and increased yields of crops in many different parts of the world.

However, the green revolution had its negative side, too. Fertilizers and pesticides are dangerous chemicals that cause cancer and pollute the environment. Also, the cost of the chemicals and the equipment to harvest more crops was far too expensive for an average peasant farmer. Consequently, owners of small farms received little benefit from the advances in agriculture. In some cases farmers were forced off the land by larger agricultural businesses.

Advances in genetics research have helped to fulfill some of the goals of the green revolution. In this new "gene revolution," resistance to pests was bred into plant strains, reducing the need for pesticides. Plants bred to tolerate poor soil conditions also reduced the need for fertilizers. The gene revolution involved some risks, including the accidental creation of disease-causing organisms. However, the revolution also brought great promises for increasing food production in a world with an expanding population.

THINK THROUGH HISTORY
C. Summarizing
What are some of the positive and negative effects of genetic engineering?

Science and technology has changed the lives of millions of people. In many cases quality of life has improved. What people produce and even their jobs have changed. These changes have altered the economies of nations. Not only have nations become linked through communications networks but they are also linked in a global economic network, as you will see in Section 2.

Section ❶ Assessment

1. TERMS & NAMES

Identify
- Hubble Space Telescope
- Internet
- genetic engineering
- cloning
- green revolution

2. TAKING NOTES

Copy the chart below and fill in information on ways science and technology has changed human life.

Science and Technology Changes Lives		
Communications	Health and Medicine	Green Revolution

Which of the three areas do you think has had the greatest global effect?

3. FORMING AND SUPPORTING OPINIONS

What is your opinion about cloning? In your judgment, is there a limit to how far cloning should go? Support your opinion with reasons.

THINK ABOUT
- the Human Genome Project
- positive effects of cloning
- negative effects of cloning

4. ANALYZING THEMES

Science and Technology
Why do you think that space exploration became an arena for cooperation between the Soviet Union and the United States?

THINK ABOUT
- goals of space exploration
- technologies involved
- images of Earth from space

Global Economic Development

TERMS & NAMES
- developed nation
- developing nation
- global economy
- multinational corporation
- free trade
- Gulf War
- ozone layer
- sustainable development

MAIN IDEA	WHY IT MATTERS NOW
The economies of the world's nations are so tightly linked that the actions of one nation affect others.	Every individual is affected by the global economy and the environment.

SETTING THE STAGE At the end of World War II, much of Europe and Asia lay in ruins, with many of the major cities leveled by bombing. The devastation of the war was immense. However, within a decade, with U.S. aid, the economies of western European nations and Japan began expanding rapidly. Their growth continued for half a century, long after the United States ceased supplying aid.

Technology Revolutionizes the World's Economy

Advances in technology caused economic growth in both Asia and the Western world. The explosion in scientific knowledge prompted great progress that quickly led to new industries. A prime example was plastics. In the 1950s, a process to develop plastics at low pressures and low temperatures was perfected. Within a few years, industries made toys, cooking utensils, containers, and a host of other products easily and cheaply out of plastics. The plastics industry boomed. Other technological advances have also changed industrial processes, lowered costs, and increased the quality or the speed of production. For example, robotic arms on automobile assembly lines made possible the fast and safe manufacture of high-quality cars.

Information Industries Change Economies Technological advances in manufacturing reduced the need for factory workers. But in other areas of the economy new demands were emerging. Computerization and communications advances changed the processing of information. By the 1980s, people could transmit information quickly and cheaply. Information industries such as financial services, insurance, market research, and communications services boomed. Those industries depended on what Professor Peter Drucker called "knowledge workers."

Car production has changed a great deal since the production of pre–World War II cars. Today, car assembly plants using efficient robots have eliminated jobs once done by people.

Global Interdependence **945**

The Effects of New Economies In the postwar era the expansion of the world's economies led to an increase in the production of goods and services so that many nations benefited. The economic base of some nations shifted. Manufacturing jobs began to move out of **developed nations**—those nations with the industrialization, transportation, and business facilities for advanced production of manufactured goods. The jobs moved to **developing nations,** that is, those in the process of becoming industrialized. Developing countries became prime locations for new manufacturing operations. Some economists believe these areas were chosen because they had many eager workers whose skills fit manufacturing-type jobs. Also, these workers would work for less money than those in developed nations. On the other hand, information industries that required better-educated workers multiplied in the economies of developed nations. The changes brought by technology changed the workplace of both developed and developing nations.

The Growth of Japan and the Pacific Rim

The Japanese began adopting modern technologies from Europe in the mid-1800s, during the Meiji era. After World War II, they continued to import and adapt the best of Western technology. For example, the Sony Corporation of Japan bought the rights to manufacture transistors, which are the basis for all electronic equipment, from an American company. Within 20 years, Sony had built a business empire based on the transistor. The company manufactured radios, stereo equipment, and televisions.

The emphasis that the Japanese and other people from Asia's Pacific Rim have placed on education has made their work force knowledgeable, creative, and flexible. This helped the region enjoy amazing economic growth from the 1950s to the present. Japanese corporations produce high-quality cars, electronic goods, and ships. The success of Japanese corporations fueled the country's high economic growth rate of 10 percent per year from 1955 through 1970. In the 1990s, averaging between 3 and 4 percent annually, Japan's growth was above that of the United States.

Four places in the Pacific Rim—South Korea, Taiwan, Hong Kong, and Singapore—followed Japan's example. In the 1970s, they set out on programs of rapid industrialization designed to make their economies both modern and prosperous. South Korea became a major exporter of automobiles and of electronic goods. Hong Kong became a world financial center. These four newly industrialized countries recorded such impressive economic growth that they became known as the Four Tigers of Asia. In the 1990s, rapidly industrializing China and Malaysia began competing with the other nations of the Pacific Rim. With Japan, the Four Tigers, China, and Malaysia, the Pacific Rim became a key arena of world trade.

Growth in East Asia

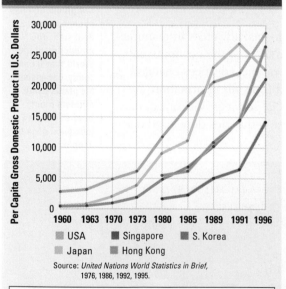

Source: *United Nations World Statistics in Brief,* 1976, 1986, 1992, 1995.

SKILLBUILDER: Interpreting Graphs
1. *Which country showed the most dramatic growth in the period from 1985 to 1991?*
2. *Which countries in 1985 were at the level of South Korea in 1991?*

Growth in World Trade

Economies in different parts of the world have been linked for centuries through trade and through national policies, such as colonialism. However, a true global economy didn't take shape until the second half of the 1800s. The **global economy** includes all the financial interactions among people, businesses, and governments that cross international borders. In recent decades, several factors hastened growth in world trade. Huge cargo ships, the length of three football fields, could inexpensively carry enormous supplies of fuels and other goods from one part of the world to another. Telephone and computer linkages made global financial transactions quick and easy. In addition, multinational corporations developed around the world.

THINK THROUGH HISTORY
C. Summarizing
What elements accelerated global trade?

Multinational Corporations Companies that operate in a number of different countries are called **multinational corporations** or transnational corporations. U.S. companies such as Ford, IBM, and Exxon; European companies such as Nestlē and Volvo; and Japanese companies such as Honda and Mitsubishi all became multinational giants.

All of these companies have established manufacturing plants in many countries. They select spots where the raw materials or labor are cheapest. This enables them to produce components of their products on different continents. They ship the various components to another location to be assembled. This level of economic integration allows such companies to view the whole world as the market for their goods. Goods or services are distributed throughout the world as if there were no national boundaries.

Vocabulary
tariff: a tax on goods imported from another country.

Expanding Free Trade After World War II, many national leaders felt that economic cooperation among countries across the world would be key to peace and prosperity. The idea of **free trade,** which is the elimination of trade barriers such as tariffs among nations, began to gain acceptance. As early as 1947, nations began discussing ways to open trade. One such agreement was GATT—General Agreement on Tariffs and Trade. Over the years, a general lowering of protective tariffs and an expansion of free trade, region by region, has expanded the global marketplace. By 1995, the World Trade Organization was established to supervise free trade.

Background
The first products to be tariff-free were iron and coal. This helped the countries develop their industries.

A European organization set up in 1951 promoted tariff-free trade among member countries. This experiment in economic cooperation was so successful that seven years later, a new organization, the European Economic Community (EEC), was formed. Over the next 40 years, most of the other Western European countries joined the organization, which now is called the European Union (EU). In another example of economic cooperation,11 European nations began using a unified currency, known as the euro, on January 1, 1999.

Regional Trade Blocs Through this economic unification, Europe exerted a major force in the world economy. The economic success of the EU inspired countries in other regions to make trade agreements with each other. The North American Free Trade

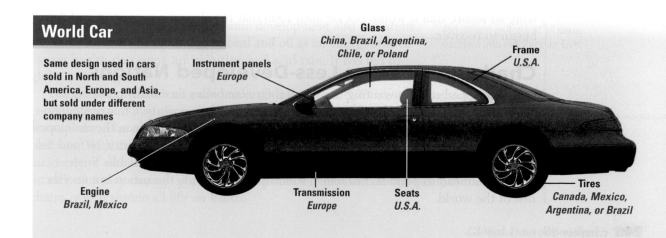

World Car

Same design used in cars sold in North and South America, Europe, and Asia, but sold under different company names

Instrument panels
Europe

Glass
China, Brazil, Argentina, Chile, or Poland

Frame
U.S.A.

Engine
Brazil, Mexico

Transmission
Europe

Seats
U.S.A.

Tires
Canada, Mexico, Argentina, or Brazil

3 Global Security Issues

TERMS & NAMES
- **Nuclear Non-Proliferation Treaty**
- **proliferation**
- **terrorism**
- **fundamentalism**
- **Universal Declaration of Human Rights**
- **civil rights movement**

MAIN IDEA	WHY IT MATTERS NOW
Since 1945, nations have used collective security efforts to solve problems.	Personal security of the people of the world is tied to security within and between nations.

SETTING THE STAGE World War II was one of history's most devastating conflicts. More than 55 million people died as a direct result of bombings, the Holocaust, combat, starvation, and disease. Near the end of the war, one of humankind's most destructive weapons, the atomic bomb, killed more than 100,000 people in Hiroshima and Nagasaki in a matter of minutes. Perhaps because of those horrors, since 1945, powerful nations have repeatedly stepped back from the brink of destruction that could result from another all-out world conflict.

SPOTLIGHT On

UN Peacekeepers

Soldiers in blue helmets, such as the one pictured above, have been sent on peacekeeping missions all over the world. They come from dozens of different nations, from Finland to Senegal, from Canada to Pakistan. As neutral soldiers they are sent to enforce peace in troubled areas.

Some missions have lasted for decades, such as the 40-year UN mission to monitor the cease-fire agreement between India and Pakistan. Other UN missions are brief. The 1962–1963 UN mission to New Guinea lasted for six months.

Some UN missions are successful in their goal of preventing the continuation of conflict, but others fail. Both kinds of missions have proved costly. More than 1,450 peacekeepers have died in the line of duty.

Nations Pursue Collective Security

In the decades since the end of World War II, the number of limited wars throughout the world increased. Such wars potentially threatened the economic, environmental, and personal security of people in all nations. So nations began to work together to pursue collective security.

Nations Unite and Take Action Many nations consider that having a strong army is important to their security. After World War II, nations banded together to make military alliances. They formed the North Atlantic Treaty Organization (NATO), the Southeast Asian Treaty Organization (SEATO), the Warsaw Pact, and others. The member nations of each of these alliances generally consider an attack on one of them to be an attack on them all. Thus, they each pledged military aid for their common defense.

In addition to military alliances to increase their security, world leaders have recognized that threats of war needed to be reduced. The United Nations (UN), an international agency established in 1945, works in a variety of ways toward increasing collective global security.

Peacekeeping Activities More than 180 nations send representatives to the UN, which has as one of its aims to promote world peace. The UN provides a public forum, private meeting places, and skilled mediators to help nations try to resolve conflicts at any stage of their development.

The UN also provides peacekeeping soldiers at the invitation of the warring parties. These forces try to prevent the outbreak of new fighting or to help enforce a cease-fire. The unarmed or lightly armed soldiers fire their weapons only in self-defense. The presence of neutral UN soldiers helps prevent aggression. In the late 20th century, the UN sent successful peacekeeping forces to such places as El Salvador in Central America, Kuwait in the Middle East, and Namibia in Africa. The UN, however, was only successful when the nations involved in a conflict maintained a commitment to working things out peacefully.

Background
A limited war is one in which only a few nations are involved and nuclear weapons are not used.

Controlling Weapons of Mass Destruction Just as nations banded together in the past five decades to try to prevent and contain conflicts, they also forged treaties to limit the manufacture, testing, and trade of weapons. The weapons of most concern are those that cause mass destruction. These include not only nuclear weapons but also chemical weapons, including poison gases and biological weapons that unleash deadly diseases.

In 1968, world nations gathered to work toward reducing their own arsenals of nuclear arms. Some signed a **Nuclear Non-Proliferation Treaty.** In this pact, nations both with and without nuclear power pledged to help prevent the **proliferation,** or spread, of nuclear weapons to other nations. In the 1970s, the United States and Russia signed the Strategic Arms Limitation Treaties. In the 1980s, both countries began to talk about deactivating some of their nuclear weapons. However, at the beginning of the 1990s, ten nations still possessed nuclear weapons.

Many nations also signed treaties promising not to produce biological or chemical weapons. Because these weapons are fairly easy to produce and are so destructive, they are called the "poor countries' nuclear bomb." Use of these weapons is not limited to international situations. Sometimes terrorist groups use them to make their demands known.

Terrorism Threatens Security In March 1995, a Japanese cult member released nerve gas in a Tokyo subway, killing 12 people and injuring thousands. A month later, an American opposed to the power of the U.S. government planted a bomb near the Federal Building in Oklahoma City, Oklahoma, killing more than 160 people. Both tragedies are examples of **terrorism,** the use of force or threats to frighten people or governments to change policies. Terrorism is a tactic used by political or ideological groups to call attention to their demands and to gain major media coverage of their positions. The ease of international travel makes every nation vulnerable to attacks. Because terrorists cross national borders or escape to countries with governments friendly to their cause, terrorism is an international problem.

THINK THROUGH HISTORY
A. Analyzing Motives Of what value would media coverage be to a terrorist group?

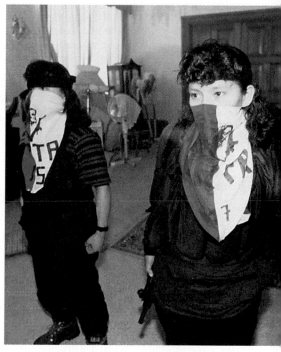

Two teenage terrorists hold hostages at the Japanese embassy in Lima, Peru. The terrorist group held hostages for over 100 days, in late 1996 and early 1997, before being forced out and killed by the Peruvian military.

Ethnic and Religious Conflicts Disrupt Peace

Conflicts among people of different racial, national, religious, linguistic, or cultural groups are not new. Some ethnic or religious conflicts have roots that reach back for decades and, in some conflicts, for centuries. Such conflicts include the "troubles" between Catholics and Protestants in Northern Ireland and the hostilities between Palestinians and Jews in the Middle East.

Some ethnic conflicts have deep historic causes that simmered under the surface until recently. Examples from the 1990s include the Hutu-Tutsi rivalry in East Africa or the Serb-Bosnian-Croat disputes in the former nation of Yugoslavia. With the removal of authoritarian rule or colonial governments, sometimes these old problems flared into violent confrontations and wars. This created problems for the security of neighboring nations and caused many refugees to seek shelter in the nearby lands.

Religious Conflicts The growth of **fundamentalism**—a strict belief in the basic truths and practice of a particular faith—also contributed to conflict among different peoples. In some countries, fundamentalist groups have worked to gain control of a government in order to impose their ideas upon an entire nation. For example, in 1997, the Taliban movement in Afghanistan gained control of that country after a long civil war. The leaders immediately imposed strict Muslim law on the land. Many opposed the fundamentalist rule even though they also were Muslim.

Ethnic and religious conflicts have often been characterized by terrible violence. People caught in these conflicts sometimes suffered torture or massacres of their whole towns or villages. An example of this is violence imposed on the Kurds, a nomadic group in southwest Asia. (See spotlight on Kurds.)

As violence escalates, communication between the conflicting groups shuts down. The Buddhist leader of Tibet, the Dalai Lama, argued that opening communication is the key to understanding differences and resolving conflicts.

A VOICE FROM THE PAST

The various religions must recognize their common responsibility. Therefore it is important that they live together and speak to each other in harmony. Certainly there is a great deal of difference between the religions. But if people openly approach each other wishing sincerely to exchange views and learn from each other they will discover that they are in agreement on many things. A large common basis, I am sure, could be found. The religions could devote this basis to the service of the world's positive development.

DALAI LAMA, quoted in *Global Trends: The World Almanac of Development and Peace*

While some have tried to find common ground through religion to ease conflict, others try to gain wide international guarantees of basic human rights.

Promoting Human Rights Worldwide

After the atrocities of the Holocaust in World War II, the newly formed United Nations resolved to work toward guaranteeing basic human rights for persons of all nations.

UN Issues a Declaration In 1948, to set human rights standards for all nations, the UN drew up and ratified the **Universal Declaration of Human Rights.** The declaration stated, "All human beings are born free and equal in dignity and rights. . . . Everyone has the right to life, liberty, and security of person." It further listed specific rights that all human beings should have. Later, in 1975, the Helsinki Accords addressed the issues of freedom of movement and freedom to publish and exchange information.

Both the declaration and the accords are nonbinding. But many people around the world became committed to ensuring that basic human rights are respected. The UN and other international nonprofit agencies, such as Amnesty International, work to track and publicize human rights violations. They also encourage people to work toward a world in which liberty and justice are available for all.

The American Civil Rights Movement The people of the United States made greater commitments to ensuring basic human rights, especially political rights, to its citizens through the civil rights movement. The **civil rights movement** was a grassroots effort by African Americans to fight discrimination and to make sure all citizens received their rights guaranteed by the U.S. Constitution. During the 1960s, the movement focused on eliminating legal segregation between African Americans and whites. Another goal was to fully empower African Americans with the right to vote and with equal public education.

During the 1950s and 1960s, thousands of Americans, both African Americans and others, organized groups and worked to change the conditions in the United States. One of the best-known leaders of the civil rights movement was Dr. Martin Luther King, Jr. Dr. King patterned his movement after Gandhi's in India, using nonviolent demonstrations to bring attention to serious injustices suffered by African Americans.

After King's assassination in 1968, people of all races and creeds continued to work to eliminate discrimination in employment, housing, and other key areas of life. The civil rights movement fueled the development of other equal rights movements by Native Americans, Hispanics, women, and people with disabilities.

Women's Status Improves

The women's rights movement grew along with the civil rights movement in the late 1950s and early 1960s. When women in Western nations entered the work force, they often met with discrimination in employment and salary. In non-Western countries, many women not only faced discrimination in jobs, they were denied access to education. In regions torn by war or ethnic conflict, they were often victims of violence and abuse. As women suffered, so also did their family members, especially children.

However, in the 1970s, with a heightened awareness of human rights, women in various parts of the world worked to improve their lives through changes in laws and government policies. In 1975, the United Nations held the first of several international conferences on women's status in the world. The fourth conference was

THINK THROUGH HISTORY
C. Making Inferences How are civil rights and women's rights related?

HISTORY MAKERS

Dr. Martin Luther King, Jr.
1929–1968
Nobel Peace Prize 1964

Dr. Martin Luther King, Jr.'s moving speeches and his commitment to active, nonviolent protest inspired people around the world. He urged them to work to end racial discrimination and toward obtaining full and equal rights for all. In his famous "I Have a Dream" speech, King urged his followers, *"Now* is the time to lift our nation from the quicksands of racial injustice to the solid rock of brotherhood."

King achieved many successes as he led a nationwide movement, organizing marches and sit-ins to demand equal justice before the law. In 1964 and 1965, the U.S. federal government passed laws protecting civil and voting rights.

During the civil rights struggles, Dr. King's home was dynamited and he and his family faced death threats. He was assassinated on April 4, 1968, in Memphis, Tennessee.

Mother Teresa
1910–1997
Nobel Peace Prize 1979

A tiny woman of boundless energy, Mother Teresa dedicated her life to helping the poor, the elderly, the disabled, and the dying. Born Agnes Gonxha Bojaxhiu, Mother Teresa joined a convent in Ireland at the age of 18. A few months later, she headed to Calcutta, India, to teach at a girls' school. Upon her arrival, she noticed many sick and homeless people in the streets. She soon vowed to devote her life to helping India's poor.

In 1948, she established the Order of the Missionaries of Charity, which committed itself to serving the sick, needy, and unfortunate. Dressed often in her trademark outfit of a plain white sari with a blue border and a cross pinned to her left sleeve, Mother Teresa soon became known throughout the world for her commitment to the downtrodden.

held in Beijing, China, in 1995. It addressed such issues as preventing violence against women and empowering women to take leadership roles in politics and in business.

One of the most highly respected activists who attended the Beijing conference was the Albanian missionary Mother Teresa. She devoted her life to caring for the poor and sick. In 1979, Mother Teresa was awarded the Nobel Peace Prize for her efforts on behalf of the homeless on the streets of Calcutta, India. Although she died in 1997, her mission continues to reach more than 25 countries worldwide.

Global Movement of People

Migration is a worldwide phenomenon that has increased in size and scope. Each year poverty, war, drought, famine, and political violence affect millions of people. To escape these life-threatening problems, many people leave their homes and migrate to other countries. Wealthy people sometimes migrate as well. In the late 1980s, some businesspeople left Hong Kong, fearing that after the Chinese regained control of the island from the British in 1997, their rights and opportunities would be limited.

Push-Pull Factors Migration sometimes takes place because people feel pushed out of their homelands. Lack of food due to drought, natural disasters, and political oppression are examples of push factors. Between 1976 and 1996, the number of refugees—people who leave their country to move to another to find safety—grew from under 3 million to almost 20 million yearly.

Not only negative events push people to migrate. Most people have strong connections to their home countries and don't leave unless strong positive attractions pull them away. They hope for a better life for themselves and for their children, and thus migrate to developed nations. For example, hundreds of thousands of people migrate from Africa to Europe and from Latin America to the United States every year. Sometimes the poorest people migrate, but often educated middle-class people migrate.

THINK THROUGH HISTORY
D. Analyzing Causes List the push and pull factors that cause people to migrate.

Effects of Immigration Immigration has both negative and positive effects on the countries receiving new people. Countries generally receive two types of immigrants—political refugees and migrants who come for economic reasons. Although a person has the right to leave a country, the country receiving the migrant does not have to accept that person. The receiving country may have one policy about accepting refugees from political situations, and another about migrants coming for economic reasons. Because of the huge volume of people migrating from war-torn, famine-stricken, and politically unstable regions, millions of immigrants have no place to go. Crowded into refugee camps under squalid conditions, immigrants face a very uncertain future. The cost of supporting these camps may cause political problems and may raise issues of prejudice and discrimination.

On the positive side, immigrants are often a valuable addition to the country where they move. They help offset labor shortages in a variety of industries. They bring experiences and knowledge that can spur the economy. In addition, they contribute to the sharing, shaping, and blending of a newly enriched culture.

Cuban boat people plead for help from a helicopter about 50 miles from Key West, Florida. Some left Cuba because of political differences, while others were looking for a better economic future.

Section ③ Assessment

1. TERMS & NAMES

Identify
- Nuclear Non-Proliferation Treaty
- proliferation
- terrorism
- fundamentalism
- Universal Declaration of Human Rights
- civil rights movement

2. TAKING NOTES

Using a chart like the one below, list collective methods employed by the nations of the world to increase world security. Give examples.

Method	Examples
1. Form military alliances	NATO, SEATO, Warsaw Pact
2.	
3.	

3. IDENTIFYING PROBLEMS

How are ethnic and religious conflicts related to problems of global security?

THINK ABOUT
- current conflicts
- political/ideological tactics of groups
- immigration

4. ANALYZING THEMES

Science and Technology In what ways have advances in science and technology increased threats to global security?

THINK ABOUT
- the destructive capability of one nuclear weapon
- the ability of less-powerful nations to produce biological or chemical weapons
- the ability to move easily across international borders

4 Cultures Blend in a Global Age

MAIN IDEA	WHY IT MATTERS NOW
Technology has increased contact among the world's people, changing their cultures.	Globalization of culture has changed the ways people live, their perceptions, and their interactions.

SETTING THE STAGE Since the beginnings of civilization, people of every culture have blended ideas and ways of doing things from other cultures into their own culture. The same kind of cultural sharing and blending continues today. But it occurs at a much more rapid pace and among people at much wider distances than ever was common in the past.

The Sharing of Cultures Accelerates

The speed and breadth of today's cultural exchanges is due to advances in technology. Twentieth-century technologies allow people from all over the world to have increasing contact with one another. Such contacts promote widespread sharing of cultures.

Cultural elements that reflect a group's common background and changing interests are called popular culture. **Popular culture** involves music, sports, movies, clothing fashions, foods, and hobbies or leisure activities. Popular culture around the world incorporates features originating in many different lands. Of all the technologies that contribute to cultural sharing, television, movies, and other media have been the most powerful.

A family in Afghanistan enjoys watching cartoons on the family TV.

Television and Mass Media More people in the United States have televisions than telephones. In fact, 98 percent of American households have televisions. Eighty-eight percent of the homes have videocassette recorders (VCRs). In Europe, too, the vast majority of households include one or more televisions. The percentages are lower for developing nations. Nevertheless, in many of these countries, the television is a family's most cherished or most wished-for possession.

Television provides a window to the world through daily newscasts and documentaries. The speed at which information about other parts of the world is presented helps create an up-to-the-minute shared experience of global events. For example, in 1991, millions of television viewers across the world watched the waging of the Persian Gulf War. Wars, natural disasters, and political drama in faraway places become a part of everyday life.

Television and other mass media, including radio and movies, are among the world's most popular forms of entertainment. Popular programs not only entertain but also show how people live and what they value in other parts of the world. Mass media is the major way popular culture spreads to all parts of the globe.

suits are standard uniforms among many people. McDonald's hamburgers and Coca-Cola soft drinks can be purchased in many countries of the world. Mickey Mouse and other Disney characters are almost universally recognized. These examples of common dress, food, and entertainment figures all originated in the West and have been picked up and incorporated by other cultures. But Western influence also has an effect on ways of thinking. The Western mindset of placing a high value on acquiring material possessions—**materialism**—has been adopted by people of many different cultures.

Non-Western Influences Travel to the West Cultural ideas are not confined to moving only from the West to other lands. Non-Western cultures also influence people in Europe and the United States. From music and clothing styles, to ideas about art and architecture, to religious and ethical systems, non-Western ideas are incorporated into Western life. The non-Western mindset of placing value on meditation and contemplation has found a home in the West. The world's fastest-growing religion—Islam—comes from non-Western roots. Cultural blending of Western and non-Western elements opens communications channels for the exchange of ideas throughout the globe.

The Arts Become International Modern art, like popular culture, has become increasingly international. Advances in transportation and technology have facilitated the sharing of ideas about art and the sharing of actual works of art. Shows and museums throughout the world exhibit art of different styles and from different places. It became possible to see art from other cultures that had not previously been available to the public. For example, art from the Forbidden City in China or artifacts from Egyptian tombs can be viewed in museums in Europe and the Americas.

Literature, too, has become internationally appreciated. Well-known writers routinely have their works translated into dozens of languages, resulting in truly international audiences. The list of recent Nobel Prize winners in literature reflects a broad variety of writers' nationalities, including Nigerian, Egyptian, Mexican, West Indian, and Japanese.

THINK THROUGH HISTORY
B. Summarizing
Name three advances that allow a greater sharing of the arts.

SPOTLIGHT ON

French Cultural Backlash

If a French organization to prevent the corruption of the French language by foreign words has its way, the term *le air bag* will officially be replaced with the term *le coussin gonflable de protection*. To a foreigner the substitute must seem awkward. Language purists argue that allowing too many English-language words into the vocabulary will eventually make the French language and culture too foreign.

Since French has no terms to cover new inventions or ideas, language specialists devise terms to help deal with such words as data bank *(banque de données)*, microchip *(puce,* which means flea), and software *(logiciel)*.

It may be a losing battle, since 80 percent of all French high school students choose to study English as their foreign language.

Future Challenges and Hopes

As the differences between peoples lessen, some worry about losing their group identity. In some lands the leaders have taken measures to preserve the unique elements of their culture.

Cultural Clashes Fear of the loss of a unique identity as a people or nation may create conflict and clashes within groups. For example, in France in the late 1990s, a bureau of the French government was responsible for removing words from the French language that are believed to corrupt the language. A French official told members of the Higher Council of the French Language that keeping language from the excesses of foreign words was "an act of faith in the future of our country." In a similar vein, recently in the United States, debates raged over the question of making English the exclusive official language of the U.S. government. A poll showed that 73 percent of the population agreed with that position.

In other parts of the world, wearing certain kinds of clothing, such as short skirts or jeans, is forbidden because it represents an intrusion of other cultures. Elsewhere, mass media is strictly censored to keep unwanted ideas from entering the land.

Sometimes groups respond to the influence of other cultures by trying to return to traditional ways. Cultural practices and rites of passage may receive even more emphasis as a group tries to preserve its identity. In some countries, native groups take an active role in preserving the traditional ways of life. For example, tribal groups, such as the Maori in New

Background
Twenty-two states have enacted English-only laws.

THINK THROUGH HISTORY
C. Recognizing Effects How do people react against greater global interdependence?

Zealand, have revived ancestral customs rather than face cultural extinction. Many Maori cultural activities are conducted in a way that preserves Maori ways of thinking and behaving. In 1987, the Maori language was made an official language of New Zealand.

Even when a nation does not have serious concerns about the impact of other cultures, it may struggle with questions of accommodation. **Accommodation** is the level of acceptance of ideas from another culture. Charles Mann, a journalist, describes the feelings of uncertainty that questions of accommodation raise.

A Samburu warrior in Kenya uses a cellular phone to stay in contact with others in his group.

A VOICE FROM THE PAST

As human . . . patterns look more and more alike . . . that unique place becomes ever harder to find. Things feel scary; people hunker down. Some retreat into their dialects, others into their national clothes, others into religion or guns. Even as the world unifies, its constituent parts fragment.

CHARLES MANN, *The Material World: A Global Family Portrait*

Global Interdependence Despite the uncertainty accompanying global interdependence, economic, political, and environmental issues do bring all nations closer together. Nations have begun to recognize that they are dependent on other nations and deeply affected by the actions of others far away. As elements of everyday life and expressions of culture become more international in scope, people across the world gain a sense of oneness with people in other areas of the world. Responses to events such as flooding in Bangladesh were international in scope. Nations from around the world sent assistance. It was as if the flooding had happened in their own country.

Technology has changed the way people, businesses, and nations view the world. Restricting cultural change is now very unlikely except in a few isolated locations.

Throughout history, human beings have faced challenges to survive and to live better. In the 21st century, these challenges will be faced by people who are in increasing contact with one another. They have a greater stake in learning to live in harmony together and with the physical planet. As Dr. Martin Luther King, Jr., stated, "Our loyalties must transcend our race, our tribe, our class, and our nation; and this means we must develop a world perspective."

Section 4 Assessment

1. TERMS & NAMES

Identify
• popular culture
• materialism
• accommodation

2. TAKING NOTES

Draw a diagram like the one below and give details that illustrate the areas of popular culture that have become very international.

International popular culture

Which of the international popular culture aspects has the greatest effect on your life? Write a paragraph to explain why.

3. ANALYZING ISSUES

You have just immigrated to the United States. You are anxious to "fit in" in your new home but don't want to lose aspects of your former culture. What do you accept about the new culture and what do you retain of your birth culture?

THINK ABOUT
• elements of your birth culture you wish to maintain, adapt, or leave behind
• practical and day-to-day concerns
• feelings about your identity

4. THEME ACTIVITY

Cultural Interaction Look at the pictures in this section and those on the opening pages of this chapter. They show types of cultural blending. Study current newspapers and magazines to see if you can find examples similar to the pictures shown. Create a scrapbook of pictures you have found. Write a caption for each picture illustrating cultural blending.

Connect to Today

THEME **Economics** *The Widening Gap*

Gross Domestic Product*

*Per Capita

In Dollars	India	United States
35,000		
30,000		$30,200
25,000		
20,000		
15,000		
10,000		
5,000	$105 $1,600	$3,536
0		

■ 1965
■ 1997

The gap is widening today between the rich and poor nations of the world. The graph to the left shows the Gross Domestic Product (GDP) of India and the United States. The GDP is the dollar value of all goods, services, and structures produced within a country during one year. In this graph, each country's GDP is divided up per capita, or per person; that is, by the number of productive workers.

Within nations, there is a widening gap between rich people and poor people. The shantytown to the left shows the existence side by side of wealth and poverty in the city of Bombay, India. Slums stand next to luxurious high-rise apartments. Many such striking contrasts exist in cities throughout the world.

THEME **Religious and Ethical Systems** *A Return to Tradition*

One growing trend that can be seen around the world is a return to more traditional religious beliefs and rituals. Among Protestant denominations this movement is called fundamentalism. This same development can be observed among Muslims, Jews, Hindus, and others. The picture to the right shows Orthodox Jews in Mea Shearim, an Orthodox community in Jerusalem. The Orthodox men wear the traditional styles of sideburns and heavy black clothes.

The picture below shows Muslims celebrating a tradition of their faith, the end of Ramadan. The celebration here takes place in the Mosque of Rome, the largest modern mosque in Europe.

Nations throughout the world continue to contend with groups bent on radical and often violent change. This is true from the Basques in Spain, to militia groups in the United States, to Marxist rebels in Central and South America.

This picture shows a car bombing in Madrid, Spain, carried out by Basque terrorists in 1992. Like many such terrorist groups, the Basques have used violent means to achieve their ends. They believe that such acts attract immediate worldwide publicity to their cause. Further, such groups often use violence because they lack faith in the political process.

THEME **Power and Authority**

A Continuing Struggle for Freedom

As the millennium changes, democracy continues to grow throughout the world. Yet many nations remain in the grip of dictatorship. In Myanmar (formerly Burma), for example, Aung San Suu Kyi leads the struggle for democracy against a repressive military regime. She received the 1991 Nobel Prize for Peace.

Such struggles continue in other parts of the world as well. The enemies of democracy include military rule, ethnic strife, one-party rule, and religious intolerance. Nonetheless, democracy continues to make its appeal to many people around the world.

EXAMINING THEMES

Economics
What might be the long-term consequences of permitting a large gap to develop between rich and poor? How would such a gap affect political stability in the world?

Religious and Ethical Systems
Why might people feel the need to return to basic religious beliefs and rituals? How might such traditional faith enrich their lives?

Revolution
What might cause people to lose faith in the political process to the extent that they would be willing to resort to violence? Is political violence ever justified?

Power and Authority
Why might people support democracy? Why might others prefer military rule?

Connect to Today

THEME **Cultural Interaction**   *Borderless Issues*

A variety of important issues in the world today bring together people from many different cultures and nations. Prominent among these are women's issues.

This photograph shows the opening ceremony of the United Nations Conference on Women held in Beijing, China, in September 1995. Women from around the world attended this conference. Issues they examined included the role of women, population growth, poverty, education, and health. Both problems and solutions were discussed.

THEME **Science & Technology**   *Advancements Spur New Questions*

Dolly is a cloned sheep who was born in July of 1996. She is an identical copy of another adult and has no father. She was cloned by a group of research veterinarians led by Ian Wilmut at the Roslin Institute near Edinburgh, Scotland. Wilmut and his fellow researchers remain opposed to the cloning of humans. Scientific advances in genetic engineering raise ethical controversies about whether scientists should do what they are capable of doing.

Challenges and Achievements

A number of serious environmental challenges face the
world community, including endangered species and
pollution. The image at the center left shows the ozone
hole (in the center within the blue boundary) in the
Southern Hemisphere. The decline in the ozone layer
is caused by the use of certain chemicals on earth.
The ozone layer helps to absorb ultraviolet-B
radiation. The ozone hole means less radiation
will be screened out, which will result in the
destruction of plant life and more cases of skin
cancer.

On the other hand, the elephants above
represent the revival of an endangered species. As
forests have been turned into farmland, migration
routes have been affected. Some conservation groups are
working to restore natural habitats. They have in some
cases been successful in establishing migratory
trails that elephants have begun using to return to
favorite haunts.

THEME Empire Building · *Internet: A New Frontier*

The computer-generated image below shows traffic on the National Science
Foundation's computer network. Volume in bytes ranges from zero (purple)
to 100 billion (white). The empires of the past were based upon military
power; the empires of the future may well be based upon information. The
old form of empire building meant the domination by one country of the
political, economic, or cultural life of others. The new form of empire might
be the domination of information processing and retrieval by a limited
number of information corporations in a few powerful nations.

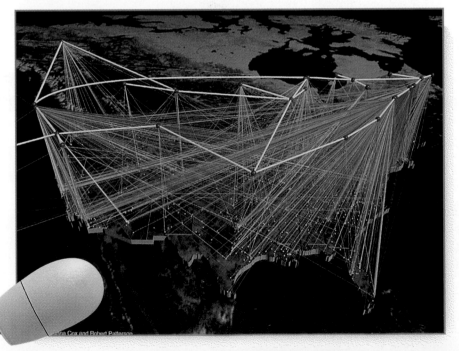

EXAMINING THEMES

Cultural Interaction
What perspective might women
bring to problems such as child-
care, health care, and education?
What special contribution might
women make to the solution to
such problems?

Science & Technology
Do you think the cloning of
human beings would be a good
or bad idea? Why?

Interaction with Environment
What is an example of an
environmental issue that the
world has addressed and begun
to solve? What is an example
of an environmental issue that
remains unsolved?

Empire Building
How might information corporations in a few powerful nations
represent a new form of empire?
What might be some of the
threats to the individual posed
by abuses of the Internet?

WORLD HISTORY
PATTERNS OF INTERACTION

Reference Section

Atlas

The atlas contains a political map of the world and both political and physical maps of the continents.

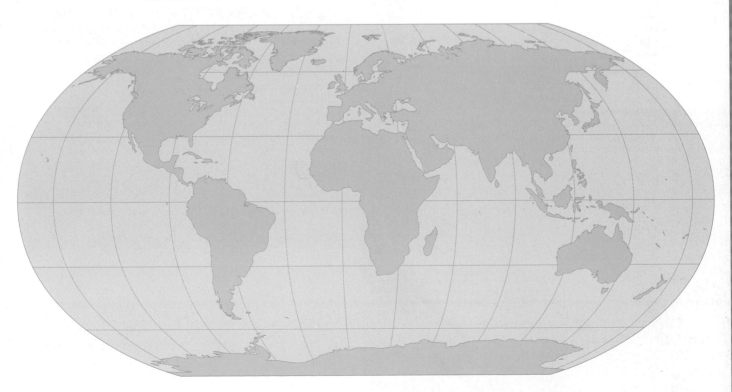

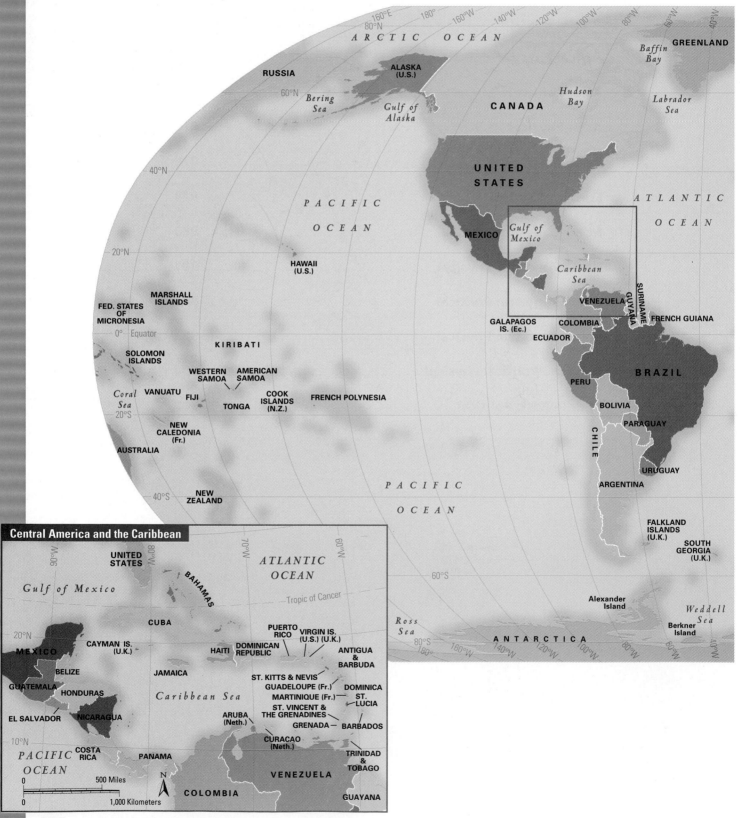

ARCTIC OCEAN

GREENLAND

Baffin Bay

RUSSIA

ALASKA (U.S.)

60°N

Bering Sea

Gulf of Alaska

CANADA

Hudson Bay

Labrador Sea

80°N

160°E 180° 160°W 140°W 120°W 100°W 80°W 60°W 40°W

40°N

UNITED STATES

ATLANTIC OCEAN

PACIFIC OCEAN

MEXICO

Gulf of Mexico

20°N

HAWAII (U.S.)

Caribbean Sea

VENEZUELA

GUYANA

SURINAME

FRENCH GUIANA

FED. STATES OF MICRONESIA

MARSHALL ISLANDS

GALAPAGOS IS. (Ec.)

COLOMBIA

ECUADOR

0° Equator

KIRIBATI

PERU

BRAZIL

SOLOMON ISLANDS

WESTERN SAMOA

AMERICAN SAMOA

BOLIVIA

Coral Sea

VANUATU

FIJI

TONGA

COOK ISLANDS (N.Z.)

FRENCH POLYNESIA

PARAGUAY

20°S

CHILE

NEW CALEDONIA (Fr.)

URUGUAY

AUSTRALIA

ARGENTINA

PACIFIC OCEAN

40°S

NEW ZEALAND

FALKLAND ISLANDS (U.K.)

SOUTH GEORGIA (U.K.)

60°S

Alexander Island

Weddell Sea

Ross Sea

Berkner Island

80°S

ANTARCTICA

180° 160°W 140°W 120°W 100°W 80°W 60°W 40°W

Central America and the Caribbean

UNITED STATES

ATLANTIC OCEAN

Gulf of Mexico

BAHAMAS

90°W 80°W 70°W 60°W

Tropic of Cancer

CUBA

20°N

MEXICO

CAYMAN IS. (U.K.)

HAITI

DOMINICAN REPUBLIC

PUERTO RICO

VIRGIN IS. (U.S.) (U.K.)

ANTIGUA & BARBUDA

BELIZE

JAMAICA

Caribbean Sea

ST. KITTS & NEVIS

GUADELOUPE (Fr.)

DOMINICA

GUATEMALA

HONDURAS

MARTINIQUE (Fr.)

ST. LUCIA

EL SALVADOR

NICARAGUA

ST. VINCENT & THE GRENADINES

ARUBA (Neth.)

GRENADA

BARBADOS

CURACAO (Neth.)

TRINIDAD & TOBAGO

10°N

PACIFIC OCEAN

COSTA RICA

PANAMA

VENEZUELA

COLOMBIA

GUAYANA

0 500 Miles

0 1,000 Kilometers

N

ATLANTIC
OCEAN

North
Sea

NORWAY

SWEDEN

DEN.

IRELAND

NETH.

UNITED
KINGDOM

GERMANY

BELG.

LUX.

CZECH REP.

PO

Bay of
Biscay

FRANCE

SWITZ.

AUS.

HUNG.

SLVN.

ROMANIA

PORTUGAL

SPAIN

ITALY

CRO.

B-H

YUGO.

BULGARIA

ALB.

MAC.

Black Sea

GEORGIA

ARMENIA

AZERBAIJAN

TURKEY

GREECE

Mediterranean Sea

SYRIA

ALGERIA

TUNISIA

CYPRUS

IRAQ

ICELAND

Norwegian
Sea

Barents
Sea

A R C T I C   O C E A N

FINLAND

NORWAY

SWEDEN

R U S S I A

UNITED
KINGDOM

GERMANY

POLAND

BELARUS

IRELAND

FRANCE

UKRAINE

Caspian
Sea

KAZAKHSTAN

MONGOLIA

AZORES
(Port.)

SPAIN

ITALY

Black Sea

TURKEY

TURKMENISTAN

UZBEKISTAN

KYRGYZSTAN

TAJIKISTAN

NORTH
KOREA

JAPAN

SOUTH
KOREA

CANARY IS.
(Port.)

MOROCCO

Mediterranean
Sea

LEBANON

SYRIA

IRAQ

IRAN

AFGHAN-
ISTAN

CHINA

BHUTAN

WESTERN
SAHARA

ALGERIA

LIBYA

EGYPT

ISRAEL

JORDAN

KUWAIT

QATAR

PAKISTAN

NEPAL

INDIA

TAIWAN

PACIFIC
OCEAN

MAURITANIA

MALI

NIGER

CHAD

SAUDI
ARABIA

U.A.E.

MYANMAR

LAOS

VIETNAM

NO.
MARIANA
IS. (U.S.)

CAPE
VERDE

ERITREA

OMAN

YEMEN

Red Sea

Arabian
Sea

BANGLA-
DESH

THAILAND

South
China
Sea

PHILIPPINES

FED. STATES OF
MICRONESIA

NIGERIA

SUDAN

DJIBOUTI

Bay
of
Bengal

CAMBODIA

PALAU

CHAD

CAMEROON

CEN.
AFR. REP.

ETHIOPIA

SOMALIA

MALDIVES

SRI
LANKA

BRUNEI

MALAYSIA

Gulf of
Guinea

GABON

CONGO

RWANDA

UGANDA

KENYA

Borneo

Sumatra

Sulawesi

Equator

PAPUA
NEW
GUINEA

DEM. REP.
OF THE
CONGO

BURUNDI

SEYCHELLES

CHAGOS
ARCH. (U.K.)

INDONESIA

Java

New Guinea

TANZANIA

MALAWI

COMOROS

ANGOLA

ZAMBIA

MADAGASCAR

MAURITIUS

INDIAN

ZIMBABWE

MOZAMBIQUE

RÉUNION
(Fr.)

OCEAN

NAMIBIA

BOTSWANA

AUSTRALIA

ATLANTIC

OCEAN

SOUTH
AFRICA

SWAZILAND

LESOTHO

N

0   2,000 Miles

0   4,000 Kilometers

KERGUÉLEN
IS. (Fr.)

SO. SANDWICH
ISLANDS (U.K.)

A N T A R C T I C A

MAURITANIA

MALI

NIGER

CHAD

SENEGAL

GAMBIA

BURKINA FASO

L. Chad

BENIN

NIGERIA

GUINEA

GUINEA-
BISSAU

CÔTE
D'IVOIRE

GHANA

TOGO

CAMEROON

CENTRAL
AFRICAN
REPUBLIC

SIERRA
LEONE

LIBERIA

ATLANTIC
OCEAN

EQUATORIAL GUINEA

Gulf of Guinea

GABON

CONGO

Equator

N

0   500 Miles

0   1,000 Kilometers

SÃO TOMÉ AND
PRINCIPE

CABINDA
(Angola)

DEM.
REP. OF
CONGO

973

EUROPE

ASIA

ATLANTIC

OCEAN

Black Sea

Caspian Sea

SOUTHWEST
ASIA

Mediterranean Sea

MADEIRA
ISLANDS
(Port.)

Tunis

Rabat • Fes
Casablanca

Oran

Algiers

TUNISIA

Tripoli

Benghazi

Alexandria

Cairo

Persian Gulf

Las Palmas de
Gran Canaria

MOROCCO

LIBYA

EGYPT

CANARY
ISLANDS
(Sp.)

• La'youn

ALGERIA

Aswan

Red Sea

Tropic of Cancer

WESTERN
SAHARA

MAURITANIA

• Nouakchott

MALI

NIGER

CHAD

Port Sudan

Khartoum

20°N

ERITREA

Asmara

Tropic of Cancer

CAPE
VERDE

Dakar

• SENEGAL

THE GAMBIA

Banjul

Bissau

GUINEA
BISSAU

GUINEA

Conakry
Freetown

SIERRA
LEONE

Niamey

BURKINA FASO

Bamako

Ouagadougou

Kano

Abuja

NIGERIA

N'Djamena

SUDAN

DJIBOUTI

Addis Ababa

Gulf of Aden

DJIBOUTI

Djibouti

CÔTE
D'IVOIRE

GHANA

TOGO

BENIN

Ibadan

Lagos

ETHIOPIA

Yamoussoukro

Lomé

Porto-Novo

LIBERIA

Monrovia

Abidjan

Accra

CAMEROON

Douala

CENTRAL AFRICAN
REPUBLIC

SOMALIA

*Gulf of
Guinea*

Malabo

Yaoundé

Bangui

UGANDA

KENYA

Mogadishu

EQUITORIAL
GUINEA

Kisangani

Kampala

Nakuru

Nairobi

SÃO TOMÉ
& PRÍNCIPE

Libreville

GABON

CONGO

DEMOCRATIC
REPUBLIC
OF THE
CONGO

RWANDA

L. Victoria

Kigali

Mwanza

Equator

INDIAN

OCEAN

Brazzaville

BURUNDI

Bujumbura

Mombasa

Kinshasa

Kananga

Mbuji-Mayi

Dodoma

Zanzibar

Luanda

TANZANIA

Dar es Salaam

Lobito

Lubumbashi

MALAWI

Moroni

COMOROS

ANGOLA

Kitwe

ZAMBIA

Lilongwe

MAYOTTE
(France)

Blantyre

Lusaka

MADAGASCAR

NAMIBIA

Harare

BOTSWANA

ZIMBABWE

Bulawayo

MOZAMBIQUE

Beira

Antananarivo

Windhoek

Gaborone

Pretoria

Maputo

Johannesburg

Mbabane

SWAZILAND

Maseru

LESOTHO

Durban

SOUTH AFRICA

Cape Town

Port Elizabeth

⊛ Capital cities

• Cities

N

0   500   1,000 Miles

0   1,000   2,000 Kilometers

Tropic of Capricorn

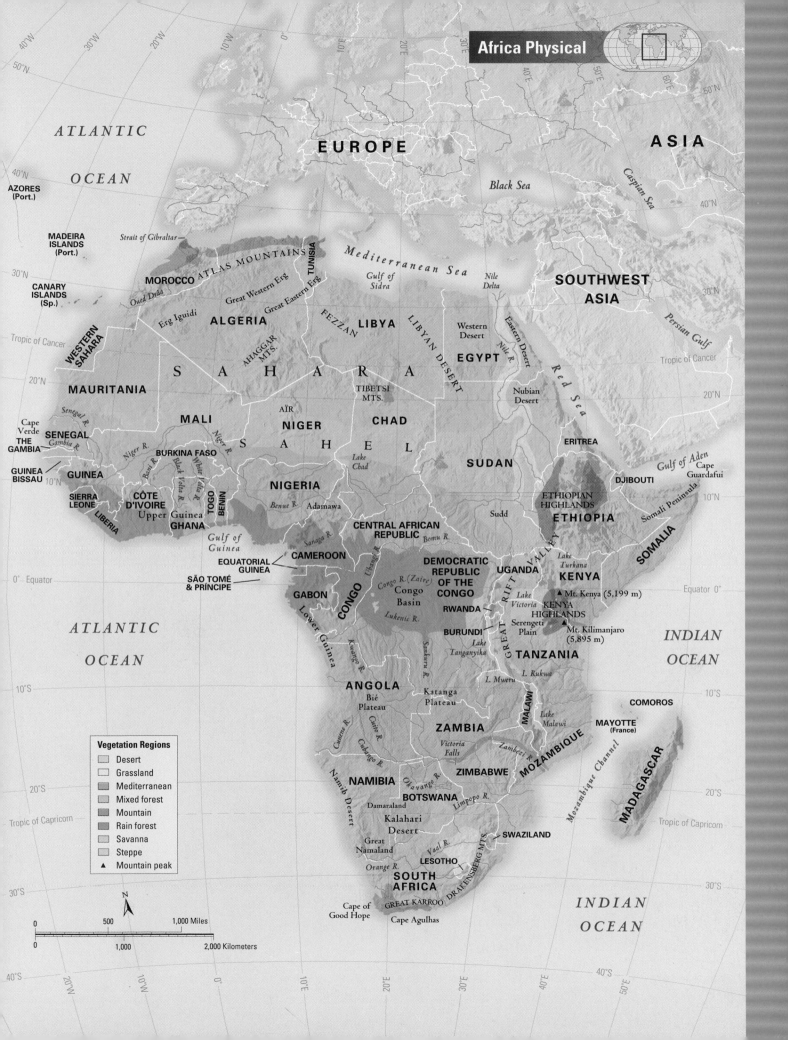

Africa Physical

ATLANTIC OCEAN

EUROPE

ASIA

Black Sea

Caspian Sea

AZORES (Port.)

MADEIRA ISLANDS (Port.)

Strait of Gibraltar

CANARY ISLANDS (Sp.)

MOROCCO ATLAS MOUNTAINS TUNISIA

Mediterranean Sea

Gulf of Sidra

Nile Delta

SOUTHWEST ASIA

Persian Gulf

Tropic of Cancer

WESTERN SAHARA

Oued Drâa

Erg Iguidi

ALGERIA

Great Western Erg

Great Eastern Erg

FEZZAN

LIBYA

LIBYAN DESERT

Western Desert

Eastern Desert

EGYPT

Nile R.

Red Sea

Tropic of Cancer

MAURITANIA

S A H A R A

AHAGGAR MTS.

TIBESTI MTS.

Nubian Desert

Senegal R.

MALI

AÏR

NIGER

CHAD

SUDAN

ERITREA

Gulf of Aden

Cape Guardafui

Cape Verde

SENEGAL

Gambia R.

THE GAMBIA

S A H E L

Lake Chad

DJIBOUTI

GUINEA BISSAU

GUINEA

BURKINA FASO

Niger R.

Bani R.

Black Volta R.

White Volta R.

NIGERIA

ETHIOPIAN HIGHLANDS

ETHIOPIA

Somali Peninsula

SIERRA LEONE

CÔTE D'IVOIRE

TOGO

BENIN

Benue R.

Adamawa

Sudd

LIBERIA

Upper Guinea

GHANA

Gulf of Guinea

Sanaga R.

CENTRAL AFRICAN REPUBLIC

Bomu R.

GREAT RIFT VALLEY

Lake Turkana

SOMALIA

Equator

EQUATORIAL GUINEA

CAMEROON

Ubangi R.

DEMOCRATIC REPUBLIC OF THE CONGO

UGANDA

KENYA

▲ Mt. Kenya (5,199 m)

Equator

SÃO TOMÉ & PRÍNCIPE

GABON

CONGO

Congo R. (Zaïre)

Congo Basin

Lukenie R.

RWANDA

Lake Victoria

KENYA HIGHLANDS

ATLANTIC OCEAN

Lower Guinea

Kwango R.

Sankuru R.

BURUNDI

Serengeti Plain

▲ Mt. Kilimanjaro (5,895 m)

INDIAN OCEAN

Lake Tanganyika

TANZANIA

ANGOLA

Bié Plateau

Katanga Plateau

L. Rukwa

L. Mweru

COMOROS

Cuanza R.

Cuito R.

ZAMBIA

Lake Malawi

MAYOTTE (France)

Cunene R.

Victoria Falls

Zambezi R.

MALAWI

MOZAMBIQUE

MADAGASCAR

NAMIBIA

Okavango R.

ZIMBABWE

Mozambique Channel

Namib Desert

BOTSWANA

Limpopo R.

Damaraland

Kalahari Desert

SWAZILAND

Tropic of Capricorn

Great Namaland

Vaal R.

DRAKENSBERG MTS.

LESOTHO

Orange R.

SOUTH AFRICA

Cape of Good Hope

GREAT KARROO

Cape Agulhas

INDIAN OCEAN

Vegetation Regions
- ☐ Desert
- ☐ Grassland
- ☐ Mediterranean
- ☐ Mixed forest
- ☐ Mountain
- ☐ Rain forest
- ☐ Savanna
- ☐ Steppe
- ▲ Mountain peak

N

0   500   1,000 Miles

0   1,000   2,000 Kilometers

PACIFIC

OCEAN

1,000 Miles
1,000 Kilometers

Capital cities
Cities

N

Bering Sea

ARCTIC OCEAN

East Siberian Sea

Laptev Sea

Yakutsk

Sea of Okhotsk

Noril'sk

Sapporo

Khabarovsk

Vladivostok

Sea of Japan

Tokyo

JAPAN

Osaka

Fukuoka

Harbin

NORTH KOREA

Pyongyang

Seoul

SOUTH KOREA

Yellow Sea

Shanghai

East China Sea

Changchun

Shenyang

Beijing

Tianjin

Qingdao

Nanjing

Wuhan

Taipei

TAIWAN

Irkutsk

Lake Baikal

Ulaanbaatar

MONGOLIA

Xi'an

CHINA

Lanzhou

Chengdu

Chongqing

Hong Kong

South China Sea

PHILIPPINES

Manila

Davao

Sulu Sea

Celebes Sea

INDONESIA

PAPUA NEW GUINEA

Arafura Sea

Banda Sea

AUSTRALIA

Novosibirsk

Ürümqi

Guangzhou

Kunming

Hanoi

Da Nang

VIETNAM

Ho Chi Minh City

LAOS

Vientiane

BRUNEI

Pontianak

MALAYSIA

Java Sea

Surabaya

Omsk

RUSSIA

Yekaterinburg

KAZAKHSTAN

Karaganda

Almaty

Bishkek

KYRGYZSTAN

Lhasa

BHUTAN

Thimphu

Mandalay

MYANMAR

THAILAND

Bangkok

CAMBODIA

Phnom Penh

Yangon

Kuala Lumpur

SINGAPORE

Palembang

Jakarta

Chelyabinsk

L. Balkhash

Aral Sea

Tashkent

UZBEKISTAN

Dushanbe

TAJIKISTAN

Islamabad

Kathmandu

NEPAL

Delhi

Kanpur

Bay of Bengal

BANGLADESH

Dhaka

Calcutta

Chennai (Madras)

SRI LANKA

Colombo

INDIAN OCEAN

Moscow

EUROPE

RUSSIA

Barents Sea

Kara Sea

Ashgabat

TURKMENISTAN

Mashhad

Herat

AFGHANISTAN

Kabul

PAKISTAN

Lahore

New Delhi

INDIA

Nagpur

Hyderabad

Mumbai (Bombay)

Ahmadabad

Karachi

Arabian Sea

Arctic Circle

Tehran

IRAN

Shiraz

GEORGIA

Tbilisi

Baku

AZERBAIJAN

Caspian Sea

ARMENIA

Yerevan

Black Sea

Istanbul

Ankara

TURKEY

CYPRUS

Nicosia

Beirut

LEBANON

ISRAEL

Jerusalem

Damascus

SYRIA

Amman

JORDAN

Baghdad

IRAQ

Kuwait

KUWAIT

SAUDI ARABIA

Riyadh

QATAR

UNITED ARAB EMIRATES

Muscat

OMAN

SOCOTRA (Yemen)

Persian Gulf

San'a

YEMEN

Gulf of Aden

Red Sea

AFRICA

Mediterranean Sea

ATLANTIC OCEAN

Vegetation Regions

- Deciduous forest
- Desert
- Evergreen forest/taiga
- Grassland
- Ice covered
- Mediterranean
- Mixed forest
- Mountain
- Rain forest
- Savanna
- Steppe
- Tundra
- No vegetation
- ▲ Mountain peak

PACIFIC OCEAN

ARCTIC OCEAN

ATLANTIC OCEAN

INDIAN OCEAN

EUROPE

AFRICA

AUSTRALIA

RUSSIA

CHINA

INDIA

MONGOLIA

KAZAKHSTAN

Central Siberian Plateau

West Siberian Plain

The Steppes

Ural Mts.

Tropic of Cancer

Arctic Circle

Equator

977

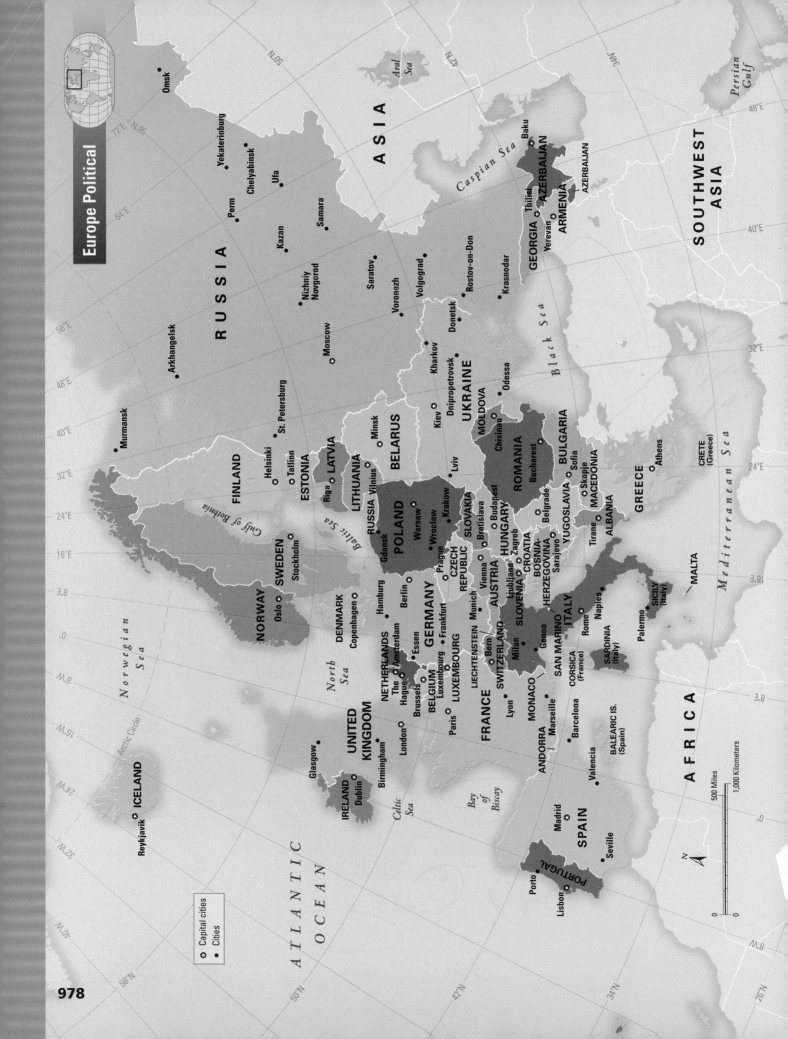

Capital cities ⊛
Cities •

ATLANTIC OCEAN

ICELAND
Reykjavik ⊛

Arctic Circle

Norwegian Sea

NORWAY
Oslo ⊛

SWEDEN
Stockholm •

FINLAND

Murmansk •

Arkhangelsk •

RUSSIA

Omsk •

Yekaterinburg •
Chelyabinsk •
Perm •
Ufa •

Nizhniy Novgorod •
Samara •
Kazan •
Saratov •
Voronezh •
Volgograd •

Moscow ⊛

St. Petersburg •

Helsinki ⊛
Tallinn •

ESTONIA
Riga ⊛
LATVIA
LITHUANIA
Vilnius ⊛

BELARUS
Minsk ⊛

Gulf of Bothnia

Baltic Sea

DENMARK
Copenhagen ⊛

Hamburg •
Berlin •
GERMANY
Essen •
Frankfurt •
Munich •

NETHERLANDS
Amsterdam ⊛
The Hague
Brussels ⊛
BELGIUM
Luxembourg ⊛
LUXEMBOURG

UNITED KINGDOM
Glasgow •
Birmingham •
London ⊛

IRELAND
Dublin ⊛

Celtic Sea

North Sea

Bay of Biscay

FRANCE
Paris ⊛
Lyon •
Marseille •

LIECHTENSTEIN
SWITZERLAND
Bern ⊛
Milan •
Genoa •

ANDORRA
MONACO

SPAIN
Madrid ⊛
Valencia •
Seville •
Barcelona •
BALEARIC IS. (Spain)

PORTUGAL
Porto •
Lisbon ⊛

POLAND
Warsaw ⊛
Gdansk •
Wroclaw •
Krakow •

CZECH REPUBLIC
Prague ⊛

SLOVAKIA
Bratislava ⊛
AUSTRIA
Vienna ⊛

HUNGARY
Budapest ⊛

SLOVENIA
Ljubljana ⊛
Zagreb ⊛
CROATIA
BOSNIA HERZEGOVINA
Sarajevo ⊛

ITALY
SAN MARINO
Rome ⊛
Naples •
Palermo •
SICILY (Italy)
SARDINIA (Italy)
CORSICA (France)

MALTA

UKRAINE
Kiev ⊛
Lviv •
Kharkov •
Dnipropetrovsk •
Donetsk •
Odessa •

Rostov-on-Don •
Krasnodar •

MOLDOVA
Chisinau ⊛

ROMANIA
Bucharest ⊛

BULGARIA
Sofia ⊛

YUGOSLAVIA
Belgrade ⊛
MACEDONIA
Skopje ⊛
ALBANIA
Tirane ⊛

GREECE
Athens ⊛
CRETE (Greece)

Black Sea

Mediterranean Sea

GEORGIA
Tbilisi ⊛
ARMENIA
Yerevan ⊛
AZERBAIJAN
Baku ⊛
AZERBAIJAN

Caspian Sea

Aral Sea

ASIA

SOUTHWEST ASIA

Persian Gulf

AFRICA

500 Miles
1,000 Kilometers

N

URAL MOUNTAINS

A S I A

Aral Sea

Persian Gulf

Caspian Sea

Caspian Depression

R U S S I A

Kama Upland

Volga R.

Ural R.

Don R.

Central Russian Upland

Dnieper R.

Sea of Azov

Black Sea

CAUCASUS MTS.

Mt. Elbrus ▲ (5,642 m)

AZER.

GEORGIA

ARMENIA

AZER.

SOUTHWEST ASIA

Barents Sea

Kanin Pen.

Kola Peninsula

White Sea

L. Onega

L. Ladoga

FINLAND

Northern European Plain

BELARUS

UKRAINE

MOLD.

Bosporus

Sea of Marmara

Dardanelles

RHODES (Greece)

CRETE (Greece)

Mediterranean Sea

North Cape

KJOLEN MTS.

Gulf of Bothnia

ESTONIA

LATVIA

LITH.

RUSSIA

Gotland

Baltic Sea

Vistula R.

POLAND

Oder R.

CARPATHIAN MTS.

Hungarian Plain

ROMANIA

Danube R.

BULGARIA

YUGO.

MACE.

ALB.

GREECE

Peloponnesus

Balkan Peninsula

Aegean Sea

Ionian Sea

SWEDEN

NORWAY

DENMARK

Jutland

Skagerrak

North Sea

NETH.

GERMANY

Elbe R.

CZECH REP.

ORE MTS.

Danube R.

SLOVAKIA

HUNGARY

AUSTRIA

SLOVENIA

CROATIA

BOSNIA-HERZE.

DINARIC ALPS

Adriatic Sea

ITALY

APENNINES

Tyrrhenian Sea

SICILY (Italy) ▲ Mt. Ebro (3,323 m)

MALTA

Norwegian Sea

Faeroe Is.

Shetland Is.

Orkney Is.

Hebrides

Highlands

GREAT BRITAIN

Irish Sea

British Isles

Celtic Sea

English Channel

BELG.

LUX.

Rhine R.

JURA MTS.

LIECH.

SWITZ.

A L P S

Matterhorn (4,478 m)

Mt. Blanc (4,807 m)

MONACO

SAN MARINO

Ligurian Sea

CORSICA (France)

SARDINIA (Italy)

Rhône R.

ICELAND

Arctic Circle

IRELAND

Bay of Biscay

FRANCE

Loire R.

Massif Central

ANDORRA

PYRENEES

Ebro R.

BALEARIC IS. (Spain)

Balearic Sea

A T L A N T I C   O C E A N

CANTABRIAN MTS.

Duero R.

Iberian Peninsula

SPAIN

PORTUGAL

Tagus R.

Strait of Gibraltar

A F R I C A

Vegetation Regions
- Deciduous forest
- Desert
- Evergreen forest/taiga
- Grassland
- Ice covered
- Mediterranean
- Mixed forest
- Mountain
- Steppe
- Tundra
- ▲ Mountain peak

N

500 Miles

1,000 Kilometers

North America Political

ASIA

ARCTIC OCEAN

North Pole

EUROPE

Norwegian Sea

Bering Strait

Beaufort Sea

ELLESMERE ISLAND

GREENLAND

Baffin Bay

Arctic Circle

Bering Sea

ALASKA

Fairbanks •

• Anchorage

Gulf of Alaska

VICTORIA ISLAND

BAFFIN ISLAND

Nuuk •

Labrador Sea

Whitehorse

Juneau •

Yellowknife •

Hudson Bay

CANADA

Happy Valley-Goose Bay

NEWFOUNDLAND

MIQUELON I. (France)

PACIFIC OCEAN

Edmonton •

Vancouver

Calgary •

Saskatoon •

Regina •

Winnipeg •

Thunder Bay •

Great Lakes

Québec •

Montréal •

Ottawa ✪

Halifax •

Seattle •

Portland •

Boise •

Billings •

Minneapolis •

Milwaukee •

Detroit •

Toronto •

Buffalo •

Boston •

New York •

Philadelphia •

Sacramento •

Reno •

San Francisco •

Salt Lake City •

Omaha •

Chicago •

Cleveland •

Cincinnati •

Baltimore •

Washington ✪

Norfolk •

BERMUDA (U.K.)

Denver •

Kansas City •

St. Louis •

Las Vegas •

UNITED STATES

Charlotte •

ATLANTIC OCEAN

Los Angeles •

San Diego •

Tijuana •

Phoenix •

Albuquerque •

Oklahoma City •

Birmingham •

Atlanta •

El Paso •

Dallas •

Ciudad Juárez •

San Antonio •

Houston •

New Orleans •

Jacksonville •

Tampa •

Miami •

BAHAMAS

Nassau ✪

VIRGIN IS. (U.S.) (U.K.)

Chihuahua •

Gulf of California

Monterrey •

Gulf of Mexico

Havana ✪

CUBA

Santiago de Cuba •

DOMINICAN REPUBLIC

San Juan

HAITI

Port-au-Prince ✪

Santo Domingo ✪

PUERTO RICO (U.S.)

LESSER ANTILLES

MEXICO

León •

Guadalajara •

México ✪

Veracruz •

Mérida •

CAYMAN IS. (U.K.)

JAMAICA

Kingston ✪

Caribbean Sea

TRINIDAD & TOBAGO

Acapulco •

BELIZE

Belmopan ✪

GUATEMALA

Guatemala ✪

San Salvador ✪

EL SALVADOR

HONDURAS

Tegucigalpa ✪

NICARAGUA

Managua ✪

COSTA RICA

San José ✪

Panamá •

PANAMA ✪

SOUTH AMERICA

PACIFIC OCEAN

Tropic of Cancer

✪ Capital cities

• Cities

N

0   1,000 Miles

0   2,000 Kilometers

PACIFIC OCEAN

Equator

EUROPE

ASIA

ARCTIC OCEAN

North Pole

Norwegian Sea

Arctic Circle

Arctic Circle

GREENLAND

Ellesmere Island

Queen Elizabeth Islands

Parry Islands

Devon I.

Baffin Bay

Beaufort Sea

Banks I.

Boothia Pen.

St. Lawrence I.

Bering Strait

BROOKS RANGE

ALASKA

Yukon R.

Victoria I.

Baffin Island

Davis Strait

Nunivak

Bering Sea

Mt. McKinley (6,194 m)

ALASKA RANGE

Foxe Basin

Labrador Sea

Aleutian Islands

Kodiak I.

Gulf of Alaska

Mt. Logan (6,050 m)

Yukon R.

MACKENZIE MTS.

Mackenzie R.

Great Bear Lake

Southampton I.

Hudson Strait

Ungava Pen.

Labrador

Alexander Archipelago

COAST MOUNTAINS

Great Slave Lake

L. Athabasca

Hudson Bay

Queen Charlotte Is.

Peace R.

ROCKY MOUNTAINS

Reindeer L.

James Bay

Newfoundland

MIQUELON I. (France)

PACIFIC OCEAN

Vancouver I.

Saskatchewan R.

GREAT PLAINS

L. Winnipeg

CANADA

Canadian Shield

Nova Scotia

CASCADES

Columbia R.

Missouri R.

L. Superior

Great Lakes

L. Huron

St. Lawrence R.

Cape Cod

Long Island

SIERRA NEVADA

Snake R.

Great Basin

Platte R.

UNITED STATES

Central Lowland

Mississippi R.

L. Michigan

L. Erie

L. Ontario

Ohio R.

APPALACHIAN MTS.

Chesapeake Bay

Cape Hatteras

BERMUDA (U.K.)

ATLANTIC OCEAN

Mt. Whitney (4,418 m)

Colorado R.

Arkansas R.

Ozark Plateau

Tennessee R.

Coastal Plain

Canadian R.

Red R.

Colorado R.

Baja California

SIERRA MADRE OCCIDENTAL

Gulf of California

SIERRA MADRE ORIENTAL

Rio Grande

Tropic of Cancer

Tropic of Cancer

BAHAMAS

VIRGIN IS. (U.S.) (U.K.)

Gulf of Mexico

DOMINICAN REPUBLIC

CUBA

HAITI

Greater Antilles

PUERTO RICO (U.S.)

Lesser Antilles

MEXICO

Yucatan Peninsula

CAYMAN IS. (U.K.)

JAMAICA

Caribbean Sea

TRINIDAD & TOBAGO

Mt. Orizaba (5,747 m)

Isthmus of Tehuantepec

BELIZE

HONDURAS

NICARAGUA

PACIFIC OCEAN

GUATEMALA

EL SALVADOR

L. Nicaragua

Isthmus of Panama

COSTA RICA

PANAMA

Orinoco R.

SOUTH AMERICA

Equator

Equator

Vegetation Regions

- Coniferous forest
- Deciduous forest
- Desert
- Grassland
- Mediterranean
- Mixed forest
- Mountain
- Rain forest
- Savanna
- Tundra
- Ice Cap
- ▲ Mountain peak

N

0   1,000 Miles

0   2,000 Kilometers

South America Political

CENTRAL
AMERICA

Barranquilla
Cartagena
Maracaibo
Barquisimeto
Caracas
Valencia
Cuidad
Guayana
TRINIDAD
& TOBAGO
Cúcuta
Bucaramanga
Medellín
Bogotá
Cali
COLOMBIA
VENEZUELA
Georgetown
GUYANA
Paramaribo
Cayenne
FRENCH
GUIANA
SURINAME

0° Equator
Quito
ECUADOR
Guayaquil
Iquitos
Piura
Trujillo
PERU
Rio
Branco
Pôrto
Velho
Macapá
Manaus
Santarém
Belém
BRAZIL
Fortaleza
Teresina
Natal
Recife
Maceió
10°S
Lima
Cuzco
Arequipa
La Paz
BOLIVIA
Oruro
Santa Cruz
Sucre
Cuiabá
Brasília
Goiânia
Belo Horizonte
Salvador

20°S
Campo
Grande
PARAGUAY
Campinas
Rio de Janeiro
Curitiba
São Paulo
Tropic of Capricorn
Antofagasta
San Miguel
de Tucumán
Asunción
CHILE
ARGENTINA
Pôrto Alegre
30°S
Córdoba
Rosario
URUGUAY
Buenos Aires
La Plata
Montevideo
Valparaíso
Santiago
Concepción
Bahía Blanca
Mar del Plata

Capital cities
Cities

Puerto Montt
40°S

N

0   500 Miles
0   1,000 Kilometers

Stanley
FALKLAND ISLANDS
(U.K.)
SOUTH
GEORGIA
(U.K.)
Punta Arenas

CENTRAL AMERICA

Cristóbal Colón (5,775 m)

Pt. Gallinas

Caribbean Sea

TRINIDAD & TOBAGO

80°W

10°N

Gulf of Panamá

L. Maracaibo

CORD. OCCIDENTAL

CORD. CENTRAL

CORD. ORIENTAL

Cauca R.

Magdalena R.

CORD. DE MERIDA

Orinoco R.

Llanos

VENEZUELA

GUYANA

SURINAME

FRENCH GUIANA

60°W

COLOMBIA

Orinoco R.

Guiana Highlands

ATLANTIC OCEAN

C. San Francisco

Branco R.

ECUADOR

Negro R.

0° Equator

0° Equator

Gulf of Guayaquil

Putumayo R.

Japurá R.

A m a z o n

Amazon R.

Marajó Island

Pariñas Pt.

Marañón R.

Amazon R.

B a s i n

Madeira R.

Tapajós R.

Xingu R.

Cape São Roque

Juruá R.

Purus R.

Araguaia R.

Parnaíba R.

Mt. Huascarán (6,768 m)

BRAZIL

Tocantins R.

PERU

10°S

10°S

A N D E S

Ucayali R.

Guaporé R.

B r a z i l i a n

São Francisco R.

SERRA DO ESPINHAÇO

Mamoré R.

Mato Grosso Plateau

H i g h l a n d s

L. Titicaca

BOLIVIA

L. Poopó

Paraguay R.

Pantanal

Atacama Desert

20°S

20°S

Cape São Tomé

Cape Frío

Tropic of Capricorn

Tropic of Capricorn

Gran Chaco

PARAGUAY

Paraná R.

Campos

SERRA DO MAR

Pilcomayo R.

PACIFIC OCEAN

Salado R.

Paraná R.

Uruguay R.

CHILE

Entre Ríos

Patos Lagoon

Mt. Aconcagua (6,960 m)

URUGUAY

30°S

30°S

Salado R.

Pampas

Río de la Plata

ARGENTINA

ATLANTIC OCEAN

Colorado R.

Negro R.

San Matías Gulf

Valdés Peninsula

40°S

40°S

Chiloé I.

Chubut R.

P a t a g o n i a

Chonos Arch.

Gulf of San Jorge

Cape Tres Puntas

N

500

1,000 Miles

Wellington I.

1,000

2,000 Kilometers

FALKLAND ISLANDS (U.K.)

Grande Bay

50°S

50°S

Strait of Magellan

Tierra del Fuego

Cape Horn

SOUTH GEORGIA (U.K.)

80°W

60°W

50°W

40°W

30°W

20°W

Vegetation Regions

- Desert
- Grassland
- Mediterranean
- Mixed forest
- Mountain
- Rain forest
- Savanna
- Steppe
- Tundra
- ▲ Mountain peak

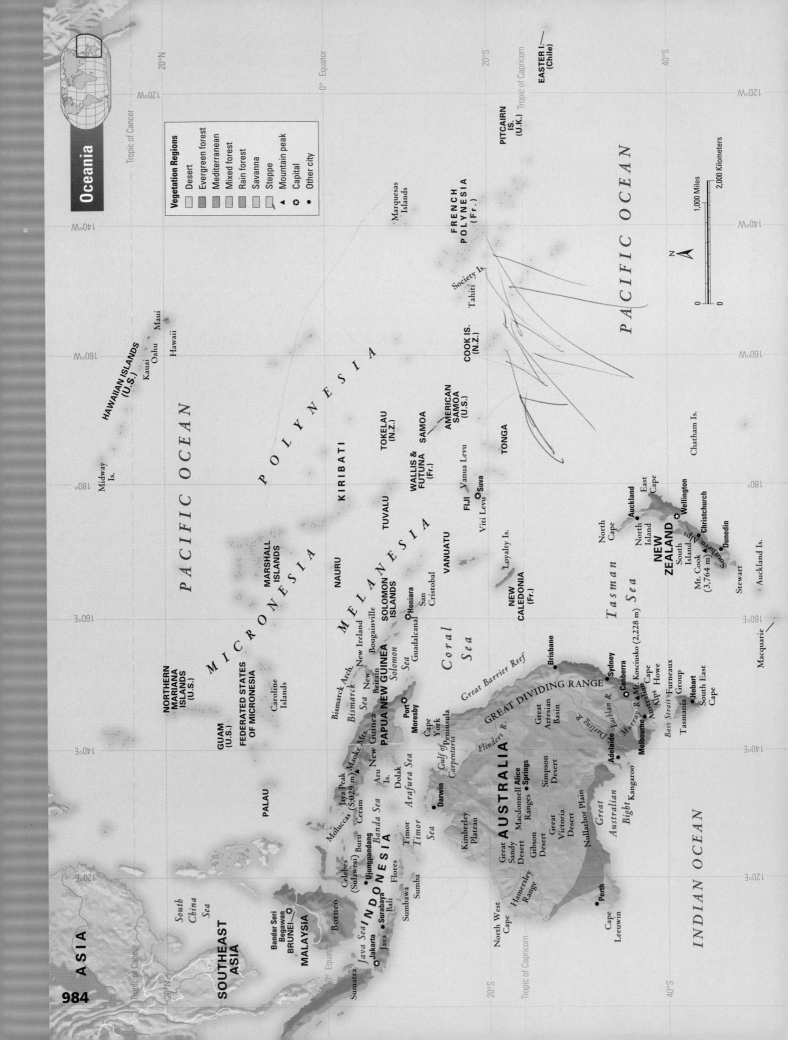

ASIA

EUROPE

AFRICA

IRAN

TURKEY

SYRIA

IRAQ

SAUDI ARABIA

EGYPT

LIBYA

OMAN

OMAN

YEMEN

KUWAIT

JORDAN

ISRAEL

LEBANON

CYPRUS

BAHRAIN

QATAR

UNITED ARAB EMIRATES

Caspian Sea

Black Sea

Mediterranean Sea

Red Sea

Persian Gulf

Gulf of Oman

Arabian Sea

Gulf of Aden

Gulf of Sidra

Strait of Hormuz

SOCOTRA (Yemen)

Mashad

Zahedan

Kerman

Bandar-e Abbas

Muscat

Salalah

Shiraz

Esfahan

Tehran

Bandar-e Bushehr

Abu Dhabi

Doha

Manama

Hofuf

Abadan

Basra

Kuwait

Riyadh

San'a

Hodeida

Aden

Mukalla

Bakhtaran

Tabriz

Mosul

Kirkuk

Baghdad

An Najaf

Medina

Jeddah

Mecca

Erzurum

Gaziantep

Aleppo

Damascus

Homs

Irbid

Amman

Ankara

Adana

Nicosia

Beirut

Tel Aviv-Yafo

Jerusalem

Qena

Aswan

Izmit

Bursa

Istanbul

Izmir

Port Said

Cairo

Suez

Giza

Alexandria

El Minya

Asyut

Tobruk

Benghazi

Tripoli

Sabha

Salalah

Tropic of Cancer

● Capital cities
● Cities

N

500 Miles

1,000 Kilometers

60°E

60°E

30°N

30°N

45°N

45°N

45°E

45°E

30°E

30°E

15°E

15°N

15°N

15°S

15°S

985

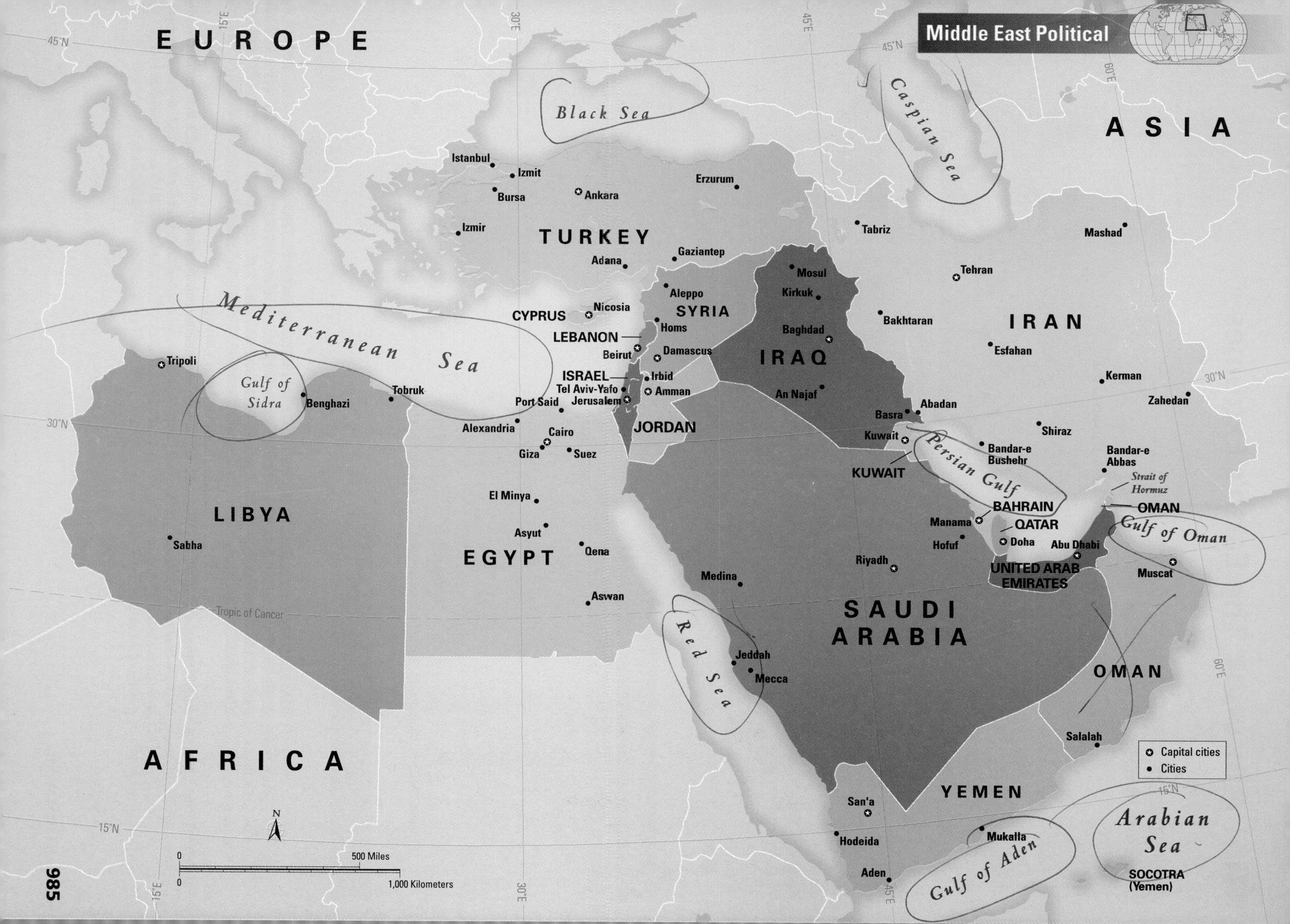

Mini Almanac The Earth's Extremes

The High and The Low

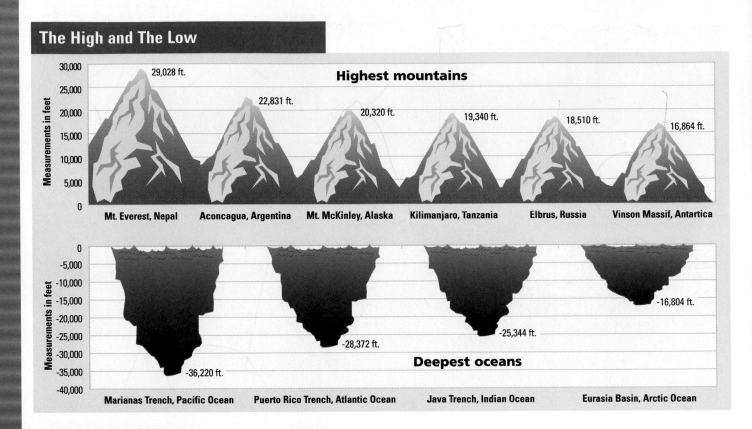

Highest mountains

Measurements in feet

29,028 ft. — Mt. Everest, Nepal
22,831 ft. — Aconcagua, Argentina
20,320 ft. — Mt. McKinley, Alaska
19,340 ft. — Kilimanjaro, Tanzania
18,510 ft. — Elbrus, Russia
16,864 ft. — Vinson Massif, Antartica

Deepest oceans

Measurements in feet

-36,220 ft. — Marianas Trench, Pacific Ocean
-28,372 ft. — Puerto Rico Trench, Atlantic Ocean
-25,344 ft. — Java Trench, Indian Ocean
-16,804 ft. — Eurasia Basin, Arctic Ocean

The Most Destructive Natural Disasters

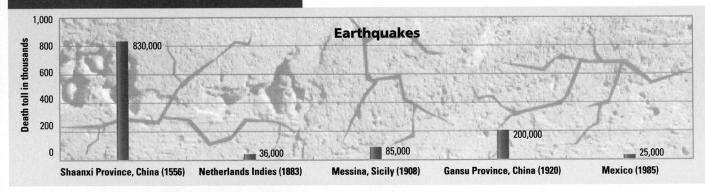

Earthquakes

Death toll in thousands

830,000 — Shaanxi Province, China (1556)
36,000 — Netherlands Indies (1883)
85,000 — Messina, Sicily (1908)
200,000 — Gansu Province, China (1920)
25,000 — Mexico (1985)

The Longest

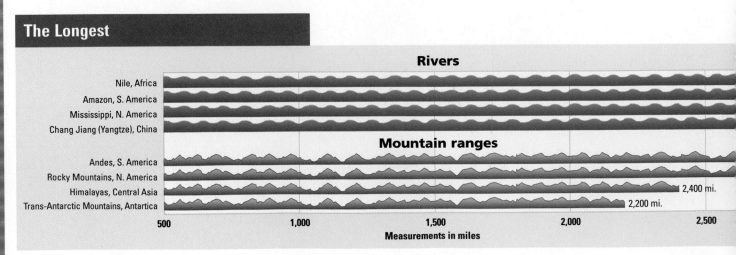

Rivers

Nile, Africa
Amazon, S. America
Mississippi, N. America
Chang Jiang (Yangtze), China

Mountain ranges

Andes, S. America
Rocky Mountains, N. America
Himalayas, Central Asia — 2,400 mi.
Trans-Antarctic Mountains, Antartica — 2,200 mi.

500   1,000   1,500   2,000   2,500

Measurements in miles

The Wet and Dry

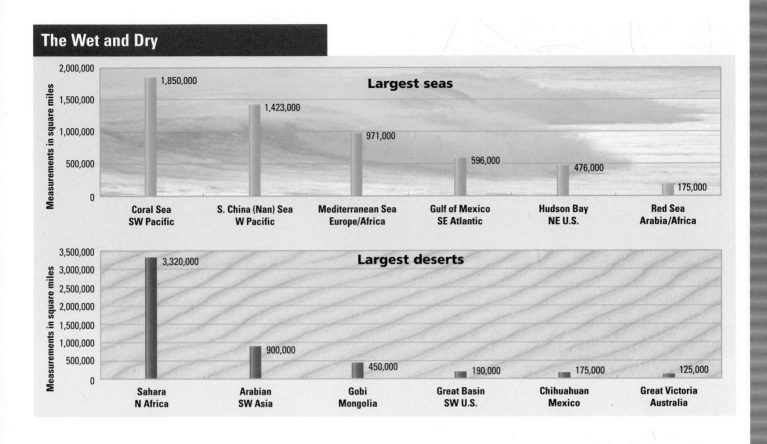

Largest seas

Measurements in square miles

- Coral Sea SW Pacific — 1,850,000
- S. China (Nan) Sea W Pacific — 1,423,000
- Mediterranean Sea Europe/Africa — 971,000
- Gulf of Mexico SE Atlantic — 596,000
- Hudson Bay NE U.S. — 476,000
- Red Sea Arabia/Africa — 175,000

Largest deserts

Measurements in square miles

- Sahara N Africa — 3,320,000
- Arabian SW Asia — 900,000
- Gobi Mongolia — 450,000
- Great Basin SW U.S. — 190,000
- Chihuahuan Mexico — 175,000
- Great Victoria Australia — 125,000

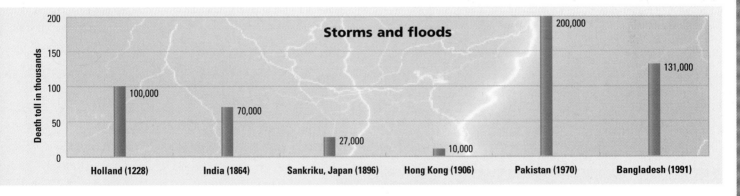

Storms and floods

Death toll in thousands

- Holland (1228) — 100,000
- India (1864) — 70,000
- Sankriku, Japan (1896) — 27,000
- Hong Kong (1906) — 10,000
- Pakistan (1970) — 200,000
- Bangladesh (1991) — 131,000

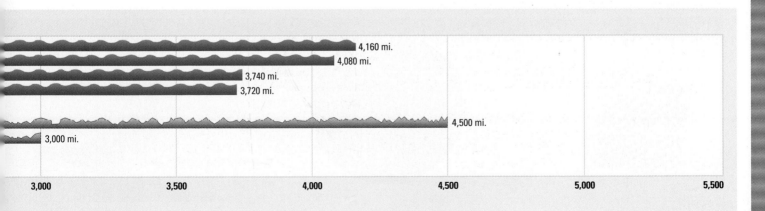

- 4,160 mi.
- 4,080 mi.
- 3,740 mi.
- 3,720 mi.
- 4,500 mi.
- 3,000 mi.

3,000   3,500   4,000   4,500   5,000   5,500

Mini Almanac The Human Panorama

Population — Projected Growth 1995-2025

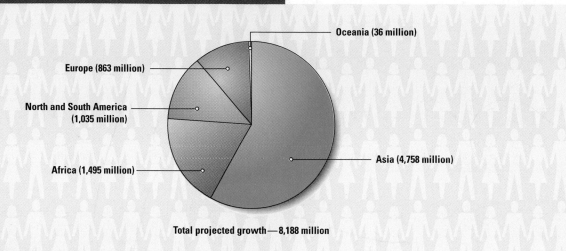

Oceania (36 million)

Europe (863 million)

North and South America (1,035 million)

Asia (4,758 million)

Africa (1,495 million)

Total projected growth — 8,188 million

Communication — Most Widely Spoken Languages

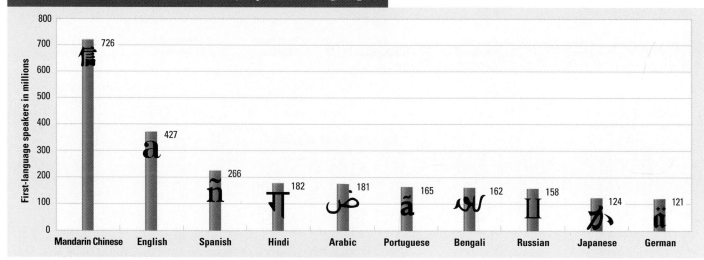

First-language speakers in millions

Mandarin Chinese	English	Spanish	Hindi	Arabic	Portuguese	Bengali	Russian	Japanese	German
726	427	266	182	181	165	162	158	124	121

Important Discoveries and Inventions

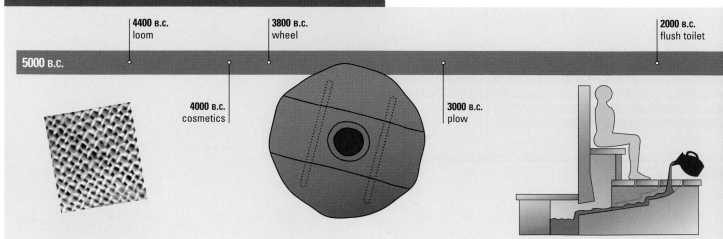

5000 B.C.

4400 B.C.
loom

4000 B.C.
cosmetics

3800 B.C.
wheel

3000 B.C.
plow

2000 B.C.
flush toilet

Technological Milestones

Longest bridges

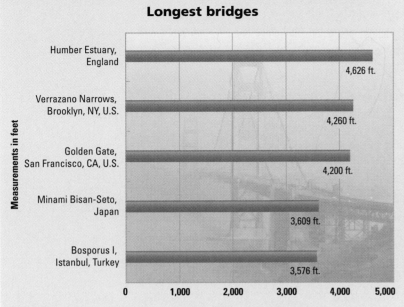

Measurements in feet

Humber Estuary, England	4,626 ft.
Verrazano Narrows, Brooklyn, NY, U.S.	4,260 ft.
Golden Gate, San Francisco, CA, U.S.	4,200 ft.
Minami Bisan-Seto, Japan	3,609 ft.
Bosporus I, Istanbul, Turkey	3,576 ft.

0   1,000   2,000   3,000   4,000   5,000

Tallest structures

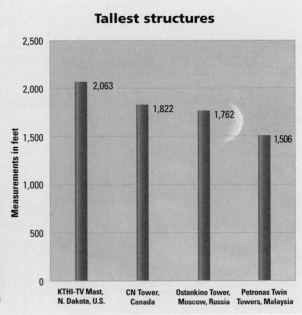

Measurements in feet

Structure	Height
KTHI-TV Mast, N. Dakota, U.S.	2,063
CN Tower, Canada	1,822
Ostankino Tower, Moscow, Russia	1,762
Petronas Twin Towers, Malaysia	1,506

Life Expectancy

Worldwide Longevity

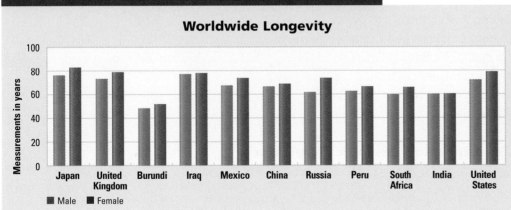

Measurements in years

Japan, United Kingdom, Burundi, Iraq, Mexico, China, Russia, Peru, South Africa, India, United States

■ Male ■ Female

Changing life expectancy in the U.S. 1850-1996

Measurements in years

1850 1870 1890 1910 1930 1950 1970 1990 2010

■ Male ■ Female

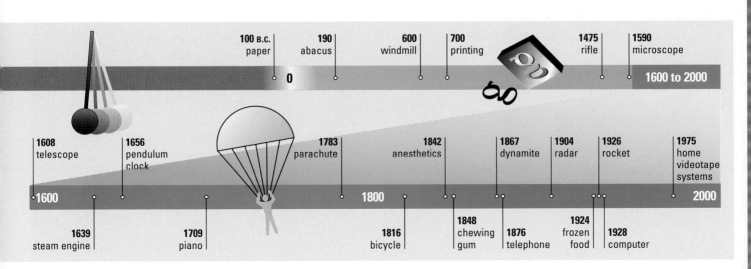

100 B.C. paper | 190 abacus | 600 windmill | 700 printing | 1475 rifle | 1590 microscope

0 ... 1600 to 2000

1608 telescope | 1656 pendulum clock | 1783 parachute | 1842 anesthetics | 1867 dynamite | 1904 radar | 1926 rocket | 1975 home videotape systems

1600 ... 1800 ... 2000

1639 steam engine | 1709 piano | 1816 bicycle | 1848 chewing gum | 1876 telephone | 1924 frozen food | 1928 computer

Skillbuilder Handbook

Refer to the Skillbuilder Handbook when you need help in answering Think Through History questions, doing the activities entitled Connect to History, or answering questions in Section Assessments and Chapter Assessments. In addition, the handbook will help you answer questions about maps, charts, and graphs.

Section 1: Understanding Historical Readings

Section 2: Using Critical Thinking

Section 3: Exploring Historical Evidence

Section 1: Understanding Historical Readings

1.1 Following Chronological Order

Chronological order is the order in which events happen in time. Historians need to figure out the order in which things happened to get an accurate sense of the relationships among events. As you read history, figure out the sequence, or time order, of events.

UNDERSTANDING THE SKILL

Strategy: Look for time clues. The following paragraph is about the rulers of England after the death of Henry VIII. Notice how the time line that follows puts the events in chronological order.

> ### HENRY'S CHILDREN RULE ENGLAND
>
> After the death of Henry VIII in 1547, each of his three children eventually ruled. This created religious turmoil. Edward VI became king at age nine and ruled only six years. During his reign, the Protestants gained power. Edward's half-sister Mary followed him to the throne. She was a Catholic who returned the English Church to the rule of the pope. Mary had many Protestants killed. England's next ruler was Anne Boleyn's daughter, Elizabeth. After inheriting the throne in 1558, Elizabeth I returned her kingdom to Protestantism. In 1559 Parliament followed Elizabeth's request and set up a national church much like the one under Henry VIII.

Look for clue words about time. These are words like *first, initial, next, then, before, after, finally,* and *by that time.*

Use specific dates provided in the text.

Watch for references to previous historical events that are included in the background.

Strategy: Order events on a time line.

If the events are complex, make a time line of them. Write the dates below the line and the events above the line.

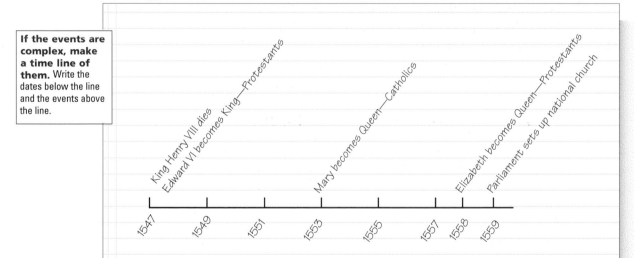

APPLYING THE SKILL

Make your own time line. Skim Chapter 35, Section 3, "Gorbachev Moves Toward Democracy," to find out about the spread of democracy in parts of Europe controlled by the Soviet Union. List the important dates and events. Start with the demonstrations in East Germany in October 1989, include events in Czechoslovakia and Romania, and end with reunification of Germany in October of 1990. Decide on a scale for your time line. Show the important dates below the line and write what happened on each date above the line.

Section 1: Understanding Historical Readings

1.2 Clarifying; Summarizing

Clarifying means making clear and fully understanding what you read. One way to do this is by asking yourself questions about the material. In your answers, restate in your own words what you have read.

Summarizing means condensing what you read into fewer words. You state only the main ideas and the most important details. In your own words, reduce the paragraph or section into a brief report of its general ideas.

UNDERSTANDING THE SKILL

Strategy: Understand and condense the text. The passage below tells about trade in West Africa between 300 and 1600. Following the description is a summary that condenses and also clarifies the key information.

Clarify: Look up words or concepts you don't know.

Summarize: Include key facts and statistics. Watch for numbers, dates, quantities, percentages, and facts.

WEST AFRICAN TRADE

The wealth of the savanna empires was based on trade in two precious commodities, gold and salt. The gold came from a forest region south of the savanna between the Niger and Senegal rivers. Working in utmost secrecy, miners dug gold from shafts as much as 100 feet deep or sifted it from fast-moving streams. Until about 1350, at least two thirds of the world's supply of gold came from West Africa.

Although rich in gold, the savanna and forest areas lacked salt, a material essential to human life. In contrast, the Sahara contained abundant deposits of salt.

Arab traders, eager to obtain West African gold, carried salt across the Sahara by camel caravan. After a long journey, they reached the market towns of the savanna. Meanwhile, the other traders brought gold north from the forest region. The two sets of merchants met in trading centers such as Timbuktu. Royal officials made sure that all traders weighed goods fairly and did business according to law.

Summarize: Look for topic sentences stating the main idea. These are often at the beginning of a section or paragraph. Restate each main idea briefly.

Clarify: Make sure you understand. Ask yourself questions and answer them. For example, who's carrying what?

Strategy: Clarify the main idea.

MAIN IDEA

Gold and salt were traded in West Africa.

Strategy: Write a summary.

Clarify and summarize: Write a summary to clarify your understanding of the main ideas.

SUMMARY

Trade in West Africa was based on gold from the south and salt from the north. Gold was mined in the forest regions. Two thirds of all the world's gold supply came from West Africa. Salt came from the desert. Arab traders met with African traders at trade centers such as Timbuktu.

APPLYING THE SKILL

Clarify and write your own summary. Turn to Chapter 30, pages 777–778, and read "Weapons of Totalitarianism." Note the main ideas. Look up any words you don't recognize. Then write a summary of the section. Condense the section in your own words.

1.3 Identifying Problems and Solutions

Identifying problems means finding and understanding the difficulties faced by a particular group of people at a certain time. Noticing how the people solved their problems is **identifying solutions.** Checking further to see how well those solutions worked is identifying outcomes.

UNDERSTANDING THE SKILL

Strategy: Look for problems and solutions. The passage below summarizes some economic problems facing Latin American nations during the early 20th century.

Look for implied problems. Problems may be suggested indirectly. This sentence suggests that a serious problem in Latin America was the uneven division of wealth.

Look for problems people face.

Look for solutions people tried to deal with each problem.

Check outcomes to the solutions. See how well the solutions worked. Sometimes the solution to one problem caused another problem.

LAND REFORM IN LATIN AMERICA

In Latin America, concentration of productive land in the hands of a few created extremes of wealth and poverty. Poor peasants had no choice but to work large estates owned by a few wealthy families. Landlords had no reason to invest in expensive farm machinery when labor was so cheap. Farming methods were inefficient and economic development was slow.

As Latin American nations began to modernize in the twentieth century, land ownership became a political issue. In response, a handful of countries began land reform programs. These programs divided large estates into smaller plots. Small plots of land were in turn distributed to farm families or granted to villages for communal farming. However, just turning over the land to the landless was not enough. Peasant farmers needed instruction, seeds, equipment, and credit. If the land and the people were to be productive, governments would have to provide assistance to the peasants.

Strategy: Make a chart.

Summarize the problems and solutions in a chart. Identify the problem or problems and the steps taken to solve them. Look for the short- and long-term effects of the solutions.

Problems	Solutions	Outcomes
A few wealthy people owned most of the land.	Land reform programs divided large estates into smaller plots.	Peasants were given land, and communal farms were set up.
Inefficient farming resulted in slow economic development.		
Peasants lacked equipment, resources, skills.	Governments would have to assist with loans and instruction.	Not stated.

APPLYING THE SKILL

Make your own chart. Turn to Chapter 31 and read "Europe After the War" on pages 801–803. Make a chart that lists the problems Germany faced after World War I. List the solutions that were tried and whatever outcomes are mentioned.

1.4 Analyzing Motives

Analyzing motives means examining the reasons why a person, group, or government takes a particular action. To understand those reasons, consider the needs, emotions, prior experiences, and goals of the person or group.

UNDERSTANDING THE SKILL

Strategy: Look for reasons why. On June 28, 1914, Serb terrorists assassinated Austria-Hungary's Archduke Franz Ferdinand and his wife when they visited Sarajevo, the capital of Bosnia. In the following passage, Borijove Jevtic, a Serb terrorist, explains why the assassination occurred. Before this passage, he explains that the terrorists had received a telegram stating that the Archduke would be visiting Sarajevo on June 28. The diagram that follows summarizes the motives of the terrorists for murdering the Archduke.

THE ASSASSINATION OF THE ARCHDUKE

How dared Franz Ferdinand, not only the representative of the oppressor but in his own person an arrogant tyrant, enter Sarajevo on that day? Such an entry was a studied insult.

28 June is a date engraved deeply in the heart of every Serb, so that the day has a name of its own. It is called the vidovnan. It is the day on which the old Serbian kingdom was conquered by the Turks at the battle of Amselfelde in 1389. It is also the day on which in the second Balkan War the Serbian arms took glorious revenge on the Turk for his old victory and for the years of enslavement.

That was no day for Franz Ferdinand, the new oppressor, to venture to the very doors of Serbia for a display of the force of arms which kept us beneath his heel.

Our decision was taken almost immediately. Death to the tyrant!

Look for motives based on past events or inspiring individuals.

Notice both positive and negative motives.

Look for motives based on basic needs and human emotions. Needs include food, shelter, safety, freedom. Emotions include fear, anger, pride, desire for revenge, patriotism, for example.

Strategy: Make a diagram.

Make a diagram that summarizes motives and actions. List the important action in the middle of the diagram. Then list motives in different categories around the action.

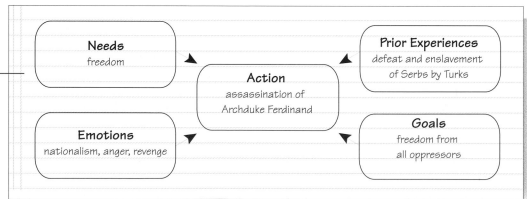

- **Needs** — freedom
- **Prior Experiences** — defeat and enslavement of Serbs by Turks
- **Action** — assassination of Archduke Ferdinand
- **Emotions** — nationalism, anger, revenge
- **Goals** — freedom from all oppressors

APPLYING THE SKILL

Make your own diagram. Turn to Chapter 27, Section 1, "Imperialists Divide Africa." Read the section and look for motives of European nations in acquiring lands in other parts of the world. Make a diagram like the one above showing the European nations' motives for taking the land.

1.5 Analyzing Causes; Recognizing Effects

Causes are the events, conditions, and other reasons that lead to an event. Causes happen before the event in time; they explain why it happened. **Effects** are the results or consequences of the event. One effect often becomes the cause of other effects, resulting in a chain of events. Causes and effects can be both short-term and long-term. Examining **cause-and-effect relationships** helps historians see how events are related and why they took place.

UNDERSTANDING THE SKILL

Strategy: Keep track of causes and effects as you read. The passage below describes events leading to the rise of feudalism in Japan. The diagram that follows summarizes the chain of causes and effects.

> **Effects: Look for results or consequences.** Sometimes these are indicated by clue words such as *brought about, led to, as a result,* and *consequently.*

> **Notice that an effect may be the cause of another event.** This begins a chain of causes and effects.

> **Causes: Look for clue words that show cause.** These include *because, due to, since,* and *therefore.*

> **Look for multiple causes and multiple effects.** The weakness of the central government caused the three effects shown here.

FEUDALISM COMES TO JAPAN

For most of the Heian period, the rich Fujiwara family held the real power in Japan. Members of this family held many influential posts. By about the middle of the eleventh century, the power of the central government and the Fujiwaras began to slip. This was due in part to court families' greater interest in luxury and artistic pursuits than in governing. ① Since the central government was weak, large landowners living away from the capital set up private armies. ② As a result, the countryside became lawless and dangerous. Armed soldiers on horseback preyed on farmers and travelers, while pirates took control of the seas. ③ For safety, farmers and small landowners traded parts of their land to strong warlords in exchange for protection. Because the lords had more land, the lords gained more power. This marked the beginning of a feudal system of localized rule like that of ancient China and medieval Europe.

Strategy: Make a cause-and-effect diagram.

> **Summarize cause-and-effect relationships in a diagram.** Starting with the first cause in a series, fill in the boxes until you reach the end result.

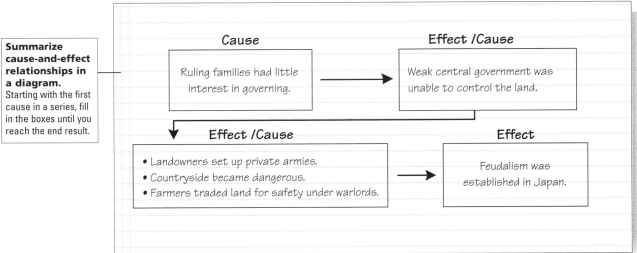

Cause

Ruling families had little interest in governing.

Effect /Cause

Weak central government was unable to control the land.

Effect /Cause

- Landowners set up private armies.
- Countryside became dangerous.
- Farmers traded land for safety under warlords.

Effect

Feudalism was established in Japan.

APPLYING THE SKILL

Make your own cause-and-effect diagram. Turn to Chapter 28, pages 730–731. Read "Juárez and *La Reforma*" and make notes about the causes and effects of Juárez's reform movement in Mexico. Make a diagram like the one shown above to summarize the information you find.

1.6 Comparing; Contrasting

Historians compare and contrast events, personalities, ideas, behaviors, beliefs, and institutions in order to understand them thoroughly. **Comparing** involves finding both similarities and differences between two or more things. **Contrasting** means examining only the differences between them.

UNDERSTANDING THE SKILL

Strategy: Look for similarities and differences. The following passage describes life in the ancient Greek city-states of Sparta and Athens. The Venn diagram below shows some of the similarities and differences between the two city-states.

Compare: Look for clue words indicating that two things are alike. Clue words include *all, both, like, as, likewise,* and *similarly.*

Contrast: Look for clue words that show how two things differ. Clue words include *unlike, by contrast, however, except, different,* and *on the other hand.*

SPARTA AND ATHENS

The Greek city-states developed separately but shared certain characteristics, including language and religion. Economically, all began as farming economies, and all except Sparta eventually moved to trade. Politically, all city-states, except for Sparta, evolved into early forms of democracies.

The leader in the movement to democracy was Athens. After a series of reforms, every Athenian citizen was considered equal before the law. However, as in the other Greek city-states, only about one fifth of the population were citizens. Slaves did much of the work, so Athenian citizens were free to create works of art, architecture, and literature, including drama.

By contrast, Sparta lived in constant fear of revolts by *helots*, people who were held in slave-like conditions to work the land. The city was set up as a military dictatorship, and Spartan men dedicated their lives to the military. In Sparta, duty, strength, and discipline were valued over beauty, individuality, and creativity. As a result, Spartans created little art, architecture, or literature.

Compare: Look for features that two subjects have in common. Here you learn that both Athens and Sparta started out as farming communities.

Contrast: Look for ways in which two things are different. Here you learn that Athens and Sparta had different values.

Strategy: Make a Venn diagram.

Compare and Contrast: Summarize similarities and differences in a Venn diagram. In the overlapping area, list characteristics shared by both subjects. Then, in one oval list the characteristics of one subject not shared by the other. In the other oval, list unshared characteristics of the second subject.

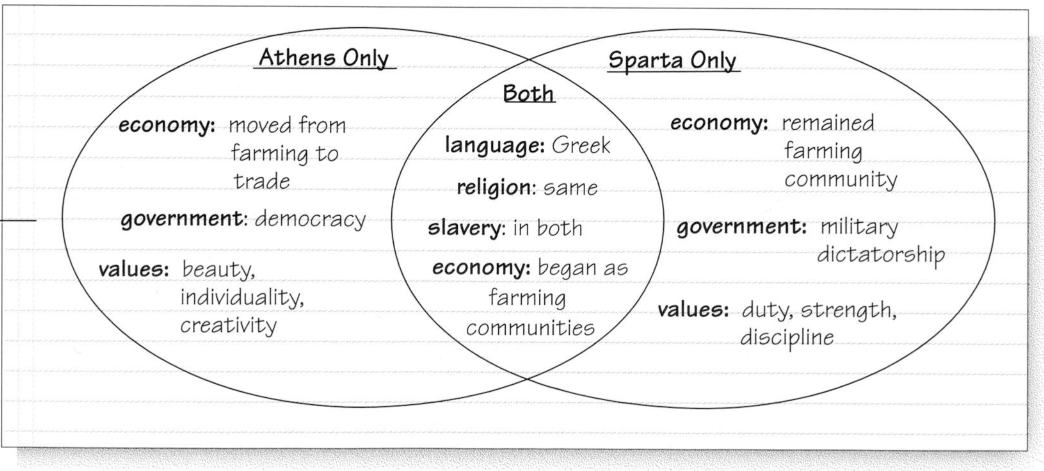

Athens Only

economy: moved from farming to trade

government: democracy

values: beauty, individuality, creativity

Both

language: Greek

religion: same

slavery: in both

economy: began as farming communities

Sparta Only

economy: remained farming community

government: military dictatorship

values: duty, strength, discipline

APPLYING THE SKILL

Make your own Venn diagram. Turn to Chapter 20, pages 493–494, and read the section called "Native American Reaction." Make a Venn diagram comparing and contrasting Dutch and English colonists' relations with Native Americans.

1.7 Distinguishing Fact from Opinion

Facts are events, dates, statistics, or statements that can be proved to be true. Facts can be checked for accuracy. **Opinions** are judgments, beliefs, and feelings of the writer or speaker.

UNDERSTANDING THE SKILL

Strategy: Find clues in the text. The following excerpt tells about the uprising of Jews in the Warsaw ghetto in 1943. The chart summarizes the facts and opinions.

THE WARSAW GHETTO UPRISING

With orders from Himmler to crush the Jews, the Nazis attacked on April 19, 1943, at the start of the holiday of Passover. Two thousand armed SS troops entered the ghetto, marching with tanks, rifles, machine guns, and trailers full of ammunition. The Jewish fighters were in position—in bunkers, in windows, on rooftops. They had rifles and handguns, hand grenades and bombs that they had made. And they let fly. . . .

Unbelievably, the Jews won the battle that day. The Germans were forced to retreat. . . . The Germans brought in more troops, and the fighting intensified. German pilots dropped bombs on the ghetto. . . .

On May 1, Goebbels [Nazi propaganda minister] wrote in his diary: "Of course this jest will probably not last long." He added a complaint. "But it shows what one can expect of the Jews if they have guns."

Goebbels' tone was mocking. But his forecast was inevitable—and correct. . . . Goebbels did not record in his diary, when the uprising was over, that the starving Jews of the ghetto, with their pathetic supply of arms, had held out against the German army for forty days, longer than Poland or France had held out.

Source: *A Nightmare in History*, by Miriam Chaikin. (New York: Clarion Books, 1987) pp. 77–78

Facts: Look for specific names, dates, statistics, and statements that can be proved. The first two paragraphs provide a factual account of the event.

Opinion: Look for judgment words that the writer uses to describe the people and events. Judgment words are often adjectives that are used to arouse a reader's emotions.

Opinion: Look for assertions, claims, hypotheses, and judgments. Here Goebbels expresses his opinion of the uprising and of the Jews.

Strategy: Make a chart.

Divide facts and opinions in a chart. Summarize and separate the facts from the opinions expressed in a passage.

FACTS	OPINIONS
On April 19, 1943, 2,000 armed SS troops attacked the Warsaw ghetto. Jewish fighters held out for 40 days.	*Goebbels:* The uprising was a jest, but showed the danger of letting Jews get hold of guns.
	Author: It is difficult to believe that Warsaw Jews with their pathetic supply of arms were able to defeat the powerful Nazis. The Jews showed greater courage and determination than did the Poles and French.

APPLYING THE SKILL

Make your own chart. Turn to Chapter 26, page 662, "Democratic Reform and Activism." Find the "Voice from the Past" from the Seneca Falls Convention. Make a chart in which you summarize the facts in your own words, and list the opinions and judgments stated. Look carefully at the language used in order to separate one from the other.

2.1 Developing Historical Perspective

Developing historical perspective means understanding events and people in the context of their times. It means not judging the past by current values, but by taking into account the beliefs of the time.

UNDERSTANDING THE SKILL

Strategy: Look for values of the past. The following passage was written by Bartolomé de Las Casas, a Spanish missionary who defended the rights of Native Americans. It challenges an argument presented by a scholar named Sepúlveda, who held that the superior Spaniards had the right to enslave the Native Americans. Following the passage is a chart that summarizes the information from a historical perspective.

Identify the historical figure, the occasion, and the date.

Explain how people's actions and words reflected the attitudes, values, and passions of the era. Las Casas challenges prejudices about Native Americans that were widely held in Europe. His language emphasizes a favorable comparison between Native American and European societies.

IN DEFENSE OF THE INDIANS (1550)
BARTOLOMÉ DE LAS CASAS

Now if we shall have shown that among our Indians of the western and southern shores (granting that we call them barbarians and that they are barbarians) there are important kingdoms, large numbers of people who live settled lives in a society, great cities, kings, judges and laws, persons who engage in commerce, buying, selling, lending, and the other contracts of the law of nations, will it not stand proved that the Reverend Doctor Sepúlveda has spoken wrongly and viciously against peoples like these? . . . From the fact that the Indians are barbarians it does not necessarily follow that they are incapable of government and have to be ruled by others, except to be taught about the Catholic faith and to be admitted to the holy sacraments. They are not ignorant, inhuman, or bestial. Rather, long before they had heard the word Spaniard they had properly organized states, wisely ordered by excellent laws, religion, and custom. They cultivated friendship and, bound together in common fellowship, lived in populous cities in which they wisely administered the affairs of both peace and war justly and equitably, truly governed by laws that at very many points surpass ours, and could have won the admiration of the sages of Athens. . . .

Look for clues to the attitudes, customs, and values of people living at the time. As a Spanish missionary, Las Casas assumes that Europeans are more civilized than Native Americans and that Native Americans need to be converted to Catholicism.

Notice words, phrases, and settings that reflect the period. Las Casas speaks from a time when Europeans looked to classical Greece as a benchmark for civilization.

Use historical perspective to understand Las Casas's attitudes. In a chart, list key words, phrases, and details from the passage. In a short paragraph, summarize the basic values and attitudes of Las Casas.

Strategy: Write a summary.

Key Phrases	Las Casas's In Defense of the Indians
• barbarians • Catholic faith • not inhuman, ignorant, or bestial • properly organized states, wisely ordered • sages of Athens	Las Casas argues that Native Americans are not inhuman and do not deserve cruelty and slavery. Rather, they are fully capable of "coming up" to the level of Spanish civilization. Although he makes the statement that Native Americans are barbarians, his language and comparisons seem to suggest that he believes them to be highly civilized in many respects. At the same time, he believes in the importance of converting them to Catholicism.

APPLYING THE SKILL

Write your own summary. Turn to Chapter 11, page 283, and read the excerpt from *The Tale of the Destruction of Riazan*. Read the passage using historical perspective. Then summarize your ideas in a chart like the one above.

Section 2: Using Critical Thinking

2.2 Formulating Historical Questions

Formulating historical questions is important as you examine primary sources—first-hand accounts, documents, letters, and other records of the past. As you analyze a source, ask questions about what it means and why it is significant. Then, when you are doing research, write questions that you want your research to answer. This step will help to guide your research and organize the information you collect.

UNDERSTANDING THE SKILL

Strategy: Question what you read. The Muslim scholar Ibn Battuta published an account of his journeys in Asia and Africa in the 1300s. Following is part of his description of China. After the passage is a web diagram that organizes historical questions about it.

Ask about the historical record itself. Who produced it? When was it produced?

Ask about the person who created the record. What judgments or opinions does the author express?

IBN BATTUTA IN CHINA, AROUND 1345

The Chinese themselves are infidels, who worship idols and burn their dead like the Hindus. . . . In every Chinese city there is a quarter for Muslims in which they live by themselves, and in which they have mosques both for the Friday services and for other religious purposes. The Muslims are honored and respected. The Chinese infidels eat the flesh of swine and dogs, and sell it in their markets. They are wealthy folk and well-to-do, but they make no display either in their food or their clothes. You will see one of their principal merchants, a man so rich that his wealth cannot be counted, wearing a coarse cotton tunic. But there is one thing that the Chinese take a pride in, that is gold and silver plate. Every one of them carries a stick, on which they lean in walking, and which they call "the third leg." Silk is very plentiful among them, because the silk-worm attaches itself to fruits and feeds on them without requiring much care. For that reason, it is so common as to be worn by even the very poorest there. Were it not for the merchants it would have no value at all, for a single piece of cotton cloth is sold in their country for the price of many pieces of silk.

Ask about the facts presented. Who were the main people? What did they do? What were they like?

Ask about the significance of the record. How would you interpret the information presented? How does it fit in with the history of this time and place? What more do you need to know to answer these questions?

Strategy: Make a web diagram.

Investigate a topic in more depth by asking questions. Ask a large question and then ask smaller questions that explore and develop from the larger question.

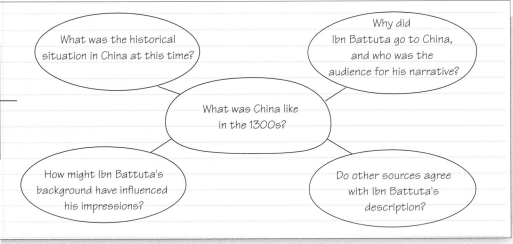

What was the historical situation in China at this time?

Why did Ibn Battuta go to China, and who was the audience for his narrative?

What was China like in the 1300s?

How might Ibn Battuta's background have influenced his impressions?

Do other sources agree with Ibn Battuta's description?

APPLYING THE SKILL

Make your own web diagram. Turn to the quotation by Bernal Díaz in Chapter 16, page 403. Use a web diagram to write historical questions about the passage.

Section 2: Using Critical Thinking

2.3 Hypothesizing

Hypothesizing means developing a possible explanation for historical events. A hypothesis is an educated guess about what happened in the past or what might happen in the future. A hypothesis takes available information, links it to previous experience and knowledge, and comes up with a possible explanation, conclusion, or prediction.

UNDERSTANDING THE SKILL

Strategy: Find clues in the reading. In studying the Indus Valley civilization, historians do not yet know exactly what caused that culture to decline. They have, however, developed hypotheses about what happened to it. Read this passage and look at the steps that are shown for building a hypothesis. Following the passage is a chart that organizes the information.

Identify the event, pattern, or trend you want to explain.

Determine the facts you have about the situation. These facts support various hypotheses about what happened to the Indus Valley civilization.

Develop a hypothesis that might explain the event. Historians hypothesize that a combination of ecological change and sudden catastrophe caused the Indus Valley civilization to collapse.

Determine what additional information you need to test the hypothesis. You might refer to a book about India, for example, to learn more about the impact of the Aryan invasions.

MYSTERIOUS END TO INDUS VALLEY CULTURE

Around 1750 B.C., the quality of building in the Indus Valley cities declined. Gradually, the great cities fell into decay. What happened? Some historians think that the Indus River changed course, as it tended to do, so that its floods no longer fertilized the fields near the cities. Other scholars suggest that people wore out the valley's land. They overgrazed it, overfarmed it, and overcut its trees, brush, and grass.

As the Indus Valley civilization neared its end, around 1500 B.C, a sudden catastrophe may have had a hand in the cities' downfall. Archaeologists have found a half-dozen groups of skeletons in the ruins of Mohenjo-Daro, seemingly never buried. Their presence suggests that the city, already weakened by its slow decline, may have been abandoned after a natural disaster or a devastating attack from human enemies. The Aryans, a nomadic people from north of the Hindu Kush mountains, swept into the Indus Valley at about this time. Whether they caused the collapse of the Indus Valley civilization or followed in its wake is not known.

Strategy: Make a chart.

Use a chart to summarize your hypothesis about events. Write down your hypothesis and the facts that support it. Then you can see what additional information you need to help prove or disprove it.

Hypothesis	Facts that support the hypothesis	Additional information needed
A combination of ecological change and sudden catastrophe caused the Indus Valley civilization to collapse	• Building quality declined • Indus River tended to change course • Unburied skeletons were found at Mohenjo-Daro • Aryan invasions occurred around same time	• What was Indus Valley culture like? • What were the geographical characteristics of the region? • How did overfarming tend to affect the environment? • What factors affected the decline of other ancient civilizations?

APPLYING THE SKILL

Make your own chart. Turn to Chapter 19, page 476, and read A Voice from the Past. Hypothesize what impact the introduction of firearms might have had on Japan. Then read the surrounding text material. List facts that support your hypothesis and what additional information you might gather to help prove or disprove it.

Section 2: Using Critical Thinking

2.4 Analyzing Issues

An issue is a matter of public concern or debate. Issues in history are usually economic, social, political, or moral. Historical issues are often more complicated than they first appear. **Analyzing an issue** means taking a controversy apart to find and describe the different points of view about the issue.

UNDERSTANDING THE SKILL

Strategy: Look for different sides of the issue. The following passage describes working conditions in English factories in the early 1800s. The cluster diagram that follows the passage helps you to analyze the issue of child labor.

> CHILDREN AT WORK
>
> **Look for a central problem with its causes and effects.**
>
> Child labor was one of the most serious problems of the early Industrial Revolution. Children as young as 6 years worked exhausting jobs in factories and mines. Because wages were very low, many families in cities could not survive unless all their members, including children, worked.
>
> In most factories, regular work hours were 6 in the morning to 6 in the evening, often with two "over-hours" until 8. It was common for 40 or more children to work together in one room—a room with little light or air. Those who lagged behind in their work were often beaten. Because safety was a low concern for many factory owners, accidents were common.
>
> In 1831, Parliament set up a committee to investigate abuses of child labor. Medical experts reported that long hours of factory work caused young children to become crippled or stunted in their growth. They recommended that children younger than age 14 should work no more than 8 hours. Factory owners responded that they needed children to work longer hours in order to be profitable. As one owner testified, reduced working hours for children would "much reduce the value of my mill and machinery, and consequently of . . . my manufacture." As a result of the committee's findings, Parliament passed the Factory Act of 1833. The act made it illegal to hire children under 9 years old, and it limited the working hours of older children.

Look for a central problem with its causes and effects.

Look for facts and statistics. Factual information helps you understand the issue and evaluate the different sides or arguments.

Look for different sides to the issue. You need to consider all sides of an issue before deciding your position.

Strategy: Make a cluster diagram.

If an issue is complex, make a diagram. A diagram can help you analyze an issue.

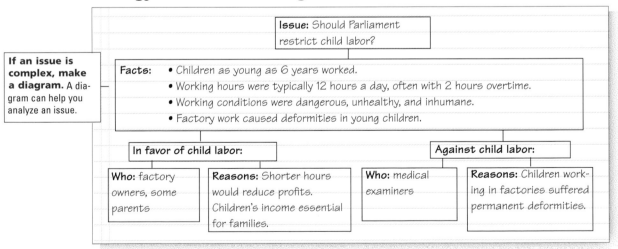

Issue: Should Parliament restrict child labor?

Facts:
• Children as young as 6 years worked.
• Working hours were typically 12 hours a day, often with 2 hours overtime.
• Working conditions were dangerous, unhealthy, and inhumane.
• Factory work caused deformities in young children.

In favor of child labor:
Who: factory owners, some parents
Reasons: Shorter hours would reduce profits. Children's income essential for families.

Against child labor:
Who: medical examiners
Reasons: Children working in factories suffered permanent deformities.

APPLYING THE SKILL

Make your own cluster diagram. Chapter 34, page 886, describes the partition of India. Make a cluster diagram to analyze the issue and the positions of the people involved.

Section 2: Using Critical Thinking

2.5 Analyzing Assumptions and Biases

An **assumption** is a belief or an idea that is taken for granted. Some assumptions are based on evidence; some are based on feelings. Whether assumptions are clearly stated or just implied, you can usually figure out what they are.

Bias is a prejudiced point of view. Historical accounts that are biased tend to be one-sided and reflect the personal prejudices of the historian.

UNDERSTANDING THE SKILL

Strategy: Think about the writer as you read. The European explorer Amerigo Vespucci reached the coast of Brazil in 1502, on his second voyage to the Americas. Below are his impressions of the people he met.

Identify the author and information about him or her. Does the author belong to a special-interest group, social class, political party, or movement that might promote a one-sided or slanted viewpoint on the subject?

Search for clues. Are there words, phrases, statements, or images that might convey a positive or negative slant? What might these clues reveal about the author's bias?

AMERIGO VESPUCCI REPORTS ON THE PEOPLE OF BRAZIL

For twenty-seven days I ate and slept among them, and what I learned about them is as follows.

Having no laws and no religious faith, they live according to nature. They understand nothing of the immortality of the soul. There is no possession of private property among them, for everything is in common. They have no boundaries of kingdom or province. They have no king, nor do they obey anyone. Each one is his own master. There is no administration of justice, which is unnecessary to them, because in their code no one rules. . . .

They are also a warlike people and very cruel to their own kind. . . . That which made me . . . astonished at their wars and cruelty was that I could not understand from them why they made war upon each other, considering that they held no private property or sovereignty of empire and kingdoms and did not know any such thing as lust for possession, that is pillaging or a desire to rule, which appear to me to be the causes of wars and every disorderly act. When we requested them to state the cause, they did not know how to give any other cause than that this curse upon them began in ancient times and they sought to avenge the deaths of their forefathers.

Examine the evidence. Is the information that the author presents consistent with other accounts? Is the behavior described consistent with human nature as you have observed it?

Strategy: Make a chart.

Make a chart of your analysis. For each of the heads listed on the left side of the chart, summarize information presented in the passage.

Vespucci's impressions of the native peoples of Brazil	
author, date	Amerigo Vespucci, 1502
occasion	exploration of coast of Brazil on second voyage to Americas
tone	judging, negative, superior
assumptions	Since the native people do not live in organized states and have no private property, they have no system of authority, laws, or moral principles. They have no apparent religious beliefs. They are warlike and cruel and seem to make war on one another for no reason.
bias	The author's comments about the soul seem to show a bias towards his own religious beliefs. He also reveals a prejudice that European customs and practices are superior to all others.

APPLYING THE SKILL

Make your own chart. Look at the quotation by the Qing emperor Kangxi in "A Voice from the Past" in Chapter 19, page 479. Summarize the underlying assumptions and biases using a chart like the one shown.

2.6 Evaluating Decisions and Courses of Action

Evaluating decisions means making judgments about the decisions that historical figures made. Historians evaluate decisions on the basis of their moral implications and their costs and benefits from different points of view.

Evaluating various courses of action means carefully judging the choices that historical figures had to make. By doing this, you can better understand why they made some of the decisions they did.

UNDERSTANDING THE SKILL

Strategy: Look for choices and reasons. The following passage describes the decisions U.S. President John Kennedy had to make when he learned of Soviet missile bases in Cuba. As you read it, think of the alternative responses he could have made at each turn of events. Following the passage is a chart that organizes information about the Cuban missile crisis.

THE CUBAN MISSILE CRISIS

During the summer of 1962, the flow of Soviet weapons into Cuba—including nuclear missiles—greatly increased. President Kennedy responded cautiously at first, issuing a warning that the United States would not tolerate the presence of offensive nuclear weapons in Cuba. Then, on October 16, photographs taken by American U-2 planes showed the president that the Soviets were secretly building missile bases on Cuba. Some of the missiles, armed and ready to fire, could reach U.S. cities in minutes.

On the evening of October 22, the president made public the evidence of missiles and stated his ultimatum: any missile attack from Cuba would trigger an all-out attack on the Soviet Union. Soviet ships continued to head toward the island, while the U.S. navy prepared to stop them and U.S. invasion troops massed in Florida. To avoid confrontation, the Soviet ships suddenly halted. Soviet Premier Nikita Khrushchev offered to remove the missiles from Cuba in exchange for a pledge not to invade the island. Kennedy agreed, and the crisis ended.

Some people criticized Kennedy for practicing brinkmanship, when private talks might have resolved the crisis without the threat of nuclear war. Others believed he had been too soft and had passed up a chance to invade Cuba and oust its Communist leader, Fidel Castro.

Look at decisions made by individuals or by groups. Notice the decisions Kennedy made in response to Soviet actions.

Analyze a decision in terms of the choices that were possible. Both Kennedy and Khrushchev faced the same choice. Either could carry out the threat, or either could back down quietly and negotiate.

Look at the outcome of the decisions.

Strategy: Make a chart.

Make a simple chart of your analysis. The problem was that Soviet nuclear missiles were being shipped to Cuba. The decision to be made was how the United States should respond.

Kennedy's choices	pros	cons	your evaluation
Publicly confront Khrushchev with navy and prepare for war.	Show Khrushchev and world the power and strong will of the U.S.; force him to back off.	Nuclear war could occur.	In your opinion, which was the better choice? Why?
Say nothing to U.S. public and negotiate quietly.	Avoid frightening U.S. citizens and avoid threat of nuclear war.	The U.S. would look weak publicly; Khrushchev could carry out plan.	

APPLYING THE SKILL

Make a chart. Chapter 31, page 815, describes the decisions British and French leaders made when Hitler took over the Sudetenland in Czechoslovakia just before World War II. Make a chart like the one shown to summarize the pros and cons of their choice of appeasement and evaluate their decision yourself.

2.7 Forming and Supporting Opinions

Historians do more than reconstruct facts about the past. They also **form opinions** about the information they encounter. Historians form opinions as they interpret the past and judge the significance of historical events and people. They **support their opinions** with logical thinking, facts, examples, quotes, and references to events.

UNDERSTANDING THE SKILL

Strategy: Find arguments to support your opinion. In the following passage, journalist Paul Gray summarizes differing opinions about the significance and impact of Columbus's voyages. As you read, develop your own opinion about the issue.

HOW SHOULD HISTORY VIEW THE LEGACY OF COLUMBUS?

In one version of the story, Columbus and the Europeans who followed him brought civilization to two immense, sparsely populated continents, in the process fundamentally enriching and altering the Old World from which they had themselves come.

Among other things, Columbus' journey was the first step in a long process that eventually produced the United States of America, a daring experiment in democracy that in turn became a symbol and a haven of individual liberty for people throughout the world. But the revolution that began with his voyages was far greater than that. It altered science, geography, philosophy, agriculture, law, religion, ethics, government—the sum, in other words, of what passed at the time as Western culture.

Increasingly, however, there is a counterchorus, an opposing rendition of the same events that deems Columbus' first footfall in the New World to be fatal to the world he invaded, and even to the rest of the globe. The indigenous peoples and their cultures were doomed by European arrogance, brutality, and infectious diseases. Columbus' gift was slavery to those who greeted him; his arrival set in motion the ruthless destruction, continuing at this very moment, of the natural world he entered. Genocide, ecocide, exploitation . . . are deemed to be a form of Eurocentric theft of history from [the Native Americans].

Decide what you think about a subject after reading all the information available to you. After reading this passage, you might decide that Columbus's legacy was primarily one of genocide, cruelty, and slavery. On the other hand, you might believe that, despite the negatives, his voyages produced many long-term benefits.

Consider the opinions and interpretations of historians and other experts. Weigh their arguments as you form your own opinion.

Support your opinion with facts, quotes, and examples, including references to similar events from other historical eras.

Strategy: Make a chart.

Summarize your opinion and supporting information in a chart. Write an opinion and then list facts, examples, interpretations, or other information that support it.

Opinion: Voyages of Columbus brought more bad than good to the Americas	
Facts:	**Historical interpretations:**
• Europeans replaced existing cultures with their own	• Europeans were arrogant and brutal
• European diseases killed many Native Americans	• Columbus's arrival set in motion ruthless destruction of environment
• Columbus enslaved Native Americans	• Through conquest and exploitation, Europeans "stole" Native Americans' history and culture

APPLYING THE SKILL

Strategy: Make your own chart. Look at the Different Perspectives on Economics and the Environment in Chapter 36, page 951. Read the selections and form your own opinion about the concept of sustainable development. Summarize your supporting data in a chart like the one shown.

Section 2: Using Critical Thinking

2.8 Making Inferences

Inferences are ideas and meanings not stated in the material. **Making inferences** means reading between the lines to extend the information provided. Your inferences are based on careful study of what is stated in the passage as well as your own common sense and previous knowledge.

UNDERSTANDING THE SKILL

Strategy: Develop inferences from the facts. This passage describes the Nok culture of West Africa. Following the passage is a diagram that organizes the facts and ideas that lead to inferences.

Read the stated facts and ideas.

Use your knowledge, logic, and common sense to draw conclusions. You could infer from these statements that the Nok were a settled people with advanced technology and a rich culture.

THE NOK CULTURE

The earliest known culture of West Africa was that of the Nok people. They lived in what is now Nigeria between 900 B.C. and A.D. 200. Their name came from the village where the first artifacts from their culture were discovered by archaeologists. The Nok were farmers. They were also the first West African people known to smelt iron. The Nok began making iron around 500 B.C., using it to make tools for farming and weapons for hunting. These iron implements lasted longer than wood or stone and vastly improved the lives of the Nok.

Nok artifacts have been found in an area stretching for 300 miles between the Niger and Benue rivers. Many are sculptures made of terra cotta, a reddish-brown clay. Carved in great artistic detail, some depict the heads of animals such as elephants and others depict human heads. The features of some of the heads reveal a great deal about their history. One of the human heads, for example, shows an elaborate hairdo arranged in six buns, a style that is still worn by some people in Nigeria today. This similarity suggests that the Nok may have been the ancestors of modern-day Africans.

Consider what you already know that could apply. Your knowledge of history might lead you to infer the kinds of improvements in life brought about by better farming tools.

Recognize inferences that are already made. Phrases like "the evidence suggests" or "historians believe" indicate inferences and conclusions experts have made from historical records.

Strategy: Make a diagram.

Summarize the facts and inferences you make in a diagram.

Stated Facts and Ideas	Inferences
• iron farming tools • iron harder than wood • tools improved life	iron tools improved agriculture and contributed to cultural development
• Nok artifacts found in 300 mile radius	Nok culture spread across this area
• heads carved in great artistic detail	Nok were skilled potters and sculptors
• sculptures included elephant heads	elephants played a role in people's lives

APPLYING THE SKILL

Make your own diagram. Read the Tamil poem from ancient India quoted in Chapter 7 on page 178. Using a chart like the one above, make inferences from the poem about its author, its subject, and the culture it comes from.

2.9 Drawing Conclusions

Drawing conclusions means analyzing what you have read and forming an opinion about its meaning. To draw conclusions, you look closely at the facts, combine them with inferences you make, and then use your own common sense and experience to decide what the facts mean.

UNDERSTANDING THE SKILL

Strategy: Combine information to draw conclusions. The passage below presents information about the reunification of East and West Germany in 1990. The diagram that follows shows how to organize the information to draw conclusions.

GERMANY IS REUNIFIED

On October 3, 1990, Germany once again became a single nation. After more than 40 years of Communist rule, most East Germans celebrated their new political freedoms. Families that had been separated for years could now visit whenever they chose.

Economically, the newly united Germany faced serious problems. More than 40 years of Communist rule had left East Germany in ruins. Its transportation and telephone systems had not been modernized since World War II. State-run industries in East Germany had to be turned over to private control and operate under free-market rules. However, many produced shoddy goods that could not compete in the global market.

Rebuilding eastern Germany's bankrupt economy was going to be a difficult, costly process. Some experts estimated the price tag for reunification could reach $200 billion. In the short-term, the government had to provide unemployment benefits to some 1.4 million workers from the east who found themselves out of work.

In spite of these problems, Germans had reasons to be optimistic. Unlike other Eastern European countries, who had to transform their Communist economies by their own means, East Germany had the help of a strong West Germany. Many Germans may have shared the outlook expressed by one worker: "Maybe things won't be rosy at first, but the future will be better."

Read carefully to understand all the facts.
Fact: Reunification brought social and political freedoms to East Germans.

Read between the lines to make inferences.
Inference: After a market economy was introduced, many industries in eastern Germany failed, which put people out of work.

Use the facts to make an inference.
Inference: Reunification put a strain on government resources.

Ask questions of the material.
What are the long-term economic prospects for eastern Germany? Conclusion: Although it faced challenges, it seemed to have a greater chance for success than other former Communist countries.

Strategy: Make a diagram.

Summarize the facts, inferences, and your conclusion in a diagram.

Facts	Inferences	Conclusion About Passage
East Germans gained freedoms.	East Germans welcomed the end of Communist rule.	Although eastern Germany was in bad shape at the time of reunification, it had the advantage of the strength of western Germany as it made the transition to democracy and capitalism.
Transportation and telephone systems were outmoded.	Rebuilding took time.	
State-run industries produced shoddy goods.	Industries couldn't compete in free-market economy.	
Unemployment skyrocketed.	Reunification put a great financial burden on Germany.	
Cost for reunification could be $200 billion.		

APPLYING THE SKILL

Strategy: Make a diagram. Look at Chapter 6, pages 146–148, on the collapse of the Roman Republic. As you read, draw conclusions based on the facts. Use the diagram above as a model for organizing facts, inferences, and conclusions about the passage.

Section 2: Using Critical Thinking

2.10 Synthesizing

Synthesizing is the skill historians use in developing interpretations of the past. Like detective work, synthesizing involves putting together clues, information, and ideas to form an overall picture of a historical event.

UNDERSTANDING THE SKILL

Strategy: Build an interpretation as you read. The following passage describes the first settlement of North and Central America. The call-outs indicate the different kinds of information that lead to a synthesis—an overall picture of Native American life.

Read carefully to understand the facts. Facts such as these enable you to base your interpretations on physical evidence.

Look for explanations that link the facts together. This statement is based on the evidence provided by baskets, bows and arrows, and nets, which are mentioned in the sentences that follow.

THE FIRST AMERICANS

From the discovery of chiseled arrowheads and charred bones at ancient sites, it appears that the earliest Americans lived as big game hunters. The woolly mammoth, their largest prey, provided them with food, clothing, and bones for constructing tools and shelters. People gradually shifted to hunting small game and gathering available plants. They created baskets to collect nuts, wild rice, chokeberries, gooseberries, and currants. Later they invented bows and arrows to hunt small game such as jackrabbits and deer. They wove nets to fish the streams and lakes.

Between 10,000 and 15,000 years ago, a revolution took place in what is now central Mexico. People began to raise plants as food. Maize may have been the first domesticated plant, with pumpkins, peppers, beans, and potatoes following. Agriculture spread to other regions.

The rise of agriculture brought about tremendous changes to the Americas. Agriculture made it possible for people to remain in one place. It also enabled them to accumulate and store surplus food. As their surplus increased, people had the time to develop skills and more complex ideas about the world. From this agricultural base rose larger, more stable societies and increasingly complex societies.

Bring together the information you have about a subject. This interpretation brings together different kinds of information to arrive at a new understanding of the subject.

Consider what you already know that could apply. Your general knowledge will probably lead you to accept this statement as reasonable.

Strategy: Make a cluster diagram.

Summarize your synthesis in a diagram. Use a cluster diagram to organize the facts, opinions, examples, and interpretations that you have brought together to form a synthesis.

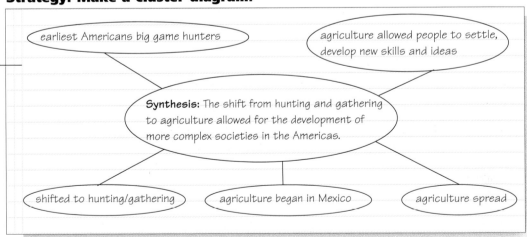

- earliest Americans big game hunters
- agriculture allowed people to settle, develop new skills and ideas
- **Synthesis:** The shift from hunting and gathering to agriculture allowed for the development of more complex societies in the Americas.
- shifted to hunting/gathering
- agriculture began in Mexico
- agriculture spread

APPLYING THE SKILL

Make your own cluster diagram. In Chapter 17 on pages 428–429, the beginnings of the Protestant Reformation are discussed. Read the passage and look for information to support a synthesis about its fundamental causes.

SKILLBUILDER HANDBOOK **1007**

Section 3: Exploring Historical Evidence

3.1 Primary and Secondary Sources

Primary sources are written or created by people who lived during a historical event. The writers might have been participants or observers. Primary sources include letters, diaries, journals, speeches, newspaper articles, magazine articles, eye-witness accounts, and autobiographies.

Secondary sources are derived from primary sources by people who were not present at the original event. They are written after the event. They often combine information from a number of different accounts. Secondary sources include history books, historical essays, and biographies.

UNDERSTANDING THE SKILL

Strategy: Evaluate the information in each type of source. This passage describes political reforms made by Pericles, who led Athens from 461 to 429 B.C. It is mainly a secondary source, but it includes a primary source in the form of a speech.

> **Secondary source: Look for information collected from several sources.** Here the writer presents an overall picture of the reforms made by Pericles and the reasons for them.

> **Primary source: Analyze the source using historical perspective.** Read the source for factual information while also noting the speaker's opinions, biases, assumptions, and point of view.

STRONGER DEMOCRACY IN ATHENS

To strengthen democracy, Pericles increased the number of public officials who were paid salaries. Before, only wealthier citizens could afford to hold public office because most positions were unpaid. Now even the poorest could serve if elected or chosen by lot. This reform made Athens one of the most democratic governments in history. However, political rights were still limited to those with citizenship status—a minority of Athens' total population.

The introduction of direct democracy was an important legacy of Periclean Athens. Few other city-states practiced this style of government. In Athens, male citizens who served in the assembly established all the important policies that affected the polis. In a famous "Funeral Oration" for soldiers killed in the Peloponnesian War, Pericles expressed his great pride in Athenian democracy:

Our constitution is called a democracy because power is in the hands not of a minority but of the whole people. When it is a question of settling private disputes, everyone is equal before the law; when it is a question of putting one person before another in positions of public responsibility, what counts is not membership of a particular class, but the actual ability which the man possesses. No one, as long as he has it in him to be of service to the state, is kept in political obscurity because of poverty.

> **Secondary source: Look for analysis and interpretation.** A secondary source provides details and perspective that are missing in a primary source. It also provides context for the secondary source.

> **Primary source: Identify the author and evaluate his or her credentials.** How is the speaker connected to the event? Here, this speaker is Pericles himself.

Strategy: Make a chart.

> **Summarize information from primary and secondary sources on a chart.**

Primary Source	Secondary Source
Author: Pericles	Author: world history textbook
Qualifications: main figure in the events described	Qualifications: had access to multiple accounts of event
Information: describes his view of Athenian democracy—power in the hands of "the whole people"	Information: puts events in historical perspective—Athens one of most democratic governments in history but limited rights to citizens

APPLYING THE SKILL

Make your own chart. Read the passage "Mehmet II Conquers Constantinople" in Chapter 18, pages 444–445, which includes a quote from the Muslim historian Oruc. Make a chart in which you summarize information from the primary and secondary sources.

Section 3: Exploring Historical Evidence

3.2 Visual, Audio, Multimedia Sources

In addition to written accounts, historians use many kinds of **visual sources.** These include paintings, photographs, political cartoons, and advertisements. Visual sources are rich with historical details and sometimes reflect the mood and trends of an era better than words can.

Spoken language has always been a primary means of passing on human history. **Audio sources,** such as recorded speeches, interviews, press conferences, and radio programs, continue the oral tradition today.

Movies, CD-ROMs, television, and computer software are the newest kind of historical sources, called **multimedia sources.**

UNDERSTANDING THE SKILL

Strategy: Examine the source carefully. Below are two portraits from the late 1700s, one of Marie Antoinette, the queen of France, and one of a woman who sells vegetables at the market. The chart that follows summarizes historical information gained from interpreting and comparing the two paintings.

A Woman of the Revolution [*La maraîchère*] (1795), Jacques Louis David

Marie Antoinette, Jacques Gautier d'Agoty

Identify the subject and source.

Identify important visual details. Look at the faces, poses, clothing, hairstyles, and other elements.

Make inferences from the visual details. Marie Antoinette's rich clothing and her hand on the globe symbolize her wealth and power. The contrast between the common woman's ordinary clothing and her defiant pose suggests a different attitude about power.

Use comparisons, information from other sources, and your own knowledge to give support to your interpretation. Royalty usually had their portraits painted in heroic poses. Ordinary people were not usually the subjects of such portraits. David's choice of subject and pose suggests that he sees the common people as the true heroes of France.

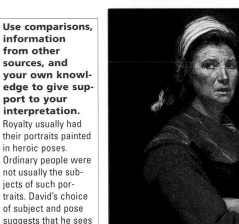

Strategy: Make a chart.

Summarize your interpretation in a simple chart.

Subject	Visual Details	Inferences	Message
Common woman	Face is worn and clothing is plain, but her head is held high and she wears the red scarf of revolution	Has worked hard for little in life, but strong, proud, and defiant	Although the details are strikingly different, the two paintings convey similar characteristics about their subjects.
Marie Antoinette	Richly dressed and made up; strikes an imperial pose	Lives life of comfort and power; proud, strong, and defiant	

APPLYING THE SKILL

Make your own chart. Turn to the detail from a mural by Diego Rivera in Chapter 16, page 403. The painting is Rivera's historical re-creation of an Aztec festival. Use a chart like the one above to analyze and interpret the painting.

3.6 Using the Internet

The **Internet** is a network of computers associated with universities, libraries, news organizations, government agencies, businesses, and private individuals worldwide. Each location on the Internet has a **home page** with its own address, or **URL.**

With a computer connected to the Internet, you can reach the home pages of many organizations and services. You might view your library's home page to find the call number of a book or visit an on-line magazine to read an article. On some sites you can view documents, photographs, and even moving pictures with sound.

The international collection of home pages, known as the **World Wide Web**, is a good source of up-to-the minute information about current events as well as in-depth research on historical subjects. This textbook contains many suggestions for navigating the World Wide Web. Begin by entering **www.mcdougallittell.com** to access the home page for McDougal Littell World History.

UNDERSTANDING THE SKILL

Strategy: Explore the elements on the screen. The computer screen below shows the home page of the history area at PBS, the public television service in Washington, D.C.

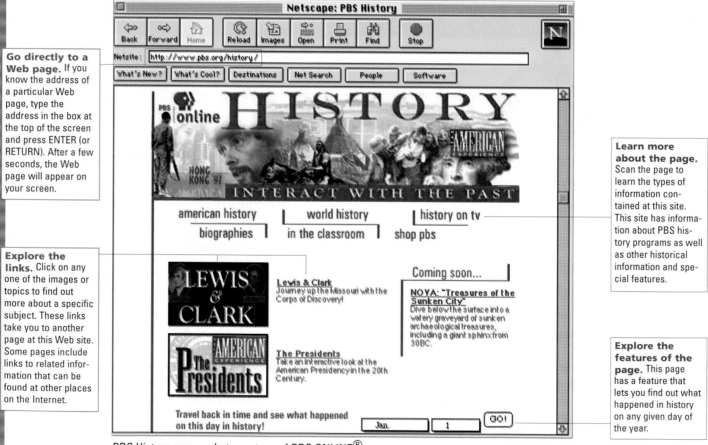

Go directly to a Web page. If you know the address of a particular Web page, type the address in the box at the top of the screen and press ENTER (or RETURN). After a few seconds, the Web page will appear on your screen.

Explore the links. Click on any one of the images or topics to find out more about a specific subject. These links take you to another page at this Web site. Some pages include links to related information that can be found at other places on the Internet.

Learn more about the page. Scan the page to learn the types of information contained at this site. This site has information about PBS history programs as well as other historical information and special features.

Explore the features of the page. This page has a feature that lets you find out what happened in history on any given day of the year.

PBS History screen shot courtesy of PBS ONLINE®.

APPLYING THE SKILL

Do your own Internet research. Turn to Chapter 34, Section 4, "Conflicts in the Middle East." Read the section and make a list of topics you would like to research. If you have a computer with Internet access, go to the McDougal Littell World History home page **www.mcdougallittell.com**. Click on "General World History Links" and then click on "Perspectives on the Present" to begin your search.

Glossary

The Glossary is an alphabetical listing of many of the key terms from the chapters, along with their meanings. The definitions listed in the Glossary are the ones that apply to the way the words are used in this textbook. The Glossary gives the part of speech of each word. The following abbreviations are used:

adj. adjective   *n.* noun   *v.* verb

Pronunciation Key

Some of the words in this book are followed by respellings that show how the words are pronounced. The following key will help you understand what sounds are represented by the letters used in the respellings.

Symbol	Examples	Symbol	Examples
a	apple [AP·uhl], catch [kach]	oh	road, [rohd], know [noh]
ah	barn [bahrn], pot [paht]	oo	school [skool], glue [gloo]
air	bear [bair], dare [dair]	ow	out [owt], cow [kow]
aw	bought [bawt], horse [hawrs]	oy	coin [koyn], boys [boyz]
ay	ape [ayp], mail [mayl]	p	pig [pihg], top [tahp]
b	bell [behl], table [TAY·buhl]	r	rose [rohz], star [stahr]
ch	chain [chayn], ditch [dihch]	s	soap [sohp], icy [EYE·see]
d	dog [dawg], rained [raynd]	sh	share [shair], nation [NAY·shuhn]
ee	even [EE·vuhn], meal [meel]	t	tired [tyrd], boat [boht]
eh	egg [ehg], ten [tehn]	th	thin [thihn], mother [MUH·thuhr]
eye	iron [EYE·uhrn]	u	pull [pul], look [luk]
f	fall [fawl], laugh [laf]	uh	bump [buhmp], awake [uh·WAYK],
g	gold [gohld], big [bihg]		happen [HAP·uhn], pencil [PEHN·suhl],
h	hot [haht], exhale [ehks·HAYL]		pilot [PY·luht]
hw	white [hwyt]	ur	earth [urth], bird [burd], worm [wurm]
ih	into [IHN·too], sick [sihk]	v	vase [vays], love [luhv]
j	jar [jahr], badge [baj]	w	web [wehb], twin [twihn]
k	cat [kat], luck [luhk]	y	As a consonant: yard [yahrd], mule [myool]
l	load [lohd], ball [bawl]		As a vowel: ice [ys], tried [tryd], sigh [sy]
m	make [mayk], gem [jehm]	z	zone [zohn], reason [REE·zuhn]
n	night [nyt], win [wihn]	zh	treasure [TREHZH·uhr], garage [guh·RAHZH]
ng	song [sawng], anger [ANG·guhr]		

Syllables that are stressed when the words are spoken appear in CAPITAL LETTERS in the respellings. For example, the respelling of *patterns* (PAT·uhrnz) shows that the first syllable of the word is stressed.

Syllables that appear in SMALL CAPITAL LETTERS are also stressed, but not as strongly as those that appear in capital letters. For example, the respelling of *interaction* (IHN·tuhr·AK·shuhn) shows that the third syllable receives the main stress and the first syllable receives a secondary stress.

A

Abbasids [uh·BAS·IHDZ] *n.* a dynasty that ruled much of the Muslim Empire from A.D. 750 to 1258. (p. 240)

Aborigine [AB·uh·RIHJ·uh·nee] *n.* a member of any of the native peoples of Australia. (p. 665)

absolute monarch [MAHN·uhrk] *n.* a king or queen who has unlimited power and seeks to control all aspects of society. (p. 517)

absolute ruler *n.* a ruler who has total power. (p. 147)

accommodation [uh·KAHM·uh·DAY·shuhn] *n.* an acceptance of the ideas and customs of other cultures. (p. 961)

acropolis [uh·KRAHP·uh·lihs] *n.* a fortified hilltop in an ancient Greek city. (p. 115)

Aksum [AHK·soom] *n.* an African kingdom, in what is now Ethiopia and Eritrea, that reached the height of its power in the fourth century A.D. (p. 199)

al-Andalus [al·AN·duh·LUS] *n.* a Muslim-ruled region in what is now Spain, established in the eighth century A.D. (p. 240)

Allah [AL·uh] *n.* God (an Arabic word, used mainly in Islam). (p. 234)

Allies [uh·LYZ] *n.* in World War I, the nations of Great Britain, France, and Russia, along with the other nations that fought on their side; also, the group of nations—including Great Britain, the Soviet Union, and the United States—that opposed the Axis Powers in World War II. (p. 748)

Almohads [AL·moh·HADZ] *n.* a group of Islamic reformers who overthrew the Almoravid Dynasty and established an empire in North Africa and southern Spain in the 12th century A.D. (p. 370)

Almoravids [AL·muh·RAHV·uhdz] *n.* an Islamic religious brotherhood that established an empire in North Africa and southern Spain in the 11th century A.D. (p. 370)

Anabaptists [AN·uh·BAP·tihst] *n.* in the Reformation, a Protestant group that believed in baptizing only those persons who were old enough to decide to be Christian and in separation of church and state. (p. 434)

Anasazi [AH·nuh·SAH·zee] *n.* an early Native American people who lived in the American Southwest. (p. 391)

Anatolia [AN·uh·TOH·lee·uh] *n.* the Southwest Asian peninsula now occupied by the Asian part of Turkey—also called Asia Minor. (p. 58)

Angkor Wat [ANG·kawr WAHT] *n.* a temple complex built in the Khmer Empire and dedicated to the Hindu god Vishnu. (p. 309)

Anglican [ANG·glih·kuhn] *adj.* relating to the Church of England. (p. 432)

animism [AN·uh·MIHZ·uhm] *n.* the belief that spirits are present in animals, plants, and other natural objects. (p. 197)

annexation [AN·ihk·SAY·shuhn] *n.* the adding of a region to the territory of an existing political unit. (pp. 709, 723)

annul [uh·NUHL] *v.* to cancel or put an end to. (p. 431)

anti-Semitism [AN·tee·SEHM·ih·TIHZ·uhm] *n.* prejudice against Jews. (p. 663)

apartheid [uh·PAHRT·hyt] *n.* a South African policy of complete legal separation of the races, including the banning of all social contacts between blacks and whites. (p. 919)

apostle [uh·PAHS·uhl] *n.* one of the followers of Jesus who preached and spread his teachings. (p. 153)

appeasement *n.* the making of concessions to an aggressor in order to avoid war. (p. 813)

aqueduct [AK·wih·DUHKT] *n.* a pipeline or channel built to carry water to populated areas. (p. 167)

aristocracy [AR·ih·STAHK·ruh·see] *n.* a government in which power is in the hands of a hereditary ruling class or nobility. (p. 115)

armistice [AHR·mih·stihs] *n.* an agreement to stop fighting. (p. 757)

artifact *n.* a human-made object, such as a tool, weapon, or piece of jewelry. (p. 7)

artisan [AHR·tih·zuhn] *n.* a skilled worker, such as a weaver or a potter, who makes goods by hand. (p. 18)

Aryans [AIR·ee·uhnz] *n.* **1.** an Indo-European people who, about 1500 B.C., began to migrate into the Indian subcontinent (p. 59). **2.** to the Nazis, the Germanic peoples who formed a "master race." (p. 831)

assembly line *n.* in a factory, an arrangement in which a product is moved from worker to worker, with each person performing a single task in its manufacture. (p. 674)

assimilation [uh·SIHM·uh·LAY·shuhn] *n.* **1.** the adoption of a conqueror's culture by a conquered people (p. 185). **2.** a policy in which a nation forces or encourages a subject people to adopt its institutions and customs. (p. 691)

Assyria [uh·SEER·ee·uh] *n.* a Southwest Asian kingdom that controlled a large empire from about 850 to 612 B.C. (p. 88)

Atlantic Charter *n.* a declaration of principles issued in August 1941 by British prime minister Winston Churchill and U.S. president Franklin Roosevelt, on which the Allied peace plan at the end of World War II was based. (p. 826)

Atlantic slave trade *n.* the buying, transporting, and selling of Africans for work in the Americas. (p. 496)

autocracy [aw·TAHK·ruh·see] *n.* a government in which the ruler has unlimited power and uses it in an arbitrary manner. (p. 100)

Axis Powers *n.* in World War II, the nations of Germany, Italy, and Japan, which had formed an alliance in 1936. (p. 813)

ayllu [EYE·loo] *n.* in Incan society, a small community or clan whose members worked together for the common good. (p. 408)

B

balance of power *n.* a political situation in which no one nation is powerful enough to pose a threat to others. (p. 593)

Balfour Declaration *n.* a statement that the British government supported the establishment of a Jewish national homeland in Palestine, made in a 1917 letter by British foreign secretary Sir Arthur Balfour. (p. 901)

Balkans [BAWL·kuhnz] *n.* the region of southeastern Europe now occupied by Greece, Albania, Bulgaria, Romania, the European part of Turkey, and the former republics of Yugoslavia. (p. 609)

Bantu-speaking peoples *n.* the speakers of a related group of languages who, beginning about 2,000 years ago, migrated from West Africa into most of the southern half of Africa. (p. 204)

baroque [buh·ROHK] *adj.* relating to a grand, ornate style that characterized European painting, music, and architecture in the 1600s and early 1700s. (p. 559)

barter *n.* a form of trade in which people exchange goods and services without the use of money. (p. 21)

Battle of Britain *n.* a series of battles between German and British air forces, fought over Britain in 1940–1941. (p. 824)

Battle of Guadalcanal [GWAHD·uhl·kuh·NAL] *n.* a 1942–1943 battle of World War II, in which Allied troops drove Japanese forces from the Pacific island of Guadalcanal. (p. 830)

Battle of Midway *n.* a 1942 sea and air battle of World War II, in which American forces defeated Japanese forces in the central Pacific. (p. 829)

Battle of Stalingrad [STAH·lihn·GRAD] *n.* a 1942–1943 battle of World War II, in which German forces were defeated in their attempt to capture the city of Stalingrad in the Soviet Union. (p. 836)

Battle of the Bulge *n.* a 1944–1945 battle in which Allied forces turned back the last major German offensive of World War II. (p. 839)

Battle of Trafalgar [truh·FAL·guhr] *n.* an 1805 naval battle in which Napoleon's forces were defeated by a British fleet under the command of Horatio Nelson. (p. 587)

Benin [buh·NIHN] *n.* a kingdom that arose near the Niger River delta in the 1300s and became a major West African state in the 1400s. (p. 377)

Beringia [buh·RIHN·jee·uh] *n.* an ancient land bridge over which the earliest Americans are believed to have migrated from Asia into the Americas. (p. 211)

Berlin Conference of 1884–85 *n.* a meeting at which representatives of European nations agreed upon rules for the European colonization of Africa. (p. 687)

Bill of Rights *n.* the first ten amendments to the U.S. Constitution, which protect citizens' basic rights and freedoms. (p. 567)

bishop *n.* a high-ranking Christian official who supervises a number of local churches. (p. 156)

blitzkrieg [BLIHTS·kreeg] *n.* "lightning war"—a form of warfare in which surprise attacks with fast-moving airplanes are followed by massive attacks with infantry forces. (p. 822)

blockade [blah·KAYD] *n.* the use of troops or ships to prevent commercial traffic from entering or leaving a city or region. (p. 589)

Boer [bohr] *n.* a Dutch colonist in South Africa. (p. 689)

Boer War *n.* a conflict, lasting from 1899 to 1902, in which the Boers and the British fought for control of territory in South Africa. (p. 689)

Bolsheviks [BOHL·shuh·VIHKS] *n.* a group of revolutionary Russian Marxists who took control of Russia's government in November 1917. (p. 770)

Boxer Rebellion *n.* a 1900 rebellion in China, aimed at ending foreign influence in the country. (p. 719)

boyars [boh·YAHRZ] *n.* landowning nobles of Russia. (pp. 275, 531)

Brahma [BRAH·muh] *n.* a Hindu god considered the creator of the world. (p. 178)

Brahmin [BRAH·mihn] *n.* in Aryan society, a member of the social class made up of priests. (p. 59)

brinkmanship *n.* a policy of threatening to go to war in response to any enemy aggression. (p. 860)

Bronze Age *n.* a period in human history, beginning around 3000 B.C. in some areas, during which people began using bronze, rather than copper or stone, to fashion tools and weapons. (p. 19)

bubonic plague [boo·BAHN·ihk PLAYG] *n.* a deadly disease that spread across Asia and Europe in the mid-14th century, killing millions of people. (p. 357)

bureaucracy [byu·RAHK·ruh·see] *n.* a system of departments and agencies formed to carry out the work of government. (p. 98)

burgher [BUR·guhr] *n.* a medieval town dweller. (p. 350)

Bushido [BUSH·ih·DOH] *n.* the strict code of behavior followed by samurai warriors in Japan. (p. 307)

C

cabinet *n.* a group of advisers or ministers chosen by the head of a country to help make government decisions. (p. 539)

caliph [KAY·lihf] *n.* a supreme political and religious leader in a Muslim government. (p. 238)

calligraphy [kuh·LIHG·ruh·fee] *n.* the art of beautiful handwriting. (p. 246)

Calvinism [KAL·vih·NIHZ·uhm] *n.* a body of religious teachings based on the ideas of the reformer John Calvin. (p. 433)

Camp David Accords *n.* the first signed agreement between Israel and an Arab country, in which Egyptian president Anwar Sadat recognized Israel as a legitimate state and Israeli prime minister Menachem Begin agreed to return the Sinai Peninsula to Egypt. (p. 903)

canon law *n.* the body of laws governing the religious practices of a Christian church. (p. 333)

capitalism *n.* an economic system based on private ownership and on the investment of money in business ventures in order to make a profit. (pp. 502, 647)

Carolingian [KAR·uh·LIHN·juhn] **Dynasty** *n.* a dynasty of Frankish rulers, lasting from A.D. 751 to 987. (p. 320)

caste [kast] *n.* one of the four classes of people in the social system of the Aryans who settled in India—priests, warriors, peasants or traders, and non-Aryan laborers or craftsmen. (p. 60)

cataract [KAT·uh·RAKT] *n.* a waterfall or stretch of rapids in a river. (p. 33)

Catholic Reformation [REHF·uhr·MAY·shuhn] *n.* a 16th-century movement in which the Roman Catholic Church sought to reform itself in response to the Protestant Reformation. (p. 435)

caudillo [kaw·DEEL·yoh] *n.* a military dictator of a Latin American country. (p. 724)

centralized government *n.* a government in which power is concentrated in a central authority to which local governments are subject. (p. 181)

Central Powers *n.* in World War I, the nations of Germany and Austria-Hungary, along with the other nations that fought on their side. (p. 748)

Chaldeans [kal·DEE·uhnz] *n.* a Southwest Asian people who helped to destroy the Assyrian Empire. (p. 90)

Chartist movement *n.* a 19th-century British movement in which members of the working class demanded reforms in Parliament and in elections, including suffrage for all men. (p. 660)

Chavín [chah·VEEN] *n.* the first major South American civilization, which flourished in the highlands of what is now Peru from about 900 to 200 B.C. (p. 221)

checks and balances *n.* measures designed to prevent any one branch of government from dominating the others. (pp. 566–567)

chivalry [SHIHV·uhl·ree] *n.* a code of behavior for knights in medieval Europe, stressing ideals such as courage, loyalty, and devotion. (p. 328)

CIS *n.* the Commonwealth of Independent States—a loose association of former Soviet republics that was formed after the breakup of the Soviet Union. (p. 928)

city-state *n.* a city and its surrounding lands functioning as an independent political unit. (p. 29)

civil disobedience *n.* a deliberate and public refusal to obey a law considered unjust. (p. 786)

civilization *n.* a form of culture characterized by cities, specialized workers, complex institutions, record keeping, and advanced technology. (p. 18)

civil rights movement *n.* a grassroots effort to fight discrimination in the United States and to make sure that all U.S. citizens receive the rights guaranteed by the Constitution. (p. 954)

civil service *n.* the administrative departments of a government—especially those in which employees are hired on the basis of their scores on examinations. (p. 183)

civil war *n.* a conflict between two political groups within the same country. (p. 146)

clan *n.* a group of people descended from a common ancestor. (pp. 197, 295)

classical art *n.* the art of ancient Greece and Rome, in which harmony, order, and balance were emphasized. (p. 121)

clergy [KLUR·jee] *n.* a body of officials who perform religious services—such as priests, ministers, or rabbis. (p. 332)

cloning [KLOH·nihng] *n.* the creation of plants or animals that are genetically identical to an existing plant or animal. (p. 944)

coalition [KOH·uh·LIHSH·uhn] **government** *n.* a government controlled by a temporary alliance of several political parties. (p. 801)

codex [KOH·DEHKS] *n.* a book with pages that can be turned, like the one you are reading now. (p. 398)

Cold War *n.* the state of diplomatic hostility between the United States and the Soviet Union in the decades following World War II. (p. 859)

collective bargaining *n.* negotiations between workers and their employers. (p. 650)

collective farm *n.* a large government-controlled farm formed by combining many small farms. (p. 777)

colony *n.* a land controlled by a distant nation. (p. 484)

Colossus of Rhodes [kuh·LAHS·uhs uhv ROHDZ] *n.* an enormous Hellenistic statue that formerly stood near the harbor of Rhodes. (p. 135)

Columbian Exchange *n.* the global transfer of plants, animals, and diseases that occurred during the European colonization of the Americas. (p. 500)

comedy *n.* a humorous form of drama that often includes slapstick and satire. (p. 123)

command economy *n.* an economic system in which the government makes all economic decisions. (p. 776)

Commercial Revolution *n.* the expansion of trade and business that transformed European economies during the 16th and 17th centuries. (p. 500)

Committee of Public Safety *n.* a committee established during the French Revolution to identify "enemies of the republic." (p. 582)

commune [KAHM·yoon] *n.* in Communist China, a collective farm on which a great number of people work and live together. (p. 864)

communism *n.* an economic system in which all means of production—land, mines, factories, railroads, and businesses—are owned by the people, private property does not exist, and all goods and services are shared equally. (p. 649)

Concert [KAHN·surt] **of Europe** *n.* a series of alliances among European nations in the 19th century, devised by Prince Klemens von Metternich to prevent the outbreak of revolutions. (p. 595)

concordat [kuhn·KAWR·dat] *n.* a formal agreement—especially one between the pope and a government, dealing with the control of church affairs. (p. 586)

Congress of Vienna [vee·EHN·uh] *n.* a series of meetings in 1814–1815, during which the European leaders sought to establish long-lasting peace and security after the defeat of Napoleon. (p. 593)

Congress Party *n.* a major national political party in India—also known as the Indian National Congress. (p. 886)

conquistadors [kahng·KEE·stuh·DAWRZ] *n.* the Spanish soldiers, explorers, and fortune hunters who took part in the conquest of the Americas in the 16th century. (p. 485)

conservatives *n.* in the first half of the 19th century, those Europeans—mainly wealthy landowners and nobles—who wanted to preserve the traditional monarchies of Europe. (p. 609)

constitutional monarchy [MAHN·uhr·kee] *n.* a monarchy in which the ruler's power is limited by law. (p. 539)

consul [KAHN·suhl] *n.* in the Roman republic, one of the two powerful officials elected each year to command the army and direct the government. (p. 142)

containment *n.* a U.S. foreign policy adopted by President Harry Truman in the late 1940s, in which the United States tried to stop the spread of communism by creating alliances and helping weak countries to resist Soviet advances. (p. 857)

Continental System *n.* Napoleon's policy of preventing trade between Great Britain and continental Europe, intended to destroy Great Britain's economy. (p. 589)

corporation *n.* a business owned by stockholders who share in its profits but are not personally responsible for its debts. (p. 645)

Council of Trent *n.* a meeting of Roman Catholic leaders, called by Pope Paul III to rule on doctrines criticized by the Protestant reformers. (p. 436)

coup d'état [KOO day·TAH] *n.* a sudden seizure of political power in a nation. (p. 585)

covenant [KUHV·uh·nuhnt] *n.* a mutual promise or agreement—especially an agreement between God and the Hebrew people as recorded in the Bible. (p. 73)

creoles [KREE·ohlz] *n.* in Spanish colonial society, colonists who were born in Latin America to Spanish parents. (p. 604)

Crimean [kry·MEE·uhn] **War** *n.* a conflict, lasting from 1853 to 1856, in which the Ottoman Empire, with the aid of Britain and France, halted Russian expansion in the region of the Black Sea. (p. 698)

crop rotation *n.* the system of growing a different crop in a field each year to preserve the fertility of the land. (p. 633)

Crusade *n.* one of the expeditions in which medieval Christian warriors sought to recover control of the Holy Land from the Muslims. (p. 343)

cultural diffusion *n.* the spreading of ideas or products from one culture to another. (p. 29)

Cultural Revolution *n.* a 1966–1976 uprising in China, led by the Red Guards, with the goal of establishing a society of peasants and workers in which all were equal. (p. 865)

culture *n.* a people's unique way of life, as shown by its tools, customs, arts, and ideas. (p. 7)

cuneiform [KYOO·nee·uh·FAWRM] *n.* a system of writing with wedge-shaped symbols, invented by the Sumerians around 3000 B.C. (p. 18)

Cyrillic [suh·RIHL·ihk] **alphabet** *n.* an alphabet for the writing of Slavic languages, devised in the ninth century A.D. by Saints Cyril and Methodius. (p. 273)

czar [zahr] *n.* a Russian emperor (from the Roman title *Caesar*). (p. 278)

D

daimyo [DY·mee·OH] *n.* a Japanese feudal lord who commanded a private army of samurai. (p. 474)

Daoism [DOW·ihz·uhm] *n.* a philosophy based on the ideas of the Chinese thinker Laozi, who taught that people should be guided by a universal force called the Dao (Way). (p. 98)

D-Day *n.* June 6, 1944—the day on which the Allies began their invasion of the European mainland during World War II. (p. 838)

Declaration of Independence *n.* a statement of the reasons for the American colonies' break with Britain, approved by the Second Continental Congress in 1776. (p. 564)

Declaration of the Rights of Man *n.* a statement of revolutionary ideals adopted by France's National Assembly in 1789. (p. 577)

delta *n.* a marshy region formed by deposits of silt at the mouth of a river. (p. 34)

demilitarization [dee·MIHL·ih·tuhr·ih·ZAY·shuhn] *n.* a reduction in a country's ability to wage war, achieved by disbanding its armed forces and prohibiting it from acquiring weapons. (p. 844)

democracy *n.* a government controlled by its citizens, either directly or through representatives. (p. 117)

desertification [dih·ZUR·tuh·fih·KAY·shuhn] *n.* a transformation of fertile land into desert. (p. 195)

destalinization [dee·STAH·lih·nih·ZAY·shuhn] *n.* Nikita Khrushchev's policy of eliminating all memory of Joseph Stalin and his programs in the Soviet Union. (p. 876)

détente [day·TAHNT] *n.* a policy of reducing Cold War tensions that was adopted by the United States during the presidency of Richard Nixon. (p. 878)

developed nation *n.* a nation with all the facilities needed for the advanced production of manufactured goods. (p. 946)

developing nation *n.* a nation in which the process of industrialization is not yet complete. (p. 946)

devshirme [dehv·SHEER·meh] *n.* in the Ottoman Empire, the policy of taking children from conquered Christian peoples to be trained as Muslim soldiers. (p. 446)

Diaspora [dy·AS·puhr·uh] *n.* the dispersal of the Jews from their homeland in Palestine—especially during the period of more than 1,800 years that followed the Romans' destruction of the Temple in Jerusalem in A.D. 70. (p. 155)

dictator *n.* in ancient Rome, a political leader given absolute power to make laws and command the army for a limited time. (p. 143)

direct democracy *n.* a government in which citizens rule directly rather than through representatives. (p. 120)

dissident [DIHS·ih·duhnt] *n.* an opponent of a government's policies or actions. (p. 918)

divine right *n.* the idea that monarchs are God's representatives on earth and are therefore answerable only to God. (p. 517)

domestication *n.* the taming of animals for human use. (p. 14)

dominion *n.* in the British Empire, a nation (such as Canada) allowed to govern its own domestic affairs. (p. 665)

domino theory *n.* the idea that if a nation falls under Communist control, nearby nations will also fall under Communist control. (p. 868)

Dorians [DAWR·ee·uhnz] *n.* a Greek-speaking people that, according to tradition, migrated into mainland Greece after the destruction of the Mycenaean civilization. (p. 113)

Dreyfus [DRY·fuhs] **affair** *n.* a controversy in France in the 1890s, centering on the trial and imprisonment of a Jewish army officer, Captain Alfred Dreyfus, who had been falsely accused of selling military secrets to Germany. (p. 663)

Duma [DOO·muh] *n.* a Russian national parliament formed in the early years of the 20th century. (p. 771)

Dutch East India Company *n.* a company founded by the Dutch in the early 17th century to establish and direct trade throughout Asia. (p. 468)

dynastic [dy·NAS·tihk] **cycle** *n.* the historical pattern of the rise, decline, and replacement of dynasties. (p. 50)

dynasty [DY·nuh·stee] *n.* a series of rulers from a single family. (p. 29)

E

Eastern Front *n.* in World War I, the region along the German-Russian border where Russians and Serbs battled Germans, Austrians, and Turks. (p. 750)

Edict of Nantes [EE·DIHKT uhv NAHNT] *n.* a 1598 declaration in which the French king Henry IV promised that Protestants could live in peace in France and could set up houses of worship in some French cities. (p. 518)

Emancipation Proclamation [ih·MAN·suh·PAY·shuhn PRAHK·luh·MAY·shuhn] *n.* a declaration issued by U.S. president Abraham Lincoln in 1863, stating that all slaves in the Confederate states were free. (p. 671)

émigrés [EHM·ih·GRAYZ] *n.* people who leave their native country for political reasons, like the nobles and others who fled France during the peasant uprisings of the French Revolution. (p. 579)

empire *n.* a political unit in which a number of peoples or countries are controlled by a single ruler. (p. 31)

enclosure *n.* one of the fenced-in or hedged-in fields created by wealthy British landowners on land that was formerly worked by village farmers. (p. 633)

encomienda [ehng·kaw·MYEHN·dah] *n.* a grant of land made by Spain to a settler in the Americas, including the right to use Native Americans as laborers on it. (p. 486)

English Civil War *n.* a conflict, lasting from 1642 to 1649, in which Puritan supporters of Parliament battled supporters of England's monarchy. (p. 537)

enlightened despot [DEHS·puht] *n.* one of the 18th-century European monarchs who were inspired by Enlightenment ideas to rule justly and respect the rights of their subjects. (p. 561)

enlightenment [ehn·LYT·uhn·muhnt] *n.* in Buddhism, a state of perfect wisdom in which one understands basic truths about the universe. (p. 64)

Enlightenment *n.* an 18th-century European movement in which thinkers attempted to apply the principles of reason and the scientific method to all aspects of society. (p. 551)

entrepreneur [AHN·truh·pruh·NUR] *n.* a person who organizes, manages, and takes on the risks of a business. (p. 636)

epics *n.* long narrative poems celebrating the deeds of legendary or traditional heroes. (p. 114)

estate [ih·STAYT] *n.* one of the three social classes in France before the French Revolution—the First Estate consisting of the clergy; the Second Estate, of the nobility; and the Third Estate, of the rest of the population. (p. 573)

Estates-General [ih·STAYTS·JEHN·uhr·uhl] *n.* an assembly of representatives from all three of the estates, or social classes, in France. (p. 575)

ethnic cleansing *n.* a policy of murder and other acts of brutality by which Serbs hoped to eliminate Bosnia's Muslim population after the breakup of Yugoslavia. (p. 929)

excommunication [EHKS·kuh·MYOO·nih·KAY·shuhn] *n.* the taking away of a person's right of membership in a Christian church. (p. 273)

existentialism [EHG·zih·STEHN·shuh·LIHZ·uhm] *n.* a philosophy based on the idea that people give meaning to their lives through their choices and actions. (p. 796)

extended family *n.* a group that includes a person's parents, children, grandparents, grandchildren, aunts, uncles, and cousins. (p. 197)

extraterritorial [EHK·struh·TEHR·ih·TAWR·ee·uhl] **rights** *n.* an exemption of foreign residents from the laws of a country. (p. 716)

factors of production *n.* the resources—including land, labor, and capital—that are needed to produce goods and services. (p. 634)

factory *n.* a large building in which machinery is used to manufacture goods. (p. 635)

fascism [FASH·IHZ·uhm] *n.* a political movement that promotes an extreme form of nationalism, a denial of individual rights, and a dictatorial one-party rule. (p. 807)

Fatimid [FAT·uh·MIHD] *n.* a member of a Muslim dynasty that traced its ancestry to Muhammad's daughter Fatima and that built an empire in North Africa, Arabia, and Syria in the 10th–12th centuries. (p. 240)

favorable balance of trade *n.* an economic situation in which a country exports more than it imports—that is, sells more goods abroad than it buys from abroad. (p. 502)

federal system *n.* a system of government in which power is divided between a central authority and a number of individual states. (pp. 567, 917)

Fertile Crescent [FUHR·tuhl KREHS·uhnt] *n.* an arc of rich farmland in Southwest Asia, between the Persian Gulf and the Mediterranean Sea. (p. 27)

feudalism [FYOOD·uhl·IHZ·uhm] *n.* a political system in which nobles are granted the use of lands that legally belong to their king, in exchange for their loyalty, military service, and protection of the people who live on the land. (p. 50)

fief [feef] *n.* an estate granted to a vassal by a lord under the feudal system in medieval Europe. (p. 324)

filial piety [FIHL·ee·uhl PY·ih·tee] *n.* respect shown by children for their parents and elders. (p. 97)

Final Solution *n.* Hitler's program of systematically killing the entire Jewish people. (p. 833)

FLN *n.* the National Liberation Front—an Algerian group that waged a guerrilla struggle for independence from France. (p. 899)

Four Modernizations *n.* a set of goals adopted by the Chinese leader Deng Xiaoping in the late 20th century, involving progress in agriculture, industry, defense, and science and technology. (p. 932)

Fourteen Points *n.* a series of proposals in which U.S. president Woodrow Wilson outlined a plan for achieving a lasting peace after World War I. (p. 760)

Franks *n.* a Germanic people who settled in the Roman province of Gaul (roughly the area now occupied by France) and established a great empire during the Middle Ages. (p. 318)

free trade *n.* commerce between nations without economic restrictions or barriers (such as tariffs). (p. 947)

French and Indian War *n.* a conflict between Britain and France for control of territory in North America, lasting from 1754 to 1763. (p. 493)

fundamentalism [FUHN·duh·MEHN·tuhl·IHZ·uhm] *n.* a strict belief in the basic truths and practices of a particular religion. (p. 953)

genetic [juh·NEHT·ihk] **engineering** *n.* the transferring of genes from one living thing to another in order to produce an organism with new traits. (p. 943–944)

genocide [JEHN·uh·SYD] *n.* the systematic killing of an entire people. (p. 833)

gentry *n.* a class of powerful, well-to-do people who enjoy a high social status. (p. 291)

geopolitics [JEE·oh·PAHL·ih·tihks] *n.* a foreign policy based on a consideration of the strategic locations or products of other lands. (p. 698)

Ghana [GAH·nuh] *n.* a West African kingdom that grew rich from taxing and controlling trade and that established an empire in the 9th–11th centuries A.D. (p. 371)

ghazi [GAH·zee] *n.* a warrior for Islam. (p. 443)

ghettos [GEHT·ohz] *n.* city neighborhoods in which European Jews were forced to live. (p. 832)

gladiator [GLAD·ee·AY·tuhr] *n.* in ancient Rome, one of the professional fighters who engaged in battles to the death in public arenas. (p. 151)

glasnost [GLAHS·nuhst] *n.* a Soviet policy of openness to the free flow of ideas and information, introduced in 1985 by Mikhail Gorbachev. (p. 921)

global economy *n.* all the financial interactions—involving people, businesses, and governments—that cross international boundaries. (p. 947)

Glorious Revolution *n.* the bloodless overthrow of the English king James II and his replacement by William and Mary. (p. 539)

glyph [glihf] *n.* a symbolic picture—especially one used as part of a writing system for carving messages in stone. (p. 398)

Gothic [GAHTH·ihk] *adj.* relating to a style of church architecture that developed in medieval Europe, featuring ribbed vaults, stained-glass windows, flying buttresses, pointed arches, and tall spires. (p. 342)

Great Depression *n.* the severe economic slump that followed the collapse of the U.S. stock market in 1929. (p. 804)

Great Fear *n.* a wave of senseless panic that spread through the French countryside after the storming of the Bastille in 1789. (p. 576)

Great Purge *n.* a campaign of terror in the Soviet Union during the 1930s, in which Joseph Stalin sought to eliminate all Communist Party members and other citizens who threatened his power. (p. 777)

Great Schism [SIHZ·uhm] *n.* a division in the medieval Roman Catholic Church, during which rival popes were established in Avignon and in Rome. (p. 357)

Great Trek *n.* a migration of Dutch colonists out of British-controlled territory in South Africa during the 1830s. (p. 689)

Greco-Roman culture *n.* an ancient culture that developed from a blending of Greek, Hellenistic, and Roman cultures. (p. 164)

green revolution *n.* a 20th-century attempt to increase food resources worldwide, involving the use of fertilizers and pesticides and the development of disease-resistant crops. (p. 944)

griot [gree·OH] *n.* a West African storyteller. (p. 197)

guerrilla [guh·RIHL·uh] *n.* a member of a loosely organized fighting force that makes surprise attacks on enemy troops occupying his or her country. (p. 590)

guild [gihld] *n.* a medieval association of people working at the same occupation, which controlled its members' wages and prices. (p. 349)

guillotine [GIHL·uh·TEEN] *n.* a machine for beheading people, used as a means of execution during the French Revolution. (p. 580)

Gulf War *n.* a 1991 conflict in which UN forces defeated Iraqi forces that had invaded Kuwait and threatened to invade Saudi Arabia. (p. 949)

Gupta [GUP·tuh] **Empire** *n.* the second empire in India, founded by Chandra Gupta I in A.D. 320. (p. 175)

Gutenberg [GOOT·uhn·BURG] **Bible** *n.* the first full-sized book printed with movable type and a printing press. (p. 426)

H

habeas corpus [HAY·bee·uhs KAWR·puhs] *n.* a document requiring that a prisoner be brought before a court or judge so that it can be decided whether his or her imprisonment is legal. (p. 538)

Hagia Sophia [HAY·ee·uh soh·FEE·uh] *n.* the Cathedral of Holy Wisdom in Constantinople, built by order of the Byzantine emperor Justinian. (p. 270)

haiku [HY·koo] *n.* a Japanese form of poetry, consisting of three unrhymed lines of five, seven, and five syllables. (p. 476)

hajj [haj] *n.* a pilgrimage to Mecca, performed as a duty by Muslims. (p. 236)

Han [hahn] **Dynasty** *n.* a Chinese dynasty that ruled from 202 B.C. to A.D. 9 and again from A.D. 23 to 220. (p. 181)

Hausa [HOW·suh] *n.* a West African people who lived in several city-states in what is now northern Nigeria. (p. 375)

heliocentric [HEE·lee·oh·SEHN·trihk] **theory** *n.* the idea that the earth and the other planets revolve around the sun. (p. 546)

Hellenistic [HEHL·uh·NIHS·tihk] *adj.* relating to the civilization, language, art, science, and literature of the Greek world from the reign of Alexander the Great to the late second century B.C. (p. 132)

helot [HEHL·uht] *n.* in the society of ancient Sparta, a peasant bound to the land. (p. 116)

heresy [HEHR·ih·see] *n.* religious beliefs or opinions that differ from the official teachings of a Christian church. (p. 157)

hieroglyphics [HY·uhr·uh·GLIHF·ihks] *n.* an ancient Egyptian writing system in which pictures were used to represent ideas and sounds. (p. 38)

Hijrah [HIHJ·ruh] *n.* Muhammad's migration from Mecca to Yathrib (Medina) in A.D. 622. (p. 235)

Hittites [HIHT·yts] *n.* an Indo-European people who settled in Anatolia around 2000 B.C. (p. 58)

Holocaust [HAHL·uh·KAWST] *n.* a mass slaughter of Jews and other civilians, carried out by the Nazi government of Germany before and during World War II. (p. 831)

Holy Alliance *n.* a league of European nations formed by the leaders of Russia, Austria, and Prussia after the Congress of Vienna. (p. 595)

Holy Roman Empire *n.* an empire established in Europe in the 10th century A.D., originally consisting mainly of lands in what is now Germany and Italy. (p. 333)

home rule *n.* a control over internal matters granted to the residents of a region by a ruling government. (p. 668)

hominid [HAHM·uh·nihd] *n.* a member of a biological group including human beings and related species that walk upright. (p. 8)

Homo sapiens [HOH·moh SAY·pee·uhnz] *n.* the biological species to which modern human beings belong. (p. 9)

House of Wisdom *n.* a center of learning established in Baghdad in the 800s. (p. 243)

Hubble Space Telescope *n.* a powerful telescope put into orbit around the earth by NASA and the European Space Agency in 1990. (p. 942)

humanism [HYOO·muh·NIHZ·uhm] *n.* a Renaissance intellectual movement in which thinkers studied classical texts and focused on human potential and achievements. (p. 418)

Hundred Days *n.* the brief period during 1815 when Napoleon made his last bid for power, deposing the French king and again becoming emperor of France. (p. 592)

Hundred Years' War *n.* a conflict in which England and France battled on French soil on and off from 1337 to 1453. (p. 359)

hunter-gatherer *n.* a member of a nomadic group whose food supply depends on hunting animals and collecting plant foods. (p. 12)

Hyksos [HIHK·sohs] *n.* a group of nomadic invaders from Southwest Asia who ruled Egypt from 1640 to 1570 B.C. (p. 83)

I

Ice Age *n.* a cold period in which huge ice sheets spread outward from the polar regions, the last one of which lasted from about 1,600,000 to 10,000 B.C. (p. 211)

I Ching [ee jihng] *n.* a Chinese book of oracles, consulted to answer ethical and practical problems. (p. 99)

icon [EYE·KAHN] *n.* a religious image used by eastern Christians. (p. 272)

iconoclast [eye·KAHN·uh·KLAST] *n.* one of the eastern Christians who destroyed religious images in churches during the eighth and ninth centuries. (p. 272)

imperialism [ihm·PEER·ee·uh·LIHZ·uhm] *n.* a policy in which a strong nation seeks to dominate other countries politically, economically, or socially. (p. 686)

impressionism [ihm·PREHSH·uh·NIHZ·uhm] *n.* a movement in 19th-century painting, in which artists reacted against realism by seeking to convey their impressions of subjects or moments in time. (p. 623)

Indo-Europeans [IHN·doh·YUR·uh·PEE·uhnz] *n.* a group of seminomadic peoples who, about 1700 B.C., began to migrate from what is now southern Russia to the Indian subcontinent, Europe, and Southwest Asia. (p. 57)

indulgence [ihn·DUHL·juhns] *n.* a pardon releasing a person from punishments due for a sin. (p. 429)

industrialization [ihn·DUHS·tree·uh·lih·ZAY·shuhn] *n.* the development of industries for the machine production of goods. (p. 634)

Industrial Revolution *n.* the shift, beginning in England during the 18th century, from making goods by hand to making them by machine. (p. 633)

inflation *n.* a decline in the value of money, accompanied by a rise in the prices of goods and services. (p. 158)

Inquisition [IHN·kwih·ZIHSH·uhn] *n.* a Roman Catholic tribunal for investigating and prosecuting charges of heresy—especially the one active in Spain during the 1400s. (p. 346)

institution *n.* a long-lasting pattern of organization in a community. (p. 18)

intendant [ihn·TEHN·duhnt] *n.* a French government official appointed by the monarch to collect taxes and administer justice. (p. 520)

Internet *n.* a linkage of computer networks that allows people around the world to exchange information and communicate with one another. (p. 943)

iron curtain *n.* during the Cold War, the boundary separating the Communist nations of Eastern Europe from the mostly democratic nations of Western Europe. (p. 857)

Iroquois [IHR·uh·KWOY] *n.* a group of Native American peoples who spoke related languages, lived in the eastern Great Lakes region of North America, and formed an alliance in the late 1500s. (p. 393)

irrigation *n.* the bringing of water to crop fields by means of canals and ditches. (p. 28)

Islam [ihs·LAHM] *n.* a monotheistic religion that developed in Arabia in the seventh century A.D. (p. 234)

isolationism *n.* a policy of avoiding political or military involvement with other countries. (p. 814)

Israel [IHZ·ree·uhl] *n.* a kingdom of the united Hebrews in Palestine, lasting from about 1020 to 922 B.C.; later, the northernmost of the two Hebrew kingdoms; now, the Jewish nation that was established in Palestine in 1948. (p. 75)

J

Jainism [JY·NIHZ·uhm] *n.* a religion founded in India in the sixth century B.C., whose members believe that everything in the universe has a soul and therefore should not be harmed. (p. 63)

janissary [JAN·ih·SEHR·ee] *n.* a member of an elite force of soldiers in the Ottoman Empire. (p. 446)

jazz *n.* a 20th-century style of popular music developed mainly by African-American musicians. (p. 797)

Jesuits [JEHZH·oo·ihts] *n.* members of the Society of Jesus, a Roman Catholic religious order founded by Ignatius of Loyola. (p. 435)

"jewel in the crown" *n.* the British colony of India—so called because of its importance in the British Empire, both as a supplier of raw materials and as a market for British trade goods. (p. 701)

joint-stock company *n.* a business in which investors pool their wealth for a common purpose, then share the profits. (p. 502)

Judah [JOO·duh] *n.* a Hebrew kingdom in Palestine, established around 922 B.C. (p. 76)

Justinian [juh·STIHN·ee·uhn] **Code** *n.* the body of Roman civil law collected and organized by order of the Byzantine emperor Justinian around A.D. 534. (p. 270)

K

kabuki [kuh·BOO·kee] *n.* a type of Japanese drama in which music, dance, and mime are used to present stories. (p. 476)

kaiser [KY·zuhr] *n.* a German emperor (from the Roman title *Caesar*). (p. 618)

kamikaze [KAH·mih·KAH·zee] *n.* during World War II, Japanese suicide pilots trained to sink Allied ships by crashing bomb-filled planes into them. (p. 841)

karma [KAHR·muh] *n.* in Hinduism and Buddhism, the totality of the good and bad deeds performed by a person, which is believed to determine his or her fate after rebirth. (p. 63)

Khmer [kmair] **Empire** *n.* a Southeast Asian empire, centered in what is now Cambodia, that reached its peak of power around A.D. 1200. (p. 309)

Khmer Rouge [roozh] *n.* a group of Communist rebels who seized power in Cambodia in 1975. (p. 870)

knight *n.* in medieval Europe, an armored warrior who fought on horseback. (p. 324)

Koryu [KAWR·yoo] **Dynasty** *n.* a dynasty that ruled Korea from A.D. 935 to 1392. (p. 311)

Kristallnacht [krih·STAHL·NAHKT] *n.* "Night of Broken Glass"—the night of November 9, 1938, on which Nazi storm troopers attacked Jewish homes, businesses, and synagogues throughout Germany. (p. 831)

kulak [koo·LAK] *n.* a member of a class of wealthy Russian peasants. (p. 777)

Kuomintang [KWOH·mihn·TANG] *n.* the Chinese Nationalist Party, formed after the fall of the Qing Dynasty in 1912. (p. 781)

Kush [kuhsh] *n.* an ancient Nubian kingdom whose rulers controlled Egypt from 751 to 671 B.C. (p. 85)

L

laissez faire [LEHS·ay·FAIR] *n.* the idea that government should not interfere with or regulate industries and businesses. (p. 647)

land reform *n.* a redistribution of farmland by breaking up large estates and giving the resulting smaller farms to peasants. (p. 912)

La Reforma [lah reh·FAWR·mah] *n.* a liberal reform movement in 19th-century Mexico, founded by Benito Juárez. (p. 730)

lay investiture [ihn·VEHS·tuh·CHUR] *n.* the appointment of religious officials by kings or nobles. (p. 334)

League of Nations *n.* an international association formed after World War I with the goal of keeping peace among nations. (p. 761)

lebensraum [LAY·buhns·ROWM] *n.* "living space"—the additional territory that, according to Adolf Hitler, Germany needed because it was overcrowded. (p. 809)

Legalism *n.* a Chinese political philosophy based on the idea that a highly efficient and powerful government is the key to social order. (p. 99)

legion *n.* a military unit of the ancient Roman army, made up of about 5,000 foot soldiers and a group of soldiers on horseback. (p. 143)

Legislative [LEHJ·ih·SLAY·tihv] **Assembly** *n.* a French congress with the power to create laws and approve declarations of war, established by the Constitution of 1791. (p. 578)

legitimacy [luh·JIHT·uh·muh·see] *n.* the hereditary right of a monarch to rule. (p. 594)

liberals *n.* in the first half of the 19th century, those Europeans—mainly middle-class business leaders and merchants—who wanted to give more political power to elected parliaments. (p. 609)

lineage [LIHN·ee·ihj] *n.* the people—living, dead, and unborn—who are descended from a common ancestor. (p. 368)

loess [LOH·uhs] *n.* a fertile deposit of windblown soil. (p. 46)

Long March *n.* a 6,000-mile journey made in 1934–1935 by Chinese Communists fleeing from Jiang Jieshi's Nationalist forces. (p. 784)

lord *n.* in feudal Europe, a person who controlled land and could therefore grant estates to vassals. (p. 324)

Lutheran [LOO·thuhr·uhn] *n.* a member of a Protestant church founded on the teachings of Martin Luther. (p. 430)

lycée [lee·SAY] *n.* a government-run public school in France. (p. 585)

M

Macedonia [MAS·ih·DOH·nee·uh] *n.* an ancient kingdom north of Greece, whose ruler Philip II conquered Greece in 338 B.C. (p. 128)

Maghrib [MUHG·ruhb] *n.* a region of western North Africa, consisting of the Mediterranean coastlands of what is now Morocco, Tunisia, and Algeria. (p. 369)

Magna Carta [MAG·nuh KAHR·tuh] *n.* "Great Charter"—a document guaranteeing basic political rights in England, drawn up by nobles and approved by King John in A.D. 1215. (p. 353)

Mahabharata [muh·HAH·BAH·ruh·tuh] *n.* a great Indian epic poem, reflecting the struggles of the Aryans as they moved south into India. (p. 60)

Mahayana [MAH·huh·YAH·nuh] *n.* a sect of Buddhism that offers salvation to all and allows popular worship. (p. 177)

maize [mayz] *n.* a cultivated cereal grain that bears its kernels on large ears—usually called corn in the United States. (p. 213)

Mali [MAH·lee] *n.* a West African empire that flourished from 1235 to the 1400s and grew rich from trade. (p. 373)

mamelukes [MAM·uh·LOOKS] *n.* Turkish slaves who served as soldiers and bodyguards in the Abbasid Empire. (p. 279)

Manchus [MAN·chooz] *n.* a people, native to Manchuria, who ruled China during the Qing Dynasty (1644–1912). (p. 471)

Mandate of Heaven *n.* in Chinese history, the divine approval thought to be the basis of royal authority. (p. 50)

manifest destiny *n.* the idea, popular among mid-19th-century Americans, that it was the right and the duty of the United States to rule North America from the Atlantic Ocean to the Pacific Ocean. (p. 670)

manor *n.* a lord's estate in feudal Europe. (p. 325)

Maori [MOW·ree] *n.* a member of a Polynesian people who settled in New Zealand around A.D. 800. (p. 665)

Marshall Plan *n.* a U.S. program of economic aid to European countries to help them rebuild after World War II. (p. 858)

martial [MAHR·shuhl] **law** *n.* a temporary rule by military authorities over a civilian population, usually imposed in times of war or civil unrest. (p. 917)

mass culture *n.* the production of works of art and entertainment designed to appeal to a large audience. (p. 674)

materialism *n.* a placing of high value on acquiring material possessions. (p. 960)

matriarchal [MAY·tree·AHR·kuhl] *adj.* relating to a social system in which the mother is head of the family. (p. 176)

matrilineal [MAT·ruh·LIHN·ee·uhl] *adj.* relating to a social system in which family descent and inheritance rights are traced through the mother. (p. 369)

Mau Mau [MOW MOW] *n.* a secret society of Kikuyu tribesmen that attempted to drive British settlers out of Kenya in the mid-20th century. (p. 897)

Mauryan [MAH·ur·yuhn] **Empire** *n.* the first empire in India, founded by Chandragupta Maurya in 321 B.C. (p. 173)

May Fourth Movement *n.* a national protest in China in 1919, in which people demonstrated against the Treaty of Versailles and foreign interference. (p. 782)

Medes [meedz] *n.* a Southwest Asian people who helped to destroy the Assyrian Empire. (p. 90)

Meiji [MAY·JEE] **era** *n.* the period of Japanese history from 1867 to 1912, during which the country was ruled by Emperor Mutsuhito. (p. 721)

Mein Kampf [MYN KAHMPF] *n.* "My Struggle"—a book written by Adolf Hitler during his imprisonment in 1923–1924, in which he set forth his beliefs and his goals for Germany. (p. 809)

mercantilism [MUR·kuhn·tee·LIHZ·uhm] *n.* an economic policy under which nations sought to increase their wealth and power by obtaining large amounts of gold and silver and by selling more goods than they bought. (p. 502)

mercenary [MUR·suh·NEHR·ee] *n.* a soldier who is paid to fight in a foreign army. (p. 159)

Mesoamerica [MEHZ·oh·uh·MEHR·ih·kuh] *n.* an area extending from central Mexico to Honduras, where several of the ancient complex societies of the Americas developed. (p. 216)

mestizo [mehs·TEE·zoh] *adj.* of mixed Spanish and Native American ancestry. (p. 486)

Middle Ages *n.* the era in European history that followed the fall of the Roman Empire, lasting from about 500 to 1500—also called the medieval period. (p. 317)

middle class *n.* a social class made up of skilled workers, professionals, businesspeople, and wealthy farmers. (p. 639)

middle passage *n.* the voyage that brought captured Africans to the West Indies, and later to North and South America, to be sold as slaves—so called because it was considered the middle leg of the triangular trade. (p. 497)

migration *n.* the act of moving from one place to settle in another. (p. 57)

militarism [MIHL·ih·tuh·RIHZ·uhm] *n.* a policy of glorifying military power and keeping a standing army always prepared for war. (p. 744)

Ming Dynasty *n.* a Chinese dynasty that ruled from 1368 to 1644. (p. 469)

Minoans [mih·NOH·uhnz] *n.* a seafaring and trading people that lived on the island of Crete from about 2000 to 1400 B.C. (p. 67)

Mississippian [MIHS·ih·SIHP·ee·uhn] *adj.* relating to a Mound Builder culture that flourished in North America between A.D. 800 and 1500. (p. 393)

mita [MEE·tuh] *n.* in the Inca Empire, the requirement that all able-bodied subjects work for the state a certain number of days each year. (p. 409)

Moche [MOH·chay] *n.* a civilization that flourished on what is now the northern coast of Peru from about A.D. 100 to 700. (p. 222)

monarchy [MAHN·uhr·kee] *n.* a government in which power is in the hands of a single person. (p. 115)

monastery [MAHN·uh·STEHR·ee] *n.* a religious community of men (called monks) who have given up their possessions to devote themselves to a life of prayer and worship. (p. 318)

monopoly [muh·NAHP·uh·lee] *n.* a group's exclusive control over the production and distribution of certain goods. (p. 185)

monotheism [MAHN·uh·thee·IHZ·uhm] *n.* a belief in a single god. (p. 73)

Monroe Doctrine *n.* a U.S. policy of opposition to European interference in Latin America, announced by President James Monroe in 1823. (p. 726)

monsoon [mahn·SOON] *n.* a wind that shifts in direction at certain times of each year. (p. 42)

mosque [mahsk] *n.* an Islamic place of worship. (p. 236)

movable type *n.* blocks of metal or wood, each bearing a single character, that can be arranged to make up a page for printing. (p. 289)

Mughal [MOO·guhl] *n.* one of the nomads who invaded the Indian subcontinent in the 16th century and established a powerful empire there. (p. 451)

mulattos [mu·LAT·ohz] *n.* persons of mixed European and African ancestry. (p. 604)

multinational corporation *n.* a company that operates in a number of different countries. (p. 947)

mummification [MUHM·uh·fih·KAY·shuhn] *n.* a process of embalming and drying corpses to prevent them from decaying. (p. 37)

Munich [MYOO·nihk] **Conference** *n.* a 1938 meeting of representatives from Britain, France, Italy, and Germany, at which Britain and France agreed to allow Nazi Germany to annex part of Czechoslovakia in

return for Adolf Hitler's pledge to respect Czechoslovakia's new borders. (p. 815)

Muslim [MUHZ·luhm] *n.* a follower of Islam. (p. 235)

Muslim League *n.* an organization formed in 1906 to protect the interests of India's Muslims, which later proposed that India be divided into separate Muslim and Hindu nations. (p. 886)

Mutapa [moo·TAHP·uh] *adj.* relating to a southern African empire established by Mutota in the 15th century A.D. (p. 381)

Mycenaeans [MY·suh·NEE·uhnz] *n.* an Indo-European people who settled on the Greek mainland around 2000 B.C. (p. 112)

myths *n.* traditional stories about gods, ancestors, or heroes, told to explain the natural world or the customs and beliefs of a society. (p. 114)

N

Napoleonic [nuh·POH·lee·AHN·ihk] **Code** *n.* a comprehensive and uniform system of laws established for France by Napoleon. (p. 586)

National Assembly *n.* a French congress established by representatives of the Third Estate on June 17, 1789, to enact laws and reforms in the name of the French people. (p. 575)

nationalism *n.* the belief that people should be loyal mainly to their nation—that is, to the people with whom they share a culture and history—rather than to a king or empire. (p. 609)

nation-state *n.* an independent nation of people having a common culture and identity. (p. 609)

NATO [NAY·toh] *n.* the North Atlantic Treaty Organization—a defensive military alliance formed in 1949 by ten Western European nations, the United States, and Canada. (p. 859)

natural rights *n.* the rights that all people are born with—according to John Locke, the rights of life, liberty, and property. (p. 551)

Nazca [NAHS·kah] *n.* a civilization that flourished on what is now the southern coast of Peru from about 200 B.C. to A.D. 600. (p. 222)

Nazism [NAHT·SIHZ·uhm] *n.* the fascist policies of the National Socialist German Workers' party, based on totalitarianism, a belief in racial superiority, and state control of industry. (p. 808)

Negritude [NEE·grih·TOOD] **movement** *n.* a movement in which French-speaking Africans and West Indians celebrated their heritage of traditional African culture and values. (p. 896)

neoclassical [NEE·oh·KLAS·ih·kuhl] *adj.* relating to a simple, elegant style (based on ideas and themes from ancient Greece and Rome) that characterized the arts in Europe during the late 1700s. (p. 559)

Neolithic [NEE·uh·LIHTH·ihk] **Age** *n.* a prehistoric period that began about 8000 B.C. and in some areas ended as early as 3000 B.C., during which people learned to polish stone tools, make pottery, grow crops, and raise animals—also called the New Stone Age. (p. 8)

Neolithic Revolution *n.* the major change in human life caused by the beginnings of farming—that is, by people's shift from food gathering to food producing. (p. 14)

New Deal *n.* U.S. president Franklin Roosevelt's economic reform program designed to solve the problems created by the Great Depression. (p. 806)

New Kingdom *n.* the period of ancient Egyptian history that followed the overthrow of the Hyksos rulers, lasting from about 1570 to 1075 B.C. (p. 83)

nirvana [neer·VAH·nuh] *n.* in Buddhism, the release from pain and suffering achieved after enlightenment. (p. 65)

Nok [nahk] *n.* an African people who lived in what is now Nigeria between 500 B.C. and A.D. 200. (p. 198)

nomad *n.* a member of a group that has no permanent home, wandering from place to place in search of food and water. (p. 12)

nonaggression [NAHN·uh·GREHSH·uhn] **pact** *n.* an agreement in which nations promise not to attack one another. (p. 821)

nonaligned nations *n.* the independent countries that remained neutral in the Cold War competition between the United States and the Soviet Union. (p. 871)

Nuclear Non-Proliferation [NOO·klee·uhr NAHN·pruh·LIHF·uh·RAY·shuhn] **Treaty** *n.* a 1968 agreement intended to reduce the spread of nuclear weapons. (p. 953)

Nuremberg [NUR·uhm·burg] **Trials** *n.* a series of court proceedings held in Nuremberg, Germany, after World War II, in which Nazi leaders were tried for aggression, violations of the rules of war, and crimes against humanity. (p. 843)

O

obsidian [ahb·SIHD·ee·uhn] *n.* a hard, glassy volcanic rock used by early peoples to make sharp weapons. (p. 400)

Old Regime [ray·ZHEEM] *n.* the political and social system that existed in France before the French Revolution. (p. 573)

oligarchy [AHL·ih·GAHR·kee] *n.* a government in which power is in the hands of a few people—especially one in which rule is based upon wealth. (p. 115)

Olmec [AHL·mehk] *n.* the earliest known Mesoamerican civilization, which flourished around 1200 B.C. and influenced later societies throughout the region. (p. 216)

Open Door Policy *n.* a policy, proposed by the United States in 1899, under which all nations would have equal opportunities to trade in China. (p. 718)

Opium War *n.* a conflict between Britain and China, lasting from 1839 to 1842, over Britain's opium trade in China. (p. 716)

oracle bone *n.* one of the animal bones or tortoise shells used by ancient Chinese priests to communicate with the gods. (p. 48)

ozone layer *n.* a layer of the earth's upper atmosphere, which protects living things from the sun's damaging ultraviolet rays. (p. 949)

P

Pacific Rim *n.* the lands surrounding the Pacific Ocean—especially those in Asia. (p. 706)

Paleolithic [PAY·lee·uh·LIHTH·ihk] **Age** *n.* a prehistoric period that lasted from about 2,500,000 to 8000 B.C., during which people made use of crude stone tools and weapons—also called the Old Stone Age. (p. 8)

Panama Canal *n.* a manmade waterway connecting the Atlantic and Pacific oceans, built in Panama by the United States and opened in 1914. (p. 727)

papyrus [puh·PY·ruhs] *n.* a tall reed that grows in the Nile delta, used by the ancient Egyptians to make a paperlike material for writing on. (p. 38)

parliament [PAHR·luh·muhnt] *n.* a body of representatives that makes laws for a nation. (p. 354)

partition *n.* a division into parts, like the 1947 division of the British colony of India into the two nations of India and Pakistan. (p. 886)

pastoralist [PAS·tuhr·uh·lihst] *n.* a member of a nomadic group that herds domesticated animals. (p. 294)

paternalism [puh·TUR·nuh·LIHZ·uhm] *n.* a policy of treating subject people as if they were children, providing for their needs but not giving them rights. (p. 691)

patriarch [PAY·tree·AHRK] *n.* a principal bishop in the eastern branch of Christianity. (p. 272)

patriarchal [PAY·tree·AHR·kuhl] *adj.* relating to a social system in which the father is head of the family. (p. 176)

patrician [puh·TRIHSH·uhn] *n.* in ancient Rome, a member of the wealthy, privileged upper class. (p. 142)

patrilineal [PAT·ruh·LIHN·ee·uhl] *adj.* relating to a social system in which family descent and inheritance rights are traced through the father. (p. 369)

patron [PAY·truhn] *n.* a person who supports artists, especially financially. (p. 418)

Pax Romana [PAHKS roh·MAH·nah] *n.* a period of peace and prosperity throughout the Roman Empire, lasting from 27 B.C. to A.D. 180. (p. 148)

Peace of Augsburg [AWGZ·burg] *n.* a 1555 agreement declaring that the religion of each German state would be decided by its ruler. (p. 430)

Peloponnesian [PEHL·uh·puh·NEE·zhuhn] **War** *n.* a war, lasting from 431 to 404 B.C., in which Athens and its allies were defeated by Sparta and its allies. (p. 123)

penal [PEE·nuhl] **colony** *n.* a colony to which convicts are sent as an alternative to prison. (p. 665)

peninsulares [peh·neen·soo·LAH·rehs] *n.* in Spanish colonial society, colonists who were born in Spain. (p. 604)

Peninsular [puh·NIHN·syuh·luhr] **War** *n.* a conflict, lasting from 1808 to 1813, in which Spanish rebels, with the aid of British forces, fought to drive Napoleon's French troops out of Spain. (p. 590)

perestroika [PEHR·ih·STROY·kuh] *n.* a restructuring of the Soviet economy to permit more local decision-making, begun by Mikhail Gorbachev in 1985. (p. 922)

Persian Wars *n.* a series of wars in the fifth century B.C., in which Greek city-states battled the Persian Empire. (p. 118)

perspective [puhr·SPEHK·tihv] *n.* an artistic technique that creates the appearance of three dimensions on a flat surface. (p. 419)

phalanx [FAY·langks] *n.* a military formation of foot soldiers armed with spears and shields. (p. 115)

pharaoh [FAIR·oh] *n.* a king of ancient Egypt, considered a god as well as a political and military leader. (p. 35)

philosophe [FIHL·uh·SAHF] *n.* one of a group of social thinkers in France during the Enlightenment. (p. 552)

philosophers *n.* thinkers who use logic and reason to investigate the nature of the universe, human society, and morality. (p. 124)

Phoenicians [fih·NIHSH·uhnz] *n.* a seafaring people of Southwest Asia, who around 1100 B.C. began to trade and found colonies throughout the Mediterranean region. (p. 68)

Pilgrims *n.* a group of people who, in 1620, founded the colony of Plymouth in Massachusetts to escape religious persecution in England. (p. 491)

plebeian [plih·BEE·uhn] *n.* in ancient Rome, one of the common farmers, artisans, and merchants who made up most of the population. (p. 142)

plebiscite [PLEHB·ih·SYT] *n.* a direct vote in which a country's people have the opportunity to approve or reject a proposal. (p. 585)

PLO *n.* the Palestine Liberation Organization—an organization dedicated to the establishment of an independent state for Palestinians in the Middle East. (p. 905)

pogrom [puh·GRAHM] *n.* one of the organized campaigns of violence against Jewish communities in late-19th-century Russia. (p. 769)

polis [POH·lihs] *n.* a Greek city-state—the fundamental political unit of ancient Greece after about 750 B.C. (p. 115)

Politburo [PAHL·iht·BYOOR·oh] *n.* the ruling committee of the Communist Party in the Soviet Union. (p. 921)

polytheism [PAHL·ee·thee·IHZ·uhm] *n.* a belief in many gods. (p. 29)

pope *n.* the bishop of Rome, head of the Roman Catholic Church. (p. 156)

Popol Vuh [POH·pohl VOO] *n.* a book containing a version of the Mayan story of creation. (p. 398)

popular culture *n.* the cultural elements—sports, music, movies, clothing, and so forth—that reflect a group's common background and changing interests. (p. 957)

potlatch [PAHT·LACH] *n.* a ceremonial feast used to display rank and prosperity in some Northwest Coast tribes of Native Americans. (p. 391)

predestination [pree·DEHS·tuh·NAY·shuhn] *n.* the doctrine that God has decided all things beforehand, including which people will be eternally saved. (p. 433)

Presbyterian [PREHZ·bih·TEER·ee·uhn] *n.* a member of a Protestant church governed by elders (presbyters) and founded on the teachings of John Knox. (p. 433)

PRI *n.* the Institutional Revolutionary Party—the main political party of Mexico. (p. 914)

printing press *n.* a machine for reproducing written material by pressing paper against arrangements of inked type. (p. 426)

proliferation [pruh·LIHF·uh·RAY·shuhn] *n.* a growth or spread—especially the spread of nuclear weapons to nations that do not currently have them. (p. 953)

propaganda [PRAHP·uh·GAN·duh] *n.* information or material spread to advance a cause or to damage an opponent's cause. (p. 756)

Protestant [PRAHT·ih·stuhnt] *n.* a member of a Christian church founded on the principles of the Reformation. (p. 430)

provisional government *n.* a temporary government. (p. 772)

psychology [sy·KAHL·uh·jee] *n.* the study of the human mind and human behavior. (p. 679)

pueblos [PWEHB·lohz] *n.* villages of large apartment-like buildings made of clay and stone, built by the Anasazi and later peoples of the American Southwest. (p. 391)

Puritans *n.* a group of people who sought freedom from religious persecution in England by founding a colony at Massachusetts Bay in the early 1600s. (p. 491)

pyramid [PIHR·uh·mihd] *n.* a massive structure with a rectangular base and four triangular sides, like those that were built in Egypt as burial places for Old Kingdom pharaohs. (p. 35)

Q

Qin [chihn] **Dynasty** *n.* a short-lived Chinese dynasty that replaced the Zhou Dynasty in the third century B.C. (p. 99)

Qing [chihng] **Dynasty** *n.* China's last dynasty, which ruled from 1644 to 1912. (p. 471)

Quetzalcoatl [keht·SAHL·koh·AHT·uhl] *n.* the Feathered Serpent—a god of the Toltecs and other Mesoamerican peoples. (p. 401)

quipu [KEE·poo] *n.* an arrangement of knotted strings on a cord, used by the Inca to record numerical information. (p. 410)

Qur'an [kuh·RAN] *n.* the holy book of Islam. (p. 236)

R

racism [RAY·SIHZ·uhm] *n.* the belief that one race is superior to others. (p. 686)

radicals *n.* in the first half of the 19th century, those Europeans who favored drastic change to extend democracy to all people. (p. 609)

radioactivity *n.* a form of energy released as atoms decay. (p. 678)

Raj [rahj] *n.* the British-controlled portions of India in the years 1757–1947. (p. 704)

rationing [RASH·uh·nihng] *n.* the limiting of the amounts of goods people can buy—often imposed by governments during wartime, when goods are in short supply. (p. 755)

realism *n.* a 19th-century artistic movement in which writers and painters sought to show life as it is rather than life as it should be. (p. 621)

realpolitik [ray·AHL·POH·lih·TEEK] *n.* "the politics of reality"—the practice of tough power politics without room for idealism. (p. 617)

recession *n.* a slowdown in a nation's economy. (p. 913)

Reconquista [reh·kawn·KEES·tah] *n.* the effort by Christian leaders to drive the Muslims out of Spain, lasting from the 1100s until 1492. (p. 346)

Red Guards *n.* militia units formed by young Chinese people in 1966 in response to Mao Zedong's call for a social and cultural revolution. (p. 865)

Red Shirts *n.* the followers of the 19th-century Italian nationalist leader Giuseppe Garibaldi. (p. 616)

Reformation [REHF·uhr·MAY·shuhn] *n.* a 16th-century movement for religious reform, leading to the founding of Christian churches that rejected the pope's authority. (p. 429)

Reign [rayn] **of Terror** *n.* the period, from mid-1793 to mid-1794, when Maximilien Robespierre ruled France nearly as a dictator and thousands of political figures and ordinary citizens were executed. (p. 582)

reincarnation [REE·ihn·kahr·NAY·shuhn] *n.* in Hinduism and Buddhism, the process by which a soul is reborn again and again until it achieves perfect understanding. (p. 63)

religious toleration *n.* a recognition of people's right to hold differing religious beliefs. (p. 174)

Renaissance [REHN·ih·SAHNS] *n.* a period of European history, lasting from about 1300 to 1600, during which renewed interest in classical culture led to far-reaching changes in art, learning, and views of the world. (p. 417)

republic *n.* a form of government in which power is in the hands of representatives and leaders are elected by the people. (p. 142)

Restoration [REHS·tuh·RAY·shuhn] *n.* the period of Charles II's rule over England, after the collapse of Oliver Cromwell's government. (p. 538)

reunification [ree·YOO·nuh·fih·KAY·shuhn] *n.* a bringing together again of things that have been separated, like the reuniting of East Germany and West Germany in 1990. (p. 924)

romanticism [roh·MAN·tih·SIHZ·uhm] *n.* an early-19th-century movement in art and thought, which focused on emotion and nature rather than reason and society. (p. 619)

Roosevelt Corollary [ROH·zuh·VEHLT KAWR·uh·lehr·ee] *n.* President Theodore Roosevelt's 1904 extension of the Monroe Doctrine, in which he declared that the United States had the right to exercise "police power" throughout the Western Hemisphere. (p. 727)

Royal Road *n.* a road in the Persian Empire, stretching over 1,600 miles from Susa in Persia to Sardis in Anatolia. (p. 94)

Russo-Japanese War *n.* a 1904–1905 conflict between Russia and Japan, sparked by the two countries' efforts to dominate Manchuria and Korea. (p. 723)

S

sacrament [SAK·ruh·muhnt] *n.* one of the Christian ceremonies in which God's grace is transmitted to people. (p. 332)

Safavid [suh·FAH·vihd] *n.* a member of a Shi'a Muslim dynasty that built an empire in Persia in the 16th–18th centuries. (p. 449)

Sahel [suh·HAYL] *n.* the African region along the southern border of the Sahara. (p. 195)

salon [suh·LAHN] *n.* a social gathering of intellectuals and artists, like those held in the homes of wealthy women in Paris and other European cities during the Enlightenment. (p. 558)

SALT *n.* the Strategic Arms Limitation Talks—a series of meetings in the 1970s, in which leaders of the United States and the Soviet Union agreed to limit their nations' stocks of nuclear weapons. (p. 879)

samurai [SAM·uh·RY] *n.* one of the professional warriors who served Japanese feudal lords. (p. 307)

sans-culottes [SANS·kyoo·LAHTS] *n.* in the French Revolution, a radical group made up of Parisian wage-earners and small shopkeepers who wanted a greater voice in government, lower prices, and an end of food shortages. (p. 579)

satrap [SAY·trap] *n.* a governor of a province in the Persian Empire. (p. 94)

savanna [suh·VAN·uh] *n.* a flat, grassy plain. (p. 195)

schism [SIHZ·uhm] *n.* a split or division—especially a formal split within a Christian church. (p. 273)

Schlieffen [SHLEE·fuhn] **Plan** *n.* Germany's military plan at the outbreak of World War I, according to which German troops would rapidly defeat France and then move east to attack Russia. (p. 747)

scholastics [skuh·LAS·tihks] *n.* scholars who gathered and taught at medieval European universities. (p. 351)

scientific method *n.* a logical procedure for gathering information about the natural world, in which experimentation and observation are used to test hypotheses. (p. 547)

Scientific Revolution *n.* a major change in European thought, starting in the mid-1500s, in which the study of the natural world began to be characterized by careful observation and the questioning of accepted beliefs. (p. 545)

scorched-earth policy *n.* the practice of burning crops and killing livestock during wartime so that the enemy cannot live off the land. (p. 590)

scribe *n.* one of the professional record keepers in early civilizations. (p. 18)

secede [sih·SEED] *v.* to withdraw formally from an association or alliance. (p. 670)

secular [SEHK·yuh·luhr] *adj.* concerned with worldly rather than spiritual matters. (pp. 319, 418)

segregation [SEHG·rih·GAY·shuhn] *n.* the legal or social separation of people of different races. (p. 672)

self-determination [SEHLF·dih·TUR·muh·NAY·shuhn] *n.* the freedom of a people to decide under what form of government they wish to live. (p. 760)

Seljuks [SEHL·JOOKS] *n.* a Turkish group who migrated into the Abbasid Empire in the 10th century and established their own empire in the 11th century. (p. 279)

senate *n.* in ancient Rome, the supreme governing body, originally made up only of aristocrats. (p. 143)

separation of powers *n.* the assignment of executive, legislative, and judicial powers to different groups of officials in a government. (p. 553)

sepoy [SEE·poy] *n.* an Indian soldier serving under British command. (p. 701)

Sepoy Mutiny [MYOOT·uh·nee] *n.* an 1857 rebellion of Hindu and Muslim soldiers against the British in India. (p. 703)

serf *n.* a medieval peasant legally bound to live on a lord's estate. (p. 324)

Seven Years' War *n.* a conflict in Europe, North America, and India, lasting from 1756 to 1763, in which the forces of Britain and Prussia battled those of Austria, France, Russia, and other countries. (p. 530)

shari'a [shah·REE·ah] *n.* a body of law governing the lives of Muslims. (p. 237)

Shi'a [SHEE·uh] *n.* the branch of Islam whose members acknowledge Ali and his descendants as the rightful successors of Muhammad. (p. 240)

Shinto [SHIHN·toh] *n.* the native religion of Japan. (p. 303)

Shiva [SHEE·vuh] *n.* a Hindu god considered the destroyer of the world. (p. 178)

"shock therapy" *n.* an economic program implemented in Russia by Boris Yeltsin in the 1990s, involving an abrupt shift from a command economy to a free-market economy. (p. 928)

shogun [SHOH·guhn] *n.* in feudal Japan, a supreme military commander who ruled in the name of the emperor. (p. 307)

Sikh [seek] *n.* a member of a nonviolent religious group whose beliefs blend elements of Buddhism, Hinduism, and Sufism. (p. 454)

Silk Roads *n.* a system of ancient caravan routes across Central Asia, along which traders carried silk and other trade goods. (p. 179)

silt *n.* the fine soil carried in the water of rivers. (p. 27)

simony [SY·muh·nee] *n.* the selling or buying of a position in a Christian church. (p. 341)

Six-Day War *n.* a brief 1967 conflict between Israel and several Arab states, during which Israel took control of Jerusalem, the Sinai Peninsula, the Golan Heights, and the West Bank. (p. 903)

skepticism [SKEHP·tih·SIHZ·uhm] *n.* a philosophy based on the idea that nothing can be known for certain. (p. 519)

slash-and-burn farming *n.* a farming method in which people clear fields by cutting and burning trees and grasses, the ashes of which serve to fertilize the soil. (p. 14)

Slavs [slahvz] *n.* a people from the forests north of the Black Sea, ancestors of many peoples in Eastern Europe today. (p. 274)

social contract *n.* the agreement by which people define and limit their individual rights, thus creating an organized society or government. (p. 551)

Social Darwinism [DAHR·wih·NIHZ·uhm] *n.* the application of Charles Darwin's ideas about evolution and "survival of the fittest" to human societies—particularly as justification for imperialist expansion. (p. 686)

socialism *n.* an economic system in which the factors of production are owned by the public and operate for the welfare of all. (p. 648)

socialist realism *n.* a style of art in which Communist values and life under communism are glorified. (p. 778)

Solidarity [SAHL·ih·DAR·ih·tee] *n.* a Polish labor union that during the 1980s became the main force of opposition to Communist rule in Poland. (p. 922)

Songhai [SAWNG·HY] *n.* a West African empire that conquered Mali and controlled trade from the 1400s to 1591. (p. 374)

soviet [SOH·vee·EHT] *n.* one of the local representative councils formed in Russia after the downfall of Czar Nicholas II. (p. 772)

Spanish-American War *n.* an 1898 conflict between the United States and Spain, in which the United States supported Cubans' fight for independence. (p. 726)

specialization *n.* the development of skills in a particular kind of work, such as trading or record keeping. (p. 18)

sphere of influence *n.* a foreign region in which a nation has control over trade and other economic activities. (p. 718)

standard of living *n.* the quality of life of a person or a population, as indicated by the goods, services, and luxuries available to the person or people. (p. 912)

Star Wars *n.* a program to protect the United States against attack by enemy missiles, proposed in 1983 by President Ronald Reagan but never implemented—formally known as the Strategic Defense Initiative. (p. 879)

stateless societies *n.* cultural groups in which authority is shared by lineages of equal power instead of being exercised by a central government. (p. 368)

steppes [stehps] *n.* dry, grass-covered plains. (p. 57)

strike *v.* to refuse to work in order to force an employer to meet certain demands. (p. 650)

subcontinent *n.* a large landmass that forms a distinct part of a continent. (p. 42)

Suez [soo·EHZ] **Canal** *n.* a manmade waterway connecting the Red Sea and the Mediterranean Sea, which was opened in 1869. (p. 699)

Suez Crisis *n.* an international crisis that occurred after Egypt seized control of the Suez Canal in 1956, when Israel, with the support of Britain and France, invaded Egypt and marched toward the canal but withdrew under pressure from the United States and the Soviet Union. (p. 902)

suffrage [SUHF·rihj] *n.* the right to vote. (p. 659)

Sufi [SOO·fee] *n.* a Muslim who seeks to achieve direct contact with God through mystical means. (p. 240)

Sunna [SUN·uh] *n.* an Islamic model for living, based on the life and teachings of Muhammad. (p. 237)

Sunni [SUN·ee] *n.* the branch of Islam whose members acknowledge the first four caliphs as the rightful successors of Muhammad. (p. 240)

surrealism [suh·REE·uh·LIHZ·uhm] *n.* a 20th-century artistic movement that focuses on the workings of the unconscious mind. (p. 797)

sustainable development *n.* economic development that meets people's needs but preserves the environment and conserves resources for future generations. (p. 950)

Swahili [swah·HEE·lee] *n.* an Arabic-influenced Bantu language that is used widely in eastern and central Africa. (p. 378)

Taiping [ty·pihng] **Rebellion** *n.* a mid-19th century rebellion against the Qing Dynasty in China, led by Hong Xiuquan. (p. 717)

Taj Mahal [TAHZH muh·HAHL] *n.* a beautiful tomb in Agra, India, built by the Mughal emperor Shah Jahan for his wife Mumtaz Mahal. (p. 454)

Tamil [TAM·uhl] *n.* a language of southern India—also, the people who speak that language. (p. 175)

technology *n.* the ways in which people apply knowledge, tools, and inventions to meet their needs. (p. 9)

Tennis Court Oath *n.* a pledge made by the members of France's National Assembly in 1789, in which they vowed to continue meeting until they had drawn up a new constitution. (p. 576)

terrorism *n.* the use of force or threats to frighten people or governments to change their policies. (p. 953)

theocracy [thee·AHK·ruh·see] *n.* **1.** a government in which the ruler is viewed as a divine figure (p. 35). **2.** a government controlled by religious leaders. (p. 433)

theory of evolution *n.* the idea, proposed by Charles Darwin in 1859, that species of plants and animals arise by means of a process of natural selection. (p. 678)

theory of relativity [REHL·uh·TIHV·ih·tee] *n.* Albert Einstein's ideas about the interrelationships between time and space and between energy and matter. (p. 795)

Theravada [THEHR·uh·VAH·duh] *n.* a sect of Buddhism focusing on the strict spiritual discipline originally advocated by the Buddha. (p. 177)

Third Reich [ryk] *n.* the Third German Empire, established by Adolf Hitler in the 1930s. (p. 814)

Third Republic *n.* the republic that was established in France after the downfall of Napoleon III and ended with the German occupation of France during World War II. (p. 663)

Third World *n.* during the Cold War, the developing nations not allied with either the United States or the Soviet Union. (p. 871)

Thirty Years' War *n.* a European conflict over religion, over territory, and for power among ruling families, lasting from 1618 to 1648. (p. 526)

three-field system *n.* a system of farming developed in medieval Europe, in which farmland was divided into three fields of equal size and each of these was successively planted with a winter crop, planted with a spring crop, and left unplanted. (p. 348)

Tiananmen [tyahn·ahn·mehn] **Square** *n.* a huge public space in Beijing, China—in 1989, the site of a student uprising in support of democratic reforms. (p. 932)

tithe [tyth] *n.* a family's payment of one-tenth of its income to a church. (p. 325)

Tokugawa Shogunate [TOH·koo·GAH·wah SHOH·guh·niht] *n.* a dynasty of shoguns that ruled a unified Japan from 1603 to 1867. (p. 475)

Torah [TAWR·uh] *n.* the first five books of the Hebrew Bible—the most sacred writings in the Jewish tradition. (p. 72)

totalitarianism [toh·TAL·ih·TAIR·ee·uh·NIHZ·uhm] *n.* government control over every aspect of public and private life. (p. 775)

total war *n.* a conflict in which the participating countries devote all their resources to the war effort. (p. 755)

totems [TOH·tuhmz] *n.* animals or other natural objects that serve as symbols of the unity of clans or other groups of people. (p. 394)

tournament *n.* a mock battle between groups of knights. (p. 328)

tragedy *n.* a serious form of drama dealing with the downfall of a heroic or noble character. (p. 123)

Trans-Siberian [TRANS·sy·BEER·ee·uhn] **Railway** *n.* a rail line built between 1891 and 1904 to connect European Russia with Russian ports on the Pacific Ocean. (p. 770)

Treaty of Kanagawa [kah·NAH·gah·wah] *n.* an 1854 agreement between the United States and Japan, which opened two Japanese ports to U.S. ships and allowed the United States to set up an embassy in Japan. (p. 720)

Treaty of Tordesillas [TAWR·day·SEEL·yahs] *n.* a 1494 agreement between Portugal and Spain, declaring that newly discovered lands to the west of an imaginary line in the Atlantic Ocean would belong to Spain and newly discovered lands to the east of the line would belong to Portugal. (p. 466)

Treaty of Versailles [vuhr·SY] *n.* the peace treaty signed by Germany and the Allied powers after World War I. (p. 761)

trench warfare *n.* a form of warfare in which opposing armies fight each other from trenches dug in the battlefield. (p. 749)

triangular trade *n.* the transatlantic trading network along which slaves and other goods were carried between Africa, England, Europe, the West Indies, and the colonies in North America. (p. 497)

tribune [TRIHB·yoon] *n.* in ancient Rome, an official elected by the plebeians to protect their rights. (p. 142)

tribute *n.* a payment made by a weaker power to a stronger power to obtain an assurance of peace and security. (p. 76)

Triple Alliance *n.* **1.** an association of the city-states of Tenochtitlan, Texcoco, and Tlacopan, which led to the formation of the Aztec Empire (p. 402). **2.** a military alliance between Germany, Austria-Hungary, and Italy in the years preceding World War I. (p. 744)

Triple Entente [ahn·TAHNT] *n.* a military alliance between Great Britain, France, and Russia in the years preceding World War I. (p. 745)

triumvirate [try·UHM·vuhr·iht] *n.* in ancient Rome, a group of three leaders sharing control of the government. (p. 147)

Trojan War *n.* a war, fought around 1200 B.C., in which an army led by Mycenaean kings attacked the independent trading city of Troy in Anatolia. (p. 113)

troubadour [TROO·buh·DAWR] *n.* a medieval poet and musician who traveled from place to place, entertaining people with songs of courtly love. (p. 330)

Truman Doctrine *n.* a U.S. policy of giving economic and military aid to free nations threatened by internal or external opponents, announced by President Harry Truman in 1947. (p. 858)

tyrant [TY·ruhnt] *n.* in ancient Greece, a powerful individual who gained control of a city-state's government by appealing to the poor for support. (p. 116)

UV

Umayyads [oo·MY·adz] *n.* a dynasty that ruled the Muslim Empire from A.D. 661 to 750 and later established a kingdom in al-Andalus. (p. 239)

union *n.* an association of workers, formed to bargain for better working conditions and higher wages. (p. 650)

United Nations *n.* an international peacekeeping organization founded in 1945 to provide security to the nations of the world. (p. 855)

Universal Declaration of Human Rights *n.* a 1948 statement in which the United Nations declared that all human beings have rights to life, liberty, and security. (p. 954)

unrestricted submarine warfare *n.* the use of submarines to sink without warning any ship (including neutral ships and unarmed passenger liners) found in an enemy's waters. (p. 754)

urbanization [UR·buh·nih·ZAY·shuhn] *n.* the growth of cities and the migration of people into them. (p. 638)

U.S. Civil War *n.* a conflict between Northern and Southern states of the United States over the issue of slavery, lasting from 1861 to 1865. (p. 671)

utilitarianism [yoo·TIHL·ih·TAIR·ee·uh·NIHZ·uhm] *n.* the theory, proposed by Jeremy Bentham in the late 1700s, that government actions are useful only if they promote the greatest good for the greatest number of people. (p. 648)

Utopia [yoo·TOH·pee·uh] *n.* an imaginary land described by Thomas More in his book *Utopia*—hence, an ideal place. (p. 425)

U-2 incident *n.* the shooting down of a U.S. spy plane and capture of its pilot by the Soviet Union in 1960. (p. 860)

vassal [VAS·uhl] *n.* in feudal Europe, a person who received a grant of land from a lord in exchange for a pledge of loyalty and services. (p. 324)

Vedas [VAY·duhz] *n.* four collections of sacred writings produced by the Aryans during an early stage of their settlement in India. (p. 59)

vernacular [vuhr·NAK·yuh·luhr] *n.* the everyday language of people in a region or country. (pp. 350, 421)

Vietcong [vee·EHT·KAHNG] *n.* a group of Communist guerrillas who, with the help of North Vietnam, fought against the South Vietnamese government in the Vietnam War. (p. 868)

Vietnamization [vee·EHT·nuh·mih·ZAY·shuhn] *n.* President Richard Nixon's strategy for ending U.S. involvement in the Vietnam War, involving a gradual withdrawal of American troops and replacement of them with South Vietnamese forces. (p. 869)

Vishnu [VIHSH·noo] *n.* a Hindu god considered the preserver of the world. (p. 178)

vizier [vih·ZEER] *n.* a prime minister in a Muslim kingdom or empire. (p. 280)

W

War of the Spanish Succession *n.* a conflict, lasting from 1701 to 1713, in which a number of European states fought to prevent the Bourbon family from controlling Spain as well as France. (p. 523)

Warsaw Pact *n.* a military alliance formed in 1955 by the Soviet Union and seven Eastern European countries. (p. 859)

Weimar [WY·MAHR] **Republic** *n.* the republic that was established in Germany in 1919 and ended in 1933. (p. 802)

Western Front *n.* in World War I, the region of northern France where the forces of the Allies and the Central Powers battled each other. (p. 748)

westernization *n.* an adoption of the social, political, or economic institutions of Western—especially European or American—countries. (p. 533)

XYZ

yin and yang *n.* in Chinese thought, the two powers that govern the natural rhythms of life (with yin representing the feminine qualities in the universe, and yang the masculine qualities). (p. 99)

Yoruba [YAWR·uh·buh] *n.* a West African people who formed several kingdoms in what is now Benin and southern Nigeria. (p. 375)

Zapotec [ZAH·puh·TEHK] *n.* an early Mesoamerican civilization that was centered in the Oaxaca Valley of what is now Mexico. (p. 218)

ziggurat [ZIHG·uh·RAT] *n.* a tiered, pyramid-shaped structure that formed part of a Sumerian temple. (p. 21)

Zionism [ZY·uh·NIHZ·uhm] *n.* a movement founded in the 1890s to promote the establishment of a Jewish homeland in Palestine. (p. 663)

Spanish Glossary

Abbasids [abasidas] *s.* dinastía que gobernó gran parte del imperio musulmán entre 750 y 1258 d.C. (pág. 240)

Aborigine [aborigen] *s.* miembro de cualquiera de los pueblos nativos de Australia. (pág. 665)

absolute monarch [monarca absoluto] *s.* rey o reina que tiene poder ilimitado y que procura controlar todos los aspectos de la sociedad. (pág. 517)

absolute ruler [gobernante absoluto] *s.* gobernante que ejerce todo el poder. (pág. 147)

accommodation [acomodación] *s.* aceptación de las ideas y constumbres de otras culturas. (pág. 961)

acropolis [acrópolis] *s.* cima fortificada de las antiguas ciudades griegas. (pág. 115)

Aksum *s.* reino africano en lo que hoy es Etiopía y Eritrea, que alcanzó su mayor auge en el siglo 4. (pág. 199)

al-Andalus *s.* región gobernada por los musulmanes en lo que hoy es España, establecida en el siglo 8 d.C. (pág. 240)

Allah [Alah] *s.* Dios (palabra árabe usada en el islamismo). (pág. 234)

Allies [Aliados] *s.* durante la I Guerra Mundial, las naciones de Gran Bretaña, Francia y Rusia, junto con otras que lucharon a su lado; también, el grupo de naciones —entre ellas Gran Bretaña, la Unión Soviética y Estados Unidos— opuestas a las Potencias del Eje en la II Guerra Mundial. (pág. 748)

Almohads [almohades] *s.* grupo de reformadores islámicos que tumbaron la dinastía de los almorávides y que establecieron un imperio en el norte de África y en el sur de España en el siglo 12 d.C. (pág. 370)

Almoravids [almorávides] *s.* hermandad religiosa islámica que estableció un imperio en el norte de África y en el sur de España en el siglo 11 d.C. (pág. 370)

Anabaptist [anabaptista] *s.* en la Reforma, miembro de un grupo protestante que enseñaba que sólo los adultos podían ser bautizados, y que la Iglesia y el Estado debían estar separados. (pág. 434)

Anasazi [anasazi] *s.* grupo amerindio que se estableció en el Suroeste de Norteamérica. (pág. 391)

Anatolia *s.* península del suroeste de Asia actualmente ocupada por la parte asiática de Turquía; también llamada Asia Menor. (pág. 58)

Angkor Wat *s.* templo construido en el imperio Khmer y dedicado al dios hindú Visnú. (pág. 309)

Anglican [anglicano] *adj.* relacionado con la Iglesia de Inglaterra. (pág. 432)

animism [animismo] *s.* creencia de que en los animales, las plantas y otros objetos naturales habitan espíritus. (pág. 197)

annexation [anexión] *s.* añadir una región al territorio de una unidad política existente. (págs. 709, 723)

annul [anular] *v.* cancelar o suspender. (pág. 431)

anti-Semitism [antisemitismo] *s.* prejuicio contra los judíos. (pág. 663)

apartheid *s.* política de Sudáfrica de separación total y legalizada de las razas; prohibía todo contacto social entre negros y blancos. (pág. 919)

apostle [apóstol] *s.* uno de los seguidores de Jesús que predicaba y difundía sus enseñanzas. (pág. 153).

appeasement [apaciguamiento] *s.* otorgar concesiones a un agresor a fin de evitar la guerra. (pág. 813)

aqueduct [acueducto] *s.* tubería o canal para llevar agua a zonas pobladas. (pág. 167)

aristocracy [aristocracia] *s.* gobierno en que el poder está en manos de una clase dominante hereditaria o nobleza. (pág. 115)

armistice [armisticio] *s.* acuerdo de suspender combates. (pág. 757)

artifact [artefacto] *s.* objeto hecho por el ser humano, como herramientas, armas o joyas. (pág. 7)

artisan [artesano] *s.* trabajador especializado, como hilandero o ceramista, que hace productos a mano. (pág. 18)

Aryans [arios] *s.* **1.** pueblo indoeuropeo que, hacia 1500 a.C., comenzó a emigrar al subcontinente de India. (pág. 59). **2.** para los nazis, los pueblos germanos que formaban una "raza maestra". (pág. 831)

assembly line [línea de montaje] *s.* en una fábrica, correa que lleva un producto de un trabajador a otro, cada uno de los cuales desempeña una sola tarea. (pág. 674)

assimilation [asimilación] *s.* **1.** adopción de la cultura del conquistador por un pueblo conquistado. (pág. 185). **2.** política de una nación de obligar o alentar a un pueblo subyugado a adoptar sus instituciones y costumbres. (pág. 691)

Assyria [Asiria] *s.* reino del suroeste de Asia que controló un gran imperio de aproximadamente 850 a 612 a.C. (pág. 88)

Atlantic Charter [Carta del Atlántico] *s.* declaración de principios emitida en agosto de 1941 por el primer ministro británico Winston Churchill y el presidente de E.U.A. Franklin Roosevelt, en la cual se basó el plan de paz de los Aliados al final de la II Guerra Mundial. (pág. 826)

Atlantic slave trade [trata de esclavos del Atlántico] *s.* compra, transporte y venta de africanos para trabajar en las Américas. (pág. 496)

autocracy [autocracia] *s.* gobierno en el cual el gobernante tiene poder ilimitado y lo usa de forma arbitraria. (pág. 100)

Axis Powers [Potencias del Eje] *s.* en la II Guerra Mundial, las naciones de Alemania, Italia y Japón, que formaron una alianza en 1936. (pág. 813)

ayllu *s.* en la sociedad inca, pequeña comunidad o clan cuyos miembros trabajaban conjuntamente para el bien común. (pág. 408)

balance of power [equilibrio de poder] *s.* situación política en que ninguna nación tiene suficiente poder para ser una amenaza para las demás. (pág. 593)

Balfour Declaration [Declaración de Balfour] *s.* declaración de que el gobierno de Gran Bretaña apoyaba el establecimiento de una patria nacional judía en Palestina, expresada en una carta de 1917 del secretario de relaciones exteriores, Sir Arthur Balfour. (pág. 901)

Balkans [Balcanes] *s.* región del sureste de Europa ocupada actualmente por Grecia, Albania, Bulgaria, Rumania, la parte eureopea de Turquía y las antiguas repúblicas de Yugoslavia. (pág. 609)

Bantu-speaking peoples [pueblos de habla bantú]

papa Pablo III, para fallar sobre varias doctrinas criticadas por los reformadores protestantes. (pág. 436)

coup d'etat [golpe de Estado] *s.* toma repentina del poder político de una nación. (pág. 585)

covenant [pacto] *s.* promesa o acuerdo mutuo, especialmente un acuerdo entre Dios y el pueblo hebreo, como los que registra la Biblia. (pág. 73)

creoles [criollos] *s.* en la sociedad española colonial, los colonos nacidos en Latinoamérica de padres españoles. (pág. 604)

Crimean War [Guerra de Crimea] *s.* conflicto de 1853 a 1856, en el cual el imperio otomano, con ayuda de Gran Bretaña y Francia, frenó la expansión rusa en la región del mar Negro. (pág. 698)

crop rotation [rotación de cultivos] *s.* sistema que cultiva distintos productos en un campo cada año para conservar la fertilidad de la tierra. (pág. 633)

Crusade [cruzada] *s.* una de las expediciones de guerreros cristianos medievales para quitarle Jerusalén y la Tierra Santa a los musulmanes. (pág. 343)

cultural diffusion [difusión cultural] *s.* proceso de difusión de ideas o productos de una cultura a otra. (pág. 29)

Cultural Revolution [Revolución Cultural] *s.* levantamiento de 1966–1976 en China, encabezado por los Guardias Rojos de Mao Tsetung, con el propósito de establecer una sociedad de campesinos y trabajadores donde todos fueran iguales. (pág. 865)

culture [cultura] *s.* forma distintiva de la vida de un pueblo, representada en sus herramientas, costumbres, artes y pensamiento. (pág. 7)

cuneiform [cuneiforme] *s.* sistema de escritura que usa símbolos en forma de cuña inventado por los sumerios hacia 3000 a.C. (pág. 18)

Cyrillic alphabet [alfabeto cirílico] *s.* alfabeto inventado en el siglo 9 por los santos Cirilo y Metodio para la escritura de los idiomas eslavos. (pág. 273)

czar [zar] *s.* emperador ruso (de la palabra latina *Caesar*). (pág. 278)

D

daimyo *s.* señor feudal de Japón que comandaba un ejército privado de samurais. (pág. 474)

Daoism [taoísmo] *s.* filosofía basada en las ideas del pensador chino Laozi, quien enseñó a guiarse por una fuerza universal llamada Tao. (pág. 98)

D-Day [Día D] *s.* 6 de junio de 1944; día elegido para la invasión aliada de Europa continental durante la II Guerra Mundial. (pág. 838)

Declaration of Independence [Declaración de Independencia] *s.* declaración de las razones de la ruptura de las colonias americanas con Gran Bretaña, aprobada por el Segundo Congreso Continental. (pág. 564)

Declaration of the Rights of Man [Declaración de los Derechos del Hombre] *s.* declaración de ideales revolucionarios adoptada por la Asamblea Nacional Francesa en 1789. (pág. 577)

delta *s.* zona pantanosa que se forma con los depósitos de légamo en la desembocadura de un río. (pág. 34)

demilitarization [desmilitarización] *s.* reducción de la capacidad bélica de un país que se logra desbandando sus fuerzas armadas y prohibiéndole que adquiera armas. (pág. 844)

democracy [democracia] *s.* gobierno controlado por sus ciudadanos, bien sea directa o indirectamente, por medio de sus representantes. (pág. 117)

desertification [desertificación] *s.* transformación de tierras fértiles en desiertos. (pág. 195)

destalinization [desestalinización] *s.* política de Nikita Khrushchev para borrar a José Stalin y sus programas de la memoria de la Unión Soviética. (pág. 876)

détente *s.* política de reducir las tensiones de la Guerra Fría, adoptada por Estados Unidos durante la presidencia de Richard Nixon. (pág. 878)

developed nation [país desarrollado] *s.* nación con las instalaciones necesarias para la producción avanzada de productos manufacturados. (pág. 946)

developing nation [país en desarrollo] *s.* nación en vías de industrialización. (pág. 946)

devshirme *s.* en el imperio otomano, política de llevarse a los niños de los pueblos cristianos conquistados para entrenarlos como soldados musulmanes. (pág. 446)

Diaspora [diáspora] *s.* dispersión de los judíos fuera de Palestina, especialmente en los más de 1800 años que siguieron a la destrucción romana del Templo de Jerusalén en 70 d.C. (pág. 155)

dictator [dictador] *s.* en la antigua Roma, líder político con poder absoluto para decretar leyes y dirigir el ejército por un tiempo limitado. (pág. 143)

direct democracy [democracia directa] *s.* gobierno en el cual los ciudadanos gobiernan directamente, no a través de sus representantes. (pág. 120)

dissident [disidente] *s.* opositor a la política oficial de un gobierno. (pág. 918)

divine right [derecho divino] *s.* noción de que los monarcas son representantes de Dios en la Tierra y, por lo tanto, sólo le deben responder a él. (pág. 517)

domestication [domesticación] *s.* entrenamiento de animales para beneficio humano. (pág. 14)

dominion [dominio] *s.* en el imperio británico, una nación (como Canadá) a la que se permitía gobernar sus asuntos internos. (pág. 665)

domino theory [teoría del dominó] *s.* noción de que si una nación cae bajo control comunista, los países vecinos también lo harán. (pág. 868)

Dorians [dorios] *s.* grupo de lengua griega que, según la tradición, emigró a Grecia después de la destrucción de la civilización micénica. (pág. 113)

Dreyfus affair [caso Dreyfus] *s.* controversia surgida en Francia en la década de 1890 por el juicio y encarcelamiento del capitán Alfred Dreyfus, oficial judío falsamente acusado de vender secretos militares a Alemania. (pág. 663)

Duma *s.* parlamento nacional ruso formado a principios del siglo 20. (pág. 771)

Dutch East India Company [Compañía Holandesa de las Indias Orientales] *s.* empresa fundada por holandeses a principios del siglo 17 para establecer y dirigir comercio por todo Asia. (pág. 468)

dynastic cycle [ciclo dinástico] *s.* patrón histórico del surgimiento, caída y sustitución de dinastías. (pág. 50)

dynasty [dinastía] *s.* serie de gobernantes de una sola familia. (pág. 29)

E

Eastern Front [Frente Oriental] *s.* en la I Guerra Mundial, región a lo largo de la frontera ruso-alemana donde rusos y servios pelearon contra alemanes, austriacos y turcos. (pág. 750)

Edict of Nantes [Edicto de Nantes] *s.* declaración en que el rey francés Enrique IV prometió que los protestantes podían vivir en paz en Francia y tener centros de veneración en algunas ciudades. (pág. 518)

Emancipation Proclamation [Proclama de Emancipación] *s.*declaración emitida por el presidente Abraham Lincoln en 1862, asentando la libertad de todos los esclavos de los estados confederados. (pág. 671)

émigrés *s.*quienes abandonan su país de origen por razones políticas, como los nobles y otros que huyeron de Francia durante los levantamientos campesinos de la Revolución Francesa. (pág. 579)

empire [imperio] *s.*unidad política en que un solo gobernante controla varios pueblos o países. (pág. 31)

enclosure [cercado] *s.*uno de los campos rodeados de cercas o de arbustos que crearon terratenientes británicos ricos en tierras que antes trabajaban los campesinos. (pág. 633)

*encomienda s.*tierras otorgadas por España a un colonizador de América, con el derecho de hacer trabajar a los amerindios que vivían en ellas. (pág. 486)

English Civil War [Guerra Civil Inglesa] *s.*conflicto de 1642 a 1649 en que los seguidores puritanos del Parlamento lucharon contra los defensores de la monarquía de Inglaterra. (pág. 537)

enlightened despot [déspota ilustrado] *s.*uno de los monarcas europeos del siglo 18 inspirados por las ideas de la Ilustración a gobernar con justicia y respeto a los derechos de sus súbditos. (pág. 561)

enlightenment [iluminación] *s.*en budismo, estado de perfecta sabiduría en que se entienden las verdades básicas del universo. (pág. 64)

Enlightenment [Ilustración] *s.*movimiento del siglo 18 en Europa que trató de aplicar los principios de la razón y el método científico a todos los aspectos de la sociedad. (pág. 551)

entrepreneur [empresario] *s.*persona que organiza, administra y asume los riesgos de un negocio. (pág. 636)

epics [epopeyas] *s.*poemas narrativos extensos que celebran las hazañas de héroes tradicionales o legendarios. (pág. 114)

estate [estado] *s.*una de las tres clases sociales existentes en Francia antes de la Revolución Francesa; el primer estado era el de la clerecía; el segundo era el de la nobleza; y el tercero era el del resto de la población. (pág. 573)

Estates-General [Estados Generales] *s.*asamblea de representantes de los tres estados, o clases sociales, de Francia. (pág. 575)

ethnic cleansing [limpia étnica] *s.*política de asesinatos y otros actos de brutalidad con que los servios quisieron eliminar la población musulmana de Bosnia después de la división de Yugoslavia. (pág. 929)

excommunication [excomunión] *s.*expulsión de una iglesia cristiana. (pág. 273)

existentialism [existencialismo] *s.*filosofía basada en la idea de que el ser humano da significado a su vida con sus decisiones y acciones. (pág. 796)

extended family [familia extensa] *s.*grupo que incluye a los padres, hijos, abuelos, nietos, tíos y primos. (pág. 197)

extraterritorial rights [derechos extraterritoriales] *s.*exención a los extranjeros de las leyes de un país. (pág. 716)

F

factors of production [factores de producción] *s.*recursos —como tierra, mano de obra y capital— necesarios para producir bienes y servicios. (pág. 634)

factory [fábrica] *s.*construcción amplia en que se manufacturan productos con maquinaria. (pág. 635)

fascism [fascismo] *s.*movimiento político que postula una forma extrema de nacionalismo, la supresión de los derechos individuales y un régimen dictatorial de un solo partido. (pág. 807)

Fatimid [fatimitas] *s.*dinastía musulmana cuyos orígenes se remontan a Fátima, hija de Mahoma, y que construyó un imperio en África del Norte, Arabia y Siria en los siglos 9 a 12. (pág. 240)

favorable balance of trade [balanza comercial favorable] *s.*situación económica en la cual un país exporta más de lo que importa, es decir, que vende más productos de los que compra en el extranjero. (pág. 502)

federal system [sistema federal] *s.*sistema de gobierno en el que el poder se divide entre una autoridad central y varios estados. (págs. 567, 917)

Fertile Crescent [Media Luna Fértil] *s.*arco de ricos terrenos de cultivo en el suroeste de Asia, entre el golfo Pérsico y el mar Mediterráneo. (pág. 27)

feudalism [feudalismo] *s.*sistema político en el cual a los nobles se les otorga el uso de tierras de propiedad del rey, a cambio de lealtad, servicio militar y protección de sus habitantes. (pág. 50)

fief [feudo] *s.*dominio concedido a un vasallo por un señor, conforme al sistema feudal de la Europa medieval. (pág. 324)

filial piety [amor filial] *s.*respeto de los hijos a los padres y a sus mayores. (pág. 97)

Final Solution [solución final] *s.*programa de Hitler de asesinar sistemáticamente a todo el pueblo judío. (pág. 833)

FLN *s.*Frente de Liberación Nacional: grupo de Argelia que libró una lucha de guerrillas buscando independizarse de Francia. (pág. 899)

Four Modernizations [cuatro modernizaciones] *s.*serie de objetivos adoptados por el líder chino Deng Xiaoping a finales del siglo 20 con miras al progreso en agricultura, industria, defensa, y ciencia y tecnología. (pág. 932)

Fourteen Points [los catorce puntos] *s.*serie de propuestas en que el presidente estadounidense Woodrow Wilson esbozó un plan para alcanzar una paz duradera después de la I Guerra Mundial. (pág. 760)

Franks [francos] *s.*pueblo germano que se asentó en la provincia romana de Galia (a grandes rasgos, donde está hoy Francia) y que formó un gran imperio durante la Edad Media. (pág. 318)

free trade [libre comercio] *s.*comercio entre naciones sin restricciones o barreras económicas (tales como aranceles). (pág. 947)

French and Indian War [Guerra contra Franceses e Indígenas] *s.*conflicto entre Gran Bretaña y Francia por control de territorio en Norteamérica, de 1754 a 1763. (pág. 493)

fundamentalism [fundamentalismo] *s.*creencia estricta en las verdades básicas y en las prácticas de una religión. (pág. 953)

G

genetic engineering [ingeniería genética] *s.*transferencia de genes de un organismo a otro para producir un organismo con nuevos rasgos. (pág. 944)

genocide [genocidio] *s.*matanza sistemática de todo un pueblo. (pág. 833)

gentry [pequeña nobleza] *s.*clase de ricos y poderosos que gozan de alto nivel social. (pág. 291)

geopolitics [geopolítica] s.política exterior basada en una consideración de la ubicación estratégica o de los productos de otras tierras. (pág. 698)

Ghana s.reino de África occidental que se enriqueció debido a recaudación de impuestos y al control del comercio, y que estableció un imperio en los siglos 9 a 11. (pág. 371)

ghazi s.guerrero del islam. (pág. 443)

ghettos s.barrios en que tenían que vivir los judíos europeos. (pág. 832)

gladiator [gladiador] s.en la antigua Roma, luchador profesional que luchaba a muerte contra un contrincante en un circo público. (pág. 151)

glasnost s.política soviética de "apertura" a la libre circulación de ideas e información introducida en 1985 por Mijail Gorbachev. (pág 921)

global economy [economía global] s.todas las interacciones financieras —entre individuos, empresas y gobiernos— que rebasan fronteras internacionales. (pág. 947)

Glorious Revolution [Revolución Gloriosa] s.derrocamiento incruento del rey Jacobo II de Inglaterra, quien fue reemplazado por Guillermo y María. (pág. 539)

glyph [glifo] s.dibujo simbólico, especialmente el usado como parte de un sistema de escritura para tallar mensajes en piedra. (pág. 398)

Gothic [gótico] adj. relacionado con un nuevo estilo de arquitectura religiosa surgido en la Europa medieval, caracterizado por bóvedas de nervadura, vitrales emplomados, contrafuertes volantes, arcos ojivales y altas agujas. (pág. 342)

Great Depression [Gran Depresión] s.crisis económica aguda que siguió a la caída del mercado de valores en 1929. (pág. 804)

Great Fear [Gran Miedo] s.ola de temor insensato que se extendió por las provincias francesas después de la toma de la Bastilla en 1789. (pág. 576)

Great Purge [Gran Purga] s.campaña de terror en la Unión Soviética durante la década de 1930, en la cual José Stalin trató de eliminar a todos los miembros del Partido Comunista y ciudadanos que amenazaban su poder. (pág. 777)

Great Schism [Gran Cisma] s.división de la Iglesia Católica Romana medieval, durante la cual había dos Papas rivales, uno en Avignon y el otro en Roma. (pág. 357)

Great Trek [Gran Jornada] s.salida de colonos holandeses de territorio controlado por los británicos en Sudáfrica durante la década de 1830. (pág. 689)

Greco-Roman culture [cultura greco-romana] s.antigua cultura producto de la mezcla de la cultura griega, helénica y romana. (pág. 164)

green revolution [revolución verde] s.esfuerzo en el siglo 20 de aumentar los alimentos en el mundo entero, a través del uso de fertilizantes y pesticidas, y de la creación de cultivos resistentes a enfermedades. (pág. 944)

griot s.narrador de África occidental. (pág. 197)

guerrilla [guerrillero] s.miembro de una unidad de combate informal que ataca por sorpresa las tropas enemigas que ocupan su país. (pág. 590)

guild [gremio] s.asociación medieval de personas que laboraban en lo mismo; controlaba salarios y precios. (pág. 349)

guillotine [guillotina] s.máquina para decapitar con que se hicieron ejecuciones durante la Revolución Francesa. (pág. 580)

Gulf War [Guerra del Golfo] s.conflicto de 1991 en que fuerzas de la ONU derrotaron las fuerzas de Iraq que invadieron a Kuwait y amenazaban invadir a Arabia Saudita. (pág. 949)

Gupta Empire [imperio gupta] s.el segundo imperio en India, fundado por Chandra Gupta I en el 320 d.C. (pág. 175)

Gutenberg Bible [Biblia de Gutenberg] s.primer libro completo impreso con tipos móviles y prensa de imprenta. (pág. 426)

H

habeas corpus s.documento que requiere que un detenido comparezca ante un tribunal o juez para que se determine si su detención es legal. (pág. 538)

Hagia Sophia [Santa Sofía] s.catedral de la Santa Sabiduría en Constantinopla, construida por orden del emperador bizantino Justiniano. (pág. 270)

haiku s.poema japonés que tiene tres versos no rimados de cinco, siete y cinco sílabas. (pág. 476)

hajj s.peregrinación a la Meca realizada como deber por los musulmanes. (pág. 236)

Han Dynasty [dinastía Han] s.dinastía china que gobernó del 202 a.C. al 9 d.C. y nuevamente del 23 al 220 d.C. (pág. 181)

Hausa [hausa] s.pueblo de África occidental que vivía en varias ciudades Estado en el actual norte de Nigeria. (pág. 375)

heliocentric theory [teoría heliocéntrica] s.idea de que la Tierra y los otros planetas giran en torno al Sol. (pág. 546)

Hellenistic [helénico] adj. relacionado con la civilización, el idioma, el arte, la ciencia y la literatura del mundo griego a partir del reino de Álejandro el Magno hasta el siglo 2 a.C. (pág. 132)

helot [ilota] s.en la antigua Esparta, campesino atado a la tierra. (pág. 116)

heresy [herejía] s.creencia u opinión religiosa que difiere de las enseñanzas oficiales de la Iglesia Católica. (pág. 157)

hieroglyphics [jeroglíficos] s.antiguo sistema de escritura egipcia en el cual se usan imágenes para representar ideas y sonidos. (pág. 38)

Hijrah s.migración de Mahoma de la Meca a Yathrib (Medina) en el 622 d.C. (pág. 235)

Hittites [hititas] s.pueblo indoeuropeo que se estableció en Anatolia hacia 2000 a.C. (pág. 58)

Holocaust [Holocausto] s.matanza en masa de judíos y otros civiles, ejecutada por el gobierno de la Alemania nazi, antes y durante la II Guerra Mundial. (pág. 831)

Holy Alliance [Alianza Sagrada] s.liga de naciones europeas formada por los dirigentes de Rusia, Austria y Prusia después del Congreso de Viena. (pág. 595)

Holy Roman Empire [Sacro Imperio Romano] s.imperio establecido en Europa en el siglo 10, que inicialmente se formó con tierras de lo que hoy es Alemania e Italia. (pág. 333)

home rule [autogobierno] s.control sobre asuntos internos que da el gobierno a los residentes de una región. (pág. 668)

hominid [homínido] s.miembro del grupo biológico que abarca a los seres humanos y especies relacionadas que caminan erguidas. (pág. 8)

Homo sapiens s.especie biológica de los seres humanos modernos. (pág. 9)

House of Wisdom [Casa de la Sabiduría] s.centro de enseñanza en Bagdad en el siglo 9. (pág. 243)

Hubble Space Telescope [telescopio espacial Hubble] *s.* potente telescopio puesto en órbita alrededor de la Tierra por NASA y la Agencia Europea del Espacio (AEE) en 1990. (pág. 942)

humanism [humanismo] *s.* movimiento intelectual del Renacimiento que estudió los textos clásicos y se enfocó en el potencial y los logros humanos. (pág. 418)

Hundred Days [Cien Días] *s.* corto período de 1815 en que Napoleón hizo su último intento de recuperar el poder, depuso al rey francés y de nuevo se proclamó emperador de Francia. (pág. 592)

Hundred Years' War [Guerra de los Cien Años] *s.* conflicto en el cual Inglaterra y Francia lucharon en territorio francés de 1337 a 1453, con interrupciones. (pág. 359)

hunter-gatherer [cazador-recolector] *s.* miembro de un grupo nómada que se alimenta de la caza de animales y la recolección de frutos. (pág. 12)

Hyksos [hicsos] *s.* grupo nómada de invasores del suroeste de Asia que gobernó Egipto de 1640 a 1570 a.C. (pág. 83)

I

Ice Age [Edad de Hielo] *s.* período de fríos en que enormes capas de hielo se desplazan de las regiones polares; la última fue de aproximadamente 1,600,000 a 10,000 a.C. (pág. 211)

I Ching *s.* libro chino de oráculos consultado para solucionar problemas éticos y prácticos. (pág. 99)

icon [icono] *s.* imagen religiosa usada por los cristianos de Oriente. (pág. 272)

iconoclast [iconoclasta] *s.* uno de los cristianos de Oriente que destruyó imágenes religiosas en iglesias durante los siglos 8 y 9. (pág. 272)

imperialism [imperialismo] *s.* política en que una nación fuerte buscar dominar la vida política, económica y social de otros países. (pág. 686)

impressionism [impresionismo] *s.* movimiento de la pintura del siglo 19 en reacción al realismo, que buscaba dar impresiones personales de sujetos o momentos. (pág. 623)

Indo-Europeans [indoeuropeos] *s.* grupo de pueblos seminómadas que, hacia 1700 a.C., comenzaron a emigrar de lo que es hoy el sur de Rusia al subcontinente hindú, Europa y el suroeste de Asia. (pág. 57)

indulgence [indulgencia] *s.* perdón que libera al pecador de la penitencia por un pecado. (pág. 429)

industrialization [industrialización] *s.* desarrollo de industrias para la producción con máquinas. (pág. 634)

Industrial Revolution [Revolución Industrial] *s.* cambio, que comenzó en Inglaterra durante el siglo 18, de la producción manual a la producción con máquinas. (pág. 633)

inflation [inflación] *s.* baja del valor de la moneda, acompañada de un alza de precios de bienes y servicios. (pág. 158)

Inquisition [Inquisición] *s.* tribunal de la Iglesia Católica para investigar y juzgar a los acusados de herejía, especialmente el establecido en España durante el siglo 15. (pág. 346)

institution [institución] *s.* patrón duradero de organización en una comunidad. (pág. 18)

intendant [intendente] *s.* funcionario del gobierno francés nombrado por el monarca para recaudar impuestos e impartir justicia. (pág. 520)

Internet *s.* vinculación de redes de computadora que permite a gente de todo el mundo comunicarse e intercambiar información. (pág. 943)

iron curtain [cortina de hierro] *s.* durante la Guerra Fría, división que separaba las naciones comunistas de Europa oriental de las naciones democráticas de Europa occidental. (pág. 857)

Iroquois [iroqueses] *s.* grupo de pueblos amerindios que hablaban lenguas relacionadas, vivían en la parte este de la región de los Grandes Lagos en Norteamérica y formaron una alianza a fines del siglo 16. (pág. 393)

irrigation [irrigación] *s.* acarreo de agua a campos de cultivo por medio de canales y acequias. (pág. 28)

Islam [islam] *s.* religión monoteísta que se desarrolló en Arabia en el siglo 7 d.C. (pág. 234)

isolationism [aislacionismo] *s.* política de evitar lazos políticos o militares con otros países. (pág. 814)

Israel *s.* reino de los hebreos unidos en Palestina, de aproximadamente 1020 a 922 a.C.; después, el reino norte de los dos reinos hebreos; actualmente, la nación judía establecida en Palestina en 1948. (pág. 75)

J

Jainism [jainismo] *s.* religión fundada en India durante el siglo 6, cuyos miembros creen que todo en el universo tiene alma y por lo tanto no debe ser lastimado. (pág. 63)

janissary [janísero] *s.* miembro de una fuerza élite de soldados del imperio otomano. (pág. 446)

jazz *s.* estilo de música popular del siglo 20 concebido principalmente por músicos afroamericanos. (pág. 797)

Jesuits [jesuitas] *s.* miembros de la Sociedad de Jesús, orden católica romana fundada por Ignacio de Loyola. (pág. 435)

"jewel in the crown" ["joya de la corona"] *s.* colonia británica de India, así llamada por su importancia para el imperio británico, tanto como proveedor de materia prima como mercado para sus productos. (pág. 701)

joint-stock company [sociedad de capitales] *s.* negocio en el que los inversionistas reúnen capital para un propósito común y después comparten las ganancias. (pág. 502)

Judah [Judea] *s.* reino hebreo establecido en Palestina alrededor del 922 a.C. (pág. 76)

Justinian Code [Código Justiniano] *s.* cuerpo del derecho civil romano recopilado y organizado por órdenes del emperador bizantino Justiniano hacia el 534 d.C. (pág. 270)

K

kabuki *s.* forma de teatro japonés en que se representa una historia con música, danza y mímica. (pág. 476)

kaiser *s.* emperador alemán (del título romano *Caesar*). (pág. 618)

kamikaze *s.* durante la II Guerra Mundial, pilotos suicidas japoneses entrenados para hundir barcos de los Aliados lanzándose sobre ellos con aviones llenos de bombas. (pág. 841)

karma *s.* en hinduismo y budismo, la totalidad de actos buenos y malos que comete una persona, que determinan su destino al renacer. (pág. 63)

Khmer Empire [imperio Khmer] *s.* imperio del sureste asiático, centrado en la actual Camboya, que alcanzó su mayor auge hacia 1200 d.C. (pág. 309)

Khmer Rouge *s.* grupo de rebeldes comunistas que tomaron el poder en Camboya en 1975. (pág. 870)

knight [caballero] *s.* en Europa medieval, guerrero con armadura y cabalgadura. (pág. 324)

Koryu Dynasty [dinastía koryu] *s.* dinastía coreana del 935 a 1392 d.C. (pág. 311)

Kristallnacht *s.* "Noche de cristales rotos": noche del 9 de noviembre de 1938, en que milicianos nazis atacaron hogares, negocios y sinagogas judíos en toda Alemania. (pág. 831)

kulak *s.* miembro de una clase de campesinos ricos en Rusia. (pág. 777)

Kuomintang *s.* Partido Nacionalista de China, formado después de la caída de la dinastía Qing en 1912. (pág. 781)

Kush *s.* antiguo reino nubio cuyos reyes gobernaron a Egipto del 751 a 671 a.C. (pág. 85)

L

laissez faire *s.* idea de que el gobierno no debe regular ni interferir en las industrias y empresas. (pág. 647)

land reform [reforma agraria] *s.* redistribución de tierras agrícolas con división de grandes latifundios y reparto de fincas a campesinos. (pág. 912)

La Reforma *s.* movimiento de reforma liberal en el siglo 19 en México fundado por Benito Juárez. (pág. 730)

lay investiture [investidura seglar] *s.* nombramiento de funcionarios de la Iglesia por reyes y nobles. (pág. 334)

League of Nations [Liga de las Naciones] *s.* organización internacional formada después de la I Guerra Mundial cuyo propósito era mantener la paz entre las naciones. (pág. 761)

lebensraum *s.* "espacio vital": territorio adicional que, según Adolfo Hitler, Alemania necesitaba porque estaba sobrepoblada. (pág. 809)

Legalism [legalismo] *s.* filosofía política china basada en la idea de que un gobierno altamente eficiente y poderoso es la clave del orden social. (pág. 99)

legion [legión] *s.* unidad militar del ejército de la antigua Roma formada por aproximadamente 5,000 soldados de infantería y grupos de soldados de caballería. (pág. 143)

Legislative Assembly [Asamblea Legislativa] *s.* congreso creado por la Constitución francesa de 1791, con poder para emitir leyes y aprobar declaraciones de guerra. (pág. 578)

legitimacy [legitimidad] *s.* derecho hereditario de un monarca a gobernar. (pág. 594)

liberals [liberales] *s.* en la primera mitad del siglo 19, europeos —principalmente empresarios y comerciantes de clase media— que deseaban darle más poder político a los parlamentos elegidos. (pág. 609)

lineage [linaje] *s.* individuos —vivos, muertos y sin nacer— que descienden de un antepasado común. (pág. 368)

loess [loes] *s.* depósito fértil de tierra traída por el viento. (pág. 46)

Long March [Larga Marcha] *s.* viaje de 6,000 millas que realizaron en 1934–35 las fuerzas comunistas de China para escapar de las fuerzas nacionalistas de Jiang Jieshi. (pág. 784)

lord [señor] *s.* en la Europa feudal, persona que controlaba tierras y por lo tanto podía dar feudos a vasallos. (pág. 324)

Lutheran [luterano] *s.* miembro de una iglesia protestante basada en las enseñanzas de Martín Lutero. (pág. 430)

lycée [liceo] *s.* escuela pública en Francia. (pág. 585)

M

Macedonia *s.* antiguo reino del norte de Grecia, cuyo rey Felipe II conquistó a Grecia en 338 a.C. (pág. 128)

Maghrib [Maghreb] *s.* región del norte de África que abarca la costa del Mediterráneo de lo que en la actualidad es Marruecos, Túnez y Argelia. (pág. 369)

Magna Carta [Carta Magna] *s.* "Gran Carta": documento de Inglaterra que garantiza derechos políticos elementales, elaborado por nobles ingleses y aprobado por el rey Juan en 1215 d.C. (pág. 353)

Mahabharata *s.* gran poema épico de India que relata las luchas arias durante su migración al sur de India. (pág. 60)

Mahayana *s.* secta del budismo que ofrece la salvación a todos y permite la veneración popular. (pág. 177)

maize [maíz] *s.* cereal cultivado cuyos granos se encuentran en grandes espigas, o mazorcas. (pág. 213)

Mali *s.* imperio de África occidental que floreció entre 1235 y el siglo 15, y se enriqueció con el comercio. (pág. 373)

mamelukes [mamelucos] *s.* esclavos turcos que sirvieron como soldados y guardaespaldas en el imperio abasida. (pág. 279)

Manchus [manchú] *s.* pueblo originario de Manchuria que gobernó en China durante la dinastía Qing (1644–1912). (pág. 471)

Mandate of Heaven [Mandato del Cielo] *s.* en China, creencia de que la autoridad real era producto de la aprobación divina. (pág. 50)

manifest destiny [destino manifiesto] *s.* idea popular en el siglo 19 en Estados Unidos de que era su derecho y obligación regir Norteamérica, desde el oceáno Atlántico hasta el Pacífico. (pág. 670)

manor [señorío] *s.* dominios de un señor en la Europa feudal. (pág. 325)

Maori [maorí] *s.* miembro de un pueblo polinesio establecido en Nueva Zelanda hacia 800 d.C. (pág. 665)

Marshall Plan [Plan Marshall] programa estadounidense de ayuda económica a países europeos para su reconstrucción después de la II Guerra Mundial. (pág. 858)

martial law [ley marcial] *s.* gobierno militar temporal impuesto a la población civil, normalmente en época de guerra o de trastornos civiles. (pág. 917)

mass culture [cultura de masas] *s.* producción de obras de arte y diversión concebidas con el fin de atraer a un amplio público. (pág. 674)

materialism [materialismo] *s.* alto interés en la adquisición de posesiones materiales. (pág. 960)

matriarchal [matriarcal] *adj.* relacionado con un sistema social en el que la madre es jefa de la familia. (pág. 176)

matrilineal *adj.* relacionado con un sistema social en el que la descendencia familiar y los derechos de herencia se trasmiten a través de la madre. (pág. 369)

Mau Mau [Mau-mau] *s.* sociedad secreta de miembros de la tribu kikuyu que trataron de expulsar a los británicos de Kenia a mediados del siglo 20. (pág. 897)

Mauryan Empire [imperio maurio] *s.* primer imperio de India, fundado por Chandragupta Mauria en 321 a.C. (pág. 173)

May Fourth Movement [Movimiento del 4 de Mayo] *s.* protesta nacional china en 1919 con manifestaciones contra el Tratado de Versalles y la interferencia extranjera. (pág. 782)

Medes [medos] *s.* pueblo del suroeste asiático que contribuyó a derrotar al imperio asirio. (pág. 90)

Meiji era [era Meiji] *s.* período de la historia japonesa entre 1867 y 1912, cuando gobernó el emperador Mutshito. (pág. 721)

Mein Kampf [Mi lucha] *s.* libro escrito por Adolfo Hitler en prisión (1923–1924), en el cual expone sus creencias y sus ideales para Alemania. (pág. 809)

mercantilism [mercantilismo] *s.*política económica de aumentar la riqueza y poder de una nación obteniendo grandes cantidades de oro y plata, y vendiendo más bienes de los que se compran. (pág. 502)

mercenary [mercenario] *s.*soldado que recibe sueldo por pelear en un ejército extranjero. (pág. 159)

Mesoamerica [Mesoamérica] *s.*región que se extiende desde el centro de México hasta Honduras, donde se desarrollaron varias de las antiguas sociedades complejas de América. (pág. 216)

mestizo *s.*mezcla de español y amerindio. (pág. 486)

Middle Ages [Edad Media] *s.*era en la historia europea posterior a la caída del imperio romano, que abarca aproximadamente desde el 500 hasta 1500, también llamada época medieval. (pág. 317)

middle class [clase media] *s.*clase social formada por trabajadores especializados, profesionales, comerciantes y granjeros acaudalados. (pág. 639)

middle passage [travesía intermedia] *s.*viaje que trajo a africanos capturados al Caribe y, posteriormente, a América del Norte y del Sur, para venderlos como esclavos; recibió este nombre porque era considerada la porción media del triángulo comercial trasatlántico. (pág. 497)

migration [migración] *s.*acto de trasladarse de un lugar para establecerse en otro. (pág. 57)

militarism [militarismo] *s.*política de glorificar el poder militar y de mantener un ejército permanente, siempre preparado para luchar. (pág. 744)

Ming Dynasty [dinastía Ming] *s.*dinastía que reinó en China desde 1368 hasta 1644. (pág. 469)

Minoans [minoicos] *s.*pueblo de navegantes y comerciantes que vivió en la isla de Creta de aproximadamente 2000 a 1400 a.C. (pág. 67)

Mississippian [misisipiense] *adj.* relacionado con una cultura constructora de túmulos que floreció en Norteamérica entre el 800 y 1500 d.C. (pág. 393)

mita *s.* en el imperio inca, obligación de todo súbdito de trabajar ciertos días al año para el Estado. (pág. 409)

Moche [moche] *s.*civilización que floreció en la actual costa norte de Perú de aproximadamente 100 a 700 d.C. (pág. 222)

monarchy [monarquía] *s.*gobierno en que el poder está en manos de una sola persona. (pág. 115)

monastery [monasterio] *s.*comunidad religiosa de hombres, llamados monjes, que ceden todas sus posesiones y se dedican a la oración y veneración. (pág. 318)

monopoly [monopolio] *s.*control exclusivo sobre la producción y distribución de ciertos bienes. (pág. 185)

monotheism [monoteísmo] *s.*creencia en un solo dios. (pág. 73)

Monroe Doctrine [doctrina Monroe] *s.*política estadounidense de oposición a la interferencia europea en Latinoamérica, anunciada por el presidente James Monroe en 1823. (pág. 726)

monsoon [monzón] *s.*viento que cambia de dirección en ciertas épocas del año. (pág. 42)

mosque [mezquita] *s.*lugar de veneración islámica. (pág. 236)

movable type [tipo móvil] *s.*bloques de metal o de madera, cada uno con caracteres individuales, que pueden distribuirse para formar una página de impresión. (pág. 289)

Mughal [mogol] *s.*uno de los nómadas que invadieron el subcontinente de India en el siglo 16 y establecieron un poderoso imperio. (pág. 451)

mulattos [mulatos] *s.*personas de ascendencia europea y africana. (pág. 604)

multinational corporation [corporación trasnacional] *s.*empresa que opera en numerosos países. (pág. 947)

mummification [momificación] *s.*proceso de embalsamamiento y secado de cadáveres para evitar su descomposición. (pág. 37)

Munich Conference [Conferencia de Munich] *s.*reunión en 1938 de Inglaterra, Francia, Italia y Alemania, en la cual Gran Bretaña y Francia aceptaron que la Alemania nazi anexara parte de Checoslovaquia, a cambio de la promesa de Adolfo Hitler de respetar las nuevas fronteras checas. (pág. 815)

Muslim [musulmán] *s.*devoto del islam. (pág. 235)

Muslim League [Liga Musulmana] *s.*organización formada en 1906 para proteger los intereses de los musulmanes de India; después propuso la división del país en dos naciones: una musulmana y una hindú. (pág. 886)

Mutapa [mutapa] *adj.* con un imperio de África del sur establecido por Mutota en el siglo 15 a.D. (pág. 381)

Mycenaeans [micénicos] *s.*grupo indoeuropeo que se estableció en Grecia hacia 2000 a.C. (pág. 112)

myths [mitos] *s.*narraciones tradicionales sobre dioses, antepasados o héroes, que explican el mundo natural o las costumbres y creencias de una sociedad. (pág. 114)

N

Napoleonic Code [código napoleónico] *s.*sistema extenso y uniforme de leyes establecido para Francia por Napoleón. (pág. 586)

National Assembly [Asamblea Nacional] *s.*congreso francés establecido el 17 de junio de 1789 por representantes del Tercer Estado para promulgar leyes y reformas en nombre del pueblo. (pág. 575)

nationalism [nacionalismo] *s.*creencia de que la principal lealtad del pueblo debe ser a su nación —es decir, a la gente con quien comparte historia y cultura— y no al rey o al imperio. (pág. 609)

nation-state [nación Estado] *s.*nación independiente de gente que tiene una cultura e identidad común. (pág. 609)

NATO [OTAN] *s.*Organización del Tratado del Atlántico Norte: alianza militar defensiva formada en 1949 por diez naciones de Europa occidental, Estados Unidos y Canadá. (pág. 859)

natural rights [derechos naturales] *s.*derechos con los que nacen todos los individuos, conforme a John Locke: vida, libertad y propiedad. (pág. 551)

Nazca [nazca] *s.*civilización que floreció en la actual costa sur de Perú de 200 a.C. a 600 d.C. (pág. 222)

Nazism [nazismo] *s.*políticas fascistas del Partido Nacional socialista de los Trabajadores de Alemania, basadas en el totalitarismo, la creencia en superioridad racial y el control estatal de la industria. (pág. 808)

Negritude movement [movimiento de negritud] *s.*movimiento de africanos de lengua francesa que celebra el legado de la cultura tradicional africana y sus valores. (pág. 896)

neoclassical [neoclásico] *adj.* relacionado con un estilo sencillo y elegante (inspirado en ideas y temas de la antigua Grecia y Roma) que caracterizó las artes en Europa a fines del siglo 18. (pág. 559)

Neolithic Age [Neolítico] *s.*período prehistórico que comenzó aproximadamente en 8000 a.C. y en algunas partes acabó desde 3000 a.C., durante el cual los grupos humanos aprendieron a pulir herramientas de piedra, hacer cerámica, cultivar alimentos y criar animales; también se llama Nueva Edad de Piedra. (pág. 8)

Neolithic Revolution [Revolución Neolítica] *s.*gran cambio en la vida humana causada por los comienzos de la agricultura; es decir, el cambio de recolectar a producir alimentos. (pág. 14)

New Deal *s.*programa de reformas económicas del presidente Franklin D. Roosevelt ideado para solucionar los problemas creados por la Gran Depresión. (pág. 806)

New Kingdom [Reino Nuevo] *s.*período de la historia del antiguo Egipto tras la caída de los gobernantes hicsos, desde 1570 hasta 1075 a.C. (pág. 83)

nirvana *s.*en budismo, la liberación del dolor y el sufrimiento alcanzada después de la iluminación. (pág. 65)

Nok [nok] *s.*pueblo africano que vivió en lo que es hoy Nigeria entre 500 a.C. y 200 d.C. (pág. 198)

nomad [nómada] *s.*miembro de un grupo que no tiene hogar permanente y que va de un lugar a otro en busca de agua y alimento. (pág. 12)

nonaggression pact [pacto de no agresión] *s.*acuerdo en que dos o más naciones prometen no atacarse. (pág. 821)

nonaligned nations [países no alineados] *s.*naciones independientes que permanecieron neutrales durante la Guerra Fría entre Estados Unidos y la Unión Soviética. (pág. 871)

Nuclear Non-Proliferation Treaty [Tratado de No Proliferación Nuclear] *s.*acuerdo de 1968 ideado para reducir la diseminación de las armas nucleares. (pág. 953)

Nuremberg Trials [juicios de Nuremberg] *s.*serie de juicios realizados en Nuremberg, Alemania, tras la II Guerra Mundial a líderes nazis por agresión, violación a las leyes de guerra y crímenes contra la humanidad. (pág. 843)

O

obsidian [obsidiana] *s.*roca volcánica dura y vítrea con que los primeros seres humanos elaboraban herramientas de piedra. (pág. 400)

Old Regime [antiguo régimen] *s.*sistema político y social que existía en Francia antes de la Revolución Francesa. (pág. 573)

oligarchy [oligarquía] *s.*gobierno en que el poder está en manos de pocas personas, particularmente un gobierno que se basa en la riqueza. (pág. 115)

Olmec [olmeca] *s.*civilización mesoamericana más antigua que se conoce, que floreció hacia 1200 a.C. e influyó sobre las posteriores sociedades de la región. (pág. 216)

Open Door Policy [política de puertas abiertas] *s.*política propuesta por E.U.A. en 1899, que postulaba que todas las naciones tuvieran las mismas oportunidades de comerciar con China. (pág. 718)

Opium War [Guerra del Opio] *s.*conflicto entre Inglaterra y China, de 1839 a 1842, por el comercio inglés de opio en China. (pág. 716)

oracle bone [hueso de oráculo] *s.*hueso de animal o caparazón de tortuga que usaban los antiguos sacerdotes chinos para comunicarse con los dioses. (pág. 48)

ozone layer [capa de ozono] *s.*capa de la atmósfera superior de la Tierra que protege a los seres vivos de los rayos ultravioleta de la luz solar. (pág. 949)

P

Pacific Rim [Cuenca del Pacífico] *s.*tierras que bordean el océano Pacífico, especialmente las de Asia. (pág. 706)

Paleolithic Age [Paleolítico] *s.*período prehistórico que abarcó aproximadamente desde 2.5 millones hasta 8000 a.C., durante el cual los seres humanos hicieron rudimentarias herramientas y armas de piedra; también se llama Antigua Edad de Piedra. (pág. 8)

Panama Canal [canal de Panamá] *s.*vía marítima que une al océano Atlántico con el Pacífico, construida en Panamá por Estados Unidos y terminada en 1914. (pág. 727)

papyrus [papiro] *s.*carrizo alto que crece en el delta del Nilo, usado por los antiguos egipcios para hacer hojas de escribir similares al papel. (pág. 38)

parliament [parlamento] *s.*cuerpo de representantes que promulga las leyes de una nación. (pág. 354)

partition [partición] *s.*división en partes, como la división en 1947 de la colonia británica de India en dos naciones: India y Paquistán. (pág. 886)

pastoralist [pastor] *s.*miembro de un grupo nómada que pastorea rebaños de animales domesticados. (pág. 294)

paternalism [paternalismo] *s.*política de tratar a los gobernados como si fueran niños, atendiendo a sus necesidades pero sin darles derechos. (pág. 691)

patriarch [patriarca] *s.*obispo principal de la rama oriental de la cristiandad. (pág. 272)

patriarchal [patriarcal] *adj.* relacionado con un sistema social en el que el padre es jefe de la familia. (pág. 176)

patrician [patricio] *s.*en la antigua Roma, miembro de la clase alta, privilegiada y rica. (pág. 142)

patrilineal [patrilineal] *adj.* relacionado con un sistema social en el que la descendencia y los derechos de herencia se trasmiten a través del padre. (pág. 369)

patron [mecenas] *s.*persona que apoya a los artistas, especialmente, en el aspecto financiero. (pág. 418)

Pax Romana *s.*período de paz y prosperidad por todo el imperio romano, de 27 a.C. a 180 d.C. (pág. 148)

Peace of Augsburg [Paz de Augsburgo] *s.*acuerdo realizado en 1555 que declaró que la religión de cada Estado alemán sería decidida por su gobernante. (pág. 430)

Peloponnesian War [Guerra del Peloponeso] *s.*guerra de 431 a 404 a.C., en la cual Atenas y sus aliados resultaron derrotados por Esparta y sus aliados. (pág. 123)

penal colony [colonia penal] *s.*colonia a donde se mandan convictos como alternativa a una prisión. (pág. 665)

peninsulares *s.*en la sociedad española colonial, colonos nacidos en España. (pág. 604)

Peninsular War [Guerra Peninsular] *s.*conflicto de 1808–1813 en que los rebeldes españoles lucharon con la ayuda de Gran Bretaña para expulsar de España las tropas de Napoleón. (pág. 590)

perestroika *s.*reestructuración de la economía soviética para permitir mayor poder de decisión local, iniciada por Mijaíl Gorbachev en 1985. (pág. 922)

Persian Wars [Guerras Pérsicas] *s.*guerras del siglo 5 a.C. entre las ciudades Estado de Grecia y el imperio persa. (pág. 118)

perspective [perspectiva] *s.*técnica artística que crea la apariencia de tres dimensiones en una superficie plana. (pág. 419)

phalanx [falange] *s.*formación militar de soldados de infantería armados con lanzas y escudos. (pág. 115)

pharaoh [faraón] *s.*rey del antiguo Egipto, considerado dios, así como líder político y militar. (pág. 35)

philosophe *s.*miembro de un grupo de pensadores sociales de la Ilustración en Francia. (pág. 552)

philosophers [filósofos] *s.*pensadores que investigan la naturaleza del universo, la sociedad humana y la moral a través de la lógica y la razón. (pág. 124)

Phoenicians [fenicios] *s.*pueblo de navegantes del suroeste de Asia, que aproximadamente en 1100 a.C. comenzó a comerciar y a fundar colonias en la región mediterránea. (pág. 68)

Pilgrims [peregrinos] *s.*grupo que en 1620 fundó la colonia de Plymouth en Massachusetts para escapar de persecución religiosa en Inglaterra. (pág. 491)

plebeian [plebeyo] *s.*en la antigua Roma, uno de los agricultores, artesanos o comerciantes comunes que conformaban la mayoría de la población. (pág. 142)

plebiscite [plebiscito] *s.*voto directo mediante el cual la población de un país tiene la oportunidad de aceptar o rechazar una propuesta. (pág. 585)

PLO [OLP] *s.*Organización de Liberación Palestina: organización dedicada a establecer un Estado independiente para los palestinos en el Medio Oriente. (pág. 905)

pogrom *s.*campaña organizada de violencia contra las comunidades judías en Rusia a finales del siglo 19. (pág. 769)

polis *s.*ciudad Estado de Grecia; unidad política fundamental de la antigua Grecia a partir de 750 a.C. (pág. 115)

Politburo [Politburó] *s.*comité dirigente del Partido Comunista en la Unión Soviética. (pág. 921)

polytheism [politeísmo] *s.*creencia en muchos dioses. (pág. 29)

pope [Papa] *s.*obispo de Roma y dirigente de la Iglesia Católica Romana. (pág. 156)

Popol Vuh *s.*libro que narra una versión de la historia maya de la creación. (pág. 398)

popular culture [cultura popular] *s.*elementos culturales —deportes, música, cine, ropa, etc.— que muestran los antecedentes comunes de un grupo y sus intereses cambiantes. (pág. 957)

potlatch *s.*fiesta ceremonial celebrada para mostrar rango y prosperidad en varias tribus del Noroeste de Norteamérica. (pág. 391)

predestination [predestinación] *s.*doctrina que postula que Dios ha decidido todo de antemano, incluso quiénes obtendrán la salvación eterna. (pág. 433)

Presbyterian [presbiteriano] *s.*miembro de una iglesia protestante gobernada por presbíteros conforme a las enseñanzas de John Knox. (pág. 433)

PRI *s.*Partido Revolucionario Institucional: principal partido político en México. (pág. 914)

printing press [prensa de imprenta] *s.*máquina para reproducir material escrito oprimiendo papel contra una bandeja de tipos móviles entintados. (pág. 426)

proliferation [proliferación] *s.*crecimiento o expansión, especialmente la expansión de armas nucleares a naciones que actualmente no las tienen. (pág. 953)

propaganda *s.*información o material distribuido para apoyar una causa o socavar una causa opuesta. (pág. 756)

Protestant [protestante] *s.*miembro de una iglesia cristiana fundada de acuerdo a los principios de la Reforma. (pág. 430)

provisional government [gobierno provisional] *s.*gobierno temporal. (pág. 772)

psychology [psicología] *s.*estudio de la mente y la conducta humanas. (pág. 679)

pueblos *s.*aldeas similares a complejos departamentales hechos de adobe, construidas por los anasazi y pueblos posteriores en el Suroeste de lo que hoy es Estados Unidos. (pág. 391)

Puritans [puritanos] *s.*grupo que, para liberarse de la persecución religiosa en Inglaterra, fundó una colonia en la bahía de Massachusetts a principios del siglo 17. (pág. 491)

pyramid [pirámide] *s.*enorme estructura de base rectangular y cuatro lados triangulares, como las que servían de tumba de los faraones del Reino Antiguo de Egipto. (pág. 35)

Q

Qin Dynasty [dinastía Qin] *s.*dinastía china que reinó brevemente y sustituyó a la dinastía Zhou en el siglo 3 a.C. (pág. 99)

Qing Dynasty [dinastía Qing] *s.*última dinastía china; reinó de 1644 a 1912. (pág. 471)

Quetzalcoatl [Quetzalcóatl] *s.*serpiente emplumada: dios de los toltecas y otros pueblos de Mesoamérica. (pág. 401)

quipu *s.*cuerda con nudos usadas para registrar información numérica por los incas. (pág. 410)

Qur'an *[Corán]* *s.*libro sagrado del islam. (pág. 236)

R

racism [racismo] *s.*creencia de que una raza es superior a otras. (pág. 686)

radicals [radicales] *s.*en la primera mitad del siglo 19, los europeos a favor de cambios drásticos para extender la democracia a toda la población. (pág. 609)

radioactivity [radioactividad] *s.*forma de energía liberada mediante la descomposición de átomos. (pág. 678)

Raj *s.*porciones de India controladas por Gran Bretaña de 1757 a 1947. (pág. 704)

rationing [racionamiento] *s.*limitación de la cantidad de bienes que la población puede comprar, generalmente impuesta por un gobierno durante una guerra debido a escasez. (pág. 755)

realism [realismo] *s.*movimiento artístico del siglo 19 en que los escritores y pintores trataron de mostrar la vida como es, no como debiera ser. (pág. 621)

realpolitik *s.*"política de la realidad"; posición política dura que no da lugar al idealismo. (pág. 617)

recession [recesión] *s.*descenso de la economía de una nación. (pág. 913)

Reconquista *s.*campaña de líderes cristianos para expulsar a los musulmanes de España, que empezó en el siglo 12 y terminó en 1492. (pág. 346)

Red Guards [Guardias Rojos] *s.*unidades de milicianos formadas por jóvenes chinos en 1966 en respuesta al llamado de Mao Zedong a llevar a cabo una revolución social y cultural. (pág. 865)

Red Shirts [Camisas Rojas] *s.*seguidores del líder nacionalista italiano del siglo 19 Giuseppe Garibaldi. (pág. 616)

Reformation [Reforma] *s.*movimiento del siglo 16 para realizar cambios religiosos que llevó a la fundación de iglesias cristianas que rechazaron la autoridad del Papa. (pág. 429)

Reign of Terror [Régimen del Terror] *s.*período entre 1793–1794 en que Maximilien Robespierre gobernó a Francia casi como dictador, durante el cual fueron ejecutados miles de personajes políticos y de ciudadanos comunes. (pág. 582)

reincarnation [reencarnación] *s.*en hinduismo y budismo, creencia de que el alma renace una y otra vez hasta alcanzar un conocimiento perfecto. (pág. 63)

religious toleration [tolerancia religiosa] *s.*reconocimiento del derecho de otros a tener creencias religiosas diferentes. (pág. 174)

Renaissance [Renacimiento] *s.*período de la historia europea de aproximadamente 1300 a 1600, durante el cual renació un interés en la cultura clásica que generó importantes cambios en el arte, la educación y la visión del mundo. (pág. 417)

republic [república] *s.* forma de gobierno en que el poder está en manos de representantes y líderes elegidos por los ciudadanos. (pág. 142)

Restoration [Restauración] *s.* en Inglaterra, período del reinado de Carlos II, después del colapso del gobierno de Oliver Cromwell. (pág. 538)

reunification [reunificación] *s.* proceso de unir dos elementos que estaban separados, como la reunificación de Alemania oriental y Alemania occidental en 1990. (pág. 924)

romanticism [romanticismo] *s.* movimiento de principios del siglo 19 en el arte y las ideas que recalca la emoción y la naturaleza, más que la razón y la sociedad. (pág. 619)

Roosevelt Corollary [corolario Roosevelt] *s.* ampliación de la doctrina Monroe, emitida por el presidente Theodore Roosevelt en 1904, en que declaró que Estados Unidos tenía el derecho de ejercer "poderes policiales" en el hemisferio occidental. (pág. 727)

Royal Road [Camino Real] *s.* carretera de más de 1,600 millas que cruzaba el imperio persa, desde Susa en Persia hasta Sardes en Anatolia. (pág. 94)

Russo-Japanese War [Guerra Ruso-Japonesa] *s.* conflicto de 1904–1905 entre Rusia y Japón, causada por el interés de los dos países de dominar Manchuria y Corea. (pág. 723)

S

sacrament [sacramento] *s.* una de las ceremonias cristianas en que se trasmite la gracia de Dios a los creyentes. (pág. 332)

Safavid [safávido] *s.* miembro de una dinastía musulmana shi'a que construyó un imperio en Persia del siglo 16 al 18. (pág. 449)

Sahel *s.* región africana a lo largo de la frontera sur del Sahara. (pág. 195)

salon [salón] *s.* reunión social de intelectuales y artistas, como las que celebraban en sus hogares señoras acaudaladas de París y otras ciudades europeas durante la Ilustración. (pág. 558)

SALT *s.* Conversaciones para la Limitación de Armas Estratégicas: serie de reuniones durante la década de 1970 en que líderes de Estados Unidos y la Unión Soviética acordaron limitar el número de armas nucleares de sus países. (pág. 879)

samurai *s.* guerrero profesional que servía a los nobles en el Japón feudal. (pág. 307)

sans-culottes *s.* en la Revolución Francesa, grupo político radical de parisienses asalariados y pequeños comerciantes que anhelaban más voz en el gobierno, bajas de precios y fin a la escasez de alimentos. (pág. 579)

satrap [sátrapa] *s.* gobernador de una provincia en el imperio persa. (pág. 94)

savanna [sabana] *s.* planicie con pastizales. (pág. 195)

schism [cisma] *s.* separación o división, especialmente la división formal de una iglesia cristiana. (pág. 273)

Schlieffen Plan [Plan Schlieffen] *s.* plan militar alemán al comienzo de la I Guerra Mundial, que preveía que Alemania derrotaría rápidamente a Francia y después atacaría a Rusia en el este. (pág. 747)

scholastics [escolásticos] *s.* académicos que se reunían y enseñaban en las universidades medievales de Europa. (pág. 351)

scientific method [método científico] *s.* procedimiento lógico para reunir información sobre el mundo natural, en que se usa experimentación y observación para poner a prueba hipótesis. (pág. 547)

Scientific Revolution [Revolución Científica] *s.* profundo cambio en el pensamiento europeo que comenzó a mediados del siglo 16, en que el estudio del mundo natural se caracterizó por cuidadosa observación y cuestionamiento de teorías aceptadas. (pág. 545)

scorched-earth policy [política de arrasamiento de campos] *s.* práctica de quemar campos de cultivo y de matar ganado durante la guerra para que el enemigo no pueda vivir de las tierras. (pág. 590)

scribe [escriba] *s.* profesional especializado en llevar registros en las civilizaciones tempranas. (pág. 18)

secede [seceder] *v.* retirarse formalmente de una asociación o alianza. (pág. 670)

secular *adj.* relacionado con lo mundano más que con los asuntos espirituales. (págs. 319, 418)

segregation [segregación] *s.* separación legal o social de gente de diferentes razas. (pág. 672)

self-determination [autodeterminación] *s.* libertad de un pueblo para decidir libremente la forma de gobierno que desea. (pág. 760)

Seljuks [seljucs] *s.* grupo turco que emigró al imperio abasida en el siglo 10 y estableció su propio imperio en el siglo 11. (pág. 279)

senate [senado] *s.* en la antigua Roma, organismo supremo de gobierno formado inicialmente sólo por aristócratas. (pág. 143)

separation of powers [separación de poderes] *s.* división de poderes del gobierno en ejecutivo, legislativo y judicial. (pág. 553)

sepoy [cipayo] *s.* soldado hindú bajo el mando británico. (pág. 701)

Sepoy Mutiny [Motín de Cipayos] *s.* rebelión de 1857 de soldados hindúes y musulmanes contra los británicos en India. (pág. 703)

serf [siervo] *s.* campesino medieval legalmente obligado a vivir en los dominios de un señor. (pág. 324)

Seven Years' War [Guerra de los Siete Años] *s.* conflicto en Europa, Norteamérica e India de 1756 a 1763, en que las fuerzas de Inglaterra y Prusia lucharon con las de Austria, Francia, Rusia y otros países. (pág. 530)

shari'a *s.* conjunto de leyes que rigen la vida de los musulmanes. (pág. 237)

Shi'a [shi'a] *s.* rama del islam que reconoce a los primeros cuatro califas como legítimos sucesores de Mahoma. (pág. 240)

Shinto [shintoísmo] *s.* religión oriunda de Japón. (pág. 303)

Shiva *s.* dios hindú considerado destructor del mundo. (pág. 178)

"shock therapy" [terapia de shock] *s.* programa económico implementado en Rusia por Boris Yeltsin en la década de 1990, que implicó un cambio abrupto de una economía de mando a una economía de mercado libre. (pág. 928)

shogun [shogún] *s.* en el Japón feudal, jefe militar supremo que regía en nombre del emperador. (pág. 307)

Sikh [sikh] *s.* miembro de un grupo religioso no violento cuyas creencias combinaban elementos del budismo, el hinduismo y el sufismo. (pág. 454)

Silk Roads [Ruta de la Seda] *s.* sistema de antiguas rutas de las caravanas por Asia central, por las que se transportaban seda y otros productos comerciales. (pág. 179)

silt [légamo] *s.* tierra que arrastran las aguas de los ríos. (pág. 27)

simony [simonía] *s.* venta o compra de una posición en una iglesia cristiana. (pág. 341)

Six-Day War [Guerra de los Seis Días] *s.* breve conflicto en 1967 entre Israel y varios países árabes, durante el cual Israel se apoderó de Jerusalén, la península del Sinaí, la meseta de Golán y Cisjordania. (pág. 903)

skepticism [escepticismo] *s.* filosofía basada en la noción de que nada puede saberse con certeza. (pág. 519)

slash-and-burn farming [agricultura de tala y quema] *s.* método agrícola de desbrozar terrenos talando y quemando árboles y pastos, cuyas cenizas sirven como fertilizante. (pág. 14)

Slavs [eslavos] *s.* pueblo de los bosques al norte del mar Negro, origen de muchos pueblos de la Europa oriental de nuestros días. (pág. 274)

social contract [contrato social] *s.* acuerdo mediante el cual el pueblo define y limita sus derechos individuales, creando así una sociedad o gobierno organizados. (pág. 551)

Social Darwinism [darvinismo social] *s.* aplicación de las teorías de Charles Darwin sobre la evolución y la "sobrevivencia del más apto" a las sociedades humanas, particularmente como justificación para la expansión imperialista. (pág. 686)

socialism [socialismo] *s.* sistema económico en el cual los factores de producción son propiedad del pueblo y se administran para el bienestar de todos. (pág. 648)

socialist realism [realismo socialista] *s.* estilo artístico que exalta los valores comunistas y la vida bajo el comunismo. (pág. 778)

Solidarity [Solidaridad] *s.* sindicato polaco de trabajadores que presentó la principal fuerza de oposición al gobierno comunista en Polonia en la década de 1980. (pág. 922)

Songhai *s.* imperio de África occidental que conquistó Malí y controló el comercio desde el siglo 15 hasta 1591. (pág. 374)

soviet *s.* consejo local de representantes formado en Rusia después de la caída del zar Nicolás II. (pág. 772)

Spanish-American War [Guerra Hispano-Americana] *s.* conflicto de 1898 entre Estados Unidos y España, en que Estados Unidos apoyó la lucha de independencia cubana. (pág. 726)

specialization [especialización] *s.* desarrollo de conocimientos para realizar determinado trabajo, como comerciar o llevar registros. (pág. 18)

sphere of influence [esfera de influencia] *s.* región extranjera en que una nación controla el comercio y otras actividades económicas. (pág. 718)

standard of living [nivel de vida] *s.* calidad de la vida de una persona o población que se mide conforme a los bienes, servicios y lujos que tiene a su disposición. (pág. 912)

Star Wars [Guerra de las Galaxias] *s.* programa para proteger a Estados Unidos de un ataque de misiles enemigos, propuesto en 1983 por el presidente Ronald Reagan pero nunca implementado; su nombre oficial es Iniciativa de Defensa Estratégica. (pág. 879)

stateless societies [sociedades sin Estado] *s.* grupos culturales en los que la autoridad es compartida por linajes de igual poder, en vez de ser ejercida por un gobierno central. (pág. 368)

steppes [estepas] *s.* llanuras secas de pastizales. (pág. 57)

strike [huelga] *s.* paro de trabajo para obligar al patrón a acceder a ciertas demandas. (pág. 650)

subcontinent [subcontinente] *s.* gran masa que forma una parte claramente diferenciada de un continente. (pág. 42)

Suez Canal [canal de Suez] *s.* canal marítimo que une al mar Rojo y al golfo de Suez con el mar Mediterráneo, cuya construcción terminó en 1869. (pág. 699)

Suez Crisis [Crisis de Suez] *s.* crisis internacional ocurrida en 1956 cuando Egipto nacionalizó el canal de Suez e Israel (con ayuda de Gran Bretaña y Francia) tomó el canal por la fuerza, pero se retiró bajo presión de Estados Unidos y la Unión Soviética. (pág. 902)

suffrage [sufragio] *s.* derecho al voto. (pág. 659)

Sufi [sufí] *s.* musulmán que busca contacto directo con Dios por medio del misticismo. (pág. 240)

Sunna [sunna] *s.* modelo islámico de vida que se basa en las enseñanzas y vida de Mahoma. (pág. 237)

Sunni [sunni] *s.* rama del islam que reconoce a Alí y a sus descendientes como sucesores legítimos de Mahoma. (pág. 240)

surrealism [surrealismo] *s.* movimiento artístico del siglo 20 que se concentra en el inconsciente. (pág. 797)

sustainable development [crecimiento sostenido] *s.* desarrollo económico que satisface las necesidades de la población pero preserva el entorno y conserva recursos para futuras generaciones. (pág. 950)

Swahili [suahili] *s.* lengua bantú con influencias árabes que se usa en África oriental y central. (pág. 378)

T

Taiping Rebellion [Rebelión Taiping] *s.* rebelión a mediados del siglo 19 contra la dinastía Qing en China, encabezada por Hong Xiuquan. (pág. 717)

Taj Mahal *s.* bella tumba en Agra, India, construida por el emperador mogol Shah Jahan para su esposa Mumtaz Mahal. (pág. 454)

Tamil [tamil o tamul] *s.* idioma del sur de India; grupo que habla dicho idioma. (pág. 175)

technology [tecnología] *s.* formas de aplicar conocimientos, herramientas e inventos para satisfacer necesidades. (pág. 9)

Tennis Court Oath [Juramento de la Cancha de Tenis] *s.* promesa hecha por los miembros de la Asamblea Nacional de Francia en 1789 de permanecer reunidos hasta que elaboraran una nueva constitución. (pág. 576)

terrorism [terrorismo] *s.* uso de la fuerza o de amenazas para presionar a personas o gobiernos a que cambien sus políticas. (pág. 953)

theocracy [teocracia] *s.* **1.** gobierno en el cual se ve al gobernante como una figura divina (pág. 35). **2.** gobierno controlado por líderes religiosos. (pág. 433)

theory of evolution [teoría de la evolución] *s.* concepto propuesto por Charles Darwin en 1859 de que las especies de plantas y animales surgen debido a un proceso de selección natural. (pág. 678)

theory of relativity [teoría de la relatividad] *s.* ideas de Albert Einstein acerca de la interrelación entre el tiempo y el espacio, y entre la energía y la materia. (pág. 795)

Theravada *s.* secta del budismo que se adhiere al énfasis original de Buda en la estricta disciplina espiritual. (pág. 177)

Third Reich [Tercer Reich] *s.* Tercer Imperio Alemán establecido por Adolfo Hitler en la década de 1930. (pág. 814)

Third Republic [Tercera República] *s.* república establecida en Francia después de la caída de Napoleón III; acabó con la ocupación alemana de Francia durante la II Guerra Mundial. (pág. 663)

Third World [Tercer Mundo] *s.* durante la Guerra Fría, naciones que no se aliaron ni con Estados Unidos ni con la Unión Soviética. (pág. 871)

Thirty Years' War [Guerra de los Treinta Años] *s.*conflicto europeo de 1618 a 1648 por cuestiones religiosas, territoriales y de poder entre familias reinantes. (pág. 526)

three-field system [sistema de tres campos] *s.*sistema agrícola de la Europa medieval en que las tierras de cultivo se dividían en tres campos de igual tamaño y cada uno se sembraba sucesivamente con un cultivo de invierno, un cultivo de primavera y el tercero se dejaba sin cultivar. (pág. 348)

Tiananmen Square [Plaza Tiananmen] *s.*plaza pública en Beijing, China; sede en 1989 de un enorme levantamiento estudiantil en favor de reformas democráticas. (pág. 932)

tithe [diezmo] *s.*pago de una familia a la Iglesia de la décima parte de sus ingresos. (pág. 325)

Tokugawa Shogunate [shogunato Tokugawa] *s.*dinastía de shogúns que gobernó un Japón unificado de 1603 a 1867. (pág. 475)

Torah *s.*cinco primeros libros de la Biblia hebrea, los más sagrados de la tradición judía. (pág. 72)

totalitarianism [totalitarismo] *s.*gobierno que controla todo aspecto de la vida pública y privada. (pág. 775)

total war [guerra total] *s.*conflicto en el que los países participantes dedican todos sus recursos a la guerra. (pág. 755)

totems [tótemes] *s.*animales u otros objetos naturales que sirven de símbolo de unidad de clanes u otros grupos. (pág. 394)

tournament [torneo] *s.*justa deportiva entre grupos de caballeros. (pág. 328)

tragedy [tragedia] *s.*obra dramática seria profunda acerca de la caída de un personaje heroico o noble. (pág. 123)

Trans-Siberian Railway [Ferrocarril Transiberiano] *s.*vía de ferrocarril construida en Rusia entre 1891 y 1904 para conectar puertos rusos con el océano Pacífico. (pág. 770)

Treaty of Kanagawa [Tratado de Kanagawa] *s.*acuerdo de 1854 entre Estados Unidos y Japón, que abrió dos puertos japoneses a los barcos de Estados Unidos y le permitió abrir una embajada en Japón. (pág. 720)

Treaty of Tordesillas [Tratado de Tordesillas] *s.*acuerdo de 1494 entre Portugal y España que estableció que las tierras descubiertas al oeste de una línea imaginaria en el océano Atlántico pertenecerían a España y las tierras al este pertenecerían a Portugal. (pág. 466)

Treaty of Versailles [Tratado de Versalles] *s.*acuerdo de paz firmado por Alemania y los Aliados después de la I Guerra Mundial. (pág. 761)

trench warfare [guerra de trincheras] *s.*forma de guerra en la que dos ejércitos contrincantes luchan detrás de trincheras cavadas en el campo de batalla. (pág. 749)

triangular trade [triángulo comercial] *s.*red comercial trasatlántica que transportaba esclavos y productos entre África, Inglaterra, Europa continental, el Caribe y las colonias de Norteamérica. (pág. 497)

tribune [tribuno] *s.*en la antigua Roma, funcionario elegido por los plebeyos para proteger sus derechos. (pág. 142)

tribute [tributo] *s.*pago de una potencia más débil a una potencia más fuerte para obtener una garantía de paz y seguridad. (pág. 76)

Triple Alliance [Triple Alianza] *s.***1.** asociación de las ciudades Estado de Tenochtitlan, Texcoco y Tlacopan, que dio origen al imperio azteca (pág. 402). **2.** alianza militar establecida entre Alemania, Austro-Hungría e Italia antes de la I Guerra Mundial. (pág. 744)

Triple Entente [Triple Entente] *s.*alianza militar entre Gran Bretaña, Francia y Rusia establecida antes de la I Guerra Mundial. (pág. 745)

triumvirate [triunvirato] *s.*en la Roma antigua, grupo de tres líderes que compartían el control del gobierno. (pág. 147)

Trojan War [Guerra de Troya] *s.*guerra, aproximadamente en 1200 a.C., en que un ejército al mando de reyes micénicos atacó la ciudad comercial independiente de Troya, ubicada en Anatolia. (pág. 113)

troubadour [trovador] *s.*poeta y músico medieval que viajaba de un lugar a otro para divertir con sus cantos de amor cortesano. (pág. 330)

Truman Doctrine [Doctrina Truman] *s.*política estadounidense de dar ayuda económica y militar a las naciones libres amenazadas por oponentes internos o externos, anunciada por el presidente Harry Truman en 1947. (pág. 858)

tyrant [tirano] *s.*en la antigua Grecia, individuo poderoso que ganaba el control del gobierno de una ciudad Estado apelando al apoyo de los pobres. (pág. 116)

U

Umayyads [omeyas] *s.*dinastía que gobernó el imperio musulmán del 661 al 750 d.C. y después estableció un reino en al-Andalus. (pág. 239)

union [sindicato] *s.*asociación de trabajadores formada para negociar mejores salarios y condiciones de trabajo. (pág. 650)

United Nations [Organización de las Naciones Unidas (ONU)] *s.*organización internacional fundada en 1945 con el propósito de ofrecer seguridad a las naciones del mundo. (pág. 855)

Universal Declaration of Human Rights [Declaración Universal de Derechos Humanos] *s.*declaración en que la ONU proclamó en 1948 que todos los seres humanos tienen derecho a la vida, la libertad y la seguridad. (pág. 954)

unrestricted submarine warfare [guerra submarina irrestricta] *s.*uso de submarinos para hundir sin alerta previa cualquier barco (incluso barcos neutrales y de pasajeros sin armamento) que se encuentre en aguas enemigas. (pág. 754)

urbanization [urbanización] *s.*crecimiento de ciudades y migración hacia ellas. (pág. 638)

U.S. Civil War [Guerra Civil de E.U.A.] *s.*conflicto entre los estados del Norte y el Sur de Estados Unidos desde 1861 a 1865, sobre el asunto de la esclavitud. (pág. 671)

utilitarianism [utilitarismo] *s.*teoría, propuesta por Jeremy Bentham a fines del siglo 18, de que las acciones del gobierno sólo son útiles si promueven el mayor bien para el mayor número de personas. (pág. 648)

Utopia [Utopía] *s.*tierra imaginaria descrita por Tomás Moro en su libro del mismo nombre; lugar ideal. (pág. 425)

U-2 incident [incidente del U-2] *s.*derribamiento en 1960 de un avión estadounidense de espionaje y captura de su piloto por la Unión Soviética. (pág. 860)

V

vassal [vasallo] *s.*en la Europa feudal, persona que recibía un dominio (tierras) de un señor a cambio de su promesa de lealtad y servicios. (pág. 324)

Vedas *s.* cuatro colecciones de escritos sagrados secretos, realizados durante la etapa temprana del asentamiento ario en India. (pág. 59)

vernacular *s.* lenguaje común y corriente de la gente de una región o país. (págs. 350, 421)

Vietcong *s.* grupo de guerrilleros comunistas que, con la ayuda de Vietnam del Norte, pelearon contra el gobierno de Vietnam del Sur durante la Guerra de Vietnam. (pág. 868)

Vietnamization [vietnamización] *s.* estrategia del presidente de E.U.A. Richard Nixon para terminar con la participación en la Guerra de Vietnam, mediante el retiro gradual de tropas estadounidenses y su reemplazo con fuerzas survietnamitas. (pág. 869)

Vishnu [Visnú] *s.* dios hindú considerado responsable de conservar al mundo. (pág. 178)

vizier [visir] *s.* primer ministro de un reino o imperio musulmán. (pág. 280)

W

War of the Spanish Succession [Guerra de Sucesión Española] *s.* conflicto de 1701 a 1713 en que varios Estados europeos lucharon para impedir que la familia Borbón controlara a España, como a Francia. (pág. 523)

Warsaw Pact [Pacto de Varsovia] *s.* alianza militar formada en 1955 por la Unión Soviética y siete países de Europa oriental. (pág. 859)

Weimar Republic [República de Weimar] *s.* república establecida en Alemania en 1919 que acabó en 1933. (pág. 802)

Western Front [Frente Occidental] *s.* en la I Guerra Mundial, región del norte de Francia donde peleaban las fuerzas de los Aliados y de las Potencias Centrales. (pág. 748)

westernization [occidentalización] *s.* adopción de las instituciones sociales, políticas o económicas del Occidente, especialmente de Europa o Estados Unidos. (pág. 533)

YZ

yin and yang [yin y yang] *s.* en China, dos poderes que gobiernan los ritmos naturales de la vida; el yang representa las cualidades masculinas en el universo y el yin las femeninas. (pág. 99)

Yoruba [yoruba] *s.* pueblo del África occidental que formó varios reinos en lo que hoy es Benin y el sur de Nigeria. (pág. 375)

Zapotec [zapoteca] *s.* civilización mesoamericana centrada en el valle de Oaxaca de lo que hoy es México. (pág. 218)

ziggurat [zigurat] *s.* estructura de gradas en forma de pirámide, que formaba parte de un templo sumerio. (pág. 21)

Zionism [sionismo] *s.* movimiento fundado en la década de 1890 para promover el establecimiento de una patria judía en Palestina. (pág. 663)

Index

An *i* preceding a page reference in italics indicates that there is an illustration, and usually text information as well, on that page. An *m* or a *c* preceding an italic page reference indicates a map or a chart, as well as text information on that page.

Judaism; Manicheanism; Zoroastrianism.
and death, 40–41
effect of printing press on, 427
in Europe (1560), m 434
influence of Greek, 135
and nationalism, c 613
in Native North America, 393
Persian, 96
reformers, 428, 431, 433, 434, 435
Roman government and, 151
spread of Indian, 180
unifying force of, 332–333
and women, 342
world, 250–264, c 250–251, c 264
religious beliefs, 18. See also religion; sacrifice.
in the Americas, 388
of ancient China, 48
in art, 221–222, i 243, 247
Aztec, 401, 403, i 404, i 405, c 406
in the Crusades, 338
effects of science on, 546
emperor worship, 151
ethical monotheism, 75
fundamentalism, 953
of heaven and hell, 96, 237
Incan, 407, 410, c 411
jaguar worship, 217
Mayan, 396, c 399
Minoan influence on Greek, 113
of Persia, 96
in prehistory, 18
Roman, 96, 138, 141, 151, 153
sports in, 127, 396
Sumerian, 29
time-keeping in, i 404–405, 410
religious conflict, 953–954
religious orders, 342
religious persecution, 203, 346. See also Christianity; Holocaust; Inquisition.
in Japan, 477
of Muslims, 929
in Spanish colonies, 488
under Stalin, 778
religious rituals, 67. See also burial rites; sacrifice.
Sumerian, 21
religious symbolism, i 252–263
cross as, i 153
religious tolerance, c 554
in Austria, 561
of Cyrus the Great, 92–93
in Edict of Nantes, 518
and French Revolution, c 585
in Indian empire, 174
limited, 538
and migration, 203
in Mughal Empire, 453
in Netherlands, 515–516
in Ottoman Empire, 446–447
reliquary, i 273
Rembrandt van Rijn, 516, 543
Renaissance, 417. See also Northern Renaissance.
art, i 416, i 419–i 421
British, 425–427
causes of, 414, 417, 423, 426–427, c 438
characteristics of, 418–422, 424–427, c 438
Chinese, 417
effects of, 427, 463

European, 414–427, c 438
Flanders, 424–425
Greek influence on, i 414
humanism, 418
Italian, 417–422
Leonardo da Vinci, 421
literature, 421
Michelangelo, 420
Muslim influence on, 247
Northern, 423–427
Petrarch, 422
Raphael, 421
Russia during the, 532
themes of, 417
values of, 416–419
women in, 419
"Renaissance men," 418–419
republic, 142
China, 781
French, 662–663
U.S., 565–566
Restoration, 538
reunification, 924
Revolution(s) c 965, 977
agricultural, 633–634
American, 542, 563–569, c 568
Bolshevik, 772–773
Chinese, 781–784
Commercial, 500–503
Cuban, 872
Cultural (Chinese), 865–866
democratic, 908
English, 536–539
and Enlightenment, i 568
failed, 610–611
French, 554, 567, 570–599, c 585
Glorious, 539
in Haiti, 603
ideas and, 606
Indian, 785–787
Industrial, m 630–655
Latin American, 590, 595, c 598, 602–609
leaders of, c 790
Mexican, 729–734
nationalist, c 624, m 600–625
role of Enlightenment on, 555, 564, c 568
Russian, m 766, 769–780, c 772, m 773
in Saint Domingue, 603
Scientific, 542, 545–550, c 548–c 549, c 568, 795
southwest Asian, 788–789
in Soviet Union, 927–928
Ricardo, David, 647, 648
Richard the Lion-Hearted, i 345
Richelieu, Cardinal, 518–519, 527
Rig Veda, 59
rights and responsibilities. See also Bill of Rights; constitution.
in Declaration of the Rights of Man, 577
in democracy, c 911–912
of habeas corpus, 538
Locke's treatise on, 551–552, c 554
under Magna Carta, 353
in Petition of Right, 536
religious freedom, c 554
Universal Declaration of Human Rights, 954
Rijn, Rembrandt van, i 516, 543
Rio de Janeiro, 938
rivers, world's longest, c 986–987
roads, 95, 100, 155, 167. See also Royal Road; Silk Roads.
during Industrial Revolution, 636

Incan, 409, c 411
Robespierre, Maximilien, 582–583, 597
Robin Hood, i 353
rock 'n' roll, 958–959
Roman Catholic Church, 272, c 273. See also Church.
absolute monarchy and, c 540
in the Americas, 487–488
authority of, 319, 320, 332–337
canon law, 333
division of, 345
during French Revolution, 573
effect of plague on, 359
effect of Renaissance on, 428
and empires, 314
in Enlightenment, 559
and fall of Roman Empire, 318
French state-controlled, 577–578
and Galileo, 547
and Holy Roman Empire, 333–337
and Huguenots, 434, 518
Inquisition in, 346
law of, 333
liberation theology in, 913
and medieval women, 331
in the Middle Ages, 332, c 362
problems in, 341
Reformation in, 435–436
reform of, 341–342
structure of, 332
weakening of, 361
Roman empire, 138–169, c 187
ancient, m 138, 139
agriculture in, 148
aquaducts, 167
army, 143–144
art and architecture, 164–166
Augustus, 148
beginnings, 141
Caesar, Julius, i 147
charioteers, 152
cities, c 317
civil wars, 146, 147
collapse of Republic, 146–167
Colosseum, i 166
cultural influence of, 134, 146, 151, c 160, 162
decline of, 150, 158–163, 317–319
economic developments of, 146, 148, 152, 158–159, c 160
education, 150
emperors, 149, c 150, 151, 162
Etruscan influence, 141–142
family life in, 150
gladiators, 151
government of, 138, 142–143, 151
Greek influence, 141
invasions into, i 161, 317
Latin language, 165
law in, 167
legacy of, 164–167
literature, 165
mercenaries, 159
Pax Romana, 148–150
political developments of, 142–149, 159, c 160
population of, c 242
Punic Wars, 144–145
reforms, 147, 159
religion in, 96, 134, 151, 153–157
republic, 143, 146
slavery in, 151
social classes, 148, 150, 151

villages
achievements of, *c 22*
become cities, 17–18
growth of, 15–16, *c 22*
Vinci, Leonardo da, *i 421*, 423, 439
Virgil, 165
Vishnu, 63, 178, 309
Fish Incarnation of, 77
vizier, 280
Vladimir, 275
Voltaire, *i 552*, 557, 563
voting, 911. *See also* suffrage.
in ancient Rome, 142

Walesa, Lech, 922, *i 923*, 930
Wang Mang, 186–187
war(s). *See also* civil war; empire(s); technology.
of 1812, 589, 643
American Revolutionary, *c 568*, 563–569
in ancient China, 48, 51
in ancient Sumer, 29, 31–32
Arab-Israeli, 902–903
of the Austrian Succession, 530
of Bantu-speaking people, 205
Boer, 689
in Bosnia, 746, 929
Chechnyan, 928
Cold, *m 852–853*, *m 857*, 859–860, 871–881, *m 881*
Crimean, 698, 702
elephants of, *i 138*
English Civil, 537
French and Indian, 493
Franco-Prussian, 618
geography's effect on, 34, 43
heroes, *i 758–i 759*
Hundred Years', 359, *c 362*, 423
Incan civil, 411
Korean, 866, *m 867*
Mexican-American, 669
monuments, *i 758–i 759*
in Nicaragua, *i 852*
Opium, 716
Peloponnesian, 123–124
Peninsular, 589–590
Persian, 118–119, *m 119*
Persian Gulf, 21, *m 28*, 815, 949
phalanx in, 115
Punic, *m 145*
religious, 518, 527
Roman civil, 146–148
of the Roses, 361
Russo-Japanese, 722, 723, *c 734*, 770
Seven Weeks', 617
Seven Years', 530
Sino-Japanese, *c 734*
Six-Day, 902–903
slave trade in, 499
Spanish-American, 726
of the Spanish Succession, 523
technology of, *i 750–i 751*
Thirty Years', 519, 526–528, *m 527*
total, 755
in Vietnam, *i 853*
warriors, feudal, 327, 328, 329
Warsaw Pact, 859
Waterloo, 592
watermills, 184
water resources, 949
Watt, James, 636
weapons, *c 289*, *i 840–841*. *See also* military

power; technology.
Assyrian, 88–89
catapult, 134
ceremonial, *i 239*
of Cold War, 859–860
of Genghis Khan, 296
"Greek Fire," 266
iron, 87
longbow, 360
in Mali, 375
seige, *i 329*
social impact of, 476
of totalitarianism, 777, *i 779*
Turkish, 43
of World War I, *i 741*, *i 750–i 751*
wedding rituals, 890–891
Weimar Republic, 802–803
welfare state, 915
West Africa. *See also* Africa.
in 1997, *m 383*
empires of (800–1500), *m 364–365*
societies in, 197–198
Western civilization. *See also* Greece; Roman empire.
effect of Enlightenment on, 555–556
Greco-Roman influence on, 135, 164–169
Greek influence on, 113
influences global culture, 958–960
Roman influence on, 162, 164–167
and Russia, 533, 535
values of, 775, 960
Western Europe
in 14th century, *m 338– m 339*
feudalism in, 323–326
formation of (800–1500), 340–363
invasions of, 317
Western Front, *i 741*
in World War I, 748, *i 749*
westernization, 533
wheel, 17, *c 19*, 24, 31, 36, *c 52*
wheelbarrow, 184
Wheel of the Law, *i 252*
Whigs, 538
Wilhelm I (kaiser), 618
Wilhelm II (kaiser), 744–745
William the Conqueror (English king), 352–353
William of Orange (Dutch ruler), 515
William of Orange, King William II of England, 522, 539
Wills, Helen, *i 799*
Wilson, Woodrow, *i 760*
Winged Victory, *i 135*
witch hunts, 430
Wollstonecraft, Mary, *c 554–i 555*
women. *See also* Queens; writers.
activists, 652, 662, *i 894*, 939
in agricultural revolution, 14
Amazons, 116
of ancient China, 48
in ancient Egypt, 38
in ancient Rome, 142
in ancient Sumer, 30–31
in Athens, 117
in Buddhist society, 65
of China, 186, 291, 473
in Crimean War, 698
in Czarist Russia, 535
in Efe society, 367
and the Enlightenment, 555, 558
equality of, *c 554*
under feudalism, 330, 331
in French Revolution, 576, 580

in Greek drama, 123
in Han Dynasty, 182, 186
in Hebrew society, 74
of India, 178, 887
and industrial reform, 652
international conferences on status of women (UN), 955
in Iran, 874
Iroquois, 394
of Japan, 475, 720
and labor laws, 651
in literature, 305
and manorialism, 325
in March Revolution, 771–772
and Marxism, 864
and medicine, 550
in the Middle Ages, 331
Minoan, 67
modern, 955, *i 968*
modern Mayan, *i 399*
Mongol, *i 297*
in Muslim culture, 243
and Napoleonic Law, 586
in New Zealand, 666
of the Reformation, 434–435
religious orders of, 342
Renaissance, 419, 421
rulers, 74, 83–84, 454, *i 525*, 562, 887–888, 893, *i 902*
in science, 555
Seneca Falls Convention, 562
slavery of, 89
Soviet, 780
in Sparta, 116
suffrage of, 660–662, 911
in Turkey, *i 766*, 788
Victorian, 660–661
of Vietnam, 310
Warrior-Women, 116
World War I, 756, 798
World War II, 845
WSPU (Women's Social and Political Union), 662
Woolley, Leonard, 20
world atlas, 971
world organizations, *c 948*
World Trade Organization, 947
World War I, *m 745*, *m 748*, *m 754*, *m 762*, 764
1914–1918, *m 740–c 765*
alliances of, 747–748
armistice, 757
aviation in, *i 752*
battlefield deaths, *c 765*
causes of, 740–747, *c 764*
and China, 781
countries at war, *m 754*
Eastern Front, 760
effect on Europe, *m 762*
effects of, 753–763, *c 764*, 785, *c 791*, 796–798
in Europe, *m 748*
Fourteen Points, 760
legacy of, 763
onset of, 746
peace treaties, 761–762
rationing, 755
and Russian Revolution, 771
science during, 795
submarine warfare, 754
technological effects of, 798–799
technology of war, *i 750*, 751, *i 752*
time line, *i 757*, *i 791*

ACKNOWLEDGMENTS

Text Acknowledgments

Title Page: Quotation from *A History of Civilizations* by Fernand Braudel, translated by Richard Mayne. Copyright © 1987 by Les Editions Arthaud; English translation copyright © 1994 by Richard Mayne. Used by permission of Penguin, a division of Penguin Books USA Inc.

Chapter 1, page 21: Excerpt *From The Poetry of Sumer: Creation, Glorification, Adoration* by Samuel Noah Kramer. Copyright © 1979 The Regents of the University of California Press. Reprinted by permission of the University of California Press.

Chapter 7, page 178: Excerpt from a Tamil poem from *The Wonder That Was India* by A. L. Basham. Published by Sidgwick and Jackson. By permission of Macmillan of London.

Chapter 10, page 243: "Quimis," from *Islam: From The Prophet Muhammad to the Capture of Constantinople*, Vol. l, by Bernard Lewis, ed. and trans. Copyright © 1974 by Bernard Lewis. Reprinted by permission of HarperCollins Publishers, Inc.

Chapter 11, page 280: Four lines from "Rumi Quatrain," from *Unseen Rain*, translated by John Moyne and Coleman Barks. Originally published by Threshold Books, 139 Main Street, Brattleboro, VT 05301. By permission of Threshold Books.

Chapter 12, page 290: "Moonlight Night," from *Tu Fu* by William Hung, Cambridge, Mass.: Harvard University Press. Copyright © 1952 by the President and Fellows of Harvard College.

Chapter 13, page 330: Seven lines from page 84 of *The Song of Roland* by Frederick Goldin, translator. Copyright © 1978 by W. W. Norton & Company, Inc. Reprinted by permission of W. W. Norton & Company, Inc.

page 337: Excerpt from "The Prologue," from *The Canterbury Tales* by Geoffrey Chaucer, translated by Nevill Coghill (Penguin Classics, 1951). Copyright © 1951 Nevill Coghill. Reprinted by permission of Penguin Books Ltd.

Chapter 19, page 476: Haiku poem, from *Matsuo Basho,* translated by Makoto Veda. By permission of Makoto Veda.

Chapter 29, page 763: Excerpt from *You Will Hear Thunder, Akhmatova,* Poems, translated by D. M. Thomas, Martin Secker & Warburg, publisher. By permission of Random House UK Limited.

Chapter 35, page 937: Excerpts from "The Coming of Mao Zedong Chic," from Newsweek, May 19, 1997, Newsweek, Inc. All rights reserved. Reprinted by permission.

Back Cover: Extract from *Millennium: A History of the Last Thousand Years* by Felipe Fernández-Armesto. Copyright © Felipe Fernández-Armesto 1995. Published by Bantam Press, a Division of Transworld Publishers Ltd. All rights reserved.

McDougal Littell Inc. has made every effort to locate the copyright holders for selections used in this book and to make full acknowledgment for their use. Omissions brought to our attention will be corrected in a subsequent edition.

Art and Photography Credits

COVERS

front *background* Copyright © 1996 Cosmo & Action/Photonica; *insets, top to bottom* Museo Nazionale, Naples, Italy/Scala/Art Resource, New York; Copyright © Jack Hollingsworth; Copyright © 1995 Archive Photos/PNI; Copyright © SuperStock; Lee Boltin; Copyright © Jack Hollingsworth; **back** *top* Copyright © Index Stock Photography, Inc.; *center* Copyright © 1996 Craig Duncan/DDB Stock Photo; *bottom* Copyright © 1992 Carl Scofield/Index Stock Photography, Inc.

FRONT MATTER

half-title page *background* Copyright © 1996 Cosmo & Action/Photonica; **title spread** *background* Copyright © 1996 Cosmo & Action/Photonica; *top row, left to right* Museo Nazionale, Naples, Italy/Scala/Art Resource, New York; Copyright © SuperStock; Copyright © 1995 Archive Photos/PNI; Lee Boltin; Copyright © 1992 Carl Scofield/Index Stock Photography, Inc.; *second row, left to right* Copyright © 1996 Craig Duncan/DDB Stock Photo; Copyright © Jack Hollingsworth; Copyright © Index Stock Photography, Inc.; *bottom* Copyright © Jack Hollingsworth; **viii** *top* Prehistoric painting, Tassili N'Ajjer, Algeria. Henri Lhote Collection, Musée de l'Homme, Paris/Erich Lessing/Art Resource, New York; *center* Pyramids, Giza, Egypt. Copyright © Robert Caputo/Stock Boston; *bottom* Stone bas-relief from palace of Ashurnasirpal II (9th century B.C.). British Museum, London/Erich Lessing/Art Resource, New York; **ix** *top* Parthenon, Athens, Greece. Copyright © SuperStock; *center, Shiva Nataraja* (13th century). Bronze, 34¼" × 27½" × 13". The Nelson-Atkins Museum of Art, Kansas City, Missouri (Purchase: Nelson Trust); *bottom* Olmec head. Archaeological Museum, Jalapa, Mexico/Art Resource, New York; **x** *top* Map by al-Idrisi (12th century). Copyright © Bodleian Library, Oxford, U.K.; *center* Mosaic portrait of Empress Theodora, S. Vitale, Ravenna, Italy. Copyright © R. Sheridan/Ancient Art & Architecture Collection; *bottom, Lady Tomoe Gozen* (about A.D. 900). E.T. Archive, London; **xi** *top* Saint Gregory and three scribes. Ivory, 20.5 cm × 12.5 cm. Kunsthistorisches Museum, Kunstkammer, Vienna, Austria/Erich Lessing/Art Resource, New York; *bottom* Sculpture of queen mother, Benin. Copyright © British Museum; **xii** *top* Inca jaguar cup. National Museum of the American Indian; *center, Shah Jahan Holding a Turban Jewel* (1617), Abu al-Hasan. Victoria & Albert Museum, London/Art Resource, New York; *bottom, Christopher Columbus,* attributed to Pedro Berruguete. Copyright © Giuliana Traverso/Grazia Neri; **xiii** *top* Detail of *Louis XIV, King of France,* Hyacinthe Rigaud. Louvre, Paris/Scala/Art Resource, New York; *center* Two of Galileo's telescopes. The Granger Collection, New York; *bottom* Painting of Simón Bolívar and Antonio José de Sucre. Mary Evans Picture Library, London; **xiv** *top* View of Sheffield, England, 1879. The Granger Collection, New York; *center* Queen Victoria. Copyright © 1994 Archive Photos/PNI; *bottom, The Siege of the Alamo* (19th-century engraving). The Granger Collection, New York; **xv** *top* British soldiers in World War I. Popperfoto; *center* Mohandas K. Gandhi. Corbis-Bettmann; *bottom* Ships afire at Pearl Harbor. UPI/Corbis-Bettmann; **xvi** *top* Fidel Castro and Nikita Khrushchev. Copyright © 1961 Seymour Raskin/Magnum Photos; *center* Nelson Mandela and F. W. de Klerk. Copyright © Mark Peters/Sipa Press; *bottom* Cuban refugees. Copyright © Hans Deryk/AP/Wide World Photos; **xviii** *left* Private collection; **xxi** *left* Detail of fresco at University of Guadalajara, Mexico (1936–1939), José Clemente Orozco; *top right* Château, Versailles, France/Giraudon/Art Resource, New York; *bottom right* Copyright © British Museum; **xxii** The Granger Collection, New York; **xxvi** *bottom left* Tony Auth, *Philadelphia Inquirer.* Copyright © 1989. Reprinted with permission of Universal Press Syndicate. All rights reserved; **xxvii** Copyright © R. Sheridan/Ancient Art & Architecture Collection; **xxviii** Palace Museum, Beijing; **xxix** *top left* The Granger Collection, New York; *center right* Copyright © Black Star; **xxx** *top left* Louvre, Paris/Alinari/Art Resource, New York; *bottom right* The Granger Collection, New York; **xxxi** *top left* Copyright © Chad Ehlers/Tony Stone Images; *bottom right* Corbis-Bettmann; **xxxii–xxxiii** Copyright © Pacific Stock/Orion Press; **xxxiii** *center left* FPG International; **xxxvi** Copyright © Stephen Alvarez/National Geographic Image Collection; **xxxvii** *top* Copyright © Kenneth Garrett; *center* Flying machine sketch from Codex Atlanticus, Leonardo da Vinci. Biblioteca Ambrosiana, Milan, Italy/Art Resource, New York; *bottom* Copyright © Warren Morgan/Westlight.

UNIT ONE

xxxviii–1 H. Armstrong Roberts; **2** *top* Sumerian hair ornaments, earrings, and necklace. British Museum, London/Werner Forman Archive/Art Resource, New York; *center* Pyramids, Giza, Egypt. H. Armstrong Roberts; *bottom* Ceramic lion detail from the Ishtar Gate, Babylon. Département des Antiquités Orientales, Louvre, Paris/Erich Lessing/Art Resource, New York; **3** Reclining Buddha, Vientiane, Laos. Copyright © 1986 John Banagan/The Image Bank.

Chapter 1

4 Copyright © Sisse Brimberg/National Geographic Image Collection; **5** *left* British Museum, London/Werner Forman Archive/Art Resource, New York; *right* Frontal articulated view of *Australopithecus afarensis,* "Lucy." Original fossil skeleton found in Hadar, Ethiopia. National Museum of Ethiopia. Copyright © 1985 David L. Brill; **6** *top, center, bottom* Copyright © 1992 W. Neeb, University of Innsbruck, Austria/Stern/Black Star; **7** Boltin Picture Library; **8** UPI/Corbis-Bettmann; **12** Copyright © Paul Hanny/Gamma-Liaison; **13** *top* Copyright © D. Johanson, Institute of Human Origins; *center* Musée de l'Homme, Paris/Erich Lessing/Art Resource, New York; *bottom* Copyright © Colorphoto Hans Hinz, Allschwil-Basel, Switzerland; **16** *left, top right, bottom right* Arlette Mellaart/Ankara Museum of Anatolian Civilizations, Turkey; **17** Copyright © Göran Burenhult Productions; **19** British Museum, London/Bridgeman/Art Resource, New York; **20** *left* Courtesy of University of Pennsylvania Museum, Philadelphia (Neg. #S4-139540); *right* Copyright © British Museum; **22** Copyright © 1992 W. Neeb, University of Innsbruck, Austria/Stern/Black Star; **23** Bruce Coleman, Inc.

Chapter 2

24 *top* Copyright © British Museum; *bottom* Louvre, Paris/Giraudon/Art Resource, New York; **25** *top* Musée Cernuschi, Paris/Giraudon; *bottom* Karachi Museum, Karachi, Pakistan/Scala/Art Resource, New York; **26** Illustration by Tom Jester; **27** Copyright © Desmond Harney/Robert Harding Picture Library; **29** Copyright © British Museum; **30–31** British Museum, London/Erich Lessing/Art Resource, New York; **31** *bottom right* Iraq Museum, Baghdad/Scala/Art Resource, New York; **32** Hirmer Verlag GmbH, Munich, Germany; **33** Copyright © Thierry Borredon/Tony Stone Images; **36** Copyright © Robert Caputo/Stock Boston; **37** Copyright © The Image Works/Topham Picturepoint; **38** *bottom left* The Granger Collection, New York; **38–39** Copyright © Victor R. Boswell, Jr./National Geographic Image Collection; **40** *top left* Corbis-Bettmann; *top right* Copyright © Steve Vidler/Tony Stone Images; *bottom center* The Granger Collection, New York; *bottom right* Louvre, Paris/E.T. Archive, London; **41** *center left* Reproduced from the collections of the Library of Congress (LC-USZ62-48427); *bottom left* Egyptian Museum, Cairo, Egypt/Scala/Art Resource, New York; *top right* Copyright © Michael MacIntyre/The Hutchison Library; **43** Copyright © P. Koch/Robert Harding Picture Library; **44** Illustration by Tom Jester; *inset* From *Civilization of the Indus Valley and Beyond,* Sir M. Wheeler (Thames and Hudson, 1966), Fig. 14.8. Reproduced by permission of Thames and Hudson Ltd.; **45** Copyright © MacQuitty International Collection; **47** Copyright © Keren Su/Tony Stone Images/PNI; **48** Academia Sinica, Taipei. Photo copyright © Wan-go H. C. Weng; **49** Musée Cernuschi, Paris/Giraudon; **51** *top, bottom* Copyright © C. M. Dixon; **52** Illustration by Tom Jester.

Chapter 3

54 Museum, Carthage, Tunisia/Erich Lessing/Art Resource, New York; **55** *top* Copyright © Suzanne Murphy/Tony Stone Images; *bottom, Story of the Cross: The Meeting of Solomon with the Queen of Sheba,* Piero della Francesca. S. Francesco, Arezzo, Italy/Scala/Art Resource, New York; **56** Detail of *Rama and Lakshmana Shooting Arrows at the Demon Ravana* (19th century), Delhi of Jaipur school. Gouache on paper. Victoria & Albert Museum, London/Art Resource, New York; **59** Copyright © R. Sheridan/Ancient Art & Architecture Collection; **60** Victoria & Albert Museum, London/Art Resource, New York; **62** Victoria & Albert Museum, London/E.T. Archive, London; **63** Robert Holmes/Corbis; **64** Copyright © 1984 Grant V. Faint/The Image Bank; **65** Copyright © 1986 John Banagan/The Image Bank; **67** British Museum, London. Photograph copyright © Michael Holford; **68** National Archaeological Museum, Beirut, Lebanon/Erich Lessing/Art Resource, New York; **70** *top left* The Bailey-Matthews Shell Museum. Photo by Sharon Hoogstraten; *top right* Copyright © British Museum; *bottom* Copyright © Nawrocki Stock Photo, Inc.; **73** *Moses with the Tablets of the Law,* Guido Reni. Galleria Borghese, Rome/Scala/Art Resource, New York; **74** Copyright © Zev Radovan, Jerusalem, Israel; **76** British Library, London/Bridgeman/Art Resource, New York; **77** Add. MS 11639, f. 521r. By permission of the British Library; **78** Detail of *Rama*

Art and Photography Credits (Cont.)

and Lakshmana Shooting Arrows at the Demon Ravana (19th century), Delhi of Jaipur school. Gouache on paper. Victoria & Albert Museum, London/Art Resource, New York.

Chapter 4

80 *top* British Museum, London. Photograph copyright © Michael Holford; *bottom* Copyright © 1990 Enrico Ferorelli/National Geographic Image Collection; **81** *top* By permission of the British Library; *bottom* Copyright © SuperStock; **82** Illustration by Patrick Whelan; **83** The Metropolitan Museum of Art, Rogers Fund and Contribution from Edward S. Harkness, 1929 (29.3.2); **84** Copyright © British Museum; **85** Courtesy of University of Pennsylvania Museum, Philadelphia (Neg. #T4-550C.2); **86** *left* Photograph by David Finn, from *Egyptian Sculpture: Cairo and Luxor* by Edna Russman, Copyright © 1989. By permission of the University of Texas Press; *right* Copyright © British Museum; **87** Staatliche Museen zu Berlin/Preussischer Kulturbesitz, Ägyptisches Museum; **88** British Museum, London. Photograph copyright © Michael Holford; **89** British Museum, London/Erich Lessing/Art Resource, New York; **91** Département des Antiquités Orientales, Louvre, Paris/Erich Lessing/Art Resource, New York; **93** *top* Copyright © R. Sheridan/Ancient Art & Architecture Collection; *bottom* SEF/Art Resource, New York; **95** *top* Copyright © British Museum; *bottom* Copyright © MacQuitty International Collection; **96** Copyright © SuperStock; **97** Bibliothèque Nationale, Paris/E.T. Archive, London; **98** *left* Copyright © Bibliothèque Nationale, Paris/Bridgeman Art Library, London/SuperStock; *right* The Granger Collection, New York; **99** Wellcome Institute Library, London; **101** *left* Copyright © 1992 Joe McNally/The Image Bank; *right* Illustration by Patrick Whelan; **102** Illustration by Patrick Whelan; **103** British Museum, London. Photo copyright © Michael Holford.

UNIT TWO

104–105 Palazzo Madama, Rome/Scala/Art Resource, New York; **106** *center left* Portrait of Paquius Proculus with his wife. Fresco from Pompeii. Museo Nazionale, Naples, Italy/Scala/Art Resource, New York; *bottom center* Luba Kifwebe mask, Congo. Copyright © Marc & Evelyn Bernheim/Woodfin Camp & Associates; **106–107** Lid of Chinese vessel, Han Dynasty. Courtesy of the Ontario Science Centre; **107** *top center* Bust of King Philip II of Macedon. Chiaramonti Museum, Vatican State/E.T. Archive, London; *bottom right* Stirrup-spout vessel, Chavín culture, South America. Copyright © R. Sheridan/Ancient Art & Architecture Collection.

Chapter 5

108 Piraeus Museum, Greece; **109** *top, The Death of Socrates* (1787), Jacques Louis David. Oil on canvas, 51" × 77¼". The Metropolitan Museum of Art, Catharine Lorillard Wolfe Collection, Wolfe Fund, 1931 (31.45); *bottom* Museo Nazionale, Naples/Scala/Art Resource, New York; **110** *left* American School of Classical Studies at Athens, Italy, Angora excavations; *center* Copyright © British Museum; *right* Copyright © SuperStock; **111** Copyright © George Grigoriou/Tony Stone Images; **112** Copyright © SuperStock; **113** The Granger Collection, New York; **114** Gift in Honor of Edward W. Forbes from his friends. Courtesy, Museum of Fine Arts, Boston; **115** Museo di Villa Giulia, Rome/Scala/Art Resource, New York; **116** Copyright © British Museum; **117** Rijks Museum van Oudheden, Leiden, The Netherlands; **118** Copyright © Elise Amendola/AP/Wide World Photos; **121** Corbis-Bettmann; **122** *top background* Copyright © SuperStock; *top foreground* National Museum, Athens, Greece/Scala/Art Resource, New York; *bottom* Copyright © SuperStock; *inset left* Copyright © R. Sheridan/Ancient Art & Architecture Collection; *inset right* Copyright © The Lowe Art Museum, the University of Miami, Florida/SuperStock; **124** Museo Archeologico Nazionale, Naples, Italy/Scala/Art Resource, New York; **125** *left* Copyright © Museo Capitolino, Rome/SuperStock; *center* Copyright © Museo Capitolino, Rome/E.T. Archive, London/SuperStock; *right* Copyright © SuperStock; **126** *center left* Museo Nazionale Romano delle Terme, Rome/Scala/Art Resource, New York; *bottom center* Photo by Sharon Hoogstraten; *bottom right* Copyright © British Museum; **127** *top left* Woodblock print by Kunisada. Photo copyright © Michael Holford; *center left* Copyright © SuperStock; *bottom left* National Archaeological Museum, Athens, Greece/Nimatallah/Art Resource, New York; *top right* Copyright © 1996 DUOMO Chris Cole; **128** Chiaramonti Museum, Vatican State/E.T. Archive, London; **129** Copyright © British Library, London/Bridgeman Art Library, London/SuperStock; **130** The Metropolitan Museum of Art, gift of Alexander Smith Cochran, 1913 (13.228.7); **132** The Granger Collection, New York; **133** The Granger Collection, New York; **134** *top* MS D'Orville 301 f. 31v. Copyright © Bodleian Library, Oxford, U.K.; *bottom left* The Granger Collection, New York; *bottom right* Smith Collection, Rare Book and Manuscript Library, Columbia University, New York; **135** Louvre, Paris/Scala/Art Resource, New York; **136** *top* Copyright © British Museum; *bottom* Copyright © SuperStock.

Chapter 6

138 Museo Archeologico Nazionale, Naples, Italy/Scala/Art Resource, New York; **139** *left* Mausoleo Galla Placidia, Ravenna, Italy/Scala/Art Resource, New York; *right* Louvre, Paris/Alinari/Art Resource, New York; **140** Illustration by Patrick Whelan; **142** Copyright © Winfield Parks/National Geographic Image Collection; **143** Copyright © British Museum; **144** Copyright © The Trustees of the British Museum; **146** Uffizi, Florence, Italy/Scala/Art Resource, New York; **147** Museo Pio Clementino, Vatican Museums, Vatican State/Scala/Art Resource, New York; **148** *left* Vatican Museums, Vatican State/Scala/Art Resource, New York; *right* Roger Wood/Corbis; **150** *top left* Charles & Josette Lenars/Corbis; *top right* Copyright © 1992 Archivi Alinari/Art Resource, New York; *bottom right* Museo Nazionale, Naples, Italy/Scala/Art Resource, New York; **151** The Granger Collection, New York; **152** Museo Archeologico Nazionale, Naples, Italy/Art Resource, New York; **153** Oviedo Cathedral/Scala/Art Resource, New York; **154** Mausoleo Galla Placidia, Ravenna, Italy/Scala/Art Resource, New York; **157** Palazzo dei Conservatori, Rome/Erich Lessing/Art Resource, New York; **158** Copyright © Mick Sharp; **159** The Granger Collection, New York; **162** Copyright © Archäologisches Landesmuseum der Christian-Albrechts-Universität, Schloss Gottorf, Schleswig, Germany; **163** *top* The Granger Collection, New York; *bottom* Charles & Josette Lenars/Corbis; **164** Galleria Borghese, Rome/Scala/Art Resource, New York; **165** North Carolina Department of Cultural Resources; **166** Illustration by Phil Colprit/Wood Ronsaville Harlin, Inc.; *top right* John Heseltine/Corbis;

167 Andrew Brown/Ecoscene/Corbis; 168 *top left* Louvre, Paris/Alinari/Art Resource, New York; *bottom right* Illustration by Patrick Whelan; 169 Vittoriano Rastelli/Corbis.

Chapter 7

170 The Nelson-Atkins Museum of Art, Kansas City, Missouri (Purchase: Nelson Trust); 171 *left* Copyright © British Museum; *right* Courtesy of the Chinese Culture Center of San Francisco; 172 Illustration by Patrick Whelan; 174 Copyright © Allan Eaton/Ancient Art & Architecture Collection; 177 National Museum, New Delhi, India/Scala/Art Resource, New York; 181 By permission of the British Library, London; 184 Tomb figures of Bactrian camel and West Asian groom (late 7th–8th century). Earthenware, camel 80 cm high, groom 67 cm high. Royal Ontario Museum, George Crofts Collection, gift of Mrs. H. D. Warren (918.22.11, 918.22.8); 185 *left* Copyright © Viktor I. Sarianidi/National Geographic Image Collection; *right* Copyright © Keren Su/Tony Stone Images; 186 Courtesy of the Ontario Science Centre; 187 *Legend of the Nine Suns,* silk painting from Han Dynasty tomb at Changsha, Hunan, China. British Museum, London/Bridgeman Art Library, London; 188 Illustration by Patrick Whelan; 189 National Museum, Beijing, China/Erich Lessing/Art Resource, New York.

Chapter 8

190 Copyright © Victor Englebert; 191 *left* Copyright © Betty Press/Woodfin Camp & Associates; *right* Copyright © Jane Taylor/Sonia Halliday Photographs; 192 Copyright © Anthony Bannister; *inset* Copyright © T. Magor/Robert Harding Picture Library; 193 Copyright © Martin Dohrn/Photo Researchers, Inc.; 194 *left* Copyright © C. & M. Denis-Huot/Peter Arnold, Inc.; *right* Copyright © Nicholas Parfitt/Tony Stone Images; 196 *center left, bottom left* Copyright © Anthony Bannister; *right* The Hutchison Library; 197 Copyright © M. & A. Kirtley/ANA; 198 Copyright © R. Sheridan/Ancient Art & Architecture Collection; 201 Werner Forman Archive/Art Resource, New York; 202 Photo by Malcolm Varon, N.Y.C. © 1993; 204 Copyright © Marc & Evelyn Bernheim/Woodfin Camp & Associates.

Chapter 9

208 *top* Boltin Picture Library; *bottom* Copyright © Nathan Benn/National Geographic Image Collection; 209 Copyright © 1988 Georg Gerster/Comstock, Inc.; 210 Illustration by Tom Jester; 212 *top* Copyright © Warren Morgan/Westlight; *bottom* Professor Tom D. Dillehay; 213 Copyright © George C. Frison; 214 Copyright © 1997 Georg Gerster/Comstock, Inc.; *bottom left insets* Photo by Sharon Hoogstraten; 216 Copyright © National Museum of Anthropology, Mexico/Explorer, Paris/SuperStock; 217 Copyright © Kenneth Garrett/National Geographic Image Collection; 218 Copyright © 1989 Editoriale Jaca Book spa, Milan, Italy. Photo by Corrado Gavinelli; 219 *bottom left* Archaeological Museum, Jalapa, Mexico/Art Resource, New York; *center* Dumbarton Oaks Research Library and Collections, Washington, D.C.; 220 Copyright © SuperStock; 221 Copyright © R. Sheridan/Ancient Art & Architecture Collection; 222 *top* Copyright © Nigel Dickinson/Tony Stone Images; *bottom* Copyright © Gary Milburn/Tom Stack & Associates; 224 Illustration by Tom Jester.

UNIT THREE

226–227 British Library, London. Photo copyright © Michael Holford; 228 *center left* Glazed earthenware horse, China, Tang Dynasty. Victoria & Albert Museum, London/Art Resource, New York; *bottom left, Saint Clare Received by Saint Francis* (13th century). S. Chiara, Assisi, Italy/Scala/Art Resource, New York; *bottom right* Sculpture of queen mother, Benin. Copyright © British Museum; 229 *top* Map by al-Idrisi (12th century). Copyright © Bodleian Library, Oxford, U.K.; *center* Bust of Yaroslav the Wise, prince of Kiev. Sovfoto; *bottom* Detail of manuscript illustration of Joan of Arc. Archives Nationales, Paris/Giraudon/Art Resource, New York.

Chapter 10

230 Bibliothèque Nationale, Paris; 231 *top* Bibliothèque Nationale, Paris; *bottom* Copyright © S. Arb/Camerapix; 232 *center left, bottom left, top right, center right* The Granger Collection, New York; 233 Copyright © Tony Waltham/Robert Harding Picture Library; 235 Copyright © I. Perlman/Stock Boston; 236 *top left* Bojan Brocelj/Corbis; *bottom right* E.T. Archive, London; 237 Copyright © 1993 C. Bruce Forster/Tony Stone Images/PNI; 238–239 By permission of the British Library; 239 *top right* The Granger Collection, New York; 243 MS Elliott, f. 192. Copyright © Bodleian Library, Oxford, U.K.; 244 Copyright © A. Duncan/Middle East Archive; 245 *center left* Copyright © Bodleian Library, Oxford, U.K.; *bottom center* The Granger Collection, New York; *top right* Istanbul University Library; 246 Michael Busselle/Corbis; 247 *left* Copyright © Peter Sanders; 248 *left* The Granger Collection, New York; *right* Copyright © 1993 C. Bruce Forster/Tony Stone Images/PNI.

World Religions

252 Copyright © SuperStock; 253 *top left* Copyright © David Hanson/Tony Stone Images; *bottom left* Oriental Museum, Durham University, England/Bridgeman Art Library, London; *top right* The Hutchison Library; *bottom right* MS Sansk 87r. Copyright © Bodleian Library, Oxford, U.K.; 254 Copyright © Rene Sheret/Tony Stone Images; 255 *top left* Copyright © 1990 Gabe Palmer/The Stock Market; *bottom left* Riverside Book and Bible House, Iowa Falls, Iowa. Style No. 220DN. Photo by Sharon Hoogstraten; *center right* Copyright © Haroldo de Faria Castro/FPG International; 256 Copyright © George Hunter/Tony Stone Images; 257 *top left* Copyright © Anthony Cassidy/Tony Stone Images; *center* Robyn Beeche with permission of Conran Octopus; *bottom left* Copyright © Bipinchandra Mistry; *bottom right* National Museum of India, New Delhi; 258 Copyright © Peter Sanders; 259 *top left* Copyright © Nabeel Turner/Tony Stone Images; *center right* Copyright © Carlos Freire/The Hutchison Library; *bottom left* From *Traditional Textiles of Central Asia* by Janet Harvey. Copyright © 1996 Thames and Hudson Ltd., London. Reproduced by permission of the publishers; *bottom right* By permission of Princeton University Press. Photo by Sharon Hoogstraten; 260 Copyright © Zev Radovan; 261 *center left* Copyright © 1989 Joseph Nettis/Stock Boston; *bottom left* Copyright © Impact Photos; *top right* Copyright © Paul Chesley/Tony Stone Images; *bottom right* Copyright © Zev Radovan; 263 *top left* Copyright © Keren Su/Pacific Stock; *center* Copyright © Orion Press/Pacific Stock; *bottom left* From *The Analects of Confucius,* edited by Chichung Huang. Copyright © 1997 by Chichung Huang. Used by permission of Oxford University Press, Inc.

Art and Photography Credits (Cont.)

Chapter 11

266 Biblioteca Nacional, Madrid, Spain/Arxiu Mas; **267** *top* Sovfoto; *bottom* Copyright © R. Sheridan/Ancient Art & Architecture Collection; **268** Scylitzes Chronicle, f. 217r. Biblioteca Nacional, Madrid, Spain/Werner Forman Archive/Art Resource, New York; **269** *top, bottom* Copyright © British Museum; **271** *left* Museo Civico dell'Eta Cristiana, Brescia, Italy/Scala/Art Resource, New York; *right* Copyright © R. Sheridan/Ancient Art & Architecture Collection; **273** Castle Armory, Kreuzenstein, Austria/Erich Lessing/Art Resource, New York; **274** Copyright © Stock Montage; **276** *left, Madonna with Child and Angels* (about 1463), Fra Filippo Lippi. Uffizi, Florence, Italy/Scala/Art Resource, New York; *right* Tass/Sovfoto/Eastfoto; **277** Tass/Sovfoto/Eastfoto; **279** The Granger Collection, New York; **280** *top* Copyright © Roger Wood/Corbis; *bottom* Or. MS 20, f. 124v. By permission of the Edinburgh University Library; **282** Scylitzes Chronicle, f. 217r. Biblioteca Nacional, Madrid, Spain/Werner Forman Archive/Art Resource, New York.

Chapter 12

284 National Palace Museum, Taipei. Copyright © Wan-go H. C. Weng; **285** *top* Denman Waldo Ross Collection. Courtesy, Museum of Fine Arts, Boston; *bottom* Art Resource, New York; **286** *top* Copyright © Science Museum, London/Science & Society Picture Library, London; *bottom* Photo by Sharon Hoogstraten; **287** Victoria & Albert Museum, London/Art Resource, New York; **288** *left* Collection, Palace Museum, Beijing. Photo copyright © Wan-go Weng Archive; *right* Wan-go Weng Archive; **290** *Buddhist Retreat by Stream and Mountains* (Northern Song Dynasty, about 960–980), attributed to Ju Ran. Hanging scroll, ink on silk, 185.4 cm high. Copyright © 1997 The Cleveland Museum of Art, gift of Katherine Holden Thayer (1959.348); **291** The Granger Collection, New York; **292** *center left* Photo by Sharon Hoogstraten; *inset* Copyright © Donna Day/Tony Stone Images; *bottom right* Copyright © James D. Wilson/Gamma-Liaison; **293** *top left* The Egyptian Museum, Cairo/Werner Forman Archive/Art Resource, New York; *top right* Courtesy of the Duckworth Collection, University of Cambridge, England. Photo copyright © G. J. Owen; *center left* Copyright © Peter Menzel/PNI; *bottom center* Copyright © Will & Deni McIntyre/Tony Stone Images; **295** *top left* The Purcell Team/Corbis; *center right* Copyright © James L. Stanfield/National Geographic Image Collection; **296–297** Illustration by Patrick Whelan; **298** Copyright © James L. Stanfield/National Geographic Image Collection; **299** Copyright © James L. Stanfield/National Geographic Image Collection; **300** *top* Copyright © Imperial Collections, Sannomaru Shozo Kan. Photograph by courtesy of the International Society for Educational Information, Inc.; *center left* Copyright © William H. Bond/National Geographic Image Collection; **301** Copyright © 1994 Archive Photos/PNI; **304** Robert Holmes/Corbis; **305** Copyright © Laurie Platt Winfrey, Inc.; **306** *left* The Metropolitan Museum of Art, Rogers Fund, 1904 (04.4.2). Photograph by Schecter Lee; *center* Museo Chiossone, Genoa, Italy/Scala/Art Resource, New York; *right* E.T. Archive, London; **309** *left* Dave Houser/Corbis; *right* Copyright © 1996 Don North/PNI; **310** From *The Warrior Queens* by Antonia Fraser, Vintage Books, a division of Random House, Inc., New York. Copyright © 1988 Antonia Fraser; **312** Photo by Sharon Hoogstraten.

Chapter 13

314 *St. George and the Dragon*, Paolo Uccello. National Gallery, London/Art Resource, New York; **315** *top, Portrait of Charlemagne*, Albrecht Dürer. Copyright © Germanisches Nationalmuseum, Nuremberg, Germany/Lauros-Giraudon, Paris/SuperStock; *bottom* Kunsthistorisches Museum, Kunstkammer, Vienna, Austria/Erich Lessing/Art Resource, New York; **316** Corbis-Bettmann; **318** The Granger Collection, New York; **319** *Saint Benedict*, Hans Memling. Uffizi, Florence, Italy/Scala/Art Resource, New York; **320** Copyright © Cathedral Treasury, Aachen, Germany/E.T. Archive, London/SuperStock; **322** Copyright © University Museum of National Antiquities, Oslo, Norway; **324** Illustration by Karen Barnes/Wood Ronsaville Harlin, Inc.; **325** *March: Two Workmen in a Garden* (about 1515), Simon Bening. Da Costa Hours, MS 399, f. 4v. The Pierpont Morgan Library/Art Resource, New York; **327** Royal Armouries; **328** Illustrations by Karen Barnes/Wood Ronsaville Harlin, Inc.; **329** Illustration by the studio of Wood Ronsaville Harlin, Inc.; **330** Copyright © Archive Photos; **332** Museo Tesoro di San Pietro, Vatican State/Scala/Art Resource, New York; **335** The Granger Collection, New York.

Chapter 14

338 The Granger Collection, New York; **339** *left* Bibliothèque Nationale, Paris/Sonia Halliday Photographs, London; *right* Manuscript illustration of Joan of Arc from Antoine Dufour's *Vie des femmes célèbres* (about 1505). Musée Dobrée, Nantes, France/Giraudon/Art Resource, New York; **340** Illustration by Patrick Whelan; **341** Bibliothèque Nationale, Paris/E.T. Archive, London; **342** S. Chiara, Assisi, Italy/Scala/Art Resource, New York; **343** *left* Copyright © Harry Bliss/National Geographic Image Collection; *center* Copyright © L. Salou/Explorer; *right* Cathedral, Chartres, France/Giraudon/Art Resource, New York; **345** *left* The Granger Collection, New York; *right* MS Roy. 14 C. VII, f. 9. By permission of the British Library; **346** The Granger Collection, New York; **347** *left* The Granger Collection, New York; *center* Copyright © Tony Stone Images; *right* Copyright © Jerry Bauer; **348** Musée Condé, Chantilly, France/Giraudon/Art Resource, New York; **350** Bibliothèque Nationale, Paris/Sonia Halliday Photographs, London; **351** The Granger Collection, New York; **352** MS Cott. Faust. B. VII, f. 72v. By permission of the British Library; **353** Photofest; **354** MS français 6465, f. 212v. Bibliothèque Nationale, Paris/AKG Photo, London; **356** The Granger Collection, New York; **357** University Library, Prague, Czech Republic/E.T. Archive, London; **358** *bottom left* Private collection; *top right, The Plague in Naples on the Piazza Mercatello* (mid-17th century), Micco Spadaro. Museo Nazionale di San Martino, Naples, Italy/G. Westermann/Artothek, Peissenberg, Germany; *inset* Reader's Digest, London; **360** MS Roy. 14 E. IV, f. 14v min. By permission of the British Library; **361** Archives Nationales, Paris/Giraudon/Art Resource, New York; **362** Illustration by Patrick Whelan; **363** By permission of the British Library.

Chapter 15

364 The Granger Collection, New York; **365** *bottom left* St. George, Lalibela, Ethiopia/Werner Forman Archive/Art Resource, New York; *top right* The Walt Disney-Tishman Collection of African Art. Photograph by Jerry Thompson; **366** Illustration by Tom Jester; **367** Copyright © Steven Winn/Anthro Photo File; **368** Copyright © British Museum; **370** Copyright © 1979 Richard Wilkie/Black Star/PNI; **371** Copyright © Lee Foster/PNI; **372** The Granger Collection, New York; **373** The Granger Collection, New York; **374** Copyright © Marc & Evelyn Bernheim/Woodfin Camp & Associates; **375** Copyright © Wendy Watriss/Woodfin Camp & Associates; **376** *center left* Staatliche Museen zu Berlin/Preussischer Kulturbesitz, Museum für Völkerkunde; *top center, right* Copyright © British Museum; **377** Photograph from *Africa: Tribal Art of Forest and Savanna* by Arnold Bamert. Copyright © Arnold Bamert; **378** Photo by Sharon Hoogstraten; **380** Copyright © SuperStock; **381** National Archives of Zimbabwe.

UNIT FOUR

384–385 Copyright © SuperStock; **386** *top* Pyramid of Kukulcan, Chichen Itza, Mexico. Copyright © Cosmo Condina/Tony Stone Images; *center* Detail of portrait of Timur the Lame. Uffizi, Florence, Italy/SEF/Art Resource, New York; *bottom* Building in Forbidden City, Beijing, China. Copyright © Bob Handelman/Tony Stone Images; **387** *top* Portrait of Elizabeth I (1588), George Gower. By courtesy of The National Portrait Gallery, London; *bottom* Engraving of Native Americans attacking a Massachusetts village during King Philip's War. The Granger Collection, New York.

Chapter 16

388 *bottom center* Museo del Templo Mayor, Mexico City/John Bigelow Taylor/Art Resource, New York; *top right* North America, New Mexico, Salado region, Mimbres culture: Cache of ritual figures, stone, wood, cotton, feathers, and pigment (about 1350). Basket 97 cm long, ritual figures 64 cm and 36 cm high, snakes 40 cm and 44 cm long, mountain lion 9 cm high, four throwing sticks each 61.5 cm long, Major Acquisitions Centennial Endowment (1979.17.1–11). Photograph copyright © 1997 The Art Institute of Chicago. All rights reserved; **389** *bottom left* National Museum of the American Indian; *top right* Copyright © 1989 Timothy O'Keefe/Index Stock Photography/PNI; **390** The Seattle Art Museum, gift of John H. Hauberg. Photograph by Paul Macapia; **391** Copyright © 1994 Tom Benoit/Tony Stone Images; **392** Maxwell Museum of Anthropology, Albuquerque, New Mexico/Werner Forman Archive/Art Resource, New York; **394** Copyright © Pat O'Hara/Tony Stone Images; **396** National Museum of Anthropology, Mexico City/Werner Forman Archive/Art Resource, New York; **397** *top right* Danny Lehman/Corbis; *left center* Charles & Josette Lenars/Corbis; *bottom* Copyright © Cosmo Condina/Tony Stone Images; **398** Copyright © British Museum; **399** Jeremy Horner/Corbis; **400** Copyright © SuperStock; **401** Nik Wheeler/Corbis; **403** Detail of *El Tajín Pyramid and Warriors* (1950), Diego Rivera. Mural. National Palace, Mexico/E.T. Archive, London; **404** *left center* National Museum of Anthropology, Mexico City, Mexico/Werner Forman Archive/Art Resource, New York; *bottom right* Copyright © J. P. Courau/Explorer; **405** *bottom left* Andromeda Oxford Ltd.; *top left* Copyright © 1994 Coco McCoy/Rainbow/PNI; *center left* Courtesy of Breitling USA. Breitling is a registered trademark of Breitling Montres S.A.; *top right* The Granger Collection, New York; **406** National Museum of Anthropology, Mexico City/Michael Zabe/Art Resource, New York; **407** The Metropolitan Museum of Art, gift and bequest of Alice K. Bache, 1974 and 1977 (1974.271.35); **409** Courtesy Department of Library Services, American Museum of Natural History (Neg. #K4673); **410** Nick Saunders/Barbara Heller Photo Library, London/Art Resource, New York; **412** *top* North America, New Mexico, Salado region, Mimbres culture: Detail of cache of ritual figures, stone, wood, cotton, feathers, and pigment (about 1350). Basket 97 cm long, ritual figures 64 cm and 36 cm high, snakes 40 cm and 44 cm long, mountain lion 9 cm high, four throwing sticks each 61.5 cm long, Major Acquisitions Centennial Endowment (1979.17.1–11). Photograph copyright © 1997 The Art Institute of Chicago. All rights reserved; *second from top* National Museum of Anthropology, Mexico City/Werner Forman Archive/Art Resource, New York; *second from bottom* National Museum of Anthropology, Mexico City/Michael Zabe/Art Resource, New York; *bottom* The Metropolitan Museum of Art, gift and bequest of Alice K. Bache, 1974 and 1977 (1974.271.35); **413** The Newberry Library, Chicago.

Chapter 17

414 *top* By courtesy of the National Portrait Gallery, London; *bottom, The School of Athens* (1508), Raphael. Stanza della Segnatura, Vatican Palace, Vatican State/Scala/Art Resource, New York; **415** Detail of *The Gates of Paradise,* Lorenzo Ghiberti. Baptistery, Florence, Italy/Scala/Art Resource, New York; **416** *The Madonna of Chancellor Rolin* (about 1434), Jan van Eyck. Louvre, Paris/Scala/Art Resource, New York; **418** *Lorenzo de' Medici* (15th–16th century), unknown artist. Painted terra cotta, 65.8 cm × 59.1 cm × 32.7 cm. National Gallery of Art, Washington, D.C., Samuel H. Kress Collection. Photograph by Philip A. Charles; **419** *top* The Granger Collection, New York; *bottom, Marriage of the Virgin* (1504), Raphael. Brera, Milan, Italy/Scala/Art Resource, New York; **420** *center left* Scala/Art Resource, New York; *bottom center,* David, Michelangelo. Accademia, Florence, Italy/Scala/Art Resource, New York; *top right* Sistine Chapel, Vatican State/Scala/Art Resource, New York; **421** *left* Self-portrait by Leonardo da Vinci. Biblioteca Reale, Turin, Italy/Scala/Art Resource, New York; *right* Detail of *The School of Athens* (1508), Raphael. Stanza della Segnatura, Vatican Palace, Vatican State/Scala/Art Resource, New York; **422** Palazzo Vecchio, Florence, Italy/Scala/Art Resource, New York; **423** *The Adoration of the Trinity* (1511), Albrecht Dürer. Oil on poplar wood, 135 cm × 123.4 cm. Kunsthistorisches Museum, Gemäldegalerie, Vienna, Austria/Erich Lessing/Art Resource, New York; **424** *Peasant Wedding* (1568), Peter Bruegel the Elder. Kunsthistorisches Museum, Vienna, Austria/Saskia/Art Resource, New York; **425** Corbis; **426** Copyright © 1990 Warner Bros., Inc./Photofest; **427** *left, right* The Granger Collection, New York; **428** *Girolamo Savonarola* (early 16th century), Alessandro Bonvicino. E.T. Archive, London; **429** *Portrait of Martin Luther* (1529), Lucas Cranach the Elder. Museo Poldi Pezzoli, Milan, Italy/Bridgeman Art Library, London; **430** The Granger Collection, New York; **431** Corbis; **432** *Elizabeth I* (1588), George Gower. By courtesy of The National Portrait Gallery, London; **433** Bibliothèque Publique et Universitaire, Geneva, Switzerland/Erich Lessing/Art Resource, New York; **434** Musée Condé, Chantilly, France/Giraudon/Art Resource, New York; **436** Louvre, Paris/Giraudon/Bridgeman Art Library, London; **437** Detail of *Portrait of Martin Luther* (1529), Lucas Cranach the Elder. Museo Poldi Pezzoli, Milan, Italy/Bridgeman Art Library, London; **438** Detail of *The Madonna of Chancellor Rolin* (about 1434), Jan van Eyck. Louvre, Paris/Scala/Art Resource, New York.

UPI/Corbis-Bettmann; **531** The Granger Collection, New York; **532** Detail of *Peter the Great, Tsar of Russia*, Sir Godfrey Kneller. The Royal Collection, copyright © Her Majesty Queen Elizabeth II; **534** *center left* RIA-Novosti/Sovfoto; *top right* Sovfoto/Eastfoto; *bottom center* Illustration from *The Art and Architecture of Russia* by George Heard Hamilton. Courtesy of Yale University Press, *Pelican History of Art*; **535** The Granger Collection, New York; **536** Title page from the King James Bible (1611). The Pierpont Morgan Library, New York/Art Resource, New York; **538** Guildhall Library, Corporation of London/Bridgeman Art Library, London; **540** Copyright © Tony Craddock/Tony Stone Images.

Chapter 22

542 Detail of *Patrick Henry Before the Virginia House of Burgesses* (1851), Peter F. Rothermel. Red Hill, The Patrick Henry National Memorial, Brookneal, Virginia; **543** *top* The Granger Collection, New York; *bottom, The Anatomy Lesson of Dr. Tulp* (1632), Rembrandt van Rijn. Mauritshuis, The Hague, The Netherlands/Scala/Art Resource, New York; **544** *Galileo Before the Holy Office in the Vatican* (19th century), Joseph Nicolas Robert-Fleury. Louvre, Paris. Copyright © Gérard Blot/Photo RMN; **545** Corbis-Bettmann; **547** The Granger Collection, New York; **548** *top left, top right* The Granger Collection, New York; **549** The Granger Collection, New York; **550** *Edward Jenner Performing the First Vaccination, 1796* (about 1915), Ernest Board. Wellcome Institute Library, London; **551** Copyright © Hulton Getty Picture Collection/Tony Stone Images; **552** The Granger Collection, New York; **553** *top, bottom* The Granger Collection, New York; **555** The Granger Collection, New York; **556** Copyright © 1995 Wood River Gallery/PNI; **557** *top* Michael Nicholson/Corbis; *bottom* "A caza de dientes" [Out hunting for teeth] from *Los caprichos* (1799), Francisco José de Goya y Lucientes. Etching and burnished aquatint, 21.5 cm × 15 cm. Gift of Paul Singer and Henry Lusardi, and the Maria Antoinette Evans Fund by exchange. Courtesy, Museum of Fine Arts, Boston; **558** *First Reading of Voltaire's "L'Orpheline de Chine" at Mme. Geoffrin's in 1755*, Anicet Charles Gabriel Lemonnier. Musée des Beaux-Arts, Rouen, France/Giraudon/Art Resource, New York; **559** *Seated Woman with Book*, Jean Baptiste Chardin. Statens Konstmuseer, Stockholm, Sweden; **560** *center left, Madame Vigée and Her Daughter*, Elisabeth Louise Vigée-Lebrun. Louvre, Paris; *bottom left, A Philosopher Giving a Lecture on the Orrery*, Joseph Wright of Derby. Oil on canvas, 58" × 80". Derby Museum and Art Gallery, England; *top right* The Granger Collection, New York; **562** The Granger Collection, New York; **563** The Metropolitan Museum of Art, gift of William H. Huntington, 1883 (83.2.228); **564** Detail of *Thomas Jefferson* (about 1805), Rembrandt Peale. Oil on canvas. Copyright © Collection of The New-York Historical Society; **566** Copyright © 1992 David Stover/PNI; **569** "El sueño de la razón produce monstruos" [The sleep of reason produces monsters] from *Los caprichos* (1799), Francisco José de Goya y Lucientes. Etching and burnished aquatint, 21.5 cm × 15 cm. Bequest of William P. Babcock. Courtesy, Museum of Fine Arts, Boston.

Chapter 23

570 *top, Portrait of Marie Antoinette*, Jean Baptiste Augustin. Aquarelle on ivory. National Museum of Art, Bucharest, Romania. Copyright © Gérard Blot/Photo RMN; *bottom* Copyright © Labat JM/Explorer, Paris; **571** *top* Mary Evans Picture Library, London; *bottom* Château de Malmaison, Rueil-Malmaison, France/Giraudon/Art Resource, New York; **572** Musée Carnavalet, Paris/Jean-Loup Charmet; **573** *Portrait of Louis XVI*, Antoine François Callet. Versailles and Trianon, France. Copyright © Photo RMN; **574** *Taille: impots et corvées* (late-18th-century engraving). Musée de la Ville de Paris, Musée Carnavalet, Paris/Giraudon/Art Resource, New York; **575** *left, La maraîchère* [Woman of the French Revolution], Jacques Louis David. Musée des Beaux-Arts, Lyon, France/Giraudon/Art Resource, New York; *right, Marie Antoinette*, Jacques Gautier d'Agoty. Château, Versailles, France/Giraudon/Art Resource, New York; **577** Musée de la Ville de Paris, Musée Carnavalet, Paris/Giraudon/Art Resource, New York; **579** *Attaque du palais des Tuileries, le 20 juin 1792: les émeutiers envahissent le palais en présence du roi et de la reine* [Attack on the Tuileries Palace, June 20, 1792: The rioters overrun the palace in the presence of the king and queen], Jean Baptiste Verité. Hand-colored engraving. Versailles and Trianon, France. Copyright © Photo RMN; **580** Musée de la Ville de Paris, Musée Carnavalet, Paris/Giraudon/Art Resource, New York; **581** Illustration by Patrick Whelan; **582** Musée Carnavalet, Paris/Bulloz; **583** Musées Royaux des Beaux-Arts, Brussels, Belgium/Giraudon/Art Resource, New York; **584** Photo by Soalhat/Sipa Press, New York; **586** Musée de l'Armée, Paris/Giraudon/Art Resource, New York; **589** Fotomas Index, Kent, England; **592** Musée de l'Armée, Paris/Giraudon/Art Resource, New York; **593** The Bettmann Archive; **594** Detail of *Masked Ball in the Redoutensaal on Occasion of the Congress of Vienna with Performance of Beethoven's Seventh Symphony and His Composition "Wellington's Victory in the Battle of Vittoria"* (around 1815), Carl Schuetz. Color print. Historisches Museum der Stadt Wien, Austria/Erich Lessing/Art Resource, New York; *inset left* Mary Evans Picture Library, London; **597** *left* Musée des Beaux-Arts, Lille, France/Giraudon/Art Resource, New York; *right* Victoria & Albert Museum, London/Art Resource, New York; **598** *far left center* Parisian sans-culotte (18th century), unknown artist. Musée de la Ville de Paris, Musée Carnavalet, Paris/Giraudon/Art Resource, New York; *left center* Model of a guillotine. Musée de la Ville de Paris, Musée Carnavalet, Paris/Giraudon/Art Resource, New York; *bottom* Musée Carnavalet, Paris/Jean-Loup Charmet.

Chapter 24

600 The Granger Collection, New York; **601** *bottom left* Copyright © 1986 R. van Butselle/Image Bank; **601** *Incontro di Teano* [Encounter at the Teano Bridge], Cesare Maccari. Palazzo Pubblico, Siena, Italy/Scala/Art Resource, New York; **602** *center left, bottom left, center, center right* Courtesy of the Flag Institute; **603** Copyright © 1991 Kathleen Marie Rohr/DDB Stock Photo; **604** The Granger Collection, New York; **605** The Granger Collection, New York; **606** *bottom left* Copyright © D. Donne Bryant; *top right* Corbis-Bettmann; **607** The Granger Collection, New York; **609** Arc de Triomphe de l'Etoile, Paris/Giraudon/Art Resource, New York; **610** *top* Historical and Ethnological Museum of Greece; *center right, George Gordon Byron, 6th Baron Byron* (1813), Thomas Phillips. By courtesy of the National Portrait Gallery, London; **611** The Granger Collection, New York; **612** Victoria & Albert Museum, London/Art Resource, New York; **614** E.T. Archive, London; **616** The Granger Collection, New York; **618** The Granger Collection, New York; **619** Illustration by Arthur Rackham from *Little Brother and Little Sister* by Jakob and Wilhelm Grimm. University of Louisville, Special Collections; **620** Copyright © Photofest; **621** Beethoven House, Bonn, Germany/Erich Lessing/Art Resource, New York; **622** *top left, The Winnowers* (1855), Gustave Courbet. Oil on canvas, 131 cm × 167 cm. Musée des Beaux-Arts, Nantes,

World War I. Copyright © Imperial War Museum/Archive Photos; *bottom* Mohandas K. Gandhi. Corbis.

Chapter 29

740 The Granger Collection, New York; **741** *top* Copyright © Imperial War Museum/Archive Photos; *bottom, Signing of the Treaty of Versailles* (1919), John Christen Johansen. National Portrait Gallery, Smithsonian Institution, Washington, D.C./Art Resource, New York; **742** The Granger Collection, New York; **743** Copyright © Hulton Getty Picture Collection/Tony Stone Images; **744** The Granger Collection, New York; **747** The Granger Collection, New York; **749** Copyright © Archive Photos/Express Newspapers; **750** *left* Popperfoto; *right* The Granger Collection, New York; **751** *left* Copyright © Archive Photos/Express Newspapers; *right* Copyright © Archive Photos; **752** *top* National Air and Space Museum, Smithsonian Institution, Washington, D.C.; *center* From the Collections of Henry Ford Museum & Greenfield Village; *bottom* Courtesy of United Airlines; **753** Copyright © Imperial War Museum/Archive Photos; **756** Roger-Viollet; **757** Copyright © Archive Photos; **758** *center* Copyright © Archive Photos; *bottom* Copyright © Ullstein Bilderdienst, Berlin; **759** *top left* Copyright © Rolf Adlercreutz/Gamma-Liaison; *top right background* Photograph copyright © Anne and Henri Stierlin; *top right foreground* Detail of Trajan's Column. Scala/Art Resource, New York; *center* Sovfoto/Eastfoto; *bottom left* Copyright © Hulton Getty Picture Collection/Tony Stone Images; **760** Copyright © Hulton Getty Picture Collection/Tony Stone Images; **764** The Granger Collection, New York.

Chapter 30

767 *top* Copyright © Vladimirov/Tass; *bottom* Copyright © Hulton Getty Picture Collection; **768** *left* Corbis; *right* UPI/Corbis-Bettmann; **769** Copyright © 1995 Elena & Walter Borowski Collection/PNI; **770** Armory Museum, Kremlin, Moscow/Bridgeman Art Library, London; **771** Copyright © Hulton Getty Picture Collection/Tony Stone Images; **772** FPG International; **773** Itar-Tass/Sovfoto; **774** Copyright © 1994 Archive Photos/PNI; **775** Sovfoto; **776** Copyright © 1994 Itar-Tass/Sovfoto/PNI; **778** Photo by Sharon Hoogstraten; **779** *top left, top right* Sovfoto/Eastfoto; *bottom center* AKG Photo; **780** David King Collection; **781** Copyright © 1994 Archive Photos/AFP/PNI; **782** *top* Photo by Sidney D. Gamble; bottom AP/Wide World Photos; **783** David King Collection; **785** Imperial War Museum, London; **786** Corbis; **787** Copyright © Mansell Collection/Time, Inc.; **788** Copyright © Hulton Getty Picture Collection/Tony Stone Images; **790** *left to right* Copyright © 1994 Archive Photos/PNI; Sovfoto; Copyright © 1994 Archive Photos/AFP/PNI; UPI/Corbis-Bettmann; Corbis; Copyright © Hulton Getty Picture Collection/Tony Stone Images.

Chapter 31

792 Copyright © the Dorothea Lange Collection, The Oakland Museum of California, The City of Oakland. Gift of Paul S. Taylor. **792–793** Richard Nowitz/Corbis; **793** *bottom* Copyright © Hulton Getty Picture Collection/Tony Stone Images; **794** *bottom* Copyright © 1995 Chicago Historical Society/PNI; **795** The Granger Collection, New York; **796** The Granger Collection, New York; **797** *The Persistence of Memory (Persistance de la mémoire)* (1931), Salvador Dali. Oil on canvas, 9½" × 13". The Museum of Modern Art, New York. Given anonymously. Photograph copyright © 1999 The Museum of Modern Art, New York; **798** *top* Copyright © 1995 Elena & Walter Borowski/PNI; *bottom* Copyright © Ullstein Bilderdienst, Berlin; **799** *top left background* The Granger Collection, New York; *top left foreground* Penguin/Corbis-Bettmann; *bottom left* Hulton-Deutsch Collection/Corbis; *center right* Corbis-Bettmann; **800** Copyright © 1994 Archive Photos/PNI; **801** The National Archives/Corbis; **802** UPI/Corbis-Bettmann; **804** Corbis-Bettmann; **806** Library of Congress; **807** Copyright © Hulton Getty Picture Collection/Tony Stone Images; **808** *center left* Copyright © Hulton Getty Picture Collection/Tony Stone Images; *bottom center* Copyright © 1995 Archive Photos/PNI; **810** Copyright © Hulton Getty Picture Collection/Tony Stone Images; **811** Copyright © Hulton Getty Picture Collection/Tony Stone Images; **812** Copyright © Hulton Getty Picture Collection/Tony Stone Images; **814** The Granger Collection, New York.

Chapter 32

818 National Archives, courtesy of USHMM Photo Archives; **819** *top* National Archives/U.S. Coast Guard; *bottom* UPI/Corbis-Bettmann; **820** Copyright © Imperial War Museum/Archive Photos; **821** Copyright © Tallandier/Archive France/Archive Photos; **823** Copyright © Archive Photos; **824** The Granger Collection, New York; **825** Itar-Tass/Sovfoto; **826** U.S. Naval Historical Center; **827** UPI/Corbis-Bettmann; **829** W. Eugene Smith/*Life* magazine. Copyright © 1945 Time, Inc.; **830** Copyright © 1994 Archive Photos/PNI; **831** Eastfoto; **832** *bottom background* Reuters/Corbis-Bettmann; *bottom foreground* Yad Vashem Photo Archives, courtesy of USHMM Photo Archives; **833** UPI/Corbis-Bettmann; **834** Courtesy of the Spertus Museum, Chicago; **835** AP/Wide World Photos; **836** UPI/Corbis-Bettmann; **837** Bildarchiv J. Piekalkiewicz; **838** National Portrait Gallery, Smithsonian Institution, Washington, D.C./Art Resource, New York; **840** *center left background* U.S. Air Force; *center left foreground* UPI/Corbis-Bettmann; *top right* AP/Wide World Photos; *bottom* Photo of aftermath of bombing of Nagasaki, August 10, 1945, by Yosuke Yamahata. Photo restoration by TX Unlimited, San Francisco; **842** William Vandivert/*Life* magazine. Copyright © Time, Inc.; **844** AP/Wide World Photos; **846** Copyright © Imperial War Museum/Archive Photos.

UNIT EIGHT

848–849 Copyright © Bernstein/FSP/Gamma-Liaison; **850** Afghan family watching TV in their tent. Copyright © 1985 Steve McCurry/Magnum Photos/PNI; **851** *top* Chinese youths celebrating Nikita Krushchev's visit to Beijing. Copyright © Brian Brake/Photo Researchers, Inc.; *bottom* Nelson Mandela and F. W. de Klerk. Copyright © Mark Peters/Sipa Press.

Chapter 33

852 *top* Bruce Shanks in the *Buffalo Evening News* (7/31/72); *bottom* Copyright © 1978 Susan Meiselas/Magnum Photos; **853** *top* Copyright © Brian Brake/Photo Researchers, Inc.; *bottom* UPI/Corbis-Bettmann; **854** *bottom* Jeremy Horner/Corbis; *inset* Copyright © Gamma-Liaison; **855** AP/Wide World Photos; **859** UPI/Corbis-Bettmann; **860** Copyright © Earl Young/Archive Photos; **861** *top left* Tass/Sovfoto; *top right, bottom left* NASA; **862** Copyright © 1997 ABC; **864** The Granger Collection, New York; **865**

Acknowledgments

Art and Photography Credits (Cont.)

UPI/Corbis-Bettmann; **866** Copyright © Archive Photos; **868** Copyright © 1967 Charles Bonnay/Black Star/PNI; **870** Chris Rainier/Corbis; **871** Art Rickerby/*Life* magazine. Copyright © Time, Inc.; **872** Copyright © 1961 Seymour Raskin/Magnum Photos; **874** *top, bottom* Copyright © Alain Mingam/Gamma-Liaison; **876** Copyright © 1991 Deborah Copaken/Contact Press Images/PNI; **877** *left* Copyright © 1994 Sovfoto/PNI; *center, right* AP/Wide World Photos; **878** Copyright © Szabo/Rothco; **879** UPI/Corbis-Bettmann; **880** Jeremy Horner/Corbis.

Chapter 34

882 *top* Copyright © Popperfoto/Archive Photos; *bottom* Copyright © Hulton Getty Picture Collection/Tony Stone Images; **883** *top* Courtesy of Nehru Memorial Museum, New Delhi, India; *bottom* Copyright © Alberto Garcia/Gamma-Liaison; **884** UPI/Corbis-Bettmann; **885** Copyright © Black Star; **886** Copyright © Archive Photos; **888** *top center* Copyright © 1979 Romano Cagnoni/Black Star; *top right, bottom right* Copyright © Gamma-Liaison; *bottom left* Margaret Bourke-White/*Life* magazine. Copyright © Time, Inc.; *bottom center* Copyright © 1968 Fred Mayer/Magnum Photos; **889** Copyright © Nickelsberg/Liaison; **890** *center left* Robyn Beeche with permission of Conran Octopus; *bottom right* Copyright © J. C. Carton/Bruce Coleman, Inc.; **891** *top to bottom* Copyright © Siegfried Tauquer/Leo de Wys, Inc.; Copyright © Black Star; Copyright © 1987 James Nachtwey/Magnum Photos; Photograph by Marilyn Silverstone; **894** Copyright © 1995 Yamamoto Munesuke/Black Star; **896** Copyright © 1984 P. Jordan/Gamma-Liaison; **897** Copyright © Black Star; **899** Copyright © Laurent Rebours/AP/Wide World Photos; **901** *top, bottom* The Granger Collection, New York; **902** Copyright © Gamma; **904** *left* AP/Wide World Photos; *right* United Press International; **905** AP/Wide World Photos; **906** UPI/Corbis-Bettmann.

Chapter 35

908 AP/Wide World Photos; **909** *bottom left* Copyright © Lee/Archive Photos; *top right* Copyright © 1988 Carlos Humberto TDC/Contact Press Images/PNI; **910** Copyright © 1989 Alon Reininger/Contact Press Images/PNI; *inset* Reuters/Corbis-Bettmann; **913** Corbis; **914** Copyright © Scott Sady/AP/Wide World Photos; **915** AP/Wide World Photos; **916** Mark Kauffman/*Life* magazine Copyright © Time, Inc.; **917** Copyright © Archive Photos; **919** Copyright © J. R. Holland/SuperStock/PNI; **920** Copyright © Mark Peters/Sipa Press; **921** Copyright © 1991 Peter Turnley/Black Star/PNI; **922** Sovfoto; **923** Copyright © 1985 W. Laski/Black Star/PNI; **924** Andreas Altwein Archiv/dpa; **925** AP/Wide World Photos; **926** Copyright © 1993 Peter Turnley/*Newsweek*/Black Star/PNI; **927** Copyright © 1992 Alexandra Avakian/Contact Press Images/PNI; **929** Copyright © Rikard Larma/AP/Wide World Photos; **932** New China Pictures/Eastfoto; **933** AP/Wide World Photos; **934** *top* Eastfoto; *center* Dominis/*Life* magazine. Copyright © Time, Inc.; *bottom* Copyright © Jeff Widener/AP/Wide World Photos; **935** Copyright © Vincent Yu/AP/Wide World Photos; **936** Copyright © 1989 Alon Reininger/Contact Press Images/PNI; **937** Tony Auth, *Philadelphia Inquirer.* Copyright © 1989. Reprinted with permission of Universal Press Syndicate. All rights reserved.

Chapter 36

938 *top* Copyright © Kevin Schafer/Tony Stone Images; *bottom* AP/Wide World Photos; **939** *top* Agence France Presse/Corbis-Bettmann; *bottom* Copyright © Gary John Norman/Tony Stone Images; **940** Copyright © Imtek Imagineering/Masterfile; **941** NASA; **943** Courtesy of National Center for Supercomputing Applications, University of Illinois, Urbana; **944** Copyright © 1994 Dan McCoy/R. Langridge/Rainbow/UCSF/PNI; **945** *left* Copyright © 1995 Culver Pictures/PNI; *right* Copyright © Kevin Horan/PNI; **947** Copyright © 1997 Ron Kimball; **950** Copyright © Ahn Young-joon/AP/Wide World Photos; **951** Copyright © Jim Morin. Reprinted with special permission of King Features Syndicate, Inc.; **952** Copyright © Scott Daniel Peterson/Gamma-Liaison; **953** Copyright © Reuters/Zoraida Diaz/Archive Photos; **955** *left* Howard Sochurek/*Life* magazine. Copyright © Time, Inc.; *right* AP/Wide World Photos; **956** Copyright © Hans Deryk/AP/Wide World Photos; **957** Copyright © 1985 Steve McCurry/Magnum Photos/PNI; **958** *left* Copyright © Archive Photos/PNI; *right* Copyright © Dominique Berretty/Black Star/PNI; **959** *top right* Copyright © 1991 Robert Holmes/PNI; *bottom center* Copyright © Jason Lauré; **961** Copyright © 1995 Sally Wiener Grotta/The Stock Market.

EPILOGUE

964 *bottom left* Fridmar Damm/Leo de Wys, Inc.; *top right* The Granger Collection, New York; **964–965** *Delhi Durbar, Celebration on the Occasion of Queen Victoria Becoming Empress of India* (1877), Alexander Caddy. Private collection/Bridgeman Art Library, London; **965** *top left* Copyright © Labat JM/Explorer, Paris; *top right* Copyright © Kenneth Garrett; *bottom right* Copyright © Alan Levenson/Tony Stone Worldwide; **966** *top* Globe Photos; *bottom background* Copyright © Livio Anticoli/Gamma; *bottom foreground* Copyright © Tony Stone Images; **967** *bottom left* Copyright © 1989 Sandro Tucci/Black Star; *top right* Copyright © Lee Brooks/Gamma; **968** *top* Copyright © Forrest Anderson/Gamma; *bottom* Copyright © Murdo MacLeod/Spooner/Gamma; **969** *top background* Copyright © Bruce Klepinger/Adventure Photo & Film; *top foreground* NASA; *bottom* Courtesy of National Center for Supercomputing Applications, University of Illinois, Urbana.

MINI ALMANAC

986 *graph background (earthquakes)* Image copyright © 1997 PhotoDisc, Inc.; **987** *graph backgrounds (seas, deserts, storms and floods)* Images copyright © 1997 PhotoDisc, Inc.; **989** *graph backgrounds (bridges, structures)* Copyright © Sense Interactive Multimedia.

SKILLBUILDER HANDBOOK

1009 *left, La maraîchère* [Woman of the French Revolution], Jacques Louis David. Musée des Beaux-Arts, Lyon, France/Giraudon/Art Resource, New York; *right, Marie Antoinette*, Jacques Gautier d'Agoty. Château, Versailles, France/Giraudon/Art Resource, New York; **1014** *frame* Netscape Communications Corporation has not authorized, sponsored, or endorsed, or approved this publication and is not responsible for its content. Netscape and the Netscape Communications Corporate Logos are trademarks and trade names of Netscape Communications Corporation. All other product names and/or logos are trademarks of their respective owners.